皮高品 著
周　榮　吳芹芳
謝泉　袁静　整理

皮高品集
（上）

荆楚文庫編纂出版委員會
武漢大學出版社

皮高品集
PIGAOPIN JI

圖書在版編目（CIP）數據

皮高品集/皮高品著；周榮，吳芹芳，謝泉，袁静整理.
—武漢：武漢大學出版社，2017.10
ISBN 978-7-307-18961-4
Ⅰ.皮…
Ⅱ.皮…
Ⅲ.圖書分類法—文集
Ⅳ.G254.1-53
中國版本圖書館 CIP 數據核字（2016）第 315162 號

責任編輯：詹　蜜　　韓秋婷　　朱金波
整體設計：范漢成　　曾顯惠　　思　蒙
責任校對：李孟瀟
出版發行：武漢大學出版社
地址：武昌珞珈山
電話：（027）87215822　　郵政編碼：430072
錄排：武漢大學出版社
印刷：湖北新華印務有限公司
開本：720mm×1000mm　1/16
印張：93.75　插頁：18
字數：1302 千字
版次：2017 年 10 月第 1 版　2017 年 10 月第 1 次印刷
定價：398.00 元（全三册）

ISBN 978-7-307-18961-4

《荆楚文庫》工作委員會

主　　　任：蔣超良

第一副主任：王曉東

副　主　任：王艷玲　梁偉年　尹漢寧　郭生練

成　　　員：韓　進　肖伏清　姚中凱　劉仲初　喻立平
　　　　　　王文童　雷文潔　張良成　馬　敏　尚　鋼
　　　　　　劉建凡　黃國雄　潘啓勝　文坤斗

辦公室

主　　　任：張良成

副　主　任：胡　偉　馬　莉　何大春　李耀華　周百義

《荆楚文庫》編纂出版委員會

顧　　　問：羅清泉

主　　　任：蔣超良

第一副主任：王曉東

副　主　任：王艷玲　梁偉年　尹漢寧　郭生練

總　編　輯：章開沅　馮天瑜

副總編輯：熊召政　張良成

編委（以姓氏筆畫爲序）：　朱　英　邱久欽　何曉明
　　　　　　周百義　周國林　周積明　宗福邦　郭齊勇
　　　　　　陳　偉　陳　鋒　張建民　陽海清　彭南生
　　　　　　湯旭巖　趙德馨　劉玉堂

《荆楚文庫》編輯部

主　　　任：周百義

副　主　任：周鳳榮　胡　磊　馮芳華　周國林　胡國祥

成　　　員：李爾鋼　鄒華清　蔡夏初　鄒典佐　梁瑩雪
　　　　　　胡　瑾　朱金波

美術總監：王開元

出版説明

湖北乃九省通衢，北學南學交會融通之地，文明昌盛，歷代文獻豐厚。守望傳統，編纂荆楚文獻，湖北淵源有自。清同治年間設立官書局，以整理鄉邦文獻爲旨趣。光緒年間張之洞督鄂後，以崇文書局推進典籍集成，湖北鄉賢身體力行之，編纂《湖北文徵》，集元明清三代湖北先哲遺作，收兩千七百餘作者文八千餘篇，洋洋六百萬言。盧氏兄弟輯録湖北先賢之作而成《湖北先正遺書》。至當代，武漢多所大學、圖書館在鄉邦典籍整理方面亦多所用力。爲傳承和弘揚優秀傳統文化，湖北省委、省政府決定編纂大型歷史文獻叢書《荆楚文庫》。

《荆楚文庫》以"搶救、保護、整理、出版"湖北文獻爲宗旨，分三編集藏。

甲、文獻編。收録歷代鄂籍人士著述，長期寓居湖北人士著述，省外人士探究湖北著述。包括傳世文獻、出土文獻和民間文獻。

乙、方志編。收録歷代省志、府縣志等。

丙、研究編。收録今人研究評述荆楚人物、史地、風物的學術著作和工具書及圖册。

文獻編、方志編録籍以 1949 年爲下限。

研究編簡體横排，文獻編繁體横排，方志編影印或點校出版。

《荆楚文庫》編纂出版委員會
2015 年 11 月

前　言

　　皮高品先生是中國著名的圖書館學家、圖書館學教育家、圖書館管理專家。先生字鶴樓，1900年9月9日出生於湖北省嘉魚縣簰洲鎮，6歲開始讀私塾，因家境貧寒，後轉入教會學校以求學，於1912年入簰洲聖公會所創辦的一所免費小學讀書。1914年簰洲聖公會以先生成績優異，將其保送進武昌文華中學（亦是教會學校，後改名聖約瑟中學）。1921年，文華中學又保送先生升入武昌私立文華大學。先生入學後先是攻讀文科，從二年級起又兼讀圖書科。1925年先生學成畢業，獲文學學士學位和圖書科畢業證書。1925年8月被分配到南開中學任圖書館主任兼英文教員。從1926年到1949年，皮高品先生歷任齊魯大學（濟南）圖書館主任、燕京大學（北京）圖書館編目部主任、國立青島大學（青島）圖書館主任、國立武漢大學（武昌）圖書館主任、文華圖書館學專科學校（重慶）教授、國立浙江大學（遵義，1946年遷回杭州）圖書館館長兼教授、國立英士大學（浙江金華）哲學教授。

　　1951年武昌文華圖書館學專科學校副校長甘蓮笙特邀皮先生重返文華，任教授。1953年院系調整，文華圖專合併到武漢大學，成立了圖書館學系，皮先生任武漢大學圖書館學系教授。此後，皮先生一直在武漢大學從事教學與研究工作，退休後也一直活躍在圖書館學界，直至1998年3月1日在哈爾濱去世。

　　皮高品先生在圖書分類學方面成就卓著，堪稱一代宗師。20世紀20年代，作爲有較深厚國學基礎，又較早接受西方圖書館學訓練的知識分子，皮高品先生深感中國傳統的"四部分類法"已不能適應知識增長和更新的需要，也深感新輸入的所謂最先進的《杜威十進分類法》也不適合中國當時的需要。從1925年在南開中學校工作時起，他就下決心要自编一本適合中國圖書館用的分類法，於是利用閑暇時間廣泛閱讀，搜集整理資料，"經常工作到夜晚十一、二點鐘"（《皮高品自傳》）。1926年在齊魯大學任圖書館主任時，他正式開始了《中國十進制分類法及索引》的編纂工作。後因時勢人情的變故，有一段時間他離職回到嘉魚老家，但仍不改初心，"預備在那極幽靜的鄉市，一心一意地完成這種工作"（沈祖榮《中國十進制分類法及索引序》）。因缺乏工具書，其困難程度可想而知。就這樣歷時八年，克服重重困難，終於編成初稿。對此，沈祖榮先生在本書的序言中多有提及，他不無感慨地說：

他從民國十五年，在齊魯大學圖書館服務的時候就動手，以後在燕京大學圖書館，青島大學圖書館，也是在繼續的編。前後八年之間，纔編成這五百餘面的一部圖書館應用工具的書籍，該是多麼不容易！

1934年《中國十進制分類法及索引》由武昌文華圖書館學專科學校出版，這本專著奠定了皮高品先生的學術地位。蔣元卿、姚明達、劉國鈞等先生都曾給予極高的評價，認爲它是增改杜威分類法的杰作。20世紀中國圖書分類學家有"北劉南杜中皮"之說，"北劉"指劉國鈞，"南杜"指杜定友，"中皮"即指皮高品。皮高品先生所創立的中國十進制分類法又被稱爲"皮氏分類法"。

關於本書的內容、特點和價值，黃宗忠、白國應、謝灼華、俞君立、程煥文等先生均有論述。據俞君立的歸納，《中國十進制分類法及索引》至少有六個方面的特點：

第一，采用中西合璧的類目體系。該分類法包括四個部分：類表、英文索引、中文索引、附錄。類表分爲十個大類：

000　總類
100　哲學
200　宗教
300　社會科學

400　語言文字學
500　自然科學
600　實業與工藝
700　美術
800　文學
900　歷史

全表類目約 13000 個，有些類目展開到 7—8 級。其類目體系的基本框架與標記制度以《杜威十進分類法》（DDC）爲基礎，但類目設置力求突出中國哲學、中國文化、中國教育、中國語言、中國文學與歷史等方面的內容，并將經學圖書集中列類。類表中所有類名與注釋均爲中英文對照。

第二，重視使用多重列類法。例如：

565.8　人類分類
　　.81　依體質分
　　.82　依區域分
　　.83　依語言分
　　.84　依組織分
　　.85　依文化分
　　.86
　　.87　依宗教分
　　.88　依種分
　　.89　依學派分

采用這種列類方法對於改善體系分類法的性能是很有意義的。本書至少有 13 處類目采用了這種多重列類法，這在當時國內所編的圖書分類法中是極少見的。

第三，較廣泛采用復分、仿分技術。本書類表中仿分方法的主要形式有："依國分""依區域分""依時代分""依朝代分""依題材分"等。仿分方法主要有臨近類目仿分、仿全表（仿十大類）分。據統計，本書中通過類目注釋指明需要采用復分方法的類目有200餘個，規定要求采用仿分方法的類目約80餘個。復分、仿分方法的使用增強了類表中類目的細化程度。

第四，大量運用"見""互見"與"參見"方法。通過"見……"注釋指明正式類目與非正式類目的位置。這種指明交替關係的"見……"注釋全書共有160餘個。此外，還較多采用了"互見"與"參見"，全書"互見"約60餘個，"參見"約70餘個。這些方法的運用，增強了類表中有關類目之間的橫向聯繫。

第五，具有較完善的類目注釋系統。本書的類目注釋類型多樣，數量豐富。其類表中采用的類目注釋類型主要有：内容範圍注釋、定義注釋、復分與仿分方法注釋、"見""互見"與"參見"注釋、宜入注釋、例注、分書方法注釋、同類書排列方法注釋等。此外，在皮氏分類法中，還設置了一些表明作者對某一事物的獨立見解與列類緣由的"考""按"，以及解釋圖書分類中疑點、難點問題的"注意"等注釋方式。據初步統計，本書中有注釋的類目有1800多個。

第六，采用數字"0"作爲擴充類目與轉換分類標準的標識。本書多處采用了這種方法。如：

980.5　世界類志

　　.501　陸地　疆域

　　.502　海洋　海峽

　　.503　島嶼　港灣

　　.504　江河　運河

　　.505　湖泊　泉井

　　.506　山嶽　峒峽

　　.507　平原　沙漠

　　.508　名勝古迹

　　.509　雜類

此例中"0"作爲擴充類目的標識符號。又如：

373　政府、行政
　.001　理論　關係
　.003　辭書　年鑒
　.004　評論
　.005　官報
　.006　會議　記録
　.007　研究
　.008　總集　小册
　.009　歷史　行政地理

此例中第一個"0"用來作爲轉換分類標準的標識。

在編製《中國十進制分類法及索引》的同時，皮高品先生還撰寫論文，就一些較複雜的圖書分類問題進行辨析，收入本集的《經書分類的研究》和《中國語言文字學書籍分類的研究》是頗見功力的兩篇力作。《經書分類的研究》發表於《説文月刊》（1944年第4卷），綜述了民國以來經書分類的幾種觀點："拆散論""拆散或不拆散論""不拆散論"，并稽古揆今，以充足的理由旗幟鮮明地提出了"經書不可拆散分類"的觀點。《中國語言文字學書籍分類的研究》發表於《圖書館學報》（1945年創刊號），該文從"語言文字學"這一名稱入手，對傳統"小學"的源流進行考辨，對"小學的範圍""小學的繫屬""小學的分目"等問題逐一厘清，率直地指出了一些分類學家"把語文與文學聯類，甚或合併"的不當之處。他説："文學要用語文表情達意，其他學問是不是要語文發揮思想？文學需要美麗的文字，其他學問又何嘗不需要美麗的文字？"他強調"圖書館分類的得當，知書是首要問題。不但要知書，還要有分類……語文分類法的編制與它類一樣有一定原則"。他也特別強調"學術是隨時代的輪子前進的，今日語文學的範圍已不是四庫時代的範圍了，語文雖分中外，但研究語文書的體例形式是不分中外的"。正是依據這些原則，他創立了皮氏的中國語言文字學書籍分類法。

值得一提的是，新中國成立後皮高品先生在武漢大學圖書館學系承擔圖書分類學課程的教學，此期間他的圖書分類思想又有所發展。經過不斷的學習，他認爲"恩格斯科學的分類和毛主席知識的分類是迄今我所知道的真正科學的分類"，以及"社會主義圖書分類法必須建立在恩格斯和毛主席唯一正確的科學的分類基礎之上。因爲他們的分類是依據物質運動形態客觀發展規律或歷史發展規律創制的"。

1954年，皮高品先生的《圖書分類法講稿》編撰完成，在講稿中他指出："社會主義圖書分類法的體系是以辨證的原理爲基礎，即以馬克思列寧主義、毛澤東思想做基礎。"1956年4月，文化部社會文化事業管理局和北京圖書館召集部分圖書館學專家在北京圖書館開會討論編製《中小型圖書館分類法》的問題，會議分三組討論，皮高品先生任第三組組長。會上皮先生提交了自編的《新中國圖書分類法簡表》，在該分類表的《緒論》中正式提出了"四分法"思想：恩格斯科學分類思想和毛澤東知識分類思想是根據物質運動形態把一切科學分爲自然科學、社會科學和哲學三大類，這個順序是按物質運動從簡單的低級的到複雜的高級的發展規律爲依據的。而圖書分類法的對象是圖書。根據圖書分類法從總到分，從一般到個別的編製原則，這個基本序列的順序就是：哲學、社會科學、自然科學。在這三類之外還有一類依寫作形式或體例編製的綜合性圖書，一共四類，即四分。至此，皮高品先生的圖書分類思想已趨於成熟，此後，他一直堅持"四分法"的分類思想，反復論證它的科學性。在1957年1月和5月的南京圖書館《中小型法》討論會上，以及後來的《關於〈中小型圖書館圖書分類表草案〉的一些問題》和《關於〈圖書分類淺說〉中的幾個問題——和劉國鈞先生商榷》等論文中，皮高品先生一再重申了"四分法"的正確性，并對當時流行的"五分法"提出了寶貴的意見。1983年皮高品先生又出版了專著《圖書分類法評論選集》，以學術評論的方式申述"四分法"的分類體系。1984年，皮先生在《八十五壽慶感想》中不無感慨地說："我更堅信，社會主義社會的圖書分類法的基本序列必須建立在恩格斯科學的分類和毛主席知識的分類這唯一科學的分類理論之上。我所發表的有關圖書分類法的文章都在維護這個觀點和它的正確性。……作爲國家標準全國圖書館統一採用的《中國圖書館圖書分類法》是關係全國圖書館的，應該認真考慮這個問題。"

在圖書分類法之外，皮高品先生的另一個重要研究領域是中國圖書史。在自編《中國圖書史講義》的基礎上，他出版了《中國圖書史綱》（吉林省圖書館學會，1986）和《中國歷代名著名家評介》（學苑出版社，1989）等重要著作。皮高品先生去世後，他的學生爲他寫了一副挽聯：皮氏分類法學貫中西問鼎世界，中國圖書史融匯古今造惠後人。這一挽聯或可作爲緬懷皮高品先生一生學術成就的一個觸碰點。

《中國十進制分類法及索引》自 1934 年出版以來一直未再版，在 1958 年以後的特定政治背景下又曾被圖書館界"一脚踢出門外"，該書今天已十分少見。所幸武漢大學圖書館尚存三本，一本存 B4 閱覽區供讀者參閱，另二本存古籍部作古籍編目工具書，三本中 B4 閱覽區的較完整，但三本都有不同程度的破損和缺漏。本次《荆楚文庫》整理重印，以 B4 閱覽區所存本作底本，并與古籍部所存二本互爲參校。《經書分類的研究》和《中國語言文字學書籍分類的研究》兩文均不見於皮先生的論文集，茲一并收入，編成《皮高品集》，以嘉惠學林。

周　榮

2016 年 9 月於珞珈山

總 目 錄

中國十進制分類法及索引 ………………………………………… 1
論文 ……………………………………………………………… 1447

沈　序

同學皮高品君，手編《中國十進分類法》一書，書成，要我做一篇序文，這是我義不容辭的一件事，也是我很願意爲他介紹的。茲將皮君對於編纂此書的本末，略述於下：

編纂這部書他是費了很長的時間的，他從民國十五年，在齊魯大學圖書館服務的時候就動手，以後他在燕京大學圖書館，青島大學圖書館，也是在繼續的編。前後八年之間，才編成這五百餘面的一部圖書館應用工具的書籍，該是多麽不容易！

談到這部書由學校出版的緣故，可以說是個機會。皮君於前年離青島大學圖書館主任的職務，回到自己的家裏，預備在那極幽靜的鄉市，一心一意地完成這種工作。不過這個當中有種困難，就是沒有應用的參考書。我們早已曉得他是在編輯這部書，究不知他的成績是如何。據我們所確知的，無論如何，在一個鄉市，沒有參考材料的地方，而想完成這部書，是很困難的。從前他有機會進行這部工作，全得力於他所服務的幾個大學圖書館。現在是到了爲山九仞之時，尤必須借用一個有參考材料的地方，以供運用。因此，我們就與他函商此項工作，並得他的同意應允來校，於一學期內編完交校付印。爲着此事，曾有幾次的討論，校內同仁，也貢給他不少的意見，幸皮君都能接納。

剛經一學期，皮君又受了武漢大學圖書館主任的聘約。幸好他的這部書已編成了功。在去年秋季開學時付印，打算最遲在今年春季就可以出版，不料在校對上，頗費周折，因爲承印的地方是在漢口聖教書局，負校對的責任還是皮君，郵寄往返，不能按期，延至今日，始得出版。我想凡關懷這部書的人，如不能明悉這種情形，一定是會責備我們的。

書已出版了，究竟書的效用如何，貢獻如何，我們不敢過於自許，聽憑採用的諸位同仁,去加以評斷。由這一部書的觀感,有一件事是我們應稱快慰的,就是見到圖書館在我國是有進步的。我常想到我與胡慶生先生所編的《仿杜威十進分類法》一書,是為我國圖書館首先的一本工具書籍。以後看來,是一本很簡單的書,而在當時所採用的實為不少。此理誠無足怪,每逢一種學術在萌芽的時候,偶而產生一種幫助的工具,是會叫人們去歡迎的,比如嚴復在中國最早仰望科學的時候,翻譯《天演論》《原富》以及《穆勒名學》等,是開闢了我國新思想一個最大的途徑。如果以現在的眼光去看他,翻譯這種的著作,是有許多的人可以應付的,而在那個時候,卻成為希世之珍。到了現在,研究科學的人,年有增加,而科學的著作,亦常有所見。圖書館之在我國進程中,亦是如此,除了《仿杜威十進分類法》那本書,在首先作一部分之貢獻外,接連杜定友,王雲五,劉國鈞,諸位先生們,隨編有圖書分類法,給國內圖書館在新進之中有一個很大啟示。近數年來,我國圖書館在各處之建設,有日新不已之勢,對於圖書館應用工具的書籍,常感缺乏,今皮君能編成這樣一部分類法的書籍以貢獻於本界,由此可以看出圖書館在中國之進步,而此書正是應運而生的。希望此書,在國內得着很大的貢獻;並希望採用此書的諸位同仁,見到書內有何缺點,多方指導,使此書得到復版的機會,再行更正,以成為一個完備的分類法,才不辜負皮君數年的心血!

本校對於此書的出版,亦是非常的快慰。近來本校同學,多有致力於編譯工作的,得使刊行多種叢書,以貢獻於本界,一方面可以見到同學愛護母校的熱忱;再一方面藉悉本校所訓練的這項專門人材,未蹈虛空。這一點,我們是應當感謝中華教育文化基金董事會,歷年所予我們以培植的機會。更希望我們的同學,努力前進,各求深造,將來不但多有編譯,並且多有創作的著作,其貢獻於國內外者,將更無有限量了。

中華民國二十三年十一月二十六日
沈祖榮序於本校創辦人韋女士舊邸

PREFACE

Mr. Pi Kao-ping, a graduate of the Boone Library School, has just completed a "Chinese Classification System" and asks me to write a preface for it. Both as a friend of his and as the Director of the Library School, I feel it my duty to comply with his request.

Mr. Pi has worked on this scheme for the past eight years. All that while it has consumed most of his free time after office hours. The Libraries of Shantung Christian University, Yenching University, and the National Tsingtao University where he served as librarian and cataloger of Chinese collections, provided him with the facilities and fitted him for this arduous task. Unfortunately, he left the last-mentioned place before the work was completed. Nevertheless, he did not give up his undertaking. He determined to finish his task at his native place during the interim before going into another position. Being aware of this, I invited him to come to our School to pursue his work, thus pushing it to completion. Here he had at his disposal the many Chinese and English classification schemes in our Library and all the help he needed from the Staff and students of the Library School, besides the practical suggestions possible from the teaching force. The manuscript was finished last July. The printing has taken longer than was expected. The numerous divisions, subdivisions, the many different kinds of type and the infinite number of minute details required processes new to the Hankow printers. The Arlington Press of the Religious Tract Society ought to be congratulated on the fine piece of work which they have produced despite these complications.

My *Adaptation of the Decimal Classification to Chinese Books* published some sixteen years ago seems to have "started something." We now have about four modern classification systems that have been worked out in this land of ours during the past ten years. This System of Mr. Pi's is the most exhausitive and the widest in scope of any because it had all these others to refer to. None of the Western systems of Classification made adequate provision for classifying Oriental books. This does not mean that this system has no defects. It has not yet been tried, so we can not say. The author states in the Preface that he will gladly welcome suggestions and criticisms from all librarians who adopt it, or who have themselves worked on classification schemes, especially our Chinese colleagues. This Classification appears also as one of the publications of the Boone Library School series, not to compete with any of the existing systems, but to make a contribution to library work in China. Indexes have been provided both in Chinese and English. This feature should make the system especially workable.

I want to express to Mr. Pi my sincere appreciation of the laborous work he has faithfully done. Also to the China Foundation, our eternal gratitude. It has entirely financed this undertaking as well as contributing partially to the maintenance of the Library School and its other publications. To all those who are always ready to give encouragement and moral support in these enterprises, our deep appreciation. Especially to Dr. Dewey, the inventor of the original system, who gave inspiration to us Chinese who have more recently come into the Library profession. His memory is green with us.

We hope the List of Subject Headings in both Chinese and English will be in finished form before long. These two tools will be indispensable to any libraries that have Oriental books, — in Western countries as well as in China. Libraries having bi-lingual collections of books will now no longer have to use two different classification systems as has hitherto been the practice.

SAMUEL T. Y. SENG

Boone Library School,
    Wuchang,
        December 5, 1934.

自　序

　　書籍分類，自昔已然。劉歆《七略》，開分類之先河；其後班《志》，鄭《經》，荀《簿》，阮《錄》，叠嬗損益，至清修《四庫》，乃集衆錄之大成，公私書目，咸奉爲圭臬矣。考學術之演進，由渾入劃，作始也簡，將畢也鉅，區區舊目，自不足以窮其變，觀之四庫內容，蕪雜凌亂，名實不給，用以部勒舊籍，猶有不可能者，矧茲學術競興，文籍大備之日乎？夫分類之要，在有體系，類有綱，綱分目，目之下更立細目，然後一一加以符號，方切實用。衡之《四庫》，不足語此！杜威，克特，國會諸分類法之因緣輸入，良有以焉。諸書中最著稱者，厥惟《杜威十進分類法》，原其法以十進部次群籍，應用之便，誠非他書所可企及也。雖然，杜法爲西書而設，初非兼中籍而並籌者；且也，類目陳舊錯列，繁省失均，逕以總貫中西載籍，其窮屈不適用，比夫《七略》《四庫》，一何以異？事非更張，理涉株守，採杜補杜固有不然，至若仿杜，而獨比附偏模，率爾就簡，亦未見其可也。蓋我國之學術，自有其特性，不容偏廢苟簡。世之作者，必悉加纂錄，詳制類目，使適中外文籍，庶云有濟。分類之匪易，誰曰不然？斯篇之作，竊取蒭蕘之誼，遑敢言他。爰綴數語，以叙作者之意云爾。

高品識於國立武漢大學
中華民國廿三年十月三十一日

誌　謝

本書之編制,始自民國十五年八月,迄至於今,逾時八載,乃克粗成。計類目易改五次,得稿共五百餘面。前後承蒙魯進修先生給予科學名詞審查會審查本,劉廷藩先生幫忙搜集佛教類材料,顧頡剛先生對於善本類,聞一多先生對於文學類,均多所教正,謹誌申謝。

本書付印之前,最後復承母校校長沈紹期先生,同學查(修)修梅先生,毛(坤)體六先生,徐(家麟)行先生審查全部一遍。沈先生,毛先生並予釐訂本書款式,及修改圖書館學,目錄學等類。又沈先生惠賜序言,毛先生指導于子強君編制索引,作者於此特別提出,敬致感謝之意。

本書於民國二十二年七月排印,原稿時祇三百餘面,後作者自任校對,乃隨校隨增,而篇幅加添幾五分之二,以故未能精細覆核,其間差錯之處,自知不免,敬乞閱者諒之,容俟再版時修改,就正於諸君子也。

作者增改印稿時,漢口聖教印書局予以各種便利,方成斯篇,附此誌謝。

AUTHOR'S PREFACE

In the past the most influential system of classification in this country was the *Four-Departmental Library Classification System*, published in 1772, when it was immediately recognized by scholars to be the best that had appeared. This authoritative position was held over one century and half, but is no longer recognized today. It is inadequate because of modern developments in various knowledge. This brings us to the necessity of opening our library field to the Western systems, systems which we employ for the purpose of evolving a system of our own. In consequence, a number of publications have made a great advance in this line, but on the other hand, have created some divergency of opinion in regard to certain aspects, such as scope of the contents, logical sequence of the main classes, etc. Thus it has brought about a growing demand for a fuller and more specific scheme adapted to books both in Chinese and in other languages. I have undertaken the present work in the attempt to contribute towards this solution.

In preparation of this work I have consulted hundreds of sources, especially the following classifications: Dewey's Decimal Classification, Cutter's Expansive Classification, The Library of Congress Classification, Brown's Subject Classification, etc. Credit is due to these and other sources for materials derived from them. I am also under obligation to the librarians of the American Museum of Natural History, The University of Minnesota, Art Institute of Chicago, and Illinois Engineering Experiment Station, from whom I have obtained information required of this work.

It becomes my pleasant duty to express thanks to Mr. Lu Chin-hsiu for sending me all the "Reports of the General Committee on Scientific Terminology". For the translations of the scientific words I have relied on these Reports greatly. To Mr. Liu Ting-fan, I am especially indebted for the help given me in gathering data on Buddhism. Appreciative thanks of obligations incurred are offered to Prof. Ku Chieh-kang and Prof. Wen Yi-to for their criticism and corrections of the divisions, "Special Collections of Book Rarities", and "Literature". Grateful acknowledgements are cordially extended to Mr. Samuel T. Y. Seng, Director of Boone Library School, my Alma Mater, Dr. Cha Hsiu, Mr. Mao K'un, Mr. Hsu Chia-ling for their courtesies in reading and criticizing the entire manuscript. Mr. Seng and Mr. Mao have corrected for me the two divisions "Library Science", and "Bibliography". They have also given much of their time and judgement regarding the form and size of the text. Finally, I wish to thank Mr. Yu Tzu-hsiang who has very kindly performed under Mr. Mao's direction the arduous task of compiling indexes both of Chinese and English. It is my desire also to extend my gratitude to the officials of the Religious Tract Society Press for their cooperation in granting me all facilities for making through the proofs additions and corrections so numerous that they form two-fifths of the main volume.

Needless to say, I am solely responsible for any errors which may remain in the text. I, therefore, take this opportunity to add that for aid in the corrections and criticisms of this piece of work will be gladly received.

Pi kao-ping

National Wu-Han University,
    Wuchang,
        Dec. 4, 1934.

目 次 Contents

第一部：類表 Tables ⋯⋯⋯⋯⋯⋯⋯⋯⋯⋯⋯⋯⋯⋯⋯⋯⋯⋯ 17
   大類　Classes ⋯⋯⋯⋯⋯⋯⋯⋯⋯⋯⋯⋯⋯⋯⋯⋯⋯⋯⋯⋯ 19
   大綱　Divisions ⋯⋯⋯⋯⋯⋯⋯⋯⋯⋯⋯⋯⋯⋯⋯⋯⋯⋯⋯ 20
   要目　Sections ⋯⋯⋯⋯⋯⋯⋯⋯⋯⋯⋯⋯⋯⋯⋯⋯⋯⋯⋯ 25
   詳表　Complete tables ⋯⋯⋯⋯⋯⋯⋯⋯⋯⋯⋯⋯⋯⋯⋯⋯ 57
      紀念藏　特藏　Memorial or special collections ⋯⋯⋯⋯⋯ 59
      總類　General works ⋯⋯⋯⋯⋯⋯⋯⋯⋯⋯⋯⋯⋯⋯⋯ 68
      哲學　Philosophy ⋯⋯⋯⋯⋯⋯⋯⋯⋯⋯⋯⋯⋯⋯⋯⋯ 95
      宗教　Religion ⋯⋯⋯⋯⋯⋯⋯⋯⋯⋯⋯⋯⋯⋯⋯⋯⋯ 138
      社會科學　Social sciences ⋯⋯⋯⋯⋯⋯⋯⋯⋯⋯⋯⋯ 189
      語言文字學　Philology　Languages ⋯⋯⋯⋯⋯⋯⋯⋯ 286
      自然科學　Natural sciences ⋯⋯⋯⋯⋯⋯⋯⋯⋯⋯⋯ 298
      實業　工藝　Productive arts　Industrial arts ⋯⋯⋯⋯⋯ 457
      美術　Fine arts ⋯⋯⋯⋯⋯⋯⋯⋯⋯⋯⋯⋯⋯⋯⋯⋯ 521
      文學　Literature ⋯⋯⋯⋯⋯⋯⋯⋯⋯⋯⋯⋯⋯⋯⋯⋯ 543
      歷史　History ⋯⋯⋯⋯⋯⋯⋯⋯⋯⋯⋯⋯⋯⋯⋯⋯⋯ 603

第二部：英文索引 Relative Index in English ⋯⋯⋯⋯⋯⋯⋯⋯ 683
第三部：中文索引 Relative Index in Chinese ⋯⋯⋯⋯⋯⋯⋯ 1085
第四部：附錄 Appendixes ⋯⋯⋯⋯⋯⋯⋯⋯⋯⋯⋯⋯⋯⋯⋯ 1375
   形式細分表　Form division ⋯⋯⋯⋯⋯⋯⋯⋯⋯⋯⋯⋯⋯ 1377
   莎士比亞文庫分類表　Tables of subdivisions for Shakespearian
      collections ⋯⋯⋯⋯⋯⋯⋯⋯⋯⋯⋯⋯⋯⋯⋯⋯⋯⋯⋯ 1380
   中國歷代帝王表　Chronological tables of the Chinese dynasty ⋯⋯ 1386
   中國縣名表　A complete list of the Chinese Districts ⋯⋯⋯⋯ 1417

大　類　Classes

0　總類　　　　　　　General works
1　哲學　　　　　　　Philosophy
2　宗教　　　　　　　Religion
3　社會科學　　　　　Social sciences
4　語言文字學　　　　Philology　Languages
5　自然科學　　　　　Natural sciences
6　實業　工藝　　　　Productive arts　Industrial arts
7　美術　　　　　　　Fine arts
8　文學　　　　　　　Literature
9　歷史　　　　　　　History

大　綱　Divisions

000　總類　　　　　　　　　**General works**
001-009　紀念藏　特藏　　　Memorial or special　collections
010　　　圖書學　目錄學　　Science of books　Bibliography
020　　　圖書館學　　　　　Library science
030　　　普通百科辭書　　　General, encyclopedias
040　　　報學　報章　　　　Journalism　General newspapers
050　　　普通雜誌　　　　　General periodicals
060　　　普通學會　　　　　General learned societies
070　　　國學　　　　　　　National literatures
080　　　叢書　　　　　　　Collections series
090　　　經學　經書　　　　The Chinese　Classics

100　哲學　　　　　　　　　**Philosophy**
110　　　東方哲學　　　　　Oriental philosophy
120　　　西方哲學　　　　　Occidental philosophy
130　　　形上學　　　　　　Metaphysics
140　　　邏輯學　　　　　　Logic
150　　　心理學　　　　　　Psychology
160
170　　　人生哲學　　　　　Philosophy of life
180　　　倫理學　　　　　　Ethics

190	美學	Esthetics

200	**宗教**	**Religion**
210	孔教	Confucianism as religion
220	道教	Taoism
230	佛教	Buddhism
240	婆羅門教	Brahmanism
250	基督教	Christianity
260	猶太教	Judaism
270	回教	Mohammedanism
280	祆教	Zoroastrianism
290	其他宗教	Other principal religions

300	**社會科學**	**Social sciences**
310	社會學	Sociology
320		
330	教育	Education
340	統計學	Statistics
350	經濟學	Economics
360	財政學	Finance
370	政治科學	Political science
380	國際政治	International politics
390	法律	Law

400	**語言文字學**	**Philology Languages**
410	中國語言文字學	Chinese philology
420	日本語言文字學	Japanese philology

430	希臘,拉丁,羅馬語言文字學	Greek, Latin, and Romance philology
440	法國語言文字學	French philology
450	英美語言文字學	English and American philology
460		
470	德國語言文字學	German philology
480	俄國語言文字學	Russian philology
490	其他各國語言文字學	Languages of other countries

500	**自然科學**	**Natural sciences**
510	數學	Mathematics
520	天文學	Astronomy
530	物理學	Physics
540	化學	Chemistry
550	地質學	Geology
560	生物學	Biology
570	植物學	Botany
580	動物學	Zoology
590	醫學	Medicine

600	**實業　工藝**	**Productive arts　Technology**
610	農業　農學	Agriculture　Agronomy
620	商業	Commerce　business
630	交通　運輸	Transportation Communication
640	工藝	Technology
650	工程	Engineering
660	化學工業	Chemical technology
670	製造工業	Manufactures

680	手工業	Mechanic trades
690	家政學	Domestic science

700　美術　　　　　　　　Fine arts

710	建築	Architecture
720	彫刻	Sculpture
730	繪畫	Arts of design
740	板刻　板畫	Engraving
750	攝影	Photography
760	工藝美術	Art applied to industry
770	音樂	Music
780	演劇	Expressive arts　Theatre
790	游藝　樂娛	Recreative arts　Amusements

800　文學　　　　　　　　Literatures

810	中國文學	Chinese literature
820	日本文學	Japanese literature
830	希臘,拉丁,羅馬文學	Greek, Latin, and Romance literature
840	法國文學	French literature
850	英國文學	English literature
860	美國文學	American literature
870	德國文學	German literature
880	俄國文學	Russian literature
890	其他各國文學	Literature of other languages

900　歷史　　　　　　　　History

910	中國史	Chinese history
920	亞洲其他各國史	History of other Asiatic countries

930	歐洲各國史	History of European countries
940	美洲各國史	Hisotry of American countries
950	非洲大洋洲各國史	History of African and Oceanian countries
960	紋章學	Heraldry
970	傳記	Biography
980	地理	Geography
990	考古學	Archaeology

要　目　Sections

總　類　General works

001-009　紀念藏　特藏　　　Memorial or special collections
　001　　黨義特藏　　　　　　The Chinese Nationalist collections
　002
　003
　004
　005
　006
　007
　008
　009　　善本特藏　　　　　　Special collections of book rarities
010　　圖書學　目錄學　　　Science of books　Bibliography
　011　　普通目錄　　　　　　General bibliography
　012　　圖書館目錄　　　　　Library catalogs
　013　　國別目錄　　　　　　National bibliography
　014
　015　　自著書目　　　　　　Personal bibliography
　016　　族姓書目　　　　　　Family author bibliography
　　　　　合著書目　　　　　　Joint author bibliography
　017　　類別書目　　　　　　Subject bibliography

018	特種書目	Bibliography, special
019	善本書目	Bibliography of book rarities
020	**圖書館學**	**Library science**
021		
022	圖書館行政與組織	Library administration and organization
023	圖書館管理	Library management
024	圖書館建築與設備	Library building
025	普通圖書館	General libraries
026	專門圖書館	Libraries on special subjects
027	圖書及圖書館使用法	Use of books and libraries
028	圖書館學校	Library school
029		
030	**普通百科辭書**	**Encyclopedias, general**
031	中國普通百科辭書	Chinese encyclopedias, general
032	亞洲其他各國普通百科辭書	General encyclopedias of other Asiatic countries
033	歐洲各國普通百科辭書	General encyclopedias of European countries
034	美洲各國普通百科辭書	General encyclopedias of American countries
035	非洲大洋洲各國普通百科辭書	General encyclopedias of African and Oceanian countries
036	索引　檢字	Indexes and indexing
037	年鑑	Yearbooks　Almanacs
038	指南　業名錄	Directories
039	其他	Others
040	**報章**	**Journalism　General newspapers**

050	普通雜誌	General periodicals
060	普通學會	General learned societies　Academics
070	國學	National literatures
080	叢書	Collections　Series　Collected works
081	中國叢書	Chinese collections
082	亞洲其他各國叢書	Collections of other Asiatic countries
083	歐洲各國叢書	Collections of European countries
084	美洲各國叢書	Collections of American countries
085	非洲大洋洲各國叢書	Collections of African and Oceanian countries
086		
087	叢論	General collected essays
088	隨筆　雜記　雜考	Polygraphy　Miscellanies　Extracts
089		
090	經學　經書	The Chinese Classics
091	易（周易）	I Ching（The Book of Changes）
092	書	Shu Ching（The Book of History）
093	詩	Shih Ching（The Book of Odes）
094	禮　三禮	Li Ching（The Book of Rites）
095	樂	Yo Ching（The Book of Music）
096	春秋	Ch'un Ch'iu（Spring and Autumn Annals）
097	孝經	Hsiao Ching（The Book of Filial Piety）
098	四書（四子書）	The Four Books（The books of the Four Philosophers）
099		

哲　學　Philosophy

100　哲學　　　　　　　　　Philosophy
101　哲學體系　　　　　　　　System of philosophy
102　本體數論　　　　　　　　According to the number of fundamental principles
103　本體質論　　　　　　　　According to the basis of organization
104　認識緣起　　　　　　　　According to the organ and instrument of knowledge
105　認識方法　　　　　　　　According to the method pursued
106　認識對象　　　　　　　　According to the relationship assumed between subject and object in knowing
107　宇宙或人類中心　　　　　According to the system of thought, belief, or action which centres about
108　世界與人生價值　　　　　According to the valuation of experience, life, and the world
109

110　東方哲學　　　　　　　Oriental philosophy
111　中國哲學　　　　　　　　Chinese philosophy
112　日本哲學　　　　　　　　Japanese philosophy
113　印度哲學　　　　　　　　Indian philosophy
114
115　波斯哲學　　　　　　　　Persian philosophy
116　土耳其哲學　　　　　　　Turkish philosophy
117　阿剌伯哲學　　　　　　　Arabian philosophy
118　小亞西亞各國哲學　　　　Philosophy of Asia Minor
119　埃及哲學及其他東方哲學　Egyptian and other Oriental philosophy

120	**西方哲學**	**Occidental philosophy**
121	希臘哲學	Greek philosophy
122	意大利哲學	Italian philosophy
123	西班牙葡萄牙哲學	Spanish and Portuguese philosophy
124	法國哲學	French philosophy
125	英國哲學	English philosophy
126	美國哲學	American philosophy
127	德國哲學	German philosophy
128	歐洲其他各國哲學	Philosophy of other European countries
129	西方其他各國哲學	Other Occidental philosophy
130	**形上學**	**Metaphysics**
131	認識論	Epistemology Theory of knowledge
132	方法論	Methology
133	本體論	Ontology
134	宇宙論　自然哲學	Cosmology　Philosophy of nature
135	心靈哲學	Philosophy of soul
136		
137	價值論	Theory of value
138		
139		
140	**邏輯學**	**Logic**
141	邏輯各論	Special topics
142	演譯	Deductive logic
143	歸納　實驗邏輯	Inductive and empirical logic
144	發生　演進邏輯	Genetic and evolutionary logic
145	象徵　數理邏輯	Symbolic and algebraic logic
146	形上邏輯	Metaphysical logic
147		

234	佛教事業	Buddhist missions
235	佛教會	Buddhist institutions and polity
236	佛教團體	Buddhist associations
237	佛教教育	Buddhist education
238	佛教生活	The Buddhist life
239	佛教宗派與歷史	Buddhism-Sects and history
240	**婆羅門教**	**Brahmanism**
241	婆羅門教哲學	Philosophy Dogmatic Brahmanism
242	婆羅門教經典	Sacred books
243	儀式	Liturgy and ritual
244	修行	
245		
246	僧侶	Brahma priests
247	廟寺	Brahma temples
248		
249	婆羅門教宗派與歷史	Brahmanism-Sects and history
250	**基督教**	**Christianity**
251	神學　教義	Doctrinal theology
252	聖經	The Bible
253	實踐神學	Practical theology
254	牧教　傳教事業	Pastoral theology
255	教會　教會制度	Church institutions and ecclesiastical polity
256	基督教會團體	Christian societies, associations, etc.
257	基督教教育	Religious education　Sunday school
258	基督徒生活	The Christian life
259	基督教宗派與歷史	Christian churches-Sects and history
260	**猶太教**	**Judaism**
261	教義　神學	Dogmatic judaism

262	經典	Sacred books
263	實踐神學	Practical Judaism
264	牧教　傳教	Pastoral Judaism
265	猶太教制度	Ecclesiastical Judaism
266	猶太教團體	Jewish associations
267	猶太教教育	Jewish education
268	猶太教徒生活	The Jewish life
269	猶太教宗派與歷史	Judaism-Sects and history
270	**回教**	**Mohammedanism Islam**
271	教義　神學	Doctrinal theology
272	聖經	Moslem scriptures
273	實踐神學	Practical theology
274	牧教　教門事業	Pastoral theology
275	教門制度	Moslem institution and polity
276	教門團體	Moslem associations
277	教門教育	Moslem education
278	教門生活	The Moslem life
279	回教宗派與歷史	Moslem sects and history
280	**祆教**	**Zoroastrianism**
281	教義　神學	Dogmatic Zoroastrianism
282	經典	Zend Avesta (Zoroastrian scripture)
283	實踐神學	Practical Zoroastrianism
284	牧教　祆教事業	Pastoral Zoroastrianism
285	祆教制度	Zoroastrian institutions and polity
286	祆教團體	Zoroastrian associations
287		
288	祆教生活	The Zoroastrian life
289	祆教宗派與歷史	Zoroastrianism-Sects and history

290	**其他宗教**	**Other principal religions**
291	神道教	Shintoism
292		
293		
294		
295		
296		
297		
298		
299		

社會科学　Social sciences

300	**社會科學**	**Social sciences**
301-309	特論	Special topics
310	**社會学**	**Sociology**
311	社會要素	Social elements
312	動態社會學	Social dynamics, or dynamical sociology
313	静態社會學	Social statics, or statical sociology
314	叙述社會學	Descriptive sociology
315	社會病理學	Social pathology
316	社會救濟學	Social welfare　Philanthropy
317	社會問題	Social problems
318	社會主義	Socialism
319	禮俗　社風	Customs　Costumes　Etiquette
320		
330	**教育**	**Education**

331	教育行政　學校行政	School government
332	學校管理	School management
333	學生生活	School life, student manners and customs
334	學則	School standardization
335	課程	Curriculum　Course of study
336	教員	Teachers　Professors　Instructors
337	教授法	Methods of instruction and study
338	學校	Schools and colleges
339	校刊	School publications
340	**統計學**	**Statistics**
341	統計法	Methods　Science of statistics
342		
343		
344		
345	國家統計　國勢調査	National statistics　Censuses
346	應用統計	Applied statistics
347		
348		
349	人口論	Demography　Population
350	**經濟學**	**Economics**
351	經濟制度　政策	Economic policy
352	生產論	Production
353	土地	Land
354	勞工　勞動	Labor and laborers
355	資本　資本主義	Capital　Capitalism
356	生產組織	Organization
357	消費論	Consumption
358	交易論	Exchange

359	分配論	Distribution
360	**財政學**	**Finance　Financial economics**
361	金融　貨幣	Money
362	銀行　儲蓄	Bank and banking　Savings
363		
364	信用　票據	Credit and credit system
365	匯兌	Exchange
366	證券	Securities
367	投資與投機	Investment and speculation
368	保險	Insurance
369	國家財政	Public finance
370	**政治科學　政治学**	**Political seiences　Politics**
371	國家學	The states
372	國民　公民學	Civics　Citizenship
373	政府　行政	Administration　Government
374		
375	政黨	Political parties
376		
377	殖民	Colonies and colonization
378		
379	軍事學	Military and naval sciences
380	**國際政治**	**International politics**
381	國際法(公法)	International law(public)
382	國際爭議	Procedure in international disputes
383	國際聯盟	League of nations
384		
385	國際關係	International relations
386	外交　使節	Diplomacy　The diplomatic service

387	條約　締約	Treaties and treaty making
388	國際問題	International problems
389		
390	**法律**	**Law**
391	憲法	Constitutional law
392	議院法　國會法	Parliamentary law
393	行政法	Administrative law
394	刑法	Criminal law
395	訴訟法	Procedure law
396	法院編制法	Law of judicial organization
397	民法	Civil law
398	商法	Commercial law
399	特別法規	Special laws and regulations

語言文字學　Philology　Languages

400	**語言文字學**	**Philology　Languages**
401	比較語言學	Comparative language
402		
403	語言類別	Differentiation and classification of languages
404		
405	世界語	Universal language
406		
407		
408		
409	語系　語言分佈學	Famillies of languages

410	中國語言文字學	Chinese philology, language
411	字源學	Etymology
412		
413	字書　字典	Dictionaries
414	聲韻學	Orthography　Phonology
415	訓詁學　方言學	Dialectology　Slang
416	文法	Grammar
417	音韻學	Prosody　Metrics　Rhythmics
418	讀本	Texts for learning the languages
419	古文字學	Paleography
420-490	其他各國語言文字學	Languages of other countries

自然科學　Natural Sciences

500	自然科學	Natural sciences
501-509	特論	Special topics
510	數學	**Mathematics**
511	算學	Arthmetic
512	代數	Algebra
513	解析學	Analysis
514	級數　連級數	Progression　Series
515	微積分　微積學	Calculus　Differential and integral calculus
516	函數　倚數	Functions
517	幾何學　形學	Geometry
518	三角學	Trigonometry

519	近世幾何學（綜合）	Modern (synthetic) geometry
520	**天文學**	**Astronomy**
521	理論天文學	Theoretic astronomy
522	實用天文學	Practical and spheric
523	叙述天文學	Descriptive astronomy
524	星球交通學	Cosmo communication
525	地球　地球物理學	Earth　Terrestrial physics
526	地形學　測地學	Figure of the earth　Geodesy
527	航海天文學	Nautic astronomy
528	律曆　曆書	Chronology　Time
529	氣象學	Meteorology (Aerology)
530	**物理學**	**Physics**
531	力學	Mechanics
532	液體　水力學	Hydromechanics　Liquids
533	氣體　氣力學	Pneumatics　Gases
534	聲學　音學	Acoustics　(Sound)
535	光學	Optics Light　(Radiant energy)
536	熱學	Thermics　(Heat)
537	電學	Electricity
538	磁學	Magnetism
539	輻射物理學	Radio-physics　Radiology
540	**化學**	**Chemistry**
541	理論化學　物理化學	Physical and theoretical chemistry
542	實驗化學	Practical and experimental chemistry
543	分析化學	Analysis　Analytic chemistry
544	定性分析	Qualitative analysis
545	定量分析	Quantitative analysis
546	無機化學	Inorganic chemistry

547	有機化學	Organic chemistry
548	應用化學	Applied chemistry
549		
550	**地質學**	**Geology**
551	自然地質學	Physical and dynamic geology
552	地面地質學	Physiography　Surface geology
553	構造地質學	Structural geology
554	地史學　地層史學	Historical（stratigraphic）geology
555		
556	應用地質學	Economic geology
557	岩石學	Lithology　Petrography
558	鑛物學	Mineralogy
559	結晶學	Crystallography　Crystals
560	**生物學**	**Biology**
561	系統與比較生物學	Systematic and comparative
562	生命　生命現象	Life　Vital phenomena
563	演化論　進化論	Genetic biology　Organic evolution
564	種源論	Origin of species
565	人類學　人種學	Anthropology　Ethnology
566	顯微學　細菌學	Microscopy
567	標本採集指南	Collectors manuals
568	應用生物學	Economic biology
569	古生物學　化石學	Palaeontology　Fossils
570	**植物學**	**Botany**
571	生理與構造植物學	Systematic botany Phytology
572	原生植物	Protophyta
573	隱花植物	Cryptogamia

574	顯花植物	Spermatophyta
575	被子植物	Angiospermae
576	雙子葉植物	Dicotyledoneae
577	離瓣類	Choripetalae
578		
579	合瓣類	Sympetalae
580	**動物學**	**Zoology**
581	生理與構造動物學	Physiological and structural Zoology
582	無脊椎動物	Invertebrate
583	關節動物	Articulata
584	節足動物	Arthropoda
585	昆蟲類	Hexapoda Entomology
586	原索動物	Chordata
587	脊椎動物	Vertebrata
588	哺乳類	Mammalia
589	靈長類	Primates
590	**醫學**	**Medicine Medical science**
591	解剖學	Anatomy
592	生理學	Physiology
593	國家醫學　衛生學	State medicine Hygiene
594	病理學	Pathology
595	醫術　治療學	Practice of medicine Therapeutics
596	藥學	Pharmacy and materia medica
597	內科	Internal medicine
598	外科	Surgery
599	獸醫學	Veterinary medicine

實業　工藝　Productive arts　Technology

600　**實業**　　　　　　　　　Productive arts
601　實業經濟　　　　　　Economics　Policies
602　實業法規　　　　　　Laws and regulations
603　實業管理　　　　　　Management of industrial enterprise
604
605　特權　　　　　　　　Patents
606
607　度量權衡　　　　　　Metric arts　Measurement
608
609

610　**農業　農學**　　　　　Agriculture　Agronomy
611　農藝　　　　　　　　The farm　Farm operations
612　農作物　　　　　　　Field crops
613　園藝　　　　　　　　Horticulture　Gardening
614　森林　　　　　　　　Forestry　Aboriculture
615　畜產業　　　　　　　Animal industries
616　蠶業　　　　　　　　Silkworms　Sericulture
617　漁業　水產業　　　　Aquatic products industries
618　鹽業　　　　　　　　Salt manufacturing
619　田獵　　　　　　　　Hunting industries

620　**商業**　　　　　　　　Commerce　Business
621　商業經濟　　　　　　Economics and policies
622　商業管理與經營　　　Business management and administration
623　商品學　　　　　　　Merchandises　Commodities
624　市場學　　　　　　　Markets

625	堆棧　貯藏	Storage and warehousing
626	商業實踐	Business practice
627	會計　簿計	Accounting　Bookkeeping
628		
629	廣告	Advertising publicity
630	**交通　運輸**	**Transportation and communication**
631	陸運	Land transportation
632	道路	Roads and highways
633	鐵路	Railways
634	水運	Water transportation
635	航空運輸	Aerial transportation
636	郵政	Postal services
637	電政　電信	Telegraphy　Telephone
638		
639	其他	Others
640	**工藝**	**Technology**
641	工藝經濟	Economics and policies
642	法規	Laws and regulations
643		
644		
645	特權	Patents
646		
647	展覽	Exhibitions
648		
649		
650	**工程**	**Engineering**
651	土木工程	Civil engineering
652		

653	衛生及城市工程	Sanitary and municipal engineering
654	水利工程	Hydraulic engineering
655	機械工程	Mechanical engineering
656		
657	電氣工程	Electrical engineering
658	鑛業工程	Mining engineering
659	其他工程	Other branch of engineering
660	**化學工業**	**Chemical technology**
661	化學藥品	Chemicals
662	電氣化學工業	Industrial electrochemistry
663	爆炸品煙火製造	Explotives and pyrotechnics
664	食物　飲料	Foods　Beverages
665	油脂工業　照明工業	Fat industries　Illuminating industries
666	窰業	Clay industries
667	漂染工業	Bleaching, dyeing, colormaking
668	其他化學工業	Other chemical industries
669	冶金學	Metallurgy
670	**製造工業**	**Manufactures**
671	金屬制品	Metal manufactures
672	木料與木製品	Lumber and woodwork
673	皮革與皮革製品	Leather industries
674	紙與紙製品	Paper manufacture and trade
675	織品	Textile industries
676	樹膠與樹膠製品	Rubber and similar products
677	麵粉製造	Flour and grain
678	煙菸製造	Tobacco industry
679	其他工業製造	Other special industries
680	**手工業**	**Mechanic trades　Handcrafts**

681	木工　竹工	Wood-working　Bamboo-working
682	鐵工,銅工,等	Iron-working, Copper-working, etc.
683	漆工	Painting, varnishing, gilding, etc.
684	裁縫	Dressmaking and tailoring
685	刺繡	Decorative needlework
686	洗衣	Laundry work
687	理髮	Hairdressing　Barber's work
688	其他手藝	Other trades
689	玩具	Amateur manuals　Toys
690	**家政學**	**Domestic science**
691	家庭管理	Household management
692	房屋　住宅	Shelter: house, home
693	衣飾　服制	Clothing
694	食物	Foods and food supply
695	烹飪	Cookery
696		
697	款待	Household entertainments
698		
699	家庭醫學	Domestic medicine

美術　Fine arts

700	**美術**	**Fine arts**
701	中國美術	Chinese fine arts
702-9	其他各國美術	Fine arts of other countries
710	**建築**	**Architecture**
711	建築設計	Plans　Execution of works

712	建築裝飾	Architectural decoration
713	建築構造	Architectural details
714		
715	宗教建築	Religious architecture
716		
717	公共建築	Public building
718	住宅	Domestic architecture
719	城市風景	Esthetics of cities
720	**彫刻**	**Sculpture**
721	彫刻材料與技術	Technique, tools, materials
722	泥塑	Plaster and clay
723	木彫	Wood carving
724	石刻　玉琢	Stone carving　Gems carving
725	金鑄	Metal carving
726	象刻　骨刻	Ivory and born carving
727	篆刻　印譜	Seal engraving　Seals
728	依人體分	Sculpture-Special forms
729	依題分	Special subjects
730	**繪畫**	**Arts of design**
731	繪畫材料與畫法	Technique
732	彩色	Color
733	素畫	Drawing　Design
734	彩畫	Painting
735	依畫面分	By surfaces
736	依派別分	By style
737	依畫題分	By subject
738	書本彩飾	Illuminating of manuscripts and books
739	書法	Calligraphy

740	**板刻　板畫**	**Engraving**
741	木板	Wood engraving　Xylography
742	金屬板	Metal engraving
743	石印	Lithography
744	五彩石印	Chromolithography
745	其他彩色印	Color printing other than lithographic
746	機器板	Photo-mechanical engraving
747	謄寫板	Mimeography
748		
749	印刷板	Printing of engravings
750	**攝影　照像**	**Photography**
751	攝影光學	Photo-optics
752	攝影化學	Photo-chemistry
753	攝影器具	Apparatus　Materials
754	攝影術	Processes　Photographing
755	陰攝法	Negative processes
756	陽攝法	Positive processes
757		
758	各種攝影	Special applications
759	照片蒐集與收藏	Collections of photos
760	**工藝美術**	**Art applied to industry**
761	美術與技藝運動	Arts and crafts movement
762	裝潢與飾品	Decoration and ornament
763	室內裝飾	Interior decoration
764	陶瓷　七寶	Ceramics
765	服裝	Costume and its accessories
766	木器	Woodwork
767	珠寶	Glyptic arts: gems, jade, etc.

768	金器	Metal-work
769	其他	Others

770　音樂　　　　　　　　Music（Literature and scores）

771	歌曲　歌唱	Song collections
772	聖樂	Sacred music　Religious
773	劇樂　舞樂	Dramatic music　Opera
774	管樂	Wind instruments
775	絃樂	Stringed instruments
776	鍵樂	Keyboard instruments
777	打樂　機械樂	Percussions and mechanical instruments
778	其他樂與樂器	Other instruments
779	管絃樂合奏	Instrumental ensemble

780　演劇　戲園　　　　　Expressive arts　Theatre

781	戲劇表演	Art of theatre　Technique
782	悲劇與喜劇	Tragedy and comedy
783	歌劇	Opera
784	話劇	Prose drama
785	滑稽戲	Farces　Operette
786	街道演劇	Pageants, masques, etc.
787	傀儡戲	Marionettes, puppet plays
788	電影	Moving pictures　Movies
789	其他	Other expressive arts

790　游藝　娛樂　　　　　Recreative arts　Amusements

791	節會	Season and day festivals
792	舞蹈	Dancing　Balls
793	運動會	Public games and sports
794	智力游戲	Games of skill

795	機遇游戲	Games of chance
796	文虎　酒令	
797	武術	Fighting sports
798	馬術　賽馬	Horsemanship　Racing
799	其他游戲	Other recreative arts

文　學　Literature

800	**文學**	**Literature**
801	詩	Poetry
802	戲曲	Drama
803	小說	Fiction
804	民間文學	Folk literature
805	兒童文學	Juvenile literature
806		
807	散文	Prose
808	其他文學	Other kinds of literature
809		
810	**中國文學**	**Chinese literature**
811	韻文	Chinese verses
812	曲　戲劇	Chinese drama
813	小說	Chinese fiction
814	民間文學	Chinese folk literature
815	兒童文學	Chinese juvenile literature
816		
817	駢散文	Chinese prose　Essays

818	其他文學	Chinese other literatures
819	滿蒙回藏等文學	Literature in the languages of Manchuria, Mongolia, Tibet, etc.
820	**日本文學**	**Japanese literature**
821	韻文	Japanese verses
822	戲曲	Japanese drama
823	小說　物語	Japanese fiction
824	民間文學	Japanese folk literature
825	兒童文學	Japanese juvenile literature
826		
827	散文　日記　隨筆	Japanese prose, journal, sayings
828	其他文學	Japanese other literatures
830	**希臘,拉丁,羅馬文學**	**Greek, Latin, and Romance literatures**
831	希臘文學	Greek literature
832	拉丁文學	Latin literature
833	意國文學	Italian literature
834		
835	西班牙文學	Spanish literature
836	葡萄牙文學	Portuguese literature
837		
838	羅馬尼亞文學	Rumanian literature
839	其他羅馬文學	Other Romance literatures
840	**法國文學**	**French literature**
841	詩	French poetry
842	戲曲	French drama
843	小說	French fiction
844	民間文學	French folk literature

845	兒童文學	French juvenile literature
846		
847	散文	French prose
848	其他文學	French other literatures
849	法國南部文學	Provencal literature
850	**英國文學**	**English literature**
851	詩	English poetry
852	戲曲	English drama
853	小說	English fiction
854	民間文學	English folk literature
855	兒童文學	English juvenile literature
856		
857	散文	English prose
858	其他文學	English other literatures
859	瑟爾文學	Celtic literatures
860	**美國文學**	**American literature**
861	詩	American poetry
862	戲曲	American drama
863	小說	American fiction
864	民間文學	American folk literature
865	兒童文學	American juvenile literature
866		
867	散文	American prose
868	其他文學	American other literatures
869	坎拿大文學	Canadian literature
870	**德國文學**	**German literature**
871	詩	German poetry

872	戲曲	German drama
873	小說	German fiction
874	民間文學	German folk literature
875	兒童文學	German juvenile literature
876		
877	散文	German prose
878	其他文學	German other literatures
879	條頓族其他各國文學	Literature of other Teutonic countries
880	**俄國文學**	**Russian literature**
881	詩	Russian poetry
882	戲曲	Russian drama
883	小說	Russian fiction
884	民間文學	Russian folk literature
885	兒童文學	Russian juvenile literature
886		
887	散文	Russian prose
888	其他文學	Russian other literature
889	斯拉夫族其他各國文學	Literature of other Slavic countries
890	**其他各國文學**	**Literature of other Languages**
891	印度支那語系各國文學	Literature of Indo-Chinese languages
892	烏拉阿爾泰語系各國文學	Literature of Ural-Altaic languages
893	印歐語系各國文學	Literature of Indo-European lauguages
894		
895	塞姆語系各國文學	Literature of Semitic languages
896	含族語系各國文學	Literature of Hamitic languages
897		

898
899

歷　史　History

900　**歷史**　　　　　　　　　　**History**
901　　史料　　　　　　　　　Historical data
902　　文化史　　　　　　　　History of civilization and culture
903
904
905
906
907
908
909　　亞洲史　　　　　　　　History of Asia
910　**中國史**　　　　　　　　**Chinese history**
911　　先秦及秦代　　　　　　Pre-Ch'in and Ch'in dynasties
912　　兩漢　　　　　　　　　Han dynasty
913　　魏晉六朝隋　　　　　　Wei, Chin, the Six dynasties and Sui
914　　唐五代　　　　　　　　T'ang and the Five dynasties
915　　宋遼金夏元　　　　　　Sung, Liao, Ching, Hsia, and Yuan dynasties
916　　明　　　　　　　　　　Ming dynasty
917　　清　　　　　　　　　　Ch'ing dynasty
918　　民國　　　　　　　　　The Republic of China
920　**亞洲其他各國史**　　　　**History of other Asiatic Countries**
921　　日本史　　　　　　　　Japanese History

922	高麗史	History of Korea
923	印度史	History of India
924	印度支那半島史	Farther India
925	波斯史	History of Persia
926	土耳其史	Turkish or Ottoman Empire
927	阿剌伯史	History of Arabia
928	小亞西亞其他各國史	History of Asia Minor
929		
930	**歐洲史**	**European history**
931	希臘史	Greek（Hells）history
932	羅馬史　意大利史	Rome　Italy
933	西班牙史　葡萄牙史	Spain　Portugal
934	法國史	France
935	英國史　大英史	England　Great Britain
936		
937	德國史	German
938	俄國史	Russia（Union of Socialist Soviet Republics）
939	歐洲其他各國史	History of other European countries
940	**美洲史**	**American history（General）**
941	美國史	History of the United States of America
942	坎拿大史	Canada　British America
943	北美洲其他各國史	History of other North American countries
944	墨西哥史	Mexico
945	西班牙美洲史　拉丁美洲史	Spanish America　Latin America
946	中美洲各國史	Central America
947	西印度群島史	West Indies

948	南美洲各國史	South America
949		
950	**非洲史**	**Africa**
951	埃及史	Egypt
952	阿比西尼亞史	Abyssinia Ethiopia
953	摩洛哥史	Morocco
954	北非東非其他各國史	History of other North and East Africa
955	西非各國史	West Africa
956	中非各國史	Central Africa
957	南非各國史	South Africa
958		
959	大洋洲史	Oceania　Polar regions
960	**紋章學**	**Heraldry**
961	國家紋章	Public and official heraldry
962	宗教紋章	Ecclesiastical and sacred heraldry
963	家庭紋章	Family heraldry
964	特殊組織紋章	Heraldry of special institution
965	特殊階級紋章	Heraldry of special classes
966	勳爵　勳位	Honor, rank, precedence, etc.
967		
968	皇室	Royalty
969	依國分	By country
970	**傳記　總傳**	**Biography, general**
971	中國傳記	Chinese biography
972-5	其他各國傳記	Biography of other countries
976		
977	系譜學	Genealogy
978		

979	別傳　個人傳記	Individual biography
980	**地理**	**Geography**
981	中國地理	Chinese geography
982	亞洲其他各國地理	Geography or other Asiatic countries
983	歐洲地理	Geography of Europe
984	美洲地理	American geography
985	非洲大洋洲地理	Geography of Africa and Oceania countries
986		
987		
988		
989		
990	**考古學**	**Archaeology**
	古物學	**Antiquities**
991	中国考古学	Chinese archaeology
992-9	其他各國考古学	Archaeology of other countries

詳 表
Complete tables

INCLUDING ALL THE
SUBSECTIONS

000 紀念藏　特藏　Memorial or special collections

001　黨義特藏　　　　The Chinese Nationalist collections

　　　　孫中山著述及國民　　Works of and on Dr. Sun Yat-sen
　　　　黨刊物單獨典藏依　　and the Nationalist Party publica-
　　　　下列分, 否則按其　　tions classified as follows, or with
　　　　性質分入各類　　　　the subject if prefer the other way.

.03　　語術　　　　　　　　Dictionaries of terms

.07　　研究　方法　　　　　Studies

.08　　總集　　　　　　　　Collected works

.088　　小冊　　　　　　　Pamphlets

.1　　孫中山　　　　　　　Sun Yatsen, Dr.

.101　　哲學　　　　　　　Philosophy

.108　　總集　全書　　　　Complete works

.11　　孫中山主義　　　　　Sunyatsenism
　　　　三民主義　　　　　　San Min Chu I

.111　　孫中山主義與世界主義　Sunyatsenism and internationalism

.112　　孫中山主義與共產主義　Sunyatsenism and communism

.114　　孫中山主義與資本主義　Sunyatsenism and capitalism

.115　　孫中山主義與帝國主義　Sunyatsenism and imperialism

.117　　孫中山主義與其他社會　Sunyatsenism in relation to other system of
　　　　主義　　　　　　　　socialism

.119　　孫中山主義與他學科　　Sunyatsenism in relation to other sciences

.12　　民族主義　　　　　　Min-ts'u(The principle of the people's nationalism)

.13　　民權主義　　　　　　Min-ch'uan(The principle of the people's sovereignty)

　　1. 選舉　　　　　　　　Suffrage

	2. 罷免		Recall
	3. 創制		Initiative
	4. 複決		Referendum
	5. 立法		Legislative
	6. 司法		Judicial
	7. 行政		Executive
	8. 監察		Censorship
	9. 考試		Civil service examination
.14	民生主義		Min-sen (The principle of the people's livelihood)
.141	平均地權		The equalization of landownership
.142	節制資本		The regulation of capital
.143	民生問題		Livelihood, problems of
.144	衣		Clothes
.145	食		Food
.146	住		Shelter
.147	行		Road
.15	建國大綱	建國方略	Principles of and plans for national reconstruction
.151	建國大綱		Principles of national reconstruction
.152	軍政時期		The period of military operations
.153	訓政時期		The period of political tutelage
.154	憲政時期		The period of constitutional government
.155	建國方略		Plans for national reconstruction
.156	心理建設		Spiritual (morally)
.157	物質建設		Material
.158	社會建設		Social
.159	國家建設		National
.16	五權憲法		The constitution of five powers
	1. 立法		Legislative
	2. 司法		Judicial

	3. 行政	Executive
	4. 監察	Censorship
	5. 考試	Civil service examination
.17	孫中山政策及宣言	Dr. Sun's policies and proclaimations
.171	對內　自由	Internal reconstruction: freedom of the people
.172	對外　平等	Foren policy: racial equality and national independence
.173	聯俄	Alliance with Soviet Russia
.174	容共	Alliance with the communist party
.175	農工	Development of agricultural and industrial enterprises
.176	國民大會	The national assembly
.177	廢除不平等條約	Abrogation of unequal treaties
.18	孫中山文集	Literary works of Dr. Sun
.181	函牘	Letters
.183	箴言	Maxims　Aphorisms
.184	演講集	Orations
.187	散文	Essays
.188	雜集	Miscellany
.189	墨迹	Autographs
.19	孫中山傳記	Biography of Dr. Sun
.191	言行錄　語錄	Words of Dr. Sun Agrapha
.192	肖像　像讚	Portraits
.193	年譜	Chronology
.194	系譜　家傳	Dr. Sun's family
.195	軼事　小傳	Narratives
.196	事業	Career
	其關係中國者	
	其關係弱小民族者	
	其關係全世界者	

.197	遺教　遺囑	Will and testament
.198	紀念	Dr. Sun's memorial services
.199	陵墓　墓誌	Epitaphy
.2	國民黨	The Kuomintang (The Nationalist party)
.201	理論　關係	Theories Relations
.202		
.203	辭書	Dictionaries
.2037	年鑑	Yearbooks
.204	評論	Criticism
.205	雜誌	Periodicals
.206	會議　紀錄	Party congresses Proceedings and transactions
.207	研究:綱要,綱目,問答,等	Study and teaching: Outlines, syllabi, questions, etc.
.208	總集　小冊	Miscellaneous printed matter
.209	黨史	History
.21	黨規　黨綱	Rules and regulations
.22	組織　制度	Organization Administration
	例　中央集權與地方分權制	e.g. Administrative centralization and separation of powers
.221	代表大會	Plenary session
.222	主席團	The chairman
.223	祕書廳	The secretariat
.224	委員會	The committees
	監察,執行,常務,等	The Control, the Executive, the Standard committees, etc.
.24	黨員　黨籍	The Party members Membership
.241	資格	Qualifications
.243	代表	Representatives
.245	選舉	Suffrage

.25	政策　宣言	Policy　Manifesto
.26	宣傳	Publicity
.27		
.28	黨徽　黨旗　關防	The Party symbolism　Emblems of the Party: flags, seals, etc.
	黨儀　黨歌	
.29	黨派	Special sects of the Party
	例　左派,右派,等	e.g. The left and right parties, etc.
.3	中央黨部　中央執行委員會	The Central Party　The Central Executive Committee
.31	組織部	Department of organization
.32	宣傳部	Department of publicity
.33	農民部	Farmers' department
.34	勞工部	Workers' department
.35	商民部	Merchants' department
.36	婦女部	Women's department
.37	青年部	Youths' department
.4	地方黨部	The Local Party
.41	省黨部	Provincial
	仿中央黨部分	subd. as The Central Party
.42	市黨部	Municipal
	仝上	subd. as above
.43	縣黨部	District
	仝上	subd. as above
.44	區黨部	
	仝上	
.45	國外分黨部	The Oversea Branch Party
	仝上	subd. as above
.5	特殊黨部	

	例　海陸軍,學校,等黨部	
.7	黨教育	The Party education
	必要時仿教育細分見 330	subd. as education when in necessity see 330
.8	黨員著述	Literary works of the Party members
	其關係黨與黨革命者	in relation to the Party and revolution
	必要時仿文學類分見 800	subd. as literature when in necessity see 800
.9	黨革命運動	History and movement of the Party revolution
.91	方法	Methods
	類如文字宣傳,政治外交活動,軍事行動,等	e.g. Propaganda, political and diplomatic activities, military operations, etc.
.92	目的	Aims
	類如國民,國家,種族平等	e.g. Freedom of the people, racial equality, national independence, etc.
.93	革命與社會	Revolution and the society
	關係經濟,教育等者	in relation to economics, education, etc.
.94	革命與政治	Revolution and the government
.95	革命與階級	Revolution and the class problem
.96	革命與種族	Revolution and the race problem
.97		
.98	革命與文藝	Revolution and literature
.99	革命與民眾　民眾運動	People's movement　Movements of farmers
.991	農民運動	Movements of farmers
.992	勞工運動	Movements of workers
.993	商民運動	Movements of merchants
.994	學生運動	Students' movements
.995	婦女運動	Women's movements

.996	青年運動		Youths' movements
.997			
.998			
.999	其他		Others

009　善本特藏　　　　　　Speial collections of book　rarities

.1	古刻本		Early printed book Incunabula
.11	原刻本		First editions
.111	宋刻本		Sung editions
.113	遼金刻本		Editions of Liao and Ching
.115	元刻本		Yuan editions
.116	明刻本		Ming editions
.117	清刻本		Ch'ing editions
.12	翻刻本		Reprint editions
.121	元覆宋本		of Sung editions at Yuan dynasty
.123	明覆宋本		of Sung editions at Ming dynasty
.125	明覆元本		of Yuan editions at Ming dynasty
.13	影印本		Photogravure editions
.15	寫刻本		Copy books in print
.151	宋		of Sung print
.153	元		of Yuan print
.156	明		of Ming print
.157	清		of Ch'ing print
.16	舊刻本		Old editions
	不詳年代之刻本類此		Books with unknown date of publishing to be clast here
.17	補修本		Repairing editions
	例　百衲本,南監本,等		
.19	國外刻本		Early foreign editions

	例　高麗,日本古刻本	e.g. Early Korea, Japan editions
.2	精刻本	Fine editions
	前清以來刻板,字體,紙質,印刷,裝訂插圖精美者類此顯微本亦類此	Books of rare type, binding, illustrations, materials, high priced, and editions deluxe. Class here also microscopic edition, dwarf books, etc.
.3	古寫本　古抄本	Early copy books
.31	定本	
.32	稿本　手稿本	Old manuscripts　Autographs
.35	影寫本	Photogravure copy books
.36	舊抄本	Old copy books
.37	精抄本	Fine copy books
.4	搨本	Rubbing editions
.5	批校本	Books with critical notes and identifications of celebrated writers
.6	逸書　孤本　禁毀等	Lost, Unique, Prohibited books
.61	逸書	Lost books
.63	孤本	Unique copies
.65	奇特	Books curiosa
.67	禁毀	Prohibited, condemned, expurgated books
	凡宗教或政府禁止之書籍以及坊間祕密私售各書均類此	Books proscribed as contrary to church faith, morality, government or social peace that condemned by religious and civil powers. Class here also obscure books sold secretly
.7		

.8	滿蒙回藏文	Books in languages of Manchurian, Mongolian, etc.
.81	滿文	Manchurian
.82	蒙文	Mongolian
.83	回文	Turki
.84	藏文	Tibetan
.86	西夏文	
.87	苗猺文	Aboriginal; Mao, T'ung, etc.
.9	外國善本	Book rarities in foreign languages
	依國分	By country
	例　英文善本書 009.95	e.g. Books rarities in English 009.95
	必要時仿上細分	May be subd. as above

010-090 總類   General works

010　圖書學　目錄學　　Science of books   Bibliography

.1　　寫本　　　　　　　The copy books
.11　　板書　　　　　　　Block volume
.12　　　瓦書　　　　　　　　of terra-cotta
.13　　　臘板　　　　　　　　of diptycha
.14　　　竹簡　　　　　　　　of bamboo
.15　　　木簡　　　　　　　　of wood
.17　　卷本　軸本　　　　Scapus volume
.18　　摺本　　　　　　　Folded roll
.19　　依國分　　　　　　By country
.3　　印本　　　　　　　The print books
.31　　木板　　　　　　　Block-books   Xylography
.33　　石印　　　　　　　Lithography
.34　　活字板　　　　　　Typography
　　　　例　鉛印,等
.37　　影印　　　　　　　Photogravure
.39　　依國分　　　　　　By country
.4　　本書　　　　　　　The text decorations and art of the
　　　　　　　　　　　　　　text
　　　封面,序跋,篇目,等之   works on the title page, preface, contents,
　　　叙述類此　　　　　　etc. to be clast here
.41　　著者　　　　　　　Author Authorship
　　　著者考證,辨偽,等
.42　　書名　　　　　　　Title
　　　書名異同,變衍,等　　The different titles of same text, its varia-
　　　　　　　　　　　　　tions, etc.
.43　　出版　　　　　　　Imprint   Publishing

		出版期,出版處,出版者,版次,版權,等	Date of publication, publishing place, publisher, edition, copyright, etc.
.44		卷册	Collation
		卷數　册數　葉數	Volumes Pages
.45		款式	Form
		行格,版框,版心,墨口,等	Columns, margins, printed edges, etc.
.46		篇幅	Size
		四開本,八開本,巾箱本,等	Quarto, octavo, minute size, etc.
.47		紙質　紙色	Sheets: Sheets of nickel, colors of sheets, etc.
.48		插圖	Illuminations, miniature paintings, etc.
.49		其他	Others
		例　字體:宋體字,黑體字,等	e. g. Capitals: Sung capitals, black-letter capitals, etc.
		卷纏	Clasps
.6		書寫	Writing
.61		漆書	Lacquer writing
.63		墨寫	Ink writing
.65		打字　見 626.7	Typewriting　see 626.7
.69		依國分	By country
.7		印刷　印刷史	Printing　Printing history
		排版,校對,印刷工作,等	Type-founding, Proof-reading, Presswork, etc.
.79		依國分	By country
		例　中國印刷史 010.791	Chinese printing-History 010.791
.8		裝潢　裝訂	Book-binding
.81		裝訂術	Arts of binding

	.82	訂本	Stabbed binding
	.84	依體制分	By forms
		例　毛裝	
	.85	依材料分	By materials used
		例　皮裝	e.g. Vellum binding
	.86	依應用分	By purposes
		例　圖書館裝	e.g. Library binding
	.88	其他	Other kinds of binding
	.89	依國分	By country
		例　中裝 010.891	e.g. Chinese binding 010.891
		和裝 010.892	Japanese binding 010.892
		高麗裝 010.893	Korea binding 010.893
	.9	國書史	History of the book
	.91	藏書記　印記	Book plates and other signs of ownership (ex-libris)
	.97	考訂(校勘　鑒別款識)	Criticisms, identifications, etc. of the book
011		普通目錄　書目彙刻	General bibliography　Catalogs
	.1	書目之書目	Bibliography of bibliography
	.3	學校出版書目	Of school publications
	.6	會社出版書目	Of society publications
	.7		
	.8	書店書目	Publishers' catalogs
	.9	譯書目錄	Translator catalogs
012		圖書館目錄	Library catalogs
	.1	分類目錄	Classified catalogs
	.2	著者目錄	Author catalogs

	.3	書名目錄	Title catalogs
	.4	標題目錄	Subject catalogs
	.5	檢字目錄	Dictionary catalogs
	.6	字母	Alphabetically
	.7	四角號碼	Four corner system
	.8	筆畫	Number of strokes
	.9	其他	Others
013		國別目錄	National bibliography
		本國人寓外國所著之書之目	Books by oversea authors
		外人用其國文字所著之書之目	Books written in the language of that country by foreigner
		關於其國之書之書	That country as subject
	.1	中國國家目錄	Chinese national bibliography
	.11	中央	Central government
	.12	地方	Local government
	.13	省	Provincial
	.14	市	Municipal
	.15	縣	District
	.19	依朝代分	By dynasty
	.2-.9	其他各國國家目錄	National bibliography of other countries
		各國皆可仿中國細分	Subd. as China
014			
015		自著書目	Personal（individual）bibliography
016		族姓書目	Family author bibliography

	合著書目	Joint author bibliography
017	類別書目	Subject (clast) bibliography
	依類分或析入各類	Class by or with the subject
	例　哲學書目	e.g. Bibliography of philosophy
018	特種書目	Bibliography, special
.1	知見　經眼	Of books recommended
.2	憶想	Of imaginary books
.3	隱名　別名	Of books by pseud authors
.4	偽書	Of books of false authors
.5	名著	Best book lists
.6	修學　參考	Lists of reference books
.7	展覽	Bibliography on exhibition
.8		
.9		
019	善本書目	Bibliography of book rarities
.1	古刻本	Of early printed books
	細分　參看　009.1	for subd. see 009.1
.2	精刻本	Of fine editions
.3	古寫本	Of early copy books
.4	搨本	Of rubbing editions
.5	批校本	Of books with critical notes and identifications of celebrated writers
.6	逸書,孤本,禁毀	Of lost, unique, prohibited books
.7		
.8	滿蒙回藏文	Of books in languages of Manchurian, Mongolian, etc.

.9	外國文	Of book rarities in foreign languages
020	圖書館學	Library science　Library economy
.1	理論　關係	Theories　Relations
.11	目的　效用	Scope　Usefulness
.15	心理	Psychology
.18	倫理	Ethics　Library morals
.19	圖書館與其他關係	Library in relation to other sciences and topics
.191	圖書館與社會	In relation to society
.193	圖書館與教育	In relation to education
.195	圖書館與個人	In relation to individual
.197	圖書館與文化	In relation to culture
.3	字典　語術	Dictionaries of library terms
.36	索引	Index
.37	年鑑	Yearbooks
.4	評論	Critiques　Criticism
.5	雜誌	Periodicals
.6	會議　協會　報告　依國分	Societies　Associations　Report　By country
	例　中國圖書館協會　020.61	e.g. The Chinese library associations 020.61
.7	展覽	Library exhibitions
.8	總集　文藝	Collected works　Library literature
.9	歷史	History
.91-.95	依國分	By country
	例　美國圖書館史 020.941	e.g. U.S.—Library history 020.941

.97 傳記 Biography
　　　其關係圖書館事業者

022 圖書館行政與組織 Library administration and organization

.1 創設與維持 Founding and maintaining
.2 法規 Library legislation
.3 董事會　委員會 Governing board　Library committees
.4 經費 Library finance
　　圖書館會計 Library bookkeeping
.5 館員　婦女館員 Personnel: librarian, staff, women in library service
　　資格,待遇,等 Qualifications, salaries, etc.
.6 規則 Library rules and regulations
.7 推廣　宣傳 Library extension, commissions Publicity works, advertising
.8
.9 檔案　印刷品 Library documents, correspondence, stationery, etc.

023 圖書館管理 Library management

.1 選購 Acquisition (selection, purchase, exchange, gifts, etc.)
.2 登錄 Accession
.3 分類 Classification
.4 編目 Cataloguing
.5 典藏 Shelving, arrangement, etc.

.6	出納	Circulation, loans, charging systems, etc.
.7	參考	Reference, consultation, etc.
.8	雜誌,小冊,雜件等之處理	Treatment of periodicals, pamphlets, and other materials
.9	裝訂,修理,保存	Binding, Repairing, Conservation
	曝書,消毒,書敵：虫蝕,水濕,等	Exposure, Enemies of books: heat, moisture, bookworms, etc.

024　圖書館建築與設備　　Library building

.1	位置　坐落	Location, site, etc.
.2	材料保護	Material, protection
.3	設計　構造	Design　Plans　Construction
.4	書庫　書架	Storage and shelving
.5	閱覽室	Reading rooms
.6	辦公室及其他各室	Administration and special rooms
.7	光線　溫度　通氣	Lighting　Heating　Ventilation
.8	用品　器具	Fixtures, furniture, fittings
.9		

025　普通圖書館　　General libraries

.1	私家藏書	Private and family
.2	學校圖書館	School libraries
.21	大學	College, university
.23	中學	Secondary
.25	小學	Primary
.3	公共圖書館	Public libraries
.31	國立	National
.33	省立	Provincial

	.34	市立	Municipal
	.35	縣立	District
	.36	鄉立	County and rural libraries
	.4	巡迴圖書館	Traveling libraries
	.5	營利圖書館	Proprietary, subscription libraries
	.6	團體,會社圖書館	Society, club libraries
	.7	特種人圖書館	Libraries for special classes
	.71	民衆	People's or popular library
	.72	兒童	Children's library
	.73	婦女	Women's library
	.74	工人	Workmen's library
	.75	戰地　隨營	Library war service
	.76	監獄	Prison library
	.77	慈善	Asylum library
	.78	殘廢　盲啞	Defectives' library
	.8	閱報室　閱書室	Free newsrooms　Reading rooms
026		專門圖書館	Libraries on special subjects
		依類分	By subjects
		例　佛教圖書館　026.23	e.g. Buddhist library　026.23
027		圖書及圖書館使用法	Use of books and libraries
	.1	閱者指導	Aids to readers
	.2	館務用具使用法	Laborsaving tools and devices
	.3	參考書用法	Use of reference books
	.4		
	.5	讀書法　互見337.9	Methods of reading, studing, etc. see also 337.9

.6

.7 　剪裁法　　　　　　　Clippings　Scrapbooks or files

.8 　筆記法　　　　　　　Notebooks, notetaking, etc.

.9 　索引檢字法　見 036　Indexing　Index rerums Etc.
　　　　　　　　　　　　see 036

028　圖書館學校　　　　Library school

.1 　行政　　　　　　　　School administration

　　　法令,制度,行政,經　Laws, systems, administration, fi-
　　　費,等　　　　　　　nance, etc.

.2 　管理　　　　　　　　Management

　　　校規,訓育,衛生,體　Rules and regulations, discipline,
　　　育,設備,等　　　　 hygiene, physical training, equip-
　　　　　　　　　　　　ment, etc.

.4 　學則　　　　　　　　School standardization

　　　入學,學年,鐘點,考　Admission, calendar year, hours, ex-
　　　試,升學,畢業,等　　aminations, promotion, graduation,
　　　　　　　　　　　　etc.

.5 　課程　　　　　　　　Curriculum Course of study

　　　教材,專修,兼修,旁　Subjects of study, single course, par-
　　　聽,等　　　　　　　allel courses, etc.

.6 　教員　　　　　　　　Teachers　Professors　Instructors

　　　任務,資格,聘任,待　Qualifications, personality, appoint-
　　　遇,教授與職業,婦女　ment, salaries, teaching as a profes-
　　　教員,等　　　　　　sion, women as teachers, etc.

.7 　教授法　　　　　　　Methods of instruction

　　　問答,實習,以及分　Art of questioning, laboratory meth-
　　　級,個性,各科,校外　od, individual instruction, floating
　　　教授法,等　　　　　schools, etc.

.8	暑期學校	Summer schools
	函授學校	Correspondence school
.9	檔案　校刊	School documents and publications
	校章,公文,指南,同學錄,文卷,雜錄,校史	Charter and statutes, directories, bulletins, alumni, thesis miscellany, and history
030	普通百科辭書	Encyclopedias, general
	專門辭書應入各專類	Technical encyclopedias to be clast with the subjects
	例　化學辭書　540.03	e.g. Encyclopedia of chemistry 540.03
031	中國普通百科辭書	Chinese encyclopedia, general
	依下例分	subd. as follows：
.2	部首	Radical system
.3	韻目	Rime system
.4	歲時	Chronological system
.5		
.6	筆畫　號碼　記數	Stroke and numeral systems
.7		
.8	類別　類書	Subject or clase system
032	亞洲其他各國普通百科辭書	General encyclopedias of other Asiatic countries
033	歐洲各國普通百科辭書	General encyclopedias of European countries
034	美洲各國普通百科辭書	General encyclopedias of American countries

035	非洲大洋洲各國普通百科辭書	General encyclopedias of African and Oceanian countries
036	索引　檢字	Indexes and indexing
	1. 依類分	1. subd. by subjects
	例　農業索引　036.61	e.g. Agricultural index 036.61
	2. 如析分	2. If prefer separately
	普通索引類此	This for general only
	專門索引各入其類	Techniques go with the subjects
	例　工程索引　650.036	e.g. Engineering index 650.036
	3. 本書索引應與該書同類	3. Indexes to particular works are classified with the works
	例　全唐詩引得	e.g. Index of the poetry of T'aug dynasty
037	年鑑	Yearbooks　Almanacs
	各類年鑑應入其類	Technical yearbooks under special subjects
	例　工業年鑑　640.037	e.g. Industrial yearbooks 640.037
.1	中國年鑑	China yearbooks almanacs
	依區域分	By local subdivision
	例　東三省年鑑　037.12	e.g. Yearbooks of the three Eastern Provinces of the Republic of China 037.12
.2	亞洲其他各國年鑑	Yearbooks of other Asiatic countries
.3	歐洲各國年鑑	Yearbooks of European countries
.4	美洲各國年鑑	Yearbooks of American countries
.5	非洲大洋洲各國年鑑	Yearbooks of African and Oceanian countries
.7	特種人年鑑	Yearbooks or almanacs for special classes of persons

例　婦女年鑑	e.g. Women almanacs
注意　專家年鑑應入各專類	Note. Technical under special subjects

.8　紀念年刊　　　　　Annuals　Keepsakes　Etc.

038　指南　業名錄　　　Directories

1. 凡研究指南及其作法諸著述類此	1. This covers only the history, description, and bibliography of directory and directory-making
2. 地方指南以及各專門指南應入各該專類	2. For form-headings see subd. directories under name of places and subjects
例　北平指南	e.g. Peiping—Directories
植物學家指南	Botanists—Directories

039　其他　　　　　　　Others

.3　手册　　　　　　　Pocketbooks, etc.
.6　訊問録　　　　　　Information bureaus
　　　　　　　　　　　　Literary agents
.8　雜訊　　　　　　　Notes and queries

040　報學　報章　　　　Journalism　General newspapers

.1　理論　　　　　　　Theories
.12　目的　效用　　　　Aim　Utility
.13　出版自由　　　　　Liberty of the press　Censorship
.15　心理　　　　　　　Psychology
.18　道德　　　　　　　Ethics　Morals
.19　報與其他關係　　　Relations to others
　　　例　報與政治關係　　　e.g. Newspaper and politics
.2

.3	主權	Ownership and control Newspaper names, Location, Patent insides, Etc.
	名稱,地址,特權,等	
.4	營業部	Business management
	職員,印刷,銷售,費用,收入,等	Staff, printing, sale, expenses, receipts, etc.
.5	編輯部	Editorial management
	社論,新聞,專號,以及通信,投稿,等	Editorials, news, special subjects, and correspondences, contributions, etc.
.6	新聞社	Press clubs　Convention
.7		
.8		
.9	歷史	History of newspapers and journalism
041-9	報章	Newspapers
	依國分	By country
	例　中國報章　041	e.g. Chinese newspapers 041
050	普通雜誌	General periodicals
	依國分	By country
	例　中國普通雜誌　051	e.g. Chinese general periodicals 051
	專門雜誌應分入各專類	Technics under special subjects
	例　哲學雜誌　100.5	e.g. Philosophical periodicals　100.5
	醫學雜誌　590.05	Medical periodicals　590.05
060	普通學會	General learned societies Academies

	專門學會應分入各類	Special under the subjects
	例　政治學會　370.6	e.g. Political societies　370.6

061　中國普通學會　　Chinese learned societies

.1

.2

.3　指南　年鑑　　Directories and lists　Yearbooks

.4　論文　　Essays

.5　雜誌　　Periodicals

.6　會議紀錄　報告　　Congresses　Proceedings and transactions

.7　捐贈　紀念　　Collections：Contributions, memoirs, etc.

.8　總集　小册　　Miscellaneous printed matter

.9

062-9　其他各國普通學會　　General learned societies of other countries

　　　　仿中國細分　　　　subd. as China

070　國學　　National literatures

此項專類闡述一國故有學術（經,史,文,哲,語言,等）者或敘明其範圍或討論其研究方法　　Under this heading is entered only matter dealing with the study of the classics, history, literature, philosophy, languages, antiquities, etc. of one country in a general and comprehensive way, such as scope, methods, and kindred subjects.

071　中國　　Sinology

　　總論　　General treatises

其專論某一類諸作則應入各該類	Treatises on one special subject go with that subject
例　經學　090	e.g. The Chinese Classics 090
072-9　其他各國國學	National literature of other countries
例　日本　072.1	e.g. Nipponology　072.1
希臘　073.1	Hellenology　073.1
埃及　079.1	Egyptology　079.1
080　叢書	Collections　Series collected work
081　中國叢書	Chinese collections
1. 幾種不同類之書籍而各該種均可單獨印行者合刻成一部依下列分	1. Distinct works of one or several authors, treating of different subjects and published in a collection
2. 如某叢書之各種分別印行各該種應按其類分	2. Collected works as mentioned above published separately as of one subject to be clast with the subject
例　胡適：中國哲學史大綱　111.8	e.g. Hu Shih: Outlines of Chinese philosophy 111.8
.04　評論	Critiques
.09　歷史	History
.1　普通叢書	General collections
彙輯他人著作(均可單獨印行)成一部者	Class here only distinct works of several authors on different subjects
例　士禮居叢書	
注意　古刻本或善本合訂應入善本	
依朝代分	By dynasty
.11　宋	Sung

.13 元　　　　　　　　　Yuan

.15 明　　　　　　　　　Ming

.17 清　　　　　　　　　Ch'ing

.18 民國　　　　　　　　The Republic of China

.3 朝代叢書　　　　　　Collected works of special dynasties

　　彙輯歷朝諸家著作成一部　Class here only distinct works of several au-
　　而於該部冠以朝代字樣者　thors on different subjects in a particular
　　　　　　　　　　　　period
　　　　例　漢魏叢書

.4 郡邑叢書　　　　　　Local collections

　　彙輯某省某邑諸家著作成　Class here only distinct works of several au-
　　一部而於該部冠以郡邑字　thors on different subjects of a particular place
　　樣者
　　　　例　湖北叢書

.5 自著叢書　　　　　　Collected works of individuals

　　合刻個人著作或間有收錄
　　他人陳著經本人注解者
　　　　例　王船山遺書

.6 族姓叢書　　　　　　Collected works of family author

　　一姓著作合刻者
　　　　例　汪氏叢書

.7 合著叢書　　　　　　Collected works of joint anthor

　　同姓或異性合著者
　　　　例　顏李叢書

.8 類別叢書　　　　　　Collected works of a particular sub-
　　　　　　　　　　　　ject

　　按叢書既以類名而其內容　Better class with the subject not here
　　又係一類似應各入其類如
　　《皇清經解》入經部《白芙
　　蓉堂叢書》入算學等是

.9 譯書叢書　　　　　　Collected works of translations
　　　外人著作譯成國文而合刻
　　　者
　　　　例　嚴譯叢書

082　亞洲其他各國叢書　Collections of other Asiatic countries

083　歐洲各國叢書　　　Collections of European countries
084　美洲各國叢書　　　Collections of American countries
085　非洲大洋洲各國叢書　Collections of African and Oceanian countries
　　　上列各國叢書皆可仿中國　subd. as Chinese collections
　　　細分

086-9　叢論　隨筆　　　General collected essays　Polygraphy　Etc.

087　叢論　　　　　　　General collected essays
　　　各學科研究論文彙集一　Class here only collected essays include several
　　　部者　　　　　　　　branches of knowledge
.1　中國　　　　　　　Chinese collected essays
.2-.9 其他各國　　　　General collected essays of other countries

088　隨筆　雜記　雜考　Polygraphy　Miscellanies　Extracts　Etc.

　　　凡不屬任何類者　　Class here works not belong to any particular classes
.1　中國　　　　　　　Chinese Miscellanies
.2-.9 其他各國　　　　Polygraphy　Miscellanies of other countries

089
090 經學　經書　　The Chinese Classics

考中國學術皆原於六經（見《莊子·天下篇》），自戰國已然，諸子著述雖各趨極端而所考信依據論難非辯，皆以六經爲的，嗣後漢武設置五經博士，經師講授蔚成專門學科，乃者離析碌裂强納近今圖書分類非惟不易殆不可能，故仍存經部立爲專類

The six Classics had been recognized early in the Warring States (B. C. 481-221) as the fountain of Chinese learning. Chuang tzu in his book "the Empire" wrote thus: "Spread over the whole world, it is focussed in the middle kingdom, and the learning of all schools renders constant homage to its power." In the reign of Emperor Wu of Han Dynasty a special Board was constituted, consisting of literate, who were put in charge of the Five Classics. Since the Han, the successive dynasties have received the Classics as law and scholars of all generations took themselves for life in the studies and discussions of these Canonical Books. It is evident to show how the Classics stand as a particular system of learning; which special branch of knowledge, to my comprehension, is quite independent of itself, inseparable or impracticable to relate the individual Classics under other system of knowledge of our decade

.01　　理論　關係　　　　Theories　Relations
　　　　例　經學與文學　　　　in relation to literature
　　　　　　經學與史學　　　　in relation to history
.02　　圖表　　　　　　　　Charts
.03　　名物考　　　　　　　Classical names
.036　　索引　　　　　　　　Index
.04　　集證　論文　　　　　Criticism and interpretation

.07	研究：綱要，綱目，問答，等	Study and teaching: Outlines, syllabi, synopses, questions, etc.
.08	總集　經解總集	Collected works　Series
	例　皇清經解	e.g. "Explanations of the Classics under the imperial Ch'ing dynasty"
	注意　各經經解，經義，翻譯，等應與本經同類	Note. Commentaries, translations, etc., either of collective or individual classics should be classified with the Classics accordingly
	例　十三經注疏類入 090.7	e.g. "The Thirteen Classics with commentary and explanations" to be clast in 090.7
.09	經學史	History
.097	經學家傳記	Biography
	其關係經學者	that in concerned with the Classics
	下列各經皆可仿上細分	Individual Classics may be subd. as above
.1	五經	The Five Classics
	按五經始於漢置五經博士所詔易，詩，書，禮，春秋	This enumeration originated in the Han Dynasty. The Five Classics are, I; Shih; Shu; Li; and Ch'un Ch'iu
	例　五經本義	e.g. The Five Classis, text and explanations
.2	六經	The Six Classics
	以上五經加周禮爲六經	By addition of Chou Li to the above Five Classics
	例　六經圖	e.g. The Six Classics, with plates
.3	七經	The Seven Classics
	易，詩，書，三禮，春秋	I; Shih; Shou; Chou Li; I Li; Li Chi; Ch'un Ch'iu

　　　　　例　七經精義　　　　　　　e.g. The Seven Classics, with the exact meaning

.4　九經　　　　　　　　　　　The Nine Classics
　　　　易,詩,書,三禮,三傳　　　I; Shih; Shu; Chou Li; I Li; Li Chi; Tso Chuan; KungYang Chuan; KuLiang Chuan

　　　　　例　九經異注　　　　　　e.g. A supplemented commentary on the Nine Classics

.5　十一經　　　　　　　　　　The Eleven Classics
　　　　以上九經加孝經論語　　　By addition of Hsiao Ching and Lun Yu to the above Nine Classics

.6　十二經　　　　　　　　　　The Twelve Classics
　　　　始於唐開平石經　　　　　This enumeration originated with the Stone cut Classics of T'ang Dynasty
　　　　见石經　　　　　　　　　see 090.9

.7　十三經　　　　　　　　　　The Thirteen Classics
　　　　以上十一經加爾雅孟子　　By addition of Erh ya and Mengtzu to the above Eleven Classics
　　　　　例　十三經注疏　　　　　e.g. The Thirteen Classics with commentary and explanations

.8　其他　　　　　　　　　　　Other collections of the Classics
　　　　　例　十四經　　　　　　　The Fourteen Classics
　　　　　　以上十三經加大戴禮　　By addition of the Rites of Senior Tai to the above Thirteen Classics
　　　　小經　　　　　　　　　　The Small Classics
　　　　　大學,中庸,論語,　　　　Ta Hsueh; Chung Yung; Lun yu;
　　　　　孟子,孝經　　　　　　　Meng tzu; Hsiao Ching

.9　石經　　　　　　　　　　　The Stone cut Classics (Classics cut in stone)

按石經有一字、三字、今字之別,現存者尚有三字石經,三石及今字石經(即唐石經,又稱十二經,無孟子),孟子之刊入始自孟蜀石經而十三經之名亦由是始孟蜀石經已殘佚不全,石經十三經今存無缺者僅清乾隆五十九年所立石經

The Classics cut in stone are of several kinds different in enumeration of forms of characters, i.e., of characters in one form, in three forms and in modern form. The Stone cut Classics that have come to us are the one in three forms (but only three tablets) and the one in modern form which also known as the Twelve Classics (without Meng Tzu), or the Stone cut Classics of T'ang Dynasty. The Thirteen Classics cut in stone (Meng Tzu included) was originated in the period of Posterior Shu, but it left behind incomplete. The Thirteen Stone cut Classics that preserved completely to our time is that carved in the reign of Ch'ien Lung of Ch'ing Dynasty.

091　易(周易)　　I Ching (The Book of Changes)

.1　四家易

The four different commentaries of "The Book of Changes"

施讎,孟喜,梁邱賀,京房

經典釋文序錄謂永嘉之亂施氏梁邱之易亡孟京費之易人無傳者,自是四家之學皆亡凡捃拾成帙或考證研究四家易諸作類此

.5　其他經師傳,注,解,等

Commentaries of "The book of Changes" by other famous classical scholars

	依朝代分		By dynasty
.6	翻譯		Translations of the "I"
	依國或文字分		By languages
	例 英譯易經 091.65		e.g. English version 091.65
.7	專篇		Individual works
.71	經		The Text
.75	傳或十翼		The Appendixes or The Ten Wings
.9	逸篇,易緯,等		Lost works, etc.
	連山,歸藏均類此		Lan Shan and Kuei Ch'an also to be clast here

092　書　　　　　　　Shu Ching (The Book of History)

.1	尚書大傳		The Great commentary
	(伏勝之今文尚書)		(Fu Sheng's modern Text)
.2	尚書孔傳		K'ung's commentary
	(孔安國之古文尚書)		(K'ung An-kuo's ancient Text)
.5	書經傳,注,解,等		Commentaries of (The Book of History)
	依朝代分		By dynasty
.6	翻譯		Translations of the "Shu"
	依國或文字分		By languages
	例　法譯尚書 092.64		e.g. French version 092.64
.7	專篇		Individual works
	考六經間有依偽,在未確定作家及依託時代前,暫仍舊説,茲附注如此,容俟再版時分別加以按語		
	例　堯典		e.g. The Canon of Yao
	禹貢		The Tribute of Yu
	洪範		The Great Plan

.9	逸書,書緯,等	Lost books, etc.
	逸周書類此	Class here "The lost Book of Chou"
093	詩	Shih Ching (The Book of Odes)
.1	三家詩	The three different texts of "The Book of Odes"
.11	魯詩故　魯故	The fragments of "The Text of Loo"
	按魯詩亡於晉,凡考證研究諸作以及掇拾成篇者類此	"The text of Loo" perished during the Chin dynasty. Studies of its fragments that remained to be clast here
.12	齊詩故　齊故	The fragments of "The text of Ch'i"
	按齊詩於魏已亡,而其考證研究或掇拾成篇諸作類此	"The text of Ch'i" perished during the Wei dynasty, Studies of its fragments that remained to be clast here
.13	韓詩　韓詩外傳	"The text of Han"
		"The illustrations of the shih"
	按韓詩亡於北宋。現存者僅其外傳而亦非全袟,至其內傳亦間有考證或掇拾成篇者均應類此	"The Text of Han" perished during Northern Sung with the exception of "The illustrations of the Shih," but imcomplete. As for his "Explanation of the text" only fragments now remained. Studies of them also to be clast here.
.2	毛傳(毛詩)	"The Text of Mao"
.3	詩序(毛詩序)	"The preface" to the "Shih" (The great and little prefaces)
.5	其他經師傳,注,解,等	Commentaries on "The Book of Odes" by other famous classical scholars
	依朝代分	By dynasty
.6	翻譯	Translations of the "Shih"

	依國或文字分	By languages
	例　德譯詩經 093.67	e.g. German version 093.67
.7	專篇	Individual works
	風	Fung (Lessons of manners)
	雅	Ya (Major and minor odes of the kingdom)
	頌	Sung (Sacrificial odes and praise odes)
.9	逸篇,詩緯,等	Lost works, etc.
094	禮　三禮	Li Ching (The Book of Rites)
	按三禮之名始於東漢鄭玄三禮注	
.1	周禮　周官	Chou Li (The Chou Rites)
		Chou Kuan (Official book of Chou)
.2	儀禮　士禮	I Li (The Decorum Rites)
		Shi Li (The Rites of Scholars)
.3	禮記	Li Chi (The Record of Rites)
	(小戴禮)	Rites of Junior Tai
.4	大戴禮	Rites of Senior Tai
.5	雜禮	Miscellany
095	樂	Yo Ching (The Book of Music)
	按樂經爲劉歆僞作,不列爲經。然樂經考亦有著述宜類此	A false canon by Liu Hsin and didn't enter as Classics, class here only works on Yo Ching
	注意　樂記一篇屬戴記非即樂經	Note. Yo Chi (The record of Music) belongs to Li Chi and is not Yo Ching
096	春秋	Ch'un Ch'iu (Spring and Autumn Annals)

.1	左傳	Tso Chuan (Commentary on the Ch'un Ch'iu by Tso Ch'iu-ming)
.2	公羊傳	KungYang Chuan (Commentary on the Ch'un Ch'iu by KungYang Kao)
.3	穀梁傳	KuLiang Chuan (Commentary on the Ch'un Ch'iu by KuLiang Ch'ih)
.4	胡氏傳	Hu's Chuan (Commentary on the Ch'un Ch'iu by Hu An-kuo)

按胡氏傳爲宋胡安國撰,有明合左,公,穀,胡稱之爲春秋四傳,故亦另列於此

| .5 | 其他經師傳,注,解,等 | Commentaries on "Spring and Autumn Annals" by other famous classical scholars |

例　毛奇齡之春秋傳　　　e.g. Commentary on "Spring and Autumn
096.58　　　　　　　　　　Annals" by Mao Chi-ling　095.58

| 097 | 孝經 | Hsiao Ching (The Book of Filial Piety) |
| 098 | 四書(四子書) | The Four Books (The Books of the Four Philosophers) |

按四書之稱始自宋朱熹　　　This arrangement originated from Chu Hsi
四書集注　　　　　　　　　"The Four Books, texts and commentaries"

| .1 | 大學 | Ta Hsueh (The Great Learning) |

.2 中庸　　Chung Yung (The Doctrine of the Mean)

.3 論語　　Lun Yu (Confucian Analects)

.4 孟子　　Meng-tzu (The Works of Mencius)

凡研究孟子哲理諸著作應入 111.114

Works on Mencius philosophy clast with 111.114

爾雅

Erh Ya (Nearing the standard) a dictionary of terms

按爾雅、説文、廣韻,自唐志列入甲部小學類,公私書目承襲不易,至有清四庫總目析爲三類 1. 爾雅 2. 説文 3. 廣韻,統屬經部小學類,兹以之彙屬諸語言文字一類,爾雅不另列此

Since the T'ang, Erh Ya, Shuo Wen and Kuang Yun operated as a distinct division "the Small Learning," the successive dynasties adopted it without the least change and in the reign of Chien Lung it was officially divided into three catagories; these are 1. Erh Ya (analogical dictionary), 2. Shuo Wen (graphical dictionary) and 3. Kuang Yun (phonetic dictionary). This triple division made accordingly stands under philology in this System and Erh Ya is not recommendable to be clast here separately

哲學　Philosophy

100　哲學　　　　　　　　　　Philosophy

　　　哲學論著之不入本篇各細類　　Works limited to none of the 9 divisions of this
　　　者列此　　　　　　　　　　class

.1　　理論　關係　　　　　　Theories　Relations
.11　　哲學與心理,倫理,等　　Relation to psychology, ethics, etc.
.12　　哲學與神學,宗教　　　 Relation to theology and religion
.13　　哲學與社會,政治,等　　Relation to sociology, political science, etc.
.15　　哲學與科學　　　　　　Relation to science
.18　　哲學與文藝　　　　　　Relation to literature
.19　　哲學與歷史　　　　　　Relation to history
.3　　辭書　　　　　　　　　Dictionaries
.37　　年鑑　　　　　　　　　Yearbooks
.4　　評論　　　　　　　　　Critiques
.5　　雜誌　　　　　　　　　Periodicals
.7　　研究　方法　　　　　　Study and teaching
　　　綱目,綱要,答問,等　　　Outlines, syllabi, synopses, questions, etc.
.8　　總集　　　　　　　　　Collected works　Polygraphy
　　　小冊　　　　　　　　　Pamphlets
.9　　歷史　　　　　　　　　History
　　　東西哲學史　　　　　　Oriental and Occidental together
　　　　東方哲學史　見 110.9　　History of Oriental philosophy prefer 110.9
　　　　西方哲學史　見 120.9　　History of Occidental philosophy prefer 120.9
　　　　參看 101-109 哲學體系　　See also 101-109 philosophic systems
.91　　古代哲學史　　　　　　Ancient
.92　　中古哲學史　　　　　　Medieval

.93	近世哲學史	Modern
.97	哲學家傳記	Biography
	其爲某一國哲學家之傳記則應入該國	Collective biographies of philosophers of a particular country clast with that country.
	例 中國哲學家傳記 111.09	e. g. Collective biographies of Chinese philosophers 111. 09
	某一哲學家之傳記則入該哲學家專類下	Biographies of individual philosophers clast with the philosophers
	例 柏拉圖傳記 121.41	e.g. Biography of Plato 121. 14
101	哲學體系	System of philosophy
	總論	General treatises
	凡研究哲學體系各論之著述依下列分	Heads 101-109 are for discussion of systems and doctrines as such
	至某哲學家著述論及下列某一類者則入該哲學家專類下不列此	Philosophical works of individual authors of these various schools better go with the individual authors, not here
	例 康德之純粹理性批評應入 127.2 不類此	e. g. Kant's Kritfk der reinen vernunft is 127. 2 and not 105. 5
102	本體數論	According to the number of fundamental principles
.1	一元論	Monism
.2	新一元論	Neo-monism
.3	二元論	Dualism
.4	新二元論	Neo-dualism
.5	多元論	Pluralism
103	本體質論	According to the basis of organization

	.1	唯物論	Materialism
	.3	唯心論	Spiritualism
	.5	並行論	Parallelism
	.7	中立論	Neutralism
	.9	同一論	Identical theory
104		認識緣起	According to the organ and instrument of knowledge
	.1	理知論	Rationalism
	.2	感覺論	Sensationalism
		或依下列分	or clast in the following manner
	.3	直知論	Intuitionalism
	.4	理智論	Intellectualism
	.5	經驗論	Empiricism
	.7	神祕論	Mysticism
105		認識方法	According to the method pursued
	.1	獨斷論	Dogmatism
	.3	懷疑論	Skepticism
	.5	批評論	Criticism
106		認識對象	According to the relationship assumed between subject and object in knowing
	.1	實在論	Realism
	.11	朴素的	Naive
	.13	批評的	Critical
	.15	新實在論	Neo-realism
	.2	觀念論	Idealism

.21	唯我論	Solipsism
.23	主觀論	Subjective
.25	客觀論	Objective
.3	實驗論	Experientialism
.4	實用主義	Pragmatism
.5		
.6	實證論	Positivism
.7	功利論	Utilitarianism
.8	現象論	Phenomenalism

107　宇宙或人類中心　　According to the system of thought, belief, or action which centres about

.1	自然主義	Naturalism
.3	人道主義	Humanism

108　世界與人生價值　　According to the valuation of experience, life, and the world

.1	樂觀論	Optimism
.3	悲觀論	Pessimism
.5	進化論	Evolutionism

109

110　東方哲學　　Oriental philosophy

111　中國哲學　　Chinese philosophy

.01　理論　　　　　　　Theories　Relations
　　例　中國哲學與佛學　　e.g. Chinese philosophy and Buddhism
　　　　中國哲學與其他學術　　In relation to other sciences

.02

.03	辭書	Dictionaries
.037	年鑑	Yearbooks
.04	評論	Critiques
.05	雜誌	Periodicals
	普通哲學雜誌　見 100.5	For general philosophical periodicals see 100.5
.06	學會	Societies
.07	研究　方法	Study and teaching
	綱目,綱要,答問,等	Outlines, syllabi, synopses, questions, etc.
.08	總集	Collected works　Polygraphy
	凡研究或彙輯某一朝哲學諸作則類入該朝	For special dynasty prefer with that dynasty
	例　明儒學案 111.6	e.g. Philosophy of Ming dynasty 111.6
	如類此亦可依朝代細分	If prefer here then subd. by dynasty
	至採用任何方法時必須前後一貫	But uniformity should be observed whichever way is adopted
.09	歷史	History
.091	古代	Ancient
.092	中古	Medieval
.093	近世	Modern
.097	哲學家傳記	Biography, collected
	別傳須與本人同類	Of single philosopher go with individuals
	例　王陽明傳記 111.63	e.g. Biography of Wang Yang-ming 111.63
	注意　如其係普通性質則入普通傳記類	Note. Unless it is too general to be clast here
.1	先秦及秦代哲學	Philosophy of Pre-Ch'in and Ch'in dynasties (B.C.? -202)

a. 下列各家間有僞託在未確定作者及其著述時代前暫仍舊說	a. The scheme under the heads 111.11-111.19 would be observed strictly unless when authorship of pseudepigrapha definitely assigned to
b. 各家著作其全集選集專篇等均依照莎士比亞者細分　見附錄二	b. For scheme of author no. for works of individual philosopher-collections, selections, and separate works see that for Shakespeare's Appendix II
例　全集	A I Complete works
c. 其爲研究各家之著述則依下列細分	c. Works on individual philosopher may be subd. as follows
1. 關係　影響	Relations　Influence
2. 圖表	Charts
3. 語言,體裁,等　　文法,等	Language, style, etc.　　grammar; pronunciation, etc.
4. 評論	Criticism and interpretation
5.	
6. 著作　作品　　稿件　　來源	Authorship　　Manuscripts　Writing Signatures　　Sources
7. 研究　　綱目,綱要,問答,等	Study and teaching　　Outlines, syllabi, synopses, questions, etc.
8. 文藝	Literature
9. 傳記　　語錄　　紀念	Biography　　Words of　　Memoirs

.11	儒家	The Confucian school
.111	孔子	Confucius (B.C. 551-479)
.112	1. 顏淵	Yen Yuan
	2. 子夏	Tzu Hsia
	3. 曾子	Tseng Tzu

	4. 子思		Tzu Szu
.114	孟子		Mencius（B.C. 372-289）
.117	荀子		Hsun Tzu（B.C.? 313-230）
.119	其他		Others
.12	道家		The Taoist school
.121	老子		Lao Tzu（B.C.? 590）
.122	1. 關尹子		Kuan Yin Tzu
	2. 文子		Wen Tzu
.124	楊朱		Yang Chu
.125	列子		Lieh Tzu（B.C.? 400）
.127	莊子		Chuang Tzu（B.C.? 369-290）
.129	其他		Others
.13	墨家		The Mocius school
.131	墨子		Mo Tzu（B.C.? 470-390）
.139	其他		Others
.15	名家 別墨		Ming Chia（Sophists）
.151	鄧析		Teng Hsi（B.C.? -501）
.152	惠施		Hui Shih（B.C.? 380-300）
.153	公孫龍		KungSun Lung（B.C.? 345-255）
.155	宋鈃		Sung Pien
	尹文子		Yin Wen Tzu
.159	其他		Others
.17	法家		Fa Chia（Philosophers on law）
.171	管子		Kuan Tzu（B.C. 706-645）
.173	慎到		Shen Tao
.174	田駢		T'ien P'ien
.175	商鞅		Shang Yang（B.C.? -338）
.176	申不害		Sheng Pu Hai（B.C.? -337）
.177	尸佼		Shih Chiao（B.B.? 380-310）
.178	韓非		Han Fei（B.C.? -233）
.179	其他		Others

.19	雜家	Miscellaneous philosophers
.191	鬻子	Yu Tzu
.192	子華子	Tzu Hua Tzu（B.C.? 550）
.193	晏子	Yen Tzu（B.C.? 493）
.195	鬼谷子	Kuei Ku Tzu
.197	呂不韋	Lu Pu Wei（B.C.? -235）
.198	孔叢子	K'nug Ts'ung Tzu（B.C.? -210）
.199	其他	Others
.2	兩漢哲學	Philosophy of Han dynasty（B.C. 206-A.D. 220）
.21	1. 陸賈	Lu Chia（B.C.? 240-177）
	3. 賈誼	Chia I（B.C.201-169）
	5. 董仲舒	Tung Ch'ung Shu（B.C.? 179-104）
.23	淮南子(劉安)	Huai Nan Tzu（B.C.178-122）
.24	1. 桓寬	Huan K'uan（B.C.? 100）
	3. 劉向	Liu Hsiang（B.C.77-6）
	4. 劉歆	Liu Hsin（B.C.53-A.D. 23）
.25	揚雄	Yang Hsiung（B.C.53-A.D. 18）
.27	王充	Wang Ch'ung（A.D. 27-97）
.28	1. 王符	Wang Fu（A.D. ? -80）
	3. 荀悅	Hsun Yueh（148-209）
	5. 仲長統	ChungCh'ang Tung（179-219）
.29	其他	Others
.3	魏晉六朝隋哲學	Philosophy of Wei, Chin, the Six dynasties, and Sui（220-618）
.33	葛洪	Ko Hung（? 253-333）
.37	文中子(王通)	Wen Chung Tzu(583-617)
.39	其他	Others

.4	唐五代哲學	Philosophy of T'ang and the Five dynasties (618-960)
.5	宋代哲學	Philosophy of Sung dynasty (960-1280)
.51	周敦頤	Chou Tun I (1017-1073)
.52	邵雍	Shao Yung (1011-1077)
.53	張載	Chang Tsai (1020-1077)
.54	二程	The Ch'eng Brothers
.541	程顥	Ch'eng Hao (1032-1085)
.542	程頤	Ch'eng I (1033-1107)
.55	其他北宋哲學家	Other philosophers of Northern Sung
.56	朱熹	Chu Hsi (1130-1200)
.57	陸九淵	Lu Chiu Yuan (1139-1192)
.58	其他南宋哲學家	Other philosophers of Southern Sung
.59	元代哲學	Philosophy of Yuan dynasty (1280-1368)
.6	明代哲學	Philosophy of Ming dynasty (1368-1644)
.63	王守仁	Wang Shou Jen (1472-1528)
.69	其他	Others
.7	清代哲學	Philosophy of Ch'ing dynasty (1644-1912)
.71	清初哲學家	Philosophers of early Ch'ing
.73	顏元	Yen Yuan (1635-1704)
.75	戴震	Tai Chen (1723-1777)
.79	其他	Others
.8	民國哲學	Philosophy of the Republic (1912-)

	民國哲學家著述以及研究其哲學諸作均類下依各哲學家姓氏分	Works of and on the philosophers of the Republic all arranged with anthor nos. of the philosophers
	注意 哲學家之文集或詩集 例胡適詩集則入文學類，前朝如唐之李翱，清之顧炎武等等著作均同此例	Note. Literary works of the philosophers better with the subjects, e.g. Collections of the poetry of Hu Shih be clast with the poetry. So also the same for those of Li Ou of T'ang and Ku Yen Wu of Ching dynasties
112	日本哲學	Japanese philosophy
113	印度哲學	Indian philosophy
	參看佛學	see also Buddhism
115	波斯哲學	Persian philosophy
116	土耳其哲學	Turkish philosophy
117	阿刺伯哲學	Arabian philosophy
118	小亞西亞各國哲學	Philosophy of Asia Minor
.1	巴比倫	Babylonian
.5	希伯來	Hebrew
.7	叙利亞	Syrian
119	埃及哲學及其他東方哲學	Egyptian and Other Oriental philosophy
120	西方哲學	Occidental philosophy
121	希臘哲學	Greek philosophy
.01	希臘哲學與希臘人生文藝之關係	Relation of philosophy to Greek life and literature
.03	希臘哲學與近世思想	Influence of Greek philosophy on modern thought

.09	希臘哲學史	History of Greek philosophy
.1	古代哲學	Early Greek philosophy
.11	愛奧尼學派	Ionic school
	此派以本質爲本體	Materialistic Things are as they seem
.111	泰理士	Thales（7th and 6th B.C.）
.112	亞諾芝曼德	Anaximander（B.C. 611-547）
.113	亞諾芝曼尼	Anaximenes（B.C. 590-525）
.115	赫拉頡利圖士	Heraclitus（B.C. 535-475）
.12	伊利亞學派	Eleatic school
	此派否認存在。	Idealistic Existence denied.
	思維方是實在	Thought is the only reality
.121	芝諾芬尼	Xenophanes（B.C. 570-480）
.123	帕門尼底士	Parmenides（B.C.? 544）
.125	芝諾	Zeno（B.C.? 519）
.127	美里瑟士	Melissus（B.C.? 550）
.13	意大利學派或畢達哥拉士學派	Italic or Pythagorean school
.131	畢達哥拉士	Pythagoras（B.C. 582-507）
.139	其他	Others
.15	亞拿薩哥拉士	Anaxagoras（B.C. 500-428）
.16	恩庇多克士	Empedocles（B.C. 488-424）
.17	原子學派	Atomistic school
.171	盧西波士	Leucippus（B.C. ? 500）
.173	德謨克拉圖士	Democritus（B.C.? 460）
.18		
.19	其他	Other early Greek
.2	蘇格拉底派與反蘇格拉底派	Socratic and Anti-Socratic schools
.21	蘇格拉底	Socrates（B.C. 469-399）
.22	詭辯學派	Sophistic school

.221　　　哥爾期亞　　　　　　　Gorgias（B.C.？485）

.222　　　普洛達哥拉士　　　　　Protegoras（B.C.480-410）

.223　　　希比亞士　　　　　　　Hippias

.225　　　普洛迭克士　　　　　　Prodicus

.23　　小蘇格拉底派　　　　　Demi-Socratic schools

.24　　　犬儒學派　　　　　　Cynic school

.241　　　安梯斯端列士　　　　　Antisthenes（B.C. 444-369）

.249　　　其他　　　　　　　　　Others

.25　　　主樂學派　　　　　　Cyrenaic school

.251　　　亞里斯梯波士　　　　　Aristippus（B.C.？455）

.259　　　其他　　　　　　　　　Others

.26　　　尚辯學派　　　　　　Megaric school

.261　　　歐几里士　　　　　　　Eukleides

.27　　　反蘇格拉底派　　　　Anti-Socratic school

　　　　斯梯爾朋,歐布里士,第　　Stilpon, Eubulides, Diodorus
　　　　阿多洛士

.28　　　伊利安學派　　　　　Elian and Eretrian

　　　　菲多,米尼底墨士,等　　　Phedo, Menedemus, etc.

.3　　柏拉圖與其學院　　　　Plato and his Old Academy

.31　　　柏拉圖　　　　　　　　Plato（B.C. 427-347）

.33　　　斯柏薛包士　　　　　　Speussipus

.34　　　芝諾克拉士　　　　　　Xenocrates

.35　　　博雷蒙　　　　　　　　Polemon

.37　　　克拉士　　　　　　　　Crates

.39　　　其他　　　　　　　　　Others

.4　　亞里斯多德及其學派　　Aristotle and his Lyceum

.41　　　亞里斯多德　　　　　　Aristotle（B.C. 384-322）

.43　　　斯特拉圖　　　　　　　Strato

.49　　　其他　　　　　　　　　Others

.5	希臘羅馬哲學	Greco-Roman philosophy
.51	伊壁鳩魯派	Epicurean school
.511	伊壁鳩魯	Epicurus（B.C. 347-270）
.513	盧克雷梯士	Lucretius
.519	其他	Other
.52	斯多亞派	Stoic school
.521	芝諾	Zeno（B.C. 342-270）
.523	克陵底士	Cleanthes（B.C. 331-251）
.525	克利西波士	Chrysippus（B.C. 281-208）
.529	其他	Others
.53	懷疑派或比羅派	Skepticism　Pyrrhonism
.531	比羅	Pyrrho（B.C.? 320）
.533	泰蒙	Timon（B.C.? 240）
.539	其他	Others
.54	折衷派:西塞祿,等	Eclecticism：Cicero（B.C. 160-13），etc.
.55	新學院派:費羅,等	New Academy：Philo（B.C.? 80），etc.
.56	新畢達哥拉士派 費鳩諾士,等	New-Pythagorean Figulus（B.C.45）,etc.
.57	畢達哥柏拉圖派 普魯達,等	Pythagorean Platonism Plutarch（B.B.? 48），etc.
.58	新柏拉圖派 普洛諾士,等	Neo-Platonic Plotinos（A.D. 204-270）
.59	其他希臘羅馬哲學	Other Greco-Roman philosophy
.6	古代基督教哲學中古哲學	Early Christian and Medieval philosophy
.61	異教派或神秘派	Gnosticism or mystic
.62	教父學派	Patristic

.622	特都里	Tertullian（160-220）
.624	克雷明	Clement（? 270）
.626	阿利堅	Origen（185-254）
.629	其他	Others
.63	經院學派	Scholastic
.633	安塞倫	Anselm（1070-1109）
.635	亞巴拉	Abelard（1079-1142）
.636	亞昆拉士	Aquinas（1225-1275）
.637	司各脫士	Scotus（1265-1303）
.65	阿剌伯哲學　見117	Arabian and Moorish philosophy Mohammedan philosophy see 117
	亞芬倍司	Avempace
	亞維塞那	Avicenna（Ibn Sina）
	亞維羅士	Averroes（Ibn Rusha）
.66	希伯來哲學　見118.5	Hebrew philosophy see 118.5
	亞維塞布諾士	Avecebronus（Ibn Gibirol）
	約瑟	Joseph（Ibn Zaddik）
.69	文藝復興時期哲學	Renaissance（1500-1600）
122	意大利哲學	Italian philosophy
123	西班牙　葡萄牙哲學	Spanish and Portuguese philosophy
124	法國哲學	French philosophy
.1	笛卡兒	Descartes（1596-1650）
.2		
.21	麥爾伯蘭基	Malebranche（1638-1715）
.22	孟德斯鳩	Montesquier（1689-1755）
.23		
.24	拉美特里	La Mettrie（1709-1751）

.25	愛爾法修	Helvetius（1715-1771）
.26	康的亞克	Condillac（1715-1780）
.27	狄戴羅	Diderot（1713-1784）
.28	霍巴昔	Holbach（1723-1789）
.29		
.3	盧梭	Rousseau（1712-1778）
.4	弗耳特耳	Voltaire（1694-1778）
.5		
.51	拉梅內	Lamennais（1782-1845）
.52	孟德比倫	Main de Biran（1765-1824）
.53	喬弗羅	Jouffroy（1796-1842）
.54	柯辛	Cousin（1792-1867）
.55		
.56	李諾維	Renouvier（1818-1903）
.57	芮農	Renan（1823-1892）
.58	聖西門	Saint Simon（1814-1896）
.6	孔德	Comte（1798-1857）
.7	柏格森	Bergson（1859-　）
.9	其他	Other French philosophers
125	英國哲學	English philosophy
.1	培根	Bacon（1561-1626）
.2	霍布士	Hobbes（1588-1679）
.3	陸克	Locke（1632-1704）
.4	柏克立	Berkeley（1685-1753）
.5	休謨	Hume（1711-1776）
.6		
.61	哈特勒	Hartley（1705-1757）

.62 弗格森　　　　　　Ferguson（1710-1776）
.63 黎德　　　　　　　Reid（1710-1796）
.64 邊沁　　　　　　　Bentham（1710-1832）
.65 斯條亞　　　　　　Stewart（1753-1828）
.66 哈密爾敦　　　　　Hamilton（1788-1856）
.67 彌爾　　　　　　　Mill, J.S.（1806-1873）
.68 格林　　　　　　　Green（1836-1882）
.69
.7 斯賓塞　　　　　　Spencer（1820-1903）
.8 羅素　　　　　　　Russell（1872-　）
.9 其他　　　　　　　Others

126　美國哲學　　　American philosophy
.1 殖民時代　　　　　Colonial
　　愛德華士　　　　　　Edwards（1745-1801）
.2 革命時代　　　　　Revolutionary
.3 十九世紀　　　　　19th century
　　愛默生　　　　　　　Emerson, R.W.（1803-1882）
.4 詹姆士　　　　　　James（1842-1910）
.5 羅益世　　　　　　Royce（1855-1916）
.6 桑他亞拿　　　　　Santayana（1863-　）
.7 杜威　　　　　　　Dewey（1859-1932）
.8 白璧德　　　　　　Babbitt（1865-1933）
.9 其他　　　　　　　Others

127　德國哲學　　　German philosophy
.1 來布尼茲　　　　　Leibnitz（1646-1716）
.19 伍爾夫　　　　　　Wolff（1679-1754）
.2 康德　　　　　　　Kant（1724-1804）

	.3	斐希特	Fichte（1762-1814）
	.4	謝林	Schelling（1775-1854）
	.5	黑格爾	Hegel（1770-1821）
	.6	叔本華	Schopenhauer（1788-1860）
	.7		
	.71	雅科俾	Jacobi（1743-1819）
	.72	詩萊爾馬哈	Schleiermacher（1768-1834）
	.73	海巴特	Herbart（1776-1841）
	.74	費希奈爾	Fechner（1801-1887）
	.75	陸宰	Lotze（1817-1882）
	.76	赫克爾	Haechel（1834-1919）
	.77	哈特曼	Hartmann（1842-1906）
	.78	馮特	Wundt（1832-1920）
	.79	其他	Others
	.8	尼采	Nietzsche（1844-1900）
	.9	其他	Others
128		歐洲其他各國哲學	Philosophy of other European countries
	.1	尼柔蘭哲學	Netherland philosophy
		斯賓諾莎	Spinoza（1632-1677）
	.4	瑞士哲學	Swiss philosophy
	.5	奧匈哲學	Austrian philosophy
	.7	斯坎第那維亞哲學	Scandinavian philosophy
	.8	俄國哲學	Russian philosophy
	.9	巴爾幹半島各國哲學	Philosophy of Balkan States
129		西方其他各國哲學	Other Occidental philosophy
130		形上學	Metaphysics

131	認識論	Epistemology　Theory of knowledge　Relation of knowledge to reality
	其關係形上學者	For Metaphysics only
.1	認識緣起	Origin and sources of knowledge
	先天論與後天論	Apriorism and aposteriorism
	理知論與經驗論	Rationalism and empiricism
.2	認識範圍	Limits of konwledge
.3	思想與實有	Thought and reality
.4	認識原理與範疇	Logical principles and fundamental categories
.5	真實與謬誤	Truth and error
.6	認識相對論	Relativity of knowledge
.8	不可知論	The unknowable
.9	信仰　信仰哲學	Belief　Faith　Faith philosophy
132	方法論　互見 141	Methology　See also 141
	知識之哲理分類	Philosophic classification of knowledge
133	本體論	Ontology
.1	"有"之自然性	Nature of being
	"有"之屬性現象論	Attributes of being Phenomenalism
.2	"有"之觀念分析　實體觀念分析	Analysis of idea of being, of substance
.21	存在	Existence
.22	本質	Essence
.3	實體　原素	Substance Monad

	實體一元論	Monism of substance, or concrete monism
.4	偶然　偶然論	Accidents
	偶然之存在	Existence of accident
.5	關係　相對	Relation
	相對之存在	Existence of real relations
.6	動作	Acts Operations
.61	靜態中"有"	being in potentiality
	動態中"有"	Being in act
.63	運動　演化	Motion Evolution
	參看 108.5 演化論	See also 108.5 Evolutionism (philosophic system)
	生物演化	Evolution in biology
.65	變化論	Becoming and change
.7	創造與非創造"有" 非物質	Created and uncreated being Immateriality
.8	"有"之超驗性	Transcendental properties of being
.81	"有"與其超驗性之區別	Distinction between being and its transcendental properties
.82	一　多	Unity　Plurality
	參看 134 宇宙論	see also 134 Cosmology
	一 "有"之超驗性	Unity, transcendental property of all being
.86	真	Truth
	真"有"之超驗性	Truth, transcendental property of all being
.88	善　惡	Goodness　Evil
	參看 180 倫理學	see also 180 ethics
	善"有"之超驗性	Goodness, transcendental property of all being
	惡　善惡相對　惡因	Evil: its relativity, its cause

.89　　美　參看 190 美學　　　　　Beauty see also 190
　　　　美 "有" 之超驗性　　　　　Beauty, transcendental property of all being

134　宇宙論　自然哲學　　Cosmology　Philosophy of nature

自然界, 宇宙, 自然律, 世界起源, 等　　Physical or inorganic from philosophic viewpoint, cosmos, nature, universe, general laws of nature, origin of the world, cosmogony, etc.

其關係哲理者類此
參看 510.1 數理哲學　　Philosophic theories and discussions only see also Philosophy of mathematic processes

.1　　機械論　　　　　Mechanism　Mechanistic theories of the universe
.11　　因果論　　　　　Cause and effect
.13　　決然論或必然論　　　Determinism or necessarianism
.2　　目的論　究竟原因論　Teleology　Final cause
.21　　宿命論　　　　　Predestination
.23　　非決然論或自由論　　Indeterminism or libertarianism
.3
.4　　空間　太虛　　　　Space　Locus　Void
.41　　空間感覺　　　　Space perception
.43　　空間與時間　　　　Space and time
.5　　時間　　　　　　Time　Duration　Eternity
　　　時間與運動之關係　　Relation of time and motion
.6　　運動　變化　變遷　Motion　Change　Transition
　　　參看 133.63　　　　see also 133.63 Motion (in ontology)
.7　　物質　物體　　　　Matter　Body
　　　物質架構　　　　　Matter, structure of
　　　原子論　參看 530.11　Atomism see also 530.11

.8	能　能力	Energy　Force　Power
	物質與運動	Matter and motion
.9	量　數　度	Quantity　Number　Extent
135	心靈哲學　理知心理學	Philosophy of soul　Rational psychology
	用思辨的方法以究討不滅的心靈之存在	To investigate the existence of the soul
.2	心靈之性質與實在	Nature and reality of the soul and mind
.3	物體與心靈	Body and soul or mind
.5	人格論	Personality
.7	心靈起源	Origin of the soul or mind
.71	先天存在	Pre-existence
.73	輪迴論	Transmigration
.8	心靈歸宿	Destiny of the soul or mind
.9	生與死之自然性	Nature of life and death
137	價值論	Theory of value
138		
139		
140	邏輯學　辯證學	Logic　Dialectics
.1	理論	Theories　Relations
.3	辭書	Dictionaries
.4	評論	Critiques　Essays
.5	雜誌	Periodicals
.6	學會	Societies
.7	研究	Studies
.8	總集	Collected works

.9	歷史	History
141	邏輯各論	Special topics
.1	命題	Propositions（Assent　Faith）
.2	論證	Reasoning　Argument　Proof
.3	三段法　省略法　連鎖法　兩難	Syllogism　Enthymeme　Sorites　Dilemma　Etc.
.4	謬誤　真與誤	Fallacies　Truth and error
.7	觀察	Observation
.71	實驗	Experiment
.73	假設	Hypotheses
.75	通則	Generalization
.77	類推	Analogy
142	演譯	Deductive logic
	演譯與歸納	Combinations of deductive and inductive
143	歸納　實驗邏輯	Inductive and empirical logic
144	發生　演進邏輯	Genetic and evolutionary logic
145	象徵　數理邏輯	Symbolic and algebraic logic
146	形上邏輯	Metaphysical logic
147		
148	機遇　或然	Logic of chance　Probability
149	職業的邏輯　應用邏輯	Logic for professional classes　Applied logic
150	心理學	Psychology
.1	理論	Philosophy　Theories　Laws

	理知心理學,形上心理學,參看135	Rational psychology, Metaphysical psychology see 135
	心理關係　見158	For relations to other subjects see 158
	應用心理學	applied psychology
.15	科學觀心理	Theories based on the pure sciences
.16	身心論　身心關係	Mind and body　Theories of Mind-body relations
.161	二元論	Dualistic theories
.162	身心交感論	Interaction
	互相,時會,因果,等關係	Mutual interaction, occasionalism, cause theory, etc.
.163	身心平行論　二面論	Parallelism The double or dual aspect theory
.165	一元論	Monistic theories
.166	唯物心理論　物質心理	Materialistic Mechanistic
	參看103.1 唯物論	see also 103.1 Materialism
	正常自動論	Conscious automaton theory　Automatism
	副象論	Epiphenomenon theory　Epiphenomenalism
.167	唯心心理論	Spiritualistics
	參看103.3 唯心論	see also 103.3 Spiritualism
	心靈一元論	Spiritual monism　Psychic monism
	心靈多元論	Panpsychism　Spiritual pluralism
	心塵論	Mind-dust or Mind stuff theory
.17	方法論	Psychologic method
	其關係實驗心理方法諸作　見150.7	General only, for methods of experimental psychology　see 150.7
.171	主觀	Subjective
.172	內省法	Introspection, observation of one's self
.173	客觀	Objective
.174	解析	Analytic
.175	綜合	Synthetic

.176		叙述　圖解	Descriptive
.177		注釋	Explanatory
.19		派別	Psychological systems or schools
		參看101-109哲學體系	see also 101-109 philosophical systems
.191		構造派	Structural or existential psychologies Structuralism
	1	官能心理　官能派	Faculty psychology
	3	精神派	Mentalism
	5	基斯塔派或完形派	Gestalt or configuration psychology
	7	身心動作心理	Psychosomatic organism or ming-body performance psychology
.193		機能派	Functional psychology
		動力心理	Dynamic psychology
		意志心理	Purposive psychology
.197		感應派	Reaction or response psychology
	1	內分泌心理	Endocrine psychology　Endocrinism
	3	行爲派或外觀派	Behaviorism　Anthroponomy
	5	反省派	Reflexology
.3		辭書	Dictionaries
.37		年鑑	Yearbooks
.4		評論　講演	Critiques, lectures, etc.
.5		雜誌	Periodicals
.6		學社	Societies
.7		研究　方法	study and teaching
.71		實驗與研究　實驗心理學	Experiment and research　Experimental psychology
.72		實驗室	Laboratories
.77		測驗	Measurements　Tests

		精神測驗, 心理測驗,才力測驗, 智力測驗, 參看330.17教育測驗	Mental tests, psychological measurements, tests or measurements of innate capacity, intelligence tests see also 330.17 Education-measurements and tests
	.8	總集	Collected works
	.9	歷史	History
151		普通心理學 正常心理	General psychology Normal psychology
	.1	感覺 知覺	sensation Sense perception
	.11	視覺 視感覺	Vision Visual sensation
	.111	眼之解剖與生理	Anatomy and physiology of the eye
	.112	視覺物理與特殊生理	Physics and special physiology of vision
	.114	視覺病理	Pathology of vision
	.115	視覺特殊現象	Special phenomena of vision
	.116	眼動與雙眼視覺	Eye movement and binocular vision
	.117		
	.118	視覺測驗	Tests and measurement of vision
	.12	聽覺 聽感覺	Hearing Auditory sensation
	.121	耳之解剖	Anatomy of the ear
	.122	聽覺物理與生理	Physics and physiology of hearing
	.124	聽覺病理	Pathology of hearing
	.126	雙聽與單聽	Binaural and monaural hearing
	.127	音樂心理	Musical psychology
	.128	聽覺測驗	Tests of auditory perception
	.13	齅覺 齅感覺	Smell Olfactory sensation
	.14	味覺 味感覺	Taste Guestatory sensation
	.15	觸覺 膚覺	Touch Tactil sensation Cutaneous senses

.16	肌覺　有機感覺	Muscular, articular or organic senses
	平衡感覺	Equilibrium
.17	知覺	Perception　Perceptual apprehension
.172	要素	Elements of perception
.173	錯誤　正常錯覺	Errors of perception　Normal illusions
	變態錯覺與幻覺	For abnormal illusions and hallucinations
	見 156.1	see 156.1
.175	特殊種類	Special classes of perception
	2　空間之知覺	Perception of space and extent
	距離,大小,形式,方向	Distance, size, form, direction
	3　時間之知覺	Perception of time (duration)
	4　運動之知覺	Perception of movement
.18	心理物理學　心理測定	Psychophysics　Psychometry
	定量心理	Quantitative psychology
.19	附感覺	Synaesthesia
.2	情緒　情感	Emotions　Sensibility　Feelings　Affections
	樂與苦	Pleasure and pain
.3	意欲　運動　運動官能	Conation and movement　Motor functions
.31	意欲與情緒	Conation and feeling
.32	運動生理	Physiology of movement
.34	運動病理	Pathology of movement
.35	運動種類	Types of movement
.351	自然動作	Automatic or involuntary movements
.352	天賦　生來	Innate
.353	習性	Acquired　Habits

.357	自意動作	Voluntary or consciously controlled movements
.36	動的發生與抑制	Dynamogenesis and inhibition
.37	本能與衝動	Instinct and impulse
	（模仿,游戲,等）	（imitation, play, etc.）
.38	特殊運動官能	Special motor functions
	言語,歌唱,寫字,繪畫,行路,眼動,等	Speech, singing, writing, drawing, walking, eye movements, etc.
.4	意志	Volition　Will
.41	意志自由	Freedom of will
	其關係心理者	Psychological treatises only
.42	人類自意動作	Voluntary human action
.43	意志鍛鍊	Training of will
	自導	Self-direction
.44	意志病理	Pathology of volition
	意志病	Diseases of the will
	錯誤與變態	Errors and abnormalities
.46	意思　本意　願望	Intentions　Motives　Desires
.48	意志測驗	Measurements of volition
.5	意識	Characters of consciousness
.51	注意　明覺　選擇	Attention, apperception, and selection
	自然反應	Physical reactions
.53	習慣　適應	Habit, accommodation and adaption
.54	遺傳與環境	Heredity and environment
.55	工作與疲勞	Work and fatigue
.57	意識之時間關係	Time relations of consciousness
.6	記憶與學習	Memory and learning　Reproductive power　Mnemonic apprehension　Theory of memory

.62	記憶程序	Memory processes
.621	聯想	Association
.623	強憶 強記	Retention Retentiveness
.625	再生 重憶	Reproduction and representation
	回憶 再記	Recall, revival, remembering
.627	認識	Recognition or identification
.64	記憶術	Memories Methods of aiding memory
.65	學習 學識	Learning or acquisition
.66	忘記	Forgetting and lapses of memory
.67	記憶病理 記憶力缺乏	Pathology of memory Memory defects
.68	測驗	Measurements
.7	想像 創造力	Imagination Creative power Invention
	靈悟心理學	Psychology of inspiration
.8	思維 思想	Thought and thinking
.81	觀念	Ideation
	概念,想象,等	Conception, concept or notion etc.
	抽象	Abstraction
.84	回想	Reflection
.85	判斷	Judgement
.86	理論 歸納 演譯 斷定	Reasoning Inductive and deductive Interence
.87	思想病理	Pathology of thought
.88	測驗	Measurements
.9	直覺 天賦理智	Intuition Innate reason
152	生理心理學 精神生理	Physiological psychology Mental psychology

		神經系構造與官能	Nervous system, structure and function
		參看150.71 實驗心理學	see also 150.71 experimental psychology
		其關係醫理者	For medical discussions
		見 590 醫學	see 590 Medicine
	.1	神經系解剖	Anatomy of nervous system
	.2	神經系生理	Physiology of nervous system
	.3	精神衛生	Mental hygiene
	.4	病理解剖	Pathological anatomy
153		精神發育與能力 精神特徵	Mental development of capacity Mental characteristics
		男性精神發育	Mental development in man
		個別心理	Differential psychology
		發生心理	Genetic psychology
		演進心理	Evolutional psychology
	.1	性別　性別心理學	As influenced by sex　Sex psychology
		婦女心理	Women psychology
		互見 312.3505	see also 312.3505
	.2	自然與社會環境之影響	As influenced by physical and social surroundings
		環境心理	Environment psychology
	.21	感覺	Sensory influences
	.22	地域	Topographic influences
	.23	氣象	Meteorological influences
	.24	住址	Residential influences
	.25	社會	Social influences
		社會心理　見 310.115	Social psychology see 310.115

.27	娛樂		Amusements
	游戲心理		Psychology of play
.28	服制		Clothing
.3	先祖遺傳		As influenced by ancestry　Mental heredity
.4	種族　種族心理		As influenced by race　Race psychology
	種族特徵		Racial characteristics
	民族心理		Folk psychology
	人種心理		Ethnic psychology
	國家心理		Psychology of nations
.5	體格		As influenced by physical structure and conditions
.6	年齡		As influenced by age
	成年與衰老心理		Adult and senescence psychology
.7	兒童研究　兒童生活 兒童心理　青春心理		Childstudy　Paidology　Child psychology　Adolescence
.71	身：兒童身體發育		Body：Physical development of child
.72	心：兒童智力發育		Mind：Intellectural development of child
.73	精神特徵		Mental characteristics
.74	兒童觀念		Children's point of view
.75	兒童描素		Delineation of children
.76	變態兒童　異常兒童		Abnormal children
.761	身體方面：殘廢		Physically defective
.762	精神方面：低能		Mentally defective
.763	道德方面：墮落		Morally defective　Delinquents
.764	野性		Wildings

.765	智童　神童	Super-normal　Exceptionals　Precocity
.766	愚童	Sub-normal　Backward children
.768	遺棄之兒童	Dependents　Homeless and abandoned children
.77	兒童問題	Child problem
	互見　312.368	see also 312.368
.773	男童	Boys　The 'gang' Boy problem
.775	女童	Girls　Girl problem
.79	依國分	By country
	研究古今中外兒童心理諸作類此	Childstudy in various countries and times class here
.8	個別心理	Psychology of types　Individual psychology
.81	人格發育與表現	Development or emergence of personality
.82	人格養成要素　特質	Constituent elements of personality　Traits
	例　自然,道德宗教,社會,等要素	e.g. Physical, moral and religious, social, etc.
.83	專長　才幹　技能	Special abilities or talents
	依十大類分	Divide like main classification
	例　音樂專長	e.g. Musical talents
.84	人格類別	Types of personality
	氣質	Temperaments
.87	人格修養　人格鍛鍊	Cultivation of personality
.88	人格測驗	Tests of personality and character
.9	天才	Genius
	偉人,才子,等	Men of superior attainments, eminent or illustrious men, supermen, etc.
.91	天才特質	Traits of genius

		生理,精神,等方面	Physical, mental, etc.
	.93	天才遺傳論	Genius as heredity
	.94	天才病理論	Genius as pathologic
	.941	天才與瘋癲	Genius and insanity
	.943	天才與疾病	Genius and disease
	.945	天才與罪惡	Genius and vice
	.947	天才與退化	Genius and degeneracy
	.97	環境與天才養成	Environment and training of genius
	.98	天才種類	Classes of genius
	.99	天才分佈	Geographical distribution of genius
		依國分	By country

154　比較心理學　生物心理　　Comparative psychology　Plant and animal behavior　Biopsychology

	.7	植物心理	Plant behavior　Phytopsychology
	.8	動物心理	Animal psychology　Zoopsychology

155　變態心理學　　Abnormal psychology

神經與精神錯亂,病理心理,精神病,心病,精神病理,畸形心理　　Nervous and mental disorders, mental derangements, pathologic psychology, mental diseases, psychopathy, psychiatry, psychopathology, teratologic psychology

其關係特殊精神官能之病理者則宜分入各該類不類此　　Class pathology of special psychologic functions with those functions

	.2	癲狂　精神病	Insanity　Mental alienation
		互見　597.84	see also 597.84
	.23	腦器質病	Organic brain diseases
	.24	腦官能病	Functional brain diseases
	.25	神經官能病	Neuroses Psychoneuroses

.251	跳舞病		Chorea Huntington's chorea
.252	迷狂症(特指女性)		Hysteria
.253	癲癇病		Epilepsy Narcolepsy
.254	失語症,語盲症,失樂症,失書症,失用症,等		Aphasia, alexia, amusia, agraphia, apraxia, etc.
.256	知覺缺乏		Anesthesia Hyperesthesia Hypesthesia
.257	先天感覺不具		Paresthesia
.259	中毒關係		Neuroses due to special poisons
.29	特殊精神病		Special psychoses and syndromes
	例　麻痺　中風		e.g. General paralysis of insane
.3	精神缺乏　精神不具		Mental deficiency
.4	精神病性		Psychopathic personality
.41	情感無常		Emotional Emotional instability
	偏癖		Eccentricity
.45	道德薄弱		Moral imbecility or insanity
.452	竊盜		Kleptomania
.453	説謊　欺騙		Pathologic liars and swindlers
.454	破壞		Destructive manias
.455	殺人　自殺		Homicidal and suicidal manias
.456	酒瘋		Dipsomania
.457	烟癖		Drug addiction
.458	色迷　花癡		Sexual manias and aberrations
	1　戀愛病		Eroticism Erotic delusions
	3　色情狂(特指女性)		Nymphomania
	5　性癖		Sexual perversions
	7　薄情		Moral impolence Frigidity
.47	智力缺乏		Intellectual defect
	例　意志薄弱		e.g. Feeblemindedness
.5	憂鬱病　精神過敏		Hypochondria Melancholia
.6	癇厥病		Catalepsy

.7	失神　喜懼反常		Ecstatics　Ecstasy
156	**精神分析**		**Depth psychology Psychoanalysis**
			Psychology of unconsciousness
.1	幻覺　錯覺		Hallucinations　Illusions
.11	幻覺		Hallucinations
.12	錯覺		Illusions
.13	重覺		Multiple consciousness
.15	恍覺　下覺		Subconscious
.17	顯現　魂魄		Apparitions　Ghosts
.3	睡與覺　夢		Sleep and wakefulness　Dreams
.32	睡與覺		Sleep and wakefulness
.321		睡境	Conditions conducive to sleep
.323		入睡之現象	Phenomena normally accompanying sleep
.325		睡之熟度	Depth and length of sleep
.33	夢　作夢		Dreams　Visions
.331		夢之種類	Classification of dreams
.332		夢相　夢境	Content of dreams
.333		夢之特徵	Characteristics and peculiarities
.334		夢之影響	Effects of dreams
.335		特殊人之夢	Dreams of special classes of persons
	1	依年齡分	Groups by age
	3	殘廢	Sensory defectives
	5	瘋癲	Insane
	7	麻醉	Drug addicts
	9	罪犯　囚犯	Criminals
.337		晝夢	Day dreams　Autistic thinking
.338		詳夢	Interpretation of dreams
		互見157.17	see also 157.17

.35	夢游病		Somnambulism Sleep walking
.36	神游		Fugues
.37	夢話		Sleep talking
.5	催眠術		Hypnotism
	動物磁術		Mesmerism Animal magnetism
.7	暗示		Suggestion
157	陰陽五行　術數		Yin, Yang, and the Five Elements Occult sciences
.097	陰陽家　先知　術士		Seers Prophets Fortune-tellers
.1	卜筮　籤語		Divination Oracles
.11	卦卜		Divination by the eight diagrams
.12	龜卜		Divination by the tortoise
.13	抽籤		Sortilage, casting lots, astragalomancy, etc.
.14	拆字		Divination by analysis of characters
.15	書卜		Bibliomancy
	翻出聖書之一節參其文以占吉凶		Omens drawn from scriptures
.16	腸卜,肝卜,等		Haruspication (inspection of entrails), Hepatoscopy (inspection of liver), etc.
	昔羅馬以祭犧牲之肝腸等用占吉凶		
.17	預兆　祥瑞		Augury and omens
	占夢		Oneiromancy Oneirocritics
.18	籤語　預言		Prophecies Oracles Sibyls
.2	星占　星命		Astrology
	星占學之關係人事方面者類此		Judicial or mundane astrology only; for

		自然星占學　見 520.1	Natural astrology see 520.1
.21		天象	Celestial bodies
.211		太陽	Sun　The greater positive
.213		太陰	Moon　The greater negative
.215		少陽	Stars　The lesser positive
.217		少陰	Planets　The lesser negative
.23		十二宮	Zodiac signs
.24		星命天宮圖	Horoscopes
.25		赤緯表	Tables of declinations
.27		普通應用	General applications
		算命　流年運氣　天干地支	Nativities　Cyclic law　Celestial and earthly cyclic characters
.28		特殊應用	Special applications
		例　醫星占學	e.g. Medical astrology
.3		相術	Physiognomy, phrenology, etc.
		命理相法合著類此	Class here material covering both nativities, physiogromy, etc.
.31		面相	Physiognomy
.32		五官　眉,髮,等	Divination by study of sensory organs, eyebrow, hair, etc.
.33		相神	Divination by expression of mentality
		神氣,體格,等	Physical features, spirits, statures, etc.
.35		骨相　肉相	Phrenology
.36		手相　掌相	Chirology　Palmistry
		由其手脉手紋等以占其命運	Divination by means of mounts, lines, and other markings of hand and fingers
.37		字相學	Graphology
		由其筆迹以占其命運	Fortune telling by means of handwriting
.4		堪輿　風水	Geomancy　Fortune of land, house, mountains, etc.

.5	術數	Occult sciences
	遁甲,太乙,九宮,六壬,等	
.6	傳心術　千里眼　順風耳	Telepathy　Clairvoyance　Clairaudience
.61	傳心術	Telepathy　Mind reading
.63	千里眼　順風耳 陰陽眼　慧眼	Clairvoyance Clairaudience 　　Crytoscopic
.67	神算	Psychoscopic　Psychometric
	能知過去未來	Supernormal knowledge of distant future or past event connected with objects at hand
.7	巫祝　魔術　妖怪	Witchcraft　Sorcery　Magic　Demonology
	法事,降神,等	Black magic, white or nature magic, necromancy, etc.
.72	魔法	Activities and practices
	魔道,念咒,現身,騰雲,等	Satanism, incantations, demoniac obsession and possession, nocturnal revels, flying in the air, etc.
.74	魔具	Instruments and apparatus
	魔書,天書,魔術棒,等	Black books, conjuring books, magician's wand, etc.
.75	符　咒	Means of help and protection
	咒語,符錄,迷魂符,等	Charms, amulets, talismans, philters, etc.
.77	妖精　妖怪	Elemental spirits, eleves, etc.
.79	妖孽	Humbugs Quackery
.9	靈學　心靈研究	Spiritualism　Psychical research
.92	魂	Animus
.93	魄	Anima

	.95	靈形現象	Objective or physical phenomena
	.951	靈之實現	Materialization of spirits
	.953	靈像學	Spirit photograph
	.955	靈成學	Dematerialization
	.96	靈神現象	Subjective or mental phenomena
	.97	靈醫治	Psychic healing
	.99	非靈論	Anti-spiritualism

158　應用心理學　　　　　　Applied psychology
　　　　總論　　　　　　　　general treatises

其關係於某類之心理宜入該類然亦可依十大類細分彙列如下

Applications to special subjects are better clast with those subjects but may be kept together here by dividing like main classification as follows：

	.2	宗教心理學　心理學與神學	Religious psychology　Relation to theology
	.33	教育心理學　心理與教育	Educational psychology　Relation to pedagogy
	.59	醫心理學	Psychology applied to medicine
	.62	商業心理學	Commercial psychology　Psychology applied to business management
	.7	美術心理學	Psychology applied to fine arts

170　人生哲學　　　　　　　Philosophy of life
171　自然主義　　　　　　　Naturalism

	.1	快樂論	Hedonism Optimism
	.2	功利論	Utilitarianism
	.5	進化論	Evolution

173　理性主義　　　　　　　Rationalism

	.1	厭世論	Passimism

.2		
.3	自律論	Autonomical theory
.4	克己論	Asceticism
.5	直覺論　良心論	Intuitionism　Moral sentiment
.7	完全論	Perfectionism
.8	幸福論	Eudaemonism

180　倫理學・道德哲學　　Ethics　Moral philosophy

.01	理論　關係	Theories　Relations
.012	倫理與宗教	In relation to religion
.015	倫理與心理	In relation to psychology
.016		
.017	倫理與人生哲學	In relation to philosophy of life
.019	倫理與美學	In relation to esthetics
.03	辭書	Dictionaries
.04	評論	Critiques　Criticism
.05	雜誌	Periodicals
.06	學會	Societies
.07	研究	Studies and teaching
	綱目,綱要,答問,等	Outlines, syllabi, questions, etc.
.08	總集	Collected works　Polygraphy
.09	歷史	History
	依國分	subd. by country
	例　中國倫理學	e.g. Chinese ethics
.091	倫理學特論	Ethical topics
.1	好壞	Goodness and badness
.2	正誤	Right and wrong

.3	真偽	True and false
.4	博愛	Altruism
.49	自私	Egoism
.5	生命	Life
.59	自殺	Suicide
.6	情慾	Passions
.61	情感	Affections
.62	友愛　友誼	Friendship
.63	恩惠	Kindness
.64	憎惡　痛恨	Hate
.65	怒	Anger
.66	懼　怯	Fear　Cowardice
.67	嫉妒　羨慕　報復	Jealousy　Envy　Revenge
.68	貪吝　貪慾	Avarice Greed
.69	淫亂及其他	Incontinence and others
.7	善	Virtues
.71	尊敬　光榮　令名	Honor　Glory　Fame
.72	真實　正直　公道	Truth　Honesty　Justice
.73	本分　義務　責任	Duty　Obligation　Responsibility
.74	勇敢　豪俠	Bravery　Courage　Gallantry
.75	欣喜	Cheerfulness
.76	信仰　希望	Faith　Hope
.77	慈悲　慈善　慷慨	Charity　Philanthropy　Mercy　Benevolence　Generosity Etc.
.78	謹慎　忍耐　謙遜	Prudence　Caution　Patience
.79	智慧　天真及其他	Wisdom　Innocence Etc.
.8	惡	Vices

.81 驕傲　誇大　　　　　Pride　Boasting
.82 名利　虛榮　　　　　Vanity
.83 頑固　剛愎　　　　　Obstinacy
.84 孤僻　　　　　　　　Sullenness
.85 殘酷　　　　　　　　Cruelty
.86 虛偽　欺詐　　　　　Lying　Deceit
.87 誹謗　責罵　　　　　Scandal　Scolding
.88 不誠實　忤逆　　　　Dishonest　Disobedience
.89 愚笨及其他　　　　　Folly and others
.9 其他　　　　　　　　Other ethical topics
.91 嘲笑　　　　　　　　Ridicule
.92 阿諛　　　　　　　　Flattery
.93 喪失　　　　　　　　Bereavement
.94
.95 安慰　　　　　　　　Consolation
.96 同情　憐憫　　　　　Sympathy　Pity
.97 悲傷　憂愁　　　　　Affliction　Sorrow
.98 快樂　　　　　　　　Happiness

181　基督教倫理　　　　Christian ethics
182　個人道德　修身　　Individual ethics
183　家庭道德　　　　　Family ethics
.1 結婚　離婚　　　　　Marriage and divorce
.2 一妻　多妻　　　　　Monogamy and polygamy
.3 父母之道　　　　　　Duties of parents
.4 兄弟之道　　　　　　Duties of brothers
.5 夫婦之道　　　　　　Duties of husbands and wives
.6 子女之道　　　　　　Duties of children

	.7	主僕之道	Masters and servants
	.8		
	.9	家庭義務	Family obligations
184		社會道德	Social ethics
	.1	禮節	Etiquette
	.2	禮貌	Courtesy
	.3	接談	Conversation Gossip
	.4		
	.5	衣冠	Dress Display
	.6		
	.7	階級	Caste Class feeling
	.8		
	.9	社會義務	Social obligations
185		國家道德	State ethics
	.1	國民之道 公民學	Duties of citizens Civics
	.2	愛國	Patriotism
	.3	官吏之道	Duties of public officers
	.4		
	.5	國家義務	Duties of state
	.6		
	.7	國際道德	International ethics
	.8	和平與戰爭	Peace and war
	.9		
186		職業道德	Professional ethics
		例 醫學道德	e.g. Medical ethics
187		性的道德	Sexual ethics

.1	貞潔		Chastity
.2	獨身		Celibacy
.3	節慾		Continence
.4			
.5	戀愛		Love
.6			
.7	淫慾		Adultery
.8	賣淫		Social evil
.9	淫畫	淫書	Immoral art Immoral literature

188　實踐道德　　　　　　Practical and applied ethics

.1	格言	箴言	Maxims Aphorisms
.2			
.3	家訓	家憲	Family instructions
.4	兒童教訓		Instructions for children
.5	婦女教訓		Instructions for women
.6	青年教訓		Instructions for young people
.7			
.8			
.9	身體修養		Ethics of the body

189　其他道德　　　　　　Other ethics

　　.7　游戲道德　　　　　Ethics of play

190　美學　　　　　　　　Esthetics

宗教 Religion

200　宗教　總類　　　　Religion General Works

- .01　多神教　　　　Polytheistic
- .02　一神教　　　　Monotheistic
- .03　天啓教　　　　Revealed
- .04　異端　　　　　Paganism Heresies
- .05　先民宗教　　　Of primitive peoples
- .06　文民宗教　　　Of civilized peoples
- .07　種族宗教　　　Ethnic
- .09　國教　　　　　National
- .1　理論　目的　關係　　Theories Aims Relations

　　　　依類分　　　　　　Subd. by subjects

　　例　宗教與哲學 .11　　　e.g. Religion and philosophy
　　　　宗教與心理 .115　　　Religion and psychology
　　　　宗教與倫理 .118　　　Religion and ethics
　　　　宗教與宗教 .12　　　Relations of religions to one another
　　　　宗教與科學 .15　　　Religion and science
　　　　宗教與文藝 .18　　　Religion and literature
　　　　宗教與歷史 .19　　　Religion and history

- .3　辭書　　　　　Dictionaries
- .37　年鑑　　　　　Yearbooks
- .4　評論　　　　　Critiques
- .5　雜誌　　　　　Periodicals
- .6　會社　　　　　Societies
- .61　宗教同盟　　　Religion alliance
- .67　反宗教同盟　　Anti-religion alliance

.7	研究	Study and teaching, Outlines, etc.
.8	總集	Collected works
.9	歷史	History
.91	古代	Ancient
.92	中古	Medieval
.93	近世	Modern
.94	年表	Religious chronology
.97	宗教家傳記	Biography
	如係某一宗教之宗教家傳記則與該宗教同類	Biography of a particular religion better go with that religion
.98	宗教地理　地圖	Religious geography　Maps
.99	宗教考古	Religious antiquities

201　自然神學　　　　　　　Natural theology

.1	神論　無神論	Theism　Atheism
.2	泛神論　一神論	Pantheism　Monotheism
.3	神性論	Nature and attributes of Deity
.31	類似論	Analogies and correspondences
.33	人形論	Anthropomorphism
.4	創造論	Creation
	地球創造說	Theory of the earth
.5	天道論	Providence
	天命論　宿命論	Fatalism　Destiny
.6	善惡論　二元論	Good and Evil　Dualism
.61	善	Good
.63	罪　惡	Sin　Evil
.7	末世論　來世論	Eschatology　Future state
.71	死	Death

.72	末日	The end of the world
.721	復活	Resurrection
.723	受審	Judgment
.725	天堂　樂土	Heaven　Paradise
.727	地獄　永刑	Hell　Eternal punishment
.73	降臨　再臨	Incarnation　Reincarnation
.75	輪迴　轉生	Transmigration　Metamorphoses
.77	靈魂論	The soul
.78	來世	Future state　Future life
.79	永生　不滅	Immortality　Eternity
.8	信條	Creed
.9	護教	Apologetics
202	聖書	Sacred books
203	實踐神學	Practical theology
204	牧教　傳道	Pastoral theology
205	宗教制度	Religious institutions and polity
206	宗教團體	Religious associations
207	宗教教育	Religious education
208	宗教事業	Missions
	實踐教宗	Practical religion
	宗教生活	Religious life
209	原始宗教	Primitive religions　Religions of primitive peoples
.1	宗教起源	Origins of religion
.2	天然崇拜	Nature-worship
.21	天體崇拜：日,月,星,辰	Cult of celestial bodies：sun, moon, stars, etc.

.22	山嶽崇拜		Cult of mountains　Litholatry
.23	土之崇拜		Cult of earth
.24	水之崇拜		Cult of water　Hydrolatry
.25	火之崇拜		Cult of fire　Pyrolatry
.26	五穀崇拜		Cult of cereal
.27	草木崇拜		Cult of plants, trees　Dendrolatry
.28	動物崇拜		Cult of animals: serpents, birds, etc. Zoolatry
.29	其他百物崇拜		Others
.3	生殖器崇拜		Sex-worship　Phallicism
.4	帝王崇拜	英雄崇拜	Emperor-worship　Hero-worship
.5	祖先崇拜	幽靈崇拜	Ancestor-worship　Worship of the dead
.6	天使崇拜	善靈崇拜	Angelolatry　Good spirits
.7	魔鬼崇拜	惡靈崇拜	Devil-worship　Evil spirits
.8	偶像崇拜	畫像崇拜	Idolatry　Image-worship
.9	神話學		The myth　Comparative mythology
	依國分		subd. by country
	例　中國神話		209.91　Chinese mythology
	日本神話		.92　Japanese mythology
	希臘　羅馬神話		.93　Greek mythology　Roman mythology

210　儒教　孔教　Confucianism as religion

1. 孔教(尊儒爲宗教者)之著述與刊物均類此
2. 於必要時仿各宗教細分

1. Class here only works and publication on Confucianism as religion
2. Works and publications on Confucianism may be subd. as other religious

220　道教(神仙)　Taoism

考道教淵源於巫祝神仙之說,而形成於張(道)陵之五斗米道,其上標老子者,蓋依以自尊也,實則老子無爲自然之哲理,與神仙餌服張陵醮事章符之教迥異,故老子,列子,莊子,等著作均應入道家

Taoism was practically and systematically formed from Chang (Tao) Ling's "The religion of five bushels of rice," and quite different from Taoist school author Lao Tsu was unauthoritatively claimed as its founder, thus works of and on Lao Tzu, Lieh Tzu, Chuang Tzu, etc. clast with the Taoist school

.1	理論　關係	Theories　Relations
.11	道教與道家	Taoism and the Taoist school
.12	道教與其他宗教	Taoism and other religions
.13	道教與社會政治	Taoism and society and politics
.14		
.15	道教與科學	Taoism and science
.16	道教與醫術	Taoism and healing
.17	道教與個人	Taoism and individuals
.18		
.19	道教與文化	Taoism and culture
.2		
.3	術語	Taoist terms
.4	評論	Critiques
.5	雜誌	Periodicals
.6	會議	Conference
.7	研究	Studies
.8	雜集	Miscellanies
.9	歷史	History
.94	靈圖	Portraits of gods, spirits, etc.

.97 傳記 仙籍 玉册 Taoist biography, list of immortals, etc.

.99 考古 Antiquities

221 教義 神仙　　Dogmatic Taoism

.1 三清 The Three Pure Ones

.11 元始天尊(玉皇上帝) Yuan Shih T'ien Tsun (Yu Huang, Ruler of the gods)

.12 太上道君 Tai Shang Tao Chun

.13 太上老君(老子) Tai Shang Lao Chun (Lao Tzu)

.2 諸神 Gods

例　文昌,關帝,等等 Wen Ch'ang Ti Chun (god of literature) Kuan Ti (god of war), etc.

.3 真人 "True Men" Divine Men

例　廣成子,孫真人,等等 Kuang Cheng Tzu, Sun Chen Jen, etc.

.4 仙人 Immortals

黃帝,彭祖,姜太公 Huang Ti, Peng Tsu, Chiang Tai Kung, etc.

八仙(鍾離權,李純陽,呂洞賓,張珍奴,藍采和,何仙姑,韓湘子,曹國舅) The eight immortals: Chun Li Chuan, Li Shun Yang (Li T'ieh Kuai), Lu Tung Ping, Chang Chen Nu, Lan Ts'ai Ho, Ho Hsien Ku, Han Hsiang Tzu, Ts'ao Kuo Ch'iu

.5

.6 冥界 Invisible world

.7 來世論 Future life

.8 信條　誡律 Creeds　Commandments

.9 護教 Apologetics

222 道書　道藏　Taoist Sacred books　The Taoist Thesaurus

按道藏分三洞四輔十二類：本文，神符，玉訣，靈圖，譜錄，戒律，威儀，方法，眾術，紀傳，讚頌，表奏，除本文爲經類此外，餘均應析分本教各專項下，如方法類應一部入修真成仙，一部入法術。

再道藏所收多非爲道教之書如洞神部之《道德真經》，《冲虛真經》，《南華真經》，及其經解經疏等等，太清部之墨子，公孫龍，尹文，韓非以及其他各洞輔之非道教著述者，率應依其性質分入各專類有如上列則應入道家，墨家，名家，法家，等等

The Taoist Thesaurus includes three principle and four subsidiary scriptures, each of which subd into twelve divisions namely: canonical works, phylactery, commentaries, spiritual portraits, chronology, commandments, liturgy and ritual, ways of attaining immortality and instruction in occult matters, alchemy, biography, panegyric, and memorial to gods. Classify here only the canon, for the rest prefer with the subjects.

The Taoist Thesaurus, however, iucludes a number of non-Taoism works such as works of, and commentaries on, Lao Tzu, Lieh Tzu, and Chuang Tzu in Tung Shen Pu; Mo Tzu, Sungsun Lung, Yin Wen, Han Fei in Tai Ch'ing Pu; all of which should be classified with the Taoist School 111. 2, Mocius school 111. 3, Min Chia 111. 4, Fa Chia 111. 5 respectively. So also with other non-Taoist works which should go with their subjects.

.1　三洞　三經　　　　Taoist three princeiple scriptures
.2　洞真部　　　　　　Tung Chen Pu
.3　洞玄部　　　　　　Tung Hsuan Pu
.4　洞神部　　　　　　Tung Shen Pu
.5　四輔　　　　　　　Taoist four subsidiary scriptures
　　太玄部　　　　　　Tai Hsuan Pu
　　太平部　　　　　　Tai Ping Pu
　　太清部　　　　　　Tai Ch'ing Pu
　　正一部　　　　　　Cheng I Pu

.7	續道藏	Taoist supplementary scriptures
.8		
.9		
223	威儀　儀式	Liturgy and ritual
.1	懺禱　許願	Purgatory
.2		
.3		
.4	頌讚	Panegyric
.5	祭醮　道場	Sacrifice　Taoist festival
	超亡　招魂　放生	Releasing the dead from hell Recalling the soul or spirit Liberating living creatures
.6		
.7	齋戒	Purification
.8	表奏(祈願文)	Memorial to gods
.9		
224	修真　成仙　長生　不死	Ways of obtaining immortality Elixirs of life
.1	內丹	Nei tan (spiritual alchemy)
.2	胎息	Selfculture
.3	養生	Deep breathing
.4		
.5	外丹	Wai tan (material alchemy)
.6	練丹	Elixir vitas
.7	丹樂：丹砂, 金丹, 玉液	Elixir of gold (pill of immortality)
.8	房中術	Communion with virgin

.9

225 法術　　　　　　　　Occultism
- .1 神咒,靈符,六甲,秘訣,等
- .2 御風
- .3 步水
- .4 隨雨
- .5 禁虎　伏虎
- .6 刻魅
- .7 拘魂
- .8 荳人
- .9

226 天師　方士,道士　　Taoist popes, magicians, priests

227 道觀,道宮　　　　　Taoist monasteries

228

229 宗派　　　　　　　　Taoist sects
　　　道教分南北二派,又分　Northern and southern sects
　　　爲真大道教,太一教,
　　　三元教

230 佛教　佛學　　　　　Buddhism
- .1 佛學與其他關係　　Buddhism in relation to
  - .11 佛學與哲學　　　Buddhism and philosophy
    - .115 佛學與心理　　Buddhism and psychology
    - .118 佛學與倫理　　Buddhism and ethics
  - .12 佛教與他宗教關係　Buddhism and other religions
  - .13 佛教與社會,教育,政治,等　Buddhism and society, education, state, etc.

.14		
.15	佛教與科學	Buddhism and science
.19	佛教與文化　種族	Buddhism and civilizations
.2		
.3	辭書	Encyclopedias　Dictionaries
.37	年鑑	Yearbooks
.4	評論	Critiques
.5	雜誌	Periodicals
.6	學會	Societies
.7	研究　方法	Study and teaching
.8	文藝	Buddhist literature
	1. 詩　3. 戲曲　4. 小說　5. 神話　傳說　7. 散文　81. 函牘　88. 雜品	Poetry　Dranma　Fiction　Folklore　Myths　Prose　Letters　Miscellanies
.9	歷史	History
.91	古代	Ancient
.92	中古	Medieval
.93	近世	Modern
.94	年表	Chronology
.97	高僧傳　像讚	Biography　Portraits
.98	地理	Geography
.99	考古	Antiquities

231　佛教哲學　教義　神學　　Philosophy of Buddhism

.1	哲學	Philosophy
.11	哲學體系	Systems of Buddhist philosophy
	例　唯心論, 虛無論, 等	e.g. Spiritualism, nihilism, etc.

.14	形上學	Metaphysics
.141	認識論	Epistemology
	例 認識緣起,範圍,性質,等	e. g. Origin and sources, limits, and nature of knowledge, etc.
.142	方法論	Methodology
.143	本體論	Ontology
	例 一切法,真如,法身,心,識,空,有,等	
.144	宇宙論	Cosmology
	例 無神論,泛神論,因果論,等	e. g. Atheism, pantheism, cause and effect, etc.
.15	心理學	Psychology
.16	因明	Hetu vidya s'astra (logic)
.18	倫理學	Ethics
.2	佛陀論	Buddhology
.21	釋家牟尼	S'akyamuni
.22	佛陀世尊	Buddho bhagavan
.23		
.24	無量壽禪	Amitayur-dhyana
.25		
.26	法身	Dharmakaya
.27	如來	
.28		
.29	釋家傳記	Life of Buddha
.291	語錄	Words of Buddha
.292	年譜 像讚	Chronology Portraits
.293	軼事 傳說	Legendary and apocryphal narratives
.294	佛陀家庭	Family of Buddha
.295	社會生活	Public life

.296	佛經上的佛陀	Buddha in Sutra
.297	美術上的佛陀	Buddha in art
.298	文學上的佛陀	Buddha in literature
.299	歷史上的佛陀	Buddha in history
.3	四諦(聲聞乘)	Aryasatyani (the four dogmas)
.31	苦諦　三明	Dukha (the dogma of misery) or Trividya
.311	無常	Anitra
.312	苦	Dukha
.313	空　無我	Anatma (no ego)
.32	集諦	Samudaya (the dogma of accumulation)
.33	滅諦	Nirodha (the dogma of extinction)
.34	道諦	Marga (the dogma of the path)
.4	八聖道	Marga (eight rules of conduct)
.41	正見	Samyagdrichti (right view)
.42	正思惟	Samyaksamkalpa (right thinking)
.43	正語	Samyagvak (right speech)
.44	正業	Samyagadjiva (right profession)
.45	正精進	Samyagvyayama (right or incessant practice of asceticism)
.46	正定	Samyaksamadhi (right steadiness)
.47	正念	Samyaksmriti (right memory)
.48	正命	Samyakkarmanta (right living)
.5	十二緣起(獨覺乘)	Nidana (twelve causes of existence)
.51	老死	Djaramavana (decrepitude and death)
.52	生	Djati (birth)
.53	有	Bhava (existence)

.54	取	Upadana (grasp)
.55	愛	Trichna (love)
.56	受	Vedana (sensation)
.57	觸	Spars'a (contact)
.58	六處或六塵	Chadayatana (the six organs of sensation, eye, ear, nose, etc.)
.59	名色	Namarupa (name and form)
	識或八識	Vidjnana (knowledge or eight forms of knowledge)
	行	Samskara (action)
	無明	Avidya (absence of perception)
.6	五蘊	Skandha (five attributes)
.61	色	Rupa (form)
.62	受	Vedana (sensation)
.63	想	Samjna (thought)
.64	行	Samskara (action)
.65	識	Vidjnana (knowledge)
.7	六波羅蜜(菩薩乘)	Paranuta (six means of passing to nirvana)
.71	布施	Dana (charity)
.72	戒	S'ila (morality)
.73	忍	Kchanti (patience)
.74	精進	Virya (energy)
.75	禪定	Dhyana (contemplation)
.76	智慧	Pradjna (intelligence)
.79	涅槃	Nirvana (absolute exemption from the wheel of transmigration)
	不死	Amata

		絕對安隱	Yogakikhema
		清淨	Sitibhava
		最高樂	Parama sukkha
	.8	三界	Trailokya (three classes of beings)
	.81	欲界	Kamadhata (the region of desire)
	.82	色界	Rupadhatu (the region of form)
	.83	無色界	Arupadbatu (the region without form or desire)
	.84	五趣	Gati (five conditions of sentient existence)
	.85	地獄	Naraka (hells)
	.86	餓鬼	Pretas (hungry demons)
	.87	傍生	Animals
	.88	人	Men
	.89	天人	Devas (spirits of heaven)
	.9	護教	Apologetics
		非難婆羅門教	Against Brahmanism
		非難其他宗教	Against other religions
232		佛經　藏經	Sutra (Buddhist scriptures)
	.01	經典	Canon
	.02		
	.03	辭書	Dictionaries
	.04	考證　論文	Critiques
	.05	古文佛經	Original texts
		巴利文一切經	Pali
		梵文一切經	Sanskrit
	.06	翻譯佛經(原文譯文本)	Versions of Sutra
		依國分	by countries

	例　中譯原文佛經之論著	e.g. Works on Chinese translation of the Sutra from the original Pali and Sanskrit
.07	經解　經疏　經義	Commentaries, concordances, etc. on whole Sutra
.08	佛經與學術	Sutra and other subjects
.081	佛經故事　神話	Sutra stories
.082	佛經奇迹　術數	Miracles in the Sutra
.084	佛經與法律	Sutra and law
.085	佛經與五明	Sutra and five vidyas
	聲明	S'abda vidya s'astra (a work on etymology)
	巧明或功明	S'ilpasthana vidya s'astra (a work on arts, ect.)
	醫方明	Tchikista vidya s'astra (a work on magic prescriptions)
	因明	Hetu vidya s'astra (a work on logic)
	內明	Addyatma vidya (esoteric luminary)
.086		
.087	佛經與個人	Sutra and individuals
	兒童, 婦女, 等	children, women, etc.
.088	佛經文學	Sutra as literature
	文法　修辭　音義	Rhetoric of the Sutra, etc.
.089	佛經與其他	Sutra and others
	雜類	Miscellanies
.09	佛經史	History of Sutra
.098	地理	Geography
.099	考古　古迹	Antiquities
	下列大小乘各經皆可仿上細分	Individual Buddhist scriptures of both Hinayana and Mahayana Sutra may be subd. as above
.1	經藏	Sutra-pitaka (Serman Basket)

.2	小乘經 阿含部	Hinayana Sutra	Agamas
.21	長阿含	Dirghagamas (long agamas)	
.22	中阿含	Madhyamagamas (middle agamas)	
.23	雜阿含	Samyuktagamas (mixed agamas)	
.24	增一阿含	Ekottaragamas (numerical agamas)	
.25	小阿含	Khuddakagamas (small agamas)	
.3	大乘經	Mahayana Sutra	
.31	般若部	Pragnaparameta	
.32	法華部	Saddbhamrapundarika	
.33	華嚴部	Avatamsaka	
.34	寶積部	Ratnakuta	
.35	涅槃部	Nirvana	
.36	大集	Mahasannepata	
.37	經集	Nikaya	
.38	密部		
.4	律藏	Vinaya-pitaka (Discipline collection)	

　　　　內有戒本,儀式,懺悔,
　　　　頌讚,等等除戒本入此
　　　　外餘均應分入各專項

.5	大乘律	Of Hinayana
.6	小乘律	Of Mahyana
.7	論藏	Abhicharma-pitaka

　　　　論藏單刻本應按其性質
　　　　分

　　　　　　　　　　(Psychological Basket)

.8	雜藏	Samyukt-pitaka

　　　　應按各部性質分

.9	僞經	Deuterocanonical Sutra

233　實踐佛學　　　　　　Practical Buddhism
　.1　聖節　香會　　　　Times and seasons
　.2　禮佛　儀式　　　　Worship　Liturgy and ritual
　.3　禮佛設備　　　　　Sacred furniture, objects, etc.
　　　袈裟,木魚,等
　.4　頌讚　　　　　　　Hymnology
　.6　念經　　　　　　　Sutra reading
　.8　受戒
　　　出家與還俗

234　傳教　傳教事業　　Buddhist missions

235　佛教會　佛教制度　Buddhist institutions and polity
　　　教化與影響　　　　Its influences and relations
　　　例 佛教與社會,個人,等　e.g. Buddhism and society, individuals, etc.
　.2　佛教行政　　　　　Buddhist polity
　.3　佛教財政　　　　　Finance　Revenues
　　　教產　　　　　　　Buddhist property
　.4　教規　教律　　　　Buddhist law　Discipline
　.5　聖職　　　　　　　Ministry
　　　例 僧侶,比丘,方丈,等　Buddhist priests, monks, etc.
　.8　佛教建築:寺,廟,庵,　Buddhist buildings: temples, monas-
　　　等　　　　　　　　　　teries, nunneries, etc.

236　佛教團體　　　　　Buddhist associations
237　佛教教育　　　　　Buddhist education
238　佛教生活　　　　　Buddhist life
239　佛教—宗派與歷史　Buddhism-Sects and history

.1	印度佛教—宗派與歷史		Indian Buddhism-Sects and history
.11	小乘		Hinayana
.111	上座部		Sthavira-vada (Theravada)
.112	一切有部		Sarvasti-vada (Vaibhasikas)
.113	大衆部		Mahasangkika-vada
.114	成實論		Satya-siddhi-castra
.115	俱舍論		Abhidharma-kaca
.116	正量論		Sammitiya-vada
.117	説出世部		Lokottara-vada
.118			
.119	其他小乘各宗		Other Hinayaua sects
.12	大乘		Mahayana
.13	法性宗		Madhyamika (Cunya-vada)
.131	宗義　宗學		Philosophy
.132	經		Sutra (general treatises)
.133	祖師		Masters
		1. 總論或彙集性宗祖師著述類此	1. General treatises on, or collections of, the masters clast here
		2. 各祖師之專論或著述應依下列分	2. Works by and about individual masters should be clast with them
		3. 凡專論某題或注解某經應依某題或某經分	3. Works on special subjects prefer with the sjbjects and commentaries of Sutra go with the Sutra
.134	馬鳴		Acvaghosa
.135	龍樹		Nagarjuma
.136	提婆		Aryadeva
.137	其他諸師		Other masters
		青目,佛護,月稱,清辨,智光,等	Pingala, Buddhapalita, Candrakirit, Bhavaviveka, Jnanaprabha, etc.
.138	支派		Madhyamika-Sects

中國十進制分類法及索引　155

.14	法相宗	Yogacara school
.141	宗義　宗學	Philosophy
.142	經	Sutra
.143	祖師	Masters
	例同法性宗	see Madhyamika
.144	彌勒	Maitreya
.145	無着　世親	Asanga　Vasu-bandhu
.146	陳那	Mahadignaga
.147	其他諸師	Other masters
	護法	Dharmapala
	安慧	Sthiramati
	戒賢	Silabhadra
	法稱	Dharmakirti
	其他	Others
.148	支派	Yogacara school-Sects
.15	淨土宗	Sukhavati or Bhakti doctrine
.16	禪宗	Dhyana
.17	密宗	Buddhist mysticism
.18	其他印度諸宗	Other Indian sects
.3	南方佛教—宗派與歷史	Southern Buddhism-Sects and history
.31	錫蘭佛教	Ceylon Buddhism
.32	緬甸佛教	Burmese Buddhism
.33	暹邏佛教	Siamese Buddhism
.39	其他南方佛教	Other Southern buddhism
.5	中國佛教—宗派與歷史	Chinese Buddhism-Sects and history
.51	三論宗（性空宗）	Three Sastra-sect, or San-lung-tsung
	成實宗	Satya-siddhi-sastra-sect, or Chen-shih-tsung

.52	法相宗(唯識宗 慈恩宗) 俱舍宗	Dharma-lakshana-sect, or Fa-hsiang-tsung Abhidharma-kosa-sastra-sect, or Chu-she-tsung
.53	華嚴宗(賢首宗)	Avatamsaka-sutra-sect, or Hua-nien-tsung
.54	律宗(南山宗)	Vinaya-sect, or Lu-tsung
.55	天台宗(法華宗)	T'ien-t'ai-tsung
.56	禪宗(心宗)	Dhyana-sect, or Ch'an-tsung
.57	真言宗(密宗)	Mantra-sect, or Chen-yen-tsung
.58	净土宗	Sukhavati-sect, or Pure-land-sect
.59	蒙藏佛教—宗派與歷史	Lamaism, or Mongolian and Tibetan Buddhism-sects and hisotry
.6	日本佛教—宗派與歷史	Japanese Buddhism-Sect and history
.61	三論宗 成實宗	Three Sastra-sect, or San-ron Satya-siddhi-sastra-sect, or Jo-jitsu
.62	法相宗 俱舍宗	Dharma-lakshana, or Hosso Abhidharma-kosa-sastra-sect, or Ku-sha
.63	華嚴宗	Avatamsaka-sutra-sect, or Kegon
.64	律宗	Vinaya-sect, or Ris-shu
.65	天台宗	Tendai
.66	禪宗	Zen
.67	真言宗(密宗)	Mantra-sect, or Shingon
.68	日蓮宗	Nichirendhu
.69	高麗佛教	Korean Buddhism
.7	歐洲各國佛教—宗派與歷史	Buddhism in European countries

	.8	美洲各國佛教—宗派與歷史	Buddhism in American countries
	.9	非洲大洋洲各國佛教	Buddhism in African and Oceanic countries
240		婆羅門教　印度教	Brahmanism　Hinduism
	.1	婆羅門教與他宗教	Brahmanism and other religions
		婆羅門教與佛教	Brahmansim and Buddhism
	.2		
	.3		
	.4	評論	Critiques
	.5	雜誌	Periodicals
	.6	學會	Conference
	.7	研究	Studies
	.8	雜集	Miscellany
	.9	歷史	History
	.97	傳記	Biography
	.99	考古　古迹	Antiquities
241		婆羅門教哲學　神學	Philosophy　Dogmatic Brahmanism
	.1	本體論	Ontology
		梵我(梵即我)	Brahman　Atman
		自性　神我	Prakrti　Purusha
	.2	認識論　知識緣起	Epistemology　Theory of knowledge　Origin and sources of knowledge
	.21	現量	Pratyaksha
	.22	比量	Anumana
	.23	譬喻量	Upamana

.24	義準量	Arthapatti
.25	聖教量	Sabda
.26	無體量	Abhava
.3	宇宙論	Cosmology
	泛神論　無神論	Theism　Pantheism　Atheism
.4	業報輪迴　因果論	Karma sansara　Teleology
.5	解脫	Mukit
	作法	Karma
	知識	Jnana
.6	二十五諦	
.61	自性	Prakrti
.62	大	Buddhi
.63	我慢	Ahamkara
.64	五唯(色聲香味觸)	Tanmtra
.65	五大(地水火風空)	Mahabhuta
.66	五知根(眼耳鼻舌皮)	Buddhindriyas
.67	五作根	Karmondriyas
.68	心平等根	Manas
.69	神我	Purusha
.7	婆羅門教神學	Dogmatic　Brahmanism
.71	婆羅門三大神	The three principle gods of Brahmanism (The Hindu Triad)
.72	婆羅門神(創造之神)	Brahma (Creator)
.73	費虛奴(護持之神)	Vishnu (Guardian)
.74	西發(毀滅之神)	Siva (Destroyer)

	.75	其他諸神	Other gods
	.77	三世論　來世論	Trailokya　Future state
	.78	靈魂論	The doctrine of soul
	.8	信條　誡律	Creed　Commandments
	.9	護教	Apologetics
242		婆羅門教經典	Sacred books
	.1	四吠陀	Catur Veda
	.11	黎俱吠陀(讀誦吠陀)	Rig-veda
	.12	耶柔吠陀(祭祀吠陀)	Yajur-veda
	.13	沙摩吠陀(歌詠吠陀)	Sama-veda
	.14	阿闥婆吠陀(禳災吠陀)	Atharva-veda
	.15	修多羅(規律教條)	Sutras of the Vedas
	.16	婆羅摩(儀式)	Bramanas of the Vedas
	.17	曼特羅(集錄)	Mantras of the Vedas
	.3	森書	Aranyaka
	.5	奧義書	Upanishad
243		儀式　祭祀	Liturgy and ritual
244		修行	
	.1	禁制	Yama
	.2	勸勉	Viyama
	.3	坐法	Asama
	.4	調息	Pranayama
	.5	制感	Pratyahara

	.6	執持	Dharana
	.7	靜慮	Dhyana
	.8	等持	Samadhi
246		僧侶	Brahma priests
247		廟寺	Brahma temples
249		婆羅門教宗派	Brahmanism-Sects and history
		正統派　六師外道	Orthodox Brahmanism Sattirthakarah
	.1	彌曼差派	Puarra Mimansa
		彌曼差經	Sutra
	.2	吠檀多派	Vedanta (Uttara Mimansa)
		梵經　或根本思維經	Bramna sutra, or, Sariraka Mimansa sutra
	.3	僧佉派(數論)	Samkhya
		僧佉經	Samkhya sutra
		僧佉頌	Samkhya karika
		諦論	Tattva samasa
		摩訶提婆	Mahadeva
	.4	瑜伽派	Yoga
		瑜伽經	Sutra
	.5	衛世師派(勝論)	Vaisesika
		衛世師經	Sutra
	.6	尼耶也派(正理派)	Nyaya, or Naiyayaka
		尼耶也經	Sutra
		反正統派	Anti-orthodox Brahmanism
	.7	尼犍子	Nirgrantha
		經典	Sutra
	.8	若提子(耆那教)	Juatiputra (Jaimism)
	.9	順世派	Lokayata

		此派思想與上列各派極端相反不信吠陀,梵神,三世,靈魂,不修行,非神祕等等	This sect unlike the above denies or disbelives vedas, brahma, trailokya, soul, etc.

250 基督教　　　　　　　　Christianity

.1	理論　關係	Theories　Relations	
.11	基督教　哲學　心理	Philosophy　Psychology	
.12	基督教與其他宗教	Relation of Christianity to other religions	
.13	基督教與社會及社會事業	Christianity in relation to society and social welfare	
.14	基督教與政治	Christianity and politics and government	
.15	基督教與科學	Christianity and science	
.16	基督教與醫學	Christianity and healing	
.17	基督教與個人	Christianity and individuals	
	兒童	Children	
	婦女	Women	
	勞動	Labors	
.19	基督教與文化種族	Christianity and culture civilization races	
.2			
.3	辭書	Dictionaries　Encyclopedias	
.4	評論	Critiques	
.5	雜誌	Periodicals	
.7	研究	Studies	
.8	基督教文藝	Christian illerature	
.81	詩	Poetry	

.82	戲曲		Drama
.83	小說		Fiction
.84	神話　傳說		Myths, superstitions, folk-lore
.86	散文		Prose
.87	函牘		Letter
.88	雜品		Miscellaneous works
.9	基督教史		History
.91	古代		Ancient
.92	中古		Medieval
.93	近世		Modern
.94	年表		Chronology
.97	傳記		Biography
.98	地理		Georaphy
.99	考古　古迹		Antiquities

251　神學　教義　　Doctrinal theology

.1	上帝　三位一體	God Doctrine of the Trinity
.11	聖父	God the Father　Creator
.12	聖子	God the Son　Redeemer
.13	聖靈	God the Holy Ghost　Sanctifier
.14	神性	Divine attributes
.141	無所不知	Omniscience
.142	無所不在	Omnipresence
.143	無所不能	Omnipotence
.144		
.145	至善	Goodness
.146	至愛	Love
.147	至正	Righteousness
.148	至惠	Grace
.149	至慧	Wisdom

.15	天國	Kingdom of God　Providence
.16	神律	Divine law
.17	神　人論	God and man　The Divine Union
.18	神現顯論　神感化説	Theophanies　Divinemanifestations Inspiration Revelation
.19	神辯	Theodicy　Vindication of the justice of God
.2	基督　基督論	Christology
.21	道成人生　彌賽亞	Incarnation　Messiah
.22	道	Logos, the Word of God
.23	贖罪	Atonement
.24	犧牲	Sacrifice
.25	復活	Resurrection
.26	二次降臨	Second coming
.27	審判	Judgment
.28	神人論	Divinity of Christ
.29	基督傳記	Life of Christ
.291	語録　未載語録	Words of Christ　Agrapha
.292	年譜　像讚	Chronology　Portraits
.293	軼事　傳説	Legendary and apocryphal narratives
.294	基督家庭	Holy family
	聖母馬利亞,聖約瑟	Mary, Mother of Christ St. Joseph
.295	社會生活	Public life
	施洗	Baptism
	受試	Temptation
	號召門徒	Calling of the Apostles
	奇迹	Miracles
	比喻　預言	Parables　Prophecies
	講道　八福	Sermon on the Mount

		祈禱	Prayers
		變形	Transfiguration
		聖餐	Last Supper
		1. 受難	Passion
		2. 受審	Trial
		3. 定罪	Condemnation
		4. 釘十字架　遺迹	Crucifixion　Relics　Cross
		5. 最後七言	Last words
		6. 死	Descent into hell
		7. 復活	Resurrection
		8. 升天	Ascension
.296		聖經上的基督	Christ in Bible
.297		美術上的基督	Christ in art
.298		文學上的基督	Christ in literature
.299		歷史上的基督	Christ in hisotry
.3	人論		Man　Doctrinal anthropology
.31	上帝造人		Creation of man
.32	亞當前有人說		Preadamites
.33	亞當時有人說		Coadamites
.34	樂園　埃甸		Earthly paradise　Eden
.35	原罪		Fall of man
.36	罪惡　本罪		Sin
.37	肉體與靈體		Natural and spiritual body
.38	自由		Freedom
.39			
.4	救世論		Salvation　Soteriology
.41	恩惠		Grace
.42	信心		Faith
		信與科學	Faith and science
		宗教上的信心	Rule of faith in theology

	宗教上的疑惑	Religious doubt
.43	救贖	Redemption
.44	重生	Regeneration
.45	悔罪	Repentance　Contrition
.46	赦免	Forgiveness　Remission of sins
.47	稱義　成聖	Justification　Sanctification
.48		
.49	預定　自救　選民　棄絕	Predestination and free will　Election　Reprobation
.6	冥界	Invisible world
.61	天使	Angels：St Gabriel, etc.
.62	諸聖	Saints
.63	魔鬼	Demons　Satan　Evil spirits
.64		
.65	僞基督	Antichrist
.66		
.67		
.68		
.69		
.7	末世論　來世論	Eschatology　Future life
.71	死	Death
.72	天地末日	End of the world
.73	復活	Resurrection of the death
.74	受審	Judgment
.75		
.76	天堂　天國	Heaven　Heavenly paradise
.77	地獄　陰府	Hell　Hades　Sheol　Gehenna
.78		

.79	來世		Future state Future life
	永生　不滅　永刑		Immortality Eternity Eternal punishment
.8	信經　信條		Creeds Confessions Covenants
.81	使徒信經		Apostles' creed
.82	尼利亞信經		Nicene creed
.83	阿塔尼西亞信經		Athanasian creed
.84	安利干信經		Anglican
.85	新教信經		Continental protestant
.86			
.87	聖約		Covenants
.88			
.89			
.9	護教		Apologetics Edivences of Christianity
.91	非難猶太教		Against the Jews
.92	非難其他宗教		Against other religions
.93	非難異端		Against heathen
.94			
.95	非難科學		Against the scientists
.96	非難其他學術		Against other specials
.97	非難反基督教運動		Against Anti-Christian movements
.98			
.99	歷史上的憑證		Evidence from history
252	**聖經**		**The Bible**
.01	經典　預言　啓示		Canon Inspiration
.02			
.03	辭書		Dictionaries
.04	評文　考證		Critiques

.05	古文聖經	Original texts and early versions
.051	迦勒底文	Chaldaic
.052	叙利亞文	Syrian
.053	希伯來文	Hebrew
.054	撒馬利亞文	Samaritan
.055		
.056		
.057	希臘文	Early Greek
.058	拉丁文	Latin
.059		
.06	翻譯聖經(原文譯文本)	Versions of Bible
	依國分	by countries
	例 中譯原文聖經之論著	e.g. Works on Chinese tr. of the Bible from the original Hebrew and Greek
.07	經解 經注 經義	Commentaries, concordances, etc. on whole Bible
.08	聖經與學術	Bible and other subjects
.081	聖經故事 神話	Bible stories The Bible story
.082	聖經奇迹	Miracles in the Bible
.083	通俗著述	Popular works about the Bible
.084	聖經與法律	Bible and law
.085	聖經與科學	Bible and science
.086	聖經與醫學	Bible and medical knowledge
.087	聖經與個人	Bible and individuals
	兒童,婦女,等	children, women, etc.
.088	聖經文學	The Bible as literature
	文法 修辭	Rhetoric of the Bible
.089	聖經與其他	The Bible and others
	雜類	Miscellanies
.09	聖經史	Biblical history Bible and history

.091		
.092		
.093		
.094	年表	Biblical chronology
.095		
.096		
.097		
.098	地理	Biblical geography
.099	考古	Biblical archeology
	下列新舊約各經皆可仿上細分	Individual scripture of both Old and New Testaments may be subd. as above
.1	舊約	Old Testament
.2	律法書	Historical books
.21	摩西五經	Pentateuch
.211	創世記	Genesis
.212	出伊及記	Exodus
.213	利未記	Leviticus
.214	民數記	Numbers
.215	申命記	Deuteronomy
.216	摩西十誡	Decalogue The Ten Commandments
.22	約書亞	Joshua
.23	士師記　路得記	Judges Ruth
.24	撒母耳	Samuel
.25	列王記	Kings
.26	歷代記	Chronicles
.27	以斯拉	Ezra
.28	尼希米書	Nehemiah
.29	以斯帖書	Esther
.3	聖詩書	Poetic books
.31	約伯記	Job

.32	詩篇	Psalms
.33	箴言	Book of Proverbs
.34	傳道	Ecclesiastes　Koheleth
.35	所羅門歌	Song of Solomen　Canticles
.4	先知書	Prophetic books　The Prophets
.41	以賽亞書	Isaiah
.42	耶利米書	Jeremiah
.43	耶利米哀歌	Lamentations
.44	以西結書	Ezekiel
.45	但以理書	Daniel
.46	何西阿	Hosea
.47	約珥書	Joel
.48	亞摩士書	Amos
.49	小先知書	The minor Prophets
.491	俄巴底亞書	Obadiah
.492	約拿書	Jonah
.493	彌迦書	Micah
.494	那鴻書	Nahum
.495	哈巴谷書	Habakkuk
.496	西番雅書	Zephaniah
.497	哈該書	Haggai
.498	撒加利亞書	Zechariah
.499	瑪拉基書	Malechi
.5	新約	New Testament
.6	四福音及使徒行傳	Gospels and Acts
.61	馬太	Matthew
.62	馬可	Mark
.63	路加	Luke
.64	約翰	John

.65	使徒行傳		Acts of the Apostles
.7	書翰　書信		Epistles
.71	羅馬人書		Romans
.72	哥林多人前書		Corinthians Ⅰ
.73	哥林多人後書		Corinthians Ⅱ
.74	加拉太人書		Galatians
.75	以弗所人書		Ephesians
.76	腓力比人書		Philippians
.77	哥羅西人書		Colossians
.78	其他聖保羅書翰		Other Pauline Epistles
.781	帖撒羅尼迦人前者		Thessalouians Ⅰ
.782	帖撒羅尼迦人後者		Thessalouians Ⅱ
.783	提摩太前書		Timothy Ⅰ
.784	提摩太後書		Timothy Ⅱ
.785	提多書		Titus
.786	腓立門書		Philemon
.787	希伯來人書		Hebrews
.79	使徒書翰		Catholic Epistles
.791	雅各書		James
.792	彼得前書		Peter Ⅰ
.793	彼得後書		Peter Ⅱ
.794	約翰第一書		John Ⅰ
.795	約翰第二書		John Ⅱ
.796	約翰第三書		John Ⅲ
.797	猶大書		Jude
.8	啓示錄		Apocalypse in canonical books
.81	舊約啓示錄		In Old Testament
.82			
.83			
.84			

.85	新約啓示錄	In New Testament
.86		
.87		
.88	約翰啓示錄	St. John's Apocalypse
.89		
.9	僞經	Deuterocanonical books Apocrypha
.91	以斯達斯第一,二書	Esdras Ⅰ, Ⅱ
.92	透比・猶狄,以斯帖	Tobit, Judith, Esther
.93	所羅門智慧	Wisdom
.94	耶穌西拉	Ecclesiasticus
.95	巴魯,耶利米書信,三聖子歌	Baruch, Epistle of Jeremy, Song of the three children
.96	蘇撒拉傳略,卑利與龍之記略,馬拿西祈禱書	Story of susanna, History of Bel and the dragon, Prayer of Manasses
.97	瑪喀比第一,二,三,四書	Maccabees Ⅰ, Ⅱ, Ⅲ, Ⅳ
.98	其他舊約僞書	Other O. T pseudepigrapha
.981	摩西升天記,以諾書	Assumption of Moses Book of Enoch
.982	約西亞書,約比利書	Book of Jasher, Book of Jubilees
.983	所羅門詩歌	Psalms and Odes of Solomon
.984	十二支派約書	Testaments of the Twelve Patriarchs
.985	先知之僞書	Other books of or on the Prophets: Elias, Jasher, etc.
.99	新約僞書	New Testament pseudepigrapha
.991	僞福音 巴拿巴書,希伯來書,雅各書,尼哥底母,彼得	Pseudepigrapha of the Gospels Barnabas, Hebrews, Book of James (Protevangelium Jacobi), Nicodemus, Peter, etc.

.993	偽行傳	Pseudepigrapha of the Acts
	雅各,約翰,多馬,保羅	Acts of James, Acts of John, Acts of Thomas, Acts of Paul and Thecla, etc.
.995	偽書翰	Pseudepigrapha of the Epistles
	阿比加書翰	Abgar epistles
	巴拿巴書翰	Epistle of Barnabas
	勞第森書翰	Epistle of Paul to the Laodiceans, etc.
.996	偽啟示錄	Pseudepigrapha of the Apocalypse
	彼得啟示錄	Apocalypse of Peter, etc.
.997	十二使徒教訓	Teaching of the Twelve Apostles
.999	耶穌言行遺墨	Apocryphal writings and sayings of Christ, Agrapha Logia

253　實踐神學　Practical theology

.1	聖節　教會節令	Times and seasons　The Church year
.11	降臨節	Advent
.12	聖誕節	Christmas　Feast of the Nativity
.13	受難　復活　升天	Good Friday, Easter, Ascension
.14	五旬節	Pentecost　Whitsunday
.15	三位一體日	Trinity Sunday
.16	諸聖日	Saints' days
.17	感謝節	Thanksgiving day
.18	禁食日	Fasts　Fast day
.19	星期日　主日	Sunday The Sabbath
.191	希伯來主日	Hebrew Sabbath
.195	基督教主日	Christian Sabbath
.199	其他聖日	Other sacred days
.2	禮拜　禮拜儀式	Rites, ceremonies and forms of public and private worship
.21	公共禮拜	Public worship

.22	家庭祈禱	Family worship
.23	個人祈禱	Personal worship
.24		
.25	主日禮拜	Sunday worship
.26	早禱　午禱　晚禱	Morning, noon, and evening services
.27		
.28	祈禱會　靈修會	Service-meetings, after-meetings
.29		
.3	禮拜設備	Sacred furniture, objects, etc.
.31	十字架	The Cross　Crucifixes
.32		
.33	聖壇	The altar
.34		
.35	聖衣　聖帶	Vestments and alter cloths
.36	聖旗	Holy banners, symbolism, etc.
.37		
.38	聖洗聖餐用品	Eucharistic vessels
.39	其他	Other liturgical functions
.4	禱文　公禱文	Prayers　Prayer books
.41	聖經禱文	Bible prayers
.42	基督禱文	The Lord's Prayer
.43		
.44	家庭禱文	Family prayers
.45	個人禱文	Private prayers
.46	兒童禱文	Children prayers
.47	特殊人禱文	Prayers for special classes
.48		
.49	禱文研究會	Prayer meetings

.5	聖詩		Hymnology Hymn-books
.57	音樂 唱詩班		Music in Divine worship Church choirs
.6	讀經		Scripture reading
.7	講經 講道		Homiletics Sermons
.71			
.72	神道方面		Doctrinal Dogmatic
.73	實踐方面		Practical Devotional
.74	學術方面		Academic Educational
.75	解經		Expository
.76			
.77	聖節講道		Sermons on times and seasons
.78	授職講道		Ordination sermons Consecration
.79	其他		Others
.791	婚姻		Marriage sermons
.793	喪葬		Funeral sermons
.795	紀念		Memorial Obituary
.797	特種人		Sermons for special class of persons
.8			
.9	聖禮 聖奠禮		Sacraments Ordinances
.91	聖洗		Baptism
.92	堅證禮		Confirmation Church fellowship
.93	聖餐		Eucharist Holy communion
.94	授職		Holy orders Ordination
.95	婚姻		Marriage
.96	懺悔		Penance Confession Absolution
.97	朝覲		Christian pilgrimages
.98	臨終聖餐,膏禮		Viaticum Unction of the sick

	.99	聖奠禮　成聖禮	Sacramentals
		聖殿,聖水,聖物,等	Dedication of churches, Holy water, Relics, etc.
254		牧教　傳教事業	Pastoral theology
	.1	佈道　宣講	Homiletics　Preaching
	.2	教區巡視	Pastoral visitations
	.3	牧教士之給養,撫恤,等	Cleric support　Celibacy
	.5	男修道　女修道	Brotherhoods　Sisterhoods
	.6	教區團體　事業	Societies for parish work
		例教育,慈善,等	e.g. Parish educational and welfare works
	.9	傳教　傳教事業	Missions　Ministrations
		各教派傳教應入各該教派	Missions of special sect go with that sect
		必要時可依人群細分	Missions work among special classes: women, children, labors, soldiers, etc.
		例:婦女,兒童,勞動,軍人,等	
		國內傳教	Home missions
		國外傳教	Foren missions
		依國分	By country
		例　中國	e.g. Missions in China
255		教會　教會制度	Church institutions and ecclesiastical polity
		教化與影響	Its influences and relations
	.01	教會與蠻族	Church vs. barbarism
	.02	教會與道德	Church and morals
	.03	教會與社會,國家	Church and society, state
	.04	教會與個人	Church and Individuals
		兒童,婦女,等	Children, women etc.

.06	教會與經濟	Church and economics
.07	教會與教育	Church and education
.08		
.09	教會與文化,思想,等	Church and civilization, modern thought, etc.
.2	教會行政　管理	Ecclesiastical polity
.3	教會財政	Church finance　Revenues
	教產	Church property　Benefices
.4	教規　教律	Church law　Discipline
	教會法庭	Courts　Trials
.5	聖職	Ministry　Religious vocations
.51	使徒	Apostolic succession
.52	羅馬教皇	Episcopacy　Prelacy
.53	主教	Bishop　Archbishop
.54	會長　牧師	Priest　Presbyter　Minister
.55	會吏　長老	Deacon　Archdeacon　Elder
.56	教士	Preachers
.57	女傳教士	Women preachers
.58	教友　奉教與反教	Laymen
.6	教區	See　Diocese
.7	教區會議	Council　Synod　Presbytery
.8	教會建築:聖堂,修道院,等	Church building: Cathedrals, Abbeys, Monasteries, etc.
.9		

256　基督教會團體　　Christian societies, associations, etc.

.1	基督教聯合會	Religious societies of both men and women

.11	救世軍	Salvation army
.13	美國基督教委員會	U.S. Christian commission
.15	基督教勵志會	United society of Christian endeavor
.16	基督教普及會	Christian society of brothers of the common life
.17		
.18	基督教友團	Christian society of brotherhoods
.2	基督教青年聯合會	Young Men's Christian unions
.3	基督教青年會	Young Men's Christian association (Y.M.C.A.)
.31	宗旨 關係	Objects, field and extension
	2. 範圍	Limits
	3. 青年會與教會	Reiation to the church
	4. 萬國青年會	International
	5. 全國青年會	National
	6. 全省青年會	State or provincial
	7. 全縣青年會	District
	8. 鄉鎮青年會	County or small towns
.32	建築	Buildings
	例如地址,材料,布置,光線,通氣,陳設,等	e.g. Location, materials, plans, size and arrangement of rooms, lighting, heating, ventilation, fixtures, fittings, etc.
.33	組織 行政	Organization Administration
	憲規	constitution and by laws
	名譽職員	Officers serving without pay
	董事,會長,司庫,書記,等常務委員會會員	Trustees, directors, president, treasurer, secretary, etc. Standing committees Membership
.34	聘任職員	Salaried officers

		總幹事	General secretary
		各部幹事	Assistant secretary
		其他	Other salaried officers
	.35	各部工作	Local work by departments
		1. 事務部	Business department
		財務,籌款,統計,印刷,等	Finance committee, budget, bookkeeping, endowments, solicitation, statistics, etc.
		2. 宗教部	Religious department
		3. 教育部	Educational department
		4. 交際部	Social department
		歡迎,招待,音樂,游戲,等	Receptions, entertainments music, amusements, etc.
		5. 體育部	Physical department
		6. 詢問部　慈善部	Information, relief, etc dept.
		7. 兒童部	Boys department
		8.	
		9. 支部	Branch
	.36	特殊青年會	Y. M. C. A. in special classes and institutions
		學校青年會	College and school
		海陸軍青年會	Army and navy
	.39	歷史	History of Y. M. C. A.
	.4	基督教女青年會	Young Women's Christian association (Y. W. C. A)
	.5	基督教婦女聯合會	Religious societies for women
	.6		
	.7	基督教兒童聯合會	Religious societies for children
257		基督教教育　主日學校	Religious education　Sunday school

258 基督教生活　　The Christian life

- .1　信徒義務　　Duties of Church members
  - 例　禮拜　　e.g. Duty of Church-going
- .2　家庭服務　　Religious work for families
- .3　社會服務　　Religious work for society
- .4　特種人服務　　Religious work and aids for special classes of people
- .5　宗教道德　　Moral theology
- .51　善德　　Virtues
- .52　信　　Faith
- .53　愛　　Love　Charity
- .54　望　　Hope
- .56　其他　　Other cardinal virtues
- .57　惡　罪惡　　Sins and vices
- .7　宗教娛樂　游藝　　Amusements and Christianity
- .8　默道　　Works of meditation and devotion
- .9　修道　　Monastic life

259　基督教宗派與歷史　　Christian Churches—Sects and history

- .01　宗學　　General works on the Sect, its doctrines, etc.
- .02　語錄　　Dialogues
- .037　年鑑　　Yearbooks
- .04　評論　　Critiques
- .05　雜誌　　Periodicals
- .06　學會　　Councils　Documents
- .07　研究　　Studies
- .08　總集　　Collected works

.09		宗派史	History	
.091		修道會派別與歷史	Religious orders and history	
	1	聖本篤派	Benedictines	529
	2	聖多明派	Dominicans	1170
	3	聖芳濟派	Franciscans	1182
	4	聖奧古司丁派	Augustinians	1256
	5	耶穌會	Jesuits	1540
	6	苦行派	Passionists	1720
	7	其他修道會	Other lesser orders	
	8	安利干修道	Anglican brotherhoods	
	9	女修道	Sisterhoods	
.092		基督教迫害史	Persecutions	
.094		異教	Heresies	
		此專指反對基督教之異教如阿利安派之否認基督爲神安提阿派之否認神律與福音爲神約或天予	only for those against Christianity, such as, Arian denying divinity of Christ, Antinomian denying force of law, under Gospel dispensation Pelagiau denying original sin and supernatural grace, etc.	
.095		東方宗派史	Oriental Church history	
.096		西方宗派史	Occidental Church history	
.1		天主教	Roman Catholic Church	
.101		關係	Relations	
.102				
.1037		年鑑	Yearbooks	
.104		評論	Criticism	
.105		雜誌	Periodicals	
.106		學會　會議	Councils　Documents	
.107		研究	Studies	
.108		總集	Collected works	
.109		歷史	History	

.11	宗義　神學	Doctrinal theology
.12	宗典	Catholic scriptures
.13	實踐神學	Practical theology
.14	教皇	Papacy
.141	聖彼得	St. Peter
.142	其他教皇	Other popes
.144	教皇與政治	Papacy and politics
.145	教皇與帝王	Papacy and emperors, kings, etc.
.146	教皇與戰爭	Papacy and wars revolutions, etc.
.148	教皇與文藝復興	Papacy and Renaissance, reformation
.149	教皇與文化	Papacy and civilization, modern thought, etc.
.16	傳教　傳教事業	Catholic missions
.18	支派	Catholic sects
	下列各宗派皆可仿天主教細分	The follows may be subd. as Roman Catholic Church
.2	耶穌教	Protestantism
.3	安利干會	Anglican church
.4	聖公會	Protestant episcopal church
.5	長老會　公禮會	Presbyterian　Congregational
.6	浸禮會	Baptist　Immersionist
.7	美美會　監理會	Methodist
.8	其他基督教宗派	Other Christian sects
.81	統一會	Unitarian
.82	普救會	Universalist
.83	路得會	Lutheran churches
.84	清教派	Puritanism
.85	教友會	Quaker　Friends　Hicksites
.86	震教派	Shaker　Mystic

.87	福音堂	London church
.88	喜信會　循道會	Swedenborgian　Swedishmissionary society
.89	其他	Other Churches and sects
	例　基督科學教會	e.g. Christian science
.9	依國分	By country
	例　中華基督教	Chinese Christian churches
	必要時可仿上列各教	May be subd. as above by churches and sects
	派細分　259.91	259.914
	例　中華基督教聖公會	

260　猶太教　希伯來教　Judaism

261　教義　神學　Dogmatic Judaism

.1	上帝　耶和華	Conception of God Jehovah
.2	彌賽亞	Doctrine of the Messiah
	猶太教之於基督	Attitude toward Christ
.3	人論　選民	Man　Chosen people
	罪惡	Sin
.6	冥界	Invisible world
.7	來世論	Future life
.8	信條	Creed
.9	護教	Apologetics
	非難基督教	Against Christianity
	例　否認基督為彌賽亞	i.e. against Christ as Messiah

262　經典　　　　　Sacred books

.1	法律書(經)	Talmud
.3	法律注釋(經外傳)	Midrash：Halacha　Haggada
.5	神秘書	Cabala：Cabala and magic

.7	猶太傳說		Jewish tradition
.9	摩西五經	十誡	Jewish laws Mosaic laws
263	實踐神學		Practical Judaism
264	牧教	傳教	Pastoral Judaism
265	猶太教制度		Ecclesiastical Judaism
266	猶太教團體		Jewish associations
267	猶太教教育		Jewish education
268	猶太教徒生活		Jewish life Spiritual life
269	猶太教宗派		Judaism Sects and history
.1	經典派		Karaites
.2	儀式派		Pharisees
.3	法律派		Sadducees
.5	苦行派		Essenes
.7	慈善派		Samaritans
.9	依國分		By country

　　　　例　中國猶太教 269.91　　　e.g. Chinese Judaism

270	回教	Mohammedanism Islam
		（清真教或天方教）
.1	理論　關係	Theories Relations

　　　　例　回教與猶太教　　　e.g. Islam and Judaism

.2		
.3	辭書	Dictionaries
.37	年鑑	Yearbooks
.4	評論	Critiques
.5	雜誌	Periodicals
.6		

.7	研究		Study and teaching, outlines, etc.
.8	文藝		Moslem literature
.9	歷史		History
.91	古代		Ancient
.92	中古		Medieval
.93	近世		Modern
.94	年表		Chronology
.97	傳記　像讚		Biography　Portraits
.98	地理		Geography
.99	考古		Antiquities　Archealogy

271　教義　神學　　Doctrinal theology

.1	阿拉	Allah (God)
.2	先知	Prophets　Revelation
.21	阿丹（亞當）上帝簡選者	Adam "Chosen of God"
.22	努海（挪亞）上帝宣傳者	Noah "Preacher of God"
.23	易卜拉欣（亞伯拉罕）上帝之友	Abraham "Friend of God"
.25	母撒（摩西）上帝之言	Moses "Spokesman of God"
.27	爾撒（耶穌）上帝之道	Jesus "Word of God"
.29	穆罕默德　上帝使者	Mohammed "Apostle of God"　Mahdi
.3	人論	Man
.4	宿命論	Predestination
.6	冥界	Invisible world
.7	末世論　來世論	Eschatology　Future life

.8	信經　信條	Creeds
.9	護教	Apologetics
272	聖經	Moslem scriptures
.1	摩西五經	Torah (Mosaic law)
.3	大衛詩篇	Zabur (David psalms)
.5	耶穌福音	Injil (Jesus's gospels)
.7	回經(可蘭)	Koran
273	實踐神學	Practical theology
274	牧教　教門事業	Pastoral theology
275	教門制度	Moslem institution and polity
276	教門團體	Moslem associations
277	教門教育	Moslem education
278	教門生活	The Moslem life
	聖戰	Holy wars
279	回教宗派與歷史	Moslem sects and history
.1	儀式方面(正宗派)	Ritual sects (Orthodox Islam)
.3	政治方面	Political sects
.5	神道方面	Theological sects
.9	依國分	By country
	例　中國回教 279.91	e.g. Chinese Moslem
280	祆教　火神教　波斯教	Zoroastrianism　Parseeism
281	教義　神學	Dogmatic Zoroastrianism
.1	上帝	Ahura Mazda (God)
.11	光	of Light
.13	真	of Truth

	.15	智	of Wisdom
	.2	左羅亞斯德	zoroaster
		救世主	Saoshyant (Savior)
	.3	人論	Man
	.6	冥界	Invisible world
	.7	來世論	Future life
	.8	信條	Creeds
	.9	護教	Apologetics
282		經典	Zend Avesta (Zoroastaian scripture)
283		實踐神學	Practical Zoroastrianism
284		牧教　祆教事業	Pastoral Zoroastrianism
285		祆教制度	Zoroastrian institutions and polity
286		祆教團體	Zoroastrian association
288		祆教生活	The Zoroastrian life
289		祆教宗派	Zoroastrianism-Sects and history
		依國分	By country
		例　中國祆教	e.g. Chinese Zoroastrianism
290		其他宗教	Other principal religions
291		神道教	Shintoism
	.1	神道　教義	Shinto　Dogmatic Shintoism
		例　伊勢神道	
	.2	經典　祝詞	Sacred books
	.21	古事記	Kojiki (Records of ancient matters)
	.23	日本義	Nihon gi (Chronicles of Japan)

.25	延喜式	Norito
.29	其他	Others
.3	實踐神學 儀式 祭典	Practical Shintoism
.4	牧教 神道事業	Pastoral Shintoism
.5	神道制度	Shinto institutions and polity
.6	神社 伊勢神宮	Shrines Imperial shrine of Ise
.8	神道生活	The Shinto life
.9	神道宗派	Shinto-Sects and history

　　　　　例　大社,金光,天理,等

292

293

294

295

296

297

298

299

社會科學　Social sciences

300　社會科學　　　　　　　Social sciences

　　　1. 總論社會,經濟,政治,法律等諸著述類此
　　　　　　　　　　　　　　1. Works dealing with subjects of sociology, economics, politics, law, etc. in a general and comprehensive way to be clast here

　　　2. 辭書,雜誌等其範圍概括社會,教育,經濟,政治等等者分列於下
　　　　　　　　　　　　　　2. All periodicals of a general, more or less mixed character, i.e., most of the contents dealing sociology, economics, etc., to be clast here

　　　3. 專類辭書,雜誌等應分入各專類
　　　　例　教育雜誌　330.5
　　　　　　　　　　　　　　3. Special periodicals are to be classified with the subject
　　　　　　　　　　　　　　e.g. Educational periodicals 330.5

　　　4. 其不明所屬之社會科學諸作類此
　　　　　　　　　　　　　　4. In case of doubt prefer here

.1　理論　關係　　　　　　Theories　Relations
　　　例　社會科學與宗教,史地等關係
　　　　　　　　　　　　　　e.g. in relations to religions, history, etc.

.2

.3　辭書　　　　　　　　　Encyclopedias　Dictionaries
.36　索引　　　　　　　　　Indexes
.37　年鑑　　　　　　　　　Yearbooks
.4　評論　　　　　　　　　Critiques
.5　雜誌　　　　　　　　　Periodicals
.6　學會　會議　紀錄　　　Societies　Congresses
　　　依國分　　　　　　　　By country
.7　研究　方法　　　　　　Study and teaching
　　　綱目,綱要,答問,等　　Outlines, syllabi, synopses, questions, etc.
.8　總集　小冊　　　　　　Collected works　Pamphlets

.9 歷史 History of the social sciences

301-309 特論 Special topics

310 社會學 Sociology

  .1 理論 Theories
      各派社會學 見318   of special schools see 318

  .2

  .3 辭書 Encyclopedias Dictionaries

  .4 評論 Critiques Criticism

  .5 雜誌 Periodicals

  .6 學會 Societies Congresses

  .7 研究 Study and teaching
      綱目,綱要,答問,等 Outlines, syllabi, questions, etc.

  .8 總集 小冊 Collected works Pamphlets

  .9 歷史 History of sociology

  .91 古代 Ancient

  .92 中古 Medieval

  .93 近世 Modern

  .97 傳記 Biography

311 社會要素 勢力 控制 Social elements, Forces, Control

  .1 環境 Environment

  .11 天然關係 Physical
      氣候,水土,交通,飲食,等 Influence of climate, acclimatization, inter-group intercourse, food, etc.

  .17 遺傳關係 Traditional
      風俗,禮儀,等 Customs, etiquette, etc.

  .2 宗教 Religions Religious sociology

	基督教社會學	Christian sociology
.28	道德	Moral　Social ethics
.29	信仰	Belief
.3	教育	Education　Educational sociology
.4		
.5	社會心理　社會行為	Social psychology　Social behavior
.51	暗示	Social suggestions
.53	模仿	Social imitations
.54	輿論	Public opinion
.55	態度	Social attitude
.57	權力與自由	Authority and freedom
.58	群眾	Crowds, tumults, etc.
.6	經濟	Economics　Economical sociology
.9	社會法	Social law
312	動態社會學	Social dynamics, or dynamical sociology
.1	社會演化　社會進化	Social evolution　Biological sociology
.2	社會起源	Origin and decent
	互見　563.2	See also 563.2
.21	社會遺傳	Transmission and inheritance
.22	社會變異	Variation
.23	社會淘汰	Social selection
	自然淘汰, 等	Natural selection, etc.
.25	社會進步	Social progress
.27	社會停滯　退化	Social regression
.29	社會不安	Social unrest
.5	社會運動	Social movement

.6	社會革命		Social revolution
.63	領袖		Leadership
.65	威信		Prestige
.8	社會改革　社會改造		Social reform　Social reconstruction
	社會改良,社會解決,		Schemes for social ameliorastism, or social solutions
	互見 317		see also 317
.9			
313	靜態社會學		Social statics, or statical sociology
	社會制度與組織,區域社會,團體社會		Social institutions and organization; communities or territorial groups, social groups; Demological sociology
.1	人類社會發生		Anthropogenicassociation (Beginnings of human society)
.2	血族社會　初民社會		Ethnogenic association　Primitive society
.3	家庭　家庭生活		Family　Family life
.31	家庭起源		Its origin
.311		古代	Ancient
.312		中古	Medieval
.313		近世	Modern
.319		依國分	By country
.32	家庭制度與組織		The family: institution and organizations
.321		家長　父系	Patriarch　Paternity
.322		父母	Parents
.323		夫婦	Husband and wife
.325		子女	Children

.327	主僕	Master and servants
.329	依國分	By country
	例　中國家庭制度	
.34	**婚姻　婚姻問題**	**Marriage**
.341	婚姻制度	Systems
	1. 一夫一妻制	Monogamy
	3. 一夫多妻制	Polygamy
	5. 一婦多夫制	Polyandry
	9. 依國分	By country
.342	戀愛　性問題	Erotica and sex relations
	1. 自由戀愛	Free love, spiritual wives
	3. 淫奔　通姦	Adultery
	5. 非法結婚	Illegitimacy
.343	求婚	Courtship
.344	許婚　婚約　背約	Betrothal　Breach of promise
.345	試婚	Trial marriage
.346	離棄	Desertion
.347	離婚	Divorce
.348	雜婚	Mixed marriages　Hetaerism　Community of wives, etc.
.349	其他	Other marriage problems
	例　獨身問題,教會與婚姻,等	e. g. Celibacy, Church and marriage, State and marriage, etc.
.35	**婦女　婦女問題**	**Woman　Feminism**
	婦女研究,摩登婦女,等	Works of feminism, the modern woman, etc.
.3501	心理	Psychology
	互見 153.11	see also 153.11
.3502	道德	Practical　Ethics
.3503	教育　互見 338.91	Education see also 338.91
.3504	衛生	Hygiene

.3507	藝術上之婦女　婦女美	Woman in art　Esthetics　Beauty in woman
.3508	文學上之婦女	Woman in literature
.3509	歷史	History of woman's work in literature
	依國分	By country
	例　中國婦女著述	e.g. Chinese-Woman's work in literature
	傳記	Female biography
.352	婦女與宗教	Woman and religion
	婦女與基督教	Woman and Christianity
	婦女與聖經	Woman and the Bible
.353	婦女與社會	Woman and society　Social relations
	婦女解放,社會生活,事業,等	Emancipation of woman, social life, social works, etc.
.354	婦女與國家	Woman and the state
	婦女政權：參政,	Political rights: Suffrage
	法權：財產,承繼,等	Legal rights: Property, inheritance, etc.
.355	婦女與經濟	Woman and economics
	婦女職業　婦女勞工	Employment, professions, occupation, labor, etc.
	互見 354.23	see also 354.23
.356	婦女會　婦女組織	Women's clubs
.359	依國分	By country
.36	兒童	Children　Child culture
	溺嬰　見 315.185	Abortion　Infanticide　see 315.185
	生育限制　見 563.57	Birth control　Limitation of offspring see 563.57
	兒童節	Child day
.361	兒童保護	Care of children
.362	兒童生活	Child life　Descriptive
	游戲	Play　Games
.363	兒童之於父母	Children's duties to parents

.364	兒童權利　兒童與國家 兒童犯罪　互見 394.2	Children's rights　The child and the state Juvenile delinquency　see 394.2
.365	兒童心理　兒童研究 互見 153.7	Psychology　Child-study see also 153.7
.367	兒童教育　互見 338.92	Education　see also 338.92
.368	青年 男 女	Youth　Both sexes Boys Girls
.369	依國分	By country
.38	**親族**	**Kindship**
.381	氏族社會	Stock group
.382	圖騰社會	Totem　Totemism
.383	血族系統	Systems of consanguinity and affinity
.384	母族系統	Female (metronymic) kinship: matriarchate
.385	父族系統	Male (agnatic) kinship: Agnation
.386	系譜　宗譜 參看 977.5	Fabricated genealogies see also 977.5
.387	繼嗣	Adoption
.388	親族組織部落,等	Kinship organization　Clans, tribe, etc.
.389	依國分	By country
.4	**鄉村　鄉村生活** 起源　演化　村落	**Rural community　Rural life** Origin　Evolution　Village community
.41	鄉村計劃	Rural planning
.411	美村	The village beautiful
.412	住宅	Housing
.413	公共建築	Public works
.414	街道	Street, roads, etc.
.415	公園	Parks
.42	人口	Rural population

	其關係統計者　見 349.07	For statistics, see 349.07
.43	衛生	Rural hygiene
	排污,自來水,等	Removal of waste, water supply, etc.
.45	精神生活	Mental and moral life
	例　宗教生活	e.g. Religious life
.46	慈善	Rural charities
.47	娛樂　游藝	Recreation　Amusements
.48	鄉村與城市及其他之關係	Country and city
.49	依國分	By country
	例　美國鄉村生活 312.496	e.g. American rural life 312.496
.5	城市　城市生活	Urban groups: the city life
	仿上細分	subd. as above
	例　城市衛生 312.53	e.g. City hygiene 312.53
.6	會社團體	Associations　Societies
.61	愛國團	Patriotic societies
.62		
.63	秘密社	Secret societies
.64		
.65	俱樂部	Social clubs
.66	朋友團	Benevolent and "Friendly" societies
.67	青年團	Young people societies
	童子軍	Boy scouts
	女童子軍	Campfire girls
.68		
.69	其他	Other societies
.7	職業團體	Trade or professional unions

.71	農業	Agricultural
.72	商業	Commercial
.74	工業	Industrial
.79	其他	Others
.8	階級團體	Classes
.81	皇族	Royalty
.82	貴族	Nobility　Aristocracy
.83	平民	Commons
.84	婢役	Servants
.85	奴隸	Slaves
.87	特殊以及變態階級	Special and abnormal classes
	例　無業流氓,等	e.g. Outcasts, etc.
.88	以財產分	Classes arising from occupation
	資本階級	Capitalist class　Bourgeosie
	勞工階級	Working class　Preletariat
.9	其他團體	Other social groups

314　社會歷史與狀況　　Social history and conditions
　　　叙述社會學　　　　Descriptive sociology

　　　社會調查　方法　統計　　Social surveys, investigation, methods, statistics

　　依國分　　　　　　By country
　　　例　印度社會歷史與狀況　　e.g. India-Social history and conditions 314.23
　　　314.23

315　社會病理學　　Social pathology
　.1　　犯罪學　　　　Criminology
　.11　　人類犯罪學　　Criminal anthropology
　.12　　犯罪種類　　　The criminal type
　.121　　　精神病性　　Insane or mental

.122	生性或本性	The born or instinctive
.123	習慣性	The habitual Recidivist
.124	職業性	The professional
.125	偶然性	The occassional
.126	感情性	The criminal by passion
.127	意外犯罪	The criminal by accident
.13	罪犯解剖　罪犯相法	Anatomy　Physiognomy
.14	罪犯測定	Criminal anthropometry
	拍照,手印,等	Bertillon method: Photo of criminals. Finger prints, etc.
.15	犯罪心理	Criminal psychology
.16	犯罪原由　罪原學	Causes of crime Criminal etiology
.161	遺傳	Heredity
.163	疾病	Influence of disease
.165	烟酒與犯罪	Alcoholism and crime
.167	環境	Environment
	氣候關係	Cosmic influences
	社會與家庭關係	Social and domestic relations
	經濟關係	Economic conditions
	例　貧窮與犯罪	e.g. Pauperism and crime Political conditions and crime
	政治狀況與犯罪	Political conditions and crime
.17	種族犯罪學	Criminal ethnography
	依國分	By country
.18	犯罪與犯法	Crimes and offenses
	此項專類研究犯罪原理,等諸作其他關係政治法律者應入349.2	Theory, etc., only—For descriptive works, history, politic cases, prefer, 349.2
.181	國家	Offenses against the state
	互見393.23	see also 393.23

	賣國,等罪	Treason, etc.
.182	法律	Offenses against justice
	見 395.08	see 395.08
	侮辱法令,等罪	Contempt of court, etc.
.183	歲入　國課	Offenses against the revenue
	假冒,私運,等罪	Counterfeiting, smuggling, ect.
.184	治安	Offenses against the public order
	非法組織,集會,暴動,等罪	Illegal organization, unlawful assemblies etc.
.185	身體	Crimes against the person
	暗殺,溺嬰,自殺,毒殺,強姦,掠奪,等罪	Homicide, Murder, Infanticide, Suicide, Poisoning and poisoners, Sexual crimes, Rape, Etc.
.186	名譽	Crimes against reputation or honor
	毀謗,讒譖,等罪	Libel and slander, etc.
.187	財產	Crimes against property
	盜竊,擅用,贋造,詐取,瞞騙,等罪	Theft, Forgery, Frauds, Humbugs, Quacks, Etc.
.188	社會道德	Offenses against public morals
	賭博,騙拐,等罪	Gambling, Imposture, Financial crime, Etc.
.189		
.19	罪犯	Crimes and criminal classes
	其性質關係或總論一國罪犯及犯罪情形者	General works and works not limited to one or two special subjects
	依國分	By country
.2	刑罰學	Penology
	互見 393.5	see also 393.5
.3	警察　公安	Police　Detectives　Constabulary
.31	警規　警章	Law　Regulation　Police codes
.32	行政	Administration　Organization

.321	中央		Central
.323	地方		Local
.324	省		Provincial
.325	市		Municipal
.326	縣		District
.33	警務 保安		Police duty　Methods of protection
.35	警庭		Police justice　Police courts
.37	偵探 偵探所		Private detectives　Detective bureaus
.39	依國分		By country
.5	監獄學 監獄改良		Prisons　Penitentiaries　Punishment and reform
.51	懲治		Forms of punishments
.52	建築		System of construction
.53	衛生		Prison hygiene
.54	飲食 服裝		Food　Dietary　Costume of prisoners
.56	宗教		Provision for religious and moral instruction
.57	教育		Provision for education of prisoners
.59	依國分		By country
.7	感化所		reformatories
.71	兒童犯罪與感化		The juvenile offender reform schools, etc.
.73	婦女犯罪與感化		Reformation and reclamation of women prisoners
.8			
.9			

316　社會救濟學　慈善事業　Social welfare　Philanthropy

	必要時下列可依國細分	the following divisions may be subd. by country
.1	紅十字會　卍字會	Red cross
.2	醫院社會服務	Hospitals social work
	生命救急法　見 593.4	For life savings　see 593.4
.3	慈善會	Charity institutions
.31	孤兒院	Orphan asylums
.33	養老院	Aged asylums
.34		
.35	殘疾所	Aid and homes for defectives
.36	癲狂癡愚院	Aid and homes for mentally defectives; nervous, etc
.37		
.38	乞丐所	Aid and homes for beggars
.4	賑濟　賑灾	Relief in case of disasters
.41	水灾	Floods
.42	火灾	Fires
.43	旱灾	Famine
.44	蝗蟲	Locusts
.45	冰雹　暴風	Hailstone, storms, etc.
.46	地震	Earthquakes
.47	瘟疫	Plague　Epedemies
.48	兵灾　匪患	Wars　Bandits (Refugees)
.5	公私卹貧	Public and private aid in general
.51	貧窮收容所	Lodgings for the poor
.53	借貸	Money aid
.55	衣物濟施	Distribution of food, clothing, and fuel
.57	工賑	Pauper labor

.59	平糶	Cheap sale of rice, etc.
.6	義田　義莊	Free farming
.7	職業介紹	Labor agencies
.8	社會保險與儲蓄	Social insurance　Savings
.9		

317　社會問題　　　　　Social problems

.1	生活問題	Problem of living
.11	衣	Clothing
.12	食	Food
.13	住	Housing
.14		
.15	生活費	Cost of living
.16	生活標準	Standard of living
.19	依國分	By country
.2	種族問題	Race problem
.3	階級問題	Class problem
	見 312.8	see 312.8
.4	奴制問題	Slavery (including slavery and serfdom, coolies)
.42	宗教之於奴制	Religion and slavery
.43	社會,經濟之於奴制	Social and economic aspects of slavery
.44	種族之於奴制	Race and slavery
.45	奴制法律	Law of slavery
.46	奴商	The slave trade
.48	奴制解放	Abolition of slavery　Anti-slavery
.49	依國分	By country
.5	婦女問題	Women's problem

		見 313.35	see 313.35
	.6	群衆問題　群衆運動	Mob problem
	.7	青年問題	Youth problem
	.8	社會清潔運動	Social purity movement
	.81	禁煙	Prohibition of drug habits (opium)
	.82	禁酒	Prohibition of alcoholism
	.83	禁賭	Prohibition of gambling
	.84		
	.85	廢妾	Abolition of concubinage
	.86	廢娼	Abolition of prostitution
	.87	纏足,束腰,文身之禁止	
	.88	鄰保事業	Social settlement
	.89	依國分	By country
	.9		
318		社會主義	Socialism
	.01	理論	Theories
	.02	政策	Policies
	.09	社會主義與教育,戰爭及其他關係	Socialism in relation to education, war, etc.
	.1	理想社會主義	Utopian socialism
		基督教社會主義	Christian socialism
		聖西門社會主義	Saint Simonism
		福利社會主義	Fourierism
	.2	國家社會主義	State socialism
		三民主義　見 001.11	Sunyatsenism　see 001.11
		法西斯主義	Febianism

.3	工團主義　基爾特主義	Syndicalism　Guild socialism
.4	無政府主義	Anarchism
.5	科學的社會主義	Scientific socialism
	馬克斯主義	Maxism
	社會民主主義	Social democracy
.6		
.7	共産主義　赤化主義	Communism　Bolshevism
.8		
.9	世界大同	Cosmopolitanism　Internationalism

319　禮俗　社風　　　　　Customs　Costumes　Etiquette
　　　歌謠俚語入民間文學

.01	理論　關係	Theories　Relations
	例　禮俗與人種學之關係	In relation to ethnology
.03	辭書	Dictionaries
.037	年鑑	Yearbooks
.04	評論	Critiques
.05	雜誌	Periodicals
.06	學會	Societies　Congresses
.07	研究　方法	Study and teaching：Outlines, etc.
.08	總集　彙集　小册	Collected works　Pamphlets
.09	歷史	History
	依國分	By country
	例　中國禮俗 319.091	e.g. Chinese customs　Etiquette 319.091
	凡總論中國禮儀風俗諸著述類此	
.1	國禮　邦禮	State ceremonies

.11	吉禮	祭祀	Sacrificial ceremonies
.111	天地		Heaven and earth
.112	社稷		Spirits of land and grain
.113	山川		Mountains Rivers
.114	日月 星辰		Sun Moon Stars
.115	百神		Worship of Gods
.116	宗廟		Ancestors
.117	謁陵		Worship at the grave
.118	祀孔		Worship of Confucius
.119	其他		Others
.12	嘉禮		Official ceremonies of royalty, nobility, etc.
	例 登極,踐祚,封爵, 等儀式		e.g. Ascension, enthrone, appointment, etc.
.13	賓禮 使儀		The diplomatic ceremonies
.15	軍禮		Customs of war
	大閱,出師,親征,凱旋, 獻俘,受俘,等		
.17	凶禮 互見319.24		Treatment of the dead Burial and funeral customs see also 319.24
	振撫,疾病,大喪,追尊, 等		
.18	雜禮		Miscellaneous customs
.19	依國分		By country
.2	家禮 家法		Family customs, etiquette
.21	誕禮 冠禮		Birth customs
.22	聘禮 婚禮		Betrothal Marriage
.23	壽禮		Birthday customs
.24	喪禮 葬禮		Burial and funeral customs

		土葬,陪葬,合葬,保葬,水葬,火葬,等	Earth burial, cremation, embalming, etc.
	.25	祭祀:祭祖,上墳,等	Sacrifice　Offering at the grave
	.26	族禮　戚禮	Customs of kinship
	.27	食禮　飲,食,烟,酒,等	Eating and drinking customs
	.29	依國分	By country
.3		社會禮節	Social etiquette
	.31	敬長　尊老	Respect of aged
	.32	謙讓　禮貌	Courtesy
	.33	投刺　介紹	Introduction and call on
	.34	見禮	Salutations　Shakehands
	.35	接談	Interlocution
	.36	款待	Entertainments
	.37		
	.38	男女交際	
	.39	依國分	By country
.4		衣冠　修飾	Dress　Costume
	.401	理論　美學	Philosophy, esthetics, etc.
	.402	圖樣	Pictorial works
	.404	法規	Laws, regulations, etc., concerning dress
	.407	展覽	Exhibitions
	.409	歷史	History
		古代,中古,近世	Ancient, medieval, modern
	.41	男服　女服　童服	Costume of men, women, children
	.42	禮服	Full dress
	.43	朝服	Court costumes
	.44	軍服	Military uniforms
	.45		

	.46	特殊階級服裝:貴族,平民,等	Costume of special classes: Nobility, commons, etc.
	.47	修飾:理髮,沐浴,等	Hairdressing, bath, etc.
	.48	飾品	Miscellaneous details and accessories
		首飾,冠冕,鞋靴,手套,扇,傘,杖,等	Ornaments, hat, footwear, gloves, fans, umbrellas, sticks, etc.
	.49	依國分	By country
	.5	住宅　用具	Houses　Dwelling　Furnitures
		房屋建築　見 651.3	For constructions　see 651.3
	.501	古代	Ancient
	.502	中古	Medieval
	.503	近世	Modern
.51-.59		依國分	By country
	.7	社會風俗	Social customs
	.71	節令	Festivals　Holidays
	.72	燕饗	Banquet　Feast
	.73	香會　燈節	Pilgrams　Lantern shows
	.75	娛樂　游藝	Amusements　Games
		跳舞	Dancing
		比武	Tournaments　Duelling
		賣藝	
	.77	野郎,游女,以及毆鬥凶殺等風俗	
	.79	依國分	By country
	.8	迷信	Superstitions
	.81	神仙,鬼怪,等	Supernatural beings, etc.
	.9	初民以及無籍流民之風俗	Customs relative to other classes: Outlaws, Gypsies, etc.

330　教育　　　　　　　　Education

.1	理論　關係	Theories　Relations
	教育思想史	History of educational theory
	.101-.109 依國分	By country
.11	教育家學說	Systems of individual educators and writers
	依國分	By country
.12	教育與國家　教育運動	Sociological aspects of education Education and the state
.122	教育政策	Educational policy
	侵略	
	自主	
.123	國民教育　公民教育	Political education and citizenship
.124	民衆教育　普通教育	People's or popular education
.125	教育通俗化	Public school question "Secularization"
	教育由宗教通俗化	Religious instruction in the public schools
.126	強迫教育	Compulsory education
.127	識字運動	Illiteracy　Analphabetism
.129	依國分	By country
.13	教育與社會,遺傳,犯罪,等	Education and society, heredity, crime, etc
.14	教育統計	Educational statistics
.15	教育心理	Educational psychology
.17	教育測驗	Educational tests
.18	教育倫理	Educational ethics
.19	教育與文化	Education and culture
.3	辭書	Encyclopedias　Dictionaries
.32	表册	Tables
.37	年鑑	Yearbooks
.38	指南	Educational directories
.4	論文　演講集	Critiques

.5	雜誌	Periodicals
	學生刊物　見 333.05	Students' publications see 333.05
	學校刊物　見 339	School publications see 339
.6	學會　會議　報告	Societies　Conventions　Reports
	依國分	By country
	例　中國教育會議	e.g. Chinese educational conventions
	330.61	330.61
	美國教育會議	U. S.—Educational conventions
	330.66	330.66
.7	研究　教育館	Study and teaching
	綱目,綱要,問答,等	Outlines, syllabi, synopses, questions, etc.
.8	總集　小册　文藝	Collected works　Pamphlets　Educational literature
.9	歷史　教育現狀	History
.91	中國教育史	History of Chinese education
.92	亞洲其他各國教育史	History of education of other Asiatic countries
.93	歐洲各國教育史	History of education of European countries
.94	美洲各國教育史	History of education of American countries
.95	非洲大洋洲各國教育史	Hisotry of education of African and Oceanian countries
.97	教育家傳記	Biography of educators
	下列各項皆可依學校細分	The following divisions may be subd. by schools
	例　大學課程　335.07	e.g. College curriculum 335.07

331　教育行政　學校行政　School government

.1　　法令　　　　　　　　　Laws　Legislation
.2　　制度　　　　　　　　　Systems
　.21　　中央集權　　　　　　State control　Centralization
　.22　　地方分制　　　　　　Local control
.3　　行政　　　　　　　　　Administration
　.31　　組織　校制　　　　　Organization
　.32　　學院　　　　　　　　Colleges
　.33　　學系　　　　　　　　Departments
　.35　　行政員　　　　　　　Administrative officers
　　.351　　行政長官　　　　　　Bureau of education
　　.352　　校董　　　　　　　　Board of trustees
　　.353　　校長　　　　　　　　Chancellar　President
　　.354　　校務長　　　　　　　Dean
　　.355　　秘書長　　　　　　　Secretary to the President
　　.356
　　.357
　　.359　　其他　　　　　　　　Others
　.36　　會議:校務,教務,院　　The committees
　　　　　務會議
.4　　經費　預算表　　　　　School finance, budgets, etc
　　　經費獨立,教育維持費
　　　等論述類此
　.41　　基金　　　　　　　　School funds, endowment, appropria-
　　　　　　　　　　　　　　　　tions and grants
　.43　　經常費　　　　　　　School budgets
　.45　　補助費:經貼,獎金,　 Scholarship
　　　　　等

.47 教育維持稅 Educational taxation
.5
.6 校產　校址 School property
.7 指導　視學 Inspection of schools
.8
.9 依國分 By country
　　　例　中國教育行政　　Chinese educational administration 331.91
　　　331.91

332 學校管理　　School management

.1 校規　校風 Rules and regulations
.11 上課與曠課 Attendance and absence　Truancy　Tardiness
.13 賞罰 Rewards and punishments
.17 學潮 Students' strike
.2 禮節　典儀 Special days　School etiquette
.3 衛生　校醫 School hygiene　School doctors
　　　互見　593.33　　see also 593.33
.31 身體測驗與檢查 Physical measurement
.32 疾病預防 Diseases control
　　　飲食,食堂,等各方面　Care of food, management of lunch room, etc.
.33 身體清潔　沐浴,等 Cleanliness　School baths, etc.
.35 攻讀衛生 Strain and overpressure　Mental capacity
.37 休息　睡眠 Recreation　Sleep
.38 空氣　光線 Fresh air　Lighting and heating
.4 訓育 School discipline
　　　個人輔導　　Personal responsible for discipline

	.5	體育　見 338.63	Physical education　see 338.63
	.6	軍事訓練	Military drills
	.7	庶務　會計	School business　School accountant
	.8		
	.9	設備	School architecture and equipment
	.91	場所：運動場，球場，等	Playgrounds, etc.
	.92	建築：講堂，試驗室，等	Buildings：Class-rooms, laboratory, etc.
	.93	器具　佈置：桌，椅，等	Equipment and supplies：Tables, etc.
	.95	學校圖書館　見 025.2	School library see 025.2
	.97	儀器	Laboratory equipment and supplies
	.99	其他用品	Other supplies
333		學生生活　學生課外組織	School life, student manners and customs
	.05	刊物	Student publications
	.06	會所	Student house　Commons　Student restaurants　Eating clubs
	.1	榮譽	Student honor　Student ethies
	.2		
	.3	游藝會	Amusement and games
	.31	音樂會	Musical clubs
	.33	演劇團	Dramatic societies
	.35	運動會	Sports
	.37	武術團	Fagging and hazing
	.38	旅行團	Traveling parties

.39	其他	Others
.4	慶祝會	Celebrations Burnings
.41	校日	School days
.45	畢業典禮	Class days　Colors　Cheers
.5	智育會	Literary societies
.51	成績展覽會	Exhibitions
.54	演講辯論會	Debates　Orations
.6	社會服務團	Social works
.63	青年會	School Y. M. C. A.
.65	義賑會	Social relief
.7	校友會	Alumni day
.8	懇親會	Parent-teacher associations
.9	社友　團契	Student fraternities and societies
334	學則	School standardization　Priciples and requirements of study
.1	入學	Admission
.11	註冊	Enrolment
	學生名單履歷	Lists of students
.15	繳費	Tuition　Fees
	免費	Free tuition　Scholarship
.17	入學禮　開學禮	Matriculation　Commencement exercises
.3	學年　校日	Calendar year　School day
.31	學年	Calendar year
.32	學期	Semesters
.33	學季	Terms
.34		
.35	校日	School day

.36 紀念日 Holidays
.37 假期 Special days　Vacations
.4 鐘點　班次　年限 Hours of study　Years required
　　例　四年制　六年制
.5 考試　計分 Examinations and marking
.6 升學　轉學　留級 Grading and promotion　Demotions
　　轉級 　　and retardation
.7 畢業　學位 Graduation　Degrees
.74 畢業論文 Thesis
.8 校徽 School symbolism
.83 校旗 School banners
.85 校歌 School songs
.87 校服 School costumes
.9

335 課程 Curriculum　Course of study
.1 教材 Subjects of study
　　依類分 By subjects
　　例　哲學在課程中的地位 e.g. Place of philosophy in the curriculum
.3 專修 Single course　Mandatory studies
.4 兼修 Parallel courses
.5 必修 Required courses
.6 選修 Optional courses　Elective system
.7 特修　旁聽 Special courses
.9 依國分 By country
　　例　中國學校課程　335.91 e.g. Curriculum for Chinese schools 335.91

336　教員　　　　　　　　　Teachers　Professors　Instructors
　.1　任務　教務　　　　　　Duties and responsibilities
　　　　例　教授學行之關於學　　　e. g. Personal influence, relations to parents, etc.
　　　　　　生,家庭,社會,等
　.2　資格　　　　　　　　　Qualifications　Personality
　.21　教員之考試問題　　　　Teacher's examination
　.25　教員證書　　　　　　　Certification of teachers
　.3　教員訓練　練習　　　　Need of training: kind and amount
　.4　聘任　任期　聘書　　　Appointment　Contract
　.5　待遇　　　　　　　　　Salary and promotion　Compensation　Amount of service
　.51　薪金　　　　　　　　　Salary: increases
　.52　養老金　　　　　　　　Pensions and insurance for teachers
　.53　住宅　　　　　　　　　Residence　Living expenses
　.55　升任　辭退　解聘　　　Promotion　Advance in rank
　.57　鐘點　　　　　　　　　Hours: Daily and weekly service
　.58　假期　年假　　　　　　Vacation　Sabbatic year
　.6　教業問題　教授與職業　Problems of the teaching Profession
　.7　婦女教員　　　　　　　Women as teachers
　.8
　.9　其他　　　　　　　　　Others
337　教授法　　　　　　　　　Methods of instruction and study
　.1　普通教授法　　　　　　General
　.11　問答法　　　　　　　　Art of questioning　Catechistic method　Socratic method

.12	演講法		Lectures: Oral and visual
.13	實驗法		Laboratory method　Field work
.14	啓發　引例法		Developing or inductive method
.15	分析　推理法		Analytic or deductive method
.17	研究法		Seminary method　Seminar　Discussion
.19	校外教授法		Floating schools or colleges
.191		旅行　遠足	Travels　Picnic
.193		調查	Surveys
.195		參觀	Trips, excursions, visits
.3	專家之教授法		Methods of individual educators
.31	設計法		Project method　Topical method
.32			Pestalozzian
.33	道爾頓制		The Dalton plan
.35	蒙鐵梭利法		Montessori system
.37			Jacctot
.38			Quincy system
.4	分級教授法		Methods of instruction　Classes
.41	單級		Monitorial system
.43	合級		Mutual system
.5	個性教授法		Individual instruction
.6	各科教授法		Methods of instruction for special subjects
		依類分或析入各類	By subjects or with the subjects
		例　英文學教授法	e.g. English literature
.7	各校教授法		Methods of instruction for special schools
		依校分或析入各校	By schools or with the schools

		例　大學授教法	e.g. College instruction
.8			
.9		修學法　讀法	Methods of reading, studying, etc.
338		學校　學校教育	Schools and colleges　School education
	.01	公立學校	Public schools and colleges
	.02	國立	National　State
	.03	省立	Provincial
	.04	市立	Municipal
	.05	縣立	District
	.07	私立學校	Private schools and colleges
	.1	蒙學教育	Preschool education
	.11	蒙養園	Nursing school
	.13	幼稚園	Kindergarten
	.131	手工	Manual work
	.133	圖畫	Drawing
	.134	游藝	Games
	.135	童話　故事	Stories
	.137	音樂　唱歌	Music and songs
	.138	寫讀	Reading
	.139	其他	Others
			Sensory training, etc.
	.19	依國分	By country
		例　中國幼稚園	e.g. Chinese kindergarten
	.2	小學教育	Primary or elementary education
	.21	初小	Lower primary school
	.23	高小	Higher primary school
	.29	依國分	By country
	.3	中學教育	Secondary or high school

.31	初中	Junior high school
.33	高中	Senior high school
.35	預備學校	Preparatory education
.39	依國分	By country
.4	職業教育	Professional or vocational
.41	鄉村　農村	Rural education
.42	林間	
.45	城市	Urban education
.47	職業學校	Vocational school
.48	職業指導	Vocational guidance
.49	依國分	By country
.5	師範教育	Normal schools　Teachers' institutes
.51	師範學校	Normal school
.53	高等師範	High normal
.55	教員訓練學校	Teachers training school
.57	師範大學	Teachers college
.59	依國分	By country
.6	專門學校	Technical schools
	依類分或析入各類	By subjects or clast with the subjects
	例　神學 338.62	e.g. Divinity school
	體育 338.63	Physical education
	法專 338.639	Law college
	語專 338.64	Lauguage school
	地質 338.655	Geological school
	醫專 338.659	Medical school
	工程 338.665	Engineering school
	美術 338.67	Art school
	其關於體育書籍可與體育教育同列如下	Works on physical education to be clast here

.63	體育學校	Physical education
.631	體操　軍操	Physical exercise　Military drills
	例　柔軟體操	e.g. Light exercises
.632	戶內游戲	Indoor games and amusement
.633	戶外游戲	Outdoor games and sports
.634	運動會：田徑賽	Athletic sports：Track and field athletic
	賽跑,跳欄,跳遠,跳高,撐高,鐵餅,標槍,等	Race, hurdles, broad-jump, high-jump, pole-vault, discus, javelin, etc.
.635	球戲　球賽	Ball games
	足球,棍球,網球,籃球,排球,板球,杓球,等	Football, baseball, tennis, basketball, volleyball, cricket, golf, polo, etc.
.636	長途競賽	Touring　Pedestrianism
.637	水上游戲　比賽	Aquatic sports
	賽船,游泳,溜冰,等	Boating, swimming and diving, ice and snow sports, etc.
.638	武術	Fighting sports
	拳術,劍術,角力,射擊,等	Boxing, fencing, wrestling, shooting, war games, etc.
.639	運動場及設備	Place and equipment of exercises
	運動場,健身所,游泳池,及各項用具	Athletic field, gymnasium, aquatic equipment, etc.
.7	大學教育	College education
.71	大學	Colleges and universities
.73	研究院	Graduate schools
.75	留學	Study abroad
.79	依國分	By country
.8	特殊教育　補習教育	Special education
.81	自修	Self-directed school
.82	家塾	Education by tutors

.83		
.84	義務　慈善	Charity schools
.85	夜校　半日學校	Evening schools　Part-time education
.86	暑期學校	Vacation schools　Summer schools
.87	函授學校	Correspondence schools
.88	讀書團	Reading circles and clubs
	公共讀書所	Community centers
	其他	Others
.89	依國分	By country
.9	特種人教育	Education of special classes of persons
.91	婦女教育	Education of women
.912	體育與智育	Physical and mental capacity of women
.913	家政	Home or domestic instruction
.914	初等	Elementary education
.915	中等	Secondary education
.916	師範	Normal school
.917	大學	College education
.918	男女同校	Co-education
.919	特殊教育	Other special education for women
	1. 性教育	Sexual education
	3. 社交教育	Social intercourse　Fashionable school
	5. 戀愛教育	Love education
	9. 其他	Others
.92	兒童教育	Children education
.93	成人教育	Adult education
.94	勞工教育	Labor education
.95	特殊階級教育	Education for special classes

.96		變態教育	Abnormal education
.961		孤兒	Orphans
.962		流荒	Outcasts
.963		赤貧	Paupers
.964			
.965		殘廢	Physically defectives
		瞽,聾,癱跛,等	Blind, deaf and dumb, crippled, etc.
.966		低能	Mentally defectives
.967		瘋癲	Nervous
.968		墮落	Morally defectives
.97		罪犯教育	Criminal education
.98		蠻民教育	Education for aboriginal : Miao, Gypsies, etc.
.99		依國分	By country

339　檔案　校刊　　　　School publications

.1	校章	Charter and statutes
.2	公文	Documents
.21	訓令	Orders and instructions
.22	公函	Official correspondences
.23	委令　聘書	Appointments
.24	呈文	Petitions
.25	佈告　啓事　通告	Notice　Announcements
.26	議案　紀錄　報告	Administration reports
.27	統計　表册	Statistics　Tables　Etc.
.28		
.29	其他	Others
.3	指南　一覽　概況	Directories　Catalogues　Annuals
.4	文卷	Lectures　Class manuals　Examination questions

.41	講義	Lectures
.42	試卷	Examination papers
.44	論文	Essays
.46	演講	Orations
.5	雜誌	Periodicals
.6	同學錄	Alumni
.7		
.8	雜錄	Miscellanies
	圖案照片等	Pictures　Class ablums　Photo Etc.
.9	校史	History and description

340　統計學　　　　　　　Statistics

.1	理論　關係	Theories　Relations
	例　統計與經濟	e.g. In relation to economics, etc.
.2		
.3	辭書	Dictionaries
.4	評論	Critiques
.5	雜誌	Periodicals
.6	學會	Societies
.7	研究	Study and teaching: Outlines, etc.
.8	總集	Collected works　Pamphlets
.9	歷史	History

341　統計法　　　　　　　Methods　Science of statistics

.1	調查法　調查程次	Methods of investigation　Procedure of investigation
.11	訪問	Inquires　Interview
.13	材料搜集	Data, collecting

.14	整理　分類		Arrangement　Analysis　Classification
.15			
.16	校勘		Correction
.17	補插法		Interpolation
.3	計算法		Statistical calculation
	例　大數,平均,差異,相關,等法		e.g. Law of great nos. average, dispersion or variation, etc.
.4	製表法		Tabulation
	例　單項,雙項,多項,等法		e.g. Single, double, trible, etc.
.5	統計圖法		Diagrams　Cartograms
	點,線,面,地圖,等法		Dots, Lines, Curves, Surface charts, Statistical maps, Etc.
.7	指數法		Index numbers
345	國家統計　國勢調查		National statistics　Censuses
			includes general statistics, censuses, population, etc.
	.1	中國統計　國勢調查	Statistics of China　Censuses
	.11	中央統計	Central
.111-.115		各院統計	The Yuans
.119		各部統計	The Departments
	.12	地方統計	Local
	.13	省	Provincial
		各廳統計	
	.14	市	Municipal
		各局統計	
	.15	縣	District

	各局統計	
.16	鄉村	Rural
.17	民間統計	Non-official
.18	華僑統計	Of Chinese emigrants
.19	（屬地殖民地統計）	
.2-.9	其他各國統計	Statistics of other countries
	仿中國細分	Subd. as Chinese

346　應用統計　　Applied statistics

　　總論　　　　　　　　　　General treatises

　　專門統計入各專類　　　　Special statistics prefer with the subjects

　　　例　教育統計 330.14　　e.g. Educational statistics 330.14

349　人口論　　Demography　Population

.01	學說	Theories
.011	馬爾薩斯	Malthusian theory
.013	新馬爾薩斯	Neo-Malthusianism
.02	人口政策	Policies
.021	人口限制	Birth control
.023	多生與無生	Fecundity and sterility
.03	人口密度與分佈	Distribution of population
.04	人地率	The man-land ratio
.05	人口與自然	Population and the nature
	與食物,環境,氣候,等關係	In relation to food, surroundings, climates, etc.
.07	人口統計	Vital statistics
.071	婚姻率	Marriages
.072	生產率　死亡率	Births　Deaths
.073	年齡別	Age
.074	性別	Sex

.075	品質別	Characteristics	
.076	職業	Professions	
.077	居住別	Domicile	
.078	其他	Others	
	變態,道德,階級,等	Abnormal, ethical, classes, etc.	
.079	國籍別	Nationality	
.1	中國人口論	Demography of China	
	仿上細分	Subd. as above	
	例　中國人地率	e.g. The man-land ratio of China	
	394.104		
	依區域分	Local subdivision	
.2-.9	其他各國人口論	Demography of other countries	
350	經濟學	Economics　Political economy	
	經濟學種類可依下列細分	Special general	
.01	私經濟學	Private economics in general	
.011	個人經濟	Personal or individual economics	
.013	家庭經濟	Family economics	
.02	區域經濟學	Economics of communities	
.024	鄉村經濟	Rural economics	
.025	城市經濟	Urban economics	
.03	公經濟學	Public economics	
.031	國家經濟	State economics	
.032	地方經濟	Municipal economics	
.04	國民經濟學　國際經濟	National or folk economics　International economics	
.05			
.06			
.08	各類經濟學	Economics of special subjects	
	依類分或析入各類	By subjects or with the subjects	
	例　社會經濟學	e.g. Sociological economics	

.09	各派經濟學	Economics of special schools
.091	重商派	Mercantile system
.092	重農派	Physiocrats
.093	古典派	Classical school
.094	歷史派	Historical school
.097	社會主義派	Socialists
.1	理論　關係	Theories　Relations
.11	經濟思想史	History of economic theory
	依國分	By country
.17	經濟與經濟行爲	Economy and economic activities
.19	經濟學與他學科關係	Relations to others
	例　經濟與政治	e.g. Economics and politics
.3	辭書	Dictionaries
.32	表册	Tables
.34	統計	Statistics
.37	年鑑	Yearbooks
.4	論文	Critiques
.5	雜誌	Periodicals
.6	學會　會議	Societies　Conventions　Reports
	依國分	By country
.7	研究	Study and teaching: Outlines, etc.
.8	總集　小册	Collected works　Pamphlets
.9	歷史　經濟狀況	History　Economic conditions
.91	中國經濟史	History of Chinese economics
.92	亞洲其他各國經濟史	History of economics of other Asiatic countries
.93	歐洲各國經濟史	History of economics of European countries

.94	美洲各國經濟史	History of economics of American countries
.95	非洲大洋洲各國經濟史	History of economics of African and Oceanian countries

351　經濟制度　政策　Economic policy

.1	實業政策	Mechanical policy
	互見 601	seel also 601
.2	農業政策	Agricultural policy
	互見 610.31	see also 610.31
.3	商業政策	Commerical policy
	互見 621	see also 621
.31	國際貿易	International trade
.32	絕對自由貿易	Absolute free trade　No tariff
.33	自由貿易	Free trade　Tariff for revenue only
.34	自由競爭	Free competition
.35	保護貿易　禁止主義　捐稅制度	Protection of trade　Licensing systems
.36	輔助貿易	Subsidies
.37	互助貿易　互惠貿易	Reciprocity　Favored nation clause
.38	其他特殊貿易	Duties on special articles
	例　原料,書籍,文具,等	e.g. Raw material, books and works of art
.39	國內貿易	Home trade
.4	工業政策	Industrial policy
	互見 641	see also 641
.5	經濟壟斷	Economic monopoly
.6	經濟侵略	Economic invasion

	.7	經濟戰爭	Economic war
	.8	經濟問題	Economic problems
	.9	依國分	By country
		細分如上	subd. as above
		例　中國經濟問題 351.918	e.g. Chinese economic problems 351.918
352		生產論	Production
		特論或經濟學特論	Special topics
	.1	慾望	Wants
		物質與非物質	Material and inmaterial
	.2	財富	Wealth
		經濟與自由	Economic and free
	.3	財貨　商品	Goods　Commodities
	.4	效用　邊際效用	Utility　Marginal utility
	.41	效用與慾望	Utility and wants
	.42	效用與區域	Utility and place
	.43	效用與時間	Utility and time
	.44		
	.45	效用遞減律	Law of diminishing utility
	.47	邊際效用	Marginal utility
	.5	競爭	Competition
		傾銷	Dumping
	.6	獨占	Monopoly
	.7	經濟恐慌　調節	Economical crises　Conciliation
	.71	過產與恐慌	Overproduction and crises
	.72	消費與恐慌	Consumption and crises
	.73	幣制與恐慌	Money and crises
	.74	銀行與恐慌	Banks and crises

.75	投機與恐慌		Speculation and crises
.76	戰爭與恐慌		War and crises
.78	各業凋蔽與恐慌		By subjects
	例 產業凋蔽與恐慌		e.g. Industrial paralysis and crises
.79	依國分		By country
	概論一國經濟恐慌者		general and comprehensive in scope of a country
.8	貧窮		Pauperism
	生產要素		Elements of production

353　土地　　　　　　　　　Land

.01	地土權	見 397.2	Ownership　see 397.2
.02	田制		Policy　Theory of distribution
.1	種類		Special types of land
.11	林地		Forest lands
.13	草地		Pasture lands
.15	場地		Yardlands
.17	鑛地		Mines
.19	荒地		Waste lands
.2	公地		Public lands
.21	國有		State ownership
.23	省有		Provincial ownership
.24	市有		Municipal ownership
.25	縣有		District ownership
.29	其他		Others
.3	私地		Private ownership
.4	土地租期		Land tenure
.41	耕種用		For farming
.43	建築用		For buildings

.5	土地生產與自然	Productivity and nature
.6	土地生產與人工	Productivity and labor
.64	耕作　見 611.4	Cultivation　see 611.4
.66	水利　見 611.6	Water rights　Irrigation　see 611.6
.67	肥田　見 611.7	Fertilizing　see 611.7
.7	土地生產漸減律	Law of diminishing productivity
.9	依國分	By country

354　勞工　勞動　　Labor and labores

.01	理論　關係	Theories　Relations
.011	勞工自由	Freedom of labor
.015	勞工心理	Psychology
.018	勞工倫理　道德　勞工神聖	Ethics　Morals　Dignity of labor
.019	關係	Relations
	例　勞工與教會	e.g. Labor and the Church
	勞工與機器	Labor and machinery
.03	辭書	Dictionaries
.032	表冊	Tables
.034	統計	Statistics
.037	年鑑	Yearbooks
.04	評論	Critiques　Criticism
.05	雜誌　刊物	Periodicals　Publications
.06	學會	Conventions　Congresses
	依國分	By country
.07	研究	Study and teaching
	綱目，綱要，答問，等	Outlines, syllabi, synopses, questions, etc.
.08	總集　小冊	Collected works　Pamphlets
		Labor literature
	勞工文藝	Labor literature

.09	歷史與狀況	Labor history and conditions
	依國分	By country
.1	勞資關係	Relations of capital to labor
.11	僱工	Labor contracts in general employment
.113	勞工介紹所	Labor supply agencies
.114	勞工資格	Equipment of workers
	人格,教育,經驗,興趣,健康,等	Personality, education, experience, tastes, health, etc.
.115	勞工選擇	Selecting workers
	具保,面試,測驗,等	Securing applicants, interviews, tests, etc.
.117	僱用方式	Engaging works
	限制與自由僱用	Closed shop and open shop policies
.13	管理與組織	Department organization
.131	制度	System
.133	職員	Staff
	經理,工人,等	Officers, employees, etc.
.135	升遷	Labor maintenance
.136	移換	Turnover
.137	期限 失業 重僱	Termination of labor Unemployment Re-employment
.15	工廠規則	Rules for workship and office employees
.16	資方法權	Jurisdiction over work Industrial and professional tribunals
.18	各業勞資關係	By industry
.19	依國分	By country
.2	勞工種類	Classification of labor and laborers
.22	依年齡分	By age

		例 童工	e.g. Children labor and laborers
.23	依性別分		By sex
		例 女工	e.g. Female labor and laborers
.25	不利勞工		Work under certain unfavorable conditions
.251		監獄勞工	Prisons　Convict labor
.252		學徒	Apprentice labor
.253		農奴	Peonage　Serfs
.254		奴僕	Slave labor
.255		苦力	Coolies
.256		賺工　僑工	Pauper labor　Cheap foreign labor
.257		血汗勞工	Sweating labor or sweating system
.258		殘廢勞工	Labors of defective
.259		其他	Others
.26	依技能分		By art
		例 粗工	e.g. Unskilled labor and laborers
.28	各業勞工		By trade
		例 手藝勞工	e.g. Handicraft
.29	依國分		By country
		例 中國勞工	e.g. Chinese labor
.3	勞工報酬		Remuneration for work
.31	工資　工資學說		Wages　Theory of wages
.311		供求工資說	The demand and supply theory of wages
.312		生活程度說	The standard of living theory
.313		工資基金說	The wages fund theory
.314		邊際生產力說	Marginal productivity theory
.315		生存說	The subsistence theory of wages or the iron law of wages
.316		剩餘說	The residual theory of wages
.317		論價說	The bargaining theory of wages
.318		函數說	The functional theory of wages

.319	其他	Others
	例　制度說	e.g. The institutional theory of wages
.32	給資,停給,索薪,等	Payment of wages stoppage, deduction, claims for wages due, etc.
.33	薪資比例	Wage scales: scale contracts, sliding scale
.337	額外給資	Extra pay
	獎金,津貼,分紅,等	Premium, bonus, profitsharing, etc.
.34	給資準則　給資方法	Bases of wages and kinds of payment
.343	按工給資	By work done
.345	按時給資	By time
	時,天,週,月,年,	Hour, day, week, month, year
.347	給資方法	Kinds of payment
.35	卹金　養老金　保險金	Pensions　Insurance　Benefit
.36	政府與工資	State and wages
	最低工資法	Minimum wage law
.38	各業工資	Wages divided by industry
.39	依國分	Wages divided by country
.4	工時　休息	Duration of work　Rest
.41	日工	Length of day
	八時制,十時制,輪流制	8-hour day, 10-hour day, shifts of work
.42	夜工	Night work
.43	星期工作	Sunday work
.45	加工	Overtime supplementary hours
.46	假期　星期休息	Vacation　Leave of absence
.467	勞工節	Labor festivals, May 1
.48	各業工時	In special industries
.49	依國分	By country

.5	工廠	Working conditions　Places of labor
.52	危險工作	Dangerous, uncomfortable, unhealthful quarters
.53	工廠衛生	Industrial hygiene
	疾病預防	Medical supervision　Prevention of occupational diseases
.54	工廠安全	Safety　Accidents　Occupational hazards
	火災預防與救護	Fires, preventive and protective measures
.55	工廠改良	Improvement of working conditions in factories, stores, etc.
	光線,通風,等	Lighting, ventilating, etc.
.56	勞工訓練	Labor training
.57	工廠道德與習慣	Morals and habits
	游戲	Amusements
.58	工廠檢查	Inspection in factories, stores, etc.
.59	依國分	By country
.6	勞資工會	Employers' and workingmen's associations　Trade-unions
	國際勞工組織 見 383.8	International labor organization see 383.8
.601	勞工運動	Labor movement
.61	僱主組織　僱主公會	Unions of employers
.63	勞工組織　勞工公會	Labor unions
.64	各業公會	By profession
	例　農業公會	e.g. Agricultural labor unions
.65	依性別分	By sex
	例　婦女勞工公會	e.g. Unions of women workers
.66	依派別分	By special schools or systems

		例　工團主義公會	e.g. Syndicalism
.68		其他特殊公會	Other special unions
.69		依國分	By country
.8		勞資爭議	Disputes between capital and labor
		勞資糾紛之和平解決與預防	Prevention and peaceful settlement of differences between capital and labor
.81		勞資問題	Problems of capital and labor
		例　生活問題,失業與無業,勞工保護,等	Cost of living, unemployment and nonemployment, protection of laborers, etc.
.83		工潮　罷工	Strikes
.831		同盟罷工	Union strikes
.833		同情罷工	Sympathetic strikes
.835		無組織罷工	Unorganized strikes
.84		勞方其他手段	Other methods of workmen
		怠業,同盟絕交,等	Sabotage boycotting, unfair list, fair list, etc.
.85		資方手段	Methods of employers
		解僱,等	Lockouts, blacklisting whitelisting, etc.
.86		仲裁　干涉　和解	Arbitration　Mediation　Conciliation
.87		聯席會議	Joint confereces
.88		各業工潮	By special industries
.89		依國分	By country
.9		其他問題	Other question
.91		勞工與國家	Labor and the state
.911		勞工法與勞工立法	Labor law and legislation
.913		勞工政治工作	Labor in politics
.915		勞工權	The right to work
.916		勞工獎勵	Encouragements to work
.919		依國分	By country

.93	勞工生活狀況	Social condition of labor
.931	生活問題	Livelihood, problems of
	1. 衣	Clothes
	2. 食	Food
	3. 住	Housing
.933	勞工教育	Labor education
.935	勞工經濟	Workingmen's budgets
.937	勞工保險	Labor insurance Social insurance
	生命,老年,疾病,殘廢,失業,等	Life, old age, sickness, defectives, unemployment, etc.
.939	依國分	By country
355	資本 資本主義	Capital Capitalism
356	生產組織	Organization
.1	公企業與私企業	Public and private enterprise
.2	單一企業	Simple enterprise
.21	個人	Individual enterprise
.23	公司	Corporative enterprise
	合名,合資,匿名,股份公司,等	Partnership, stock and joint-stock partnership, etc.
.3	聯合企業	Combinative enterprise
	合拼,信託,買股信託公司,等	Fusion, trust, trust by holding company
.4	企業協定	Cartell
.5	企業聯盟	Syndicate
.6		
.7	合作論 合作社	Cooperation
.71	生產合作:工廠合作社	Cooperative production: Cooperative factories
.73	消費合作:商店合作社	Cooperative consumption: Cooperative stores

.75	交易合作：合作銀行	Cooperative exchange; Cooperative banks
.77	分配合作	Cooperative distribution
.8		
.9	分工論	Division of labor

357 消費論　　　　　　　Consumption

.1	必需的或生活的	Necessity
.2		
.3	有益的或生產的	Useful
.4		
.5	無益的或奢侈的	Luxury
.6		
.7	有害的	Harmful
.8		
.9		

358 交易論　　　　　　　Exchange

價值與價格　　　　　　Value and price

現貨,貨樣,定期,現款,信用交易,等

359 分配論　　　　　　　Distribution

總論地租,工資,利息,利潤,諸作類此　　General works on rent, wages, interest, profit together to be clast here

財產均分　　　　　　　Equalization of wealth

360 財政學　　　　　　　Finance　Financial economics

Private finance

361 金融　貨幣　　　　　Money

.01	理論	Theories

.1	法律　造幣律		Money legislation　Laws
.2	幣制		Money system
.21	單本位		Monometallism
		金本位,銀本位,銅本位,等	Gold, silver, copper, etc.
.22	複本位		Bimetallism
.23	新複本位		Neo-bimetallism
.25	跛行本位		Limping or humpbacked
.26	金匯兌本位		Gold exchange
.28	國際本位		International standard
.5	貨幣		Commodities
.6	錢幣		Coins
.61	正幣		Principle coins
.63	輔幣		Subsidiary coins or tokens
.7	紙幣		Paper money
.71	代表紙券:金證券,銀證券		Representative paper money: Gold and silver certificates
.73	信用紙幣:兌換券		Fiduciary paper money
.75	強制紙幣:不兌換券		Fiat paper money: Inconvertible paper money
.8			
.9	依國分		By country
		例　中國金融 361.91	e.g. Chinese money 361.91

362　銀行　儲蓄　　Bank and banking　Savings

.05	雜誌	Periodicals
.06	會議	Conventions
.1	種類	Special classes of banks

.11	私立	Private
.12	公立	Public
	中央,地方,等	Central, local, etc.
.13	各業:農業,商業,工業銀行,等	Of business: Agricultural, Commercial, etc.
.14	票據交換所 票據銀行	Clearing house Clearing banks
.15	信託公司	Trust company
.16	金融公司	Finance company
.17	兌換銀錢	Money exchange
.18	借貸	Loan institutes Money lending
.19	典當	Pawnbroking Pawn shops
.2	組織與制度	Banking organization and institution
.3	銀行管理	Administration and management
.4	基金:資本金,公積金	Funds: Capital Reserved fund
.5	存款	Deposit
	定期,活期,通知,儲蓄,存票,以及特殊存款,等	Fixed, current, demand or call, saving, certificate of deposit, etc.
.6	貼現與利息	Discount and interest
.7	貸款	Loan
	信用,活期,保證,臨時,以及抵押放款:例珍珠,證券,股票,票據,商品,等	Fiduciary, overdraft or over drawn, cash credit, call loan, and property loan: precious metals, public bonds, bills, commodities, etc.
.8	銀行問題	Problems of banks and banking
	例 銀行循環,恐慌,破產,倒票,等	e. g. Banks cycle theory, crises, bankruptcy, fall notes, etc.

	.9	儲蓄　儲蓄銀行	Savings
	.91	有獎儲蓄	Savings with prize
	.92	無獎儲蓄	Savings without prize
	.93	儲蓄銀行	Savings and savings banks
	.94	官營儲蓄銀行	Official savings institutions
		中央,地方,等	National , local, etc.
	.95		
	.96	學校儲蓄銀行	Scholl savings banks
	.97	郵政儲蓄銀行	Postal savings banks
	.98	鐵路儲蓄銀行	Railways savings banks
	.99	其他	Others
363			
364		信用　票據	Credit and credit system
	.1	鈔票　莊票	Bank bill　Notes
	.2	支票：橫線,保付,透支,等	Checks：Cross, certified, and perfroted checks
	.3		
	.4	匯票	Bill of exchange
	.5	期票	Promissory note
	.6		
	.7	賒賬　記賬	On credit
	.8		
	.9		
365		匯兌	Exchange
		國際,國內匯兌,票匯,信匯,電匯,逆匯,押匯,等	International , home exchanges, remittance by draft, circular letter of credit, cable transfer, advance, and documentary draft

366　證券　　　　　　　　　Securities
　.1　　債券　　　　　　　　Bonds
　.2　　抵押品　　　　　　　Mortgages
　.3　　股票　　　　　　　　Stocks
　.4
　.5　　國家證券　　　　　　Public securities
　.6
　.7　　工商證券　　　　　　Industrial securities
　.9　　依國分　　　　　　　By country
　　　　例　中國債券　366.91　　　e.g. Chinese bonds 366.91

367　投資與投機　　　　　　Investment and speculation
　.1　　投資　　　　　　　　Investment
　.11　　　國內投資　　　　　Domestic investments
　.13　　　國外投資　　　　　Foren investments
　.15　　　證券投資　　　　　By form: Bonds, mortgages, stocks, etc.
　.18　　　各業投資:工業投資，等　By class: Industrial securities, etc.
　.19　　　依國分　　　　　　By country
　.3　　投機　　　　　　　　Speculation
　.31　　　投機與賭博及其他　Speculation and gambling, business, etc.
　.38　　　各業投機　　　　　By class: Speculation in stocks, etc.
　.39　　　依國分　　　　　　By country
　.5　　彩票(獎券)　　　　　Lotteries

368　保險　　　　　　　　　Insurance
　.01　　理論　　　　　　　　Theories

	例　數理保險	e.g. Mathematical insurance
.1	火險	Fire insurance
.2	水險　海上保險	Marine insurance
.3	生命	Life insurance
	人壽保險	Age insurance　Annuities, etc.
.4		
.5	財產	Casualty insurance
	例　農業保險	e.g. Agricultural
	信用債券保險	Insurance of bank deposits, etc.
.6	社會保險：失虞,疾病,等	Social insurance　Workingmen's insurance
.7	各廠保險：火柴,玻璃廠,等	Against breakage or damage Matches, glass, etc.
.8		
.9	政府經營保險	Government control
	例　紐約州保險公司	e.g. Insurance in New York
	依國分	By country

369　國家財政　　　Public finance

其性質係概論或比較各國國家財政者列下　　General works only, works limited to one country see that country

.001	理論　關係	Theories　Relations
.003	辭書	Dictionaries
.0032	表冊	Tables
.0034	統計	Statistics
.0037	年鑑	Yearbooks
.004	評論	Critiques
.006	會議	Conventions　Congresses
.007	研究	Study and teaching: Outlines, etc.

.008	總集	Collected works
.009	歷史	History
.02	財務行政　預決算論	Financial administration
.021	法令	Law　Legislation
.022	制度	Systems
	中央,地方	Central vs local
.023	行政	Administration
.024	預算論	The budget
.029	決算論	Settling of account or control of budget
.03	歲出論	Public expenditure
.04	歲入論	Public revenue
.05	賦稅	Tax and taxation
.06	關稅	Customs　Tariff
	稅則	The tariff
	海關	Custom duties
.08	國債論	Public debt　Credit loan
.1	中國國家財政	China　Public finance
	按國家財政書籍多係統計表冊其關某項者應與該項同例	
	例　中國國家預算表 369.124	
.12	財務行政	Financial administration
.121	法令	Law　Legislation
.122	制度	Systems
.123	行政　組織	Administration
.124	預算論	The budget　Income and expenditure
.125	現計	Actual account or execution of budget
	收入與支出	Receipts and disbursements
.126	會計年度	Fiscal year
.127	金庫制度	Treasury system

	例　國家金庫制,委託保管金庫制,銀行存款制,等	e.g. Independent treasury system, custody system, deposit system, etc.
.129	決算	Settling of account or control of budget
	核計,審計,議定	Estimating or calculating, audit, voting, etc.
.13	歲出　公共經費	Public expenditure
	憲法,政務,國防,財務,公債,等	Expenditures Constitutional, civil service, the cost of defence, financial administration
.14	歲入　公共收入	Public revenue
.141	官產	State monopolies
	動產,不動產:土地,森林,鑛山,等	Personal estate, real estate, forests, etc.
.142	官業	Government enterprise
	工業,商業,交通:鐵路,郵政,電政,航政;鹽業,漁業,水利,等	Industries; Commerce; Communication: railways, postal service, etc.
.143	政務收入:規費	Administrative revenue
.145	沒收　罰款	Confiscated Fines
.146	捐贈　補助金	Subsidy
.147	賠款　進貢	Indemnity Tribune
.149	其他雜收入	Miscellanies
.15	賦稅	Tax and taxation
.151	財產稅　收益稅	Property tax Betterment tax
	田賦,土產,房屋,地價,遺產稅,等	Farming tax, excise, building, land, inheritance
.152	國產稅	Taxes on internal commodities
	鹽,茶,糖,絲,棉,菸酒稅,等	Salt, tea, sugar, silk, cotton, tobacco and wine, etc.
.153	營業稅	Business tax
	商業,工業,屠宰,落地稅,等	Commercial, industrial, butchery, pawnshop, etc.

.155	所得稅：人頭稅	Income tax　Capitation or poll tax
.156	印花稅	Stamp duties
.157	奢侈稅	Taxes on luxury
	骨牌，花捐，等	Taxes on dominos, brothels, etc.
.158		
.159	其他	Other tax and taxation
.16	關稅	Customs Tariff
.1606	會議	Tariff conventions
.161	稅則	The tariff
.1611	國定：關稅自主	Tariff autonomy
.1613	協定	Conventional tariff
.1615	複關	Double or duel tariff system
	最低或特惠關稅	Mutual concessions of duties
	最高或無條約國關稅	Non-treaty duties
.1617	關稅轉嫁	Tariff shifting
.1619	附加稅	Surtax
.162	制度	Systems
.163	行政	Administration
.164	政策	Tariff policy
	1. 自由關稅	Free tariff
	3. 保護關稅	Protective tariff
	6. 關稅同盟	Tariff alliance
.165	常關(內地稅)	Native custom
.166	厘金	Likin
.167	海關	Custom duties
	1. 進口	Import duty
	3. 出口	Export duty
	5. 通過或子口稅	Transit duty
	7. 從價　從量	Ad valorem　Specific duty
.168	關稅問題	Tariff problems
	關稅戰爭	Tariff war

.18		國債論　公債論	Public debt　Credit loan
.181		內債	Domestic
.182		外債	Foren
.183		擔保與無擔保公債	Secured and unsecured debts
.184		年金公債	Annunity loan
.185			
.186		公債募集	Creation of debt
.187		公債借換	Conversion of debt
.188		公債清理	Funding system
		失效與償還	Bankruptcy　Repudiation　Sinking fund
.19		地方財政	Local finance
		依區域分	By regions
		下列各國均依中國細分	Public finance of any country may be subd. as China
.2		日本	Japan　Public finance
.3		希臘　意國　西班牙	Public finance of Greek　Italy　Spain
.4		法國	France　Public finance
.5		英國	Great Britain　Public finance
.6		美國	U. S.　Public finance
.7		德國	Germany　Public finance
.8		俄國	Russia　Public finance
.9		其他各國	Public finance of other countries

370　政治科學　政治學　Political science　Politics

.1	理論　關係	Theories　Relations
	例　政治與社會,歷史等關係	e.g. In relation to history, etc.
.3	辭書	Dictionaries
	年鑑	Yearbooks

.4	評論	Critiques Essays
.5	雜誌	Periodicals
.6	學會 會議	Societies Conventions
	依國分	By country
.7	研究	Studies
.8	總集	Collected works
.9	歷史	History
.91-.95	依國分	By country
.97	政治家傳記	Biography
.98	政治地理	Political geography

371 國家學　　　　　　　　　The states

.01	國家起源 演進	Origin of the state
.011	神權説	The Divine theory
.012	強權説	The force theory
.013	民約説 社約説	The contract theory The social coutract theory
.014	有機體説	The organic theory
.015		
.016	家族與國家起源	Kinship and state origin
.017	宗教與國家起源	Religion and state origin
.018	其他如經濟,戰爭與國家起源	Others, such as, war, economic life, etc.
.019	國家演進	Evolution of the state
.02	國家要素 性質 範圍	Elements, nature, entity, concept, of the state
.021	三要素説(人民,土地,主權)	The three elements theory (Population, territory, sovereignty)
.022	四要素説(人民,土地,組織或經濟,主權)	The four elements theory (Population, territory, organization or economy, sovereignty)

.023	五要素說(人民,土地,政府,主權,法律)	The five elements theory (Population, territory, government, sovereignty, law)
.025	人民　互見 372	Population　see also 372
.026	土地	Territory
	領土,領海,領空	Land, sea, air
.027	主權	Sovereignty
.029	忠順與愛國	Allegiance　Loyalty　Patriotism
.03	**國家主義**	**Nationalism**
.031	領土擴張與喪失	Nation and territory: Expansion　Acquisition of territory
.033	國界　邊疆	Frontiers
.035	帝國主義	Imperialism
.036	世界主義	Cosmopolitanism
.04	**國體　政體**	**Form of state　Forms of government**
.041	君主	Monarchy
.043	貴族	Aristocracy
.045	立憲	Constitutional or limited monarchy
.046	民主　共和	Democracy　Republic
.047		
.048	政體	Forms of government
.0482	專制	Despotism
.0483	憲政	Constitutional government
.049	國體政體之變更	Change of form of the state and government
.0491	革命	Revolutions
.0493	倒戈	Coups d'etat
.0495	正統	Legitimation; de facto governments
.06	**國家功用　關係**	**Purpose, functions, and relations of the state**
.061	國家與道德	The state and morality
.062	國家與宗教教會	The state and the church, religion
.063	國家與教育	The state and education

.064		
.065	國家與地土,生產,等	The state and land, production, etc.
.066	國家與社會團體	The state and social groups
	家庭,會社,階級,等	The family, society, class, etc.
.067	國家與個人	The state and the individual
	權利與義務　見 372.1	Rights and duties of the indiviual see. 372.1
.068	國家與文藝	The state and literature
.069	國家與其他關係	The state and others
.07	國家研究　方法	Studies of the state
.071	生物學方法	Biological analogy
.072	比較方法	Comparative
.073	實驗方法	Experimental
.074	歷史方法	Historical
.075	心理學方法	Psychological
.079	其他	Others
.08	國徽　國旗　關防	Symbolism, emblems of the state: arms, flag, seal, etc.
	依國分	By country
.09	歷史	History
	依國分	By country
	例　中國國家史 371.091	e.g. History of the state of China 371.091
.1	原始國家	Primative state
.11	家族	Family patriarchy
.13	部落	Tribal institutions
.15	村市	Village community
.2	封建國家	Feudal institutions　Feudal state
.3	帝國	Empire

.4	民主國 共和國	Democracy Republic	
.5	理想國 烏托邦	The ideal state Utopia	
.6	依組織分	By institutions	
.61	單一國	Simple state	
.63	混合國	Mixed state	
.64	聯邦	Federal state	
.65	聯盟	Confederation of state	
.7	依主權分	By sovereignty	
.71	獨立國	Sovereign state Independent	
.73	附屬國	Part-sovereign state	
.75	保護國	Protectoral	
.8	中立國	Neutral state	
.9	其他如印第安等國家	Others, such as, American Indians, etc.	

372　國民　公民學　　Civics　Citizenship

.1	民權	Rights of citizens
.11	人格權	Personality
	生命,身體,名譽	Life, body, fame
.12	財產權	Property
.13	自由權	Liberty
.131	行動	Freedom of action
.132	思想	Freedom of conscience
.133	言論	Freedom of speech
.134	信仰 宗教	Freedom of belief
.135	教育	Freedom of education
.136	職業	Freedom of profession
.137	集會結社	Freedom of assembly
.14	平等權	Right of equality
	例 法律,法庭平等	e.g. Before law, courts

.15	請願權	Right of petition
.16	參政權　選舉權	Suffrage　Elections
	見 372.5	see 372.5
.17	罷免權	Right of recall
.18	創制權	Right of initiative
.19	複決權	Right of referendum
.2	義務	Duties and obligations of citizens
	納稅　當兵	
.3	國籍與入籍	Nationality and naturalization
.4	民權喪失	Limitations and suspension of individual rights and guarantes
.41	戒嚴時期	Martial law
.43	被圍時期	State of siege
.45	國籍開除時期	Loss of citizenship or naturalization
.5	參政　選舉	Suffrage　Elections
.51	資格	Qualifications and conditions of suffrage
	年齡,性別,財產,教育,國籍,居住年限,等	Age, sex, property, education, nationality, residence, etc.
.52	制度　方法	Electoral systems　Voting
.521	全體選舉制	Universal suffrage
.522	限制選舉制	Partial suffrage
.523	特殊選舉制	Special suffrage
	複數,强迫,郵寄,等	Plural, compulsory, voting by mail, etc.
.524	單區選舉制	Single member constituency
.526	大區選舉制	Multimember constituency
.527	比例選舉制	Proportional representative
	名簿,海爾投票法	List system, Hare system, etc.
.528	少數代表制	Minority representative

		限制,積聚投票法	Limited, cumulative, graduated votes
.54		候選	Selection of candidates
.55		手續　選舉票	Voting procedure　The ballot
.551		程序　規則	Voting procedure
		注册,地點,時間,等	Registration, place, time, etc.
.553		選舉　投票	The ballot
		公開,秘密：澳制,空白,等	Public, secret: Australian, blanket, etc.
.555		覆選	Second ballot
.557		計票	Count of ballot
.558		宣示	Announcement of vote
.56		選舉院	Electoral college and indirect voting
.57		賄選與爭選	Corruption　Election contests
.58		選舉改善問題	Problem of suffrage reform
.7		婦女選舉　互見313.354	Women suffrage see also 313.354
.8		地方選舉	Local suffrage
.9		依國分	By country

373　政府　行政　　Administration　Government

1. 下列概爲總括性質其關係一國者應入各該國如關係某國一院,一部,或地方政府者亦應入各該國院,部,或地方行政各機關

1. General works only. For special country prefer with that country. Works dealing with the special functions of the department clast by subject

2. 憲法與憲法史　見391

2. Constitutional law and history　see 391

.001	理論　關係	Theories　Relations
.003	辭書	Dictionaries
	年鑑	Yearbooks
.004	評論	Critiques
.005	官報	Official publications

.006	會議　紀錄	Conventions　Congresses
.007	研究	Study and teaching: Outlines, etc.
.008	總集　小册	Collected works　Pamphlets
.009	歷史	History
	行政地理	Administrative geography
.01	中央政府　行政	**Administration of central government**
.011	元首(帝王,總統,主席)	Sovereigns (Emperor, President, Chairman)
	登極,權柄,任期,退位,等	Inauguration, powers, terms of office, retired, etc.
.012	官規	Regulation and control
.013	官制	Official organization
.014	官吏	Officials
.015	官爵	Ranks
.016	官錄	Salaries
.017	任免	Appointments and removals
.018	封贈　榮典　賞卹	Decorations　Pension
.019	其他	Others
.02	中央行政委員　常務委員	The Executive committee　The Standard committee
.03	立法院	The Legislative
.031	議院法　互見392	Parlimentary law see also 392
.032	立法	Legislation
	1. 法律解釋	Interpretation of law
	2. 法律統一	Uniform laws
	例　統一省憲	e.g. Uniformity of law on same subject in different provinces
	4. 編制	Codification
	5. 立法權　法權	Legislative powers
	7. 創制	Initiative
	8. 複決	Referendum

.033	議院　國會		Legislatures
	上議院　下議院		Upper and lower houses
.034	議員		Membership　Election
		1. 資格	Conditions of membership, eligibility
		2. 俸錄	Compensation
		3. 代表	Representation
		省,市,縣,殖民地	of provinces, district, colonies, etc.
		各界	of special classes
		5. 額數	Number of members
		7. 選舉	Methods of appointment
.035	議院權限		Prerogatives and powers　Restrictions
.036	會議		Sessions
.037	議院組織		Internal organization and discipline
.038	立法手續		Legislative procedure
	讀,議,辯,決,等		
.039	議院制		Form of legislature
	一院制,兩院制,等		One and two chambers
.04	司法院		The Judiciary
	大理院,高等與地方法院		Supreme, high, and district courts
.05	行政院		The Executive
	其性質關係政務者		N.B.　Only material relating purely to administrative theory and to civil service
.0501	集權制		Administrative centralization
.0502	分權制		Separation of powers
.0503	元首制		The sovereigns: President, Emperor, Chairman, etc.
.0504			
.0505	內閣制		Cabinet
.0506	院部制		Departments
.051	內務部		Interior department

.052	外交部	Department of forein affairs
.053	軍政部	Department of military affairs
.054	財政部	Department of finance
.055	交通部	Department of communications
.056	農礦部	Department of agriculture and mining
	工商部	Department of commerce and industry
.057	教育部	Department of education
.058	衛生部	Department of public health
.059	其他特殊委員會	Special commissions
	1. 建設委員會	The national reconstruction commission
	3. 禁煙委員會	The national opium suppression commission
	9. 蒙藏委員會	The commission for Mongolian and Tibetan afftairs
.06	監察院	The Control Yuan
.061	監察委員	Members of the Control Yuan
.065	審計院	Board of Audit
.07	考試院	The Examination Yuan
.071	典試委員會	The commission for the conduct of examination
.075	銓叙部	The ministry of public service qualifications
.08	地方政府與行政	Administration of local government
.081	省政府與行政	Administration of provincial government
	1. 民政廳	Department of civil affairs
	2. 財政廳	Department of finance
	3. 建設廳	Department of reconstruction
	4. 教育廳	Department of education
	5. 農礦廳	Department of agriculture and mining
	6. 工商廳	Department of industry, labour and commerce
	9. 秘書長	The secretariat

.082	市政府與行政	Administration of municipal government
	1. 財政局	Bureau of finance
	2. 土地局	Land bureau
	3. 社會局	Bureau of social affairs
	4. 工務局	Bureau of public works
	5. 公安局	Bureau of public safety
	6. 衛生局	Bureau of public health
	7. 教育局	Bureau of education
	8. 港務局	Bureau of harbors affairs
.083	縣政府與行政	Administration of district government
	1. 公安局	Bureau of public safety
	2. 財務局	Bureau of finance
	3. 建設局	Bureau of reconstruction
	4. 教育局	Bureau of education
	5. 衛生局	Bureau of public health
	6. 土地局	Land bureau
.084	區　村　里	Section　Villages　Li
.087	殖民地政府與行政	Administration of colonial government
.09	政府財產, 建築, 等	Government property, building, supplies, etc.
.091	國都	The Capital, central
.092	省會	The Capital, local
.093	公共建築	Public buildings
.094	中央	Central
.095	地方	Local
.096	財產	Government property
.097	設備	Supplies
.099	其他	Others
.1-.9	各國政府與行政	Administration　Government of individual country

概仿上列細分	Under each country the above divisions may be used
例　中國內務部 373.151	e.g. Interior department of the Republic of China 373.151

375　政黨　　　　　Political parties

.01	理論　關係	Theories　Relations
	例　政黨職責	e.g. Responsibility of political parties
	政黨與國民	Parties and the individual citizen
.03	辭書	Dictionaries
.037	年鑑	Yearbooks
.04	評論	Critiques　Criticism
.05	雜誌	Periodicals
.06	學會	Societies
.07	研究	Studies and teaching
.08	總集	Collected works　Polygraphy
.09	歷史	History
.097	傳記	Biography
.1-.9	依國分	By country
.1	中國政黨	Chinese political parties
	例	e.g.
.6	美國政黨	U. S. Political Parties
.61	聯邦黨	Federalist
.62	共和黨或民主共和黨	Republican Democratic
.63	惠格黨	Whigs
.64	自由土黨	Free Soil
.65	不知道黨	Know Nothing
.66	人民黨	Populist or People's Party
.67	禁酒黨	Prohibition
.68	工黨	Labor

.69 　其他 　　　　　　　　　Others
　　　　例　社會黨,等　　　　　　e.g. Socialist, etc.
.7
.8
.9

376
377 殖民　移民　移住　Colonies and colonization　Emigration　Immigration

.01 　理論　關係 　　　　　　Theories　Relations
　　　　例　殖民與土著之關係　　　e.g. In relation to the natives
.04 　評論 　　　　　　　　　Critiques
.05 　雜誌 　　　　　　　　　Periodicals
.06 　會議 　　　　　　　　　Conventions　Congresses
.07 　研究 　　　　　　　　　Study and teaching: Outlines, etc.
.08 　總集　小冊 　　　　　　Collected works
.09 　歷史 　　　　　　　　　History
.1 　殖民地 　　　　　　　　Colonies and colonization
　　　　發現,經濟,租借,襲佔,割　Colonies of exploitation, Commercial settle-
　　　　讓,保護國,等　　　　　ments, Leased, Conquest, Cession, Protectorate, etc.
.2 　殖民緣因　政策 　　　　Colonial policy　Colonial movement
　　　　宗教,種族,人口,社會,經　Religious, Racial, Colonization and popula-
　　　　濟,政治,等　　　　　　tion, Social, Economical, etc.
.3 　殖民地行政 　　　　　　Colonial administration
　　　　見 373.087　　　　　　see 373.087
.4
.5 　移民(移出) 　　　　　　Emigration
.6 　移住(移入) 　　　　　　Immigration

	1. 法規		Laws and regulation
	2. 獎勵		Promotion and assistance
	3. 禁制		Restriction and exclusion
	5. 檢查注册		Registration
	7. 分佈		Distribution
	9. 同化		
.7	殖邊　國內移民		
.8			
.9	依國分		By country
	例　中國國內移民		
	377.917		
	美國移住禁例		
	377.9663		

378

379　軍事學　　　　　　　　　Military and naval sciences

	1. 中國軍政部　見 373.153		1. For War department of the Republic of China see 353.153
	2. 各國軍政部均同上例		2. Apply same to War department of other country
	3. 戰事入各國戰事史		3. Special wars of a country prefer with the hisotry of that country
.01	理論　關係		Theories　Relations
.011	軍國主義		Militarism
.019	軍事與社會,國家,等之關係		In relation to society, state, etc.
.03	辭書　術語		Military terms
.032	表册		Tables
.034	統計		Statistics
.037	年鑑		Yearbooks
.04	評論		Critiques

.05	雜誌	Periodicals
.06	會社　會議	Societies　Conventions
	例　軍人俱樂部,青年會	e.g. Army clubs　Army and navy clubs Army and navy Y. M. C. A.
.07	軍官學校　軍事教育	Military education
	可仿教育細分	subd. as education
.08	總集　小冊	Collected works
	戰事文藝小品	Military literature, etc.
.09	歷史	History
	依時代分	By period
.097	軍事家傳記	Biography
.098	軍事地理　地圖	Military geography, maps Geographical works from military point of view
.099	戰地調查	War conditions surveys
.1	各國軍事學	Military and Naval sciences of special country
	例　中國軍事學 　　379.11	e.g. Chinese Military and Naval sciences 　　379.11
.2		
.3	軍事行政	Military administration
.31	軍法　軍令	Military law　Military orders
	軍事法庭	Military courts
.32	制度	Organizatioin of military forces
	軍備	Armaments
	國防	National defense
.33	軍官　司令　行政員	Military officers　Military hierarchy
	任免	Appointment, promotion, retirement, removal, etc.
	檢閱	Inspection and inspectors

.34	宿兵　募兵	Corpulsory service　Conscription and exemption
.349	裁兵	Disbandment
.36	守備與戰地工作	Garrison and field service
	演習,動員,偵探,巡哨,防禦,等	Grand maneuvers, instruction camps, mobilizatiion, recon-naissance, scouting, patrol, guard duty, etc.
.37	軍需　軍用品	Military equipment and supplies
.371	軍糧	Military food
.372	軍餉	Rations Pay and allowances
.373	軍服	Uniforms
.375	軍械	Arms Ammunitions
.377	軍廠	Arsenals
.379	其他	Others
	軍醫　看護	Medical and sanitary services　Nursing
.38	軍徽,軍符,番號,口號,信號,等	Military symbolism: arms, flags, seals, etc.
.39	軍人生活	Military life, manners and customs, etc.
	入伍與退伍,平時戰時生活,名譽,道德,等	Service periods and retirement, military life in peace and war, military honor, morality, etc.
.4	戰略　戰術	Tactics and strategy
	治軍,行軍,攻,守,進,退,以及偵探,等等	Logistics and field service, siege and defense warfare, etc.
.5	陸軍	Military science　Army
.52	陸軍行政	Administration
	細分如上	subd. as above
.53	陸軍戰略	Starategy　Tactics　Land operatioins
.54	軍隊	Armies　Special branches of services

.55	步隊	Infantry
.56	馬隊	Cavalry
.57	砲隊	Artillery
.58	工程, 輜重, 運輸, 等隊	Engineering Transportation Etc.
.6	海軍	Naval science
.62	海軍行政	Administration
	細分如上	subd. as above
.63	海軍戰略	Strategy Tactics Naval operations
.64	艦隊	War ships
.65	主要軍艦	Capital ships
.651	戰鬥艦	Battleships
.652	戰鬥巡洋艦	Battle cruisers
.653	航空母艦	Aircraft carriers
.655	巡洋艦	Cruisers
.656	驅逐艦	Destroyers
.657	潛水艇	Submarines
.658	水雷艇	Torpedo
	水雷母艦	Torpedo depotship
	水雷驅逐艦	Torpedo destroyer
.66	輔助軍艦	Auxiliaries
.661	埋雷艦	Minelayers
.663	掃雷艦	Minesweepers
.665	裝甲邊防艦	Armoured coast defense vessels
.667	礮船	Gunboats
.669	其他	Others
.7	空軍	Military aviation Aeronautics
.72	空軍行政	Organization Administration
	細分如上	subd. as above
.73	空戰戰略	Aerial operations

.74	空隊　飛艇		Airships　Aeroplanes
	戰鬥機,驅逐機,偵察機,爆擊機,等		
.8	鄉團　義勇隊		Militia and volunteers
.9	古代兵器		Arms, ancient
.91	刀劍　劍術		Swords　Fencing
.92	槍戟		Spear
.93	棍櫚		Staff
.94	弓矢　射術		Bows and arrows　Archery
.95	盔甲		Armor
.96	盾牌		Shields
.97	兵車		Chariot
.98	旗,鼓,及其他		Flags　Drums　Etc.
.99	依國分		By country
380	**國際政治**		**International politics**
	國際　國際社會		The family of nations　International community　International society
.1	理論　關係		Theories　Relations
	例　與社會學關係		e.g. Relation to sociology
	與經濟學關係		Relation to economics
	與政治學關係		Relation to political science
	與法律關係		Relation to law
	與歷史關係		Relation to hisotry
.3	辭書		Encyclopedias　Dictionaries
.37	年鑑		Yearbooks
.4	評論		Critiques　Criticism
.5	雜誌		Periodicals
.6	國際會議		Societies　Congresses

	常設會議	Permanent congresses
	依會議地點分	By place or country
	例　海牙會議	e.g. Hague conferences
	巴黎和會	Paris peace conference
.8	總集	Collections
	其不屬任何類者	of a general and miscellaneous character not belong elsewhere
	條約　見387	For treaties　see 387
.9		

381　國際法（公法）　International law（Public）

.01	理論　關係	Theories　Relations
	例　國際法與國內法	e.g. International law and law
.02	法源	Sources of international law Sanctions
.021	條約　見387	Treaties　see 387
.023	慣例	Customs and usages
.025	官書	International documents　State papers
	例　國際抗議,談判,通知,等	
.026	會議條例	Statutes
.027	仲裁院之裁決書	Decisions
.029	法典	Codes
	國際法之編纂	Codification of international law
	官修　依時期分	Official, by date
	民纂　依編纂人分	Non-official, by editor
.07	研究	Studies
.09	歷史　派別	History and development of international law
.091	古代國際法	Ancient international law
.092	中古國際法	Medieval international law
.093	近代國際法	Modern international law

.099	派別	Systems of international law
	1. 自然法派	The law of nature
	3. 意志法派	The volumtary law
	5. 格羅法派	The Grotians
	9. 其他	Others
.1	國家　國際法人	The state as an international person
.11	主權國	Sovereign states
.12	非主權國	Non-sovereign states
	半主權國,屬國,保護國,等	Semisovereign, dependent, vassal and protected states
.13	永久中立國	Permanently neutralized states
.15	國家承認	Recognition of states
.16	國家承繼	"Statensuccession"
.17	國家分裂　内戰	State dismemberment　Civil war
.18	國家解體與消滅	Dissolution of a state
.19	其他特論	Other special topics
.191	共管	Condominium
.193	隸屬	Servitudes
.195	國家破産	State bankruptcy
.2	國家主權	The fundamental rights
.21	獨立權　獨立保障	Independence　Means of protecting independence
	非干涉	Non-interference
.22	自衛權	Self-preservation
	領土外自衛	Exterritorial self-defense
.23	平等權	International equality
.25	法權	Jurisdiction　Competence
	治外法權　見 386.5	Exterritoriality　see 386.5
.27	國家國際責任	Responsibility and obligations

.28		國際禮貌	International courtesy Comitas Courtoisie Precedence
.3		領土	Territory
.31		領土取得	Acquisition of territory
.311		添附	By accretion
.312		時效	By prescription
.313		佔領	By occupation and possession
.314		發現	By discovery
.315		割讓	By cession Annexation
.317		征服	By conquest
.319		其他	Other specials
		1. 殖民地	Colonies
		3. 勢力範圍	Spheres of influence
		4. 利益範圍	Spheres of interest
		5. 租借地 租界	Leases
		7. 委任統治地	Mandates
.32		領土喪失	Loss of territory
.321		自然喪失	Physical loss of territory
.323		領土放棄	Dereliction
.33		國界	Boundaries
.331		自然界限	Natural boundaries
		山,河,湖,岸,等	Mountains, rivers, lakes, coast, etc.
.333		人定界限	Artificial boundaries
.34		領陸	Land domain
.35		領河 國際河	Fluvial domain International rivers
.36		領海	Maritime domain
.37		國際海洋 運河	Interoceanic canals
.38		領空	Aerial domain
.39		國際地役	International servitude
.5		戰爭法	Law of war

.51	最後通牒	Ultimatum
.52	外交決裂	Rupture of diplomatic relations
.53	宣戰與開戰	Declaration and outbreak
	宣戰前敵對行爲	Hostilities prior to declaration
.54	交戰法規	Law of belligerency
.541	交戰承認	Recognition of belligerency
.542	聯軍,援軍,等	Alliance, succor, etc.
.543	交戰國與非交戰國	Belligerents and noncombatants
.545	戒嚴令	Martial law
.547	交戰國商務	Effect on commercial relations of belligerents
.548	交戰國財產	Property of belligerents in war
.55	陸戰法規	Laws and customs of war on land
.551	侵伐　軍事佔領	Invation　Belligerent occupation
.552	蹂躪	Permissible violence　Devastation
.553	轟炸與圍困	Bombardments and sieges
.554	游擊	Guerrilla warfare
.555	戰鬥器	Arms and instruments of war
	違禁戰鬥器	Prohibited instruments or methods
.556	傷兵待遇	Treatment of wounded
.557	俘虜　人質	Prisoners of war　Hostages
	俘虜交換	Cartels
	逃亡	Deserters
.558	戰時交涉	Intercourse of belligerents
	1. 停戰	Flag of truce
	3. 通行狀	Safe-conduct
	5. 投降	Surrender　Capitulations
.56	海戰法規	Laws and customs of war on sea
.561	封鎖	Blockade
.565	捕獲審檢所	Prize law
.57	空戰法規	Laws and customs of aerial war

.58	戰爭終局	End of war
	和約　互見　387.5	Treaty of peace　see also 387.5
.6	中立法	Law of Neutrality
.61	中立權利	Neutral rights
.62	中立義務	Neutral duties and obligations
.63	中立國財產與商務	Neutral property and trade
.64	繼續航海	Continous voyage or "Ultinate destination"
.65	敵性之中立	Unneutral service
.66	中立之破壞	Infractions of neutrality
.67	中立區戰艦	War vessels in neutral ports
.68	交戰國之搜索權與送護權	Right of visit and search　Right of convey
.7	海上法　公海法權	Maritime law　Jurisdiction over the High seas
.71	海上開放與鎖閉	The open and closed sea
.72	航海法	Navigation law
.73	海上衝突	Collisions at sea
.75	海船失虞救護	Shipwreck, salvage
.76	海上保險　見368.2	Marine insurance see 368.2
.79	海盜	Piracy
.8	國際私法	International private law
	法則區別論,法律抵觸論,領土外法律效力論,外國法適用論,私國際法,等	Theory of statute, conflict of law, extraterritorial authority of law, application of foreign law, private international law, etc.
.801	理論　範圍　關係	Theories　Scopes　Relations
	例　海牙會議與國際私法	e.g. The Hague conference and international private law

.802	法源	Sources and sanctions
	法典　國際私法之編纂	Codes　Codification of international private law
.807	研究	Studies
.809	歷史　派別	History and systems
.81	**國籍法**	**Nationality**
.811	本籍	Nationality by birth
.812	歸化	Naturalization
.813	婚姻與國籍	Marriage and nationality
.815	除籍	Expatriation
.816	復籍	Repatriation
.818	住所與居所	Domicile and residence
.82	**外國人地位**	**Alienage**
	放逐　流刑	Expulsion　Deportation
.821	土地權	Ownership of land
.822	居住權	Right of domicile
.824	逮捕與監禁	Arrest and imprisonment
.825	工作　職業	Labor　Occupation　Professions
.826	僑民保護	Protection of citizens abroad
.828	國外旅行	Travellers in foreign countries
.829	其他	Other special topics
	例　當兵	e.g. Military service
.83		
.84	**國際民法**	**Civil law (international)**
.842	財產法　物權	Property
.843	債權法	Obligation
.844	契約	Contract
.845	親屬法	Consanguinity　Family
	結婚, 離婚, 等	Marriage, divorce, etc.
.846	承繼法	Inheritauce and succession
	遺囑	Wills and other testamentary instruments

	國家沒收外人所有權	The state's right of succession to property of aliens
.85	國際商法	Commercial law (international)
	海商法　參看　381.7	Maritime law　see also 381.7
.87	國際訴訟法(私法)	Procedure in international private law
	華洋訴訟	Procedure in the trial of cases to which aliens are parties
.88	國際刑法	Criminal law (international)
	國際引渡	Extradition
.9	國際特別法	Special international laws
.93	殖民法	Law of colonization
.95	航空法(平時航空法)	Aviation law (of peace)
382	國際爭議	Procedure in international disputes
.1	國際息爭　國際仲裁	Settlements of internatioinal disputes　International arbitration
.2	和平解決	Compromisory clause
.21	自衛	Self-help
.22	直接交涉	Direct negotiation
.23	斡旋	Good offices
.24	調停	Mediation
.26	國際調查委員會	International commission of inquiry
.27	常設國際委員會	Permanent international Commission
.28	仲裁	Arbitration
.3	強制解決	Compulsive arbitration
.31	報復	Retorsion
.32	報仇	Reprisals

	.33	平時封鎖	Pacific blockade
	.34	戰時封鎖	Blockade in war
	.36	經濟絕交或封鎖	Economic boycott or blockade
	.38	武力裁制	Application of organized international force
	.4	法庭判決	Adjudication
	.41	國際常設法庭	Permanent courts of international justice
	.43	常設仲裁法庭	Permanent courts of arbitration
		仲裁條約　見　387.7	Arbitration treaties see 387.7
	.45	國際仲裁訴訟	Procedure in international arbitration
	.5	國際爭議與國際聯盟	International disputes and the League of Nations
		參看　383	see also 383
		和解委員會	Council of conciliatioin
	.6		
	.7	國際警察	Police, international
	.8		
	.9	其他特殊問題	Other special topics
		例　國家榮譽　382.91	e.g. "Vital interest," "National honor" 382.91
		婦女與國際和平 382.95	Women and peace movements 382.95
383		國際聯盟	League of nations
	.01	理論　關係	Theories　Relations
		例　國聯與世界和平	e.g. League of nations and the world peace
	.02	盟約	Covenant
	.04	評論	Critiques　Criticism

.05	雜誌　刊物	Periodicals　Publications
.06	會議	Congresses and conferences
.07	研究	Studies
.08	總集	Collected works
.09	歷史	History
.1	代表大會　常年大會	The assembly
	盟員國與非盟員國	Member states and Nonmember states
.2	理事會　行政院	The council
	常任理事	Permanent members of the council
	非常任理事	Non-permanent members of the council
.3	秘書廳	The secretariat
.4	專門組織	Technical organizatons
.41	經濟財政組織	Economical and financial organization
.43	交通運輸組織	Communications and transit organization
.45	衛生組織	International health organization
.5	諮詢委員會	Permanent advisory commissions
.51	國際法典編纂委員會	Advisory committee for progressive codification of international law
.53	軍備研究委員會	Permanent advisory committee on armaments
.54	委任統治委員會	Permanent mandates commission
.56	鴉片委員會	Advisory committee on traffic in opium
.58	兒童及青年保護委員會	Advisory committee for protection of children and young people

.6	國際學院	International research council International academic union
.61	國際智識合作學院	International institute of intellectual cooperation
.63	國際統一私法學院	International institute of unification of private law
.65	國際教育電影學院	Educatiional cinematographic institute
.7	國際局所	International bureaus
.71	國際救濟局	Bureau international d'assistance
.73	國際航線測量局	Bureau international bydrographique
.75	國際航空委員會	Comite international de la navigation aerienne
.8	國際勞工組織	International labor organization
.9	其他國際組織	Other international organization

384

385　國際關係　　　　　International relations

　　　國際問題之可供國際法之材料者　　International question treated as sources of or contribution to theory of international law

　　　至若世界大事或戰爭外交史等者入歷史類　　All history of events, diplomatic history of war, etc. go in history

　　依國分　　　　　By country
　　　　例　中國國際關係 385.1　　e.g. Chinese foreign relations 385.1
　　　　中日關係 385.11　　　　Sino-Japanese relations 385.11

386　外交　使節　　　Diplomacy The diplomatic service

.01	理論	Theories
.03	語術	Diplomatic languages, style, etc.
.04	評論	Critiques Criticism
.05	雜誌	Periodicals
.06	會議	Congresses Conferences
.07	研究	Studies
.08	總集	Collected works
.09	歷史	History
.1		
.2	使節	The diplomatic service
.21	任命	Appointment
.22	國書	Credentials Reception
.23	非法交涉	Unauthorized negotiations (including works on their criminal aspects)
.24		
.25	使權 特權	Powers and priviledges Immunities
.26	任務	Duties Functions
.27	使儀	Ceremonials Precedence
.28	使服	Dress
.3	外交行政	Organization Administration
.31	元首	Sovereigns
.32	外交部 外交部長	Department of foreign affairs The Minister of foreign affairs
.33	外交官吏	Diplomatic agents
	大使,公使,等	Ambassadors, plenipo, tentiaries, envoys, etc.
.34	外交團	Diplomatic corps
.35	領事 見 386.6	Consuls see 386.6

.36	外交專員		Special political agents
.38	國際委員會		International commissions
.4	國際交涉		Diplomatic negotiation
.41	直接談判 參看 382.22		Direct negotiation see also 382.22
.43	宣言		Declaration
.45	通告 照會		Notification
.47	抗議		Protest
.5	治外法權		Extraterritoriality
	元首,國際代表,外交官吏,軍隊,戰艦,軍用飛機,等		Sovereigns, international delegation, diplomatic agents, armies, war vessels, etc.
.6	領事　領事制度		Consuls　Consular system
	領事制度與治外法權		Consular system in relation to jurisdictional sovereignty
	領事裁判權		Consular jurisdiction
.7			
.8	外交問題		Diplomatic questions
.9	依國分		By country
387	條約　締約		Treaties and treaty making
	其關係普通或混合性者		Only treaties of general character or miscellaneous provision
	若限於一國之條約則應入該國		Collections of treaties of one particular country go under that country
.1	締交與通商條約		Treaties "of amity and commerce"
	關稅條約		Tariff treaties
.2			
.3	政治經濟條約		Political and economical
	例　引渡條約		e.g. Extradition treaties

		國界條約	Boundary treaties
	.4	軍事條約	Military
		和約	Treaty of peace
	.6	國際私約　國際密約	Private　Secret
	.7	仲裁條約	Arbitration treaties
	.9	依國分	By country
	.91	中國	Chinese treaties
		例　中日條約 387.911	e.g. Sino-Japanese treaties 387. 911

388	國際問題		International problems
	.1	亞洲問題	Problems of Asia
	.11	東方政策	Eastern policy
	.12	近東問題	Near east problems
	.13	中東問題	Mid east problems
	.14	遠東問題	Far east problems
	.15	滿蒙問題	Mongo-Manchurian
	.18	西比利亞問題	Siberia, prolems of
	.19	太平洋問題	Pacific problems
	.2	歐洲問題	Problems of Europe
	.21	巴爾幹問題	Balkan question　Balkan pivot
	.25	地中海問題	Mediteranian questioin
	.3	美洲問題	Problems of America
	.31	加拿大問題	Canadian question
	.35	大湖問題	Great lakes question
	.4	非洲大洋洲問題	Problems of Africa and Oceania
	.41	非洲問題	African question
	.47	菲力賓問題	Philippine question
	.5	社會問題	Social problems (international)

.51	第一國際	First international
	參看　帝國主義 371.035	see also Imperialism 371.035
.53	第二國際	Second international
	參看　資本主義　355	see also Capitalism 355
.55	第三國際　少年國際	Third international
	參看　社會主義　318	see also Socialism 318
.57	第四國際　幼稚病國際	Fourth international
	參看　工團主義 318.3	see also Syndicalism 318.3
.59	其他社會問題	Other social problems
.6	經濟問題	Economical problems (international)
.61	生產問題	International production
.62	勞工問題	International labor problem
.63	資本問題	Capital question
.64	市場問題	International market
.65	漁業問題	Fisheries question
.67	石油問題	Petroleum question
.69	其他	Others
.7	政治問題	Political problems (international)
.71	國界問題	Boundary
.72	國際平等	International equality
.73	國際共管　見 381.191	Condominium　see 381.191
.74		
.75	政治獨立	Independence
.76	領土保全	Territorial integrity
.77	海上自由	Freedom of the sea

.79	其他	Others
.8	軍事問題	Military problems (international)
.81	軍備問題	Problems of armament
.82	裁軍問題　軍縮問題	Problems of disarmament
.84	戰債問題	War debts
.87	軍械問題	Ammunitions, allowable
	毒氣,轟炸,毒彈,等之廢止	prohibition in warfare: poisons, explosive dum-dum bullets, etc.
.89	非戰運動	Anti-war movements
.9	其他問題	Other problems (international)

389

390 法律　　　　　　　Law

	種類	Classification
.001	成文法與不成文法	Written law and unwritten law
.002	固有法與繼受法(母法與子法)	Native law and adopted law
.003	普通法與特別法	General law and special law
.005	強行法與任意法	Imperative law and dispositive law
.007	實體法與程序法	Substantive law and adjective law
.008	公法與私法	Public law and private law
.009	國內法與國際法	Municipal or national law and international law
.01	法理學	Philosophy　Spirit of the law
.011	立法學	Science of legislation
.015	法律心理學	Psychology of law
.016	法律倫理學	Ethics of law
.017	法律教育學	Education of law
.019	依派別分	By schools or systems
	1. 哲學派	Philosophical schools
	2. 形上學派	Metaphysical schools

	希臘法理派	Greek
	羅馬法理派	Roman
	3. 神學法派	Theological schools
	4. 自然法派	School of the law of nature
	6. 社會學派	Sociological schools
	7. 分析派	Analytical schools
	8. 比較法學派	School of comparative jurisprudence
	9. 歷史學派	Historical schools
.02	法源	Sources of law
.021	習慣法	Customary law
.023	判例法	Case law　Judge-made law
.025	成文法	Written law
.029	法典　法典編纂	Codes　Codification
.03	辭書	Dictionaries
.037	年鑑	Yearbooks
.04	評論	Critiques　Criticism
.05	雜誌	Periodicals
.06	學會　會議	Societies　Congresses and conferences
.07	法律公布,解釋,廢止,等	Promulgation, interpretation, abrogation of law etc.
.08	總集　彙集　提要	Collected works　Digests
	其爲普通性質者	General digests, all series and state digests go with the books digested, all special digests go with their subjects.
	某書之提要應與該書同類	
	某類之提要應入各該類	
.09	歷史	History
.091	古代法時代	Archaic law
.092	嚴格法時代	Strict law
.093	自然法與衡平法時代	Natural law and equity
.094	法律成熟時代	Maturity of law

	.095	法律社會化時代	Socialization of law
	.097	法學家傳記	Biography
	.1	中國法系	Chinese law
	.2	印度法系	Indian law
	.3	回教法系	Moslem law
	.4	猶太法系	Jewish law
	.5	羅馬法系	Roman law
	.6	日爾曼法系	German law
	.7	斯拉夫法系	Slavic law
	.8	英吉利法系	English law
	.9	其他法系	Other systems of law

391　憲法　　　　　　　　　　　Constitutional law
　　　依國分　　　　　　　　　　By country
　　.1　中國憲法　　　　　　　　Chinese constitutional law
　　　　臨時約法,約法,憲法　　　Provisional constitutional law　Constitutional law
　　.2　日本憲法　　　　　　　　Japanese constitutional law
　　　　皇室典範　　　　　　　　Imperial household law
.3-.9　其他各國憲法　　　　　　　Constitutional law of other countries

392　議院法　國會法　　　　　　Parliamentary law
　　　依國分　　　　　　　　　　By country
　　　　例 美國國會法 392.6　　　e.g. Parliamentary law of U.S.A. 392.6

393　行政法　　　　　　　　　　Administrative law
　　　依國分　　　　　　　　　　By country
　　.1　中國行政法　　　　　　　Chinese administrative law
　　.11　行政組織法　　　　　　　Government organization
　　　　　例 中央組織法,地方組織法,等　　　e.g. Organic law of central and local governments, etc.

.13	行政行爲(法律行爲)	Legal act
.15	行政訴訟法	Law of administrative procedure
.17	訴願法	Law of petition
.19	其他行政法	Others
.2-.9	其他各國行政法	Administrative law of other countries
	仿中國行政法細分	Subd. like Chinese administrative law

394　刑法　　　　　　　　　Criminal law

.1	原則	Principles
	例　動機,意志,豫謀,等	e.g. Motive, intent, malice, etc.
.2	犯罪與罪犯	Crime and criminals
	兒童犯罪	Juvenile delinquency
.21	法定犯　政治犯　見 371.049	Political offenses　see 371.049
	例　革命,倒戈,等	e.g. Revolution, coupe d'etat, etc.
.23	國事犯　互見 315.181	Offenses against the state see also 315.181
	例　賣國	e.g. Treason
.25	因事犯　常事犯	Ordinary offenses
	互見　315.18	see also 315.18
.3	不法行爲	Torts
.5	刑罰	Punishments
.51	主刑	Principal punishments
.511	生命刑　死刑	Punishment of death　Capital
	斬首,絞刑,槍斃,電斃,等	Beheading, garrote, shooting, electrocution, etc
	身體刑　笞,杖,等	Punishment of the body
.513	自由刑　徒刑	Punishment of imprisonment
.515	財産刑　罰金	Pecuniary punishment
.517	名譽刑	Ignominious punishment

	.53	從刑	Accessory punishment
		褫奪公權,沒收,等	To be deprived of public right, to be confiscated, etc.
	.55	緩刑	Conditional execution
	.57	假釋	Provisional release
	.58	時效	Prescription
	.6	特別刑法	Special criminal law
	.61	少年刑法	Juvenile
	.63	婦女刑法	Women
	.65	變態刑法	Abnormal
	.9	依國分	By country
		例　中國刑法　394.91	e.g. Chinese criminal law 394.91
395		訴訟法	Procedure law
	.02	訴訟	Pleading practice
	.03	庭審	Trial practice
		當事人,通知,訴狀,出庭,審問,辯論,判決,抗告,再審,上訴,宣判與執行,等	Parties, notices, motive petitions, appearance, pleadings, examination, right to begin and reply, judgments, new trials, appeal, execution, etc.
	.04	陪審官	Jury
	.05	證據　證人	Evidence　Witness
	.06	法庭職員法	Laws of forms for all public officers
	.07	律師	Lawyers
	.08	侮辱法令	Contempt of courts
	.09	裁判權	Jurisdiction
		包括一切訴訟問題,判決,抵觸,未決訴訟,在決訴訟,既決訴訟,等	Including all questions of bar by suit, conflict of decisions, Lis pendens, Res judicata, stare decisis, etc.
	.1	民事訴訟法	Civil procedure law

	.2	刑事訴訟法	Criminal procedure law
	.3	特別訴訟法	Special procedure law
	.9	依國分	By country
		例　中國訴訟法 395.91	e.g. Chinese procedure law 395.91
396		法院編制法	Law of judicial organization
		依國分	By country
		例　美國大理院	e.g. U. S. Supreme court
397		民法	Civil law
	.1	總則	Generalia
	.11	自然人	Natural person
	.12	法人	Legal person
	.13	物	Things
	.15	法律行爲	Legal act
	.17	期間	Time
	.18	時效	Prescription
	.2	物權法	Property law
	.23	特權法	Patent law
	.3	債權法	Obligation law
	.4	契約　互見 398.51	Contract　see also 398.51
		贈予,買賣,交換,貸借,委任,存寄,等	Donation, gift, sale, exchange, loan, mandate, deposit, etc.
	.5	親屬法　家法	Consanguinity law　Family law
	.51	夫妻	Husband and wife
		結婚,婚姻,離婚,遺棄,財產,居住,等	Marriage, promises, divorce, desertion, property, settlements, etc.
	.52	父母與子女	Parents and children
	.53	監護	Guardian and ward

.54	主僕	Master and servant
.55	管家	Agency
.57	奴隸	Slavery
.6	承繼法	Inheritance and succession law
	遺囑	Will and other testamentary instruments
.9	依國分	By country
	例　中國民法 397.91	e.g. Chinese civil law 397.91
	中國親屬法 397.915	Chinese consanguinity law 397.915
	日本物權法 397.922	Japanese property law 397.922

398　商法　　Commercial law

.1	商人通例	General regulations on traders
.2	公司條例	Corporation law
.23	合資公司	Partnership
.3	商行爲法	Business transaction
.38	交易	Exchange
.4	委託與運送法	Bailments and carriers
.41	委託	Bailments
	存放, 貸借, 等	Deposit, loan, etc.
.43	載物	Carriers of things
.44	載人	Carriers of persons
.45	運送法	Methods of carriage
.49	經理	Agencies
.5	票據法	Bill law
.51	契約　契據　互見 397.4	Contract　see also 397.4
.6	保險法	Insurance law

.7	海商法　參看 381.7	Maritime law　see also 381.7
.8	其他	Others
.81	破產法	Bankruptcy
.9	依國分	By country
	例　中國商法 398.91	e.g. Chinese commercial law 398.91

399　特別法規　　　　　　　　Special laws and regulations

特別法規之彙置於下者係因法學圖書館而計設其他普通圖書館可按其性質析入各專類不列此

The followings are given in the manner to fill out the scheme for a law library. General library better prefer with subjects not grouped here

.2	教會法　見 255.4	Ecclesiastical law　see 255.4
.3	勞工法　見 354.911	Labor law　see 354.911
.4	戒嚴法　見 372.41	Martial law　see 372.41
.5	海陸軍法　見 379.31	Military and naval law　see 379.31
.6	國際法　見 381	International law　see 381
.7	法醫學　見 593.8	Medical jurisprudence　see 593.8
.9	其他	Other specials
	例　農業法規　見 610.32	e.g. Agricultural laws and regulations see 610.32

語言文字學   Philology   Languages

400   語言文字學   Philology   Languages

         語言與文學合論類此   works treating of language and literature conjointly to be clast here

     .1   理論   關係   Theories   Relations
     .2
     .3   辭書   Dictionaries
     .4   評論   Critiques   Criticism
     .5   雜誌   Periodicals
     .6   學會   Societies
     .7   研究   Studies
     .8   總集   Collected works
     .9   歷史   History of philology
         語言起源   Origin of language

401   比較語言學   Comparative language

         下列係比較研究其專論某國語言者應入各該國   The follows are of general and comparative study. Every thing about an individual language put with that language

     .1   字源學   Etymology
         文字源流   Origin of words by derivation
     .2
     .3   字書   成語   Dictionaries   Lexicography
         專門字典應入各專類   Generally the dictionary of any science of art will go under that science or art
         兩種以上語言之字典依第一語言分   Prefer to put dictionary of two or more languages under the first languages
     .4   聲韻學   Orthography   Phonology
         語音自然律   Natural laws of language

		音譯學	Transliteration
	.5	方言學	Dialectology
	.6	文法	Grammar
		文法,聲韻,音韻合論類此	401.6 includes general works covering also orthography and prosody
	.7	音韻學	Prosody　Metrics　Rhythmics
	.8	讀本	Texts for learning the language
	.9	古文字學	Paleography
		見 990.8	see also 990.8
		契文	Hieroglyphics
402			
403	語言類別		Differentiation and classification of languages
		孤立語,附着語,曲折語,抱合語,緝合語,等	Isolating, agglutinative, inflectional, incorporating, polysynthetic, etc.
404			
405	世界語		Universal language
			Artificial: Volapuk　Esperanto
406			
407			
408			
409	語系　語言分佈學		Families of languages
		語係比較研究類此	Only such general works of comparative study on the families of languages put here.
		其關係某國語言之一切著述應入該國不列此	For other works on individual language of particular country prefer with that country

.7	亞非利加語系	African
	班篤語	Bantu
	非洲語之屬於塞含兩語系者則應入該兩語系	For other languages spoken in Africa, see Semitic and Hamitic
.8	亞美利加語系	American aboriginal languages
	例　印第安語	e.g. Indians
	愛斯基慕語	Eskimo
	亞爾哥金語	Algonkin
.9	其他語系	Other families of languages
410	中國語言文字學	Chinese philology, language
411	字源學	Etymology
.1	說文解字	The Shuo Wen
	按說文解字實係一部說明字源之字書宜列此	An etymological dictionary explains the graphic origin of each character
.11	關係　影響	Relations　Influence
.12	圖表	Diagram　Charts
.13	聲訓　音義	Orthography
.14	評論	Criticism and interpretation
.15	傳說　注解	Commentaries
.17	研究	Study and teaching: outlines, question, etc.
.18	雜說	Miscellanies
.3	六書	The Six scripts
.31	象形	Representation of objects
.32	指事	Indications of actions of states
.33	會意	Suggestive compounds
.34	諧聲	Phonetic aggregates
.35	假借	Borrowed figures

	.36	轉注	Mutable significations
413		字書　字典	Dictionaries
	.1	譯文　中外合璧	Dictionaries of Chinese-foreign languages
		例　四體清文鑑	e.g. Ssu t'i ch'ing wen ch'ien a tetraglot dictionary (Chinese, Manchu, Mongol, Tibetan)
		中外對譯之字典依下列分	Chinese dictionaries with foreign equivalents should be clast accordingly as follows:—
	.11	中印	Chinese-Indic
	.12	中日	Chinese-Japanese
	.13	中希	Chinese-Greek
	.14	中法	Chinese-French
	.15	中英	Chinese-English
	.17	中德	Chinese-German
	.18	中俄	Chinese-Russian
	.3	成語	Idioms
	.4	同意字　反意字	Synonyms　Homonyms　Antonyms
	.5	同源字　雙關字	Paronyms
	.7	新字	New words
	.8	雜字	Miscellanies
	.9	異字　外來字	Foren words and phrases
414		聲韻學	Orthography　Phonology
	.1	字母	Alphabet
		例　三十六字母	e.g. The thirty-six alphabets
	.2	聲(子音)	Consonants
	.3	韻(母音)	Vowels
	.5	切音　拼音	Phonetic spelling　Spelling reform

.9 依朝代分　　　　　　　By dynasty

　　例　孫愐:唐韻　414.94　　　e.g. Sun Mien: T'ang Yun　414.94

　　　　陳彭年:大宋重修　　　　Ch'en Peng-nieu: The Sung revised

　　　　廣韻　414.95　　　　　　Kuang Yun　414.95

　　　　洪武正韻　414.96　　　　Hung Wu Cheng yun　414.96

415　訓詁學　方言學　　Dialectology　Slang

.1　爾雅　　　　　　　　Erh Ya (Nearing the standard)

　　按"爾雅乃一部解釋因
　　時代不同地域不同而轉
　　變之各種異代殊域之語
　　文字書"

　　依說文解字細分　　　　　subd. like the Shuo Wen

　　　例　郭璞:爾雅圖贊　　　e.g. Kuo P'o: Erh Ya, with plates 415.12
　　　　　415.12

.2　群雅　　　　　　　　Other kinds of Ya

　　例　劉熙:釋名(逸雅)　　　e.g. Liu Hsi: Shih Ming (defines the Chi-
　　　　　　　　　　　　　　　nese words by homophones)

　　　　張揖:廣雅(博雅)　　　Chang I: Kuang Ya

.5　揚雄方言　　　　　　Fang Yen of Yang Hsiung

　　　　　　　　　　　　　(a collections of dialect words from different
　　　　　　　　　　　　　parts of China)

.9　方言　依區域分　　　By regions

　　　例　蜀方言　　　　　　e.g. The Shu (Szechuan) dialect

416　文法　　　　　　　Grammar

.1

.2　名詞類　　　　　　　Parts of speech

		名字,代名字,形容字, 動字,等	Nouns, pronouns, adjectives, verbs, etc.
	.3	章句法	Syntax
	.4	標點法	Punctuation
	.5	省寫法	Abbreviations
	.6		
	.7	會話	Conversations
	.8	修辭學　文章法	Rhetoric
	.83	文言	Literary
	.85	白話	Vulgar
	.9		
417		音韻學	Prosody　Metrics　Rhythmics
418		讀本	Texts for learning the language
		研究文法之課本列此其關係 文學方面者則入文學類	Including only books for learning the lauguage, with grammatic or philologic notes, etc. For other works see literature of the language
	.1	訓蒙　識字	Elementary vocabulary
		例　蒼頡篇	e.g. Ts'ang hsieh p'ien
	.2	拼音讀本	Spelling books
	.5	初級讀本	Elementary readers
	.6	高級讀本	Secondary readers
	.7	選本	Selections
	.9	外人用	For foreigners
419		古文字學	Paleography
		參看 990.81	see also 990.81
		例　史籀篇	e.g. Shih Chou p'ien
		孫詒讓:契文舉例	Sung Yi-jang; The hieroglyphics with illus- trations

	下列各國語言文字均仿中國細分	The follows subd. like Chinese
420	日本語言文字學	Japanese philology, language
430	希臘,拉丁,羅馬語言文字學	Greek, Latin, and Romance philology, languages
431	希臘語言文字學	Greek
432	拉丁語言文字學	Latin
433	意國語言文字學	Italian
434		
435	西班牙語言文字學	Spanish
436	葡萄牙語言文字學	Portuguese
437		
438	羅馬尼亞語言文字學	Rumanian
439	其他羅馬語言文字學	Other Romance
440	法國語言文字學	French philology, language
450	英美語言文字學	English and American philology, language
460		
470	德國語言文字學	German philology, language
480	俄國語言文字學	Russian philology, language
490	其他各國語言文字學	Languages of other countries
491	印度支那語系	Indo-Chinese

.1	暹羅語言文字學	Siamese
.3	緬甸語言文字學	Burmese
.4	安南語言文字學	Annamese
.9	其他	Others
492	烏拉阿爾泰語系	Ural-Altaic
.1	芬蘭語言文字學	Finnic
.2	拉柏蘭語言文字學	Lappish
.5	匈牙利語言文字學	Hungarian
.6	土耳其語言文字學	Turkic
.9	其他	Others
493	印歐語系	Indo-European
.1	印度語言文字學	Indian
.3	波斯語言文字學	Persian
.9	其他	Others
494		
495	含族語系	Semitic
.1	阿剌伯語言文字學	Arabian
.9	其他	Others
496	塞姆語系	Hamitic
.1	埃及語言文字學	Egyptian
.9	其他	Others
497		
498		
499		

自然科學　Natural sciences

500　自然科學　　　　　　Science　Natural sciences

按 500.1-500.9 各項純係科學之普通或總括性其關於一類者則依該類分

All the follows are of a general, more or less mixed character, For specials go under the subjects

例　化學雜誌號碼爲 540.05 非 540.5

.1	理論　關係		Theories　Relations
	例　科學與宗教之關係		e.g. Science and religion
.2			
.3	辭書		Dictionaries
.37	年鑑		Yearbooks
.38	指南		Scientists' directories
.4	評論		Critiques
.5	雜誌		Periodicals
.6	會社　會議　紀錄		Societies　Reports
.7	研究		Study and teaching
	綱目,綱要,問答,等		Outlines, syllabi, questions, etc
.8	總集		Collected works
.81	文藝		Literature, arts, science readers, etc.
.87	游戲		Scientific recreations
.88	小册		Pamphlets
.9	歷史		History
.91	古代		Ancient
.92	中古		Medieval
.93	近世		Modern
.97	傳記		Biography

.98	游記		Voyages and expeditions
501-9	特論		Special topics
510	數學		Mathematics

周髀算經,九章算術等類此。茲將九章錄下其分論諸作入各類

方田,粟米,衰分,少廣,商功,均輸,盈不足,方程,句股

.01	理論 關係		Theories Relations
.011	數理哲學		Philosophy of mathematics
.015	心理		Psychology
.016	數理邏輯		Logic, mathematical or Symbolic
	參見 512.016		see also 512.016
.019	關係		
.02			
.03	辭書		Dictionaries
.037	年鑑		Yearbooks
.04	評論		Critiques Criticism
.05	雜誌		Periodicals
.06	學社		Societies
.07	研究		Studies
	綱目,綱要,答問,等		Outlines, syllabi, questions, etc.
.08	總集 小冊		Collected works Pamphlets
.09	歷史		History
	每一類之專史應入其類		The history of each subject may be put under the subject
	例 代數史 512.09		e.g. History of algebra
.091-.095	依國分		By country

　　　　　　　例　希臘數學史　　　e.g. History of Greek mathematics
　　　　　　　　510.0931

.097　　疇人傳　　　　　　　Biography of mathematicians
.1
.2　　數學表　　　　　　　　Mathematical tables
.21　　算學表　　　　　　　 Arithmetical
.211　　九九表　乘數表　　　 Multiplication
.213　　因數表　　　　　　　 Fector tables
.215　　反數表　　　　　　　 Reciprocals
.22
.23　　對數　三角對數　自   Logarithmic and circular (Trigono-
　　　　然對數　　　　　　　 metrical)　Natural
.24
.25　　指數表　　　　　　　 Exponential
.26　　雙曲對數（訥氏對   Hyperbo-lic logarithms (Napier's
　　　　數）　　　　　　　 log.)
.27　　布氏對數　　　　　　 Conversion of Briggsian and hyperbol-
　　　　　　　　　　　　　　　 ic logarithms
.28　　反對數　　　　　　　 Antilogarithms
.29　　其他　　　　　　　　 Other
.3　　 公理　公式　　　　　 Mathematical theorems, expres-
　　　　　　　　　　　　　　　 sions, forms, etc.
　　　　二項式公理　　　　　 Binomial theorem
.4　　 記號論　　　　　　　 Theory of symbols　Pasigraphy
.5　　 命數法與記數法　　　 Numeration and notation
.6　　 算法式　　　　　　　 Algorisms (Algorithms)
.7　　 算術　　　　　　　　 Calculation　Numerical computation
.71　　十進算術　　　　　　 Decimal

.72	十二進算術		Duodecimal
.73	六十進算術		Sexagesimal
.74			
.75	心算　暗算		Mental
.76	器械算術		Instrumental
	珠算,尺算,滑尺,等		Abacus and measure calculations, slide scale, etc.
.77	表算　圖算		Tabular and graphic
.78	應用算術		Applied
	例　政治算術,等		e.g. Political, etc.
.79			
.8	問題與解法		Problems and solutions
.9	數學游戲		Mathematical recreations
511	**算學**		**Arithmetic**
	算學有純理,應用,高等,初等之別必要時可以 01-09 細分		Special treatises on theoretical, applied, higher, and elementary arithmetics may be classed accordingly as follows:
	例　高等算學　511.07		e.g. Higher arithmetic
.1	數理		Theory of numbers
	見 512.4		see 512.4
.2	四基法　四則		Four fundamental rules
.21	加		Addition
.22	減		Subtraction
.23	乘		Multiplication
.24	除		Division
.3	命分,比例,等		Fractions, proportion, etc.
.31	命分		Fractions　Decimal
.32			
.33	比例		Proportion

.34
　.35　　百分　　　　　　　　　Percentage
　.36
　.37　　利息　　　　　　　　　Interest
　.38
　.39
　.4　　解析：順列與錯列　　　Analysis：Permutation and combination
　.5　　開方與乘方　　　　　　Evolution and involution
　.6
　.7　　方程式　　　　　　　　Equations
　.8　　問題與解法　　　　　　Problems and solutions
　.9　　算學與代數　　　　　　Arithmetic and algebra together

512　代數(舊名借方根)　Algebra
　　　　大衍，天元類此

　.01　　理論　　　　　　　　　Theories　Relations
　.015　　心理　　　　　　　　　Psychology
　.016　　邏輯　代數邏輯　　　　Algebra of logic Symbolic and algebraic logic

　.02　　圖解代數　　　　　　　Graphic algebra
　.1　　代數量之數理論　　　　Arithmetical theory of algebraic quantities

　.2　　代數式　　　　　　　　Algebraic forms（Algebraic configuration：Quantics）

　.21　　二元式　　　　　　　　Binary forms
　.22　　不變式與共變式　　　　Invariants and covariants
　.23
　.24　　海斯行列式　　　　　　Hesse's determinant

.25	函數(耶柯)行列式	Functional (Jacobean) determinant
.26	二元二次式	Quadratic forms; Bilinear
.27	三元二次式	Ternary quadratic
.28	三元四次式	Ternary quartic form
.29	其他	Others
.3	行列式	Determinants
.31	對稱行列式	Symmetric
.32	反稱行列式	Skew symmetric
.33		
.34	函數行列式	Functional
.35	得數式	Resultant
.36	判別式	Discriminant
.37	方列式	Matrices
.38		
.39	消元法	Elimination
.4	數論	Theory of numbers
.41	數之原理	Elementary theory
	質數,完數,等	Prime numbers, perfect numbers, etc.
.43	數之解析	Analytical theory of numbers
.44	算學函數	Arithmetical functions
.47	代數數與超越數	Algebraic and transcendental numbers
.49	其他	Others
.5		
.6	大代數　高等代數	Linear algebra　Higher algebra
.61	複數論	Complex numbers
.62	四元	Quaternions
.63		Ausdehnungslehre

.65	向量解析	Vector analysis
.66		
.67	群論	Theory of groups
.68		
.69		
.7	方程式論	Theory of equations
.71	根數　對稱函數	Roots　Symmetric functions
.73	方程式解法	Solution of equations
.77	代數方程式　極大極小論	Algebraic equations　Maxima and minima
.8	問題與解法	Problems and solutions
.9	公算論及其他	Claculus of probability and allied problems
.91		
.93	誤差法　最小二乘法	Theory of errors　Method of least squares
.95	數學統計	Mathematic statistics
.97	人壽保險	Life insurance

513　解析學　　　　　　　Analysis

　　解析學特論依 .01-.09 細分　　Special topics
　　例　極限論 513.03　　　　　e.g. Theory of limits 513.03
　　　　十八世紀前解析學　　　　Early works before 1800. 513.08
　　　　513.08

514　級數　連級數　　　Progression　Series

　　垛積類此

.1	算學級數或等差級數	Arithmetic progression
.2	幾何級數或等比級數	Geometric progression

	.3	代數級數或調和級數	Harmonic progression
	.4	三角級數	Trigonometrical progression
	.41	指數級數	Exponential
	.43	對數級數	Logarithmic
	.5		
	.6	收歛級數與發散級數	Convergent and divergent
	.7		
	.8		
	.9	連級數	Series
515		微積分　微積學	Calculus　Differential and Integral calculus
	.1	微數解析學	Infinitesimal analysis（Infinitesimal calculus）
	.2	微分學(正流數)	Differential calculus
	.3	積分學(反流數)	Integral calculus
	.4	變分學	Calculus of variations
	.5	差分學　有限差法	Calculus of finite differences
	.6	運分學　虛分學	Calculus of operations
	.7	方程式	Equations
	.71	微分方程式	Differential equations
	.73	微分方程式之積分	Integral of differential equations
	.75	積分方程式	Integral equations
	.77	極大極小論	Maxima and minima
	.8	問題與解法	Problems and solutions
	.9		
516		函數　倚數	Functions

.1	解析函數	Analytic functions
.11	實元函數	Real variable
.13	複元函數	Complex variables
.2	代數函數　常函數	Algebraic functions
.3	越函數	Transcendental variable
.31	指數函數	Exponential
.33	對數函數	Logarithmic
.35	圓函數　三角函數	Circular or trigonomical
.4	反函數	Inverse functions
.41	橢圓函數	Elliptic funcitons and integrals
.42	雙曲函數	Hyperbolic functions
.43	雙曲橢圓函數	Hyperelliptic functions
.44		
.45	亞柏林函數	Abelian functions
.46		
.47	狄他函數	Theta functions
.48		
.49		
.5	疊函數	Function of functions or compound functions
.6	微數函數：微分積分	Infinitesimal functions: Differential and integrable
.7	特殊函數	Special functions Functions in union with groups
.8	解析法之關於物理問題者	Analytical methods connected with physical problems
.81	調和解析	Harmonic analysis

.82	佛爾連級數	Fourier's series
.83	拉柏雷斯與黎干得函數(球圓調和)	Laplace's and Legeudre's function (spherical harmonics)
.84	柏塞爾函數(柱圓調和)	Bessel's functions (cylindrical)
.85	雷姆函數(橢圓調和)	Lame's functions (ellipsoidal harmonics)
.86		
.87	涂瑞朵函數	Toroidal harmonics
.88		
.89		
.9		

517　幾何學　形學　geometry

.1	幾何學基礎與原理	Fundation and principles
	凡總論歐几里與非歐几里幾何者類此,其專論一類者,則一入平面幾何學,一入非歐几里幾何學	Euclidean and Non-Euclidean (general discussions). For special treatment see plane geometry and Non-Euclidean geometry
.2		
.3	平面幾何學	Plane geometry (Planimetry)
.31	正線	Right line
.32	交線	Intersecting lines
.33	平行線	Parallel lines
.34	三角形	Triangle
.35	四邊形	Quadrilaterals
.36	多邊形	Other polygons
.37	相似	Similarity
.38	極大極小論	Maxima and minima

	.39		
	.4	曲線幾何學	Curves　Curvilinear geometry
	.41	圓線	Circle
		圓周率類此	
	.43	圓錐曲線	Conic sections
	.44	橢圓	Ellipse
	.45	雙曲	Hyperbola
	.46	拋物線	Parabola
	.5	立體幾何學	Solid geometry (Stereometry)
	.51	線與平面	Lines and planes
		交線, 平線平面	Intersecting and parallel planes
	.53	多面體	Polyhedrons
		稜錐體　稜柱體	Pyramids　Prisms
	.55	曲面體	With curved surfaces
		球體　圓錐體　圓柱體	Sphere　Cone　Cylinder
	.6	測量求數法　分體學	Mensuration　Stereotomy
	.7	高等幾何畫	Higher geometrical drawing
	.8	難解問題	Insoluble problems
	.81	圓方論	Quadrature of the circle (Circle squaring, cyclotomy)
	.83	角三分論	Trisection of the angle
	.85	重立方論	Duplication of the cube
	.9	幾何與三角	Geometry and trigonometry
518		三角學	Trigonometry
		割圓重差類此	
	.1	平面三角學	Plane trigonometry
	.2	球面三角學	Spherical trigonometry

.3	解析三角學	Analytical trigonometry
.4	假球面三角學	Pseudospherical trigonometry
.5	雙曲三角學	Hyperbolic trigonometry
.6		
.7	方程式	Equations
.8	問題與解法	Probiems and solutions
.9		

519 近世幾何學（綜合）　Modern（synthetic）geometry

.01	點素幾何學	Geometry of the points
.02	線素幾何學	Geometry of the lines
.03	面素幾何學	Geometry of the surfaces
.04	截斷線論	Theory of transversals
.05	反轉幾何學	Inversion
.06	乘方幾何學	Involution
.07	三角幾何學	Geometry of the triangle
.08	圓幾何學	Geometry of the circle
.09	其他	Others
.1	實際幾何學　構造幾何學	Practical geometry（Constructive geometry；geometrography）
.2	形位學　位置幾何學	Geometry of position（Carnot）
.3	畫法幾何學　投影幾何學	Geometry of transformation（Descriptive and projective geometry）
	數學畫	Mathematic drawing
.31	投影法	Projection　Projectivity
	中央,斜面等投影法	Central, oblique, etc.
.32		
.33	畫法幾何學	Descriptive geometry

.34	正投影	Orthogonal projection
	均等,類似投影	Isometric and analogous projections
.35	球面投影	Spherical projection　Map projection
.36	直線投影	Linear perspective
.37	影　影面	Shades and shadows
	其關係幾何者	Geometric only
.38		
.39	投影幾何學	Projective geometry
.4	解析幾何學	Analytical geometry
	積分幾何學	Integral geometry
	代數幾何學	Algebraic geometry
.41	平面解析幾何學	Analytical geometry (Plane)
.42	空間解析幾何學	Analytical geometry (Space)
.43	坐標	Coordinate geometry
.44	軌迹	Loci
.45	曲線論	Theory of curves
.451	平面曲線	Plane curves
.452	圓錐曲線	Curves of the 2nd order (Conics; conic sections)
.454	代數平面曲線	Algebraic plane curves
.455	雙曲橢圓曲線	Hyperelliptic curves
.457	三面曲線(立體)	Plane curves of 3rd order (Cubic curves)
.458	四面曲線	Plane curves of 4th order (Quartic curves)
.46	曲面論	Theory of surfaces
.461	二面曲面	Surfaces of the 2nd order
.463	代數曲面　拗扭曲面	Algebraic surfaces and algebraic gauche curves

.465	三面曲面 （立體）	Surfaces of the 3rd order (Cubic surfaces)
.467	四面曲面	Surfaces of the 4th order (Quartic surfaces)
.47	特殊曲線曲面	Special curves and surfaces
.471	超越曲線	Transcendental curves
.473	特殊曲面	Special surfaces
.48	問題與解法	Problems and solutions
.49	計算幾何學	Enumerative geometry (Denumerative geometry)
.5		
.6	雙曲空間	Hyperspace
.61	N次空間	Geometry of n-dimensional space
.62		
.63	四次空間	Fourth dimension
.64		
.65		
.66		
.67	複數範圍	Complex domain
.68		
.69		
.7	微數幾何學 微分幾何	Infinitesimal geometry Differential geometry
.71	微分方程式之幾何原理	Geometrical theory of differential equations
.72	曲線曲面之微數原理	Infinitesimal theory of curves and surfaces
.73	微分方程式之近似積分	Approximate integration of differential equations

	.74		
	.75	N次空間之微數幾何	Infinitesimal geometry in space of n-dimensions
	.76		
	.77		
	.78	動力幾何幾	Kinematic geometry
	.79		
	.8	非歐几里幾何學	Non-Euclidean geometry
			Absolute geometry
			Imaginary geometry
	.83	歐几里之第五假定	Euclid's postulate V
	.85	雙曲線幾何學	Hyperbolic geometry
	.86	拋物線幾何學	Parabolic geometry
	.87	橢圓幾何學	Elliptical geometry
	.88		
	.89		
	.9		
520		天文學	Astronomy
		天算類此	Mathematics and astronomy together
	.01	關係	Relations
		例　天文與數學,物理等之關係	e.g. to mathematics and physics, etc.
	.02		
	.03	辭書	Dictionaries　Astronomical terms
	.037	年鑑	Yearbooks
	.04	評論	Critiques　Criticism
	.05	雜誌	Periodicals
	.06	學社	Societies

	.07	研究	Studies
	.071	綱目　綱要	Outlines　Compends
	.072	圖表	Tables　Charts
			Pictorial works, etc.
	.08	總集　小冊	Collected works　Pamphlets
		文藝	Astronomical myths, legends and superstitions, etc.
	.09	歷史	History
		依國分	By country
		例　希臘天文史 520.0931	e.g. History of Greek astronomy
	.097	傳記	Biography of astronomers
	.098	地理	Astronomical geography
	.1-.9	特論	Special treatises
		例　占星術	e.g. Astrology, etc.
		參看 157.2	see also 157.2
521		理論天文學	Theoretic astronomy
		天體(例太陽係)運動之數理觀	Mathematic investigation of celestial motions, specially of the solar system
		各個天體運動應入各該天體	For individuals see the subject
	.1	天體力學	Celestial dynamics
	.11	平衡與運動律	General laws of equilibrium and motion
	.12	重力與運動之關係日球者	Law of universal gravition and motion
	.13	三天體論（日，月，地球）	Problem of 3 bodies
	.14		
	.15	天體運動	Rotation of heavenly bodies

.2	天球中心 太陽中心	Geocentric and heliocentric place
.21	太空中軌道平面	Plane of orbit in space
.22	平面上軌道位置	Position of orbit in its plane
.23	軌道上天體位置	Position of body in its orbit
.24	太空中天體位置	Position of body in space
.25	太陽經緯	Heliocentric longitude and latitude
.26	地球經緯	Geocentric longitude and latitude
.27	升降變遷論	Variations of right ascension and declination
.28	經緯變遷論	Variations of longitude and latitude
.29		
.3	軌道:軌道之確定	Orbits: Definition of orbits
.4		
.5	攝動	Perturbations
.51	行星互動	Mutual action of planets
.53	衛星行動	Action of satellites
.55	行星非球形論	Nonsphericity of planets
.57	間 阻力論	Resisting medium
.6		
.7	星論　衛星論	Theory of planets　Theory of satellites
	行星,流星,彗星各論 見 523.4, 523.5, 523.6	Stars, comets, etc. see each name
.8	蝕論	Theory of eclipses
	月蝕,日蝕各論 見 532.38, 523.78	Solar eclipse, lunar eclipse see each name
.9	歲差與章動	Precession and nutation

		見 522.84, 522.85	see each name
522	實用天文學 天體測量		Practical and spheric
	.1	天文台	Observatories
	.2	天文鏡	Telescopes　Objectives
	.3	子午儀	Meridional instruments　Transit
	.4	太陽, 赤道, 天極儀	Heliometer, equatorial, zenith telescope, etc.
	.5	其他儀器	Auxiliary instruments
		天文鐘, 電記時器, 度微器, 象天儀	Sidereal clock and chronometer, electrochronography, micrometers, celestial globes, etc.
	.6	光鏡	Optical apparatus Observation methods
		測光鏡, 攝光鏡, 偏光顯微鏡, 分光鏡	Astro-photometry, astrophotography, polarization, astro-spectroscope, etc.
	.7	天體測量	Spherical astronomy
	.71	天球	Celestial sphere
	.72	天球坐標	Spheric coordinates
	.73		
	.74	子午線　子午圈	Meridian line
	.75	天赤道	Celestial equator
	.76	天球經緯	Celestial latitude and longitude
	.77	黃道	Ecliptic
		春秋分點	Vernal and autumnal equinoxes
		十二空　二十八宿	Zodiac
	.8	星球測量法	Corrections

	.81	視差法	Parallax
	.82	蒙氣法	Refraction
	.83	光行差法	Aberration
	.84	歲差法　見 521.9	Precession see 521.9
	.85	章動差法　見 521.9	Nutation see 521.9
	.86	像片比較法	
	.87	光帶線比較法	
	.88	儀器差法	
	.89		
	.9		
523		叙述天文學	Descriptive astronomy
		天文物理學	Astrophysics
	.1	宇宙	Universe
	.11	宇宙構造	Structure of the universe
	.12	宇宙演化論	Theory of cosmic evolution
	.13	星雲假設	Nebular hyphothesis
	.14	世界多數論	Plurality of worlds
	.15	太空　太空溫度	Space and its temperature
	.16		
	.17	天塵	Cosmic dust
	.18	拒力	Repulsive force
	.19		
	.2	太陽系	Solar system
	.21	行星分佈律	Distributive laws of planets
	.22		
	.23	行星相會與相距	Conjunctions and oppositions
	.24	太陽系之太空運動	Motion of solar system in space
	.26	太陽系之構成	Constitution of planerary system

.27	太陽系固定論	Stability of solar system
.28		
.29		
.3	月球　太陰	Moon
.301	理論　關係	Theories　Relations
	例　月球與生物	e.g. The Moon and living matter
.302	圖表	Charts, photos, etc.
.31	質量, 大小,	Constants: size, mass,
	距離與視差	distance and parallax
.32	光射　溫度	Heat and light
.33	軌道與運動	Orbit and motions: Sidereal month, tropical, sun and earth's attraction, etc.
.34		
.35	月面景物	Features of surface: mountain,
	天然態狀	plains, etc.
.36	月球大氣	Atmosphere
.37		
.38	月蝕	Eclipses
.39		
.4	行星　行星論	Planets　Planetary system
.41	水星	Mercury and intramercurial
.42	金星	Venus
.43	地球　見525	Earth as a planet
.44	火星	Mars
.45	木星	Jupiter
.46	土星	Saturn
.47	天王星	Uranus
.48	海王星	Neptune and transneptunian

.49	小行星	Minor planets　Asteroids
.5	流星　黃道光	Meteors and zodiacal light
.51	隕石	Meteorites
.52	火球	Fireballs
.53	星雨	Meteoric showers, radiant points, etc.
.54	流星系	Systems of meteors
.55		
.56	流星與彗星相關論	Connection of comets and meteors
.57	黃道光　南北極光	Zodiacal light　Aurora
.58		
.59		
.6	彗星	Comets
.7	日球　太陽	Sun
.701	理論　關係	Theories　Relations
	例　日球與生物	e.g. The Sun and living matter
.702	圓表	Charts, photos, etc.
.71	質量，大小，距離與視差	Constants, dimensions, distance and parallax
.72	光射　熱度	Heat and light; theories as to source
.73	軌道與運動	Orbit and motions
.74		
.75	日斑　黑點	Sun spots, faculae, and other features of surface
.76	光球　色球　日冠	Prominences, chromosphere, corona
.77		
.78	日蝕	Eclipses
.79		
.8	星　星宿	Stars　Fixed stars (Sidereal systems)

	.81	白光星	White colored-stars
		星雲　星團　天河	Nebulae, star clusters, milky way (galaxy)
		星群　複星	Multiple, double stars
	.82	黃光星	Yellow colored-stars
	.83	赤光星	Red colored-stars
	.84	暗光星	Pale colored-stars
	.85	變光星	Variable stars
	.86	近極星	Polaris, etc.
	.87	新星	New stars
	.88	未見星	Invisible stars
	.89		
	.9	經過子午綫　陰蔽	Transits and occultations
524		星球交通學	Cosmo-communication
525		地球　地球物理學	Earth　Terrestrial physics
	.01	地球物理	Terrestrial physics
	.02	圖表	Charts, photos, etc.
	.1	質量, 大小, 距離與視差	Constants; mass, weight, dimensions, distance, etc
	.2	光射　溫度	Heat　Light
	.3	軌道與運動	Orbit and motions
	.4	坐標：經緯測定	Geographic coordinates: Finding latitude and longitude
	.5	晝夜　四季	Day and night　Seasons
	.6	潮夕	Tides
	.7	黃昏與黎明	Sunset and twilight
	.8		
	.9		

526	地形學　測地學	Figure of the earth　Geodesy
.7	測量	Surveying
527	航海天文學	Nautic astronomy
	航海通書	Nautic almanacs　Ephemerides
528	律曆　曆書	Chronology　Time
.1	恒星，太陽，太陽平均，日	Sidereal and solar day: apparent and mean time, causes of inequality, etc.
.2		
.3	恒星，回歸，近日，年	Sidereal, tropical, and auomalistic year
.4		
.5	計時學	Horology
.51	子午計時法	Finding time by trausit
.52	時候分配	Distribution of time
.53	時候差式	Equation of time
.54		
.55	恒星時	Sidereal time
.56	天文時	Cosmic time
.57	標準時	Standard time
.58	地方時	Local time
.59	計時器	Instruments of measuring
	例　羅盤計，日晷，表，等	e.g. Compass, sundials, levels, clocks, etc.
.6	日曆	Calendars
	陰曆　陽曆　古代日曆	Lunar, solar, aucient calendars
.61	天文用曆	Cosmic
.62	宗教曆	Religious

	.63	佛教	Buddhist
	.64		
	.65	基督教	Christian
	.66	回教	Moslem
	.67	公曆	General and perpetual
	.68		
	.69		
	.7		
	.8		
	.9	依國分	By country

   例 中國曆書 528.91   e.g. Chinese chronology
     希臘曆書 528.931   Greek chronology

529		氣象學	Meteorology (Aerology)
	.01		
	.02		
	.03	辭書	Dictionaries
	.04	評論	Critiques　Criticism
	.05	雜誌	Periodicals
	.06	學會	Societies
	.07	研究	Studies: Outlines, syllabi, questions, etc.
	.08	總集	Collected works
	.09	歷史	History
	.1	大氣物理學	Physics of the atmosphere
		氣象力學	Dynamic meteorology
	.11	空氣熱動學	Thermodynamics of the air
	.12		
	.13	空氣傳導	Conductivity

.14	大氣灰塵	Atmospheric dust
.15	空氣成分	Composition of the air
.16	大氣高度	Height of the atmosphere
.17	溫度與輻射	Temperature and radiations
.18	日差與夜差	Diurnal and nocturnal variations
.19		
.2	氣壓與流動	Pressure and circulation
	氣壓分配　日間變化	Distribution of pressure　Diurnal changes
	流動	Circulation
.3	風　風暴	Winds and storm
.301	理論	Theories : Convectional
.302	圖表	Wind tables　Diagrams　Windrose
.31	風之種類	Classification of winds
	信風，四季風，等	Planetary　Trade-winds　Monsoons Etc.
.32		
.33	風暴　颶風	Wind storms　Hurricanes
.34		
.35	颶風	Cyclonic storms
.36		
.37	颶風與反颶風	Cyclonic and anticyclonic winds
.38		
.39	地方風暴	Local storms
.4	濕氣　凝結與雨水	Atmospheric moisture Condensation and precipitations
.41	露	Dew　Dew point
.42	霜	Frost
.43	霧	Fog　Fog-breakers
.44	雲	Clouds

.45	雨水	Precipitation Rainfall
.46	雪	Snow
.47	雹	Hail
.48		
.49	其他	Others
.5	氣象電學	Atmospheric electricity
	參看 537.7	see also 537.7
.51	雷	Thunder
.52		
.53	電光　閃電	Lightning
.54		
.55	極光	Aurora
	參看 523.57	see also 523.57
.56		
.57		
.58		
.59		
.6	氣象光學	Meteorological optics
.61	折光現象	Refraction phenomena
.62	青空	Color of the sky
.63	朝紅與夕陽	Sunrise, sunset and twilight phenomena
.64	虹	Rainbows Fog bows, etc.
.65	暈　光環	Coronae Halos Parhelia
.66	彩雲　霞	Luminous clouds
.67	蜃氣	Mirage Fata Morgana
.68	破鏡	Brocken spectre
.69		

.7	實用氣象　天氣	Practical meteorology　Weather
.71	天氣推測	Methods of observation　Computation
.72	氣象臺	Meteorological observatories
.73	測候所	Weather bureaus
.74		
.75	風暴警報　天氣預報	Storm signals　Weather warnings
.76	天氣圖	Weather maps
.77		
.78	應用氣象學	Applied meteorology
	農林, 商務	Application to agriculture and commerce, etc.
.79		
.8	氣候學	Climatology　Climate
.81	週期變差	Periodic variations
.82	長年差	Secular variation
.83	地質氣候	Geological climates
.84		
.85	地勢與地境之影響	Effects of topography and local conditions
	例　海洋影響	Influence of the ocean
.86		
.87	氣候與植物	Relation to vegetation
.88	氣候與動物人類	Relation to animals and man
.89	氣候分佈	Climatic distribution
	依國分	By country
.9		

530 物理學 Physics

.01	理論　關係	Theories　Relations
	例　物理與數學	e.g. Physics and mathematics
	物理與天文	Physics and astronomy
	天文物理　見 523	Astrophysics　see 523
	地球物理　見 525	Geophysics　see 525
.02		
.03	辭書	Dictionaries
.04	評論	Critiques　Criticism
.05	雜誌	Periodicals
.06	學社	Societies
.07	研究　綱目，綱要，答問，等	Studies: Outlines, syllabi, questions, etc.
.072	實驗　試驗室	Laboratories
.073	方法	Methods
.074	儀器	Apparatus
.077	量度	Physical measurements Weights and measures
.079	物理表	Physical units, tables
.08	總集　小册	Collected works　Pamphlets
.09	歷史	History
.1	物質組織與物性學	Constitutions and properties of matter
.11	以太與物質構造	Structure of matter and ether
	分子與原子物理學	Molecular and atomic physics
.2	物質動理	Kinetic theory of matter
.3	特殊物性學	Special properties of matter
	壓縮性，彈性，等	Compressibility, elasticity, etc.
.4	物質不滅論	Conservation of matter

.5		物理定律	Physical laws
.6			
.7		相對論　量子論	Theory of relativity
			Quantum theory
.71		相對論	Theory of relativity
		空間與時間	Space and time
		能子論	Theory of energy
.73		量子論	Quantum theory
.75		新量子論	New quantum theory
		得氏波群論	De Broglie waves
		斯氏波動力學	Schrodinger wave mechanics
		海氏量子力學	Heisenberg quantum mechanics
.8			
.9		物理異説	Physical paradoxes
531		力學	**Mechanics**
.1		理論力學	Rational mechanicss
.11		哲理	Philosophical
.12		數理	Mathematical
.13		物理	Mechanical and physical
.14			
.15			
.16			
.17			
.18			
.19		其他特殊原理	Special principles
.2		動學	Kinematics
.21		運動　運動律	Motion　Laws of motion
.22		點動學	Kinematics of a point

.221	直線運動		Rectilinear motion
.223	曲線運動		Curvilinear motion
.225	發射物運動		Motion of a projectile
.23	單面動學		Uniplanar kinematics
.24	固形動學		Kinematics of a rigid figure
.241	旋動		Rotation
.243	平面運動		Plane motion
.245	曲折運動		Crank motion
.25			
.26	變形動學		Kinematies of a deformable figure
.27	流體動學		Kinematics of fluids
.28			
.29	機械動學		Kinematics of mechanism
.3	應用力學		Applied mechanics
.32	生理力學		Physiological mechanics
.37	游藝力學		Mechanics of games and sports
.4	工藝力學		Technieal mechanics
	見 工程力學 650.3		See Engineering 650.3
.41	物料強度		Strength of material
.43	構造力學		Structural mechanics
.5	解析力學		Analytical mechanies
.6	分子與固體力學		Dynamics of a particle and of a rigid body
.61	靜力學		Statics
.62	平衡		Equilibrium
.63	引力與靜勢		Attraction and potential
.64	重力		Gravity
.65	物墜律		General gravitation
.66	圖解靜力		Graphic statics

.67		
.68		
.69	分子動力學	Kinetics of a particle or a rigid system
.691	物力與運動	Force and motion
.692	惰性	Inertia
.693	動力與勢能	Kinetic and potential energy Work and energy
.694	摩擦力	Friction
.695	旋動	Rotating bodies　Rotation
.696	向心力　離心力	Centrifugal and centripetal
.697	衝動　衝力	Impulse　Impact
.698	射發學	Ballistics
.7		
.8	彈體力學	Dynamics of elastic solids
.81	彈性	Elasticity
.82	張力	Tension
.83	牽引力	Traction
.84		
.85	轉扭力	Torsion
.86		
.87	擺動　振動	Elastic vibration　Oscillation
.88		
.89		
.9	單減機械　傳力	Simple machines　Transmission of force
.91	桿秤	Lever and balance
.92	輪軸	Wheel and axle
.93	繩索	Cord and catenary

	.94	滑車	Pulley
	.95	斜面	Inclined plane
	.96	楔	Wedge
	.97	螺旋	Screw
	.98		
	.99		
532		液體　水力學	Hydromechanics Hydraulics　Liquids
	.1	液體動學	Dynamics of liquids
	.11	毛管引力	Capillary attraction
	.12	溶解	Solubility
	.13	混合與分離	Miscibility and immiscibility
	.14	擴散	Diffusion
	.15	滲透與吸收	Osmose　Absorption
	.17	內摩擦力　黏力	Internal friction
	.2		
	.3	液體靜力學	Hydrostatics
	.31	密度	Density
	.32	比重　比重計	Specific density
	.33	壓力	Pressure
	.34	張力	Tension
	.35	平衡	Equilibrium
	.36	浮力　浮體	Buoyant effects
	.37	壓縮	Compressibility
	.38		
	.39		
	.4		
	.5	液體動力學	Hydrokinetics

.51	水動方程式	Hydrodynamic equations
.52	液體流動	Movement of liquids
	流體運動	
.53	流出	Efflux Discharge
.54		
.55	衝力	Impact
.56	阻力	Resistance
.57	浮體運動	Motion of vessels and other floating bodies
.58	固體在液體中之運動	Motion of a rigid body in a incompressible liquids
.59		
.6		
.7	膠質物理	Viscous fluids
.8		
.9	水力學	Hydraulics
	見　水利工程 654	see hydraulic engineering 654
	水力機械	Hydraulic appliances
	例　水力機,水車,等	e.g. Motors, waterwheels, etc.

533　氣體　氣力學　　Pneumatics　Gases

.1	氣體動學	Aerodynamics
.11	動能	Dynamic energy
.13	溶解與吸收	Solubility and absorption
.15	擴散	Diffusion
.17	內摩擦力　黏力	Internal friction
.2		
.3	氣體靜力學	Statics Aerostatics
.31	密度	Density

.32	比重	Specific gravity
.33	彈力	Elasticity
.34	壓力　張力	Pressure　"Tension"
.35	平衡	Equilibrium
.36	壓縮　壓縮律	Compression
.37	壓力減除　真空	Reduction of pressure　Vacua
.38	溫度與壓力	Temperature and pressure
.381	大氣壓力	Atmospheric pressure
.383	壓力傳導	Transmission of pressure
.39	壓計	Measurement of pressure
.4		
.5	氣體動力學	Kinetics　Aerokinetics
.51	氣體動力論	Kinetic theory of gases
.52	氣體運動	Motion of gases
.53	流出	Effusion
.54	衝力與阻力	Resistance to air movement
.55	氣體流動	Flow of gases
.56		
.57	固體在氣體中之運動	Movement of rigid bodies in gases
.58		
.59		
.6		
.7	大氣	Atmosphere
	航空力學	Aeronautics
.8		
.9	氣力機械	Pneumatic apparatus
	見　氣力機　655.5	see Pneumatic engines 655.5
	例　風扇機，抽氣機，等	e.g. Air motor, air pump, etc.

中國十進制分類法及索引　| 331

534　聲學　音學　　Acoustics (Sound)

.1　　數理論　　　　　　　Mathematical theory
.2　　波動論　　　　　　　Kinematics of vibration and wave motion　Undulations
.3　　音波　　　　　　　　Sound waves
.31　　振幅　波長　　　　Amplitude　Wave length
.32
.33　　縱波　疎密波　　　Longitudinal wave
.34　　橫波　高低波　　　Transverse wave
.35　　波界　　　　　　　Wave front
.36
.37　　波形　　　　　　　Wave form
.38
.39
.4　　音之波及　　　　　　Propagation of sound
.41　　速度　　　　　　　Velocity
　　　　　氣體，液體，固體　　In gases, liquids, and isotropic solids
.43　　回音　回響　　　　Reflexion　Echo
.45　　屈拆　　　　　　　Refraction
　　　　　風　　　　　　　　By wind
　　　　　溫度之變遷　　　　By varying temperature
.47　　迴拆　　　　　　　Interference　Diffraction
.5　　振動　發音體　　　　Vibrations
.51　　周波與音節　　　　Frequency and pitch
.511　　　測定法　　　　Instruments for determining
.512　　　圖解法　　　　Graphic method
.513　　　斷續活動法　　Strobosocopic method
.515　　　耀焰法　　　　Manometric flames
.52　　共鳴　　　　　　　Resonance

.53		解析	Analysis　Measurement of vibration
.531		週期曲線　和音曲線	Periodic curve　Harmonic curve
.532		圖解	Graphic representation
.533		聲之強度	Measurement of intensity of sound
.535		複振動之解析	Analysis of compound vibrations
.537		複振動之投射	Projection of compound vibrations
.54		絃振動	Vibration of stretched strings or wires
.541		和音　陪音	Harmonies　Overtones
.543		彈性之於絃振動	Influence of elasticity
.545		縱振動	Longitudinal vibration
.546		橫振動	Tranverse vibration
.55		棒振動	Vibration of rods
.56		盤振動	Vibration of plates (discs) and membranes
.57		管振動	Vibration in pipes and other cavities
.58		熱之於振動	Vibrations maintained by heat
.59			
.6		波之重疊	Superposition of waves
.61		干涉	Interferance
.63		拍子	Pulsation　Beats
.65		和音中拍子	Beats between harmonics (overtones)
.67		合調	Combination tones
.7		樂音　音調感覺	Physical basis of music Sensations of tone
.71		音色　音質	Tone color (Timbre　Quality)
.72			
.73		音程	Intervals
.74		音階	Scales

.75	音之調和與不調和	Consonance and dissonance
.76		
.77	音節准則	Standards of pitch
.78		
.79		
.8		
.9	生理音學　聲與耳	Physiological acoustics Voice and ear
.91	聲調	Tones of the voice
.93	音之綜合	Synthesis of the vowels
.95	耳　音之認知	The ear　Perception of sound
.99	測音器	Phonographs Gramophones microphones
535	**光學**	**Optics Light (Radiant energy)**
.1	光理學　解析光學	Theories of light　Analytical theory of light
.11	光微子論	Corpuscular theory
.13	光波論	Wave theory
.2	光性學	Nature of light
.21	振動	Oscillation　Vibration
.23	白光之分析	Analysis of white light
.25	同性放射	Homogeneous radiation
.3	物理光學	Physical optics
.31	傳導　速度	Propagation　Velocity
.32	反線	Reflexion (Catoptrices)
.33	屈線　收差	Refraction　Aberration
.34	撓線　干涉	Interference
.35	迴線	Diffraction

.36		雙屈線	Double refraction
.37		偏光	Polarized light　Polarization
.38		吸收與分散	Absorption and dispersion
.39		光色	Color
.391		光色感覺	Sensations of color
.392		實驗與測定	Experiments and determinations
.393		物體光色	Colors of bodies
.395		光色混合	Mixture of colors
.397		光色消沒	Achromasy
.4		分光學	Spectroscopy
.41		分光鏡	Spectroscope
.42		其他光鏡	Other apparatus
		例　攝光鏡	e.g. Spectrophotography
.43		分光計　測光器	Photometry　Spectrometry
.44		光帶之性質與構造	Nature and structure of the spectrum
.441		放射光帶	Emission spectra
.443		連續光帶	Continuous spectra
.444		不連續光帶	Discontinuous spectrs
.445		吸收光帶	Absorption spectra
.447		複數光帶	Plurality of spectra
.45		光帶之產生	Production of spectra
		火焰，電光帶，熱光帶，發光	Flame, electric spectra, heat spectra, luminescence, etc.
.46		天文光帶	Astronomical spectra
.47		大氣光帶	Atmospheric spectra
		極光，電，火球	Aurorae, lightning, etc.
.48		單色射線取法	Methods of obtaining monochromatic rays
		分光法，吸收法，重反射法	Spectrum method, absorption method, multiple reflexion method, etc.

	.49		
	.5	光線　射線	Transformation of radiant energy Radiation
	.51	發光	Luminescence
	.52	氟光	Fluorescence
	.53	X 光線	Rontgen rays (X-rays)
	.54	N 光線	N-rays
	.55		
	.56	燐光	Phosphorescence
	.57	輻射能之化學作用	Chemical action of radiant energy
	.58	輻射之熱動學	Thermodynamics of radiation
	.59	黑體輻射	Black-body radiation
	.6		
	.7	幾何光學	Geometrical optics
	.8	光學儀器	Optical instruments
		望遠鏡, 輻射能測量, 等	Telescope, measurement of radiant energy, etc.
	.9	生理光學	Physiological optics
		眼　視	The eye　Sight　Vision
536		熱學	Thermics (Heat)
	.1	溫度	Temperature
	.11	測熱法　見 536.31	Calorimetry　see 536.31
	.13	溫度計	Thermometer　Thermometry
	.14	高溫計	Measurement of high temperature Pyrometry
	.15	低溫計	Measurement for very low temperature
	.16	恒溫計	Thermostat
	.17	顯溫計	Thermoscopy

.18
.19
.2   膨脹   Expansion
         固體，液體，氣體   Solids, liquids, gases
.3   比熱   Specific heat   Thermal capacity
.31   計熱　測熱法   Measurement   Calorimetry
.32
.33   固體比熱測定法   Solids
.34   液體比熱測定法   Liquids
.35   氣體比熱測定法   Gases and vapors
.36
.37   原子與分子重量   Atomic and molecular weights
.38
.39
.4   傳熱　傳導與輻射   Transmission（Conduction and radiation）
.41   傳導   Conduction   Conductivity
.411   數理論   Mathemetical treatment
.412   擴散   Diffusivity
.413   放射   Emissivity
.415   物理論   Physical treatment   Conductive capacity
.417   固體傳熱   Conduction in solids
.418   液體傳熱   Conduction in liquids
.419   氣體傳熱   Conduction in gases
.42   輻射   Radiation   Emission
.43   反射   Reflexion
.44   屈射   Refraction
.45   撓射　干涉   Interference
.46   迴射   Diffraction

.47	雙屈輻射	Double refraction
.48	偏射	Polarization
.49	吸收　分散	Absorption　Diathermacy
.5	熱力論	Mechanical theory of heat
.51	數理	Mathematical treatment
.53	熱電學	Thermoelectricity
.55	內熱反應	Endothermic reaction
.57	能之變成熱能	Energy changes into heat energy
	熱源　體溫	Sources of heat　Animal heat
.6	熱動學	Thermodynamics
.61	第一律	First law
.62	第二律	Second law
.63	週期變化論	Theory of cyclic transformation
.64	逆反原理	Principle of reversibility
.65	熱函數	Entropy
.66	熱動位	Thermodynamic potential
.67	熱動力	Thermodynamic motivity
		Dissipation of energy
.68	熱彈性	Thermoelasticity
.69	熱動力之應用	Application of thermodynamics
.7	物態變化	Change of state
		(Change of phase)
.71	固體與流體	Solid and fluid state　Fusion Solidification
.711	溶點與凝點	Melting and freezing point
.713	溶解	Latent heat of fusion
.715	凝固	Solidification
.72	流體　液體與氣體	Liquid and gaseous state
.721	沸點	Boiling　Boiling point

.722	氣化	Vaporization
.723	臨界點	Critical point
.725	熱分解	Dissociation
.727	蒸溜	Distillation
.728	凝結	Condensation (liquefaction) of gases
.73		
.74	混合流體之凝結與氣化	Condensation and vaporization of mixed fluids
.75	飽和蒸氣	Saturated vapor Steam
.76		
.77	過熱蒸氣	Superheated vapor
.78		
.79		
.8		
.9	應用熱力學	Technical thermodynamics
	見 655.25 655.42	see 655.25 655.42
	汽機，煤氣機，等	Machines：Steam-engine, gas-enging, etc.

537　電學　電磁　Electricity　Electricity and magnetism together

.01	電理	Theories of electricity
.011	流體說	Fluid
.013	幾何說	Geometrical
.015	力學說	Mechanical
.017	以太說	Edlund's ether
.02		
.03	辭書	Dictionaries
.037	年鑑	Yearbooks
.04	評論	Critiques Criticism

.05	雜誌		Periodicals
.06	學會		Societies
.07	研究　問答		Studies：Outlines, syllabi, questions, etc.
.072		實驗　試驗室	Laboratories
.075		電機	Apparatus and machines
.077		量度　測定	Electrical measurement
		静電計　電流計等	
.08	總集　小册		Collected works
.09	歷史		History
.1	静電學		Electrostatics
.11	以太應力		Ether stress
.12			
.13	電化　發電		Electrification
.14	電場		Electrical field
.141		指力線	Lines of force
.143		電應力	Electrical stress
.145		電位	Potential
.15			
.16			
.17	電數理論		Mathematical theory
.18	無體傳電		Dielectrics
.19			
.2	流電學		Electric current
.21	電池　蓄電池		Voltaic (Galvanic) cell　Voltaic element
.22	線流電		Linear current
.23	面流電		Surface current
.24	三面流電		Tridimensional current

.25	週期流電	Periodic (irregular) current
.26		
.27	傳電與阻電	Electric conduction and resistance
.28		
.29	電解傳電	Electrolytic conduction
.3	動電學	Electrokinetics　Electrodynamics
.31	流電動理	Dynamical theory of the currents
.32		
.33	流電互相作用	Mutual action of currents
.34	電感應	Induction　Inductance
.35	交流電流	Alternating currents
.36		
.37	氣體中之電道	Passage of electricity through gases
.371	數理	Mathematical theory
.372	電離　游子　電子	Ionization and electrizations　Ions　Electrons
.373	氣體中流電	Electric currents in gases
.374	游子遷移	Migration of ions
.375	游子輻射	Ionic radiation
.377		
.379	物理與化學作用	Physical and chemical effects
.4		
.5		
.6	熱電學	Thermoelectricity
.7	空中電學	Atmospheric electricity
.71	避電學	Applications to lightning rods
.8	應用電學	Electrical technology
.9		

538　磁學　　　　　　　Magnetism

.1	磁石　磁鐵	Magnets
.11	天然	Natural
.12		
.13	人造	Artificial
.14		
.15	磁極	Poles　Directive force
.16	磁石互吸作用	Mutual action of magnets
.17	振動	Oscillation
.18		
.19		
.2	磁化　磁力吸引	Magnetization
.24	磁場	Fields
.3	磁測量　磁計	Magnetic measurements
.4	磁感應	Magnetic induction
.41	理論方面	Theoretical
.42	磁流與磁路	Magnetic current and circuit
.43	分子説	Molecular theory
.44		
.45	實驗方面	Experimental
.46	特殊現象	Particular phenomena
.47	殘留磁學	Residual magnetism　Hysteresis, etc.
.48		
.49		
.5	逆磁學　正磁學	Diamagnetism
		Paramagnetism
.59	結晶磁學	Crystal magnetism
.6	物理關係	Physical relations

.61	關係力學者	To mechanics	
	磁壓	Magnetostriction	
.64	關係音學者	To sound	
	振動影響	Influence of Vibration	
.65	關係光學者　光磁學	To light　Magneto-optics	
	磁反射	Magnetic reflexion	
.66	關係熱學者　熱磁學	To heat　Thermomagnetism	
	溫度影響	Influence of temperature	
.7	地磁學	Terrestrial magnetism	
.71	磁原素	Magnetic elements	
.72			
.73	磁線	Magnetic lines	
.74			
.75	地磁觀測	Magnetic observations	
.751	週期磁變	Periodic phenomena	
	日變，歲變，常年變，等	Diurnal, annual, secular, etc.	
.752	磁變律	Laws of magnetic disturbances	
.753	地磁與日斑	Terrestrial magnetism and sunspot period	
.754	地磁與蝕	Terrestrial magnetism and eclipses	
.755	地磁與氣象	Terrestrial magnetism and meteorological phenomena	
.756			
.757	地磁與地質構造	Terrestrial magnetism and geological structure	
.758	地磁與地震	Terrestrial magnetism and earthquakes	
.76			
.77	地磁路	Earth circuits	
.78			
.79			
.8	電磁	Electromagnetism	

	.81	電磁石	Electromagnets
	.82	磁性	Magnetic quantities
	.83	磁石上流電作用	Action of the current on magnet
	.84	流電上磁石作用	Action of magnet on electric current
	.85	電磁感應	Electromagnetic induction
	.86	電磁能之移傳	Transference of electromagnetic energy
	.861	電振動　電波	Electric oscillations　Electric waves
	.862	傳道	Propagation
	.863	反射	Reflexion
	.865	屈射	Refraction
	.867	分極	Polarization
	.87	電磁旋動與振動	Electromagnetic rotation and vibration
	.88		
	.89	電磁機械	Electromagnetic machinery
	.9		
539		輻射物理學	Radio-physics　Radioactivity　Radiology
540		化學	Chemistry
		生理化學　見 592.4	Physiological chemistry see 592.4
		醫化學　見 596.4	Medical and pharmacentical chemistry see 596.4
		農業化學　見 610.54	Agricultural chemistry see 610.54
		工藝化學　見 660 或 548	Chemical technology see 650 or 548 if prefer
	.01	關係	Relations
		例　生物化學　參看 562.4	e.g. Bio-Chemistry　see also 562.4

.02			
.03	辭書	Dictionaries Nomenclature	
.037	年鑑	Yearbooks	
.04	評論	Critiques Criticism	
.05	雜誌	Periodicals	
.06	學會	Societies	
.07	研究	Studies	
	綱要, 問答, 等	Outlines, syllabi, question, etc.	
.08	總集 小冊	Collected works Pamphlets	
.09	歷史	History	
.097	化學家傳記	Biography of chemists	
.1-.9	特論	Special treatises	
	例 點金術	e.g. Alchemy Philosopher's	
	點金石 540.1	stone 540.1	
	參看 224	see also 224	
	萬物溶化術	Alkahest Universal	
	溶媒 540.3	Solvent 540.3	
	化學游戲 540.7	Chemical recreations 540.7	
541	理論化學 物理化學	Physical and theoretical Chemistry	
	近世化學	Modern chemic theories	
.01	原子論	Atomic theory	
	其關係成分, 結構, 重量, 等者	Laws of chemical combination: weights, etc.	
	原子物理學 見 530.11	For atomic physics See 530.11	
.02	元素	Chemical elements	
	性質	Nature and properties	
.03	化合物	Chemical compounds Structure and formulas	

	酸，鹽基，鹽，合金，等	Acids, bases, salts, alloys, etc.
.04	分子	Molecular types
.05		
.06	立體化学	Stereochemistry
.061	化學變化律	Conditions and laws of chemical change
.063	化學动學	Chemical dynamics
.064	化學靜學	Chemical statics
.065	化學平衡	Chemical equilibrium
.067	化合力　親合力	Chemical affinity
.07	同素	Allotropy
	化學構造方式之不入 541.03 者類此	Class here material on structure not included in 541.03
.08		
.09	化學律，週期律，化學表	Formulas　Periodic law　Stoichiometry　Tables
.1	固態	Solid state
	參看 536.715	see also 536.715
.2	液態	Liquid state
	參看 536.728	see also 536.728
.21	有機液態	Organic liquids
.23	無機液態	Inorganic liquids
.3	氣態	Gaseous state
	參看 536.722	see also 536.722
.4	溶態	Solute state　Solubility
.41	溶解律	Laws
.42	溶解表	Tables of solubility
.43	溶解　滲透壓	Solubility, osmotic pressure, diffusion, etc.
.44	冰點與蒸氣壓	Freezing points and vapor pressure

	分子重量測定	Determination of molecular weight
.45	過飽和溶液	Supersaturated solutions
.46	溶媒	Solvents
.47		
.48	膠質化學	Colloidal state　Colloidal chemistry
.49	乳質化學	Emulsions
.5	光化學	Photochemistry
	光之於化學作用，化學構造，等	Relation of light to chemic action, of polarized light to chemic structure, etc.
541.6	熱化學	Thermochemistry
.61	高低溫度之化學	Chemistry of high and low temperatures (general)
.62	燃燒，發焰，爆裂	Combustion, flame, explosion
.63	熱分解	Dissociation
.64	溶點與沸點	Melting and boiling points
.65	分別蒸餾	Fractional distillation
.66		
.67	蒸氣密度	Vapor densities
.68	氣液化	Liquefaction of gases
.69		
.7	電化學	Electrochemistry
	電解化學	Electrolysis
.71	電解分解	Electrolytic dissociation
.73	電解物傳導	Conductivity of electrolytes
.8	磁化學	Magnetochemistry
.9		
542	實驗化學	Practical and experimental chemistry

		其關係分析方面者 見 543	For analysis see 543
	.1	試驗室	Laboratories
		內部建築與設備	Interior construction and installation
	.2	儀器與用法	Apparatus and manipulations
		試驗準備，程序，等	Arrangements Procedure Preparation of substances etc.
	.3	量度儀器	Measuring apparatus
		重量，密度，容量，等之測定	Determination of weights and density, and of volume
	.4	蒸餾法	Heating Distillation
		煤，油，氣，電，等燃料蒸餾	Heating with coal, liquid fuels, gas, etc.
	.5	火酸法 吹管法	Flames Blowpipes
		參看乾式分析法 544.2	see also Dry methods of analysis 544.2
542.6		液體法	Aqueous and liquid treatment
	.61	溶解 溶解法	Dissolving Solution
	.62	溶度測定	Determination of solubility Supersaturation
	.63	擴散	Diffusion
	.64	滲透 滲透器	Dialysis Dializers
	.65	凝結	Solidification
	.66	徐注	Decantation
	.67	濾清 濾水器	Filtration and filters
	.68	搾擠	Expression and presses
	.69	洗	Washing
	.7	氣體法	Gas manipulation

		成氣法，集氣法，洗氣法，貯氣法，量氣法，抽氣法，壓氣法，液氣與固氣法	Gas production, collecting and decanting, washing and dissolving, storage, measurement, rarefaction, compression, liquefaction and solidification
	.8	電與流電法	Electric and galvanic manipulations
	.9	其他	Other operations
		脂酸，瓦斯法:酸化與復原	Attacks by acids and gases: oxidations, etc.
543		分析化學	Analysis Analytic chemistry
		定性定量分析	Class here general works covering both qualitative and quantitative analysis
	.1	食物飲料分析	Analysis of food and drink
	.13	酪物分析　牛乳	Dairy products Milk
	.15	水分析	Water
	.2	農物分析	Agricultural analysis
	.21	土壤	Soils
	.22	肥料	Fertilizers
	.23		
	.24	田作物	Field corps
	.25	蔬菜	Vegetables
	.26	果物	Fruits
	.27		
	.28	畜產	Animal products
	.29		
	.3		
	.4	藥物分析	Analysis of drugs and medicines
	.49	毒劑　互見 593.9	Poisons see also 593.9
	.5	岩礦分析	Analysis of rocks and ores

	.6	無機物分析	Analysis of inorganic products in general
	.61	空氣分析	Analysis of the air
	.64	金類分析	Analysis of metals
	.7	有機物分析	Analysis of organic products in general
	.8		
	.9	其他	Others
544		定性分析	Qualitative analysis
	.03	原素定性法	Determination of chemic elements of substances
	.1	濕式分析法	Wet method
	.11	試藥	Chemical reagents
	.12	鹽基定性法	Determination of bases
	.15	酸定性法	Determination of acids
	.2	乾式分析法	Dry method
	.3	吹管分析法	Blowpiping
	.4	瓦斯分析法	Gas analysis　Reactions
	.41	純粹瓦斯確定法	Identifying an isolated gas
	.43	瓦斯混合物分析法	Analysis of gaseous mixture
	.5	滲透分析法	Dialysis
	.57	電滲透法	Electric dialysis
		互見　542.8	see also 542.8
	.6	色度分析法	Spectrum analysis　Colorimetric
		互見 535.4	see also 535.4
	.7	偏光分析法	Polariscopic analysis
		互見 535.37	see also 535.37
	.8	顯微鏡分析法	Microscopic examinations

.9	其他	Other methods
.93	電分析法	Electroanalysis
.95	毛管分析法	Capillary analysis
545	**定量分析**	**Quantitative analysis**
.1	濕式分析法	Wet method
	滴定法，鹼質定量，酸定量	Titration solution, alkalimetry, acidimetry
.2	乾式分析法	Dry method
	吹管定量，灰吹法	Quantitative analysis with blowpipe, cupellation
.3	重量分析法	Gravimetric
	秤衡定量，樣品選取，等	Analysis by weighing, sampletaking, etc.
.4	容量分析法	Titrometric methods
.41	液體	Volumetric analysis of liquids
.43	氣體　瓦斯	Volumetric analysis of gases
	瓦斯容量測定	Endiometry and eudiometers
.5	電分析法	Electric methods
.51	定量電流分析	Constant current analysis
.53	定量電壓分析	Constant voltage analysis
.57	接觸作用	Catalytic analysis
.6	色度分析法	Spectrum analysis
		Colorimetric
.7	偏光分析法	Polarimetric
.8	顯微分析法	Microscopic examinations
.89	其他	Others
.9	綜合化學	Synthesis　Synthetic chemistry
.97	電綜合化學	Electric synthesis

546　　無機化學　　　　　　　Inorganic chemistry

	1.凡專論某一元素者應分入下列某元素類	1.Works treating of the compounds of a single element clast accordingly as follows
	2.凡專論某屬元素者應入該屬元素類	2.Works treating of the compounds of a group elements are to be placed with the group
	3.凡總論二種或二種以上元素者則分入第一種元素類	3.Works treating of compounds consisting of two or more elements are to be placed under the first element

.1	非金屬元素	Nonmetallic elements
.11	氫	Hydrogen H1
.12		
.13	造鹽元素	Halogen group
.131	氯	Chlorin Cl 17
.133	溴	Bromin Br 35
.135	碘	Iodin I 53
.137	氟	Fluorin F 9
.14	氮元素	Nitrogen group
.141	氮	Nitrogen N 7
.143	磷	Phosphorus P 15
.145	砷	Arsenic As 33
.15	氧元素	Oxygen group
.151	氧	Oxygen O 8
.153	硫	Sulphur S 16
.155	硒	Selenium Se 34
.157	碲	Tellurium Te 52
.16	碳元素	Carbon group
.161	碳	Carbon C 6
.163	矽	Silicon Si 14

.17	硼元素	Boron group
	硼	Boron B 5
.18	氦元素	Helium group
.181	氦	Helium He 2
.182	氖	Neon Ne 10
.183	氬	Argon A 18
.185	氪	Crypton Kr 36
.186	氙	Xenon Xe 54
.187	氡	Radon (or Niton) Rn (Nt) 86
.19		
.2	金屬元素	Metals
.21	鹻金元素	Alkali group
.211	鉀	Potassium K 19
.213	鈉	Sodium Na 11
.215	鋰	Lithium Li 3
.217	銣	Rubidium Rb 37
.219	鎧	Caesium Cs 55
.22	鹻土金元素	Alkalin earths
.221	鈣	Calcium Ca 20
.223	鍶	Strontium Sr 38
.225	鋇	Barium Ba 56
.227	鐳	Radium Ra 88
.23	鎂元素	Magnesium group
.231	鉛	Glucinum or Beryllium Gl
.233	鎂	Magnesium Mg 12
.235	鋅	Zinc Zn 30
.237	鎘	Cadmium Cd 48
.24	鉛 銀元素	Lead and silver group
.241	鉛	Lead Pb 82
.243	鉈	Thallium Tl 81
.25	銀元素	Silver group

.251	銅	Copper Cu 29
.253	銀	Silver Ag 47
.255	銾	Mercury Hg 80
.26	鈰元素 希土金元素	Cerium group　Rare earths
.261	釔	Yttrium Yt 39
.263	鈰	Cerium Ce 58
.265	鑭	Lanthanum La 57
.267	鐠	Praseodymium Pr 59
.269	錂	Neodymium Nd 60
.27		
.271	鉺	Erbium Er 68
.272	鐿	Ytterbium Yb 70
.273	鋱	Terbium Tb 65
.274	鋁	Aluminum Al 13
.275	銦	Indium In 49
.277	鎵	Gallium Ga 31
.28		
.29	其他希土金元素	Other metals of rare earths
.291	鈧	Scandium Sc 21
.292	釤	Samarium or decipium Sa 6
.293	釓	Gadolinium Gd 64
.294	鍺	Germanium Ge 32
.295	銪	Europium Eu 63
.297	銩	Thulium Tm 69
.3	鐵元素	Iron group
.33	錳	Manganese Mn 25
.35	鐵	Iron Fe 26
.37	鈷	Cobalt Co 27
.39	鎳	Nickel Ni 28

.4	鉻元素	Chromium group
.41	鉻	Chromium Cr 24
.43	鉬	Mohybdenum Mo 42
.45	鎢	Tungsten or Wolfram W 74
.47	鈾	Uranium U 92
.5	錫元素	Tin group
.53	錫	Tin Sn 50
.54	鈦	Titanium Ti 22
.55	鋯	Zirconium Zr 40
.57	釷	Thorium Th 90
.58	錒	Actinium Ac 89
.6	釩元素	Vanadium group
.61	釩	Vanadium V 23
.62	銻	Antimony Sb 51
.63	鉍	Bismuth Bi 83
.64	鉭	Tantalum Ta 73
.65	鈮或鈳	Niobium or Columbium Cb 41
.67	鏷	Polonium Po 84
.7	鉑元素	Platinum group
.71	金	Gold Au 79
.73	鉑	Platinum Pt 78
.75	銥	Iridium Ir 77
.77	鋨	Osmium Os 76
.8	釕元素	Ruthenium group
.81	釕	Ruthenium Ru 44
.83	銠	Rhodium Rh 45
.87	鈀	Palladium Pd 46
.9	想像或推定元素	False and putative elements

		依字母次第列下	Arrange alphabetically
547		有機化學	Organic chemistry
	.1	碳氫化物　脂肪族	Hydrocarbons　Fatty compounds
	.11	矯質烷屬　石蠟	Paraffins
	.12	嬴質烯屬或成油氣屬	Olefins
	.13	亞嬴質炔屬	Acetylenes
	.2	芳香族	Aromatic compounds
		燏屬	Benzenes
	.3	醇類	Alcohols　Phenols
	.4	醚類　醇精質	Ethers
	.5	醛類　間質	Aldehydes
	.6	酮類　擬間質	Ketones　Quinones
	.7	酸類	Acids
	.8	碳水化物	Carbonhydrates
	.81	糖類	Saccharine　Dextrine　Glucose　Sugar
	.83	澱粉類	Starch
	.85	纖維類	Cellulose
	.9	其他化物	Other compounds
	.91	蛋白質類	Albuminoids
	.92	蛋白質	Proteids
	.93	膠質	Gelatines
	.94	膽質	Biliary substances
	.95		
	.96		
	.97	醶類	Alkaloids
	.98		
	.99	化物之有金屬者	Compounds with metals

548	應用化學	Applied chemistry
	必要時可類此	clast here if prefer
	子目 見 660	Subdivisions see 660
549		
550	地質學	Geology
.01	理論　關係	Theories　Relations
.03	辭書	Dictionaries　Nomenclature
.037	年鑑	Yearbooks
.038	指南	Directories
.04	論文	Critiques　Criticism
.05	雜誌	Periodicals
.06	會社	Societies
.07	研究：綱目，綱要，答問，等	Studies：Outlines, syllabi, questions, etc.
	模型，圖解，等	Models, diagrams, etc.
	調查　測量	Field work
.08	總集	Collected works
.09	歷史	History
	依洲分	By continent
	例　亞洲地質	e.g. Asia
	北極地質	Arctic regions
.1	中國地質	Chinese geology
	依區域分	By regions
	例　北平地質	e.g. Geology of Peiping
.2	亞州其他各國地質	Geology of other Asiatic countries
.3	歐洲各國地質	Geology of European countries
.4	美州各國地質	Geology of American countries
.5	非州大洋州各國地質	Geology of African and Oceanian countries

551 自然地質學 動力地質 Physical and dynamic geology

.1	地球結構	Structure of earth
	地球形體與大小	Form and size of earth
	見 525.1	see also 525.1
.11	地心	Interior of the earth
.12	狀態	Conditions
	氣體,液體,固體,鐳體,説	Gases, liquids, solids, radian
.15	地殼	Earth's crust
.16	密度 堅鬆	Density
.17	運動	Movement of earth's
	其關係陸海成因者	crust in relation to the formation of land and sea
.3	地震學	Seismology Earthquakes
.31	震因	Structure of earthquake
.311	天體攝動	Perturbations of heavenly bodies
.313	地殼收縮與變遷	Oscillations of the earth's crust
.315	火山爆發	Volcanic action
.32		
.33	震源 震波	Hypocentrum Focus (of earthquake) Earthquake waves:
	前震 主震 後震	preliminary tremor, main and end waves
.34	地震測候 地震預兆	Observatiories Earthquake phenomena
.37	大陸地震	Continental
.38	海洋地震	Oceanic
.39	依國分	Local distribution By country
	例 日本地震 551.392	e.g. Japanese earthquakes 551.392

.4	火山	Volcanoes
.41	火山成因	Structure
	地心膨脹與地殼破裂	
.42	火山種類	Types of volcanoes
	活火山，睡眠火山，	Active, dormant, extinct, etc.
	死火山，等	
.44	火山測候	Observatories
.47	大陸火山	Continental volcanoes
.48	海洋火山	Submarine volcanoes
.49	依國分	Local distribution　By country
	例　意國火山　551.593	e.g. Volcanoes of Italy 515.593
.5	沸泉　溫泉	Hot springs　Geysers
.6		
.7	浸蝕與沈澱	Erosion and deposition
.71	風化	Aerial erosion
.72	雨蝕	Aqueous erosion
.73	雪崩	Icebergs
.74	電擊	Thunder-stroke
.75		
.76	冰河　冰河現象	Glaciers and glacial phenomena
.77	大陸冰河	Continental glaciers
.78	海洋冰河	Oceanic glaciers
.8		
.9	地質由成之要素	Agents of geologic work
.92	霜	Frost
.93	水	Water
.94	大氣	Atmosphere
.95	地質化學	Geochemistry

	變質作用	Chemic changes; heat
.97	植物	Plants
.98	動物	Animals
	珊瑚礁	Coral reefs
.99	分結與結核	Segregation and concretion
552	地面地質學	Physiography　Surface geology
	其爲文獻之紀述則入類志	This subject properly belongs in geography.
	其性質關係海，陸，湖，泊，等之成因，剝蝕，沉積，變遷，等者類此	But when its structure, erosion and deposition treated it is included here
.1	大陸	Continents
.2	海洋	Oceans
.3	島嶼　洲渚	Isands
.4	江河	Rivers
	溺河，順河，逆河，先成河，等	
.5	湖泊　泉	Lakes
	剝湖，冰湖，火山湖，等	
	泊	Mere
	泉	Springs　Ground water
.6	山　峒　谷	Mountains　Orology　Valleys
.7	平原　沙漠	Plains　Deserts
553	構造地質學	Structural (Tectonic Geotectonic) geology
.1	地層	Stratification
.2	彎曲層　撓屈層	Curvature and contortion

.3	波痕　乾裂		Ripple marks and sun cracks
.4	節理　岩極		Joints　Polarity in rocks
.5	傾斜　露層　層向		Dip　Outcrop　Strike
.6	外斜層　內斜層		Anticlinal　Synclinal
.7	斷層　縐縐		Faults and folds
.8	脉　岩脉　岩頸 岩瘤		Veins　Dykes　Necks　Bosses

554　　地史學　地層史學　Historical (Stratigraphic) geology

　　　　　　　　　　　　　　Geogony, age of the earth, geological climates, etc.

.1	玄古代	Archaean age
	地殼始固結	
.2	無生代	Azoic age
	無水時代	Anhydritic era
	海洋時代	Oceanic era
.3	有生代	Zoic age
.4	始生代	Archaeozoic or eozoic era
.5	古生代	Palaeozoic era
.51	震旦紀	Sinian period
	由中國得名 藻類植物	
.52	寒武紀	Cambrian period
	由英地方得名 三葉蟲	
.53	奧陶紀	Ordovician period
	仝上	
.54	志留紀	Silurian period
	仝上　始有魚	

.55　　　泥盆紀　　　　　　　　Denonian period
　　　　　　仝上　魚類最多
.56　　　石炭紀　　　　　　　　Carboniferous period
　　　　　　由煤最多得名
　　　　　　始有爬行動物
.57　　　二疊紀　　　　　　　　Dyas or Permian period
　　　　　　生物起極大變化
.58
.59
.6　　中生代　　　　　　　　　Mesozoic era
.61　　　三疊紀　　　　　　　　Triassic period
　　　　　　始有哺乳類
.63　　　侏羅紀　　　　　　　　Jurassic period
　　　　　　由瑞士山得名
　　　　　　始有鳥　裸子植物
.65　　　白堊紀　　　　　　　　Cretaceous period
　　　　　　由白堊岩得名
　　　　　　生物再起大變化
.7　　新生代　　　　　　　　　Cainozoic era
.71　　　第三紀　　　　　　　　Tertiary period
　　　　　　哺乳類特別發育
　　　　　　被子植物
.73　　　第四紀　　　　　　　　Quaternary period
　　　　　　動植物始形似現代者
　　　　　　始有人類
.8
.9

555
556　　應用地質學　　　　　　　Economic geology

.1	鑛物地質學	Mining geology
.2	軍用地質學	Military geology
.3	農林地質學	Agriculture geology
.5	工程地質學	Engineering geology
557	**岩石學**	**Lithology　Petrography　Petrology**
.1	火成岩	Igneous rocks
.2	火山岩　噴出岩	Volcanic rocks
.21	熔岩	Lavas
.22	火山灰　凝灰岩	Volcanic ashes
.23	黑曜岩　浮岩　松脂岩	Obsidian　Pumis　Pitchstone
.24	粗面岩	Trachyte
.25	流文岩	Rhyolite
.26	安山岩　響岩	Andesite　Dacite　Phonolite
.27	晶基長英斑岩	Felsites
.28	玄武岩	Basalt
.29		
.3	深成岩	Plutonic rocks
.31	斑岩　珍岩	Porphyry　Porphyrite
.32	正長岩	Syenite
.33	花綱岩	Granit
.34	輝綠岩　輝長岩	Diabase and gabbro
.35	粗輝綠岩	Dolerite
.36	閃長岩	Diorite
.37	加紫蘇輝長岩	Norite
.38	橄欖岩	Peridotite
.39		
.4	變成岩	Metamorphic rocks

.41		
.42	片麻岩	Gneiss
.43	片岩	Schists
.44	板岩　粘土岩　千枚岩	Slates　Argillite　Phyllite
.45	石英岩　密砂岩	Quartzite　Novaculite　Itacolumite
.46	大理岩　結晶石灰岩	Marble　Crystallin limestone
.47	蛇紋岩	Serpentine
.48	纖維蛇紋岩	Chrysolitic rocks
.49	其他	Other metamorphic rocks
.5	水成岩	Sedimentary rocks
.51	碎屑岩	Clastic rocks
.52	黏土岩	Clayey rocks
.521	陶土	Porcelain earth
.522	泥土	Mud
.523	黏土	Clay
.525	頁岩	Schale
.527	黏板岩	Clay slate
.53	砂礫岩	Psephite and psammite rocks
	礫，砂，角礫岩，礫岩，砂岩，硅岩，等	Pebble, sand, breccia, conglomerate, sandstone, quartzite, etc.
.55	沉澱岩	Precipitate rocks
	岩鹽，石膏，硼砂，燐鈣岩，硫黃岩	Rock salt, gypsum, etc.
.56	炭酸鹽岩	Carbonate rocks
.561	石灰岩	Limestone
.562	鯯狀石灰岩	Oolitic limestone
.563	白堊	Chalk
.564	白雲岩	Dolomite

.565	泥灰岩	Marl
.566	黄土	Loess
.567	壚坶	Lohm
.568	黑土	Black earth
.57	可燃岩　有機岩	Inflammable rocks
	石灰，煤炭，石墨，石油，等	Lime, coal, graphite, petroleum, etc.
.6	隕石　見 523.51	Meteorites　see also 523.51
.7	岩石腐化	Decay of rocks
.8	岩石顯微學	Microscopic petrography
.9	岩石分佈	Local distribution of rocks

558　礦物學　Mineralogy

.1	叙述礦物　礦物	Descriptive mineralogy　Minerals
.11	礦藏　礦床	Ore deposits
	例　胎凝礦，水成礦，氣成礦，以及礦脈，等	
.12	炭系礦	Carbon series
.121	泥炭	Peat
.122	褐炭	Lignite
.123	油炭	Cannel coal
.124	瀝青炭	Bituminous coal
.125	無烟炭	Anthracite
.126	石墨　筆鉛	Graphite　Plumbage
.127	地瀝青炭　地臘	Asphaltic coal
.128	石油	Petrolium
.13	鐵礦	Ores of iron
.14	其他金屬礦	Ores of metals other than iron
.141	金礦	Ores of gold
.142	銀礦	Ores of silver

.143	銅鑛	Ores of copper
.144	鉛鑛	Ores of lead
.145	鋅 錫 錄鑛	Ores of zinc, tin and mercury
.146	錳鑛 鉻鑛	Ores of manganese and chromium
.147	銻鑛 砷鑛	Ores of antimony and arsenic
.148	鎳鑛 鈷鑛	Ores of nickel and cobalt
.149	其他	Other metallic ores
.15	石鑛	Building stones
	其性質爲建築用者	Stone for building purpose
	例 大理石,花綱石,等	e.g. Marbles, granites, etc.
.16	土屬鑛	Earthy economic minerals
	例 磚土,陶土,砂,等	e.g. Brick clays, potter's clays, sand, etc.
.17	鑛泉	Mineral waters
	鹼,鹹,硫,鈣,等泉	Alkalin, salin, chalybeate, ironbearing, sulphuric, calcic, etc.
.18	寶石	Gems　Precious stones
.181	寶石彫琢術	Lapidary work (glyptics)
.182	人造寶石	Artificial
.183	金剛石	Diamonds
.184	紅寶石 青玉 黃玉	Rubies　Sapphires
.185	玉髓 瑪瑙	Chalcedony　Agates
.186	琉璃	Lapis-lazuli
.187	琥珀	Amber
.188	真珠 琲翠	Pearls　Jade
.19	其他鑛物	Other minerals
.2	鑛物鑑定	Determinative mineralogy
	分析:物理方面,化學方面	Analysis: physical and chemical
.3	鑛物物理學	Physical mineralogy

		其關係鑛物性質，形態，光澤，顏色，比重，溶度，等者	Its property, shape, color, specific gravity, solubility, etc.
.4	鑛物化學		Chemical mineralogy
		同分異性，同分同像，等	Isomerism, isomorphism, etc.
.5	鑛物生理學		Physiological mineralogy
		其關係鑛物生成，產狀，等者	Its growth, etc.
.6			
.7	綜合鑛物學		Synthetic mineralogy
.8			
.9	鑛物分佈		Geographical distribution
	依國分		By country
		例　中國鑛物學 558.91	e.g. Chinese mineralogy 558 91

559　結晶學　　　　　　　　　Crystallography　Crystals

.1	數理結晶學	Mathematical and geometrical crystallography
.11	結晶計算法	Calculation (crystallometry)
.13	結晶畫法　投影法	Drawing　Projection (axonometry)
.3	物理結晶學	Physical properties of crystals
.31	液體結晶	Fluid crystals
.35	光結晶學	Optical crystallography
.36	熱結晶學	Thermal crystallography
.37	電結晶學	Electrical crystallography
.38	磁結晶學	Magnetic crystallography
.39	顯微結晶學	Micro-crystallography
.4	化學結晶學	Chemical crystallography
.6	結晶形態學（構造與生長）	Morphological (structure and growth)

.61	構造	Theories of structure
.63	生長	Theories of growth
.7	人造結晶	Artificial production Pseudomorphs

560 生物學　　　　　Biology

.01	理論　關係	Theories　Relations
	例　生物與社會，地質等關係	e.g. In relation to societies, geology, etc.
.03	辭書	Dictionaries
.037	年鑑	Yearbooks
.04	評論	Critiques　Criticism
.05	雜誌	Periodicals
.06	學社	Societies
.07	研究	Studies
	綱目，綱要，答問，等	Outlines, syllabi, questions, etc.
.08	總集　文藝	Collected works
.09	歷史	History
.097	生物學家傳記	Biography
.099	生物考古	Archaeology
	互見569與990.6	see also 569 and 990.6
.1-.9	特論	Special treatises

561　系統與比較生物學　Systematic and comparative

.1	形態學　解剖學	Morphology　Anatomy
.11	原形態學	Promorphology　Type of structure
.12	數理論	Mathematical
.13	同形	Symmetry

		例 左右同形	Bilateral, etc.
.15	差等與類似		Homology and analogy
.17	組織形態學		Textology (Structural morphology)
		原形質與細胞構造	Protoplasmic and cellular structure
.2	組織學		Histology
.3	畸形學		Teratology (Malformations)
		例 雌雄同體	e.g. Hermaphroditism
.4	生理學		Physiology
		例 新陳代謝	e.g. Metabolism
		能子交換	Interchange of energy
			Performance of work
		感覺	Sensation
.5	細胞學		Cytology Cell-theory Microbiology
.51	原形質		Protoplasm Cytoplasm
.52	細胞構造		Cell structure
		細胞核	Nucleus "Germinal vesicle".
.53			
.54	細胞分裂		Cell division (Cleavage Segmentation)
		中心體	Centrosome
		細胞膜	Cellular membrane
.55	物理特質		Physical properties
		滲透, 腫脹, 等	Osmosis, turgescence, etc.
.56			
.57	生理特質		Physiological properties
		熱, 光, 電之產生	Production of heat, light, electricity
.58	細胞生長		Cell growth
.59	細胞死亡		Pathological changes: death
.6	生殖學　胎生學		Reproduction Embryology

.61	無性生殖	Asexual
.611	自然發生 參看 562.71	Abiogenesis see also 562.71
.613	分裂生殖	Fission
.615	發芽生殖	Gemmation (Budding) Sporulation
.62	有性生殖	Sexual
.621	接合生殖	Conjugation Zygosis
.622	受精生殖	Spermatization
.623	多胚生殖	Heterogenesis
.625	世代交番	Metagenesis (Alternation of generation)
.626	人工生殖	Artificial fertilization
.627	雜種生殖	Hybridization
.63	近世胎生學	Modern embryology
.64	原種論 胚種論	Germ-layer theory
.65	形態胎生學	Morphological embryology
.66	性別論 性原論	Sex differentiation Origin of sexual characters
.661	性定論	Determination of sex
.663	性遺傳論 見 563.37	Inheritance of sex see 563.37
.67	實驗胎生學 (發生力學 生物力學)	Experimental embryology (Developmental mechanics Bio-mechanics)
.7	發育論 先胎發育論	Development Post-embryonic development
.71	發育生理	Physiology of development
.72		
.73	發育加速律	Law of acceleration Earlier inheritance
.74	發育減退	Theory of abbreviations "Short cuts"
.75	畸異發育	Heterochrony

.76	發育過剩	Excess of development	
.77			
.78	退化論	Degeneration (Ontogenetic)	
.79	衰謝律	Law of decay	
.8	生態學	Ecology	
.9	地方生物學	Local distribution of biology	
.902	大陸生物	Terrestrial	
.904	海洋生物	Oceanic	
.905	淡水生物	Inland water	
.907	空中生物	Aerial	
.91-.99	依國分	By country	

562　生命　生命現象　Life　Vital phenomena　Living matter

.1			
.2			
.3	生物物理學	Bio-physics	
	生命理論	Theories of life	
.31	機械論	Mechanical theory　Physico-chemical	
.32	活力論	Vitalism　Neo-vitalism	
.33	生長力	Bathmism (growth force)	
.34	生產能	Genetic energy	
.35	自適論　見 363.76	Self-adaptation　see 363.76	
.36	支配力	Directive force	
.37	生活原理	Vital principle	
.38	生活質	Vital substance	
.39			
.4	生物化學	Bio-chemistry	

		互見 541.9	See also 541.9
.5			
.6		生物測定	Biometrics
.7		生物發生論	Biogenesis
		生命始原	Origin of life
.71		自然論	Abiogenesis (Spontaneous generation)
.74		創造論	Special creation
.75		演化論　見563	Evolution　see 563
.77		來自星球論	From other planets
.8		生命論	Properties of living matter
.81		有生物與無生物	Living and dead matter
.82			
.83		生命要件	Conditions of life
		水氣，空氣，食物，等	Moisture, temperature, food, etc.
.85		植物與動物	Difference between plants and animals
.87		性自然論	Sex in nature
.9		死亡論	Death
563		**演化論**	**Genetic biology**
		進化論	Organic evolution
.1		個體發育	Ontogeny
.11		選擇與保存	Selection and preservation
.13		相互關係	Mutual relations
.14		擬態　模仿　染色	Mimetic resemblance
			Mimicry　Coloration
		保護色	Protective colors
		攻擊色	Aggressive colors
		警戒色	Warning colors

.17	性擇	Sexual selection
.19	環境關係	Relations to environment (Hexiology)
.191	無機方面	Inorganic environment
.192	有機方面	Organic environment
.194	生存競爭	Struggle for existence
.195	選擇終止　雜合	Cessation of selection　Panmixia
.197	適應　適合	Accommodation
.2	系統發育	Phylogeny　Origin and descent Descendenzlehre
.3	遺傳學	Heredity　Inheritance
.31	胚種原素	Germinal elements
.32	物理基質	Physical basis
.33	胚種連續論	Doctrine of germinal continuity
.34	混雙作用	Amphimixis
.35	胚質淘汰	Germinal selection
.36	祖先遺傳律	Laws of ancestral inheritance
.37	性遺傳	Heredity of sex
.38	生殖淘汰	Reproductive (Genetic) selection
.39	其他	Others
.391	生育遺傳	Fertility
.393	色素遺傳	Color heredity
.395	歸先現象	Reversion (Atavism)
.397	實驗研究	Empirical study of heredity
.4		
.5	優生學　遺傳漸化	Eugenics　Genetics
.51	育種學	Breeding
.52	雜種學	Hybridity　Cross-breeding
	人工雜種	Artificial hybrids

.53 隔絕說 Isolation Segregation
　　無區別繁殖 Indiscriminate (Apogamy) Separate breeding
　　區別繁殖 Discriminate (Homogamy) Segregate breeding
.54
.55 性教育 Sexual education
.56
.57 生育限制與優生學 Birth control and eugenics
.58
.59 優境學 Euthenics
.6 變異論 Variation Deviation
.61 先天與後天變異 Congenital variation and acquired characters
.62 連續變異 Continuous (Fluctuating)
.63 不連續變異　驟變 Discontinuous (Definite) Mutation (Sports)
.64 適時變異 Seasonal
.65 性變異 Sexual
.66 變異律 Laws of variation
.67 實驗變異 Experimental variation
.68
.69 變化　自然變異 Modification Ontogenetic variation
.7 適應論 Adaptation
.71 因變異適應　遺傳的 Through variation (hereditary)
.72 因變化適應　後天的 Through modification (acquired)
.73
.74 連帶適應 Co-adaptation

.75	輻合適應	Convergence　Parallelism
.76	自適	Self-adaptation
.77	適應與世代	Adaptation and regeneration
.78		
.79		
.8	退化論	Degeneration（Phylogenetic）
.9	絕種論	Extinction
564	種源論	Origin of species
	特殊演化學說	Particular evolutionary theories
	自然發生　見 562.71	For abiogenesis　see 562.71
.1	拉馬克學說	Lamarck's theory　Lamarckism
.2	達爾文學說	Darwinism
.21	自然淘汰	Natural selection
.23	適存論	Survival of the fittest
.29	非達爾文學說	Anti-Darwiniana
.3	新達爾文學說	Neo-Darwinism（Ulta-Darwinism）
.31	華雷斯之主張	Wallace's exposition
.33	魏司曼學說	Weismanism
	主張以胚子原形質為遺傳之基質	
.37	遞減發育	Retrogressive development
	萎縮演化	Evolution by atrophy
.4	非淘汰學派	Anti-selection school
.5	新拉馬克學說	Neo-Lamarckism
	例　貝力之"相異生存說"	e.g. Bailes（"Survival of the unlike"）
.6	直進演化	Orthogenetic evolution
	動理演化	Kinetogenesis　Dynamical evolution
.7	實驗演化	Experimental evolution

.8			
.9	人類出生		Evolution of man
	人類演化 見人類學		see Authropology
565	**人類學　人種學**		**Anthropology　Ethnology**
.01	理論　關係		Theories　Relations
.011	人類之於自然界		Man's place in nature
.012	人類中心論		Anthropocentrism
	人形主義		
.019	關係		Relations
	例　與社會學之關係		e.g. In relation to sociology, etc.
.03	辭書		Dictionaries
.04	評論		Critiques　Criticism
.05	雜誌		Periodicals
.06	學社		Societies
.07	研究：綱目，綱要，問答，等		Studies: Outlines, syllabi, questions, etc.
.08	總集		Collected works
.09	歷史　人類史		History
.099	人類考古		Archaeology
.1	人類自然史		Natural history of man
.2	人體學		Anthropography
	體質人類學		(Somatology　Physical characters)
.21	身材		Stature　Bodily form
.22	身材比例		Proportions of the body
.23			
.24	顱骨		Cranium　Head
.25	軀幹　四肢		Trunk and limbs
.26	色素		Pigmentation

	皮膚，髮，等	Skin, hair, iris
.27		
.28	畸形	Deformities
.29		
.3	人體測定學	Anthropometry (Measurement)
.31	測定器	Instruments for measuring
.32	測驗	Tests
.33	顱骨測定	Craniometry Cephalometry
.34		
.35	軀幹　四肢測定	Trunk and limbs
.36	身材長短表	Tables of height
.37	外部生殖器測定	External sexual organs
.38		
.39		
.4	生理人類學	Physiological anthropology
.41	體力	Bodily strength
.42	運動	Movement
.43	血液循環	Circulation
.44		
.45	覺官	Senses
.46	情表	Expression of the emotions
.47		
.48	病理人類學	Pathological anthropology
.49		
.5	人類發生論	Anthropogeny (Zoological anthropology)
.6		
.7	人種學	Ethnology (Volkerkunde)

.71	人類行動與演化	Actiology and evolution
.72	人類始源	Origin of man
.724	創造說	Special creation theory
	見 362.74	see 362.74
.725	演化說　見 563	Evolution theory　see 563
.73	人種混合	Specific unity of the human race
.731	一源說	Monogenetic
.733	多源說	Polygenetic
.74	人類分化	Varietal diversity of the Hominidae
.75	人類遷移	Migration of man
.76		
.77	自然之於人類	Physical influences to mankind
.771	氣候	Climate
.773	土壤	Soil
.775	環境	Surrounding
.79	初民文化	Primative culture
	（風俗與制度）	（Customs and institutions）
.791	初民物質生活	Material life of primitive people
	衣，食，住，等	Clothes, food, shelter, etc.
.792	初民精神生活	Psychic life of primitive people
	宗教，語言，文藝，等	Religion, language, literature, etc.
.793	初民家庭生活	Family life
.795	初民社會生活	Social life
	風俗，游藝	
.799	初民與初民關係	Exterior relations with other primitive people
.8	人類分類	Ethnography (Races of men)
.81	依體質分	Somatological (physical) grouping
.82	依區域分	Geographical grouping
.83	依語言分	Linguistic grouping

.84	依組織分	By institutions and social organization
.85	依文化分	By arts and culture
.86		
.87	依宗教分	By religion
.88	依種分	Ethnic groups
.881	黑種	Negroid type (black)
.882	黃種	Mongolian type (yellow)
.883	紅種	American (red race)
.884	白種	Caucasic (white race)
.89	依學派分	By special schools
.9	地方人類學　人種學	Local anthropology and ethnology
	依國分	By Country
	例　中國人類學　人種學　565.91	e.g. Chinese anthropology and ethnology 565.91
	必要時可仿上細分	May be subd. as above
	例　北平人種	e.g. Peiping man
566	**顯微學　細菌學**	**Microscopy**
.1	顯微儀器與用法	Microscopical technique
.11	顯微鏡	Microscopes
.12	其他儀器	Other apparatus
	例　測微器	e.g. Photomicroscope
.13	配製	Preparation
.131	顯微截斷　顯微截斷器	Section cutting　Microtomy
.133	硬固　保存	Fixing　Hardening
.135	染色	Stains and staining
.138	其他	Other operations
	如石灰質之除去與軟柔	Decalcification　Softening
.14	裝置	Mounting

.15	特殊物質之處理	Special treatment for particular substances
.16	顯微截斷研究與方法	Methods for study of sections
.17		
.18	顯微照相術	Photomicrography
.19		
.2	叙述顯微學	Micrography Descriptive microscopy
	例	e.g.
.24	顯微化學	Microchemistry
.25	地質顯微學	Microgeology
.26	岩石顯微學 見 557.8	Micropetrology see 557.8
.27	鑛物顯微學	Micromineralogy
.28	結晶顯微學 見 559.39	Microcrystallography see 559.39
.29	古生物顯微學	Micropalaeontology
.3	生物顯微學	Microbiology
.4	植物顯微學	Microbotany
.5	動物顯微學	Microzoology
.6	應用顯微學	Technological and economic
.61	農業	Agriculture
.63	森林	Foresty
.65	工藝	Chemical technology
.67	製造	Manufactures
.69	衛生	Sanitation
.7	顯微法理學	Nomological (legal) microscopy
.8	醫科顯微學	Medical microscopy
.81	解剖	Anatomy

.82	生理	Physiology
.84	病理	Pathology (diseases)
.85	治療	Therapeutics
.86	醫藥　藥物	Pharmacy　Drugs　Medicines
.9	微生學　細菌學	Bacteriology
.91	形態	Morphology
.92	生理	Physiology
.921	生機	Vitality
.922	滋養　生長	Nutrition　Growth
.923	繁殖	Propagation　Reproduction
.924	運動	Movement
.925	生態	Ecology　Oekology
	與光之關係	Relation to light
	與熱之關係	Relation to heat
	共生	Symbiosis
.926	酵素　酶酵	Enzymes　Fermentation
.927	霉爛，氧化酸化，硝化，等	Putrefaction, oxidation, nitrification
.928	新陳代謝產物	Products of metabolism
.929	毒素與抗毒素	Toxins and antitoxins
.93	無機物細菌	Bacteria of inorganic substances
	鐵細菌，硫細菌，等	Iron, sulphur bacterias
.94	細菌與無生物之關係	Relation to non-living substances
	空氣，水，土壤，食物，飲料，等	Air, water, soil, aliments, beverages
.95	衛生細菌	Bacteria of hygiene and sanitation
.96	細菌與動物界之關係	Relation to the animal kingdom
.961	特殊官能細菌	Bacteria of particular organs
.962	寄屍細菌	Saprophytic microorganisms
.963	無病菌	Non-pathogenic

	.964	病菌	Pathogenic orga nisms
	.965	免疫質	Immunity　Immunization
	.966	白血病	Leucocytosis
	.967	殺菌	Bacteriolysis
	.968	消毒　防腐	Disinfection　Antiseptics
	.97	細菌與植物之關係	Micro-organisms in relation to plants
	.98	動物之菌病	Micro organic diseases to animals
567		標本採集指南	Collectors manuals
	.1	骸骨配製	Preparing skeletons
	.2	流體硬固與保存	Preservatives and hardening fluids
	.3	注射法	Injections
	.4	剝製術	Taxidermy
	.5	標本裝置	Mounting specimens
	.6	標本採集	Collecting
	.7	標本陳列	Arrangement of specimens in museums
	.8	標本保存	Preservation of specimens
568		應用生物學	Economic biology
569		古生物學　化石學	Palaeontology　Fossils
	.1	古植物學	Palaeobotany
	.2	隱花植物　胞子植物	Cryptogamia
	.21	原生植物　始震旦紀	Protophyta
	.22	菌藻植物　始寒武紀	Thailophyta
	.23	蘚苔植物　始第三紀	Bryophyta
	.24	羊齒植物　始泥盆紀	Pteriodophyta
	.3	顯花植物　種子植物	Phanerogamia　Spermatophyta
	.4	裸子植物　始侏羅紀	Gymnospermae
	.5	被子植物　始第三紀	Angiospermae

.51	單子葉		Monocotyledonae
.55	雙子葉		Dicotyledonae
.6	古動物學		Palaeozoology
.7	無脊椎動物		Invertebrates
.71	原生動物	始寒武紀	Protozoa
.72	腔腸動物	始寒武紀	Coelenterata
.73	刺泡動物	始奧陶紀	Cnidaria
.74	棘皮動物	始奧陶紀	Echinodermata
.75	軟體動物	始奧陶紀	Mollusca
.76	假軟體動物	仝上	Molluscoidea
.77	節足動物		Arthoropoda
.8	脊椎動物		Vertebrates
.83	魚類	始志留紀	Pisces　Fishes
.84	兩棲類	始石炭紀	Amphibia
.85	爬蟲類	始石炭紀	Reptils
.86	鳥類	始侏羅紀	Birds
.87	哺乳類	始三疊紀	Mammalia
.88	兩手類	始第三紀	Bimana
.9	依國分		By country

例　中國古生物學 569.91　　e.g. Chinese palaeontology 569.91

570　植物學　　　　　　Botany

.01	理論　關係	Theories　Relations
.02		
.03	辭書	Dictionaries
.04	評論	Critiques　Criticism
.05	雜誌	Periodicals
.06	學社	Societies
.07	研究：綱目，綱要，答問，等	Studies：Outlines, syllabi questions, etc.

.08	總集　文藝	Collected works
.081	植物神話	Plant lore
.083	花語	Language of flowers　Floral emblems
.087	國花	National flowers
.09	歷史	History
571	生理與構造	Systematic botany
	植物學	Phytology　Life of plants
.1	組織學（內部形態學）	Histology (Internal morphology)
.11	植物細胞	Plant cell
.111	原形質	Protoplasm
.112	含液小體	Vacuoles
.113	細胞核	Nucleus
.114	色素體	Plastids (Chromatophores)
.115	中心體	Centrosomes
.116	細胞膜	Cellular membrane
.117	細胞構成與分裂	Cell formation　Cell division
.13	細胞組織	Tissues
.15	組織系統	Tissue systems
.17	特殊植物組織	Histology of particular plant forms
.2	形態學　植物軀幹	Morphology　Plant body
.21	普通形態	General morphology
.211	軀幹分裂	Segmentation of plant-body
.213	單細胞植物	Unicellular plants
.215	纖維植物	Filamentous plants
.216	脈管植物	Vascular plants
.217	同形	Symmetry
	例　放射狀同形	e.g. Radial
.23	原形態學	Promorphology
.24	差等與類似	Homology and analogy

.25		組織形態學	Tectology (Structural morphology)
.26			
.27		特殊形態　植物器官學	Special morphology　Organography
.271		葉狀體	Thallus
.272		葉根	Leafy shoot
.273		根	Root (Hypercotyl)　Epitropism
.274		莖	Stem (Cauloma, Hypocotyl)
.275		葉	Leaf (Foliage leaf)
.276		花	Flower (Floral leaf)
.277		生殖器官	Reproductive organs　Reproduction
.278		果　種子	Fruit　Seed
.3			
.4		生理學	Physiology
.41		細胞與細胞組織	Cell and cellular tissue
		見 571.1	see 571.1
.42		滋養物	Nutrition　Food
.43		呼吸	Respiration
.44		新陳代謝	Metabolism
.45		生長　發芽	Growth
.46		化學之於植物	Chemical agents affecting plants
		毒素，瓦斯，等	Poisons, gases, etc.
.47		物理之於植物	Physical agents affecting plants
		熱，光，電，等	Heat, light, electricity
.48		刺激與運動	Irritability and movement
.49			
.5		病理學	Phytopathology
		病原學　畸形學	Aetiology　Teratology
.6		生殖學　胎生學	Reproduction　Embryology

.61	無性生殖	Vegetative (Asexual)
.63	有性生殖	Sexual (Parturital)
.65	世代生殖	Alternation of generation
.67	種子分佈	Distribution of seeds
.7	生態學	Ecology　Oekology
.71	寄屍植物　互見 566.962	Saprophytism　see also 566.962
.72	防旱	Protection against drouth
.73	防冷	Protection against cold
.74	防禦動物	Protection against animal
.75	食蟲植物	Carnivorous plants Insectivorous plants
.76	共生植物	Symbiosis
.77	植物演化	Evolution of plants
.771	遺傳	Heredity
.773	變異	Variation
.775	自然與人工淘汰	Natural and artificial selection
.777	退化	Degeneration
.8	應用與醫藥植物學	Economic and medical botany
.9	地方植物學	Phytogeography
	植物分佈	Geographical distribution
.901	林木　喬木　灌水	Sylvae　Trees　Shrubs general treatises
.902	陸生植物	Terrestrial plants
.903	高山植物	Alpine plants
.904	海洋植物　海濱植物	Oceanic　Seaside plants
.905	淡水植物　湖沼植物	Inland water　Freshwater Mere and lake plants
.908	熱帶植物	Tropical plants
.909	寒帶植物	Arctic plants
	依國分	By country

例　中國植物學　571.91　　　e.g. Chinses botany 571.91

572　原生植物　　　　　　Protophyta

.1	分生植物	Schizophyta　Fission fungi
.11	分生菌綱　細菌綱	Schizomycetes　Bacteria
.12	真細菌目	Eubacteria
.121	桿狀細菌科	Bacteriaceae(Bacterium)　Rod bacteria
.122	螺旋細菌科	Spirillaceae(Spirillum)
.123	線狀細菌科	Chlamydobacteriaceae　Iron bacteria
.125	球狀細菌科	Coccaceae (Micrococcus　Streptococcus)
.127	黏液細菌科	Myxobacteriaceae
.15	硫黃細菌目	Thiobacteria　Sulphur bacteria
.151	紫色細菌科	Beggiatoaceae　Purple bacteris
.153	紅色細菌科	Rhodobacteriaceae　Red bacteria
.17	分生藻綱　藍藻綱	Schizophyceae　(Cyanophyceae) Blue green algae
.171	顫藻科	Oscillatoriaceae
.172	單列藍藻科	Scytonemataceae
.173	多列藍藻科	Stigonemataceae
.174	念珠藍藻科	Nostoceae
.175	端毛藍藻科	Rivlularirceae
.176	球狀藍藻科	Chroococcaceae
.177	離生藍藻科	Chamaesiphonaceae
.2	膠質植物	Phytosarcodina (Myxothallophyta　Myxomycetes　Mycetozoa)
.21	膠滴菌綱	Aerasiales
.213	膠滴菌科	Guttulinaceae
.215	分枝滴菌科	Dictyosteliaceae
.23	寄生菌綱	Plasmodiophorales
.25	真黏液菌綱	Myxogasteres
.26	外子目	Extosporeae

.27	內子目	Endosporeae
	紅管菌科，網狀黏菌科，黑絲黏菌科，灰質黏菌科，其他	Liceaceae, clathroplychiaceae cribrariaceae, trichiaceae, stamonitaceae, physaraceae, etc.
.3	蟲菌植物	Flagellata
.31	無口目	Pantostomatinales
	全毛蟲菌科，根毛蟲菌科	Holomastigaceae, Rhizomastigaceae
.32	兩口目	Distomatinales
.33	單口目	Protomastigales
	單毛蟲菌科，雙毛蟲菌科，等	Oicomonadaceae, bicoecaceae, etc.
.34	黃色蟲菌目	Chrysomonadales
	染色蟲菌科，赭色蟲菌科，等	Chromulinaceae, Ochromonadaceae, etc.
.35	隱色蟲菌目	Cryptomonadales
.36	綠色蟲菌目	Chloromonadales
.37	綠藻蟲菌目	Euglenales
.38		
.39		
.4	蟲藻植物	Peridinieae (Dinoflagellatae)
	夜光藻科，原蟲藻科，被膜蟲藻科，等	Gymnodiniaceae, prorocentraceae, peridiniaceae, etc.
.5	矽質蟲藻植物	Silicoflagellatae
.51	管皮目：單毛矽藻科	Siphonotestales: Dictyochaceae
.53	固皮目：二毛矽藻科	Stereotestales: Ebriaceae
.6	矽藻植物	Diatomeae (Bacillariales) Diatoms
	矽藻科，盤狀亞科，筒狀亞科，等	Bacillariaceae, discoideae, sclenioideae, etc.

.7	接藻植物	Conjugatae Desmids
.8		
.9		
573	**隱花植物**	**Cryptogamia**
.1	菌藻植物	Thallophyta
	葉狀植物	
.2	藻類植物	Alage Seaweeds
.21	綠藻植物	Chlorophyceae Green algae
	原藻綱，絲藻綱，管藻綱，等	Protococcales, confervales, siphoneae, etc.
.23	輪藻植物	Charales Stoneworts
.25	褐藻植物	Phaeophyceae Brown algae
	褐子目，圓子目，海團扇目，等	Phaeosoporeae, cyclosporeae dictyotales, etc.
.26	紅藻植物	Rhodophyceae(Florideae) Red algae
.261	紫菜綱	Bangiales
	紫菜科，紅毛海苔科，等	Bangiaceae, rhodochaetaceae, etc.
.265	正紅藻綱	Florideae
	石花菜目，杉海苔目，頭髮菜目，海羅目，等	Nemalionales, gigatinales, rhodymeniales, cryptonemiaceae, etc.
.28	藻菌植物	Phycomycetes Algae-fungi
.29		
.3	菌類植物	Eumycetes (Mycomycetes)
	真菌植物	Fungi Mycology
.31	囊子菌綱	Ascomycetes
.32	半囊子菌綱	Hemiascales
.33	真囊子菌綱	Euascomycetes
.34		

.35	擔子菌綱	Basidiomycetes
	半擔子目，銹菌目，木耳目，白木耳目，等	Hemibasidiales (Smuts), uredineineae, auricularineae, tremellineae, etc.
.36		
.37	高等擔子綱菌	Autobasidiomycetes Mushrooms
	淚蕈科，貝殼蕈科，雞瓜蕈科，等	Dacryomcetaceae, thelephoraceae, clavariaceae
.38		
.39	不完全菌綱	Fungi imperfecti
.4	地衣類	Lichenes　Lichens
.41	囊子地衣	Ascolichenes (Discolichenes)
	核果地衣，裸果地衣，蝌蚪紋地衣，圓果地衣，	Pyrenocarpeae, gymnocarpeae, graphideae, cyclocarpineae, etc.
.47	擔子地衣 帽狀地衣	Basidiolichenes： Hymenolichenes
.5	苔蘚植物	Archegoniatae (Cormophyta) Bryophyta (Muscineae)
.6	苔類植物　苔蘚	Hepaticae　Liverworts
	地錢目，角苔目，鱗苔目，等	Marchantiales, anthocerotales, jungermanniales, etc.
.7	蘚類植物	Musci　Mosses
	水蘚目，頂果蘚目，腋果蘚目，等	Sphagnales, acrocarpi, pleurocarpi, etc.
.8	羊齒植物	Pteridophyta (Vascular cryptogams)
	羊齒綱，木賊綱，石松綱，水韭綱，等	Filicales (Ferns), equisetincae, lycopodiales, isoetales, etc.
574	顯花植物 種子植物	Spermatophyta (Phanerogamia Siphonogamia)

.1	裸子植物	Gymnospermae
.2	鳳尾松綱	Cycadales
	鳳尾松科	Cycadaceae
.3	銀杏綱	Ginkgoales
	銀杏科	Ginkgoaceae
.4	松柏綱	Coniferae
.41	紫杉科	Taxaceae
.43	松柏科	Pinaceae
.5	麻黃綱	Gnetales
	麻黃科	Gnetaceae
575	被子植物	Angiospermae (Metaspermae)
.1	單子葉植物	Monocotaledoneae
.2	榮蘭綱	Pandanales
.21	香蒲科	Typhaceae
.23	榮菌科	Pandanaceae
.25	黑三稜科	Sparganiaceae
.3	沼生綱	Helobiae (Fluviales)
.31	眼子菜科	Potamogetonaceae
.32	茨藻科	Najadaceae
.33	荇蔆科	Butomaceae
.34	喜望峯眼子菜科	Apononogetonaceae
.35	芝菜科	Juncaginaceae
.36	澤瀉科	Alismataceae
.37	水鱉科	Hydrocharitaceae
.4	本鄉草綱	Triuridales
	本鄉草科	Triuridaceae
.41	穎花綱	Glumiflorae
		Grasses　Sedges

.42	禾本科	Gramineae
.43	莎草科	Cyperaceae(Carices)
.47	合花綱	Synanthae
.48	巴拿馬草科	Cyclanthaceae
.5	棕櫚綱	Principles
.51	棕櫚科	Palmae（Palms）
.53	蒐花綱	Spatheflorae（Spadiciflorae）
.54	天南星科	Aracaceae
.55	浮萍科	Lemnaceae
.6	黃眼草綱	Xyridales
.61	黃眼草科	Xyridaceae
.63	苔草科	Mayacaceae
.7	粉狀胚乳綱	Farinosea
.71	山藤科	Flagellariaceae
.72	穀精草科	Eriocaulaceae
.73	鳳梨科	Bromeliaceae
.74		
.75	鴨跖草科	Commelinaceae
.76	雨久草科	Tontederiaceae
.77	田蔥科	Philydraceae
.78		
.79		
.8	百合花綱	Liliales
.81	燈心草科	Juncaceae
.82	百部科	Stemonaceae
.83	百合科	Liliaceae
.84	血草科	Haemodoraceae
.85	石蒜科	Amaryllidaceae

	.86	田代薯科	Taccaceae
	.87	薯蕷科	Dioscoraceae
	.88	鳶尾科	Iridaceae
	.89		
	.9	芭蕉綱	Scitamineae
	.91	芭蕉科	Musaceae
	.92	蘘荷科	Zingiberaceae
	.93	曇華科　美人蕉科	Cannaceae
	.94		
	.95	箭根草科	Marantaceae
	.96		
	.97	微子綱	Microspermae
	.98	雛錫杖科	Burmanniaceae
	.99	蘭科	Orchidaceae
576		雙子葉植物	Dicotyledoneae
	.1	無瓣類(元始花)	Apetalae（Archichlamydeae）
	.2	輪生綱	Verticillatae
	.21	木麻黃科	Casuarinaceae
	.25	胡椒綱	Peperales
	.26	三白草科	Saururaceae
	.27	胡椒科	Piperaceae
	.28	珠蘭科	Chloranthaceae
	.3	楊柳綱	Salicales
	.31	楊柳科	Salicaceae
	.35	楊梅綱	Myricales
	.36	楊梅科	Myricaceae
	.4	橡子木綱	Balanopsidales
	.41	橡子木科	Balanopsidaceae

.43	絞望綱	Garryales
.44	絞木科	Garryaceae
.47	塞子木綱	Leitneriaceae
.48	塞子木科	Leitneriaceae
.5	胡桃綱	Juglandales
.51	胡桃科	Juglandaceae
.55	白襖綱	Batidales
.56	白襖科	Batidaceae
.6	絮木綱	Julianiales
.61	絮木科	Julianiacene
.65	山毛櫸綱	Fagales
.66	樺木科	Betulaceae
.67	山毛櫸科	Fagaceae
.7	蕁麻綱	Urticales
.71	榆科	Ulmaceae
.72	麻科	Cannabiuaceae
.73	桑科	Moraceae
.74	蕁麻科	Urticaceae
.77	山茂樫綱	Porteales
.78	山茂樫科	Porteaceae
.8	檀香綱	Santales（Hysterophyta）
.81	檀香科	Santalaceae
.83	幌幌木科	Olacaceae
.85	桑寄生科	Loranthaceae
.87	蛇菰科	Balanophoraceae
.9	馬兜鈴綱	Aristolochiales
.91	馬兜鈴科	Aristolochiaceae
.92	大花草科	Rafflesiaceae

.93	奴草科	Mitrastemonaceae
.95	蓼綱	Polygonaceae
.96	蓼科	Polygonaceae
577	**離瓣類（後生花）**	**Choripetalae（Mesachlamydeae）**
.1	中子綱	Centrospermae
.11	藜科	Chenopodiacea
.13	莧科	Amaranthaceae
.15	紫茉莉科	Nyctaginaceae
.17	結節草科	Illecebraceae
.19	小熊草科　大和草科	Cynocrambaceae
.2	落葵科	Basellaceae
.21	商陸科	Phytolacaceae
.23	蕃蓓科	Aizoaceae
.25	馬齒莧科	Portulacaceae
.27	石竹科	Caryophyllaceae
.3	毛茛綱	Ranales（Polycarpicae）
.31	睡蓮科	Hymphaceae
.32	金魚藻科	Ceratophyllaceae
.33	桂科　白果科	Circidiphyllaceae
.35	雲葉科	Trochodendraceae
.36	毛茛科	Ranunculaceae
.37	木通科	Lardizabalaceae
.38	小蘗科	Berberidaceae
.4	己防科	Menispermaceae
.41	木蘭科	Magnoliaceae
.42	臘梅科	Calycanthaceae
.43	蕃荔枝科	Anonaceae
.44	肉荳蔻科	Myristicaceae

.45	樟科	Lauraceae
.47	蓮葉桐科	Hernandiaceae
.5	罌粟綱	Rhoeadales
.51	罌粟科	Papaveraceae
.53	荷包牡丹科	Fumariaceae
.55	白花菜科	Capparikaceae
.57	十字花科	Cruciferae
.58	木犀草科	Resedaceae
.6	瓶子草綱	Sarraceniales（Insectivorae）
.61	瓶子草科	Sarraceniaceae
.63	豬龍草科	Nepeuthaceae
.65	茅蒿菜科	Droseraceae
.7	薔薇綱	Rosales（Saxifraginae　Rosiflorae）
.71	川草科	Podostemaceae
.72	景天科	Crassulaceae
.73	土瓶草科	Cephalotaceae
.74	虎耳草科	Sexifragaceae
.75	海桐花科	Pittosporaceae
.76	金縷梅科	Hamamelidaceae
.77	篠懸木科	Plantanaceae
.78	薔薇科	Rosaceae
.79	豆科	Leguminosae
.8	簫綱	Pandales
.81	簫科	Pandaceae
.85	牻牛兒苗綱	Geraniales（Gruinales）
.86	牻牛兒苗科	Geraniaceae
.87	酢漿草科	Oxalidaceae
.88	金蓮花科	Tropaeolaceae

.89	亞麻科	Linaceae
.9	古柯科	Erythroxylaceae
.91	蒺藜科	Zygophyllaceae
.92	芸香科	Rutaceae
.93	樗科　苦木科	Simarubaceae
.94	橄欖科	Burseraceae
.95	楝科	Meliaceae
.96	金虎尾科	Malpighiaceae
.97	遠志科	Polygalaceae
.98	大戟科	Euphorbiaceae
.99	水馬鹵科	Callitrichaceae
578.1	無患子綱	Sapindales（Celastrales）
.11	黃楊科	Buxaceae
.12	嚴高蘭科	Empteraceae
.13	假人魚草科	Limnanthaceae
.14	黃精鈎吻科	Coriariaceae
.15	漆樹科	Anacardiaceae
.16	鞣木科	Cyrillaceae
.17	冬青科	Aquifoliaceae（Ilicineae）
.18	衛矛科	Celastraceae
.2	杜仲科	Eucommiaceae
.21	茶茱萸科	Icacinaceae
.22	省沽油科	Staphyleaceae
.23	槭樹科	Aceraceae
.24	七葉樹科	Hippocasianaceae
.25	無患子科	Sapindaceae
.26	清風藤科	Sabiaceae
.27	鳳仙花科	Balsaminaceae

.3	鼠李綱	Rhamuales（Frangulinae）
.31	鼠李科	Rhamnceae
.33	葡萄科	Vitaceae（Ampelideae）
.4	錦葵綱	Malvales（Columniferae）
.41	膽八樹科	Elaeocarpaceae
.43	田麻科	Tiliaceae
.45	錦葵科	Malvaceae
.47	木錦科	Bombacaceae
.48	梧桐科	Sterculiaceae
.5	側膜胎座綱	Parietales（Cistiflorae　Passiflorineae）
.51	獼猴桃科	Dilleniaceae
.52	茶科	Theaceae（Ternstroimiaceae）
.53	金絲桃科	Guttiferae（Hypericaceae）
.54	龍腦香科	Dipterocarpaceae
.55	溝繁縷科	Elatinaceae
.56	檉柳科	Tamaricaceae
.57	紅木科	Bixaceae
.58	嚴茨科	Cistaceae
.59	堇堇菜科	Violaceae
.6	椅科	Elacouritaceae
.61	旌節花科	Stachyuraceae
.62	西蕃蓮科	Passifloraceae
.63	蕃瓜樹科	Caricaceae
.64	刺蓮花科	Loasaceae
.65	秋海棠科	Begoniaceae
.67	仙人掌綱	Opuntiales
.68	仙人掌科	Cactaceae
.7	桃金孃綱	Myrtiflorae（Thymelaeinae）

.71	瑞香科	Thymelacaceae
.72	胡頹子科	Elaeagnaceae
.73	千屈菜科	Lythraceae
.74	野藪木科	Sonneratiaceae
.75	安石榴科	Punicaceae
.76	玉蕊科	Lecythidaceae
.77	紅樹科	Rhizophoraceae
.78	八角楓科	Alangiaceae
.8	使子君科	Combretaceae
.81	桃金孃科	Myrtaceae
.82	野牡丹科	Melastomataceae
.83	柳葉菜科	Onagraceae
.84	待宵草科	Oenotheraceae
.85	菱科	Hydrocaryaceae
.86	蟻培科	Halorrhagidaceae
.87	蘊藻科	Hippuridaceae
.9	繖形綱	Umbelliflorae
.91	五加科	Araliaceae
.93	繖形科	Umbelliferae
.95	山茱萸科	Cornaceae

579　合瓣類(後生花)　Sympetalae　Monopetalae　Metachlamydeae

.1	杜鵑花綱	Ericales
.11	山柳科	Clethraceae
.13	鹿蹄草科	Pirolaceae
.15	杜鵑花科	Ericaceae
.17	岩梅科	Diapensiaceae
.2	櫻草綱	Primulales

.21	紫金牛科	Myrsinaceae
.23	櫻草科	Primulaceae
.25	磯松科	Plumbaginaceae
.3	柿樹綱	Ebenales（Diospyrineae）
.31	赤鐵科	Sapotaceae
.33	柿樹科	Ebenaceae
.35	白檀科	Symplocaceae
.37	安息香科	Styracaceae
.4	捩花綱	Contortae
.41	木犀科	Oleaceae
.42	馬錢科	Loganiaceae
.43	龍膽科	Gentianaceae
.45	夾竹桃科	Apocynaceae
.47	蘿藦科	Asclepiadaceae
.5	管花綱	Tubiflorae（incl. Personatae）
.51	旋花科	Convolvulaceae
.52	花葱科	Polyemoniaceae
.53	幌菊科	Hydrophyllaceae
.54	紫草科	Borraginaceae
.55	馬鞭草科	Verbenaceae
.56	南菜科	Nolanaceae
.57	脣形科	Labiatae
.58	茄科	Solanaceae
.6	紫威科	Bignoniaceae
.61	胡麻科	Pedaliaceae
.62	角胡麻科	Martyniaceae
.63	列當科	Orobanchaceae
.64	苦苣苔科	Gesneriaceae

.65	狸藻科	Lentibulariaceae
.66	爵牀科	Acanthaceae
.67	苦檻籃科	Myoporaceae
.68	透骨草科	Phrymaceae
.7	車前綱	Plantaginales
.71	車前科	Plantaginaceae
.8	茜草綱	Rubiales
.81	茜草科	Rubiaceae
.82	忍冬科	Caprifoliaceae
.83	五福花科	Adoxaceae
.85	敗醬科	Valerianaceae
.87	山蘿蔔科	Dipsacaceae
.9	鐘花綱	Campanulatae
.91	葫蘆科	Cucurbitaceae
.92	山梗菜科	Lobeliaceae
.93	桔梗科	Campanulaceae
.95	山羊草科	Goodeniaceae
.97	菊科	Compositae

580 動物學　　Zoology

.01	理論　關係	Theories　Relations
	例　動物與人類	Animals in reation to mankind
.02		
.03	辭書	Dictionaries
.038	指南	Directories
.04	評論	Critiques　Criticism
.05	雜誌	Periodicals
.06	學會	Societies
.07	研究：綱目，綱要，答問，等	Studies：Outlines, syllabi, questions, etc.

.072	試驗	Laboratories
.075	採集與保存	Collecting and preservation
.077	動物園	Zoological gardens
.078	水族館	Aquariums
.08	總集　文藝	Collected works
.082	聖經上動物	Bible zoology
.089	動物神話	Animal lore
.09	歷史	History
.091	古代動物	Animals in the ancient world
.097	動物學家傳記	Biography of zoologists
.099	動物游記	Voyages and expeditions

.1-9.

581　生理與構造動物學　Physiologyical and structural zoology

.1	形態學	Morphology
	比較解剖學	Comparative anatomy
	總論比較解剖著述以及各個器官之解剖諸作均類此，其關係某一種或某個動物之解剖者則類入該種或該動物類下	Here are classified general works on comparative anatomy and special works on the anatomy of individual organs; for works on the anatomy of special groups of animals, see subjects
	例　蛙之胎生學	e.g. Embryology of the frogs
	其他如組織，生理，病理，生殖，等例仝上	Same examples for the use in the systematic classification.
.101	原形質構造　細胞構造	Protoplasmic structure　Cellular structure
.103	多細胞構造	Multicellular structure
.107	保持與防禦構造	Supportiug and defensive structures
.11	血循環系	Vascular system (Circulatory system)
.12	呼吸系	Respiratory system

.13	消化系	Digestive system
.14	腺及淋巴系	Glandular and lymphatic system
.16	泌尿生殖系	Genito-urinary system
.17	運動與皮膚系	Motor and integumentary systems
.18	神經系	Nervous system
.19	部位解剖	Regional anatomy
.2	組織學	Histology
.21	細胞	Cell
.22	胚種	Primary germinal layer　Body wall
.23	皮膚組織	Tegumentary (cutaneous) tissue
.24	特殊組織	Specialized tissue
.25	連續組織	Connective tissue
.26	骨組織	Osseous tissue (bone and dentine)
.27	脉管組織	Vascular tissue
.28	液體組織	Liquid tissue
.29	生殖組織	Reproductive tissue
.4	生理學	Physiology
.401	活力論　生活力	Vitalism　"Vital force"
.402	新活力論	Neovitalism
.403	生活要素	Conditions of life
.404	生活力學	Vital processes and functions　Vital mechanics
.407	細胞生理	Cellular physiology
.408	組織生理	Physiology of the tissues
.41	血循環系	Circulation (Vascular system)
.411	腔液	Coelomic fluid
.412	水	Water
.413	血	Blood
.414	血淋巴	Haemolymph

.415	淋巴	Lymph
.417	乳糜	Chyle
.42	呼吸系	Respiration
.421	血色素及其化物	Haemoglobin and its compounds
.423	鰓呼吸	Branchial respiration
.424	鰓氣管呼吸	Tracheo-branchial respiration
.425	氣管呼吸	Tracheal respiration
.427	肺呼吸	Pulmonary respiration
.429	局部呼吸	Localized respiration
.43	體溫	Animal heat
.44	分泌系　腺生理	Secretion (and excretion) Physiolegy of the glands
.443	物理作用	Physical processes
.444	化學作用	Chemical processes
.446	外部分泌	External secretion
.447	內部分泌	Internal secretion
.45	導管生理	Physiology of the ductless glands
.46	神經系	Nervous system Physiology of nerve and muscle
.47	電生理學	Electro-physiology
.49	生理化學	Physiological chemistry
.491	化學成分	Chemical composition of the animal body
.492	化學作用	Chemical processes
.493	滲透	Osmosis
.494	膠質	Colloids
.495	蛋白質	Proteids
.496	酵素	Enzymes
	毒素與抗毒素	Toxins and antitoxin
.497	色素	Coloring matters　Pigments
.498	炭水化物	Carbohydrates

.499	其他	Others
	酸脂，醇類，等	Fatty acids, alcohols, amido-acids, etc.
.5	病理學	Pathology
	病原學　畸形學	Aetiology　Teratology
.6	生殖學　胎生學	Auxology (Reproduction Embryology)
.61	無性生殖	Asexual reproduction (agamogenesis)
.611	分裂	Fission　Schizogony
.613	發芽	Gemmation (Budding)
.615	單性生殖	Parthogenesis
.62	有性生殖	Sexual reproduction (gamogenesis)
.621	生殖腺	Genital gland (Germ gland)
.623	受精生殖	Coajugation　Impreguation　Fertilization
.624	生卵	Oviposion　Spawning
.625	卵生	Oviparity
.626	熟卵生殖	Ovoviviparity
.627	胎生	Viviparity
.66	性　性別論	Sex　Sexual differentiation
.661	性定論	Sex determination
.663	男性優勝	Androrhopy (Male preponderance)
.665	副雄論	Complemental males
.667	性之副徵	Secondary sexual characters
.69	胎生學	Embryology
.691	細胞分裂	Segmentation
.692	胚種與器官之分別	Differentiation of layers and organs
.693	發育不全　不全器官	Vestigial structures　Rudimentary organs
.694	實驗胎生	Experimental embryology
.695	先胎發育	Post-embryological development (ontogenesis)

.696	退化	Degeneration
.697	復生　重生	Regeneration
.698	老衰　還童　長生	Senescence and rejuvenescence　Longevity
.699		Life history　Life cycle
.7	**生態學**	**Ecology　Oekology**
.701	動物心理學	Animal psychology
.702	本能	Instinct
.703	方向本能	Orientation
	遷移	Migration
	歸家	Homing
.705	意識　覺	Consciousness
.706	精神官能與現象	"Psychic" functions and phenomens
.708	動物倫理	Animal ethics
.71	習性	Habits
.72	行爲	Habitats
.73	行動	Locomoton and attachment
.75	防禦　防禦器	Defense
	刺，叉棘，震毛，擬態，保護色，等	Spines, pedicellariae, avicularia, mimicry, protective coloration, etc.
.76	社會生活	Social life　Social relations
.761	性關係：性認識	Sexual relations　Sex recognition
.762	親屬關係	Parental relations
.763	共生　共棲	Commensalism　Symbiosis
.765	敵對與依附	Antagonistic　Parasitism
.766	群居	Gregarious life
.767	移住	Colony formation
.77	變異，適應，及其他	Variation, adaptation, etc.
.771	變異	Variation

	季變異，性變異，色變異，質變異，等	Seasonal, sexual, color variation, substantive, etc.
.775	適應	Adaptation
.777	環境關係	Hexiology (Environment effects)
	1.力學方面：動力，大氣，壓力	Mechanical: gravity, atmosphere, etc.
	3.物理方面：光與黑暗 溫度	Physical: light and darkness Temperature
	4.化學方面	Chemical
	5.食物	Food Diet
	6.水勢	Currents of water
	7.風之作用	Action of wind
	8.氣候	Climate Phaeuology
	9.種之消滅	Extinction of races
.8	應用動物學	Economic zoology
	有益動物與有害動物	Useful animals: Pets
		Noxions animals: Pests
.9	地方動物學	Geographical zoology
	動物分佈	Geographical distribution
.902	陸生動物	Terrestrial: alpine, cave
.904	水生動物	Aquatic: marine, crenic
.907	空生動物	Aerial
.908	熱帶動物	Tropical
.909	寒帶動物	Arctic
	依國分	By country
	例　中國動物學　581.91	e.g. Chinese zoology 581.91
582	無脊椎動物	Invertebrata
.1	原生動物	Protozoa
.11	偽足類	Sarcodina (Gymnomyxa)
.12	菌蟲類	Mycetozoa (Myxomycetes Myxogastres)

.13	有孔類	Foraminifera（Reticularia Testacea）
.15	根足類	Rhizopoda
	葉狀類	Lobosa
	絲狀類	Filiosa
.16		
.17	太陽蟲類	Heliozoa
.18	放射蟲類	Radiolaria
.19		
582.2	胞子蟲類	Sporozoa
.21	晚生胞子蟲類	Telosporidia
.22	簇蟲類	Gregarinida
.23	球蟲類	Coccidiiae
.24	血液胞子蟲類	Haemosporidia
.26	早生胞子蟲類	Nesosporidia
.27	膠胞子蟲類	Myxosporidia
.28	肉胞子蟲類	Sarcosporidia
.3	鞭毛蟲類	Mastigophora
.31	真鞭毛蟲類	Flagellata（Euflagellata）
.33	矽質鞭毛蟲類	Silicoflagellata
.35	硬皮鞭毛蟲類	Dinoflagellata
.37	囊狀鞭毛蟲類	Cystoflagellata
.4	纖毛蟲類	Infusoria（Ciliophora）
.5	海綿動物	Porifera（Parazoa） Sponges
.51	鈣質海綿類	Calcarea（Calcispongiae）
	等腔類	Homocoela
	異腔類	Heterocoela
.53	膠質海綿類	Myxcspongiae
.54	矽質海綿類	Hexactinellida（Hyalospongiae）

.55	八軸海綿類	Octactinellida
.56	多軸海綿類	Heteractinellida
.57	普通海綿類	Demospongiae
	四針類	Tetraxonida（Tetractiuellida）
	單針類	Monaxonida
.6	複細胞動物	Metazoa
.7	腔腸動物	Coelenterate（Coelentera Enterocoela）
.71	水螅水母類	Hydrozoa（Hydromedusae）
.711	水螅蟲類	Eleutheroblastea
.713	水螅珊瑚類	Milleporina（Hydrocorallina）
.715	硬水母類	Trachomedusae
.717	管水母類	Siphonophora
.73	真水母類	Scyphozoa（Scyphomedusae） Jelly-fish
.75	珊瑚類　花形蟲類	Anthozoa（Actinozoa）　Corals
.751	八出珊瑚類	Alcyonaria
.753	六放珊瑚類	Zoantharia
582.77	櫛水母類	Ctenophora
.771	有觸手類	Tentaculata
.772	氣球水母類	Cydippidea
.773	兜水母類	Lobata
.774	帶水母類	Cestoidea
.777	無觸手類	Nuda
.778	瓜水母類	Reroidea
.8	體腔動物	Coelomata（Coelomocoela）
.9	棘皮動物 放射動物	Echinodermata　Radiata
.91	海盤車類	Asteroidea　Starfishes

.92	蛇尾類　陽遂足類	Ophiuroidea　Brittle stars
.93	海膽類	Echinoidea　Sea urchins
.94	海參類	Holothuroidea　Sea cucumbers
.95	海百合類	Crinoidea　Sea lilies
.96		
.97		
.98	海林禽類	Cystoidea
.99	海蕾類	Blastoidea

583　關節動物　　　　　　　　Articulata

.1	蠕形動物	Vermes
.2	蠕態類	Helminthes　Parasiti
.3	扁蟲類	Platyhelmia（Platyhelmintha）
.31	渦蟲類	Turbellaria（Planaria）
.32	截頭類	Temnocephaloidea
.33	吸蟲類	Trematoda
.34	條蟲類	Cestoidea（Cestoda）
.35		
.36	直游類	Orthonectida
.37	紐蟲類	Nemertea（Nemertini）
.4	圓蟲類	Nemathelmia（Nemathelminthes）
.41	線蟲類	Nematoidea（Nematoda）Thread-worms
.42	髮蟲類	Nematomorpha
.43	釣頭蟲類	Acanthocephala
.45	輪蟲類	Trochelmia（Trochelminthes）
.46	車輪蟲	Rotifera（Rotatoria）
.47	腹毛類	Gastrotricha
.48	動嘴類	Kinorphyncha（Echinoderidae）

.5	軟體動物	Mollusca
.51	原軟體類	Amphineura（Isopleura）
.511	多板類	Polyplacophora
.513	無板類	Aplacophora（Solenogastres）
.53	腹足類	Gasteropoda（Gastropoda）
.531	前鰓類	Streptoneura（Prosobranchiata）
	楯鰓類	Scutibranchia
	櫛鰓類	Pectinibranchia
.535	後鰓類	Opisthobranchia
	覆鰓類，裸鰓類，翼足類	Tectibranchia, nudibranchia, pteropoda
.537	有肺類	Pulmonata
.54	掘足類	Scaphopoda（Solenoconcha）
.55	斧足類　無頭類	Pelecypoda　（Lamellibranchiata　Acephala）
.551	原鰓類	Protobranchia
.552	絲瓣鰓類	Filibranchia
.553	擬瓣鰓類	Pseudolamellibranchia
.555	正瓣鰓類	Eulamellibranchia
.557	隔鰓類	Septibranchia
.57	頭足類	Cephalopoda
.571	四鰓類	Tetrabranchia
.573	二鰓類	Dibranchia
.6	有環類　環蟲類	Annelida（Annulata　Annulosa）
.61	毛足類	Chaetopoda
.611	貧毛類	Oligochaeta
.612	多毛類	Polychaeta
.613	顯頭類	Phanerocephala
.615	隱頭類	Cryptocephala
.616	始原環蟲類	Haplodrili（Archiannelida）
.617	吸口蟲類	Myzostomida

.63	蛭類	Hirudinea（Discophora）
.65	螠類　棘毛類	Echiuroidea
.67	星蟲類	Gephyrea
.7	假輭體動物	Molluscoidea
.8	苔蘚蟲類	Polyzoa（Bryozoa）
.81	內肛類	Entoprocta
.83	外肛類	Ectoprocta
.84	裸喉類	Gymnolaemata
.85	被喉類	Phylactolaemata
.9	箒蟲類	Phoronidea
.93	腕足類	Brachiopoda
.94	無關節類	Ecardines(Inarticulata　Tretenterata)
.95	有關節類	Testicaridines（Articulata Clistentertata）
.97	毛顎類	Chaetognatha
.98	箭蟲，鋤蟲，鑱蟲，等	Segitta, spedella, krohnia, etc.

584　節足動物　　　　　　　　Arthropoda　Articulata
　　　節肢動物

.1	擬足類	Hyparthropoda
.2	原足類	Protarthropoda
	有爪類	Onychophora（Protracheata）
.3	真足類	Euarthropoda
.4	多足類	Myriapoda
	原脣足類，脣足類，(蜈蚣類)，擬多足類，脣鄂類(馬陸類)，等	Protosyngnatha, chilopoda（Syngnatha）archipolypoda, chilognatha（diplopoda）, etc.
.6	蜘蛛類	Arachnida

.61	三葉類	Trilobitae
.63	海蜘蛛類	Pantopoda
	蜻蛛，砂海蛛，海蜘蛛	Nymphonomorpha, ascorhynchomorpha, pycnogonomorpha
.65	真蜘蛛類	Euarachnida　Spiders
.66	水生蜘蛛類	Delobranchia (Hydropneustea)
	劍尾類，等	Xyphosura, etc.
.67	陸生蜘蛛類	Embolobranchia (Aeropneustea)
.671	蠍類	Scorpionidea
.672	觸脚類	Pedipalpi (Thelyphonidae)
.673	直蜘蛛類	Araneida (Araneae)
.674	鬚脚類	Falpigradi (microthelyphonida)
.675	避日類	Solpugida (Solifugae Mycetophorae)
.676	擬蠍類	Pseudoscorpiones (Chelonethi)
.678	盲蜘類	Opiliones (Phalangidea)
.679	壁蝨類	Rhynchostomi
.8	甲殼類	**Crustacea (Branchiata)**
.81	軟甲類	Malacostraca
.82	胸甲類	Thoracostraca
.821	漣蟲類	Cumacea
.823	口脚類	Stomatopoda
.825	裂脚類	Schizopoda
.827	十脚類	Decapoda
	蝦，蟹，等	Shrimps, lobsters and crabs
.83	節甲類	Arthrostraca
	端脚類，等脚類	Amphipoda, Isopoda
.85	狹甲類	Leptostraca
.86	切甲類	Entomostraca
.861	葉脚類	Phyllopoda
.863	鰓足類	Branchiopoda (Euphyllopoda)

.865	介形類	Ostracoda
.867	撓脚類	Copepoda
.87	蔓脚類	Cirripedia（Thyrostraca）
.88	大甲類	Gigantostraca
	廣翼類，等	Eurypterida

585　昆蟲類　昆蟲學　　Hexapoda（Insecta）　Entomology

.1	不變態類（無翅類）	Ametabola（Aptera　Apterygota）
	跳蟲類，蟬尾類，食毛類，隱翅類，等	Collembola, thysanura, mallophaga, anoplura（pediculina parasitica）etc.
.3	不完全變態類（外翅類）	Hemimetabola（Exopterygota）
.31	直翅類	Orthoptera
	革翅類，蜚蠊類，螳螂類，竹節蟲類，跳躍類：蝗，螽斯，蟋蟀，等	Dermaptera, blattodae, mantoidea, phasmodae, sallatoria: acrididae, locustidae, cryllidae, etc.
.33	大翅類	Amphibiotica
	襀翅類，蜻蛉類，蜉蝣類，等	Plecoptera（perlidae）odonata, ephemeridae（agnathi）, etc.
.35	擬脈翅類	Pseudoneuroptera（Corrodentia）
	白蟻，嚙蟲，等	Embiidae, termitidae, psocidae, etc.
.37	總翅類	Thysanoptera（Physopoda）
.38	半翅類	Hemiptera（Rhynchota）
	異翅類，等	Heteroptera, etc.
.5	完全變態類（內翅類）	Metabola（Holometabola　Endopterygota）
.51	脉翅類	Neuroptera

		駱駝蟲，草蜻蛉，等	Rhaphididae, chrysopidae, etc.
	.53	鱗翅類	Lepidoptera
	.531	蝶類	Rhopalocera Butterflies
	.535	蛾類	Heterocera Moths
	.54	鞘翅類	Coleoptera
	.55		
	.56	撚翅類	Strepsiptera
	.57	雙翅類	Diptera
		長形類（蚊），圓形類（蠅），蠅蝨類	Orthorhapha, cyclorhapha, pupipara
	.58	膜翅類	Hymenoptera
		有椎類	Parasitica
		有劍類：蜜蜂，黃蜂，蟻，等	Aculeata：Bees, wasps and ants
	.8	應用昆蟲學	Economic entomology
586		原索動物	Chordata
	.1	擬索類	Hemichordata（Adelochorda）
	.2	原索類	Protochordata
	.3	尾索類	Urochorda（Tunicata）
	.4	頭索類	Cephalochordata（Acrania Leptocardii）
587		脊椎動物	Vertebrata（Craniata）
	.1	圓口類　囊鰓類	Cyclostomata（Marsipiobranchii）
	.11	穿口蓋類	Hypotreta（Myxinoides）
	.13	完口蓋類	Hyperoartia（Petromyzontes）
	.2	函皮類　有函類	Ostracodermi（Ostracophori）
	.3	魚類	Pisces Fishes Ichthyology
	.4	板鰓類	Elasmobranchii（Plagiostomi Chondtopterygii）

.41	橫口類	Plagiostoma
	肋鰭類，魟類，等	Pleuropterygii　Raiae（rays）,etc.
.43	全頭類	Holocephali
.45	肺魚類	Dipnoi（Dipneusti）
	櫛齒類，角齒類，節頸類	Ctenodipterini, sirenoidei, arthrodira
.47	真口類	Teleostomi　Ganoids and bony fishes
.471	總鰭類	Crossopterygia
.473	硬鱗類　光鱗類	Actinopterygia　Ganoids
.474	軟骨硬鱗類	Choudrostei
.475	硬骨硬鱗類	Aetheospondyli
.477	硬骨類	Teleostei　Bony fishes
	1.固顎類	Plectospondyli
	3.總鰓類	Lophobranchii
	5.喉鰾類	Physostomi
	7.軟鰭類	Anacanthinii
	9.硬鰭類	Acanthopterygii
.49	海洋魚類學	Ocean ichthyology（General works）Deep-sea fishes
.6	兩棲類　兩生類	Amphibia
.63	堅頭類	Stegocephalia（Labyrinthodontia）
.66	無足類　裸蛇類	Ophiomorpha（Apoda　Gymnophiona）
.67	有尾類	Urodela（Caudata）
.68	無尾類	Anura（Ecaudata　Salicentia）
	蛙類	Batrachia（Frogs）
.7	蜥形類	Sauropsida（Reptilia and Aves）
.8	爬蟲類	Reptilia　Reptiles　Herpetology
.81	獸形類	Synapsida
.811	距齒類	Cotylosauria（Pareiasauria）
.812		

.813		異齒類	Anomodontia
.814		楯齒類	Placodontia
.815		鰭龍類	Sauropterygia
.817		龜類	Testudinata（Chelonia）
		稜龜類，鼈類，等	Atheca, trionychia, etc.
.83	蜥龍類		Diapsida
.831		蜥龍類	Diaptosauria
.833		槽齒類	Parasuchia（Thecodontia）
		鷲龍，箭齒龍，等	Aetosauria（pseudosuchia）, phytosauria
.835		魚龍類	Ichthyosauria（Ichthyopterygia）
.836		鱷類	Crocodilia（Loricata Cataphracta Emydosauria）
.837		恐龍類	Dinosauria
		獸脚類，龍脚類，直脚類，等	Theropoda, opisthocoelia, orthopoda, etc.
.85	有鱗類　鱗蜥類		Squammata（Lepidosauria Plagiotremata）
.851		蛇形類　滄龍類	Pythonomorpha（Mosasauri）
.853		蜥蜴類	Lacertilia
.855		變色龍類	Rhiptoglossa
.857		蛇類	Ophidia（Serpentes）　Snakes
.87	翼龍類　鳥蜥類		Pterosauria（Ornithosauria）
.9	鳥類		Aves　Birds　Ornithology
.91	古鳥類　蜥尾類		Saururae（Archaeornithes Saurornithes）
.92	真鳥類　新鳥類		Eurhipidurae（Neornithes Ornithurae）
.93	走禽類		Dromaeognathi
.94	平胸類		Ratitae
.941		鴯鶓類	Rheiformes（Rheae）

.942　　　　鴕鳥類　　　　　　Struthioniformes
.943　　　　鶓鶓類　　　　　　Casuariiformes（Megistaues）
.945　　　　恐鳥類　　　　　　Didornithiformes（Immanes）
.946　　　　隆鳥類　　　　　　Aepyornithiformes
.947　　　　幾維類　　　　　　Apterygiformes
.95　　　齒鳥類　　　　　　　Odontolcae（Odontornithes）
　　　　　例　黃昏鳥　　　　　　e.g. Hesperornithidae
.97　　　正鳥類　　　　　　　Euornithes
.971　　　　突胸類　　　　　　Carinatae
　　　　　孔雀，雞，等　　　　　Peacocks, domestic fowls, etc.
.972　　　　鴿類　　　　　　　Columbinae
.973　　　　水禽類　　　　　　Natatores（Swimmers）
　　　　　鴨，鵝，鷗，等　　　　Duchs, geese, swans, etc.
.974　　　　涉禽類　　　　　　Grallatores（Waders）
　　　　　鷺，鶴，等　　　　　　Herons, storks, etc.
.975　　　　攀禽類　　　　　　Scansores（Climbers）
　　　　1.鸚鵡類　　　　　　　Psittacidae（Parrots）
　　　　3.啄木鳥類　　　　　　Picidae（Woodpeckers）
　　　　5.杜鵑類　　　　　　　Cuculidae（Cuckoos）
　　　　7.鷞鴗類　　　　　　　Rhamphastidae（Cockatoos）
.976　　　　鳴禽類　燕雀類　　Passeres（Insessores　Perchers）
.977　　　　叫禽類　　　　　　Clamatores
.978　　　　鳴禽類　　　　　　Ossines
.979　　　　猛禽類　　　　　　Raptores（Birds of prey）
　　　　1.神鷹類　　　　　　　Cathartidae（King vulture）
　　　　3.晝禽類　　　　　　　Accipitres（Falcons）
　　　　5.夜禽類　　　　　　　Striges（Owls）

588　　哺乳類　　　　　　　Mammalia
.1　　　原獸類　　　　　　　Prototheria
.11　　　原齒類　　　　　　　Protodonta
.13　　　異獸類　　　　　　　Allotheria（Multituberculata）

.15	單孔類	Monotremata（Ornithodelphia）
.2	真獸類	Eutheria
.21	二子宮類　後獸類	Didelphia
.22	有袋類	Marsupialia
.23	齧齒有袋類	Rhizophaga
.24	食草有袋類	Diprotodontidae
.25	食果有袋類	Carpophaga
.26	食肉有袋類	Polyprodontidae
.28	足手有袋類	Pedimana
.3	單子宮類	Monodelphia
.31	正關節類	Effodientia（Fodientia Tubulidentata）
.32	貧齒類	Edentata（Bruta）
.321	光齒類	Ganodonta（Stylinodonta）
.323	異關節類	Xenarthra
.33	有蹄類	Ungulata
.331	偶蹄類	Artiodactyla
.332	不反芻類	Bunodonta
.333	反芻類	Solenodonta
.334	叉角羚類	Antilocapridae
.335	牛類	Bovidae Ox, sheep, etc.
.336	駱駝類	Camelidae
.337	鹿類	Cervidae Deer
.338	長頸鹿類	Giraffidae（Camelopardidae）
.34	奇蹄類	Perissodactyla
.342	馬類	Equidae　Horse
.343	鼠狸類	Hyracotheriinae
.345	古獏類	Lophiodontidae（Helaletidae）
.346	馬獏類	Palaeotheriidae
.347	犀類	Rhinocerotidae（Caenopidae）
.348	獏類	Tapiridae

.349	雷獸類	Titanotheriidae (Palaeosyopinae)
.35	原有蹄類	Condylarthra
	例 彊狼，等	e.g. Mioclaenidae, etc.
.36	蹄兔類	Hyracoidea
.37	鈍脚類	Amblypoda
	兜齒獸，等	Coryphodontidae, etc.
.38	象類　長鼻類	Proboscidea
.381	兇猛獸類	Dinotheriidae
.382	象類	Elephantidae
.385	曲脚類	Ancylopode (Ancylodactyla)
.386	砂擴類，等	Chalicotheriidae etc.
.39	南美有蹄類	Notoungulata
.391	焦獸類	Pyrotheria
.393	滑距骨類	Liopterna
.395	箭齒類	Toxodontia
.397	印齒獸類	Typotheria
.4	海牛類	Sirenia
.41	儒艮類	Dugongidae (Halicoridae)
.42	海豕類	Halitheriidae
.43		
.44	海牛類	Trichechidae (Manatidae)
.47	游水類　鯨類	Cete (Cetacea)　Whales
.471	原鯨類	Archaeoceti
.473	鬚鯨類	Mysticeti (Mystacoceti)
.474	露骨鯨類	Balaenidae
.475	鰮鯨類	Balaenopteridae
.477	齒鯨類	Odontoceti (Denticeti)
.5	食肉類	Ferae (Carnivora)
.51	陸棲食肉類	Fissipedia
.511	貓類	Felidae　Cat

		貓，豹，虎，獅，等	Cats, leopards, tigers, lions, etc.
.512			
.513		鬣狗類	Hyaenidae
.514		土狼類	Protelidae
.515		靈貓類	Viverridae
.516		犬類	Canidae　Dog
.517		鼬鼠類	Mustelidae
.518		熊類	Ursidae　Bear
.53		水棲食肉類	Pinnipedia
.533		海象類	Odobenidae
.535		海驢類	Otariidae
.537		海豹類	Phocidae
.55		肉齒類	Creodonta
.6		齧齒類	Glires（Rodentia）
.61		單齒類	Simplicidentata
.611		海貍類	Castoridae（Mylagaulidae）
.612		擬松鼠類	Pseudosciuridae
.613		松鼠類	Sciuridae
.614		跳鼠類	Dipodidae
.615		鼠類	Muridae
.616		豚鼠類	Caviidae（Hydrochoeridae）
.617		豪豬類	Hystricidae
.63		重齒類	Duplicidentata
.64		兔類	Leporidae
.7		裂齒類	Tillodontia
.8		食蟲類	Insectivora
.81		皮翼類	Dermoptera
		貓猴類	Galeopithecidae
.85		食蟲類	Leptictidae（Ictopsidae）
		昏蒙獸，猬類，等	Amphidozotherium, Erinaceidae, etc.

	.9	翼手類	Chiroptera
	.91	大蝙蝠類	Megachiroptera
	.95	小蝙蝠類	Microchiroptera
589		靈長類	Primates
	.1	指猴類	Chiromyoidea
	.3	擬猴類　狐猴類	Lemuroidea (Prosimiae)
	.31	烈武猴	Adapidae
	.33	人齒猴	Anaptomorphidae
	.35	狐猴	Lemuridae (Nycticebidae)
	.37	跗猴	Tarsiidae
	.5	人猿類	Anthropoidea
	.51	古猿類	Archaeopithecidae
	.53	狨類	Callitrichidae (Hapalidae　Mididae)
	.55	卷尾猴類	Cebidae
		卷尾猴，吼猴，等	Cebiuae, mycetinae, etc.
	.57	獼猴類	Cercopithecidae
		犬猿，天狗猴，等	Cynopithecidae, semnopithecinae, etc.
	.7	類人猿	Simiidae (Anthropomorphidae)
	.9	二手類	Hominidae (Bimana)
590		醫學	Medicine　Medical science
	.01	理論　關係	Theories　Relations
	.012	醫學之重要	Essentials of medicine
	.018	醫道德	Medical ethics
		婦女行醫	Women as physicians
	.03	辭書	Dictionaries
	.037	年鑑	Yearbooks
	.04	評論	Critiques　Criticism
		醫士爭執	Controversies and quarrels of physicians

.05	雜誌	Periodicals
	醫藥雜誌　見 596.05	Pharmaceutic journals see 596.05
.06	學社	Societies
.07	研究　教育	Studies　Medical education
.077	醫科學校	Medical school
.078	女醫學校	Medical school for girls
.079	看護學校	Nurse school
.08	總集　文藝	Collected works　Anecdotes, humor, etc.
.081	奇醫　行醫奇談	Curiosities of medicine
.082	手稿	Manuscripts
.084	報章剪裁	Broadsides　Newspaper cuttings
.09	歷史	History of medicine
.091	古代醫學	Ancient systems of medicine
.097	醫士傳記	Biography
.1-.9	依國分	By country
	例　中國醫學　590.1	e.g. Chinese medicine 590.1

591　解剖學　　　　　　　Anatomy

	顯微解剖　見 566.81	Microscopic anatomy see 566.81
	外科解剖　見 598.11	Surgical anatomy see 598.11
.1	解剖術	Dissection
.3	畸形學　畸胎學	Teratology　Abnomalies
.5	個體發生學　胎生學	Ontogeny　Embryology
.51	生殖細胞	Germinative cells
.511	精液	Sperm
.513	卵	Ovum
.52	授胎	Copulation　Fecundation　Fertilization
.53	胚種	Germ layers
.54	內葉器官	Entodermic, entoblastic or hypoblastic organs

.55	外葉器官	Ectodermic, epiblastic or ectoblastic organs
.56	中葉器官	Mesodermic organs
.57	胚外形	External form of embyro
.58	實驗胎生學	Experimental embryology
.7	組織學	Histology
.71	細胞學	Cells　Cytology
.72	結締組織	Connective tissue
.73	軟骨組織	Cartilaginous tissue
.74	骨骼組織	Bone or osseous tissue
.75	血液	Blood
	淋巴	Lymph
.76	肌組織	Muscular tissue
.77	皮膚組織	Epithelial tissue
.78	神經組織	Nervous tissue
.8	部位解剖學	Regional anatomy
.81	頭	Head
.82	面	Face
.83	頸	Neck
.84	胸	Thorax
.85	腹	Abdomen
	腹上,腹中,腹下,腰,盆骨,會陰,等	Epigastric, mesogastric, hypogastric, lumbar, pelvic and perineal regions
.86	四肢	Extremities
.87	上肢	Upper extremities
	肩,臂,肘,前臂,手腕,手,指,等	Shoulder or axilla, arm, elbow, forearm, wrist, hand, fingers, etc.
.88	下肢	Lower extremities

	髖,臀,股,膝,膕窩,腿,踝,足,趾,等	Hip, nates, thigh, knee, popliteal space, leg, ankle, foot, toes, etc.
.89	尾	Tail
.9	比較解剖學	Comparative anatomy
	宜入 581.1	Usually better clast in 581.1
592	**生理學**	**Physiology**
.1	生死自然論 生活力	On the nature of life and death Vitalism
	凡欲彙列生理學及其相關諸作於一處者類此,否則各入其類	This place is provided for the one who prefers to keep related topics with his subjects
.11	真死徵	Signs of real death
.12	刑屍之實驗	Experiments on executed persons
.13	生命與靈魂	Theories of life and the soul
.14	動植物生命比較論	Comparisons of animals and plants
.15	有機無機物質比較論	Organism and inanimate matter
.16	生活力　見 592.1	Vital energy　see 592.1
.17	生活器官之驗徵	Experiments on surviving organs
.2	細胞與生機生理學	General physiology of cells and organisms
.24	細胞化學	Chemistry of cells
.25	細胞生理形態	Physiologic morphology of cells
.26	細胞生理特性	Physiologic characteristics of cells
.28	環境之影響細胞與生機	Influence of environment on cells and organisms
	氣壓,電,冷熱,光,聲,毒劑與化學質,動力,等	Effects of barometric pressure, electricity, heat and cold, light, sound, poisons and chemic substances, etc.
.3	病理生理學	Pathologic physiology

.4	生理化學	Physiologic chemistry in general
.41	酵素	Ferments
	氧分解，水分解，蛋白質，脂肪，澱粉，糖，醇，等	Oxydants, hydrolytic, proteolytic, lipolytic, amylolytic and sucroclastic glycolytic, etc.
.43	身軀與其產物之成分	Normal composition of the body and its products
.45	色素質　色素	Staining substances and pigments
.47	滋養　新陳代謝	Nutrition　Metabolism
.471	飢　渴　滋養缺乏	Hunger　Thirst　Inanition
.473	食物	Food
.475	刺激品	Condiments and stimulants
.477	生長期須要食品	Ration or food requirement during growth
.478	成年期須要食品	Ration or food requirement of adults
.5	體溫	Animal heat
.51	起源　生熱	Sources　Thermogenesis
	滋養作用	Influence of alimentation
	呼吸作用	Effect of respiration
.52	散熱	Loss of heat　Radiation
	皮膚放射，肺蒸發，皮膚蒸發，等	Cutaueous radiation, loss by pulmonary evaporation and cutaneous evaporation
.54	其他之影響於體溫者	Other conditions affecting temperature and thermogenesis
	沐浴，滋養缺乏，毒劑，等	Effect of baths, inanition, etc.
.55	生熱與調節之變異	Variations in production and regulation of heat
	熱病	In disease: fevers
.56	體溫度	Temperature of body

.57	冬眠動物	Hibernation animals	
.58	冷熱之關係生物	Heat and cold; effect on organism	
.6	生殖　發育　生長	Reproduction and generation Development	
.8	實驗生理學	Experimental physiology	
	活體解剖	Vivisection	
.9	比較生理學	Comparative physiology	

593　國家醫學　衛生學　State medicine　Hygiene

.1	個人衛生	Personal hygiene
.11	空氣與光線	Air and light
.111	氣候	Climate Acclimation
.112	休養所　山澗　海濱	Health resorts　Mountain　Sea-shore
.113	四季	Seasons　Time of day
.114	瘧　濕氣　地氣	Malaria　Moisture　Ground air
.115	空氣清潔	Purification of air
.117	溫度	Temperature
.118	日光	Sunlight
.12	食品　飲食學	Food　Dietetics
.121	食物	Dietaries
.122	嬰兒食品	Food for infants
.123	病人食品	Food for the sick
.124	禁食　飢餓　餓死	Fasting　Famine　Starvation
.125	餘食	Excess of food
.126	菜蔬	Vegetable food
.127	菓品	Fruits
.128	魚肉	Animal food; meats, fish, oysters, etc.
.13	飲料	Beverages
.14	身體清潔　沐浴	Cleanliness of body　Clothing
.15	居住　設備	Human habitation and resort

.16	休息　睡眠	Hygiene of recreation and sleep
	運動　游戲	Amusement or play
.19	子嗣衛生	Hygiene of offspring　Heredity
	優生　見 563.5	Eugenics　see 563.5
.2	公共衛生	Public health
	衛生行政	Board of health
.21	人口注册　人口統計	Registration and vital statistics
.22	食品，飲料，藥物，菸，等檢查	Inspection of articles liable to affect public health
.23	普通傳染病	Contagious and infectious diseases: general
.231	病原	Causes and origin
.232	症候分佈學	Geographic distribution
	依國分	By country
.233		
.234	病媒	Modes of propagation and communication
.235	預防法	Prevention and restriction
	1.隔離法	Isolation, lazarettos
	3.檢疫法	Quarantine, etc.
	5.接種防禦法	Protective inoculation
	6.種痘	Vaccination
	7.反對種痘	Antivaccination
.236	消毒法	Disinfection
.237	流行病　瘟疫	Epidemics　Plagues
.24	特殊傳染病	Contagious and infectious diseases: special
	其性質只關係公共衛生者至治療方法之討論　見 595	These heads are for public health discussion only. For treatment, etc. see 595

.26	屍體埋葬	Disposal of the dead
.27	空氣與地土衛生	Hygiene of the air and ground
	清道與障礙物之處置	Nuisances
.28	動物衛生	Hygiene of animals
.3	其他衛生	Others
.33	學校衛生	School hygiene
.34	海上衛生	Marine hygiene
.35	海陸軍衛生	Military and naval hygiene
.36	監獄衛生	Prison hygiene
.37	工作衛生　職業衛生	Labor hygiene
.4	生命救急法	Protection of human life from accidents casualties, etc.
.41	溺死	Drowning
	淹溺救急法	Rescue of the drowning
	溺斃復蘇法	Resuscitation of the drowned　First help
.43	窒息　悶死	Suffocation
.44	炸傷	Explosions
.45	火傷	Fires
.46	房屋建築律	Building laws
	房屋檢查	Inspection of building
.48	旅行保護	Protection of travelers
.481	陸行	Travel on land, highways
.482	水行	Travel on water
.483	燈塔	Lighthouses, buoys, etc.
.485	引航	Pilots
.487	救生船	Boats, life preservers, rescue of shipwreck, etc.
.5	熱帶醫學	Tropical medicine

	.6	家庭醫學	Domestic medicine
	.7	行醫管理	State control of medicine
	.71	解剖及活體解剖律	Anatomy and vivisection laws
	.72	行醫注册　行醫證書	Registration of physicians, etc. License to practice
	.73	行醫規則	Regulation of medical practice
	.75	庸醫　偽醫	Quackery and malpractice
	.76	藥品專賣權	Nostrums and patent medicines
	.77	醫院	Hospitals　Dispensaries
	.8	法醫學	Medical jurisprudence
	.9	毒藥學　毒物學	Toxicology　Poisons
	.91	無機物	Inorganic poisons
	.92	有機物	Organic poisons
	.93	瓦斯	Gaseous poisons
	.97	菜蔬	Vegetable poisons
	.98	動物	Animal poisons
	.99	食品	Food poisoning　Ptomaines Botulism
594		病理學	Pathology
	.05	雜誌	Periodicals
	.09	歷史	History
	.1	病理解剖與組織學	Pathological anatomy and histology
	.2	病因學	Etiology (Causation of disease)
	.21	遺傳	Hereditary diseases
	.23	週期	Periodicity and periodical diseases
	.24	年齡	Influence of age
	.25	性別	Influence of sex
	.27	刺激	Infection　Immunity and immunization
	.28	氣候	Temperature changes

.29	其他	Others
.3		
.4	化理病理學	Chemical pathology
.5	普通病理學	General pathology
.6	餘病　續發病	Sequels of disease
.7		
.8	特殊病理學	Special pathology
.81	炎症　膿潰	Inflammation　Suppuration
.82	脂肪變性	Fatty degeneration
.84	其他變性病	Other degeneration
.85	壞疽	Necrosis
.86		
.87	新陳代謝違和	Disorders of metabolism　Pathological conversion of nitrogen, etc.
.88	其他特殊病理學	Other special pathology
.9	傳染病及他通行病	Contagious and infectious diseases
.91	疹	Special infectious diseases
.911	疹熱	Eruptive fevers
.912	天花	Small pox
.913	牛痘	Cowpox
.914	水痘	Chickenpox
.915	麻疹	Measles
.916	風疹	Rubella, rubeola, rotheln
.918	猩紅熱	Scarlet fever, scarlatina
.92	熱症	General works on fevers
.921	登革熱	Dengue, breakbone fever
.922	鼠疫	Plague
.923	飢熱	Relapsing fever　Famine fever
.924	脊髓熱	Cerebrospinal fever

.925	稽留熱	Simple continued fever
.926	腸熱　傷寒	Typhus　Typhoid fever
.927	黃熱	Yellow fever
.928	瘧熱	Malarial fever
.93	白喉　瀉病	Diphtheria　Cholera
.931	白喉	Diphtheria
.933	霍亂症	Cholera
.934	亞洲霍亂	Asiatic cholera
.935	嬰兒霍亂	Infant cholera
.937	流行腹瀉	Epidemic diarrhea
.938	痢疾　赤疾	Dysentery
.94	膿毒病	Septic diseases
.941	潰瘍	Phagedena
.943	丹毒	Erysipelas
.945	膿毒血病	Pyemia
.947	敗血病	Septicemia
.95		
.96	動物傳染	Diseases due to lower animals
.961	瘋犬	Hydrophobia
.962	癰　炭疽	Anthrax　Charbon
.963	鼻疽	Glanders
.965	馬痘	Horsepox
.967	脾熱	Splenic fever
.97	寄生病	Diseases due to parasites
.971	動物寄生	Animal parasites
.972	內寄生蟲	Entozoa
	吸蟲，嘵蟲，帶蟲，線蟲，圓蟲，旋毛蟲，鈎頭蟲，等	Trematoda, cestoda, tapeworms, nema-toda, round worms, trichinae, acanthocephala, etc.
	昆蟲寄生:蠋蛆寄生	Insecta parasitica
.973	外寄生蟲	Ectozoa

.974		昆蟲寄生:蚊蟲，臭蟲，蚤，蝨，等寄生	Insecta parasitica: mosquitoes, lice, etc.
.975		蜘蛛寄生:鼠，壁蝨，等寄生	Arachnida parasitica: mites, ticks, etc.
.976		吸蟲寄生:水蛭寄生	Suctoria parasitica, looches
.978		植物寄生	Vegetable parasites
.98		中毒	Effects of poisons
.99		其他諸病	Other diseases Constitutional diseases
.991		風濕 風濕熱	Rheumatism
.993		腫:皮脂囊腫，癌，等	Tumors: cysts, wens, cancer, etc.
.994		結節	Tubercle
.995		斯科夫拉病 佝僂病	Scrofula Rickets
.996		水腫 克汀病	Myxedema Cretinism
.997		痲瘋 癩	Leprosy
595		**醫術 治療學**	**Practice of medicine Therapeutics**
.1		臨床醫學	Clinical medicine
.2		診斷學	Diagnosis
.21		舌診法	Tongue
.22		面，眼，皮膚診斷法	Facial, eye, skin, etc.
.23		觸診法	Palpation
.24		脉診法	Pulse Sphygmography Sphygmomanometer
.25		看熱	Temperature Thermometry
.26		聽診法	Auscultation Stethoscope Phonendoscope
.27		自然診斷法	Physical diagnosis
.271			
.273		電診	Electro-diagnosis
.275		鐳電診斷	Radiography
.277		X光線診斷	X-ray apparatus

.278	顯徵診斷	Microscopic diagnosis
.29	化理檢驗法	Chemical examination
	尿分析，血液分析，驗屍	Urine analysis, examination of the blood, autopsies, etc.
.3	症候學	Symptomatology
	病症預測	Prognosis
.4	不治病　絕症	Incurable diseases
.5	不知病	Unknown diseases
	僞病	Pseudo-diseases
.7	藥療學　醫方	Experimental therapeutics Pharmacotherapy
.71	藥性學	Action of remedies
.72	施藥學	Administration of medicines
.73	互攻法　逆療法	Antagonism of medicines
.74	順療法	Law of similars　Homeopathy
.75	年齡藥療法	Influence of age
.76	性別藥療法	Influence of sex
.77	特性藥療法	Influence of idiosyncrasy
.8	其他治療法	Remedies other than drugs　Physiothorapy
.81	手術療法	Operative
.811	放血　静脉切開術	Blood-letting　Cupping
.813	線束	Setons and issues
.814	繃帶　縛線	Bandages　Ligatures
.815	打針　注射	Acupuncture　Injection
.817	吸引	Pneumatic aspiration
.82	食物療法	Alimentation　Diet
.83	水療法	Hydrotherapy and balneology Washing and cleansing

.84	空氣療法	Climate cures (Aerotherapy)
.85	日光療法	Light cure (Finsinism)
.86	熱療法	Thermotherapy
.87	電療法　射線療法	Electrotherapy　Radiotherapy
.88	音樂療法	Mechanotherapy; music
.89	看護	Nursing
.9	特殊醫術	Special therapeutics
		Suggestive therapeutics
.91	相手療法	Palmistry, phrenology, etc.
		(Medical aspects only)
.92	宗教醫學	Religious therapeutics
	神醫	Pastoral medicine
.94	折衷療法	Eclectic medicine
.96	致病醫病療法	Homeopathy
.98	按摩療法	
.99	他其特殊療法	Special not otherwise provided for
596	**藥學**	**Pharmacy and materia medica**
.01	理論　關係	Theories　Relations
.02		
.03	辭書	Dictionaries
.04	評論	Critiques　Criticism
.05	雜誌	Periodicals
.06	學社	Societies
.07	研究	Studies
.08	總集	Collected works
.09	歷史	History
.091	古代藥物	Early works on pharmacy, drugs, etc.
.099	藥物分佈	Geographical distribution

.1	藥物　藥材		Pharmaceutical substances　Drugs
.11	動物		Animal drugs
.12	植物		Vegetable drugs　Botanic
.13	本草		Herbals
.15	礦物		Mineral drugs
.2	化學藥品		Chemical medicines
.3	藥性　忌物		Pharmacology
			Physiological action, incompatibility
.4	藥化學		Medical and pharmaceutical chemistry
	重量		Weights and measures
.5			
.6	製藥學　練藥　練丹		Pharmaceutical preparations　Elixirs
.7	藥局		Pharmacy　Dispensatories
.71	藥局方　藥方		Pharmacopoeias, formularies
.73	配藥		Practical pharmary
.75	賣藥		Patent medicines
.8			
.9	法藥學		Pharmaceutical jurisprudence

597　內科　Internal medicine
　　　　　　　　　　　　Systematic medicine

.1	血循環系		Circulatory system
.11	血循環系解剖學		Anatomy of the circulatory system
.111	心包		Pericardium
.112	心		Heart: Left heart, right heart
.115	動脉		Arteries
.116	靜脉		Veins

.117			
.118	毛細管		Capillaries
.12	血循環系生理學		Physiology of the circulatory system
.121	血素質		Properties of blood
	1.赤血球		Red corpuscles
	2.白血細胞		Leucocytes and ameboid cells
.122	血化學性		Chemic properties of blood
.123	血循環壓理		Hydranlic principles of circulation
.124	血液壓力		Blood pressure
.125	血循環速度		Rapidity of circulation
.126	脉　病脉		Pulse　Pulse in disease
.127	心　病心		Heart　Heart in disease
.128	血管舒縮		Vasomotors
.129	其他		Action of special organs on circulation
.14	血循環系病理學		Diseases of the circulatory system
.141	心膜		Membranes of the heart
.142	心　心痛		Heart　Angina pectoris
.145	動脉		Arteries
.146	靜脉		Veins
.147	血液		Blood
.15	血循環系治療學		Therapeuties of the circulatory system
.16	血循環系藥學		Drugs acting on the circulatory system
	刺激藥，制阻藥，等		Stimulants, depressants
.17	血循環系手術		Surgery of the circulatory system
.2	呼吸系		Respiratory system
.21	呼吸系解剖學		Anatomy of the respiratory organs
.211	鼻　見 598.491		Nose　see 598.491
.212	喉　見 598.495		Larynx　see 598.495
.213	氣管　支氣管		Trachea and bronchi
.215	肺		Lungs, or pulmones
.216	胸膜		Pleura

.217	膈膜	Diaphram
.218	縱膈膜	Mediastinum
.22	呼吸系生理學	Physiology of the respiratory organs
.221	呼吸動作	Respiratory movements　Mechanics of respiratory
.223	呼吸換氣　呼吸化學	Respiratory exchange of gases　Respiratory chemistry
.224	血內換氣	Gaseous exchange of the blood
.225	肺呼吸	Lung capacity
.226	肺呼出之水	Exhalation of water from lungs
.227	內部或組織呼吸	Internal of tissue respiration
.24	呼吸系病理學	Diseases of the respiratory system
	哮吼,草氣喘,窒息,等	Croup, hay asthma, asphyxia, etc.
.241	鼻：鼻涕,鼻炎　見 598.491	Nose：catarrh, etc.　see 598.491
.242	喉　　見 698.495	Larynx　see 598.495
.243	氣管：氣喘	Trachea：bronchi
.245	肺	Lungs
	肺炎,充血,出血,膿腫,壞疽,癆,肺癆,癆瘵,栓塞,氣腫,虛脫,等	Pneumonia, congestion, hemorrhage, abscess, gangrene, phthisis, tuberculosis, consumption, embolism, emphysema, collapse, etc.
.246	胸膜：胸膜炎	Pleura　Pleurisy
.25	呼吸系治療學	Therapeutics of the respiratory system
.26	呼吸系藥學	Drugs acting on the respiratory system
	祛痰劑,發鼻液,打嚏	Expectorants, errhines
.27	呼吸系手術	Surgery of the respiratory system
.3	消化系	Digestive system
	其關係齒之解剖,生理,等者　見 598.2	Anatomy, physiology, etc. of the teeth see 598.2

.31	消化系解剖學	Anatomy of the digestive system
.311	口	Mouth
	舌，腭，涎管，唇，頰，等	Tung, palate, salivary glands, lips, cheeks, etc.
.312	咽　小舌　食管	Pharynx　Esophagns　Tonsil
.313	腹　胃腺	Stomach　Gastric glands
.314	腸	Intestine
	小腸，盲腸，大腸，結腸，直腸，等	Small intestine, cecum, large intestine, colon, rectum, etc.
.315	肝　膽汁導管	Liver　Bile ducts
.316	胰腺　胰管	Pancreas
.317	腹膜　腸系膜	Peritoneum　Mesentery
.318	脂肪體	Adipose bodies
.32	消化系生理學	Physiology of the digestive system
.321	口　涎腺生理	Mouth　Salivary glands
	咀嚼，嚥，涎，食管，等	Mastication, deglutition, saliva, esophagus, etc.
.322	胃　胃液	Stomach　Gastric juice
.324	腸　腸液	Intestine　Intestine juice
.325	肝　膽	Liver　Bile
.326	胰腺　胰汁	Pancreas　Pancreatic juice
	例　肝於已化食物之作用	e.g. Effect of liver on absorbed food
.327	大腸　大便	Large intestine　Defecation
	例　排泄物成分　大腸動作	e.g. Chemic composition of excrements　Movements of large intestine
.329	吸收	Absorption
	吸入，滲透，擴散，等	Imbibition, osmosis, diffusion, etc.
.33	消化系衛生學	Hygiene of the digestive system
.34	消化系病理學	Diseases of the digestive system
.341		

.342	食管炎	Esophagus
.343	胃病	Stomach
	胃炎，食滯，嘔吐，等	Gastritis, dyspepsia, vomiting, etc.
.344	腸病	Intestines
	赫尼亞，腸瀉，等	Hernia, diarrhea, constipation, colic
.345	直腸:痔	Rectum: piles
.347	腹膜炎	Peritoneum Peritonitis
.349	飲食病	Dietetic diseases
	脹，飢，壞血病	Surfit, starvation, scurvy, dyspepsia
.35	消化系治療學	Therapeutics of the digestive system
.36	消化系藥學　藥劑	Drugs acting of the digestive system
.361	吐劑　嘔藥	Emetics
	吐根，芥子，阿浦嗎啡，等	Ipecac, mustard, apomorphine, etc.
.362	瀉藥	Cathartics
	瀉鹽，水瀉，汞毒，等	Salines, hydragogs, drastics, mercurials, etc.
.363	驅蟲藥	Authelmintics
.365	助消藥	Aids to digestion
	苦味健胃藥	Bitters, tonics
	酶:酸酶，胰腺酶	Ferments, pepsin, pancreatin, etc.
	酸:解酸劑	Acids, antacids
.367	潤藥　潤滑藥	Demulcents, emollients, etc.
.37	消化系手術	Surgery of the digestive system
.4	腺及淋巴系	Glandular and lymphatic system
.41	腺系解剖學	Anatomy of the glandular and lymphatic system
.411	脾　脾小體　脾囊	Apleen, malpighian bodies
.412	淋巴管　毛細管	Lymphatic vessels and capillaries
.413	胸腺	Thymus
.414	甲狀腺	Thyroid gland

.415	腎上腺	Suprarenal capsules or bodier
.416	淋巴腺	Lymphatic glands
.417	頸動脉腺	Carotid gland or body
.418	尾骨腺	Coccygeal gland
.42	腺系生理學　分泌排除	Physiology of the glandular system　Secretion
	腺與血循環，等之互相關係	Effect of glands and circulation on each other
.44	腺系病理學	Diseases of the glandular system
.45	腺系治療學	Therapeutics of the glandular system
.46	腺系藥學	Drugs acting of the glandular system
.461	催涎劑	Sialagogs (Saliva)
.463	利膽劑	Cholagogs (Bile)
.465	發汗	Diaphoretics (Perspiration)
	熱，運動	Heat, exercise
.466	退熱劑　解瘧劑	Antipyretics　Antiperiodics
	金雞納霜，冰冷法，沐浴，等	Quinin, Cold, baths, etc.
.47	腺系手術	Surgery of the glandular system
.6	泌尿生殖系	Genito-urinary system
	花柳病　見 598.6	For Veneral diseases　see 598.6
	女生殖器解剖，生理，病理，等　見 598.7	Anatomy, physiology, etc. of female genital organs see 598.7
.61	泌尿生殖系解剖學	Anatomy of the genito-urinary system
.611	腎　輸尿管	Kidneys　Ureter
.612	膀胱　尿道	Bladder　Urethra
.615	男生殖器	Male genital organs
	睾丸，副睾，輸精管，射精管，精囊，陰囊，精索，等	Testicles, epididymia, vas deferens, ejaculatory ducts, seminal vesicles, scrotum, spermatic cord, etc.
.617	陰莖	Penis

.62	泌尿生殖系生理學	Physiology of the genitourinary system
.621	男生殖官能	Male functions of generation
.623	交媾與授胎	Copulation and fecundation
.63	泌尿生殖系衛生學	Hygiene of the genito-urinary system
.64	泌尿生殖系病理學	Diseases of the genito-urinary system
.641	腎病	Kidneys Bright's disease
.642	膀胱(尿泡)	Bladder
	石　結石	Calculus
.643	尿病　糖尿病	Urinary disorders Diabetes
.645	男生殖官能病	Functional diseases of male generative organs
	精溢　陽痿	Matorrhea, impotence
.65	泌尿生殖系治療學	Therapeutics of the genito-urinary system
.66	泌尿生殖系藥學	Drugs acting on genito-urinary system
	利尿劑	Diuretics
	水，醋劑，毛地黃，咖啡素，等	Water, acetates, digitalis, etc.
.67	泌尿生殖系手術	Surgery of the genito-urinary system
.7	運動系	Locomotor system
	皮膚解剖，生理，病理，等 見 598.5	Anatomy, physiology, etc. of skin see 598.5
.71	運動系解剖學	Anatomy of the locomotor system
.711	骨骼學	Osteology Skeleton
	1.脊柱	Spinal colum
	2.肋骨　胸堂	Ribs Thorax
	3.胸骨	Sternum or breast bone
	4.頭骨	Bones of head Skull
	頭頂，顱座，眼眶，鼻腔	Calvaria cranium, base of cranium, etc.

	5. 顱骨	Cranium, cranial bones
	後頂，蝶骨，顳骨，頂骨，等	Occipital, sphenoid, temporal, parietal, etc.
	6. 面骨：頜骨，腭骨，舌骨，等	Bones of face or visceral cranium
	7. 上肢骨	Bones of upper extremity
	肩胛骨，鎖骨，腕骨，指骨，等	Scapula, clavicle, carpus, metacarpus, etc.
	8. 下肢骨	Bones of lower extremity
	臗骨，股骨，脛骨，蹠骨，趾骨，等	Hip bone, femur, tibia, metatarsal, phalanges of foot, etc.
.713	韌帶　關節	Classes of joints
.715	肌學	Muscular system　Myology
.716	腱筋	Tendons　Fasciae
.717	腱囊	Bursae　Sheaths of tendons
.718	結締組織	Connective tissue
.72	運動系生理學	Physiology of the locomotor system
.721	原形質	Protoplasm
.723	行走	Locomotion
.725	聲音　言語	Voice and speech
.74	運動系病理學	Diseases of the locomotor system
.75	運動系治療學	Therapeutics of the locomotor system
.76	運動系藥學	External agencies
.77	運動系手術	Surgery of the locomotor system
.8	神經系	Nervous system
	眼，耳，解剖，生理，病理，等　見598.3　598.4	Anatomy, physiology, etc. of eye, ear　see 598.3　598.4
.81	神經系解剖學	Anatomy of the nervous system
.811	腦	Brain　Encephalon

中國十進制分類法及索引　443

	1.構造	General structure of brain
	2.部位	Localizations
	3.主腦　前腦　半腦	Prosencephalon, forebrain Hemispheres
	4.間腦	Diencephalon　Interbrain
.811	5.中腦	Mesencephalon, midbrain or mesencefal
	6.腦峽	Isthmus rhombencephali
	7.後腦　小腦	Metencephalon of epencephalon, hindbrain
	8.末腦　髓	Myelencephalon, metencefal, or afterbrain
	9.腦膜　大腦膜	Meninges and cerebral meninges
.813	脊髓　髓質　髓膜	Spinal cord, or myel
.816	周圍神經系	Peripheral nervous system
	神經	Nerves
.817	交感神經系	Sympathetic nervous system
.818	五官	Sense organs
.819	神經節瘤	Ganlions
.82	**神經系生理學**	Physiology of the nersous system
.821	周圍神經系	Peripheral nervous system
	感覺與運動神經之差別	Distinction between sensory and motor nerves
.823	神經中樞　腦經	Nervous centers　Brain
.825	生理心理學　見 152	Physiologic psychology see 152
.827	交感神經系	Sympathetic nervous system
.83	**神經系衛生學**	Hygiene of the nervous system
	酒精，鴉片，咖啡素，烟草，蒅，其他麻醉藥，不寐藥	Alcohol, opium　Caffeine, tobacco and other narcotics　Insomnia
.84	**神經系病理學**	Diseases of the nervous system
.841	脊髓血循環病	Diseases relating to cerebrospinal circulation

	中風	Apoplexy
.842	脊髓膜	Diseases relating to cerebrospinal meninges
.843	腦索構造病	Structural diseases of brain and cord
.844	腦索官能病	Functional diseases of brain and cord
	1.眩暈	Vertigo
	3.麻痺	Paralysis
	5.神經衰弱	Neurasthenia
	6.脊髓刺激	Spinal irritation
	7.驚厥　搐搦	Eclampsia, convulsions
.845	神經官能病	Neuroses
	1.舞蹈病	Chorea, St. Vitus dance
	2.迷狂症	Hysteria
.845	3.癲癇病	Epilepsy
	4.破傷風　牙關鎖閉病	Tetanus, lackjaw
	5.失語症	Aphasia
	6.麻木　過敏	Anesthesia, hyperesthesia
	7.偏頭病　頭病	Megrim, headake
.846	神經病　神經痙攣	Diseases of nerves Neuralgia, cramp
.847	交感神經病	Diseases of sympathetic nervous system
.85	神經系治療學	Therapeutics of the nervous system
.86	神經系藥學	Drugs acting on the nervous system
.861	蒙汗藥:醚	Anesthetics;ether, etc.
.863	安眠藥:臭化氫	Hynotics;chloral, bromids
.865	止痛藥:鴉片	Analgesics;opium
.866	散瞳藥:蘋茄	Mydriatics;belladonna
.867	興奮藥	Excitants;strychnin
.869	其他	Other drugs
.87	神經系手術	Surgery of the nervous system
598	外科	Surgery

.01	理論　關係	Theories　Relations
.03	辭書	Dictionaries
.04	評論	Critiques　Criticism
.05	雜誌	Periodicals
.06	學社	Societies
.07	研究：綱目，綱要，問答，等	Studies. Outlines, syllabi, questions, etc.
.08	總集	Collected works
.09	歷史	History
.1	普通外科	General surgery
.11	外科解剖學	Surgical anatomy
.12	外科細菌學	Surgical bacteriology
.13	外科衛生學	Surgical hygiene
.14	外科病理學	Surgical pathology
		Surgical; diseases
.141	震盪	Shock
.142	發炎	Inflammation
.143	膿　瘻管　瘺	Abscess　Sinus　Fistula
.144	潰瘍　瘡	Ulcers　Sores
.145	壞疽　脫疽	Mortification　Gangrene
.146	傷熱	Traumatic fever
.147	破風傷	Tetanus
.15	外科治療學	Surgical therapeutics
.155	手術麻醉	Surgical anesthesia
.157	防腐手術	Asepsis and antisepsis
.16	損傷	Wounds, injuries and accidents
.161	火傷　燙傷	Burns and scalds
.162	電擊	Lightning and electric shock
.163	挫傷　擦傷	Contusions and abrasions
.164	傷痕	Wounds

	割傷，打傷，裂傷，刺傷，鎗傷，等	Incised, contused, lacerated, punctured, gunshot, etc.
.165	骨折	Fractures
.166	脫位　挫位	Dislocations
.167	捩傷	Sprains
.169	其他	Other injuries
.17	畸形外科	Orthopedic surgery　Deformities
	其關係畸形諸作均類此	The whole subject of deformities is clast here
.171	發育不全　生長不全	Incomplete development or growth
.172	局部煤素不全：脣裂	Incomplete coalescencet of parts: harelip
.173	局部煤素	Coalescene of parts
.174	胎兒煤素：暹羅國雙胎	Coalescence of fetuses: Siamese twins
.175	局部餘多：雙指，雙趾，等	Supernumerary parts or organs: extra fingers, toes, etc.
.176	生長不均	Disproportionate growth of parts
.177	局部移生或錯生	Transposition or displacement of parts
.178	先天捩轉：畸足	Congenital distortions, including talipes, club foot, etc.
.18	手術	Clinical and operative surgery
	部位手術	Regional surgery
.19	應用外科	Technique surgery
.1901	外科器件	Surgical instruments
.1903	矯形器件：夾板，等	Orthopedic appliances: splints, trusses, etc.
.1905	外科敷料	Surgical dressings
.1907	截斷術	Amputation　Resection
.1908	換補術	Plastic surgery
.195	海陸軍外科	Military and naval surgery
.197	鐵路外科	Railroad surgery
.2	牙科　齒科	Dentistry

.201	理論	Principles of dentistry
	8　倫理	Ethics
.205	雜誌	Periodicals
.207	研究	Studies: Outlines, syllabi, questions, etc.
.208	總集	Collected works
.209	歷史	History
.21	牙解剖學	Dental anatomy
.22	牙生理學	Dental physiology
.23	牙衛生學	Derntal hygiene
.24	牙病理學　牙病	Dental pathology　Diseases
.241	齒髓	Diseases of dentallpulp
.242	齒質	Diseases of dentin and cementum
.243	齒骨	Diseases of dental periosteum
.245	齒錯位與畸形	Malposition and malformation of teeth
.247	齒痛	Odontalgia, toothake
.25	牙治療學　醫藥	Dental therapeutics Medicines
.27	牙手術	Operative dentistry
.271	麻醉	Anesthetics
.273	手術	Operative technique and methods
.275	移牙	Replantation, implantation, transplantation of teeth
.276	取牙折牙	Dislocation and fracture of teeth
.277	填牙	Filling: plastic filling, amalgam, etc.
.28	補牙　鑲牙	Mechanical dentistry　Prosthetic dentistry
.284		
.286	牙冶金學	Dental metallurgy
.288	假牙	Artificial teeth
.29	牙科器件	Instruments and appliances

.3	眼科	Ophthalmology Disease of the eye	
	眼，耳，鼻，喉合論類此	Treatises for eye, ear, nose throat together	
.301	理論：盲	Theories: blindness	
.309	歷史	History	
.31	眼解剖學	Anatomy of the eye	
.32	眼生理學	Physiology of the eye	
.33	眼衛生學	Hygiene of the eye	
.34	眼病理學 眼病	Pathology of the eye Diseases	
.341	結合膜，角膜，硬結，眼炎	Conjunctiva, cornea, scleretic, ophthalmia	
.342	虹膜，眼脈絡膜，睫狀體	Iris, choroid, ciliary body	
.343	眼神經　網膜	Optic nerve Retina	
.344	鏡與鏡被膜，玻璃狀液體眼球病，內障	Lens and its capsule vitreous humor, affections of the globe, cataract	
.345	視病	Disorders of vision	
	近視，遠視，散光，色盲，雙視	Myopia, shortsightedness astigmatism, colorblindness	
.346	淚器	Lacrimal apparatus	
.347	眼瞼	Eyelids	
.348	眼眶	Orbit and neighboring parts	
.35	眼治療學 醫藥	Therapeutics of the eye Medicines	
	電療治	Electrotherapy	
.37	眼科手術	Operative ophthalmology	
	麻醉	Auesthetics	
.38	假眼	Artificial eyes	
.39	驗目器	Instruments and applications	
.399	配鏡　眼鏡	Refraction and optical defects Spectacles and eye-glasses	

.4	耳科		Otology　Rhinology　Laryngology
	耳，鼻，喉合論類此		Treatises on ear, nose, and throat together
.401	理論		Theories
	聾		Deafness
.409	歷史		History
.41	耳解剖學		Anatomy of the ear
.42	耳生理學		Physiology of the ear
.43	耳衛生學		Hygiene of the ear
.44	耳病理學　耳病		Pathology of the ear　Diseases
.441		外耳	Affections of external ear
.442		耳郭	Auricle
.443		耳道	Auditory canal
.444		中耳	Affections of middle ear
.445		鼓膜	Membrana tympani
.446		耳咽管	Eustachian tubes
.447		耳骨	Boues
.449		內耳	Affections of internal ear
.45	耳治療學　醫藥		Therapeutics of the ear　Medicines
	電療治		Electrotherapeutics
.47	耳科手術		Operative otology
.48	假耳		Artificial ear
.489		驗耳器　助聽器	Instruments and applications
.49	鼻科　喉科		Rhinology　Laryngology
.491		鼻科	Rhinology
.495		喉科	Laryngology
.5	皮膚科		Dermatology
.501		理論	Principles of dermatology
.509		歷史	History
.51	皮膚解剖學		Anatomy of the skin

.52	皮膚生理學	Physiology of the skin
.53	皮膚衛生學	Hygiene of the skin
.54	皮膚病理學	Pathology of the skin
	皮膚病	Skin diseases
.541	炎性病	Inflammatory affections
	瀾漫，丘診，鱗，風疹塊，蕁麻疹，等	Diffuse, papular, scaly, nettlerash, hives, etc.
.542	卡他性　皰狀　膿皰狀　濕疹　帶狀疱疹	Catarrhal, vesicular, pustular Eczema, shingles
.543	皮脂腺病	Disorders of sebaceous glands
.544	胞大　萎縮	Hypertrofies　Atrofies
	雞眼，瘊，白髮，頹頭，等	Corns, warts, white hair, baldness, etc.
.545	新結構　色毒變遷	New formation
		Pigmentary changes
	白化病，雀斑	Albinism, freckles
.546	汗腺病	Disorders of sweat glands
.547	寄生病	Parasitic diseases
.548	其他	Other skin diseases
	凍瘡，皮膚輝裂，等	Chilblain, frostbite, chaps, etc.
.55	皮膚治療學　醫藥	Therapeutics of the skin Medicines
.57	皮膚科手術	Operative dermatology
.58	皮膚科器件	Instruments and applications
.59	髮　鬚　甲	Hair　Beard　Nails
.6	花柳科　花柳病	Veneral diseases
.7	婦科	Gynecology
	婦科，產科，小兒科，合論類此	Treatises on gynecology, obstetrics, pediatrics together clast here
.71	婦女生殖器解剖學	Anatomy of the female generative organs

.72	婦女生殖器生理學	Physiology of the female generative organs
.721	發身	Puberty
.723	月經　行經	Menstruation
.725	卵之生成與出發	Ovulation
.727	月經完止	Menopause
.73	婦女生殖器衛生學	Hygiene of the female generative organs
.74	婦女生殖器病理學	Diseases of the female generative organs
.741	卵巢	Ovary
.742	輸卵管	Fallopian tube
.743		
.744	子宮　子宮頸	Uterus and cervix
.745	陰道	Vagina
.746	女陰	Vulva
.747	官能與交感神經病	Functional and symptomatic disorders
	1.月經病	Diseases of menstruation
	3.白帶	Leucorrhea
	5.無生殖能	Sterility
.749	乳病	Diseases of the breast
.75	婦科治療學　醫藥	Therapeutics of the female generative organs　Medicines
.77	婦科手術	Operative gynecology
.79	變態婦科	Abnormal gynecology
.795	瘋癲婦科	Gynecology among insane
.8	產科	Obstetrics
.81	腹孕　生理	Pregnancy　Physiology
.811	診斷　孕徵	Diagnosis　Signs of pregnancy
.813	孕期	Duration

.815	孕期衛生	Hygiene management
.817	多孕：雙孕，等	Multiple pregnancy: twins, etc.
.82	**腹孕病理學**	**Pathology of pregnancy**
.821	異位妊娠　子宮外孕	Ectopic gestation Extrauterin pregnancy
.824	卵病理學	Pathology of ovum
	死胎與胎留滯	Death and retention of fetus
.827	胎附件病理學	Pathology of fetal appendages
	1.蛻膜	Decidua
	3.胎盤	Placenta
	5.羊膜	Amnion
	7.臍帶	Umbilic cord
.828	小産　死胎産　血胎	Abortion　Miscarriage　Stillbirtb,
	打胎	etc.
.83	**分娩　生産　生理**	**Parturition　Labor　Physiology**
.831	分娩機例	Mechanism of labor
.833	産式	Presentations　Positions
.835	臨床程次與方法	Clinic courses and phenomena
.837	正産法與處理	Conduct of normal labor　Management
.84	**分娩病理學**	**Pathology of labor**
.841	異常生産　錯産	Abnormal labor from faults
	1.使力關係	Of expellent forces
	3.岐路關係　障礙	Of passages　Mechanical obstacles
	關係	to expulsion
	5.胎兒關係	Of child Abnormalities of fetus
	例　畸形胎兒	e.g. Deformities
.843	併發病症	Complications
.844	出血	Hemorrhage
.845	破裂	Rupture of laceration of genital tract
.846	胎盤留滯	Retention of placenta
.847	子宮內翻	Inversion of uterus
.848	臍帶脫垂	Prolapsus funis

.849		其他	Other complications
.85	產後 生理		Puerperal state　Physiology
.86	產後病理學		Pathology of puerperal state　Puerperal diseases
.861		乳病：乳熱，乳房炎，等	Diseases of lactation：milk fever, mastitis, etc.
.862		產褥熱	Puerperal fever
		子宮炎，腹膜炎，蜂窩織炎，敗血病，膿毒血病，等	Metritis, peritonitis, cellulitis, septicemia, pyemia, etc.
.863		驚厥	Convulsions
.864		產後躁狂	Puerperal mania
.866		静脉炎	Phlebitis, venous thrombosis, phlegmasia dolens
.867		其他静脉病	Other puerperal affections
.868		產後暴死	Sudden death after delivery
.87	產科手術		Operative obstetrics
.871		助產槓杆與鉗子用法	Application of lever and forceps
.872		胎倒轉術	Version
.873		胎兒截割法	Embryotomy
.874		口與頸擴張術	Dilatation of os and cervix
.875		恥骨切開術	Symphyseotomy
.876		開腹產術	Caesarian section
.877		胎盤移動術	Removal of placents
.878		引產術　卵移動術	Induction of labor　Removal of ovum
.879		產科防毒劑　子宮内注射	Intra-uterin injections　Antiseptics in midwifery
.9	小兒科		Pediatrics
.91		胎教　優生　遺傳	Prenatal culture　Stirpiculture　Heredity

.93	小兒衛生		Hygiene of children
	小兒飲食　滋養		Feeding of children
			Nutrition of infants
.94	產兒病理學　產兒病		Diseases of new-born infants
.941	呼吸停止		Asphyxia
.942	浮腫		Edema
.943	出血		Hemorrhages
.944	黃疸病		Jaundice
.945	乳房炎		Mastitis
.946	眼炎		Ophthalmia　Conjunctivitis
.947	中風		Paralysis
.948	產兒受傷		Injuries of new-born infants
.95	小兒病		Childhood diseases
.96	小兒治療　醫藥		Therapeutics and materia medica
.97	小兒外科		Surgery of children
599	**獸醫學　家畜獸學**		**Veterinary medicine**
.1	獸解剖學		Anatomy of the domesticated animals
.2	獸生理學		Physiology of the domesticated animals
.3	獸衛生學		Hygiene of the domesticated animals
.4	獸病理學　獸病		Veterinary pathology　Diseases
.41	馬		Horses
.42	牛		Cattle
.43	羊		Sheep, goats
.44	豬		Swine
.45	家禽:雞、鴨、鵝、等		Poultry: chickens, ducks, etc.
.46	鳥		Birds
.47	犬		Dogs

.48	貓	Cats
.49	其他	Others
.5	獸治療學　醫學	Veterinary therapeutics　Medicines
.7	獸外科	Veterinary surgery
.8	獸產科	Veterinary obstetrics

實業　工藝　Productive arts　Industrial arts

600　　實業與工藝　　　　Productive arts and technology
　.1　　理論　關係　　　　Theories　Relations
　　　　例　與經濟，政治，　e.g. In relation to economics, politics, etc.
　　　　　　等關係
　.2
　.3　　辭書　　　　　　　Dictionaries
　.37　　　年鑑　　　　　　Yearbooks
　.4　　評論　　　　　　　Critiques　Criticism
　.5　　雜誌　　　　　　　Periodicals
　.6
　.7　　研究　教育　　　　Studies　Education
　.8　　總集　　　　　　　Collected works
　.9　　歷史　　　　　　　History
　　　　依國分　　　　　　　　By country
　　　　　例　中國實業史　600.91　　e.g. History of Chinese industrial arts

601　　實業經濟　　　　　Economics　Policies
　　　　實業政策

602　　實業法規　　　　　Laws and regulations
　.3　　契約　合同　　　　Contracts and specifications

603　　實業管理　　　　　Management of industrial enterprise

604

605　　特權　　　　　　　Patents
　.1　　發明　　　　　　　Inventors and inventions

.3	意匠		Designs and models
.5	商標		Trade marks
606			
607	度量權衡		Metric arts Measurement
608			
609			
610	農業 農學		Agriculture Agronomy
.01	理論 關係		Theories Relations
	例 農業與國家		e.g. Agriculture and the state
.03	辭書		Dictionaries
.037	年鑑		Yearbooks
.04	評論		Critiques Criticism
.05	雜誌		Periodicals
.06	學社		Societies
.07	研究 教育		Studies Education
	綱要，答問，等		Outlines, syllabi, questions, etc.
.077	農業學校		Schools Colleges
.078	農事試驗場		Experiment stations
.079	展覽		Exhibitions
.08	總集		Collected works
.081	文藝		Literature
.088	小冊		Pamphlets
.09	歷史		History
.091	古代		Ancient
	古代田制		Ancient land systems
.092	中古		Middle ages
.093	近世		Modern
.097	農業調查 游歷		Agricultural missions, voyages, etc.

.098	熱帶農業	Tropical agriculture
.099	依國分	By country
	例　中國農業	e.g. Chinese agriculture
	610.0991	
.1	農業社會	Agricultural sociology
.11	農業組織	Agricultural organizations
.12		
.13	農業階級	Agricultural classes
.14		
.15	農村生活	Rural life
.16	農民遷移	Rural exodus
.17	農村改良	Improvement of country life conditions
.18	農賑	Provision of famines
.3	農業經濟　農業政策	Agricultural economics
.31	農業政策	Agricultural policies
.311	制度	Agricultural system
.312	大農制	Large farm
.313	小農制	Small farm
.314	集約制	Intensive farming
.315	放任制	Extensive farming
.317	墾殖	Methods and systems of exploitation Land settlement
.318	賦稅	Rents, taxes, valuation, etc.
.32	農業法規	Laws and regulations
.33	農場管理	Agricultural management
.35	農業金融	Agricultural finance
.355	農業銀行	Agricultural bank
.357	農業簿記	Agricultural bookkeeping
.358	市場	Markets, marketing, etc.

.37	農村副業	
.4		
.5	農業基礎科學	Basal sciences in agriculture
.51	農業數學	Agricultural mathematics
.52	農業氣象學	Agricultural meteorology
.527	農業與氣候	Agriculture and climate
.53	農業物理	Agricultural physics
.54	農業化學	Agricultural chemistry
.541	解析與實驗	Analysis and experiments
.56	農業顯微學	Agricultural microscopy
.57	農業植物學	Agricultural botany
.58	農業動物學	Agricultural zoology
.6	農業工程　農具建築	Farm machinery and farm engineering
.61	耕耘用具	Clearing and soil working: general tools
	鋤，鍬，犂，耙，轆轤，耕耘機，等	Spade, shovel, plows, harrows, rollers, hoe, cultivators, etc.
.62	栽種用具	Seeding and sowing machinery
	播種機，栽種機，移植機，等	Seed sowers, planters, transplanters, etc.
.63	防禦用具	Equipment for care of plants, trees, etc.
	接枝器，修樹剪刀，花房，架，花托，等	Grafting, pruning, greenhouses, supports, receptacles, etc.
.64	收穫用具	Harvesting
	刈草，割禾機，等	Mowers, reapers, etc.
.65	貯藏用具	Tools used in preparing for storage or transport

		打穀機，簸揚器，等	Threshers, cleaning, etc.
.66		運輸用具	Transport　Power, power transmission appliances
		拖車，輓具，等	Tractors, etc.
.67		農事建築	Farm buildings
.8		農產製造	Agricultural manufactures
.9		農產物利用	Farm products utilizations
611		**農藝**	**The farm　Farm operations**
.1		農時　時令	Seasons
.2		農田	Type of farms
.21		穀田	Crop farm
.23		菜田	Vegetable farm
.25		菓田	Fruit farm
.27		林地	Woodlands
.28		牧場	Stock farm
.3		土壤學	Land, soil
.31		化學	Soil chemistry
		分析與實驗	Analysis and experiments
.33		物理	Soil physics
.331		比重	Specific weight (gravity) of soil
.333		濕潤　濕度	Humidity
.335		溫度	Temperature
.34		土壤種類	Soil classification
		鹼質土壤，特質土壤，等	Alkali lands, soils for special crops, etc.
.35		土壤生產力：保存與消耗	Soil fertility: maintenance, exhaustion
.36		土壤細菌學	Soil bacteriology

.37	土壤測驗	Soil surveys
.38		
.39	歷史	History
.4	耕種　耕作	Farm operations
.5	選種　育種　種苗	Selection, breeding, etc.
.57	繁植	Methods of plant multiplication
	輪栽, 移植, 等	Seedage, transplanting, etc.
.6	灌溉　排水　給水	Irrigation　Water supply
.7	肥料　肥田	Fertilizers and improvement of the soil
.8	收穫	Harvesting
.9	害農與益農	Hindrances　Protection
	其關係動物病理者應入599	That relating to diseases of animals is better clast in 599
.91	天災	Elemental destruction
.911	低溫, 霜, 凍	Low temperature, frost, freezing
.912	炎熱　乾旱	Excessive heat and drought
.913	冰雹	Hail
.914	雷電	Lightning
.915	風雨	Wind and rain
.916	水	Floods, inundations
.917	火	Fires: forest and prairie
.919	其他	Other destructive agents
	例如　地震, 瓦斯, 等	e.g. earthquakes, gas, etc.
.93	鳥獸	Gall　Cecidiology
.94	蟲害	Bacteria and bacterial diseases
.95	病菌	Fungi
.97	草木	Parasitic and injurious plants

.971	雜草		Weeds
.977	毒草		Plants injurious to animals
.99	益農		Means of protection
.991	方法與用具		Methods and apparatus
	噴水，拂塵，燻烘		Spraying, dusting, fumigating
.993	防禦		Preparations and materials
	殺蟲，殺菌，防腐		Insecticides, fungicides, antiseptics
.995	害物之天然敵		Natural enemies of pests
.997	其他防禦		Other means of protection
	警報，遮蔽，等		Warnings, covering, etc.

612　農作物　　　　　　　Field crops: grains, grasses, fibers, etc.

.1	禾穀作物	Cereals　Grains
.11	小麥	Wheat
.12	蕎麥	Buckwheat
.13	燕麥	Oats
.14	裸麥	Rye
.15	玉蜀黍　高粱	Corn, maize
.16	大麥	Barley
.17	黍　粟　稷	Millet, sorghum, etc.
.18	稻　陸稻	Rice, upland rice
.19	其他	other
.2	芻秣作物：牧草類	Forage crops: grasses
.21	早熟禾	Blue grass　Poa
.22	鴨茅	Archard grass　Dactylis
.23	糠穗	Red top, bent grass　Asrestis
.24	大粟草	Timothy　Phleum
.25		

.27	其他栽植草類	Other cultivated grasses
.271	狗牙根	Bermuda grass　Cunodon
.272	雀麥	Brome grass　Bromus
.273	黑麥草	Rye grass　Lolium
.275	大蟹釣	Oat grass　Arrhenatherum
.277	雀稗	Paspalum
.278	藺草	Phalaris
.29	其他草類	Other grasses
.291	結縷草	Zoysicae
.292	高粱草	Andropogonae
.293	稷草	Paniceae
.294	稻草	Oryzeae
.295	虎尾草	Chlorideae
.296	三芒草	Aristida
.297	畫眉草	Eragiostis
.3	芻秣作物：豆菽類	Forage crops：legumes, etc.
.31	扁豆	Dolichos
.32	毛豆	Eriosema
.33	大豆	Soybean　Glycine
.34	豇豆	Cajanus
.35	落花生	Peanut　Arachis
.36	豌豆	Edible podded pea　Pisum
.37	蠶豆	Vetches　Vicia
.38	其他	Other legumes
.381	苜蓿	Alfalfa　Medicago
.382	白翹搖	Clovers, berseem　Trifolium
.383	藜豆	Velvet bean　Mncuna
.384	胡支子	Japan clover　Lespedeza
.385	舞草	Beggar weed　Meibomia

.386	草木犀	Sweet clover Melilotus	
.387	含羞草	Minora	
.388	白合歡	Leucaena	
.389			
.39	其他芻秣作物	Other forage crops	
.4	根菜作物	Roots crops	
.41	甘藷	Beet Beta vulgaris	
	恭菜	Mangel and mangel wurzel	
.42	蕪菁	Turnip Brassica apa	
	蕓薹	Rutabaga Brassica campestris	
.45	胡蘿蔔	Carrot Daucus carota	
.47	防風草	Parsnip Pastinaca sativa	
.48	球莖類	Tubers and bulbs	
.481	馬鈴薯	Potato Salunum tuberosum	
.483	甘薯	Sweet potato Ipomaea batatas	
.485	菊芋	Jerusalem artichoke	
		Helianthus tuberosie	
.5	纖維作物	Textil fibers, cordage, plaiting, basket, etc.	
.51	棉	Cotton Gossypium	
.52	大麻	Flax Linum	
.53	苧麻	Hemp Cannabis	
.54	黃麻	Jute Corchorus	
.55	莔麻 亞麻	Ramie, China grass Bochmeria	
.56			
.57	其他細纖維作物	Other soft fibers	
	例 中國黃麻	e.g. China jute Abutilon	
.58	硬纖維作物	Hard fibers	
	例 新西蘭大麻	e.g. New Zealand hemp Phormium	

.59		編織用纖維	Fibers for plaiting, basket and wicker work
	.591	椰子皮纖維	Coir, coconut fiber　Cocos
	.592	棕櫚葉纖維	Raffia　Raphia
	.593	編織草帽纖維	Hat fibers
	.594	蘆葦	Reeds　Arundo
	.595	竹	Bamboo
	.596	杞柳	Osier, willow　Salix
	.599	其他	Other fibers
.6		糖　澱粉作物	Sugar plants and starch
	.61	甘蔗	Cane Saccharum
	.62	蘆粟	Sorghum　Andropozon sorghum brot.s. vulgare linn
	.63	甜菜	Sugar beets　Beta
	.64	楓械	Maple　Acer saccharum marsh
	.65	佛肛竹	
	.66	棕櫚	Palm
	.67	其他製糖作物	Other sugar plants
	.68	澱粉	Starch
612.7		刺激作物	Alkaloidal plants
	.71	菸草	Tobacco　Nicotiana
	.72	茶	Tea　Canellia thea link
	.73	咖啡	Coffee　Coffea
	.74	椰子	Cacao, coco, chocolate　Thesbroma
	.75	罌粟(鴉片)	Poppy (opium) Papaver
	.76	可樂	Kola or cola
	.77	冬青茶	Mate　Ilex　Jesuits tea
	.78	萄苣	Chicory, succory　Cichorinm
	.79		

.8	香料作物	Perfumes, spices, condiments, etc.
.81	芬芳植物	Perfumery
.811	花:玫瑰,素馨,等	Floral: rose, jasmin, violet
.813	草:迷迭香,天竺葵,等	Herbal: lavendar, rosemary, etc.
.815		
.817	木:檀香,香椿	Woods: sandalwood, cedar
.818	根:鳶尾,等	Roots: orris, vetiver
.83	香液 香膏	Balms and gums
	没藥,安息香,等	Myrrh, benzoin
.85	香氣	Flavoring
	嘩呢拉,薄荷,鹿蹄草,黃樟,等	Vanilla, mints, wintergreen, sassafras, etc.
.87	丁香 荳蔻	Spices Allspice
.88	香料	Condiments
	胡椒,芥子,等	Pepper, mustard, etc.
.89		
.9	其他特用作物	Other special plants
.91	染料作物	Vegetable dyes, dye plants
.92		
.93	鞣皮作物	Tanning material
	鹽膚本,等	Sumac Canaigre
.94		
.95	藥料作物	Medicinal plants
.96		
.97	油漆作物	Oil producing plants
.98		
.99		
613	**園藝**	**Horticulture Gardening**

.1	菜蔬　菜園	Olericulture　Kitchen gardening
.11	根菜類	Roots edible
	蘿葡，胡蘿葡，等	Turnip, carrot, etc.
.12	塊莖類	Tubers, edible
	薑，等	Ginger, etc.
.13	球莖類　鱗莖類	Bulbs edible
	蒜，葱，韭，等	Garlic, leek, shallot, etc.
.14	嫩莖類	Corms ediblee
.15		
.16	葉菜類	Leaves edible
	蘆荀，菠薐草，等	Asparagus, Polansia, etc.
.17	花菜類	Flowers edible
	花椰菜，等	Cabbage, etc.
.19	雜類	Miscellany
.2	瓜菜　葫蘆類	Fruits edible
.21	甜瓜	Melons　Cucumis
.22	西瓜	Watermelon　Citrullus
.23	南瓜	Squashes　Cucurbits
.24	黃瓜	Cucumbers
.25	冬瓜	Benincasa
.26	絲瓜	Luffa
.27	苦瓜	Momordia
.3	豆菽類	Seeds edible　Peas
	雞豆，扁豆，等	Chick pea, lentils, etc.
.4	香菜　香草	Condimentaland sweet herbs
	薄荷，茴香，等	Mints, anis, etc.
.5	蕈　菌	Mushrooms
	麥蕈，等	Truffies, etc.

.7	果類　果園	Pomiculture　Pomology
		Fruits gardening
.71	仁果類	Pomaceous fruits
.711	蘋果	Apple　Pyrus malus
.712	梨	Pear　Pyrus
.715	榲桲	Qnince　Cydouia
.717	枇杷	Loquat, Japan plum
		Eriobotrya Japonica
.72	核果類	Drupaceous or stone fruits　Prunus
.721	杏	Apricot　Prunophora
.723	李	Plum　Prunophora
.725	櫻桃	Cherry　Cerasus
.727	桃	Peach　Prunus　Persica
.73	柑橘類	Citrous fruits: orange family, etc.
.731	橘　橙　香橙	Orange　Citrus aurantium
.733	金橘	Fortunella
.735	香櫞	Citron　Var. genuina
.737	檸檬	Lemon
.74	漿果類	Moraceous fruits
.741	無花果	Fig　Ficus carica
.743	桑子	Mulberry　Morus
.745	麵包果	Bread fruit　Artocarpus incisa
.75	葡萄	Grapes　Vinyards　Viticulture
.76	堅果類	Nut fruits　Nuciculture
.761	胡桃	Walnut　Juglans
.762	栗	Chestnut　Castanea
.763	榛子	Filbert, cobnut　Corylus
.765	杏仁　扁桃	Almond　Prunus
.766	茘枝	Litchi, leechee
		Nephelium litchi
.767	銀杏	Ginkgo　G. biloba

.77	棕櫚類	Palmaceous fruits
.771	椰子	Coconut, coco palm Cocos nucifera
.773	棗椰子	Date palm Phoenix dactylifera
.775	阿列布	Olive Olea Europea
.776	柘榴	Pomegranate Punica granatum
.777	萬壽果	Papaw Carica
.778	棗	Jujube Zizyphus
.78	灌木　草果類	Bush and herblike fruits
	例　樹苺，苺，芭蕉，鳳梨，等	e. g. Brambles, strawberry, banana, pineapple, etc.
.79	其他果類	Miscellaneous fruits
.8	花卉　養花　花園	Floriculture Flowers
	其關係與花及其研究諸作類此	Class here works on methods of raising flowers.
.801	養花經濟	Economics and operations
.803	花卉品評	Flower shows and methods of judging
.805	養花自然要素及其區分	Special conditions of growth
	1.依氣候分	Climate
	熱帶，寒帶，高山，等花木	Tropic, arctic, alpine plants, etc.
	2.依季節朝夕分	Season and hour of flowering
	春季，夏季，秋季，冬季，朝，夕，等	Spring, summer, autumn, winter, morning, evening, etc.
	3.依光暗分	Environment as related to light: Sunny, shady
	4.依土壤分	Soil
	濕地，乾地，沙地，等	For moist, dry, sandy soils, etc.
	5.依顏色分	Color
	白，紫，青，黃，紅，等	White, violet, blue, yellow, red, etc.
	6.依香氣分	Odor

	7.依感覺分	Feeling: roughleaved, irritant
.806	應用花草	Purpose
	1.家用　盆栽	House plants　Potted plants
	3.展覽	Flower shows　Exhibits
	5.裝飾	Decoration
	7.其他	For other purposes
.808	花房　苗圃	Under glass: greenhouses
.809	花卉保存及繁殖	Preservation and reproduction of flowers, etc.
.81	一二年性草花類	Annual and biennial plants
	朝顏, 罌粟, 等	Opium poppy, etc.
.82	多年性草花類	Perennial plants
	菊, 蘭, 芍藥, 萬年青, 等	Chrysanthemum, cymbidium, paconiaalbiflora, phodea, etc.
.83	球根性草花類	Bulbous plants
	百合, 鈴蘭, 水仙, 等	Lilium Japonicum, poet's narcissus, etc.
.84	其他草花類	Other herbaceous plants
.85	常青性灌木花類	Evergreen shrubs, hedges
	躑躅, 瑞香, 等	Daplane odora, etc.
.86	落葉性灌木花類	Deciduous shrubs, hedges
	薔薇, 牡丹, 等	Rosa, paeonia montan, etc.
.87	常青性喬木花類	Evergreen trees
	山茶, 茶梅, 等	Thea Japonica, thea sasanqua, etc.
.88	落葉性喬木花類	Deciduous trees
	楓, 梅, 櫻, 等	Liquidambar formosana, prunus mume, etc.
.89	其他	Othe flowers
.9	造園學	Landscape gardening
614	森林	Forestry　Aboriculture

.01	理論	Theories
	重要	Value　Importance
.02		
.03	辭書	Dictionaries
.04	評論	Critiques　Criticism
.05	雜誌	Periodicals
.06	學會	Societies
.07	研究	Studies
.08	總集	Collected works
.09	歷史	History
	依國分	By country
.1	森林經濟	Economics
.11	影響：自然方面	Forest influence: geophysic
.111	氣候	On climate
.112	土壤	On soil
.113	雨水　河流	On water resources and stream flow
.115	浸蝕	On erosion
.117	雪崩	On avalanches
.12	影響：社會方面	Forest influence: social
.123	衛生	On public health
.125	道德	On ethics and morals
.127	美學	On esthetics
.128	園圃	Forest parks
.13		
.14	工業方面	Relation to industries
.15	森林政策　林政	Forest policy
	國有　國家經營	State ownership
.16	林源	Forest resources
.17	森林管理與行政	Forest management and administration

.18			
.19	森林法規		Laws and regulations
.2	森林工程		Engineering
.23	測量		Surveying
.25	建築		Construction engineering
			Forest improvements
.27	水利		Hydraulic engineering
.3	森林植物學		Forest botany
.31	樹木學		Dendrology
.37	森林生態學		Ecology　Oekology
.38	森林地理		Geographical distribution
	森林分佈		
		依種分	By species
.4	造林學		Silviculture
.41	天然生產		Natural production systems
		清晰法	Clear cutting
		選擇法	Selection method
.43	插木		Intermediate cuttings
.45	標記		Marking
.47	矮林處置		Brush disposal
.48	林事		Forestation
.481		用具	Tools and equipments
.482		種子	Seed
.483		直播	Direct seeding
.484		育苗	Nursery practice
.485		植樹	Planting
.487		植幼	Underplanting
.489		樹木栽培與育種	Tree breeding
.5	害林與益林		Hindrances　Protections

.6	森林分類	Taxonomic forestry
	森林原理之應用於各別樹木者	Forestry Principles applied to individual tree species
.7	森林利用	Forest product utilization
.71	伐木	Logging
.72	製材	Rough-wood products
.73	特種材木	Other lumber: by uses
	其關係森林者類此	Lumbering viewpoint only
	其關係樹木工業及其應用者入專類	For lumbering industry and technic of use better clast with special topic
.74		
.75	樹皮製造	Bark products
.76	樹液	Saps
.77	果　種　核	Fruits　Seeds　Nuts
.78	副產物	Other forest products
.781	簇葉	Foliage
.783	寄生物之利用	Parasite utilization　Abnormalities
.785	餘廢利用	Wastes
.79		
.8		
.9	其他森林利用	Other uses
.91	農務方面	Farming
.92	森林牧場	Forest pasture　Forest grazing
.93	田獵　漁場	Hunting and fishing
.94	娛樂方面	Recreation uses
.95	飲料方面	Potable water protection
.96		
.97	田園森林	Farm forestry
.98		

.99

615 畜產業   Animal industries
                                      Animal culture

.01   畜產經濟　畜政   Economics and policies
.02   馴養   Zootechny
.03   育種   Breeding　Reproduction
.04   保護   Care of animals
.05   飼養   Feeding
.06   飼料   Food　Foods　Forage
.07
.08   衛生   Hygiene, diseases, etc.
.09
.1   家畜   Domestic animals
.11   馬   Horse
.12   牛   Cattle
.13   羊   Sheep, goats
.14   豚   Swine
.15   犬   Dogs
.17   猫   Cats
.18
.19
.2   家禽   Poultry　Domestic birds
         雞，鴨，鵝，等   Fowls, ducks, goose, etc.
.3   飛鳥   Birds
.4   養蜂   Bee keeping　Apiculture
.5   白蠟蟲   Wax
.6   其他益蟲   Other useful insects
         例　臙脂蟲   e.g. Cochineal, etc.

	.7	酪農	Dairy and dairy products
	.71	牛乳	Milk
	.72	乳酪	Cream
	.73	牛酪	Butter
	.74	乾酪	Cheese
	.8	畜産製造	Animal technology
	.9	畜産利用	Utilization of animals and animal products
616		蠶業	Silkworms Silk industries Sericulture
	.1	蠶業經濟 蠶業政策	Economics and policies
	.2	蠶體學	Natural history of silkworm
	.21	叙述解剖學 器官學	Descriptive anatomy Organography
	.22	生理學	Physiology
	.24	病理學	Pathology
	.25		
	.27	生態學	Ecology
	.271	習性	Habits
	.274	食物	Foods
	.277	時季	Season
	.28		
	.29	蠶分佈學 依國分	Geographic distribution By Country
	.3	蠶種 蠶子	Silkworm eggs
	.4	養蠶 育蠶	Silk-raising
		害蠶與益蠶	Hindrances and protections

.5	蠶室　蠶牀　蠶具	Silkcultural room and implements
.6	栽桑	Mulberry culture
	貯桑法	Preservation of mulberry leaves
.7	繭	Cocoon
	殺蛹法	Stifling cocoons
	乾繭法	Drying cocoons
	貯繭法	Storing cocoons
.8		
.9	蠶之利用	Utilization of silkworms
.91	醫藥	Medicines
.92		
.93		
.94	食物	Foods
.95		
.96	製絲	Silk
.97		
.98		
.99	其他	Other uses
617	**漁業　水產業**	**Aquatic products industries**
.1	漁業經濟	Economics and policies
	漁業政策	
.2	水產基礎科學	Basal sciences in fishery
.24	水產化學	Fisheries chemistry
.25	水質	Hydrology for fishery
.26	水產海洋學, 湖沼學	Fisheries oceanography, limnology, etc.
.27	水產植物學	Aquatic botany
.28	水產動物學	Aquatic zoology

	.3	養魚法	Pisciculture Fish culture
	.4		
	.5	捕魚	Fisheries Fishing
	.51	淡水	Fisheries in fresh water
	.53	沿岸	Coasting fisheries
	.55	海洋	Fisheries in ocean
	.57	深海	Deep sea fisheries
	.6	漁船　漁具	Fishing boats and implements
	.7	蛙　鼈水產業	Frogs, oysters Shelfish
	.8	其他水產業	Other sea food
		例　海藻，等	e.g. seaweeds, etc.
	.9	依國分	By country
618		鹽業	Salt manufacturing
619		田獵	Hunting industries
	.1	獵獸	Animal hunting
	.2	獵鳥	Bird hunting
	.3		
	.4	鳥獸保養法	Animal and bird preservation and protection
	.5		
	.6		
	.7	田獵生活	Outdoor life
	.8		
	.9	依國分	By country
620		商業	Commerce Business
	.01	理論　關係	Theories Relations
	.013	擇業	Choosing a business
			Success literature

.015		商業心理	Business psychology
.018		商業倫理	Business ethics
.019		關係	Relations
	例	商業與實業	e.g. Commerce and industry
.03		辭書	Dictionaries
.037		年鑑	Yearbooks
.04		評論	Critiques　Criticism
.05		雜誌	Periodicals
.06		會社　商會	Chambers of commerce and industry
.07		研究　訓練	Studies　Training
.08		總集	Collected works
.09		歷史	History
.091		古代商業	Ancient
.092		中古商業	Medieval
.093		近世商業	Modern
.097		傳記	Biography
.098		商業地理	Commercial geography
.1-.9	依國分		By country
	例	中國商業　620.1	e.g. Chinese commerce
621	商業經濟　商業政策		Economics and policies
.1		國有　政府經營	State control of business
.3		商業組合	Commercial association
.5		商業興信所	Mercantile agency
.9		商業法規	Laws and regulations
622	商業管理與經營		Business management and administration
.1		事務管理	Office economy

.15	事務能率	Business efficiency
.2	商店組織與管理	Shop organization and management
.3	店員	Personnel　Employee
.4	經理　經紀	Commission business Agencies, etc.
.5	販賣	Buying and selling
.51	購買	Buying
.52	銷售	Selling
.53	零賣	Retail business
.54	批發	Wholesale business
.55	招徠	Canvassing
.56	行商　小販	Peddling and pedlars
.57	通信販賣	Mail order business
.58	拍賣	Auctions, fairs, etc.
.6	發送　裝包	Shipping　Packing
.7	百貨商店	Department stores
.8	聯號	Branch and chain stores
.9	各種販賣	Specific industries
	專業販賣應入該業	Business having special no. prefer in that no.
	其在他處未備號碼者類此	Mercantile business not having special no. clast here
623	商品學	Merchandises　Commodities
624	市場學	Markets
.1	市場觀察與分析	Market surveys and analysis
.3	市情預測	Commercial forecasts
.5	市價	Trade cycles　Commercial fluctuations

	.6	商業破產	Commercial bankruptcy
	.7	商業仲裁	Commercial arbitration
625		堆棧　貯藏	Storage and warehousing
626		商業實踐	Business practice
	.1	商業數學	Business mathematics
	.18	數表	Tables: discount, etc.
	.2	商業函牘	Business correspondences
	.3	商務文件整理	Filing and indexing
	.7	打字	Typewriting
	.8	速記	Short hand
627		會計　簿計	Accounting　Bookkeeping
628			
629		廣告	Advertising　Publicity
	.1	圖畫與廣告	Pictures and advertising
	.2	彩色與廣告	Colors and advertising
	.3	商標與廣告	Trade marks and advertising
	.4	戶外廣告	Outdoors advertising
		招貼，傳單，路車，等	Postcards, circulars, street-car advertising
	.5	戶內廣告	Indoors advertising
		展覽，陳列，電影，等	Exhibitions, motion pictures, etc.
	.7	書報廣告	Magazines　Newspapers
	.8	各業廣告	Special lines of business
	.9	國外廣告	Advertising in foreign countries
630		交通　運輸	Transportation and communication
	.01	理論　關係	Theories　Relations
		例　交通與農業	e.g. Transportation and agriculture

.02
.03 辭書 Dictionaries
.04 評論 Critiques Criticism
.05 雜誌 Periodicals
.06 會社 Societies
.07 研究 Studies
.08 總集 Collected works
.09 歷史 History
.091 古代 Ancient
.092 中古 Medieval
.093 近世 Modern
.094
.095
.096
.097
.098 地理　路線 Geography Trade routes
.099
.1-.9 依國分 By country
例　中國交通　630.1　　e.g. Chinese transportation and communication

631 陸運 Land transportation
632 道路 Roads and highways
.1 驛站 Stage lines
.2 轎輿 Sedan chair
.3 乘馬 Hacks
.4 馬車 Carriages, coaches, omnibuses, etc.
.5
.6 汽車 Motor vehicles, cars

	.7	電車	Tramcars
	.8		
	.9	依國分	By country
633		鐵路	Railways Railway transport
	.1	鐵路與政府　政策	Railways and the state Policy
	.11	法規	Laws and regulations
	.12	條例	Cases
	.13	政府援助	State aid
	.14		
	.15		
	.16		
	.17	國有鐵路	Government ownership
	.18	私有鐵路	Private ownership
	.19	國際鐵路	International railway agreement
	.2		
	.3	鐵路管理與經營	Administration and management
	.4		
	.5	鐵路 　運輸與貿易	Railways 　Transportation and traffic
	.6		
	.7	載便鐵路	Quick transport railways 　Street railways
	.8		
	.9	依國分	By country
634		水運	Water transportation
	.1	航政 　法規, 稅率, 貿易, 　等	Waterways and the state Policy 　Laws and regulations, taxation, 　traffic, etc.

	.2		
	.3	運輸公司	Transportation agencies, navigation, co., etc.
	.4		
	.5	擺渡	Ferries
	.6	漕運	Inland canals　Inland navigation
	.7	海運	Maritime transport
	.8		
	.9	依國分	By country
635		航空運輸	Aerial transportation
			Aerial navigation
636		郵政	Postal services
	.1	法規　章程	Postal law
	.2		
	.3	郵務行政與管理	Administration and management
	.31	國有	Government post
	.32	私有	Private post
	.33		
	.34	郵務公會	Post union
	.35	人員	Personnel
	.36		
	.37	郵運	Transport by mail
	.38	郵匯	Banking by mail
	.39		
	.4	郵票	Postage stamps
	.48	郵票蒐集	Stamp collections　Philately
	.5	郵件	Special Mails

	.51	免費郵件	Free delivery
	.52		
	.53	航空郵件	Aerial delivery
	.54		
	.55	掛號郵件	Registered mail
	.56	快遞郵件	Express mail
	.57		
	.58		
	.59	無法投遞之信件	Dead letters
	.6	包裹	Parcels post
	.7		
	.8	國際郵便	International postal service
	.9	依國分	By country
637		郵政　電信	Telegraphy　Telephone
	.03	電碼	Codes
	.1	電報	Telegraphy
	.2	海底	Submarine　Cables
	.3	無線	Wireless
	.7	電話	Telephone
	.9	依國分	By country
638			
639		其他	others
	.1	信號	Signaling
	.7	鴿傳信	Carrier pigeons
640		工藝	Technology
	.1	理論　關係	Theories　Relations
	.2		

	.3	辭書	Dictionaries
	.37	年鑑	Yearbooks
	.4	評論	Critiques　Criticism
	.5	雜誌	Periodicals
	.6	學會	Societies
	.7	研究　教育	Studies　Education
	.8	總集	Collected works
	.9	歷史	History
		依國分	By country
641		工業經濟　政策	Economics and policies
642		法規	Laws and regulations
	.3	契約　合同	Contracts and specification
643			
644			
645		特權	Patents
	.1	發明	Inventors and inventions
	.3	意匠	Designs and models
	.7	商標	Trade marks
646			
647		展覽	Exhibitions
648			
649			
650		工程	Engineering
		建築之關係美術者應入美術類	For artistic part prefer with the arts
	.01	理論　關係	Theories　Relations

.02		
.03	辭書	Dictionaries
.037	年鑑	Yearbooks
.04	評論	Critiques Criticism
.05	雜誌	Periodicals
.06	學會	Societies
.07	研究 教育	Studies Education
.08	總集	Collected works
.09	歷史	History
	依國分	By country
.1	工程數學	Engineering mathematics
.2	工程圖表 圖算	Engineering tables and callations Graphics
.3	工程力學	Mechanics of engineering
.4	工程材料	Materials of engineering and construction
.41	材料強度與試驗	Strength and testing of materials
.42		
.43		
.44		
.45	木料	Wood
.46	石料	Stone
.47	磚瓦陶磁	Brick, tile, terra cotta, glasses, etc.
.48	鋼鐵及其他金屬	Iron and steel, alloys, and other matels
.49	其他如紙, 布, 等	Others as paper, cloth, etc.
.5		

	.6		
	.7	風壓之於工程	Wind pressure in relation to engineering
	.8	工程用具	Engineering machinery, tools, and implements
	.9	測量	Surveying
651		土木工程	Civil engineering
	.1	建築工程	Structural engineering (General)
	.11	建築構造	Systems of construction
	.115	木造	Wooden construction
	.116	石造	Masonry construction
	.118	鋼鐵構造	Iron and steel
	.119	其他構造	Other
	.12	建築設計	Plans Execution of works
	.122	圖樣	Architectural drawings
	.123		
	.124	價格	Estimates Costs
	.125	合同	Contracts Agreements
	.126		
	.127	監督	Superintendence
	.13	基礎工事	Foundations
	.135	臺架工事	Scaffolding
	.14	土工術 土夫	Earthwork
	.143	掘鑿法	Excavations Rock excavation
	.15	木工術 木匠	Carpentry and joinery
	.16	石工術 瓦工術	Masonry
		琢石, 砌磚, 蓋瓦	Stonecutting, bricklaying, etc.
	.17	圬工 油漆匠	Plastering, paintings works
	.18	鋼鐵術	Metal-works (Cutting, bending, etc.)

.19		其他建築小工	Minor works
.2			
.3		房屋建築	Building construction
.4			
.5		橋樑工程	Bridge engineering
.501		橋樑種類　依材料分	Bridges according to the material used
	5.木橋		Wooden bridges
	6.石橋		Masonry bridges
	8.鐵橋		Bridges of metal
	9.其他		Bridges of other materials
.502		橋樑種類　依用途分	Bridges according to purpose
	1.路橋　步道橋		Road bridges
	3.棧道		Viaducts
	5.水道橋		Canal and aqueduct bridges
	7.軍用橋		Military and temporary bridges
.503		橋樑種類　依形式分	Bridges according to outline or type
		直橋，曲橋，等	Right, curved bridges
.505		橋樑設計	Determination and computation of bridges
		圖案，荷重，等	Designs, loads, etc.
.506		橋樑位置　路線	Location　Approaches
.507			
.508		橋樑細部構造	Bridge details
		基礎，橋脚，橋墩，等	Foundations, piers and abutments
.51		桁樑　桁樑橋	Girders and girder bridges
.52		鐵樑橋	Metal lattice bridges
.53		鐵管式橋　箱樑橋	Metal tubular bridges
.54		吊橋	Suspension, bridges
.55		拱橋	Archt bridges
.56		混合建築	Bridges of composite construction

.57	移動橋	Movable and shifting bridges
.571	跳橋　摺橋	Bascule: folding, etc.
.573	旋轉橋	Swing: turning, etc.
.575	昇降橋	Lifting
.577	浮橋	Pontoon bridges: floating, raft, etc.
.579	其他	Other movable bridges
.58	特殊橋樑	Special bridges
	例　公園, 等橋樑	e.g. Park and ornamental bridges, etc.
.6	隧道工程	Tunnel engineering Tunneling
.7	道路工程	Roads and pavements
.71	材料　設計	Materials for road-making
.73	基礎工事	Constructive details
		Foundations
	陰溝, 排水, 輾轉, 等	Culverts, drainage, rolling, etc.
.75	鋪路	Pavements
	木, 石, 磚, 等	Wood, brick, stone, asphalt, concrete, etc.
.76	道路種類 依材料分	Roads, according to the materials used
.761	砂土	Earth and sand
.762	砂礫	Gravel
.763	碎石	Broken stone
.765	混合土	Concrete roads
.767	黑油	Tarred roads
.77	道路種類　依用途分	Roads according to the importance or purpose
.771	鄉村道路　村路 寬路, 狹路, 等	Rural roads Wide, narrow, etc.
.773	城市道路	City or town roads
	大路　街　街中大路	Thoroughfares, avenues, boulevards, etc.

	小路　狹街　衖衕	Narrow streets, alleys, etc.
.78	道路維持與修補	Road maintenance and repair
.79	清道	Cleaning, sweeping
.8	鐵道工程	Railway engineering
	鐵道管理與運用 見 633.3	For railways managements and operation see 633.3
.81	鐵道建築	Railway construction
.811	路線	Route
	測量	Locating surveys
.812	路基　軌道	Roadbed Permanent way
.813	鐵軌及其附件	Rails and accessories
	鐵軌鑽桿, 等	Rail braces, etc.
.814	車輛	Rolling stock
	機車　見 655.27	For locomotives　see 655.27
.816	信號, 避綫, 等	Signals, turnouts, etc.
.817	鐵路設備	Road equipments
	欄杆, 閘門, 月台 站, 車站, 等	Fences, gates, platforms, stations, etc.
.818	鐵路維持與修補	Railroad maintenance and repair
.82	登山鐵道	Inclined and mountain railways
.83	吊懸鐵道	Suspension railways
.84	單軌鐵道	Single-rail railways
.85	綱索鐵道　齒軌鐵道	Cable railways　Rack railways
.86	高架鐵道	Elevated railways
.87	地底鐵道	Underground railways
.88	電氣鐵道	Electric railways
.89	其他鐵道	Others
	城市鐵道, 工場鐵道, 等	Municipal and street, industrial railways, etc.
.9		

653 衛生及城市工程　　Sanitary and municipal engineering

.1	自來水　給水 （工業與家用）	Water-supply for industrial and domestic purpose
.11	水率	Water-rates
.12	水質	Qualities of water
.13	水之檢驗與分析	Examination and analysis of water
.14	水源 井，泉，江河，等	Sources of water-supply Wells, rivers, lakes, ponds, etc.
.15		
.16	貯水池	Reservoirs
.17	水道	Aqueducts, conduits, etc.
.18	水之清净與蒸溜	Purification and filtration of water-supply
.19	農用給水與其他	Water-supply for farms, country houses, etc.
.2	路燈	Street light
.3	排污工事 公共衛生	Sewerage and municipal refuse
.31	溝渠污物及其處理	Sewerage systems
.32	乾溝	Dry sewerage systems
.33	水溝	Water carriage systems
.34	陰溝	Sewers
.35	糞便處理 公共厠所	Sewage disposal Public closets, etc.
.36	塵埃及其他廢物	Municipal refuse and waste
.37	大氣污物	Pollution of atmosphere
.4	工場衛生工程	Industrial and factory sanitation

.5	房屋衛生工程	Sanitary engineering of building
.6	鄉村衛生工程	Rural sanitary engineering
.7	洗店衛生工程	Wash-houses and public laundries
.8		
.9	其他衛生工程	Other sanitary engineering
	公園，浴室，等衛生工程	Parks, public baths, etc.

654　水利工程　　　　Hydraulic engineering

　　　　給水　見 653.1　　　　　For water-supply　see 653.1

.1	應用水力學	Technical hydraulics
	互見水力學	see also hydaulics
.11	靜力	Hydrostatics
.12	動力	Hydrodynamics
.18	測水器	Hydraulic instruments, meters, registers, etc.
.2	海岸工程	Coast protective works
	防波堤，海岸石垣，等	Breakwaters, sea-walls, embankments, dunes, etc.
.3	港灣工程	Harbor works
.31	船渠	Docks
.33	棧橋	Piers
.35	岸壁	Quays
.36	碼頭	Wharves
.37	乾船渠	Dry-docks
.38	浮船渠	Floating docks
.4	燈塔	Light-houses (Construction, and equipment)
.41	位置	Location
.42	圖案	Design

.43	基礎工事	Foundations
.44	上部建築	Superstructure
.45		
.46	浮標	Lighted beacons and buoys
.47	燈船	Light-ships
.48	霧靄警報	Fog signals
.49	其他	Others
.5	湖泊工程	Lake protective works
.6	江河工程	River protective works
.61	測量	Surveying, sounding
.62	堤防	Levees, jetties
.63	挖泥　起石	Dredging and rock removal
.64	分水嶺	Watersheds
.65		
.66	冲蝕防護	Erosion and erosion protection
.67	洪水防護	Floods and flood protection
.68	閘堰	Dams
.69	其他	Others
.7	運河工程	Canal engineering
.8	灌漑工程	Irrigation engineering
	填築工程	Reclamation
.81	起水灌漑	Irrigation by pumping
.82	灌漑斜槽及其水道	Irrigation flumes and conduits
.83	水門構造	Gates and other incidental structures
.85	沙漠荒地之灌漑	Flooding of deserts and waste lands
.87	排水	Drainage
	陸地排水	Land drainage
	淤泥，沼澤，湖泊，等之填築	Reclamation of bogs, swamps, lakes, etc.

655　機械工程　　　　　Mechanical engineering

	總論機械電氣工程諸	Mechanical and electrical engineering
	作類此	conbined
.1	機械學	Mechanics applied to machinery
.11	機構原理	Principles of mechanism
	機動學	Kinematics of machinery
.12	機械動轉	Mechanical movements
.13	機械設計　圖案	Machine design and drawing
.15	機械模型	Mechanical models
.16	裝置機件	Erecting work
.17	原動力　熱力機	Prime movers in general Heat engines
	畜力機，其他	Animal motors, etc.
.2	汽機工程	Steam engineering
.21	蒸汽	Steam (including heated fluids)
.22	蒸汽生發　汽鍋	Steam generation　Boilers
.221	燃料　燒燃	Fuels　Combustion
.223	火爐	Furnace　Stoves
.225	汽鍋　汽罐	Boilers
	1.構造	Construction　Setting
	2.種類	Types
	5.附件	Accessories
	水表，浮尺，等	Watergages, floaters, etc.
.227	蒸汽傳導　裝管	Steam transmission and distribution Piping
.23	汽力發電所	Steam boiler and power plants
.25	汽機　種類及其構造	Types of engines: structural
.251	原式機	Primitive
.252	單動機	Single acting
.253	雙動機	Double acting
.254	依傳力分	According to transmission of motion

	直接與間接傳力機	Direct and indirect
.255	依位置分	According to position
	平置，直立，擺動，斜置，等	Horizontal, vertical, inclined, etc.
.256	依壓力分	According to terminal pressure
	低壓，高壓機	Condensing, noncondensing, etc.
.257	依膨脹分	According to expansion
	單段，二段，三段，四段膨脹機	Single, double, triple, quadruple expansions
.258	其他	Other
.259	細部構造	Steam engines—Design and construction
	汽筒，蒸汽圍套，活塞，叉頭，曲柄，軸，整速輪，嚚鍵，調速器，凝汽器，等	Cylinder, steam-jacket, piston, crand, shaft, fly-wheel, valve-gears, governors, condensers, etc.
.26	輪船汽機　見 659.16	Marine engines　see 659.16
.27	機車　車頭	Locomotives
.271	理論	Theory of the locomotive
	拖力　馬力	Tractive force, horsepower, etc.
.272	種類	Types
	貨車頭，礦用車頭，等	Freight engines, mining engines, etc.
.273	機車汽鍋	Locomotive boilers
.274	機車機關　汽機	Engine of the locomotive
.275	煤水車	Tenders
.278	機車保存與修理	Locomotive maintenance and repair Lubrication
.279	機車廠	Locomotive works and shops
.29	其他汽機	Other steam engines
.291	牽輓汽機	Traction engines
.292	便移汽機	Portable engines
.293	農用汽機	Farm engines

.295		汽輪機	Steam turbines
.298		特式往復汽機	Reciprocating engines of unusual form
.299		其他特式汽機	Steam engines of other forms not reciprocating
		水蒸汽力機，等	Eolipiles, etc.
.3	水力機		Hydraulic engines or motors
.31		水力發電所	Hydraulic power plants
.33		水車	Water-wheels
.331		上射水車　汲水車	Overshot or bucket wheels
.332		下射水車　浮水車	Undershot or impulse wheels and floating wheels
.335		水輪機	Turbines
.35		水壓機　蓄水機	Water pressure engines Accumulators
.36		水力機械與其應用	Hydraulic machinery and appliances
		水力引重機，起重機，昇降機，等	Funicular engines, hoists, elevators, etc.
.37		汲水機	Pumps and pumping engines
		手吸水機，自動起水機，等	Hand-pumps, hydraulic rams, etc.
.4	空氣機，瓦斯機，等		Air and gas engines, etc.
.41		熱風機	Hot air engines
.42		瓦斯機	Gas engines
.43		內燃機	Internal combustion engines
.44		石油機	Oil and gasoline engines
.45		火酒機	Alcohol motors
.46		其他內燃機	Others
.48		風車	Windmills
.49		日光機	Solar engines—Utilization of energy in sun's rays

.5	氣力機械	Pneumatic machinery
.51	空氣制動機	Air-brakes
.52	抽氣機	Air-pumps
.53	送風機　扇風機	Blowers and fans　Exhausters
.55	氣壓機	Compressed air
	噴沙機	Sand blast
.56	真空汲筒及機械	Rarefied air and vacuum appliances
.57	氣管與傳導	Pneumatic tubes and carriers
.58	管中瓦斯流動	Flow of gases in pipes
	空氣計	Air meters
.6	製冷機械	Mechanical refrigeration
.67	製冰　見 664.8	Icemaking　see 664.8
.7	機械　機械廠	Machinery, machine-shops and machine-shop practice
.71	馬力及其傳導	Power and power transmission
.72	驗力器	Measurement of power Dynamometers
.73	馬力調節	Regulation and control of power Governors
.74	軸動　軸	Shafting
.75	軸承	Bearings
.76	添油與摩擦	Lubrication and friction
.77	調帶裝置	Bell gearing　Belt transmission
.78		
.79	機械廠	Machine-shops and machineshop practice
.791	建築	Building and arrangement
.793	管理	Management of machine-shops

.795		機廠工事	Machine-shop practice
.797		機件，用具	Machine and hand tools
.799		其他	Others
.8		舉重與運輸機械	Hoisting and conveying
.81		舉重機	Hoisting machinery
.82		起重車　吊車	Cranes and derricks
.83		昇降機	Elevators
.84		其他	Others
.85		運輸機	Conveying machinery
.86		運煤機	Coal-handling machinery
.87		五穀起運機	Grain-elevator machinery
.88		其他	Others
.89			
.9		其他特殊機械	Other special machinery
.91		縫紉機	Sewing machines
.92			
.93			
.94			
.95		包裹機	Wrapping machinery
.96			
.97		書寫　印刷等機	Machines for writing, shorthand, printing, stamping, etc.
.98			
.99			
657		電氣工程	Electrical engineering
		電學　見 537	For electricity in general, see 537
		工藝電化學　見 662	For industrial electrochemistry, see 662
.1		電氣測定	Electric measurements and testings

.11	電氣單位	Electric units
.12	電氣計	Electric meters
.13	電阻測定：誘導	Resistances meters: inductance, capacity
.14	電位測定：電壓	Potential meters: voltage
.15	強度測定：電流	Intensity meters: current
.16	電量測定	Quantity or work meters
.17	電能與電力測定	Energy and power meters
.18	周波測定　記振器等	Frequency meters Oscillographs etc.
.19	其他測定	Other electric measurements
.2	生電　發電	Production of electric energy or power
.21	電力傳導	General transmission (transformation) of power
.22	熱力發電	Production from heat
.221	汽力發電	Production from steam
.223	瓦斯發電	Production from gas
.225	其他	Production from other sources of heat
.23	水力發電	Production from waterpower
.24	風力發電	Production from wind-power
.25	化學作用發電	Direct production from chemical action
.26	依電流分	Production clast by character of the electric current
	直流	Direct-current engineering
	交流	Alternating-current engineering
.27	海潮利用發電	Production from tide
.28	太陽利用發電	Production from sun

.29	發電所　總發電所　變電所	Power-plants Central stations Substations
.3	電氣機械與附件	Dynamo-electric machinery and auxiliaries
.4	動電機(直流, 交流)	Dynamo-electric machinery (both D.C. and A.C.)
.401	理論	Theory of dynamo-electric machinery
.402	整電與電刷阻電	Commutation and brush-resistance
.403	標準	Standards
.404	測定	Testing
.407	構造	Design and contruction
.408	種類	Types
.409	其他	Miscellaneous Special
.41	發電機(直流, 交流)	Generators—General (D. C. and A. C.)
.42	電動機(直流, 交流)	Motors—General (D.C. and A.C.)
.43	變壓機(直流, 交流)	Transforming machinery (D.C. and A. C.)
.44	直流電氣機械	Direct-current machinery
.441	理論	Theory
.442	測定	Testing
.443	構造	Design and construction
.444	種類	Types
.446	直流發電機	Direct-current generators or dynamos
.447	直流電動機	Direct-current motors
.448	直流變壓機	Direct-current transforming machinery
.449	其他直流機械	Other D.C. machinery
.45	交流電氣機械	Alternating-current machinery
.451	理論	Theory
.452	測定	Testing

.453		構造	Design and coustruction
.454		種類	Types
.456		交流發電機	Alternating-current generators
.457		交流電動機	Alternating-current motors
.458		交流變壓機	Alternating-current transforming machinery
.459		其他交流機械	Other A.C. machinery
.48		動電機附件	Apparatus auxiliary to dynamo-electric machinery
		配電盤，開閉器，整流器，變流器，繼電機，等	Switchboards, switches, regulators, converters, relays, etc.
.6		傳電　配電	Distribution or transmission of electric power
.61		電路	The electric circuit
.62		配電測定	Testing of distribution systems
.63		配電系統	Systems
.631		直流系統	Direct-current systems
.633		交流系統	Alternating-current systems
.639		其他	Other systems
.65		電線與傳電體	Lines and conductors
.651		天線	Overhead or aerial lines
.652		地線	Underground lines
.653		海底電線	Cables and conductors
.655		屋內電線	Interior or indoor wiring
.659		其他	Other
.67		絕緣與絕緣物	Insulation and insulators
.68		安全裝置	Protective devices
.687		避電線	Line lightning arresters
.69			

.8	電力應用	Applications of electric power
.81	電燈	Electric lighting
.811	電燈發電所	Central stations for lighting
.812	電燈機械	Machinery for lighting
.813		
.814	電燈系統	Systems of electric lighting
	1.電燈	Electric lamps
	3.弧光燈	Arc lighting
	5.白熱電燈	Incandescent lighting
	7.放電電燈	Neon gas lighting
.816	特用電燈	Special uses of electric lighting
	探海燈，路燈，以及劇場，鋪店，家用電燈	Search light, street lighting, theatre, store, and house lighting
.817	電熱	Electric heating
	電熱器，電爐，等	Electric heaters, furnaces, etc.
.818	電燃燒	Electric ignition
.82		
.83	電報　電信	Electric telegraphy
.831	發電所　電報所	Telegraphy plants　Stations
.832	按線　接線	Construction　Connections
	天線，地線，等	Overhead lines, underground lines, etc.
.833	電信器	Instruments of telegraphing
	1.傳電器	Transmitting: keys, etc.
	3.繼電器	Intermediate and accessory
	5.受信器	Receiving instruments
	7.自動傳電受信器	Automatic transmitting and receiving instruments
.835	電信系統	Telegraphy　Systems
	1.針指電信	Needle telegraphy, etc.

		2.手動電碼電信	Hand operated code telegraphy
		3.自動電碼電信	Automatic code telegraphy
		5.印刷電信	Printing telegraphy
		7.書寫電信	Writing telegraphy
		8.光線電信	Facsimile telegraphy
		9.其他	Other wire systems
	.837	海底電信	Submarine telegraphy
	.838	無線電信	Wireless telegraphy Radiotelegraphy
.85		電話	Electric telephony
	.851	電話局	Telephone plants Stations
	.852	按線 接線	Construction Connections
	.853	電話器	Systems and instruments for transmitting sound
	.857	自動電話	Automatic and semi-automatic telephone systems
	.858	非電電話	Non-electric telephony
.86			
.87		電相	Phototelegraphy Picture telegraphy The electric eye
.88			
.89			
.9		其他電氣應用	Other applications of electricity
.91			
.92			
.93		家庭電汽裝置	Domestic electric installation
		電鈴，電氣警報，電鐘，電氣信號，等	Electric bells, alarms, clocks, signaling, etc.
.94			
.95		電氣鐵道	Electric traction
.96			

.97	電氣自動車	Electric vehicles
.98		
.99	其他電氣工業	Miscellaneous electrical industries
658	**鑛業工程　鑛業**	**Mining engineering　Mineral industries**
	鑛物　見　鑛物學	For minerals, see mineralogy
.02	鑛毒	Mineral pollution
.05	雜誌	Periodicals
.09	歷史	History
.1	鑛業經濟	Mining economics
	鑛業政策	Mining policy
.2	探鑛　探鑛法	Prospecting　Practical prospecting
.21	鑛床	Ore deposit
.23	評價	Mine examination and valuation Selling
.25	測量	Mine surveying
.3	開鑛工事	Practical mining operations
.31	掘鑿	Excavating and quarrying
.32	錐鑽　爆炸	Drilling and blasting
.33		
.35	隧道　橫坑道	Tunneling, drifting
.36	窒塞	Stoping
.37	架構	Timbering
.4	安全工事	Safety measures
.41	通風　光線	Ventilation and lighting of mines
.43	排水	Mine drainage
.45	失虞	Dangers and accidents in mines and quarries

	.47	救急	Rescue work, first aid, etc.
	.5	鑛務鐵道與運輸	Mine transportation, haulage, and hoisting
	.6	鑛務機械	Mining machinery, tools, etc.
	.7	鑛務電氣工程	Electrical engineering in mines—General
	.8	採鑛	Special kinds of mining Exploitation
		鐵鑛，金鑛與銀鑛，銅鑛，等	Iron, gold and silver, copper mining, etc.
	.9	選鑛	Ore dressing and milling
659		其他工程	Other branches of engineering
	.1	船舶工程　航海術	Naval architecture and Nautics
		戰艦潛水艇構造見 659.39	War vessels, submarine see 659.39
	.101	理論	Theory of the ship
	.105	雜誌	Periodicals
	.109	歷史	History
	.11	船舶設計與構造	Design and construction
	.114	木船構造	Wooden ships
	.116	鐵船構造	Steel and iron ships
	.13	船舶	Special types of vessels
		快艇，小舟，划船，帆船，以及其他特用船舶	Yachts, boats, rowboats, sailboats, and vessels for special uses
	.15	船舶裝設	Structural arrangements of ships
		電燈，裝管，等	Lighting, heating of ships, etc.
	.16	船舶機械	Marine engines
	.163	汽鍋	Marine boilers
	.165	航馳器	Resistance and propulsion of ships

.167		機械附件	Accessories to marine engines
.17		船舶用具	Appliances pertaining to ships
		錨，繩纜，等	Anchors, cables, etc.
.18		船廠	Marine building, shops, etc.
.19		航海術	Nautics Navigation Shipping
.191		航海天文　見　天文學	Navigation and nautical astronomy see astronomy
.192		航海用具:指南針, 等	Nautical instruments; Ships' compasses
.193		航線測量	Hydrographic surveying
.194		駕駛	Shipping
.195		引航	Sailing directions Pilot guides
.196		航海燈塔　信號	Lighthouse, signals, etc.
.197		失虞與救護	Shipwrecks and fires Life-saving Salvage
.198		潛水術	Diving
.199		其他	Others
.3	海陸軍工程		Military and naval engineering
.31		堡壘　礮臺	Fortifications
.32		圍攻工程　地雷	Siege operations Mines
.33		防禦工程	Defensive operations
.34		造兵廠　火藥局	Arsenals Firearms, ordnance and projectiles
.35		鎗礮製造	Gunnery
.36		軍用道路，橋樑與建築	Military roads, bridges and buildings
.37		軍用信號	Military signals
.38			
.39		戰艦　水雷　等	War vessels Torpedoes Etc.
.4	航空工程		Aeronautics Aviation
		航空力學	Mechanics of flight Aerodynamics
.41		航空	Air navigation

.42	航空指南	Sailing directions
.43	航空機械構造	Construction of flyingmachines, etc.
.44	飛船　飛機	Air-ships　Aeroplanes
	氣球　飛下傘	Balloons　Parachutes
.45		
.46	航空燃料	Fuel for airship engines
.47	飛機場　航埠	Landing-fields, airports, etc.
.48	飛機貯藏處	Hangars
.49	紙鳶　風箏	Kites
.5		
.6		
.7	自動車工程	Motor vehicles　Cycles
.71	汽車	Automobiles（by power）
.72	蒸汽	Steam automobiles
.73	瓦斯	Gasoline automobiles
.74	火酒	Alcohol automobiles
.75	電氣	Electric automobiles and their batteries
.76		
.77	自行車	Cycles　Bicycles
.78	自動自行車　摩托車	Motor-cycles
.79		
.8		
.9	其他	Other special engineering
660	化學工業	Chemical technology
.5	雜誌	Periodicals
.7	研究	Studies

.9	歷史	History
661	**化學品　化學藥品**	**Chemicals**
.1	無機化學藥品	Inorganic chemicals
.2	原素及其化合物	Chemical elements and compounds
.3	酸類	Acids
	硫酸，鹽酸，硝酸	Sulphuric, hydrochloric, nitric
.4	鹼類	Alkalies
	炭酸鉀，炭酸鈉或蘇打，阿摩尼亞	Potash, soda, ammonia
.5	鹽類	Salts
	鹽化物，硝酸鹽，硫酸鹽	Ammonia salts, nitrates and sulphates
.6	酸化物	Oxides
.7	瓦斯　煤氣	Gases
.8	其他無機化學藥品	Other inorganic chemicals
.9	有機化學藥品	Organic chemicals
.97	植物	Vegetable products
.98	動物	Animal products
662	**電氣化學工業**	**Industrial electrochemistry**
	電化學	Chemistry
.1	電解工業	Electrolytic technology
.2	水之電解	Electrolysis of water
.3		
.4		
.5	電熱化學工業	Electrothermal technology
.6		

	.7	電鍍工業	Electroplating technology
	.73	電鍍物品	Electroplated ware
	.75	鍍銀　鍍金	Silver-plating, gold-plating, etc.
	.8		
	.9		
663		爆炸品　烟火製造	Explotives and pyrotechnics
	.1	火藥	Explosives
	.11	黑色火藥	Gunpowder
	.13	無烟火藥	Smokeless powder
	.15	綿火藥	Nitrocellulose compounds Guncotton
	.17	炸藥	Nitroglycerine compounds Dynamite
	.2		
	.3	導火線　信管	Fuses, caps, fulminates
	.4	火藥貯藏	Storage and handling Thaw houses
	.5	烟火製造	Pyrotechnics
	.6	火柴	Matches
	.7	燃料	Fuel
		木柴，煤炭，等	Wood, coal, etc.
	.8	燃燒副料	By-products of combustion
	.9	其他	Others
664		食物　飲料	Foods　Beverages
	.1	糖工業	Sugar manufacturing and refining
	.2	澱粉工業	Starch manufacturing
	.3	糊精工業	Dextrine manufacturing
	.4	香料工業	Flavoring extracts
	.41	醬油	Chinese and Japanese soy
	.43	醋	Vineger

.45	味精	
.49	其他	Others
.5	醱酵工業　酒　醇	Fermentation industries　Beverages　Alcohol
.51	酒　釀酒	Wines and wine-making
.53	啤酒麥酒釀造	Brewing and malting
	啤酒，麥酒，米酒，等	Beer, ale, rice-beer, etc.
.55	蒸溜酒	Distilling
	醇　酒精　火酒	Alcohol
	白蘭地，威士忌，等	Brandy, whiskey, etc.
.57	菓子露	Fruit juice
.6	非醇飲料	Non-alcoholic beverages
.61	人造鑛泉	Artificial mineral waters
.63	蘇打	Soda-water
.66	檸檬，等	Lemond-water, etc.
.7	茶類	Tea
	可可，咖啡，等	Cocoa, coffee, etc.
.8	製冰業	Refrigeration and icemaking
.9		
665	**油脂工業　照明工業**	**Fat industries　Illuminating industries**
.1	油脂解析	Oil analysis
.2	植物油脂	Vegetable oils
	棉油，麻油，松脂，橦油，等	Cottonseed oil, linseed oil, rosin-oil, tung-oil, etc.

	.3	動物油脂	Animal fats, oils, etc.
	.4	蜂臘	Beeswax
	.5	鑛油	Mineral oils and waxes
		石油，煤油，石臘，等	Petroleum, gasoline, paraffin, etc.
	.6		
	.7	照明工業	Illuminating industries
	.71	火炬	Torches
	.72	燭	Candles
	.73	燈	Lamps
	.75	瓦斯照明	Illuminating and fuel gas
	.77	鈣光	Calcium light
	.79	其他	Others
	.8		
	.9		
666		窰業	Clay industries
	.1	陶磁	Ceramic technology
	.11	陶器	Potteries Earthenwares
	.13	磁器	Porcelains Stoneware
	.15	土器	Terra-cotta
	.2		
	.3	磚瓦	Bricks and brick-making
			Tiles(clay, cement, etc.)
	.4		
	.5	玻璃	Glass and glass-making
	.6	琺瑯	Glazes, enamels, etc.
	.7	人造寶石	Artificial gems

	.8	水泥　石灰　等	Cementindustries Cement, lime, mortar, etc.
	.9		
667		漂染工業	Bleaching, dyeing, color-making, etc.
	.1	漂白	Bleaching, cleaning, etc.
	.2	染料　染色	Dyes　Dyeing
	.3		
	.4		
	.5	印花	Textile printing, calicoprinting, cotton dyeing
	.6		
	.7	顏料，墨水，漆，等	Paints, pigments, inks, varnishes, etc.
	.71	顏料	Paints and pigments
	.73	墨水	Ink—Manufacture
	.74	畫家墨水	Printers' ink
	.75	漆	Varnishes　Lacquer
	.77	靴墨	Blacking
	.8		
	.9	其他	Others
668		其他化學工業	Other chemical industries
	.1	化粧品	Perfumery and cosmetics
	.11	香料　香水	Perfumes　Essences
	.12	皮膚滋潤品：雪花膏，等	Nutriments of skin

.13	毛髮滋潤品：生髮油，等	Nutriments of hair
.15	口齒滋潤品	Nutriments of mouth
.16	容顏，粉，胭脂，眉墨，等	Face powdering, etc.
.17	染髮油	Dyes of hair
.2	肥皂	Soaps and soap-making
.3	樹膠　樹脂	Glue and gelatine Resins in general
.4	纖維化學工業	Cellulose in general
.41	人造象牙	Celluloid
.43	人造絲	Artificial silk (Rayon)
.5	木材乾溜	Wood distillation
.6	石炭油　油脂	Coal-tar and coal-tar products
.7	肥料	Fertilizers
.77	人造肥料	Artificial fertilizers
.8	塗料	Plastic materials
.9	其他	Others
669	**冶金學**	**Metallurgy**
.1	鍛鍊工事	General factors of smelting, refining, etc.
.11	鎔礦爐	Blast furnaces
.13	驗熱器	Pyrometry
.15	鎔渣	Slags
.17	冶金廠	Plants
.2	化學工事	Chemical preparation
.21	混合	Amalgamation

.23	氯化	Chlorination
.25	靖化	Cyanide process
.27	鎔化	Flux
.3		
.4	電氣冶金學	Electric metallurgy
.5	試金學	Assaying
.6	合金學	Alloy
.7	金相學	Metallography
.8		
.9	特殊金屬	Metallurgy of special metals
.91	金　銀	Gold and silver
.92	鐵　鋼	Iron and steel
.93	銅	Copper
.94	鉛	Lead
.95	汞	Mercury
.96	錫	Tin
.97	鋅	Zine
.99	其他	Other metals
.991	銻	Antimony
.992	鎘	Cadmium
.993	鉻	Chromium
.994	鈷	Cobalt
.995	鎂	Magnesium
.997	錳	Manganese
.999	鎳，鉑，鎢，等	Nickel, platinum, tungsten, etc.

670	製造工業		Manufactures
		凡製造品不屬任何其他類者列此，特殊製造品例如汽機等者應入其類	These heads are for such that are not of more interest elsewhere, Special topics, e.g. steam engine, go with the subjects
671	金屬製品		Metal manufactures
.1	鋼鐵製品		Of iron and steel
		鎗，礮，鐘，表，等	Pistols, guns, watches, clocks, etc.
.3	銅製品		Of brass and bronze
.5	金銀製品		Of gold and silver
		首飾	Jewelry
.9	其他金屬製品		Other metal manufactures
672	木料與木製品		Lumber and woodwork
		器具及其他	Furniture, etc.
673	皮革與皮革製品		Leather industries
	鞣製		Tanning
		皮鞋，皮箱，等	Shoes, trunks, etc.
674	紙與紙製品		Paper manufacture and trade
.1	羅紋　水印		Water-marks, etc.
.2	草紙		Papyrus
.3	素紙		Cellulose
.5	羊皮紙		Parchment
.6	木質纖維紙		Wood-pulp industry
.9	文具：筆，等		Stationary: Pens, etc.
675	織品		Textile industries
.02	圖案		Textile design

.03	紡績	Spinning
.04	配列　大小	Sizing
.05	織法	Weaving
.06		
.07	麥塞法	Mercerization
.08	防水法	Waterproofing
.09	紡織機	Textile machinery
.1	麻與麻織品	Flax manufactures
.2	棉與棉織品	Cotton manufactures
.3	毛與毛織品	Woolen manufactures
.4	絲與絲織品	Silk manufactures
	人造絲與其絲織品	Artificial silk and manufactures
.5	其他纖維織品	Other fiber industries
.6	特殊織品	Special fabrics
.7	繩索, 飾帶, 等	Cordage　Rope making　Trimmings　Passementerie
.8		
.9	織品副業	Industries auxiliary to textile industries
676	樹膠與樹膠製品	Rubber and similar products
677	麵粉製造	Flour and grain　Milling industry
678	烟菸製造	Tobacco industry
679	其他製造工業	Other special industries
680	手工業　手藝	Mechanic trades Handcrafts Miscellaneous arts
	其關係製造方面者 見 670	For manufactures and allied industries see 670
681	木工　竹工	Wood-working　Bamboo-work

682	鐵工　銅工　等	Iron-working　Copper-work　Lead-work Etc.
683	漆工	Painting, varnishing, gilding, etc.
684	裁縫	Dressmaking and tailoring Clothing manufacture
685	刺繡	Decorative needlework
686	洗衣	Laundry work
	例　汽機洗衣	e.g. Steam-laundry work
687	理髮	Hair-dressing　Barbers' work
688	其他手藝	Other trades
.1	眼鏡	Optician's trade
.3	帽	Hat-making
.4	扇	Fan-making
.5	傘	Umbrella-making
689	玩具	Amateur manuals　Toys
690	家政　家政學	Domestic science
.9	歷史	History
691	家庭管理	Household management
	家庭經濟	Home economics
	家庭簿記, 預算, 等	Bookkeeping, budgets, accounts, etc.
692	房屋　住宅	Shelter: house, home
	地址, 佈置, 光線, 通風, 煖屋, 器具, 裝飾, 等	Location, plan, light, ventilation, heat, furniture, decoration, etc.

693		衣飾　服制	Clothing　Toilet
	.1	衣料：棉，絲，毛，等	Materials：cotton, silk, fur, etc.
	.3	冠帽　首飾	Millinery　Headgear
	.4	洗濯	Cleaning
	.5	修飾　美容	Toilet　Cosmetics
		結髮，修指，等	Care of hair, nails, etc.
	.6	服制　依性別分	Clothing divided by sex
		男服，女服，童服，等	Clothing for men, women, children, etc.
	.7	服制　依季節分	Clothing divided by seasons
	.8	服制　依用途分	Clothing divided by purpose
	.9	服制　依國分	Clothing divided by country
694		食物	Foods and food supply
	.1	肉食	Animal foods
	.2	菜蔬	Vegetable foods
	.3	香料	Condiments, spices, etc.
	.4	飲料	Beverage
	.5	食物保存：鑵頭	Preservation of foods：Canning, etc.
	.7	飲食主義　美食	Gastronomy, pleasures of the table, dining, etc.
	.9	依國分	By country
695		烹飪	Cookery
696			
697		款待	Household entertainments
698			

699 家庭醫學   Domestic medicine
衛生，看護，育嬰，   Domestic hygiene, home nursing,
等   care of children, etc.

皮高品 著
周 榮 吳芹芳
謝 泉 袁 静 整理

皮高品集
（中）

荆楚文庫編纂出版委員會
武漢大學出版社

美術　Fine arts

700	美術	Fine arts
.1	理論　關係	Theories　Relations
.11	美學　互見190	Esthetics　see also 190
.12	美術解剖	Art anatomy
.13	裸體畫	The nude in art
.15	美術心理	Art psychology
.16	美術鑑賞	Principles of art criticism
	風格，風味，調合，等	Style, Taste, Symmetry, Proportion, Rhythm, etc.
.18	自然美	Beautiful in nature
.19	美術與其他	Art in relation to others
	例　與倫理，音樂，等之關係	e.g. to ethics, music, etc
.2		
.3	辭書	Dictionaries
.37	年鑑	Yearbooks
.4		
.5	雜誌	Periodicals
.6	藝術社	Art societies　Arts clubs
.7	美術館	Art museums, galleries, etc.
.8	總集	Collected works
.9	歷史	History
.91	古代	Ancient
.92	中古	Medieval
.93	近世	Modern
.97	傳記	Biography of the artists

.99	考古	Fine arts-Archeology
701	中國美術	Chinese fine arts
702-9	其他各國美術	Fine arts of other countries
710	建築	Architecture
	其關係工程方面者應入 651.1	For the mechanic part see structural engineering 651.1
.01	美學　關係	Esthetics　Relations
.03	辭書	Dictionaries
.037	年鑑	Yearbooks
.04	評論	Critiques　Criticism
.05	雜誌	Periodicals
.06	學會	Societies
.07	研究	Studies
.08	總集	Collected works
.09	歷史	History
.091	古代	Ancient
.092	中古	Medieval
.093	近世	Modern
.097	傳記	Biography
.1	中國建築	Chinese architecture
.2-.9	其他各國建築	Architecture of other countries
711	建築設計	Plans　Execution of works
.2	圖樣	Architectural drawing
.3	模型	Models and modeling
.7	建築音響學	Architectural acoustics
.8	建築法式	Orders and styles of architecture
712	建築裝飾	Architectural decoration

.1	繪畫	Painted decoration
.2	彫刻	Decoration in relief　Sculptured decoration
.3	灰泥	Decorative plaster
.5	陶器	Terra cotta
.6	嵌石　鑲木	Incrustation　Veneering
.9	其他木工, 鐵工等裝飾	Woodwork, ironwork, etc.

713　建築構造　　　　　Architectural details, motives, etc.

.1	基礎	Foundations
.2	柱墩	Piers　Colums
.3	旋拱	Archt constructions
.4	墻壁	Walls
.5	屋頂	Roofs
.6	地板	Floors and flooring
.7	樓板	Ceilings
.8	門窗	Doors　Gates　Windows
.9	其他	Others

714

715　宗教建築　　　　　Religious architecture

.1	孔教建築:孔廟	Confucian
.2	道教建築:道觀　道宮	Taoist
.3	佛教建築:佛寺	Buddhist
.5	基督教建築:聖殿	Christian

	.6	猶太教建築：會堂	Jewish
	.7	回教建築：清真寺	Moslem
	.9	其他宗教建築	Other religious architecture
	.91	神社	Shrines
	.97	墓地	Mortuary (religious)
716			
717		公共建築	Public building
	.1	政府建築	Governmental
	.2	教育建築	Educational and scientific
	.3	慈善建築	Hospitals and asylums
	.4	監獄建築	Prisons and reformatories
	.5	商務建築	Business and commercial
	.6	運輸建築	Transportation and storage
	.7	工廠建築	Factories　Mills　Etc.
	.8	游藝建築	Refreshment　Recreation
	.9	其他	Other public buildings
718		住宅　別墅	Domestic architecture
			Houses　Dwellings
			Residences
	.2	皇宮	Palaces　Castles
	.3	城市住宅	City house
	.4	俱樂部	Club houses
	.5	旅館	Hotel　Inns　Restaurants
			Apartment houses
			Flats　Tenement house
	.6		

	.7	鄉村住宅	Country homes Villas
			Country seats, manor houses
	.8	海濱山澗住宅	Seaside and mountain cottages
	.9	其他	Minor buildings, etc.
		下房, 厨房, 等	Lodges Servants' quarters
			Kitchens Stables Etc.
719		城市風景	Esthetics of cities
	.1	公園	Public parks and gardens
	.2	公場	Public squares and promenades
	.3	路道	Walks Drives
	.4	紀念碑 墓碑	Monuments
	.5	牌坊 凱旋門	Memorial and triumphal arches
	.6	噴泉	Fountains
	.7	樹木	Trees Hedges Shrubs
	.8	花草	Plants Flowers
720		彫刻	Sculpture
	.01	美學	Esthetics
	.07	研究	Studies
	.08	總集	Collected works
	.09	歷史	History
	.1	中國彫刻	Chinese sculpture
	.2-.9	其他各國彫刻	Sculpture of other countries
721		彫刻材料與技術	Technique, tools, materials
	.1	模型	Models and modeling
	.2	顏色	Color Polychrome
	.7	陽文彫刻	Sculpture in relief

中國十進制分類法及索引 | 525

722	泥塑	Plaster and clay
723	木彫	Wood carving
724	石刻　玉琢	Stone carving
		Gems carving
725	金鑄	Metel carving
		Bronze carving
726	象刻　骨刻	Ivory and born carving
727	篆刻, 印章, 印譜	Seal engraving　Seals
728	依人體分	Sculpture-Special forms
	像, 半身像, 假面, 等	Statues, busts, masks, etc.
729	依題分	Special subjects
.2	宗教	Religious
.3	神話	Mythological
.5	人物	Human
.7	植物	Plants
.8	動物	Animals
.9	其他	Others
730	繪畫	Arts of design　Graphic arts
		Drawing　Design Painting
	書畫類此	
.01	美學	Esthetics
.05	雜誌	Periodicals
.07	研究	Studies
.08	總集	Collected works
.09	歷史	History
.1	中國畫	Chinese drawing, painting, etc.

		凡中國畫家之作品，	Works of and criticism on Chinese artists
		評傳，等均類此	to be clast here
		依朝代分	By dynasty
	.2-.9	其他各國畫	Drawing, painting, etc. of other countries
731		繪畫材料與畫法	Technique
	.1	圖畫解析	Art anatomy
	.3	配景法	Perspective
	.4	透視法	Projection
	.5	陰影法	Shadow
	.7	儀器畫法	Geometic drawing
732		彩色	Color
733		素畫	Drawing　Design
	.1	木炭畫	Charcoal
	.3	堊筆畫	Crayon
	.5	鉛筆畫	Lead pencil
	.7	墨筆畫	Pen and ink
	.9	其他	Others
734		彩畫	Painting
	.1	水彩畫	Water-color painting
	.2	胡粉畫	Gouache
	.3	單色彩畫	Water monochrome
	.4	蠟畫	Encaustic
	.5	膠畫　漆畫	Pastel　Lacquer
	.7	油畫	Oil painting
735		依畫面分	By surfaces
	.1	墻畫	Walls and ceilings, mural painting

.11	壁畫		Fresco painting
.13	石膏		Gesso
.3	象牙		Ivory
.4	陶磁		Pottery Porcelain
.5	玻璃		Glass
.6	扇		Fans
.7	織繡		Textile fabrics
.8			
.9	全景及其他		Panoramas, etc.

736　依派別分　　　　By style

　　　　1.其性質不指定一國　　1.Not belongs to any particular country
　　　　　之畫派者

　　　　2.國畫宜類入各國　　　2.National styles go under individual country

.1	理想派	Idealist
.2	自然派	Naturalist
.3	寫實派	Realist
.4	象徵派	Symbolist
.5	古典派	Classical
.6	浪漫派	Romantic
.9	其他	Others

737　依畫題分　　　　By subject

.1	自然畫	Sketching from nature
.11	海濱畫　海景	Marine
.12	山水畫　風景	Landscapes
.13	花果　樹木	Flowers and fruit　Trees
.15	静物畫	Still life
.16	建築	Architectural

	.18	動物畫　鳥	Animals and birds
	.3	人物畫	Human figures
	.31	畫像	Portraits
	.33	微小畫像	Portrait miniatures
	.5	宗教畫	Religious　Mythological
	.7	世情　風俗畫	Genre　Epic
	.77	諷刺畫	Caricature　Pictorial humor and satire
	.9	歷史畫	Historical
	.95	戰爭畫	Battle scenes
738		書本彩飾	Illuminating of manuscripts and books
739		書法	Calligraphy
	.1	中國書法	Chinese calligraphy
		下列均可依朝代細分	The follows may be subd. by dynasty
	.12	碑銘	Inscriptions on tablets
	.13	法帖	Copy plates
	.15	墨迹	Autographs　Handwritings
	.17	依字體分	By forms of script
	.171	古文　蝌蚪文	Paleographs　The tadpole characters
	.172	篆字	The seal characters
	.173	隸書	The official text
	.174	楷書	The plain characters
	.175	行書	The cursive hand
	.176	草書	The "grass" characters
	.177	飛白	
	.19	文房	Materials and instruments
		紙，筆，墨，硯，等	Papers, brush pens, ink sticks, ink-stone, etc.

	.2-.9　其他各國書法	Calligraphy of other countries
740	板刻　板畫	Engraving
741	木板	Wood engraving　Xylography
742	金屬板	Metal engraving
.1	銅板	Copper
.2	鋼板	Steel
.4	線刻	Line
.5	點刻	Stipple
.7	蝕刻(水蝕)	Mezzotint and aquaint
.8	蝕刻(乾蝕)	Etching　Dry point
743	石印	Lithography
744	五彩石印	Chromolithography
745	其他彩色印	Color printing other than lithographic
746	機器板	Photo-mechanical engraving
.1	珂羅板	Collotype
.3	石印影板	Photo-lithography
.5	鋅印影板	Zincography
.7	攝影板	Photogravure
747	謄寫板　複寫板	Mimeography
748		
749	印刷板	Printing of engravings
750	攝影　照像	Photography
751	攝影光學	Photo-optics
752	攝影化學	Photo-chemistry

753		攝影器具	Apparatus Materials
	.7	攝影機	Cameras and accessories
754		攝影術	Processes Photographing
755		陰攝法	Negative processes
	.1	濕板　底片	Wet plates
	.2	乾板　照片	Dry plates and films
	.3	顯影	Development
	.4	定影	Fixing
	.5	強烈與縮小攝影	Intensification and reduction
	.7	暗室攝影	Dark rooms
	.8	修片	Re-touching
756		陽攝法	Positive processes
	.1	銀板攝影	Daguerrotypes
	.3	鐵板攝影	Ferrotype (tin types)
	.5	銀鹽陽畫	Silver prints
	.7	藍色板攝影	Blue prints
758		各種攝影	Special applications
	.1	電攝影	Telephotography
	.2	空中攝影	Aerial photography
	.3	彩色攝影	Color photography
	.4	正色攝影	Orthochromatic photography
	.7	活動攝影	Panoramic photography
	.8	幻燈攝影	Lantern slide making
	.9	顯微攝影	Stereoscopic photography
759		照片蒐集與收藏	Collections of photos

760	工藝美術	Art applied to industry　Decoration and ornament
761	美術與技藝運動	Arts and crafts movement
762	裝璜與飾品　圖案	Decoration and ornament　Design
763	室內裝飾	Interior decoration　House decoration
.1	畫品	Special subjects for design
.2	家具	Furniture
.3	地毯	Rugs　Carpets
.4	屏風	Screens
.5	掛綿	Tapestries
.6	壁軸	Upholstery　Well hangings
.7	壁紙	Wall-papers
.9	其他	Others
764	陶磁　七寶	Ceramics　Art pottery, porcelain and cloisonne
765	服裝	Costume and its accessories　Acuary and textile arts
.3	刺繡	Art needle work, embroidery
.5	染色	Dyeing　Artificial colors
766	木器	Woodwork
.2	彫刻	Wood-carving
	參看　723	see also 723
.5	油漆　蒔繪	Lacquer
.7	鏤鑲	Marquetry　Inlaying

767	珠寶		Glyptic arts: Gems, jade, ivory carving, etc.
768	金器		Metal-work: Army and armor, gold and silver, brasses, iron-work, pewter, etc.
769	其他		Others
.1	烙畫		Pyrography
.2	鏤花		Stencil work
.3	印畫		Transfer pictures (decalcomania)
770	音樂		Music (Literature and scores)
.01		哲理與物理音學	Philosophy and physics of music
.011		音響與物理	Acoustics and physics
.012		生理	Physiology
		手	Hand
		聲與術生	Voice and hygiene
.015		心理	Psychology
.017		美學	Esthetics
		欣賞	How to hear, to understand, to enjoy music
.019		關係　影響	"Influence" of music
		音樂與道德, 國家, 婦女, 等	Moral influence of music, the State and music, women and music, etc.
.02		音樂演奏	Technique of music
.021		音素	Elements
.022		符號	Notation and its history
.023		拍子	Time, mensurable music
.024		旋律	Melody
		節奏	Rhythm

.025	和聲　和絃法	Harmony and thorobase (harmony and composition together)
.026	譜曲	Composition
	對位法及其他	Counterpoint, canon, fugue, etc.
.027	樂式	Musical forms
	聲樂，器樂，舞樂，等式	Vocal forms, instrumental forms, dance forms, etc.
.028	樂式與譜曲之分析	Analysis of forms and composition
.029	導演	Interpretation, conducting, etc.
.03	辭書　樂譜　樂典	Dictionaries　Musical terms
.037	年鑑	Yearbooks
.038	指南	Directories
.04	評論	Critiques　Criticism
.05	雜誌	Periodicals
.06	學會	Societies
.07	研究　教學	Instruction, training, study
.073	耳之訓練	Ear training, perception of pitch
.074	眼之訓練	Eye training, music reading
.075	聲之訓練	Singing and voice culture
.077	樂器教學法	Instrumental technics
770.08	總集　文藝	Collected works　Musical fiction, etc.
.09	歷史	History
.091	古代	Ancient
.092	中古	Medieval
.093	近世	Modern
.097	傳記	Biography
.1	中國音樂　邦樂	Chinese music
	參看　柯林之英文中國辭書樂器篇	See Samuel Couling: "The encyclopaedia Sinica" musical instruments

.11	匏：笙	Gourd instruments: the Chinese reed-organ
.12	土：塤或壎	Clay instruments: the Chinese ocarina, etc.
.13	革：晉鼓，應鼓，搏拊，魚鼓，等	Skin instruments: the large drum, the barrel-shaped drum, etc.
.14	木：木魚，拍板，梆子，魚梆，等	Wooden instruments: Mu Yu, P'ai pan or castanets, Pang tzu or wooden drum, etc.
.15	石：玉笛，玉簫，等	Stone instruments: jade flute, etc.
.16	金：鐘，鈴，點子，鑼，鐺子，金鼓，響板，磬，等	Mental instruments: bells, bells with clappers, gongs, flat gong, Chin ku, metal plates, Ch'ing or brass bowl, etc.
.17	絲：風箏，琴，瑟，月琴，琵琶，三絃，胡琴，等	Stringed instruments: Feng cheng, Ch'in, Se, Yueh ch'in or moonguitar, P'i pa, San hsien, etc.
.18	竹：排簫，籥，篪，管，胡笳，等	Bamboo instruments: Pandean pipes, bamboo flute, Ch'ih, Kuan or pipe of wood, Hu chia or double-reed pipe
.19	其他	Others
.2-.9	其他各國音樂	Music of other countries
	聲樂	Vocal music
771	歌曲　歌唱　歌唱團	Song collections Concerted vocal music
.2	民歌	Folk songs Children's songs

	.3	國歌　戰歌	National, patriotic, political, war songs
	.4	讌歌	Festival, society songs
	.5	校歌	School and college songs
	.7	歌唱團	Concerted vocal music
	.71	重唱	Glees Madrigals
	.72	輪唱	Round and catches
	.73	吟誦	Arias　Recitative
	.74	獨唱	Solos
	.75	二人合唱	Duets
	.76	三人合唱	Trios
	.77	四人合唱	Quartets
	.8	歌唱樂室	Chamber vocal music
772		聖樂	Sacred music　Religious
773		劇樂　舞樂	Dramatic music Opera Dance music
		器樂	Instrumental music
774		管樂	Wind instruments
		木管樂器	Wood-wind
	.1	橫笛	Flute family
	.2	豎笛	Oboe family
	.3	單簧樂器	Single reed: Clarinet, etc.
	.4	複簧樂器	Double reed: Oboe, etc.
	.5	其他木管樂器	Other wood-wind instruments
		金屬管樂器	Brass-wind
	.6	喇叭	Trumpet
	.7	滑動喇叭	Trombone

	.8	號筒	Horn
	.9	其他金屬管樂器	Other brass-wind instruments
775		絃樂	Stringed instruments
		彈絃樂器	Plectoral
	.1	豎琴	Harp
	.2	洋琵琶	Lute
	.3	琪塔	Guitar
	.4	其他彈絃樂器	Other plectoral instruments
		例 曼獨鈴，曼獨拉，等	e.g. Mandorin, mandola, etc.
		擦絃樂器	Bowed
	.5	瓔珴琳	Violin
	.6	瓔珴拉 大提琴	Viola
	.7	低音瓔珴琳	Violoncello
	.8		
	.9	其他擦絃樂器	Other bowed instruments
776		鍵樂	Keyboard instruments
	.1	鋼琴	Piano Pianoforte
		豎鋼琴，平鋼琴，變調鋼琴，自動鋼琴，等	Cabinet piano, grand piano, transposing piano, pianola, etc.
	.7	風琴	Organ
		簧風琴，管風琴，等	Harmonium (reed-organ), pipe-organ, etc.
777		打樂 機械樂	Percussions and mechanical instruments
		打樂器	Percussions

	.1	鼓	Drum
	.2	鐃鈸	Cymbals
	.3	三角	Triangle
	.4	其他打樂器	Other percussions
		機械樂器	Mechanical
	.5	手風琴	Barrel-organ
	.6	自動演奏器	Music-box
	.8	蓄音器	Phonographs and records
	.9	其他機械樂器	Other mechanical instruments
778		其他樂與樂器	Other instruments
		其性質不屬任何類者入此	Not belongs to elsewhere
		例 口笛，口琴，等	e.g. Whistling, harmonica, etc.
779		管絃樂合奏　樂團	Instrumental ensemble
			Orchestral music
	.1	朔拿大	Sonata
	.2	交響樂	Symphony
	.3	序曲	Overture
	.4	組曲	Suite
	.5	競奏曲	Concerto
	.6	標題音樂	Program music
	.7	室樂	Chamber music
		三樂合奏，四樂合奏，五樂合奏，六樂合奏，七樂合奏，八樂合奏，九樂合奏	Trios, quartets, quintets, sextets, septets, octets, nonets
	.8		

	.9	聲樂附管絃樂	Music for orchestra with voice
780		演劇　戲園	Expressive arts Theatre
	.01	理論　關係	Theories Relations
	.011	美學	Esthetics
	.015	心理	Psychology
	.019	關係	Relations
		與文學，音樂，宗教，等關係	to literature, music, religion, etc.
	.04	評論	Critiques Criticism
	.05	雜誌	Periodicals
	.07	研究	Studies
	.09	歷史	History
	.1	中國演劇	Chinese theatre
	.2-.9	其他各國演劇	Theatre of other countries
781		戲劇表演	Art of theatre Technique
	.1	排劇　編劇	Dramatic composition
	.11	三一律	The unities
	.15	情節	The plot
	.17	腳色	The characters
	.2	優伶　扮演	Actors and acting
	.22	像片	Iconography Portrait album
	.27	傳記	Biography
	.3	服裝	Costume, make-up
		依國分	By Country
	.4		
	.5	舞臺	Stage and accessories
	.51	佈景	Scenery
	.53	用具佈置	Stage setting

	.55	光線	Lighting
	.6	導演	Stage direction
	.7	音樂	Dramatic music
	.8	管理	Organization and management
		廣告，門票，戲單，等	Advertising, tickets, play bills, etc.
	.9		
782		悲劇與喜劇	Tragedy and comedy
	.1	悲劇	Tragedy
	.2	喜劇	Comedy
783		歌劇	Opera
		例　京劇，崑劇，等	
784		話劇	Prose drama
		例　文明戲	
785		滑稽戲	Farces　Operette
	.5	諷刺歌曲	Burlesques
	.8	小調	Vaudeville　Minstrels
786		街道演劇	Pageants, masques,
		學校演劇等	amateur and college theatricals, and other outdoor plays
787		傀儡戲	Marionettes, pantomines, shadow, puppet plays
788		電影	Moving pictures　Movies
789		其他	Other expressive arts
	.3	馬戲	Circuses
790		游藝　娛樂	Recreative arts　Amusements
791		節會	Season and day festivals

792		舞蹈	Dancing　Balls
	.1	國舞	National dances
	.2	宗教舞	Religious dances
	.3	交際舞	Social dances
		通常與旋轉舞及其他	Minuet, waltz, etc.
	.5	劍舞	Sword dance
	.6	劇舞　舞曲	Theatrical dancing, ballet
	.7	化裝舞	Masked balls, fancy balls
	.8	朝舞	Court balls, State balls
	.9	其他	Others
793		運動會	Public games and sports
794		智力遊戲	Games of skill
		奕棋,撞球,等	Chess, billiards, etc.
795		機遇游戲	Games of chance
		麻雀,撲克,等	Mahjong, poker, etc.
796		文虎　酒令	
797		武術	Fighting sports
	.1	鬥雞走狗	Animal fights: cock, dog, bull, etc.
	.2	決鬥	Dueling
	.3	拳術	Boxing
	.4	劍術	Fencing
	.5	馬上比武	Tournament
	.6	角力	Wrestling
	.7	射擊	Shooting
	.8	戰爭遊戲	War games

.9	其他	Others
798	馬術　賽馬	Horsemanship　Racing
799	其他游藝	Other recreative arts

文學   Literature

800	文學		Literature (General and universal)
.1	理論　關係		Theories　Relations
.18	派別		Systems of literature
.181		理想派	Idealism
.182		寫實派	Realism
.183		浪漫派	Romanticism
.185		自然派	Naturalism
.187		象徵派	Symbolism
.188			
.189		其他文學	Other forms of literature
		1.漁澤文學	Piscatory literature
		2.田園文學	Gardens
		3.山林文學	Mountains
		5.酒色文學	Anacreontic literature
		7.戀愛文學	Erotic literature
.19	關係, 運動, 與時文		Special relations, movements, and currents of literature
.3	辭書		Dictionaries
.4	文藝批評		Literary criticism
		1.其關係詩評詞評等者則入詩詞等類	Criticism on special branches of literature clast with the subject
		2.其關係一國之文評者則入各該國	Criticism on the literature of a particular country clast with that country
.42	文藝著述		Authorship
		著述職業論	Authorship as a profession
.44	批評		Art of criticism
.442		文法方面	Grammatical qualities of style: correctness, etc.

.444	文章　文體方面	Rhetorical qualities of style
.445	創作　個性方面	Personal qualities of style: individuality, etc.
.447	字句方面	Rhetorical technique
.449	其他	Others
.45	剽竊　抄襲	Plagiarism
.46		
.47	文學家之故里	Literary landmarks Homes and haunts of authors
.48	文學家之逸話，爭論，快事，等	Anecdotes, quarrels, and amenities of authors, etc.
	見　800.97	see 800.97
800.5	雜誌	Periodicals
.6	學社	Societies
.7	研究	Studies
	綱目，綱要，答問，等	Outlines, syllabi, questions, etc.
.8	總集	Collected works
	精華錄　備忘錄	Literary extract Commonplace books, etc.
.9	歷史	History
.91	古代	Ancient
.92	中古	Medieval
.93	近世	Modern
.97	文學家傳記	Biography of literate
	1.其有文藝價值者，否則入傳記類	That is, biography regarded as literature
	2.其關係一國之文學家傳記則入各該國	Biography of literate of one country clast with that country

		比較文學	Comparative literature By form
		下列係比較研究	General and comparative
801		詩	Poetry
	.1	牧歌　田園詩	Pastoral poetry: Idyll, eglogue
	.2	宗教詩	Religious poetry
	.3	劇詩	Dramatic poetry
		舞曲，等	Ballet, etc.
	.4	抒情詩（琴歌）	Lyric poetry
	.41	哀歌	Elegiac
	.43	頌歌	Ode
	.45	山歌	Cantate
	.49	其他	Others
	.5	敘事詩（史詩）	Epic (Epic-didactic)
	.6	幽默詩　諷刺詩	Humorous poetry　Satirical poems
	.7		
801.8		短歌	Fugitive poetry
		八行詩，十四行詩，循環詩，三解詩，等	Triolet, sonnet, rondeaux, ballade, etc.
	.9	其他	Others
		描寫，幻想，神秘，戀愛，等詩歌	Poetry of color, dreams, mysticism, platonism, etc.
802		戲曲	Drama
	.1		
	.2	歌劇	Opera
		滑稽歌劇，等	opera bouffe, etc.
	.3	話劇	Prose drama
	.4		

	.5	傀儡劇	Marionettes, Punch and Judg, etc.
		影子戲	Shadow plays
	.6	啞劇　無言劇	Pantomimes
	.7	電影	Moving-picture shows
	.8		
	.9	依性質分	Special forms of plays
	.91	史劇	Historical plays
	.92	宗教劇	Religious plays
	.93	悲劇	Tragedy
	.94	喜劇	Comedy
	.95	樂劇　傳奇劇	Melodrama
	.96	滑稽劇	Farces, burlesques, mimes
	.97	插戲	Interludes, masques, etc.
	.98	雜演	Vandeville　Varieties
803		小說	Fiction
	.1		
	.2	講史	Historical
	.3	筆記	Memoire
	.4	異聞	Mythical
	.5	社會	Social
803.6		家庭	Family
	.7	言情	Epic　Romantic
	.8	武俠　偵探	Chivalric　Detective
	.9	其他	Others
804		民間文學	Folk literature
	.1		

	.2	說本　歌本	Chap-books and chap-book literature
		一種通俗書本記載英雄傳神話等者	Folk tales and legends, etc.
	.3	寓言	Fables　Fairy tales
		以鳥獸或無生物擬人之談話者	
	.4	傳奇　艷事	Prose romances, etc.
	.5	諺語　俚諺	Proverbs　Local songs
	.6	謎語	Folk riddles
	.7	小曲	Chanson-nette
	.8	雜品	Centos　Pasticcios
	.9	其他	Others
805		兒童文學	Juvenile literature
	.1	童歌	Verses for children
	.2	童劇	Juvenile drama
	.3	童話	Conte
	.4	童畫	Juvenile pictural works
	.5	科學　工藝故事	Science and industry tales
	.6		
	.7		
	.8		
	.9	歷史，地理，傳記故事	Historical, geographical and biographical tales
806			
807		散文	Prose
808		其他文學	Other kinds of literature

	.1	函牘文學　書說類	Correspondence, letters
		其有文學價值者，某一類之尺牘則應入該類。尺牘之重在傳記方面者則入傳記類	That is, literary and miscellanious letters, Letters on any one subject go with the subject. A correspondence whose interest is chiefly biographical should be put in biography
	.2	幽默諷刺文學	Humorous and satirical literature
	.3	箴銘類　格言　金言	Maxims, apothegms, mottoes, etc.
	.4	論辯文學　演講錄	Speeches　Orations
	.5	序跋類	Foreward, preface, etc.
		題辭，引言，序文，楔子，書後，等	Dedications, introduction, preface, prologue, epilogue, etc.
	.6		
	.7	傳誌文學　哀祭類	Biographical literature Sacrificial
	.8	游記文學	Travels　Voyages
		日記　回憶錄	Journal, sayings, thought
	.9	雜記　雜事瑣語	Miscellany
810		中國文學	Chinese literature
	.01	理論　關係	Theories　Relations
	.011	哲理　文藝	Philosophy　Esthetics
	.019	關係，運動，與時文	Special relations, movements and currents of literature
		例　文學與美術	e.g. Literature and arts
	.03	辭書	Dictionaries
	.04	文藝批評	Literary criticism
	.05	雜誌	Periodicals
	.06	學社	Societies
	.07	研究	Studies

.08	總集　文學總集	Collections (general)
	歷朝諸家之韻文與	Collections of verses and prose togeth-
	無韻文合刻類此	er in general clast here
	其關係一朝代之文學	
	總集則	
	依朝代分	By dynasty
.081	先秦及秦代(前？—202)	Pre-Ch'in and Ch'in dynasties
.082	兩漢(202—後 220)	Han dynasty
.083	魏晉六朝隋(220—618)	Wei, Chin, the Six dynasties, and Sui
.084	唐五代(618—960)	T'ang and the Five dynasties
.085	宋(960—1280)	Sung dynasty
	遼金(907—1234)	Liao and Ching dynasties
	元(1280—1368)	Yuan dynasty
.086	明(1368—1644)	Ming dynasty
.087	清(1644—1912)	Ch'ing dynasty
.088	民國(1912—　)	The Republic
.09	歷史	History
.091	古代	Ancient
.092	中古	Medieval
.093	近世	Modern
.097	文學家傳記	Biography of literate
	文學別集	Individual collections
	個人之韻文與散文合	of verses and prose together
	刻類此	
	依朝代分	By dynasty
.1	先秦及秦代(前？—202)	Pre-Ch'in and Ch'in dynasties
.2	兩漢(202—後 220)	Han dynasty
.3	魏晉六朝隋(220—618)	Wei, Chin, the Six dynasties, and Sui

.31	魏(220—265)	Wei
810.32	晉(265—420)	Chin
.33	劉宋(420—479)	Sung(House of Liu)
.34	齊(479—502)	Ch'i
.35	梁(502—557)	Liang
.36	陳(557—589)	Ch'en
.37	北朝(386—581)	Northen dynasties
.38	隋(581—618)	Sui dynasty
.4	唐五代(618—960)	T'ang and the Five dynasties
.41	初唐(618—713)	Early period
.42	盛唐(713—780)	Period of glory
.45	中唐(780—847)	Mid period
.48	晚唐(847—907)	Later period
.49	五代(907—960)	The Five dynasties
.5	宋遼金元(960—1368)	Sung, Liao, Ching, and Yuan dynasties
.51	北宋(960—1127)	Northern Sung
.57	南宋(1127—1280)	Southern Sung
.58	遼金(907—1234)	Liao and Ching dynasties
.59	元(1280—1368)	Yuan dynasty
.6	明(1368—1644)	Ming dynasty
.7	清(1644—1912)	Ch'ing dynasty
.71	清初(1644—62)	Early period
.72	康熙時代(1662—1723)	K'ang Hsi period
.75	乾隆時代(1736—96)	Ch'ien Lung period
.78	道光時代(1821—51)	Tao Kuang period
.79	清末(1851—1911)	Later period
.8	民國(1912—)	The Republic

811 韻文 Chinese verses

詩詞歌賦合刻類此

.1 詩 Chinese poetry

.101	理論　關係		Theories　Relations
.103	詩典　詩韻		Dictionary of terms　Rhymes
.104	詩評　詩話		Poetic critiques
.105	雜誌		Periodicals
.106	詩社		Societies
.107	詩法　試帖		Poetic formulas
.108	詩總集		Collected works, general

歷朝詩家各體各派合刻，類此一朝之詩合刻

依朝代分　　　　　　　By dynasty

811.108　　1.先秦及秦代(前?—202)　Pre-Ch'in and Ch'in dynasties

2.兩漢(202—後220)　Han dynasty

3.魏晉六朝隋(220—618)　Wei, Chin, the Six dynasties, and Sui

4.唐五代(618—960)　T'ang and the Five dynasties

5.宋遼金元(960—1368)　Sung, Liao, Ching, and Yuan dynasties

6.明(1368—1644)　Ming dynasty

7.清(1644—1912)　Ch'ing dynasty

8.民國(1912—　)　The Republic

.109　　詩史　　　　　　　History

詩別集(個人詩集)　Individual collections

詩詞合刻諸書不另立類，如作者以詩名則以之入詩，以詞名則以之入詞，其於二者並著，如蘇軾之詩詞然者則入詩

.11　　先秦及秦代(?前—202)　Pre-Ch'in and Ch'in dynasties

.12　　兩漢(202—後220)　Han dynasty

		李陵(124—74)，	Li Ling,
		蘇武(143—60)，等	Su Wu, and others
.13		魏晉六朝隋(220—618)	Wei, Chin, the Six dynasties, and Sui
.131		魏(220—265)	Wei
		曹植(後 192—232)，等	Ts'ao Chih, and others
.132		晉(265—420)	Chin
		2. 陸機(261—303)	Lu Chi
		3. 陸雲(262—303)	Lu Yun
		4. 潘岳(？—303)	P'an Yo
		5. 左思	Tso Ssu
		6. 其他西晉詩家	Other poets, of Western Chin
		7. 陶潛(365—427)	T'ao Chien
		9. 其他東晉詩家	Other poets, of Eastern Chin
.133		劉宋(420—479)	Sung (House of Liu)
		1. 謝靈運(385—433)	Hsieh Ling-yun
		3. 顏延之(384—456)	Yen Yen-chih
		5. 鮑照(421—465)	Pao Chao
		9. 其他	Others
.134		齊(479—502)	Ch'i
		謝朓(464—499)，等	Hsieh T'iao, and others
.135		梁(502—557)	Liang
		沈約(441—513)，等	Shen Yo, and others
.136		陳(557—589)	Ch'en
		徐陵(507—583)，等	Hsu Ling, and others
.137		北朝(386—581)	Northern dynasties
		庾信(513—581)，等	Yu Hsin, and others
.138		隋(581—618)	Sui
811.14		唐五代(618—960)	T'ang and the Five dynasties
.141		初唐(618—713)	Early period
		1. 學士派	Poetry of the Eighteen scholars
		魏徵(580—643)，等	Wei Cheng, and others

	2. 上官體	ShangKuan style
	上官儀(？—664)	ShangKuan Yi
	3. 四傑	The Four heroes
	王勃(618—675), 等	Wang Po, and others
	4. 二大家	The Two great poets
	沈佺期,	Shen Ch'uan-ch'i and
	宋之問	Sung Chih-wen
	5. 陳子昂(656—698)	Ch'en Tse-ang
	7. 四友	The Four friends
	杜審言, 等	Tu Shen-yen, and others
	8. 燕許	Dukes of Yen and Hsu
	蘇頲(670—727),	Su T'ing and
	張說(667—730)	Chang Yueh
	9. 其他	Others
.142	盛唐(713—780)	Period of glory
	王維(699—759),	Wang Wei,
	孟浩然(689—740), 等	Meng Hao-jan, and others
.143	李白(699—762)	Li Po
.144	杜甫(712—770)	Tu Fu
.145	中唐(780—847)	Mid period
	1. 大歷十才子	The Ten genius of Ta-Li period
	韓翃, 等	Han Hung, and others
	2. 韋應物	Wei Ying-wu
	3. 劉長卿	Liu Ch'ang-ch'ing
	4. 韓愈(768—824)	Han Yu
	5. 柳宗元(773—819)	Liu Chung-yuan
	6. 劉禹錫(772—842)	Liu Yu-hsi
	7. 元稹(779—831)	Yuan Chen
	8. 白居易(772—846)	Po Chu-yi
	9. 其他	Others
.148	晚唐(847—907)	Later period
	1. 杜牧(803—852)	Tu Mu

	2. 溫庭筠	Wen Ting chun
	3. 李商隱(813—858)	Li Shang-yin
	4. 段成式(?—863)	Tuan Cheng-shih
	5. 皮日休(?—881)	P'i Jih-hsiu
	6. 陸龜蒙(?—881)	Lu Kuei-meng
	7. 司空圖(837—908)	SsuK'ung T'u
	8. 魚玄機	Yu Hsuan-chi
	9. 其他	Others
.149	五代(907—960)	The Five dynasties
811.15	宋遼金元(960—1368)	Sung, Liao, Ching, and Yuan dynasties
.151	北宋(960—1127)	Northern Sung
	1.西崑體	The Hsi K'un style
	楊億(974—1020),等	Yang Yi, and others
	3.白體	Po Chu-yi's style
	王禹偁(954—1001),等	Wang Yu-ch'eng, and others
	5.晚唐體	Late T'ang style
	寇準(961—1023),等	K'ou Chun, and others
	7.理學詩	Poetry of the philosophers
	周敦頤(1017—73),等	Chou Tun I, and others
.152	歐陽修(1007—72)	OuYang Hsiu
.153	蘇軾(1036—1101)	Su Shih
.154	黃庭堅(1045—1105)	Huang Ting-chien
.156	其他北宋詩家	Other Northern Sung poets
.157	南宋(1127—1280)	Southern Sung
	1.南宋初	Early period
	葉夢得(1077—1148),等	Yeh Meng-te, and others
	2.朱熹(1130—1200)	Chu Hsi
	4.四大家	The Four great poets
	陸游(1125—1210),等	Lu Yu, and others
	5.四靈	The Four Lings
	徐照,等	Hsu Chao, and others

	6.嚴羽	Yen Yu
	7.江湖派	The Wandering poets
	戴復古，等	Tai Fu-ku, and others
	8.遺民詩	The Patriotic poets
	文天祥(1236—82)，等	Wen T'ien-hsiang, and others
	9.其他	Other Southern Sung poets
.158	遼金(907—1234)	Liao and Ching
	元好問(1190—1257)，等	Yuan Hao-weu, and others
.159	元(1280—1368)	Yuan
	虞集(1272—1348)，等	Yu Chi, and others
.16	明(1368—1644)	**Ming dynasty**
.161	明初(1368—1425)	Early period
	劉基(1311—75)，等	Liu Chi, and others
.162	吳中四傑	The Four poets, of Wu-chung
	高啓(1336—74)，等	Kao Chi, and others
.163	臺閣體	The Cabinet's style
	楊士奇(1365—1444)，等	Yang Shih-ch'i, and others
.164	明中(1425—1573)	Mid period
	李夢陽(1472—1529)，等	Li Meng-yang, and others
.166	七才子	The Seven genius
	王世貞(1526—90)，等	Wang Shih-chen, and others
.167	公安體	The Kung An style
	袁宏道，等	Yuan Hung-tao, and others
.168	竟陵體	The Ching Ling style
	鍾惺(1574—1624)，等	Chung Hsing, and others
.169	明末(1573—1644)	Later period
	艾南英(1609—71)，等	Ngai Nan-yin, and others
811.17	清(1644—1912)	**Ch'ing dynasty**
.171	清初(1644—62)	Early period
	錢謙益(1582—1664)，等	Ch'ien Chien-yi, and others
.172	康熙時代(1662—1723)	K'ang Hsi period

	朱彝尊(1629—1709), 等	Chu Yi tsun, and others
.173	漁洋派	Yu Yang style
	王士禎(1634—1711), 等	Wang Shih-chen, and others
.174	反漁洋派	Anti Yu Yang style
	沈德潛(1746—69), 等	Shen Te-chien, ane others
.175	乾隆時代(1736—96)	Ch'ien Lung pariod
	厲鶚(1692—1752), 等	Li O, and others
.177	吳中七子	The Seven poets of Wu-chung
	王鳴盛(1722—97), 等	Wang Ming-shen, and others
.178	道光時代(1821—51)	Tao Kuang period
	鄭珍(1806—61), 等	Cheng Chen, and others
.179	清末(1851—1912)	Later period
	譚獻(1832—1901), 等	T'an Hsien, and others
.18	民國(1912—　)	The Republic
	民國詩集依作家姓氏號碼分	Works of the poets of the Republic to be arranged in accordance with author numbers of the poets
.2		
.3	騷賦	Chinese poetic compositions
.31	楚辭	Elegies of Ch'u
.311	屈原(? 前 340—285)	Ch'u Yuan
.312	宋玉(? 前 290—220)	Sung Yu
.319	其他	Others
.32	漢賦	Of Han dynasty
	賈誼(前 201—169), 等	Chia I, and others
.33	魏晉六朝隋(220—618)	Of Wei, Chin, the Six dynasties, and Sui
	曹植(後 192—232), 等	Ts'ao Chih, and others
.34	唐五代(618—960)	Of T'ang and the Five dynasties
.35	宋遼金元(960—1368)	Of Sung, Liao, Ching, and Yuan dynasties

.36	明(1368—1644)	Of Ming dynasty
.37	清(1644—1912)	Of Ch'ing dynasty
.38	民國(1912—　)	Of the Republic
.4		
.5	樂府	Chinese poetic songs
	按樂府之爲詞者應入詞類	
.6		
811.7	詞(長短句　詩餘)	Chinese poetry of irregular syllables
.701	理論　關係	Theories　Relations
.703	詞典　詞韻	Dictionary of terms　Rhymes
.704	詞評　詞話	Critiques
.705	雜誌	Periodicals
.706	詞社	Societies
.707	研究	Studies
.708	總集	Collected works
.709	歷史	History
.71	唐五代詞(618—960)	Of T'ang and the Five dynasties
.711	唐(618—907)	T'ang
.713	五代(907—960)	The Five dynasties
.714	後唐(923—936)	Later T'ang
	李存勗(885—926),等	Li Ts'un-hsu, and others
.715	南唐(937—975)	Southern T'ang
	李煜(936—977),	Li Yu,
	馮延巳(?—960),等	Feng Yen-chi, and others
.717	前蜀(908—925)	Former Shu
	王衍(854—925),	Wang Yen,
	韋莊(?860—910),等	Wei Chuang, and others
.718	後蜀(931—965)	Posterior Shu
	孟知祥(?—935),等	Meng Chih-hsiang, and others

.72	宋遼金元詞(960—1368)	Of Sung, Liao, Ching, and Yuan dynasties
.73	宋(960—1280)	Sung
.731	北宋(980—1127)	Northern Sung
.732	柳永(? 1000)	Liu Yung
.733	張先(990—1078)	Chang Hsien
.734	晏幾道(? 1010)	Yen Chi-tao
.735	歐陽修(1007—72)	OuYang Hsiu
.736	蘇軾(1036—1101)	Su Shih
.737	周邦彥(1060—1125)	Chou Pang-yen
.738	北宋其他詞家	Others
.739	南宋(1127—1280)	Southern Sung
	1. 李易安(1082—? 1140)	Li Yi-an
	3. 朱敦儒(? 1080—1155)	Chu Tun-ju
	4. 陸游(1125—1210)	Lu Yu
	5. 辛棄疾(1140—1207)	Hsin Ch'i-chi
	6. 辛派詞家	Hsin's school
	7. 姜夔(? 1155—1235)	Kiang Kuei
	8. 姜派詞家	Kiang's school
	9. 南宋其他詞家	Others
.74	遼金(907—1234)	Liao and Ching
.75	元(1280—1368)	Yuan
811.76	明代詞家(1368—1644)	Of Ming dynasty
.77	清代詞家(1644—1912)	Of Ch'ing dynasty
.78	民國詞家(1912—)	Of the Republic
812	**曲　戲劇**	**Chinese drama**
.01	理論　關係	Theories　Relations
.03	曲譜　曲韻　互見770.03	Rhymes　see also 770.03
.04	曲評　曲話	Critiques
.05	雜誌	Periodicals

.06	劇社	Societies
.07	戲園 見 780	Theatre see 780
.08	曲總集 曲選	Collections Selections
	依朝代分	By dynasty
.09	曲史	History

曲別集　　　　Individual works

.1	古代至宋（？—1280）	From Ancient to Sung dynasty
.2	元（1280—1368）	Yuan dynasty
.3	蒙古時代（1206—1280）	The Mongol period
.31	關漢卿（？1200—1285）	Kuan Han-ch'ing
.32	王實甫（？1200）	Wang Shih-fu
.33	白樸（？1226）	Po P'u
.34	馬致遠（？1220）	Ma Chih-yuan
.39	其他	Others
	楊顯之，等	Yang Hsien-chih, and others
.4	統一時代（1280—1368）	The period of Union
.41	鄭光祖	Cheng Kuang-tsu
.42	喬吉甫（？—1345）	Ch'iao Chi-fu
.43	宮天挺	Kung Tien-t'ing
.46	金仁傑（？1330）	Ching Jen-chien
.49	其他	Others
	秦簡夫，等	Ch'in Chien-fu, and others
.5	無名氏	By unknown authors
.6	明（1368—1644）	Ming dynasty
.7	清（1644—1912）	Ch'ing dynasty
.8	民國（1612— ）	The Republic

813　　小說　　　　　　　　　Chinese fiction

　　　　　　小說號碼可以 F 代表之　　A more usual and better mark is F

.01	理論　關係	Theories　Relations
.04	評論	Critiques　Criticism
.05	雜誌	Periodicals
.06	學會	Societies
.07	研究	Studies
.08	總集	Collected works
.09	歷史	History
	別集	Individual works
	凡研究個人小說一種或	Works of and on individual authors
	數種者依下列朝代分	may be clast as follows:—
	例　水滸傳　813.591	e.g. Shui Hu Chuan: a tale of brigandage 813.591
	聊齋志異　813.73	Liao Chai Chih I (Liao library records strange) 813.73
	紅樓夢　813.75	Dream of the Red Chamber 813.75
.1	先秦及秦代（前？202）	Pre-Ch'in and Ch'in dynasties
.2	兩漢(202—後220)	Han dynasty
.21	虞初(？170)	Yu Ch'u
.23	東方朔(？160)	TunFang Shuo
.25	伶元(？55)	Ling Yuan
.27	郭憲(？50)	Kuo Hsien
.29	其他	Others
.3	魏晉六朝隋(220—618)	Wei, Chin, the Six dynasties, and Sui
.31	張華(232—300)	Chang Hua
.32	葛洪(253—333)	Ko Hung
.35	郭璞(276—824)	Kuo P'u

.37	干寶	Kan Pao
.38	王嘉	Wang Chia
.39	其他	Others
	劉義慶(403—444)，等	Liu Yi-ch'ing, and others
.4	唐五代(618—960)	T'ang and the Five dynasties
	元稹(779—831)，	Yuan Chen,
	杜光庭(850—933)等	Tu Kuang-ting, and others
813.5	宋遼金元(960—1368)	Sung, Liao, Ching, and Yuan dynasties
.51	宋(960—1280)	Sung
	樂史(930—1007)，等	Lo Shih, and others
.58	遼金(907—1234)	Liao and Ching
.59	元(1280—1368)	Yuan
.591	施耐庵	Shih Nai-an
.6	明(1368—1644)	Ming dynasty
.63	吳承恩(1510—30)	Wu Ch'eng-en
.65	王世貞(1526—90)，等	Wang Shih-chen, and others
.7	清(1644—1912)	Ch'ing dynasty
.71	董若雨(1620—?)	Tung Jo-yu
.72	金聖嘆(1627—65)	Ching Shing-t'an
.73	蒲松齡(1630—1715)	Pu Sung-ling
.74	吳敬梓(1701—54)	Wu Chin-hsin
.75	曹雪芹(? 1719—64)	Ts'ao Hsueh-ch'in
.76	袁枚(1716—97)	Yuan Mei
.77	紀昀(1721—1805)	Chi Chun
.78	俞樾(1821—1906)	Yu Yueh
.79	其他	Others
	曾孟樸, 等	Tseng Meng-p'u, and others

.8	民國(1912—)	The Republic	
	依體制分	By form	
.82	講史	Historical	
.827	傳記小說	Biographical	
.828	游記小說	Geographical	
.829	其他	Others	
.83	筆記	Memorie	
.84	異聞	Mythical	
.85	社會	Social	
.853	教育小說	Educational	
.857	政治小說	Political	
.859	其他	Others	
.86	家庭	Family	
.87	言情	Epic　Romantic	
.871	哀情	Tragic	
.873	苦情	Miserable	
.875	慘情	Melancholic	
.876	艷情	Winsome	
.877	愛情	Love	
.879	其他	Others	
.88	武俠　偵探	Chivalric　Detective	
.89	其他	Others	

814　民間文學　　　　　　Chinese folk literature

.01	理論　關係	Theories　Relations
.04	評論	Critiques
.05	雜誌	Periodicals
.06	學社	Societies
.07	研究	Studies
.08	總集	Collected works

.09	歷史	History
.2	説本　歌本	Chap-books and chap-book literature
.3	寓言	Fables　Fairy tales
.4	傳奇　艷事	Prose romances, etc.
.5	諺語　俚諺	Proverbs　Local songs
.6	謎語	Folk riddles
.7	小曲　鼓詞　彈詞	Chanson-nette
.8	雜品	Centos　Pasticcios
	寶卷, 道情, 竹枝詞, 等	
9.	其他	Others

815　兒童文學　　Chinese juvenile literature

兒童文學號碼之前宜置一J字以易識別也　　A more usual and better mark is J prefixed to the ordinary class mark

.01	理論　關係	Theories　Relations
.04	評論	Critiques
.05	雜誌	Periodicals
.07	研究	Studies
.09	歷史	History
.1	童歌	Verses for children
.2	童劇	Juvenile drama
.3	童話	Conte
.4	童畫	Juvenile pictural works
.5	科學　工藝故事	Science and industry tales
.9	歷史, 地理, 傳記故事	Historical, geographical, and biographical tales

816

817	駢散文		Chinese prose Essays
.01	理論　關係		Theories　Relations
.04	評論		Critiques
.07	研究		Studies
.08	總集		Collected works
	歷朝諸家各體各派		By dynasty
	合刻類此依朝代分		
.081	先秦及秦代(前？—202)		Pro-Ch'in and Ch'in dynasties
.082	兩漢(202—後220)		Han dynasty
.083	魏晉六朝隋(220—618)		Wei, Chin, the Six dynasties, and Sui
.084	唐五代(618—960)		T'ang and the Five dynasties
.085	宋遼金元(960—1368)		Sung, Liao, Ching, and Yuan dynasties
.086	明(1368—1644)		Ming dynasty
.087	清(1644—1912)		Ch'ing dynasty
.088	民國(1912—　)		The Republic
.09	歷史		History
	文別集		Individual works
.1	先秦及秦代		Pre-Ch'in and Ch'in dynasties
	(前？—202)		
	李斯(？前—208)，等		Li Shih, and others
.2	兩漢(202—後220)		Han dynasty
.23	賈誼(201—169)		Chia I
.25	揚雄(前53—後18)		Yang Hsiung
.29	其他		Others
.3	魏晉六朝隋(220—618)		Wei, Chin, the Six dynasties, and Sui
.31	曹植(192—232)		Ts'ao Chih
.37	陶潛(365—427)		T'ao Chien
.39	其他		Others

	.4	唐五代(618—960)	T'ang an the Five dynasties
	.41	初唐(618—713)	Early period
		王勃(648—675),等	Wang Po, and others
	.42	盛唐(713—780)	Period of glory
		張九齡(673—740),等	Chang Chiu-ling, and others
	.45	中唐(780—847)	Mid period
		呂溫(772—811)	Yu Wen, and others
	.46	韓愈(768—824)	Han Yu
	.47	柳宗元(773—819)	Liu Chung-yuan
	.48	晚唐(847—907)	Later period
	.49	五代(907—960)	The Five dynasties
817.5		宋遼金元(960—1368)	Sung, Liao, Ching, and Yuan dynasties
	.51	北宋(960—1127)	Northern Sung
	.511	初期	Early period
		王禹偁(950—1001),等	Wang Yu-ch'eng, and others
	.512	歐陽修(1007—72)	OuYang Hsiu
	.513	蘇洵(1009—66)	Su Hsun
	.514	蘇軾(1036—1101)	Su Shih
	.515	蘇轍(1039—1112)	Su Ch'e
	.516	曾鞏(1019—83)	Tseng Kung
	.517	王安石(1021—86)	Wang An-shih
	.519	末期	Later period
	.57	南宋(1127—1280)	Southern Sung
	.571	朱熹(1130—1200)	Chu Hsi
	.572	陸九淵(1139—92)	Lu Chiu-yuan
	.573	呂祖謙(1137—81)	Yu Tsu-ch'ien
	.574	王十朋(1112—71)	Wang Shih-p'eng
	.575	陳亮	Ch'en Liang
	.576	葉適(1150—1223)	Yeh Shih

.577	魏了翁(1178—1237)	Wei Liao-weng
.578	真德秀(1178—1235)	Chen Te-hsiu
.579	其他	Others
	文天祥(1236—82)	Wen T'ien-hsiang, and othrs
.58	遼金(907—1234)	Liao and Ching
.581	黨懷英(1134—1211)	Tang Huai-ying
.583	趙秉文(1159—1232)	Chao Ping-wen
.585	耶律楚材(1190—1243)	YehLu Ch'u-ch'ai
.587	元好問(1190—1257)	Yuan Hao-wen
.589	其他	Others
.59	元(1280—1368)	Yuan
	金履祥(1232—1303),等	Ching Li-hsiang, and others
.6	明(1368—1644)	Ming dynasty
.61	明初(1368—1425)	Early period
.611	劉基(1311—75)	Liu Chi
.612	宋濂(1310—81)	Sung Lien
.613	方孝儒(1357—1402)	Fang Hsiao-ju
.615	楊士奇(1365—1444)	Yang Shih-ch'i
.619	其他	Others
.64	明中(1425—1573)	Mid period
	李夢陽(1472—1529),等	Li Meng-yang, and others
	歸有光(1506—71)	Kuei Yu-kuang
	唐順之(1507—60)	T'ang Shun-chih
	王世貞(1526—90)	Wang Shih-chen
.69	明末(573—1644)	Later period
	黄道周(1585—1616),等	Huang Tao-chou, and others
817.7	清(1644—1912)	Ch'ing dynasty
.71	清初(1644—62)	Early period
.711	錢謙益(1582—1664)	Ch'ien Chien-yi
.713	顧炎武(1613—82)	Ku Yen-wu

.715	侯方域(1616—54)	Hou Fang-yu
.719	其他	Others
.72	**康熙時代(1662—1725)**	K'ang Hsi period
.721	施閏章(1618—83)	Shih Jen-chang
.722	汪琬(1624—90)	Wang Wan
.723	陳其年(1625—82)	Ch'en Ch'i-nien
.725	姜宸英(1628—99)	Kiang Chen-yin
.726	朱彝尊(1629—1709)	Chu Yi-tsun
.727	尤侗(1618—1704)	Yu Tung
.728	毛奇齡(1623—1716)	Mao Chi-ling
.729	其他	Others
.73	**乾隆時代(1736—96)**	Ch'ien Lung period
.731	惠棟(1697—1758)	Hui Tung
.733	全祖望(1705—55)	Chuan Tsu-wang
.734	戴震(1723—77)	Tai Chen
.735	盧文弨(1717—95)	Lu Wen-ch'ao
.736	錢大昕(1728—1804)	Ch'ien Ta-hsin
.737	章學誠(1738—1805)	Chang Hsueh-cheng
.738	崔述(1740—1816)	Tsui Shu
.739	其他	Others
	彭紹升(1740—96),	P'ang Shao-sheng,
	汪中(1744—94),等	Wong Chung, and others
.74	**桐城派**	Tung Ch'eng school
.741	方苞(1668—1749)	Fang Pao
.742	劉大魁(1698—1780)	Liu Ta-k'uei
.743	姚鼐(1731—1815)	Yao Nai
.749	其他	Others
.75	**陽湖派**	Yang Hu school
.751	惲敬(1757—1817)	Yun Chin
.752	張惠言(1761—1803)	Chang Hui-yen
.759	其他	Others

.76	駢文八大家	The eight great terse antithetic prose writers
.761	邵齊燾(1718—69)	Shao Ch'i-tao
.762	袁枚(1716—97)	Yuan Mei
.763	劉星煒(1718—72)	Liu Hsing-wei
.764	洪亮吉(1716—1809)	Huang Liang-chi
.765	吳錫麒(1746—1818)	Wu Hsi-ch'i
.766	孫星衍(1753—1818)	Sun Hsing-yen
.767	孔廣森(1752—86)	K'ung Kuang-sen
.768	曾燠(1760—1831)	Tseng Ao
.77		
817.78	道光時代(1821—51)	Tao Kuang period
.781	龔自珍(1792—1841)	Kung Tzu-chen
.783	曾國藩(1811—72)	Tseng Kuo-fan
.785	魏源(1791—1856)	Wei Yuan
.789	其他	Others
.79	清末(1851—1912)	Later period
.791	王闓運(1832—1916)	Wang K'ai-yun
.793	康有爲(1858—1927)	K'ang Yu-wei
.795	王國維(1877—1927)	Wang Kuo-wei
.799	其他	Others
.8	民國(1912—)	The Republic
	民國文集依作家姓氏號碼分	Works of the prose writers of the Republic all arranged accordingly by author numbers

818　其他文學　　Chinese other literatures

.1	函牘文學　書說類	Correspondence, letters
	其有文學價值者，某一類之尺牘則應入該類。尺牘之重在傳記方面者則入傳記類	That is, literary and miscellanious letters, Letters on any one subject go with the subject. A correspondence whose interest is chiefly biographical should be put in biography

	.2	幽默諷刺文學	Humorous and satirical literature
	.3	箴銘類　格言 金言　銘言	Maxims, apothegms, mottoes, etc.
	.4	論辯文學　演講錄	Speeches　Orations
	.43	訓辭	Instructions
	.45	頌辭	Panegyrics
	.5	序跋類	Foreward, preface, etc.
	.51	題辭　題獻	Dedication
	.52	導言　引言	Introduction
	.53	序文	Preface
	.54		
	.55	楔子	Prologue
	.56	書後	Epilogue
	.59	其他	Others
	.6		
818.7		傳誌文學 　　哀祭類	Biographical literature 　　Sacrificial
	.71	傳狀	Biography
	.73	碑，誌，銘，表，志，等	Inscriptions, epitaphs, monumental legends, etc.
	.75	哀祭 　　訃聞，祭文，誄 　詞，哀辭，等	Sacrificial orations 　　obituaries, laments, dirges, etc.
	.79	其他	Others
	.8	游記文學 　筆記　日記　回憶錄	Travels　Voyages Journal, sayings, thought
	.9	雜記　雜事瑣語	Miscellany

中國十進制分類法及索引　569

819	滿蒙回藏等文學	Literature in the languages of Manchuria, Mongolia, Tibet, etc.
820	日本文學	Japanese literature
821	韻文	Japanese verses
.1	詩	Poetry
.2	和歌	Waka　Japanese old poems
	長歌，短歌，旋頭歌，雜歌，等	
.21	上古時代(？—710)	Ancient period
.22	奈良時代(710—794)	Nara period
.23	平安時代(794—1192)	Heian period
.24	鎌倉時代(1192—1333)	Kamakura period
.25	室町時代(1335—1573)	Muromachi peiod
.26	江戶時代(1603—1868)	Edo period
.27	明治及明治以後(1863—)	Meiji and Post-Meiji period
.3	連歌	Renka
.4	俳諧　俳句	Haikai　Haiku
.5	歌謠	Ballads
.51	神樂歌	Kagura-uta
.52	催馬樂	Saibara
.53	東游歌	Azuma-asobi-uta
.54	風俗歌	Fuzoku-uta
.55	朗詠集	Roei
.56	今樣歌	Imayo-uta
.59	其他	Others

	.7	劇詩	Dramatic poetry
		宴曲，舞曲，等	Enkyoku, Bukyoku, Etc.
	.9	其他	Others
822		戲曲	Japanese drama
823		小説　物語	Japanese fiction
	.1	上古時代(？—710)	Ancient period
	.2	奈良時代(710—794)	Nara period
	.3	平安時代(794—1192)	Heian period
	.31	竹取物語	Taketori monogatari
	.32	伊勢物語	Ise monogatari
	.33	大和物語	Yamato monogatari
	.34	宇津保物語	Utsubo monogatari
	.35	落窪物語	Ochikubo monogatari
	.36	源氏物語	Genji monogatari
	.37	狹衣物語	Sagoromo monogatari
	.38	今昔物語	Konjaku monogatari
	.39	其他	Others
		例　唐物語，等	e.g. Kara monogatari, etc.
823.4		鎌倉時代(1192—1333)	Kamakura period
	.5	室町時代(1335—1573)	Muromachi period
	.6	江戸時代(1603—1868)	Edo period
	.61	假名草紙	Kana-zoshi
	.62	浮世草紙	Ukiyo-zoshi
	.63	八文字屋本	Hachimonjiya-bon
	.64	草雙紙	Kusa-zoshi
		赤本，黑本，黄表紙，等	
	.65	讀本	Yomibon
	.66	實録物	Jitsurokumono

.67	灑落本(蒟蒻本)	Sharebon
.68	人情本	Ninjobon
.69	滑稽本	Kokkeibon
.7	明治及明治以後（1868— ）	Meiji and Post-Meiji period
824	民間文學	Japanese folk literature
	例 伽噺，俚諺，謎語，等	e.g. Fables, local songs, riddles, etc.
825	兒童文學	Japanese juvenile literature
.1	童歌	Verses for children
.2	童劇	Juvenile drama
.3	童話	Conte
.4	童畫	Juvenile pictural works
.5	科學　工藝故事	Science and industry tales
.9	歷史, 地理, 傳記故事	Historical, geographical, and biographical tales
826		
827	散文　日記　隨筆	Japanese prose, journal, sayings
	按日本散文多爲日記隨筆類,故均列此	
.1	上古時代(？—710)	Ancient period
.2	奈良時代(710—794)	Nara period
.3	平安時代(794—1192)	Heian period
.31	土佐日記	Tosa nikki
.32	更科日記	Sarashina nikki
.33	紫式部日記	Murasaki-shikibu nikki
.34	蜻蛉日記	Kagero nikki
.35	和泉式部日記	Izumi-shikibu nikki

.36	讚岐典侍日記	Sanuki-no-suke-no nikki
.38	枕草紙	Makura-no-soshi
.39	其他	Others
827.4	鎌倉時代（1192—1333）	Kamakura period
.41	方丈記	Hojoki
.42	辨內侍日記	Ben-no-naishi nikki
.43	中務內侍日記	Nakatsukasa-no-naishi nikki
.44	十六夜日記	Izayoi nikki
.45	海道記	Kaidoki
.46	東關紀行	Tokan kiko
.49	其他	Others
.5	室町時代（1335—1573）	Muromachi period
	從然草，太平記，等	
.6	江戶時代（1603—1868）	Edo period
.7	明治及明治以後（1868—　）	Meiji and Post-Meiji period
828	其他文學	Japanese other literatures
.1	函牘文學	Correspondence, letters
.2	幽默諷刺文學	Humorous and satirical literature
	狂詩，狂歌，狂句，笑話，等	Kyoshi, kyoka, kyoku, jokes, etc.
.3	箴銘類　格言　金言	Maxims, apothegms, mottoes, etc.
.4	論辯文學　演講類	Speeches　Orations
.5	序跋類	Foreward, pretace, etc.
	題辭，引言，序文，楔子，書後，等	Dedications, introduction, preface, prologue, epilogue, etc.
.7	傳記文學	Biographical literature
	哀祭類	Sacrificial

.8	雜記　雜事瑣語	Miscellany
829	朝鮮, 臺灣, 琉球, 等文學	Literature of Korea, Formosa, Loochoo, etc.
830	希臘, 拉丁, 羅馬文學	Greek, Latin, and Romance literatures
831	希臘文學	Greek literature
.1	詩(通論)	Greek poetry in general
.11	提奧格力士	Theognis
.13	亞拉圖	Aratu
.19	其他	Others
	賴科夫綸, 等	Lycophron, and others
.2	劇詩	Greek dramatic poetry
.21	伊斯奇士(前 525—457)	Eschylus
.22	索福客士(前？495—406)	Sophocles
.23	幼里庇底士(前 480—406)	Euripides
.24	亞理士多芬(前？448—380)	Aristophanes
.29	其他	Others
	麥南德, 等	Menander, and others
.3	史詩	Greek epic poetry
.31	荷馬(前？900)	Homer
.32	希西阿(前？776)	Hesiod
.39	其他	Others
	奧匹安, 等	Oppian, and others
.4	情詩	Greek lyric poetry
.41	忒提阿士	Tyrtaeus
.42	薩福(前？600)	Sappho
.43	亞那克里溫(前？563—478)	Anacreon

.44	施蒙尼迪士（前？556—468）	Simonides of Ceos
.45	品得（前？522—？448）	Pindar
.49	其他	Others
	擺溫，等	Bion, and others
.7	散文	Greek prose
.8	其他文學	Greek other literatures
.81	函牘	Greek letters
	忒密斯托克士（前？527—460），等	Themistocles, and others
.82	幽默	Greek satire and humor
	亞基洛克士，等	Archilochus, and others
.84	論辯　演講	Greek oratory
.842	黎西亞士（前458—378）	Lysias
.844	伊索克雷士（前436—388）	Isocrates
.845	伊斯啓泥士（前389—314）	Eschines
.846	狄摩西尼士（前384—322）	Demosthenes
.849	其他	Others
.88	類雜	Greek miscellany
.881	希羅多德（前？484—425）	Herodotus
.882	都昔的底士（前471—400）	Thucydides
.886	伊索（前？560）	Esop
.887	盧西安（？120—200）	Lucian
.889	其他	Others
.9	中古與近世希臘文學	Medieval and modern Greek
832	**拉丁文學**	**Latin literature**
.1	詩（通論）	Latin poetry in general
.11	魯克理細阿士（前95—55）	Lucretius Carus, Titus
.12	奧維德（前48—後17）	Ovid (Publius Ovidius Naso)
.13	其他	Others

.2	戲曲	Latin drama
.23	普魯塔士(前? 254—184)	Plautus, Titus, Maccius
.25	忒棱士(前? 190—159)	Terence (Publius Terentius Afer)
.29	其他	Others
	辛尼加(前? 4—後 65),等	Seneca, Lucius Annaeus, and others
.3	史詩	Latin epic poetry
.31	維吉爾(前 70—19)	Virgil (Publius Virgilius or Vergilius Maro)
.32	魯干洛士(前 39—65)	Lucanus, Marcus Annaeus
.39	其他	Others
.4	情詩	Latin lyric poetry
.42	加圖魯士(前 87—54)	Catullus, Caius Valerins
.43	秦布魯士(前? 51—18)	Tibullus, Albius
.44	普帕細阿士(前? 50—15)	Propertius, Sextus Aurelius
.45	賀拉士(前 65—8)	Horace (Quintus Horatius Flaccus)
.49	其他	Others
.7	散文	Latin prose
.8	其他文學	Latin other literatures
.81	函牘	Latin letters
	普林尼(? 62—114)	Pliny (Caius Plinius Caecilius Secundus), and others
.82	幽默	Latin satire and humor
.826	馬四亞爾(? 40—120)	Martial (Marcus Valerius Martialis)
.827	朱維那爾(? 60—140)	Juvenal (Decimus Junius Juvenalis)
.829	其他	Others
.84	論辯　演講	Latin oratory
.841	西塞祿(前 106—43)	Cicero, Marcus Tullius

.846	昆體良（？35—100）	Quintilian (Marcus Fabius Quintilianus)
.849	其他	Others
.88	類雜	Latin miscellany
.881	愷撒（前100—44）	Caesar, Caius, Julius
.882	薩魯斯特（前86—34）	Sallust (Caius Sallustius Crispus)
.884	李維（前59—後17）	Livy (Titus Livius Patavinus)
.886	荅四圖士（？55—117）	Tacitus, Caius Cornelius
.889	其他	Others
.9	中古與近世拉丁文學	Medieval and modern Latin
833	**意國文學**	**Italian literature**
.1	詩	Italian poetry
.11	初期　丹第時代	Early Italian　Age of Dante
	（後1375）	
.115	丹第（1265—1321）	Alighieri, Dante
.118	佩特拉克（1304—74）	Petrarca, Francesco
.119	其他	Others
.12	經學時代（1375—1492）	Period of Classic learning
.123	麥地奇（1448—92）	Medici, Lorenzo dei
.124	坡利齊阿諾（1454—94）	Poliziano Angelo
.129	其他	Others
.13	黎阿第十時代	Ago of Leo the Tenth
	（1492—1542）	
	亞立斯托（1471—1533），等	Ariosto, Lodovico, and others
.14	十六世紀後期	Later 16th century
	（1542—85）	
	塔索（1544—95），等	Tasso, Torquato, and others
.15	浸衰時代（1585—1748）	Period of decline
.152	瑪利里（1569—1625）	Mariui, Giovambattista
.155	基第（1650—1712）	Guidi, Alessandro
.159	其他	Others

.16		革新時代(1748—1814)	Period of renovation
.17		十九世紀前期 (1814—59)	Early 19th century
.18		十九世紀後期 (1859—1900)	Later 19th century
.19		二十世紀(1900—)	20th century
.2		戲曲	Italian drama
.3		小説	Italian fiction
.4		民間文學	Italian folk literature
.5		兒童文學	Italian juvenile literature
.7		散文	Italian prose
.8		其他文學	Italian other literatures
.81		函牘	Italian letters
.82		幽默　諷刺	Italian satire and humor
.84		論辯　演講	Italian oratory
.88		雜類	Italian miscellany

834

835　西班牙文學　　　　　Spanish literature

.1	詩	Spanish poetry
.2	戲曲	Spanish drama
.3	小説	Spanish fiction
.4	民間文學	Spanish folk literature
.5	兒童文學	Spanish juvenile literature
.7	散文	Spanish prose
.8	其他文學	Spanish other literatures
.81	函牘	Spanish letters
.82	幽默　諷刺	Spanish satire and humor

.84	論辯　演講	Spanish oratory
.88	雜類	Spanish miscellany
836	葡萄牙文學	Portuguese literature
837		
838	羅馬尼亞文學	Rumanian literature
839	其他羅馬文學	Other Romance literatures
	法國文學　見840	For French literature　see 840
840	法國文學	French literature
841	詩	French poetry
.1	古代(842—1400)	Early French
.11	羅蘭歌　武勳歌	Chanson de Roland
		Chanson de geste
.19	其他	Others
.2	變遷時代(1400—1500)	Transition period
.21	沙對(1368—1458)	Chartier, Alain
.22	奧爾良(1391—1465)	Orleans, Charles duc d'
.23	柯基拉(1421—1510)	Coquillart, Guillaume
.29	其他	Others
.3	文藝復興時代(1500—1600)	Renaissance
.31	多臘(1510—88)	Daurat, Jean
.32	杜拔里(1524—60)	Du Bellay, Jaochim
.33	柏羅(1528—77)	Belleau, Remy
.34	龍沙(1524—85)	Ronsard, Pierre de
.39	其他	Others
.4	經學時代(1600—1715)	Classic period
.41	馬雷布(1555—1628)	Malherbe, Francois de

.42	美涅德(1582—1646)	Maynard, Francois
.44	沙普郎(1595—1674)	Chapelain, Jean
.45	拉封騰(1621—95)	La Fontaine, Jean de
.49	其他	Others
.5	十八世紀(1715—89)	18th century
.51	盧梭(1670—1741)	Rousseau, Jean Baptiste
.52	拉辛(1692—1763)	Racine, Louis
.56	史立野(1762—94)	Chenier, Andre Marie de
.59	其他	Others
.6	革命與帝國時代(1789—1815)	Revolution and empire
	封達侖(1757—1821),等	Fontanes, Louis and others
.7	君主立憲時代(1815—48)	Constitutional monarchy
.71	白蘭佳(1780—1857)	Beranger, Pierre Jean de
.72	拉馬丁(1792—1869)	Lamartine, Alphonse Marie Louis de Prat de
.73	威尼(1799—1863)	Vigny, Alfred Victor, comte de
.74	穆塞(1810—57)	Musset, Louis Charles Alfred be
.76	囂俄(1802—85)	Hugo, Victor Marie, comte
.79	其他	Others
.8	十九世紀後期(1848—1900)	Later 19th century
.81	拉普勒(1812—83)	Laprade, Pierre Marin Victor Richard de
.82	杜滂(1821—70)	Dupont, Pierre
.83	邦威爾(1820—91)	Banville, Theodore Faullain de
.84	卜呂敦(1839—1907)	Sully Prudhomme, Rene Francois Armand

.85	柯楓(1842—1908)	Coppee, Francis Edouaro Joachim
.86	赫勒底亞(1842—1905)	Heredia, Jose Maria de
.89	其他	Others
.9	二十世紀(1901—)	20th century

842　　戲曲　　　　　　　　　French drama

.1	古代(842—1400)	Early French
.2	變遷時代(1400—1500)	Transition period
.3	文藝復興時代(1500—1600)	Renaissance
.4	經學時代(1600—1715)	Classic period
.41	柯奈耶(1606—84)	Corneille, Pierre
.42	穆里爾(1622—73)	Moliere, Jean Baptiste Poquelin
.44	保耳索(1638—1701)	Boursault, Edme
.45	拉辛(1639—99)	Racine, Jean
.46	卜呂亞士(1640—1723)	Brueys, David Augustin de
.47	杜弗勒里(1648—1724)	Dufresny, Charles Riviere
.48	巴郎(1653—1729)	Baron, Michel Boyron
.49	其他	Others
.5	十八世紀(1715—89)	18th century
.51	拉穆特(1672—1731)	La Motte, Antoine Houdart de
.52	客勒比勇(1674—1762)	Crebillon, Prosper Jolyot de
.54	馬利弗(1688—1763)	Marivaux, Pierre Carlet de Chamblain de
.55	皮隆(1689—1773)	Piron, Alexis
.56	弗耳特耳(1694—1778)	Voltaire, Francois Marie Arouet de
.57	塞登(1719—97)	Sedaine, Michel Jean
.58	博馬舍(1732—99)	Beaumarchais Pierre Augustin Caron de

.59	其他	Others
.6	革命與帝國時代（1789—1815）	Revolution and empire
.61	杜西士(1733—1816)	Ducis, Jean Francois
.63	拉哈普(1739—1803)	La Harpe, Jean Francois de
.69	其他	Others
.7	君主立憲時代（1815—48）	Constitutional monarchy
.73	威尼(1799—1863)	Vigny, Alfred Victor, comte de
.74	穆塞(1810—57)	Musset, Louis Charles Alfred de
.75	大杜馬(1806—70)	Dumas, Alexandre, the elder
.76	囂俄(1802—85)	Hugo, Victor Marie, comte
.79	其他	Others
.8	十九世紀後期（1848—1900）	Later 19th century
.81	拉比士(1815—88)	Labiche, Eugene Marin
.82	逢沙(1824—67)	Ponsard, Francois
.83	奧基亞(1822—89)	Augier, Guillaume Victor Emile
.84	小杜馬(1824—95)	Dumas, Alexandre, fils
.86	沙都(1831—1908)	Sardon, Victorien
.87	巴勒農(1831—99)	Pailleron, Edouard
.88	柯楓(1842—1908)	Coppee, Francis Edouard Joachim
.89	其他	Others
.9	二十世紀(1901—)	20th century
843	**小說**	**French fiction**
.1	古代(842—1400)	Early French
.2	變遷時代(1400—1500)	Transition period

.3	文藝復興時代 （1500—1600）	Renaissance
.4	經學時代（1600—1715）	Classic period
.5	十八世紀（1715—89）	18th century
.51	勒薩日（1668—1747）	Le Sage, Alain Rene
.52	馬利弗（1688—1763）	Marivaux, Pierre Carlet de Chamblain de
.53	卜勒浮（1697—1763）	Prevost d'Exiles, Antoine Fraucois
.54	弗耳特耳（1694—1778）	Voltaire, Francois Marie Arouet de
.56	盧梭（1712—78）	Rousseau, Jean Jacques
.59	其他	Others
.6	革命與帝國時代 （1789—1815）	Revolution and empire
.62	斯達埃爾夫人 （1766—1817）	Stael Holstein, Anne Louise Germaine (Necker) baronne de
.65	沙多勃良（1768—1848）	Chateaubriand, Francois Auguste Rene, vicomte de
.69	其他	Others
.7	君主立憲時代 （1815—48）	Constitutional monarchy
.71	培爾（1783—1842）	Beyle, Marie Henri (de Stendhal)
.72	巴爾札克（1799—1850）	Balzac, Honore de
.73	蘇維斯忒（1806—54）	Souvestre, Emile
.75	大杜馬（1806—70）	Dumas, Alexandre, the elder
.76	囂俄（1802—85）	Hugo, Victor Marie, comte
.79	其他	Others
.8	十九世紀後期 （1848—1900）	Later 19th century

	.81	麥里美(1803—70)	Merimee, Prosper
	.82	杜德峯(桑德) (1804—76)	Dudevant, Amantine Lucile Aurore Dupin (George Sand)
	.84	弗洛貝爾(1821—81)	Flaubert, Gustave
	.85	都德(1840—97)	Daudet, Alphonse
	.86	左拉(1840—1902)	Zols, Emile
	.87	莫泊桑(1850—93)	Maupassant, Guy de
	.89	其他	Others
	.9	二十世紀(1901—)	20th century
		羅曼羅蘭(1868—),等	Romain Rolland, and Others
844		民間文學	French folk literature
845		兒童文學	French juvenile literature
846			
847		散文	French prose
	.1	古代(842—1400)	Early French
	.2	變遷時代(1400—1500)	Transition period
	.3	文藝復興時代 (1500—1600)	Renaissance
		蒙旦(1538—1592)	Montaigne, Michel Eyquem de
	.4	經學時代(1600—1715)	Classic period
	.41	杜發(1556—1621)	Du Vair, Guillaume
	.43	白勒(1647—1706)	Bayle, Pierre
	.49	其他	Others
	.5	十八世紀(1715—89)	18th century
	.51	封得乃爾(1657—1757)	Fontenelle, Bernard le Bovier de
	.52	孟德斯鳩(1689—1755)	Montesquieu, Charles le Secondat, baron de

.53	亞蘭柏(1717—83)	Alembert, Jean le Rond d'
.59	其他	Others
.6	革命與帝國時代 (1789—1815)	Revolution and empire
.62	朱伯爾(1754—1824)	Jubert, Joseph
.63	古里野(1772—1825)	Courier de Mere, Paul Louis
.69	其他	Others
.7	君主立憲時代 (1815—48)	Constitutional monarchy
	聖布菲(1804—69)	Sainte Beuve, Charles Augustin
.8	十九世紀後期 (1848—1900)	Later 19th century
	芮農(1823—92)	Renan, Ernest
.9	二十世紀(1900—)	20th century
848	其他文學	French other literatures
.1	函牘文學　書說類	Correspondence, letters
	其有文學價值者，某一類之尺牘則應入該類 尺牘之重在傳記方面者則入傳記類	That is, literary and miscellaneous letters, Letters on any one subject go with the subject. A correspondence whose interest is chiefly biographical should be put in biography
.2	幽默諷刺文學	Humorous and satirical literature
.3	箴銘類　格言　金言	Maxims, apothegms, mottoes, etc.
.4	論辯文學　演講錄	Speeches　Orations
.5	序跋類	Foreward, preface, etc.
	題辭，引言，序文，楔子，書後，等	Dedications, introduction, preface, prologue, epilogue, etc.
.7	傳誌文學　哀祭類	Biographical literature　Sacrificial

	.8	游記文學	Travels　Voyages
		日記　回憶錄	Journal, sayings, thought
	.9	雜記　雜事瑣語	Miscellany
849		法國南部文學	Provencal literature
850		英國文學	English literature
851		詩	English poetry
	.1	古代(450—1350)	Early English
	.11	比武爾夫	Beowulf
		盎格諾薩克森時代之史詩	An old epic or heroic poem
	.12	希得曼	Caedmon
	.13	琴武爾夫	Cynewulf
	.15	羅亞曼(1150—1207)	Layamon
	.19	其他	Others
		明諾特(1313—52),等	Minot, Lawrence, and others
	.2	先以利沙伯時代 (1350—1558)	Pre-Elizabethan
	.21	郎格蘭(1332—99)	Langland, William
	.22	巴伯(1316—95)	Barbour, John
	.23	綽塞(1340—1400)	Chaucer, Geoffrey
	.24	答格拿士(1474—1522)	Douglas, Gavin
	.25	夏威斯(1483—1509)	Hawes, Stephen
	.26	林瑟(1490—1555)	Lyndsay, Sir David
	.27	威阿特(1503—42)	Wyatt, Sir Thomas
	.28	蘇瑞(1517—47)	Surrey, Henry Howard, earl of
	.29	其他	Others
	.3	以利沙伯時代 (1558—1625)	Elizabethan
	.31	斯賓塞(1553—99)	Spenser, Edmund

	.32	錫德尼(1554—86)	Sidney, Sir Philip
	.33	但以理(1562—1619)	Daniel, Samuel
	.34	德敦(1563—1631)	Drayton, Michael
	.37	夫勒拆(1585—1650)	Fletcher, Giles and Phineas
	.38	赫伯特(1593—1632)	Herbert, George
	.39	其他	Others
	.4	後以利沙伯時代(1625—1702)	Post-Elizabethan
	.43	赫立克(1591—1674)	Herrick, Robert
	.45	駱甫雷斯(1618—58)	Lovelace, Richard
	.46	柯雷(1618—67)	Cowley, Abraham
	.47	密爾頓(1608—74)	Milton, John
	.48	德來登(1631—1700)	Dryden, John
	.49	其他	Others
	.5	安麗時代(1702—45)	Queen Anne
	.53	頗普(1688—1744)	Pope, Alexander
	.54	藍母則(1686—1758)	Ramsay, Allan
	.55	楊愛德華(1684—1765)	Young, Edward
	.56	湯姆生(1700—48)	Thomson, James
	.57	柯林士(1721—59)	Collins, William
	.59	其他	Others
851.6		十八世紀後期(1745—1800)	Later 18th century
	.61	格雷(1716—71)	Gray, Thomas
	.63	查忒敦(1752—70)	Chatterton, Thomas
	.64	戈爾斯密(1728—74)	Goldsmith, Oliver
	.65	顧伯(1731—1800)	Cowper, William
	.67	本斯(1759—96)	Burns, Robert

.68	懷特(1785—1806)	White, Henry Kirke
.69	其他	Others
.7	十九世紀前期 (1800—37)	Early 19th century
.71	威斯衛司(1770—1850)	Wordsworth, William
.72	顧勒理治(1772—1834)	Coleridge, Samuel Taylor
.73	騷德(1774—1843)	Southey, Robert
.74	司各脫(1771—1832)	Scott, Sir Walter
.75	穆爾(1779—1852)	Moore, Thomas
.76	擺倫(1788—1824)	Byron, George Gordon Noel, 6th lord
.77	薛理(1792—1822)	Shelley, Percy Bysshe
.78	濟士(1795—1821)	Keats, John
.79	其他 洪德(1784—1859),等	Others Hunt, Leigh, and others
.8	維多利亞時代 (1837—1900)	Victorian period
.81	丁尼生(1809—92)	Tennyson, Alfred, 1st baron
.82	勃勞寧女士(1809—61)	Browning, Elizabeth Barrett
.83	勃勞寧(1812—89)	Browning, Robert
.84	洛塞諦(1828—82)	Rossetti, Dante Gabriel
.85	安勞(1822—88)	Arnold, Matthew
.86	莫理士(1834—96)	Morris, William
.87	斯文本(1837—1909)	Swinburne, Algernon Charles
.89	其他	Others
.9	二十世紀(1900—)	20th century
852	戲曲	English drama
.1	古代(450—1350)	Early English

	.2	先以利沙伯時代 （1350—1558）	Pre-Elizabethan
	.3	以利沙伯時代 （1558—1625）	Elizabethan
	.31	格麟(1561—92)	Greene, Robert
	.32	馬邏(1561—93)	Marlowe, Christopher
	.33	莎士比亞(1564—1616) 莎士比亞之戲劇，詩，文，以及研究莎氏諸作均類此，詳細分類表見附錄二	Shakespeare, William Class here all works of and on Shakespeare. For subdivision see Appendix II
	.34	江孫(1574—1637)	Jonson, Ben
	.35	白蒙得(1584—1616)	Beanmont, Francis
	.36	夫勒拆(1579—1625)	Fletcher, John
	.39	其他	Others
852.4		後以利沙伯時代 （1625—1702）	Post-Elizabethan
	.43	克藍(1644—99)	Crowne, John
	.44	尉柝力(1640—1715)	Wycherly, William
	.45	德來登(1631—1700)	Dryden, John
	.46	孔格雷夫(1670—1729)	Congreve, William
	.49	其他	Others
	.5	安麗時代(1702—45)	Queen Anne
	.51	丹尼斯(1657—1734)	Dennis, John
	.52	騷鄧(1660—1746)	Southerne, Thomas
	.54	習柏(1671—1757)	Cibber, Colley
	.59	其他	Others
	.6	十八世紀後期 （1745—1800）	Later 18th century

.61	嘉立克(1716—79)	Garrick, David
.62	佛特(1721—77)	Foote, Samuel
.64	霍姆(1724—1808)	Home, John
.66	薛立敦(1751—1816)	Sheridan, Richard Brinsley
.69	其他	Others
.7	十九世紀前期(1800—37)	Early 19th century
	貝勒(1762—1851),等	Baillie, Joanna, and others
.8	維多利亞時代(1837—1900)	Victorian period
	勃勞寧(1812—89),等	Browning, Robert, and others
.9	二十世紀(1900—)	20th century
853	**小說**	**English fiction**
.1	古代(450—1350)	Early English
	亞勒弗烈之"盎格諾薩克森傳"	Alfred the Great: Anglo Saxon Chronicle
.2	先以利沙伯時代(1350—1558)	Pre-Elizabethan
	莫爾之"烏托邦"	More's Utopia
.3	以利沙伯時代(1558—1625)	Elizabethan
	黎里之"攸菲斯或智能之解剖"	Lyly's Euphues
.4	後以利沙伯時代(1625—1702)	Post-Elizabethan
.42	班燕(1628—88)	Bunyan, John
.49	其他	Others
.5	安麗時代(1702—45)	Queen Anne

.51	第福(1661—1731)	Defoe, Daniel
.53	斯尉夫特(1667—1745)	Swift, Jonathan
.55	菲爾丁(1707—54)	Fielding, Henry
.59	其他	Others
.6	十八世紀後期 (1745—1800)	Later 18th century
.61	理查孫(1789—61)	Richardson, Samuel
.62	司騰(1713—68)	Sterue, Laurence
.64	戈爾斯密(1728—74)	Goldsmith, Oliver
.65	麥肯基(1745—1831)	Mackenzie, Henry
.69	其他	Others
853.7	十九世紀前期 (1800—37)	Early 19th century
.71	路伊斯(1775—1818)	Lewis, Matthew Gregory
.72	愛治衛司(1767—1849)	Edgeworth, Maria
.73	司各特(1771—1832)	Scott, Sir Walter
.74	奧斯騰(1775—1817)	Austen, Jane
.75	坡爾忒(1776—1850)	Porter, Jane
.76	皮各克(1785—1866)	Peacock, Thomas Love
.79	其他	Others
.8	維多利亞時代 (1837—1900)	Victorian period
.82	塔刻立(1811—63)	Thackeray, William Makepeace
.83	迭更士(1812—70)	Dickens, Charles
.85	金斯黎(1819—75)	Kingsley, Charles
.86	伊利阿(1819—80)	Cross, Mary Ann (Evans) Lewes 〔George Eliot〕
.87	特洛普(1815—82)	Trollope, Anthony

.88	史蒂芬生(1850—94)	Stevenson, Robert Louis
.89	其他	Others
	布拉克摩(1825—1900),等	Blackmore, Richard Doddridge, and others
.9	二十世紀(1900—)	20th century
854	民間文學	English folk literature
855	兒童文學	English juvenile literature
856		
857	散文	English prose
.1	古代(450—1350)	Early English
.2	先以利沙伯時代(1350—1558)	Pre-Elizabethan
	馬洛利之"阿德之死"	Thomas Malory: Morte d'Arthur
.3	以利沙伯時代(1558—1625)	Elizabethan
	培根(1561—1626),等	Bacon, Francis, and others
.4	後以利沙伯時代(1625—1702)	Post-Elizabethan
.43	勃勞理(1605—82)	Browne, Thomas
.45	華爾頓(1593—1683)	Walton, Isaac
.49	其他	Others
.5	安麗時代(1702—45)	Queen Anne
.51	莎慈白利(1671—1713)	Shaftsbury, Anthony Ahley Cooper, 3rd, earl of
.52	愛迭孫(1672—1719)	Addison, Joseph
.53	斯提爾(1671—1729)	Steele, Sir Richard
.55	頗普(1688—1744)	Pope, Alexander
.59	其他	Others

.6	十八世紀後期 （1745—1800）	Later 18th century
.63	約翰孫(1709—84)	Johnson, Samuel
.64	戈爾斯密(1728—74)	Goldsmith, Oliver
.67	吉本(1737—94)	Gibbon, Edward
.69	其他	Others
857.7	十九世紀前期 （1800—37）	Early 19th century
.71	馬金叨斯(1765—1832)	Mackintosh, Sir James
.72	斯密司(1771—1845)	Smith, Sydney
.75	藍姆(1775—1831)	Lamb, Charles
.76	藍姆女士	Lamb, Mary
.79	其他	Others
.8	維多利亞時代 （1837—1900）	Victorian period
.81	第昆栖(1785—59)	De Quincey, Thomas
.82	喀萊爾(1795—1881)	Carlyle, Thomas
.83	馬可黎(1800—1859)	Macaulay, Thomas Babington
.84	赫爾普士(1817—75)	Helps, Sir Arthur
.85	安勞(1822—88)	Arnold, Matthew
.86	羅斯金(1818—1900)	Ruskin, John
.89	其他	Others
.9	二十世紀(1900—　)	20th century
858	其他文學	English other literatures
.1	函牘文學	Correspondence, letters

	其有文學價值者，某一類之尺牘則應入該類。尺牘之重在傳記一方面者則入傳記類	That is, literary and miscellaneous letters, Letters on any one subject go with that subject. A correspondence whose interest is chiefly biographical should be put in biography
.2	幽默諷刺文學	Humorous and satirical literature
	依時代分	By period
	例 蒲特烈(1612—1680) 858.242	e.g. Butler, Samuel 858.242
	頗普(1688—1744) 858.255	Pope, Alexander 858.255
.3	箴銘類　格言　金言	Maxims, apothegms, mottoes, etc.
.4	論辯文學　演講錄	Speeches　Orations
.42	柏克(1729—97)	Burke, Edmund
.43	法克思(1719—1806)	Fox, Charles James
.44	薛立敦(1751—1816)	Sheridan, Richard Brinsley
.46	皮維廉(1759—1806)	Pitt, William
.5	序跋類	Foreward, preface, etc.
	題辭　題獻	Dedication
	導言　引言	Introduction
	序文	Preface
	其他	Others
.7	傳誌文學	Biographical literature
.8	游記文學	Travels　Voyages
	筆記　日記　回憶錄	Journal, sayings, thought
.9	雜記　雜事瑣語	Miscellany
859	瑟爾文學	Celtic literatures
.1	蘇格蘭文學	Scottish
.3	愛爾蘭文學	Irish
.5	威爾斯文學	Welsh
.9	其他	Others

860		美國文學	American literature
861		詩	American poetry
	.1	殖民時代(1607—1776)	Colonial
	.12	布勒斯特里(1612—72)	Bradstreet, Anne
	.13	威格斯衛司(1631—1705)	Wigglesworth, Michael
	.14	格林(1706—80)	Green, Joseph
	.15	李溫士敦(1723—10)	Livingston, William
	.19	其他	Others
		弗格森(1739—1801)	Ferguson, Elizabeth, and others
	.2	後革命時代 (1776—1830)	Post-revolutionary
	.21	春布爾(1750—1831)	Trumbull, John
	.22	代特(1752—1817)	Dwight, Timothy
	.23	巴羅(1755—1812)	Barlow, Joel
	.24	夫勒諾(1752—1832)	Freneau, Philip
	.25	亞爾索(1761—1841)	Alsop, Richard
	.27	德那(1787—1879)	Dana, Richard Henry
	.29	其他	Others
		司普格(1791—1875)	Sprague, Charles, and others
	.3	十九世紀中期 (1830—61)	Middle 19th century
	.31	愛倫坡(1809—49)	Poe, Edgar Allan
	.32	愛默生(1803—82)	Emerson, Ralph Waldo
	.33	布頓安(1791—1878)	Bryant, William Cullen
	.34	郎匪羅(1807—82)	Longfellow, Henry Wadsworth
	.35	惠特亞(1807—92)	Whittier, John Greenleaf
	.36	霍謨士(1809—94)	Holmes, Oliver Wendell
	.37	羅威爾(1819—91)	Lowell, James Russell

	.38	惠特曼(1819—92)	Whitman, Walt
	.39	其他	Others
		黎德(1822—72)，藍泥爾(1842—81)，等	Read, Thomas Buchanan, Lanier, Sidney, and others
	.4	十九世紀後期(1861—1900)	Later 19th century
	.41	斯托德(1825—1903)	Stoddard, Richard Henry
	.42	赫因(1831—86)	Hayne, Paul Hamilton
	.43	斯忒德曼(1833—1908)	Stedman, Edmund Clarence
	.44	文特(1836—1918)	Winter, William
	.45	密勒(1841—1913)	Miller, Cincinnatus Hiner (Joaquin)
	.46	泰羅(1825—78)	Taylor, Bayard
	.47	亞爾德赤(1836—1907)	Aldrich, Thomas Bailey
	.49	其他	Others
	.5	二十世紀(1900—)	20th century
862		戲曲	American drama
		依時代分	By period
863		小說	American fiction
	.1	殖民時代(1607—1776)	Colonial
	.2	後革命時代(1776—1830)	Post-revolutionary
	.22	布郎(1771—1810)	Brown, Charles Brockdon
	.23	伊爾文(1783—1859)	Irving, Washington
	.24	庫柏(1789—1851)	Cooper, James Fenimore
	.26	保羅鼎(1779—1860)	Paulding, James Kirke
	.29	其他	Others

.3	十九世紀中期	Middle 19th century
	（1830—61）	
.31	愛倫坡(1809—49)	Poe, Edgar Allan
.32	甘涅底(1795—1870)	Kannedy, John Pendleton
.33	何桑(1804—64)	Hawthorne, Nathaniel
.35	習姆士(1806—70)	Simms, William Gilmore
.37	司徒(1812—96)	Stowe, Harriet Beecher
.39	其他	Others
.4	十九世紀後期	Later 19th century
	（1861—1900）	
.41	亞爾科特(1832—88)	Alcott, Louisa May
.42	克力門士(1835—1910)	Clemens, S.L.(Mark Twain)
.43	豪厄爾士(1837—1920)	Howells, William Dean
.45	哈特(1839—1902)	Harte, Francis Bret
.46	赫黎士(1848—1908)	Harris, Joel Chandler
.49	其他	Others
.5	二十世紀(1900—　)	20th century

864	民間文學	American folk literature
865	兒童文學	American juvenile literature
866		
867	散文	American prose
.1	殖民時代(1607—1776)	Colonial
.2	後革命時代	Post-revolutionary
	（1776—1830）	
.21	佛蘭克林(1706—90)	Franklin, Benjamin
.22	韋白斯特(1758—1843)	Webster, Noah
.23	伊爾文(1783—1859)	Irving, Washington

.29	其他	Others
.3	十九世紀中期 （1830—61）	Middle 19th century
.31	霍蘭(1819—81)	Holland, Josiah Gilbert
.32	愛默生(1803—82)	Emerson, Ralph Waldo
.36	霍謨士(1809—94)	Holmes, Oliver Wandell
.37	羅威爾(1819—91)	Lowell, James Russell
.38	惠特曼(1819—92)	Whitman, Walt
.39	其他	Others
.4	十九世紀後期 （1861—1900）	Later 19th century
.5	二十世紀(1900—)	20th century
868	其他文學	American other literatures
.1	函牘文學	Correspondence, letters
	其有文學價值者，某一類之尺牘則入該類。尺牘之重在傳記一方面者則入傳記類	That is, literary and miscellaneous letters, Letters on any one subject go with that subject. A correspondence whose interest is chiefly biographical should be put in biography
	依時代分	By period
.2	幽默諷刺文學	Humorous and satirical literature
	依時代分	By period
	例 伊爾文(1783—1859) 868.223	e.g. Irving, Washington 868.223
	霍謨士(1809—94) 868.236	Holmes, Oliver Wendell 868.236
.3	箴銘類 格言 金言 銘言	Maxims, apothegms, mottoes, etc.
.4	論辯文學 演講錄	Speeches Orations

	.5	序跋類	Foreward, preface, etc.
	.51	題辭　題獻	Dedication
	.52	導言　引言	Introduction
	.53	序文	Preface
	.59	其他	Others
	.7	傳誌文學	Biographical literature Sacrificial
	.8	游記文學	Travels　Voyages
		筆記　日記　回憶錄	Journal, sayings, thought
	.9	雜記　雜事瑣語	Miscellany
869		坎拿大文學	Canadian literature
870		德國文學	German literature
871		詩	German poetry
	.1	前十字軍時代	Before the Crusades
		（後？—1150）	
	.11	喜爾得布藍斯歌	Hildebrandslied
	.13	路易斯歌	Ludwigslied
	.19	其他	Others
	.2	中盛時代(1150—1300)	Middle high
	.21	尼柏隆歌	Nibelungenlied
	.22	谷德倫歌	Gudrun
	.23	海因立哈(？—1200)	Heinrich von Veldeke
	.24	烏弗蘭	Wolfram von Eschenbach
	.29	其他	Others
	.3	浸衰時代(1300—1517)	Period of decline
	.4	革新時代(1715—1625)	Reformation; new high
	.44	薩克斯(1494—1576)	Sachs, Hans

.49	其他	Others
.5	模仿時代（1625—1750）	Period of imitation
.6	經學時代（1750—1830）	Classic period
.62	克洛卜斯托克（1724—1803）	Klopstock, Friedrich Gottlieb
.64	赫德爾（1744—1803）	Herder, Johann Gottfried von
.69	其他	Others
.7	後經學時代（1625—1756）	Postclassic period
.75	海奈（1799—1856）	Heine, Heinrich
.79	其他	Others
.8	十九世紀後期（1856—1900）	Later 19th century
.9	二十世紀（1900— ）	20th century
872	戲曲	German drama

　　　　依時代分　　　　　　　　By period
　　　例　經學時代　　　　　　　e.g. Classic period
　　　　歌德（1749—1832）　　　　Gothe, Johann, Wolfgany
　　　　872.62　　　　　　　　　　von 872.62
　　　　席勒爾（1759—1805）　　　Schiller, Johann Christoph
　　　　872.63　　　　　　　　　　Friedrich 872.63

873	小說	German fiction
874	民間文學	German folk literature
875	兒童文學	German juvenile literature
876		
877	散文	German prose
878	其他文學	German other literatures

879		條頓族其他　各國文學	Literature of other Teutonic countries
	.1	哥德文學	Gothic
	.2	斯坎第那維亞文學	Scandinavian
	.21	挪威文學	Norwegian literature
	.22	瑞典文學	Swedish literature
	.23	丹麥文學	Danish literature
	.24	冰島文學	Icelandic literature
	.3	法里森文學	Frisian
	.8	荷蘭文學	Dutch literature
	.9	其他	Others
880		俄國文學	Russian literature
881		詩	Russian poetry
882		戲曲	Russian drama
883		小說	Russian fiction
884		民間文學	Russian folk literature
885		兒童文學	Russian juvenile literature
886			
887		散文	Russian prose
888		其他文學	Russian other literatures
889		斯拉夫族其他各國文學	Literature of other Slavic countries
		波蘭文學	Polish literature
		捷克文學	Czech literature
		其他	Others

890		其他各國文學	Literature of other languages
891		印度支那語系各國文學	Literature of Indo-Chinese languages
	.1	暹羅文學	Siamese literature
	.3	緬甸文學	Burmese literature
	.4	安南文學	Annamese literature
	.9	其他	Others
892		烏拉阿爾泰語系各國文學	Literature of Ural-Altaic languages
	.1	芬蘭文學	Finnic literature
	.2	拉柏蘭文學	Lappish literature
	.5	匈牙利文學	Hungarian literature
	.6	土耳其文學	Turkic literature
	.9	其他	Others
893		印歐語系各國文學	Literature of Indo-European languages
	.1	印度文學	Indian literature
	.3	波斯文學	Persian literature
	.9	其他	Others
895		塞姆語系各國文學	Literature of Semitic languages
	.1	阿剌伯文學	Arabian literature
	.9	其他	Others
896		含族語系各國文學	Literature of Hamitic languages
	.1	埃及文學	Eygptian literature
	.9	其他	Others
899			

歷史 History

900	歷史		History
	史地合論類此		History and geography together
.1	歷史哲學		Philosophy of history
.2			
.3	辭書		Dictionaries
.37	年鑑		Yearbooks
.4	史評		Critiques　Criticism
.5	雜誌		Periodicals
.6	學會		Societies
.7	研究		Studies
	綱目，綱要，答問，等		Outlines, syllabi, questions, etc.
.8	總集		Collected works
.85	史稿		Historical manuscripts
.86	史鈔		Historical excerpta
.88	小册		Pamphlets
.9	史學		Historiography
			Historiology

凡研究歷史性質，原理，意義，用意，價值，以及各史之研究方法，史學家之義務與態度，歷史修辭，考證義例，歷史關係與影響等等者屬之

General studies to history, its nature, principles, idea, use and misuse, value, etc., and separately study of history, duties and character of the historians, canons of historical criticism, etc.

.97	史學家傳記		Biography
	其關係評傳者		General criticism and biography only
.98	史學地理		Historical geography
	互見 980.19		see also 980.19
	其關係疆界國土者		General work on boundaries; history of territorical expansion, etc.
.99	史學史		History of historiography

901	史料		Historical data when treated collectively
	考古學　見990		Archeology see 990
	其關係一國者　見該國		For individual country go under that country
.1	古文書學		Diplomatics
	古文字學(與古文書學)見990.8		Paleography (and diplomatics) see 990.8
	凡研究古代公文,勅令,特許狀,奏議,等等之可供史料者屬之		Collections of ancient documents, edicts, memorials and petitions, statecraft, etc. for study
.2	公文檔案		Archives Public documents
.21	詔令		Edicts
.23	奏議		Memorials and petitions
.25	實錄		Statecraft
.27	函牘		Public correspondences
.29	其他		Others
.5	璽印　關防		Seals
	其關係美術者　見727		For fine arts see 727
	其關係考古者　見990.16		For archeology see 990.16
.9	其他		Other public documents
	依類分		By subject
902	文化史		History of civilization and culture
.1	民族史		Races Nationalities
.3	世界現狀		Social conditions and customs of the world
.4	世界交通史		History of communications
.7	世界政治外交史		Political and diplomatic history
.8	世界戰爭史		History of War

	總論戰事者類此,其以軍事立場專論兵事方面者入軍事學	General excepting those works which are written from a purely military standpoint for a purely military purpose
	世界大戰　見 930.7	The Great War see 930.7
909	亞洲史	History of Asia
910	中國史	Chinese history
	史地合論類此	Class here works on history and geography together
.01	歷史哲學	Philosophy of history
.03	辭書	Dictionaries
.04	史評	Critiques Criticism
.05	雜誌	Periodicals
.06	學社	Societies
.07	研究	Studies
	綱目,綱要,問答,等	Outlines, syllabi, questions, etc.
.08	總集	Collected works
.085	史稿	Historical manuscripts
	其為一朝代之史稿則入該朝	For that of individual dynasty prefer under that dynasty
	例　清史稿 917.085	e.g. Historical manuscripts of Ch'ing dynasty 917.085
.086	史鈔	Historical excerpta
.088	小冊	Pamphlets
.089	雜著	Miscellanies
.09	史學　史學史	Historiography Historiology
.092	年表	Chronological tables
.097	傳記	Biography
.098	歷史地理	Historical geography
	互見 981.19	see also 981.19
.1	史料	Historical data, general
.2	文化史	History of civilization and culture

.21	民族史	Races Nationalities
.23	民俗史	Social life and customs
.24	交通史	History of communications
.25	興亡史	History of rise and decline
.27	政治制度史　政治交外史	Political history and institutions Political and diplomatic history
	其關係歷代政迹使節等等者	History of periods, and administration, relations with other countries
	至關於一朝之政迹使節等等者則入各該朝	Of individual dynasty prefer with that dynasty
	例　班超之使西域 912.327	e.g. Pan Ch'ao's mission to Hsi Yueh 912.327
.28	戰爭史	History of War
.281	戰事	Battles Special campaigns
.282	國內	Civil wars
	依朝代分或分入各朝	By dynasty or with the dynasty
	例　垓下之戰(前202)	e.g. Battle of Hai Hsia (B.C.202)
.283	國外	Foren wars
	依朝代分或分入各朝	By dynasty or with the dynasty
	例　甲午之戰(1891—95)	e.g. Sino-Japanese war(1894-1895)
.285	俘虜　降卒	Prisoners　Surrenders
.286	和議　盟約	Armistice　Peace
	其關係和戰倍償疆界等者	
.289	將帥	Generals Commanders in chief
.29	革命史	History of revolution
.4	別史	Historiete narratives

凡分別敘述歷朝帝王之文治武功以及其弒‚放‚俘‚質‚等;宗室;后妃;外戚;宦官;權臣;黨獄;教案;盜匪;之關係國之興亡治亂諸著述得依 1~9 次第類列於下

.5　雜史　　　　　　　　　Miscellanies

.6　方隅史　　　　　　　　Local history and description
　　　參看981.5　　　　　　　see also 981.5
　　　凡記載地方之歷史者屬之
　　　例　華陽國志

.7　邊記　外記　　　　　　History of bordering states of China
　　　一朝之外記則入該朝
　　　　例　明夷待訪錄
　　　　　　916.7

.71　滿　　　　　　　　　　Manchuria
　　　凡總論契丹‚遼‚金‚清　　General works on Khitan, Liao, Ching, and
　　　等諸作屬之　　　　　　　　Ch'ing dynasties

.72　蒙　　　　　　　　　　Mongolia
　　　匈奴　胡　　　　　　　Hsiung Nu, and Hu tribes

.73　新疆　青海　　　　　　Sinkiang Chinghai
　　　西域　　　　　　　　　Hsi Yueh

.74　西藏　　　　　　　　　Tibet
　　　回部　　　　　　　　　Mohammedans

.77　苗‚猺‚獞‚等　　　　　History of Miao tribes, or aboriginal Chinese, etc.

910.9　通史　　　　　　　　General history
　　　其限于朝代者則入斷代史　　For individual history of different dynasties put under the dynasties

	例　五代史 914.3	e.g. History of the Five dynasties 914.3
.91	依體裁分	By forms
	斷代紀傳,編年,紀事本末等則入各該朝	Historical records, annals, complete records, etc. of individual dynasty to be clast under that dynasty
	例　明史紀事本末 916.098	e.g. Complete records of Ming dynasty 916.098
	紀傳	Historical records
.911	史記	"Historical records" of SzeMa Ch'ien
	1. 關係　影響	Relations Influence
	2. 圖表	Charts
	3. 體裁	Style, etc.
	文法	Grammar, etc.
	4. 評論	Criticism and interpretation
	7. 研究	Studies
	綱目,綱要,問答,等	Outlines, syllabi, synopses, etc.
	8. 文藝	Literature
	編年	Annals
.913	竹書紀年	"Bamboo books"
	可仿上細分	may be subd. as above
	例　著作 910.9136	e.g. Authorship 910.9136
	其他各史皆可仿上細分	other history books may also be subd. as above
.915	資治通鑑	"National history" or Comprehensive Mirror of SzeMa Kuang
	紀事本末	Complete records
.918	通鑑紀事本末	"Complete records of the National history" of Yuan Shu
.919	其他	Others
.92		
.93	十史	The Ten histories

.94	十七史	The Seventeen histories
.95	十八史	The Eighteen histories
.96	二十一史	The Twenty-one histories
.97	二十二史	The Twenty-two histories
.98	二十四史	The Twenty-four histories
.99	其他	Others
	斷代史	History of individual dynasty
	列朝史皆可仿下細分	History of individual dynasty may be subd. in accordance as follows
	1. 史料	Historical data
	2. 文化史	History of civilization and culture
	4. 別史	Historiette narrtives
	5. 雜史	Miscellanies
	6. 方隅史	Local history and description
	7. 邊紀	History of bordering states
	9. 代時代分	By reigns
	見 附錄三	see Appendix III
	中國歷代帝王表	Chronological tables of the Chinese dynasties
911	先秦及秦代	Pre-Ch'in and Ch'in dynasties
.1	傳說時代	Mythical and legendary period
	凡研究三皇五帝諸作類此	studies of the three primordial sovereigns and the five ancient emperors to be clast here
.3	三代 （？前2205—255）	The three dynasties of antiquity, or ancient
.4	夏（？2205—？1766）	Hsia dynasty
.5	商（殷） （？1766—？1122）	Shang, or Yin dynasty

.6	周（？1122—255）	Chou dynasty
.61	西周（？1122—770）	Western Chou
.62	東周（776—255）	Eastern Chou
.63	春秋時代（772—481）	Age of Feudalism
	五霸類此	History of the "Five leaders" to be clast here
.631	齊	The state of Ch'i
.632	魯	The state of Lu
.633	宋	The state of Sung
.634	鄭	The state of Cheng
.635	晉	The state of Chin
.636	秦	The state of Ch'in
.637	楚	The state of Ch'u
.639	其他春秋各國史乘	History of other I'cudal states
	1.衛	The state of Wei
	3.陳	The state of Ch'en
	5.曹	The state of Ts'ao
	9.其他	Others
.65	戰國時代（481—221）	Age of War, or Age of the Seven States
.651	齊（田齊）（386—221）	The state of Ch'i (House of T'ien)
.652	楚	The state of Ch'u
	見 911.637	see 911.637
.653	燕	The state of Yen
.654	三晉	The three divisions of the state of Chin
.655	韓（403—233）	The state of Han
.656	趙（403—228）	The state of Chao
.657	魏（403—225）	The state of Wei
.658	秦	The state of Ch'in
	見 911.636	see 911.636
.7	秦（221—206）	Ch'in dynasty

	.8	楚(項羽)(206—202)	Ch'u
912		兩漢(202—後220)	Han dynasty
	.1	西漢(202—後9)	Western or Former Han
	.2	新莽(9—23)	The New dynasty
	.3	東漢(25—220)	Eastern or Later Han
	.4	三國(220—280)	The three kingdoms
	.5	魏	The kingdom of Wei
		見 913.1	see 913.1
	.6	蜀(221—263)	Shu Han, or Minor Han
	.7	吳(孫吳)(222—280)	The kingdom of Wu(House of Sun)
913		魏晉六朝隋(220—618)	Wei, Chin, the Six dynasties and Sui
	.1	曹魏(220—265)	Wei(House of Ts'ao)
	.2	兩晉(265—420)	Chin
	.3	西晉(265—317)	Western Chin
	.4	東晉(317—420)	Eastern Chin
	.5	五胡(304—439)	The "Five tribes of Hu"
	.51	匈奴(304—439)	Hsiung Nu, or Mongols
	.52	氐(304—403)	Ti, or Tibetan tribe
	.53	羯(319—351)	Ch'ieh or Tungustic tribe
	.54	鮮卑(349—431)	Hsien Pei, or Tungustic tribe
	.55	羌(348—417)	Ch'iang, or Tibetan tribe
	.58	十六國	The Sixteen kingdoms
	.581	成漢(巴蠻)(304—347)	Cheng Han
	.582	前趙(匈奴)(315—329)	Former Chao
	.583	後趙(羯)(319—351)	Posterior Chao

	.584	前燕(鮮卑)(337—370)	Former Yen
	.585	前涼(漢)(346—376)	Former Liang
	.586	前秦(氐)(351—394)	Former Ch'in
	.587	後燕(鮮卑)(384—409)	Posterior Yen
	.588	後秦(羌)(389—403)	Posterior Ch'in
	.589	西燕(鮮卑)(385—394)	Western Yen
	.591	後涼(氐)(389—403)	Posterior Liang
	.592	西秦(鮮卑)(394—413)	Western Ch'in
	.593	南涼(鮮卑)(397—414)	Southern Liang
	.594	北涼(匈奴)(397—439)	Northern Liang
	.596	西涼(漢)(400—421)	Western Liang
	.597	夏(匈奴)(407—431)	Hsia
	.598	北燕(漢)(409—436)	Northern Yen
.6	南北朝(420—589)		Southern and Northern dynasties
.7	南朝(420—589)		Southern dynasties
	.71	劉宋(420—479)	Sung(House of Liu)
	.72	齊(479—502)	Ch'i(House of Hsiao)
	.73	梁(502—557)	Liang(House of Hsiao)
	.74	陳(557—589)	Ch'en
.8	北朝(386—581)		Northern dynasties
	.81	北魏(386—535)	Northern Wei
	.82	東魏(534—549)	Eastern Wei
	.83	西魏(535—556)	Western Wei
	.85	北齊(550—577)	Northern Ch'i
	.86	北周(557—581)	Northern Chou
.9	隋(581—618)		Sui dynasty
914	唐五代(618—960)		T'ang and the Five dynasties
	.1	唐(618—907)	T'ang dynasty

.3	五代（907—960）	The Five dynasties
.4	後梁（907—923）	Later Liang
.5	後唐（923—936）	Later T'ang
.6	後晉（936—947）	Later Chin
.7	後漢（947—951）	Later Han
.8	後周（951—960）	Later Chou
914.9	十國（907—979）	The Ten kingdoms
.91	吳（886—937）	Wu
.92	閩（873—947）	Ming
.93	楚（907—951）	Ch'u（House of Ma）
.94	吳越（907—978）	Wu Yueh
.95	前蜀（908—925）	Former Shu
.96	南漢（916—971）	Southern Han
.97	荊南（924—963）	Ching Nan
.98	後蜀（938—965）	Posterior Shu
.99	南唐（933—975）	Southern T'ang
.991	北漢（950—979）	Northern Han
915	宋遼金夏（960—1280）	Sung, Liao, Ching, and Hsia dynasties
.1	宋（960—1280）	Sung dynasty
.2	北宋（960—1127）	Northern Sung
.3	南宋（1127—1280）	Southern Sung
.4	遼（907—1211）	Liao dynasty
.5	契丹（907—1124）	Khitan
.6	西遼（1124—1211）	Western Liao
.7	金（1115—1234）	Ching dynasty

	.8	西夏(1036—1227)	Western Hsia
	.9	元(1280—1368)	Yuan dynasty
	.91	蒙古時代 (1206—80)	The Mongol period, the period before the conquest of China
	.92	統一時代 (1280—1368)	The period of Union
	.94	四大汗國 (1280—1368)	The Four grand empires, or khanates
	.95	奇卜察克 (1238—1783)	Kipchack khanate
	.96	察罕臺(1224—1369)	Jargatai khanate
	.97	諤格德(1224—1306)	Ogdai khanate
	.98	伊兒(1256—1368)	Il khanate
916		明(1368—1644)	Ming dynasty
917		清(1644—1912)	Ch'ing dynasty
	.991	太平天國(1850—64)	T'ai Ping T'ien Kuo, or the T'ai Ping Rebellion
918		民國(1912—)	The Republic of China
		亞洲其他各國史	History of other Asiatic countries
		亞洲史　見909	History of Asia see 909
921		日本史	Japanese history
	.1	史料	Historical data, general
	.2	文化史	History of civilization and culture
	.21	民族史	Races Nationalities
	.23	民俗史	Social life and customs
	.27	政治外交史	Political and diplomatic history
	.28		

.29	革命史	History of revolution
.4	別史	Historiette narratives
.8	斷代史	Individual history
		By period
.81	古代	Ancient history
.811	神話時代	Mythologic period
.812	傳說時代	Prehistoric (or legendary) period
	（前660—後480）	
	神武至開代	Jummu-Kaikwa
	（前? 600—98）	
	崇神至雄略	Sujin-Yuryaku
	（98—後480）	
.815	古史（480—645）	Early historic period
	清寧至宣化	Seinei-Senkwa
	（480—539）	
	欽明至皇極	Kimmei-Kogyoku
	（539—645）	
.82	中古	Medieval history
.821	大化革新時代	Taikwa reform
	（645—710）	
	孝德,齊明,天智,弘文,天武,持統,文武	Kotoku, Saimei, Empress (Kokyoku restored), Tenji, Kobun, Temmu, Jito, Empress Mommu
.823	奈良時代（710—794）	Nara period
	元明	Gemmyo, Empress
	元正	Gensho, Empress
	聖武,孝謙	Shomu, Kokeu, Empress
	淳仁,稱德	Junnia, Shotoku, Empress
	光仁	(Koken restored), Konin
.825	平安時代（794—1192）	Heian period

	桓武,平城,嵯峨,淳和,仁明,文德,清和,陽成,光孝,宇多,醍醐,朱雀,村上,冷泉,圓融,華山,一條,三條,後一條,後朱雀,後冷泉,後三條,白河,堀河,鳥羽,崇德,近衞,後白河,二條,六條,高倉,安德	Kwammu, Heizei, Saga, Junna, Nimmyo, Montoku, Seiwa, Yozei, Koko, Uda, Daigo, Shujaku, Murakami, Reizei, Enyu, Kwazan, Ichijo, Sanjo, Go-Ichijo, Go-Shujaku, Go-Reizei, Go-Sanjo, Shirakawa, Horikawa, Toba, Sutoku, Konoe, Go-Shirakawa, Nijo, Rokujo, Takakura, Antoku
.83	幕府時代	Feudal ages Shoguns
	近古	Early modern history
.831	鎌倉時代(1192—1333)	Kamakura period
	後鳥羽,土御門,順德,仲恭,後堀河,四條,後嵯峨,後深草,龜山,後宇多,伏見,後伏見,後二條,花園,後醍醐	Go-Toba, Tsuchimikado, Juntoku, Chukyo, Go-Horikawa, Shijo, Go-Saga, Go-Fukakusa, Kameyama, Go-Uda, Fushimi, Go-Fushimi, Go-Nijo, Hanazono, Go-Daigo
.832	建武中興(1333—39)	Imperial restoration
.833	吉野時代(1339—92)	Yoshino(Southern dynasty)
	後村上,長慶,後龜山	Go-Murakami, Chokei, Go-Kameyama
.834	室町(足利)時代(1392—1464)	Muromachi(Kyoto)period(Northern dynasty)
	光嚴,光明,崇光,後光嚴,後圓融,後小松,稱光,後花園	Kogon, Komyo, Suko, Go-Kogon, Go-Enyu, Go-Komatsu, Shoko, Go-Hanazono
.835	戰國時代(1467—1573)	The period of War
	後土御門,後柏原,後奈良	Go-Tsuchimikado, Go-Kashiwabara, Go-Nara
.836	安土(織田)時代(1573—1582)	Oda period

		正親町	O-Gimachi
.837		桃山(豐臣)時代(1582—1603)	Momoyama period
		後陽成	Go-Yozei
.84		江戶(德川)時代 近世(1603—1868)	Edo period Tokugawa shoguns Modern history
.841		創業時代(1603—51)	Foundation
		後陽成(慶長八年)	Go-Yozei
		後水尾	Go-Minoo
		明正	Myosho, Empress
		後光明	Go-Komyo
.843		興盛時代(1651—1837)	Prosperity
.844		元祿時代(1651—1709)	
		後西院,靈元,東山	Go-Saiin, Reigen Higashiyama
.845		享保時代(1709—45)	
		中御門	Nakamikado
		櫻町(延享二年)	Sakuramachi
.846		田沼時代(1745—86)	
		櫻町(延享二年)	Sakuramachi
		桃園	Momozono
		後櫻町	Go-Sakuramachi
		後桃園	Go-Momozono
		光格(天明六年)	Kokaku
.847		化政時代(1786—1837)	
		光格(天明七年)	Kokaku
		仁孝(天保七年)	Ninko
.848		衰弱時代(1837—68)	Fall
		仁孝(天保八年)	Ninko
		孝明	Komei

	.85	皇室復興時代　近代	Imperial power reestablished
		（1868—　）	
	.86	明治（1868—1912）	Meiji period Emperor Mutsuhito
	.863	清日之戰（1894—95）	Sino-Japanese war
	.865	日俄之戰（1904—05）	Russo-Japanese war
	.867	韓國之亡（1908—12）	The Fall of Korea
	.87	大正（1912—26）	Taisho period Emperor Yoshihito
	.88	昭和（1926—　）	Showa period Emperor Hirohito
	.9	台灣，琉球，澎湖史	History of Formosa, Loochoo, etc.
922		高麗史	History of Korea (Ch'ao-Sien)
	.1	史料	Historical data, general
	.2	文化史	History of civilization and culture
	.21	民族史	Races Nationalities
	.23	民俗史	Social life and customs
	.25	興亡史	History of rise and decline
	.27	政治外交史	Political and diplomatic history
	.4	別史	Historiette narratives
	.5	雜史	Miscellanies
	.8	斷代史	History of special period
	.81	箕氏時代	
		（？前—149）（朝鮮）	
	.82	衛滿至石渠時代	
		（149—108）	
	.83	混亂時代	
	.84	三國時代	
	.841	高句麗（37—後668）	
	.843	百濟（14—後668）	
	.845	新羅（57—後935）	

.85	王氏時代(918—1392)	
	（後高麗）	
.86	李氏時代(1392—1910)	
	（後朝鮮）	
.87	日屬時代(1910—　)	
	獨立運動(1917—1931)	

923　印度史　　　　　　　　History of India

.1	史料	Historical data, general
.2	文化史	History of civilization and culture
.21	民族史	Races Nationalities
.23	民俗史	Social life and customs
.27	政治外交史	Political and diplomatic history
.28		
.5	雜史	Miscellanies
.6	方隅史	Local history and description
	參看 982.35	see also 982.35
.8	斷代史	History of special period
.81	獨立時代	Hindus Early history
	（前？—後 997）	
.82	回屬時代(997—1205)	Mohammedan conquests
.83	阿富汗帝國時代	Patan or Afghan empire
	（1205—1397）	
.84	蒙古帝國時代	Mongol conquests
	（1526—1748）	
.85	法國經營時代	Early French settlements
	（1664—1761）	
.86	英屬時代(1861—　)	British conquests

按英于一八五八年逐印
帝於仰光印度係亡

.9 錫蘭 不丹 尼泊爾史 History of Ceylon, Bhotan, Nepal, etc.

924 印度支那半島各國史 Farther India

.1 印度支那史(越南) Indo-China

.2 交趾支那(南圻) Cochin China

.3 安南(中圻) Anam

.4 柬蒲塞(高綿) Cambodia

.5 東京(北圻) Tonkin

.6 老撾(辽國) Laos

.7 緬甸史 Burma

.79 英屬緬甸史 British Burma

.8 暹羅史 Siam

.9 馬來半島史 Malay peninsula

925 波斯史 History of Persia

可依各國細分 subd.like others

.9 阿富汗史 俾路支史 Afghanistan Baluchistan

926 土耳其史 Turkish or Ottoman Empire

可依各國細分 subd.like others

.9 西土耳其史 History of Turkey in Europe

927 阿剌伯史 History of Arabia

可仿各國細分 subd.like others
凡總論世界回教帝國史類此 Mohammedan empire in general throughout the world

.9 漢志史 History of Hejaz

928　小亞西亞其他各國　History of Asia Minor
　　　史
　.1　　巴比倫　　　　　　Babylonia
　.2　　亞述　　　　　　　Assyria
　.3　　腓尼基　　　　　　Phoenicia
928.4　猶太　　　　　　　Judia
　.481　　古代(前？—63)　　Early period
　.482　　羅馬時代　　　　Romans
　　　　（前63—後136）
　　　　耶路撒冷滅亡以後時　　After the fall of Jerusalem
　　　　代
　.483　　中古　　　　　　Medieval period
　.485　　各國猶太史　　　History of Jews in countries out of Palestine
　　　　依國分　　　　　　may be subd. by countries
　　　　　例　英國猶太史　　　e.g. Jews in English
　　　　　　　德國猶太史　　　Jews in Germany
　.7　　叙利亞　　　　　　Syria
　.9　　其他　　　　　　　Others
930　歐洲史　　　　　　　　European history
　.1　　史料　　　　　　　Historical data, general
　.2　　文化史　　　　　　History of civilization and culture
　.21　　民族史　　　　　　Races Nationalities
　.27　　政治外交史　　　　Political and diplomatic history
　.28　　戰爭史　　　　　　History of War
　　　　世界大戰　　　　　　The Great War or The World
　　　　見930.7　　　　　　War see 930.7
　.4　　古代史(？—後476)　Ancient Europe
　　　　止於西羅馬帝國之滅亡　To fall of the Western empire (Rome)
　.5　　中古史(476—1453)　Medieval Europe

	拜占庭帝國	For Byzantine empire
	見 931.86	see 931.86
.51	新國建立時代	Rise of new nations
	（476—800）	
.53	封建時代（800—1100）	Age of feudalism
.55	武士道時代	Age of chivalry
	（1100—1453）	
	止於東羅馬帝國之滅亡	To fall of the Eastern empire (Constantinople)
.57	十字軍時代	Crusades
	（1096—1270）	
.6	近世史（1453—　）	Modern Europe
.61	文藝復興時代	Renaissance period
	（1453—1517）	
.62	宗教革興時代	Age of the reformation
	（1517—1789）	
.63	卅年戰爭時代	30 years war
	（1618—1648）	
.65	拿皇時代	Napoleonic period
	（1789—1815）	
.67	十九世紀	19th century
	（1815—1914）	
.68	神聖同盟	Holy alliance
	（1815—1830）	
.7	世界大戰	The Great War
		The World War
	下列均限於關係大戰者，否則宜各入其類	Conditions and events mentioned below are to be clast here only when considered distinctly in relation to the war, otherwise under their own numbers

.705		雜誌	Periodicals
.706		會議	Congresses Conferences
.708		雜集	Collected works
		文藝	War poetry, satire, caricuture, etc.
		圖片	Pictorial works
		小冊	Pamphlets
.709		傳記	Biography
.71	史料		Historical data
.72	政治史		Political history
.721		大戰原因	Causes
		歷史, 政治, 外交方面	Historical, political and diplomatic causes
		經濟方面	Economic causes
.723		大戰善後	Efforts to preserve or restore peace
.725		協約	Results: terms of peace
.726		歐洲改造	Reconstruction
.727		大戰之影響於世界	Effect on world conditions
.728		大戰之影響於各國	Effect on special countries
.73	外交史		Diplomatic history
.75	國團		Groups of countries: allies and neutrals
.751		德聯	Entente
.753		國聯	Teuton allies, Central powers
.755		中立國	Neutrals
.76	戰事		Battles Special campaigns
.761		陸戰	Land operations
.763		海戰	Naval warfare
.765		空戰	Air warfare or operations
.77	俘傷 死亡		Prisoners The death
		戰區住民災民之保護與救濟	Welfare works for refugees
.78	慶祝 紀念		Celebrations Commemorations

.8	二十世紀（1914— ）	20th century
931	希臘史	Greek (Hellas) history
.1	史料	Historical data, general
.2	文化史	History of civilization and culture
.21	民族史	Races Nationalities
.23	民俗史	Social life and customs
.25	興亡史	History of rise and decline
.27	政治外交史	Political and diplomatic history
.28		
.5	雜史	Miscellanies
.6	方隅史	Local history and description
	參看 983.15	see also 983.15
.8	斷代史	Period divisions
.81	傳說時代	Mythical or heroic age
	（？前—776）	
.82	建國時代（776—479）	Growth of states
	統一時代（500—479）	Union of Greece
	波斯戰爭	Persian wars
.83	盟主時代（479—323）	The period of the supremacy
.831	雅典（479—404）	Athenian supremacy
	半島之戰（431—404）	Peloponnesian war
.833	斯巴達　塞拜	Spartan and Theban supremacy
	（404—362）	
.835	馬其頓（362—323）	Macedonian supremacy
	世界之征服	Conquest of the world
	（334—323）	
.84	羅馬征服時代	Roman conquest of Greece
	（323—後323）	

.85	復興時代(323—716)	Greek revival(Medieval Greece)	
	(中古史)		
.86	拜占庭帝國時代	Byzantine empire	
	(716—1453)		
.861	極盛時期(716—1057)	Period of prosperity	
.863	衰亡時期(1057—1204)	Period of decline	
.865	希臘復存時期	Period of survival	
	(1204—1453)		
.87	土耳其征服時代	Turkish occupation	
	(1453—1821)		
.88	獨立時代(1821—)	Greek independence	
	(近世史)	(Modern Greece)	
.881	帝制時期(1827—1924)	Empire	
.883	共和時期(1924—)	Republic	

932　羅馬史　意大利史　Roma Italy

.1	史料	Historical data, general
.2	文化史	History of civilization and culture
.21	民族史	Races Nationalities
.23	民俗史	Social life and customs
.27	政治外交史	Political and diplomatic history
.28		
.6	方隅史	Local history and description
	參看983.25	see also 983.25
.8	斷代史	Period divisions
.81	羅馬時代	Period of Rome
.82	列王時期	Kings
	(前753—509)	
.83	共和時期(509—31)	Republic

	意大利之征服 (509—264)	Conquest of Italy
	世界之征服(264—31)	Conquest of the world
	內訌(164—31)	Civil strife
.84	帝制時期 (31—後476)	Empire
.841	憲政(31—後284)	Constitutional
.843	專制(284—476)	Absolute
.845	帝國之分裂 (395—476)	Division of empire
.846	西羅馬之滅亡(476)	Fall of the Western empire
.847	東羅馬帝國(476—1453)	Eastern empire(Constantinople)
.848	近代(1453—)	Modern Rome
	意大利首都羅馬 (1870—)	Capital of Italy
.85	意大利時代	Period of Italy
.86	古代(476—1300)	Early Italy
.861	高盧,倫巴時期 (476—774)	Gothic and Lombard kingdoms
.863	法皇時期(774—961)	Frankish emperors
.865	德皇時期(961—1122)	German emperors
.867	市政時期(1100—1300)	Age of the commune
.87	中世(1300—1870)	Medieval Italy
.871	暴君時期(1300—1492)	Age of the despots
.873	侵犯時期(1492—1527)	Age of invasions
.875	西奧統治時期 (1527—1796)	Spanish-Austrian ascendancy
.877	獨立運動時期 (1796—1870)	Struggle for independence
.88	統一時期(1870—)	United Italy

933	西班牙史 葡萄牙史	Spain Portugal	
.1	史料	Historical data, general	
.2	文化史	History of civilization and culture	
.21	民族史	Races Nationalities	
.23	民俗史	Social life and customs	
.27	政治外交史	Political and diplomatic history	
.28			
.5	雜史	Miscellanies	
.6	方隅史	Local history and description	
	參看 983.35	see also 983.35	
.8	斷代史	Period divisions	
.81	古代（ —後711）	Early history	
.811	羅馬時代	Roman dominion	
.813	高盧時代	Gothic kingdom	
.82	回屬時代(711—1479)	Moorish kingdom	
.83	腓得南五世與以色巴拉時代(1479—1516)	Ferdinand 5 and Isabella	
.84	查理一世與腓力二世時代(1516—1598)	Charles I and Philip 2	
.85	腓力三世至查理四世時代(1598—1808)	Philip 3-Charles 4	
.859	半島之戰(1808—1814)	Peninsular war	
.86	布邦復辟時代(1814—1868)	Bourbon restoration	
.87	革命與第二次復辟時代(1868—1931)	Revolution and 2nd restoration	

.88	共和時代(1931—)	The Republic
.9	葡萄牙史	Portugal
.981	古代	Early history
	羅馬時代	Roman dominion
	高盧時代	Gothic kingdom
.983	回屬時代	Moorish kingdom
.984	爵臣主政時代(1095—1139)	Counts
.985	西屬時代(1580—1640)	Spanish rule
.986	獨立時代(1640—1910)	Portugal independence
.987	共和時代(1910—)	The Republic

934　法國史　France

.1	史料	Historical data, general
.2	文化史	History of civilization and culture
.21	民族史	Races Nationalities
.23	民俗史	Social life and customs
.27	政治外交史	Political and diplomatic history
.28	戰爭史	History of war, general
.29	革命史	History of revolution, general
	總論法國革命史類此	
.5	雜史	Miscellanies
.6	方隅史	Local history and description
	參看 983.45	see also 983.45
.8	斷代史	Period divisions
.81	古代(—987)	Early history
.811	古瑟爾時期(—前59)	Ancient Kelts
.813	羅馬時期(59—後418)	Roman dominion
.815	馬諾芬時期(418—752)	Merovingian dynasty
.817	加諾林時期(752—987)	Carolingian

.82	卡白與華洛時代	Capet and Valois
	卡白至亨利三世	Hugh Capet to Henry 3
.83	布邦時代	Bourbon
	（1589—1789）	
	亨利四世至路易十六	Henry 4-Louis 16
.84	革命時代	Revolution
	（1789—1804）	
.841	國會時期(1789—92)	National assembly
.843	第一次共和(1792—99)	First republic
.844	國會時期(1792—95)	Convention
.845	恐怖時期(1799—1804)	Reign of terror
.846	五執政內閣時期	Directory
	（1795—99）	
.847	拿皇執政時期	First consulate, Napoleon
	（1799—1804）	
.85	拿皇稱帝時代	First empire
	（1804—14）	
.86	光復時代(1814—48)	Restoration
	路易十八至腓力	Louis 18-Louis Philippe
.87	二次共和與二次帝制	Second republic and second empire
	（1848—70）	
	拿破崙(路易)至拿破崙三世	Louis Napoleon-Napoleon 3
.88	三次共和(1870—)	Third republic

935	英國史　大英史	England Great Britain
.1	史料	Historical data, general
.2	文化史	History of civilization and culture
.21	民族史	Races Nationalities
.23	民俗史	Social life and customs

.27	政治外交史	Political and diplomatic history
.28	戰爭史	History of war, general
.6	方隅史	Local history and description
	參看 983.55	see also 983.55
.8	斷代史	Period divisions
.81	盎格諾 薩克森時代 （前 55—後 1066）	Anglo-Saxon
	先史, 羅馬, 布列顛, 等時期	Prehistoric, Roman, British, Danish
.82	諾爾曼時代 （1066—1154）	Norman
	威廉一世, 威廉二世, 亨利一世, 史蒂芬	William 1, William 2, Henry 1, Stephen
.83	普郎大那時代 （1154—1399）	Plantagenet
	亨利二世, 理查一世, 約翰, 亨利三世, 愛德華一世, 愛德華二世, 愛德華三世, 理查二世	Henry 2, Richard 1, John, Henry 3, Edward 1, Edward 2, Edward 3, Richard 2
.84	蘭約兩黨執政時代 （1399—1485）	Lancaster and York
	亨利四世, 亨利五世, 亨利六世, 愛德華四世, 愛德華五世, 理查三世,	Henry 4, Henry 5, Henry 6, Edward 4, Edward 5, Richard 3
.85	都鐸爾時代 （1485—1603）	Tudor
	亨利七世, 亨利八世, 愛德華六世, 瑪利, 以利沙伯	Henry 7, Henry 8, Edward 6, Mary, Elizabeth

.86	斯圖亞時代 （1603—1704）	Stuart
	詹姆斯一世,查理一世, 共和黨時代,查理二世, 詹姆斯二世,威廉三世, 安麗	James 1, Charles 1, Commonwealth, Charles 2, James 2, William 3, Anne
.87	漢諾威時代 （1714—1837）	Hanover
	喬治一世,喬治二世,喬 治三世,喬治四世,威廉 四世	George 1, George 2, George 3, George 4, William 4
.88	漢諾威後期(1837—　)	Later Hanoverian Windsor
	維多利亞,愛德華七世, 喬治五世	Victoria, Edward 7, George 5
.9	蘇格蘭,愛爾蘭,威爾 斯,專史	History of Scotland, Ireland, Wales
.91	蘇格蘭	Scotland
.911	高爾時代(　—1097)	Gaelic period
.912	英國時代(1097—1314)	English period
.913	獨立時代(1314—1424)	Independent kingdom
.914	詹姆斯氏時代 （1424—1557）	The Jameses
.915	革新時代(1557—1603)	Reformation
.916	聯治時代(1603—1707)	Union of crowns and parliaments
.917	漢諾威時代 （1707—1837）	Hanover
.918	漢諾威後期(1837—　)	Later Hanoverian Windsor
.93	愛爾蘭	Ireland
.931	初期(　—1086)	Early history
.933	列國時代(1086—1172)	Separate kingdoms
.935	英治時代(1172—1801)	English domain

		自亨利二世之征服起	Conquest by Henry 2—Closing with the
		至喬治三世時聯治止	union
.937		十九世紀(1801—1900)	19th century
.938		二十世紀(1900—)	20th century
.95		威爾斯	Wales

937　　德國史　　　　　　　　　　German

　　　　德奧匈史合著類此　　　　Germany, Austria, and Hungary together

.1	史料	Historical data, general
.2	文化史	History of civilization and culture
.21	民族史	Races Nationalities
.23	民俗史	Social life and customs
.27	政治外交史	Political and diplomatic history
.28	戰爭史	History of war, general
.5	雜史	Miscellanies
.6	方隅史	Local history and description
	參看 983.75	see also 983.75
.8	斷代史	Period divisions
.81	建國時代(　—後843)	Formative period
	羅馬戰爭	Wars with Rome
	查理曼大帝(800—814)	Charlemagne
.82	宗教革新前之帝國	Empire before the reformation
	(843—1519)	
	路易二世至馬克西米連一世	Louis 2—Maximilian 1
.83	宗教革新後之帝國	Reformation
	(1519—1618)	
	查理五世至馬提亞	Charles 5—Matthias
.84	分裂時代	Disintegration
	(1618—1705)	

		斐迪南二世至利歐破爾一世	Ferdinand 2—Leopold 1
.85		普魯士興盛時代（1705—1789）	Rise of Prussia
		約瑟一世至約瑟二世	Joseph 1—Joseph 2
.86		拿皇戰征時代（1789—1815）	Napoleonic wars
		利歐破爾二世至法蘭西斯二世	Leopold 2—Francis 2
.87		改造時代（1815—1866）	Reorganization
.88		新帝國時代（1866—1918）	New German empire
		威廉一世至威廉二世	William 1—William 2
.89		共和時代（1918—　）	German republic
.9		條頓族其他各國史	History of other Teutonic countries
.91		尼柔蘭（比國與荷蘭）	Netherlands(Belgium and Holland)
.92		比國史	Belgium
.93		荷蘭史	Holland(Dutch)
.931		初期（　—1476）	Early history
.932		奧治時代（1476—1507）	Austrian dominion
.933		西治時代（1507—66）	Spanish dominion
.934		獨立戰爭時代（1566—1648）	Wars for independence
.935		興盛時代（1648—1795）	Age of prosperity
.936		革命時代（1795—1830）	Revolutionary
.937		十九世紀（1830—1900）	19th century
.938		二十世紀（1900—　）	20th century
.94		瑞士史	Switzerland
.941		初期（　—1300）	Early history
.942		獨立戰爭時代（1300—1499）	Struggle for independence

.943	革新時代(1499—1648)	Reformation
.944	和平時代(1648—1789)	Period of tranquillity
.945	革命時代(1789—1815)	Period of revolution
.947	十九世紀(1815—1900)	19th century
.948	二十世紀(1900—)	20th century
.95	奧匈史	Austria Hungary
.96	捷克史	Czechoslovakia
.97	波蘭史	Poland
.98	斯坎第那維亞史	Scandinavia
	挪威,瑞典,丹麥合史	Norway, Sweden, Denmark together
.981	傳說時代(—800)	Legendary period
	移民時代(800—1397)	Consolidation Migration
.982	三國統一時代(1397—1523)	Union of the 3 kingdoms
.983	革新時代(1523—1618)	The reformation
	浸衰時代(1648—1792)	The decline
.984	拿皇戰征時代(1792—1818)	Napoleonic wars
	挪威瑞典之合併 1814	Union of Norway and Sweden
.985	十九世紀(1818—1900)	19th century
	二十世紀(1900—)	20th century
.986	挪威史	Norway
.987	瑞典史	Sweden
.988	丹麥史	Denmark
.989	冰島史	Iceland Faroe islands
.99	其他	Others
938	俄國史	Russia(Union of Socialist Soviet Republics)

.1	史料	Historical data, general
.2	文化史	History of civilization and culture
.21	民族史	Races Nationalities
.23	民俗史	Social life and customs
.27	政治外交史	Political and diplomatic history
.28	戰爭史	History of war, general
.5	雜史	Miscellanies
.6	方隅史	Local history and description
	參看 983.85	see also 983.85
.8	斷代史	Period divisions
.81	初期（ —1237）	Primitive Russia
.82	蒙古侵略時代（1237—1462）	Mongolian invasion
.83	伊桓三世至五世（1462—1689）	Ivan 3—Ivan 5
.84	大彼得時代（1689—1725）	Peter the Great
.85	格得運一世至二世（1725—96）	Catharine 1—Catharine 2
.86	保羅一世至尼古拉一世(1796—1855)	Paul 1—Nicholas 1
.87	亞力山大二世至尼古拉二世(1855—1917)	Alexander 2—Nicholas 2
.88	蘇聯共和時代（1917— ）	Republic

939　歐洲其他各國史　　　History of other European countries

　　.1　芬蘭史　　　　　　　Finland

	.2	拉柏蘭史	Lapland
	.5	巴爾幹半島各國史	Balkan states
	.51	羅馬尼亞	Rumania
	.53	亞爾巴尼亞	Albania
	.55	巨哥斯拉夫（南斯拉夫）	Jugoslavia
	.57	塞國	Serbia
	.58	布加利亞	Bulgaria
	.7	波羅的海各國史	Baltic provinces
	.71	愛沙尼亞	Esthonia
	.73	拉脫維亞	Latvia
	.75	立陶宛	Lithuania
	.9	其他	Others
		西土耳其	For Turkey in Europe
		見 929.6	see 929.6
940		美洲史	American history (General)
941		美國史	History of the United States of America
	.1	史料	Historical data, general
	.2	文化史	History of civilization and culture
	.21	民族史	Races Nationalities
	.23	民俗史	Social life and customs
	.27	政治外交史	Political and diplomatic history
	.28	戰爭史	History of war, general
	.5	雜史	Miscellanies
	.6	方隅史	Local history and description
		參看 984.15	see also 984.15

.8　　　斷代史　　　　　　　　Period divisions

.81　　　發現時代　　　　　　　Discovery
　　　　（　—後 1607）

.811　　　先科倫布時代　　　　　Precolumbian
　　　　　例　阿刺伯,中國等　　　e.g. Arabs, Chinese, etc.
　　　　　　　之發現美洲

.813　　　科倫布時代　　　　　　Columbus

.815　　　後科倫布時代　　　　　Postcolumbian
　　　　　西班牙　葡萄牙　　　　Spanish and Portuguese
　　　　　英國　　　　　　　　　English
　　　　　法國　　　　　　　　　French
　　　　　其他　　　　　　　　　Other nations

.82　　　殖民時代　　　　　　　Colonial period
　　　　（1607—1775）

.83　　　革命時代　　　　　　　Revolution and confederation
　　　　（1775—89）

.84　　　憲政時代　　　　　　　Constitutional period
　　　　（1789—1809）

.841　　　華盛頓　　　　　　　　George Washington
　　　　　　　　　　　　　　　　30 Ap.1789—4 Mar.1797

.842　　　亞當士　　　　　　　　John Adams
　　　　　　　　　　　　　　　　4 Mar.1797—4 Mar.1801

.843　　　哲斐孫　　　　　　　　Thomas Jefferson
　　　　　　　　　　　　　　　　4 Mar.1801—4 Mar.1809

.85　　　十九世紀初期　　　　　Early 19th century
　　　　（1809—61）

.851　　　馬迪孫　　　　　　　　James Madison
　　　　　　　　　　　　　　　　4 Mar.1809—4 Mar.1817

.852　　　孟祿　　　　　　　　　James Monroe

			4 Mar.1817—4 Mar.1825
941.853		亞當士(昆稷)	John Quincy Adams
			4 M.1825—4 M.1829
.854		哲克孫	Andrew Jackson
			4 M.1829—4 M.1837
.855		梵柏稜	Martin Van Buren
			4 M.1837—4 M.1841
.856		哈禮孫	William Henry Harrison
			4 M.1841—4 April.1841
.857		泰勞	John Tyler
			4 April 1841—4 M.1845
.858		坡克	James Knox Polk
			4 Mar 1845—4 M.1849
.859		泰羅	Zachary Tylor
			5 M.1849—9 July 1850
	1.	斐爾摩	Millard Fillmore
			9 July 1850—4 M.1853
	2.	皮爾司	Franklin Pierce
			4 M.1853—4 M.1857
	3.	布卡南	James Buchanan
			4 M.1857—4 M.1861
.86		內戰時代(1861—65)	War of secession
.861		林肯	Abraham Lincoln
			4 M.1861—15 April 1865
.87		十九世紀後期 （1865—1901）	Later 19th century
.871		約翰孫	Andrew Johnson
			15 Ap.1865—4 M.1869
.872		格蘭特	Ulysses Simpson Grant
			4 M.1869—4 M.1877
.873		赫斯	Rutherford Birchard Hayes

.874	嘉菲爾	4 M.1877—4 M.1881 James Abram Garfield 4 M.1881—19 Sep.1881
.875	阿德	Chester Alan Arthur 19 Sep.1881—4 M.1885
.876	克力非蘭(第一任)	Grover Cleveland, 1st.term 4 M.1885—4 M.1889
.877	哈禮孫(便雅憫)	Benjamin, Harrison 4 M.1889—4 M.1893
.878	克力非蘭(第二任)	Grover Cleveland, 2nd term 4 M.1893—4 M.1897
.879	馬金烈	William McKinley 4 M.1897—14 Sep.1901
.88	二十世紀(1901—)	20th century
.881	羅斯福	Theodore Roosevelt 14 Sep.1901—4 M.1909
.882	泰福	William Howard Taft 4 M.1909—4 M.1913
941.883	威爾遜	Woodrow Wilson 4 M.1913—4 M.1921
.884	哈丁	Warren Gamaliel Harding 4 M.1921—2 Aug.1923
.885	顧里治	Calvin Coolidge 2 Aug.1923—4 M.1929
.886	胡佛	Herbert Clark Hoover 4 M.1929—4 M.1933
.887	羅斯福(佛蘭克林)	Franklin Delano Roosevelt 4 M.1933—
942	**坎拿大史**	**Canada British America**
.81	法屬時代 (1497—1763)	French regime

	.811	發現及佔領時代 (1497—1632)	Discovery and early settlement
	.813	英國浸入時代 (1632—1763)	Extension of English rule
	.815	英法戰爭時代 (1755—63)	Struggle with England for supremacy
	.82	戰後至立憲時代 (1763—91)	End of 7 years war to constitutional act 1791
	.83	立憲至聯治時代 (1791—1841)	1792 to Union act 1841
	.85	聯治至聯盟時代 (1841—67)	Union 1841 to Confederation 1867
	.86	英屬時代(1867—)	Dominion of Canada
943	北美洲其他各國史		History of other North American countries
		印第安史,其他	Aboriginal America The Indians, etc.
944	墨西哥史		Mexico
	.81	古代(—1516)	Ancient civilization
	.82	發現與西治時代 (1516—1810)	Discovery and Spanish rule
	.83	獨立戰爭時代 (1810—22)	Independence
	.84	第一帝國時代 (1822—45)	First empire
	.85	美墨戰爭時代 (1845—48)	War with the United States
	.86	立憲與革新時代 (1848—61)	Constitution of 1857 Reform
	.87	法國干政時代	French intervention

		（1861—67）	
	.88	十九世紀後期	Later 19th century
		（1867—1900）	
	.89	二十世紀(1900—)	20th century
945		西班牙美洲史	Spanish America
		拉丁美洲史	Latin America
		墨西哥,中美洲,西印度,南美洲合史類此	Mexico, Central America, West Indies and South America; all of three of them combined
		西班牙與拉丁之影響及於美洲者其論著類此	Spanish or Latin influence in America Spaniards in North America(general)
946		中美洲各國史	Central Ameria
	.1	危地馬拉	Guatemala
	.2	英領洪都拉斯	British Honduras Belize
	.3	洪都拉斯	Honduras
	.4	薩爾瓦多	San Salvador
	.5	尼加拉瓜	Nicaragua
	.6	哥斯達黎加	Costa Rica
	.8	巴拿馬	Panama
947		西印度群島史	West Indies
	.1	古巴	Cuba
	.2	牙買加	Jamaica
	.3	聖多明谷	Santo Domingo
	.4	海地	Hayti
	.5	波爾多黎各	Porto Rico
	.6	巴哈馬	Bahamas
	.7	利溫群島	Leeward islands

	.8	文德瓦德群島	Windward islands Barbados
	.9	百慕群島	Bermudas
948		南美洲各國史	South America
	.1	巴西	Brazil
	.2	阿根廷	Argentina
	.29	巴塔哥尼亞	Patagonia
	.3	智利	Chile
	.4	玻利維亞	Bolivia
	.5	秘魯	Peru
	.6	哥倫比亞共和國	U.S. of Colombia
	.69	厄瓜多爾	Ecuador
	.7	委內瑞拉	Venezuela
	.8	基阿那	Guiana
	.9	巴拉圭	Paraguay
	.99	烏拉圭	Uruguay
		非洲大洋洲	History of Africa and Oceania
950		非洲史	Africa
		北非與東非	North and East Africa
951		埃及史	Egypt
	.1	史料	Historical data, general
	.2	文化史	History of civilization and culture
	.21	民族史	Races Nationalities
	.23	民俗史	Social life and customs
	.27	政治外交史	Political and diplomatic history
	.28	戰爭史	History of war, general
	.5	雜史	Miscellanies

	.6	方隅史	Local history and description
		參看 985.15	see also 985.15
	.8	列代史	Period divisions
	.81	古帝國時代	Ancient Egypt
		（前 3180—525）	
		古代與中古帝國	Old and middle kingdoms
		（第一朝至第十七朝）	1st-17th dynasties
		新帝國	New kingdoms
		（第十八朝至第二十六朝）	18th-26th dynasties
	.82	波斯時代(525—332)	Persian rule
	.83	希臘時代(332—30)	Greek rule Alexander and Ptolemies
		埃及女王克力奧佩特	Cleopatra
	.84	羅馬時代	Roman rule
		（30—後 638）	
	.85	回屬時代(638—1684)	Mohammedan rule
	.86	土耳其時代	Turkish rule
		（1684—1882）	
		法蘭西侵略時代	French invasion
		（1798—1801）	
	.87	英屬時代	British domain
		（1882—1922）	
	.88	獨立時代(1922—)	Egypt independence
952		阿比西尼亞史	Abyssinia Ethiopia
953		摩洛哥史	Morocco
954		北非東非其他各國史	History of other North and East Africa
	.8	亞爾基里亞史	Algeria

955	西非各國史	West Africa
.5	里比利亞史	Liberia
956	中非各國史	Central Africa
.5	剛果自由邦史	Kongo Free State
957	南非各國史	South Africa
.6	鄂蘭吉自由邦史	Orange Free State
959	大洋洲史	Oceania Polar regions
.1	南洋群島史	Malaysia
.2	巽他群島史	Sunda
.3	澳大利亞史	Australia
.4	新西蘭史	New Zealand
.5	美拉尼西亞(沿岸群島)史	Malanesia
.59	新幾內亞史	New Guinea
.6	密克羅尼西亞(細島)史	Micronesia
.7	波里尼西亞(多島)史	Polynesia
.8	夏威夷群島史	Hawaii
.9	南北極史	Polar regions
.91	南冰洋	Antarctic regions
.95	北冰洋	Arctic regions
960	紋章學	Heraldry
.01	理論 關係	Theories Relations
	紋章學與美術,等	Heraldry and art, etc.
.02	圖案	Heraldic drawing, design
.08	文藝	Literary illustrations, verses, etc.

		游藝	Heraldic recreations, games, etc.
	.09	歷史	History of heraldry
	.1	盔飾	Crests
	.2	花字	Monograms
	.3	花樣	Devices
	.4	袖章	Badges
	.5	警句	Mottoes
	.6	吶喊	Battle-cries War-cries
	.7	旗幟	Flags, banners, and standards
	.8	賜授　佩戴	Law, grants of arms, etc. Right to bear arms
961		國家紋章	Public and official heraldry
962		宗教紋章	Ecclesiastical and sacred heraldry
963		家庭紋章	Family heraldry
964		特殊組織紋章	Heraldry of special institutions
965		特殊階級紋章	Heraldry of special classes
966		勳爵　勳位	Honor, rank, precedence, etc.
968		皇室(勳章　皇冠　寶器)	Royalty (Insignia Crown, regalia, etc.)
		僭擅	usurpation of titles, etc.
	.9	武士道	Chivalry and knighthood
969		依國分	By country
		例　中國旗幟　969.107	e.g. Chinese flags, banners and standards 969.107
970		傳記　總傳	Biography, general
	.03	人名辭書	Biographical dictionaries

	.09	傳記史	History of biography
	.1	言行錄　語錄	Words of Agrapha
	.2	肖像　像讚	Portraits Iconography
	.3	人名錄	Who's who Directories
	.4	評傳	Biographical critiques
	.6	軼事　傳說	Personal narratives
	.7	烈女傳	Female biography
			Biography of women
	.8	兒童傳	Biography of children
971		中國傳記(總傳)	Chinese biography (general)
		仿上細分	subd. like above
		例　中國烈女傳 971.7	e.g. Biography of Chinese women 971.7
972-5		其他各國傳記	Biography of other countries
977		系譜學	Genealogy
	.1	皇族	Royalty, ruling families, imperial house
	.2	貴族	Nobility
	.3	世家	Gentry
	.4	平民	Commoners
	.5	家譜　族譜	Family history
		姓氏,名字,小名,等	Surnames, forenames, soubriquets, etc.
	.9	依國分	By country
979		別傳　個人傳記	Individual biography
		除下列外別傳(不論國籍)率應類此依被傳者姓氏號碼大小次第排列	Individual biography of persons of all nations clast here in a single alphabet except the follows which go under their special class

	1.篇內已經列出者	1.Those marked in the text
	2.專家傳記之關係專門學術者	2.Specialist's that distinctly illustrate a subject
	注意 別傳分類號碼可用 B 字代表	Note."B" may be used for the class number of individnal biography

980　地理　地理學　Geography

.01	理論　關係	Theories Relations
.03	辭書	Dictionaries Geographic terms
.031	地名表	Gazetteers
.032	路程表	Tables.Distance, geographical positions, etc.
.033	世界京城商埠一覽	Capitals, metropolis, etc.of the world
.04	評論	Critiques Criticism
.05	雜誌	Periodicals
.06	學社	Societies
.07	研究	Studies
	綱要, 答問, 等	Outlines, syllabi, questions, etc.
.08	總集	Collected works
	神話, 等	Geographical myths, imaginary voyages, etc.
.09	歷史	History
.091	古地理	Ancient geography
.093	今地理	Modern geography
.1	專門地理	Special geography
	專門地理應按其性質分入各類	Special geography better clast with the subjects,
	如類此則依下列分	if prefer here, then subd. as follows
.11	自然地理	Physical geography
.111	數理地理	Mathematical geography
.113	海洋地理	Oceanography
.116	生物地理	Biological geography

.117		植物地理	Botanical
.118		動物地理	Zoological
.13		人文地理	Cultural geography
.14		社會地理	Social geography
.15		經濟地理　實業地理	Vocational and economical geography
.151		農業地理	Agricultural
.152		商業地理	Commercial
.154		工業地理	Industrial
.17		政治地理	Political geography
.175		軍事地理	Military
.178		國際地理	International
.19		歷史地理	Historical geography
980.3		地圖　地圖學	Maps, atlases, cartography
		各國地圖如類此可分列如下然後依各該國區域細分或析分入各國	Subd. like follows, or prefer with individual countries
.303		圖繪	Map making
.305		陸地地圖	Continental atlases
.306		海洋地圖	Maritime atlases
.308		專門地圖	Technical atlases
		依類分	By subject
.309		各洲地圖	By continent
.31		中國地圖	Chinese maps, atlases, etc.
		或入 981.2	or clast in 981.2
.32		亞洲其他各國地圖	Maps, atlases, etc. of other Asiatic countries
.33		歐洲各國地圖	Maps, atlases, etc. of European countries

.34	美洲各國地圖		Maps, atlases, etc. of American countries
.35	非洲大洋洲各國地圖		Maps, atlases, etc. of African and Oceanian countries
.5	世界類志		Surface geography (general)
		例　見上	
.501	陸地　疆域		Territories Boundaries
.502	海洋　海峽		Seas Oceans Straits
.503	島嶼　港灣		Islands Bays
.504	江河　運河		Rivers Canals
.505	湖泊　泉井		Lakes Springs Wells
.506	山嶽　峒峽		Mountains Caverns
.507	平原　沙漠		Plains Plateaus Valleys Deserts
.508	名勝古迹		Descriptions of famous places of scenery Historical ruins
.509	雜類		Miscellanies
.51	中國類志		Surface geography of China
	或入 981.3		or clast in 981.3
.52	亞洲其他各國類志		Surface geography of other Asiatic countries
.53	歐洲各國類志		Surface geography of European countries
.54	美洲各國類志		Surface geography of American countries
.55	非洲大洋洲各國類志		Surface geography of African and Oceanian countries
980.7	游記		Travels and descriptions (Collectively)
	例全前類此或析入各國		
.703	游覽指南		Traveler's manuals, guidebooks
	例　鐵路指南		e.g. Railway guides
.705	航海記　發現		Drifting Discoveries

	.707	探險記	Explorations, adventures shipwrecks, buried treasure, etc.
		海盜 海賊	Pirates, buccaneers, filibusters, etc.
		海洋生活	Ocean life
	.709	各洲游記	Circumnavigations Expeditions
		步行	Walking, pedestrian
	.71	中國游記 或入 981.4	Travels and descriptions—China or clast in 981.4
	.72	亞洲其他各國游記	Travels and descriptions of others Asiatic countries
	.73	歐洲各國游記	Travels and descriptions of European countries
	.74	美洲各國游記	Travels and descriptions of American countries
	.75	非洲大洋洲各國游記	Travels and descriptions of African and Oceanian countries
981		中國地理	Chinese geography
	.01	理論 關係	Theories Relations
	.03	辭書	Dictionaries
	.031	地名表	Gazetteers
	.032	路程表	Tables. Distance, geographical positions, etc.
	.04	評論	Critiques Criticism
	.05	雜誌	Periodicals
	.06	社會	Societies
	.07	研究	Studies
	.08	總集	Collected works
	.09	歷史	History
	.091	古地理	Ancient geography
	.093	今地理	Modern geography

.1	中國專門地理	Special geography—China
	可仿980.1 細分	May be subd.like 980.1
	例　中國人文地理 981.13	e.g. Chinese cultural geography 981.13
.2	中國地圖	Chinese maps
	依區域分	subd.by regions
.3	中國類志	Surface geography of China
.31	疆域　境界	Boundaries Territories—state domain
	依朝代分	By dynasty
.32	海洋　海峽	Seas Oceans Straits
	渤海,黃海,東海,南海,等	Puhai, Yellow sea, East sea, South sea, etc.
.33	島嶼　港灣	Islands Bays
.34	江河　運河	Rivers Canals
.341	長江　揚子江	Yangtze river
	岷江,漢水,等	Ming river, Han river, etc.
.342	黃河	Yellow river
	汾水,渭水,等	Fen river, Wei river, etc.
.343	珠江	Chu Kiang
	東江,北江,西江	Tung Kiang, Peh Kiang, Si Kiang
.345	黑龍江	Amur river (Heilungkiang)
	松花江,烏蘇里江,等	Sungari river, Ussuri river, etc.
.347	淮水	Hwai Ho
	潁水,汝水,等	Ying river, Yu river, etc.
.348	其他江河	Other rivers
	錢塘江,閩江,等	Tsian Tang Kiang, Min river, etc.
.349	運河	Grand canal
.35	湖泊　泉井　瀑布	Lakes Springs Wells Waterfalls
.351	洞庭湖	Tung-ting lake
.352	鄱陽湖	Po-yang lake
.353	太湖	Tai Hu
.354		

.355	其他	Other lakes
.356	泉	Springs
.357	井	Wells
.358	瀑布	Waterfalls
.36	山嶽　峒峽	Mountains, gorges, caverns
.361	泰山	Taishan
.362	華山	Huashan
.363	衡山	Hengshan
.364	恒山	Huanshan
.365	嵩山	Sungshan
.366	廬山	Lushan
.367	莫干山	Mokanshan
.368	其他	Other mountains
	天台山,等	Tien Tai Shan, etc.
.369	峒峽	Caverns Gorges
.37	平原　沙漠	Plains Plateaus Valleys Deserts
.38	名勝古迹	Descriptions of famous places of scenery Historical ruins
.381	宮殿	Palaces
.382	苑囿	Parks
.383	亭臺　樓閣	Pavelions and galleries
.384	廟宇	Temples
.385	宗祠	Ancestral halls
.386	陵墓	Tombs
.387	洲渚	Inlets
.388	城郭	Citadels
.389	其他	Other historical ruins
.39	雜類　雜記	Miscellanies
.4	中國游記	Travels and descriptions China
	依區域分	By regions

	注意 江,湖,山等游記及指南應與江,湖,山等同類	Note. Travels and descriptions on rivers, lakes, mountains, etc. prefer with the subjects
981.5	中國地志	Regional geography of China
	1.總志一統志類此	1.Class here regional geography of China in general
	例 大明一統志	e.g. Regional geography of Ming dynasty
	2.方志依下列各省分	2. Regional geography of individual provinces clast as follows
	例 湖北通志 981.73	e.g. Regional geography of Hupeh 981.73
	3.各省之府,縣,等志均可依下列細分	3.Regional geography of prefecture, district, etc. of one province subd. accordingly as follows
	4.全國縣名表 見附錄四	4.For classified gazetteer of Chinese districts see appendix IV
.51	首都	National capital
.52	省會	Provincial capitals
.53	特別市 商埠	Special cities, treaty ports, etc.
.55	府道	Prefecture(Fu) Circuit(Tao)
.56	州廳	Department (Chou) sub-prefecture (T'ing)
.57	縣	District(Hsien)
.58	鄉鎮 鄉土志	Village
.59	私志	Private topography
981.6	中國北部	The Northern provinces
.61	河北省	Hopei(Chihli)
.62	山東省	Shantung
.63	河南省	Honan
.64	山西省	Shansi

.65	陝西省	Shensi
.66	甘肅省	Kansu
.67	寧夏省	Ninghsia
.68	青海省	Chinghai or Kokonor
981.7	中國中部	The Central provinces
.71	四川省	Szechuan
.72	西康省(川邊)	Sik'ang
.73	湖北省	Hupeh
.74	湖南省	Hunan
.75	江西省	Kiangsi
.76	安徽省	Anhwei
.77	江蘇省	Kiangsu
.78	浙江省	Chekiang
.8	中國南部	The Southern provinces
.81	福建省	Fukien
.83	廣東省	Kwangtung
.85	廣西省	Kwangsi
.86	雲南省	Yunnan
.87	貴州省	Kweichow
.9	中國藩部	The outer territories of China
.91	滿州　東三省	Manchu The three Eastern provinces
.911	遼寧省(奉天)	Liaoning (Fengtien)
.913	吉林省	Kirin
.915	黑龍江省	Heilungkiang
.93	蒙古	Mongolia
.94	內蒙古	Inner Mongolia
.941	熱河省	Jehol
.943	察哈爾省	Charhar
.945	綏遠省	Suiyuan

.95	外蒙古		Outer Mongolia
.951	車臣汗部		Tsetsen khanate
.952	土謝圖汗部		Tushetu khanate
.953	三音諾顏汗部		Sain Noin khanate
.955	札薩克圖汗部		Dzarssaktu khanate
.956	科布多		Cobdo
.957	唐努烏梁海		Tangno Ulianghai
.97	新疆省		Sinkiang (Chinese Turkistan)
.98	西藏		Tibet
.981	前藏		Anterior Tibet
.983	後藏		Ulterior Tibet
.985	中藏		Central Tibet
.987	阿里(西藏)		Ngari, or Western Tibet

982　亞洲其他各國地理　Geography of other Asiatic countries

.1	日本地理		Japanese geography
.15	地志		Regional geography of Japan
.16	日本本部		Japan proper
.161	關東地方		Kanto district
	1.東京府　伊豆七島, 小笠原島		Tokyo prefecture
	2.武藏國		
	3.神奈川縣　武模國		Kanagawa
	4.千葉縣　安房,上總國		Chiba
	5.下總國		
	6.茨城縣　常陸國		Ibaragi
	7.琦玉縣		Saitama
	8.群馬縣　上野國		Gumma
	9.栃木縣　下野國		Tochigi

.162 奧羽地方　　　　　　　　Ou district
　　　1.福島縣　岩代國　　　　Fukushima
　　　2.盤城國
　　　3.宮城縣　　　　　　　　Miyagi
　　　4.陸前,陸中,陸奧國
　　　5.岩手縣　　　　　　　　Iwate
　　　6.青森縣　　　　　　　　Aomori
　　　7.秋田縣　　　　　　　　Akita
　　　8.羽後國
　　　9.山形縣　羽前國　　　　Yamagata
.163 中部地方　　　　　　　　Chubu district
　　　1.新潟縣　越後,佐渡國　　Niigata
　　　2.富山縣　越中國　　　　Toyama
　　　3.石川縣　能登,加賀國　　Ishikawa
　　　4.福井縣　越前,若狹國　　Fukui
　　　5.岐阜縣　飛驒,美濃國　　Gifu
　　　6.長野縣　信濃縣　　　　Nagano
　　　7.山梨縣　甲斐國　　　　Yamanashi
　　　8.靜岡縣　伊豆,駿河,遠江國　Shizuoka
　　　9.愛知縣　三河,尾張國　　Aichi
.164 近畿地方　　　　　　　　Kinki district
　　　1.京都府　山城,丹後國　　Kyoto
　　　2.丹波國

	3.大阪府　河内,和泉國	Osaka
	4.攝津國	
	5.兵庫縣　但馬,播磨,淡路國	Hyogo
	6.和歌山縣　紀伊國	Wakayama
	7.奈良縣　大和國	Nara
	8.三重縣　伊賀,伊勢,志摩國	Mie
	9.滋賀縣　近江國	Shiga
982.165	中國　四國地方	Chugoku, Shikoku district
	1.鳥取縣　因幡,伯耆國	Tottori
	2.島根縣　出雲,石見,隱岐國	Shimane
	3.山口縣　長門,周防國	Yamaguchi
	4.廣島縣　安藝,備後國	Hiroshima
	5.岡山縣　美作,備中,備前國	Okayama
	6.香川縣　讚岐國	Kagawa
	7.德島縣　阿波國	Tokushima
	8.愛媛縣　伊豫國	Ehime
	9.高知縣　土佐國	Kochi
.166	九州地方	Kyushu district
	1.福岡縣　築前,築後,豐前國	Fukuoka
	2.佐賀縣	Saga
	3.肥前國	
	4.長崎縣　臺岐,對馬國	Nagasaki

5. 熊本縣　肥後國　　　　Kumamoto
6. 大分縣　豐後國　　　　Oita
7. 宮崎縣　日向國　　　　Miyazaki
8. 鹿兒島縣　薩摩,　　　Kagoshima
   大隅國
9. 冲繩縣　琉球　　　　　Kyukyu(Loochoo)

.167　北海道地方　　　　　　　Hokkaido
1. 函館,檜山支廳
   渡島國
2. 後志支廳　後志國
3. 札幌,空知支廳
   石狩國
4. 室蘭,浦河支廳
   擔振,日高國
5. 上川,留萌支廳
   天鹽國
6. 宗谷,綱走支廳
   北見國
7. 釧路,河四支廳
   釧路,十勝國
8. 根室支廳　根室國,
   千島列島
9. 樺太島　　　　　　　　Karafuto(Saghalien)

982.2　高麗地理　　　　　Geography of Korean(Chosen)
.25　　地志　　　　　Regional geography of Korean

京幾道,黃海道,平安　　Kieki, Kokai, South Heian, North Heian,
南道,平安北道,咸鏡　　South Kankyo, North Kankyo, Kogen,
南道,咸鏡北道,江原　　South Chusei, North Chusei, South Zenra,
道,忠清南道,忠清北　　North Zenra, South Keisho, North Keisho
道,全羅南道,全羅北
道,慶尚南道,慶尚北
道

.3	印度地理	Geography of India
.35	地志	Regional geography of India
.36	東北部	Northeast
	孟加拉州	Bengal
	俄利薩,阿薩密	Orissa, Assam
.37	中部	Central
	合拼州	United provinces
	中央諸州	Central provinces
.38	西北部	Northwest
	本若州	Punjab
	克什米爾	Kashmir
.39	西南部　東南部	Southwest and Southeast
	孟買州	Bombay
	信地	Sind
	瑪德拉斯	Madras
	達梵科爾,賣索爾	Travancore, Mysore
	海得拉巴	Hyderabad
	錫蘭　不丹 尼泊爾地理	Geography of Ceylon, Bhotan, Nepal, Sikkim
.4	印度支那半島地理	Geography of Farther India
.41	印度支那地理(越南)	Indo-China
.42	交趾支那(南圻)	Cochin China
.43	安南(中圻)	Anam
.44	柬埔寨(高緜)	Cambodia
.45	東京(北圻)	Tonkin
.46	老撾(遼國)	Laos
.47	緬甸地理	Burma
	英屬緬甸地理	British Burma
.48	暹邏地理	Siam
.49	馬來半島地理	Malay peninsula

	.5	波斯地理	Geography of Persia
	.51	阿富汗地理	Afghanistan
	.58	俾路支地理	Baluchistan
	.59	土耳其斯坦地理	Turkestan
982.6		土耳其地理	Geography of Turkey
	.65	地志	Regional geography of Turkey
	.66	東土耳其	Turkey in Asia
	.661	亞訥多里亞	Anatolia
		何達溫的格雅,科里,伊丁,加士他年尼,昂哥拉	Khodavendigar, Kouieh, Aidin, Kastamuni, Angora
	.662	加拉馬尼亞	
	.663	亞達那	Adana
	.664	西威斯	Sivas
	.665	德比孫	Trebizond
	.666	亞美尼亞:挨爾斯倫	Armenia; Erzerum
	.667	古爾的斯丹	Kurdistan
		比特里斯,地亞比克溫尼,哈其利	Bitlis, Diarbekir Van,
	.668	美索波達美亞	Mesopotamia
		摩蘇爾,白格達,巴索拉,索爾,亞勒伯	Mosul, Bagdad, Basra, Aleppo
	.67	叙利亞,腓尼基,巴勒士登	Syria, Phenicia, Palestine
		見 982.8	see 982.8
	.69	西土耳其	Turkey in Europe
	.7	阿剌伯地理	Geography of Arabia
	.75	地志	Regional geography of Arabia
	.76	西部	West provinces
		麥加	Mecca

		黑德斯	
	.77	南部	South provinces
		葉門	Yemen
		哈達拉穆	Hadramaut
		馬拉	Mahrah
	.78	東部　中部	East and Central provinces
		阿曼	Oman
		哈薩	Hasa
		內惹德	Nejd
	.79	漢志地理	Geography of Hejaz
	.8	小亞細亞其他各國地理	Geography of Asia Minor
	.81	巴比倫	Babylonia
	.82	亞述	Assyria
	.83	腓尼基	Phoenicia
	.84	猶太	Judia, Palestine, Holy Land
	.85	希伯來	Hebrew
	.87	叙利亞	Syria
	.89	其他	Others
983		歐洲地理	Geography of Europe
		仿世界地理細分	subd. like world geography
	.1	希臘地理	Greek geography
	.15	地志	Regional geography of Greek
	.16	希臘北部	North states
		馬其頓,帖撒利,伊庇魯斯,阿刻內尼亞,挨陀利亞,羅格里斯,多立斯,佛西斯,伊大卡,波的亞,麥加利,優卑亞,亞的加	Macedonia, Thessaly, Epirus, Acaruania, Aetolia, Locris, Doris, Phocis, Ithaca, Boeotia, Megaris, Euboea, Attica

.17	希臘南部：伯羅奔尼撒	South states Peloponnesus
	哥林的亞,亞該亞,伊利斯,亞加的亞,亞哥利斯,美塞尼亞,拉哥尼亞	Corinthia, Achaia, Elis, Arcadia, Argolis, Messenia, Laconia
.18	希臘多島	Grecian archipelago
.19	伊奧尼亞群島	Ionia islands
.2	意大利地理	Italian geography
.25	地志	Regional geography of Italy
.26	意大利北部	North Italy
	辟門,利高里亞,倫巴底,威尼西亞,伊爾尼亞,多斯加納,瑪撒斯,安布里亞,來土穆	Piedmont, Liguria, Lombardy, Venetia, Emilia, Tuscany, Marches, Umbria, Latium
.27	意大利南部：那不斯	South Italy：Naples
	亞布魯索,摩里斯,干巴尼亞,亞浦里亞,波西利加大,加拉布里亞	Abruzzo, Molise, Campania, Apulia, Basilicata, Calabria
.28	西西里,撒丁	Sicily, Malta, Sardinia and Corsica
.3	西班牙　葡萄牙地理	Geography of Spain　Portugal
.35	地志	Regional geography of Spain
.36	西北部	Northwest
	加黎薩,亞斯都利亞,列翁,義斯得勒馬都拉	Galicia, Asturias, Leon, Estremadura
.37	東北部	Northeast
	亞拉岡,北斯開灣諸省,加達魯尼亞,瓦稜薩,巴里亞利克群島	Aragon, Basque provinces, Catalonia, Valencia, Balearic iles

.38	中部　南部	Central and South
	舊加塞爾,新加塞爾,木爾西亞,安達盧四亞,加那列群島	Old Castile, New Castile, Murcia, Andalusia, Canary iles
.39	葡萄牙地理	Geography of Portugal
983.4	法國地理	French geography
.45	地志	Regional geography of France
.46	西北　北部	Northwest and North
.461	布勒塔尼:非尼斯特勒,摩爾比韓,下羅亞爾,伊裏維勒內	Brittany: Finistere, Morbihan, Loire Inferieure, Ille et Vilaine
.463	賣內:邁恩,薩爾多	Maine: Mayenne, Sarthe
.464	安如:賣內羅亞爾	Anjou: Maine et Loire
.465	諾爾滿的:滿士加爾瓦多斯,奧內,與勒,下塞納	Normandy: Manche, Calvados, Orne, Eure, Seine Inferieure
.466	比加底:索美	Picardy: Somme
.467	亞爾多亞:巴的加雷	Artois: Pas de Calais
.468	諾爾	French Flanders: Nord
.47	東北　東部	Northeast and East
.471	賞巴尼亞:亞爾德內斯,馬爾內,高馬爾內	Champagne: Ardennes, Marne, Haute Marne
.473	伊里德佛蘭薩:哀斯尼,俄義斯,塞納俄義斯,巴黎塞納馬爾內	He de France: Aisue, Oise, Seine et Oise, Paris Seine et Marne
.474	羅勒:米于塞,木爾德莫塞勒,佛日	Lorraine: Meuse, Meurthe et Moselle, Vosges
.475	不爾疳尼亞:約內,哥德多爾,索內羅亞爾,亞英	Burgundy: Yonne, Cote d'Or, Saone et Loire, Ain

.477 佛蘭斯官德:高索爾,比爾佛德,都伯,汝拉　　Franche Comte: Haute Saone, Belfort, Doubs, Jura

.478 撒歪:撒歪,上撒歪　　Savoy: Savoie, Haute Savoie

.48 　中部　　Central

.481 奧里亞斯:與勒洛亦爾,羅挨勒,洛亦爾捨爾　　Orleans: Eure et Loir, Lciret, Loir et Cher

.482 都勒內:音德勒洛亦爾　　Touraine: Indre et Loir

.483 北利:音德勒,捨爾　　Berry: Indre, Cher

.484 尼威爾內:尼甫勒　　Nivernais: Nievre

.485 不爾波內:亞列爾　　Bourbonnais: Allier

.486 里疴內:羅挨勒,羅內　　Lyonnais: Loire, Rhome

.487 疴維爾內:不伊德多美,干達爾　　Auvergne: Puy de Dome, Cantal

.488 馬爾也:克留斯　　Marche: Creuse

.489 黎木性:高維也納,哥勒塞　　Limousin: Haute Vienne, Correze

.49 　西南　東南部　　West, South, and Southeast

.491 波亞都:維也納,塞威勒,枉德,下砂蘭德,砂蘭德　　Poitou: Vienne, Deux Sevres, Vendee, Charente Inferieure, Charente

.492 圭也:日倫大,多爾多內,羅特,亞維倫,達爾尼加羅內,羅加羅內　　Guienne: Gironde, Dordogne, Lot, Aveyron, Tarn et Garonne, Lot et Garonne

.493 加斯可內:蘭德,惹爾,高比里牛斯　　Gascony: Landes, Gers, Hautes Pyrenees

.494 伯爾尼:下比里牛斯　　Bearn: Basses Pyrenees

.495 郎吉德:高羅亞爾,羅塞勒,亞爾德世,迦爾,尼羅爾德,達爾尼,高加羅內,疴德　　Languedoc: Haute Loire, Lozere, Ardeche, Gard, Herault, Tarn, Haute Garonne, Aude

.496	佛克史：亞列吉，東比里牛斯	Foix：Ariege，Pyrenees Orientales
.497	不羅溫薩：不世德羅內，窩哥律師，瓦爾，沿海阿爾卑斯，下阿爾卑斯	Prevence：Bouches du Rhone，Vaucluse，Var，Alpes Maritimes，Basses Alpes，Monaco，Monte Carlo
.498	多飛：高阿爾卑斯，多羅美，義塞勒	Dauphiny：Hautes Alpes，Drome，Isere
.5	英國地理	Geography of Great Britain
.55	地志	Regional geography of Great Britain
.56	英格蘭	England
.561	中薩克斯　倫敦	Middlesex London county
.562	東南部：塞來，肯德，塞薩克斯，漢斯，威地島，波克斯	Southeast：Surrey，Kent，Sussex，Hants，Isle of Wight，Berks
.563	西南部：威耳斯，多塞特，海峽群島，得文，康瓦爾，索美審特	Southwest：Wilts，Dorset，Channel islands，Devou，Cornwall，Somerset
.564	中地西部：哥羅塞斯德，蒙穆夫，希爾佛爾，刹洛波，斯達佛爾，瓦色斯德，窩爾維克	West Midland：Gloucester，Monmouth，Hereford，Salop，Stafford，Worcester，Warwick
.565	中地北與南部：德彼，諾特斯，林肯，里色斯特，羅得蘭，諾桑波，亨庭敦，裴德福，牛律，巴京汗，赫德福，劍橋	North and South Midland Derby，Notts，Lincoln，Leicester，Rutland，Northampton，Huntingdou，Bedford，Oxford，Buckingham，Hertford，Cambridge
.566	東部：諾福克，薩福克，厄塞克斯	East：Norfolk，Suffolk，Essex
.567	西北部：折縣，蘭加縣	Northwest：Cheshire，Lancashire
.568	約克縣	Yorkshire

	.569	北部：都汗，諾森伯蘭，昆布蘭，西摩蘭，人島	North: Durham, Northum-berland, Cumberland, Westmoreland, Isle of Man
	.57	蘇格蘭	Scotland
	.58	愛爾蘭	Ireland
	.59	威爾斯	Wales
983.7		德國地理	Geography of Germany
	.75	地志	Regional geography of Germany
	.76	普魯士及德國北部	Prussia and Northern Germany
		東普魯士，西普魯士，但澤，波森，細勒西亞，巴郎敦堡，波美拉尼亞，梅格林堡，盧卑克，普魯士薩克森，安哈忒	East Prussia, West Prussia, Danzig, Posen, Silesia, Brandenburg, Pomerania, Mecklenburg, Lubeck, Prussian Saxony, Anhalt
	.77	中部　南部	Central and Southern Germany
		薩克森，條倫吉亞，薩克森威瑪，薩克森阿爾丁堡，薩克森高塔科堡，薩克森買寧根，士發次堡，壘斯，黑森丹摩斯大得，萊因普魯士，萊因巴威，亞爾薩斯，羅測林，巴登，瓦敦堡，巴威，霍亨索倫	Saxony, Thuringia, Saxe-Weimar, Saxe-Alteuburg, Saxe-Gotha-Cobury, Saxe-Meiningen, Schwartzburg, Reuss, Hesse Darmstadt, Rhenish Prussia, Rhenish Bavaria, Alsace, Lorraine, Baden, Wurtemburg, Bavaria, Hohenzollern
	.78	西北部	Northwest Germany
		什列斯疛爾斯德音，漢堡，布勒門，鄂爾敦堡，漢諾威，不倫瑞克，里卑，西發里亞，瓦爾得克，黑森拿騷	Schleswig-Holstein, Hamburg, Bremen, Oldenburg, Hanover, Brunswick, Lippe, Westphalia, Waldeck, Hesse-Nassau

.79	條頓族其他各國地理	Geography of other Teutonic countries
.791	尼柔蘭(比國與荷蘭)	Netherlands(Belgium and Holland)
.792	比國地理	Belgium
.793	荷蘭地理	Holland(Dutch)
.794	瑞士地理	Switzerland
.795	奧匈地理	Austria Hungary
	下奧,上奧,薩爾斯堡,的羅爾,士的里亞,克倫地亞,喀尼鄂拉,伊斯的里亞,達爾馬提亞匈:匈牙利,斯拉窩尼亞,哥羅地亞,波斯尼亞,黑塞哥維亞	Lower Austria, Upper Austria, Salzburg, Tyrol, Styria, Carinthia, Carniola, Istria, Dalmatia, Transleithania; Hungary, Slavonia, Croatia Bosnia, Herzegovina
983.796	捷克地理	Czechoslovakia
	波希米亞,摩拉維亞,細勒四亞,加理細亞,布哥維亞	Bohemia, Moravia, Silesia, Galicia, Bukowina
.797	波蘭地理	Poland
.798	斯坎葉那維亞	Scandinavia
	6.挪威地理	Norway
	基里士特利亞,基里士信山,貝爾根,哈馬,特倫折穆,德琅索	Oslo(Christiania), Christiansand, Bergen, Hamar, Threndhjem, Tromso
	7.瑞典地理	Sweden
	哥士蘭,式威蘭,諾爾蘭	Gothland, Svealand, Norrland
	8.丹麥地理	Denmark
	9.冰島地理	Iceland Farce ilands

	.799	其他	Others
.8		俄國地理	Geography of Russia (Union Socialist Soviet Republics)
	.85	地志	Regional geography of Russia
	.86	大俄	Great Russia
	.87	西俄	West Russia
	.88	小俄　南俄　高加索	Little Russia　South Russia　Caucasia
	.89	東俄　西比利亞	East Russia　Siberia
.9		歐洲其他各國地理	Geography of other European countries
	.91	芬蘭地理	Finland
	.92	拉柏蘭地理	Lapland
	.95	巴爾幹半島各國地理	Balkan states
	.951	羅馬尼亞	Rumania
	.952	亞爾巴尼亞	Albania
	.953	巨哥斯拉夫	Jugoslavia
	.955	塞國	Serbia
	.957	布加利亞	Bulgaria
	.97	波羅的海沿岸各國地理	Baltic provinces
		愛沙尼亞, 拉脫維亞, 立陶宛	Esthonia, Latvia Lithuania
	.99	其他	Others
		西土耳其地理	For geography of Turkey in Europe
		見 982.69	see 982.69

984　美洲地理　　American geography (general)

可仿世界地理細分　　subd. like the geography of the world

.1　美國地理　　Geography of the United States

.15	地志	Regional geography of the United States
.16	大西洋諸州	Atlantic
.161	緬因,新罕木什爾	Maine, New Hampshire
.162	威爾滿,馬薩諸塞	Vermont, Massachusetts
.163	羅德島,康涅狄格	Rhode Island, Conuecticut
.164	紐約,彭士法尼亞	New York, Pennsylvania
.165	新澤西,德拉瓦	New Jersey, Delaware
.166	馬里蘭,哥倫比亞華盛頓城	Maryland, District of Columbia Washington (city)
.167	西維基尼亞,維基尼亞	West Virginia, Virginia
.168	北卡羅林納,南卡羅林納	North Carolina, South Carolina
.169	佐治亞,佛羅里達	Georgia, Florida
.17	中部諸州	Central
.171	阿拉巴瑪,密士失必	Alabama, Mississippi
.172	路易斯安那,得克薩斯	Louisiana, Texas
.173	印第安地俄克拉何馬	Indian Territory Oklahoma
.174	阿肯色,田納西	Arkansas, Tennessee
.175	阡塔基,俄亥俄	Kentucky, Ohio
.176	印第安納,伊里諾亞	Indiana, Illinois
.177	密執安,威斯康星	Michigan, Wisconsin
.178	明尼蘇達,伊阿華	Minnesota, Iowa
.179	密蘇里	Missouri
.18	西部諸州	Western of Mountain
.181	堪薩斯	Kansas
.182	內布拉斯加	Nebraska
.183	南達科他	South Dakota
.184	北達科他	North Dakota
.185	蒙大拿	Montana

	.186	歪俄明	Wyoming
	.187	科羅拉多	Colorado
	.188	新墨西哥	New Mexico
	.19	太平洋諸州	Pacific
	.191	亞利桑那	Arizona
	.192	烏台	Utah
	.193	內華達	Nevada
	.194	加利佛尼亞	California
	.195	俄勒阿	Oregon
	.196	伊達荷	Idaho
	.197	華盛頓	Washington
	.198	阿拉斯加	Alaska
984.2		坎拿大地理	Canada British America
	.25	地志	Regional geography of Canada
	.26	西北部	Northwest territories
		育空,馬更基,佛蘭克林,等	Yukou, Mackenzie, Franklin, etc.
	.27	西南部	Southwest territories
		英屬哥倫比亞,亞爾伯特,薩斯喀特撒溫,克瓦丁,馬尼多巴	British Columbia, Alberta, Saskatchewan, Keewatin, Manitoba
	.28	東南部	Southeast territories
		安剔鰲阿,魁北克,新布隆斯威克,那佛斯科的亞,布里敦島,愛德華太子島,紐芬蘭,拉布剌多	Ontario, Quebec, New Brunswick, Nova Scotia, Cape Breton (island), Prince Edward Island Newfoundland, Labrador
	.29	東北部	Northeast territories
	.3	北美洲其他各國地理	Geography of other North American countries

.4	墨西哥地理	Mexico
.46	北部	Northern states
	新雷汪,科亞赫拉,濟華花,都郎額,西拿羅亞,索諾拉,下加利佛尼亞	Nuevo Leon, Cohahuila, Chihuahua, Durango, Sinaloa, Sonora, Lower California and islands
.47	內部	Interior states
	薩加得加,聖路易斯波多塞,亞哥斯科林特斯,瓜那寂阿多,給勒打羅,希德爾哥,布委巴拉,達拉斯喀拉,摩勒羅,墨西哥	Zacatecas, San Louis Potosi, Aguascalientes, Guanajuato Queretaro, Hidalgo, Puebla, Tlascala, Morelos, Mexico
.48	墨西哥灣	Gulf states
	達毛黎巴,委拉古盧斯,達巴斯哥,干伯徹,于加敦	Tamaulipas, Vera Cruz, Tabasco, Campeche, Yueatan
.49	南部	Southern states
.5	西班牙美洲地理	Spanish America
	拉丁美洲地理	Latin America
984.6	中美洲各國地理	Central America
.61	危地馬拉	Guatemala
.62	英領洪都拉斯	British Honduras Belize
.63	洪都拉斯	Honduras
.64	薩爾瓦多	San Salvador
.65	尼加拉瓜	Nicaragua
.66	哥斯達黎加	Costa Rica
.68	巴拉馬	Panama
.7	西印度群島地理	West Indies

.71	古巴	Cuba
.72	牙買加	Jamaica
.73	聖多明谷	Santo Domingo
.74	海地	Hayti
.75	波爾多黎各	Porto Rico
.76	巴哈馬	Bahamas
.77	利溫群島	Leeward islands
.78	文德瓦德群島	Windward islands Barbados
.79	百慕群島	Bermudas
.8	南美洲各國地理	South America
.81	巴西	Brazil
.82	阿根廷	Argentina
.829	巴塔哥尼亞	Patagonia
.83	智利	Chile
.84	玻利維亞	Bolivia
.85	秘魯	Peru
.86	哥倫比亞共和國	U.S. of Colombia
.869	厄瓜多爾	Ecuador
.87	委內瑞拉	Venezuela
.88	基阿那	Guiana
.89	巴拉圭	Paraguay
.899	烏拉圭	Uruguay

985　非洲大洋洲地理　　Geography of Africa and Oceania countries

	北非與東非	North and East Africa
.1	埃及	Egypt
.15	地志	Regional geography of Egypt

.16	埃及本部	Egypt proper
.161	下埃及	Lower Egypt
.162	中埃及	Middlw Egypt
.163	上埃及	Upper Egypt
.17	英屬埃及蘇丹	Anglo-Egyptian Sudan
.171	努比亞	Nubia Northern
.173	當哥拿	Dongola
.175	中部：喀土穆	Central：Khartum, etc.
.176	西部：哥爾多番	West：Kordofau,
	達爾夫耳	Darfur
.178	東部與南部	East and South
	塞那爾，等	Sennar, etc.
.2	阿比西尼亞地理	Abyssinia Ethiopia
.3	摩洛哥地理	Morocco
.4	北非東非其他各國地理	Geography of other North and East African countries
.41	索巴蘭	Somaliland
	意屬	Italian, French,
	英屬	British
.42	德屬東非	German East Africa
.43	桑給巴爾	Zanzibar
.44	莫三比克	Mozambique Portuguese East Africa
.45	迪里斯	Tunis
.46	的黎玻里	Tripoli Libia Italiana
	非三	Fezzan
.47	撒哈拉	Sahara
.48	亞爾基里亞	Algeria

	.49		
	.5	西非地理	West Africa
	.51	蘇丹（法屬）	Sudan (French)
	.53	塞內岡比亞	Senegambia Senegal
	.55	里比利亞	Liberia
985.57		上幾內亞	Upper Guinea
		亞干的	
		達疴美	
	.58	下幾內亞	Lower Guinea
		喀麥隆	Kamernu (French)
		安哥拉	Angola (Portuguese)
	.6	中非地理	Central Africa
	.65	剛果自由邦	Kongo Free State
	.66	法屬剛果	French Kongo
	.67	比屬剛果	Belgian Kongo
	.7	南非地理	South Africa
	.71	英屬南非	British
	.72	德屬南非	Germany
	.73	索法拉	
	.74	德蘭士瓦	Transvaal
	.76	鄂蘭吉自由邦	Orange Free State
	.77	好望角	Cape of Good Hope
	.78	馬達加斯加島	Madagascar and islands of South Indian Ocean
	.9	大洋洲地理	Geography of Oceanian countries
	.91	南洋群島	Malaysia
	.911	菲力賓群島	Philippine islands
	.912	呂宋	
	.915	婆羅洲	Borneo

.916	西里伯	Celebes
.917	摩鹿加丁香群島	Moluccas or Spice islands
.92	巽他群島	Sunda
.921	蘇門答剌	Sumatra
.923	爪哇	Java
.93	澳大利亞地理	Australia
.935	地志	Regional geography of Australia
.936	西澳	Western Australia
.937	南澳	South Australia
.938	北澳	North Australia
.939	東澳	East Australia
	1.昆士蘭	Queensland
	2.新南威爾斯	New South Wales
	3.維多利亞	Victoria
	5.大斯馬尼亞	Tesmania
.94	新西蘭地理	New Zealand
985.95	美拉尼西亞(沿岸群島)地理	Melanesis
.951	新喀里多里亞群島　忠島	New Caledonia, Loyalty islands
.952	新希不力斯群島	New Hebrides
.953	所羅門群島	Solomon islands, etc.
.954		
.955	新不列顛島	New Britain
.956	卑斯馬克群島	Bismark islands
.957	亞得米拉爾群島	Admiralty islands
.959	新幾內亞	New Guinea
.96	密克羅尼西亞(細島)地理	Micronesia
.961	加羅林群島	Caroline

.963	馬利亞納群島		
.965			
.967	馬紹爾群島	Marshall islands	
.968	吉爾貝特群島	Gilbert islands	
.97	波里尼西亞(多島)地理	Polynesia	
.971	斐濟群島	Figi islands	
.972	佛林得里群島	Friendly islands	
.973	三毛亞群島		
.974	科克群島	Cook's islands	
.975	會島	Society islands	
.976	低島	Low Archipelage	
.977	馬貴斯群島	Marquesas islands	
.979	其他	Others	
.98	夏威夷群島	Hawaii	
.99	南北極地理	Polar regions	
.991	南冰洋	Antarcitic regions	
.995	北冰洋	Arctic regions	

990　考古學　古物學　Archaeology　Antiquities

.01	理論　關係	Theories Relations
.018	考古倫理	Ethics of archaeology
.019	關係	Relations
	例　與人類學,等關係	e.g. In relation to anthropology, etc.
.03	辭書	Dictionaries
.04	評論	Critiques Criticism
.05	雜誌	Periodicals
.06	學會	Societies
.07	研究	Studies
.071	方法	Methology

	層位學的方法	Stratigraphical
	型式學的方法	Typological
	土俗學的方法	Ethnographical
.072	圖表　統計	Tables Illustrations
.073	調查　測量	Exploration Surveying
.074	發掘　採集	Excavation Collections
.075	鑒別　考釋	Identifications
	題跋　欵識	Legend
.076	摹　拓　影　模造	Reproductions　Rubbings　Photographing Modelling
.077	偽造　贋器	Forgeries of antiquities
.079	博物院	Museums
	1.古物保存	Preservation and conservation
	3.古物修理	Restoration
	7.古物陳列　展覽	Exhibition
.08	總集　小册	Collected works
.09	歷史	History
.098	考古游記	Travels and descriptions
.1	遺物　遺迹	Historical remains Historical ruins
	凡比較研究各國遺物遺迹諸作類此	General and comparative
.11	甲骨	Bone remains
.12	吉金	Metal remains
.13	石　古玉	Stone remains
.14	土器	Terra-cotta
.15	竹木	Bamboo and wooden remains
.16	鉨印　符契	Seals Sigillography
.17	其他遺物	Other historical remains
.18	遺迹	Historical ruins

990.2	宗教考古		Religious archaeology
	總論宗教博物諸作類此可仿宗教細分或析入各教宗類		General and comparative may be subd. by religions or put with the religious
	例	佛教考古	e.g. Buddhist archaeology
		990.23 或 230.99	990.23 or 230.99
		基督教考古	Christian archaeology
		990.25 或 250.99	990.25 or 250.99
.5	生物考古		Biological archaeology
	互見 560.099		see also 560.099
.7	美術考古		Archaeology of fine arts
	互見 770.99		see also 770.99
.8	文字考古		Paleography
	古文字學		
.81	中國文字考古		Chinese paleography
	互見 419		see also 419
.811	甲骨文		of ancient bones
.812	金文		of metal remains
	鐘鼎文		of bells, tripods
	彝器文		of sacrificial vessels
.813	石刻文		of stone remains
.814	土器文		of terra-cotta
.815	竹簡文		of document straps
.816	符契 鑈印文		of tallies, seals
.82-.85	其他各國文字考古		Paleography of other countries
.9	史前考古學		Prehistoric archaeology
	可依舊石器,新石器,銅器,鐵器,等時代細分		Subd. by periods—Paleolithic, neolithic, bronze age, iron age, etc.

991 中國考古學　古物學　Chinese archaeology　antiquities

	遺物　遺迹	Historical remains Historical ruins
.1	甲骨	Bone remains
.2	吉金	Metal remains
.21	鐘	Bells Campanology
.22	鼎	Tripods
.23	彝器　禮器	Sacrificial vessels
.24	古泉　泉幣	Numistics
.26	古兵	Ancient weapons
.27	古鏡	Ancient mirrors
.29	其他吉金類	Other metal remains

991.3　石　古玉　　Stone remains

.31	古玉	Ancient jades
.32		
.33	石鼓	Ancient stone-drums
.34	碑碣	Ancient tablets
.35		
.36	古硯	Ancient ink-stones
.37		
.39	其他	Other stone remains
.4	土器	Terra-cotta
.41	古磚	Ancient bricks
.42	瓦當	Ancient tiles
.43	古陶	Ancient pottery, stoneware
.44	古磁	Ancient porcelain
.49	其他	Others
.5	竹木	Bamboo and wooden remains

.51	竹簡		Document straps
.53	漆器		Lacquer remains
.6	鉩印　符契		Seals Sigillography
.61	古鉢　古印		Ancient seals
.611	官印		Stamp (Official)
.613	私印		Signet (private)
.615	封泥		Cachet
.617	花押		Signature
.619	其他		Others
.62	印質		Seal (the impression) materials
	金,銀,臘,膠,等		Gold, silver, wax, wafer, etc.
.63	印形		Form
	圓,橢圓,八方,尖穹,		Round, oval, octagonal, ogival, shield shape,
	楯形,菱形,套印		lozenge, counter seal
.64	印色		Color
.65	銘制		Seal inscriptions
.66	畫像		Seal iconography
.68	其他		Others
	裝飾		Attachment
	垂飾		Pendant
.69	符契　符牌		Tallies
991.7	其他遺物		Other historical remains
.71	明器		Mortuary remains
.72	像　造像		Statues
.721	金人　銅像		Of metal
.722	石像		Of stone
.723	木偶		Of wood
.724	泥塑　土俑		Of clay
.726	畫像		Portraits

.728	其他		Others
.73	樂器		Musical instrument
	例　箜篌,羯鼓,面具,等		
.74	車器　馬飾		Chariot and the instruments
.75	服御諸器		Household, agricultural, etc. instruments, ornaments
.76	織繡及紙類		Silk, skin, papers, etc.
.77	權度		Weights and measures
.78	刻板		
.79	其他		Others
.8	遺迹		Historical ruins
.81	都市　城寨		City Citadel
.82	宮殿　住宅		Palace Residence
.83	苑囿　亭臺		Parks Paveline
.84	寺院		Temples
	見 990.2 宗教考古		see 990.2 religions archaeology
.841	廟		Buddhist temple
.842	石窟寺		Cavern
.843	塔(浮屠)		Pagoda
.845	觀		Taoist temple
.846	祠堂		Ancestral hall
.847	書院		School and College
.85	紀念牌		Ancient monuments
	石柱,石碑,石臺,牌坊,凱旋門,等		Monoliths, cromlechs, memorial and triumphal arches
.86	墓地　墳墓考古		Archaeology of sepulchre
.88	工藝場所		Industrial quarters
	例　石場,淘窯,等		e.g. Stone quarry, kiln, etc.

.9 　地方考古　　　　　Local archaeology
　　　地方金石志
　　　依區域分　　　　By regions
992-999 其他各國考古學　Archaeology of other countries

PREFACE

The relative index in English now prepared is a part of the original plan, as stated in the preface to the main volume of this work. The first index compiled by Mr. Yu Tzu-ch'iang was not altogether satisfactory, as it did not fully index the tables of the classification, not to mention the relative topics, synonyms or alternative topics, as are expected in an index of this kind. The first half of the index from A-L was prepared by the author, while the latter half by Mr. Lo Chi-chu, an assistant of the Boone Library School, under the supervision of Mr. Mao Kun. To both of them the writer expresses his deep appreciation. This thoroughly revised and rewritten work has therefore caused considerable delay.

Numerically, this index is very small when compared with Dr. Dewey's memorable work. It contains not more than 20000 entries. It, however, indexes all important topics, necessary to accomplish its purpose. It will serve as a great time-saving device to the readers of the classification table, or in other words serve as the first aid in applying for topics, "which might be thought to fall indifferently under diverse sections of the classification." This index also gives names of persons, places, trees, animals, etc, as they appear in the table.

When using, it should be borne in mind that this index is arranged in alphabetical order, with a class number accom-panying each topic, except when a cross reference is given. Find the topic wanted first in the index for class number, then look up this number in the table where the desired and allied subjects will be found. If this is strictly followed, it will make the index really useful and the classification as well.

P'I KAO-PING.

April, 1937.

A B C telegraphy	657. 8351
Abaca agriculture	612. 58
Abacus calculation	510. 76
Abandoned children see Dependents	
Abbeys Christ. hist.	259. 091
Abbreviations	626.8
Chinese grammar	416.5
other languages	
in special topics　see subjects	
Abcesses veneral diseases	598.6
Abdomen anatomy	591.85
Abelard medieval philos.	121.635
Abelian functions	516.45
Aberration	
astronomy	522.83
mental disease	597.84
insanity	155.2
optics	535.33
sexual	155.458
Abies botany	574.43
Abhava Hinduism	241.26
Abhidharma-kaca Buddhism	239.115
Abhidharma-kosa-sastra	
Chinese Buddhism	239.52
Indian Buddhism	239.115
Japanese Buddhism	239.62
Abhidharma-pitake Sutra	232.7
Abilities psychology	153.83
Abiogenesis	
animals	581.61
biology	561.611
biogenesis	562.61
plants	571.61
Abjuration	
oath naturalization	372.3
Abnormal	
children	153.76
criminal law	394.65
education	338.96
gynecology	598.79
labor obstetrics	598.841
psychology	155
Abolition of slavery	317.48
Aborigines	
Chinese	910.77
other nations	
Abortion	
botany	571.5
crimes and offenses	315.185
ethics	183.5

law	394.25	old Gk. philos.	121.3
pathology of pregnancy	598.828	Acanthaceae botany	579.66
Abrasions wounds	598.163	Acanthocephala zoology	588.43
Abruzzo Italy geography	983.27	Acanthopterygii zoology	587.4779
Abscess		Accession book lib. science	023.2
in lungs	597.245		
surgery	598.143	Accessories see for subjects	
Absolute free trade	351.32		
geometry	519.8	Accessory punishment	394.53
ontology	133	Accidents	
Absolutism pol. sci.	371.0482	industrial economics	354.54
Absorption		pub. safety	593.4
optics	535.38	insurance	368.6
liquids	532.15	medicine	598.16
physiology	597.329	miners	658.45
thermics	536.49	ontology	133.4
Abstraction psychology	151.81	Accipitres zoology	587.9793
Abutilon agriculture	612.57	Acclimatization	
Abyssinia geography	985.2	animals	581.7778
history	952	forest botany	614.376
Academies	338	Acclimatization (cont.)	
architecture	717.2	hygiene	593.111
female	338.91	man	565.771
learned	060	mental influence	153.23
of special subjects see subjects		ontogeny	563.19
		plants agric.	610.527
Academy, new Gk. philos.	121.55	botany	571.776
		Accommodation	569.197

and adaptation	
habitudes	151.53
ontogeny	563.197
social psychology	311.5
Accounting in business	627
Accumulators	
chemical electricity	657.94
hydraulic	655.35
physics	537.21
Aceology therapeutics	595
Acephala zoology	583.55
Acer agriculture	612.64
Aceraceae botany	578.23
Acetylene	
chemic technology	665.7
heat prac. chem.	542.4
Acetylenes organic	
chem.	547.13
Acetates medicine	597.66
Achaia, Greece	
geography	983.17
Achinotrocha worm	583.67
Achlamydosporeae	
botany	576.8
Achlorophyllaceae	
botany	572.11
Achromatiaceae botany	572.155
Achromasy optics	535.397
Acidimetry chemistry	545.1
Acids	
aids to digestion	597.365
chemic technology	661.3
organic chemistry	547.7
physiological chemistry	581.499
qualitative analysis	544.15
theoretic chemistry	541.03
Acipenseridae zoology	587.474
Acology medicine	595
Acoustics physics	534
Acquisition	
learning	151.65
library	023.1
of colonies	377.1
territory intern law	381.3
pol. sci.	371.031
Acrania zoology	586.4
Acraseae botany	572.21
Acrasiales botany	572.21
Acrididae zoology	585.31
Acrocarpi botany	573.7
Acting theatre	781.2
Actinium inorganic	
chem.	546.58
Actinopterygia zoology	587.473

Actinotherapy medicine	595.85	animals	581.775
Actinozoa zoology	582.75	forest botany	614.376
Actiology ethnology	565.71	plants agric.	610.527
Action		botany	571.776
cosmology	134.6	Addison, Joseph Eng.	
freedom of	372.131	essays	857.52
psychology	151.3	Addition arithmetic	511.21
voluntary will	151.42	Addresses	
Active		Chinese literature	818.4
being ontology	136.61	other literatures	
Actors theatre	781.2	on education	330.4
Acts ontology	133.6	spec. topics see topic	
Acts of Apostles Bible	252.65	Addyatma vidya	
Actuarial science		Buddhism	232.085
insurance	368	Adelochorda zoology	586.1
Aculeata zoology	585.58	Adelphia deformities	598.174
Acupuncture		Adenology	597.4
therapeutics	595.815	Adipose bodies anatomy	597.318
Acvaghosa Buddhism	239.134	Adjudication intern. law	382.4
Ad valorem duty	369.0677	Adjustment	
Chinese	369.1677	biology	563.7
other nations		habitudes	151.53
Adana, Turkey		Administration	
geography	982.663	library	022
Adaptation	563.7	of medicines	595.72
and accommodation		political science	373
		central government	373.01
habitudes	151.53	colonial government	373.087

district government	373.083
local government	373.08
provincial government	373.081
railway	633.3
school	331.3
spec. subjects,	
see subjects	
Administrative	
Aspects	
spec. topics,	
see subjects	
buildings architecture	717.1
law	393
revenue	369.043
Admiralty islands	985.957
Admission school	334.1
Adolescence childstudy	153.7
Adopted law	390.002
Adoption	313.387
family law	397.5
Adoxaceae botany	579.83
Adult education	338.93
Adultery ethics	187.7
crime and	
offenses	315.185
law	394.25
sex relations	313.3423
Advent	

Anglican festivals	253.11
second Christology	251.26
Adverse possession law	397.2
Advertising business	629
Advisory committee for	
progressive	
codification of	
international law	383.51
Advisory committee for	
protection	
of children and young	
people	383.58
Advisory committee on	
traffic in	
opium	383.56
Aeluroidea zoology	587.51
Aeolic dialect Gk.	
language	431.51
Aepyornithiformes	
zoology	587.946
Aerasiales botany	572.21
Aeration	
brewing	664.53
plant respiration	571.43
water purification	653.18
Aerial	
bridges engineering	651.576
delivery	636.53

domain	381.38
ecosion	551.71
lines elec. eng.	657.651
navigation	635
operations	379.73
photography	758.2
transportation	635
Aerodromes	659.47
Aerodynamics physics	533.1
Aerokinetics physics	533.5
Aerolites astronomy	523.51
geology	557.6
Aerology meteorology	529
physics	533.7
Aerometers prac. chem.	542.3
Aeronautics	
engineering	659.4
physics	533.7
Aerophytes botany	573.4
Aeroplanes aviation	659.44
Aeropneustea zoology	584.67
Aerostatics physics	533.3
Aerostation aviation	659.47
Aerotherapy therapeutics	595.84
Aeschines Gk. oratory	831.843
Aeschylus Gk. drama	831.21
Aesop Gk. literature	831.886

Aesthetics, see Esthetics	
Aether, see Ether	
Aetheopspondyli zoology	587.475
Aetiology botany	571.5
Aetolia, Greece	
geography	983.16
Affections	
ethics	180.61
psychology	151.2
Affinity chemistry	541.067
family law	397.5
Affliction ethics	180.97
Afghanistan geography	982.51
history	925.9
Africa geography	985
history	950
Afterbrain anatomy	597.8118
Agamas sutra	232.2
Agamogenesis biology	561.61
botany	571.61
zoology	581.61
Age	
child labor	354.22
mental characteristics	153.6
of animals	581.698
chivalry Europ.	
history	930.55

feudalism Chinese hist.	911.63	geologic		554
Europ. history	932.52	Agglutinative languages		403
legislators	373.0341	Agnathi zoology		585.33
man natural history	565.72	Agricultural		
physiology	592.6	analysis		543.2
statistics	349.073	bank		610.355
the despots Ital. hist.	932.871		or,	362.13
the reformation Europ. hist.	930.62	bookkeeping		610.357
the seven states Chinese hist.	911.65	botany		610.57
the world geology	554.9	chemistry		610.54
voters suffrage	372.51		or,	543.2
psychology of	153.6	classes		610.13
school	334.4		or,	313.71
therapeutics	595.76	Agricultural (cont.)		
Aged asylums	316.33	econemics		610.3
Agencies			or,	350.086
business	632.4	education		610.077
labor economics	354.113	experiment stations		610.078
social weltare	398.49	finance		610.35
law	398.49	geography		980.151
student aid	334.9	geology econ. geol.		556.3
teachers	336.45	soil		611.3
Agents, geologic	551.9	implements		910.6
Ages, archaeologic	990.9	insurance		368.5
		law		610.32
		machinery		610.6
		management		610.33
		manufacture		610.8

mathematics	610.51	public	316.5
meteorology	610.52	societies charity	316.3
microscopy	510.56	Aids to digestion	597.365
mission	610.097	memory	151.64
organization	610.11	Aids to readers	027.1
Pests agriculture	611.9	Ain, France geography	983.475
botany	571.8	Air	
zoology	581.8	analysis chemistry	543.61
physics	610.53	baths, hot hygiene	593.146
policies	610.31	battles world war	930.765
or,	351.2	brakes mech. eng.	655.51
social statics	313.71	compressors mech. eng.	655.55
sociology	610.1	composition of	529.15
system	610.311	craft aeronautics	659.44
zoology	610.58	disinfection cont.	
Agriculture	610	diseases	593.236
Agronomy	610	engines mech. eng.	655.4
Aguascalientes, Mex.		gun manufacture	671.1
geography	984.47	hygiene personal	593.11
Ahamkara Hinduism	241.63	public health	593.27
Ahom languages	409.124	meteorology	529
Ahura Mazda Parseeism	281.1	navigation	659.41
Aichi, Japan geography	982.1639	operations military sci.	379.73
Aid		world war	930.765
funds economics	354.17	passages respiratory	
insurance economics	354.35	system	597.2
medical social welfare	316.2	planes aeronautics	659.44
private	316.5	pneumatics	533

pollution public health	593.27
sanitary eng.	653.37
pressure of meteorology	529.2
pumps	655.52
radiation	529.17
ships engineering	659.44
military sci.	379.74
territory intern. politics	381.38
politics	371.026
thermodynamics	529.11
transport communication	635
enginering	659.4
warfare world war	930.765
Airdromes aviation	659.47
Airports aviation	659.47
Aisne, France geography	983.473
Aizoaceae botany	577.23
Akita, Japan geography	982.1627
Alabama, U. S.	
geography	984.171
Alangiaceae botany	578.87
Albania geography	983.952
history	939.53
Albanian languages	409.35
Alberta, Canada	
geography	984.27
Albuminoids organic	
chem.	547.91
Alcohol	
as a food physiology	592.473
engines	655.45
Alcohol (cont.)	
heating prac. chemistry	542.4
hygiene	597.83
mental hygiene	152.3
motor vehicles	659.74
narcotic poisons	593.95
stimulants	597.16
Alcoholic	
drink physiology	592.473
ferments botanic chem.	571.46
phys. chem.	592.41
liquors manufacture	664.55
Alcoholism	
and crime	315.165
genius	153.945
diseases	597.8458
mind and body	155.259
prohibition	317.82
Alcohols organic	
chemistry	547.3
Alcoran Islam	272.7
Alcott, L. M. Am. fiction	863.41
Alcyenaria zoology	582.751
Aldehydes organic	
chem.	547.5

Aldrich, T. B. Am. poet.	861.47
Alembert. J. le R. d' Fr.	847.53
essays	
Ales manufacture	664.533
Alexia medicine	597.8455
psychology	155.254
Alfalfa forage crops	612.381
Algae botany	573.2
Algebra	512
graphic	512.02
higher	512.02
linear	512.6
Algebraic	
configuration	512.2
equations	512.77
forms	512.2
functions	516.2
gauche curves	519.463
geometry	519.4
plane curves	519.454
surfaces	519.463
Algeria geography	985.48
history	954.8
Algorisms mathematics	510.6
Algorithms mathematics	510.6
Aliens	
clas'n of workers	354.256
international law	381.82
naturalization intern. law	381.812
pol. sci.	372.3
owners of land	381.821
right of domicile	381.822
Alighteri. Dante Ital.	
poet.	833.115
Alimentation	
therapeutics	595.82
Alimony law	397.5
Alismataceae botany	575.36
Alkalies	
chemic technology	661.4
inorganic chemistry	546.21
Alkalin earths inorganic	
chem.	546.22
Alkaloidal plants	612.7
Alkaloids chemistry	547.97
Alkoran Islam	272.7
Allah Islam	271.1
Allegiance political	
science	371.029
Alliances	
internat. law	381.542
political science	371.65
Allier, France geography	983.485
Allies	
central world war	930.753

entente world war	930.751
Allodium land	
ownership	353.3
law	397.2
Allopathy therapeutics	595.7
Allotheria zoology	588.13
Allotropy chemistry	541.07
Alloys	
metallurgy	669.6
tests	650.48
theoretic chemistry	541.03
Allspice agriculture	612.87
Alluvium geology	551.72
Almanacs	
astrologic	157.2037
chronology	528.67
for teachers	330.37
general	037
nautic	527
statistical	340
of special topics see subjects	
Almond pomiculture	613.765
Alpes Basses, France geography	983.497
Alpes (cont.)	
Hautes, France geography	983.498
Maritimes. France geog.	983.497
Alphabet	
Chinese orthography	414.1
other languages	
Alphabetic catalogs	012.6
Alpine plants botany	571.903
Alsop, Richard Am. poet.	861.25
Altaic languages	409.25
Alternate	
generation biology	561.625
botany	571.65
zoology	581.65
Alternating-current	
generators	657.456
machinery	657.45
motors	657.457
systems	657.633
transforming machinery	657.458
Altruism ethics	180.4
Aluminum inorganic chem.	546.274
Alumni asssociated	339.6
Alumni day	333.7
Amalgamation	
immigration	377.69

metallurgy	669.21
Amaranthaceae botany	577.13
Amaryllidaceae botany	575.85
Amata Buddhism	231.79
Amateur manuals	
handcrafts	689
Ambassadors internat.	
law	386.33
Amber mineralogy	558.187
Amblypoda zoology	588.37
America geography	984
history	940
central geography	984.6
history	946
south geography	984.8
history	948
west Indies geography	984.7
history	947
American	
aborigines	943
antiquities	994
bibliography	013.41
civil war U. S. hist.	941.86
colleges	338.794
American (cont.)	
constitution	391.6
constitutional history	391.69
encyclopedias	034
fiction	863
folk literature	864
geography	984
history	940
independence U. S. hist.	941.83
Indians	943
juvenile literature	865
language	450
literature	860
newspapers	046
painting	730.6
periodicals	056
philosophy	126
poetry	861
political parties	375.6
prose	867
rebellion U. S. hist.	941.86
revolution U. S. hist.	941.83
statutes law	390.8
Americana history	940
Ametabola zoology	585.1
Amitayur-dhyana	
Buddhology	231.24
Ammonia	
chemic technology	661.4
salts chem. tech.	661.5
stimulants	597.16
Amnion obstetrics	598.8275

Amos, book of Bible	252.48
Ampelideae botany	578.33
Amphibia palaeozoology	569.84
zoology	587.6
Amphibiotica zoology	585.33
Amphidozoteerium	
zoology	588.85
Amphimixis heredity	563.34
Amphineura zoology	583.51
Amphioxides zoology	586.4
Amphipoda zoology	584.83
Amputation surgery	598.1907
Amur river	981.345
Amusements	790
children's	313.362
customs	319.75
ethics	189.7
hygiene	593.16
Amusements (cont.)	
of laboring classes	354.932
rural life	313.47
school	333.3
the Christian life	258.7
Amusia medicine	597.8455
psychology	155.254
Anacanthinii zoology	587.4777
Anacardiaceae botany	578.15
Anacreon Gk. poet.	831.43
Anacreontic literature	800.1795
Analgesics medicine	597.865
Analogy	
comparative anatomy	581.1
logic	141.77
plants	571.24
theology	201.31
Analysis	513
air chemistry	543.61
arithmetic	511.4
being ontology	133.2
beryllium inorganic	
chem.	546.231
blowpipe chemistry	544.3
capillary chemistry	544.95
catalytic chemistry	545.57
character psychology	153.8
chemic	543
colorimetric	
qualitative	544.6
quantitative	545.6
constant current	545.51
voltage	545.53
decipium inorganic	
chem.	546.292
drugs chemistry	543.4
electro qualitative	544.93

quantitative	545.5	Analytic	
food chemistry	543.1	chemistry	543
zootechny	615.06	functions	516.1
gas chemistry	544.4	geometry	519.4
liquids, volumetric	545.41	mechanics	531.5
logic	140	method	
market	624.1	education	337.15
metals chemistry	543.64	psychology	150.174
microscopic	566	trigonometry	518.3
milk agriculture	615.71	Anam	
chemistry	543.13	geography	982.43
mineralogy	558.2	history	924.3
polarimetric chem.	545.7	language	409.14
		literature	891.4
Analysis (cont.)		Anapsida zoology	587.811
polariscopic chem.	544.7	Anaptomorphidae	
psycho	156	zoology	589.33
qualitative chem.	544	Anarchism socialism	318.4
quantitative chem.	545	Anatma Buddhism	231.313
rocks chemistry	543.5	Anatolia, Turkey	
soils	611.31	geography	982.661
sounds acoustics	534.53	Anatomy	
spectrum		art	700.12
astronomy	522.6	comparative animals	599.1
chemistry qual.	544.6	biology	561.1
quan.	545.6	medicine	591.9
optics	535.4	plants	571.2
water chemistry	543.15	zoology	581.1
white light optics	535.23		

dental	598.21
descriptive microscopy	566.2
human	591
laws	593.71
microscopic	566.81
pathologic	594.1
regional	591.8
Anatomy(cont.)	
surgical	598.11
Anaxagoras Gk. philos.	121.15
Anaximander Gk. philos.	121.112
Anaximenes Gk. phiols.	121.113
Ancestor-worship	209.5
Ancylodactyla zoology	588.385
Ancylopoda zoology	588.385
Andesite lithology	557.26
Andropogonae forage crops	612.292
Andropozon agriculture	612.62
Anesthesia	
disease	597.845
hypnotism	156.5
psychology	155.256
Anesthetics medicine	597.861
Angelolatry	209.6
Angels Christian doctrine	256.61
Anger ethics	180.65
Angina pectoris diseases	597.142
Angiocarpa botany	373.41
Angiospermae botany	575
palaeobotany	569.5
Anglican church	259.3
brotherhoods	259.0918
creed	251.84
missions	259.36
ordination	259.339
persecution	259.0943
ritual	259.32
sects	259.38
sisterhoods	259.0919
Anglicisms English language	455
Anglo-Egyptian Sudan geog.	985.17
Anglo-Saxon	
history	935.81
language	409.383
laws	390.8
literature	850.1
poetry	851.1
Angora, Turkey geography	982.661
Anguilla zoology	587.477
Annalt, Germany	

geography	936.76	sculpture	729.8
Anhwei, China		habitats	581.72
geography	981.76	habits	581.71
Anhydrids		heat	
organic chemistry	547.7	physiol. zoology	581.43
theoretic chemistry	541.03	physiology	592.5
Anilin colors	667.2	thermics	536.57
Anima spiritualism	157.93	industries	615
Animal		instincts comp.	
behavior	581.71	psychology	581.702
chemistry		kingdom	580
analysis	543.78	lore	580.089
organic chem.	547	magnetism hypnotism	156.5
diseases		motors engineering	655.17
medicine	599.4	oils chem. technology	665.3
public health	593.283	parasites diseases	594.971
zoology	581.5	poisons toxicology	593.9
drugs	596.11	products	
electricity		chemistry	543.28
hypnotism	156.5	chem. technology	661.98
zoology	581.75	psychology comp. psych.	154.8
fats	665.3	zoology	581.791
food		worship	209.28
domestic science	694.1	Animals	
hygiene	593.128	agents of geol. work	551.98
physiology	592.473	Bible	252.0858
forms		or,	580.082
painting	737.18	Animals (cont.)	

care of	593.28	botany	578.93
or,	615.04	Anitra Buddhism	231.311
cruelty to ethics	189.58	Anjou, France geography	983.464
or,	581.708	Annals, Spring and Autumn	
diseases		Ch. classics	096
vet. medicine	599.4	Annelida zoology	583.6
zoology	581.5	Annexation	
domestic	615.1	intern. politics	381.315
evolution	563	pol. science	371.0315
feeding	615.05	Annihilation Buddhism	231.79
gati Buddhism	231.87	Anniversaries	
geographic distribution	581.9	special days edu.	334.37
hunting	619.1	student life	333.4
hygiene pub. health	593.28	world war	930.78
injurious agriculture	611.98	Annonaceae botany	577.43
zoology	581.8	Annotations for readers	027.1
painting	737.18	Announcement of vote	372.558
palaeontology	569.6	Annuals	073.8
plants injurious to	611.977	astrology	157.2037
psychology		Annuals (cont.)	
comp. psych.	154.8	floriculture	613.81
zoology	581.791	statistical	340
sculpture	729.8	special, see subject	
sports	797.1	Annulata zoology	583.6
Animism metaphysics	135	Annulosa zoology	583.6
Animus spiritualism	157.92	Annunities	
Anis		insurance	368.3
agriculture	613.4		

mathematics	512.97	Anthelmintics medicine	597.363
public finance	369.084	Anthocerotales botany	573.6
Chinese	369.184	Anthozoa zoology	582.75
other nations		Anthracene organic	
Annunciation		chem.	547.28
Christology	251.294	Anthracite mineralogy	558.125
Anomodontia zoology	587.813	Anthrax infectious	
Anonaceae botany	577.43	diseases	594.962
Anonales botany	577.43	Anthorpocentrism	
Anoplura zoology	585.1	anthropology	565.012
Anselm medieval philos.	121.633	Anthropogenic	
Anseres zoology	587.973	association	313.1
Ant		Anthropogeny	
bird zoology	587.977	anthropology	565.5
eaters zoology	588.32	Anthropography	
entomology	586.58	anthropology	565.2
Antaganism of		Anthropoidea zoology	589.5
medicines	595.73	Anthropology	565
Antagonistic		Anthropometry	
parasitism animals	581.765	anthropology	565.3
Antarctic		Anthropomorphidae	
explorations travels	985.991	zoology	589.7
ocean physiography	552.29	Anthropomorphism	
regions geography	985.991	natural theology	201.33
history	959.91	Anti-Darwiniana	
Anterior Tiber, China		evolution	564.29
geography	981.981	Anti-religion alliance	200.67

Anti-selection school		Antivaccination pub.	
evolution	564.4	health	593.2357
Anti-Socratic school		Anumana Hinduism	241.22
Gk. philos.	121.17	Anura zoology	587.68
Anti-spiritualism	157.99	Aomor, Japan geography	982.1626
Anti-war movements	388.89	Apes zoology	589.7
Antichrist Christ.	251.65	Apetalae botany	576.1
Anticlinal geology	553.6	Aphaniptera zoology	586.57
Antilocapridae zoology	588	Aphasia	
Antilogarithms math.	510.28	diseases	597.8455
Antimony		mental derangements	155.254
inorganic chemistry	546.62	Aphelion astronomy	521.3
metallurgy	669.991	Aphid zoology	585.38
Antiperiodics medicine	597.446	Apiary science	615.4
Antipyretics medicine	597.446	Apiculture	615.4
Antiquities	990	Aplacophora zoology	583.513
biblical	252.099	Apleen anatomy	597.411
see also special subjects		Apeocalypse in canonical	
Antiquity of man	565.099	books	252.8
Antiseptics		Apocrypha Bible	252.9
agriculture	611.993	Sutra	232.9
bacteriology	566.968	Apocynaceae botany	579.45
obstetrics	598.879	Apocynales botany	579.45
public health	593.236	Apoda zoology	587.66
surgery	598.157	Apogamy genetics	563.53
Antislavery sociology	317.48	Apologetics natural	
Antisthenes Gk. philos.	121.241	theology	201.9

Christian	251.9	
Aponogetonaceae botany	575.34	
Apoplexy diseases	597.841	
Apostles		
acts of canonical	252.6	
pseudepigrapha	252.993	
calling of Christology	251.2953	
creed	251.81	
Apostolic succession	255.51	
Apothecary pharmacy	596.73	
Apparatus		
physical	530.074	
practical chemistry	542.2	
witchcraft	157.74	
see also special subjects		
Apparitions		
psychoanalysis	156.17	
Appendicitis diseases	597.344	
Appendix anatomy	597.314	
physiology	597.327	
Apperception psychology	151.51	
Appetite physiology	592.471	
Appetites mental faculty	151.37	
Apple pomiculture	613.711	
Applicants		
securing economics	354.115	
Applications of electric		
power	657.8	
to lightening rods	537.71	
Applied		
arts	600	
chemistry	548	
or,	660	
mechanics	531.3	
or,	655.1	
meteorology	529.78	
psychology	158	
science	600	
statistics	346	
Appointment		
civil service officers	373.017	
diplomatic service officers	386.21	
teachers	336.4	
Appreciation of music	770.017	
Apprehension		
direct	151.9	
imaginal	151.7	
Apprehension(cont.)		
mnemonic	151.6	
perceptural	151.17	
Apprentice labor	354.252	
Approaches		
bridgebuilding	651.506	

Appropriations	
library finances	022.41
school finances	331.41
Apraxia	
medicine	597.8455
psychology	155.254
Apricot pomiculture	613.712
Apterygidae zoology	587.947
Aptera zoology	585.1
Apterygiformes zoology	587.947
Apterygota zoology	585.1
Apulia, Italy geography	983.27
Aquariums	580.078
Aquatic	
animal products	617.28
animals geog.	
distribution	581.904
carnivora zoology	587.53
plants geog. distribution	571.905
sports	338.637
vegetable products	617.27
Aqueducts municipal	
engin'g	653.17
Aqueous	
erosion geology	551.72
rocks geology	557.5
treatment prac. chem.	542.6
Aquifoliaceae botany	578.17
Aquinas medieval	
philos.	121.636
Aquivascular	
respiration zoology	581.422
Arabia	
geography	982.7
history	927
Arabic	
discovery of America	941.811
literature	895.1
philosophy	117
Arabs in Spain Span.	
hist.	933.82
Aracaceae botany	575.54
Arachis agriculture	612.35
Arachnida zoology	584.6
Arachnida paraditics	
diseases	594.975
Aragon, Spain geography	983.37
Arales botany	575.53
Araliaceae botany	578.91
Aramaic language	409.57
Araneae zoology	584.673
Araneida zoology	584.673
Aranyaka Hinduism	242.3
Aratu Gk. poet.	831.13
Arbitration	

capital and labor	354.86
commercial	624.7
international law	382.86
treaties	387.7
Arboriculture	614
Arc lighting elec.	
engin'g	657.8143
Arcadia, Greece	
geography	983.17
Archaean age geology	554.1
Archaeoceti zoology	588.471
Archaeology	990
Archaeopithecidae	
zoology	589.51
Archaeornithes zoology	587.91
Archaeozoic geology	554.4
Archaic law	390.091
Archard grass	
agriculture	612.22
Archbishop Christ.	255.53
Archegoniatae botany	573.5
Archegony	
biology	561.611
botany	571.61
zoology	581.61
Arches	
architectural	
construction	713.3
engineering	651.55
triumphal architecture	719.5
Chinese antiq.	991.85
Archiannelida zoology	583.616
Archichlamydeae botany	576.1
Archipelago, Greece	
geography	983.18
Archipolypoda zoology	584.4
Architectural	
acoustics	711.7
decoration	712
drawing	711.2
Architecture	710
Archives	901.2
Archt	
construction architecture	713.3
bridges	651.55
Arctic	
alpine regions botany	571.909
zoology	581.909
Arctic (cont.)	
explorations	985.995
ocean physical	
geography	552.2
regions geography	984.82
history	948.2
Ardeche, France	

geography	983.495
Ardennes, France	
geography	983.471
Argentina	
geography	984.82
history	948.2
Argillite geology	557.44
Argolis, Greece	
geography	983.17
Argon inorganic	
chemistry	546.183
Argument logic	141.2
Aria vocal music	771.73
Aristide agriculture	612.296
Aristippus Gk. philos.	121.251
Aristocracy	
education	338.95
form of state	371.043
social classes	313.82
Aristolochiaceae botany	576.91
Aristolochiales botany	576.9
Aristophanes Gk.	
dramatic poet.	831.24
Aristotelian Gk. philos.	121.4
Aristotle Gk. philos.	121.41
Arithmetic	511
Arithmetical	

functions	512.44
progression	514.1
tables	510.21
Arizona, U. S. geography	984.191
Arkansas, U. S.	
geography	984.174
Armament, problems of	388.81
Armature manuals	
handcrafts	689
Armenia, Turkey	
geography	982.666
Armies	
military engineering	695.3
science	379.5
Chinese history	910.28
war customs	319.15
world war	930.7
Armor and arms, antique	379.95
Arms military science	379.375
Army military science	379.5
Arnold, Matthew Eng.	
essays	857.85
poet.	851.85
Aromatic compounds	
chem.	547.2
Arrest and imprisonment	381.824
Arrhenatherum	

agriculture	612.275	religions	715
Arsenals		textile	765
military engineering	659.34	useful	600
science	379.377	woman in	313.3507
Arsenic inorganic chem.	546.145	Arteries	
Art		anatomy	597.115
acuary	765	blood pressure	597.124
anatomy drawing	731.1	circulation in	597.123
theory	700.12	diseases of	597.145
ceramic	764	Arthapatti Hinduism	241.24
decorative	762	Arthrodira zoology	587.45
domestic	690	Arthropoda	
embroidery	765.3	palaeozoology	569.77
expressive	780	zoology	584
fine	700	Arthrostraca zoology	584.83
galleries	700.7	Articulata zoology	583
glyptic	767	Artificial	
graphic	730	boundaries	381.333
history	700.9	or,	371.033
household	690	Artificial(cont.)	
industrial useful arts	600	colors chem. technol.	667.2
interior decoration	763	crystals	559.7
museums fine arts	700.7	decoration and ornam.	765.5
needlework	765.3	ear	598.48
pottery	764	eyes	598.38
productive	600	fertilization	
psychology	700.15	biology	561.626
recreative	790	botany	571.626

zoology	581.623
fertilizers	668.77
fuel chem. technol.	663.7
gems chem. technol.	666.7
mineralogy	558.182
hybrids	563.52
ice chem. technol.	664.8
light projective geometry	519.37
lights chem. technol.	665
dom. science	692
limbs	598.18
magnets	538.13
mineral waters	664.61
silk	668.43
stone chem. technol.	666.4
teeth	598.288
Artillery military science	379.57
Artiodactyla zoology	588
Artois, France geography	983.467
Arts	
and crafts	761
fine	700
graphic	730
industrial	600
productive	600
Arundo agriculture	612.594
Arupadbatu Buddhism	231.83
Aryadeva Buddhism	239.136
Aryasatyani Buddhism	231.3
Asafetida medicine	597.869
Asama Hinduism	244.3
Asanga Buddhism	239.145
Ascension Christology	251.2958
Asceticism	173.4
Asclepiadaceae botany	579.47
Asclepiadae botany	579.47
Ascolichenes botany	573.41
Ascomycetes botany	573.31
Ascorhynchomorpha	
zoology	584.63
Ascosporeae botany	573.31
Ascus fungi botany	573.31
Asepsis surgery	598.157
Asexual reproduction	
biology	561.61
botany	571.61
zoology	581.61
Ashes	
fertilizers agriculture	611.731
removal of sanitary engin'g	653.36
volcanic geology	557.22
Asia	
geography	980.9
history	909

Asia Minor	
geography	982.8
history	928
Asiatic cholera	
pathology	594.934
Asparagus olericulture	613.16
Asphaltic coal	558.127
chemic technology	665.5
mineralogy	558.127
pavements	651.75
Asphyxia pediatrics	598.941
Aspiration pneum.	
therapeutics.	595.817
Asrestis agriculture	612.23
Ass zoology	588.342
Assam, India geography	982.36
Assassination criminal law	394.25
Assault and battery crim. law	394.25
Assaying metallurgy	669.5
Assembly, freedom of pol. sci.	372.137
Assembly, the league of nations	383.1
Assent logic	141.1
Association psychology	151.621
Association psychology	313.6
anthropogenic	313.1
business cooperation	356.7
charitable	316.3
ethnogenic	313.2
library	020.6
parent-teacher	333.8
religions Y. M. C. A.	256.3
workingmen's	354.63
see also special subjects	
Assumption of Moses	
apocrypha	252.981
Assyria	
geography	982.82
history	928.2
Asteroidea zoology	582.91
Asteroids astronomy	523.49
Astigmatism	
ophthalmology	598.345
Astragalomancy	
divination	157.13
Astral body spiritism	157.95
Astrolatry	
nature-worship	209.21
Astrology	
astronomy	520.1
judicial	157.2
medical	157.28

mundane	157.2
natural	520.1
occult sciences	157.2
Astronomical	
almanacs chronology	528.61
clocks	
astronomy	522.5
chronology	528.59
manufacture	671.1
instruments	522
observations	522.1
physics	521
spectra	535.46
Astronomy	520
descriptive	523
nautic	527
physical	521
practical	522
spherical	522.7
theoretic	521
Astrophysics astronomy	523
Asylums	
architecture	717.3
libraries	025.77
sociology	316.3
Atavism heredity	563.395
Athanasian creed Christ.	251.83
Atheca zoology	587.817
Atheism natural theol	201.1
Atharva-veda Hinduism	242.14
Athenian supremacy	
Gk. hist.	931.831
Athletic sports	338.634
Atlantic	
ocean phys. geography	552.22
surface geography	980.5022
states	984.16
Atlases maps	980.3
Atman Hinduism	241.1
Atmosphere	551.7
erosion	551.7
geologic agent	551.94
ground hygiene	593.114
height of	529.16
hexiology	581.7771
meteorology	529.1
moon	523.36
physics of	529.1
pneumatics	533.7
Atmospheric	
currents	529.3
dust	529.14
electricity meteorology	529.5
physics	537.7
moisture	529.4
pressure meteorology	529.2

physiology	592.28
pneumatics	533.381
spectra	535.47
vibrations sound	534.5
Atomic theory chem.	541.01
Atomistic school Gk.	
philos.	121.17
Atonement Christology	251.23
Attachment zoology	581.73
Attack	
means of zoology	581.75
military engineering	659.32
science	379.4
Attacks	
on laborers	354.82
Attainments	
superior psychology	153.9
Attendance	
church	258.6
school	332.11
Attention	
and learning	151.65
psychology	151.51
Attica, Greece geography	983.16
Attitudes reflection	151.84
Attraction	
capillary	532.11
chemical affinity	541.067
magnetism	538
mechanics	531.63
sun and earth	523.33
Attributes of God Christ.	251.14
Auctions business	622.58
Aude, France geography	983.495
Audiences psychology	311.58
Audiphone acoustics	534.99
Auditing public finance	369.029
Auditory	
anatomy physiology	598.41
psychology	151.121
canal ear diseases	598.443
hygiene	598.43
pathology	
physiology	598.44
psychology	151.124
perception	
acoustics	534.95
psychology	151.228
physiology	598.42
psychology	151.122
sensations psychology	151.12
therapeutics physiology	598.45
testing psychology	151.128
Augier, G. V. E. Fr.	
drama	842.83
Augury divination	157.17

Augustinian monks	259.0914
Auricle otology	598.442
Auricles of heart	598.1125
Auricularineae botany	573.35
Auroras	
astronomy	523.57
meteorology	529.53
Auscultation	
therapeutics	595.26
Austen, Jane Eng.	
fiction	853.74
Australia	
geography	985.93
history	959.3
Australian ballot	
suffrage	372.553
Austria	
geography	983.795
history	937.95
Authocerotales botany	573.6
Author	
bibliographies	
false authors	018.4
family authors	016
individual authors	015
joint authors	016
library catalogs	012.2
pseud authors	018.3
Authorship	
Bible	252.01
Chinese classics, the	090.06
literary criticism	800.42
Autistic thinking	
psychoanalysis	156.337
Autobasidiomycetes	
botany	573.37
Autobiography	970
Autocracy form of state	371.047
Autoelectrolytic processes	
practical chemistry	542.8
Autographs book rarites	001.189
handwritings	739.15
Autohypnotism	156.58
Autolysis biology	562.94
Automatic	
movement psychology	151.351
speaking spiritualism	157.96
telephone systems	657.857
telegraphy	657.8353
transmitters	657.8337
writing spiritualism	157.96
Automobiles engineering	659.71
Autonomy	173.3

Autopsy therpeutics	595.29	Avesta, Zend Parseeism	282
Autumn		Aveyron, France	
customs	319.71	geography	983.492
flowering	613.8052	Aviation	
Auxology zoology	581.6	engineering	659.4
Avarice ethics	180.68	law	381.95
Avatamsaka-sutra-sect		physics	533.7
Chinese Buddhism	239.53	Avicenna medieval	
Japanese Buddhism	239.63	philos.	121.65
Avecebronus medieval		Avicplture	615.3
philos.	121.66	Axle physics	531.92
Avempace medieval		Axonometry	
philos.	121.65	crystallography	559.13
Averroes medieval		Azoic age geology	554.2
philos.	121.65	Azuma-asobi-uta Jap.	
Aves zoology	587.9	ballads	821.53

Babbitt Am. philos.	126.8
Babylon	
geography	982.81
history	928.1
language	495.2
philosophy	118.1
Bachelors celibacy	187.2
Bacillariaceae botany	572.6
Bacillariales botany	572.6
Bacillariophyta botany	572.6
Backbone anatomy	597.711
Backward	
children childstudy	153.766
Bacon English essays	857.31
philos.	125.1
Bacteria	
agriculture	611.94
botany	572.11
fermentation	664.5
Bacteriaceae botany	572.121
Bacterial diseases	611.94
Bacteriales botany	572.11
Bacteriology	566.9
Bacteriolysis	566.967
Bacterium botany	572.121
Baden, Germany	
gergraphy	983.77
Badges heraldry	960.4
Bahamas	
geography	984.76
history	947.6
Bailments law	398.41
Baking	
cookery	695.1
powder	664.46
Balaenidae zoology	588.474
Balaenopteridae zoology	588.475
Balance	
bridge engineering	651.52
machines	531.91
metrology	607
of power polit. science	370.1
sense of psychology	151.16
Balances, chemic	542.3
Balanophoraceae botany	576.87
Balanopsidaceae botany	576.41
Balanopsidales botany	576.4
Baldness dermatology	598.544
Balkan	
league World war	
causes	930.721
pivot	388.21
question	388.21
states	
geography	983.95

history	939.5
Ball games	338.635
Ballade poetry	801.8
Ballet poetry	801.3
Ballistics physics	531.698
Ballot suffrage	372.553
Ballots, count of suffrage	372.557
Balms field crops	612.83
Balsaminaceae botany	578.27
Baltic provinces	
geography	983.97
history	939.7
Baluchistan	
geography	982.58
history	925.9
Balzac, Honore de	
Fr. fiction	843.72
Bamboo	
botany	575.428
raising	612.595
"Bamboo books"	
Chinese hist.	910.913
Bamboo instruments	770.18
Banana	
botany	575.91
horticulture	613.78
Band music	774
Bandages therapeutics	595.814
Bangiaceae botany	573.261
Bangiales botany	573.261
Bangioideae botany	573.261
Banishment crim. law	394.519
Banjo	775.4
Bank	
notes	364.1
of China	362.121
the U. S.	362.129
Banking	
by mail postal service	636.38
finance	362
Bankruptcy law	398.81
Banks	
and banking	362
crises	352.74
Banks (cont.)	
bankruptcy	362.8
cooperative cooperation	356.75
political economy	362
savings banking	362.9
Banners	
flowers botany	570.087
heraldry	960.7
Chinese	969.109
sacred ornaments	
Christianity	253.36

Banquets	
domestic economy	697.5
social customs	319.72
student life	333.4
Bantu languages	409.71
Banville, T. F. de	
Fr. poet.	841.83
Baptism	253.91
of Christ	251.2951
infants	253.91
sacrament	253.91
Baptist Christianity	259.6
Barbarians	
antiquitles see country	
customs	319.9
Barbour, John Eng. poet.	851.22
Bargaining	
of wages theory	354.317
Barium inorganic chem.	546.225
Barley agriculture	612.16
Barlow, Joel Am. poet.	861.23
Barnacles zoology	584.87
Barou, M. B. Fr. drama	842.48
Barrel-organ	777.5
Baruch apocrypha	252.95
Basalt geology	557.28
Bascule bridges	651.571
Baseball games	338.635
Basellaceae botany	577.2
Bases	
qualitative analysis	544.12
theoretical chemistry	541.03
wage political econ.	354.34
Basidiales botany	573.35
Basidiolichenes botany	573.47
Basidiomycetes botany	573.35
Basins physical	
geography	552.6
Basket	
ball games	338.635
fibers	612.59
Basque	
language	409.399
literature	889.9
provinces	
geography	983.97
history	939.7
Basses	
Alpes, France	
geography	983.498
Pyrenees, France	
geography	983.494
Bathing	
customs	319.47
domestic economy	693.4

hygiene	593.14	Beaumarchais, P. A. C. de	
school hygiene	332.33		
sport	338.637	Fr. drama	842.58
Bathmism biology	562.33	Beaumout, Francis	
Batidaceae botany	576.56	Eng. drama	852.35
Batidales botany	576.55	Beautiful in nature	700.18
Batrachia		Beauty	
paleontology	569.84	esthetics	190
zoology	587.68	fine arts	700.1
Battles		ontology	133.89
Chinese history	910.28	Becoming and change	133.65
see also history of other countries		Bee	
		apiculture	615.4
military science	379.4	entomology	586.58
World war 1914—19	930.7	keeping	615.4
Battleships	379.651	wax	
Bayle, Pierre Fr. essays	847.43	animal culture	615.5
Bean		chem technol.	665.4
botany	577.79	Beech	
family fruits culture	613.3	botany	576.67
field crops	612.3	pomiculture	613.712
Bearings machinery	655.75	Beef	
Bearn, France geography	983.494	cattle	615.12
Bears zoology	587.518	food	694.1
Beasts		Beer	
agriculture	615	analysis, chemic	543.17
of prey	587.5	manufacture	664.53
zoology	588	Beets	

field crops	612.41
horticulture	613.11
Beggar weed forage	
crops	612.385
Beggars	
charity ethics	180.77
pauperism	352.8
relief	316.38
Beggiatoaceae botany	572.151
Beginnings	
of life biology	562.7
Begonia botany	578.65
Begoniaceae botany	578.65
Behavior	
ethics	184
of animals psychology	154.8
zoology	581.72
plants botany	571.7
psychology	154.7
Behaviorism psychology	150.1973
Beheading punishments	
crim. law	394.51
Being	
nature of ontology	133.1
Bel and the dragon	
apocr.	252.96
Belgian Kongo	
geography	985.67
history	956.7
Belgium	
geography	983.792
history	937.92
Belief	
epistemology	131.9
freedom of	372.134
salvation	251.42
Beliefs reasoning	151.86
Belleau, Remy Fr. poet.	841.33
Belles-lettres	800
Belligerents, right of	
intern. law	381.543
Benedictines monks	259.0911
Benevolence ethics	180.77
Benevolent societies	313.66
Bengal, India geography	982.36
Benincasa fruits edible	613.25
Bentham Eng. philos.	125.64
Benzenes organic	
chemistry	547.2
Benzoin perfume plants	612.83
Benzole light chem.	
tech.	665.75
Beowulf Eng. poet.	851.11
Beranger, P. J. de	

Fr. poet.	841.71
Berberidaceae botany	577.38
Berberidales botany	577.38
Bereavement ethics	180.93
Bergson Fr. philos.	124.7
Berkeley Eng. philos.	125.4
Bermuda grass forage crops	612.271
Bermudas	
geography	984.79
history	947.9
Beroidea zoology	582.778
Berries pomiculture	613.78
Berry, France geography	983.483
Berseem forage crops	612.382
Bessel's functions	516.844
Best	
book lists	018.5
reading	027.5
Beta sugar plants	612.63
Beta vulgaris roots crops	612.41
Betrothal	313.344
Betterment tax	369.051
Betulaceae botnay	576.66
Beverages	
adulterations	593.22
alcoholic hygiene	597.83
hygiene	593.13
Beverages (cont.)	
manufacture	664.5
water hygiene	593.131
Beyle, M. H. Fr. fiction	843.71
Bhakti Indian Buddhism	239.15
Bhava Buddhism	231.53
Bhotan	
geography	982.399
history	923.9
Bible	
and law	252.084
science	252.085
antiquities	252.099
dictionaries	252.03
geography	252.098
history	252.09
omens	157.15
prayers	253.41
revision Chinese	252.061
stories	252.081
zoology	580.082
Bibliography	010
family author	016
general	011
joint author	016
national	013
of bibliography	011.1

book rarities	019
subject	017
Bibliomancy divination	157.15
Bibliomania	
bibliography	010
Bicarpellatae botany	579
Bicoecaceae botany	572.33
Bicycles engin'g	659.77
Biennials floriculture	613.81
Bigamy	
ethics	183.2
ethnogenic assoc.	313.3413
Bignonia botany	579.6
Bignoniaceae botany	579.6
Bilateral promorphology	561.13
Bile	
ducts anatomy	597.315
physiology	597.325
therapeutics	597.463
Biliary substances	
org. chem.	547.94
Bill law	398.5
of exchange	364.4
Bimana	
palaeozoology	569.88
zoology	589.9
Bimetallism	361.22

Binary	
forms	512.21
stars astronomy	523.81
Binaural	
hearing psychology	151.126
Binding, book	023.9
Binocular	
optics	535.9
physiology	598.345
psychology	151.116
Binomial theoren math.	510.3
Bio-chemistry	
biology	562.4
chemistry	541.9
physiology	592.4
Biogenesis	562.7
Biography	970
of special subject	
see subject	
Biological	
analogy	371.071
archaeology	990.5
chemistry	
biology	562.4
chemistry	541.9
physiology	592.4
geography	980.116
Biology	560

Biomagnetism hypnotism	156.5	physiology	592.63
Biometrics	562.6	customs	319.21
Bion Gk. lyric poet.	831.49	growth after	592.65
Bio-mechanics		obstetrics	598.8
embryology	561.67	population statistics	349.072
Bionomics		rates public health	593.211
biology	561.8	Birthday customs	319.23
botany	571.7	Births	
zoology	581.7	registration public	
Biophysics	562.3	health	593.21
Biopsychology	154	statistics	349.072
Biotypology psychology	153.84	Bishops	255.53
Birds		Bismark islands	985.956
agricultural aids	611.995	Bismuth	
diseases of	599.46	drugs digestive system	597.367
divination	157.17	inorganic chemistry	546.63
eggs	587.9	Bisulca zoology	589.331
flight migration	581.703	Bituminous coal	558.124
Brids(cont.)		Bixaceae botany	578.57
hunting	619.2	Bixales botany	578.57
nests of zoology	587.9	Bixinea botany	578.57
palaeontology	569.86	Black	
poultry	615.3	art magic	157.7
Birth		body radiation	535.59
control		books witchcraft	157.74
ethics	183.5	death plague	593.237
eugenics	563.57	earth lithology	557.568
demography	349.021	friars Dominicans	259.0912

magic	157.7	asylums	
monks		architecture	717.3
Augustinians	259.0914	philanthropy	316.35
Benedictines	259.0911	childstudy	153.761
race		education of	338.65
ethnography	565.881	libraries for	025.78
psychology	153.411	schools for	338.965
Blacking chem.		Blindness	598.301
technology	667.77	Block-books	010.31
Blacklisting		Blockade	
labor strikes	354.85	economic	382.36
Blacksmithing	682	internat. law	381.561
Bladder		in war	382.34
anatomy	497.612	pacific	382.33
diseases	597.642	Blood	
physiology	597.627	changes in respiration	597.224
Blade		diseases	597.147
leaf morphology	571.275	examination	595.29
Blankets manuf.	675.36	histology	591.75
Blast furnace	669.11	letting therapeutics	595.811
Blastoidea zoology	582.99	physiology	597.12
Blattodae zoology	585.31	poisoning discases	594.94
Bleaching chemic		pressure physiology	597.124
technology	667	purification	597.224
Bleeding		vessels anatomy	597.11
therapeutics	595.811	zoology	581.413
wounds	598.164	Blowers engineering	655.53
Blind		Blowpiping	

experimental chem.	542.5	development childstudy	153.71
qualitative analysis	544.3	physiol.	592.6
quantitative analysis	545.2	ethics of	188.9
rock analysis chem.	543.5	growth childstudy	153.71
Blue		measurements of	565.3
books		natural and spiritual	251.175
lists of officers	373.014	proportions of	565.22
Chinese	373.13	structure	153.71
grass cherapeutics	595.85	temperature of	592.56
green algae	573.21	weight anthropometry	565.3
grass agriculture	612.21	Bohemia see Czeck	
prints photography	756.7	Boilers engin'g	655.225
Board		Boiling	
of audit	373.065	heat	536.721
trustees	331.352	points chemistry	541.64
Boats		Boko, Japan geography	982.18
life preservers	593.487	Bolivia	
shipbuilding	659.13	geography	984.84
Bochmeria fibers	612.55	history	948.4
Bodily strength	565.41	Bolshevism	318.7
Body		Bombacaceae botany	578.47
and mind	135.3	Bombaceae botany	578.47
astral spiritualism	157.951	Bombay, India	
care of childstudy	153.71	geography	982.39
hygiene	593.1	Bombs chem. technology	663.1
school hygiene	332.3	Bonaparte, Napolon	
cleanliness of hygiene	593.14	consulate	935.847
cosmology	134.7	empire	934.85

Bondage slavery	317.4
Bonds	
finance	369.08
Chinese	369.18
insurance of	369.81
investment	367.15
securities	366.1
Bones	
descriptive anatomy	581.17
diseases of	597.74
human anatomy	597.71
of ear anatomy	598.41
psychology	151.121
physiology	597.72
skeleton	597.711
Book	
binding	010.8
buying lib. manag.	023.1
cases lib. building	024.8
catalogs	010
clubs	338.88
collecting	023.1
illustration inserted	
plates	010.91
keeping accounts	627
of Changes Chinese	
classics	091
Enoch apocrypha	252.981
Filial Piety Chinese	
classics	097
Four Philosophers	
Ch. classics	098
History Chinese	
classics	092
Jasher apocrypha	252.982
Jubilees apocrypha	252.982
Music Chinese	
classics	095
Odes Chinese	
classics	093
Proverbs Bible	252.33
Rites Chinese	
classics	094
ownership	010.91
rarities	009
stacks	024.4
worm	023.9
Bookkeeping	627
Books	
and reading	027.5
bibliography	010
black witchcraft	157.74
Books (cont.)	
censorship prohibition	009.67
classification of	023.3
condemned	009.67

curiosa	009.65
deuterocanonical	
Buddhism	232.9
Christianity	252.9
dwarf	009.2
early copy	009.3
printed	009.1
editions de luxe	009.2
enemies of lib. economy	023.9
expurgated	009.67
fine editions	009.2
first editions	009.11
incunabula	009.1
library economy	020
lists of best	018.5
lost	009.6
microscopic editions	009.2
obscure, sold secretly	009.67
old editions	009.16
omens	157.15
photogravure editions	009.13
prohibited	009.67
reference	023.7
repairing editions	009.17
reprint editions	009.12
unique copies	009.6
Booksellers catalogs	011.8
Borage botany	579.54
Boraginaceae botany	579.54
Boraginales botany	579.54
Borneo	
geography	985.915
history	959.15
Boron inorg. chemistry	546.17
Borraginaceae botany	579.54
Bosses geology	553.8
Botany	
agricultural	610.57
forestry	614.3
fossil	569.1
geographical distribution	571.9
medical	596.12
structural	571.2
systematic	571.1
Boundaries	
national	
foreign relations	387.3
internat. law	381.33
political science	371.033
for special country	
see that	
country	
Bourbon	
family	
France history	934.83
restoration	934.86

Spain history	933.854
restoration	933.86
Bourbonnasis, France		
geography	983.485
Boursault, Edme Fr.		
drama	842.44
Bovidae zoology	588
Bows		
and arrows shooting	379.94
Boxer		
uprising Chinese history	917.4
Boxing	797.3
Boy		
problem childstudy	153.773
scouts societies	313.67
Boycotting labor strikes	354.84
Boys		
childstudy	153.773
dept. Y. M. C. A.	256.357
libraries	025.72
religions societies	256.7
societies sociology	313.67
Brachiopoda zoology	588.93
Brachycera insects	586.57
Bradstreet, Anne Am.		
poet.	861.12
Brahma		

god	241.72
priests	246
temples	247
Brahmanism	240
Brain		
anatomy	597.811
functional diseases		
abnormal psychology	155.24
medicine		
mental derangements		
abnormal psychology	155
medicine	597.84
Brain (cont.)		
organic diseases		
abnormal psychology	155.23
medicine	597.84
physiology	597.82
mental	152.2
structural diseases of	597.843
Bramanas of the Vedas	242.16
Bramble fruits	613.71
Branches		
retail selling	622.8
Branchial respiration	581.423
Branchiata zoology	584.8
Branchiopoda zoology	584.863
Brandy		
hygiene	593.13

manufacture	664.55	man	597.22
stimulant	597.16	plants	571.43

Brass
    instruments music   774
    manufacture   671.3

Brasses monmental
    ecclesiology   253.34
    sculpture   725

Brassica campestris
    roots crops   612.42
        rapa roots crops   612.42

Bravery ethics   180.74

Brazil
    geography   984.81
    history   948.1

Bread
    adulterations   593.22
    as food physiology   592.473
    cookery   695.6
    fruit   613.745

Breakage insurance   368.7

Breakwaters hydraulic
    engin'g   654.2

Breast
    anatomy   598.719
    diseases of   598.749

Breathing
    animals   581.42

Breccia lithology   557.53

Breeding
    animal culture   615.03
    eugenics   563.51
    plants   611.5

Brewing chemic tech.   664.53

Bribery
    criminal law   394.25
    electoral fraud   372.57

Brick
    chemic tech.   666.3
    clays mineralogy   558.16
    construction masonry   651.16
    pavement   651.75
    strength of materials   650.47

Bridges
    building   651.5
    engineering   651.5
    military eng.   659.36

British
    America
        geography   984.2
        history   942
    Burma
        geography   982.479
        history   924.79

colonies polit. science	377.95
constitution	391.5
empire	
geography	983.5
history	935
Honduras	
geography	984.62
history	946.2
India	
geography	982.3
history	923
philosophers	125
regime, Canada	
geography	984.2
history	942
Somaliland	
geography	985.41
history	954.1
Britons	
geography	983.5
history	935
Brittany, France	
geography	983.461
Brittle stars zoology	582.92
Brocken spectre	
meteorology	529.68
Brome forage crops	612.272
Bromeliaceae botany	575.73
Bromin inorganic chem.	546.133
Bromus forage crops	612.272
Bronchi	
anatomy	597.213
pathology	597.243
Bronze	
age prehist. archaeology	990.9
fine arts	725
manufacture	671.3
remains prehist arch.	990.9
Chinese	991.2
Broomsticks	
riding on witchcraft	157.72
Brothels ethics	187.8
Brotherhoods monks	254.5
Brown, C. B. Am. fiction	863.22
Brown	
algae	573.25
coal	558.122
flowers	613.8055
race ethnography	565.883
psychology	153.453
Browne, Thomas Eng.	
essays	857.43
Browning,	
E. B. Eng. poet.	851.82
Robert Eng. poet.	851.83
Brueys, D. A. de Fr.	

drama	842.46
Brush disposal	
silviculture	614.47
Bruta zoology	588.32
Bryant, W. C. Am. poet.	861.33
Bryophyta botany	573.5
palaeobotany	569.23
Bryozoa zoology	583.8
Buckwheat field crops	612.12
Buddha life of	231.29
Buddhi	241.62
Buddhindriyas	241.65
Buddhism	
and science	230.15
evidences	231.9
history	
Chinese	239.5
Indian	239.1
Japanese	239.6
other countries	
Buddhist	
apologetics	231.9
architecture	715.3
art	230.89
associations	236
Buddhist(cont.)	
calendars chronology	528.63
doctrines	231
education	237
ethics	231.18
evidences	231.9
iconography	
rel. art	230.89
sculpture	729.23
institutions	235
life	238
logic	231.16
monasteries	235.8
monks	235.5
nunneries	235.8
philosophy	231.1
psychology	231.15
sects	239
scriptures	232
Sutra	232
temples	235.8
Buddho bhagavan	
Buddhism	231.22
Buddhology	231.2
Budget	
financial administration	369.024
Chinese	369.124
other nations	
laboring classes	354.935
Buffalo zoology	588.335

Building	
architecture	710
construction	651.3
laws	
protection of life	593.46
rent of land for	353.43
stones mineralogy	558.15
Buildings	
farm	610.67
inspection of	593.46
library	024
military engineering	659.36
public	
administration	373.093
architecture	717
Y. M. C. A.	256.32
Bulbous plants	613.83
Bulbs edible	613.13
Bulgaria	
geography	983.958
history	939.58
Bundestaat pol. sci.	371.64
Bunodonta zoology	588.332
Bunyan, John Eng.	
fiction	853.42
Buoyant effects	532.36
Buoys	
harbor engin'g	654.46

protection of life	593.483
Burgundy, France	
geography	983.475
Burial	
cemeteries	719.4
ceremonies	319.17
church rituals	253.98
customs	319.24
insurance	368.6
public health	593.26
Burke, Edmund Eng.	
oratory	858.42
Burlesques	
drama	802.86
expressive arts	785.5
Burma	
geography	982.47
history	924.7
Burmannia botany	575.98
Burmanniaceae botany	575.98
Burmese	
Buddhism	239.32
language	409.133
literature	891.3
Burning	
the dead customs	319.24
Burns and scalds	
surgery	598.161

Burns, Robert Eng. poet.	851.67
Bursae anatomy	597.717
Burseraceae botany	577.94
Bush fruits	613.78
Business	
building architecture	717.5
commerce	620
cooperation	356.7
correspondence	626.2
cycles	624.5
ethics	186
or,	620.018
law	398
or,	621.9
management	622
manuals	620.02
mathematics	626.1
Business (cont.)	
practice	626
psychology	620.015
state control of	621.1
tax	369.053
Chinese	369.153
other nations	
transaction law	398.3
Busts sculpture	728
Butomaceae botany	575.33
Butter dairy	615.73
Butterflies zoology	586.531
Buxaceae botany	578.11
Buying business	
methods	622.51
Buzzard bird	587.979
By-products	
forestry	614.78
of combustion	663.8
Byron, G. G. N. Eng.	
poet.	851.76
Byzantine empire	931.86

Cabala Judaism	262.5
Cabbage olericulture	613.17
Cabinet	
council	373.0505
officers in legis. bodies	373.003
piano	776.1
Cable	
metal manufacture	675.72
roads city transit	633.7
railway engin'g	651.85
Cables	
electric engin'g	657.653
manufacture	675.7
submarine	
communication	637.2
engineering	657.837
telegraphy	
business	637.2
engineering	657.837
Cacao alkaloidal plants	612.74
Cachet seals	991.615
Cactaceae botany	578.68
Cactales botany	578.68
Cacteae botany	578.68
Cadmium	
inorganic chem.	546.237
metallurgy	669.992
Caedmon Eng. poet.	851.12
Caenopidae zoology	588.347
Caesar, C. J. Latin literature	832.881
Caesarian section	
obstetrics	598.876
Caesium inorganic chem.	546.219
Cainozoic ere geology	554.7
Cajanus forage crops	612.34
Cake cookery	695.6
Calabria, Italy	
geography	983.27
Calais, France	
geography	983.467
Calcarea zoology	588.51
Calcispongiae zoology	582.51
Calcium	
inorganic chem.	546.221
light chem. tech.	665.77
Calculation mathematics	510.7
Calculus	
diseases	597.642
mathematics	515
Calendar year school	334.31
Calendars chronology	528.6
California	
Lower geography	984.46

U. S. geography	984.194	Campaigns	
Calligraphy	739	political	375
Callitrichaceae botany	577.99	Chinese history	910.281
Callitrichidae zoology	589.53	World war	930.76
Caloric		Campanales botany	579.93
engines	655.41	Campania, Italy	
physics	536	geography	983.27
Calorimetry		Campanology antiquities	990.121
physics	536.31	Chinese	991.21
physiology	592.51	Campanulaceae botany	579.93
Calvados, France		Campanulatae botany	579.9
geography	983.465	Canada	
Calvinism Christianity	259.22	geography	984.2
Calvinistic		history	942
baptist church	259.61	literature	869
methodist church	259.72	Canal engineering	654.7
Calycanthaceae botany	577.42	Candidates suffrage	372.54
Calyciflorae botany	577.7	Candles chemic tech.	665.72
Cambodia		Cane agriculture	612.61
geography	982.44	Canidae zoology	588.516
history	924.4	Cannabinaceae botany	576.72
Cambrian period geology	554.52	Cannabis fibers	612.53
Camel zoology	588.336	Cannaceae botany	575.93
Camelidae zoology	588.336	Cannel coal mineralogy	558.123
Camelopardidae zoology	588.338	Canon	
Camera	753.7	of scripture	252.01
Cameralistic science	369	Cantate poetry	801.45

Canticles Bible	252.35
Canvassing sales methods	622.55
Capacity	
conductive thermics	536.415
for knowing	
childstudy	153.72
psychology	153
mental	
of women psychology	153.1
sensory intelligence	
tests	150.77
suffrage qualifications	372.51
thermal thermics	536.3
Cape of Good Hope	985.77
Capet	
House of French history	934.82
Capillaries	
blood anatomy	597.118
lymph anatomy	597.412
Capillary	
analysis chemistry	544.95
attraction of liquids	532.11
Capital	
and income econ.	355
labor econ.	354.1
punishment law	394.511
ships navies	379.65
Capitalism	355
Capitation tax	369.055
Chinese	369.155
other nations	
Capitulations intern. law	381.5585
Capparidaceae botany	577.55
Capparidales botany	577.55
Capparidineae botany	577.55
Caprifoliaceae botany	579.82
Captures intern. law	381.577
Carbon	
compounds organ. chem.	547
group inorgan. chem.	546.16
inorganic chemistry	546.161
series mineralogy	558.12
Carbonate rocks	
lithology	557.56
Carbonhydrates	
in blood physiology	597.122
nutrition physiology	592.476
organic chemistry	547.8
Carboniferous period	
geology	554.56
Card	
catalog	023.4
playing amusements	795
Care	

animals	615.04	Carpets	
body		decoration	763.3
childstudy	153.71	design	735.73
hygiene	593.14	manufacture	675.33
children		Carpoascomycetes	
dom. econ.	699.1	botany	573.33
sociology	313.361	Carpomyceteae botany	573.33
plants agriculture	611.90	Carpophaga zoology	588.25
Carica pomiculture	613.777	Carriages	632.4
Caricaceae botany	578.63	Carrier pigeons	639.7
Caricature drawing	737.77	Carriers law	398.44
Carices botany	575.43	Carrot olericulture	613.11
Carinate zoology	587.971	roots crops	612.45
Carlyle, Thomas Eng.		Cartell pol. econ.	356.4
essays	857.82	Cartilaginous tissue	591.73
Carnegie institution	331.44	Caryophyllaceae botany	577.27
Carniola, Austria		Case law	390.023
geography	983.795	Castanea pomiculture	613.762
Carnivals customs	319.79	Caste ethics	184.7
Carnivora mammals	588.5	Casting ots	157.13
Carnivorous plants	571.75	Castles architecture	718.2
Carnot geometry	519.2	Castoridae zoology	588.661
Carol sacred music	253.58	Casualties insurance	368.5
Caroline island	985.961	Casuariiformes zoology	587.943
Carolingians Fr. history	934.817	Casuarinaceae botany	576.21
Carotid gland	597.417	Cat	
Carpentry	651.45	diseases of medicine	599.48

domestic animals	615.17
zoology	588.511
Catabolism botany	571.43
Catalepsy abnormal psych.	155.6
Catalogs, general	011
see also Bibliography, For special subject see subject	
Cataloguing	023.4
Catalysis chemistry	541.068
Catalytic analysis	545.57
Cataphracta zoology	587.836
Catarrh	
diseases	597.241
epidemic diseases	598.542
Cathartics drugs	597.362
Cathartidae zoology	587.9791
Catholic church, Roman	259.1
epistles New Testament	252.79
Catoptrices optics	535.32
measurement of radiant energy	535.8
Cats see Cat	
Cattle	
domestic animals	615.12
veterinary medicine	599.42
Catullus, C. V. Latin lyric poet.	832.42
Catur Veda Hinduism	242.1
Caucasia, Russia	
geography	983.88
Caucasic race	565.884
Caudata zoology	587.67
Cauliflower olericulture	613.17
Cauloma botany	571.274
Causality philosophy	134.11
Causation philosophy	134.11
Cause and effect philosophy	134.11
Causes	
contagious diseases	593.231
Causes (cont.)	
final philosophy	134.2
of crime	315.16
World war 1914-19	930.721
Cavalry military science	379.56
Caviidae zoology	588.616
Caxton editions rarities	009.95
Cebidae zoology	589.55
Cedar sugar plants	612.817
Ceilings architecture	713.7
Celastraceae botany	578.18

Celastrales botany	578.18	Cellular membrane	571.116
Celebes, Malaysia		Celluloid chemic tech.	668.41
geography	985.916	Cellulose	
Celebrations		chemic technology	668.4
military	379.39	manufacture	674.3
student life	333.4	organic chemistry	547.85
World war 1914-19	930.78	Celtic language	409.37
Celestial		literatures	859
bodies	157.21	Celts French history	934.811
cyclic characters	157.27	Cements	
dynamics	521.1	engineering materials	650.46
equator	522.75	manufacture	666.8
latitude and longitude	522.76	Censorship	
signs divination	157.17	press	
sphere	522.71	journalism	040.13
Celibacy ethics	187.2	political science	372.138
Cell		Sunyatsenism	001.138
division		or,	001.164
biology	561.54	see also Books, censorship	
plant growth	571.117	Censuses statistics	345
formation	571.117	Central	
growth	561.58	Africa	
structure		geography	985.6
biology	561.52	history	956
botany	571.117	America	
histology	591.71	geography	984.6
zoology	581.21	history	946
Cells see Cell		provinces, India geog.	982.37

stations	657.81
Centralization	
administrative	373.0501
school government	331.21
Centrifugal	
force physics	531.696
Centripetal	
force physics	531.696
Centrosomes	571.115
Centrospermae botany	577.1
Cephalopoda zoology	583.57
Cephalotaceae botany	577.73
Ceramics	
eng. materials	650.47
fine arts	764
manufacture	666.1
Cerasus pomiculture	613.725
Ceratophyllaceae botany	577.32
Cercopithecidae zoology	589.57
Cereals agriculture	612.1
Cerebellum anatomy	597.8117
Cerebral meninges	
anatomy	597.8119
Cerebrospinal fever	594.924
Cerebrum anatomy	597.811
Ceremonies customs	319.1
Cerium inorganic chem.	546.263
Certification of teachers	336.25
Cervidae zoology	588
Cessation of selection	563.195
Cession of territory	
intern law	381.315
pol. sci.	371.031
Cestoidea zoology	582.774
Cestoda zoology	583.34
Cetacea zoology	588.47
Cete zoology	588.47
Ceylon	
Buddhism	239.31
geography	982.399
history	923.9
Chadayatana Buddhism	231.58
Chaetognatha zoology	583.97
Chaetopoda zoology	583.61
Chalcedony gems	558.185
Chalicotheriidae zoology	588.386
Chalk lithology	557.563
Cham Austronesian	
language	409.181
Chamaesiphonaceae	
botany	572.177
Chamber	
music	779.7
vocal music	771.8

Chambers			Change	
form of legislature	373.039		cosmology	134.6
Chameleon zoology	587.855		of air hygiene	593.112
Champagne			form of state	371.049
chemic technology	664.51		phase thermics	536.7
France geography	983.471		seasons	525.5
Chance			Changes, Book of Ch.	
game of			classics	091
amusements	795		Changes of blood,	
ethics	189.75		respiration	597.223
metaphysics	134.13		Chanson de	
probabilities	512.9		geste Fr. poetry	841.11
vs cause metaphysics	134.11		Roland Fr. poetry	841.11
Chancellar education	331.353		Chanson-nette	
Chances mathematics	512.9		folk literature	804.7
Ch'an-tsung Chinese			Chinese	814.7
Buddhism	239.56		Chao Ping-wen Chinese	
Chang Hsien Chinese			prose	817.583
poet.	811.733		Chap-books	804.2
Chang Hsueh-cheng Ch.			Chapelain, Jean Fr.	
prose	817.737		poet.	841.44
Chang Hua Chinese			Character	
fiction	813.31		analysis	
Chang Hui-yen Chinese			divination	157.14
prose	817.752		economics	354.114
Chang Tsai Chinese			psychology	153.8
philos.	111.53		ethics	180
			of consciousness	151.5

special subject see subject		
psychology	153.8	
qualifications		
economics	354.114	
library	022.5	
tests	153.88	
Characteristics		
mental childstudy	153.73	
psychology	153	
racial	153.41	
visions	156.333	
Characterology		
psychology	153.8	
Characters		
inheritance biology	563.394	
theatre	781.17	
Charales botany	573.23	
Charbon diseases	594.962	
Charcoal		
chemic technology	663.7	
drawing	733.1	
Charging systems lib. sci.	023.6	
Charhar, China		
geography	981.943	
Chariot ancient arms	379.91	
Charity		

bureaus	316.53
entertainments	316.5
ethics	180.77
institutions	316.3
schools	338.84
sociology	316
Charlatanry quackery	157.79
Charlemagne	
age of	
European history	930.53
French history	934.817
German history	937.81
Charms occultism	157.75
Charophyta botany	573.23
Chartier, Alain Fr. poet.	841.21
Charts	
education	337.12
geography	980.3
illustrative	
of spec. topics, see subj.	
maps	980.3
of earth astronomy	525.02
moon astronomy	523.302
statistics	341.5
sun astronomy	523.702
special topic see subject	
Chase hunting industries	619

Chastity ethics	187.1	disinfectants	593.236
Chateaubriand, F. A. R. V. de	843.65	dynamics	541.063
		elements	
Chatterton, Thomas Eng. poet.	851.63	chem. tech.	661.2
		chemistry	541.02
Chaucer, Geoffrey Eng. poet.	851.23	equations	541.09
		Chemical (cont.)	
Checks		equilibrum	541.065
banks	364.2	examination of blood	595.29
commercial law	398.5	industries	660
Cheeks anatomy	591.82	laboratories	542.1
Cheerfulness ethics	180.75	manipulation	542.2
Cheese dairy	615.74	medicines	596.2
Chekiang, China		mineralogy	558.4
geography	981.78	nomenclature	540.03
Chelonethi zoology	584.676	physics	541
Chelonia reptils	587.817	physiology	
Chemical		biology	561.49
action of radiant energy	535.57	botany	571.49
affinity	541.067	physiology	592.4
agents, affecting plants	571.46	zoology	581.49
analysis	543	properties of blood	597.192
apparatus	542.2	living matter	562.8
composition of animal body	581.491	reagents	544.11
		recreations	540.7
compounds	541.03	statics	541.064
crystallography	559.4	technology	660

Chemicals	661	qualitative	544
Chemistry		quantitative	545
agricultural	610.54	stereo	541.06
analytic	543	synthetic	545.9
and physics	541	theoretical	541
applied	548	thermo	541.6
or,	660	Ch'en Ch'i-nien Chinese	
bio	562.4	prose	817.723
economic		Ch'en Liang Chinese	
botany	571.84	prose	817.575
zoology	581.84	Chen-shih-tsung Ch.	
electro	541.7	Buddhism	239.51
experimental	542	Chen Te-hsiu Chinese	
industrial chem. tech.	660	prose	817.578
inorganic	546	Ch'en Tse-ang Chinese	
magnets	541.8	poet.	811.1415
medical	596.4	Chen-yen-tsung Ch.	
of cells	592.24	Buddhism	239.57
soil	611.31	Cheng Han Chinese	
organic	547	history	913.581
photo	541.5	Ch'eng Hao Chinese	
physical	541	philos.	111.541
physiological		Ch'eng I Chinese philos.	111.542
botany	571.49	Cheng Kuang-tsu	
physiology	592.4	Chinese drama	812.41
zoology	581.49	Chenier, A. M. de Fr.	
Chemistry (cont.)		poet.	841.56
practical	542		

Chenopodiinae botany	577.11
Cher, France geography	983.483
Cherry pomiculture	613.725
Chess amusements	794
Chest	
anatomy	591.84
diseases	597.24
surgery	598.184
Chestnut pomiculture	613.762
Chi Chun Chinese	
fiction	813.77
Chia I	
Chinese philos.	111.123
prose	817.23
Ch'iao Chi-fu Chinese	
drama	812.42
Chiba, Japan geography	982.1614
Chick pea seeds edible	613.3
Chicken	
farming	615.2
pox diseases	594.914
Chicory field crops	612.78
Ch'ien Ch'en-yi Chinese	
prose	817.711
Ch'ien Ta-hsin Chinese	
prose	817.736
Child	
and the state	313.364
culture	313.36
day	313.3606
insurance	368.36
labor	354.22
life	313.362
Child (cont.)	
psychology	153.7
or,	313.365
Childbirth obstetrics	598.8
Childhood	153.7
diseases	598.95
mental characteristics	153.73
Children	
abandoned child study	153.768
abnormal child study	153.76
education	338.961
aid	316.31
asylums	316.31
backward	153.766
care of	313.361
clothing for dom. econ.	693.6
costume of customs	319.41
cruelty to ethics	180.85
delineation of	153.75
diseases of	598.95
dreams of	156.3351
duties of	183.6

education of	338.92
games of	793.1
hospitals for	316.2
hygiene of	598.93
instructions for ethics	188.4
labor of	354.22
mental characteristics	153.73
protection	313.36
psychology	153.7
or,	313.365
sub-normal	153.766
super-normal	153.765
surgery of	598.97

Children's
duties to parents	313.363
ethics	183.6
library	025.72
point of view	153.74
rights	313.364
songs	771.2

Childstudy	153.7

Chile
geography	984.83
history	948.3

Chilognatha zoology	584.4
Chilopoda zoology	584.4

Ch'in dynasty Chinese
history	911.7

China
administration	373.1
agriculture	610.0991
antiquities	991
archaeology	991
architecture	710.1
archives	910.12
army	379.115
biography	971
botany	571.91
boundaries	371.0331
Buddhism	239.5
calligraphy	739.1
census	345.1
church	259.91
civilization	910.2
climate	529.891
colleges	338.7911
constitutions	391.1
defenses	379.11
description and travel	980.71
or,	981.4
diplomatic and consular service	386.91
directories	038.1
drawing	730.1
economic conditions	350.91
education	330.91

emigration	377.95	maps		980.31
encyclopedia	031		or,	981.2
ethnology	565.91	medicine		590.1
finance	369.1	militia		379.81
fine arts	701	music		770.1
flag	371.081	national bibliography		013.1
the Kuomintang	001.28	nationality		372.93
foreign relations	385.1	navy		379.116
—Japan	385.11	numismatics		991.24
genealogy	977.91	painting		730.1
geography	981	paleography		419
regional	981.5		or,	990.81
geology	550.1	philology		410
government	373.1	philosophers		111
central	373.11	police		315.391
local	373.18	population		349.1
government publications	373.105	race question		317.21
heraldry	969.1	revenue		369.14
history	910	schools, public		338.011
immigration	377.95	sculpture		720.1
language	410	seal		371.081
China(cont.)		antiquities		991.6
law	390.1	the Kuomintang		001.28
learned institutions and		statistics		345.1
societies	061	vital		349.17
libraries	020.91	tariff		369.16
literature	810	taxation		369.15
local governmental	373.18	theatre		780.1

travel	980.71
or,	981.4
treaties	387.91
universities	338.7911
year books	037.1
zoology	581.91
Ch'ing dynasty Chinese history	917
Ch'ing editions	009.117
Ching Jen-chien Chinese drama	812.46
Ching Nan Chinese history	914.97
Ching Shing-t'an Chinese fiction	813.72
Chinghai, China geography	981.68
Chirology palmistry	157.36
Chiromancy palmistry	157.36
Chiromyoidea zoology	589.1
Chiroptera zoology	588.9
Chivalry. age of Europ. history	930.55
Chlamydobacteriaceae botany	572.123
Chloranthaceae botany	576.28
Chlorideae forage crops	612.295
Chlorin inorganic chem.	546.131
Chlorination metallurgy	669.23
Chloromonadales botany	572.37
Chlorophyceae botany	573.1
Cholagogs drugs	597.463
Cholera diseases	594.933
Chondrostei zoology	587.474
Chondtopterygii zoology	587.4
Chordata zoology	586
Chorea abnormal psychology	155.251
diseases	597.8451
Choripetalae botany	577
Chosen geography	982.2
history	922
Chou dynasty Chinese history	911.6
Chou Kuan Chinese classics	094.1
Chou Li Chinese classics	094.1
Chou Pang-yen Chinese poet.	811.737
Chou Tun I Chinese philos.	111.51
Christ	

中國十進制分類法及索引 749

doctrinal theology	251.2
life of	251.29
Christening baptism	252.91
Christian	
apologetics	251.9
architecture	715.5
associations	256
brothers monks	254.5
calendars	528.65
church	255
doctrines	251
education	257
ethics	181
evidences	251.9
father	254.5
iconography sculpture	729.25
institutions	255
life	258
Christian (cont.)	
philosophy	121.6
pilgrimages	253.97
Sabbath	253.195
science	259.89
sects	259
sisters	254.5
socialism	318.15
societies	256
sunday	253.195
union	259
unions, young men's	256.2
Christianity	250
and science apologetics	251.95
evidences	251.9
history	259.09
Christmas celebration	253.12
Christology	251.2
Chromatophores histology	571.114
Chromium	
inorg. chem.	546.41
metallurgy	669.993
mineralogy	558.146
group inorganic chem.	546.4
Chromolithography	
engraving	744
Chromosphere sun	523.76
Chronicles Bible	252.26
history see special subj.	
Chronography	
astronomy	522.5
instruments	528.59
Chronograms horology	528.6
Chronology astronomy	528
Chroococcaceae botany	572.176
Chrysanthemum	
floriculture	613.82

Chrysippus Gk. philos.	121.525
Chrysolitic rocks lithology	557.48
Chrysomonadales botany	572.34
Chrysopidae zoology	585.51
Chu Hsi	
Chinese philos.	111.56
poet.	811.157
prose	817.571
Chu-she-tsung Ch. Buddhism	239.52
Chu Yi-tsun Chinese prose	817.726
Ch'u Yuan Chinese poet.	811.311
Chuan Tsu-wang Chinese prose	817.733
Chuang Tzu Chinese philos.	111.127
Chubu, Japan geography	982.163
Chugoku, Japan geography	982.165
Ch'un Ch'iu Chinese classics	096
Chung-Ch'ang Tung Ch. philos.	111.285
Chung Yung Chinese classics	098.2
Church	
and clergy law	255.4
education	255.07
state	
eccl. polity	255.03
ethics	185.2
persecutions	259.092
polit. science	371.062
architecture	715.5
attendance	253.2
calendar	253.1
Christian	255
decoration sacred orn.	253.3
discipline eccl. polity	255.4
fellowship	253.92
festivals worship	253.2
tinance	255.3
furniture	253.3
government	255
history	259
membership ordinances	253.92
of England	259.3
Rome	259.1
polity	255.2
property	255.3
rates cleric support	254.3
religious history	259

rites	253.2
sacraments	253.9
sects	259
services pub. worship	253.2
unity	259
vestments	253.35
work	255
Chyle zoology	581.417
Cibber, Colley Eng.	
drama	852.54
Cicero, M. T.	
Greek philos.	121.54
orations	832.841
Cichorium sugar plants	612.78
Ciliary body	
eye diseases	598.342
Ciliata zoology	581.41
Ciliophora zoology	582.4
Circidiphyllaceae botany	577.33
Circle squaring geometry	517.81
Circles plane geometry	517.41
Circular functions	516.35
Circulation	
and blood	597.1
hydraulic principles of	597.123
in animals zoology	581.41
library science	023.6
money	360
physiological	
anthropology	565.43
pressure in	597.124
rapidity of	597.125
Circulatory system	597.1
Circumnavigations	980.709
Circuses amusements	789.3
Cirripedia zoology	584.87
Cistaceae botany	578.58
Cistiflorae botany	578.5
Cities	
administration	373.082
ancient antiquities	990.181
Chinese	991.81
beautification	313.511
growth of statistics	345.14
Citizens	
duties of ethics	185.1
Citizenship	
law	397.11
political science	372
Citron pomiculture	613.735
Citrullus fruits edible	613.22
Citrus aurantium	
pomiculture	613.731
City	
governments adminis.	373.082

houses architecture	718.3
libraries	025.34
life	313.5
planning	313.51
property local gov.	373.095
roads	651.773
ruins antiquities	990.181
Civics	
ethics	185.1
pol. science	372
Civil	
authority local gov.	373.08
engineering	651
Civil (cont.)	
government pol. science	370
law	397
international	381.84
liberty	372.13
lists	373.014
pensions	373.018
procedure law	395.1
rights constitutional law	391
service administration	373
trials	395.03
war	
China history	910.282
U. S. history	941.86
Clairaudience occult	
sciences	157.63
Clairvoyance occult	
sciences	157.63
Clamatores birds	587.977
Clans	
genealogy	977.5
political science	371.12
Clarinet wind instru.	774.3
Class	
colors	333.45
days	333.45
feeling ethics	184.7
problem	317.3
representation pol. sci.	373.0343
room	332.92
system suffrage	372.523
Classes	
hours of educ.	334.4
of genius	153.98
joints	597.713
social	
pol. sci.	371.066
sociology	313.8
Classics	
Chinese, the	090
Greek literature	831
Latin	832
Classification	

library	023.3	dom. econ.	693.4
of books	023.3	roads and pavements	651.79
dreams	156.331	Cleanliness	
knowledge		of body hygiene	593.14
methodology	132	clothing hygiene	593.14
labor	354.2	school hygiene	332.33
languages	403	Cleanthes Greek philos.	121.523
soils	611.34	Clearing	
Classification (cont.)		banks banking	362.14
of statistical data	341.14	house banking	362.14
winds	529.31	Cleavage geology	553.4
workers economics	354.2	Clemens, S. L. Am. fiction	863.42
special subject see subject			
philosophy	132	Clement medieval philos.	121.624
Clastic rocks lithology	557.51	Clergy	
Clathrophychiaceae		canon law	255.4
botany	572.27	celibacy	
Clavariaceae botany	573.37	ethics	187.2
Clay		pastoral theo.	254.3
chemic technology	666.3	ethics	187.2
industries chem. tech.	666	pastoral work	254
instruments	770.12	Cleric support	254.3
petrography	557.523	Clethraceae botany	579.11
slate	557.527	Climate	
Clayey rocks lithology	557.52	animal effects ecology	581.7778
Cleaning		effects of	
chem. tech.	667.2	diseases	594.28
		mental charac.	153.23

therapeutics	595.84	adapted to season	693.7
forest effects	614.111	care of children	699
hygiene	593.111	distribution of	316.55
Climate (cont.)		domestic economy	693
influence on		hygiene	593.14
living matter	562.83	manufacture	684
man	565.771	psychological effects	153.28
meteorology	529.8	social problems	317.11
seasons	525.5	Clouds	
Climatology	529.8	meteorology	529.44
Climbers birds	587.975	worship	209.21
Clinics		Clover forage crops	612.382
obstetrics	598.835	Club houses architec.	718.4
surgery	598.18	Clubs	
therapeutics	595.1	boys sociology	313.671
in special subject see subject		girls sociology	313.673
		student sociology	333.06
Clippings	027.7	for special purposes see subject	
Clistentertata zoology	583.95	Clusters, star astronomy	523.81
Clocks		Cnidaria palaeozoology	569.73
chronology	528.59	Coach local transit	632.4
electric manuf.	671.1	Coadamites Christian	
manufacture	671.1	theology	251.33
sidereal	522.5	Coal	
Cloisonne ceramics	764	fuel chem. tech.	663.7
Clothes dom. economy	693	Coal (cont.)	
making trade	684	gas illuminating	665.77
Clothing			

heating prac. chem.	542.4
mineralogy	558.12
mining	658.8
oil	
chem. tech.	665.5
mineralogy	558.128
petrology	557.57
tar	
colors chem. tech.	667.2
products chem. tech.	668.6
washing ore dressing	658.9
Co-adaptation	563.74
Coalescence	
fetuses deformities	598.174
incomplete deformities	598.172
of parts deformities	598.173
Coast	
changes erosion	551.72
defense military eng.	659.33
frontier intern. law	381.33
pol. science	371.033
protective works hyd. eng.	654.2
survey geodesy	526
tides	525.6
Cobalt	
inorganic chem.	546.37
metallurgy	669.994
Cobdo, China geography	981.956
Coccaceae botany	572.125
Coccidiiae zoology	582.23
Coccygeal gland	597.418
Cochin China, India	
geography	982.42
history	924.2
Cochineal	
agriculture	615.6
dyeing	667.2
Cock fighting	
amusements	797.1
Cockatoo zoology	587.9757
Coco	
adulterations	593.22
agriculture	612.74
beverages	694.4
manufacture	664.7
palm pomiculture	613.771
Coconscious	
psychology of	156
Coconut pomiculture	613.771
Cocoon silkworms	616.7
Codes	
international law	381.029
law	390.029
telegraphic	637.03

Codification	
legislation	373.0324
of international law	381.029
law	390.029
Co-education	338.918
Coelenterata	
palaeontology	569.72
zoology	582.7
Coelomata zoology	582.8
Coelomic fluid	581.411
Coelomocoela zoology	582.8
Coffee	
adulterations	593.22
agriculture	612.73
beverages	694.4
hygiene	593.13
manufacture	664.7
stumulants	597.16
Coffins	
burial customs	319.24
pub. health	593.26
Cognition psychology	151.8
Cohesion physics	530.3
Coinage	361.6
Coins	361.6
Coir agriculture	612.591
Cold	
antipyretics	597.466
baths hygiene	593.14
drinks hygiene	593.13
physics	536
physiological effects	592.58
physiothorapy	595.83
psychological effects	153.23
storage	
business	664.8
domestic science	694.5
Colds catarrh	597.241
Coleoptera zoology	585.54
Coleridge, S. T. Eng.	
poet.	851.72
Collected	
biography	970
works, see subject	
Collecting	
biology	567.6
book lib. science	023.1
Collections	080
of photos	759
other topics, see subject	
Collectors manuals	567
College	
banners	334.83
cheers student customs	333.45
degrees	333.7

education, cost of	331.48	theoretical chemistry	541.49
electoral suffrage	372.56	Collotype engraving	746.1
entrance requirements	334.1	Colonial	
libraries	025.21	history, U. S.	941.82
life	333	system political science	377
societies students		Colonies	
customs	333.9	acquisition of territory	381.3191
song	334.85	political science	377
sports	333.35	Colonization political	
Y. M. C. A.	333.63	science	377.1
Colleges		law of intern. law	381.93
administration	331.3	Color	
agricultural	610.077	blindness	598.345
or,	338.661	Color (cont.)	
and universities	338.71	heredity	563.393
architecture	717.2	of the sky	529.62
for women	338.917	optics	535.39
hygiene	593.33	painting	732
Collembola zoology	585.1	photography	758.3
Collins, William Eng.		sense	151.11
poet.	851.57	suffrage	372.51
Collisions at sea intern.		tone acoustics	534.71
law	381.73	Colorado, U.S. geography	984.187
Colloids		Colorimetric analysis	
physiological chemistry		qualitative	544.6
biology	561.494	quantitative	545.6
botany	571.494	Coloring	
zoology	581.494		

dyeing	667.2
matters	
organic chemistry	547
physiological chemistry	
biology	561.497
physiology	591.497
zoology	581.497
Colors	
and advertising	629.2
artificial chem. tech.	667.2
college	333.45
manufacture of paints	667.7
military science	379.38
painting	732
practical theology	253.36
Colossians epistles	252.77
Colum, spinal osteology	597.7111
Columbus discov. of Amer.	941.813
Columbinae zoology	587.972
Columbium inorg. chem.	546.65
Columniferae botany	578.4
Combretaceae botany	578.8
Combustion	
chemistry	541.62
engines, internal	655.43
steam generation	655.221
Comets astronomy	523.6
Commelinaceae botany	575.75
Commemorations	
Great war 1914-19	930.78
military science	379.39
Commensalism	581.763
Commentaries, Bible	252.07
see also distinctive name	
Commerce	620
Commercial	
agencies credit	364
arbitration	624.7
arithmetics	626.1
association	621.3
bankruptcy	624.6
buildings architecture	717.5
fluctuations	624.5
forecasts	624.3
geography	620.098
or,	980.152
industry state control	621.1
law	398
international	381.85
morals	620.018
policy	351.3
or,	621
psychology	158.62
or,	620.015
Committees	

library	022.3	Comparative	
see also distinctive name		anatomy	
Commodities		animals	581.1
commerce	623	plants	571.1
finance	361.5	embryology zoology	581.6
political econ.	352.3	language	401
Commons, house of	373.033	medicine	599
Commonwealth		mythology	209.9
English history	935.86	physiology	581.4
Rome history	932.83	or,	592.9
Commonwealths, ideal	370.1	psychology	154
Communal marriage	319.22	wages pol. econ.	354.3
Communes		Compensation	
age of, in Italy	932.867	labor pol. science	354.3
Communication	630	legislatures	373.0342
Communion		Competition	
close baptists	259.6	prices	352.5
holy sacraments	253.93	wages	354.3
with virgin	224.8	Complex	
Communism	318.7	domain	519.67
Community		numbers	512.61
centers	338.88	ores	699
international	380	variables	513.13
of land pol. econ.	353.27	Complications in labor	598.843
wives	313.348	Compositae botany	579.97
rural	313.4	Composition	
urban	313.5	of the air meteorology	529.15
village	313.4	Compounds	

chemic	541.03
with metals	547.99
Compressed air	
engines	655.42
machinery	655.55
Compressibility of air	532.37
Compression of gases	533.36
Compromisory clause	
intern. law	383.2
Compulsive arbitration	
intern. law	382.3
Compulsory	
education	330.126
insurance	354.937
labor	354.259
vaccination pub health	593.2356
voting political science	372.523
Computation	
bridge engin'g	651.505
mathematics	510.7
Comte Fr philos	124.6
Conation psychology	151.3
Concept	
of state	371.02
psychology	151.811
Conception	
immaculate Christology	251.22
of Jehovah Judaism	261.1

physiology	598.81
psychology	151.811
Concerted vocal music	771.7
Concerto orchestral	
music	779.5
Concerts amusements	791
Conchology zoology	583.5
Concrete	
bridge engineering	651.5016
chemic technology	666.8
construction	651.116
engineering material	650.46
pavements engineering	651.75
roads engineering	651.765
see also special structures	
Concretion geologic	
agent	551.99
Concubinage	
abolition of	317.85
marriage system	313.3413
Condemned books	009.67
Condensation	
of gases	536.728
mixed fluids	536.74
Condillac Fr. philos.	124.26
Condimental	
herbs field crops	612.88
garden crops	613.4

Condiments		Cone solid geometry	517.55
adulterations	593.22	Confederation	
chem. technology	664.46	Canadian history	942.86
domestic science	694.3	form of state	371.65
physiological chem.	592.475	North German	937.88
Conditional execution		of the Rhine	937.86
crim. law	394.55	U. S. history	941.83
Conditions		Conference meetings,	
influencing animal		church	253.49
temperature	592.54	Conferences	
of chemic change	541.061	library	020.6
Condominium intern.law	381.191	see also special subject	
or,	388.73	Confervales botany	573.21
Conduct		Confession	
of life ethics	180	and absolution	
normal labor		sacraments	253.96
obstetrics	598.837	Augsburg creeds	251.85
Conduction		auricular sacraments	253.96
electricity	537.27	Confessional Roman	
heat	536.41	church	259.1
Conductivity		Confessions creeds	251.8
of air	529.13	Configuration, algebraic	512.2
electrolytes	541.73	Confinement	
rocks	551.18	obstetrics	598.83
Conductors electric		punishment	
engineering	657.65	crim. law	394.5
Condylarthra zoology	588.35	schools	332.13
		solitary	

crim. law	394.513
prison discipline	315.51
Confimation sacraments	253.92
Conflict of laws intern.	
law	381.8
Confucian Analects Ch.	
classics	098.3
school Chinese	
philos.	111.11
Confucianism as religion	210
Confucius Chinese	
philos.	111.111
Congenital	
defects of body	
hygiene	593.19
teratology	591.3
distortions surgery	598.178
variation biology	563.61
Congestion of the lungs	597.245
Conglomerate lithology	557.53
Congo, see Kongo	
Congregation eccle.	
polity	255.7
Congregational	
church	359.5
creed	251.86
Congregationalism sects	259.5

Congress	
of nations intern.	
politics	380.6
U. S. legisl bodies	373.633
Congresses, library	020.6
see also special subject	
Congreve, William Eng.	
drama	852.46
Conic sections	
analytic geometry	519.452
geometry	517.43
Conicoids analytic	
geometry	519.467
Conics analytic	
geometry	519.452
Coniferae botany	574.4
Conjugatae botany	572.7
Conjunctions solar	
system	523.23
Conjunctive eye	
diseases	598.341
Connecticut, U. S.	
geography	984.163
Connection of comets	523.56
Connective tissue	
anatomy	597.718
diseases	597.74

histology		
physiology	591.72	
zoology	581.25	
Conquest		
Norman Eng. history	935.82	
of Greece by Rome	931.84	
territorial		
international law	381.317	
political science	371.031	
Consanguinity		
law	397.5	
international	381.845	
physiology	592.607	
Conscience, freedom of	372.132	
Consciousness		
philosophy	135.5	
psychology	151.5	
comparative	581.705	
Conscription mil.		
science	379.34	
Consecration Christianity	253.99	
sermons	253.78	
Conservation of		
energy physics	531.693	
matter physics	530.4	
moisture agric.	611.6	
Consolation ethics	180.95	
Consonance acoustics	534.75	
Consonants language	401.42	
Chinese	414.2	
Conspiracies		
crim. law	394.23	
criminology	315.181	
Constant		
current analysis chem.	545.51	
voltage analysis chem.	545.53	
Constantine the Great	931.86	
Constantinople		
history	932.847	
Latin conquest	931.863	
Turkish conquest	931.865	
geography	982.69	
Constantinopolitan creed	251.81	
Constants		
earth	525.1	
moon	523.31	
sun	523.71	
Constipation pathology	597.344	
Constituency		
multimember	372.526	
single member	372.524	
Constituent elements		
of personality	153.82	
Constitution		
Chinese law	391.1	
day school observ.	334.37	

English law	391.5
Japanese law	391.2
of five powers	
Sunyatsenism	001.16
matter metaphysics	134.7
physics	530.1
1857 Mex. history	944.86
planetary system	523.26
U. S. history	941.84
law	391.6
Constitutional	
act, Canada under	942.83
conventions	391
diseases	594.9
government	371.0483
history	391
Constitutional (cont.)	
law	391
monarchy pol. science	371.045
Construction	
aircraft aviation	659.43
architectural	713
boilers	655.2251
building civil	
engineering	651.3
library buildings	024.3
light-houses hyd.	
engin'g.	654.4
railway railway engin'g.	651.81
shipbuilding	659.11
systems of civil	
engineering	651.11
see also special subject	
Constructive geometry	519.1
Consular	
jurisdiction intern. law	386.67
system intern. law	386.6
Consuls intern. law	386.6
Consumption	
and crises	352.72
cooperative	356.7
final pol. economy	357
lung diseases	597.245
Contagious diseases	
pathology	594.9
public health	
general	593.23
special	593.24
Contempt of courts	395.08
Continence ethics	187.3
Continental	
atlases	980.305
earthquakes	551.37
heraldry	960
protestant sects	251.85
volcanoes	551.47

Continents phys. geology	552.1
Continuation schools	338.8
Continuous	
spectra physics	535.443
variation biology	563.62
voyage intern. law	381.64
Contortae botany	579.4
Contract labor pol. econ.	354.25
Contracts	
law	397.4
or,	398.51
Contracts (cont.)	
international law	381.844
marriage	397.51
teachers	336.4
wage scales	354.33
Contravariants algebra	512.22
Contributions	
election suffrage	372.57
Control, social	311
Contusion surgery	596.163
Convention	
eccles. polity	255.7
French history	934.444
Conventional tariff	369.0613
Chinese	369.1613
other nations	
Conventions pol. parties	362.06
see also special subjects	
Convergence adaptation	563.75
Convergent progression	514.6
Conversation ethics	184.3
Conversion	
of Briggsian	510.27
debt	369.087
Chinese	369.187
other nations	
monastic life	258.9
Conveying machinery	655.85
Convict labor pol. econ.	354.251
Convicts criminal law	394.2
Convolvulaceae botany	579.51
Convulsions	
diseases	597.8447
puerperal	598.863
Cook	
books dom. science	695
Cookery dom. science	695
Cook's islands	985.974
Coolies	354.255
Cooper, J. F. Am. fiction	863.24
Cooperation pol. econ.	356.7
Cooperative	
banks	356.75
consumption	356.73

distribution	356.77
exchange	356.75
factories	356.71
production	356.71
stores	356.73
Coordinates	
analytical geometry	519.4
geographic	525.4
spheric astronomy	522.72
Copepoda zoology	584.867
Copernican theory	
astronomy	521
Coppee.E. E. J.	
Fr. drama	842.88
poet.	841.85
Copper	
coins money	361.63
drugs	596.153
engraving	742.1
inorganic chemistry	546.251
manufacture	671.3
metallurgy	669.93
money system	361.21
ores mineralogy	558.143
Coptic language	409.65
Copulation	
embryology	591.52
physiology	597.623

Copy	
books	010.1
early	009.3
plates Chinese	
calligraphy	739.13
rights publishing	010.43
Coquillart, Guillaume	
Fr. poet.	841.23
Coral reefs geology	551.98
Corallines algae	573.2
Corals zoology	582.75
Corchorus fibers	612.54
Cord	
machine physics	531.93
spinal anatomy	597.813
diseases	
functional	597.844
structural	5978.43
Cordage	
fibers agriculture	612.5
manufacture	675.7
Corea see Korea	
Coriariaceae botany	578.14
Corinthians	
1 epistles	252.72
2 epistles	252.73
Cormophyta botany	573.5
Corms edible	613.14

Corn			optics	535.11
cereals	612.15		Correction, houses of	315.7
duty on	369.052		Corrections	
Chinese	369.152		astronomy	522.8
other nations			of orbit astron.	521.35
Cornaceae botany	578.95		Corr-spondence	
Cornea eye-diseases	598.341		autobiography	970
Corneille, Pierre Fr.			business	626.2
drama	842.41		Chinese literature	818.1
Cornish language	409.378		library administration	022.9
Corns dermatology	598.544		logic	141.77
Corona of sun	523.76		natural theology	201.33
Coronae meteorology	529.65		schools	338.87
Corporations			Corrodentia zoology	585.35
business	620		Corruption	
charitable	316.3		electoral suffrage	372.57
law of	398.2		official ethics	185.3
mining	658		Corylus pomiculture	613.763
Corparative enterprise	356.23		Coryphodontidae zoology	588.37
Corpulence diseases	597.349		Cosmic dust	
Corpulsory service mil.			astronomy	523.17
sci.	379.34		calendar	528.61
Corpuscles			philosophy metaphysics	134
chemistry	541.01		time horology	528.56
red physiology	597.1211		Cosmo-communication	524
white physiology	597.1212		Cosmogony	
Corpuscular theory			metaphysics	134
			natural theology	201.4

Cosmography			textile arts	765
physiography	552		Costumes	319.4
Cosmology			Cottages	
metaphysics	134		laborers archit.	718.78
natural theology	201.4		mountain archit.	718.8
Brahamanism	241.3		seaside archit.	718.8
Buddhism	231.44		Cotton	
Cosmopolitanism			agriculture	612.51
political science	371.036		clothing hygiene	593.14
socialism	318.9		domestic science	693.1
Cosmos methaphysics	134		dying chem. tech.	667.5
Cost			manufacture	675.2
keeping accounts	627		mills archit	717.7
of college education	331.48		Cotylosauria zoology	587.811
living	317.15		Coughs and colds	597.241
pol. economy	352		Council	
Costa Rica			ecclesiastic polity	255.7
geography	984.66		history, Christian	259
history	946.6		Council(cont.)	
Costume			league of nations	383.2
academic	334.87		of conciliation	382.5
court	319.32		Counterpoint music	770.026
ecclesiastic	253.35		Counters library science	023.6
fashion magazine	693.05		Country	
hygiene	593.14		and city	313.48
military	319.44		homes archit.	718.7
or,	379.373		laboring class in	
stage	781.3		special	354.29

life	313.4
schools	338.41
seats archit.	718.7

County
government admin.	373.084
libraries	025.36
Y. M. C. A.	256.318

Coups d'etat pol. science	317.0493
Courage ethics	180.74

Courier de Mere, P. L.
Fr. essays	847.63

Courses
curriculum	335
of reading lib. sci.	027.5

Court
balls	792.8
costumes	319.43
etiquette	319.12
supreme law	396

Courtesy social ethics	184.2
etiquette	319.32

Courts
administration	373.04
authority of	390
contempt of	395.08
ecclesiastical	255.4
military	379.31
of arbitration	382.43
international justice	382.41
Courtship marriage	313.343
Cousin Fr. philos.	124.54
Covariants algebra	512.22

Covenants religious
creeds	251.87
Cowardice ethics	180.66

Cowley, Abraham Eng.
poet.	851.46

Cowper, William Eng.
poet.	851.65
Cowpox diseases	594.913

Cows
diseases of	599.42
domestic animals	615.12
zoology	588.355

Crabs
fishery	617.7
zoology	584.827
Cramming examinations	334.5
Cramp diseases	597.846
Cranberry pomiculture	613.78

Cranes and derricks
engin'g	655.82
Cranial bones osteology	597.7115
Craniata zoology	587

Craniology

anthropography	565.24
Craniometry	565.33
Cranium	
anatomy	597.7115
anthropography	565.24
Crank motion mechanics	531.245
Crassulaceae botany	577.72
Crates Greek philos.	121.37
Crayon drawing	733.3
Cream dairy	615.72
Creation	
biogenesis	562.74
metaphysics	134
natural theology	201.4
of debt	369.086
man Christian theol.	251.31
Creative power	
psychology	151.7
Creator Christian theol.	251.11
Crebillon, P. J. de Fr.	
drama	842.52
Credentials	
academic	334.7
diplomacy	386.22
legislative bodies	373.037
Credit and credit system	364
Creeds	
Christianity	251.8
see also other religions	
Cremation	
of the dead customs	319.24
public	
health	593.26
Creodonta zoology	588.55
Crests heraldry	960.1
Cretaceous period	
geology	554.65
Cretinism diseases	594.996
Creuse, France	
geography	983.488
Cribrariaceae botany	572.27
Cries, battle war customs	319.15
Crime	
and illiteracy edu.	330.127
Crime(cont.)	
law	394
suffrage disqualification	372.51
Crimes and punishments	394.5
Criminal	
anthropology	315.11
anthropometry	315.14
classes	315.19
courts administration	373.04
education	338.97

ethnography	315.17
etiology	315.16
law	394
international	381.88
procedure	395.2
psychology	315.5
trials criminal law	395.23
Criminals	
dreams of	156.3359
education of	338.97
juvenil	
childstudy	153.763
law	394.6
Criminology	315.1
Crinoidea zoology	582.95
Crippled education	338.965
Crises	
bank	362.8
commercial	624.6
economical	352.7
Critical philosophy	105.5
Criticism	
philosophy	105.5
see also special subjects	
Crocodilia zoology	587.836
Crop	
farming	612
farms	611.21
Crops	
agricluture	612
tools for cleaning	610.65
Cross. M. A. L. Eng.	
fiction	853.86
Cross	
Christology	251.2954
sacred furniture	253.31
Crossbreeding	
animal culture	615.03
eugenics	563.52
Crossing plant breeding	611.53
Crossings railway	
engin'g	651.816
Crossopterygia zoology	587.471
Crowne, John Eng.	
drama	852.43
Cruciferae botany	577.57
Crucifixes sacred	
furniture	253.31
Crucifixion Christology	251.2954
Cruelty ethics	180.85
Cruisers naval science	379.655
Crusades European	
history	930.57
Crust of the earth	
geology	551.15

Crustacea zoology	584.8
Cryllidae zoology	585.31
Cryptocephala zoology	583.615
Cryptogama botany	573
palaeobotany	569.2
Cryptogams, vascular botany	573.8
Cryptomonadales botany	572.35
Crypton inorganic chem.	546.185
Cryptonemiaceae botany	573.265
Crystal magnetism	538.59
Crystalline	
aggregations	559.4
limestone	557.46
state chemistry	541.07
Crystallization	
practical chemistry	542.65
Crystallizers prac. chem.	542.65
Crystallorgraphy	559
Crystalloids chemistry	541.4
Crystals	559
Ctenodipterini zoology	587.45
Ctenophora zoology	582.77
Cuba	
geography	984.71
history	947.1
Cubic	
curves analytic geom.	519.457
surfaces analytic geom.	519.465
Cuckoos zoology	587.9755
Cuculidae zoology	587.9755
Cucumbers fruits edible	613.24
Cucumis fruits edible	613.21
Cucurbitaceae botany	579.91
Cult	
of animals	209.28
celestial bodies	209.21
cereal	209.26
Cult(cont.)	
of earth	209.23
moon	209.21
mountains	209.22
plants	209.27
stars	209.21
sun	209.21
trees	209.27
water	209.24
Cultivation	
land geog. distribution	611.09
of personality psychology	153.87
rent for	353.64
Cultivators farm	
machinery	610.61
Cultural geography	980.13
Culture	

and religion	200.19	Chinese calligraphy	739.175
see also special religions		Cursores birds	587.93
history of	902	Curvature geology	553.2
primitive	565.79	Curve	
self education	338.81	harmonic acoustics	534.531
vocal music	770.075	periodic acoustics	534.531
Cumacea zoology	584.821	Curves	
Cumulative		algebraic gauche	519.463
vote suffrage	372.528	analytical geometry	519.451
Cunodon forage crops	612.271	cubic	519.457
Cunya-vada Indian		geometry	517.4
Buddhism	239.13	of 2nd order	519.452
Cupping therapeutics	595.811	3rd order	519.457
Curative		4th order	519.458
electricity therap.	595.87	plane	519.451
gymnastics therap.	595.97	quartic	519.458
Cures, miraculous		theory of	519.45
miracles	251.16	transcendental	519.471
therapeutics	595.92	Curvilinear	
Curiosa books	009.65	geometry	517.4
Currency banking	361.7	motion physics	531.223
Currents		Custom duties	369.06
atmospheric meteorology	529.3	Customary law	390.021
electric physics	537.2	Customs	
oceanic physiography	552.2	and duties tariff	369.06
of water animal ecology	581.7776	manners	319
Curriculum	335	usages intern. law	381.023
Cursive writing		of kinship	319.26

primitive man	565.79
war	319.15
student life	333
taxation	369.06
Cutaneous	
diseases pathology	598.54
evaporation animal heat	592.52
glands physiology	598.522
radiation animal heat	592.52
respiration physiology	598.523
secretion physiology	598.522
sensibility physiology	598.524
Cyanids chem. tech.	669.25
Cyanophyceae botany	572.17
Cycadaceae botany	574.2
Cycadales botany	574.2
Cyclanthaceae botany	575.48
Cyclic transformation, theory of	536.63
Cycles engineering	659.77
Cyclocarpineae botany	573.41
Cyclones meteorology	529.37
Cyclopedias, general	030
special, see subject	
Cyclops zoology	584.86
Cycloshapha zoology	585.57
Cyclosporeae botany	573.25
Cyclostomata zoology	587.1
Cyclotomy geometry	517.81
Cydippidea zoology	582.772
Cydonia pomiculture	613.715
Cylinders solid geometry	517.55
Cymbals music instrument	777.2
Cymbidium floriculture	613.82
Cynewulf Eng. poet.	851.13
Cynic school Greek philos.	121.24
Cynocrambaceae botany	577.19
Cynopithecidae zoology	589.57
Cyperaceae botany	575.43
Cyrenaic school Greek philos.	121.25
Cyrillaceae botany	578.16
Cystoflagellata zoology	582.37
Cystoidea zoology	582.98
Cysts diseases	594.993
Cytinaceae botany	577.63
Cytisin organ. chem.	547.2
Cytology biology	561.5
Czechoslovakia	
geography	983.796
history	937.96

Dacites lithology	557.26	Daniel Bible	252.45
Dacryomcetaceae botany	573.37	Daniel, Samuel Eng.	
Dactylis forage crops	612.22	poet.	851.33
Daguerrotypes		Danish	
photography	756.1	England Eng. history	935.81
Dairy		language	409.3823
cattle dairying	615.7	literature	879.23
products		Daplane odora	
chemical analysis	543.13	floriculture	613.85
dairy	615.7	Dark	
Dalton plan, the		ages Europ. history	930.5
education	337.33	rooms photography	755.7
Daltonism eye diseases	598.345	Darwinism biology	546.2
Dams river engineering	654.68	Dante Alighieri Italian	
Dana Buddhist paranuta	231.71	poet.	833.115
Dana, R. H. Am. poet.	861.27	Dantzig, German	
Dances		geography	983.76
amusements	792	Darfur, Egypt geography	985.176
customs	319.75	Date palm pomiculture	613.773
Dancing		Daucus carota roots	
amusements	792	crops	612.45
customs	319.75	Daudet, Alphonse Fr.	
ethics	189.73	fiction	843.85
Dangers		Dauphiny, France	
mining engineering	658.45	geography	983.498
to life protection against	593.4	Day	
workmen political		and night	525.5
econ.	354.52	dreams	156.337

of judgement Christian theol.	251.74	of fetus pregnancy	598.824
schools	334.35	penalty criminal law	394.511
Day (cont.)		rates public health	593.21
sidereal and solar	528.1	signs of real	592.11
Deacon	255.55	Deaths	
Dead		public health	593.21
disposal of the pub. health	593.26	De Broglie waves physics	530.75
list of Great war	930.787	Debt, public	369.08
ministry of sacraments	253.98	Chinese	369.18
treatment of the	319.24	other nations	
Dead letters	636.59	Decalcomania arts	769.3
Deaf and dumb		Decalogue Bible	252.216
childstudy	153.761	Decantation prac. chem.	542.66
education of	338.965	Decapitation	
institutions	316.35	punishments	394.511
Deafness diseases	598.44	Decapoda zoology	584.827
Death		Decay of rocks lithology	557.7
after delivery obstetrics	598.868	Decidua pregnancy	598.8271
and resurrection nat. theol.	201.721	Deciduous	
Christian doctrine	251.71	hedges floriculture	613.86
biology	562.9	shrubs floriculture	613.86
from		trees floriculture	613.86
cold physiology	592.582	Decimal	
heat physiology	592.581	system	
nature of	592.1	classification	023.3
		mathematics	510.71

Decipium inorganic
  chem. 545.292
Decision
  of character ethics 180
Decisions
  international law 381.027
  mathematics 512.94
Declaration
  diplomatic negotiation 386.4
  of independence U. S. 941.83
  war intern. law 381.53
Declination, variations of 521.27
Decoration
  and ornament 762
  architectural 712
  design 730
  domestic economy 692
  house 763
  in relief architecture 712.2
  interior 763
  sculptured architecture 712.2
Decorations
  heraldry 960
  presentations
    government 373.018
    Great war 930.784
Decorative
  art 730
  needlework 685
  plaster 712.3
Decorum ethics 184.2
Dedication
  church ordin. 253.99
  sermons 253.78
Deduction psychology 151.86
Deductive logic 142
Deep sea fisheries 617.57
De facto governments 371.0495
Defectives
  aid and homes for 316.35
  education 338.96
  library 025.78
  psychology 155.4
    childstudy 153.76
Defects of body
  congenital
    hygiene 593.19
    surgery 597.17
    teratology 591.3
Defense
  means of 581.75
  of religion apologetics 201.9
    see also special religion
Defenses fortifications 659.31

Defensive operations	659.33
De Foe, Daniel Eng	
fiction	853.51
Deformities	
anatomy	591.3
anthropography	565.28
surgery	597.17
Degeneration	
biology	561.78
botany	571.777
zoology	581.696
Degrees, academic	334.7
Deism natural theology	201.1
Delaware, U. S.	
geography	984.165
Delineation of children	153.75
Delinquents	
education	338.97
institutions	315.7
juvenile	394.2
or,	313.364
psychology	155.4
social pathology	315.19
Delobranchia zoology	584.66
Deluge	
Genesis	252.211
geologic agents	551.93
Delusions	157.7
Demand and supply	
wages	354.311
Dematerialization	157.955
Dementia abnormal	
psychology	155.2
Demi-Socratic schools	
Gk. philos.	121.23
Democracy	
form of government	371.046
state	371.4
social	318.55
Democratic party U. S.	375.62
Democritus Greek	
philos.	121.173
Demography statistics	349
Demonetization	361.1
Demoniac possession	251.63
Demonology	
Christian dogmatics	251.63
witchcraft	157.7
Demons	251.63
Demonspongiae zoology	582.57
Demulcents therapeutics	597.367
Demosthenes Greek	
oratory	831.846
Dendrology	614.31
Dengue diseases	594.921

Denmark			Deodorizers contag.	
geography	983.7988		diseases	593.236
history	937.988		Deontology ethics	180
Dennis, John Eng.			Department	
drama	852.51		stores business	622.7
Denominations, Christian	259		Departments	
Denonian period geology	554.55		government	373.0506
Density			Chinese	373.1506
gases	533.31		U. S.	373.6506
gravity	531.64		Dependents	
liquids	532.31		childstudy	153.768
of blood	597.122		education	338.96
earth	551.16		institutions	316.31
Dental			Deposit bank and	
anatomy	598.21		banking	362.5
hygiene	598.23		Deposition geology	551.7
metallurgy	598.286		Depositions evidence	395.05
pathology	598.24		Depravity	
periosteum, diseases of	598.243		natural theology	201.63
physiology	598.22		Depravity (cont.)	
pulp, diseases of	598.241		pessimism	108.3
Denticeti zoology	588.477		total Christian theology	251.36
Dentine diseases			Depressants	
dentistry	598.242		circulatory drugs	597.16
Dentistry	598.2		nervous drugs	597.868
Dentists, registration of	593.72		Depressions	
Denudation geology	551.7		trade	
Denumerative geometry	519.49			

commerce	624.6
production	352.7
Depth psychology	156
De Quincey, Thomas	
Eng. essays.	857.81
Derangement, mental	155
Derby, England	
geography	983.565
Dereliction intern.	
politics	381.323
Dermaptera zoology	585.31
Dermatology	598.5
animals	581.17
operative	598.57
Dermoptera zoology	588.81
Descartes Fr. philos.	124.1
Descendenzlehre	
evolution	563.2
Descent	
genealogy	977
into hell Christology	251.295
of man evolution	563.2
rules of law	397.5
Description	980.7
Descriptive	
anatomy	
botany	571.27

human	591
sericulture	616.21
zoology	581.1
astronomy	523
geometry	519.33
microscopy	566.2
mineralogy	558.1
sociology	314
Desertion marriage	313.346
Deserts	
physiography	552.7
reclamation	611.69
Design	
architectural	711
arts of	730
metaphysics	134.2
of library buildings	024.3
shipbuilding	659.11
Designing decoration	762
Designs technology	654.3
Desmids botany	572.7
Despotism form of state	371.0482
Despots Italian history	932.871
Destiny of mind	135.8
soul	135.8
Destroyers naval science	379.656
Destruction	
elemental agriculture	611.91

Destructive manias
 abnormal psychology   155.454
Determination
 of acids   544.15
  bases   544.12
  chemic elements   544.03
  earth's figure   526.1
  orbits astron.   521.3
  sex   561.661
  solubility chem.   542.62
Determinative
 mineralogy   558.2
Determinism
 cosmology   134.13
 natural theology   201.5
Deuterocanonical Books   252.9
 see also special subject
Deuteronomy Bible   252.215
Devas Buddhist gati   231.89
Devastation intern. law   381.552
Development
 incomplete defornities   598.171
 of embryo, abnormal
  anatomy   591.3
  surgery   598.17
  anatomy   591.5
  physiology   592.6
 personality psychology   153.81

 photographing   755.3
 physiology   592.6
 post-embryonic   561.7
 theory biology   561.7
Deviation biology   563.6
Devil
 personal theology   251.63
 worship   209.7
Devils Christian
 dogmatics   251.63
Devon, England
 geography   983.563
Devonian period geology   554.55
Devotional
 exercises pub. worship   253.21
 sermons   253.73
 theology   253
Dew meteorology   529.41
Dewey Am. phhilos.   126.7
Dextrine chem.
 technology   664.3
Dextrose chem.
 technology   664.3
Dharana Hinduism   244.6
Dharmakaya Buddhism   231.26
Dharma-lakshana
 Chinese Buddhism   239.52

Japan Buddhism	239.62	Diaphoretics	
Dhyana Chinese		therapeutics	597.465
Buddhism	239.56	Diaphragm anatomy	597.217
Indian Buddhism	239.16	Diapsida zoology	587.83
Japanese Buddhism	239.66	Diaptosauria zoology	587.831
Dhyana		Diarrhea	
Paranuta Buddhism	231.75	epidemic diseases	594.937
Diabase lithology	557.34	pathology	597.344
Diabetes diseases	597.643	public health	593.237
Diagnosis		Diathermacy heat	536.49
of pregnancy	598.811	Diatomeae botany	572.6
therapeutics	595.2	Diatoms botany	572.6
Dialectics logic	140	Dibranchia zoology	583.573
Dialectology	401.5	Dice games	795
Chinese language	415	Dickens, Charles Eng.	
see also other languages		fiction	853.83
Dials chronology	528.59	Dicotyledonae	
Dialysis		botany	576
practical chemistry	542.64	palaeontology	569.55
qualitive chemistry	544.5	Dictatorship pol. science	371.0482
Dializers prac. chem.	542.64	Dictionaries	401.3
Diamagnetism		Chinese language	413
magnetism	538.5	see also other languages special, see subject	
Diameter of earth	525.1		
Diamonds mineralogy	558.183	Dictionary catalogs	012
Diapensiaceae botany	579.17	Dictyochaceae botany	572.51

Dictyosleliaceae botany	572.215	Diffuse affections of skin	598.541
Dictyotales botany	573.25	Diffusion	
Didactic poetry	801.5	of gases physics	533.15
Didactics education	337	liquids physics	532.14
Didelphia zoology	588.21	physiology of absorption	597.329
Diderot Fr. philos.	124.27	practical chemistry	542.63
Didornithiformes zoology	587.945	theoretical chemistry	541.43
Didymium inorganic chem.	546.266	Diffusivity thermics	536.412
Diencephal anatomy	597.8114	Digestion	
Diencephalon anatomy	597.8114	aid to therapeutics	597.365
Dietaries hygiene	593.121	animals	581.13
Dietetic diseases pathology	597.349	Digestion(cont.)	
		history of	597.309
Differences, finite calculus	515.5	human physiology	597.3
		practical chemistry	542.61
Differential		theories of	597.301
calculus	515.2	Digestive	
equations calculus	515.71	secretion in animals	581.447
psychology	153	system	
Differentiation		anatomy of	597.31
biology	563.6	animals	581.13
of languages	403	diseases of	597.34
layers and organs	581.692	drugs acting on	597.36
Diffraction		human physiology	597.3
optics	535.35	hygiene of	597.33
thermics	536.46	physiology of	597.32
		surgery of	597.37

therapeutics of	597.35
Digests	
of cases	
international law	381.08
law	390.08
Digging tools	610.61
Digitalis	
diuretics	597.66
stimulants	597.16
Digits, extra deformities	598.175
Dignity of	
labor polit. econ.	354.018
Dikes	
engineering	654.62
reclamation	611.69
Dilatation operative	
obstet.	598.874
Dilleniaceae botany	578.51
Dimension, fourth	
modern geo.	519.63
Dimensions of	
earth	525.1
moon	523.31
sun	523.71
Dining domestic science	694.7
Dinners	
family domestic sci.	697.1
public domestic sci.	697.45
Dinoflagellata zoology	582.35
Dinosauria zoology	587.837
Dinotheriidae zoology	588.381
Diocese ecclesiastic	
polity	255.6
Diodorus Greek philos.	121.27
Diogenes Greek philos.	121.243
Dioi language	409.127
Dioptrics optics	535.33
Diorite lithology	557.36
Dioscoraceae botany	575.87
Diospyrineae botany	579.3
Dip of rocks geology	553.5
Diphtheria diseases	594.931
Diplomacy intern.	
politics	386
Diplomas school records	334.7
Diplomatic	
agents	
diplomacy	386.33
extraterritoriality	386.5
ceremonies customs	319.13
corps diplomacy	386.34
history	
genera	902.7
Chinese	910.27

Great war	930.73
see also other nations	
negotiation diplomacy	386.4
Diplopoda zoology	584.4
Dipneusti zoology	587.45
Dipnoi zoology	587.45
Dipodidate zoology	588.614
Dippers	
baptist sect	259.6
birds	587.976
Diprotodontidae zoology	588.24
Dipsacaceae botany	579.87
Dipsomania abnor.	
psychology	155.456
Diptera insects	585.57
Dipterocarpaceae botany	578.54
Direct	
current	
machine	657.44
systems	657.631
legislation polit. science	373.0326
negotiation	
diplomacy	386.41
intern. arbitration	382.22
probabilities	
mathematics	512.91
seeding agriculture	614.483
taxation	

public finance	369.05
Chinese	369.15
see also other nations	
Directive force	
biophysics	562.36
Directories	038
special, see subject	
Directories library	
adminis.	022.5
Directory French history	934.846
Dirghagamas Sutra	232.21
Disabilities, inherited	
mental	593.192
Disarmament arbitration	388.82
Disbandment military	
science	379.349
Discharge	
from military service	379.33
of pupils school gov't	332.13
teachers	336.55
water sanitary engin'g	653.1
Disciples of Christ sect.	259.66
Discipline	
civil service	373.018
ecclesiastic polity	255.4
prison	315.5
school	332.4

Discoideae botany	572.6
Discolichenes botany	573.41
Discomycetes botany	573.31
Discophora zoology	583.63
Discount banking	362.6
Discourses Christian	
theology	253.7
see subject	
Discoveries	
geography	980.705
science, history	500.9
Discovery	
of America U. S. history	941.81
Canada history	942.811
territorial	
international law	381.314
political science	371.031
Discriminants algebra	512.36
Discussion, freedom of	372.133
Diseases	
animals	
veterinary med.	599.4
zoology	581.5
bacterial agriculture	611.94
causation of	594.2
classification of	594.02
communication	
to man	594.96
animal hygiene	593.28
pathology	594.9
public health	593.23
Diseases (cont.)	
contagious	
of domestic animals	593.28
special public health	593.24
dietetic	597.349
hereditary pathology	594.21
incurable therapeutics	595.4
inherited hygiene	593.193
mental	
abnormal psychology	155
medicine	597.84
of children pediatrics	598.95
ear otology	598.44
eye ophthalmology	598.34
new-born infants	
pediatrics	598.94
plants	
agriculture	611.9
botany	571.5
gregnancy	598.82
teeth dentistry	598.24
women	598.74
pathology	594
periodical pathology	594.23
pseudo therapeutics	595.5

sequels of pathology	594.6
unknown therapeutics	595.5
Diseases veneral	598.6
Dishonest ethics	180.88
Disinfectants	
contagious diseases	593.236
Disinfection	
bacteriology	566.968
contagious diseases	593.236
of sewage	653.35
the dead pub. health	593.26
Disintergration	
geologic agents	551.9
German history	937.84
Dislocations	
geology	553.7
of teeth dentistry	598.276
surgery	598.166
Disorders	
of metabolism pathology	594.87
sebaceous glands	
dermatology	598.543
sweat glands	598.546
vision ophthalmology	598.345
Dispensatories pharmacy	596.7
Dispersion optics	535.38
Displacement	
of parts deformities	598.177
water shipbuilding	659.11
Display ethics	184.5
Disposal of	
sewage san. engin'g	653.35
the dead pub. health	593.26
wastes san. engin'g	653.36
Disproportionate growth	598.176
Disputes between capital	
and labor	354.8
Dissection	
anatomy	
animal	581.1
human	591.1
experimental physiology	592.81
law	593.71
Dissipation of energy	536.67
Dissociation	
chemical affinity	541.067
theory of solution chem.	541.43
thermics	536.725
thermochemistry	541.63
Dissolution of	
state intern. politics	381.18
Distance of earth from	
sun	525.1
moon	523.31
sun	523.71
Distillation	

coal-tar chem. tech.	668.6
practical chemistry	542.4
thermics	536.727
wood chem. tech.	668.5
Distilling	
air pollution	593.27
beverages	664.55
Distomatinales botany	572.32
Distortions, congenital	
surgery	598.178
Distribution	
of animals	581.9
earthquakes	
seismology	551.9
electric power	657.6
fertilizers agric.	611.7
food philanthropy	316.55
plants	571.9
population	
demography	349.03
pressure	529.2
Distribution (cont.)	
of seeds reproduction	571.67
time chronology	528.52
volcanoes	551.49
political economy	352
tide astronomy	525.63
wealth polit. economy	359
Distributive	
cooperation	356.77
laws solar system	523.21
Diurnal	
changes	529.2
variations	529.18
Divers birds	587.973
Divination occult	
sciences	157.1
Divine	
attributes	251.14
humanity	251.28
law	251.16
manifestations	251.18
providence	251.15
natural	201.5
theory of	
kings	371.04
the origin of state	371.011
service pub. worship	253.21
union	215.17
Diving	
nautics	659.198
submarine	659.39
Divinity of Christ	251.28
Division	
arithmetic	511.24
of empire, Rome hist.	932.845

labor polit. economy	356.9	Documents, public	373.005
Divorce		special, see subject	
ethics	183.1	Dog	
law	397.51	diseases of	599.47
sociology	313.347	domestic animals	615.15
Djaramavana Buddhism	231.51	fighting amusements	797.1
Djati Buddhism	231.52	zoology	588.516
Docks harbor		Dogma, Christian	251
engineering	654.31	see also other religions	
Dockyards harbor		Dogmatic	
engin'g	654.31	Brahmanism	241.7
Doctrinal		Christianity	251
sermons, Christian	253.72	Judaism	261
see also other		Taoism	221
religions		Zoroastrianism	281
theology, Christian	251	other religions	
see also other		Dogmatics, Christian	251
religions		see also other religions	
Doctrine of		Dogmatism philosophy	105.1
germinal continuity	563.33	Dolerite lithology	557.35
Messiah		Dolichos forage crops	612.31
Christianity	251.21	Dolomite lithology	557.564
Judaism	261.2	Domestic	
soul	201.77	animals infect. diseases	615.1
see also special		architecture	718
religions		duties ethics	183
Doctrine of the Mean		economy	690
Chinese classics	098.2	education	338.913

electric installation	657.93
investments	367.11
mammals	588.33
medicine	
domes. science	699
public health	593.6
relations	
law	397.5
political science	371.06
science	690
trade	351.39
Domicile	
legal capacity	
law	397.12
international law	381.818
statistics	349.077
suffrage qualifications	372.51
Dominicans mon. orders	259.091
Dominion of Canada	
history	942.86
Dominoes games	795
Dongola, Egypt	
geography	985.173
Donkeys dom. animals	615.18
Doors arch. construction	713.82
Dordogne, France	
geography	983.492
Dorset, England	
geography	983.563
Dosology materia med.	596.72
Double	
acting engines	655.253
curvature anal. geometry	519.467
reed wind instrum.	774.4
refraction optics	535.36
thermics	536.47
standard coins money	361.22
stars astronomy	523.81
tariff system	369.0615
Chinese	369.1615
other nations	
Doubs, France geography	983.477
Doubt metaphysics	131.9
Douglas, Gavin Eng.	
poet.	851.24
Dower law	397.51
Draft horse	615.11
Drafts games	794
Dragon flies insects	585.35
Drainage	
agriculture	611.69
engineering	654.87
house	653.5
of cities	653.3
mines	658.43
public health	593.27

road engineering 651.73
Drains
  reclamation agriculture 611.69
                engineering 654.87
Drake, Francis
  discovery of America 941.8155
Drama 802
  American literature 862
Drama (cont.)
  Chinese literature 812
  English literature 852
  French literature 842
  German literature 872
  Greek literature 831.2
  Italian literature 833.2
  Japanese literature 822
  Latin literature 832.2
  religious 802.92
    Christian 250.82
    see also other
      religions
  Russian literature 882
  Spanish literature 835.2
  see also other
    literatures
Dramatic
  amusements 780
  art theatre 780
  composition 781.1
  music 773
  theatre 781.7
  poetry literature 801.3
  societies student life 333.33
Draughts games 794
Drawbridges engin'g. 651.57
Drawing 730
  elementary educ. 338.133
  see also special
    applications
Drawings
  architectural 711.2
  crystals 559.13
  engineering 650.2
    mechanical 655.13
    structural 651.122
Drayton, Michael Eng. 851.34
  poet.
Dreams psychoanalysis 156.33
Dredging hydraulic 654.63
  engin'g.
Dress
  costume 319.4
  diplomatic 386.28
  ecclesiastic
    Buddhism 233.3
    Christianity 253.35

see also other religions	
ethics	184.5
fashion	319.401
Dresses domestic science	693
Dressing	
hair	319.47
Dressing (cont.)	
of stone	651.16
ore mining engin'g.	658.9
Dressmaking	684
Drift, glacial geology	551.76
Drifting	
discoveries	980.705
mining engineering	658.35
Drilling	
mining engineering	658.32
Drink chem. analysis	543.1
Drinks see Beverages	
Drives esthetics of cities	719.3
Driving amusements	798
Dromaeognathi zoology	587.93
Drome, France	
geography	983.498
Droop system suffrage	372.527
Droseraceae botany	577.65
Drought	
agriculture	611.912
meteorology	529.45
philanthropy	316.43
Drowning protection of life	593.41
Drug	
addiction	155.457
addicts	156.3357
habits, prohibition of	317.81
Drugs	596.1
adulteration of	593.22
analytic chemistry	543.4
economic botany	571.8
Drum musical instrum.	777.1
Drunkenness crim. law	394.25
Drupaceous pomiculture	613.72
Dry	
cleaning dom. science	693.4
docks engineering	654.37
films photography	755.2
method	
qualitative analysis	544.2
quantitative analysis	545.2
plates photography	755.2
point engraving	742.8
sewerage systems	653.32
Dryden, John Eng.	

drama	852.46
poet.	851.48
Drying	
food preservation	694.5
practical chemistry	542.69
Dryplate processes	
photography	755.2
Dualism	
natural theology	201.6
ontology	133
philosophy	102.3
psychology	150.161
Du Bellay, Jaochim Fr.	
poet.	841.32
Ducis, J. F. Fr. drama	842.61
Ducks	
poultry	615.2
zoology	587.973
Ducts	
bile	597.315
ejaculatory	597.615
kidney	
anatomy	597.611
diseases	597.641
Dudevant. AL. AD. Fr.	
fiction	843.82
Duel tariff system	369.0615
Chinese	369.1615
other nations	
Dueling	
criminal law	394.25
customs	319.75
fighting sports	797.2
student life	333.37
Duets vocal music	771.75
Dufresny, C. R. Fr.	
drama	842.47
Dugongidae zoology	588.41
Dukha Buddhism	231.31
Dumas, A. fils Fr. drama	842.84
A. D. pere Fr.	
drama	842.75
fiction	843.75
Dumb	
asylums	316.35
education	338.965
Duns Scotus medieval	
philos.	121.637
Duodecimals	
mathematics	510.72
Duplication of the cube	517.85
Duplicidentata zoology	588.63
Dupont, Pierre Fr. poet	841.82
Durange, Mexico	
geography	984.46

Duration obstetrics	598.813
Duration of work pol.	
econ	354.4
Durham, England	
geography	983.569
Dust	
air poliution	593.27
cosmic descrip astron	523.17
Dusting	
protection against pests	611.991
Dutch	
geography	983.793
history	937.93
language	409.388
literature	879.8
Duties	
custom	369.067
moral	180
of brothers	183.4
children	183.6
church members	258.1
citizens	185.1
or,	372.2
husbands and wives	183.5
parents	183.3
public officers	185.3
servants	183.7
state	185.5
teachers	336.1
social ethics	184
stamp public finance	369.056
Duty ethics	180.73
Du Vair, Guillaume Fr.	
essays	847.41
Dwarfs anthropology	565.27
Dwellings	
architecture	718
hygiene	593.15
laboring classes	354.9313
sanitation	653.5
Dwight, Timothy Am. poet.	861.22
Dyas period geology	554.57
Dyeing	
chemic technology	667.2
decoration	765.5
Dyes	
agriculture	612.92
chem. tech.	667.2
perfumery and cosmetics	668.17
Dykes engineering	654.62
Dynamical	
electricity	537.3
energy pneumatics	533.11
engineering	655
geology	551

sociology	312	protection of life	593.44
Dynamics		Dynamo-electric	
celestial	521.1	machinery	657.3
electro	537.3	Dynamogenesis	
of elastic solids	531.8	psychology	151.36
liquids	532.1	Dysentery diseases	594.938
particle	531.6	dietetic diseases	597.349
rigid body	531.6	digestive diseases	597.343
social	312	Dzarssaktu, China	
Dynamite		geography	981.955
chem. tech.	663.17		

Ear
  anatomy   598.41
  artificial   598.48
  care of   598.43
  deaf and dumb asylums   316.35
  diseases   598.44
  education for deaf and
     dumb   338.965
  physics   534.95
  physiology   598.42
  psychology   151.12
  training music   770.073
Early
  Christian philosophy   121.6
  copy books   009.3
  education, elementary   338.2
  Greek philosophy   121.1
  institutions pol. science   371.1
  printed books   009.1
Earth
  as a planet astronomy   523.43
  astronomy   525
  attraction of moon
     astronomy   523.33
  burial of dead
     customs   319.24
     pub. health   593.26
  circuits magnetism   538.77
  figure of astronomy   526
  interior of geology   551.11
  physical geology   551
  rotation of astronomy   525.3
  structure of phys.
     geology   551.1
Earthenwares chem.
     tech.   666.11
Earthly paradise
  Christianity   251.34
Earthquakes
  agriculture   616.919
  geology   551.3
  philanthropy   316.46
Earths
  alkalin inorg. chem.   546.22
  rare inorg. chem.   546.26
Earth's crust geology   551.15
Earthworks
  foundations
     architec.   713.1
     engin'g.   651.14
  railway engineering   651.812
  roadmaking   651.73
Earthworms zoology   583.1
Earthy aconomic
     minerals   558.61
East

Indies geography	982.3
Prussia geography	983.76
Russia geography	983.89
Turkistan geography	981.97
Easter Anglican calendar	253.13
Eastern	
Chin Chinese history	913.4
Chou Chinese history	911.62
empire Rome history	932.847
Han Chinese history	912.3
policy intern. politics	388.11
Wei Chinese history	913.82
Eating	
customs	319.27
hygiene	613.2
pleasures of	694.7
Ebenaceae botany	579.33
Ebenales botany	579.3
Ebriaceae botany	572.53
Ecardines zoology	583.94
Ecaudata zoology	587.68
Eccentricity	
in manners ethics	184
of orbit of earth	525.3
seasons	525.5
psychology	155.41
Ecclesiastes Bible	252.34
Ecclesiasticus apocrypha	252.94
Echinoderidae zoology	583.48
Echinodermata	
paleontology	569.74
zoology	582.9
Echinoidea zoology	582.93
Echiuroidea zoology	583.65
Echo acoustics	534.43
Eclampsia diseases	597.8447
Eclectic medicine	595.94
Eclecticism philosophy	121.54
Eclipses	
of moon	523.38
sun	523.78
theory	521.8
Ecliptic spherical astron.	522.77
Ecology	
aboriculture	614.37
bacteriology	566.925
Ecology (cont.)	
biology	561.8
botany	571.7
sericulture	616.27
zoology	581.7
Economic	
biology	568

blockade intern. politics	382.36
botany intern. politics	571.8
boycott intern. politics	382.36
chemistry intern. politics	660
or,	548
entomology zoology	585.8
geology	556
invasion pol. econ.	351.6
monopoly pol. econ.	351.5
policy pol. econ.	351
sociology pol. econ.	311.6
war pol. econ.	351.7
zoology	581.8

Economics

aboriculture	614.1
animal culture	615.01
aquatic products	617.1
business	621
family	350.013
floriculture	613.801
folk	350.04
individual	350.011
international	350.05
municipal	350.032
national	350.04
of communities	350.02
personal	350.011
political economy	350
private	350.01
public	350.03
rural	350.024
sericulture	616.1
state	350.031
urban	350.025
war	350.0837

Economy

domestic	690
ethics	186
library	020
political	350
Ecstasy abnormal psy	155.7
Ecstatics abnormal psy	155.7

Ectoblastic organs

embryology	591.55

Ectodermic organs

embryology	591.55

Ectopic gestation

obstetrics	598.821
Ectoprocta zoology	583.83
Ectozoa animal parasites	594.973

Ecuador

geography	984.869
history	948.69
Eczema dermatology	598.542
Edema pediatrics	598.942

Eden orig. home of man	565.76
Edentata mammals	588.32
Edgeworth, Maria Eng.	
fiction	853.72
Edible	
bulbs horticulture	613.13
corns horticulture	613.14
flowers horticulture	613.17
fruits horticulture	613.2
leaves horticulture	613.16
podded pea forage crops	612.36
roots horticulture	613.11
seeds horticulture	613.3
stems horticulture	613.18
tubers horticulture	613.12
Edicts archives	901.21
Editorial work	
journalism	040.5
Edlund's ether	
electricity	537.017
Education	
freedom of	372.135
of women	338.91
suffrage qualifications	372.51
special, see subject	
Educational	
buildings architecture	717.2
cinematographic institute	383.65
ethics	330.18
psychology	158.33
or,	330.15
statistics	330.14
taxation	331.47
tests	330.17
Eels zoology	587.477
Effect	
and cause metaphysics	134.11
Effects of poison	
pathology	594.98
Effigies, monumental	719.4
Efflux hydraulics	532.53
Effodientra zoology	588.31
Effusion pneumatics	533.53
Egg embryology	581.625
Eggs	
dietetics	593.128
food value	694.1
oology	587.9
physiology of nutrition	592.473
poultry	615.2
Egoism ethics	180.49
Egypt	
geography	985.1
history	951
language	409.61
philosophers	119

Egyptian Sudan	
geography	985.17
Egyptology	079.1
Ehime, Japan geography	982.1658
Eight hour law pol.	
econ.	354.41
Ejaculatory ducts	
anatomy	597.615
Ejectment law	397.2
Ekottaragamas Sutra	232.24
Elacouritaceae botany	578.6
Elaeagnaceae botany	578.72
Elaeocarpaceae botany	578.41
Elasmobranchii fishes	587.4
Elastic vibration physics	531.87
Elasticity	
mechanics	531.81
pneumatics	533.33
pulmonary physiology	597.221
Elatinaceae botany	578.55
Elbow anatomy	591.87
Elders ecclesiastic polity	255.55
Eleatic school Gk.	
philos.	121.12
Election	
Christian theology	251.49
frauds suffrage	372.57

to legislative body	373.034
Elective	
franchise	372.5
system education	335.6
Electoral	
college suffrage	372.56
frauds suffrage	372.57
lists suffrage	372.551
systems suffrage	372.52
Electric	
automobiles	659.75
Electric (cont.)	
communication engin'g.	657.8
conduction physics	537.27
crystallography	559.37
current physics	537.2
in gases physics	537.373
dialysis qual. analysis	544.5
engineering	657
in mines	658.7
execution of criminals	394.511
field physics	537.14
furnaces	657.817
heaters	
engineering	657.817
practical chemistry	542.4
ignition	657.818
installation, domestic	657.93

lamps	657.8141
light engineering	657.81
machinery engineering	657.3
machines physics	537.075
manipulations chem.	542.8
measurements	
engineering	657.1
physics	537.77
metallurgy	669.4
meters	657.12
methods	
qualitative analysis	544.93
quantitative analysis	545.5
oscillations physics	538.861
phenomena physics	537.7
power	
stat ons engin'g.	657.29
transmission engin'g.	657.6
railways	651.88
resistance physics	537.27
shock surgery	598.162
signals	657.93
storms physics	538.7
stress physics	537.143
synthesis chemistry	545.97
telegraphy	
communication	637.1
engineering	657.83
telephone	
communication	637.7
engineering	657.85
Electric (cont.)	
testing engineering	657.1
traction engineering	657.95
units engineering	657.11
vehicles engineering	657.97
waves physics	538.861
Electricity	537
animal hypnotism	156.5
applied	
engineering	657.8
physics	537.8
atmospheric	
electricity	537.7
meteorology	529.5
generation	657.2
hygiene	593.116
therapeutics	595.87
Electrification	537.13
Electrizations	537.372
Electro—	
analysis	
qualitative	544.93
quantitative	545.5
ballistic machines	659.35
biology	

animal mag.	156.5
biology	562.8
blasting mining	658.32
chemistry	541.7
chronography astronomy	522.5
diagnosis	595.273
dialysis qual. analysis	544.5
dynamics	537.3
kinetics	537.3
magnetism	538.8
magnets	538.81
motors machines	657.42
physiology	
animal mag.	156.5
biology	562.8
zoology	581.47
plated ware	662.73
plating chem. tech.	662.7
statics	537.1
thermal technology	662.5
Electrocution crim. law	394.511
Electrolysis	
electrochemistry	541.7
Electrolysis (cont.)	
of water chem. tech.	662.2
qualitative analysis	544.93
quantitative analysis	545.5
Electrolytic	

analysis chemistry	545.5
conduction physics	537.29
dissociation chemistry	541.71
technology	662.1
Electrons	
chemistry	541.01
physics	537.372
Embryology	
animals	581.69
botany	571.6
experimental	591.58
human	591.5
Embryotomy obstet.	
oper.	598.873
Emergencies surgery	598.16
Emerson, R. W. Am.	
essays	867.32
Emetics drugs	597.361
Emigration pol. science	377.5
Emilia, Italy geography	983.26
Emission spectra optics	535.441
Emissivity thermics	536.413
Emollients drugs	597.367
Emotions	
instability psychology	155.41
Empedocles Greek philos.	121.16
Emperor	

sovereigns	377.011
worship	209.4
Emphysema lung	
diseases	597.245
Empire	
Eastern	
Greek history	931.86
Rome history	932.847
French	
1st history	934.85
2nd history	934.87
political science	371.3
Rome history	932.84
Western, fall of history	932.846
Empirical study	
of heredity	563.397
Empiricism philosophy	104.5
in medicine	593.75
Employees	
associations	354.63
classification of	354.2
Employers	
and employed pol. econ.	354.1
liability	354.5
insurance	354.937
unions of	354.61
Employment	
agencies	354.113
of children pol. econ.	354.22
women pol. econ.	354.23
Empteraceae botany	578.12
Emulsions chemistry	541.49
Emydosauria zoology	587.836
Enamel	
arch. decoration	712.6
chem. technology	666.6
painting	735.5
Encaustic painting	734.4
Encephalon anatomy	597.811
Encyclopedias, general	030
special, see subject	
Endbrain anatomy	597.8113
Electrotherapy	595.87
Elegiac poetry	801.41
Elegies of Ch'u Chinese	
poet.	811.31
Elemental	
destruction agriculture	611.91
eleves occult sciences	157.77
spirits occult sciences	157.77
Elementary	
education	338.2
readers Chinese	
language	418.5
schools	338.2

theory of numbers	512.41
vocabulary Chinese	
language	418.1
Elements	
chemical	
chemic technology	661.2
chemistry inorganic	546
theoretical	541.02
false chemistry	546.9
nonmetallic chemistry	546.1
of music	770.021
perception psychology	151.172
state political science	371.02
putative chemistry	546.9
Elephantidae zoology	588.385
Eleutheroblastea zoology	582.711
Elevated	
ground hygiene	593.112
railways engin'g.	651.86
Elevators mech. engin'g.	655.83
Eleven classics, the Ch.	
classics	090.5
Elian philosophers	121.28
Elimination algebra	512.39
Eliot, George Eng.	
fiction	853.86
Elixir of gold	224.7
vitas	224.6

Ellipse geometry	517.44
Elliptic functions	516.41
geometry	519.87
Emancipation	
of slavery	317.48
woman	313.353
Embalming	
customs	319.24
public health	593.26
Embankments	
reclamation	611.69
hydraulic engineering	654.2
Embassadors diplomacy	386.33
Embiidae zoology	585.35
Emblems	
ecclesiology	253.36
military	379.38
state	371.08
Embolobranchia zoology	584.67
Embroidery	765.3
Embryo, external form	
of	591.57
Endemic diseases	594
Endless punishment	
theology	201.727
special religions	
Endocrine psychology	150.1971

Endocrinism psychology	150.1973
Endopterygota zoology	585.5
Endosmose liquids	532.15
Endosporeae botany	572.27
Endothermic reaction	536.55
Endowments	
library finance	022.4
school finance	331.41
special, see subjects	
Enemies of pests	
agriculture	611.995
Energy	
changes into heat energy	536.57
conservation of	531.693
metaphysics	134.8
meters engin'g.	657.17
radiant optics	535
transformation of	535.5
vital physiology	592.16
Engineering	650
bridge	651.5
canal	654.7
civil	651
dynamic	655
electrical	657
in mines	658.7
farm	610.6
forestry	614.2
geology	556.5
hydraulic	654
industrial	653.4
irrigation	654.8
materials	650.4
mathematics	650.1
mechanical	655
mechanics of	650.3
military	659.3
mining	658
municipal	653
railway	651.8
sanitary	653
rural	653.6
steam	655.2
structural	651.1
tunnel	651.6
Engines	655.25
special, see subject	
England	
administration	373.5
antiquities	995
archaeology	995
architecture	710.5
archives	935.12
army	379.155
biography	973.5
botany	571.95

calligraphy	739.5	law	390.8
census	345.5	learned institutions and	
church	259.3	societies	065
England (cont.)		libraries	020.935
colleges	338.7951	literature	850
constitutions	391.5	local government	373.58
defenses	379.15	maps	980.335
diplomatic and consular		or,	983.52
service	386.956	militia	379.85
directories	038.5	music	770.5
drawing	730.5	national bibliography	013.5
economic conditions	350.935	navy	379.156
education	330.935	painting	730.5
encyclopedia	033.5	paleography	459
finance	369.5	or,	990.835
fine arts	705	philology	450
flag	371.0835	philosophers	125
foreign relations	385.5	police	315.395
genealogy	977.95	population	349.5
geography	983.5	revenue	369.54
geology	550.35	schools, public	338.015
government	373.5	sculpture	720.5
central	373.51	seal	371.0835
local	373.58	statistics	345.5
government publications	373.505	vital	349.57
heraldry	969.5	England (cont.)	
history	935	tariff	369.56
language	450	taxation	569.55

theatre	780.5
travel	980.735
or,	983.54
treaties	387.95
universities	338.7951
yearbooks	037.35
zoology	581.95

English
art	705
discovery of America	941.8155
ophemerides	527.5
language	450
literature	850
newspapers	045
periodicals, general	055
philology	450
philosophy	125

Engraving	740
Enoch, book of apocrypha	252.981
Enrolment school	334.11
Entente Great war 1914—19	930.751
Enterocoela zoology	582.7

Entertainments
etiquette	319.36
private dom. science	697.41
public dom. science	697.45

Enthusiasm
psychology	151.2
religious	258.8
Enthymeme logic	141.3

Entity
of state pol. science	371.02
Entoblastic organs	591.54
Entodermic organs	591.54
Entomostraca zoology	584.86
Entoprocta zoology	583.81

Entozoa parasitic
diseases	594.972
Entropy physics	536.65
Enumerative geometry	519.49

Environment
criminal etiology	315.167
evolution	563.19
influence of	
physiology	592.28
therapeutics	595.78

Environment (cont.)
influence on	
animals	581.777
man	565.775
plants	571.773
psychology	153.2
social elements	311.1
Envy ethics	180.67

Enzymes chem.	566.926
Eocene	
fossils palaeotology	569
period geology	554.71
Eozoic era geology	554.4
Epencephalon anatomy	597.8117
Ephemeridae zoology	585.33
Ephemerides astronomy	527
Ephesians Bible	252.75
Epic	
painting	737.7
poetry	801.5
Epicurean school Gk.	
philos.	121.51
Epicurus Greek philos.	121.511
Epidemic diarrhea	
diseases	594.937
Epidemics	
contagious diseases	594.9
public health	593.237
Epigenesis origin of life	562.72
Epilepsy	
abnormal psychology	155.253
diseases	597.8453
institutions	316.36
Episcopacy	
ministry	255.52
sects	259.4
Episcopal church	259.4
Epistemology	
metaphysics	131
Epistles	
Bible	252.7
monuments	719.4
of Dr. Sunyatsen	001.199
Epithelial tissue	
histology	591.77
Epitropism botany	571.273
Equador see Ecuador	
Equality	
right of	372.14
social ethics	184.7
Equation of time	
chronology	528.53
Equations	
algebraic	512.77
arithmetic	511.7
calculus	515.7
chemical	541.09
differential	515.71
approximate	
integration of	519.73
geometrical theory of	519.71
integral of	515.73
integral	515.75

theory of	512.7
trigonometric	518.7
Equidae zoology	588.342
Equilibrium	
astronomy laws	521.11
chemical	541.065
hydraulics	532.35
mechanics	531.62
pneumatics	533.35
sense of psychology	151.16
Equinoxes astronomy	522.77
Equipment	
military	379.37
of workers	354.114
Equisetineae botany	573.8
Eragrostis forage crops	612.297
Erbium inorganic chem.	546.271
Erecting work mech. engin'g.	655.16
Erection physiology	597.621
Eretrian philosophers	121.28
Erh Ya Chinese dialectology	415.1
Ericaceae botany	579.15
Ericales botany	579.1
Erinaceidae zoology	588.85
Eriocaulaceae botany	575.72
Eriosema forage crops	612.32
Erosion	
geology	551.7
hydraulic engineering	654.66
Erotic	
delusions abnormal psy.	155.4581
literature	800.1897
Erotica	
ethics	187.5
sociology	313.342
Eroticism abnormal psychology	155.4581
Errhines drugs	597.26
Error, sources of logic	141.4
Errors	
of perception psychology	151.173
popular demonology	157.79
theory of probability	512.93
Eruptions volcanoes	551.4
Eruptive fevers diseases	594.911
Erysipelas diseases	594.943
Erythroxylaceae botany	577.9
Erzerum, Turkey in Asia geog.	982.666
Eschatology	
natural theology	201.7
Christian	251.7

other religions		
Esdras apocrypha	252.91	
Esophagus		
anatomy	597.312	
diseases	597.342	
physiology	597.321	
Esperanto language	405	
Essays		
Chinese literature	817	
special topic, see subject		
Essence metaphysics	133.22	
Essences chem. tech.	668.11	
Essenes Judaism	269.4	
Essex, England		
geography	983.566	
Estates		
law	397.2	
intern.	381.842	
social classes	371.066	
Esther		
apocrypha	252.92	
Bible	252.29	
Esthetics		
architecture	710.01	
fine arts	700.11	
gastronomy	694.7	
literature	800.1	
music	770.017	

of cities	719	
painting	730.01	
philosophy	190	
sculpture	720.01	
theatre	780.011	
Esthonia		
geography	983.971	
history	939.71	
Etching engraving	742.8	
Eternity metaphysics	134.5	
Ether		
anesthetics	597.861	
Edlund's	537.017	
light	535.1	
physics	530.11	
stress	537.11	
Ethers organic chem.	547.4	
Ethics	180	
special topic, see subject		
Ethiopia		
geography	985.2	
history	952	
Ethnic		
groups ethnography	565.88	
psychology	153.5	
religion	200.07	
Ethnogenic association	313.2	
Ethnography	565.8	

Ethnology	565.7	evolution	563.5
Etiology		hygiene	593.194
criminal	315.16	Euglenales botany	572.38
pathology	594.2	Eukleides see Euclid	
Etiquette		Eulamellibranchia	
customs	319	zoology	583.555
ethics	184.1	Eumycetes botany	573.3
Etymology comp.		Euornithes zoology	587.97
philology	401.1	Euphorbiaceae botany	577.98
Euarachnida zoology	584.65	Euphyllopoda zoology	584.863
Euarthropoda zoology	584.3	Eurhipidurae zoology	587.92
Euascomycetes botany	573.33	Euripides Greek drama	831.23
Eubacteria botany	572.12	European history	930
Eubulides Gk. philos.	121.27	Eurypterida zoology	584.88
Eucharist sacrament	253.93	Evangelic alliance	
Eucharistic vessels	253.38	religion	200.61
Euclid Greek philos.	121.261	Evangelist ministry	255.55
Euclidean geometry	517.1	Evangelistic work	
Euclid's postulate V	519.83	Christian	254.2
Eucommiaceae botany	578.2	Evaporation	
Eudaemonism	173.8	custaneous physiology	592.52
Eudiometers quan.		food preservation	694.5
analysis	545.43	heat chemistry	542.4
Eudiometry quan.		meteorology	529.45
analysis	545.43	physics	536.722
Euflagellata zoology	582.31	pulmonary physiology	592.52
Eugenics		vacuum chemistry	542.7

Evening		
prayers	253.26	
schools	338.85	
Evergreens		
coniferae botany	574.4	
hedges floriculture	613.85	
shrubs floriculture	613.85	
trees floriculture	613.87	
Evidence		
circumstantial	395.05	
law	395.05	
logic	141.1	
Evidences		
Bible	252.01	
of Christianity	251.9	
other religions		
Evil		
eye	157.7	
metaphysics	133.88	
natural theology	201.63	
origin of	201.63	
sin		
natural theology	201.63	
Christian	251.36	
other religions		
spirits	251.63	
theodicy	251.19	
Evolution		

apologetics	251.95	
Evolution (cont.)		
arithmetic	511.5	
biology	563	
by atrophy	564.37	
dynamical	564.6	
experimental	564.7	
natural theology	201.4	
of man	564.9	
plants	571.77	
origin of		
life	562.75	
man	565.725	
orthogenetic	564.6	
philosphy of life	171.5	
social	312.1	
theory of state	371.019	
Evolutional psychology	153	
Evolutionism philosophy	108.5	
Ex-libris	010.91	
Examination		
chemical	595.29	
of credentials suffage	372.552	
teachers education	336.21	
water engin'g.	653.13	
school education	334.5	
Yuan, the government	373.07	
Chinese	373.17	

other nations		Excrements physiology	597.327
Examinations school	334.5	Excretion	
Excavation		biliary physiology	597.325
foundations engin'g.	651.143	physiological zoology	581.44
mining	658.31	physiology	597.42
Excavations antiquities	990.074	Excretions, respiratory	597.223
Excess of		Execution criminal law	394.511
food hygiene	593.125	Executive, the	
development biology	561.76	government	373.05
Exchange		Chinese	373.15
bills of law	397.4	other nations	
money	364.4	Exercise hygiene	593.16
business transaction	398.38	physical education	338.631
international money	365	Exhalation	
of prisoners		of vapor zoology	581.428
Great war	930.77	water vapor	
international law	381.557	physiology	597.226
of professors	336.8	Exhibitions	
stock	366.3	of arts	700.7
territorial		special, see subject	
international law	381.316	Exile	
political science	371.031	punishments	394.514
Excise tax	369.051	social ethics	184.9
Chinese	369.151	Existence of being	
other nations		metaphysics	133.21
Excitants drugs	597.867	Exodus Bible	252.212
Excommunication		Exopterygota zoology	585.3
eccles. polity.	255.4		

Expansion	
heat physics	536.2
territorial intern, law	381.31
political sci.	371.031
Expatriation Intern. law	381.815
Expectorants drugs	597.26
Expedition, see special name	
Expeditions	
history of	980.709
scientific	500.98
Expellent forces	
obstetrics	598.8411
Expenditure	
public finance	369.03
Chinese	396.13
other nations	
Expenses	
allowance to teachers	336.54
domestic science	691
library finance	022.4
living teachers salaries	336.53
of students	331.48
Experientialism	
philosophy	106.3
Experiment stations	
agric.	610.078
Experimental	
chemistry	542
embryology	
biology	561.67
physiology	591.58
zoology	581.694
evolution	564.7
physiology	592.8
psychology	150.71
therapeutics	595.7
variation	563.67
Experiments	
chemical	542
fertilizer	611.7
on executed persons	592.12
surviving organs	592.17
physics	530.072
soil agriculture	611.31
Exploitation mining	658.8
Explorations	
history of	980.709
scientific	500.98
Explosives	
chemic technology	663.1
military engineering	659.34
mining dangers	658.45
protection of life	593.44

Exponential	
functions	516.31
tables	510.25
trigonometrical	
progression	514.41
Export duties customs	369.0673
Chinese	369.1673
other nations	
Expository sermons	253.75
Exposure	
of children customs	319.21
dead customs	319.24
to cold protec. of life	593.49
Express mail	636.56
Expression	
facial art anatomy	700.12
physiognomy	157.33
of emotions	
anthropology	565.46
practical chemistry	542.68
Expressions,	
mathematical	510.3
Expressive arts	780
Expulsion school	
management	332.13
Expurgated books	009.67
Extatics mental	
deficiency	155.7
Extensive farming	610.315
Extent metaphysics	134.9
External	
agencies drugs	597.76
ear anatomy	598.411
diseases	598.441
physiology	598.421
form of embryo	591.57
secretion comp.	
physiology	581.446
sexual organs	
anthropometry	565.37
Extinct	
animals palaeontology	569.6
plants palaeontology	569.1
Extinction	
of animal races	581.7779
fire protec. of life	593.45
species	563.9
painless, of animal life	593.287
Extosporeae botany	572.26
Extra	
fingers or toes surgery	598.175
pay wage scales	354.337
Extraction	
mining	658.5
of teeth	598.276

Extracts	
flavoring chem. tech.	664.4
on special subjects,	
see subject	
Extradition	
international law	381.88
treaties	387.3
Extraterritoriality	386.5
Extra-uterin pregnancy	598.821
Extreme unction	
Christian	253.98
Extremities anatomy	591.86
lower	
anatomy	591.88
bones of	597.7118
surgery	598.188
upper	
anatomy	591.87
bones of	597.7117
surgery	598.187
Eye, see Eyes	
Eyes	
anatomy	
ophthalmology	598.31
psychology	151.111
artificial surgery	598.38
asylums for blind	316.35
care of hygiene	598.33
diagnosis therapeutics	595.22
diseases of surgery	598.34
education for blind	338.965
glasses	598.399
optics	535.9
physiology	
ophthalmology	598.32
psychology	151.111
psychology	151.11
Ezekiel Bible	252.44
Ezra Bible	252.27

Fa Chia Chinese philos.	111.17	Faculae sun	523.75
Fables		Faculty	
folk literature	804.3	intuitive	151.86
Chinese	814.3	psychology	150.1911
other literatures		schools	331.36
Fabricated genealogies	313.386	Fagaceae botany	576.67
or,	977.5	Fagales botany	576.65
Face		Fagging student life	333.37
anatomy	591.82	Fair list pol. econ.	354.84
bones	597.7116	Fairy tales	
powdering chem. tech.	668.16	folk literature	804.3
surgery	598.182	Chinese	814.3
Facial		other literatures	
angel craniology	565.24	Faith	
diagnosis	595.22	Christian theology	251.42
Facsimile telegraphy	657.8358	confessions of creeds	251.8
Factor tables		cure Christian	254.8
mathematics	510.213	therapeutics	595.92
Factories		ethics	180.76
architecture	717.7	logic of assent	141.1
cooperative pol. econ.	356.71	moral theolotg Christian	258.52
sanitation in	653.4	philosophy	131.9
technology	670	Falcons zoology	5879.793
Factors and brokers law	398.49	Falcoury hunting	619.2
Factory		Fall notes finance	362.8
inspection pol. econ.	354.58	Fall of man Christian	
laws pol. econ.	354.15	theology	251.35
system labor and wages	354.38	Fallacies logic	141.4

Fallen, parish care of	254.8
Falling bodies	
deviation astron.	525.27
laws physics	531.65
Fallopian tube	
gynecology	598.742
False elements	
chemistry	546.9
Falsehood ethics	180.3
Fame ethics	180.71
Family	
author bibliography	016
customs	319.2
devotions Christianity	253.22
ethics	183
ethnogenic association	313.3
etiquette	319.2
form of state	371.11
genealogies	313.386
or,	977.5
heraldry	963
histories	977.3
intructions ethics	188.3
law	397.5
international	381.845
libraries	025.1
life	313.3
or,	565.793
meals dom. science	697.1
medicine	593.6
obligations ethics	183.9
patriarchs form of state	371.11
prayers Christianity	253.22
relations customs	319.2
to state	317.066
religious work for	258.2
worship Christianity	253.22
Famine hygiene	593.124
Famine fever disease	594.923
Famines	
provision of	610.18
relief of philanthropy	316.43
Fancy psychology	151.7
Fancywork	765.3
Fang Hsiao-ju Chinese	
prose	817.613
Fang Pao Chinese prose	817.741
Fang Yen of Yang	
Hsiung	
Chinese dialectology	415.5
Fans	
blowing engines	655.53
mining engineering	658.41
painting	753.6
Fantasms occult sci.	157.1
Fantoms occult sci.	157.1

Far East history	909	Fascial anatomy	597.716
problems intern. politics	388.14	diseases of	597.746
Faradization		Fascination animals	581.75
electrotherapy	595.87	Fascism sociology	318.2
Farces		Fashionable edu. of	
drama	802.96	women	338.9193
theatre	785	Fashions customs	319.4
Farewell sermons		Fast-day Christianity	253.18
Christian	253.793	Fasting hygiene	593.124
Farinosea botany	575.7	Fasts Christianity	253.18
Farm		Fat	
buildings	610.67	diseases	597.349
engines	655.293	industries chem. tech.	665
forestry	614.97	Fatalism natural	
machinery	610.6	theology	201.5
operations	611.4	Fathers duties	183.3
products utilizations	610.9	of the church	254.5
systems	610.311	Fatique hygiene	593.16
types	611.2	psychology	151.55
Farming tax	369.051	school hygiene	332.35
Chinese	369.151	Fats	
other nations		adulterations	593.22
Farmsted	611	animal chem. tech.	665.3
Fare amusements	795	nurtition	592.474
Farming agiculture	614.91	organic chemistry	547.1
Farther India		physiology	592.474
geography	982.4	vegetable chem. tech.	665.2
history	924		

Fatty	
compounds organic	
chem.	547.1
degeneration pathology	594.82
Faults structural geology	553.7
Fauna zoology	581.9
Favored nation clause	351.37
Fear	
ethics	180.66
psychology	151.2
school incentive	332.13
Feasts Anglican calendar	253.12
social customs	319.72
Features of surface:	
moon	523.35
sun	523.75
Fechner German philos.	127.74
Fecundation biology	561.622
botany	571.63
comp.	
embryology	581.623
embryology	591.52
physiology	597.623
Fecundity demography	349.023
physiology	598.724
Federal	
government pol. sci.	371.64
party, U. S.	375.61
state pol. sci.	371.64
Federalism pol. sci.	371.64
Feeble-minded	
asylums for	316.36
childstudy	153.762
education of	338.966
Feeding of animals	
zootechny	615.05
children	
pediatrics	598.93
Feelings emotions	151.2
Fees tuition	334.15
Feet costumes	319.48
human anatomy	591.88
weights and measures	607
Felidae zoology	588.511
Fellowship, church	253.92
Fellowships school	331.45
Felsites lithology	557.27
Female	
biography	970.7
colleges education	338.917
education	313.3503
or,	338.91
employments	313.355
or,	354.23
functions of generation	598.72
kinship matriarchate	313.384

labor	313.355	artificial biology	561.626
or,	354.23	biology	561.622
sex biology	562.87	botany	571.63
duties	183	embryology	591.52
suffrage	313.354	Fertilization(cont.)	
or,	372.7	physiology	596.623
Feminism	313.35	zoology	581.623
Fences agriculture	610.67	Fertilizers	
Fencing amusements	797.4	agriculture	611.7
Fenianism pol. assoc.	313.62	chemic tech.	668.7
Ferae zoology	588.5	chemistry	543.22
Ferguson Eng. philos.	125.62	Festivals	
Fermentation		amusements	791
chemic tech.	664.5	Anglican church	253.1
yeasts, etc.	572.11	labor holidays	354.467
Fermented beverages		of song music	771.4
adulterations	593.22	social customs	319.71
chem tech.	664.53	Fetal appendages	
Ferments physiol. chem.	592.41	pathology	598.827
Ferns botany	573.8	Fetus	
palaeobotany	569.24	abnormalities of	598.8415
Ferries transportation	634.5	death and retention of	598.824
Ferrotype photography	756.3	Fetuses	
Fertility		coalescence of deform.	598.174
fecundity	598.724	Feudal institutions	371.2
heredity	563.391	state	371.2
soil	611.35	Feudalism, age of	
Fertilization		Europ. history	930.53

political science	371.2	animal amusements	797.1
		sports amusements	797
Fever		physical educ.	338.638
animal heat	592.55	Figi islands geography	985.971
lung diseases	597.245	history	959.71
typhoid diseases	594.926	Figs agriculture	613.741
Fevers, eruptive diseases	594.911	Figulus Greek philos.	121.56
general works on		Figure	
diseases	594.92	human in art	737.3
Fiat paper money	361.75	of earth astron.	525.1
Fiber crops agriculture	612.5	geodesy	526
Fibers		Figureheads carving	728
agriculture	612.5	Figures	
connective tissue		correlation of geometry	519.097
histology	591.72	of heavenly bodies	
Fichte German philos.	127.3	astron.	521.14
Fiction		Filamentous plants	571.215
literature	803	Filbert pomiculture	613.763
Chinese	813	Filial duty ethics	183.6
other literatures		Piety, book of Ch.	097
Ficus carica pomiculture	613.741	classics	
Fiduciary paper money	361.73	Filibranchia zoology	583.552
Field crops		Filicinae botany	573.8
agriculture	612	Filiosa zoology	582.15
analytic chemistry	543.24	Filling	
Fielding, Henry Eng.		teeth dentistry	598.277
fiction	853.55	fibers for agric.	612.599
Fighting		Filth diseases pathology	594.93

Filtration		
practical chem.		542.67
water supply		653.18
Final causes		
metaphysics		134.2
Finance		
agricultural		610.35
company		362.16
dom. science		691
library economy		022.4
private		360
public		369
Financial		
administration civil serv.		369.02
Chinese		369.12
other nations		
crises pol. econ.		352.7
economics		360
institutions		360
markets		366
Finding		
latitude		525.4
longitude		525.4
meridian line astron.		522.74
time by transit		528.51
Fine arts		700
Fine copy books rarities		009.37
editions rarities		009.2
Finger		
prints anthropometry		565.35
rings costumes		319.48
Fingers anatomy		591.87
extra deformities		598.175
Finite and infinite		
metaphysics		134.3
differences calculus		515.5
Finland geography		983.91
history		939.1
Finnic language		409.231
literature		892
Finno-Ugrian language		409.23
Finsinism therapeutics		595.85
Fire		
alarms signals		638
arms ordnance		659.34
manufacture		671.1
balls meteors		523.52
chemistry		541.62
clay minerals		558.16
engines prot. of life		593.45
insurance		368.11
physics		536.78
worship		209.25
Fireproofing structural engin'g.		651.16
Fires		

agricultural hindrances	611.917
protection of life	593.45
relief philanthropy	316.42
First	
cause metaphysics	134.11
consulate Fr. history	934.847
editions rarities	009.11
international	388.51
law thermics	536.61
Fish	
as food domestic sci.	594.1
hygiene	593.128
culture	617.3
diseases of	599.49
fresh, inspection of	593.22
preservation dom. sci.	694.5
Fisheries	617.5
chemistry	617.24
coasting	617.53
deep sea	617.57
Fisheries (cont.)	
in fresh water	617.51
ocean	617.55
limnology	617.26
oceanography	617.26
Fishes paleontology	569.83
zoology	587.3
Fishing aquatic products	617.5
sports	799
Fishways fish culture	617.3
Fission	
biology	561.613
physiological zoology	581.611
Fissipedia zoology	588.51
Fistula surgery	598.143
Five classics, the Ch.	
classics	090.1
dynasties Chinese	
history	914.3
"Five tribes of Hu" Ch.	
history	913.5
Flag day school	334.37
of truce intern. law	381.5581
Flagellariaceae botany	575.71
Flagellata botany	572.3
zoology	582.31
Flags	
college	334.83
heraldry	960.7
military	379.38
ancient	379.98
state	371.08
Flames	
physics	536.78
practical chemistry	542.5
thermochemistry	541.62

Flanders geography	983.792
history	937.92
Flattery ethics	180.92
Flanbert, Gustave Fr	
fiction	843.84
Flavoring	
extracts chem. tech.	664.4
field crops	612.85
horticulture	613.4
Flax	
agriculture	612.52
manufacture	675.1
Fleas	
animal parasites	594.974
insects	586.57
pests	611.94
Fleets	
naval engin'g.	659.39
science	379.64
Fletcher, G. and P. Eng.	
poet.	851.37
John Eng. drama	852.36
Fleur de lis heraldry	960
Flexible bridge engin'g.	651.54
Flies insects	586.57
pests agric.	611.94
public health	593.234
artificial fishing	617.5
Flight of birds migration	581.703
Floating	
bodies physics	532.57
bridge engin'g.	651.577
docks engin'g.	654.38
schools	337.19
Flooding of deserts	654.85
mines	658.45
Floods	
agriculture	611.916
meteorology	529.45
protection against	654.67
relief philanthropy	316.46
Floors and flooring	
archit.	713.6
Flora, geographic	571.9
Floral perfume plants	612.811
leaf	571.276
Floriculture	613.8
landscape gardening	613.9
Florida, U. S. geography	984.169
Florideae botany	573.265
Flour manufacture	677
Flow	
of blood physiology	597.125
gases physics	533.55
in pipes	655.58
liquids physics	532.52

streams meteorology	529.45
Flower	
garden	613.8
shows	613.803
Flowering plants botany	574
Flowerless plants botany	573
Flowers	
agriculture	613.8
botany	571.276
drawing	737.13
Flowers (cont.)	
edible	613.17
landscape gardening	613.9
language of	570.083
national	570.087
seasoning	613.8052
Fluid crystals	559.31
Fluids physics	532
preservative biology	567.2
Fluorescence light	535.52
Fluorine inorganic	
chem.	546.137
Flute musical instrum.	774.1
Fluvial domain intern.	
law	381.35
Fluviales botany	575.3
Fluxes metallurgy	669.27
Fluxious calculus	515
Fly see Flies	
Flycatcher birds	587.976
Flying	
animal locomotion	581.73
fish zoology	587.477
machines aeronautics	533.7
engineering	659.44
Fodientia zoology	588.31
Foetal, foetus, see	
Fetal, Fetus	
Fog meteorology	529.43
signals engineering	654.48
Fog-breakers	
meteorology	529.43
Foix, France geography	983.496
Folding bridge engin'g.	651.571
Folds geology	553.7
Foliage	
aboriculture	614.781
botany	571.275
Folk literature	804
Folly ethics	180.89
Fontenelle, B. le B. de	
Fr. essays	847.51
Food	
adulterations public	

health	593.22	Foot	
animal domestic science	694.1	ball physical edu.	338.635
hygiene	593.128	bridges engin'g.	651.5021
chemical analysis	543.1	human anatomy	591.88
technology	664	measures	607
children's hygiene	593.122	wear clothing	319.48
cures therapeutics	595.82	Foote, Samuel Eng.	
digestion and nutrition	592.473	drama	852.62
domestic science	694	Forage crops grasses	612.2
hexiology animals	581.7775	legumes	612.3
Food(cont.)		Foraminifera zoology	582.13
hygiene	593.12	Force	
inspection adulterations	593.22	and motion kinetics	531.691
of animals zootechny	615.06	centrifugal and	
infants	593.122	centripetal	531.696
laboring classes	354.9312	directive bio-physics	562.36
plants	571.42	magnetism	538.15
prisoners	315.54	growth bio-physics	562.36
the sick	593.123	metaphysics	134.8
silkworms	616.274	repulsive astron.	523.18
physiology	592.473	tractive locomotives	655.271
poisoning	593.99	transmission of physics	531.9
preservation	594.5	Forceps obstetrics	598.871
silkworms	616.94	surg. instrum.	598.190
stuffs dom. sci.	694	Forearm anatomy	591.87
vegetable dom. sci.	694.2	Forebrain anatomy	597.811
hygiene	593.126	Forces, social	311
zoology	581.7775	Foreign see Foren	

Foreknowledge of God	
Christian theol.	251.141
Foren	
banks pol. econ.	362.11
Foren (cont.)	
elements Chinese	
language	413.9
investments pol. econ.	367.13
labor pol. econ.	354.29
loan of China	369.182
missions Christianity	254.9
relations intern. politics	385
trade pol. econ.	351.31
wars of China	910.283
words and phrases Ch.	
language	413.9
Forest	
botany	614.3
grazing	614.92
lands pol. econ.	353.11
parks	614.128
pasture	614.92
product utilization	614.7
resources	614.16
Forestation forestry	614.48
Forestry	
agriculture	614
farm	614.97
taxonomic	614.6
Forests meteorology	529.78
state ownership	614.15
Forgery criminology	315.187
law	394.25
of antiquities	990.077
Forging blacksmithing	682
Forgiveness of sin	
Christ. theol.	251.46
Form	
external, of embryo	591.57
of government	371.048
legislature	373.039
state	371.04
ontology	133.2
Former Chao Chinese	
history	913.582
Ch'in Chinese	
history	913.586
Liang Chinese	
history	913.585
Shu Chinese	
history	914.95
Yen Chinese	
history	913.584
Formosa geography	982.17
Forms	
algebraic	512.2

binary algebra	512.21	Four fundamental rules	
laws of	395.06	arithmetic	511.2
musical	770.027	Fourierism socialism	318.17
of punishments	315.51	Fourier's series	
suffrage	372.52	functions	516.82
Formulas		Fourth dimension	
recipes, see special subject		geometry	519.63
		Fowling hunting	619.2
theoretical chemistry	541.09	Fowls animal culture	615.2
Formularies materia med.	596.71	Fox, C. J. Eng. oratory	858.43
Fortifications mil. engin'g.	659.31	Foxes zoology	588.514
		Fractional distillation	541.65
Fortunella horticulture	613.733	Fractions arithmetic	511.31
Fortune-tellers	157.097	Fractures surgery	598.165
Fortune-telling	157	France	
Fossils paleontology	569	administration	373.4
Foundations		antiquities	994
architec. construction	713.1	archaeology	994
bridge engineering	651.508	architecture	710.4
light-houses engin'g.	654.43	archives	934.12
structurai engin'g.	651.13	army	379.145
Founding of libraries	022.1	biography	973.4
Fountains esthetics of cities	719.6	botany	571.94
		calligraphy	739.4
		census	345.4
Four books, the Ch. classics	098	colleges	338.7941
		constitutions	391.4

defenses	379.14
diplomatic and consular service	386.946
directories	038.4
drawing	730.4
economic conditions	350.934
education	330.934
encyclopedia	033.4

France (cont.)

finance	369.4
fine arts	704
flag	371.0834
foreign relations	385.4
genealogy	977.94
geography	983.4
geology	550.34
government	373.4
central	373.41
local	373.48
government publications	373.405
heraldry	969.4
history	934
language	440
law	390.54
learned institutions and societies	064
libraries	020.934
literature	840
local government	373.48
maps	980.334
or,	983.42
militia	379.84
music	770.4
national bibliography	013.4
navy	379.146
painting	730.4
paleography	449
or,	990.834
philology	440
philosophers	124
police	315.394
population	349.4
revenue	369.44
schools, public	338.014
sculpture	720.4
seal	371.0834
statistics	345.4
vital	349.47
tariff	369.46
taxation	369.45
theatre	780.4
travel	980.734
or,	983.44
treaties	387.94
universities	338.7941
yearbooks	037.34

zoology	581.94
Franche Comte, Fr.	
geography	983.477
Franchise, elec. suffrage	372.5
Franciscan monks	259.0913
Frangulinae botany	578.3
Frankish emperors Ital. history	932.863
Franklin, Benjamin Am. essays	867.21
Franks history	937.81
Fraud	
electoral suffrage	372.58
law	394.25
Frauds	
antiquities	990.077
art	700.77
literary	800.45
Freckles dermatology	598.545
Free	
baptists Christian sects	259.6
cities Italian history	932.867
coinage of silver	361.6
competition pol. econ.	351.34
delivery mails	636.51
farming philanthropy	316.6
hand drawing	733
love ethics	187.5
sociology	313.3421
news and reading rooms	025.8
public libraries	025.3
religion	201.1
soil party, U. S.	375.64
speech pol. sci.	372.133
tariff	369.0641
Chinese	369.1641
other nations	
thought rationalism	201.1
trade	351.33
wealth	352.2
will Christian theology	251.49
metaphysics	134.23
psychology	151.41
Freedmen	
education of	338.95
slavery	317.48
Freedom	
and emancipation	
slavery	317.48
women	313.353
metaphysics	134.23
of action	372.131
Freedom (cont.)	
of assembly	372.137
belief	372.134

conscience	372.132
education	372.135
labor	354.011
man Christianity	251.38
press journalism	040.13
profession	372.136
speech	372.133
the sea intern. law	388.77
teaching education	336.6
personal pol. science	372.13
political liberty	372.1
religious salvation	251.49

Freezing

agricultural hindrances	611.911
artificial chem. tech.	664.8
ice machines	655.67
food preservation	694.5
points chemistry	541.44
physics	536.711

Freight

boat shipbuilding	659.13
locomotives steam engin'g.	655.272
transportation	630

French

art	704
Cochin China geography	982.42
history	924.2

discovery of America	941.8154
Guinea geography	985.58
Kongo geography	985.66
language	440
literature	840
newspapers	044
periodicals, general	054
philology	440
philosophy	124
regime Canadian history	942.81
republic, 1st history	934.843
2nd history	934.87
3rd history	934.88
revolution	934.84
Somaliland geography	985.41
Sudan geography	985.51

Freneau. Philip Am.

poet.	861.24

Frequency

and pitch acrustics	534.51
maters elec. engin'g.	657.18

Fresco painting	735.11
Friction physics	531.694

Friendly

islands geography	985.972
societies	313.66

Friends, society of sects	259.85
Friendship ethics	180.62

Frigidity psychology	155.4587
Frisian	
language	409.383
literature	879.3
Frobel's system	
education	338.13
Frogs	
aquatic products	617.7
zoology	587.68
Frontiers	
intern. law	381.33
pol science	371.033
Frost	
actions geology	551.92
bite skin diseases	598.548
hindrances and	
protection	611.911
meteorology	529.42
Fruit	
culture	613.7
drinks adulterations	593.22
dom. science	694.4
hygiene	593.13
farms agriculture	611.25
mice chem. tech.	664.57
pomiculture	613.7
Fruits	
analysis	543.26
and seeds aboriculture	614.77
organography	571.278
as food hygiene	593.127
edible horticulture	613.2
painting	737.13
Fuel	
chemic technology	663.7
steam engin'g.	655.221
Fugues psychoanalysis	156.36
Full development,	
period of	598.72
Fukien, China geography	981.81
Fukui, Japan geography	982.1634
Fukuoka, Japan	
geography	982.1661
Fukushima, Japan	
geography	982.1621
Fumariaceae botany	577.53
Function of functions	516.5
Functional	
determinant	512.34
Jacobean	512.25
diseases of brain and cord	
medicine	597.844
psychology	155.24
women	598.747
psychology	150.193
theory of wages pol. econ.	354.318

Functions	516
Abelian	516.45
algebraic	516.2
analytic	516.1
arithmetical	512.44
Bessel's	516.84
compound	516.5
elliptic	516.41
function of	516.5
hyperbolic	516.42
hyperelliptic	516.43
in union with groups	516.7
infinitesimal	516.6
inverse	516.4
Lame's	516.85
Laplace's	516.83
Legendre's	516.83
nervous medicine	597.8
of generation female	598.72
male	597.621
symmetric	512.71
Theta	516.47
Fund, wage pol. econ.	354.313
Funding system finance	369.083
Funds finance	362.4
Funeral sermons	253.793
rites customs	319.24
sermons	253.793
Fungi	573.3
fission	572.1
imperfecti	573.39
pests agriculture	611.95
Funis, prolapsus	
obstetrics	598.848
Furnaces steam engin'g.	655.223
Furniture	
domestic science	692
ecclesiastic	253.3
interior decoration	763.2
library science	024.8
school	332.93
Fuses explosives	663.3
Future	
events probabilities	512.9
judgment natural theology	201.723
life natural theology	201.78
punishment natural theology	201.727
state natural theology	201.78
Fuzoku-uta Japanese ballads	821.54

Gabbro plutonic rocks	557.34
Gadolinium inorganic chem.	546.293
Gaelic language	409.372
Galatians Bible	252.74
Galaxy astronomy	523.81
Galeopithecidae zoology	588.81
Gall	611.93
Gallantry ethics	180.74
Galleries, art	700.7
Gallia language	409.371
Gallium inorganic chem.	546.277
Gallows criminal law	394.511
Galvanic batteries	
manipulation	542.8
physics	537.21
Gambling	
amusementa	795
ethics	189.75
prohibition of	317.83
Game sports	793
Games	
amusements	790
customs	319.75
ethics	189.7
hygiene	593.16
kindergarten	338.134
of chance	
amusements	795
ethics	189.75
skill	
amusements	794
ethics	189.74
public	793
school	338.63
Gamopetalae botany	579
Ganglions anatomy	597.819
Gangrene	
lung diseases	597.245
surgery	598.145
Ganodonta zoology	588.321
Ganoids fishes	587.473
Garden crops	613.1
Gardening	
elem. education	338.13
flower agriculture	613.8
fruits	613.7
horticulture	613
kitchen	613.1
Gardening (cont.)	
landscape	613.9
market	613.1
Gardens	
botanical	570.077
public	719.1

zoological	580.077
Gardianship law	397.53
Garlic olericulture	613.13
Garrick, David Eng.	
drama	852.61
Garryaceae botany	576.44
Gas	
analysis	544.4
engines	
engin'g.	655.42
physics	536.9
exchange	
respiration	597.223
in blood respiration	597.224
fuel chem. tech.	663.7
heating prac. chem.	542.4
manipulation prac.	
chem.	542.7
manufacture	665.75
suffocation by prot. of	
life	593.493
Gascon, France	
geography	983.493
Gases	
agricultural hindrances	611.919
and vapors	536.35
chemic technology	665
chemicals	661.7
expansion thermics	536.2
pneumatics	533
qualitative analysis	544.4
quantitative analysis	545.43
respiratory exchange	597.223
volumetric analysis	545.43
Gasoline	
automobiles	659.73
engines	655.44
Gasteropoda zoology	583.53
Gastric	
glands	597.313
juice	597.321
Gastritis diseases	597.343
Gastronomy	694.7
Gastropoda zoology	583.53
Gastrotricha zoology	583.47
Gates	
architectural	
construction	713.8
irrigation engineering	654.83
Gati Buddhism	231.84
Gautama Buddhology	231.2
Gazetters	983.031
special country, see	
country	
Geese hunting	619.2
poultry	615.2

zoology	587.973
Gelatines	
chem. tech.	668.3
chemistry	547.93
Gemmation biology	561.615
botany	571.61
zoology	581.613
Gems	
carving	724
glyptic arts	767
mineralogy	558.18
Geneagenesis zoology	581.615
Genealogy	977
General	
see special subjects	
Generalization logic	141.75
Generation	
alternation of	
biology	561.625
botany	571.65
biology	561.6
of electricity	657.2
physiology	592.6
spontaneous biology	562.71
steam	655.2
zoology	581.6
Generators	
alternating-current elec. eng.	657.456
direct-current elec. eng.	657.446
general elec. eng.	657.41
Genesis Bible	252.211
Genetic	
biology	563
energy	562.34
selection	563.38
logic	144
psychology	153
Genetics biology	563.5
Genito-urinary system	
physiology	597.6
zoology	581.16
Genius psychology	153.9
Genji monogatari	
Japanese lit.	823.36
Genre painting	737.7
Gentianaceae botany	579.43
Gentry genealogy	977.3
Geocentric	
latitude astronomy	521.26
longitude astronomy	521.26
place astronomy	521.2
Geochemistry geology	551.95
Geodesy	526
Geognosy geology	551
Geographic	

coordinates	525.4
distribution	
agriculture	611.09
animals	581.9
forest	614.38
minerals	558.9
of contag. diseases	595.232
genius	153.99
plants	571.9
silkworms	616.29
Geography	980
see special names	
Geological climates	529.83
Geology	550
agriculture	556.3
applied	556
dynamic	551
economic	556
engineering	556.5
geotectonic	553
historical	554
military	556.2
mining	556.1
physical	551
stratigraphic	554
structural	553
surface	552
tectonic	553

Geomancy occult	
sciences	157.4
Geometric	
drawing	731.7
optics	535.7
Germetric (cont.)	
progression	514.2
theory of differential	
equations	519.71
electricity	537.013
Geometrography	519.1
Geophysics astronomy	525.01
Georgia, U. S. geography	984.169
Gephyrea zoology	583.67
Geraniaceae botany	577.86
Geraniales botany	577.8
Germ	
cells embryology	591.51
continuity, doctrine of	563.33
elements heredity	563.31
layers embryology	591.53
selection heredity	563.35
theory biology	561.64
vesicle cytology	561.52
German	
art	707
discovery of America	941.8157

East Africa	985.42	drawing	730.7
emperors Ital. history	932.865	Germany(cont.)	
empire, new	937.88	economic conditions	350.937
language	470	education	330.937
literature	870	encyclopedia	033.7
painting	730.7	finance	369.7
philology	470	fine arts	707
philosophy	127	flag	371.0837
republic	937.89	foreign relations	385.7
Germanium inorganic		genealogy	977.97
chem.	546.294	geography	983.7
Germany		geology	550.37
administration	373.7	government	373.7
antiquities	997	central	373.71
archaeology	997	local	373.78
architecture	710.7	government publications	373.705
archives	937.12	heraldry	969.7
army	379.175	history	937
biography	973.7	language	470
botany	571.97	law	390.6
calligraphy	739.7	learned institutions and	
census	345.7	societies	067
colleges	338.7971	libraries	020.937
constitutions	391.7	local government	373.78
defenses	379.17	maps	980.337
diplomatic and consular		or,	983.72
service	386.976	militia	379.87
directories	038.7	music	770.7

national bibliography	013.7
navy	379.176
painting	730.7
paleography	479
or,	990.837
philology	470
philosophers	127
schools, public	338.017
sculpture	720.7
seal	371.0837
statistics	345.7
vital	349.77
tariff	369.76
taxation	369.75
theatre	780.7
travel	980.737
or,	983.74
treaties	387.97
universities	338.7971
yearbooks	037.37
zoology	581.97
Germinal	
elements	563.31
selection	563.35
vesicle cytology	561.52
Germinative cells	591.51
Gesneriaceae botany	579.64
Gesso painting	735.13
Gestalt psychology	150.1915
Gestation	
ectopic obstetrics	598.821
obstetrics	598.8
Ghost, Holy Christian	
dogmatics	253.13
Ghosts spiritualism	157.9
Giant humbugs	157.79
Giants nat. hist. of man	565.27
Gibbon. Edward Eng.	
essays	857.67
Gifu, Japan geography	982.1635
Gigantostrace zoology	584.88
Gigatinales botany	573.265
Gilbert islands	985.968
Ginger olericulture	613.12
Ginkgo pomiculture	613.767
Ginkgoaceae botany	574.3
Ginkgoales botany	574.3
Gipsies outcast races	319.9
Girder bridges engin'g.	651.51
Girders engin'g.	651.51
Girl problem child	
culture	313.368
psychology	153.775
Girls	
child culture	313.368

counsels ethics		183.6
education		338.91
	or,	313.3503
psychology		153.775
religious societies		256.5
societies sociology		313.356
Giroude, France		
geography		983.492
Glacial drift erosion		551.76
period		554.73
Glaciers geology		551.76
Glanders diseases		594.963
Glandular system		597.4
comparative		581.14
Glass		
apparatus prac.		
chemistry		542.2
making		666.5
manufacture		666.5
painting		735.5
Glazes chemic tech.		666.6
Glees vocal music		771.71
Glires zoology		588.6
Globe of eye diseases of		598.344
Globes, celestial		
astronomy		522.5
Globular of blood, see Corpuscles		
Glossaries languages		401.3
Chinese		411.3
Gloves		
clothing		693.3
costume		319.48
Glucinum inorganic chem.		546.231
Glucose chem. tech.		664.1
Glue chem. tech.		668.3
Glumaceae botany		575.41
Glumiflorae botany		575.41
Glycine forage crops		612.33
Glycolytic ferments physio. chem.		592.41
Glyptics carving		767
Gneiss lithology		557.42
Gnetaceae botany		574.5
Gnetales botany		574.5
Gnomic poetry Gk. literature		831.1
Gnosticism philosophy		121.61
Gnostics heresy		259.094
Goats		
dairy		615.714
diseases of comp. med.		599.43

domestic animals	615.13
zoology	588.335
God Christian doctrines	251.1
Gods	
ethnic religions	209
Hinduism	241.71
mythology	209.9
Taoism	221.2
Gold	
coinage	361.6
exchange money system	361.26
inorganic chem.	546.71
manufacture	671.5
metallurgy	669.91
mineralogy	558.141
money system	361.21
Goldsmith, Oliver Eng.	
essays	857.64
fiction	853.64
poet.	851.64
Goldsmithing	671.5
Golf amusements	793
Gonorrhea veneral	
diseases	598.6
Good	
Friday	253.13
Hope, Cape of geography	985.77
offices intern. politics	382.23
Goodeniaceae botany	579.95
Goodness	
ethics	180.1
natural theology	201.61
ontology	133.88
Goods pol. econ.	352.3
Gorgias Greek philos.	121.221
Gospels	
Bible	252.6
pseuds.	292.991
Gossypium fibers	612.51
Gothic, J. W. German	
drama	872.62
Gothic	
kingdom	
Ital. history	932.861
Span. history	933.813
language	409.381
literature	879.1
Gouache painting	734.2
Gourd instruments	770.11
Government	
buildings	717.7
or,	373.09
central	
administration	373.01
Chinese	373.11
church	255

control insurance	368.9
divine Christ. theology	251.16
family ethics	183
forms of	371.048
change of	371.049
loans	
finance	369.08
Chinese	369.18
local	
administration	373.08
Chinese	373.18
political science	373
school education	331
science of pol. sci.	373
Grace Christian theology	251.41
Grades schools	334.6
Graduate schools	338.73
Graduated	
system suffrage	372.528
Graduation schools	334.7
Grain-elevator	
machinery	655.87
Grains agriculture	612.1
Grallatores zoology	587.974
Gramineae botany	575.42
Grammar	
comparative	401.6
universal	401.6
Grammars Chinese lang.	416
Gramophones acoustics	534.99
Grand canal	981.349
Granit plutonic rocks	557.33
Grants to schools	331.41
Grapes pomiculture	613.75
Graphic	
algebra	512.02
arts fine arts	700
statics	531.66
Graphideae botany	573.41
Graphite mineralogy	558.126
Graphology physiognomy	157.37
Grasses	
agriculture	612.2
botany	575.41
ornamental	719.8
Grasshoppers zoology	585.31
Grave	
mounds hist. ruins	990.186
stones monuments	719.4
yards	719.4
Gravel	
diseases	597.642
petrology	557.53
roads engin'g.	651.762
Graves cemeteries	719.4

Gravimetric anal. chem.	545.3
Gravitation	
celestial dynamics	521.12
general	531.65
Gravity mechanics	531.64
Gray, Thomas Eng. poet.	851.61
Great Britain	
administration	373.5
antiquities	995
Great Britain (cont.)	
colonies	373.587
constitutions	391.5
government	373.5
heraldry	969.5
history	935
see also England	
Great learning, the Ch.	
classics	098.1
Great Russia	983.86
Great war, the	930.7
Grecian, see Greek	
Greco-Roman philosophy	121.5
Greece	
administration	373.31
antiquities	993.1
architecture	710.31
archives	931.12
army	379.1315
biography	973.1
botany	571.931
calligraphy	739.31
census	345.31
colleges	338.79311
constitutions	391.31
defenses	379.131
diplomatic and consular	
service	386.9316
directories	038.31
drawing	730.31
economic conditions	350.931
education	330.931
finance	369.31
fine arts	703.1
flag	371.0831
foreign relations	385.31
genealogy	977.931
geography	983.1
geology	550.31
government	373.31
government publications	373.3105
heraldry	969.31
history	931
law	390.51
learned institutions and	
societies	063.1
libraries	020.931

literature	831	Greek	
local government	373.318	archipelago	983.18
maps	980.331	calendar	528.931
or,	983.12	classics	831
Greece(cont.)		dialects	431.5
militia	379.831	independence	931.88
music	770.31	language	431
national bibliography	013.31	literature	831
navy	379.1316	mythology	209.931
painting	730.31	paleography	431.9
paleography	431.9	philosophy	121
or,	990.831	sculpture	720.31
philology	431	Green Eng. philos.	125.68
philosophers	121	Green, Joseph Am. poet.	861.14
population	349.31	Greene, Robert Eng.	
revenue, public	369.314	drama	852.31
schools	338.0131	Gregarinida zoology	582.22
sculpture	720.31	Gregariousness of	
seal	371.0831	animals	581.766
statistics	345.31	Ground	
vital	349.317	air hygiene	593.114
tariff	369.316	hygiene of	593.27
taxation	369.315	water physiography	552.5
travel	980.731	Groups, theory of	512.67
or,	983.14	Growth	
treaties	387.931	biology	562.81
yearbooks	037.31	Growth(cont.)	
zoology	581.931	botany	571.45

disproportionate deform.	598.176
force vitalism	562.33
incomplete deform.	598.171
Gruinales botany	577.85
Guanajuato, Mex.	
geography	984.47
Guardianship law	397.53
Guatemala	
geography	984.61
history	946.1
Gudrun German poet.	871.22
Guerrilla warfare	381.554
Guiana	
geography	984.88
history	948.8
Guidance, vocational	338.48
Guidebooks	038
traveler's	980.703
Guidi, Alessandro	
Italian poet.	833.155
Guienne, France	
geography	983.492
Guild socialism	318.3
Guilds pol. econ.	354.6
Guillotine crim. law	394.511
Guinea	
Lower, Africa geography	985.58
New	
geography	985.959
history	959.59
Upper, Africa geography	985.57
Guitar music	775.3
Gulf states, Mex	
geography	984.48
Gullet, diseases of	597.342
Gumma, Japan	
geography	982.1618
Gunboats naval science	379.667
Gunnery mil. engin'g.	659.35
Gunpowder explosives	663.11
Guns	
manufacture	671.1
mil. engin'g.	659.35
Gunshot wounds surgery	598.164
Guttiferae botany	578.53
Gymnocarpeae botany	573.41
Gymnodiniaceae botany	572.4
Gymnolaemata zoology	588.84
Gymnomyxa zoology	582.11
Gymnophiona zoology	587.66
Gymnospermae	
botany	574.1
palaeobotany	569.4
Gynecology	598.7
Gypsies	319.9
Gypsum lithology	557.55

Habakkuk Bible	252.495	agriculture	611.913
Habit psychology	151.353	meteorology	529.47
Habitations		Hair dressing customs	319.47
animals	581.703	handcrafts	687
human	593.17	toilet	693.5
Habitats, animal	581.72	dyes toilet	693.5
Habits		Halicoridae zoology	588.41
animals zoology	581.71	Halitheriidae zoology	588.42
customs	319	Hallucinations	
laboring classes	354.57	psychoanalysis	156.11
psychology	151.353	Halogen group	
Habitudes will	151.53	inorganic chem.	546.13
Hachimonjiya-bon Jap.		Haloids organ. chem.	547.7
fiction	823.63	Halorrhagidaceae botany	578.86
Hacks transporation	632.3	Hamamelidaceae botany	577.76
Hades		Hamburg, Ger.	
natural theology	201.727	geography	983.78
Buddhism	231.85	Hamilton, Sir W.	
Christianity	251.77	Eng. philos.	125.66
Hadramant, Arabia		Hamitic language	409.6
geography	982.77	Han dynasty Chinese	
Haechel German philos.	127.76	hist.	912
Haemodoraceae botany	575.84	Han Fei Chinese philos.	111.178
Haemosporidia zoology	582.24	Han Yu Chinese poet.	811.454
Haggai Bible	252.497	prose	817.46
Haikai Haiku Jap. poet.	821.4	Hand	
Hail		chirology	157.36

human anatomy	591.87	Harp music	775.1
operated code telegraphy	657.8352	Harris, J. C. Am. fiction	863.46
Handbooks of travel	980.703	Harrows	610.61
of special subject, see subject		Harte, F. B. Am. fiction	863.45
Handcrafts mechan.		Hartley Eng. philos.	125.61
trades	680	Hartmann German philos.	127.77
Hangars aeronautics	659.48	Haruspication divination	157.16
Hanover		Harvesting machines	610.64
Germany geography	983.78	operations	611.8
House of Eng. history	935.87-935.88	Hasa, Arabia geography	982.78
		Hat fibers agriculture	612.593
Hapalidae zoology	589.53	Hat-making handcrafts	688.3
Haplodrili zoology	583.616	Hate ethics	180.64
Happiness ethics	180.98	Hats clothing	693.3
Harbor works		costume	319.48
engineering	654.3	Haute	
Hard fibers agriculture	612.58	Garonne, France	
Harmonic analysis	516.81	geography	983.495
progression	514.3	Loire, France geography	983.495
Harmonies		Marne, France geography	983.471
ellipsoidal	516.85	Saone, France geography	983.477
spherical	516.83	Savoie, France geography	983.478
toroidal	516.87	Vienne, France geography	983.489
Harmony		Hautes	
acoustics	534.541	Alpes, France geography	983.498
music	770.025	Pyrenees, France	
Harness dom. animals	615.11	geography	983.493

Hawaii			public	593.2
geography	985.98		resorts hygiene	593.112
history	959.8		Healths	
Hawes, Stephen Eng.			drinking of customs	319.72
poet.	851.25		Hearing	
Hawthorne, Nathaniel			acoustics	534.9
Am. fiction	863.33		anatomy	598.41
Hay agriculture	612.2		diseases	598.44
fever diseases	597.24		physiology	598.42
Hayne, P. H. Am. poet.	861.24		psychology	151.12
Hayti			Heart	
geography	984.74		anatomy	597.112
history	947.4		diseases	597.142
Head			physiology	597.127
ake diseases	597.8457		Heat	
anatomy	591.81		agriculture	611.912
art anatomy	700.12		animal physiology	592.5
bones of	597.7114		thermics	536.57
craniology	565.24		diaphoretics	597.465
diseases	594		engines	655.41
dress customs	319.48		geologic agents	551.95
phrenology	157.35		Heat (cont.)	
surgery	598.181		of earth	525.2
Headakes diseases	597.8457		moon	523.32
Headstones monuments	719.4		sun	523.72
Health			physics	536
laws hygiene	593		physiologic effects	592.58
of students	332.3		thermochemistry	541.6

Heating	
domestic economy	692
libraries	024.7
practical chemistry	542.4
steam plants	655.23
Heaven	
Christian theology	251.76
natural theology	201.725
Heavenly bodies	
figures of	521.14
rotation of	521.15
Hebrew	
geography	982.84
history	928.4
language	409.55
philosophy	121.66
or,	118.5
religion	260
Sabbath	253.191
Hebrews epistles	252.787
Hedjaz see Hejaz	
Hedonism	171.1
Hegel German philos.	127.5
Height of atmosphere meteor.	529.16
Heilungkiang, China	
geography	981.915
Heine, Heinrich German poet.	871.75
Heinrich von Veldeke	
Ger. poet.	871.23
Heirs law	397.6
Heisenberg quantum mechanics	530.75
Hejaz geography	982.79
history	927.9
Helaletidae zoology	588.345
Helianthus tuberosis roots crops	612.483
Heliocentric	
longitude and latitude	521.25
place	521.2
Heliometer astronomy	522.4
Heliozoa zoology	582.17
Helium group inorganic chem.	546.18
Helium inorganic chem.	546.181
Hell	
Christian theology	251.77
natural theology	201.727
Hellenic language	409.341
Helminthology zoology	583.2
Helminthes zoology	583.2
Helobiae botany	575.3
Helps, Sir Arthur Eng.	

essays	857.84	Herbals drugs	596.13
Helvetius Fr. philos	124.25	Herbart German philos.	127.73
Hematology see Blood		Herbert, George Eng.	
Hemiascales botany	573.32	poet.	851.38
Hemibasidiales botany	573.35	Herblike fruits	613.78
Hemichordata zoology	586.1	Herbs garden crops	613.4
Hemimetabola zoology	585.3	Herder, J. G. von Ger.	
Hemiptera zoology	585.38	poet.	871.64
Hemorrhage		Heredia, J. M. de Fr.	
in labor obstetrics	598.844	poet.	841.86
of the lungs diseases	597.245	Hereditary	
pediatrics	598.943	diseases hygiene	594.21
Hemp		genius mental charac.	153.93
agriculture	612.53	succession law	397.6
see also		pol. science	371.041
distinguishing name		Heredity	
manufacture	675.1	criminal etiology	315.16
Hengshan	981.363	evolution	563.3
Hens diseases of	599.45	of plants	571.771
poultry	615.2	Heredity (cont.)	
Hepaticae botany	573.6	hygiene	593.19
Hepatology physiology	597.325	mental	153.3
Heraclitus Greek philos.	121.115	osex	563.37
Heraldry	960	psychology	151.54
Herault, France		Heresies	295.094
geography	983.495	Hermaphroditism	
Herbal perfume plants	612.813	teratology	561.3

Hermits art alchemy chem.	540.1
Taoism	224
Hernandiaceae botany	577.47
Hernia diseases	597.344
Herniotomy surgery	598.185
Herodotus Greek literature	831.881
Heroism ethics	180.74
Herons zoology	587.974
Herpetology zoology	587.8
Herrick, Robert Eng. poet.	851.43
Hesiod Gk. epic. poet.	831.32
Hesperornithidae zoology	587.95
Hesse—	
Darmstadt Ger. geography	983.77
Nassau Ger. geography	983.78
Hetaerism marriage	313.348
Heteractinelida zoology	582.56
Heterocera zoology	585.535
Heterochrony development	561.75
Heterocoela zoology	582.51
Heterogenesis reproduction	561.623
Heteroptera zoology	585.38
Hetu vidya s'astra Buddhism	231.16
Hexacorolla zoology	582.753
Hexactinellida zoology	582.54
Hexagons geometry	517.36
Hexapoda zoology	585
Hexateuch Bible	252.21
Hexiology evolution	563.19
Hibernating animals	592.57
Hierachy, military	379.33
Hieroglyphics	401.9
Chinese	419
High	
church Anglican church	259.3
German language	409.385
normal schools	338.53
treason law	394.23
Higher	
algebra	512.6
Higher (cont.)	
education	338.7
of women	338.917
geometrical drawing	517.7
Highways transportation	632
Hildebrandslied German poet.	871.11

Hinayana		biology	561.2
sects	239.11	botany	571.1
Sutra	232.2	human anatomy	591.7
Hindbrain anatomy	597.8117	of practicular plant	
Hindi language	409.317	forms	571.17
Hindrances		Historical books Bible	252.2
aboriculture	614.5	"Historical records" of	
farming	611.9	SzeMa Ch'ien	910.911
Hindu		Historical geology	554
language	409.31	ruins	990.18
philosophy	113	remains	990.1
religion	240	Historiography	900.9
Hinduism	240	Historiology	900.9
Hindustan history	923	History	900
Hip anatomy	591.88	of special topics, see	
bone	597.7118	subject	
surgery	598.188	History, book of Ch.	
Hippias Greek philos.	121.223	classics	092
Hippocasianaceae		Hives apiculture	615.4
botany	578.24	skin diseases	598.541
Hippology zoology	588.342	Hobbes Eng. philos.	125.2
Hippuridaceae botany	578.87	Hog diseases of	599.44
Hiroshima, Japan		domestic animals	615.14
geography	982.1654	zoology	588.617
Hirudianea zoology	583.63	Hoisting machinery	
Histology		engin'g.	655.81
animals	581.2	Hojoki Japanese essays	827.41

Hokkaido, Japan	
geography	982.167
Holbach Fr. philos.	124.28
Holidays	
customs	319.71
laboring classes	354.46
school education	334.36
Holland	
geography	983.793
history	937.93
Holland, J. G. Am.	
essays	867.31
Holmes, O. W. Am.	
essays	867.36
humor	868.236
poet.	861.36
Holocephali zoology	587.43
Holomastigaceae botany	572.31
Holometabola zoology	585.5
Holothuroidea botany	572.94
Holy	
alliance European hist.	930.68
banners	253.36
communion	253.39
ghost Christian theology	251.13
land geography	982.84
history	928.4
orders church	253.94
Roman empire	937
scriptures	252
spirit Christian theology	251.13
water sacramentals	253.99
Homage feudalism	371.2
Home, John Eng. drama	852.64
Home	
customs	319.2
domestic economy	690
economics	691
education of girls	338.913
self-education	338.81
vs school	338.82
life	313.3
missions church	254.9
trade economics	351.39
women in	313.357
Homeopathy therap.	595.96
Homer Gk. epic poet.	831.31
Homicide	
abnormal psychology	155.455
crimes	315.185
criminal law	394.25
ethics	180.59
Homiletics	
sermons	253.7
theology	254.1

Hominidae zoology	589.9
Homocoela zoology	582.51
Homocopathy therap.	595.96
Homogamy genetics	563.53
Homogeneous radiation	535.25
Homologies biology	561.15
botany	571.24
zoology	581.1
Homometabola zoology	586.5
Honan, China geography	981.63
Honduras	
British	
geography	984.62
history	946.2
Central America	
geography	984.63
history	946.3
Honesty ethics	180.72
Honeymoon customs	319.22
Honolulu	
geography	985.98
history	959.8
Honor ethics	180.71
heraldry	966
military	379.39
student	333.1
Hookworm diseases	594.972
Hooping cough diseases	597.24
Hopei, China geography	981.61
Horace Latin lyric poet.	832.45
Horn wind instrument	774.8
Horology astronomy	528.5
Horoscopes astrology	157.24
Horse	
diseases veterin. med.	599.41
domestic animals	615.11
pox diseases	594.965
racing amusements	798
training domestic	
animals	615.11
zoology	588.342
Horsemanship	
amusements	798
Horsepower, locomotive	655.271
Horticulture	613
Hosea Bible	252.46
Hospice of St. Bernard	
protec. of life	593.49
Hospitality ethics	184.2
Hospitals	
and asylums arch.	717.3
institutions	316.2
medicine	593.77
Hosso Japanse	

Buddhism	239.62	tenement	718.5
Hostages intern. law	381.557	Houses	
Hostilities, see War		accounts dom. econ.	691
Hot air engines	655.41	customs	319.5
Hot springs	551.5	farm	610.67
air baths hygiene	593.14	hygiene	593.15
engines	655.41	lower legislatures	373.033
drinks hygiene	593.13	upper legislatures	373.033
houses floriculture	613.808	wash	653.7
springs geology	551.5	Housewifery	690
Hotels architecture	718.5	Housing	
Hou Fang-yu Chinese		livelihood	317.13
prose	817.715	laboring classes	354.9313
Hours		rural community	313.412
of labor pol. econ.	354.41	urban community	313.512
service teachers	336.57	Howells, W. D. Am.	
school	334.4	fiction	863.43
House		Hsia dynasty Chinese	
building engin'g.	651.3	history	911.4
domestic science	692	Hsiao Ching Ch. classics	097
drainage sanitary		Hsieh Ling-yun Chinese	
engin'g.	653.5	poet.	811.1331
fortune of	157.4	Hsin Ch'i-chi Chinese	
of commons	373.033	poet.	811.7395
plants floriculture	613.806	Hsun Tzu Chinese	
tax	369.051	philos.	111.117
Chinese	369.151	Hsun Yueh Chinese	
other nations			

philos.	111.283
Huai Nan Tzu Chinese philos.	111.23
Hua-nien-tsung Ch. Buddhism	239.53
Huan K'uan Chinese philos.	111.241
Huang Ting-chien Ch. poet.	811.154
Hugo, V. M. Fr. drama	842.76
fiction	843.76
poet.	841.76
Hui Shih Chinese philos.	111.152
Hui Tung Chinese prose	817.731
Human	
anatomy	591
body art anatomy	700.12
temperature	592.56
and mind	150.16
faculties psychology	150
figures drawing	737.3
habitations hygiene	593.15
life protec. from accidents	593.4
mind psychology	150
physiology	592
race ethnology	565.7
resorts hygiene	593.15
rights pol. science	372.1
sculpture	729.5
Humanism philosophy	107.3
Humbugs demonology	157.79
Hume Eng. philos.	125.5
Humidity soil	611.333
Humor	
literature	808.2
American	868.2
Chinese	818.2
English	858.2
Hunan, China geography	981.74
Hung Liang-chi Chinese prose	817.164
Hungarian	
language	409.235
literature	892
Hungary geography	983.795
history	937.95
Hunger and thirst physiology	592.471
Hungtze lake	981.354
Hunting industries	619
Hupeh, China geography	981.73
Hu's Chuan Chinese classics	096.4
Hurricanes meteorology	529.33

Husband and wife	
ethics	185.3
family life	313.323
law	397.51
Husbandry agriculture	610
Husbands, duties of	
ethics	183.5
Hwai Ho	981.347
Hyaenidae zoology	588.513
Hyalospongiae zoology	582.54
Hybridity eugenics	563.52
Hybridization biology	561.627
Hybrids eugenics	561.627
Hydraulic	
engineering	654
aboriculture	614.27
engines mech. engin'g.	655.3
physics	532.9
instruments engin'g.	654.18
machinery engin'g.	655.36
meters engin'g.	654.18
motors mech. engin'g.	655.3
physics	532.9
power plants engin'g.	655.31
principles of circulation	597.123
ram engineering	655.37
registers engin'g.	654.18
Hydraulics	

science	532.9
technical	654.1
Hydrocarbons chemistry	547.1
Hydrocaryareae botany	578.85
Hydrocharitaceae botany	575.37
Hydrochoeridae zoology	588.616
Hydrocorallina zoology	582.713
Hydrodynamics	
hydraulic engin'g.	654.12
physics	532.1
Hydrogen chemistry	546.11
Hydrogeology	551.93
Hydrograpic surveying	659.193
Hydrokinetics	532.5
Hydrology	552.2
Hydromechanics	532
Hydromedusae zoology	582.71
Hydropathy therap.	595.83
Hydrophobia diseases	594.961
Hydrophyllaceae botany	579.53
Hydropneustea zoology	584.66
Hydrostatics engin'g.	654.11
physics	532.3
Hydrotimetry chem. anal.	543.15
Hydrozoa zoology	582.71
Hygiene	593
industrial	354.53

labor	593.37	Hymnology	253.5
managements pregnancy	598.815	Hymphaceae botany	577.31
marine	593.34	Hyogo, Japan geography	982.1645
mental	152.3	Hyparthropoda zoology	584.1
military	593.35	Hyperbolic functions	516.42
naval	593.35	geometry	519.85
of air and ground	593.27	logarithms	510.26
animals pub. health	593.28	trigonometry	518.5
veter. med.	599.3	Hypercotyl botany	571.273
zootechny	615.08	Hyperelliptic curves	519.455
children	598.93	functions	516.43
offspring	593.19	Hyperemia diseases	597.14
pregnancy	598.815	Hyperesthesia diseases	597.8456
recreation and sleep	593.16	Hypericaceae botany	578.53
woman feminism	313.3504	Hypericinea botany	578.53
personal	593.1	Hyperoartia zoology	587.13
prison	593.36	Hyperspace modern	
or,	315.53	geometry	519.6
public	593.2	Hypertrofies skin	
rural	313.43	diseases	598.544
school education	332.3	Hypnotics drugs	597.863
public health	593.33	Hypnotism	
vocal	770.012	psychoanalysis	156.5
Hydrometry meteorology	529.45	Hypocentrum seismology	551.33
Hymenolichenes botany	573.47	Hypochondria	
Homenomycetes botany	573.32	medicine	597.8452
Hymenoptera zoology	585.58	mental diseases	155.5
Hymn-books hymnology	253.5		

Hypocotyl botany	571.274
Hypotheses logic	141.73
Hypotreta zoology	587.11
Hyracoidea zoology	588.36
Hyracotheriinea zoology	588.343
Hyrax zoology	588.36
Hysteria medicine	597.8452
mental diseases	155.252
Hysteresis magnetism	538.47
Hysterophyta botany	576.8
Hysterotomy obstetrics	598.876
Hystricidae zoology	588.617

I Ching Chinese classics	091	Icemaking	655.67
		chem. tech.	664.8
I Li Chinese classics	094.2	Ichnology palaeozoology	569.8
Ibaragi, Japan geography	982.1616	Ichthyology zoology	587.3
Ibn Gibirol medieval philos.	121.66	Ichthyoperygia reptiles	587.835
		Ichthyosauria reptiles	587.835
Ibn Rusha medieval philos.	121.65	Iconography	781.22
		biography	970.2
Ibn Sina medieval philos.	121.65	Ictopsidae zoology	588.85
		Idaho, U. S. geography	984.196
Ibn Zaddik medieval philos.	121.66	Ideal state pol. science	371.5
		Idealism philosophy	106.2
Ice		Ideation psychology	151.81
age geology	554.73	Identitical theory	103.9
erosion and deposition	551.76	Idioms Chinese language	413.3
frost geologic agents	551.92		
manufacture	655.67	Idiosyncrasy	
chem. tech.	664.8	influence of therapeu.	595.77
meteorology	529.49	Idiots asylums	316.36
Icacinaceae botany	678.21	childstudy	153.766
		schools	338.966
Icebergs physical geology	551.73	Idolatry image-worship	209.8
Iceland		Idyll poetry	801.1
geography	983.7989	Igneous rocks lithology	557.1
history	937.989	Ignominious punishment	394.517
language	409.3824	Ile de France, Fr. geography	983.473
literature	879.24		

Ilex sugar plants	612.77
Ilicineae botany	578.17
Ille et Vilaine, Fr.	
geography	983.461
Illecebraceae botany	577.17
Illegal voting suffrage	372.57
Illegitimacy marriage	313.3425
Illiteracy education	330.127
Illuminati society	313.63
Illuminating	
engineering	653.2
gas chem. tech.	665.75
industries chem. tech.	665.7
Illumination	
electric engin'g.	657.81
engineering	653.2
house lighting	692
Illusions, mental	156.12
Image worship idolatry	209.8
Imaginary	
books, bibliography of	018.2
geometry	519.8
quantities algebra	512.1
Imagination	
in art	700.1
science	500.1
psychology	151.7
Imayo-uta Japanese	
ballads	821.56
Immaculate conception	
of Christ	251.21
Mary	251.294
Immanes zoology	587.945
Immersionists sects	259.6
Immigration	377.6
Immoral	
art ethics	187.9
literature ethics	187.9
Immortality	
Christian theology	251.79
natural theology	201.79
of animals	581.698
Immortals Taoism	221.4
Immunity bacteriology	566.965
Immunigation	
bacteriology	566.965
Impact	
hydraulics	532.55
mechanics	531.697
Imperative law	390.005
Imperialism pol. science	371.035
Implements, agricultural	610.6
Imponderable remedies	595.8
Importance	

of labor pol. econ	354.018	public finance	369.04
Imports, duty on	369.0671	Chinese	369.14
Chinese	369.1671	student	311.48
other nations		tax finance	369.055
Impostors humbugs	157.79	Chinese	369.155
Impotence diseases	597.645	Imcomplete	
Impregnation		coalescence deform.	598.172
physiology	598.81	development deform.	598.171
zoology	581.623	Incontinence ethics	180.69
Imprisonment		Incorporating languages	403
punishment	394.513	Incrustation architec.	
Impulse		decoration	712.6
mechanics	531.697	Incunabula bood rarities	009.1
of water hydraulics	532.55	Incurable diseases	595.4
Inarticulata zoology	583.94	Indemnity	369.147
Inaugurations		Independence	
ceremonies	373.011	Am. U. S. history	944.83
or,	319.12	state intern. law	381.21
Incandescent lighting	651.8145	Indeterminism cosmology	134.23
Incantations occult		Index	
sciences	157.72	making	036
Incarnation Christology	251.21	or,	027.9
Incised wounds surgery	598.164	numbers statistics	341.7
Inclined		rerums	027.9
plane	531.95	Indexes, see subject	
railways	651.82	indexed	
Income		India	

administration	373.931
antiquities	999.31
architecture	710.931
botany	571.9931
British history	923
Farther history	924
finance	369.931
geography	982.3
geology	550.23
history	923
language	493.1
laws	390.2
literature	893
philosophy	113
zoology	581.9931

Indian
archipelago geography	982.49
Buddhism sects	239.1
corn agriculture	612.15
philosophers	113
religions	240
territory, U. S. geography	984.173

Indiana, U. S. geography	984.176

Indians
American	943
education of	338.98
ethnography	565.883
language	409.8
literature	898

Indies, East
Dutch geography	982.49
history	924.9
Indigestion medicine	597.343
Indigo chem. tech.	667.2
Indium inorganic chem.	546.275

Individual
enterprise pol. econ.	356.21
ethics	182
instruction education	337.5
psychology	153.8
rights pol. science	372.1
soul, origin of	135.7

Individualism pol.
science	371.067

Individuals
and the state	371.067

Indo—
China geography	982.41
history	924.1
Chinese languages	409.1
European languages	409.3
Indoor amusement	338.632
Indoors advertising	629.5
Indre, France geography	983.483
et Loire, France geography	983.482

Induction	
electricity	537.34
electromagnetic	538.85
logic	143
magnetic	538.4
of labor obstetrics	598.878
reasoning psychology	151.86
Inductive	
logic	143
reasoning	151.86
science	500
Industrial	
arbitration	354.86
arts	600
classes pol. econ.	354
social groups	313.74
diseases, see Occupations	
economy	350
electrochemistry	662
geography	980.154
history	600.9
hygiene	354.53
insurance	368
policy	351.4
or,	641
public health	593.37
sanitation	653.4
securities	366.7
statistics	354.034
tribunals	354.16
Industries	
chem. tech.	660
manufacture	670
productive arts	600
Inertia mechanics	531.692
Infancy, psychology of	153.7
Infant	
baptism	253.91
cholera	594.935
Infant (cont.)	
education	338.11
therapeutics	595.75
Infanticide	
customs	319.21
ethics	183.5
law	394.25
social pathology	315.185
Infantalism pediatrics	598.9
Infantry army	379.55
Infants	
diseases of	598.94
feeding of	598.93
nutrition of	598.93
stillbirth obstetrics	598.828
Infection	
etiology	594.27

public health	593.23
Infectious diseases	
pathology	594.9
public health	593.23
special	593.24
Infinite metaphysics	134.3
Infinitesimal	
analysis	515.1
calculus	515.1
functions	516.6
geometry	519.7
in space of	
n-dimensions	519.75
Inflammable rocks	
lithology	557.57
Inflammation	
pathology	594.81
surgery	598.142
Inflammatory	
affec. of skin	598.541
Inflectional languages	403
Influence	
personal, of teachers	336.1
Influenza diseases	597.24
Information bureaus	039.6
Infractions	
of neutrality intern. law	381.66
Infusoria zoology	582.4

Inheritance	
evolution	563.3
law	397.6
international	381.846
laws of ancestrial	563.36
Inheritance (cont.)	
of sex embryology	561.663
evolution	563.3
soul metaphysics	135.72
tax	369.051
Chinese	369.151
other nations	
see also Heredity	
Inherited	
diseases hygiene	593.193
pathology	594.21
mental disability	
hygiene	593.192
Initiative, right of	
legislative	373.0327
pol. science	372.18
Sunyatsenism	001.133
Injections	
collectors manuals	567.3
intra-uterin obstetrics	598.879
medicine	595.72
therapeutics	595.815
Injil Moslem scriptures	272.5

Injuries			Inner Mongolia China	
agriculture	611.9		geography	981.94
of new-born infants	598.948		Inns	
surgery	598.16		architecture	718.5
torts	394.4		domestic science	690
Injurious			Inorganic	
animals			chemicals	661.1
agriculture	611.98		chemistry	546
zoology	581.8		of soil	611.31
insects agriculture	611.98		drugs	596.15
plants			liquids physical chem.	541.23
agriculture	611.97		poisons toxicology	593.91
botany	571.8		substances, analysis of	543.6
Ink			Insane	
manufacture	667.73		asylums architecture	717.3
writing	010.63		criminology	315.121
Inland			dreams of	156.3355
canals transportation	634.6		education	338.967
navigation			hospitals	316.36
engin'g.	654.7		Insanity	
transportation	634.6		law	394.65
water			nervous diseases	597.84
biology	561.905		psychology	155.2
botany	571.905		Inscriptions	
zoology	581.905		literature	808.73
Inlay decoration	766.7		Chinese	818.73
Innate ideas	151.352		on tablets calligraphy	739.12
reasons	151.9		Insecta	

entomology	585	Institutions		
parasitica pathology	594.974	Christian	256	
Insecticides agriculture	611.993	educational	330	
Insectivarae botany	577.6	sociology	313.6	
Insectivora zoology	588.8	see special topics		
Insects		Instructions		
injurious agriculture	611.98	education	330	
library science	023.9	family ethics	188.3	
zoology	581.9	for children ethics	188.4	
zoology	585	women ethics	188.5	
Insessores birds	587.976	young people ethics	188.6	
Insignia		methods	337	
college	334.8	Instrumental		
heraldry	968	calculation mathematics	510.76	
military	379.38	ensemble music	779	
Inspection of		errors prac. astronomy	522.88	
buildings	593.46	music	770	
explosions	593.44	Instruments		
factories, etc.	354.58	astronomic	522	
Inspection of (cont.)		chronologic	528.59	
food, etc. pub. health	593.22	drawing	731.7	
schools	331.7	engineering	650.8	
Inspiration		for determining	534.511	
psychology of	151.7	measuring	565.31	
Instinct		telegraphing	657.833	
psychology	151.37	mathematical	510.76	
zoology	581.702	musical	770	
Instinctive knowledge	151.37	optical	535.8	

surgical	598.1901
witchcraft	157.74
for other purposes, see subject	
Insular	
faunas zoology	581.906
floras botany	571.906
Insulators elec. engin'g.	657.67
Insurance	368
law	398.6
Integral	
calculus	515.3
Integral (cont.)	
equations	515.75
of differential	515.73
geometry	519.4
Intellectual	
defect abnor. psychology	155.47
development	
education	330.1
of child	153.72
life self education	338.81
philosophy	150
Intellectualism	
philosophy	104.4
Intensification	
photography	755.5
Intensity meters elec.	
engin'g.	657.15
Intensive farming	610.314
Interaction mind and	
body	150.162
Interbrain anatomy	597.8114
Intercollegiate	
contests athletic	333.35
literary	333.34
Intercommunication	630
Intercourse of	
belligerents	381.558
Interest	
and usury law	397.4
calculation of arithmetic	511.37
finance	362.6
Interference acoustics	534.47
optics	535.34
thermics	536.45
waves	534.61
Interior	
decoration	763
department	
administration	373.051
Chinese	373.151
of earth geology	551.11
wiring elec. engin'g.	657.655
Interlibrary loans	023.68
Interlocution customs	319.35
Interludes drama	802.97

Intermarriages		
law		397.51
international		381.845
of families hygiene		593.194
races ethics		183.1
sociology		313.34
Intermediate		
cuttings silviculture		614.43
Intermediate (cont.)		
education		338.3
elec. telegraphy		657.8333
Interment customs		319.24
public health		593.26
Intermitent fever		
pathology		594.928
Internal		
affairs administration		373.051
combustion engines		655.43
ear anatomy		598.419
diseases		598.449
physiology		598.429
friction		
hydraulics		532.17
pneumatics		533.17
heat geology		551.13
medicine		597
relations pol. science		371.06
respiration physiology		597.227
secretion comp.		
physiology		581.447
International		
academic union		383.6
arbitration		382.1
association, the		318.7
bureau		383.7
coinage		361.28
commissions diplomacy		386.38
community		380
congresses		380.6
on special topics, see subject		
courtesy		381.28
delegation		386.5
disputes		382.5
procedure in		382
equality		381.23
ethics		185.7
exchange		365
extradition		381.88
geography		980.178
labor organization		383.8
law		381
	or,	399.6
private		381.8
library loans		023.68
police		382.7

politics	380	psychoanalysis	156.338
postal service	636.8	law	390.07
problems	388	legislation	373.0321
International (cont.)		Interschool	
railways	633.19	contests athletic	333.35
relations	385	literary	333.54
research council	383.6	Intersecting lines	
rivers	381.35	geometry	517.32
servitude	381.39	Intervals sound	634.73
standard money system	361.28	Intervention intern. law	382.1
technical organizations	383.4	Intestines	
trade	351.31	anatomy	597.314
Y. M. C. A.	256.314	diseases	597.344
Internationalism		physiology	597.324
international politics	380	Intimidation	
political science	371.036	electoral corruption	372.57
socialism	318.9	labor strikes	354.84
Interoceanic canals		Intoxicants, see Alcohol;	
engineering	654.7	Liquors; Stimulants	
international law	381.37	Intra-uterin injections	598.879
Interpolation		Intrenchments mil.	
methods		engin'g.	659.31
calculus	515.5	Intuition psychology	151.9
statistics	341.17	Intuitionalism philosophy	104.3
spherical astronomy	522.73	philos. of life	173.5
Interpretation		Inundations	
musical	770.029	agriculture	611.916
of dreams divination	157.17		

meteorology	529.45
protection engin'g.	654.67
relief of	316.41
Invariants algebra	512.22
Invation intern. law	381.551
Inventions patents	
industrial	605.1
technology	645.1
Inverse functions	516.4
probabilities	512.91
Inversion geometry	519.05
of uterus	598.847
sexual	155.4585
Invertebrates	
paleonzoology	569.7
zoology	582
Investments	367
Invisible	
stars	523.88
world	
Christianity	251.6
other religions	
Involuntary movement	
psych.	151.351
Involution	
arithmetic	511.5
modern geometry	519.06
Iodin inorganic chem.	546.135
Ionia islands, Greece	
geography	983.19
Ionic radiation electricity	537.375
school Gk. philos.	121.11
Ionization electricity	537.372
Ions electricity	537.372
Ipomaea batatas roots	
crops	612.483
Iranic language	409.32
Ireland	
geography	983.58
history	935.93
Iridaceae botany	575.88
Iridium inorganic chem.	546.75
Iris eye diseases	598.342
Irish	
discovery of America	941.8155
language	409.373
literature	859.3
Iron	
age prehistoric arch.	990.9
Iron (cont.)	
bridges engineering	651.5018
inorganic chemistry	546.35
manufacture	671.1
materia medica	596.152
metallurgy	669.92

mineralogy	558.13	Islam Mohammedanism	270
mining	658.8	Islands	
ores mineralogy	558.13	physical geography	552.3
ships	659.116	for special islands,	
strength of meterials	650.48	see name	
structures engineering work	651.118	Isle de France	
		geography	983.473
manufacture	671.1	Isocrates Greek oratory	831.844
mechanic trades	682	Isoetales botany	573.8
ornamental	768	Isoeteae botany	573.8
structural engin'g.	651.18	Isogonic lines	
Irrigation		magnetism	538.73
agriculture	611.6	Isolation	
engineering	654.8	eugenics	563.53
sewage	653.3	in contag. diseases	593.2351
Irritability		Isolating languages	403
in plants botany	571.48	Isomerism chemistry	541.07
Irritation, spinal		Isometric projections	
diseases	597.8446	geometry	519.34
Irving Washington Am.		Isopleura zoology	583.51
essays	867.23	Isopoda zoology	584.83
fiction	863.23	Issues therapeutics	595.813
Isaiah Bible	252.41	Isthmus rhombencephali	
Ise monogatari Jap.		anatomy	597.8116
fiction	823.32	Itacolumite lithology	557.45
Isere, France geography	983.498	Italian	
Ishikawa, Japan		art	703.2
geography	982.1633		

discovery of America	941.8152	fine arts	703.2
language	433	flag	371.0832
literature	833	foreign relations	385.32
painting	730.32	genealogy	977.932
philosophy	122	geography	983.2
republics history	932.867	geology	550.32
sculpture	720.32	government	373.32
Italic school Gk. philos.	121.13	publications	373.3205
Italy		heraldry	969.32
administration	373.32	history	932
antiquities	993.2	law	390.5
architecture	710.32	learned institutions and	
archives	932.12	societies	063.2
army	379.1325	libraries	020.932
biography	973.2	local government	373.328
botany	571.932	maps	980.332
calligraphy	739.32	or,	983.22
census	345.32	Italy (cont.)	
college	338.79321	militia	379.832
constitutions	391.32	music	770.32
defenses	379.132	national bibliography	013.32
diplomatic and consular		navy	379.1326
service	386.9326	paleography	432.9
diretories	038.32	or,	990.832
drawing	730.31	philology	432
economic conditions	350.932	philosophers	122
education	330.932	population	349.32
finance	369.32	revenue	369.324

schools, public	338.0132	Itch parasitic diseases	594.975
seal	371.0832	Ithaca, Greece geography	983.16
statistics	345.32	Ivory	
vital	349.327	carving	726
tariff	369.326	glyptic ar	767
taxation	369.325	painting	735.3
travel	980.732	Iwate, Japan geography	982.1625
or,	983.24	Izayoi nikki Japanese	
treaties	387.932	prose	827.44
universities	338.79321	Izumi-shikibu nikki Jap.	
yearbooks	037.32	prose	827.35
zoology	581.932		

Jackass dom. animals	615.18
Jacobins monastic orders	259.0912
Jacotot's system of education	337.37
Jade	
glyptic arts	767
mineralogy	558.188
Jail fever pathology	594.926
Jails	
architecture	717.4
prisons	315.5
Jaimism Hindu sect	249.8
Jamaica	
geography	984.72
history	947.2
James, St epistle	252.791
James Am. philos.	126.4
James, acts of apocrypha	252.993
book of apocrypha	252.991
Japan	
administration	373.2
antiquities	992
architecture	710.2
archives	921.12
army	379.125
biography	972.1
botany	571.92
Buddhism	239.6
calligraphy	739.2
census	345.2
clover	612.384
colleges	338.7921
constitutions	391.2
defenses	379.12
diplomatic and consular service	386.926
directories	038.2
economic conditions	350.921
education	330.921
encyclopedia	032.1
fauna	581.92
finance	369.2
fine arts	702
flag	371.0821
foreign relations	385.2
genealogy	977.92
geography	982.1
geology	550.21
government	373.2
publications	373.205
Japan (cont.)	
heraldry	969.2
history	921
learned institutions and societies	062
libraries	020.921

local government	373.28
militia	379.82
music	770.2
national bibliography	013.2
navy	379.126
plum	613.717
police	315.392
population	349.2
revenue	369.24
schools, public	338.012
seal	371.0821
statistics	345.2
vital	349.27
theatre	780.2
travel	980.721
or,	982.14
treaties	387.92
universities	338.7921
yearbooks	037.21
zoology	581.92
Japanese	
art	702
language	420
literature	820
painting	730.2
philosophy	112
sculpture	720.2
Jasher, book of apocrypha	252.982

Jasmin perfume plants	612.811
Jaundice pediatrics	598.944
Java geography	985.923
Jealousy ethics	180.67
Jehol, China geography	981.941
Jehovah	
Christianity	251.11
Judaism	261.1
Jelly fish zoology	582.73
Jeremiah Bible	252.42
Jerusalem	
artichoke	612.485
city	
geography	982.84
history	928.4
Jesuits	
religious orders	259.0915
tea agric.	612.77
Jesus Christology	251.2
Jetties engineering	654.62
Jewelry	
customs	319.48
glyptic arts	767
manufacture	671.5
toilet	693.3
Jewish	
architecture	715.6

calendar	528.65
languages	409.55
law	390.4
laws Mosaic	262
literature	895.84
philosophy	118.5
or,	121.66
religion	260
tradition scripture	262.7
Jews	
apologetics against	251.91
disabilities of	260
ethnology	565.9284
geography	982.84
history	928.4
Jitsurckumono Japanese	
fiction	823.66
Job Bible	252.31
Joel Bible	252.47
John, St. Bible	252.64
1　epistle	252.794
2　epistle	252.795
3　epistle	252.796
Johnson, Samuel Eng.	
essays	857.63
Joinery structural	
engin'g.	651.15
Joints	
anatomy	597.713
geology	553.4
Jo-jitsu Japanese	
Buddhism	239.61
Jonah Bible	252.492
Jonson, Ben Eng. drama	852.34
Joshua Bible	252.22
Joubert, Joseph Fr.	
essays	847.62
Journalism	040
Journeys	
around the world	980.709
Juatiputra Hinduism	249.8
Jubilees, book of	
apocrypha	252.982
Judaism	260
Jude Bible	252.797
Judge	
made law	390.023
Judges	
book of Bible	252.23
procedure law	395.06
Judgement	
Christology	251.27
eschatology	201.723
Christianity	251.74
psychology	151.85

trial practice	395.03	Julianiales botany	576.6
Judia		Juncaceae botany	575.81
geography	982.84	Juncaginaceae botany	575.35
history	928.4	Jungermanniales botany	573.6
Judicial		Junior high school	338.31
astrology	157.2	Jupiter	
chemistry		astronomy	523.45
law	399.7	worship	209.21
medical	593.8	Jura, France geography	983.477
control		Jurassic period geology	554.63
administration	373.04	Jurisdiction	
Chinese	373.14	international law	381.25
other nations		over work	354.16
organization, law of	396	procedure law	395.09
Judith apocrypha	252.92	suffrage	372.552
Juglandaceae botany	576.51	Jurisprudence	399.7
Juglandales botany	576.5	medical	593.8
Juglans pomiculture	613.761	Jurists, see Lawyers	
Jugoslavia		Jury procedure law	395.04
geography	983.953	Justice	
history	939.53	ethics	180.72
Juice		pol. science	372.14
fruit chem. tech.	664.57	Justification Christian	
gastric physiology	597.322	theol.	251.47
intestine physiology	597.324	Jute	
pancreatic physiology	597.326	agriculture	612.54
Jujube pomiculture	613.778	manufacture	675.1
Julianiaceae botany	576.61		

Juvenal Latin literature	832.827	criminals		313.364
Juvenile			or,	394.2
books	027.55	literature		805
see also subject		offender		315.71
courts	315.71	reformatories		315.71
criminal law	394.61			

Kabala Jewish philos.	118.5	Kansu, China geography	981.66
Kafir agriculture	612.17	Kant German philos.	127.2
Kagawa, Japan geography	982.1656	Kanto, Japan geography	982.161
Kagero nikki Jap. essays	827.34	Karfuto, Japan geography	982.1679
Kagoshima, Japan geography	982.1668	Karaites Jewish sects	269.1
Kagura-uta Jap. ballads	821.51	Karenko, Japan geography	982.177
Kaiodoki Japanese essays	827.45	Karma sansara Hinduism	241.4
Kairin drugs	597.466	Karmondriyas Hinduism	241.67
Kale horticulture	613.17	Kartum, see Khartum	
Kaleidoscope optics	535.8	Kashmir, India geography	982.38
Kalendar	528.6	Kastamuni, Turkey geography	982.661
Kalifs Moslem sects	279.1		
Kamadhata Buddhist trailokya	231.81	Kchanti Buddhist paranuta	231.73
Kan Pao Chinese fiction	813.37	Keats, John Eng. poet.	851.78
Kanagawa, Japan geography	982.1613	Keepsakes	037.8
Kana-zoshi Jap. fiction	823.61	Keewatin, Canada geography	984.27
K'ang Yu-wei Chinese prose	817.793	Kegon Japanese Buddhism	239.63
Kangaroo zoology	588.23	Keltic languages	409.37
Kannedy, J. P. Am. fiction	863.32	Kent, England geography	983.562
Kansas, U. S. geography	984.181	Kentucky, U. S.	

geography	984.175
Kepler's problem astron.	521.37
Keramics	
art	764
chem. tech.	666.1
Kerosene	
chem. tech.	665.5
heating chemistry	542.4
Ketones chemistry	547.6
Keyboard instruments	776
Khitan Chinese history	915.5
Khmer language	409.173
Khodavendigar, Turkey	
geog.	982.661
Kuddakagames Sutra	232.25
Kiang Chen-yin Chinese	
prose	817.725
Kiang Kuei Chinese	
poet.	811.7397
Kiangsi, China	
geography	981.73
Kiangsu, China	
geography	981.77
Kidneys	
anatomy	597.611
diseases	597.641
Kindergarten education	338.13
Kindness ethics	180.63
Kinematic geometry	519.78
Kinematics	
machinery	655.11
physics	531.1
Kinetic theory of gases	533.51
matter	530.2
Kinetics physics	533.5
Kinetics of a particle	531.69
Kinetogenesis biology	564.6
King vulture zoology	587.9791
Kingdom of	
God Christian theology	251.15
Wei Chinese history	912.5
or,	913.1
Wu Chinese history	912.7
Kings	
absolute monarchy	371.041
book of, Bible	252.25
constitutional monarchy	371.045
divine right pol. sci.	371.011
evil diseases	594.995
Kingship pol. science	371.041
Kingsley, Charles Eng.	
fiction	853.85
Kinki, Japan geography	982.164
Kinship	

and state origin	371.016
customs	319.26
ethnogenic ass'ns	313.38
genealogy	977.5
pchack khanate Ch.	
history	915.95
Kirin, China geography	981.913
Kissing customs	319.2
Kitchen	
Kidomestic science	692
gardening	613.1
Kitchens architecture	718.9
Kite flying	
aeronautics	659.49
meteorology	529.3
sports	799
Kites aeronautics	659.49
Kleptomania mental	
diseases	155.452
Klepstock, F. G. German	
poet.	871.62
Knee anatomy	591.88
Kneipp cure	
therapeutics	595.83
Knightage heraldry	968.9
Knighthood	
orders heraldry	968.9

Know nothing party,	
U. S.	375.65
Knowledge, theory of	131
Kodaks photography	375.7
Ko Hung Chinese	
fiction	813.32
philos.	111.33
Kochi, Japan geography	982.1659
Koheleth Bible	252.34
Kojiki Shintoism	291.21
Kokkeibon Japanese	
fiction	823.69
Kola agriculture	612.76
Kongo	
Belgian geography	985.67
Free State	
geography	985.65
history	956.5
French geography	985.66
Konieh, Turkey	
geography	982.661
Konjaku monogatari Jap.	
fiction	823.38
Koran Moslem scripture	272.7
Kordofan, Egypt	
geography	985.176
Korea	

Buddhism	239.69
geography	982.2
history	922
language	429
literature	829
Kosmos univ. language	405
Krishna Hinduism	241.73
Krohnia zoology	583.98
Krypton inorganic chem.	546.185
Ku Klux Klan pol. ass'ns	313.62
Ku-sha Japanese Buddhism	239.62
Ku Yen-wu Chinese prose	817.713
Kuan Han-ching Chinese drama	812.31
Kuan Tzu Chinese philos.	111.171
Kuei Ku Tzu Chinese philos.	111.195
Kuei Yu-kuang Chinese prose	817.65
KuLiang Chuan Ch. classics	096.3
Kumamoto, Japan geography	982.1665
K'ung Kuang-sen Chinese prose	817.767
KungSun Lung Chinese philos.	111.153
Kung Tien-t'ing Chinese drama	812.43
K'ung Ts'ung Tzu Ch. philos.	111.198
Kung Tzu-chen Chinese prose	817.781
KungYang Chuan Ch. classics	096.2
K'ung's commentary Ch. classics	092.2
Kuo Hsien Chinese fiction	813.27
Kuo P'u Chinese fiction	813.35
Kurdish language	409.327
Kurdistan, Turkey geography	982.667
Kusa-zoshi Japanese fiction	823.64
Kwangsi, China geography	981.85
Kwangtung, China geography	981.83
Kweichow, China	

geography	981.87	geography	982.1669
Kyoto, Japan geography	982.1641	Kyushu, Japan	
Kyukyu, Japan		geography	982.166

Labels library supplies	024.8
Labia majora anatomy	598.716
minora anatomy	598.716
Labiatae botany	579.57
Labiche, E. M. Fr. drama	842.81

Labor
and laborers	354
machinery	354.019
the state	354.91
agencies soci. welfare	316.7
apprentice	354.252
cheap foren	354.256
children	354.22
compulsory	354.259
conduct of normal	
obstetrics	598.837
contracts	354.11
convict	354.251
dignity of	354.018
education	354.933
or,	338.94
female	354.23
festivals	354.467
freedom of	354.011
hygiene	593.37
in politics	354.913
induction of obstetrics	598.878
insurance	354.937
land pol. econ.	353.6
laws	354.911
or,	399.3
maintenance	354.135
mechanism of obstetrics	598.831
movement	354.601
obstetrics	598.83
occupations	381.825
of children	354.22
party English	375.58
U. S.	375.68
other nations	
pathology of obstetrics	598.84
pauper	354.256
political economy	354
skill	354.26
slave	354.254
social condition of	354.93
statistics	354.034
supply econ.	354.113
sweating	354.257

Labor(cont.)
training	354.56
turnover	354.136
unions	354.63
unskilled	354.26
vacations	354.467
women	354.23

Laboratories		art needle work	765.3
architecture	717.2	handcrafts	685
biological	560.7	Lacerated wounds surg.	598.164
chemic	542.1	Laceration	
method of instruction	337.13	of genital tract obstetrics	598.845
defectives	354.258	Lacertilia reptils	587.853
psychology	150.72	Laconia, Greece	
savers	027.2	geography	983.17
school building	332.92	Lacquer work	
equipment	332.97	chem. technology	667.75
state adulterations	593.21	decoration and ornament	766.5
Laboratory		handcrafts	683
method of instruction	337.13	painting	734.5
technic chemistry	542	remains archaeology	990.153
Laborers		Chinese	991.53
cottages architecture	718.78	writing	010.61
domestic	691.3	Law (cont.)	
occupation hygiene	593.37	codification of	390.029
political econ.	354	international	381.029
Laboring		intern. private	381.802
classes education of	354.933	pol. sci.	373.0324
or,	338.94	college	338.639
pol. econ.	354	commercial	398
sociology	313.88	international	381.85
Labrador, Canada		consanguinity	397.5
geography	984.28	international	381.845
Labyrinthodontia zoology	587.63	constitution of five	
Lacemaking		powers	391.1

constitutional	391
Chinese	391.1
Japanese	391.2
other nations	
continental	390.5
corporation	398.2
criminal	394
international	381.88
special	394.6
divine Christianity	251.16
ecclesiastical	399.2
or,	255.4
education of	390.017
eight hour pol. econ.	354.41
ethics of	390.016
extraterritorial authority	
of	381.8
family	397.5
international	381.845
first thermics	536.61
inheritance and	
succession	397.6
international	381.846
insurance	398.6
international	381
or,	399.6
private	381.8
interpretation of	390.07

or,	373.0321
the iron, of wages	354.315
judge-made	390.023
labor	399.3
or,	354.911
making	373.032
maritime	398.7
international	381.7
martial	399.4
or,	372.41
military and naval	399.5
or,	379.31
Law (cont.)	
moral ethics	180
national	391
navigation	381.72
obligation	397.3
international	381.843
of acceleration biology	561.73
belligerency	381.54
colonization	381.93
decay biology	561.79
diminishing	
productivity	353.7
utility	352.45
judicial organization	396
nature metaphysics	134
science	501

neutrality	381.6
similars therapeutics	595.74
slavery	317.45
universal gravitation & motion	521.12
war	381.5
parliamentary	392
or,	373.031
patent	397.23
penal	394
periodic chemistry	541.09
police	315.31
procedure	395
in intern. private	381.87
promulgation of	390.07
property	397.2
international	381.842
psychology of	390.015
second thermics	536.62
social	311.9
sources of	390.02
international	381.02
intern. private	381.802
spirit of the	390.01
systems of	
Chinese	390.1
English	390.8
German	390.6
Indian	390.2
Jewish	390.4
Moslem	390.3
Roman	390.5
Slavic	390.7
ten hour pol. econ.	354.41
uniformity of	373.0322
Lantern	
slide making	758.8
shows sociology	319.73
Lanthanum chemistry	546.256
Lao Tzu Chinese philos.	111.121
Laos, Asia	
geography	982.46
history	924.6
Laotian languages	409.122
Lapidary work	
minerology	558.181
Lapis-lazuli minerology	558.186
Laplace's function	516.83
Lapland	
geography	983.92
history	939.2
Lappish	
language	409.232
literature	892
Laprade, P. M. V. R. de	
Fr. poet.	841.81

Lardizabalaceae botany	577.37
Large	
farm agric.	610.312
intestine anatomy	597.314
physiology	597.327
Laryngology	598.495
Laryngoscope	598.495
Laryngoscopy	598.495
Larynx	
acoustics	534.9
anatomy	598.41
diseases of	598.44
physiology	598.42
Last supper Christology	251.295
words Christology	251.2955
Latent heat of fusion	536.713
Later	
Chin Chinese hist.	914.6
Chou Chinese hist.	914.8
Han Chinese hist.	914.7
Hanoverian Eng. hist.	935.88
hist. of Scotland	935.918
Liang Chinese hist.	914.4
Tang Chinese hist.	914.5
Latin	
America geography	984.5
history	945
antiquities	993.2
biography	972.32
Latin (cont.)	
church	259.1
classics	832
drama	832.2
epic poetry	832.3
letters	832.81
inscriptions	432.9
language	430
families	409.343
literature	832
lyric poetry	832.4
mythology	209.93
oratory	832.84
prose	832.7
satire and humor	832.82
Latitude	
celestial	522.76
finding	525.4
geocentric	521.26
heliocentric	521.25
variations of	521.28
Latium, Italy geography	983.26
Lattice bridges engin'g.	651.52
Latvia	
geography	983.97
history	939.73
Laughter	

emotions	151.2	life	593.46
hysteria abnor. psy.	155.252	conflict of	381.8
diseases	597.8452	library lib. econ.	022.2
Laundry work	686	medical license	593.72
Lauraceae botany	577.45	practice	593.73
Lavas lithology	557.21	of ancestral inheritance	563.36
Lavender perfume plants	612.813	chemical change	541.061
Law		combination	541.01
abrogation of	390.07	equilibrium and	
administrative	393	motion	521.11
Chinese	393.1	language, natural	401.4
other nations		magnetic disturbances	538.752
application of foren	381.8	motion physics	531.21
aviation	381.95	nature, general	134
bill	398.5	planets, distributive	523.21
canon	399.2	solubility chem.	541.41
or,	255.4	variation evolution	563.66
case	390.023	physical physics	530.5
church	399.2	uniform legislation	373.0321
or,	255.4	Lawyers	395.07
civil	397	Layamon Eng. poet.	851.15
international	381.84	Laymen Christianity	255.58
Laws		Lazarettos cont. diseases	593.2351
aeronautics	381.57	Le Sage, A. R. Fr. fic.	843.51
anatomy and vivisection	593.71	Lead	
and regulations		chemistry	546.24
see distinctive name		drugs	596.154
building protection of		metallurgy	669.94

mineralogy	558.144	Legal		
ores	558.144	act administration	393.13
pencil drawing	733.5	civil law	397.15
Leadership soclology	312.63	capacity of persons law	397.12
Leaf botany	571.275	chemistry	399.7
Leafy shoot botany	571.272	or,	593.8
League of nations	383	medicine jurisprudence	399.7
Learned societies	060	or,	593.8
Learning psychology	151.65	microscopy	566.7
Leases territory	381.3195	person	397.12
Least square, method of		status of woman	313.354
computing orbits	521.36	tender paper money	361.77
probabilities	512.93	Legends folk literature	804.2
Leather industries	673	mythology	209.9
Leaves edible	613.16	see also distinctive name	
Lectures methods of instruction	337.12	Legendre's function calculus	516.83
on special topic, see subject		Legislation	373.032
		see also qualifying term	
Lecythidaceae botany	578.76	Legislative	
Leechee pomiculture	613.766	constitution of five	
Leek olericulture	613.13	powers	001.161
Leeward islands		political science	373.03
geography	984.77	Legislatures pol. science	373.033
history	947.7	Legitimacy family law	397.52
Left heart anatomy	597.112	Legitimation pol. science	371.0495
Leg anatomy	591.88	Legs, artificial surgery	598.188

Legumes forage crops	612.3	Letters literature	808.1
Leguminosae botany	577.79	see also special subject	
Leibnitz German philos.	127.1	Lettic languages	409.397
Leicester, England		Lettish languages	409.395
geography	983.565	Leucaena forage crops	612.388
Leinster, Ireland		Leucippus Greek philos.	121.171
geography	983.58	Leucocytes physiology	597.1212
Leipzig, German		Leucocytosis animal	
geography	983.77	diseases	566.966
Leitneriaceae botany	576.47	Leucorrhea gynecology	598.7473
Lemnaceae botany	575.55	Levees hydraulic eng.	654.62
Lemons pomiculture	613.737	Lever	
Lemond-water chem.		application obstetrics	598.871
tech.	664.66	mechanics	531.91
Lemuridae zoology	589.35	Leviticus Bible	252.213
Lemuroidea zoology	589.3	Lewis, M. G. Eng. fic.	853.71
Lens eye diseases	598.344	Lexicography,	
Lenses optics	535.8	comparative	401.3
Lentibulariaceae botany	579.65	Chinese language	413
Leon, Spain geography	983.36	Lexicons see Language	
Leopards zoology	588.511	on special topics, see	
Lepidoptera zoology	585.53	subject	
Lepidosauria zoology	587.85	Li Chi Chinese classics	094.3
Leprosy diseases	594.997	Li Ching Chinese	
Leptocardii zoology	586.4	classics	094
Leptostraca zoology	584.85	Li Ling Chinese poet.	811.12
Lespedeza forage crops	612.384	Li Meng-yang Chinese	

essays	817.64
poet.	811.164
Li O Chinese poet.	811.175
Li Po Chinese poet.	811.143
Li Shang-yin Chinese poet.	811.1483
Li Shih Chinese prose	817.1
Li Tsun-hsu Chinese poet.	811.714
Liability	
insurance pol. eco.	354.35
to military service	379.34
Liang dynasty Chinese hist.	913.73
Liao dynasty Chinese history	915.4
Liaoning, China	
geography	981.911
Lias geology	554.65
Liberia	
geography	985.55
history	955.5
Liberating	
creatures	223.5
Libertarianism metaphys.	134.23
Liberty	
civil law	397.12
pol. science	372.13
metaphysics	134.23
of press journalism	040.13
pol. science	372.138
will psychology	151.41
personal law	397.12
pol. science	372.13
salvation	251.49
Libia	
geography	985.46
history	954.6
Librarian qualifications	022.5
Libraries	
architecture	717.28
asylum	025.78
children's	025.72
club	025.6
college	025.21
county	025.36
defective's	025.78
district	025.35
family	025.1
municipal	025.34
national	025.31
people's	025.71
popular	025.71
prison	025.76
private	025.1

proprietary	025.5	science	020
provincial	025.33	war service	025.75
public	025.3	Librations moon	523.33
rural	025.36	Librettos opera	773
school	025.2	Lice animal parasites	594.974
society	025.6	entomology	585.1
subscription	025.5	pests	611.94
traveling	025.4	Liceaceae botany	572.27
women's	025.73	License	
workmen's	025.74	of dentists	593.72
university	025.21	pharmacists	593.72
Library		physicians	593.72
administration	022	teachers	336.25
associations	020.6	Licensing systems	
bookkeeping	022.4	economics	351.35
building	024	Lichens botany	573.4
catalogs	012	Lieh Tzu Chinese	
Library (cont.)		philos.	111.125
committees	022.3	Life	
economy	020	and death biology	562.81
exhibitions	020.7	animal painless	
extension	022.7	extinction	593.287
finance	022.4	army	379.39
legislation	022.2	biology	562
management	022	boats protection of life	593.487
morals	020.18	shipbuilding	659.13
rules and regulations	022.6	child	313.362
school	028	city	313.5

conditions of biology	562.83	social	313.353
contingencies math.	512.97	tables life insurance	368.3
elixis of archemy	540.1	theories of	
Taoism	224	biology	562.3
ethics	180.5	physiology	592.13
family	313.3	**Lifting**	
future Christian theology	251.79	bridge engineering	651.575
natural theology	201.78	**Light**	
insurance	368.3	and air hygiene	593.1
labor	354.937	shadow geometric	519.37
probabilities	512.97	calcium chem. tech.	665.77
metaphysics	133	cure therapeutics	595.85
Life (cont.)		effect on plants	571.47
nature of physiology	592.1	electric engineering	657.81
navy	379.39	houses engineering	654.4
of Buddha	231.29	navigation	659.196
Christ	251.29	protec. of life	593.483
plant botany	571	of earth	525.2
origin of biology	562.7	moon	523.32
personality	372.11	sun	523.72
preservers protec. of life	593.487	optics	535
properties of living		photochemistry	541.5
matter	562.8	polarization of	535.37
protection from		production of	
accidents	593.4	microbiology	561.57
rural	313.4	shelter dom. sci.	692
saving service nautics	659.197	street engineering	653.2
school	333	therapeutics	595.85

zodiac astronomy	523.57
Lighthouse	
hydraulic engineering	654.4
naval architecture	659.196
protection of life	593.483
Lighted bacons river prot.	
works	654.46
Lighting	
electric engineering	657.81
library buildings	024.7
mines engineering	658.41
school buildings	332.92
shipbuilding	659.15
systems	692
theater	781.55
Lightning	
agriculture	611.914
arresters elec. line	657.687
meteorology	529.53
physics	535.47
rods, applications to	537.71
shock surgery	598.162
Lights	
chem. tech.	665
dom. econ.	692
Light-ships shipbuilding	654.47
Lignite mineralogy	558.122
Liguria, Italy geography	983.26
Liliaceae botany	575.83
Liliales botany	575.8
Liliiflorae botany	575.8
Liliineae botany	575.8
Lyly botany	575.8
Limbs anatomy	591.86
anthropography	565.25
anthropometry	565.35
Limes	
building materials	650.49
chemic technology	666.8
economic geology	556.1
lithology	557.57
Limestone lithology	557.46
Limitations individual	
rights	372.4
Limited	
monarchy pol. sci.	371.045
representatives suffrage	372.528
Limits of knowledge	
epistemology	131.2
Limnanthaceae botany	578.13
Limousin, Fr. geography	983.489
Limping money	361.25
Linaceae botany	577.89
Lincoln, England	
geography	983.565

Line	
electric engineering	657.687
engraving	742.4
meridian astronomy	522.74
Linear	
algebra	512.6
current	537.22
perspective	519.36
Lines divination by	
means of	157.36
elec. eng.	657.65
geometry of	519.02
plane	517.31
solid	517.51
magnetic	538.73
of force electricity	537.141
Linguistics	400
Ling Yuan Chinese	
fiction	813.25
Linseed	
oil chem. tech.	665.2
Linum fibers	612.52
Lions zoology	588.511
Lippe, German	
geography	983.78
Lips anatomy	593.311
Liquefaction of gases	
chem.	541.68
physics	536.728
Liquid	
physics	536.72
state chemistry	541.2
physics	536.72
tissue zoology	581.28
Liquids	
physics	532
specific heat	536.34
volumetric analysis	545.41
Liquors	
manufacture	664.5
prohibition	317.83
taxation	369.052
List of immortals Taoism	220.97
system suffrage	372.527
Lists	
electoral suffrage	372.552
of reference books	018.6
Litchi gardening	613.766
Literary	
addresses	808.4
on special topics, see topic	
club education	338.88
criticism	800.4
art of	800.44
extract	800.8

frauds and forgeries	800.45
Literary (cont.)	
history	800.9
landmarks	800.47
periodicals	800.5
plagiarism	800.45
societies student life	333.5
Literature	800
anacreontic	800.1895
ancient	800.91
and scores music	770
children delineated in	313.3608
classic (Greek and Latin)	831
erotic	800.1897
immoral ethics	187.9
medieval	800.92
modern	800.93
national	070
piscatory	800.1891
woman delineated in	313.3508
Lithium inorg. chem.	546.215
Lithography	
engraving	743
printed books	010.33
Litholatry	209.22
Lithology geology	557
microscopic	566.26
Lithophytes zoology	582.75
Lithotomy surgery	597.68
Lithuania	
geography	983.975
history	939.75
Lithuanian language	409.398
Litopterna zoology	588.393
Little Russia geography	983.88
Liturgies Buddhism	233.2
Christianity	253.2
other religions	
Liu Ch'ang-ch'ing Ch. poet.	811.1453
Liu Chi Chinese poet.	811.161
prose	817.811
Liu Chung-yuan Ch. poet.	811.1455
prose	817.47
Liu Hsiang Chinese philos.	111.243
Liu Hsin Chinese philos.	111.244
Liu Hsing-wei Chinese prose	817.763
Liu Ta-k'uei Chinese prose	817.742
Liu Yu-hsi Chinese poet.	811.1456
Liu Yung Chinese poet.	811.732

Live-forever botany	577.72
Live stock agriculture	615
Livelihood, problem of	
labor and laborers	354.931
sociology	317.1
Sunyatsenism	001.143
Liver	
anatomy	597.315
divination	157.16
physiology	597.325
Liverpool, England	
geography	983.567
Liverworts botany	573.6
Living	
and dead matter biology	562.81
cost of dom. science	691
sociology	317.15
expenses teachers	336.53
matter biology	562
properties of	562.81
standard of sociology	317.16
wages	354.312
Livingston, W. Amer.	
poet.	861.15
Livy Latin literature	832.884
Lizards reptiles	587.853
Lo Chih Chinese fiction	813.51
Loan	

banks finance	362.7
funds, for poor	316.53
student	331.45
institutes	362.18
system lib. econ.	023.6
Loans	
law bailments	398.41
contract	397.4
library economy	023.6
private finance	362.18
public finance	369
Loasa botany	578.64
Loasaceae botany	578.64
Lobata zoology	582.773
Lobeliaceae botany	579.92
Lobosa zoology	588.15
Lobsters zoology	584.827
Local	
anthropology	565.9
archaeology	
Chinese	991.9
other nations	
bank finance	362.12
Local (cont.)	
distribution of	
biology	561.9
botany	571.9
diseases	593.232

earthquakes	551.39	library building	024.1
forestry	614.39	light-house	654.41
genius	153.99	newspaper	040.3
minerals	558.9	railway engin'g.	651.811
rocks	557.9	Loci modern geometry	519.44
volcanoes	551.49	Locke English philos.	125.3
zoology	581.9	Lockjaw diseases	597.8454
finance, Chinese	369.19	Lockouts capital and	
governments	373.08	labor	354.85
histories see name of place		Locomotion	
national statistics see name of place		animal	581.73
		physiology	597.723
official savings institution	362.94	psychology	151.38
		Locomotive	
storms	529.39	boilers	655.273
songs	804.5	maintenance	655.278
Chinese	814.5	works	655.297
other nations		Locomotives steam eng.	655.27
suffrage	372.8	Locomotor system	597.7
taxes	369.159	Locris, Greece geography	983.16
time horology	528.58	Locus metaphysics	134.4
Localizations anatomy	597.8112	Locustidae zoology	585.31
Locating		Locusts pests	611.94
surveys	651.811	relief philanthropy	316.44
Location		zoology	585.31
of bridges engin'g.	651.506	Lodgings for the poor	316.51
college or universities	331.6	Loess lithology	557.566
house dom. sci.	692		

Logania botany	579.42
Loganiaceae botany	579.42
Logarithmic	
function	516.33
progression	514.43
Logarithms	510.23
Briggsian's	510.27
hyperbolic	510.26
Napier's	510.26
natural	510.23
Logging forestry	614.71
Logia sayings of Jesus	251.291
Logic	140
Logos Christology	251.22
Lohm lithology	557.567
Loi language	409.128
Loir et cher, Fr.	
geography	983.481
Eure et	983.481
Indre et	983.482
Loire, Fr. geography	983.486
Haute	983.495
Inferieure	983.461
Maine et	983.464
Saone et	983.475
Loiret, Fr. geography	983.481
Lokayata Hinduism	249.9
Lokottara-vada Indian Budd.	239.117
Lolium forage crops	612.273
Lolo languages	409.135
Lombardy, Italy	
geography	983.26
London	
church	259.87
England geography	983.561
Longevity animals	581.698
life insurance	368.3
probabilities	512.97
statistics	349.072
Longfellow, H. W. Am. poet.	861.34
Longipennes birds	587.973
Longitude	
determinations geodesy	526.62
geocentric theor. astron.	521.26
heliocentric theor. astron.	521.25
methods of finding	525.4
variations theor. astron.	521.28
Longitudinal	
vibration	534.545
wave	534.33
Looches diseases	594.976

Looking glasses		Louisiana, U. S.	
optics	535.8	geography	984.172
toilet	693.5	Lousefly entomology	586.57
Loon birds	587.973	Love	
Lophiodontidae zoology	588.345	ethics	187.5
Lophobranchii fishes	587.4773	education	338.9195
Loquat fruit culture	613.717	of God Christian theol.	251.146
Loranthaceae botany	575.85	psychology	151.2
Lord's day	253.195	Lovelace, Richard Eng.	
prayer	253.42	poet	851.45
supper	253.93	Low	
Loricata zoology	587.836	Archipelago	985.976
Lorraine, Fr. geography	983.474	Frankish language	409.388
Germany		lterature	879.8
geography	983.77	Low(cont.)	
Lory birds	587.9751	German language	409.387
Loss of		temperature elemental	
animal heat physiology	592.52	destruc.	611.911
citizenship	372.4	Lowell, J. R. Amer. poet.	861.37
territory intern. law	381.32	prose	867.37
pol. science	371.031	Lower	
Lost books	009.6	California, Mex.	
Lot, France geography	983.492	geography	984.46
et Garonne	983.492	Canada geography	984.28
Lots occult sci	157.13	Egypt geography	985.161
Lotteries	367.5	empire Byzantine	931.86
Lotze German philos.	127.75	extremities anatomy	591.88
		Guinea geography	985.58

primary school	338.21
Loyalty pol. science	371.029
state ethics	185.1
Loyalty island	
geography	985.951
history	959.51
Lu Chi Chinese poet.	811.1322
Lu Chia Chinese philos.	111.211
Lu Chiu-yuan Chinese	
philos.	111.57
prose	817.572
Lu Kuei-meng Chinese	
poet.	811.1486
Lu Pu-wei Chinese	
philos.	111.197
Lu-tsung Chinese	
Buddhism	239.54
Lu Wen-ch'ao Chinese	
prose	817.735
Lu Yu Chinese poet.	811.1574
Lu Yun Chinese poet.	811.1323
Lubeck, Germany	
geography	983.76
Lubrication	
mechanical engineering	655.76
steam engineering	655.278
Lucanus, M. A. Latin	
liter.	832.32
Lucian Greek literature	831.887
Lucretius Greek philos.	121.513
Latin poet.	832.11
Ludwigslied Ger. poet.	871.13
Luffa gardening	613.26
Lugworm zoology	583.611
Luke Bible	252.63
Lumber manufacture	672
Luminescence optics	535.51
spectra	535.45
Luminous	
clouds meteorology	529.66
Lun Yu Chinese	
classics	098.3
Lunar	
calendar chronology	528.6
eclipses astronomy	523.38
methods find'g.	
longitude	525.4
tables	523.33
Lung fish zoology	587.45
Lungs	
anatomy	597.215
capacity of physiology	597.225
diseases of	597.245
exhalation of water from	597.226

functions of	597.2	glands anatomy	597.416
Lute music	775.2	system	597.4
Lutheran churches	259.83	anatomy	597.41
Luxury economics	357.5	vessels anatomy	597.412
Lyceum Gk. philos.	121.4	Lymphatics anatomy	597.412
Lycophron Gk. poet.	831.19	Lyndsay, David Eng.	
Lycopodiales botany	573.8	poet.	851.26
Lying ethics	180.86	Lyonnais, France	
pathologic	155.453	geography	983.486
Lyly, John Eng. fiction	853.3	Lyons, France geography	983.486
Lyly's Euphues Eng.		Lyric poetry literature	801.4
fiction	853.3	Lysias Greek oratory	831.842
Lymph anatomy	591.75	Lythraceae botany	578.73
Lymphatic		Lytton, E. G. B. Eng fic.	853.84

Ma Chih-Yuan Chinese	
drama	812.34
Macaulay, T. Eng. essays	857.83
Maccabees Bible	252.97
Macedonia, Greece	
geography	983.16
Macedonian supremacy	
Gk. hist.	931.835
Macedorumanian	
language	430
literature	830
Machiavelli, N.	
Ital. essays	833.07
drama	833.2
Machines	655.2
design	655.13
drawing	655.13
engineering	655.1
engraving	746
farm	610.6
for lighting	657.812
printing	655.97
stamping	655.97
writing	655.97
hydraulic	654
irrigating	611.6
mechanics	531.9
modulus of physics	531.43

shorthand	626.8
washing dom. econ.	693.4
Mackenzie, Canada	
geography	984.26
Henry Eng.	
fic.	853.65
Mackintosh, Sir James	
Eng. essays	857.71
Madagascar	
geography	985.78
history	957.8
Madhyamagamas sutra	232.22
Madhyamika Indian	
Buddhism	239.13
Madness abnormal psy.	155.2
Madras, India	
geography	982.39
Madrid	
geography	983.38
Maeterlinck, M.	
Belg. drama	842.91
essays	847.91
Magazines	
general periodicals	050
Magic witchcraft	157.7
Magician's wand	
witchcrart	157.74

Magnesium		Buddhism	239.113
group chemistry	546.23	Mahasannepata sutra	232.36
metallurgy	669.995	Mahayana Buddhism	239.12
Magnetic		Mail order business	622.57
circuit	538.42	Main de Biran Fr.	
crystallorgraphy	559.38	philos.	124.52
current	538.42	Maine, France	
elements	538.71	geography	983.463
induction	583.4	Maine et Loire, France	
lines	538.73	geography	983.463
machines	538.89	Maine	983.464
measurements	538.3	U. S. geography	984.161
observations	538.75	Maitreya	239.144
seperation of ore	658.9	Maize field crops	612.15
surveys mining	658.2	Majority	
telegraphy business	637	election suffrage	372.528
quantities	538.82	to legisl. body	343.0347
Magnetism		vote legislative	
animal hypnotism	156.5	proceedure	373.038
electromagnetism	538.8	Makura-mo-soshi	
terrestrial	538.7	Japanese	
Magnetization	538.2	essays	827.38
Magnetochemistry	541.8	Malacology zoology	583.5
Magnets, properties of	538.1	Malacostraca zoology	584.81
Magnoliaceae botany	577.41	Malanesia	
Mahabhutas Hinduism	241.6	geography	985.95
Mahadignaga Buddhism	239.146	history	959.5
Mahasangkika-vada Indian			

Malaria	
hygiene	593.114
marshes	593.27
Malarial fever	
diseases	594.928
public health	593.24
Malay	
language	409.183
peninsula geo.	982.49
hist.	924.9
Malaysia	
geography	985.91
history	959.1
Male	
functions of generation	597.621
genital organs	597.615
kinship	313.385
preponderance zoology	581.663
Malebranche Fr. philos.	124.41
Malechi Bible	252.499
Malformation of teeth	598.245
Malherbe Fr. poetry	841.41
Mallophaga zoology	585.1
Malory, Thomas Eng.	
essays	857.2
Malpighiaceae botany	577.96
Malposition of teeth	598.245
Malta, Italy geography	983.28
Malthusian theory	349.011
Malvaceae botany	578.45
Malvales botany	578.4
Mammalia paleontology	569.87
zoology	588
Man	
anatomy	591
antiquity prehist. arch.	569
nat. hist. of	
man	565.1
christianity	251.3
Isle of, England	
geography	983.569
ethnography	565.8
mammals	589
mental characteristics	153
faculties	150
nature history of	565.1
origin of	
christian doctrine	251.31
Man(cont.)	
evolution	564.9
nat. hist.	565.5
theol.	201.33
physiology	592
zoroastriamism	281.3
Man-land ration	

population	349.04	chemistry	546.33
Management		metallurgy	669.997
business	622	ores minerology	558.146
cooperative economics	354.13	Mangel roots cropt	612.41
engineering	622	wurzel roots crops	612.41
farm economics	610.33	Manipulation	
industrial	622	practical chemistry	542.2
library economics	023	therapeutics	595.8
of household	691	Manitoba, Canada	
industrial enterprise	603	geography	984.27
machine shops	655.793	Manly exercises sports	793
school	332	Manners and customs	319
Managers		Manometric flames	534.515
offis offis economy	622.4	Man's place in nature	565.011
Y. M. C. A.	256.34	Mansions architecture	718.3
Manas Hinduism	241.68	Mantoidea zoology	585.31
Manatidae zoology	588.44	Mantra-sect	
Manche, France		Chinese Buddhism	239.57
geography	983.465	Japanese Buddhism	239.67
Manchuria, China		Mantras of the Vedas	242.17
foreign relations	381.91	Manual	
geography	981.91	training	335.1
history	910.71	work education	338.131
language	409.28	Manufactories	
literature	819	architecture	717.7
Mandates intern. law	381.3197	engineering	653.4
Maneuvering machinery	659.34	Manufactures	670
Manganese			

chemisc technology	670		economical geology	556.1
military resources	379.377		lithology	557.46
miscroscopy	566.67		mineralogy	558.15
production	354.5		sculpture	724
public health	593.37		Marchantiales botany	573.6
state control	373.056		Marche, France	
Manures fertilizers agri.	611.7		geography	983.488
Manuscripts			Marches, Italy geography	983.26
Bible	252.05		Marching sport	793
book rarites	009.3		Marga Buddhism	231.4
copyright	010.43		Marginal	
library administration	022.9		productivity theory	354.314
Manx language	409.375		utility	352.47
Mao Chi-ling Chinese			Marine	
prose	817.728		animals	581.904
Map			architecture	
cases library admin.	023.8		naval eng.	659.3
drawing in schools	980.7		ship building	659.18
making	980.303		bollers	659.163
projection geometry	519.35		botany	571.904
geodesy	526.8		building	659.18
Maple sugar plants	612.64		engines	659.16
Maps	980.3	or,		655.26
astronomic, general	526		fauna zoology	581.904
museum economy	990.079		flora botany	571.904
school apparatus	332.97		hygiene	593.34
Marantaceae botany	575.95		insurance	381.76
Marble		or,		368.2

law	398.7	architecture	717.5
plants	571.904	agriculture	610.358
sketching	737.11	commerce	624
surveying	527	Marking	
zoology	581.904	forestry	614.45
Marionettes		system education	334.5
amusements	787	Marl lithology	557.565
drama	802.5	Marlowe, C. Eng. drama	852.32
Maritime		Marne, France	
atlases	980.306	geography	983.471
affairs naval science	379.6	Haute	983.471
discovery	980.113	Seine et	983.473
domain	381.36	Marquesas islands	
law	398.7	geography	985.977
or,	381.7	history	959.77
surveying	527	Marquetry woodwork	766.7
transport business	634.7	Marriage	
Mariui, Giovambattista		and divorce ethics	183.1
Ital. poet.	833.152	customs	319.22
Marivaux, P. C. de C. de		ethics	183.1
French drama	842.54	family	313.34
fiction	843.52	law	381.813
Mark Bible	252.62	of poor	316.57
Market		sacraments	253.95
analysis	624.1	sermons	253.79
surveys	624.1	vital statistics	349.071
Marketing agric.	610.358	Mars planets	523.44
Markets		Marshall islands	

geography	985.967
history	959.67
Marshes	
hygiene of pub. health	593.27
physical geology	552.5
Marsipiobranchii	
zoology	587.1
Marsupialia zoology	588.22
Martial Latin satire	832.826
Martial law	
jurisprudence	372.41
of war	381.545
Martyniaceae botany	579.62
Maryland, U. S.	
geography	984.166
Masefield, J.	
Eng. drama	852.9
poet	851.9
Mashonaland history	957
Masked balls	792.7
Masks	
amusem'ts	790
theater	781
Masonry	
bricklaying	651.16
bridges archt.	651.5016
construction	651.116
stonecutting	651.16

Massachusetts, U. S.	
geography	984.162
Master and servant	
family ethics	183.7
law	397.54
sociology	313.327
Mastication physiology	597.321
Mastigophora zoology	582.3
Mastitis	
obstetrics	598.861
pediatrics	598.945
Masts shipbuilding	659.17
Matches	
chem. tech.	663.6
mil. engin'g	654.34
sports	794
Mate agriculture	612.77
Materia medica	
medicine	590
Material	
protection lib. econ.	024.2
Materialism philosophy	103.1
Materialistic psychology	150.166
Materialization of spirits	157.951
Materials	
building	710
bridge engineering	651.5

clothing dom. econ.	693.1	Matorrhea diseases	597.645
for road-making	651.71	Matrices algebra	512.37
of construction	650.4	Matriculation school	334.17
engineering	650.4	Matter	
offis economy	626	and motion metaphysics	134.8
library building	024.2	metaphysics	134.7
Mathematical		physical chemistry	541
biology	561.12	physics	530.1
crystallography	559.1	properties of living	562
drawing geometry	519.3	structure of metaphysics	134.7
expressions	510.3	Matthew Bible	252.61
forms	510.3	Maturity	
geography	980.111	of law	390.094
mechanics	531.12	physiology	592.6
recreations	510.9	Maupassant, Guy de	
tables	510.2	Fr. fic.	843.87
theorems	510.3	Maxima and minima	
theory		algebra	512.7
acountics	534.1	calculus	515.77
electrostatics	537.17	geometry	517.38
electrodynamics	537.371	Maxims	
of music	770.011	ethics	188.1
Mathematical (cont.)		literature	808.3
treatment		Chinese	818.3
mechanical theory of		Maxism socialism	318.53
heat	536.51	Mayacaceae botyny	575.63
transimission	536.411	Mayenne, France	
Mathematics	510	geography	983.463

Maynard, F. Fr. poetry	841.42
Meals domestic	
economy	694
Merns	
of help	157.75
protection agri.	611.99
witchcratf	157.75
Measles diseases	594.915
Measurement	
heat	536.31
for low temperature	536.15
of high temperature	536.14
intensity of sound	534.533
power mechanical eng.	655.72
pressure aerostatics	533.39
Measurements	
child study	153.7
Measurements (cont.)	
educational	330.17
electric	
engineering	657.1
physics	537.077
learning	151.68
of volition	151.48
practical chemistry	542.3
psychology	150.77
thinking	151.88
tests	150.77
Measuring apparatus	
prac. chem.	542.3
Meat	
as food dom. econ.	694.1
hygiene	593.128
physiology	593.22
cookery	675
Mechanic arts and	
trades	680
Mechanical	
dentistry	598.28
drawing	733
electricity	537.015
engineering	655
models	655.15
movements	655.12
musical instruments	777
policy	351.1
productive arts	601
refrigeration engin'g.	655.6
remedies therapeutics	595.8
theory of	
heat	536.5
life bio-physics	562.31
trades	680
Mechanics	
applied	531.3
to machinery	655.1

of games	531.37	school	590.077
sports	531.37	for girls	590.078
physics	531	societies	590.6
Mechanism		zoology	581
of labor obstertrics	598.831	Medici, L. de Ital poet.	833.123
philosophy of nature	134.1	Medicinal plants	
Mechanistic theories of		agriculture	612.95
universe	134.1	materia medica	596
Mechanotherapy	595.88	Medicine	590
Mecklenburg, Ger.		chemic analysis	543.4
geography	983.76	dental	598.2
Mediastinum anatomy	597.218	preventive pub. health	593.235
Mediation intern.		Medicines silk worms	616.91
politics	382.24	Medieval	
Medicago forage crops	612.381	architecture	710.3
Medical		art, history of	703
analysis chemistry	543.4	commerce	620.092
astrology	157.28	customs costumes	319
chemistry	596.4	designs	730.3
botany materia medica	596	Europe history	930.5
education	590.7	Greek	931.85
ethics	186	international law	381.092
inspection of schools	332.3	Italy	932.87
jurisprudence	399.7	Latin	832.9
or,	593.8	philosophy	100.92
microscopy	566.8	Mediteranian	
practice pathology	594	question	388.25
science	590	sea poultry	599.45

Medgachiroptera zoology	588.91
Meetings attendance lib.	
econ.	022.3
Megaric Gk. philosophy	121.26
Megaris, Greece	
geography	983.16
Megistanes zoology	587.943
Meibomia forage crops	612.385
Melancholia abnormal	
psy.	155.5
Melastomataceae botany	578.82
Meliaceae botany	577.95
Melilotus forage crops	612.386
Melissus Gk. philos.	121.127
Melodrama literature	802.95
Melancholy mind &	
body	155.5
Melody theory of univer.	770.024
Melons horticulture	613.21
Melting	
prac. chem.	536.711
points thermochemistry	541.64
Membership	
election	373.034
Kuomintang	001.241
legislative bodies	373.034
Membrana tympani ear	
diseases	598.445
Membranes of the heart	
diseases	597.141
Memorial	
esthetics of cities	719.5
Memoire	
fiction	803.3
Chinese	813.83
Memory	
defects	151.67
forgetting and lapses of	151.66
games	794
in animals zoology	581.7
pathology	151.67
processes	151.62
psychology	151.6
theory of	151.6
Menander, Gk. dramatic	
poet.	831.29
Mencius Chinese philos.	111.114
Menedemus Greek	
philos	121.28
Meng Hao-jan Chinese	
poet.	811.142
Meng-tze Chinese	
classics	098.4
Meninges of brain	

anatomy	597.8119
Menispermaceae botany	577.4
Menopause physiology	598.727
Menstruation gynecology	598.723
Menauration geometry	517.6
Mental	
alienation	155.2
and moral life	313.45
characteristics	153
childstudy	153.73
deficiency	155.3
Mental(cont.)	
derangements	155
development education	330
of capacity	153
diseases	155
disorders	155
faculties	150
heredity psy.	153.3
hygiene	152.3
mathematics	510.75
phenomena spiritualism	157.96
philosophy	153
science	153
tests	
child study	153.7
psychology	150.77
Mentalism psychology	150.1913
Mercantile	
agency	621.5
system econ. theory	350.091
Mercerization	
manufacture	675.07
Merchandices commerce	623
Mercurials drugs	597.362
Mercury	
chemistry	546.255
metallurgy	669.95
planets	523.41
Mercy ethics	180.77
Meridian line prac.	
astrom.	522.74
Meridional instruments	522.3
Merimee, Prosper Fr.	
Fic.	843.81
Mesachlamydeae botany	577
Mesencephalon anatomy	597.8115
Mesentery anatomy	597.317
Mesmerism hypnotism	156.5
Mesodermic organs	
embry.	591.56
Mesopotamia Turkey	
geography	982.668
history	926.68
Mesozoic period geology	554.6

Messenia, Greece	
geography	983.17
Metabola zoology	585.5
Metabolism physiology	591.47
Metachlamydeae botany	579
Metagenesis embryology	561.625
Metal	
beams bridge engin'g.	651.501
carving	725
Metal (cont.)	
engraving	742
lattice bridges	651.52
manufactures	671
pavements engin'g.	651.75
remains	
archaeology	990.12
Chinese	991.2
tubular bridges	651.53
Metallography	669.7
Metallurgy	669
Metals	
history	669
inorganic chemistry	546.2
manuf. ctures	670
organic chemistry	547.99
Metamorphic rocks geol.	557.4
Metamorphoses nat.	
theology	201.75
Metaphysical	
logic	146
psychology	135
or,	150.1
schools law	390.0192
Metaphysics philosophy	130
Metaspermae botany	575
Metazoa zoology	582.6
Metencephalon anatomy	597.8117
Meteoric	
points astron.	523.53
showers astron.	523.53
Meteorites	
astronomy	523.51
lithology	557.6
Meteorological	
influences	153.23
observatories	529.72
optics	529.6
Meteorology	529
Meteors	
and comets	523.56
zodiacal light	523.5
astronomy	523.5
systems of	523.54
Meter	
music	770.02
weights and measures	607

Methodist	
church	259.7
episcopal church	259.7
Methodology	
metaphysics	132
Methods	
for study of sections	
miscro.	566.16
of appointment	
legistative	373.0347
carriage law	398.45
education	337
employers	354.85
exploitation agri.	
econ.	610.317
individual educators	337.3
instructioin	
and study	337
classes	337.4
library school	028.7
for special subjects	337.6
schools	337.7
investigation	341.1
least squares algebra	512.93
observation	529.71
obtaining	
monochromatic rays	535.48
plant multiplication	611.57
reading	
education	337.9
library economy	027.5
studying	
education	337.9
library economy	027.5
statistics	341
protective agriculture	611.991
Methology	
logic	141
metaphysics	132
Metric arts metrology	607
Metritis obstetrics	598.862
Metrology	607
Meurthe et Moselle, Fr.	
geography	983.474
Meuse, Fr. geography	983.474
Mexico	
geography	984.4
history	944
state geography	984.47
Mezzotint engraving	742.7
Miao languages	409.15
Micah Bible	252.493
Michigan	
geography	984.177
Microbiology biology	561.5
or,	566.3

Microbotany	566.4
Microchemistry	566.24
Microchiroptera entomol.	588.95
Micrococcus botany	572.125
Microcrystallography	566.28
or,	559.39
Microgeology	566.25
Micrography	566.2
Micromineralogy	566.27
Micronesia	
geography	985.96
history	959.6
Micro-organic diseases	
to animals	566.98
Micro-organisms in	
relation to plants	566.97
Micropalaeontology	566.29
Micropetrology	566.26
Microphotography	
microscopy	566.11
photography	758
Microscopes	566.26
Microscopic	
diagnosis	595.278
examinations	
analysis qual.	544.8
quan.	545.8
petrography	557.8
Microscopy	566
animal histology	581.2
human histology	591.7
lithology	557.8
Microspermae botany	575.97
Microthelyphonidae	
zoology	584.674
Mid east problems	
intern. pol.	388.13
Midbrain	
anatomy	597.8115
Middle	
ages European history	930
ear anatomy	591.82
diseases of	598.444
Egypt	
geography	985.162
history	951.62
High	
German language	470
Kongo	
Belg. geography	985.67
French geography	985.66
Middlesex, Eng.	
geography	983.561
Mididae zoology	589.53
Midrash Jewish	

scripture	262.3
Mie, Japan geography	982.1648
Migration	
of animals	581.703
ions	537.374
man ethnology	665.75
political science	377
Militarism	379.011
Military	
Academies	379.07
administration	379.3
aeronautics	379.7
and naval arts	379
antiquities	379.09
architecture, buildings	659.3
balloons engin'g.	629.44
bridges	651.5027
building	659.36
discipline	332.6
drill	332
education	379.07
engineering	659.3
equipment	379.37
food	379.371
geography mil. science	379.089
geology	556.2
hiararchy	379.33
history	379.09
honor	379.39
hospitals	379.38
hygiene	593.35
law	399.5
courts martial	379.31
orders	379.31
life	379.39
manners	379.39
morality	379.39
music	774
officers	379.33
organization in schools	332.6
political geography	980.175
railways	651.89
roads mil. engin'g.	659.36
science	379.5
signaling	379.38
signals	659.37
supplies	379.37
Military (cont.)	
surgery	598.195
symbolism	379.38
telephony mil. eng.	659.37
treaty of peace	387.4
uniforms costume	319.44
Militia military sci.	379.8
Milk	
agriculture	615.71

analysis		
adulterations	593.22	
chemistry	543.13	
as food physiology	592.473	
cure therapeutics	596.82	
dairy	615.71	
depots	694.5	
fever obstetrics	598.861	
physiology	592.6	
Milky way astronomy	523.81	
Mill, J. S. British philos.	125.67	
Mill		
architecture	717.7	
gearing and machinery	655.85	
work engineering	655.8	
Milleporina zoology	582.713	
Miller, Joaquin Am.		
poet.	861.45	
Millet field crops	612.17	
Millinery		
clothing	693.3	
trade	684	
Milton, John Eng. poet.	851.47	
Mimeography engraving	747	
Mimetic resemblance	563.14	
Mimicry biology	563.14	
zoology	581.75	
Min-ch'uan		
Sunyatsenism	001.13	
Min-sen Sunyatsenism	001.14	
Min-ts'u Sunyatsenism	001.12	
Mind	150	
and body	150.16	
child study	153.72	
dust theory psychology	150.167	
educational psychology	330.15	
physiologic psychology	597.852	
psychology	150	
reading occult sci.	157.61	
stuff theory psychology	150.167	
Mine		
cars engineering	658.5	
drainage	658.43	
examination engineering	658.23	
haulage	658.5	
hoisting	658.5	
surveying	658.25	
transportation	658.5	
valuation	658.23	
Minelayers naval science	379.661	
Mineral		
drugs	596.15	
foods psysiology	597.473	
industries	658	
oils		
chemic tech.	665.5	

econom. geology	556.1	geology	556.1
pollution	658.02	machinery	658.6
spring econom. geol.	556.1	engines. steam eng.	655.272
waters	558.17	laws	658.007
econom. geol.	556.1	practical	658.3
wax	655.5	tools hydraulic	655.36
Mineralogy	558	Minister eccles. pol.	255.54
determinative	558.2	Ministry	
Minerals mineralogy	558.1	Buddhism	235.5
Mines		ecclesiastic polity	255.5
economics	353.17	lay	255.58
military engineering	659.32	parish work	254.6
mining	658.23	political science	373.078
Minesweepers military sci.	379.663	religion	255.5
		Minnesota, U. S.	
Minima and maxima		geography	984.178
algebra	512.77	Minor	
geometry	517.38	planets	523.49
Minimum wage law		Prophets	252.49
economics	354.36	Minora forage crops	612.387
Ming Chia Chinese philos.	111.15	Minority representation	372.528
		Minot, L. Eng. poet.	851.19
Ming dynasty Chinese history	916	Mints horticulture	613.4
		Mioclaenidae zoology	588.35
Mining		Miracle plays	
dangers and accidents	658.45	English literature	852.1
economics	658.1	religion	252.082
engineering	658	theater	792.6

Miracles			Miyazaki, Japan	
in the Bible	252.082		geography	982.1667
Sutra	232.082		Mnemonic apprehension	
Mirage astron.	529.67		psychology	151.6
Miscarriage obstetrics	598.828		Mnemonies psychology	151.64
Miscellanies see subjects			Mo Tzu Chinese philos.	111.131
Miscibility hydraulics	532.13		Mob problem sociology	317.6
Missions			Mocius school Chinese	111.13
city	254.9		philos.	
home and foreign	254.9		Modeling archit.	711.3
practical religion	208		Models	
religious life	208		art study	700.7
Roman catholic	259.16		architecture	711.3
Mississippi, U. S.			sculpture	721.1
geography	984.171		Modern	
river description	980.74		analytic geometry	519.4
discovery U. S. hist.	941.815		architecture	710.3
state			commerce	620.093
admission U. S. hist.	941.852		costumes and customs	319
Missouri state			embryology	561.63
geography	984.179		European history	930.6
Mitrastemonaceae			geometry	517.56
botany	576.93		synthetic	517
Mixed			Greek	
marriages	313.348		language	431.1
state	371.63		literature	831.9
Mixture of colors optics	535.395		history	930.6
Miyagi, Japan geography	982.1623		Latin literature	832.9

philosophy	100.93
Rome	932.848
woman feminism	313.35
Modes	
Communication	593.234
of propagation	593.234
Modesty ethics	180.79
Modification inheritance	563.69
Mohammed	
Mohammedanism	271.29
Mohammedan	
architecture	715.7
conquests	923.82
rule history	951.82
Mohammedanism	270
Mohybdenum inorganic	
Chem.	546.43
Moisture	
hygiene	593.114
physical geography	552.8
Mokiere, J. B. P. Fr.	
drama	842.42
Mokanshan	981.367
Molecular	
physics	538.43
theoretic chemistry	541.04
Molecules displacement	
of	538.43
Molise, Italy geography	983.27
Mollusca	
paleontology	569.75
zoology	583.5
Molluscoidea	
paleontology	569.76
zoology	583.7
Mollusks fishery	617.7
Moluccas islands	
geography	985.917
history	959.17
Momordia horticulture	613.26
Mon language	409.171
Monaco. Fr. geography	983.497
Monarchy pol. sci.	371.041
Monasteries	
architecture	715.2
theology	255.8
Monastic life	258.9
Money	361
aid	316.53
anderiss	352.73
deposit by lib. borrower	022.6
exchange	362.17
legislation	361.1
lending	362.18
making ethics	186

paper	361.7
soliciting library rules	022.6
system	361.2
Mongolia	
Buddhism	236.59
foreign relations	381.91
geography	981.93
history	910.72
language	409.23
literature	819
Mongolian	
collection	009.82
invasion	938.82
type (yellow)	565.882
Monism philosophy	102.1
Monistic theories	150.165
Monitorial system of educ.	337.41
Monkeys zoology	589.1
Mon-khmer language	409.17
Monmouth, England	
geography	983.564
Monocotyledoneae	
botany	575.1
palaeobotany	569.51
Monodelphia zoology	588.3
Monogamy	
family	
ethics	183.2
sociology	313.3411
Monograms heraldry	960.2
Monometallism	361.21
Monopetalae botany	579
Monopoly	
economy	351.5
trade	352.6
Monotheism nat. theology	201.2
Monotremata zoology	588.15
Montaigue, M. E. de Fr.	
essays	847.3
Montana, U. S.	
geography	984.185
Montesquier Fr. philos.	124.22
Montesquieu, Fr. essays.	847.52
Montesori system	
education	337.35
Monuments	
American revolution	992.418
antiquities	991.85
cemeteries	719.4
Great War 1914-19	992.307
prehistoric	990.9
Moon astronomy	523.3
Moore, Thomas Eng.	

poet.	851.75	geography	984.47
Moorish kingdom		More's Utopia Eng.	
Spanish history	933.82	fiction	853.2
Portugal history	933.983	Morning prayer	
Moraceous fruits	613.74	Anglican ritual	253.26
Moral		family devotions	253.22
education	330.18	personal religion	253.23
heredity metaphysics	135.7	services	253.26
imbecility psychology	155.45	Morocco, Africa	
impolence	155.4587	geography	985.3
insanity	155.45	history	953
philosophy	180	Morphin habit ethics	180.89
science ethics	180	Morphological	
sentiment	173.5	crystallography	559.6
social ethics	313.28	embryology	561.65
systems	180.07	Morphology	
Morally defectives	338.968	bacteriology	566.91
Morals		biology	561.1
and church	255.02	botany	571.2
history of ethics	180.9	zoology	581.1
of the press		Morris. W. Eng. poet.	851.86
ethics	189	Mortality	
journalism	040.18	law of insurance	368.3
war ethics	185.3	statistics	349.078
Moravia, Czecho.		Mortgages	
geography	983.796	finance	366.2
Morbihan, Fr. geography	983.461	law	397.2
Morelos, Mexico		Mortification surgery	598.145

Mortuary	
building architecture	715.97
customs	319.24
remains Chinese	
antiquities	991.71
statistics population	349
Mortar	
engineering	650.49
mounts ordnance	659.34
Mortars	
ordnance	659.34
prehistoric archeology	990.9
Morus pomiculture	613.743
Mosaic law Bible	252.216
Mosaics arch. decoration	712
Mosasuari zoology	587.851
Moscow	
geography	983.88
Moslems	
associations	276
building architecture	715
chronology	528.66
education	277
history	279
institution	275
law	390.3
life	278
polity	275
scriptures	272
sects	279
Mosquitoes	
animals parasites	581.5
parasitic diseases	594.974
zoology	585.3
Mosses	
botany	573.7
sea algae	573.2
Mother ethics	183.3
Moths zoology	585.535
Motion	
laws of	
astronomy	521.11
physics	531.21
metaphysics	133.63
of a projectile	531.225
earth astronomy	525.3
liquids hydraulics	532.58
gases	533.52
solar system	523.24
vessels	532.57
pictures, see Moving	
Motives psychology	151.46
Motor	
bicycle	659.77
cars elec. traction	632.6
engines see motors	

system anatomy	581.17	physiology	597.321
vehicles	632.6	**Movable bridges**	
cycles	659.78	civil eng.	651.57
Mottoes		mil. engineering	651.5027
heraldry	960.5	**Movement**	
literature	808.3	anthropology	565.42
Mounds prehistoric		muscular animal heat	592.54
arch.	990.9	of liquids hydraulics	532.52
Mountain		gases	533.57
cottages architecture	718.8	farmers	001.991
guns gunnery	659.34	merchants	001.993
hygiene	593.112	students	001.994
mounts ordnance	659.34	women	001.995
railways	651.82	worker	001.992
Mountains		youths	001.996
etiquette	319.113	psychology	151.3
geography		**Mozambique, Africa**	
Chinese	981.36	geography	985.44
physical	552.6	history	954.4
general	980.506	**Mucuna forage crops**	612.383
literature	800.1893	**Mud lithology**	557.522
volcanic	551.4	**Mulberry**	
Mounting		culture	616.6
microscopy	566.14	fruit	613.743
mounts ordnanoe	659.34	leaves	616.6
specimens	567.5	**Mule domestic animal**	615.1
Mouth		**Multicellular structure**	581.103
anatomy	597.311	**Multimember**	

constituency suffrage	372.526
Multiple	
consciousness	156.13
integrals calculus	515.3
pregnancy obstetrics	598.817
stars astronomy	523.81
Multiplication	
arithmetic	511.23
mathematics	510.211
of plants	611.57
Multituberculata zoology	588.13
Mundane astrology	157.2
Municipal	
economics	350.032
engineering local gov't.	373.095
goverment admin.	373.082
law	390.009
local party	001.42
police	315.325
refuse	653.36
statistics of China	354.14
waste	653.36
Municipalities admin.	373.082
Munitions of war mil.	
eng.	659.34
Munster, Ireland	
geography	983.57
Murasaki-shikibunikki	
Jap. prose	827.33
Murcia, Spain geography	983.38
Murder criminal law	394
Muridae zoology	588.615
Murmurs	
arterial physiology	597.115
cardiac physiology	597.127
muscle physiology	598.52
Musaceae botany	575.91
Musaceous fruits	613.78
Musci botany	573.7
Muscle	
histology	591.76
wave physiology	598.52
Muscles	
anatomy	591.76
chemic composition of	598.52
effect of nervous on	597.817
physiology	598
structure anatomy	591.76
Muscular	
arteries anatomy	597.115
contraction	
Muscular (cont.)	
chem. effect	598.52
physiology	598.52
disorders eye diseases	598.345
movement and animal	

heat	592.54
respiration	597.22
psychology	151.16
sense	
localization of	597.8
physiology	597.8
system anatomy	597.715
tissue histology	591.76
Museum	
library buildings	024.6
material lib. admin.	023.8
Museums	
architecture	717.2
art fine arts	700.7
education	330.7
medical	590.07
school equipment	332.96
rooms	332.92
other museums, see subjects	
Music	
art	770
dance	773
dramatic	773
ecclesiology	253.57
education	338.137
halls architecture	717.9
library administration	023.8
orchestral	779
public worship	253.57
room	
domestic econ.	690.692
library building	024.6
sacred	772
vocal	771
chamber	771.8
concerted	771.7
Musical	
forms	770.027
instrument	991.73
school	332.99
psychology	151.127
sensations physiology	770.012
sounds acoustics	770.011
terms	770.03
Muskoka	
dist. Ont	942.87
lakes Ont geography	984.287
Muspilli German poet.	871.14
Musset, L. A. de Fr. dram.	
French drama	842.74
poetry	841.74
Mustelidae zoology	588.517
Mutiny maritime law	399.4
Mutton sheep	615.13

Mutual		
action of currents		537.33
magnets		533.16
planets		521.51
aid societies pol. econ.		356.78
concessions of duties		369.1615
insurance pol. econ.		356.78
or,		368
relations		563.13
system education		337.43
Mycel anatomy		597.813
Mycetinai zoology		589.55
Mycetophorae zoology		584.675
Mycetozoa		
botany		572.2
zoology		582.12
Mycology botany		573.3
Mycomycetes botany		573.3
Mydriatics		
physiology		598.342
therapeutics		597.866
Myel anatomy		597.813
Myelencefal anatomy		597.8117
Myelencephalon		
anatomy		597.8118
Mylaganlidae zoology		588.611
Myology anatomy		597.715

Myopia	
eye diseases	598.345
physiology	597.866
Myoporaceae botany	579.67
Myrana univ. language	405
Myriapodo zoology	584.4
Myricaceae botany	576.36
Myricales botany	576.35
Myrrh perfume plants	612.83
Myrsinaceae plants	579.21
Myrtaceous fruits	613.79
Myrtales botany	578.81
Myristicadeae botany	577.44
Myrtaceae plants	578.81
Myrtiflorae	
(Thymelaeinae)	578.7
Myrtle family fruits	613.79
Mysore India geography	982.39
Mystacoceti zoology	588.473
Mysterits	
drama see Mystery plays	
occultism	255
Mystery plays	
English literature	852.1
history	802.9
religion	253.73
theater	781

Mystic philosophers	121.61	botany	572.127
Mysticeti zoology	588.473	Myxogastores	
Mysticism philosophy	104.7	botany	572.25
Myth	209.9	zoology	582.12
Mythological sculpture	729.3	Mysomycetes	
Mythology	209.9	botany	572.2
archaeology	990.071	zoology	582.12
comparative	250.84	Myxospongiae zoology	582.53
metaphysics	132	Myxosporidia zoology	582.27
Myxedema diseases	594.996	Myxostonida zoology	583.617
Myxinoides zoology	587.11	Myxothallophyta botany	572.2
Myxobacteriaceae			

N dimensional space	
geography	519.61
infinitesimal geometry	519.75
rays physics	535.54
Nagano, Japan geography	982.1636
Nagarjuma Buddhism	239.135
Nagasaki, Japan	
geography	982.1644
Nahum Bible	252.494
Najadaceae botany	575.32
Nails	
strength of materials	650.41
care of toilet	693.5
Naive philosophy	106.11
Naiyayaka Hinduism	249.6
Nakatsukasa-no-	
naishinikki	827.43
Namarupa Buddhism	231.59
Nantes	
geography	983.461
Napier's logarithms	
math.	510.26
Naples, Italy	
geography	983.27
history	932.7
Napoleonic	
period European hist.	930.65

wars	
Ger. hist.	937.86
Scand. hist.	937.984
Naraka Buddhism	231.85
Narcolepsy abnor.	
psychology	155.253
Narcotics	
action of hygiene	597.83
therapeutics	597.86
Natal, Africa	
geography	985.7
history	957
Natatores zoology	587.973
Nates anatomy	591.88
Nation pol. sci.	371.031
National	
and state universities	338.71
assembly	001.176
French revolution	934.841
banks	362.12
bibliography	013
capital	981.51
cemeteries	719.4
costumes	319.4
customs, special	319
dances amusements	792.1
National (cont.)	
defense	379.32

economics	350.04
flowers	570.087
forest policy	614.15
law	390.009
libraries	025.3
literature	070
music	771.3
object Y. M. C. A.	256.316
opiums suppression commission	373.3503
parks	719.1
polities	
China	375.1
England	375.5
U. S. A.	375.6
reconstruction	
commission	373.0591
plans for	001.155
Sunyatsenism	001.159
religion	200.09
savings bank	362.94
songs music	771.3
statistics	345
Nationalism pol. sci	371.03
Nationalities	
history of civilization	902.1
China	910.21
Egypt	951.21
England	935.21
Europe	930.21
France	934.21
Germany	937.21
Greece	931.21
India	923.21
Japan	921.21
Korea	922.21
Rome	932.21
Russia	938.21
Spain	933.21
U. S. A.	941.21
suffrage	372.51
Nationality	
by birth inter'l pol.	381.811
civics	372.3
International politics	381.81
vital statistics	349.079
Native	
custom	369.165
law	390.002
Natural	
ability workers econ.	354.114
astrology astronomy	520.1
body doctrinal theol.	251.31
boundaries intern'l pol.	381.331
drainage mining	658.43
enemies of pests	611.995

gas		
chem. technology	661.7	
economical geology	556.1	
history		
collectors handbks	567	
of man	565.1	
silkworm	616.2	
zoology	580	
law	390.093	
magic	157.7	
magnets physics	538.11	
person	397.11	
philosophy	134	
production systems	614.41	
religion	201	
science	500	
selection		
biology	564.21	
evolution	571.775	
sociology	312.23	
theology	201	
Naturalism		
philosophy	107.1	
of life	171	
system of literature	800.185	
Naturalization		
civics	372.3	
international politics	381.812	

lost of	372.45	
suffrage	372.3	
Nature		
and attributes of deity	201.3	
language	401.4	
land economics	353.5	
magic occult sci.	157.7	
metaphysics	134	
of being metaphysics	133.1	
life and death		
metaphysics	135.9	
light optics	535.2	
soul and mind		
metayphsics	135.2	
the spectrum physics	535.44	
state pol. sci.	371.02	
Nature(cont.)		
population	349.05	
study		
biology	560.07	
elem. educ.	338.139	
general	507	
worship	209.2	
Nautical		
almanacs estronomy	527	
astronomy	527	
instruments	659.192	
navigation	659.191	

Nautics		transportation	634.3
navigation shipping	659.19	Navy	
Naval		administration	379.62
architecture engin'g	659.1	Near East	
battles	379.1	problems	388.12
engineering	659.3	questions	
gunnery	659.35	Balkan states	939.5
history	379.09	W. war causes	930.721
world war	930.7	Nebraska U. S.	
hygiene	593.35	geography	984.182
law	399.5	Nebulae astron.	523.81
mounts ordnance	659.34	Nebular	
nautics	659.1	hyphothesis astron.	523.13
operations	379.63	Necessarianism	
ordnance	659.34	metaphysics	134.13
school	379.07	Necessity econ.	357.1
science	379.6	of grace chri. doctr.	251.41
shipping	659.19	Neck anatomy	591.83
surgery	598.195	Necks geography	553.8
surveying	379.099	Necrology colleges	338.7
war	379.1	Necromancy witchcraft	157.7
Navarce		Necrosis pathology	594.85
geography	983.38	Need	
Navigation		of training	336.3
aerial see aerial navigation		Needle	
		telegraphy	657.8351
astronomy	659.191	work art	765.3
law	381.72		

Negative		
processes photography	755	
Negro		
education	338.98	
race	317.2	
slavery	317.4	
Negroid		
type ethnology	565.881	
Nehemiah Bible	252.28	
Neighboring		
part diseases	598.348	
Nemalionales botany	573.265	
Nemathelmia zoology	583.4	
Nemathelminthes		
zoology	583.4	
Nematoda zoology	583.41	
Nematoidea zoology	583.41	
Nematomorpha zoology	583.42	
Nemertea zoology	583.37	
Nemertini zoology	583.37	
Neo-Darwinism		
evolution	564.3	
Neo-dualism philosophy	102.4	
Neo-Lamarckism		
evolution	564.5	
Neo-Malthusianism		
demography	349.013	
Neo-monism philosophy	102.2	
Neo-platonic Gk. philos.	121.58	
Neo-realism philosophy	106.15	
Neodymium chemistry	546.269	
Neolithic		
age prehis. arch.	990.9	
Neon		
gas lighting	657.8147	
inorganic chemistry	546.182	
Neopersian		
language	493.3	
literature	893.3	
Neornithes zoology	587.92	
Nepal		
geography	983.39	
history	923.9	
Nepeuthaceae botany	577.63	
Nephelium pomiculture	613.766	
Neptune astronomy	523.48	
Nervous		
abnormal education	338.967	
centers	597.823	
physiology	597.823	
system		
central physiology	597.823	
comparative anatomy		
zool.	581.18	
diseases of	597.84	

drugs acting on	597.86	physiologic zoology	581.46
human anatomy	597.88	Neuroptera insects	585.51
physiology	597.88	Neuroses	
hygiene	597.83	diseases	597.845
pathology	597.84	due to special poisons	155.259
physiology zoology	581.46	psychology	155.25
surgical operations	597.87	Neurotic	
sympathetic		poisons toxicology	593.9
anatomy	597.817	Neutral	
physiology	597.827	duties and obligations	
tissue histology	591.78	intern. law	381.62
Nesosporidia zoology	582.26	property and trade	
Nests		intern. law	381.63
birds zoology	587.9	rights intern. law	381.61
Netherlands		state pol. sci.	371.8
geography	983.791	Neutralism philosophy	103.7
history	937.91	Neutrality	
language	479.388	international law	381.6
literature	879	Neutrals World war	930.755
philosophy	128.1	Nevada, U. S. geography	984.193
Nets		New	
biology	567.6	academy Gk. philos.	121.55
manufactures	675.6	Britain geography	985.955
toilet	693.5	Brunswick, Can.	
Neuralgia diseases	597.846	geography	984.28
Nettlerash dermatology	598.541	Caledonia geography	985.951
Neurology		Castile, Spain geography	983.38
morphology	581.1	Dynasty, the Chinese	

hist.	912.2	Newborn infants		
formations dermatology	598.545	disease	598.94	
German empire	937.88	physiology	592.6	
Guinea		Newfoundland		
geography	985.959	geography	984.28	
history	959.59	Newspapers journalism	040	
Hampshire, U. S.		News room		
geography	984.161	free	025.8	
Hebrides geography	985.952	library building	024.6	
Jersey, U. S.		Ngai Nan-yin Chinese		
geography	984.165	poet.	811.169	
Mexico geography	984.188	Ngari, China geography	981.987	
platonism Gk. philos.	121.57	Nibelungenlied German		
quantum theory physics	530.75	poet.	871.21	
South Wales, Australia		Nicaragua		
geo.	985.9352	geography	984.65	
stars astronomy	528.87	history	946.5	
Testament		Nice		
Bible	252.5	geography	983.498	
pseud-pigrapha	252.99	Nicene		
trials law	395.03	creed	251.82	
York, U. S. geography	984.164	Nichirendhu Buddhism	239.68	
Zealand		Nickel		
geography	985.94	coinage econ.	261.21	
hemp fibers	612.58	inorganic chemistry	546.39	
history	959.4	metallurgy	669.999	
New-Pythagorean Gk.				
philos.	121.56	ores econ. geol.	558.148	

sheets of sci. of bks	010.47
Nicodemms aprocrypha	252.991
Nicotiana alkaloidal plants	612.71
Nidana Buddhism	231.5
Nietzsche German philos.	127.8
Nievre, Frence geography	983.484
Night work laboring class	354.42
Nihon-gi Shintoism	291.23
Niigata, Japan geography	982.1631
Nikaya Buddhism	232.37
Nine Classics, the Chinese classics	090.4
Ninghsia, China geography	981.67
Ninjobon Japanese fic.	823.68
Niobium inorg. chem.	546.65
Nipal, India geography	982.39
Nirgrantha Hinduism	249.7
Nirodha Buddhism	231.33
Nirvana Buddhist philosophy	231.79
Mahayana sutra	232.35
Niton inorg. chem.	546.187
Nitrates chemicals	661.5
Nitrocellulose compounds chem. tech.	663.15
Nitrogen fertilizers agric.	611.7
group inorg. chem.	546.14
Nitroglycerine compounds chem. tech.	663.17
Nivernais, France geography	983.484
Nobility ceremonies	319.1
genealogy	977.2
social class	313.82
Nobles see Nobility	
Nocturnal revels witchcraft	157.22
variations meteology	529.18
Nolanaceae botany	579.56
Nomenclature theor. chem.	541.09
Nominations suffrage	372.54
Nomological microscopy	566.7
Non-alcoholic beverages chem. tech.	664.6

Non-electric	
telephony electric	
enging.	657.858
Non-Euclidean	
geometry	519.8
Non-sovereign	
states intern. law	381.12
Nonmetallic	
elements chem.	546.1
poisons therapeutics	593.9
Nonsphericity	
of planets astronomy	521.55
Nord, France	
geography	983.465
Norfold, England	
geography	983.566
Norite lithology	557.37
Norito Shintoism	291.25
Normal	
composition of the body	592.43
illusions	151.173
psychology	151
school	338.5
of special class	338.916
Norman	
conquest Eng. hist.	935.82
Normandy, Fr.	
geography	983.465
Normans Eng. hist.	935.82
Norrland, Sweden	
geography	983.7987
Norse	
language	479.21
literature	879.21
Norseman, Scand.	
geography	983.7986
North	
Carolina, U. S.	
geography	984.168
Dakota, U. S. geography	984.184
Northampton, England	
geography	983.565
Northern	
Ch'i Chinese hist.	913.85
Chou Chinese hist.	913.86
Dynasties	
Chinese history	913.8
Han Chinese history	914.991
Liang Chinese history	913.594
Sung Chinese	915.2
Wei Chinese history	913.81
Yen Chinese history	913.598
Northumberland, England	
geography	983.569
Norway	
administration	373.37

botany	571.937	geography	983.565
finance	350.937	Nova Scotia, Canada	
geography	983.7986	geography	984.28
geology	550.37	Novaculite lithology	557.45
history	937.986	Novels literature	803
maps	980.337	Novgorod, Russia	
school, public	338.7937	geography	983.895
statistics	345.37	Novilatiin univ. lang.	405
Norwegian		Noxious	
language	409.3821	animai econ. zoology	581.8
literature	879.21	plants econ. botany	571.8
Nose		Nubia, Egypt geo.	985.171
anatomy	597.211	Nuciculture pomiculture	613.76
disease	597.241	Nucleus	
physiology	597.22	histology	571.113
Nostoceae botany	572.174	of cell biology	591.71
Nostrums medicine	593.76	Nuda zoology	582.777
Notation		Nude in art	700.13
arithmatic	510.5	Nudibranchia zoology	583.535
music	770.022	Nuevo Leon, Mexico	
Notebooks	027.8	geography	984.46
Notices		Number	
trial law	395.03	metaphysics	134.9
Notification intern. law	386.45	of members	373.0345
Nottingham, Eng.		strokes	012.8
geography	983.565	Numbers	
Notoungulata zoology	588.39	book of Bible	252.214
Notts, England			

theory of algebra	512.4	physiology	
Numeration arithematic	510.5	bacteriology	566.922
Numeric		biology	561.47
computation		botany	571.4
mathematics	510.7	human	592.47
equations, higher	512.6	zoology	581.4
Numistics archaeology	990.124	Nutriments	
Chinese	991.24	of hair	666.13
Nurse		mouth	668.15
school	590.079	skin	668.12
training of	599.079	Nuts pomiculture	613.76
Nut		Nyaya Hinduism	249.6
culture	613.7	Hyctaginaceae botany	577.15
fruits	613.76	Nycticebidae zoology	589.35
Nutation		Nymphomania abnormal	
astron. correc.	522.85	psy.	155.4583
theoret. astron.	521.9	Nymphonomorpha	
Nutrition		zoology	584.53

Oat grass forage crops	612.275	volcanoes	551.44
Oats field crops	612.13	Observing	
Obadiah Bible	252.491	chairs astron.	522.28
Obedience ethics	183.9	powers educ.	338.139
Object		Obstetrics gynecology	598.8
teaching education	338.139	Occidental philosopy	120
Objective		Occult sciences	157.5
philosophy	106.25	Occultations	
phenomena occult sci.	157.95	and transit astron.	523.9
psychology	150.173	Occultism	157.5
Obligations		Occupational hazards	354.54
civil law(intern'l)	381.843	Occupations	
ethics	180.73	dangerous economics	354.54
family ethics	183.9	woman	313.355
law	397.3	Ocean	
neutrality	381.62	biology	561.904
rights politics	381.27	botany	571.904
Odes of Solomon		currents phys. geog.	552.2
spocrypha	252.983	geography	980.502
Oboe musical instru.	774.2	China	981.32
Observation		glaciers	551.78
logic	141.7	ichtyology zoology	587.49
mental faculty	151	seismology	551.38
of one's self psy.	150.172	Oceanian	
Observatories		geography	985.9
astronomy	522.1	history	959
meteorologic	529.72	Oceans physical	
semismology	551.34	geography	552.2

Ochikubo monogatari Jap. fic.	823.35
Ochromonadaceae botany	572.34
Octactinelida zoology	585.55
Ode poetry	801.43
Odobenidae zoology	588.533
Odonata zoology	585.33
Odontalgia dentistry	598.247
Odontoceti zoology	588.477
Odontolcae zoology	587.95
Odontornithes zoology	587.95
Oekology see Ecology	
Oenotheraceae botany	578.84
Offenses	
against justice	315.182
public	315.188
the public orders	315.184
revenue	315.183
state	394.23
Offering	
at the grave	319.25
Office	
economy	622.1
equipment and methods	622.1
Official	
ceremonies of royalty	319.12
correspondences	339.22
organization	373.013
savings institutions	362.94
heraldry	961
text calligraphy	739.173
Ofthalmology	
anatomy	598.31
diseases	598.34
physiology	498.32
Ohio, U. S. geography	984.175
Ogdai Khanate Chinese hist.	915.97
Oicomonadaceae botany	572.33
Oil	
analysis	665.1
and gasoline engines	655.44
painting art	734.7
producing plants	612.97
Oil cloth manuf.	679
Oils	
industries	655.3
manufacture	679
Oise, France geography	983.473
Seine et	983.473
Oita, Japan geography	982.1666
Okayama, Japan geography	982.1555
Oklahoma, U. S.	

geography	984.173	Omnipotence doct.	
Olacaceae botany	576.83	theology	251.141
Old		Ominpresence doct.	
academy	121.3	theology	251.142
age insurance pol. econ.	354.937	Ominscence doct.	
Castile, Spain geography	983.38	theology	251.143
copy books	009.36	Oneirocritics occult sci.	157.17
editions	009.16	Oneiromancy occult sci.	157.17
English languages	409.383	Onagraceae botany	578.83
French languages	440	Ontario, Canada	
High German languages	470	geography	984.28
Manuscripts	009.32	Ontogenetic	
Persian languages	409.322	variation biology	563.69
Prussian languages	499.396	Ontogeny	
Testament	252.1	anatomy	591.5
Oldenburg, Ger.		biology	561.3
geography	983.78	Ontology	
Olea Europea		metaphysics	133
pomiculture	613.775	Onychophora zoology	584.2
Oleaceae botany	579.41	Oolitic	
Olefins organic chem.	547.12	limestone lithology	557.562
Olericulture gardening	613.1	Open	
Olfactory sensation psy.	151.13	sea maritime law	381.71
Oligochaeta zoology	583.611	arc elec. lighting	657.8143
Olive pomiculture	613.775	Opera	
Omens occult sci.	157.17	amusement	783
Omnigraphy engraving	740	dramatic music	802.2

Operative	
dentistry	598.27
dermatology	598.57
gynecology	598.77
obstetrics	598.87
opthalmology	598.37
otology	598.47
remedies	598.81
surgery	598.18
Ophidia reptils	587.857
Ophiomnorpha zoology	587.66
Ophuroidea invertebrata	582.92
Ophtalmia	
Ophthalmology	598.341
pediatrics	598.946
ophthalmology	598.3
Opiliones articulata	584.678
Opisthobranchia	
articulata	583.535
Opisthocoelia zoology	587.837
Opium	
agriculture	612.75
narcotic poisons	597.83
Oppian Greek poet.	831.39
Opposition	
of good and evil hersey	259.094
solar system	523.23
Optic	
crystallography	559.35
instrument manuf.	688.1
nerve eye diseases	598.343
Optical	
apparatus	522.6
crystillography	559.35
defects	598.399
instruments	535.8
Optician's trade	688.1
Optics physics	535
physiology	598.32
Optimism philosopy	108.1
Optional courses	
education	335.7
Opuntiales botany	578.67
Oracles occult sci.	157.18
Oral	
examinations edcation	334.5
Orange	
family agric.	613.731
free state	
geography	985.76
history	957.6
Orations literature	808.4
Orbit	
of comets	523.6
earth	525.3
eye, etc. disease	598.348

moon astron.	523.33	
part disease	598.348	
Orbits		
of heavenly bodies	521.3	
plane of, in space		
astron.	521.21	
position of, in plane		
astron.	521.22	
Orchestral music	779	
Orchidaceae botany	575.99	
Orchids gardening	716.2	
Order school	339.21	
Orders architecture	711.8	
Ordinances		
city	373.082	
religion	253.9	
Ordination		
Christianity	253.94	
sermons	253.78	
Ordnance military		
engin'g	659.34	
Ordovician period		
geology	554.53	
Ore		
deposit econ. geol.	558.11	
prospecting	658.21	
dressing mining		
engineering	658.9	

Oregon, U. S. geography	984.195
Ores	
chemic analysis	543.5
iron econ. geol.	556.1
metallurgy	669
mineralogy	558
mining	658
of antimony	558.147
copper	558.143
gold	558.141
iron	558.13
Ores(cont.)	
lead	558.144
manganese and	
chromium	558.146
metals	558.14
nickel and cobalt	558.148
silver	558.142
zinc, tin and mercury	558.145
Organ musical instru.	776.7
Organic	
brain diseases	155.23
chemicals	665.9
chemistry	547
drugs materia medica	596.1
environment	563.192
evolution biology	563
liquids	541.21

poisons	593.92
senses	151.16
theory state	371.014
Organism physiology	592.15
Organization	
arts theater	781.8
christian societies	256
city local government	373.082
cooperation	356.7
diplomacy	386.3
Kuomintang	001.22
laboring class	354.6
library economy	022
military	
aviation	379.72
force	379.32
political economy	356
school	331.31
technical league of nations	383.4
Y. M. C. A.	256.33
Organography botany	571.27
Organs	
embryonic, human	591.5
of generation anatomy	597.61
respiratory physiology	597.23
Oriental philosophy	110
Orientation zoology	581.703
Origin	
and descent evolution	563.2
sources of knowledge	131.1
English language	451
language	400.9
Origin (cont.)	
life biology	562.7
of man anthropology	565.72
sexual characters	561.66
species evolution	564
the soul or mind	135.7
state pol. sci.	371.01
words language	401
printing	749
Origins	
of religion	209.1
Orleans, C. duc d' Fr.	
poet.	841.22
Orleans, France	
geography	983.481
Ornament	
carved arch. decoration	712.2
painted arch. decoration	712.1
Ornamental	
flowers esthetics of cities	719.8
gardening esthetics of cities	719
plasterwork masonry	651.17

Ornaments	
domestic science	693
toilet	693.5
Orne, Fr. geography	983.465
Ornithodelphia zoology	588.15
Ornithology zoology	587.9
Ornithosauria zoology	587.87
Ornithurae zoology	587.92
Orobanchaceae botany	579.63
Orology phys. geol.	552.6
Orphan asylums	
philanthropy	316.31
Orris perfumes	612.818
Orthochromatic	
photography	758.4
Orthogenetic evolution	564.6
Orthogonal projection	519.34
Orthography	
comparative language	401.4
Orthonectida zoology	583.36
Orthopedic	
appliances	598.1903
surgery deformities	598.17
Orthopoda zoology	587.837
Orthoptera zoology	585.31
Orthorhapha zoology	585.57
Oryzeae forage crops	612.294
Osaka, Japan geography	982.1643
Oscillation	
magnetism	538.17
optics	535.21
Oscillations	
of earth's crust	551.313
Oscillography electric	
eng'ing	657.18
Oscillatoriaceae botany	572.171
Osier fiber	612.596
Oslo, Norway geography	983.7986
Osmium inorg. chem.	546.77
Osmose	
of liquids	532.15
Osmosis	
cytology	561.55
physiological chemistry	581.493
Osmotic	
pressure chemistry	541.43
Ossines zoology	587.978
Osteology human	
anatomy	597.711
Ostracoda zoology	584.865
Ostracodermi zoology	587.2
Ostracophori zoology	587.2
Otariidae mammalia	588.535
Otology	598.4
Ottoman	
empire Turkish hist.	926

Ou, Japan geography	982.1621
Ou Yang Hsiu	
Chinese poetry	811.735
prose	817.512
Outcasts education	338.962
sociology	313.87
Outcrop geology	553.5
Outdoor	
advertising	629.4
games	338.633
life hunting industries	619.7
plays theater	786
sports	338.633
Outer	
Mongolia, China	
geography	981.95
Ovary gynecology	598.741
Overdrawn bank and	
banking	362.7
Overdraft bank and	
banking	362.7
Overhead	
lines elec. trans.	657.651
Overpopulation	
demography	349
Overpresure school	
hygiene	332.35
Overshot	
wheels mech. eng.	655.331
Overture orchestral	
music	779.3
Ovid Latin poetry	832.12
Oviparity zoology	581.625
Oviposion zoology	581.624
Ovoviviparity zoology	581.626
Ovulation physiology	598.725
Ovum	
anatomy	591.513
embryology	591.5
physiology	592.6
Owls zoology	587.9795
Ownership	
land pol. econ.	353.01
of land inter'l private	
law	381.821
Ox zoology	588.335
Oxalidaceae botany	577.87
Oxford, England	
geography	983.565
Oxides	
chem. tech.	661.6
theoretic chem.	541.03
Oxygen	
chemistry	546.151
group inorganic chem.	546.15
Oysters fishers	617.7
Ozone chemistry	546.151

Pacific	
blockade intern. law	382.33
islands, Polynesia	
geography	985.97
history	959.7
problems intern. pol.	388.19
ocean, physical geology	552.2
packing business meth.	622.6
Paconia albiflora	
floriculture	613.82
Paganism theology	200.04
Pageants	
dramatic theater	786
Paidology Psychology	153.7
Pailleron, E. Fr. drama	842.87
Painted	
decoration archite.	712.1
Painting	
arts	734
handcrafts	683
porcelain	735.4
Paintings	
collection of	734
engravings from	745
works engineering	651.17
Paints	
chemical technology	667.7
painting	734
Palaces	
architecture	718.2
historic ruins	990.182
China	991.82
Palaeobotany	569.1
Paleolithic	
age prehist. arch.	990.9
Palaeontology	569
Palaeotheriidae zoology	488.346
Palaeozoic ere geology	554.5
Palaeozoology	569.6
Palate anatomy	593.311
Pale	
colored-stars astronomy	523.84
Paleography	
archaeology	990.8
philology	409
China	419
Palestine	
geography	982.67
Pali languages	409.313
Palladium inorgan.	
chem.	546.87
Palm	
botany	575.51
plants agriculture	612.66
Palmaceous fruits	613.77

Palmae botany	575.51
Palmistry	
occult sci.	157.36
therapeutics	595.91
Palpation diagnosis	595.23
Palpigradi zoology	584.674
Pamphlets library	
science	023.8
Pamir languages	409.328
P'an Yo Chinese poet.	811.1324
Panama	
geography	984.68
history	946.8
Pancreas	
anatomy	597.316
physiology	597.326
Pancreatic	
juice physiology	597.326
Pancreatin drugs	597.365
Pandaceae botany	577.81
Pandales botany	577.8
Pandanaceae botany	575.23
Paniceae forage crops	612.293
Panmixia biology	563.195
Panoramas drawing	735.9
Panoramic	
photography	758.7
Panpsychism psychology	150.167
Pantheism theology	201.2
Pantopods zoology	584.64
Pantostomatinales	
botany	572.31
Pao Chao Chinese poet.	811.1335
Papacy	259.14
and civilization	259.149
emperors	259.145
politics	359.144
Renaissance reformation	259.148
wars	259.146
Papaver alkaloidal	
plants	612.75
Papaveraceae botany	577.51
Papaw pomiculture	613.777
Paper	
manufacture	674
money	361.7
trade	674
Papers	
historic remains	991.76
matarials office econ.	626
Papular dermatology	598.541
Papyrus manufacture	674.2
Parabola	517.46
geometry	519.86

Paraffins chem. techol.	665.5
Chemistry	547.11
Paraguay	
geography	984.89
history	948.9
Parallax	
practical astron.	522.81
terrestrial astron.	525.01
Parallel	
courses education	335.4
lines geometry	517.33
planes geometry	517.51
Parallelism	
philosophy	103.5
psychology	150.163
Paralysis	
diseases nervous system	597.8443
pediatrics	598.947
Parama Buddhism	231.79
Paramagnetism	538.5
Parasite	
utilization	614.783
Parasites	
animal diseases	597.84
pathology of animals	581.5
Parasiti zoology	583.2
Parasitic	
diseases	598.547
plants	611.97
Parasitica zoology	585.58
Parasitism zoology	581.765
Parasuchia zoology	587.833
Parazoa zoology	582.5
Parcels	
post postal services	636.6
Parchment manufacture	674.5
Pareiasauria zoology	587.811
Parent-teacher	
associations	333.8
Parents	
and children	397.52
teachers	333.8
Parents(cont.)	
duties of ethics	183.3
family life	313.322
Paresthesia abnormal	
psy.	155.257
Parhelia meteorology	529.65
Parietales botany	578.5
Paris, France	
geography	983.473
peace conference	380.6
Parish	
educational work	254.6
work	254.6

Parks	
public landscape garden	719.1
rural planning	313.415
Parliamentary	
law	392
political science	373.031
Parmentides Gk. philos.	121.123
Parrots zoology	587.9751
Parsnip roots crops	612.47
Part-	
sovereign state pol. sci.	371.73
Parthogeresis intern. law	381.615
Parties law	395.03
Parturition obstetrics	598.83
Parties, political	375
Pasigraphy mathematics	510.4
Paspalum forage crops	612.277
Passage	
of electricity	537.37
Passementerie	
manufacture	675.7
Passeres birds	587.976
Passifloraceae botany	578.62
Passiflorineae botany	578.5
Passimism philosiophy	173.1
Passion	
of Christ christology	251.2951
Passions ethics	180.6
Passionists christianity	259.0916
Pastel painting	734.5
Pastinaca	
sativa roots crops	612.47
Pastoral	
Judaism	264
medicine	595.92
poetry	801.1
Pastoral (cont.)	
theology	
Christianity	254
Mohammedan	274
visitations	254.2
Zoroastrian	284
Pasture	
lands	353.13
Patagonia	
geography	984.829
Patan	923.83
Patent	
industrial arts	605
law	379.23
medicines state control	593.75
Patents technology	645
Paternity sociology	313.321
Pathogenic	
organisms	566.964

Pathological		
anatomy		
medical science	594.1	
psychology	152.4	
anthropology biology	565.48	
changes biology	561.59	
liars abnor. psy.	155.453	
physiology	592.3	
psychology	155	
Pathology		
medical science	594	
microscopy	566.84	
of fetal appendage		
obstetrics	598.827	
hearing psychology	151.124	
labor obstetrics	598.84	
memory psychology	151.67	
ovum obstetrics	598.824	
pregnancy	598.82	
puerperal state	598.86	
the ear otology	598.44	
eye ophthalmology	598.34	
skin dermatology	598.54	
thought psychology	151.87	
vision psychology	151.114	
volition psychology	151.44	
silkworms	616.24	
zoology	581.5	
Patience ethics	180.78	
Patriotic		
societies sociology	313.61	
Patriotism ethics	185.2	
Paul		
epistle apocrapha	252.995	
Paulding, J. K. Am.		
humor	863.26	
Pauper		
labor	316.57	
political economy	354.256	
Pauperism economics	352.8	
Pavements		
road engineering	651.75	
Pawn		
shops finance	362.19	
Pea garden crops	613.3	
Peace		
and war	185.8	
Peach pomiculture	613.727	
Peacock, T. L. Eng fic.	853	
Peacocks zoology	587.971	
Peanut forage crops	612.35	
Pear pomiculture	613.727	
Pearls precious stone	558.188	
Peat mineralogy	558.121	
Pebble lithology	557.53	

Pectinibranchia zoology	583.531
Pecuniary	
punishment	394.515
Pedaliaceae botany	579.61
Peddling commerce	622.56
Pedestrianism education	338.036
Pediatrics	598.9
Pedicellariae zoology	581.75
Pediculina parasitica	
zoology	585.1
Pedimana zoology	588.28
Pedipalpi arthropoda	584.672
Pegu languages	409.171
Peking, China	
geography	981.61
Pelecypoda articulata	583.55
Peloponuesus	
geography	983.17
Penalties criminal law	394
Penance theology	253.96
Penis anatomy	597.617
Penitentiaries sociology	315.5
Pennsylvania, U. S.	
geography	984.164
Penology social	
pathology	315.2
Pens manuf.	674.9
Pensions	
insurance	354.35
teachers	336.52
Pentateuch Bible	252.21
Pentecost practical	
theol.	253.14
Peonage working	
conditions	354.253
People's	
library	025.71
movement	001.99
popular education	330.124
primitive religions	209
party, U. S.	375.66
Peperales botany	576.25
Pepsin drugs	597.365
Percentage arithmetic	511.35
Perception	
of movement psychol.	151.1754
space psychol.	151.1752
time psychol.	151.1753
psychology	151.17
Perceptual	
apprehension psychology	151.17
Perchers zoology	587.976
Percussions	
instruments music	777

Perennial		Peritonitis	
plants horticulture	613.82	diseases of	597.347
Perfectionism	173.7	obstetrics	598.862
Performance psychology	150.1917	Perlidae zoology	585.33
Perfumery		Permanent	
agriculture	612.81	advisory commissions	383.5
chemical technology	668.1	on armaments	383.53
Perfumes		congresses	380.6
agriculture	612.8	courts of Arbitration	
chem. tech.	668.11	treaties	382.43
Pericardium anatomy	597.111	international	
Peridiniaceae botany	572.4	justice	382.41
Peridotite lithology	557.38	international commission	382.27
Periodic		mandates commission	383.54
current electricity	537.25	Perman languages	409.234
curve acoustics	534.531	Permissible	
phenomena magnetism	538.751	violence intern. law	381.552
variations astron.	529.81	Persecutions christianity	259.092
Periodicity		Persian languages	409.323
diseases pathology	594.23	literature	893
Peripheral		philosophy	115
nervous system		Persica gardening	613.727
anatomy	597.816	Personal	
physiology	597.821	bibliography	015
Perissodacryla zoology	588.34	hygiene	593.1
Peritoneum		narratives	970.6
anatomy	597.317	economics pol. sci.	350.011
diseases	597.347	qualities of style liter.	800.445

worship	253.23	Peru	
Personality		administration	373.84
constituent elements of psy.	153.82	botany	571.984
		finance	350.984
cultivation of psychology	153.87	geography	984.85
development or emergence of psychology	153.81	geology	550.84
		history	948.5
		school	338.7984
for library service	028.6	Pessimism philosophy	108.3
library staff	022.5	Pests	
metaphysics	135.5	agriculture	611.9
political science	372.11	grape culture	613.75
psychopathic	155.4	Peter, St.	
teachers education	336.2	apocryphe	252.996
tests of psychology	153.88	epistle 1	252.792
types of psychology	153.84	2	252.793
workers economics	354.114	gospel	252.991
Personatae botany	579.5	Petiton, right of pol. sci,	372.15
Personnel		Petrarca. F. Ital. poetry	833.118
business	622.3	Petrography geology	557
estate	369.141	Petroleum	
library service	022.5	chemic tech.	665.5
post services	636.35	economical geology	556.1
responsible for discipline	332.4	lithology	557.57
		mineralogy	665.5
Perturbations		Petrology geology	557
of heavenly bodies	551.311	Petromyzontes zoology	587.13
theoretic astronomy	521.5	Phaeophyceae botany	573.25

Phaeosoporeae botany	573.25	Phasmodae zoology	585.31
Phagedena diseases	594.941	Phedo Gk. philos.	121.28
Phalaris forage crops	612.278	Phenicia	
Phalangidea zoology	584.678	geography	982.67
Phallicism sex worship	209.3	history	926.7
Phanerocephala zoology	583.613	Phenols organic chem.	547.3
Phanerogamia		Phenomenalism	
botany	574	philosophy	106.8
palaeobotany	569.3	Philanthropy ethics	180.77
Pharisees Judaism	269.2	sociology	316
Pharmaceutical		Philemen Bible	252.786
jurisprudence	593.9	Philippians epistles	252.76
preparations	596.6	Philippine	
chemistry	596.4	islands	985.911
substances	596.1	question	388.47
Pharmacology materia		Philo Greek. philos.	121.55
medica	596.3	Philology	400
Pharmacotherapy		Philosophical	
therapeutics	595.7	mechanics physics	531.11
Pharmacy		Philosophy	100
materia medica	596	natural	530
medical microscopy		of life	170
biology	566.86	soul	135
Pharynx		special topics see	
anatomy	597.312	subject	
diseases of	597.34	Philters witchcraft	157.75
physiology	597.32	Philydraceae botany	575.77

Philanthropy sociology	316
Phlebitis obstetrics	598.866
Phlegmasia doleus obstetrics	598.866
Phleum forage crops	612.24
Phocidae zoology	588.537
Phocis, Greece geography	983.16
Phodea floriculture	613.82
Phoenicia	
geography	982.83
history	928.3
Phoenician languages	409.53
Phonendoscope therapeutics	595.26
Phonographs	
acoustic phys.	534.99
instru. music	777.8
Phonolite lithology	557.26
Phonology philology	401.4
Phormium fibers	612.58
Phoronidea zoology	583.9
Phosphorescence optics	535.56
Phosphorus inorg. chem.	546.143
Photo—	
chemistry photography	752
theor. chem.	541.5
optics	751
lithography	746.3
mechanical engraving	746
Photography	750
Photogravure	
bibliography	010.37
copy books	009.35
editions	009.13
engraving	746.7
Photomicrography	566.18
Phototelegraphy	657.87
Phrenology occult. sci.	157.3
therapeutics	595.91
Phrymaceae botany	579.688
Phthisis diseases	597.245
Phycomycetes botany	573.28
Phylactolaemata zoology	583.85
Phyllite lithology	557.44
Phyllopoda zoology	584.861
Phylogeny biology	563.2
Phyllite lithology	557.44
Physaraceae botany	572.27
Physical	
agents plants	571.47
effects	537.379
chemistry	541
basis	563.32

of music	534.7	Physiocrats economics	350.092
diagnosis	595.27	Physiognomy occult sci.	157.3
education	338.63	Physiography geology	552
school	332.5	Physiological	
exercise	338.631	acoustics	534.9
environment social		action	596.3
control	311.11	anthropology	565.4
geography	980.11	botany	571
Physical(cont.)		chemistry	
hexiology	581.7773	biology	561.49
influences to mankind	565.77	botany	571.49
laws	530.5	general	592.4
loss of territory	381.321	zoology	581.49
measurements	332.31	mechanics	531.32
physics	530.077	mineralogy	558.5
mineralogy	558.3	morphology of cells	592.25
optics	535.3	optics	535.9
paradoxes	530.9	properties of cells	561.56
phenomena spiritualism	157.95	psychology	152
properties of cell		zoology	581
cytology	561.55	theory of music	770.01
crystals	559.3	Physiology	
Physics	530	bacteriology	566.92
of hearing	151.122	biology	561.4
the atmosphere	529.1	botany	581.4
vision	151.112	medical microscopy	566.82
terrestrial	525.01	science	592
theory of music	770.01	music	770.012

obstetric	598.81
Physiology (cont.)	
of development	561.71
hearing	151.122
labor obstetrics	598.83
movement	151.32
nerve and muscle	581.46
the circulatory system	597.12
digestive system	597.32
domesticated animals	599.2
ductless glands	581.45
ear	598.42
eye	598.32
female generative organs	598.72
genitourinary system	597.62
glands	581.44
glandular system	597.42
locomotor system	597.72
nervous system	597.82
respiratory organs	597.22
skin	598.52
tissues	581.408
vision	151.112
silkworms	616.22
zoology	581.4
Physopoda zoology	585.37
Physostomi zoology	587.4775
Phytogeography botany	571.9
Phytolacaceae botany	577.21
Phytology botany	571
Phytopathology botany	571.5
Phytopsychology comp. psy.	154.7
Phytosarcodina botany	572.2
Phytosauaia zoology	587.833
P'i Jih-hsiu Chinese poet.	811.1485
Piano music	776.1
Pianoforta music	776.1
Pianola music	776.1
Picardy, Fr. geography	983.466
Picidae zoology	587.9753
Picture telegraphy	657.87
Piedmont, Italy geography	983.26
Piers	
architecture	713.2
hydraulic engineering	654.33
Pigmentary dermatology	598.545
Pigments chem. tech.	667.71
Pilots	
nautics	659.195

protection of travelers	593.485	Plagiostomi zoology	587.4
Pinaceae botany	574.43	Plagiotremata zoology	587.85
Pindar Gk. lyric poet.	831.45	Plague	594.922
Pingala Buddhism	239.137	pathology	594.922
Pinnipedia zoology	588.53	sociology	316.47
Piperaceae botany	576.27	Plains	
Pipe-organ music	776.7	geography	980.507
Pipes steam		China	981.37
transmission	655.227	physical geology	552.7
Piping steam		Planaria zoology	583.31
engineering	655.227	Plane	
Piracy maritime law	381.79	curves	519.451
Pirolaceae botany	579.13	of 3rd order	519.456
Piron, Alexis Fr. drama	842.55	4th order	519.458
Pisces palaeozoology	569.83	geometry	517.3
zoology	587.3	motion	531.243
Pisciculture fish culture	617.3	of orbit in space	521.21
Pistols manufactures	671.1	Planetry system	
Piston steam eng.	655.259	astronomy	523.4
Pisum forage crops	612.36	Planets	
Pitchstone lithology	557.23	astronomy	523.4
Pitt, W. Eng. liter.	858.46	lesser negative astrology	157.217
Pittosporaceae botany	577.75	Planimetry geometry	517.3
Pity ethics	180.96	Plans	
Placenta obstetrics	598.8273	architecture	711
Placodontia zoology	587.814	of national	
Plagiostoma zoology	587.41	reconstruction	001.155
		Plant	

and animal behavior	154
behavior	154.7
body morphology	571.2
cell	571.11
lore	570.081
Plantaginaceae botany	579.71
Plantaginales botany	579.7
Plantanaceae botany	577.77
Planters agriculture	610.62
Plants	
affecting	571.47
botany	570
esthetics of cities	719.8
geologic	551.97
geography distribution	571.96
injurious to animals	611.977
metallurgy	669.17
paleontology	569.1
sculpture	729.7
terrestrial	571.902
Plasmodiophorales	
botany	572.23
Plastic	
materials	668.8
surgery	598.1908
Plastids botany	571.114
Platesus	
geography	980.507
China	981.37
Platinum	
group chem.	546.7
inorganic chemistry	546.73
Plato Gk. philos.	121.3
Platonism Gk. philos.	121.57
Platium metallurgy	669.999
Platyhelmia zoology	583.3
Platyhelmintha zoology	583.3
Plautus, Latin drama	832.23
Play amusements	790
Playgrounds school	332.91
Pleadings law	395.02
Pleasure	
and pain psychology	151.2
Plecoptera zoology	585.33
Plectospondyli zoology	587.4771
Plectral	
stringed instrum. music	775
Pleura	
anatomy	597.216
disease	597.246
Pleurisu diseases	597.246
Pleurisy diseases	597.246
Pleurocarpi botany	573.7
Pleuropterygii zoology	587.41
Pliny Latin letters	832.81

Plotins Gk. philos.	121.58	poet	861.31
Plum fruits gardening	613.723	Poetic	
Plumbage mineralogy	558.126	books Bible	252.3
Plumbaginaceae botany	579.25	Poetry	801
Plural		American literature	861.1
vote electoral systems	372.523	Chinese literature	811.1
Pluralism philosophy	102.5	English literature	851.1
Plurality		French literature	841
of spectra	535.447	German literature	871.1
worlds	523.14	Greek literature	831.1
ontology	133.82	Italian literature	833.1
Plutarch Greek philos.	121.57	Japanese literature	821
Plutonic rocks geology	557.3	Latin literature	832.1
Pneumatic		Spanish literature	835.1
apparatus phys.	533.9	Poisons	
aspiration therapeutics	595.817	chemic analysis	543.49
engines eng'ing	655.5	medical jurisprudence	593.9
machinery eng'ing	655.5	toxicology	593.9
Pneumatics physics	533	Poitou, France	
Po Chu-yi Chinese		geography	983.491
poet.	811.1458	Poland	
Po P'u Chinese drama	812.33	geography	983.797
Poa forage crops	612.21	history	937.97
Pocketbooks	039.3	Polansia olericulture	613.16
Podostemaceae botany	577.71	Polar regions	
Poe, E. A.		geography	985.99
Am. fiction	863.31	history	959.9
		Polaris stars	523.86

Polariscopic analysis	544.7
Polarization	
magnetism	538.867
of light optics	535.37
transmission	536.48
Polarized	
light optics	535.37
Polemon Gk. philos.	121.35
Poles magnetism	538.15
Police	
courts	315.35
duty	315.33
international	382.7
justice	315.53
sociology	315.3
Policy	
Kuomintang, the	001.25
land pol. econ.	353.02
Polish languages	409.393
Political	
education	330.123
geography	980.17
pol. sci.	370.98
history	
diplomatic	902.7
China	910.27
Egypt	951.27
England	935.27
Europe	930.27
France	934.27
Germany	937.27
Greece	931.27
India	923.27
Japan	921.27
Korea	922.27
Political (cont.)	
Rome	932.27
Russia	938.27
Spain	933.27
U. S. A.	941.27
offenses	394.21
parties	375
problems intern. pol.	388.7
science	370
treaties	387.3
war songs	771.3
Politics	370
Poliziano A. Ital. poet.	833.124
Pollution	
of atmosphere hygiene	653.37
Polonium inorganic	
chem.	546.67
Polyandry marriage	313.3415
Polycarpicae botany	577.3
Polychaeta zoology	583.612
Polyemoniaceae botany	579.52

Polygalaceae botany	577.97	Pope, Alexander	
Polygamy		Eng. poetry	851.53
ethics	183.2	prose	857.55
marriage	313.3413	satire	858.255
Polygenetic biology	565.733	Popliteal space anatomy	591.88
Polygonaceae botany	576.95	Poppy alkaloidal plants	612.75
Polyhedrons geometry	517.53	Population	
Polynesia		demography	349
geography	985.97	state pol. sci.	371.025
history	959.7	Populists	
Polyplacophora		party pol. sci.	375.66
articulata	583.511	Porcelain	
Polyprodontidae zoology	588.26	art	735.4
Polyzoa zoology	583.8	earth	557.521
Pomaceous		Porcelains	
fruits gardening	613.71	clay industries	666.13
Pomegranate gardening	613.716	Porifera zoology	582.5
Pomerania, Germany		Porphyrite lithology	557.31
geography	983.76	Portable	
Pomiculture gardening	613.7	engines engineering	655.292
Pomology agriculture	613.7	Porteaceae botany	573.78
Ponard, F. French		Porteales botany	576.77
drama	842.82	Porterm, J. Eng. fic.	853
Ponds		Porto Rico	
water supply	653.14	geography	984.75
Pontoon		history	947.5
bridges eng.	651.577	Portrait	

miniatures	737.33
Portraits	
biography, general	970.2
Dr. Sun	001.192
human figure	737.31
Portugal history	933.9
Portuguese	
discovery of America	941.815
East India	
geography	985.44
history	954.4
languages	409.363
literature	836
philosophy	123
Portulacaceae botany	577.25
Posen, Ger. geography	983.76
Position of	
body in orbit	521.23
space	521.24
plane	521.22
Positivism philosophy	106.6
Post union	636.34
Postage stamps	636.4
Postal	
law	636.1
Postal (cont.)	
savings banks	362.97
services	636
Posterior	
Chao Chinese history	913.583
Ch'in Chinese history	903.588
Liang Chinese history	913.591
Shu Chinese history	914.98
Yen Chinese history	913.587
Potable	
water protection	614.95
Potamogetonaceae	
botany	575.31
Potassium inorg. chem.	546.211
Potato agriculture	612.481
Potteries clay industries	666.11
Pottery	
arts of design	735.4
Poultry	
domestic	615.2
veterinary medicine	599.45
Power	
metaphysics	134.8
plants	657.29
steam	655.23
transmission	655.71
appliances agr.	610.66
Powers	
central government	373.011
legislative pol. sci.	373.035
separation of	373.0502

Pracrit languages	409.315	
Practical		
chemistry	542	
Buddhism	233	
devotional Christianity	253.73	
ethics	188	
sociology	313.3502	
geometry	519	
Judaism	263	
meteorology	529.7	
mining operation	658.3	
pharmacy	593.73	
prospecting	658.2	
Shintoism	291.3	
theology	203	
Christianity	253	
Mohammedanism	273	
Roman Catholic Church	254.13	
Zoroastrianism	283	
Practice		
of medicine	595	
trial law	395.02	
Pradjna Buddhism	231.76	
Pragmatism philosophy	106.4	
Pragmaparameta Sutra	232.31	
Prakrti Hinduism	241.61	
Pramayama Hinduism	244.4	
Praseodymium inorg. chem.	546.267	
Paratyahara Hinduism	244.5	
Pratyaksha Hinduism	241.21	
Prayer		
books	253.4	
meetings	253.49	
of Manasses Apocrypha	252.96	
Prayers		
practical theology		
Christianity	253.4	
Preachers ministry	255.56	
Preadamites doctrinal anthro.	251.32	
Precession		
practical astron.	522.84	
theoretic astron.	521.9	
Precipitate rocks		
geology	557.55	
Precipitation		
meteorology	529.45	
Precocity		
child study	153.765	
Predestination		
Christianity	251.49	
metaphysics	134.21	
Mohammedan	271.4	

Pre-existence	
metaphysics	135.7
Preface	
to the "Shih" Chinese	
classics	093.3
Preformation biology	562.73
Pregnancy obstetrics	598.81
Prehistoric	
archaeology	990.9
Prelacy Christianity	255.52
Preletariat sociology	313.88
Prenatal	
culture pediatrics	598.91
Preparation	
microscopy biology	566.13
Preparatory	
education	338.35
Preparing	
skeletons biology	567.1
Presbyter	
ministry Christianity	255.54
Presbyterian	
church Christianity	259.5
Presbytery Christianity	255.7
Preschool	
education	338.1
Prescription	
civil law	397.18
criminal law	394.58
Presentations obstetrics	598.833
Preservation	
biology	563.11
museums	990.079
of flowers	613.809
foods	694.5
mulberry leaves	616.6
specimens	567.8
President government	373.0503
Press	
clubs journalism	040.6
Pressure	
hydrostates	532.33
meteorology	529.2
temperature	533.38
"Tinsion" physics	533.34
transimission of	533.383
Prestige sociology	312.65
Pretas Buddhism	231.86
Preventive	
measure labor	354.54
Prevost d'Exiles French	
fic.	843.53
Pride ethics	180.81
Priest ministry	
Christianity	255.54

Primary			history	010.7
education	338.2		of engravings	749
germinal layer zoology	581.22		mark hist. of printing	010.7
libraries	025.25		telegraphy	657.8355
Primates zoology	589		textile chem. tech.	667.5
Primative			Prisms geometry	517.53
culture ethnology	565.79		Prison	
religions	200.05		hygiene prisons	315.53
state pol. sci.	371.1		library	025.76
Primulaceae botany	579.23		Prisons	
Primulales botany	579.2		political economy	354.251
Principal			public building	717.4
punishments crim. law	394.51		sociology	315.5
Principle			Private	
coins money	361.61		aid sociology	316.5
of reversibility thermics	536.64		detectives police	315.37
Prince Edward Island, Canada			economics in general	350.01
			enterprise organization	356.1
geography	984.28		international law	381.8
Principles			law	390.008
of mechanism	655.11		libraries	025.1
national			ownership	353.3
reconstruction	001.15		railways	633.18
study education	334		post	636.32
Print books biblo.	010.3		prayers	253.45
Printers' ink. chem. tech.	667.74		schools and colleges	338.07
			worship Christianity	253.2
Printing			Privileges diplomacy	386.25

Prize law	381.565
Probability	
logic	148
calculus of algebra	512.9
Problem	
of living sociology	317.1
suffrage reform pol.	
sci.	372.58
3 bodies astronomy	521.13
Proboscidea zoology	588.38
Procedure	
international arbitration	382.41
disputes	382
private law	381.87
of investigation	341.1
law	395
Prodicus Gk. philos.	121.225
Production pol. economy	352
Productive arts	600
Productivity economics	353.5
Products	
of metabolism	566.928
Professional	
education	338.4
ethics	186
type criminology	315.124
union trade	313.7
Profession	
education	336.6
vital statistics	349.076
Professors'	
education	336
salaries education	336.5
Prognosis therapeutics	595.3
Progression mathematics	514
Prohibited	
books rarities	009.6
Profect	
prognosis	595.3
Projection	
arts of design	731.4
modern geometry	519.31
of compounds vibrations	
phys.	534.537
Projective	
geometry	519.39
Projectivity geometry	519.31
Promenades esthetics	
of cities	719.2
Promorphology	
biology	561.11
botany	571.23
Propagation	
magnetism physics	538.862
microscopy biology	566.923
of sound	534.4

optics	535.31	Prosobranchiata zoology	583.531
Properties		Prosody	
of blood	597.121	comparative language	401.7
living matter	562.8	Prospecting	
Propertius Lat. lyric		mining eng'ing	658.2
poetry	832.44	Prostitution sociology	317.86
Property		Protarthropoda zoology	584.2
civil law	381.842	Protected states intern.	
law	397.2	law	381.12
loan banks	362.7	Protection	
of belligerents in war	381.548	against animal botany	571.74
political science	372.12	cold botany	571.73
tax public finance	369.151	drouth botany	571.72
woman feminism	313.354	methods of police	315.33
Prophecies occult sci.	157.18	of citizens abroad	381.826
Prophetic Books Bible	252.4	human life	593.4
Prophets Bible	252.4	silkworn agriculture	616.4
occult sci.	157.097	trade economics	351.35
Prophyrite lithology	557.31	travelers	593.48
Proportion arithmetic	511.33	Protective	
Proportional		coloration biology	563.14
representative suffrage	372.527	zoology	581.75
Proprietary libraries	025.5	inoculation public	
Propulsion shipbuilding	659.165	health	593.2355
Prorocentraceae botany	572.4	measures pol. econ.	354.54
Prose literature	807	tariff finance	369.1643
Prosencephalon anatomy	597.8113	Protectoral	
		sovereignty pol. sci.	371.75

Protegoras Greek philos.	121.222
Proteids	
organic chemistry	547.92
physiological chem.	
zoology	581.495
Protelidae mammalia	588.514
Protest diplomatic	
negotiation	386.47
Protestant	
episcopal church	259.4
Protestantism	
Christianity	259.2
Protobranchia zoology	583.551
Protochordata zoology	586.2
Protococcales botany	573.21
Protodonta mammalia	588.11
Protomastigales botany	572.33
Protophyta	
botany	572
palaeonotology	569.21
Protoplasm	
botany	571.111
cytoxlogy	561.51
physiology	
locomotor system	597.721
Protosyngnatha zoology	584.4
Prototheria mammalia	588.1
Protozoal	
palacontology	569.71
zoology	582.1
Protracheata zoology	584.2
Provencal	
languages	409.365
literature	849
Providence theology	201.5
Christianity	251.15
Province France	
geography	983.497
Provision	
for education of	
prisoners	315.57
religious instruction	315.56
of famines agri.	610.18
Provisional	
release criminal law	394.57
Prudence ethics	180.78
Prunophora gardening	613.723
Prunus gardening	613.727
Prussia, Ger. geography	983.76
East	983.76
Rhenish	983.77
Prussian Saxony, Ger.	
geography	983.76
Psalms	

of Solomon New		healing occult sci.	157.97
Testament	252.983	life of primitive people	565.792
Old Testament	252.32	monism psychology	150.167
Psammite lithology	557.53	research occult. sci.	157.9
Psanniute		Psychoanalysis	
rocks lithology	557.53	psychology	156
Psephite		Psychological	
rocks lithology	557.53	measurements	150.77
Pseudepigrapha		schools	150.19
of the Apocalypse	252.996	systems	150.19
Epistles	252.995	Psychology	150
Gospels	252.991	abnormal	155
Pseudo diseases	595.5	abolescence	153.7
Pseudolamellibrancha		adult	153.6
zoology	583.553	animal	154.8
Pseudoneuroptera		or,	581.701
zoology	585.35	applied	158
Pseudosciuridae zoology	588.612	bio.	154
Pseudoscorpiones		child	153.7
zoology	584.676	or,	313.365
Pseudospherical		comparative	154
trigonometry	518.4	configuration	150.1915
Pseudosuchia zoology	587.833	depth	156
Psittacidae zoology	587.9751	differential	153
Psocidae zoology	585.35	dynamic	150.193
Psychiatry abnor. psy.	155	endocrine	150.1971
Psychic		Psychology(cont.)	
		environment	153.2

ethnic	153.4	reaction	150.197
evolutional	153	response	150.197
existential	150.191	senescence	153.6
experimental	150.71	sex	153.1
faculty	150.1911	social	310.115
folk	153.4	structural	150.191
functional	150.193	teratologic	155
general	151	women	153.1
genetic	153	or,	313.3501
gestalt	150.1915	zoology	154.8
individual	153.8		
mental	152		
metaphysical	150.1		
or,	135		
mind-body performance	150.1917		
normal	151		
of inspiration	151.7		
nations	153.4		
types	153.8		
unconsciousness	156		
pathologic	155		
physiological	152		
phyto.	154.7		
purposive	150.193		
quantitative	151.18		
race	153.4		
rational	150.1		
or,	135		

special subject see
   subject

Psychoneuroses abnor.
  psychology   155.25

Psychopathic
  personality abnor. psy.   155.4

Psychopathology abnor.
  psy.   155

Psychopathy abnor.
  psychology   155

Psychophysics
  psychology   151.18

Psychoscopic
  knowledge occult
    science   157.67

Pteriodophyta
  botany   573.8
  palaeontology   569.24

Pteropoda zoology	583.535
Pterosauria zoology	587.87
Pu Sung-ling Chinese fic.	813.73
Puarra sutra	249.1
Puberty gynecology	598.721
Public	
administration	373
aid sociology	316.5
bank	362.12
bonds	362.7
building architecture	717
closets	653.35
debt	369.08
China	369.18
economics	350.03
enterprise	356.1
expenditure	369.03
China	369.13
finance	369
games	793
health	593.2
forest effect	614.123
heraldry	961
lands	353.2
law	390.008
libraries	025.3
opinion social control	311.54
parks esthetics of cities	719.1
promenades esthetics of cities	719.2
revenue	369.04
China	369.14
school	330.125
and college educ.	338.01
securities finance	366.5
sports	793
squares esthetics of cities	719.2
worship Christianity	253.21
Publicity	
works library	022.4
Publishers' catalogs	011.8
Puebla, Mexico	
geography	984.47
Puerperal	
diseases obstetrics	598.86
fever pathology	598.862
mania obstetrics	598.864
state obstetrics	
Pulley mechanics	531.94
Pulmonary	
animal heat	592.52
respiration	581.427
Pulmonta zoology	583.537
Pulmons anatomy	597.215

Pulsation acoustics	534.63	Purposive psychology	150.193
Pulse		Purusha Hinduism	241.69
in diseases	597.126	Pycnogonomorpha	
physiology	597.126	zoology	584.63
therapeutics	595.24	Pyemia diseases	594.945
Pumis lithology	557.23	obstetrics	598.862
Pumping		Pyramids geometry	517.53
engines engin'g	655.37	Pyrenocarpeae botany	573.4
mechanical engineering	655.37	Pyrenees Fr. geography	
Pumps		Basses	983.494
engineering	655.37	Haute	983.493
Punicaceae botany	578.75	Orientales	983.496
Punishment		Pyrography	
of death criminal law	394.511	decoration and	
body criminal law	394.511	ornament	769.1
imprisonment		Pyrolatry nature worship	209.25
criminal law	394.513	Pyrometry metallurgy	669.13
Punishments law	394.5	temperature	536.14
Punjab, India		vibrations	536.14
geography	982.38	Pyrotechnics chem.	
Pupipara zoology	585.57	tech.	663.5
Pure-land-sect Chinese		Pyrotheria zoology	588.391
Buddhism	239.58	Pyrrho Greek philos.	121.531
Purification		Pyrrhoinsm Greek	
of air pubic health	593.115	philos.	121.54
water-supply engin'g	653.18	Pyrus	
ritual Taoism	223.7	pomiculture	613.712
Puritanism Chistianity	259.84		

malus pomiculture	613.711	philos.	121.57
Pythagoras Greek philos.	121.31	Pythonomorpha zoology	587.851
Pythagorean Greek			

Quackery	
delusions	157.79
medical state control	593.75
Quadratic forms algebra	512.26
Quadrature	
integral calculus	515.3
of circle geometry	517.81
Quadrilaterals plane geom.	517.35
Quadrupes zoology	588
Quaker Christianity	259.85
Qualifications of	
library staff	022.5
Kuomintang	001.243
teachers	
education	336.2
library economy	028.6
voters suffrage	372.51
workers economics	354.114
Qualitative analysis	544
Quality	
metaphysics	133
of water sanitary eng'ing	653.12
Quantitative analysis	545
psychology	151.18
Quantity	
metaphysics	134.9
meters elec. engin'g	657.16
Quantum theory physics	530.73
Quarantine public health	593.2353
Quartets vocal music	771.77
Quartic	
curves modern geometry	519.458
surfaces modern geometry	519.467
Quartzite lithology	557.45
Quaternary period geology	554.73
Quaternions mathematics	512.62
Quays habor engineering	654.35
Quebec, Canada geography	984.28
Queensland, Australia geography	985.939
Queretaro, Mexico geography	984.47
Questioning, art of educat.	337.11
Questions	
on special subject see subject	
Quick transport railways	633.7

Quicksilver, see Mercury
Quilier-Couch, A. T.
    Eng. Fict.   853.91

Quince pomiculture   613.715
Quinones organic chem.   547.6
Quintilian Latin oratory   832.846

Rabbits
   dom. animals   615.19
   zoology   588.64
Race
   and slavery   317.44
   horse amusement   798
      domestic animals   615.19
   problem sociology   317.2
   psychology   153.4
Races
   history of civilization   902.1
      China   910.21
      Egypt   951.21
      England   935.21
      Europe   930.21
      France   934.21
      German   937.21
      Greece   931.21
      India   923.21
      Japan   921.21
      Korea   922.21
      Rome   932.21
      Russia   938.21
      Spain   933.21
      U. S. A.   941.21
   of men ethnography   565.8
Racial characteristics
   psychology   153.41

Racine, L. Fr. poetry   841.52
Racing
   amusement   798
   boat   798
   horse   798
   dog   798
Rack railway eng.   651.85
Racline, J. Fr. drama   842.48
Radiant
   energy physics   535
   of sun astronomy   523.72
   transformation of   535.5
   points meteors   523.53
Radiata zoology   582.9
Radiation
   meteorology   529.17
   of heat physics   536.42
   optics   535.5
   physiology   592.52
   transmission   536.4
      physics   536.42
Radio
   engineering   657.838
   transportation   637.3
Radioactivity physics   539
Radiography diagnosis   595.275
Radio-physics   539
Radiolaria zoology   582.18

Radiology physics	539
Radiotelegraphy elec. eng.	657.838
Radiotherapy therapeutics	595.87
Radium inorgan. chem.	546.227
Radon inorgan. chem.	546.187
Raffia fibers	612.592
Rafflisiaceae botany	576.92
Raft	
bridge engin'g	651.577
Raiae fishes	587.41
Railroad	
engineering	651.8
elevated	651.86
maintenance eng.	651.818
repair	651.818
surgery	598.197
transportation	633
Rails	
railroad engineering	651.813
Railway	
construction	651.81
engineering	651.8
transport	633
Railways	
and the state	633.1
communication	633
savings banks	362.98
traffic	633.5
Rain	
agric. hindrances	611.915
protection against agric.	611.9
worship	209.29
Rainbows meteorology	529.64
Rainfall meteorology	529.45
Ram hydraulic eng.	655.37
Ramie fibers	612.55
Ramsay, A. Eng. poet.	851.54
Ranales botany	577.3
Ranks	
government	373.015
heraldry	966
Ranunculaceae botany	577.36
Rape roots crops	612.42
Raphia fibers	612.592
Raptores birds	587.979
Rare	
binding book rarities	009.2
books rarities	009
earths inorgan. chem.	546.26
printing book rarities	009.1
Rarefied	
air and vacuum	655.56

Rasores birds	597	library economy	027.5
Rat		rooms lib. econ.	024.5
dom. animals	615.19	Reagents chem. anal.	544.11
zoology	588.615	Real	
Rational		estate public finance	369.141
mechanics	531.1	property law	397.2
psychology	135	taxation	369.151
or,	150.1	variable functions	516.11
Rationalism		Realism	
philosophy	104.1	philosophy	106.1
of life	173	Reapers agriculture	611.8
Ratitae birds	587.94	Reasoning	
Ratnakuta sutra	232.34	logic	141.2
Raw		psychology	151.86
silk manuf.	675.4	Recall	
Rayon chem. tech.	668.43	psychology	151.625
Rays fishes	587.41	right of pol. sci.	372.17
N physics	535.54	Sunyatsenism	001.132
rontgen physics	535.53	Receivers	
X physics	535.53	telephone	637.1
Reaction psychology	150.197	telegraph	637.7
Read, T. B. Amer. poet.	861.39	Reciprocals	
Readers		mathematics	510.215
aids lib. econ.	027.1	Reciprocating engines	655.298
rule lib. econ.	022.6	Reclamation	
Reading		drainage eng.	654.87
education	337.9	irrigation agric.	611.6
kindergarten	338.138	engin'g	654.8

of bogs	654.87	Reeds fibers	612.594
women prisoners	315.73	Reemployment econ.	354.137
Recognition	381.541	Reference library	023.7
of belligerency intern.		Referendum	
law	381.541	legislative	373.0328
states intern. law	381.15	Referendum(cont.)	
psychology	151.627	right of pol. sci.	372.19
Records mech.		Sunyatsenism	001.134
instruments	777.8	Reflections	
Recreation		light	535.32
building arch.	717.8	mental faculty	151.84
school	332.37	Reflexion	
uses forestry	614.94	acoustics	534.43
Recreative arts	790	heat	536.43
Rectilinear		magnetism	538.863
Motion physics	531.221	transmission	536.43
Rectum		Reflexology psychology	150.1976
anatomy	597.314	Reform	
diseases	597.345	prison sociology	315.5
Red		social sociology	312.8
bacteria botany	572.153	Reformation	
colored stars astronomy	523.83	of women prisoners	315.73
corpuscles physiology	597.1211	Reformatories	
cross philanthropy	316.1	architecture	717.4
top forage crops	612.23	sociology	315.7
Redemotion theology	251.43	Refraction	
Reduced		acoustics	534.45
wages pol. econ.	354.32	astronomy	522.82

heat	536.44
magnetism	538.865
ophthalmology	598.399
optics	535.33
phenomena meteorology	529.61
surgery	598.399
Refreshment	
buildings architec.	717.8
Refrigeration	
making chem. tech.	664.8
mech. engineering	655.6
Refugees	
world war hist.	930.77
Regalia heraldry	968
Regeneration	
embryology	581.697
physiology	592.6
theology	251.44
Regiment mil. sci.	379.54
Regional	
anatomy	591.8
surgery	598
zoology	581.19
Registered mail	636.55
Registration	
immigration	377.65
of physicians	593.72
Statistics	340
public health	593.21
Regulation	
of capital	001.142
medical practice	593.73
power governors	655.73
Reid Eng. philosophy	125.63
Reign	
of terror Fr. hist.	934.845
Reindeer domestic	
animals	615.1
zoology	588.337
Reinforced	
concrete engineering	650.46
Rejuvenscence zoology	581.698
Relapsing	
fever	594.924
Relations	
international intern.	
politics	385
of capitital to labor	
economics	354.1
Relativity	
of knowledge	
metaphysics	131.6
physics	530.7
Releasing	
dead from hell Taoism	223.5
Relics	

sacramentals	
Christianity	253.99
Religion	200
Religions	
of primitive people	209
social control	311.2
Religious	
archaeology	990.2
or,	200.99
architecture	715
calendars	528.62
ceremonies	
ritual Christianity	253.2
sacraments	
Christianity	253.99
chronology	528.62
or,	200.94
dances	792.2
education	207
christianity	257
history	200.9
life	208
Religious(cont.)	
music	772
plays	802.92
poetry	801.2
population	377.2
psychology	158.2
sculpture	729.2
sociology	311.2
therapeutics	595.92
work	
and aids Christianity	258.4
families Christianity	258.2
society Christianity	258.3
Remedies therapeutics	595.8
Remembering	
psychology	151.625
Removal	
of ovum obstetrics	598.878
of placents obstetrics	598.877
Remuneration	
for work pol. econ.	354.3
Renaissance	
European history	930.61
philosophy	121.69
Renan	
Fr. essays	847.8
philos.	124.57
Renka Japanese poetry	821.3
Renouvier Fr. philos.	124.56
Rents	
farm economy	610.318
political economy	353.4
Rapairing editions	009.17
Repatriation intern. law	381.816

Repentance christian doctrine	251.43
Replantation dentistry	598.275
Representation	
legislatures	373.0343
psychology	151.625
of objects etymology	411.31
Reprisals intern'l law	382.32
Reproduction	
Bacteriology	566.923
biology	561.6
botany	571.6
of flowers agric.	613.809
physiology	592.6
psychology	151.625
zoology	581.6
embryo.	581.69
Reproductive	
genetic biology	563.38
power psych.	151.6
Reptiles	
zoology	587.8
palaeonology	569.85
Republic	
French history	934.87
German history	937.89
Greek history	931.883
of China history	918
political science	371.4
Portugal history	933.987
Roman history	932.83
Russian history	938.88
Spanish history	933.88
Republican-Democratic	
U. S. parties	375.62
Repulsive force	
astronomy	523.18
Requirements	
of study education	334
Rescue	
of the drowning	593.41
shipwreck	593.487
work mining eng'ing	658.47
Resedaceae botany	577.58
Reservoirs	
forest eng.	614.2
irrigation agric.	611.6
water-supply	653.16
Residual	
magnetism physics	538.47
theory of wage pol. econ.	354.16
Resistance	
meters elec. engin'g	657.13
of materials	650.41
water hydraulics	532.56

ships eng.	659.165	Restriction		
to air movement phys.	533.54	election legislative	373.034	
Resisting medium		of contagious diseases	593.235	
astronomy	521.57	on legislation	373.035	
Resonance acoustics	534.52	political science	377.63	
Respiration		Resultant algebra	512.35	
animals	581.42	Resurrection		
botany	571.143	christology	251.25	
effect	592.51	doct. theol.	251	
physiology	597.22	life of Christ	251.2957	
Respiratory		natural theology	201.721	
chemistry	597.223	of the death	251.73	
Respiration (cont.)		Resuscitation of the		
exchange gases	597.223	drowned	593.41	
movements physiol.	597.221	Retail business	622.53	
organs	597.223	Retention		
system	597.2	of placenta	598.846	
anatomy	597.21	psychology	151.623	
diseases of	597.24	Retentiveness		
drugs acting on	597.26	psychology	151.623	
physiology	597.22	Reticularia zoology	582.13	
zoology	581.12	Retina		
Responsibility ethics	180.73	anatomy	598	
Response psychology	150.197	eye disease	598.343	
Rest		physiology	598.32	
and sleep hygiene	593.16	Retired sovereigns		
labor classing	354.4	govern.	373.011	
Restaurants architecture	718.5	Retirement		

from military services	379.39	Rheumatism diseases	594.991
officers	379.33	Rhinocerotidae zoology	588.347
Reuss, Germany		Rhinology	
geography	983.77	anatomy	598.41
Revenge ethics	180.67	diseases	598.44
Revenue finance	369	physiology	598.42
Revelations		surgery	598.49
Christianity	251.18	Rhiptoglossa zoology	587.855
Mohammedan	271.2	Rhizomastigaceae	
Reversion heredity	563.395	botany	572.31
Revival psychology	151.625	Rhizophaga zoology	588.23
Revolution		Rhizopoda zoology	588.15
American history	941.83	Rhizophoraceae botany	578.77
form of state	371.04	Rhode Island, U. S.	
Rewards		geography	984.163
and punishments		Rhodium inorg. chem.	546.83
education	332.13	Rhodobacteriaceae	
Rhamnceae botany	578.31	botany	572.153
Rhamphastidae zoology	587.9757	Rhodochaetaceae botany	573.261
Rhamuales botany	578.3	Rhodophyceae botany	573.26
Rhaphididae zoology	585.51	Rhodymeniales botany	573.265
Rheae zoology	587.941	Rhoeadales botany	577.5
Rheiformes zoology	587.941	Rhone, France	
Rhenish. Ger.		geography	983.486
Geography		Bouches du	983.497
Bavaria	983.77	Rhoplocera zoology	585.531
Prussia	983.77	Rhpnchostomi zoology	584.679

Rhynchota zoology	585.38
Rhyolite lithology	557.25
Rhythm music	770.024
Rhythmics	
comparative languages	401.7
Chinese language	417
Ribs anatomy	597.7112
Rice	
corn field crops	612.18
Richardson, S. English	
fic.	853.61
Riches economics	352.2
Rickets diseases	594.995
Ridicule ethics	180.91
Rifle	
military engineering	659.35
shooting amusements	797.7
Rifled	
ordnance mil.eng.	659.34
Rifling mil.eng.	659.35
Rig-veda Hinduism	242.11
Right	
ethics	180.2
line geometry	517.31
of citizens	372.1
domicile	381.82
equality	372.14
initiative	372.18
parties	001.29
petition	372.15
recall	372.17
referendum	372.19
trial law	395.03
visit and search	381.68
to work pol.econ.	354.915
Rights	
and liberties const.law	391
civil see civil rights	
land pol.econ.	353.66
of citizens	372.1
individual pol.sci.	372.4
political science	372
Riots	
internal relations	385
law	394
Ripple marks geology	553.3
Ris-shu Jap.Buddhism	239.64
Rites	
book of, the Chinese	
classics	094
Chou, the Chinese	
classics	094.1
decorum, the Chinese	
classics	094.2
of Junior Tai Chinese	
classics	094.3

Senior Tai Chinese classics	094.4	importance	651.77
		materials used	651.76
Record of, the Chinese classics	094.3	military mil.eng.	659.36
		rural life	313.414
River		stone eng.	651.763
boats shipbuilding	659.13	transport	632
engineering	654.6	Rock	
protective works	654.6	analysis chem.	543.5
Rivers		minerals	558.19
engineering	654.6	salt lithology	557.55
frontiers	319.113	structure lithology	557
international pol.	381.331	workship	209.29
geography	980.504	Rocks	
China	981.34	lithology	557.53
hydraulics	532.9	polarity in geology	553.4
physical geograbhy	552.4	Rodentia zoology	
water supply	663.14	Rods	
Rivulariaceae botany	572.175	glass prac.chem.	542.2
Road	001.147	strength of materials	650.41
bed engin'g	651.812	Roei Japanese poetry	821.55
bridges engin'g	651.5021	Rolland, Romain Fr.	
equipments eng.	651.817	fiction	843.9
maintenance eng.	651.78	Rollers farm machinery	610.62
political econ.	354.931	Rolling stock eng.	651.503
Roads		bridge engineering	651.503
agriculture	651.771	Rolls	
and pavements engin'g	651.7	of honor mil.	379.39
engineering	651	school	333.1

Romaic	
language	431.9
literature	831.9
Roman	
architecture	710.832
art	708.32
catholic church	259.1
conquest of Greece	931.84
dominion	
France	934.813
Spain	933.811
empire	932.84
history	932
law	390.5
literature	830
mythology	209.93
republic history	932.883
rule	951.84
sculpture	720.832
Romance	
languages	430
literatures	830
Romanish	
language	438.9
literature	838.9
Romans epistles Bible	252.71
Romantic	
orchestral	736.6
music	779
piano music	776.1
Romany language	409.318
Rome history	932
Ronsard, P. de Fr. poet.	841.34
Rontgen rays physics	535.53
Roofs	
architecture	713.5
construction architec.	731.5
Root	
botany	571.273
corps	612.4
Roots	
algebra	512.71
crops	612.4
edible	613.11
perfumes	612.818
Rope	
making manuf.	675.7
Rosales botany	577.7
Rosiflorae botany	577.7
Rosin	
oil chem. tech.	665.2
Rossetii, D. G. Eng. poet.	851.84
Rotifera zoology	583.46
Rotating	
bodies physics.	531.695

Rotation	
mechanics physics.	531.24
of heavenly bodies astron.	521.15
physics	531.695
Rotatoria zoology	583.46
Rotheln diseases	594.916
Rough-wood	
products forestry	614.72
Round	
and catches music	771.72
Rousseau, J.B. Fr.poet.	841.51
Rousseau, J.J. Fr.fiction	843.56
Rousseau, J.J. Fr.philos.	124.3
Route	
canal engineering	654.7
engineering	651.8
railroad eng.	651.811
Rowboats	
boat building	659.13
Rowing sport	793
Royalty	
classes sociology	313.81
heraldry	968
genealogy	977.1
Royce Amer.philos.	126.5
Rubbet	
manufactures	676
Rubbings archaeology	990.076
Rubella diseases	594.916
Rubeola diseases	594.916
Rubiaceae botany	579.81
Rubiaceae botany	579.8
Rubidium inorganic chem.	546.217
Rubies econ.geol.	558.184
Rugs house decora.	763.3
Ruins	
antiquities	990
Ruling families genealogy	977.1
Rules	
Kuomingtang	001.21
library	022.6
Rules(cont.)	
for offce employees	354.15
workship	354.15
school	332.1
Rumania	
geography	983.915
history	939.51
Rumanian	
language	438
literature	838
Running	
horse dom.animals	615.11
sports	793

Rupa Buddhism	231.61
Rupadhatu Buddhism	231.82
Rupture	
of diplomatic relations	381.52
genital tract obstetrics	598.845
Rural	
architecture	718.7
charities	313.46
community	313.4
education	383.41
economics	350.024
agriculture	610.3
exodus agric.	610.16
hygiene	313.43
libraries	025.36
life agric.	610.15
sociol.	313.4
planning	313.41
population	313.42
roads eng.	651.771
sanitary engin'g.	653.6
sports	793
water supply	653.19
Ruskin, J. Eng. prose	857.19
Russell Eng. philos.	125.8
Russia	
administration	373.38
archaeology	993.8
botany	571.38
education	330.938
finance	369.18
geography	983.8
geology	550.38
heraldry	969.38
history	938
Russia (cont.)	
maps	980.338
schools	338.7938
statistics	345.38
travel	980.7383
treaties	387.938
Russian	
drama	882
fiction	883
folk literature	884
juvenile literature	885
language	480
literature	880
music	770.8
philosophy	128.8
philology	480
poetry	881
prose	887
Russo—	
Japanese war Japanese	

hist.	921.865	group	546.8
Russian hist.	938.87	inorganic chemistry	546.81
Rutabaga		Rutland, England	
field crops	612.42	geography	983.565
Rutaceae botany	546.8	Rye	
Ruth Bible	252.23	field crops	612
Ruthenium		grass forage cross	612.273

Sabbath	253.19
Christian	253.195
Hebrew	253.191
Sabbatic year education	336.5
Sabda Hinduism	241.25
S'abda vidya s'astra	
Buddhism	232.085
Sabiaceae botany	578.26
Sabotage labor and	
laborers	354.84
Saccharine org.chem.	547.81
Sachs, Hans Ger.poetry	871.44
Sacramentals prac.theol.	253.99
Sacred	
books	202
Brahmanism	242
Judaism	262
Shintoism	291.2
Taoist	222
days Christianity	253.199
music	772
Sacrifice	
Christology	251.24
family customs	319.25
Taoism	223.5
Sacrificial	
ceremonies	319.11
vessels Chinese arch.	991.23
Saddhamrapundarika	
sutra	232.32
Sadducees Judaism	269.3
Safe-conduct intern.	
law	381.5583
Safety	
measures miging	
engineering	658.4
working condition	354.54
Saga, Japan geog.	982.1662
Sagoromo monogatari	
Jap.fiction	823.37
Sahara	
geography	985.47
Saibara Japanese ballads	821.52
Sailboats engineering	659.13
Sailing directions	659.42
navigation	659.195
Sain Noin khanate, China	
geography	981.953
Saint	
Bartholomew massacre	259.092
Gabriel Christianity	251.61
Louis city, Mo	
geography	984.179
Petersburg, Fla.	

geography	984.165
Saint (cont.)	
Simon Fr.philos.	124.58
Simonism socialism	318.16
Vitus dance diseases	597.8451
Sainte Benve, C.A.	
Fr.essays	847.7
Saints'	
days Christianity	253.16
Saitama, Japan geog.	982.1617
S'akyamuni Buddhology	231.21
Salaries	
library	
school	028.5
service	022.5
officers	
government	373.016
Y.M.C.A.	256.34
of teachers	336.5
political economy	354.3
Sale catalogues of book	011.8
Sales business	622.52
Salesman	
training	622.52
Salicaceae botany	576.31
Salicales botany	576.3
Salines	
drugs	597.362
mineralogy	558.17
Saliva	
physiology	597.321
Salivary	
glands	
anatomy	597.311
physiology	597.321
Salix fibers	612.596
Sallatoria zoology	585.31
Sallust Latin lit.	832.882
Salop, England geography	983.564
Salt	
lithology	557.55
manufacture	618
rock	557.55
tax finance	369.052
Salts	
chemical teachnology	661.5
theoretic chemistry	541.03
Salunum tuberosum roots	
crops	612.481
Salutations customs	319.34
Salvage	
maritine law	381.75
nautics eng.	659.197
Salvation	
army	256.11

doctrinal Christian	251.4	San Louis Potosi, Mexico	
Salzburg, Austria		geography	984.47
geography	983.795	San-lun-tsung Chinese	
Sama-veda Hinduism	242.13	Buddhism	239.51
Samadhi Hinduism	244.8	San Min Chu I	
Samaritan Bible	252.054	Sunyatsenism	001.11
Samaritans Judaism	269.5	San-ron Japanese	
Samarium inorg.chem.	546.292	Buddhism	239.61
Samjna Buddhism	231.63	San Salvador	
Samkhya Hinduism	249.3	geography	981.64
Rarika Hinduism	249.3	history	946.4
Sammitiya-vada Indian		Sanctions	
Buddhism	239.116	codes inter'l private law	381.802
Samoyed-ostiak lang.	409.22	public law	381.02
Samskara Buddhism	231.64	Sand	
Samudays Buddhism	231.32	building stone	558.16
Samuel Old Testameat	252.24	filteration water supply	653.18
Samyagadjiva Buddhism	231.44	lithology	557.53
Samyagdrichti Buddhism	231.41	Sandalwood	
Samyagvak Buddhism	231.43	field crops	612.817
Samyagvyayama Buddhism	231.45	Sandstone	
Samyakkarmanta Buddhism	231.48	economical geography	556.1
Samyaksamkalpa Buddhism	231.48	lithology	557.53
Samyaksamadhi Buddhism	231.46	Sanitary	
Samyaksmriti Buddhism	231.47	affairs public health	593.2
Samyukt-pitaka Sutra	232.8	engineering	653
Samyuktagamas Sutra	232.23	building	653.5
		Sanitation	

microscopy biology	566.69
public	593.2
working conditions	354.5
Sanrornithes zoology	587.91
Sanskrit language	409.312
Santaceae botany	576.81
Santales botany	576.8
Santayana Am. philos.	126.6
Santo Domingo	
geography	984.73
history	947.3
Sanuki-no-suke-no-nlkki	
Jap.prose	827.36
Saone, France geography	983.477
et Loire	983.475
Saoshyant Parseeism	281.2
Sapindaceae botany	578.25
Sapindales botany	578.1
Sapotaceae botany	579.31
Sapphires	
precious stone	
Sappho Gk, lyric poetry	381.42
Saprophytic micro-	
organisms	566.962
Saprophytism botany	571.71
Saps forestry	614.76
Sarashina nikki Jap.prose	827.32
Sarcodina sporozoa	582.28
Sardinia, Italy	
geography	983.28
Sardou, Victorien	
Fr.dram.	842.86
Sarraceniaceae botany	577.61
Sarraceniales botany	577.6
Sarthe, France	
grography	983.463
Sarvasti-vada Indian	
Buddhism	239.112
Saskatchenan, Canada	
geography	984.27
Satan Christianity	251.63
Satanism witchcraft	157.72
Satellites, theory of	
astronomy	521.7
Saturated vapor thermics	536.75
Saturn descrip.astron.	523.46
Satrya-siddhi-sastra	
Chinese Buddhism	239.51
Indian Buddhism	239.114
Japanese Buddhism	239.61
Sauropsida reptiles	587.7
Sauropterygia Buddhism	587.815
Saururaceae botany	576.26
Saururae birds	587.91

Savings	
banks	362.93
finance	362.9
social welfare	316.8
with prize	362.91
without prize	362.92
Savoie, France geography	983.478
Haute	983.478
Savoy, France	
geography	983.478
Saxe, Germany geography	
Altenburg	983.77
Gotha-Cobury	983.77
Meiningen	983.77
Weimar	983.77
Saxifraginas botany	577.7
Saxony, Germnay	
geography	983.77
Prussian	983.76
Scaffolding civil eng'ing	651.135
Scale	
contract wages	354.33
sliding	
mathematics	510.76
vages	354.33
Scales	
piano instruction	776.1
practical chemistry	542.3
wages economy	354.33
weights and measure	530.077
Scaly dermatology	598.541
Scandal ethics	180.87
scandinavia	
geography	983.798
history	937.98
Scandinavian	
language	409.382
literature	879.2
Scandium inorgan.chem.	546.291
Scansores zoology	587.975
Scaphopoda zoology	583.54
Scapus volume	010.17
Scarlatina diseases	597.918
Scarlet fever diseases	594.918
Scenery art of theatre	781.51
Schale rocks	557.525
Schelling Ger.philos.	127.4
Schiller, J.C.F. Ger.	
drama	872.63
Schists lithology	557.43
Schizophyceae botany	572
Schizomycetes botany	572.11
Schizophyta botany	572.1
Schizopoda zoology	584.825
Schleiermacher Ger.	

philos.	127.72
Schleswig-Holstein,	
Ger.geo.	983.78
Scholarships	
school finance	331.45
tuition	334.15
School	
administration	
education	331
lib.economy	028.1
accountant	332.7
and college	338
songs	771.5
architecture	332.9
banners	334.83
budgets	331.43
calendar	
education	334.3
lib.economy	028.4
costumes	334.87
day	334.35
discipline	332.4
equipment	332.9
etiquette	332.2
examinations	
education	334.5
lib.economy	028.4
finance	331.4
funds	331.41
government	331
graduation	
education	334.7
lib.economy	028.4
hygiene	
education	332.3
medicine	593.33
School(cont.)	
hours	
education	334.4
lib.economy	028.4
libraries	025.2
life	333
management	332
promotion	
education	334.6
lib.economy	028.4
property	331.6
publications	339
savings banks	362.96
songs	334.85
standardization	
education	334
library	028.4
symbolism	334.8
Y.M.C.A.	333.63
year	

education	334.31		occult	157
lib.economy	028.4		Scientific	
Schools			building architecture	717.2
agricultureal	610.077		management business	622
and colleges	338		recreations	500.87
architecture	332.9		Scitamineae botany	575.9
education	338		Sciuridae zoology	588.613
hygiene	332.3		Scolding ethics	180.87
library training	028		Scorpionidea zoology	584.671
public	338.01		Scotch	
Schopenhauer Ger.philos.	127.6		language	409.372
Schrodinger			philosophy	129
wave mechanics physics	530.75		poetry	859.1
Schwartzburg.Ger.			Scotland	
geography	983.77		administration	373.35
Science			antiquities	993.5
mental	150		architecture	710.35
natural	500		botany	571.935
of books biblio.	010		constitutional law	391.35
legislation	390.011		education	330.935
religion	200.11		finance	369.35
statistics	340		geography	983.57
political	370		geology	550.35
sanitary	653		history	935.91
social sociology	300		laws	390.5
Sciences			statistics	345.35
classification of	501		zoology	581.933
natural	500		Scott, Walter	

Eng. fiction	853	
poetry	851.74	

Scottish, see Scotch

Scotus
Duns philos.	121.637	
Erigena philos.	121.637	

Scouts
boy	313.67	
girl	313.67	

Scrap
books lib. econ.	027	
for special see subject		

Screw
cutting mech. engin'g	655.88	
gears mech. engin'g	655.88	
jacks mech. engin'g	655.88	
physics	531.97	
strength of materials	650.41	

Scripture
of special religion see the religion

Scriptures, holy Bible	252
Scrofula diseases	594.995
Scrotum anatomy	597.615
Sculpture	720
in relief	721.7
Scurvy diseases	597.349
Scutibranchia zoology	583.531
Scyphomedusae zoology	582.73
Scyphozoa zoology	582.73
Scytonemataceae botany	572.172

Sea
aqueous erosion geology	551.72
baths hygiene	593.14
cucumbers zoology	582.94
fishing sports	799
food fishery	617
laws	381.7
lilies zoology	582.95
moses algae	573.2
shore resorts hygiene	593.112
songs music	771.3
territory pol. sci.	371.026
urchins zoology	582.93
weeds	
botany	573.2
fertilizers	611.7

Seal
engraving	727
emblems of	371.08
iconography arch.	991.66
inscriptions arch.	991.65

Seals
heraldry	901.5
historic remains	990.16
military pol. sci.	379.38

Seas

geography	980.502
China	981.32

Search

right of intern.law	381

Seaside

cottages architecture	718.8
resorts hygiene	593.112

Seashore

games	799
resorts hygiene	593.112

Season

festivals amusement	791

Seasons

astronomy	525.5
farm	611.1
hygiene	593.113

Seaweeds botany	573.2

Second

advent of Christ	251.26
ballot suffrage	372.555
coming christology	251.26
empire Fr.history	934.87
international problem	388.53
law	536.62
republic Fr.hist.	934.87

Secondary

education	338.915
school	338.3
for girl	338.915
public	338.9

sexual characters zoology	581.667
Secret societies soci.	313.63

Secretion

physiology	597.42
zoology	581.44

Section

observation magnetism	538.75

Secular variation

meteorology	529.82
Secularization educ.	330.125

Secured debts public

finance	369.183
Securing applicants econ.	354.115
Securities finance	366
Sedaine, M.J. Fr.drama	842.57
Sedan chair transport.	632.2
Sedges botany	575.41
Sedimentary rocks lithol.	557.5
See eccles.polity	255.6

Seed see also seeds

Seedage agric.	611.57
Seeding machinery agric.	610.62

Seeds

edible	613.3
floriculture	613.8

forestry	614.482
sowers farm machinery	610.62
Seers occult sci.	157.097
Segitta zoology	583.98
Segmentation	
embryology zoology	581.691
of plant body botany	571.211
Segregation	
and concretion	
agents of geologic work	551.99
eugenics biology	563.53
Seine France geography	
et marne	983.473
et Oise	983.473
Inferieure	983.465
Seismology geology	551.3
Selection	
anti-evolution	564.4
cessation of evolution	563.195
germinal heredity	563.35
natural evolution	564.21
of books lib.econ.	023.1
candidates suffrage	372.54
plants	611.5
workers econ.	354.115
reproductive heredity	563.38
sexual evolution	563.17
Selenium inorganic chem.	546.155
Self	
adaptation	
bio-physics	562.35
organic evolution	563.76
culture Taoism	224.2
defense intern.public law	381.22
directed school educ.	338.81
direction psychology	151.43
education	338.93
government pol.sci.	371.4
help intern.disputes	382.21
preservation intern.law	381.22
Selfishness ethics	180.8
Selling	
business methods	622.52
mine engineering	658.23
Semesters school admin.	334.32
Seminal vesicles anatomy	597.615
Seminar	
discussion edu.	337.17
educational methods	337.17
Semisovereign states	
intern.law	381.12
Seminaries	
architecture	717.2
education	338.915
for special topic see subject	
Semitic language	409.5

Semnopithecinae zoology	589.57	Sensory		
Senators		defectives psychology	156.3353	
election pol.sci.	373.034	influence psychology	153.21	
Seneca, L.A. Latin drama	832.81	Septibranchia zoology	583.557	
Senegal, Africa geography	985.53	Septic diseases pathology	594.94	
Senegambia, Africa		Septicemia		
geography	985.53	diseases	598.862	
Senescence		pathology	598.947	
psychology	153.6	Sequels of disease		
comparative	581.698	pathology	594.6	
Senior high class	338.33	Serbia		
Sennar, Egypt geography	985.178	geography	983.955	
Sensation		history	939.57	
mental faculties	151.1	Serfs		
physiologic psychology	597.825	economics	354.253	
Sensationalism philosophy	104.2	slavery	317.4	
Sensations of color optics	535.391	social classes	371.066	
tone physics	534.7	Sericulture	616	
Sense organs		Series mathematics	514.1	
anatomy	597.818	Sermons		
mental faculties	151.1	homiletics Christianity	253.7	
physiology	597.828	public worship Christianity	253.21	
Sense perception		Serpentine		
psychology	151.1	economical geology	556.1	
Sensibllity		lithology	557.47	
mental faculties	151.2	Serpents zoology	587.857	
physiologic psychology	597.825	Servants		

ethics	183.7
social class	313.84
Sessions	
the legislative	373.036
school	334.4
Setons therapeutics	595.813
Setting type printing	010.7
Settlements intern.	
disputes	382.1
Settling	
of account	369.029
Seven	
Classics, the Chinese	
classics year war	090.3
Canadian hist.	942.815
German hist.	937.85
U.S. hist.	940.82
Seventeen histories, the	910.94
Sevres, Deux, France	
geography	983.491
Sewerage	
refuse engineering	653.3
systems engineering	653.31
Sewers engineering	653.34
Sewing	
clothing manuf.	684
domestic economy	691
element'y manual training	338.914

machine	655.91
Sex	
customs	319.41
determination of	
biology	561.661
zoology	581.661
differentiation	
biology	561.66
zoology	581.66
heredity of	563.37
in education	338.9191
nature biology	562.87
inheritance of	561.663
	or, 563.37
origin of biology	562.75
psychology	153.1
woman's labor econ.	354.23
Sex (cont.)	
mental characters psych.	153.1
recognition ecology	581.761
vital statistics	349.074
Sex-worship	209.3
Sexagesimal calculation	
math.	510.73
Sexifragaceae botany	577.74
Sexual	
characters, origin of	
biology	561.62

education	338.9191	peoetry	811.1412
or,	563.55	Shang dynasty Chinese	
ethics	187	hist.	911.5
manias and aberrations		Shang Yang Chinees	
abnormal psychology	155.458	philos.	111.175
organs anatomy	597.6	Shansi, China geography	981.64
perversions abnor.		Shangtung, China	
psych.	155.4585	geography	981.62
relations ecology	581.761	Shao Chi-tao Chinese	
reproduction biology	561.62	prose	817.761
botany	571.63	Shao Yung Chinese	
zoology	581.62	philos.	111.52
selection biology	563.17	Sharebon Japanese	
variation		fiction	823.67
animals	581.771	Shaw, G.B. Eng.drama	852.9
biology	563.65	H.W. Am.Humor	868.2
Shades modern geometrys	519.37	Sheaths of tendons	
Shadows mod.geom.	519.37	anatomy	597.717
Shaftsbury, earl of Eng.		Sheep	
essays	857.51	diseases of compar.med.	599.43
Shakehands customs	319.34	domestic animals	615.13
Shaker christian churches	259.86	hunting	799
Shakespear, William Eng.		zoology	588.335
drama	852.33	Shel	
Shallot olericulture	613.13	fish	
Shan language	409.123	fishery	617.5
Sham language	409.12	zoology	587.3
ShangKuan yi Chinese			

Shelley, P.B. Eng.poet.	851.77
Shels	
armor piercing ordnance	659.34
eleugated ordnance	659.34
paleontology	569.83
prehistoric archaeology	990.9
projectils	659.34
Shelter	
domestic science	692
of laboring class pol.econ.	354.931
Shelving	
library	
buildings	024.4
management	023.5
Shemitic languages	409.5
Shen Ch'uan-chi Chinese	
poet.	811.1414
Shen Tao Chinese philos.	111.173
Shen Te-chien Chinese	
poet.	811.174
Shen Yo Chinese poet.	811.135
Shensi, China geography	981.65
Sheridan, R.B.	
English	
drama	852.66
oratory	858.44
Shields	
heraldry	960
weapons	379.96
Shifting bridge civil eng.	651.57
Shifts of work pol.econ.	354.41
Shiga, Japan geo.	982.1649
Shih Chiao Chinese	
philos.	111.177
Shih Ching Chinese	
Classics	093
Shih Jen-chang Chinese	
prose	917.721
Shih Nai-an Chinese	
fiction	813.591
Shimanem Japan	
geography	982.1652
Shinchiku, Japan	
geography	982.172
Shingles dermatology	598.542
Shingon Japanese	
Buddism	239.67
Shinto Shintotism	291.1
Shintoism	291
Ship	
building eng.	659.11
equipment shipbuilding	659.15
Shipping	
business	622.6

laws	398.45
navigation engin'g	659.19
Ships	
naval architecture	659.11
transportation	659.192
Ships' compasses engin'g	659.192
Shipwreck	
engineering	659.197
maritime law	381.75
Shizuoka, Japan	
geography	982.1638
Shock surgery	598.141
Shoes	
costume	319.48
manufacture	673
Shop	
engineering works	655.279
management	622.2
organization	622.2
Shooting	
criminal law	394.511
game sport	799
gunnery	659.35
target	799
sport	797.7
Short cuts	
thory of biology	561.74
Shorthand business	626.8
Shortsightedness eye dis.	598.345
Shoulder anatomy	591.87
Shovel	
crop cleaning	610.66
digging tools	610.61
plow	610.61
Shows	
entertainments	780
public customs	319.7
Shrimps zoology	584.827
Shrines	
Imperial	291.6
of Ise	291.6
religious architecture	715.91
Shrubs	
botany	571.901
esthetic of cities	719.7
floriculture	613.86
Shu Ching Chinese	
classics	092
Shu Han, dynasty Chinese	
hist.	912.6
Shuo Wen, the Chinese	
philology	411.1
Sialagogs therapeuties	597.461
Siam	
geography	982.48

history	924.8
Siamese	
Buddhism	239.33
language	409.121
literature	891
twins surgery	598.174
Siberia, Russia geography	983.89
Sibyls	
divination	157.18
Sicily, Italy geography	983.28
Sick	
food for hygiene	593.123
headache disease	597.8457
hospitals for	316.2
Sickness	
insurance	
business	368.6
economics	354.937
labor	354.937
pensions econ.	354.35
Sidereal	
chronology	528.3
clock and chronometer	522.5
day chronology	528.1
month	
astronomy	523.33
chronology	528.1
systems astronomy	523.8
time chronology	528.3
year astronomy	528.3
Sidney, Philip Eng. poet.	851.32
Sidewalks	
pavement road eng.	651.75
Siege	
artillary mil. engin'g	659.34
guns gunnery	659.35
mounts ordnance	659.34
operations mil. eng.	659.32
welfare mil. science	379.4
Sight	
anatomy	598.31
diseases of	598.34
mental faculties	151.11
Sight (cont.)	
optics	535.9
physiology	598.32
Sigillography	
archaeology	990.16
Chinese	991.6
see other countries	
Signals	
communication	639.1
in navigation	659.196
military mil. eng.	659.37
railway engineering	651.816
Signs	

of real death physiol.	592.11
Sik'ang, China geography	981.72
Sikkim, Japan geography	982.39
S'ila Buddhism	231.72
Silabhadra Buddhism	239.147
Silage agriculture	612.3
Silesia, Czechoslovakia geography	983.76
Silicates mineralogy	558.4
Silicoflagellata zoology	582.33
Silicoflagellatae botany	572.5
Silicon inorgan.chem.	546.163
Silk	616.96
book rarities	009.2
braid manuf.	675.4
cordage manuf.	675.7
culture	616.5
domestic economy	693.1
dye chem.tech.	667.2
implements	616.5
industries	616
lacing	767.54
manufaculture	675.4
ribbon manuf.	675.4
raising	616.4
tax public finance	369.052
worm agriculture	616
eggs	616.3
S'ilpasthana vidya s'astra Buddhism	232.085
Silurian period geology	554.54
Silver	
certificates money	361.71
group	546.25
inorganic chemistry	546.253
Silver(cont.)	
metallurgy	669.91
mineralogy	558.142
mining	658.8
money finance	361.21
ores of	558.142
plating	662.75
prints	756.5
seal Chinese arch.	991.62
Silverware	
art industry	768
manufacture	671.5
Silvics forest botany	614.4
Silviculture forestry	614.4
Simiidae zoology	589.7
Similarity plane geom.	517.37
Simms.W.G.Am.fiction	863.35
Simonides of Ceos Greek lyrics	831.44
Simpathetic	

nervous system	
anatomy	597.827
diseases	597.847
Simpathy emotions	151.2
Simple	
continued fever	594.925
enterprise pol.econ.	356.2
machines physics	531.9
state pol.sci.	371.61
Simplicidentata zoology	588.61
Simptoms diagnosis	595.2
Sin	
Christian doctrine	251.36
natural theology	201.63
Sinaloa, Mexico	
geography	984.46
Sind, India geography	982.39
Singapore	
geography	982.49
Singing	
function psychology	151.38
games	793
vocal music	770.075
Single	
acting engines	655.252
course curriculum	335.3
curved	
lines descr.geom.	519.33
surface descr.geom.	519.33
Single (cont.)	
member constituency	
pol.sci.	372.54
rail railways	651.8
methods statistics	341.4
reed wind instrum.	774.3
standard coinage	361.6
vote suffrage	372.524
Sinian period geology	554.51
Sinkiang, China	
geography	981.97
Sino-Japanese War	
Chinese hist.	910.283
	or, 917.2837
Japanese history	921.863
Sins	
against Holy Ghost Chris.	
doctr.	258.87
Sinus surgery	598.143
Siphoneae botany	573.21
Siphonogamia botany	574
Siphonophora zoology	582.717
Siphonotestales botany	572.51
Siphons prac.chem.	542.66
Sirenia mammals	588.4
Sirenoidei zoology	587.45

Sistematic
   biology 561
   botany 571
   catalogs bibliography 018.9
   medicine 597
Sistems
   consanguinity and affinity 313.383
   construction shipbuilding 651.11
   customs 369.162
   economics 350.091
   electrical engineering 657.53
   engineering 657.835
   electoral suffrage 372.527
   for transmitting sound
      eng. 657.853
   irrigation 611.6
   licensing econ.policy 351.35
   manuals see subject
   marriage 313.341
   of aerial lines 657.651
      construction 651.11
      electric
         lighting 657.814
         traction 657.95
         transmission 657.63
Sistems(cont.)
   individual educators 330.11
      writers 330.11

   meteors 523.54
   philosophic 101
   public
      finance 369.022
         Chinese 369.122
         see other countries
   road engineering 651.56
   school 331.2
   suffrage 372.527
Sisterhoods pastoral work 254.5
Site
   library buildings 024.1
   school 332.92
Sithe see Syth
Sitibhave Buddhism 231.79
Siva Hinduism 241.74
Sivas,Turkey geography 982.664
Sivs
   crop cleaning 610.65
   practical chemistry 542.22
Six
   Classics,the Chinese
   classics 090.2
   scripts,the philology 411.3
Sixteen kingdoms,the
   Ch.hist. 913.58
Size
   perception of space psy. 151.1752

Sizes
   of book lib.econ.   023.9
   type printing   010.7
Skandha Buddhism   231.6
Skeleton, human   597.711
Skepticism
   Greek philos   121.53
   philosophy   105.3
Sketching
   from nature drawing   737.1
Skewsymmetric algebra   512.32
Skild labor pol.econ.   354.26
Skill
   amusements   790
   games of   794
Skin
   anatomy   598.51
   diagnosis   595.2
   pigmentation biology   565.26
Skin (cont.)
   diseases   598.54
   function physiology   598.52
Skull bones   597.7114
Sky worship   209.29
Slags metallurgy   669.15
Slang
   Chinese language   415
   comp.language   401.5
   English language   455
Slate
   building stones   558.16
   lithology   557.44
Slaughtering
   methods of animal
   hygiene   593.128
Slave
   labor pol.econ.   354.254
   law, fugitive slavery   317.46
   trade slavery   317.46
Slavery
   abolition of   317.48
   anti-   317.48
   consanguinity   397.57
   social problems   317.4
Slaves social classes   313.85
Slavic
   language   409.391
   law   390.7
   Lettish
   language   409.39
Slavonia, Austria
   geography   983.795
Sleep
   and rest hygiene   593.16
   education   332.37

psychology	156.3	Snow	
talking psychoanalysis	156.37	meteorology	529.46
walking psychoanalysis	156.35	sports	793
Slide scale		Soap	
mathematics	510.76	laundry	686
wages	354.33	making chemic tech.	668.2
Small		Soaps chemic tech.	668.2
editions rare book	009.2	Social	
farm agriculture	610.313	amelioratism, schemes of	312.8
intestine anatomy	597.314	aspects of slavery soci.	
pox diseases	594.912	patho.	317.43
Smell		attitude soci.psychology	311.55
anatomy	597.818	behavior	311.5
physiology	597.828	clubs	313.56
senses	151.13	conditions of labor econ.	354.93
Smelting metallurgy	669.1	the world hist.	902.3
Smoke		sociology	314
nuisance sanitation	593.22	control	311
Smoking hygiene	597.83	customs	319.7
Smith, Sydney Eng.essays	857.72	dances amusements	792.3
Smokeless powder Chem.		democracy socialism	318.55
tech.	663.13	department Y.M.C.A.	256.354
Smuggling		dynamics sociology	312
criminal law	394.25	elements	311
offense	315.183	ethics	184
tariff	369.159		or, 311.28
Smuts botany	573.35	etiquette	319.3
Snakes zoology	587.857	evil ethics	187.8

evolution sociology	312.1
forces	311
geography	980.14
history and conditions	314
imitations	311.53
influences psychology	153.25
insurance	
finance	368.6
sociology	316.8
Social (cont.)	
intercourse customs	319.38
investigation	314
law	311.9
life	
primitive culture	565.795
special country see that	
country zoology	581.76
movement	312.5
obligations ethics	184.9
pathology	315
plans for reconstruction	001.158
problems	317
international	388.5
progress	312.25
psychology	311.5
	or, 153.25
purity movement	317.8
reconstruction	312.8
reform	312.8
regression	312.27
relations	
woman	313.352
zoology	581.76
revolution	312.6
sciences	300
selection	312.23
settlements	317.88
solutions	312.8
statics	313
statistics	314
surveys	
sociology	314
travel	980.71-5
suggestions	311.51
theories pol.sci.	370.1
unrest	312.29
welfare	316
Socialism sociology	318
Societies	
special see subject	
Society	
ethics	184
island geog.	985.975
libraries lib.econ.	025.6
Sociolization of law	390.095
Sociology	310

Socrates Gk phil.	121.21
Socratic philosophy	121.2
Soda	
chemic technology	664.63
water chem.tech.	664.63
Sodium inorg.chem.	546.213
Soil	
bacteriology	611.36
chemistry	611.31
classification	611.34
fertility	611.35
influences to mankind	
ethnology	565.773
physics	611.33
surveys	611.37
Soils	
agriculture	611.3
chemic analysis	543.21
floriculture	613.8054
for crops	611.34
forest botany	614.3
Solanaceae botany	573.58
Solar	
calendar chronology	528.6
day chronology	528.1
engines engin'g	655.49
parallax, transit of Venus	523.92
physics	523.7
spectrum astronomy	523.77
system discrip.astron	523.2
year chronology	528.3
Soldiers	
food for hygiene	593.35
military science	379
Solenodonta mammalia	588
Solenioideae botany	572.6
Solenoconcha zoology	583.54
Solenogastres zoology	583.513
Solid and fluid state	
geometry	517.5
physics	536.71
state chem.	541.4
Solidification heat	536.715
prac.chem.	542.65
Solids heat	536.33
Solifugae zoology	584.675
Solipsism philosophy	106.21
Solomon	
islands	985.953
song of apocrypha	252.983
Solos	
vocal music	771.74
Solpugida zoology	584.675
Solubility	
hydraulics	532.12

pneumatics	533.13
theoretic chemistry	541.43
Solute state chemistry	541.4
Solution	
chemic	542.62
of equations	512.73
plane triangles trigo.	518.1
spheric triangles trigo.	518.2
trigonometric equations	518.8
Solutions	
mathematic	510.8
quantitative analysis	545.41
special topics see subject	
Solvents prac.chem.	541.47
Somaliland geography	985.41
Somatology anthropology	565.2
Somerset	
geography	983.563
Somme, France geography	983.466
Somnambulism psychology	156.35
Sonata	
music composition	779.1
organ music	776.7
piano music	776.1
Song	
collections music	771
of Solomon apocrypha	252.35
the three children	
apocrypha	252.95
Sonora, Mexico geography	984.46
Sophistic school Gk.	
philos.	121.22
Sophocles Greek poet.	157.7
Sorcery witchcraft	157.7
Sores surgery	598.144
Sorghum	
field crops	612.17
plants	612.62
Sorites logic	141.3
Sorrow ethics	180.97
Sortilage occult sci.	157.13
Soul	
future life Christian doct.	251.7
metaphysics	135
natural theology	201.77
Soul (cont.)	
origin metaphysics	135.7
philosophy of	135
theories physiology	592.13
Sound	
music theory	770.01
physics	534
sensibility to physiol.	597.825
wave	534.3
Sounding hydraulic eng.	654.61

Soup cookery	695
Surces	
codes intern.law	381.02
Sources of animal heat	592.51
international law	281.02
law	390.02
water-supply eng.	
South	
Africa	
geography	985.7
history	957
America	
geography	981.8
history	948
Australia	
grography	985
Carolina, U.S.	
geography	984.168
Dakota, U.S.geography	984.183
Russia geography	983.88
Southern	
and Northern dynasties	
Chinese hist.	913.6
Han Chinese history	914.96
Liang Chinese history	913.953
Sung Chinese histor	915.3
T'ang Chinese hist.	914.99
Southerne, Thomas Eng.	
drama.	852.52
Souvestre, Emile Fr.	
fiction	843.73
Sovereign state	
international politics	381.11
political science	371.71
Sovereigns	
executive, the pol.sci.	373.3503
Sovereignty pol.sci.	371.027
Sowing machinery agric.	610.62
Soybean forage crops	612.33
Space	
and time metaphysics	134.43
Space (cont.)	
astronomy	523.15
metaphysics	134.4
perception metaphysics	134.41
Spadiciflorae botany	575.53
Spain	
administration	373.33
antiquities	993.3
architecture	710.33
botany	571.933
finance	369.33
geography	369.33
geology	550.33
history	933
maps	980.333

schools	338.7933
statistics	345.33
treaties	387.933
zoology	581.933

Spanish
America	
geography	984.5
history	945
Austrian ascendencey	932.875
dominion	937.933
drama	835.2
fiction	835.3
folk literature	835.4
juvenile literature	835.5
letters	835.81
literature	835
folk	835.4
juvenile	835.5
miscellany	835.81
oratory	835.84
poetry	835.1
prose	835.7
rule history	933.985
satire and humor	835.82

Spans horsemanship	798
Sparganiaceae botany	575.25

Sparrows
agriculture	615.3
zoology	587.976
Spars'a Buddhism	231.57
Sparta, Greece geography	983.17

Spartan supremacy Gk.
history	931.833
Spatheflorae botany	575.53
Spawning zoology	581.624
Spear arms	379.92

Special
abilities or talents psycho.	153.83
creation	
biology	562.74
theory ethnology	565.724
curves and surfaces	519.47
days	
school	334.37
etiquette	332.2
education	338.8
functions	516.7
infectious diseases	594.91
procedure law	395.3
types education of	338.9
Specialization of libraries	025.7

Species
origin of biology	564

Specific
customs taxation	369.1677
density physics	532.32

duty taxation	369.1677
gravity	
chemistry	542.3
liquids phys.	532.32
physics	531.64
pneumatics	533.32
heat phys.	536.3
industries	622.9
unity human race	565.73
weight of soil agric.	611.331
Spectacles	
manufacture	679
optics	535.8
Spectroscope optics	535.41
Spectroscopy optic	535.4
Spectrum	
analysis	
chemistry	544.6
optics	535.1
qualitative	544.6
of comets astron.	523.6
meteors astron.	523.5
moon astron.	523.3
star astron.	523.8
sun astron.	523.7
Speculation	
economics	352.75
finance	367.3
Spedella zoology	583.98
Speech	
freedom of pol.sci.	372.133
organs of accoustic	534.9
philology	400
physiology	597.725
Speeches	
oratory	808.4
Chinese	818.4
U.S.	868.4
Spencer Eng.philos.	125.7
Spenser.Edward Eng.	
poetry	851.31
Sperm	
anatomy	591.511
cells development	591.7
embryology	591.511
physiology	592.2
Spermatic cord anatomy	597.615
Spermatization biology	561.622
Spermatophyta botany	574
Speusippus Gk.philos.	121.33
Sphagnales botany	573.7
Sphere geometry	517.55
Spheres of	
influence intern.law	381.3193
interest intern.law	381.3194

Spheric	
astronomy	522.7
coordinates astron.	522.72
geometry	517.55
harmonics calculus	516.83
projection descr.geom.	519.35
trigonometry	518.2
Sphygmography diagnosis	595.24
Sphygmomanometer	
diagnosis	595.24
Spice islands, Malaysia	
geography	985.917
history	959.17
agriculture	612.87
chemic technology	664.45
Spiders zoology	
Spinal	
column	597.7111
cord	
anatomy	597.813
Spinal (cont.)	
functional disease of	597.844
physiology	597.823
membranes anatomy	597.813
nerves anatomy	597.813
irritation	597.8446
Spines zoology	
Spinning	

machines	675.03
manufacture	675.03
Spinoza Netherland philos.	128.1
Spirillaceae botany	572.122
Spirillum botany	572.122
Spirit	
doctrinal theology	251.63
photograph occult sci.	157.953
Spiritism occultism	157.9
Spirits	
elemental witchcraft	157.77
of grain	319.112
land	319.112
Spiritual	
body doctrinal theology	251.31
monism phychology	150.167
pluralism psychology	150.167
Spiritualism	
metaphysics	103.3
occultism	157.9
Splenic fever pathology	594.967
Sponge zoology	582.5
Spontaneous	
combustion chemistry	541.62
generation biology	562.71
Sporozoa zoology	
Sports	
education	333.35

outdoor amusem. 796
Sprague, charles Amer.
    poet. 861.29
Sprains surgery 598.167
Spring
    and Autumn Annals
    Chinese classics 096
    flowering floriculture 613.8052
Springs
    hot physic.geol. 551.5
    mineral econ.geol. 556.1
    physical geography 551.5
    strength of materials 650.41
    waterworks 653.14
Squadron military aci. 379.54
Squammata zoology 587.85
Squares
    least, method of 512.93
    tables of 510.2
Squaring the circle
    geometry 517.81
Squashes gardening 613.23
Ssu K'ung Tu Chinese
    poet. 811.1487
"Staaten succession" intern.
    polit. 381.16
Stabbed binding book-
    binding 010.82
Stabilitity of solar system 523.27
Stables
    architecture 718.9
    farm building agric. 610.67
Stachyuraceae botany 578.61
Stacks lib.econ. 024.4
Stael Holstein, A.L.G.
    Fr.fic. 843.62
Staff
    library economy 022.5
    military science 379.93
Stafford, England
    geography 983.564
Stage
    coach game 799
    direction theatre 781.6
    lines comm. 632.1
    setting theatre 781.53
    theater 781.5
Staining
    chemic technology 668.9
    substances, physiolo.
    chem. 592.45
Stains microscopy 566.135
Stamonitaceae botany 572.27
Stamp

collections	636.48
duties public finance	369.056
Stamps	
postage postal service	636.4
Standard	
clock system horology	528.57
library lib.econ.	025.79
of living pol.econ.	354.312
theory soci.	317.16
Standards	
of pitch acoustics	534.77
Staphyleaceae botany	578.22
Star	
clusters astronomy	523.81
fishes zoology	582.91
worship nat.worship.	209.21
Starch	
chemistry of food	547.83
manufacturing	664.2
plants	612.68
Stars	
astrology	157.217
descriptive astronomy	523.8
worship nat.worship	209.21
Starvation diseases	597.349
State	
aid railways	633.13
and church religion pol.sci.	371.062
individual duty pol.sci.	371.067
individual rights pol.sci.	371.067
wages economics	354.36
as an international person	381.1
bankruptcy intern.law	381.195
ceremonies customs	319.1
control school	331.21
of business	621.1
medicine	593.7
dismemberment intern.law	381.17
economics	350.031
education	330.12
ethics	185
government	371.049
labor wages	354.3
libraries	025.3
medicine	593
monopolies public finance	369.041
of Chao Chinese history	911.656
Ch'en Chinese history	911.6393
Cheng Chinese history	911.634
Ch'i Chinese history	911.651
	or, 911.631
Chin Chinese history	911.635
Ch'in Chinese history	911.658
	or, 911.636
Ch'u Chinese history	911.652
Han Chinese history	911.655

Lu Chinese history	911.632	
siege pol.sci.	372.43	
Sung Chinese history	911.633	
Ts'ao Chinese history	911.6396	
Wei Chinese history	911.6391	
Yen Chinese history	911.653	
political science	371	
properties finance	369.04	

State (cont.)

religion	200.09
saving banks	362.94
socialism sociology	318.2
trial criminal law	394
universities	338.71
Statecraft archives	901.25

State's rights constitution

law	391

Statics

chemic	541.3
forest finance	614.1
mechanics	531
pneumatics	533.3

Stationary

library

correspondence	022.9
printing	022.9

Stations

central elec.engineering	657.29
railway passenger eng.	651.817

Statistical

calculation statistics	341.3
methods statistics	341

Statistics 340

central	345.11
library administration	022.4
local	345.12
military	379.034
national	345
of China	345.1
school education	331
see also special subjects	
Statutes intern.law	381.026

Steam

automobiles eng.	659.72
boilers eng.	655.23
distribution	655.227
locomotives	655.27
engineering	655.2
engines	655.259
mech.eng.	655.2
physics	536.9
generation engin'g	655.22
heating boiler plants	655.23
jecket engin'g	655.259
physics	536.75
	or, 536.721

pipes engin'g	654.227
Steam (cont.)	
power plants	655.23
pumps eng.	655.37
ships naval arch.	659.13
transmission eng.	655.227
turbines eng.	655.295
vessels shipbuilding	659.13
Stedman, E.C. Am. poet.	861.43
Steel	
building materials	650.48
bridge archt.	651.5018
engraving	742.2
manufacture	671.1
metallurgy	669.92
piers and columns arch.	713.2
ships eng.	659.116
strength of materials	650.41
structures architec.	713.9
works architec.	713.9
Steele, Richard Eng.	
essays	857.53
Stegocephalia zoology	587.63
Stem botany	571.274
Stemonaceae botany	575.82
Stencil work art	769.2
Sterculiaceae botany	578.48
Stereochemistry	541.06
Stereometry geometry	517.5
Stereoption optics	535.8
Stereoscopic photography	758.9
Stereoscopes optics	535.8
Stereotestales botany	572.53
Stereotomy geometry	517.6
Sterility diseases	598.7475
Sterne, Laurence Eng. fict.	853.62
Sternum anatomy	597.7113
Stethoscope diagnosis	595.26
Stevenson, R.L. Eng. essay	853
Stewary Eng. philos.	125.65
Sthavira-vada Buddhism	239.111
Sthiramati Buddhism	239.147
Stigonemataceae botany	572.173
Stillbirth obstetrics	598.828
Stilpon Gk. philos.	121.27
Stimulants drugs	597.16
Stipple engraving	742.5
Stirpiculture pediatrics	598.91
Stock	
farm agric.	611.28
group kindship	313.381
Stoddard, R.H. Am. poetry	861.41
Stoic school Gk. philos.	121.52
Stoichiometry Chemistry	541.09
Stomach	

anatomy	597.313
disease	597.343
physiology	597.322
Stomatopoda zoology	584.823

Stone
age, early prehistoric archaeo.	990.9
late prehistoric archaeo.	990.9
artifical building materials	650.46
building materials	650.46
carving sculpture	720
ceiling arch.construc.	713.7
columns arch.construc.	713.2
constructions mansonry	651.16
cut, classics, the Chinese classics	090.9
pavements engineering	651.75
quarries archaeology	990.188

Stone
remains archaeology	990.13
walls architecture	713.4
ware chem.tech.	666.13
Stonecutting civil eng.	651.16

Stones
building	558.15
ornamental	558.18
Stoneworts botany	573.23
Stoping mining eng.	658.36

Stoppage
of wages econ.	354.32

Storage
building architecture	717.6
business	625
chemical technology	663.4
library	024.4
Storks zoology	587.974
Storm signals meteorology	529.75

Storms
meteorology	529.3
wind meteorology	529.33
Story of Susanna apocrypha	252.96

Stoves
kitchen equipment	695
manufactures	679
mechanical steam eng.	655.22

Stowe, Mrs Harriet Am.
fic.	863.37

Strategy
military science	379.53
naval science	379.63
Stratification geol.	553.1
Stratigraphic geology	554
Strato Gk.philos.	121.43

Straw	
matting manuf.	679
mats manuf.	679
Straw berry	
fruit culture	613.78
tree fruit culture	613.78
Street	
cleaning	653.9
light	653.2
railways engineering	651.89
sociology	313.414
Streets	
engineering	651.7
local administration	373.0816
Strength of	
materials engin'g	650.41
molecular physics	531.41
Strepsiptera zoology	585.56
Streptococcus botany	572.125
Streptoneura zoology	583.531
Stresses bridge engin'g	651.5
Striges birds	587.9795
Strike geology	553.5
Strikes	
labor pol.econ.	354.83
student school	332.17
Stringed instruments	
music	775
Chinese	770.17
Strobosocopic method	
acoustics	534.513
Strontium inorg.chem.	546.223
Structural	
arrangements of	
botany	571
ships eng.	659.15
diseases of	
brain	597.843
cord	597.843
engineering	651.1
geology	553
mechanics	531.43
Structural (cont.)	
psychologies	150.191
zoology	581
Structuralism psychology	150.191
Structure	
of atomic physics	530.1
earth physical geology	551.1
earthquake seismology	551.31
formulae chemistry	541.03
matter physics	530.11
molecular physics	530.1
the universe astron.	523.11
volcanoes geol.	551.41
Structures	

composition architec.	713.9	
iron architec.	713.9	

Struggle
    for existence evolution   563.194
Struthioniformes zoology   587.942
Strychnin drugs   597.867
Stuart English history   935.86
Student
    ethic   333.1
    fraternities   333.9
    life and custom   333
    movements   001.94
    self-government   333.9
    societies   333.9
    songs music   771.7
    strikes school   332.17
Study
    abroad laboring classes   338.75
    methods school   337.7
    rooms lib.econ.   025.8
    of special topics see subjects
Style
    costume   319
    domestic science   693
Stylinodonta zoology   588.321
Styracaceae botany   579.37
Styria, Austria geography   983.795
Su ch'e Chinese prose   817.515

Su Hsun Chinese prose   817.515
Su Shih
    Chinese
    poetry   811.153
        of irregular syllables   811.736
    prose   817.514
Su Wu Chinese poet.   811.12
Su T'ing Chinese poet   811.1418
Subconscious psychology   156.15
Subject
    bibliography   017
    catalogs   012.4
Subjective
    phenomena occult sci.   157.96
    philosophy   106.23
    psychology   150.171
Subjects
    of study curriculum   335.1
Submarine
    cables comm.   637.2
    telegraphy eng.   657.837
    volcanoes geol.   551.48
Submarines naval sci.   379.657
Subscription
    libraries lib.econ.   025.5
Subsidiary
    coins money   361.63
    tokens money   361.63

Subsidies econ.policy	351.36
Substance metaphysics	133.3
Substantive law	390.007
Substations	
electric engineering	657.29
Substitutions algebra	512
Subtraction math.	511.22
Subways road eng.	651.773
Succession law	397.6
Succor, see Aid	
Suctoria	
parasitica diseases	594.976
Sudan, France geograph	985.51
Sudden death surgery	598.868
Suffocation protec.of life	593.43
Suffold, England geography	983.566
Suffrage	
civics	372.16
Kuomintang	001.245
political science	372.5
Sugar	
beets agric.	612.63
cane agric.	612.6
manufacturing chem.tech.	664.1
organic chemistry	547.81
refining chem.tech.	664.1
Sugar(cont.)	

plants agric.	612.6
starch agric.	612.6
Suggestion	
psychology	156.7
therapeutics	595.9
Sui dynasty	
history	913.9
Suicide	
criminology	315.185
ethics	180.59
Suite music composition	779.4
Suiyuan, China geography	981.945
Sukhavati	
Chinese Buddhism	239.58
Sukhavati doctrine	
Buddhism	239.15
Indian doctrine Buddhism	239.15
Sulfates chem.tech.	661.5
Sulfur	
chemistry	546.153
waters	558.17
Sulfur inorgan.chem.	546.153
Sulfuric acid chem.tech.	661.3
Sullenness ethics	180.84
Sully-Frudhomme, Rane	
F.poct.	841.84
Sulphate see sulfates	

Sulphids mineralogy	558.4
Sulphur, see sulfur	
Sumac field crops	612.92
Sumatra geography	985.921
Summer	
house	717.9
school	
library economy	028.8
self-education	338.86
Sun	
astrology	157.211
cracks geology	553.3
customs	319.114
descriptive astronomy	523.7
dials chronology	528.1
effects on tides	525.6
light hygiene	593.118
pictures	523.702
spots	523.75
worship	209.21
Sun Hsing-yen Chines	
prose	817.766
Sunda	
geography	985.92
history	959.2
Sunday	
practical theology	
Christianity	253.19
school Christianity	257
work Christianity	354.43
workship Christianity	253.25
Sung	
dynasty Chinese history	915.1
editions rarities	009.111
(House of Liu) Chinese hist.	913.71
Sung Chih-wen	
Chinese poetry	811.1414
Sung Lien Chinese prose	817.612
Sung Pien Chinese philos.	111.155
Sung Yu Chinese poet.	811.312
Sunrise	
meteorology	529.63
terrestrial physics	525.7
sunset	
meteorology	529.63
terrestrial physics	525.7
Sunyatsenism	001.11
Superheated vapor heat	536.77
Supernatural beings	
superstitions	319.81
Supernaturalism occult. sci.	157
Supernumerary	
organs deformities	598.175

Supersaturated solutions	
chem.	541.45
Supersaturation chem.	542.62
Superposition	
of waves acoustics	534.6
Superstitions	
occult sci.	157
folklore	319.8
Superstructure hydraulic	
eng.	654.44
Supporting	
structures zoology	581.107
Suprarenal	
capsules glandular system	597.415
Surface	
current electric current	537.23
features of earth geol.	552
geology	552
of the 2nd order mod.	
geom.	519.461
3rd order mod.	
geom.	519.465
4th order mod.	
geom.	519.467
Surfit diseases	597.349
Surgery	598
of children	598.97
the circulatory system	597.17
digestive system	597.37
genito-urinary system	597.67
glandular system	597.47
locomotor system	597.77
nervous system	597.87
respiratory system	597.27
Surgical	
anatomy	598.11
anesthesia	598.115
bacteriology	598.12
diseases	598.14
dressings	598.1905
hygiene	598.13
instruments	598.1901
operations	598.18
therapeutics	598.15
Surrender intern. law	381.5585
Surrey, earl of Eng. poet.	851.28
Surrey, England geography	983.562
Surtax tariff	369.0619
Surveying	
engineering	650.9
forestry eng.	614.23
geodesy	526.7
hydraulic	654.61
Surveys floating schools	337.193
Survival	
of the fittest evolution	564.23

unlike evolution	564.5	history	937.987
Suspension		laws	390.7
bridges engin'g.	651.54	statistics	345.37
railways engin'g.	651.83	zoology	581.937
Sussex England		Swedenborgian christianity	259.88
geography	983.562	Swedish	
Sutra Buddhism	232	language	409.3822
Svealand, Sweden		literature	879.22
geography	983.7987	missionary society	
Swamps physical		Christianity	259.88
geography	552.5	Sweet	
Swans		clover field crops	612.483
domestic birds	615.3	potato	
zoology	587.973	field crops	612.483
Sweat see Swet		garden crops	613.13
Sweating		Swet	
labor pol.sci.	354.257	effect on temperature	
system pol.sci.	354.257	physio.	592.28
Sweden		Swift, Jonathan Eng.	
administration	373.37	fiction	853.53
antiquities	993.7	Swimmers zoology	587.973
architecture	710.37	Swinburne, A.C. Eng.poet.	851.87
botany	571.937	Swine	
constitutional law	391.37	domestic animals	615.4
education	330.937	veterinary pathology	599.44
finance	369.37	Swing	
geography	983.7987	bridges engin'g	651.573
geology	550.37	Swinging amusement	799

Swiss philosophy	128.4
Switzerland	
administration	373.379
antiquities	993.79
architecture	710.379
constitutional law	391.379
education	330.9379
finance	369.379
geography	983.794
geology	550.379
history	937.94
laws	390.79
Sword	
dance recreative arts	792.5
Swords arms	379.91
Syenite	
metamorfic rocks	557.41
plutonic rocks	557.32
Syllogism logic	141.3
Symbiosis botany	571.76
botany	571.76
zoology	581.763
Symbolic logic	145
Symbolism	
political science	371.08
literature	800.187
Symbolist arts of design	736.4
Symmetric	
determinants	512.31
functions algebra	512.71
Symmetry	
biology	561.13
botany	571.217
Sympathetic	
nervous system	
anatomy	597.817
physiology	597.827
strikes political econ.	354.833
Sympathy ethics	180.96
Sympetalae botany	579
Symphony orchestral	
music	779.2
Symphyseotomy	
obstetrics	598.875
Symplocaceae botany	579.35
Symptomatology	
therapeutics	595.3
Symptoms diagnosis	595.2
Synaesthesia psychology	151.19
Synanthae botany	575.47
Synapsida vertebrata	587.81
Synclinal geology	553.6
Syndicalism	
political economy	354.66
sociology	318.3

Syndicate pol.econ.	356.5	Syphilis diseases	594.99
Syngnatha zoology	584.4	Syria	
Synod Christianity	255.7	geography	982.67
Synthesis		history	928.7
chemistry	545.9	Syrian	
electric chemistry	545.97	philosophy	118.7
of the vowels	534.93	System	
logic	140	labor organization	
quantitative analysis	545.9	pol.econ.	354.131
Synthetic		of philosophy	101
chemistry	545.9	Systematic, Systems, see	
mineralogy	558.7	Sistematic, sistems	
modern geometry	519	Szechuan, China	
psychology	150.175	geography	981.71

Ta Hsueh Chinese classics	098.1
Tabasco, Mexico geography	984.48
Tables	
business	626.18
life life insurance	368.3
mathematical	510.2
of declinations	157.25
height anthropometry	565.36
solubility chemistry	541.42
physics	530.079
Tabular mathematics	510.77
Tabulation statistics	341.4
Taccaceae botany	575.86
Tacitus, C.C. Latin liter.	832.866
Tactics	
land	379.53
military	379.4
naval	379.63
political science	379.4
Tactil sensation psychology	151.15
Tadpole	
characters Chinese calligraphy	739.171
Tai Chen	
Chinese philos.	11175
prose	817.734
Tai Fu-ku Chinese poet.	811.1577
Tai Shang Lao Chun Taoism	221.13
Tai Shang Tao Chun Taoism	221.12
Taichu, Japan geography	982.173
Taihoku, Japan geography	982.171
Tail	
regional anatomy	591.89
Tainan Japan geography	982.174
Taito, Japan geography	982.176
Taiwan, Japan geography	982.17
Takao, Japan geography	982.175
Taketori	
monogatari Japan fiction	823.31
Talismans witchcraft	157.75
Tallies Chinese archaeology	991.59
Talmud	
sacred books Judaism	262.1
Tamaricaceae botany	578.56
Tamaulipas, Mexico geography	984.48
T'an Hsien Chinese poet.	811.179
T'ang dynasty	
Chinese history	914.1
Tang Huai-ying Chinese	

prose	817.581
T'ang Shun-chih Chinese	
prose	817.66
Tanguo Ulianghai, China	
geo.	981.957
Tanmtra Hinduism	241.64
Tanning	
manufactures	673
material agric.	612.93
T'ao Chien	
Chinese essays	817.57
verse	811.1327
Taoism	220
Taoist	
architecture	715.2
festival	223.5
four subsidiary scriptures	222.5
monasteries	227
popes	226
sacred books	222
school Chinese philos.	111.12
three principle scriptures	222.1
Tapestries art industry	763.5
Tapiridae zoology	588.348
Tar	
chemical technology	668.3
coal chem.tech.	668.6
Tariff	369.06
alliance	369.0646
autonomy	369.0611
conventional	369.0613
conventions	369.0606
customs	369.061
free	369.0641
policy	369.064
protective	369.0643
shifting	369.0617
treaties intern.law	387.2
war	369.068
Tarn, France geography	983.495
et Garonne	983.492
Tarred	
road engineering	651.767
Tarsiidae primates	589.767
Tartar language	409.2
Tasso, Torquato Italian	
poet.	833.14
Taste	
sensation psychology	151.14
Tattva samasa	249.3
Tax	
public finance	369.05
China	369.15
Taxation	369.05
China	369.15
Taxaceae botany	574.41

Taxes
    farm economy   610.318
    on dominos, brothels, etc. 369.157
        internal commodities 369.152
        luxury   369.157
Taxidermy
    collectors manuals biology 567.4
Taxonomic
    forestry   614.6
Tactile
    sensation psychology   151.15
Taylor, B. Am. poet.   861.46
Tchikista vidya s'astra
    Buddhism   232.085
Tea
    culture   612.72
    chemical technology   664.7
    tax   369.152
Teachers
    college   338.57
    examination   336.21
    institutes educ.   338.5
    library   028.6
    normal school   338.5
    training school   338.55
Teaching
    as a profession library   028.6
    of the Twelve Apostles   252.997

Technical
    atlases geog.   980.308
    hydraulics engin'g   654.1
    mechanics zoology   581.4
    organizations league of
        nations   383.4
    schools education   338.6
    thermodynamics heat   536.9
Technique
    arts of design   731
    of music   770.02
    sculpture   721
    surgery   598.19
Technologic school   640.7
Technologic miscroscopy   566.6
Technology   640
    chemical   660
Tectibranchia zoology   583.535
Tectology botany   571.25
Tectonic geology   553
Teeth
    artificial dentistry   598.288
    dentistry   598.2
    disease of   598.24
    human anatomy   598.21
    physiology   598.12
Telegraphic
    instruments engin'g   657.833

Telegraphy	
electric engineering	657.835
communication	637.1
plants eng.	657.831
wire eng.	657.8358
wireless eng.	657.838
Teleology metaphysics	134.2
Teleostei fishes	587.477
Teleostomi fishes	587.47
Telepathy ocult sci.	157.6
Telephone	
communication	637.7
instruments	657.853
plants	657.851
Telephotography	758.1
Telescopes	
astronomy	522.2
optics	535.8
Tellurium inorganic chem	546.157
Telosporidia zoology	582.21
Temnocephaloidea zoology	583.32
Temperaments psychology	153.84
Temperature	
and pressure gases	533.38
radiations meteorology	529.17
agriculture	611.335
heat	536.1
hygiene	593.117
decripture astronomy	523.15
measurement physics	536.15
of body	592.56
physical zoology	581.7773
therapeutics	595.25
varying refraction	534.45
Temporary	
bridges eng.	651.5027
Temptation doct.theol.	251.295
Ten	
histories Chinese history	910.93
hours day pol.econ.	354.41
kingdoms Chinese hist.	914.9
Tendai Chinese Buddhism	239.65
Tenders locomotives	655.275
Tendons	
anatomy	597.71
diseases	597.74
physiology	597.72
Tenement house	
architecture	718.5
Teng Hsi Chinese	
philos.	111.151
Tennessee, U.S.	
geography	984.174
Tennyson, A. Eng.poet.	851.81
Tension	
hydraulic	532.34

mechanics	531.82
Tentaculata zoology	582.771
Tepegraphy communication	637
Tenure of	
land.pol.econ.	353
Teratologic psychology	155
Teratology	
anatomy	591.3
animals	581.5
biology	561.3
plants	571.5
Terbium inorganic chem.	546.273
Terence Latin drama	832.25
Termination	
of labor pol.econ.	354.137
Termitidae zoology	585.35
Ternary	
quadratic algebra	512.27
quatric form	512.28
Ternstroimiaceae botany	578.52
Terra cotta	
antiquitic	990.14
China	991.4
architecture	712.5
Chinese paleography	990.814
clay industries	666.15
copies biblio.	010.12
Terrestrial	
biology	561.902
integrity	388.76
magnetism	538.7
Terrestrial(cont.)	
and earthquake	538.758
eclipses	538.754
magnetism	
geological structure	538.757
meteorological	
phenomena	538.755
sunspot period	538.753
physics	525.01
plants botany	571.902
zoology	581.902
Territory	371.026
acquisition pol.sci.	371.031
rights internat.pol.	381.3
Tertiary period geology	554.71
Tertullian Greek philos.	121.622
Tesmania, Australia	
geography	985.9395
Testacea zoology	582.13
Testament	
new Bible	252.5
old Bible	252.1
Testaments of	
12 Patriarchs apocrypha	252.984
Testicles	

anatomy	597.615
physiology	597.62
Testicardines zoology	583.95
Testing	
direct-current	657.442
enineering	657.404
of distribution systems	657.62
materials	650.41
Tests	
and measurement vision	151.118
chemic analysis	543
of auditory perception	151.128
labor economy	354.115
Testudinata zoology	587.817
Tetanus	
nervous system	597.8454
surgery	598.147
Tetrabranchia mollusks	583.571
Tetractinellida zoology	582.57
Teuton allies world war	930.753
Texax, U.S.	
geography	984.172
Text	
of Ch'i Chinese classics	093.12
of Han Chinese classics	093.15
Loo Chinese classics	093.11
Mao Chinese classics	093.2
Textile	
design	675.02
fabrics	735.7
manufactures	675
fibers	612.5
industries	675
machinery	675.19
printing	667.5
Textology	561.17
Thackeray, W.M.Eng.fic.	853
Thai language	409.12
Thales Greek philos.	121.111
Thallium inorg.chem.	546.243
Thallophyta	
cryptophyta	573.1
palaeobotany	569.22
Thallus botany	571.271
Thanksgiving day	
Christianity	253.17
Thaw houses	
pyrotechnics chem.tech.	663.4
Thea cultivation	612.72
Theaceae botany	578.52
Theatre	780
Theban	
supremacy Gk.history	931.833
Thecodontia zoology	587.833
Theism natural theology	201.1

Thelyphonidae zoology	584.672
Themistocles Gk.letters	831.81
Theodicy Christian doctrine	251.19
Theognis Greek poet.	831.11
Theology	
natural religion	201
Theophanies Christian doctrine	251.18
Theoretic	
astronomy	521
chemistry	541
Theory of	
relativity	530.71
special subject see subject	
Therapeutics	595
Theravada Buddhism	239.111
Thermal	
capacity thermics	536.3
crystallography	559.36
Thermics heat	536
Thermochemistry	541.6
Thermodynamic	
motivity	536.67
potential	536.66
Thermodynamics	
mechanical	536.6
of radiation	535.58
the air meteorology	529.11
technical	536.9
Themoelectricity	
electricity	537.6
mechanical theory of heat	536.53
thermodynamics	536.68
Thermogenesis	
conditions affect'g physiol.	592.54
physiology	592.51
Thermometer physics	536.13
Thermometry	
pathology	595.25
physics	536.13
Thermoscopy physics	536.17
Thermostat physics	536.16
Thermotheraphy	
therapeutics	595.86
Theropoda zoology	587.867
Thesaurus Taoist scripture	222
Thessaly, Greece	
geography	983.16
Thesis	
library school	028.9
school	334.74
Thessalonians	

I New Testament	252.781	Throat		
II New Testament	252.782	anatomy	597.212	
Theta		diseases	597.242	
functions	516.47	Thrombosis, Venous		
Thigh anatomy	591.88	obstetrics	598.866	
Thiobacteria botany	572.15	Throndhjem, Norway		
Third		geography	983.7986	
international problems	388.55	Thucydides Gk.liter.	831.882	
republic Fr.history	934.88	Thulium inorg.chem.	546.297	
Thirteen Classics, the		Thunder meteorelogy	529.51	
Ch.classics	090.7	Thuringia, Germany		
Tho languages	409.126	geography	983.77	
Thomas, A.Amer.drama	862	Thymelacaceae botany	578.71	
Thomson, J.Eng.poetry	851.56	Thymelaeinae botany	578.7	
Thoracostraca zoology	584.82	Thymus		
Thorax		anatomy	597.413	
anatomy	597.7112	diseases	597.44	
histology	591.84	physiology	597.42	
Thorium inorganic chem.	546.57	Thyroid		
Thought		body		
and reality metaphysics	131.3	anatomy	597.413	
thinking psychology	151.8	diseases of	597.44	
pathology of psychology	151.87	physiology	597.42	
Thread-worms zoology	583.41	gland	597.414	
Three		Thyrostraca zoology	584.87	
kingdoms, the Chinese hist.	912.4	Thysanoptera zoology	585.37	
Threshers agric.		Thysanura zoology	585.1	

Ti see Tibetan	
Tibet, China	
geography	981.98
history	910.74
Tibetan	
families of languages	409.131
tribe	913.52
Tibeto-Burmese languages	409.13
Tibullus, A. Latin lyric poet.	832.43
Tides	
astronomy	525.6
physical geography	551.2
T'ien P'ien Chinese philos.	111.174
T'ien t'ai tsung Chinese Buddhism	239.55
Tigers zoology	588.511
Tiliaceae botany	578.43
Tillodontia zoology	588.7
Timber	
building materials	650.45
forestry	614
Timbering mining engin'g	658.37
Time	
chronology	528
metaphysics	134.5
music	770.023
of day hygiene	593.113
psychology	151.57
Timon Gk. philos.	121.533
Timothy	
I New Testament	252.783
II New Testament	252.784
forage crops	612.24
Tin	
chemistry	546.53
groups chem.	546.5
manufactures	671.9
metallurgy	669.96
mining	658
ores econ. geology	558.145
Tissues	
animal histology	581.408
botany histology	571.13
Titanium inorganic chem.	546.54
Titanotheriidae zoology	588.349
Titrometric methods chem.	545.4
Titus Bible	252.785
Latin poet.	832.11
Tlascala, Mexico geography	984.47
Tobacco	

agriculture	612.71	dentistry	598.247
industry	678	Topical	
Tobit Apocrypha	252.92	method education	337.31
Tochigi, Japan geography	982.1619	Torches illuminating	
Toes		industries	665.71
anatomy	591.88	Toroidal	
extra deformities	598.175	harmonics functions	516.87
Toilet dom.sci.	693.5	Torpedoes	
Tokan kiko Japanese		maval mil.engin'g.	659.39
prose	827.46	Torsion mechanics	531.85
Tokushima, Japan geog.	982.1657	Torts criminal law	394.3
Tone		Tosa nikki Japanese prose	827.31
color acoustics	534.71	Tottori, Japan geography	982.1651
Tongue		Touch	
anatomy	597.311	sensation psychology	151.15
diagnosis	595.21	Touraine, Fr. geography	983.482
diseases of	597.34	Tournaments	
physiology	597.32	fighting sports	797.5
Tonics drugs	597.365	Toxicology poisons	593.9
Tonkin, Indo-China		Toxins bacteriology	566.929
geography	982.45	Toxodontia zoology	588.395
Tonsils		Toyama, Japan	
anatomy	597.312	geography	982.1632
disease of	597.34	Trachea	
physiology	597.32	anatomy	597.213
Tontederiaceae botany	575.76	diseases of	597.243
Toothake		Trachomedusae inverte-	

brata	582.715
Trachyte lithology	557.24
Traction	
engines	655.291
mechanics	531.84
Trade	
advertising business	629.3
cycles markets	624.5
patents technology	645.7
neutrality law	381.63
Trade (cont.)	
unions	
labor and laborers	354.6
sociology	313.7
Trades	
mechanic	680
Traffic	
railways	633.5
Tragedy	
drama	802.93
theater	782
Trailokya	
Brahmanism	241.77
Buddhism	231.8
Training	
of will psychology	151.43
Traits	
of genius psychology	153.91
Tramcars communication	632.7
Transcendental	
curves modern geom.	519.471
properties of being	
ontology	133.8
variable functions	516.3
Transference	
of electromagnetic energy	538.86
Transformation	
of radiant energy	535.5
Transforming	
machinery engin'g.	657.43
Transit	
circle astron.instrum.	522.3
duty tariff	369.1675
instrument	522.3
Transition metaphysics	134.6
Transits astron.	523.9
Transleithania, Austria	
geography	983.795
Transliteration	
comparative philology	401.4
Transmigration	
eschatology	201.75
rational psychology	135.73
Transmission	
heat	536.4
of force mechanics	531.9

pressure pneumatics	533.383
Transneptunian astronomy	523.48
Transplantation	
of teeth dentistry	598.275
Transport	
agriculture	610.66
by mail	636.37
Transportation	
agencies	634.3
mechanic trade	680
public building	717.6
railways	633.5
Transposition	
of parts orthopedic surgery	598.177
Transvaal, Africa	
geography	985.74
history	957.4
Transverse	
vibration acoustics	534.546
wave acoustics	534.34
Traumatic	
fever diseases	598.146
Travancore, India	
geography	982.39
Travel	
on land hygiene	593.481
water hygiene	593.482
Traveler's manuals	980.713
Traveling	
libraries lib.econ.	025.4
parties education	333.38
Travels	
general	980.7
school educ.	337.191
special, see subject	
Treaties	
commerce	387.1
diplomacy	387
making	387
tariff	387.1
international law	381.021
Treatment	
of periodicals	023.8
the dead	319.17
wouded	381.556
Trebizond, Turkey	
geography	982.665
Trees	
botany	571.901
esthetics of cities	719.7
forestry	614.489
fruit culture	613.8
ornamental floriculture	613.87
Trematoda zoology	583.33
Tremellineae botany	573.35

Tretenterata zoology	583.94
Trial	
christology	251.2952
civil	395
criminal	394
jury	395.04
marriage	313.345
practice law	395.03
Trials	
civil law	395
criminal law	394
Triangle	
geometry	517.34
mechanical instruments	
music	777.3
plane	
geometry	517.3
trigonometry	518.1
practical chemistry	542.2
spheric trigonometry	518.2
Triassic period geology	554.61
Tribal	
institutions state	371.13
Trichechidae zoology	588.44
Trichiaceae botany	572.27
Trichna Buddhism	231.55
Tridimensional	
current electricity	537.24
Trifolium forage crops	612.382
Trigonometrical	
progression mathematics	514.4
Trigonometry	518
Trilobitae zoology	584.61
Trimmings manuf.	675.7
Trinity Sunday prac.theol.	253.15
Trionychia vertebrata	587.817
Trios vocal music	771.76
Tripods	
Chinese antiquities	991.22
physical chemistry	542.2
Tripoli, Africa	
geography	985.46
history	954.6
Trips methods of	
instruction	337.195
Trisection	
of the angle geometry	517.83
Triumphal	
esthetics of cities	719.5
Triuridales botany	575.4
Trividya Buddhism.	231.31
Trochelmia zoology	583.45
Trochelminthes zoology	583.45
Trochodendraceae botany	577.35

Trolapsus funis obstetrics	598.848	and error logic.	141.4
Trollope, A. Eng. fic.	853.87	ethics	180.72
Trombone wind instrum.	774.7	ontology	133.86
Trominences descriptive		theory of knowledge	131.5
astron.	523.76	Ts'ao Chih	
Tromso, Norway		Chinese poetic comp.	811.33
geography	983.7986	poetry	811.131
Tropaeolaceae botany	577.88	prose	817.31
Tropical		Ts'ao Hsuen-ch'in	
agriculture	610.098	Chinese fic.	813.75
zoology	581.908	Tseng Ao Chinese prose	817.77
medicine	593.5	Tseng Kung Chinese	
orbit moon	523.33	prose	817.516
plants botany	571.908	Tseng Kuo-fan Chinese	
year chronology	528.3	prose	817.783
Trucks		Tseng Meng-p'u Chinese	
farm transport	610.66	fiction	813.79
True		Tseng Tzu Chinese	
ethics	180.3	philos.	111.1123
Men Taoism	221.3	Tsetsen khanate, China	
Truffles gardening	613.5	geog.	981.951
Trumbull, J. Amer. poet.	861.21	Tso Chuan Chinese	
Trumpet wind instrum.	774.6	classics	096.1
Trunk		Tso Ssu Chinese poetry	811.1325
anthropography	565.25	Tsui Shu Chinese prose	817.738
anthropometry	565.35	Tu Fu Chinese poetry	811.144
Truth		Tu Kuang-ting Chinese	

fiction.	813.4
Tu Mu Chinese poetry	811.1481
Tu Shen-yen Chinese poet.	811.1417
Tuan Cheng-shih Chinese poet.	811.1484
Tubercle diseases	594.994
Tuberculosis diseases	597.245
Tubers	
field crops	612.48
garden crops	613.12
Tubiflorae botany	579.5
Tubulidentata zoology	588.31
Tudor Eng. history	935.85
Tuition	
fees school	334.15
Tumors disease	594.993
Tung Fang Shuo Chinese fic.	813.23
Tung Chen Pu Taoist scripture	222.2
Tung Ch'ung Shu Chinese philos.	111.215
Tung Hsuan Pu Taoist scripture	222.3
Tung Jo-yu Chinese fic.	813.71
Tung oil	
chemical technology	665.2
Tung Shen Pu Taoist scripture	222.4
Tungsten	
inorganic chemistry	546.45
metals metallurgy	669.999
Tungusic language	409.28
Tunicata zoology	586.3
Tunis, Africa geography	985.45
Tunnel	
engineering	651.6
Tunneling	
engineering	651.6
mining engin'g	658.35
Turanian language	409.2
Turbellaria zoology	583.31
Turbines engin'g	655.335
Turkey	
Asia	
geography	982.66
history	926.6
Europe	
administration	373.26
botany	571.26
finance	350.25
geography	982.69
geology	550.269
history	926.9

Turkey (cont.)	
maps	980.3269
schools	338.7982
statistics	354.26
Turkish	
empire history	926
language	409.26
literature	892
occupation Greek hist.	931.87
philosophy	116
rule Egypt history	951.86
Turkman language	409.26
Turning	
bridges engin'g.	651.573
Turnip	
field crops	612.42
gardening	613.11
Turnover, labor econ.	354.136
Turpentine chem.tech.	665.2
Tuscany, Italy	
geography	983.26
Tushetu khanate, China	
geog.	981.952
Twelve Classics, the Ch.	
classics	090.6
Twenty-	
four histories, the	910.98
one histories, the	910.96
two histories, the	910.97
Twilight	
meteorology	529.63
terrestrial physics	525.7
Twins obstetrics	598.817
Siamese orthopedic	
surgery	598.174
Tympanum	
anatomy	598.41
ear disease	598.44
physiology	598.42
Types	
locomotives engin'g.	655.272
of engines	655.25
movement	151.84
personality	153.84
structure	561.11
volcanoes	551.82
psychology	153.8
steam engineering	655.2252
Typewriting	626.7
Typhaceae botany	575.21
Typhoid	
fever pathology	594.926
Typhus	
fever pathology	594.926
Typotheria zoology	588.397
Tyrol, Austria geography	983.795

Tyrtaeus Greek lyric poet.	831.41	philos.	111.192
Tzu Hsia Chinese philos.	111.1122	Tzu Szu Chinese philos.	111.1124
Tzu Hua Tzu Chinese			

Ukiyo-zoshi Japanese fiction	823.62
Ulcers surgery	598.144
Ulmaceae botany	576.71
Ulster, Ireland Geography	983.58
Ulta-Darnwinism biology	564.3
Ulterior Tibet, China geography	981.983
Ultimatum intern.law	381.51
Umbelliforae botany	578.9
Umbilic cord obstetrics	598.8277
Umbrella-making handcrafts	688.5
Umbria, Italy geography	983.26
Unconsciousness psychology	156
Unction of the sick Christianity	253.98
Under-ground lines electric eng'ing.	657.652
railways	751.87
Understanding psychology	151.8
Undulations acoustics	534.2
Unemployment economics	354.137
insurance	354.937
Unfair list pol.econ.	354.84
Ungulata mammals	588.33
Unicellular plants botany	571.213
Uniform laws	373.0322
Uniforms domestic	693
employees econ.	354.155
military dress	319.44
equipment	379.373
Union strikes pol.econ.	354.831
Unions of employers	354.61
Uniplanar kinematics	531.23
Unique copies rarities	009.63
Unitarian church Christianity	259.81
United Italy	932.88
society of christian	256.15
United States of America administration	373.6
antiquities	996
architecture	710.6
army	379.161
bank political econ.	361.1241
biography	976
botany	571.96
boundaries	984.1
christian commission	256.13

United State of America (cont.)
- colleges 338.7961
- constitution 391.6
- education 330.96
- encyclopedia 034
- finance 369.6
- fine arts 706
- geography 984.1
- geology 550.6
- government
  - central 373.61
  - local 373.68
- history 941
- language 450
- laws 390.6
- libraries 020.96
- literature 860
- local government 373.68
- maps 980.341
  - or, 984.12
- music 770.6
- national bibliography 013.6
- navy 379.166
- painting 730.6
- patriotic societies 313.6141
- philosophy 126
- political parties 375.6
- schools, public 338.061
- statistics 345.41
- travels 984.14
  - or, 980.76
- treaties 387.96
- universities 338.7961
- yearbooks 037.36
- zoology 581.96

United States of Colombia
- geography 984.86
- history 948.6

Unity
- metaphysics 133.82
- of God Christian doctrine 251.1
  - human race 565.73
  - knowledge 131
  - language 400.9
- theatre 781.11

Universal
- gravitation, law of mech. 531.64
- history 909.9
- language 40

Universalists Christianity 259.82

Universe
- astron. 523.1
- mechanistic theories of
  - metaphys. 134.1

Universities
- education 338.71

women education	338.917	geography	985.57
Unknowable metaphysics	131.8	history	955.7
Universology cosmology	134	house legis.bodies	373.033
Unneutral service intern.		Ural	
law	381.65	Altaic	
Unorganized strikes pol.		language	409.2
econ.	354.835	literature	809.2
Unwritten law	390.001	Uranium chemistry	546.47
Upadana Buddhism	231.54	Uranus planets	523.47
Upamana Hinduism	241.23	Urban	
Upanishad Hinduism	242.5	economics	350.025
Upholstery decoration &		education	338.45
ornament	763.6	sociology	313.5
Upland rice field crops	612.18	Uredineineae botany	573.35
Upper		Urethra	
Austria		female anatomy	598.71
Geography	983.795	male anatomy	597.6
history	937.95	Urinary	
Canada		disorders diseases	597.643
geography	984.28	organ anatomy	597.6
history	942.8	Urine analysis	
chamber legis.bodies	373.033	therapeutics	595.29
Egypt		Urochorda zoology	586.3
geography	985.163	Urodela zoology	587.67
history	951.63	Ursidae zoology	588.518
extremities anatomy	591.87	Urticaceae botany	576.74
Guinea		Urticales botany	576.7

Uruguay	
geography	984.899
history	948.99
Use of	
books and libraries	027
reference books	027.3
Useful	
arts	600
economics	357.3
Usefulness of	
animals econ.zoology	581.8
plants econ.botany	571.8
Utah, U.S.	
geography	984.192
Uterus	
anatomy	598.71
disease	598.744
physiology	598.72
Utilitarianism	
ethics	171.2
philosophy	106.7
Utilization	
of animals zootechy	615.9
silkworms	616.9
Utopian socialism	318.1
Utopia political science	371.5
Utsubo monogatari	823.34
Uttara Mimansa Hinduism	249.2
Unveal tract	
anatomy	598.31
physiology	598.37

Vacations
    laboring class   354.46
    school education   336.58
Vaccination
    public health   593.2356
Vacuum
    lamps elec.lighting   657.8145
    lump chem.apparatus   542.7
Vagina
    anatomy   598.71
    diseases of women   598.745
Vaibhasikas Indian
    Buddhism   239.112
Vaisesika Hinduism   249.5
Valencia, Spain
    geography   983.37
Valerianaceae botany   579.85
Valleys phys.geography   552.6
Valois, house of Fr.history   934.82
Valuation
    farm economics   610.317
    forests forestry   614.01
Value
    of money   361
    political economy   350.1
    standards of money   361
Value, theory of

    metaphysics   137
Vanadium group
    chemistry   546.6
Vanity ethics   180.82
Vapor
    densities   541.67
    lamps elec.lighting   657.8145
    pressure chemistry   541.44
    saturated   536.75
    superheaded   536.77
Vaporization
    heat   536.722
    practical chemistry   542.4
Var, France geography   983.497
Variable
    complex algebra   512.7
        calculus   515.8
    real functions   516.11
    stars astronomy   523.85
    transcendental functions   516.3
Variation
    evolution   571.773
    calculus of   515.4
    congenital   563.61
    continuous   563.62
Variation(cont.)
    discontinuous   563.63
    experimental   563.67

genetic biology	563.6
laws of	563.66
of animal heat	592.55
longitude and latitude	521.28
right ascen.and declin.	521.27
ontogenetic	563.69
seasonal	563.64
sexual	563.65
sociology	312.22
zoology	581.77
Varnishes chem.technol.	667.7
Varnishing.	
painting	734.5
mechanic trade	683
Vascular	
plants botany	571.216
system anatomy	581.11
tissue physiology	581.27
Vas deferens anatomy	597.615
Vases pottery	764
Vasomotors physiology	597.128
Vasu-bandhu Buddhism	239.145
Vaucluse, France	
geography	983.497
Vaudeville farces	785.8
Vector analysis algebra	512.65
Vedana	
Nidana Buddhism	231.56
Skandha Buddhism	231.62
Vedanta Hinduism	249.2
Vedic language	409.311
Vegetable	
chemistry	543.25
drugs	596.12
dye plants agric.	612.91
farm	611.23
food	
dom.econ.	694.2
hygiene	593.126
physiol.	592.473
fats chem.tech.	665.2
oils chem.tech.	665.2
parasites diseases	594.978
poisons toxicology	593.97
products	661.97
world botany	570
gardening	613
Vegetables	
chemistry	543.25
field crops	612.4
garden crops	613
Vegetation botany	570
Vehicles	
farm transport	610.66
motor	659.7
Veins	

anatomy	597.116	school building	332.92
diseases	597.146	sanitary eng.	653.5
geology	553.8	working conditions	354.55
Velocity		Venus	
of light optics	535.31	planets	523.42
liquids	534.41	transits astron.	523.92
sound acoustic	534.4	Vera Cruz, Mexico	
Velvet		geography	984.48
bean	612.383	Verbenaceae botany	579.55
cotton manuf.	675.2	Vermes zoology	583.1
ribbon manuf.	675.7	Vermont, U.S.	
silk manuf.	675.4	geography	984.162
special fabrics manuf.	675.6	Verona, Italy	
Vendee, France		geography	983.26
geography	983.491	Versailles, France	
Veneral diseases	598.6	geography	983.471
Venetia, Italy geography	983.26	Version	
Venezuela		obstetrics	598.872
geography	984.87	of Bible	252.06
history	948.7	Sutra	232.06
Venice, Italy		Vertebrata zoology	587
geography	983.26	Vertebrates	569.8
Venous thrombosis		paleontology	569.8
anatomy	598.866	zoology	587
Ventilation		Verticillatae botany	576.2
library economy	024.7	Vertigo	
mining engineering	658.41	diseases	597.8441
of house dom.econ.	692	physiology	597.823

Vesicular skin diseases	598.542	Vicia forage crops	612.37
Vessels shipbuilding	659.39	Victoria, Austria	
Vestments ecclesiology	253.35	geography	985.9393
Vetches agriculture	612.37	Victoria, Queen	
Veterinary		Eng.hist.	935.88
medicine	599	Scot.history	935.918
obstetrics	599.8	Viejnana Buddhism	231.65
pathology	599.4	Vienna, Austria	
surgery	599.7	geography	983.795
therapeutics	599.5	Vienne, France	
Viaducts bridges	651.5023	geography	983.491
Viaticum Christianity	253.98	Haute	983.489
Vibration		Vignettes engraving	740
in pipes	534.57	Vigny, A.V.	
light	535.21	Fr.poet.	841.73
longitudinal	534.545	drama	842.73
of membranes	534.56	Vilaine, Ille et	
poates	534.56	France geography	983.461
rods	534.55	Village	
stretched strings	534.54	beautiful	313.411
wires	534.54	community	371.15
tranverse	534.546	pol.sci.	371.15
Vibrations acoustics	534.5	sociology	313.4
maintained		homes architecture	718.7
by heat	534.58	Villas architecture	718.7
Vices		Vinaya	
crime	394	—pitaka Sutra	232.4
ethics	180.8	—sect Chinese Buddhism	239.54

Japanese Buddhism	239.64	organs of	598.31
Vine		physiology	598.32
culture pomiculture	613.75	Visions psychoanalysis	156.33
Vineger chemic.tech.	664.43	Visitations Eng.heraldry	966.5
Vinyards pomiculture	613.75	Visual	
Viola stringed instruments	775.6	instruction education	337.13
Violaceae botany	578.59	sensation	151.11
Violin stringed		Vitaceae botany	578.33
instruments	775.7	Vital	
Violoncello stringed		energy	592.1
instruments	775.5	functions	
Virgil Latin epic poet.	832.31	animals	581.404
Virgin island		man	592.1
geography	984.167	force	581.401
Virginia, U.S.		mechanics	581.404
geography	984.167	phenomena biology	562
West	984.167	principle	562.37
Virtues		processes and functions	581.404
christian doctrine	258.51	statistics	349.07
ethics	180.7	substance	562.32
Virya Buddhism	231.74	Vitalism biology	562.38
Viscous fluids hydraulics	532.7	physiology	581.401
Vishnu Hinduism	241.73	Vitality biology	566.921
Vision		Viticulture pomiculture	613.75
disorders disease of eye	598.345	Vitis fruit raising	613.75
mental faculty	151.11	Vitreous humor	
optics	535.9	eye diseases	598.344
		physiology	598.321

Viverridae zoology	588.515	Volkerkunde ethnology	565.7
Viviparity zoology	581.627	Volley ball sports	333.35
Vivisection		Volition	151.4
experimental phys.	592.81	pathology of	151.44
laws medicine	593.71	measurements of	151.48
Viyama Hinduism	244.2	Voltaic	
Vocal		cell	537.21
chamber music	771.8	element	
forms	770.027	physics	537.21
music	771	electricity	657.14
organs diseases of	598.495	Voltaire, F.M.	
human anatomy	597.212	French drama	842.56
Vocational		fiction	843.54
and economical		philos.	124.4
geography	980.15	Volumetric	
education	338.4	analysis of gases	
guidance	338.48	chemistry	545.43
school	338.47	liquids chemistry	545.41
Voice acoustics physic	534.9	Voluntary	
Void metaphysis	134.4	human action	151.42
Volapuk language	405	Volunteers military sci.	379.8
Volcanic		Vomiting diseases	597.343
action	515.315	Vosges, France geography	983.474
Volcanic (cont.)		Vote	
ashes	557.22	announcements	372.558
rocks	557.2	legislative procedure	373.038
Volcanoes physical geol.	551.4	majority legis.bod.	373.038
Volkalied vocal music	771.2	plural suffrage	372.5

Voting			scientific	500.98
	political science	372.52	travels	980
	procedure	372.55	zoology	580.099
	suffrage	372.5	Vulva	
Voyages			anatomy	598.71
	round the world	980.709	diseases of women	598.746

Wadding cotton manuf.	675.2
Waders zoology	587.974
Wage	
fund pol.econ.	354.313
living pol.econ.	354.935
minimum pol.econ.	354.36
scales pol.econ.	354.33
Wagers ethics	189.7
Wages	
attachment of	398
base of econ.	354.34
economics	354.3
for state labor	354.36
in special countries	354.39
industries	354.48
labor and polit.econ.	354
theory of	354.31
work at reduced	354.25
Wagons farm transport	610.66
Wai tan Taoism	224.5
Waka	
Japanese poems	821.2
Wakayama, Japan	
geography	982.1646
Waldeck, Germany	
geography	983.78
Wales	
geography	983.59
history	935.95
language	493.9
Walking	
School hygiene	332.3
Walks	
esthetics of cities	719.3
Wallace's exposition	564.31
Walls	
architectural construc.	713.4
painted decora.	735.1
Walnut nut raising	613.761
Walton, Isaac Eng.essays	857.45
Waltz dance	792.3
Wan wei Chinese prose	811.142
Wang An-shih Chinese	
prose	817.517
Wang Chia Chinese	
fiction	813.38
Wang Ch'ung Chinese	
philos.	111.27
Wang Fu Chinese philos.	111.281
Wang K'ai-yun Chinese	
prose	817.791
Wang Kuo-wei Chinese	
prose	817.795
Wang Ming-sheu Chinese	
poet	811.177

Wang Po	
Chinese poet.	811.1413
Chinese prose	817.41
Wang Shin-chen(Ming)	
Chinese fiction	813.65
Chinese poet.	811.166
Chinese prose	817.6
Wang Shih-chen(Ching)	
Chinese poet.	811.173
Wang Shih-fu Chinese	
drama	812.32
Wang Shih-p'eng Chinese	
prose	817.574
Wang Shou-Jen.Chinese	
philos.	111.63
Wang Wan Chinese prose	817.722
Wang Wei Chinese poet.	811.142
Wang Yu-Ch'eng	
Chinese poet.	811.1513
prose	817.511
Wants	
and utilily econom.	352.41
immaterial	352.1
material	352.1
War	
and crises pol.econ.	352.76
debts intern.pol.	388.84
ethics	185.8
games	797.8
law of	390.008
Mexican U.S.history	944.85
of secession U.S.history	941.86
science and art of	379.5
ships	379.64
vessels	659.39
in neutral ports	381.67
Warsaw,Poland	
geography	983.86
Warships ship building	659.11
Warts dermatology	598.544
Warwick,England	
geography	983.564
Washing	
house cleaning	653.7
laundry	686
public municipal eng.	653.7
practical chemistry	542.69
Washington,U.S.(City)	984.166
geography	984.197
Wasps zoology	585.58
Waste	
land pol.econ.	353.19
removal of sociology	313.43
sanitary eng'ing	653.36
sociology	313.43

sewage disposal	653.35
Watches manufactures	671.1
Water	
baths prac.chemistry	542.4
buffalo	615.12
carriage	653.33
chemical analysis	543.15
colors painted	734.1
cure therap.	595.83
engines mech.eng.	655.3
falls	981.358
filters sanitary eng.	653.18
fows.zoology	587.971
gages	655.2255
geologic action	551.93
hydraulics	532
in soil	611.333
inorganic chemistry	546.11
marks	674.1
meteorology	529.4
monochrome painting	734.3
municipal engineering	653
physical geography	552.5
power	
hydraulic engin'g	654.69
mech.eng.	655.35
pressure engines	655.35
pumps	655.37
ram	
engineering	655.37
hydraulics	532.9
resources	
forestry	614.113
municipal engineering	653.14
supply	
agriculture	611.6
industries	653.1
sanitary engin'g	653.19
source of	653.14
towers water-works	653.16
transportation	634
tube boilers	655.225
underground phy.geog.	552.5
vapor exhalation physiol.	597.226
Water(cont.)	
wheels	
hydraulics	532.9
mech.eng.	655.33
works	653.1
worships hydrolatry	209.24
Watermelon gardening	613.22
Watersheds hydraulic eng.	654.64
Waterways transportation	634.1
Watt	
hour meters elec.eng.	657.19

meters elec.eng.	657.17
Wave	
form	534.37
front	534.35
theory	
optics	535.13
sound	534.3
Waves	
De Broglie physics	530.75
theory of hydraulics	532.59
Wax	
bee keeping	615.4
flowers	765.3
Ways	
of obtaining immortality	
Taoism	224
Weak current engineering	657.19
Wealth pol.ecom.	352.2
Weather	
bureau	529.73
maps	529.76
meteorology	529.7
warnings	529.75
Weaving	
machinery	675.09
manufactures	675.05
Webster, Noah Amer.	
essays	867.22
Wedding customs	319.22
Wedge physics	531.96
Weeds injurious plants	611.97
Wei Cheng Chinese poet.	811.1411
Wei Dynasty Chinese	
history	913
Wei Liao-weng Chinese	
prose	817.577
Wei Ying-wu Chinsse	
poet	811.1452
Wei Yuan Chinese prose	817.785
Weight	
chemical apparatus	542.3
of earth	525.1
Weights	
and measures	530.077
Chinese antiquities	991.77
medical chem.	596.5
atomic theor.chem.	541.01
Wells	
water supply	653.14
agriculture	611.6
engines	653.1
Welsh	
geography	983.59
history	935.95
language	409.376

literature	859.5
Wen Chung Tzu Chinese philos.	111.37
Wen Ting-chun Chinese poet.	811.482
Wen Tian-hsiang	
Chinese poet.	811.1578
prose	817.579
Wen Tsu Chinese philos.	111.1222
Wens diseases	
West	
Africa	
geography	985.5
history	955
Indies	
geography	984.7
history	947
Spanish America	945
Prussia	
geography	983.76
history	937.6
Russia	
geography	983.87
history	938.7
Virginia	
geography	984.167
Western	
Australia	
geography	985.936
history	595.36
Chin Chinese history	913.3
Ch'in Chinese history	913.592
Chou Chinese history	911.91
church Roman catholic	259.1
Han Chinese history	912.2
hemisphere	
geography	980.74
phys.geog.	552.1
Western (cont.)	
Hsia Chinese history	915.8
Liang Chinese history	913.596
Liao Chinese history	915.6
Tibet China geography	981.987
Wei Chinese history	913.83
Yen Chinese history	913.589
Westmoreland, England	
geog.	983.569
Westphalia, Germany	
geography	983.78
Wet	
method	
qual.chem.anal.	544.1
quan.chem.anal.	545.1
plates	755.1
Whales fisheries	617.5
zoology	588.47

Wharves engineering	654.36
Wheat field crops	612.11
Wheel	
and axle	531.92
hoe	610.61
vehicles agric.	610.66
Wheelbarrows farm trans.	610.66
Wheels	
cog mech.eng.	655.8
water hydraulics	532.9
mech.eng.	655.33
wooden manufactures	672
Whigs U.S.pol.parties	375.63
Whirlpools geology	552.2
Whirlwinds meteorology	529.3
Whiskey chem.tech.	664.55
Whitsunday Christianity	253.14
White	
colored-stars astronomy	523.81
corpuscles physiology	597.1212
hair dermatology	598.544
Nile	
geography	985.175
swine	615.14
White,H.K.Eng.poet.	851.68
White Tai languages	409.125
Whitelisting pol.econ.	354.85
Whitman,Walt Am.poet.	861.38
Whittier,J.G.Am.poet.	861.35
Wholesale business	622.54
Who's who biography	970.3
Wigglesworth,M.Am.poet.	861.13
Wight,Isle of	
England geography	983.562
Wild	
animals hunting	619.1
fowl sports	799
goose	615.2
silk textil manuf.	675.4
Wildings childstudy	153.764
Will	
diseases of	151.44
freedom of	151.41
of god ethics	181
psychology	151.4
heology Christianity	251.49
training of	151.43
Willow botany	567.31
fibers	612.596
Wilts,Eng.geography	983.563
Wind	
agriculture hindrances	611.915
anticyclonic meteorology	529.37
cyclonic meteorology	529.37
instruments music	774

meteorology	529.3
mills	655.48
planetary meteorology	529.31
storm	529.33
refraction physics	534.45
trade meteorology	529.31

Windward islands.

geography	984.78
history	947.8

Wine

at table temper.	180.89
chemical tech.	664.51
making	664.51
manufacture	664.51
tax	369.152
temperance	180.89

Winter, W.Amer.poet.	861.44

Wire

manufacture	671.1

Wireless

communication	637.3
telegraphy	657.838

Wiring

central station engin'g	657.29
electrical transmission	657.6
house elec.engin'g.	657.816

Wisconsin, U.S.geography	984.177

Wisdom

apocrypha	252.93
doctrinal theology	251.149
ethics	180.79
Witchcraft occult science	157.7
Wives'duties family ethics	183.5
Wolff Ger.philos.	127.19

Wolfram

inorgan.chem.	546.45
v.Eschenbach Ger.poet.	871.24

Woman

beauty in	313.3507
customs	319.41
or,	338.91
education	313.3503
feminism	313.35
in art	313.3507
home	313.357
literature	313.3508
modern, the	313.35
position and treatment	313.35
psychology	153.1
or,	313.3501
sociology	313.35
suffrage feminism	313.354
pol.sci.	372.7

Woman's

exchange sociology	313.353
rights	313.354

Women
  as librarian   022.5
    teachers   336.7
      library   028.6
  costume of etiquette   319.41
  disease of   598.7
  dutes of
    family ethics   183.5
    social ethics   184
  emancipation of
    feminism   313.353
  labors of
    feminism   313.355
    pol.econ   354.23
  law for   394.63
Women's
  Christians asso.Christianity   256.4
  cloths
    domestic econ.   693.6
    manufactures   684
Women's(cont.)
  clubs feminism   313.356
  hats
    domestic econ.   693.3
    manufactures   688.3
  library   025.73
  religious societies
    Christianity   256.5
  rights feminism   313.354
  unions pol.econ.   354.65
  work in church Christianity   254.9
Wood
  alcohol chem.tech.   661
  ashes agri.   611.7
  beams bridge eng.   651.5023
  building material   650.45
  buildings library   024.2
  bridges, archt.engin'g.   651.5015
  carving   723
    industries   766.2
  city house   718.3
  construction   651.115
    carpentry   651.15
    shipbuilding   659.114
  distillation   668.5
  engraving   741
  implements manufac.   672
  pavements road eng.   651.7
  pulp manufac.   674.6
  Ships shipbuilding   659.11
  village house   718.7
  wind music   774
  work
    arch.decoration   712.9
    joints carpentry   651.15
    art industry   766

manufactures	672
Working	
manufactures	672
mechanic trade	681
Wooden	
bridges	651.5015
ceilings arch.construc.	713.7
construction	651.115
doors arch.construc.	713.8
floors arch.construc.	713.6
manufactures	675.3
roofs arch.construc.	713.5
ships	659.114
Wooden(cont.)	
shoes manufac.	672
walls arch.construc.	713.4
Woodlands farm econ.	611.27
Woodpeckers zoology	587.9753
Woods	
economic botany	571.8
forestry	614
perfume	612.817
Wool	
cloths manufac.	675.2
domestic economics	693.1
dyeing chem.tech.	667.9
manufactures	675.3
Worcester,England	
geography	983.564
Cape of Good Hope	985.77
Words	
of Agrapha	970.1
Christ	251.291
Dr.Sun	001.191
slang English	455
Work	
and energy mechanics	631.693
fatigue psychology	151.55
duration of pol.econ.	354.4
Jurisdiction over pol.econ.	354.16
remuneration for pol.econ.	354.3
Workers	
economics	354
departments	001.34
offis.economy	622.1
selecting	354.115
unions of women	354.65
Working	
class pol.econ.	354.4
conditions	354.5
of farm systems	610.3
soil	611.4
Workingmen's	
associations	354.6
budgets	354.935
insurance	368.6

Workmen
    accident compensation   354.35
    cottage, for architec.   718.7
    disputes   354.8
    insurance
        compulsory   354.35
        law   398.8

Workmen (cont.)
    transport.econ.   354.9
    libraries
        lib.econ.   025.94
        pol.econ.   354.933
    temments for architec.   718.5

Workshop
    receits tech.   660

World
    atlass of   980.3
    voyages round   980.7
    war   930.7

Worms
    diseases   594.972
    palaeontology   569.6
    zoology   583.1

Worship
    at the grave   319.117
    Buddhism   233.2
    family   253.22
    natural theology   201

    of
        Gods   319.115
        humans   209.5
        nature   209.2
        primitive religions   209
        public Christianity   253.21

Wounds
    injuries and accidents   598.16
    reparation of surgery   598.16

Woven
    carpets manufact.   675.6
    fabrics manufact.   675.6
    glass manufact.   675.5
    straw manufact.   675.5

Wrapping machinery   655.95

Wrestling sports   797.6

Wrist anatomy   591.87

Writing
    machines business   626.7
    materials   622
    music   770

Written
    examinations law   390.025
    law   390.001

Wrong ethics   180.2

Wu Ch'eng-en Chinese
    fiction   813.63

Wu Chih-hsin Chinese

fiction	813.74	Wundt German philos.	127.78
Wu Dynasty Chinese hist.	914.91	Wurtemburg, Germany geo.	983.77
Wu Hsi-ch'i Chinese prose	817.763	Wyatt, T. Eng. poetry	851.27
		Wycherly, W. Eng. drama	852.44
Wu Yueh Chinese history	914.94	Wyoming, U.S. geography	984.186

X-ray		Xenon inorganic chem.	546.186
diagnosis	595.277	Xenophanes Gk.philos.	121.121
electricity	537.3	Xiphodontidae paleon-	
optics	535.53	tology	569.877
radioactivity	539	Xylography engraving	741
Xenarthra zoology	588.323	Xyphosura zoology	584.66
Xenacanthina paleontology	569.83	Xyridaceae botany	575.61
Xenocrates Gk.philos.	121.34	Xyridales botany	575.6

Yacht clubs architecture	717.8	Yearbooks	037
Yachting recreation	799	statistics	340
Yachts		see subject	
engine driven shipbuilding	659.13	Yeast	
sailing driven shipbuilding	659.13	chemic technology	664.5
Yajur-veda Hinduism	242.12	fungi botany	573.3
Yamagata, Japan		protophyta botany	572.1
geography	982.1629	Yeh-Lu Ch'u-ch'ai	
Yamaguchi, Japan		Chinese prose	817.585
geography	982.1653	Yeh Meng-te Chinese	
Yamanashi, Japan		poet.	811.1571
geography	982.1637	Yeh Shih Chinese prose	817.576
Yamato monogatari		Yellow	
Japanese fiction	823.33	colored-star	523.82
Yang Chu Chinese philos.	111.124	fever	
Yang Hsien-chih Chinese		diseases	594.927
drama	812.39	public health	593.24
Yang Hsiung		vegetable dye plants	612.91
Chinese philos.	111.25	Yemen, Arabia	
prose	817.25	geography	982.77
Yang Shih-ch'i		history	927.7
Chinese poet.	811.163	Yen Chi-tao Chinese	
prose	817.615	poet.	811.734
Yang Yi Chinese poet.	811.1511	Yen Tze Chinese philos.	111.193
Yao Nai Chinese prose	817.745	Yen Yen-chih Chinese	
Yardlands land	353.15	poet.	811.1333
Year Chronology	528.3	Yen Yu Chinese poet.	811.1576

Yen Yuan Chinese philos.	111.73	geography	983.568
Y.M.C.A.		Young, E. Eng. poet.	851.55
building	256.32	Young	
architecture	715.9	childstudy	313.365
Y.M.C.A. (cont.)		education of elem. educ.	338.2
committees		Men's Christian ass'n	256.3
special	256.35	men's Christian unions	256.2
standing	256.33	people societies	313.67
departments	256.35	Women's Christian ass'n.	256.4
extension	256.31	Ytterbium inorg. chem.	546.272
general secretary	256.34	Yttrium inorg. chem.	546.261
history	256.39	Yu chi Chinese poet.	811.159
institutes	256.36	Yu Chu Chinese fiction	813.21
local work by dep'ts	255.35	Yu Hsin Chinese poet.	811.137
membership	256.33	Yu Hsuan-chi Chinese	
officers		poet.	811.1488
salaried	256.34	Yu Tsu-ch'ien Chinese	
unsalaried	256.33	prose	817.573
organization	256.33	Yu Tung Chinese prose	817.727
reports	256.39	Yu Tzu Chinese philos.	111.191
Yo Ching Chinese		Yu Wen Chinese prose	817.45
classics	095	Yu Yueh Chinese fiction	813.78
Yoga Brahmanism	249.4	Yuan Chen Chinese poet.	811.1457
Yogacara school Indian		Yuan dynasty Chinese	
Buddhism	239.14	history	915.9
Yomibon Japanese fiction	823.65	Yuan editions book	
Yonne, France geography	983.475	rarities	009.115
Yorkshire, England			

Yuan Hao-wen		prose	817.762
Chinese poet.	811.158	Yucatan, Mexico geography	984.48
prose	817.578	Yukon, Canada geography	984.26
Yuan Hung-tao Chinese poet.	811.167	Yun Chin Chinese prose	817.751
Yuan Mei		Yunnan, China geography	981.86
Chinese fiction	813.76		

Zacatecas, Mezico	
geography	984.47
Zanzibar, Africa	
geography	985.43
history	954.3
Zechariah Bible	252.498
Zen Japanese Buddhism	239.66
Zend	
Avest	
Persian lit.	893.3
religion	280
Avesta (Zoroastaian scripture)	282
language	493.3
Zenith telescope	
astronomy	522.4
Zeno	
Apostolo Italy dram.	833.2
early Greek philos.	121.125
Stoic philosopher	121.521
Zephaniah Bible	252.496
Zinc	
inorganic chemistry	546.235
metallurgy	669.97
ores	558.145
Zincography photography	746.5
Zingiberaceae botany	575.92
Zirconium inorg.chem.	546.55
Zodiac	
light astronomy	523.57
signs occult science	157.23
Zoic age geology	554.3
Zola, Emile Fr.fict.	843.86
Zoolatry nature worship	209.28
Zoological anthropology	565.5
gardens	580.077
physical geography	980.118
Zoology	580
agriculture	610.58
Zoopsychology	154.8
Zootechny	615.02
Zoroaster Parseeism	281.2
Zoroastrianism	280
Zoysicae forage crops	612.291
Zululand	
geography	985.75
history	957.5
Zygophyllaceae botany	577.91
Zyosporeae	
algae	573.2
lichens	573.4

皮高品 著
周　榮　吳芹芳
謝　泉　袁　静　整理

皮高品集
（下）

荊楚文庫

荊楚文庫編纂出版委員會
武漢大學出版社

中國十進分類法中文索引說明

（一）本書索引分中文西文兩部，茲爲中文部分，西文部分另有說明。

（二）本索引係採分類表中各種重要之名稱——學名人名地名等——編排而成。於可能範圍內，雖分類表中無有是項地位，或是項名稱者，亦擇要編入於正目或副目之中，使其略具有相關索引之優點。

（三）本索引按照王雲五氏發明之四角號碼檢字法排列，體例如下：

（A）單字注四角及附角之號碼於本字之前。

   例如 00104 主

（B）同首字下之各名辭，其排列次序仍按依四角號碼之次序，但其號碼概不注出。

   例如 主席

      主權國

      主日禮拜

（C）正目中所包含之各名詞，謂之副目，在正目下退一格印刷。副目次序仍按依四角號碼排列。

（四）每條後所注數碼，代表分類表中之類號。

   例如 童子軍 313.67

（五）四角號碼檢字法詳見次頁。

（六）本索引之編製謄寫校對，係由于子強、尤明軒、張正義、駱繼駒、范禮煌、田清濂諸先生，及本校一九三六級同學諸君合力成之；但編製之體例不善，及名詞之選擇不精，仍應由予全任其咎。

             中華民國二十四年雙十節毛坤

第二次改訂四角號碼檢字法

王雲五發明

第一條　筆畫分爲十種,各以號碼代表之如下:

號碼	筆名	筆形	舉例	說明	注意
0	頭	亠	言 主 广 疒	獨立之點與獨立之橫相結合	0456789各種均由數筆合爲一複筆。檢查時遇單筆與複筆並列,應盡量取複筆;如 乂作0不作3,寸作4不作2,厂作7不作2,丷作8不作32,小作9不作33
1	橫	一 亅 乚	天 土 地 江 元 風	包括橫,刁與右鉤	
2	垂	丨 丿 丨	山 月 千 則	包括直,撇與左鉤	
3	點	丶 ㇏	六 衤 宀 厶 之 衣	包括點與捺	
4	乂	十 乂	草 杏 皮 刈 大 筓	兩筆相交	
5	插	扌	扌 戈 申 史	一筆通過兩筆以上	
6	方	口	國 鳴 目 四 甲 由	四邊齊整之形	
7	角	丁 厂 ⺁	羽 門 灰 陰 雪 衣 學 罕	橫與垂相接之處	
8	八	八 丷 人 厶	分 頁 羊 余 災 余 定 ⺈	八字形與其變形	
9	小	小 ⺌ 丬 忄	尖 糹 舞 呆 惟	小字形與其變形	

第二條　每字祇取四角之筆,其順序:

(一)左上角　(二)右上角　(三)左下角　(四)右下角

(例)　(一)左上角……　端　……(二)右上角
　　　(三)左下角……　　　……(四)右下角

檢查時按四角之筆形及順序,每字得四碼。

(例)　$_2^0$頑$_8^1$=0128　$_5^4$截$_5^3$=4325　$_8^6$睬$_9^7$=6789

第三條　字之上部或下部,祇有一筆或一複筆時,無論在何地位,均作左角,其右角作0。

(例)　^{3}宣^0　^{4}直^0　^{8}首^0　$_2$冬　$_5$軍^0　$_9$宗^0　$_5$母^0

每筆用過後,如再充他角,亦作0。

(例)　^{1}干^6　$_3$之$_0$　^{5}持　掛$_0^3$　^{4}大^0　^{5}十$^e_0$　^{5}車^0　^{6}時$^0_0$

第四條　由整個口門鬥所成之字,其下角取內部之筆,但上下左右有他筆時,不在此例。

（例）　因 = 6043　閉 = 7724　鬭 = 7712　茵 = 4460　瀾 = 3712

附　　則

I　字體均照楷書如下表

正	住[0] 匕[1] 反[1] 礻[3] 戶[3] 安[3] 心[3] 卜[3] 斥[3] [3]刀 [8]业[2] [3]亦[3] [4]草[4] 真[4] 執[4] [4]禺 [7]衣
誤	住[5] 匕[2] 反[2] 礻[1] 戶[1] 安[5] 心[1] 卜[4] 斥[4] 刀[5] [2]业[3] [2]亦[3] [1]草[1] [2]真[1] 執[5] [2]禺 [1]衣[4]

II　取筆時應注意之點

(1) 宀戶等字,凡點下之橫,右方與他筆相連者,均作 3,不作 0。

(2) 尸皿門等字,方形之筆端延長於外者,均作 7,不作 6。

(3) 角筆之兩端,不作 7,如 [1]冖[7]。

(4) 交义之筆,不作 8,如 [4]美[2]。

(5) 业小中有二筆,水小旁有二筆,均不作小形。

III　取角時應注意之點

1　獨立或平行之筆,不問高低,概以最左或最右者為角。

（例）　[1]非[1] [1]俾[1] 疾 浦[3] [2]帝[2]

2　最左或最右之筆,有他筆蓋於其上或承於其下時,取蓋於上者為上角,承於下者為下角。

（例）　×宗× ×幸× ×寧× 共×

3　有兩複筆可取時,在上角應取較高之複筆,在下角應取較低之複筆。

（例）　功ˣ　ˣ盛ˣ頗ˣ鴨ˣ奄

4 斜撇爲他筆所承,取他筆爲下角。

（例）　ˣ春ˣ　奎ˣ　碓ˣ　衣

5 左上之撇作左角,其右角取右筆。

（例）　勾ˣ　鉤ˣ　侔　鳴

IV 四角同碼字較多時,以右下角上方最貼近而露鋒芒之一筆爲附角;如該筆業已用過,則附角作 0。

（例）　芒=44710　元₁　洋₂　是₃　疝₄　歆₅　畜₆　殘₇　主₈ 難₁　霖₂　毹₃　拼₄　蠻₅　覽₆　功₇　郭₈　癥₉　愁₁₀　金₁₁　速₁₂ 仁₁　見₂。

附角仍有同碼字時,得按各該字所含橫筆(即第一種筆形,包括橫刁及右鉤)之數順序排列。

例如市、帝二字之四角及附角均同,但市字含有二橫,帝字含有三橫,故市字在前帝字在後,餘照此類推。

主 童 立 症 瘧 癱 瘟

00104 主

主席	373.011
主席團	001.222
主要軍艦	379.65
主刑	394.51
主僕	
家庭	313.327
家法	397.54
倫理	183.7
主樂學派	121.25
主權	
報學	040.3
國家	371.027
主權國	381.11
主顧	150.171
主顧論	106.23
主教	255.53
主日	253.19
主日禮拜	253.25
主腦	597.8113

00105 童

童話	
兒童文學	805.3
學校教育	338.135
（各國童話見各國文學下）	
童子軍	313.67
童歌	805.1
童劇	805.2
童畫	805.4

00108 立

立憲	371.045
立法	
五權憲法	001.161
行政	373.032
民權主義	001.135
立法手續	373.038
立法權	373.0325
立法院	373.03
立法學	390.011
立體幾何學	517.5
立體化學	541.06
立陶宛	
語言	409.398
地理	983.97
歷史	939.75

00111 症

| 症候學 | 595.3 |
| 症候分佈學 | 593.232 |

00111 瘧

| 瘧 | 593.114 |
| 瘧熱 | 594.928 |

00114 癱

| 癱 | 594.962 |

00114 瘟

| 瘟疫 | |

瘋 痢 疹 病 痛 瘺 癇 疾 瘊 瘻 疲 瘡 癌

社會救濟	316.47	病原學	571.5
公共衛生	593.237	公共衛生	593.231
00117 瘋		病脈	597.126
瘋癲		病人食品	593.123
特殊教育	338.967	**00127 痛**	
精神分析	156.3355	痛恨	180.64
瘋癲婦科	598.795	**00127 瘺**	
瘋犬	594.961	瘺	598.143
00120 痢		**00127 癇**	
痢疾	594.938	癇厥病	155.6
00122 疹		**00134 疾**	
疹	594.91	疾病	354.937
00127 病		凶禮	319.17
病理學	594	社會病理	315.163
動物	581.5	疾病預防	
植物	571.5	學校管理	332.32
細菌	566.84	工廠	354.53
蠱	616.24	**00134 瘊**	
病理解剖	594.1	瘊	598.544
精神生理學	152.4	**00144 瘻**	
病理生理學	592.3	瘻管	598.143
病理人類學	565.48	**00147 疲**	
病心	597.127	疲勞	151.55
病媒	593.234	**00167 瘡**	
病菌		瘡	598.144
農業	611.95	**00172 癌**	
細菌學	566.964	癌	594.993
病因學	594.2		

癲 癇 痲 亭 鹿 魔 產 塵 競 庵 竟 贏 序 齊 齋 方

00186 癲
 癲   594.997
00186 癇
 癲癇病
  變態心理   155.253
  神經系   597.8453
 癲狂   155.2
 癲狂癡愚院   316.36
00194 痲
 痲瘋   594.997
00201 亭
 亭臺
  名勝   981.383
  遺跡   991.83
00211 鹿
 鹿蹄草
  植物學   579.13
  農作物   612.85
 鹿類   588.337
00213 魔
 魔鬼   251.63
 魔術   157.7
00214 產
 產科   598.8
 產兒病理學   598.94
00214 塵
 塵埃   653.36

00214 競
 競奏曲   779.5
00216 庵
 庵   235.8
00216 竟
 竟陵體   811.168
00217 贏
 贏質烯屬   547.12
00222 序
 序曲   779.3
00222 齊
 齊
  春秋時代史   911.612
  戰國時代史   911.651
  南北朝   913.72
   文學   810.34
   韻文   811.134
 齊詩故   093.13
00223 齋
 齋戒   223.7
 齋明   921.821
00227 方
 方言   401.5
  中國方言   415
 方列式   512.37
 方程式   511.7
  三角   518.7

市 帝 旁 育 盲 商

微積分	515.7	畜產業	615.03
算學	511.7	農藝	611.5
方程式解法	512.73	育苗	614.484
方向	151.1752		

00227 盲
方向本能	581.703
盲啞圖書館	025.78

方法論

00227 商
形上學	132	商朝(？1766？1122)	911.5
佛學	231.142	商店合作社	356.73
心理學	150.17	商務文件整理法	626.3
方士	226	商行爲法	398.3
方丈記	827.41	商業	620
方苞(1668—1749)	817.741	建築	717.5
方孝儒(1357—1402)	817.613	倫理	620.018

00229 市
市價	624.5	官營	369.142
市場學		法律	398
商業	624	法規	621.9
國際經濟	388.64	數學	626.1
市黨部	001.42	團體	313.72
市情預測	624.3	銀行	362.13

00227 帝
		商業破產	624.6
		商業函牘	626.2
帝王崇拜	209.4	商業政策	621
帝國	371.3	商業稅	369.153
帝國主義	371.035	商業經濟	621

00227 旁
		商業仲裁	624.7
旁聽	335.7	商業組合	321.3

00227 育
		商業心理	620.015
育種	563.51	商業心理學	158.62

高　庸　廟　膏　庶　應

商業實踐	626	高架鐵道	651.86
商業地理	620.098	高中	338.33
商業興信所	321.5	高馬爾內	983.471
商業管理	622	高等幾何畫	517.7
商標	629.3	高等代數	512.6
實業	605.5	高等法院	373.04
工業	645.7	高等師範	338.53
商書	092.73	高等擔子綱菌	573.37
商鞅	111.175	高小	338.23
商品學	623		

00227 庸

庸醫	593.75

商陸科	567.21		
商民運動	001.993		

00227 廟

廟宇	
佛教	235.8
名勝	981.384
遺迹	991.841
婆羅門教	247

00227 高

高部日耳曼語	409.385
高麗	
文學	829
語言	429
佛教	239.69
地理	982.2
歷史	922
高比里牛斯	983.493

00227 膏

膏體	253.98

00231 庶

庶務	332.7

高低波	534.34
高低溫度之化學	541.61

00231 應

應鼓	770.13
應用水力學	654.1
應用電學	537.8
應用統計	346
應用外科	598.18

高山植物	576.903
高僧傳	230.97
高粱	612.15
高溫計	536.14
高加索	983.88

應用動物學	581.8		夜差	529.18
應用生物學	568		夜禽類動物	587.9795
應用化學	548	**00247 度**		
應用心理學	158		度量衡	607
應用邏輯學	149	**00247 庾**		
應用花草	613.806		庾信	811.137
應用熱力學	536.9	**00247 廢**		
應用力學	531.3		廢妾	317.85
應用地質學	556		廢物	653.36
應用顯微學	566.6		廢娼	317.86
應用昆蟲	585.8		廢除不平等條約	001.177
應用氣象學	529.78	**00252 摩**		
00232 康			摩鹿加丁香群島	985.917
康語	409.378		摩訶提婆	249.3
康德	127.2		摩西五經	
康的亞克	124.26		基督教	252.21
康友爲(1858—1927)	817.793		猶太教	262.9
00232 豪			回教	272.1
豪豬類動物	588.617		摩西升天記	252.981
豪厄爾士(1837—1920)	863.43		摩西十誡	252.216
00241 庭			摩爾比韓	983.461
庭審	395.03		摩登婦女	313.35
00242 底			摩洛哥	
底片	755.1		文學	896
00247 夜			語言	496
夜工	354.42		地理	985.3
夜校	338.85		歷史	953
			摩拉維亞	983.796

庫 店 唐 廣 麻 忘 烹 意

摩托車	659.78	心理學	156.3357
摩擦力	531.694	麻織品	675.1
摩里斯	983.27	麻科	576.72

00256 庫
庫爾德語	409.327
庫拍(1789—1851)	863.24

00261 店
店員	622.3

00267 唐
唐朝
文學	810.4
哲學	111.4
歷史	914.1
唐順之(1507—1560)	817.66
唐努烏梁海	981.957

00286 廣
廣西省	981.85
廣翼類動物	584.88

廣告
顏色	629.2
戲劇	781.9
陳列法	629.5
廣東省	981.83

00294 麻
麻疹	594.915
麻痺	597.8443
牙科治療	598.271

麻油	665.2
麻本	597.8456
麻黃綱植物	574.5
麻雀	795

00331 忘
忘記	151.66

00336 烹
烹飪	695

00336 意
意識
生態學	151.5
心理學	581.705
時間關係	151.57
意外犯罪	315.127
意志	151.4

意大利
文學	833
語言	433
建築	710.32
統計	345.32
動物	581.932
條約	387.932
憲法	391.132
法系	390.32
游記	983.2

文 辛 章

大學	338.7932	文字考古	990.8
地理	983.2	文法	401.6
地圖	980.332	中國語文	416
地質	550.32	文學	800.442
哲學	122	文藝	
考古	993.2	紋章學	960.08
植物	571.932	初民文化	565.79
教育	330.932	歷史	910.9118
財政	369.32	文藝批評	800.4
歷史	932	文中子	111.37
意思		文明戲	784
意匠		文體	800.444
工藝	645.3	文學	800
實業	605.3	文學上的基督	251.298
意欲	151.3	文學家	

00400 文

文章	800.444	傳記	800.97
文言	416.83	逸話	800.48
文章法	416.8	故里	800.47
文天祥	811.157	文具	674.9
文子	111.1222	文民宗教	200.06
文虎	796		

00401 辛

辛棄疾(1140—1207)	811.7395
辛派詞家	811.7396

文特(1836—1918)   861.44

文德瓦德群島

00406 章

地理	984.78	章動	522.82
歷史	947.8	章動差法	521.9
文房	793.19	章程	636.1
文字源流	401.1	章句法	416.3

交 離 弈 辯 辨 牽 言

章學誠(1738—1805)	817.737

00408 交
交線	
平面幾何	517.32
立體幾何	517.51
交響樂	779.2
交流	
電動機	657.42
變壓機	657.43
電流	637.35
機械	657.45
交通	
歲入	369.142
實業	630
運輸組織	383.43
歷史	910.24
交通部	373.055
交媾	597.623
交感神經病	
病理	597.847
生理	598.747
交感神經系	
解剖	597.817
生理	597.827
交易論	358
交趾支那	
地理	982.42
歷史	924.2

交戰國	381.54
交際舞	792.3

00414 離
離葉	313.346
離瓣類植物	577
離生藍藻科植物	572.177
離心力	531.696
離婚	
倫理	183.1
社會	313.347
法律	397.51
國際法	381.845

00430 弈
弈棋	794

00441 辯
辯證學	140

00041 辨
辨內侍日記	827.42

00503 牽
牽引力	531.83
牽輓汽機	655.291

00601 言
言語	
生理	599.725
心理	151.38
言論自由權	372.133
言行錄	970.1

音 盲 畜 注 諺 訪 諦

孫中山	001.191
言情小說	803.7
中國小說	813.87

00601 音

音韻學	401.6
比較	401.7
中國	417
音調感覺	534.7
音樂	770
聖詩	253.57
幼稚園	338.137
戲劇	781.7
青年會	256.354
音樂療法	595.88
音樂心理學	151.127
音樂演奏	770.02
學校	333.31
音德勒	983.483
音德勒洛亦爾	983.482
音程	534.73
音色	534.71
音響	770.011
音之調和	534.75
音之認知	534.95
音之綜合	534.93
音之波及	534.4
音波	534.3
音素	770.021
音階	534.74
音質	534.71
音學	534
音義	
佛經	232.088
文字學	411.13
音節準則	534.77

00601 盲

盲蜘類動物	584.678

00603 畜

畜產	543.28
製造	615.8
經濟	615.01
利用	615.9
畜產業	615
畜政	615.17
畜力機	655.17

00614 注

注冊	
選舉	372.551
學校	334.11

00622 諺

諺語	804.5
中國諺語	814.5

00627 訪

訪問	341.11

00627 諦

衣 玄 哀 衰 六 棄 京 雜

諦論	249.3

00732 衣
衣
民生主義	001.144
社會問題	317.11
初民文化	565.791
勞工狀況	354.9311
衣物濟施	316.55

衣冠
道德	184.5
禮俗	319.4

衣飾	693
衣料	693.1

00732 玄
玄武岩	557.28
玄古代	554.1

00732 哀
哀歌	801.41
哀辭	818.75

00732 衰
衰謝律	561.71

00800 六
六塵	231.58
六放珊瑚類動物	582.753
六壬	157.7
六經	090.2
六處	231.58
六樂合奏	779.7
六波羅密	231.7
六十進算術	510.73
六書	411.3
六甲	225.1
六年制	334.4

00904 棄
棄絕	251.49

00906 京
京劇	783
京都府	982.164

00914 雜
雜誌	050
雜訊	039.8
雜記	818.9
雜歌	821.2
雜種生殖	561.627
雜種學	563.52
雜件管理法	023.8
雜家	117.19
雜字	413.8
雜演	802.98

雜禮
經學	094.5
禮俗	319.18

雜婚	333.348
雜考	088
雜藏	232.8

顫 龍 顏 誹 訂 評 語 諧 襲 龔 端 刻 訓

雜草	611.971
雜史	910.5
雜事瑣語	808.9
雜品	
基督教文藝	250.88
中國民間文學	814.8
民間文學	804.8
雜阿含	232.23
雜合	563.195

01186 顫
顫藻科植物	572.171

01211 龍
龍沙(1524—85)	841.89
龍樹	239.135
龍腦香科植物	578.54
龍膽科植物	579.43
龍腳類動物	587.837

01286 顏
顏元	111.73
顏延之(384—456)	811.1335
顏色	721.2
顏淵	111.1121
顏料	667.7

01611 誹
誹謗	180.87

01620 訂
訂本目錄	010.82

01649 評
評價	658.23
評傳	970.4

01661 語
語言	565.792
(初民文化)	
語言學	400
分佈	409
類別	403
語盲症	155.254
語系	409
語術	001.03
語錄(基督教)	251.291

01662 諧
諧聲	411.34

01732 襲
襲佔	377.1

01801 龔
龔自珍(1792—1841)	817.83

02127 端
端毛藍藻科植物	572.175
端腳類動物	584.83

02200 刻
刻魅	225.6
刻板	991.78

02600 訓
訓育	332.4

證　訴　誘　誕　話　新

訓詁學	415
訓政時期	001.153
訓辭	818.43
訓蒙	418.1
訓令	339.21

02618 證

證人	395.05
證據	395.05
證券	366
證券投資	367.15

02621 訴

訴訟法	395
訴願法	393.17
訴狀	395.03

02627 誘

誘導	657.13

02641 誕

誕禮	319.21

02664 話

戲劇	802.3
演劇	784

02921 新

新一元論	102.2
新二元論	102.4
新不列顛島	985.955
新西蘭	
地理	985.94

歷史	959.4
新疆省	981.97
新畿內亞	
地理	985.959
歷史	959.59
新結構(皮膚病)	598.545
新生代	554.7
新約	252.5
新約偽書	252.99
新約啟示錄	252.85
新鳥類動物	587.92
新字	413.7
新實在論	106.15
新活力論	581.402
新達爾文學說	564.3
新澤西	981.165
新罕木什爾	984.161
新瀉縣	982.193
新複本位	361.23
新希不力斯群島	985.952
新南威爾斯	985.9392
新莽(9—23)	911.2
新加寨爾	983.38
新柏拉圖派	121.58
新教信經	251.85
新拉馬克學說	564.5
新星	523.87
新羅(57—後935)	922.845

鷲 卟 試 識 熟 計 謝 謹 訥 誇 誌 讌 詩

新量子論	530.75
新墨西哥	984.188
新畢達哥拉士派	121.56
新喀里多里亞群島	985.951
新馬爾薩斯	349.013
新陳代謝	
生理	592.47
植物	571.44
新陳代謝產物	566.928
新陳代謝違和	594.87
新聞社	040.6
新學院派哲學	121.55
新竹州	982.172

03327 鷲

鷲龍	587.833

03600 卟

卟聞	818.75

03640 試

試帖	811.107
試婚	313.345
試藥	544.11
試驗室	
化學	542.1
學校	332.92
試金學	669.5

03650 識

識	231.65
識字	418.1

識字運動	330.127

04331 熟

熟卵生殖	581.626

04600 計

計票	372.558
計熱	536.31
計時器	528.59
計時學	528.5
計分	334.5
計算幾何學	519.49
計算法（統計）	341.3

04600 謝

謝靈運(380—433)	811.133
謝林(1775—1854)	127.4
謝朓(464—499)	811.134

04614 謹

謹慎	180.78

04627 訥

訥氏對數	510.26

04627 誇

誇大	180.81

04631 誌

誌	818.75

04631 讌

讌歌曲	771.4

04641 詩

詩	

譁 諸 諾 讀 讚 請 講

意大利文學	833.1
文學	801
西班牙文學	835.1
經典	093
俄國文學	881
德國文學	871
希臘文學	831.1
拉丁文學	832.1
基督教文藝	250.81
英國文學	851
中國文學	811.1
日本文學	821.1
美國文學	861
詩序(毛詩序)	093.3
詩評	811.104
詩話	811.104
詩韻	811.1043
詩緯	093.9
詩總集	811.108
詩法	811.107
詩社	811.106
詩萊爾馬哈	127.72
詩史	811.109
詩典	811.103
詩篇(基督教)	253.32
詩餘	811.7

04654 譁
譁尼拉	612.85

04660 諸
諸聖	251.62
諸聖日	253.16
諸神	221.2

04664 諾
諾爾	983.468
諾爾蘭	983.7987
諾爾滿的	983.465
諾福克	983.566
諾森伯蘭	983.569

04686 讀
讀經	253.6
讀岐典侍日記	827.36
讀本	
文字學	401.8
中文语言學	418
日本文学	823.65
讀書法	027.5
讀書團	338.88

04686 讚
讚岐國	982.165

05627 請
請願權	372.15

05645 講
講經	253.7
講道	253.7
講史	

中國十進制分類法及索引 | 1105

誅 謁 諤 誤 譯 韻 課 親 望 郭 訊 諷 詭 讒 記

小說	803.2
中國小說	813.82
講堂	333.92

05690 誅

誅詞	818.75

06627 謁

謁陵	319.117

06627 諤

諤格德(1224—1306)	915.97

06634 誤

誤差法	512.93

06641 譯

譯文字典	413.1
譯書叢書	081.9
譯書目錄	011.9

06686 韻

韻母	414.3
韻文	811
韻目類書	031.3

06694 課

課程	335

06910 親

親族	313.38
親征	319.15
親屬法	397.5
國際民法	361.845
親屬關係	581.762

親合力	541.067

07104 望

望	
倫理	180.76
基督徒生活	258.54
望遠鏡	535.8

07427 郭

郭璞	813.35
郭憲	813.27

07610 訊

訊問錄	039.6

07610 諷

諷刺詩	801.6
諷刺文學	
意大利文學	833.82
西班牙文學	835.2
諷刺歌曲	785.5
諷刺畫	737.77

07612 詭

詭辨學校	121.22

07613 讒

讒譖	315.186

07617 記

記振器	657.18
記賬	364.7
記號論	510.4
記憶病理	151.67

詞 詢 調 謬 部 認 設

記憶術	151.64	部位解剖學	591.8
記憶程序	151.62	部位手術	598.18
記憶力缺乏	151.67	部落	371.13
記憶與學習	151.6	部首類書	031.2

07620 詞

詞	811.7
詞評	811.704
詞話	811.704
詞韻	811.703
詞社	811.706
詞典	811.703

07620 詢

詢問部(青年會)	256.356

07620 調

調息	249.4
調和解析	516.01
調和級數	514.3
調速器	655.259
調查	337.193
調查程次	341.1
調查法	341.1
調帶裝置(機械)	655.77
調節	352.7

07622 謬

謬誤	141.4

07627 部

部位解剖	581.19

07632 認

認識	151.627
認識論	
哲學	131
佛教	231.141
婆羅門教	241.2
認識方法	105
認識緣起	
哲學	104
形上學	131.1
佛教	231.141
婆羅門教	241.2
認識對象	106
認識相對論	131.6
認識原理	131.4
識認範圍	131.2

07647 設

設計	
土木工程	651.71
圖書館建築	024.3
設計教學法	337.31
設備	
政府	373.097
國家醫學	593.15

詔 諮 施 旌 旅 族 放 敵 旋 旗 詐 說

學校	332.9	放射光帶	535.441
07662 詔		放生	223.5
詔令	901.21	放血	595.811
07668 諮		放款	362.7
諮詢委員會	383.5	**08240 敵**	
08212 施		敵性中立	381.65
施耐庵	813.591	**08281 旋**	
施藥學	595.72	旋頭歌	821.2
施蒙尼迪士	831.44	旋動	
施閏章(1618—83)	817.721	力學	531.241
08214 旌		固禮	531.695
旌節花科	578.61	旋律	770.024
08232 旅		旋花科	579.51
旅行	337.191	旋拱	713.3
旅行保護	593.48	旋轉橋	651.573
旅行團	333.38	旋轉舞	792.3
旅館	718.5	旋風	529.35
08234 族		**08281 旗**	
族譜	977.5	旗幟	
族禮	319.26	軍事	379.98
族姓叢書	081.6	紋章	960.7
族姓書目	016	**08611 詐**	
08240 放		詐取	315.189
放任制	610.315	**08616 說**	
放射	536.413	說文解字	411.1
放射動物	582.9	說謊	155.453
放射蟲類	582.18	說出世部	239.117

診　論　謙　許　詳　議　譜　謎　談

08622 診			
診斷學	592.2	詳夢	156.338
08627 論		08655 議	
論辯文學	818.4	議員	373.034
論語	098.3	議院	373.033
論證	141.2	議院制	373.039
論價說	354.317	議院組織	373.037
論藏	232.7	議院法	392
08637 謙		議院權限	373.035
謙讓	319.32	08661 譜	
謙遜	180.78	譜曲	770.026
08640 許		09639 謎	
許婚	313.344	謎語	814.6
許願	223.1	09689 談	
08651 詳		談	381.025

一　工

10000 一

一二年性草花類	613.81
一元論	102.1
一多	133.82
一源說	565.731
一神論	201.2
一神教	200.02
一婦多夫制	313.3415
一切有部	239.112
一妻制	183.2
一夫一妻制	313.3411
一夫多妻制	313.3413
一院制	373.039

10100 工

工廠	
建築	717.7
習慣	354.57
改良	354.55
衛生	354.53
安全	354.54
道德	354.57
檢查	354.58
規則	354.15
工商廳	373.0816
工商證券	366.7
工務局	373.0824
工程	650
電氣	657
水利	654
航海	659
軍事學	556.5
力學	650.3
橋樑	651.5
機械	655
材料	650.4
地質學	556.0
城市	653
數學	650.1
圖表	650.2
用具	650.8
鑛學	658
鐵路	651.8
工作	
普通心理	151.55
國際私法	381.825
工作衛生	593.37
工業	
政策	351.4
經濟	641
稅收	351.4
社會學	313.74
森林	614.14
地理	980.154
工潮	354.83
工資	
基金	354.313

二

學說	354.31
分配	359
工藝	645
力學	531.4
考古	991.88
故事	805.5
中國	815.5
日本	825.5
顯微學	566.65
美術	760
工場衛生	653.4
工團主義	318.3
工賑(慈善會)	316.57
工時	354.4
各業工時	354.48
工人	
特種人團	025.74
勞資	354.133
工黨(美國)	375.68

10100 二

二元論	
心理學	150.161
哲學	102.3
二元二次式	512.26
二元式	512.21
二面論	150.163
二面曲面	519.461
二子宮類	588.21

三

二毛矽藻科	572.53
二手類	589.9
二程(程灝,程頤)	111.54
二鰓類	583.573
二次降臨	251.26
二十五諦	241.6
二十一史	910.96
二十二史	910.97
二十四史	910.98
二疊紀	554.57
二人合唱	771.75

10101 三

三音諾顔汗部	981.953
三論宗	239.51
三元二次式	512.27
三元四次式	512.28
三一律	781.11
三面流電	537.24
三面曲面(立體)	519.465
三要素說(人民)	371.021
土地(主權)	
三晉(戰國)	911.654
三天體論	521.13
（日　月　地球）	
三聖子歌	252.95
三絃	770.17
三毛亞群島	985.973
三位一體	251.1

正

三位一體日	253.15	三民主義	001.11
三重縣	982.1648	三段法	141.3
三經(道教)	222.1	三人合唱	771.76

10101 正

三樂合奏	779.7		
三代	911	正瓣鰓類	583.555
(？前 2205—255)		正產法與處理	598.837
三白草科	576.26	正語	231.43
三解詩	801.8	正誤(倫理學)	180.2
三角	777.3	正親町	921.836
三角形	517.34	正理派	249.6
三角函數	516.35	正磁學	538.5
三角幾何學	519.07	正統(國家學)	371.0495
三角級數	514.4	正紅藻綱	573.265
三角對數	510.23	正線	517.31
三角學	518	正色攝影	758.4
三家詩	093.1	正鳥類	587.97
三河	982.1639	正定(八聖道)	231.46
三次共和(1870—)	934.88	正業(八聖道)	231.44
三清(道教)	221.1	正直	180.72
三洞	222.1	正投影	519.34
三世論	241.77	正見(八聖道)	231.41
三芒草	612.298	正量部	239.116
三葉類	584.61	正思惟(八聖道)	231.42
三葉蟲	554.52	正長岩	557.32
三界	231.8	正關節類	588.31
三疊紀	554.61	正念(八聖道)	231.47
三明	231.31	正命(八聖道)	231.48
三體	094	正常自動	150.166

歪 玉 壐 王 至 埜 噩 五

正常心理	151
正常錯覺	151.173
正精進(八聖道)	231.45
正幣(金融)	361.61

10101 歪
歪俄明	984.186

10103 玉
玉琢	724
玉皇上帝	221.11
玉液	224.7
玉蕊科	578.76
玉蜀黍	612.15
玉髓	556.185
玉册	220.97
玉笛	770.15
玉簫	770.15

10103 壐
壐印	
考古	990.16
史料	901.5
美術	727

10104 王
王充	111.27
王維(699—759)	811.142
王禹偁(954—1001)	817.511
王衍	811.717
王安石(1021—86)	817.517
王守仁	111.63
王寶甫(？1200)	812.32
王通	111.37
王嘉	813.38
王十朋(1112—71)	817.574
王勃(648—674)	817.41
王士禎(1634—1711)	811.173
王世貞(1526—90)	
駢文	817.67
小説	813.65
王國維(1877—1927)	817.795
王鳴盛(1722—97)	811.177
王氏時代(918—1392)	922.85
王闓運(1832—1916)	817.791
王符	111.281

10104 至
至正	251.147

10104 埜
埜筆畫	733.3

10106 噩
噩狠	588.35

10107 五
五要素説	371.023
(人民,土地,政府,	
主權,法律)	
五經	090.1
五彩石印	744
五樂合奏	779.7
五旬節	353.14

互 亞

五作恨	241.67
五官	
神經系	597.818
相術	157.32
五福花科	579.83
五大（地 水 火 風 空）	241.65
五蘊	231.6
五執政內閣（1795—99）	934.846
五權憲法	001.16
五加科	578.91
五胡（304—439）	913.5
五趣	231.84
五穀崇拜	209.26
五穀起運機	655.87
五唯（色,聲,香,味,觸）	241.64
五知根（眼,耳,鼻,舌,皮）	241.66

10107 互

互攻法	595.73
互助貿易	351.37

10107 亞

亞麻	612.55
亞該亞	983.17
亞立斯托（1474—1533）	833.13
亞摩士書	252.48
亞贏質炔屬	547.13
亞納多里亞	982.661
亞諾芝曼德	121.112
亞諾芝曼尼	121.113
亞千的	985.57
亞哥利斯	983.17
亞爾多亞	983.467
亞爾科特（183—288）	863.41
亞爾伯特	984.27
亞爾德內斯	983.471
亞爾德赤（1836—1907）	861.47
亞爾索（1761—1844）	861.25
亞爾基里亞	
地理	985.48
歷史	954.8
亞爾巴尼亞	
文學	893.35
語言	409.35
地理	983.952
歷史	939.53
亞非利加語系	409.7
亞列爾	983.485
亞理士多芬（前？448—380）	831.24
亞那克里溫（前？563—478）	831.43
亞維倫	983.492

豆 巫 靈

亞利桑那	984.191	亞巴拉	121.635
亞利安語系	409.3	亞美利加語系	409.8
亞伯林函數	516.45	亞美尼亞	982.666
亞伯拉罕	271.23	亞美尼亞語	409.33
亞得米拉爾群島	985.957	亞含姆	409.124
亞的加	983.16	亞拉薩哥拉士	121.15
亞洲		亞當	271.21
地理	982	亞當士	941.842
歷史	909	亞當士（昆稷）	941.853

10108 豆

亞洲霍亂	594.934	豆科植物	577.79
亞浮司太語	409.321	豆菽類	613.3
亞述		豆人（法術）	225.8
地理	982.82		

10108 巫

| 　歷史 | 928.2 | 巫祝 | 157.7 |
| 亞達那 | 982.663 | | |

10108 靈

亞力山大二世		靈元	921.844
（1855—1917）	938.87	靈形現象	157.95
亞布魯索	983.27	靈魂論	
亞斯都利亞	983.36	自然神學	201.77
亞英	983.475	婆羅門教	241.78
亞基洛克士	831.82	靈貓類	588.515
亞蘭柏(1717—83)	847.53	靈像學	157.953
亞加的亞	983.17	靈修會	253.28
亞拉圖	231.13	靈之寶現	157.951
亞拉岡	983.37	靈神現象	157.96
亞里斯多德學派	121.251	靈成學	157.955
亞里斯梯波士	121.251	靈圖	220.94
亞昆拉士	121.636		

琉 疏 瓌 露 雪 丁 哥 元 死

靈長類動物	589
靈學	157.9
靈醫	157.97
靈符	225.1
靈悟心理學	151.7

10113 琉
琉璃	558.186
琉球	
文學	829
地理	982.1669
歷史	921.9

10113 疏
疏密波	534.33

10132 瓌
瓌珴琳	775.5
瓌珴拉	775.6

10164 露
露	529.41
露層	553.5
露骨鯨類動物	588.474

10167 雪
雪	529.46
雪崩	
森林	614.117
地震學	551.73

10200 丁
丁香	612.87
丁尼生(1809—92)	851.81

10201 哥
哥德多爾	983.475
哥勒塞	983.489

10211 元
元(1280—1368)	
文學	810
哲學	111.59
歷史	915.9
元刻本	009.115
元正	921.823
元覆宋本	009.121
元稹(779—831)	
韻文	811.1457
小說	813.4
元始天尊	221.11
元始花	576.1
元好問(1190—1257)	
韻文	811.158
駢散文	817.587
元素	541.02
元明	921.823
元首	
外交行政	386.31
治外法權	386.5
中央政府	373.011
元首制	373.0503

10211 死

霍 兩 雨 爾 霧 下 汞

死	
心靈論	135.9
冥界	251.71
基督論	251.2956
末世論	201.71
死亡	
生物學	562.9
世界大戰	930.77
人口論	349.072
死刑	394.511
死胎	598.824
死胎產	598.828
死火山	551.42

10214 霍
霍謨士(1809—94)	867.36
霍亂症	594.933
霍布士	125.2
霍蘭(1819—81)	867.31
霍姆(1724—1808)	852.64
霍巴昔(1723—89)	124.28

10227 兩
兩手類	569.88
兩生類	587.6
兩漢哲學	111.2
兩難(邏輯)	141.3
兩棲類	
脊椎動物	587.6
古生物	569.84
兩口目植物	572.32
兩院制	373.039

10227 雨
雨水	
森林	614.113
氣象學	529.45
雨久草科植物	575.76
雨蝕	551.72

10227 爾
爾撒(耶穌)	271.27
爾雅	415.1

10227 霧
霧	529.43
霧靄警報	654.48

10230 下
下議院	373.033
下砂蘭德	983.491
下幾內亞	985.58
下射水車	655.332
下總國	985.1615
下埃及	982.161
下羅亞爾	983.461
下野國	982.1619
下阿爾卑斯	983.497
下肢	519.88
下肢骨	597.7118
下覺	156.15

10232 汞

震 夏 憂 覆 霞 惡 干 耳 平

汞	669.95

10232 震

震毛	581.75
震源	551.33
震波	551.33
震盪	598.141
震教派	259.86
震因	551.31
震旦紀	554.51

10247 夏

夏書	092.72
夏威斯	851.25
（1483—1509）	
夏威夷群島	
地理	985.98
歷史	959.8

10247 憂

憂愁	180.97
憂鬱病	155.5

10247 覆

覆鰓類動物	583.535
覆選	372.555

10247 霞

霞	592.66

10331 惡

惡	
神學	201.63
倫理	180.8
基督徒道德	258.57

10400 干

干寶	813.37
干涉	
音學	534.61
熱學	536.34
光學	535.34
勞資	354.86
干巴尼亞	983.27

10400 耳

耳	534.95
耳郭	598.442
耳科	
病理	598.44
手術	598.47
衛生	598.43
生理	598.42
解剖	
心理	151.121
醫學	598.41
法療	598.45
耳之訓練	770.073
耳道	598.443
耳咽管	598.446
耳骨	598.447

10409 平

平面	517.51

天

三角	518.1
幾何	517.3
解析幾何	519.41
平面上軌道位置	521.22
平面運動	531.243
平面曲線	519.451
平行綫	517.33
平衡	
液體	532.35
分子與固體	531.62
氣體	533.35
平衡感覺	151.16
平衡與運動律	521.11
平線平面	517.51
平糴	316.59
平均地權	001.141
平時航空法	381.95
平時封鎖	382.33
平原	
地理學	980.507
地質學	552.7
中國地理	981.37
平民	
系譜學	977.4
社會學	313.83
平胸類動物	587.94
平鋼琴	776.1
平等權	
國際法	381.23
公民學	372.14

10430 天

天塵	523.17
天主教	259.1
天文台	522.1
天文物理學	523
天文時	528.56
天文學	520
天文用曆	528.61
天文鏡	522.2
天文光帶	535.46
天干	157.27
天元	512
天王星	523.47
天武	921.821
天球	522.71
天球經緯	422.76
天球中心	521.2
天球坐標	522.72
天師	226
天災	611.91
天台山	981.368
天台宗(法華宗)	
中國	239.55
日本	239.65
天然磁石	838.11
天然生產	614.41

霉 更 石

天然崇拜	209.2	天體運動	521.15
天使	251.61	天體測量	522.7
天使崇拜	209.6	天體力學	511.1
天線		天體攝動	551.311
電力應用	657.832	天鹽國	982.1675
傳電	657.651	天人(五趣)	231.89
天象	157.21	天命論	201.5
天河	523.81	天氣預報	529.75
天道論	201.5	天竺葵	612.813
天啓教	200.03	天氣推測	529.71
天才		天氣圖	529.76
病理	153.94	天智	921.821
種類	153.98	天堂	
特質	153.91	自然神學	201.725
心理	153.9	神學	151.625

10505 霉

霉爛	566.927

10506 更

更科日記	827.32

10600 石

石	
病理學	597.642
音樂	770.15
道路工程	651.75
古物學	991.3
考古學	990.13
石膏	735.13
石刻	724

天南星科植物	575.54
天赤道	522.75
天花	594.912
天真	180.79
天極儀	523.4
天地末日	251.72
天狗猴	589.57
天國	
神學	251.15
末世論	251.76
天體崇拜	209.21

百　西

石刻文	990.813
石工術	651.16
石碑	991.85
石經	090.9
石炭紀	554.56
石炭油	668.6
石川縣	982.1633
石像	991.722
石窟寺	991.842
石造	651.116
石油	
礦物學	558.128
礦油	665.5
石油機	655.41
石柱	991.85
石臺	991.85
石橋	651.5016
石狩國	982.167
石鼓	991.33
石英岩	557.45
石蒜科	575.85
石蠟	547.11
石墨	558.126
石灰	666.8
石灰岩	557.561
石蠟	665.5
石印	
板刻	743
圖書學	010.33
石印影板	746.3
石鑛	558.15
石竹科	577.27
石料	650.46

10600 百

百部科	575.82
百貨商店	622.7
百科辭書	030
百濟(14—後665)	922.843
百衲本	009.17
百神	319.115
百慕群島	
地理	984.79
歷史	947.9
百分(算學)	511.35
百合花	
植物學	575.8
圖藝	613.83

10601 西

西摩蘭	983.569
西康省(川邊)	981.72
西夏文	009.86
西西里	983.28
西班牙	
文學	835
語言	435
建築	710.33

西

統計	345.33
動物	581.933
條約	387.933
游記	983.3
大學	338.7933
地理	983.3
地圖	980.333
地質	550.33
哲學	123
考古	993.3
植物	571.933
教育	330.933
財政	369.33
歷史	933
西班牙(美洲)	
地理	984.5
歷史	945
西發(毀滅之神)	241.74
西維基尼亞	984.167
西番雅書	253.496
西比利亞	983.89
國際問題	388.18
西崑體	811.1511
西俄	983.87
西奧統治(1527—1796)	932.875
西塞禄(前106—43)	
文學	832.841
哲學	121.54
西治(1507—1566)	937.933
西奧	985.936
西土耳其	
地理	982.69
歷史	926.9
西域	910.73
西藏	
文學	819
語言	909.13
地理	981.98
歷史	910.74
佛教	239.59
經典	232
西蕃蓮科	578.62
西威斯	982.664
西里伯	985.916
西羅馬之滅亡(476)	932.846
西瓜	613.22
西印度	945
西印度群島	
地理	984.7
歷史	947

10601 面

面	
統計圖法	341.5
解剖學	591.82
醫學	595.22

晉 雷 硫 可 哥 碲 釀 醇 碎 礆

面試	354.115
面流電	537.23
面相	157.31
面素幾何學	519.03
面骨	597.7116

10601 晉
晉鼓	770.13

10603 雷
雷	529.51
雷電	611.914
雷姆函數	516.85
雷獸類	588.349

10613 硫
硫	546.153
硫酸	661.3
硫酸鹽	661.5
硫黃細菌目	572.15

10620 可
可拉	612.76
可蘭經	272.7
可燃岩	557.57

10621 哥
哥爾期亞	121.221
哥德	
文學	879.1
語言	409.381
哥倫比亞共和國	
地理	984.86
歷史	948.6
哥布底語	409.65
哥林的亞	983.17
哥斯達黎加	
地理	984.66
歷史	946.6
哥林多人後書	252.73
哥林多人前書	252.72
哥羅四人書	252.77
哥羅塞斯德	983.561

10627 碲
碲	546.157

10632 釀
釀酒	664.51

10647 醇
醇	
有機化學	547.3
飲料	664.55

10648 碎
碎石	651.763
碎屑岩	557.51

10648 礆
礆	671.1
礆船	379.667
礆臺	659.31
礆隊	379.57

電

10716 電

電
- 電學　　　　　537
- 生物學　　　　561.57
- 熱學　　　　　537

電離　　　　　　537.372
電療法　　　　　595.87
電應力　　　　　537.143
電話
- 電政　　　　　637.7
- 電氣工程　　　657.85
- 非電　　　　　657.858

電話器　　　　　657.853
電話局　　　　　657.851
電診　　　　　　595.273
電碼　　　　　　637.03
電理　　　　　　537.01
電子　　　　　　537.372
電政
- 交通　　　　　637
- 財政　　　　　369.142

電磁　　　　　　538.8
電磁旋動　　　　538.87
電磁石　　　　　538.81
電磁能之移轉　　538.86
電磁機械　　　　538.89
電磁感應　　　　538.85
電磁振動　　　　588.87

電位　　　　　　537.145
電信
- 電政　　　　　637
- 電氣工程　　　657.83

電信系統　　　　657.835
電信器　　　　　657.833
電位測定　　　　657.14
電能　　　　　　657.17
電綜合化學　　　545.97
電動機　　　　　657.42
電化學
- 工業化學　　　662
- 化學　　　　　541.7

電結晶學　　　　559.37
電生理學　　　　481.47
電線與傳電體　　657.65
電解
- 傳電　　　　　537.29
- 傳導　　　　　541.73
- 分解　　　　　541.71

電解工業　　　　662.1
電流　　　　　　657.15
電滲透法　　　　544.57
電法　　　　　　537.21
電波　　　　　　538.861
電力應用　　　　657.8
電力傳導　　　　657.21
電力測定　　　　657.17

電機	537.075	電學	537
電熱	657.817	電與流電法	542.8
電熱化學工業	662.5	電阻測定	657.13
電熱器	657.817	電鐘	657.93
電相	757.87	電分析法	
電報		定量	545.5
交通	657.83	定性	544.93
工程	657.83	電氣	659.72
接線	657.832	工程	657
電報所	657.831	化學工業	662
電場	537.14	自動車	657.97
電車	632.7	測定	657.1
電振動	538.861	冶金學	669.4
電攝影	758.1	機械附件	657.3
電感應	537.34	鐵道	657.95
電擊		工程	651.88
外科	598.162	電氣計	657.12
自然地質學	551.74	電氣單位	657.11
電數理論	537.17	氣電信號	657.93
電量測定	657.16	電鍍工業	662.7
電影		電氣警報	657.93
廣告	629.5	電鈴	657.93
戲曲	802.7	電光	529.53
演劇	788	電光帶	535.45
電路	657.61	電爐	657.817
電匯	365	電燈	657.81
電壓	657.14	發電所	657.811
電刷阻電	657.402	系統	657.814

瓦　雲　函　賈　頁　不

船上	659.15	西班牙	835.81
機械	657.812	孫中山	001.181
電燃燒	657.818	基督教	250.87
電斃	394.511	中國	818.1

10717 瓦

瓦爾	983.497	日本	828.1
瓦工術	651.16	美國	868.1
瓦稜薩	983.37	英國	858.1
瓦色斯德	983.564	公文檔案	901.27
瓦斯		函皮類	587.2
發電	657.223	函授學校	
化學藥品	661.7	補習教育	338.87
容量測定	545.43	圖書館學校	028.8
毒物	593.93	函數	516
照明	655.75	函數説	354.318
分析	544.4	函數(耶柯)行列式	
容量	545.43	耶柯	512.25
混合	544.43	普通	512.34
瓦斯機	655.42	函館	982.1671
瓦書	010.12		
瓦當	991.42		

10806 賈

賈誼(201—168)	
韻文	811.32
哲學	111.213
駢散文	817.23

10731 雲

雲	529.44
雲南省	981.86
雲葉科	577.35

10806 頁

頁岩	557.525

10772 函

函牘文學	808.1
意國	883.81

10900 不

不爾疴尼亞	983.475
不爾波内	983.485

票 栗 霜 北 豇 非

不可知論	131.8
不列顛語	409.377
不變態類	585.1
（無翅類）	
不變式	512.22
不動產	369.141
不完全變態類	585.3
（外翅類）	
不完全菌綱	573.39
不滅	
神學	251.79
自然神學	201.79
不治病	595.4
不法行為	394.3
不連續變異	563.63
不連續光帶	535.444
不世德羅內	983.497
不成文法	390.001
不羅溫薩	983.497
不明所屬語	409.19
不反芻類	588.332
不丹	
地理	982.39
歷史	923.9
不兌換券	361.75
不知病	595.5
不知道黨	375.65

10901 票

票據	364
票據交換所	362.14
票據法	398.5
票據銀行	362.14
票匯	965

10904 栗

栗	
農作物	612.17
園藝	613.762

10963 霜

霜	
地質	551.92
農藝	611.911
氣象	529.42

11110 北

北孤語	409.171
北卡羅林納	984.168
北利	983.483
北宋詞家	811.738
北冰洋	
地理	985.995
歷史	959.55
北達科他	984.184
北澳	985.938
北見國	982.167

11110 豇

豇豆	612.34

11111 非

玩 琲 班 斑 疆 琥 珂 巧 瑪 琢

非主權國	381.12
非靈論	157.99
非電電話	657.858
非醇飲料	664.6
非物質	133.7
非洲	
經濟史	350.95
佛教	239.9
游記	980.75
地理	985
歷史	950
非法交涉	386.23
非達爾文學說	564.29
非法組織	315.184
非法結婚	313.3425
非決然論	134.23
非淘汰學派	564.4
非難	
科學	251.95
宗教	251.92
猶太教	251.91
異端	251.93
反基督教運動	251.97
學術	251.96
非戰運動	388.89
非盟員國	383.1
非尼斯特勒	983.461
非歐几里幾何學	519.8

非金屬元素	546.1
非常任理事	383.2

11111 玩
玩具	689

11111 琲
琲翠	558.188

11114 班
班燕	853.42
班篤語	409.7

11116 斑
斑岩	557.31

11116 疆
疆域	981.31

11117 琥
琥珀	558.187

11120 珂
珂羅板	746.1

11127 巧
巧明(佛經)	232.085

11127 瑪
瑪瑙	558.185
瑪利里(1569—1625)	833.152
瑪德拉斯	982.39
瑪拉基書	252.499
瑪喀比第一,二, 三,四,五書	252.97

11132 琢

頭　頸　琴　脊　彌　張　頑　預

琢石	651.16

11186 頭
頭	591.81
頭病	597.8457
頭素類動物	586.4
頭足類動物	583.57
頭骨	597.7114

11186 頸
頸	391.83
頸動脈腺	597.417

11207 琴
琴	771.017
琴武爾夫	851.13

11227 脊
脊柱	597.7111
脊椎動物	
生物	569.8
動物	587
脊髓	597.813
脊髓血循環病	597.841
脊髓熱	594.914
脊髓刺激病	597.8446
脊髓膜	597.842

11227 彌
彌爾	125.67
彌賽亞	
基督教	254.21
猶太教	261.21
彌迦書	252.493
彌勒	239.144
彌曼差經	249.1

11232 張
張說（667—730）	811.1118
張先（990—1078）	811.733
張力	
水力學	532.34
力學	531.82
張九齡（673—740）	817.42
張載	111.53
張華（232—300）	813.31
張惠言（1761—1803）	817.752

11286 頑
頑固	180.83

11286 預
預言	
陰陽五行	157.18
聖經	252.07
預備學校	338.35
預定	251.49
預兆	157.17
預決算	369.02
預防法	593.235
預算論	
國家財政	369.024
中國	369.124

悲 瑟 斐 碼 研 硬 硒 琵 登 瑞 聯

11331 悲
悲劇
  戲曲 802.93
  演戲 782.1
悲傷 180.97
悲觀論 108.3

11331 瑟
瑟 770.17
瑟爾
  文學 850
  語言 409.37

11400 斐
斐爾摩 941.8591
斐濟群島 985.971
斐希特 127.3

11627 碼
碼頭工程 654.26

11645 研
研究院 338.73

11646 硬
硬水母類動物 528.715
硬織維作植物 612.58
硬結 598.341
硬鱗類動物 587.473
硬皮鞭毛蟲類 582.35
硬固 566.133
硬骨類 587.477

11660 硒
硒 546.155

11711 琵
琵琶 770.17

12108 登
登山鐵路 651.82
登極 373.011
登草熱 594.921
登錄 023.2

12127 瑞
瑞香
  花卉 613.35
  植物學 578.71
瑞士
  地理 983.794
  哲學 128.4
  歷史 937.94
瑞典
  文學 879.22
  語言 409.3822
  地理 983.7987
  歷史 937.987

12172 聯
聯席會議 354.87
聯軍交戰法規 381.542
聯想 151.621
聯邦國 371.64

列 引 卐 水

聯邦黨	375.61
聯號	622.8
聯盟國	371.65
聯合企業	356.3

12200 列

列王記	252.25
列子	111.125
列翁	983.36
列當科植物	579.63

12200 引

引言	818.52
引產術	598.878
引航	
航海	659.195
救急法	593.485
引例法	337.14
引力	531.63

12217 卐

卐字會	316.1

12230 水

水	
電解	662.2
崇拜	209.24
生理	581.412
地質	551.93
蒸餾	653.18
農藝	611.916
分析	653.13
水痘	594.914
水率	653.11
水療法	595.83
水產	
動物	617.28
化學	617.24
湖沼	617.26
海洋	617.26
植物	617.27
水產業(漁業)	617
水族館	580.078
水雷	659.39
水雷艇	379.658
水雷母艦	379.658
水雷驅逐艦	379.658
水力引重機	655.36
水力機	655.3
水力學	532
水行(旅行)	593.482
水上游戲	338.937
水仙	613.83
水利	
土地	353.66
森林	614.27
財政	369.142
水利工程	654
水彩畫	734.1
水動方程式	532.51

弧　發

水產動物	581.904
水生蜘蛛	584.66
水災	316.41
水源	653.14
水溝	653.33
水泥	666.8
水運	634
水道	653.17
水道橋	651.5025
水葬	319.24
水棲食肉	588.53
水表	655.2255
水車	655.33
水蛭寄生	594.976
水成岩	557.5
水螅珊瑚	582.713
水螅水母	582.71
水螅虫	582.711
水輪機	655.335
水星	523.41
水馬齒科植物	577.99
水壓機	655.35
水質	
水產業	617.25
衛生	653.12
水腫	594.996
水印	674.1
水門構造	654.83

水險	368.2
水氣	562.83
水分析	543.15
水禽	587.973
水鼈	575.37

12230 弧

弧光燈	657.8143

12247 發

發育	
生理	592.6
生物	561.7
發音體	534.5
發電	
電氣	657.2
靜電	537.13
發電機	657.41
發電所	
電報	657.831
生電	657.29
發現	
殖民	377.1
地理	980.705
領土	381.314
發射運動	531.225
發生（邏輯）	144
發生力學	561.67
發鼻液	597.26
發身	598.721

烈 刑 延 孔 飛 形

發汗	597.465	孔德	124.6
發送貨物	622.6	孔叢子	111.198
發芽		孔格電夫(1670—1729)	852.46
生殖	581.613	孔教	210
生理	571.45	孔教建築	715.1
發散級數	514.6	孔雀	587.971
發掘古物	990.074		

12413 飛

發明		飛下傘	659.44
工藝	645.1	飛艇	379.74
實業	605.1	飛白書法	739.177
發光		飛鳥	615.3
光帶	535.45	飛船	659.44
光線	535.51	飛機	659.44
發炎(外科)	598.142	飛機場	659.47
發焰	541.62	飛機貯藏	659.48
		飛驒	982.1635

12330 烈

烈武猴	589.31
烈女傳	970.7

12422 形

		形位學	519.2

12400 刑

刑法	394	形上邏輯	146
刑事訴訟	395.2	形上學	130
刑罰	394.5	佛學	231.14

12401 延

		形態	581.1
延喜式經典	291.25	微生	566.91

12410 孔

		解剖	561.1
孔廟	715.1	植物	571.2
孔廣森(1752—86)	817.767	胎生	561.65
孔子	111.111	形容字	416.2
		形學	517

孤 孫 副 醱 磯 碳 裂 剽 恥 豌 球 武

12430 孤
 孤立語   403
 孤本
  特藏   009.6
  書目   019.6
 孤兒院   336.31

12453 孫
 孫中山
  文集   001.18
  傳記   001.19
  宣言   001.17
 孫星衍(1753—1818)   817.766

12600 副
 副象論   150.166
 副雄論   581.665

12647 醱
 醱酵   566.926
 醱酵工業   664.5

12655 磯
 磯松科   579.25

12689 碳
 碳   546.161
 碳元素   546.16
 碳水化物   547.8
 碳氫化物   547.1

12732 裂
 裂齒類   588.7
 裂脚類   584.825

12900 剽
 剽竊文學   800.45

13100 恥
 恥骨切開術   598.875

13112 豌
 豌豆   612.36

13132 球
 球面三角學   518.2
 球面投影   519.35
 球戲   338.635
 球狀細菌   572.125
 球狀藍藻   572.176
 球賽   338.635
 球莖類植物
  農藝   612.48
  園藝   613.13
 球根性草花類   613.83
 球場   332.91
 球蟲類   582.23
 球體   517.55

13140 武
 武術
  游藝   797
  教育   338.638
 武術團   333.37
 武俠偵探小說   813.88

職 弘 強 殘 酸 功 琺 聽

武勳歌	841.11
武士道	968.9
武力裁製	382.38
武藏國	982.1612
武模國	982.1613

13150 職
職業
衛生	593.37
道德	186
犯罪	315
教育	338.4
指導	338.48
團體	313.7
國際私法	381.825
學校	338.47
人口	349.076
介紹	316.7
公民	372.136
職員	354.133

13202 弘
弘文	921.821

13236 強
強度測定	657.15
強烈攝影	755.5
強行法	390.005
強迫教育	330.126
強姦	315.185
強權說	381.012

強憶	151.623

13253 殘
殘廢
心理	156.3353
圖書館	025.78
勞工	354.937
殘疾所	316.35
殘留磁學	538.47

13647 酸
酸化物	661.6
酸類
工業	661.3
有機	547.7
酸定量	545.1
酸定性法	544.15

14127 功
功利論
認識	106.7
人生	171.2

14127 琺
琺瑯	666.6

14131 聽
聽診法	595.26
聽覺
病理	151.124
生理	151.122
物理	151.122

玻 琪 殖 豬 硅 確 醛 破 酵 醋 聘 珠 建

測驗	151.128		醛類	547.5
心理	151.12		**14647 破**	
14147 玻			破產法	398.81
玻璃			破傷風	
繪畫	735.5		外科	598.147
窯業	666.5		神經系	597.8454
玻璃廠	368.7		破鏡	529.68
玻璃狀液體	598.344		**14647 酵**	
玻利維亞			酵素	
地理	984.84		微生	566.926
歷史	948.4		生理	
14181 琪			動物學	581.496
琪塔(絃樂)	775.3		醫學	592.41
14217 殖			**14661 醋**	
殖邊	377.7		醋	664.43
殖民	377		**15121 聘**	
殖民緣因	388.2		聘任(教員)	336.4
殖民法	381.93		聘禮	319.22
殖民地	377.1		**15190 珠**	
14264 豬			珠寶	767
豬	599.44		珠江	981.343
豬籠草科	577.63		珠蘭科	576.28
14614 硅			珠算器械	510.76
硅	546.163		**15400 建**	
14614 確			建設廳	373.0813
確度	991.77		建設委員會	373.0591
14614 醛			建設局	373.0833

砷 磚 碘 聖

建國方略	001.155	聖職	
建國大綱	001.15	佛教	235.5
建築		基督教	255.5
音響	711.7	聖子	251.12
設計	711	聖經	272
工程	651.1	文學	252.088
裝飾	712	禱文	253.41
構造		奇迹	252.082
土木	651.11	基督教	252
美術	713	回聖	272
體式	711.8	歷史	252.09
15606 砷		聖樂	772
砷	546.145	聖彼得	259.141
砷礦	558.147	聖物	253.99
15646 磚		聖餐	253.93
磚瓦	666.3	聖約	251.87
磚瓦陶磁	650.47	聖約瑟	251.294
15681 碘		聖奧古司丁派	259.0914
碘	546.135	聖多明派	259.0912
16104 聖		聖多明谷	
聖誕節	235.12	地理	984.73
聖詩	253.5	歷史	947.3
聖詩書	252.3	聖衣	253.35
聖旗	253.36	聖洗	53.91
聖靈	251.13	聖洗用品	253.38
聖西門	124.58	聖禮	253.9
聖水	253.99	聖壇	253.33
聖武	921.823	聖帶	253.35

聖芳濟派	259.0913	社會主義	318.1
聖教量	241.25	理想國	371.5
聖本篤派	259.0911	理事會	383.2
聖書	202	理髮	
聖戰	278	理俗	319.47
聖殿	253.99	手工	687
聖馬利亞	251.294	理學詩	811.1517
聖父	251.11	理知論	104.1
聖奠禮	253.9	理智論	104.4
聖公會	259.4	理性主義	137
聖節	233.1		

16132 環

聖節講道	253.77	環境	
聖堂	255.8	病理	315.167

16110 現

現計財務	369.125	天才	153.97
現款交易	358	動物	581.77
現貨交易	358	心理	153.2
現身	157.72	演化	563.19
現象論		社會	311.1
認識	106.8	人種	565.775
本體	133.1	環蟲類	583.6
理論			

16256 彈

化學	541	彈詞	814.7
力學	531.1	彈絃樂器	775
理查孫(1689—1761)	853.61	彈力	533.33
理想派		彈體力學	531.8
文學	800.181	彈性力學	531.81

16610 硯

繪畫	736.1	硯	739.19

碑 魂 孟 羽 耶 鄧 蛋 珊 弓 刀 鴉 帚 鴝

16640 碑

碑	818.73
碑碣	991.34
碑銘	739.12

16713 魂

| 魂 | 157.92 |
| 魂魄 | 156.17 |

17107 孟

孟子
    哲學   111.114
    四書   098.4
孟德比倫   124.52
孟德斯鳩(1689—1755)
    文学   847.52
    哲学   124.22
孟浩然(689—740)   811.142
孟禄   941.852
孟加拉州   982.39
孟買州   982.39
孟知祥(？—935)   811.718

16120 羽

| 羽後國 | 982.1628 |
| 羽前國 | 982.1629 |

17127 耶

耶柔吠陀(祭祀吠陀)	242.12
耶穌言行遺墨	252.999
耶穌西拉	252.94
耶穌福音	272.5
耶穌教	259.2
耶穌會	249.0915
耶利米書信	252.95
耶利米哀書	252.43
耶利米書	252.42
耶律楚材(1190—1243)	817.585
耶和華	261.1

17127 鄧

| 鄧析 | 111.151 |

17136 蛋

蛋白質
    化學   547.92
    動物   581.495

17145 珊

| 珊瑚礁 | 551.98 |
| 瑚珊類動物 | 582.75 |

17207 弓

| 弓矢 | 379.94 |

17220 刀

| 刀劍 | 379.91 |

17227 鴉

| 鴉片 | 597.865 |

17227 帚

| 帚蟲類 | 583.9 |

17227 鴝

| 鴝鵒類 | 587.943 |

中國十進制分類法及索引 | 1139

鶯 承 恐 忍 子 孕 兔 群 那 吊(弔) 習

17227 鶯
  鶯子 111.191

17232 承
  承繼法
    國際法 381.846
    民法 397.6

17331 恐
  恐龍類動物 587.837
  恐鳥類動物 587.945

17332 忍
  忍冬科 579.82

17407 子
  子夏 111.122
  子宮 598.744
  子宮頸 598.744
  子宮外孕 598.82
  子宮內翻 598.847
  宮子內注射 598.879
  子宮炎 598.862
  子法 390.002
  子華子 111.192
  子口稅 369.675
  子思 111.1124
  子嗣衛生 593.19
  子午計時法 528.51
  子午線 522.74
  子午儀 522.3
  子午圈 523.74

17407 孕
  孕徵 598.811
  孕期 588.813
  孕期衛生 598.815

17413 兔
  免疫質 566.965
  兔類 588.64

17501 群
  群論 512.67
  群衆心理 311.58
  群衆運動 317.6
  群雅 415.2
  群馬縣 982.1618

17527 那
  那佛斯科的亞 984.28
  那鴻書 252.494

17527 吊(弔)
  吊橋 651.54
  吊懸鐵道 651.83

17602 習
  習柏(1671—1757) 852.54
  習姆士(1806—70) 836.35
  習性
    動物 581.71
    心理 151.353
    蠶業 616.271

君 配 司 矽 砌 硼 酮 郡 邵 酪 歌

習慣	151.53
習慣法	390.021
習慣性	315.122

17607 君
君主國	371.041

17617 配
配電系統	657.63
配電測定	657.62
配電盤	657.48
配列	657.04
配製	566.13
配藥	596.73
配景法	731.3
配鏡	598.399

17620 司
司徒(1812—96)	863.37
司各特(1771—1832)	
詩	851.74
小說	853.73
司各脫士	121.637
司騰(1713—68)	853.62
司空圖(837—908)	811.1487
司法	
五權	001.162
民權	001.136
司法院	373.04
司令	379.33

17620 矽
矽質海綿類	582.54
矽質鞭毛蟲類	582.33
矽質蟲藻植物	572.5
矽藻植物	572.6

17610 砌
砌甎	651.16

17620 硼
硼元素	546.17

17620 酮
酮類	547.6

17627 郡
郡邑叢書	081.4

17627 邵
邵雍	111.52
邵齊燾(1718—69)	817.761

17664 酪
酪物分析	543.13
酪農	615.7

17682 歌
歌詠吠陀	242.13
歌謠	821.5
歌劇	
戲曲	802.2
演劇	783
歌本	
中國民間文學	814.2
民間文學	804.2

己 翼 瑜 珍 玫 政 玫 酢 磁

歌曲	717.1	財產	373.09
歌唱		政務	369.13
音樂	771	政務收入	269.143
心理	151.38	政治	
歌唱樂室	771.8	外交	910.27
歌唱團	771.7	條約	387.3

17717 己

己防科植物	577.4	地理	980.17
		獨立	388.75

17801 翼

翼龍類	587.87	歷史	930.72
翼手類	538.9	小說	813.857
翼足類	583.535	政治家傳記	370.97
		政治犯	394.21

18121 瑜

瑜伽經	249.4	政財學	360
		政體	371.048

18122 珍

政策

珍岩	557.37	工藝	641

18140 玫

玫讀衛生	332.35	孫中山	001.17
		經濟	351

18140 政

政府	373	移民	377.2
建築	717.1	社會主義	218.02
中央	373.09	國民黨	001.25
公共	717.1	關稅	369.164
經營	621.1	政黨	375
保險	368.9		
行政	373		

18140 玫

玫瑰	612.811

援助 633.13

18611 酢

酢漿草科	577.87

18632 磁

鹼 砂 硝 醚 磷

磁	537
磁計	538.3
磁石	538.1
磁石互吸	538.16
磁石流電	538.83
磁變律	538.725
磁化	538.2
磁化學	541.8
磁結晶學	559.38
磁線	538.73
磁流	538.42
磁測量	538.3
磁力吸引	538.2
磁極	538.15
磁場	538.24
磁感應	538.4
磁器	666.13
磁原素	538.71
磁學	538
磁鐵	538.1

| 磁性 | 538.82 |

18686 鹼
| 鹼類 | 547.97 |

19620 砂
砂礫	651.762
砂礫岩	557.53
砂海蛛	584.63
砂土	651.761
砂蘭德	983.491
砂擴類	588.386

19627 硝
硝酸	661.3
砂酸鹽	661.5
硝化	566.927

19639 醚
| 醚類 | 547.4 |

19659 磷
| 磷 | 546.143 |

垂 重 黍 住 禿 位 停 傍 喬 辭 愛

20104 垂
垂飾　991.68

20104 重
重立方論　517.85
重商派　350.091
重齒類　588.63
重生
　救世論　251.44
　胎生學　581.697
重力　531.64
重力與運動之關係　521.12
重農派　350.092
重量分析法　545.3
重唱　771.71
重反射法　535.48
重覺　156.13
重憶　151.625

20132 黍
黍　612.17

20214 住
住
　社會問題　317.13
　民生問題　001.146
　人種學　565.791
　勞工生活狀況　354.9313
住宅
　建築　718
　鄉村生活　313.412

家政學　692
社俗　319.5
遺迹　991.82
教員　336.53
住址　153.24
住所　381.818

20217 禿
禿頭　593.544

20218 位
位置
　水利工　654.41
　圖建築與設備　024.1
位置幾何學　519.2

20221 停
停戰　381.5581

20227 傍
傍生　231.87

20227 喬
喬治一世二世
　三世四世　935.87
喬治五世　935.88
喬吉甫　812.42
喬木　571.901
喬弗羅　124.53

20241 辭
辭退教員　336.55

20247 愛

倍　信

愛		
佛教		231.55
基督教		258.53
愛爾法修		124.25
愛爾蘭		
文學		859.1
語言		409.373
地理		983.58
歷史		935.98
愛德華七世		935.88
愛德華太子島		984.28
愛奧尼學派		121.11
愛治衛司		853.72
愛迭孫		857.52
愛沙尼亞		939.71
愛媛縣		982.165
愛國		
倫理		185.2
國家		371.029
愛國團		313.61
愛默生		
詩		861.32
散文		867.32
哲學		126.3
愛知縣		982.1639
愛情		813.877

20261 倍

倍根(1561—1626)等	857.3

20261 信

信	258.52
信託	356.3
信託公司	
儲蓄	362.15
生產組織	356.3
信經	
基督教	251.8
回教	271.8
信徒義務	258.1
信仰	
形上學	131.9
政治科學	372.134
倫理學	180.76
社會學	311.29
信仰哲學	131.9
信條	
自然神學	201.8
祆教	281.8
婆羅門教	241.8
道教	221.8
猶太教	261.8
信心	251.42
信濃縣	982.163
信地	982.39
信號	
電政	639.1
船舶工程	659.196

焦 鯨 千 委 受 雙

軍事學	379.38	國民黨	001.224
鐵道工程	651.816	圖行政與	
信匯	365	組織	022.3
信風	529.31	委令	339.23
信用		**20407 受**	
交易	358	受	
票據	362.7	五蘊	231.56
紙幣	361.73	十二線覺	231.62
貨款	346	受信器	657.8335
信管	663.3	受審	
20331 焦		自然神學	201.723
焦獸類	588.391	冥界	251.74
20396 鯨		基督論	251.2952
鯨類	588.47	受難	253.13
20400 千		受戒	233.8
千島列島	982.1678	受精生殖	
千葉縣	982.1614	動物學	561.622
千枚岩	557.44	生物學	581.523
千里眼	157.63	**20407 雙**	
千屈菜科	578.73	雙聽	151.126
20404 委		雙孕	598.817
委託	398.4	雙子葉	569.55
委任統治委員會	383.54	雙子葉植物	76
委任統治地	381.3197	雙動機	655.253
委內瑞辣		雙翅類	585.57
地理	984.7	雙指	598.175
歷史	948.7	雙曲	517.45
委員會		雙曲三角學	518.5

雞　雛　航　手

雙曲函數	516.42	機械構造	659.43
雙曲線幾何學	519.85	氣力學	533.7
雙曲空間	519.6	燃料	659.46
雙曲橢圓函數	516.43	航空法	381.95
雙曲橢圓曲線	519.455	航空指南	659.42
雙曲對數	510.26	航空母艦	379.653
雙趾	598.173	航海記	980.705
雙關字	413.5	航海天文	659.191
雙屈線	535.36	航海天文學	527
雙屈輻射	536.47	航海術	659.1

20414 雞

雞		航海法	381.72
畜產業	615.2	航海通書	527
正鳥類	587.971	航海用具	659.192
獸醫學	599.45	航海燈塔	659.196
雞豆	613.3	航埠	659.47
雞眼	598.544	航馳器	659.165

20414 雛

20500 手

雛錫杖科	575.98	手工業	680

20417 航

航政		手稿本	009.32
水運	634.1	手術	598.18
中國國家財政	396.142	手術麻醉	598.155
航線測量	659.193	手術療法	595.81
航空		手動電碼電信	657.8352
工程	659.4	手藝	680
郵件	636.53	手藝勞工	354.28
運輸	635	手相	157.36
		手吸水機	655.37
		手冊	039.3

舌 看 香 毛 爵 乘 系

手風琴	777.5

20604 舌
舌診法	595.21
舌骨	597.7116

20604 看
看護	595.89
看護學校	590.079
看熱	595.25

20609 香
香膏	612.83
香水	668.11
香川縣	982.165
香液	612.83
香橙	613.731
香蒲科	575.21
香草	613.4
香菜	613.4
香椿	612.817
香櫞	613.735
香會	
實踐佛學	319.73
社會風俗	233.1
香氣	612.85
香料	
化學工業	668.11
家政	694.3
農業	612.88
香料工業	664.4
香料作物	612.8
香粉	668.16

20714 毛
毛詩	093.2
毛豆	612.32
毛織品	675.3
毛傳	093.2
毛細管	
血循環系	597.118
腺系解剖學	597.412
毛奇齡	817.728
毛茛綱	577.3
毛足類	583.61
毛顎類	583.97
毛髮滋潤品	668.13
毛管引力	532.11
毛管分析法	544.95

20746 爵
爵狀科	579.66

20901 乘
乘法	511.23
乘方幾何學	519.06
乘數表	510.211
乘馬	632.3

20903 系
系譜	
孫中山傳記	001.194
静態社會學	313.386

禾 集 統 維 纏 紡 締 稿 絃 紋 絞 順

系譜學	977
系統發育	563.2

20904 禾
禾穀作物	612.1
禾本科	575.42

20904 集
集諦	231.32
集約制	610.314
集權制	373.0501
集會	315.184
集會結社	372.137

20913 統
統計	
各院	345.111-115
各部	345.119
統計法	341
統計圖法	341.5
統計學	340
統一會	250.81
統一省憲	373.0322

20914 維
維多利亞	
澳大利亞地理	985.9393
維多利亞時代	
詩	851.8
戲曲	852.8
散文	857.8
小說	853.8
維吉爾	832.31
維也納	983.491
維基尼亞	981.167

20914 纏
纏足	317.87

20927 紡
紡織機	675.09
紡績	675.03

20927 締
締交	387.1
締約	387

20927 稿
稿本	009.32

20932 絃
絃樂	775
絃振動	534.54

20940 紋
紋章學	960

20948 絞
絞刑	394.511
絞望綱	576.43
絞本科	576.44

21086 順
順療法	595.74
順列	511.4
順河	552.4
順世派	249.9

上 止 黏 步 仁 俳 能 征 虛 軀

| 順風耳 | 157.6 | 止痛藥 | 597.865 |

21100 上
21160 黏

上座部	239.111	黏液細菌科	572.127
上帝		黏土	557.523
祆教	281.1	黏土岩	557.52
基督教	251.1	黏板岩	557.527
猶太教	261.1	黏力	
上帝使者	271.29	液體	532.17
上帝之友	271.23	氣體	533.17
上帝造人	251.31		

20201 步

上訴	395.03	步水（法術）	225.3
上課與曠課	332.11	步道橋	651.5021
上部建築	654.44	步隊	379.55
上議院	373.033		

21210 仁

| 上川 | 982.1675 | 仁果類 | 613.71 |
| 上幾內亞 | 985.57 | | |

21211 俳

上總國	982.1614	俳諧	821.4
上官議	811.1412	俳句	821.4
上官體	811.1412		

21211 能

上古時代		能登	982.1633
韻文	821.21	能子論	530.71
散文	827.1		
小說	823.1		

21211 征

| 上埃及 | 985.163 | 征服 | 381.317 |

21212 虛

| 上墳 | 319.25 | 虛分學 | 515.6 |
| 上野國 | 982.1618 | | |

21216 軀

| 上肢 | 591.87 | 軀幹 | |

21100 止

伍 虎 盧 何 行

體質人類學	565.2
人體測定學	565.3
軀幹分裂	571.211

21217 伍
伍爾夫	127.19

21217 虎
虎尾草	612.295
虎耳草科	577.74

21217 盧
盧文弨(1717—95)	817.735
盧西安	831.887
盧西波土	121.171
盧上	981.366
盧克雷梯士	121.513
盧梭	124.3

21220 何
何西阿	252.46
何達温的格雅	982.661
何桑(1804—64)	863.33

21221 行
行	
佛學哲學	231.64
民生問題	001.147
行商	622.56
行列式	512.3
行政	
五權憲法	001.163

政府	373
基督教會團體	256.33
教育行政	331.3
圖書館學校	028.1
財務行政	369.123
關稅	369.163
民權主義	001.137
公安	315.32
行政訴訟法	393.15
行政行為	393.13
行政組織法	393.11
行政法	393
行政員	331.35
軍事行政	379.33
教育行政	331.35
行政院	
中央政府	373.05
國際聯盟	383.2
行政長官	331.351
行經	598.723
行動	
生態學	581.73
公民學	572.131
行為	581.72
行為派	150.1973
行軍	399.4
行走	597.723
行書	739.175

中國十進制分類法及索引 | 1151

行星論	523.4		21221 衛	
行星互動	521.51		衛	911.6391
行星非球形論	521.55		衛矛科	578.18
行星相距	523.23		衛生	
行星相會	523.23		畜產業	615.08
行星分佈律	523.21		細菌學	566.69
行路	151.38		鄉村生活	313.43
行醫			森林經濟	614.123
注書	593.72		婦女問題	313.3504
注冊	593.72		學校管理	332.3
規則	593.73		監獄學	315.53
管理	593.7		衛生部	373.058
21221 街			衛生及城市工程	653
街道	331.414		衛生細菌	566.95
街道演劇	786		衛生組織	383.45
21221 術			衛生局	
術語	220.3		市政府與行政	373.0826
術士	157.097		縣政府與行政	373.0825
術數	157.5		衛生學	593
佛經	232.082		衛滿至石渠時代	
陰陽五行	157		（149—108）	922.82
21221 衡			衛世師派（勝論）	249.5
衡山	981.363		衛世師經	249.5
21221 衝			衛星論	521.7
衝動			衛星行動	521.53
水力學	532.55		**21227 儒**	
分子動力學	531.697		儒家	111.11
氣力學	535.54		儒教	210

肯 膚 卡 虞 便 優 歲 佔 穎 偵 傾 價 顱 魟

儒艮類	588.41

21221 肯
肯德	983.562

21227 膚
膚覺	151.15

21231 卡
卡地性	598.542

21234 虞
虞集(1272—1318),等	811.159
虞初	813.21
虞書	092.71

21246 便
便移汽機	655.292

21247 優
優生	598.91
優生學	563.5
優卑亞	983.16
優伶	781.2
優境學	563.59

21253 歲
歲變	538.751
歲出	369.13
歲出論	369.03
歲時	031.4
歲入	
社會病理學	315.183
國家財政	369.14
歲入論	369.04
歲差	521.9
歲差法	522.84

21260 佔
佔領	381.313

21286 穎
穎水	981.347

21286 偵
偵察機	379.74
偵探	
公安	315.37
游記文學	807.8
偵探所	315.37

21286 傾
傾斜	553.5
傾銷	352.5

21286 價
價值論	137
價值與價格	358
價格	651.124

21286 顱
顱骨	
骨骼學	597.7115
人體學	565.24
顱骨測定	565.33

21310 魟
魟類	587.41

21316 鱷			比較	
鱷類	587.836		語言學	401
21331 態			生理學	592.9
態度	311.55		生物學	561
21331 熊			解剖學	591.9
熊木縣	982.1665		心理學	154
熊類	588.518		法學派	390.0198
21360 齣			比較方法	371.072
齣狀石灰岩	557.562		比量	341.22
21550 拜			比國	937.92
拜占庭帝國時代	931.86		地理	983.792
21600 占			歷史	937.92
占語	409.181		德國	983.791
占夢	157.17		條頓族	937.91
21710 比			比羅	121.531
比爾佛德	983.47		比屬剛果	985.67
比武	319.75		**21727 師**	
比武爾夫	851.11		師範	338.916
比重			師範大學	338.57
天文學	532.32		師範教育	338.5
農藝	611.331		師範學校	338.51
比重計	032.32		**21772 齒**	
比例選舉制	372.527		齒痛	598.247
比特里斯	982.667		齒鯨類	588.477
比斯開灣諸省	983.37		齒科	598.2
比熱	536.3		齒鳥類	587.95
比加底	983.466		齒軌鐵道	651.85
			齒質	598.242

齒髓	598.241
齒骨	598.243
齒錯	598.245

21806 貞
貞潔	187.1

21903 紫
紫色細菌科	572.151
紫杉科	514.41
紫式部日記	827.33
紫草科	579.54
紫菜綱	573.261
紫茉莉科	577.15
紫威科	579.6
紫金牛科	579.21

21910 紅
紅毛海苔科	573.261
紅種	565.883
紅色細菌科	572.153
紅寶石	558.184
紅木科	578.57
紅十字會	316.1
紅藻植物	573.26
紅樹科	578.77

21911 經
經	
佛教	239.132
中國考古學	991.71
經注	232.07
經疏	232.07
經理	354.133
商業管理	622.4
公司條例	398.49
勞工	354.133
經集	232.37
經緯變遷論	521.28
經緯測定	525.4
經解	
佛經	232.07
聖經	252.07
經紀	622.4
經濟	
主權	371.022
壟斷	351.5
殖民地	377.1
恐慌	352.7
政策	351
行為	350.17
制度	351
自由	352.2
侵略	351.6
絕交	382.36
社會學	311.66
封鎖	382.36
地理	980.15
思想史	350.11
戰爭	351.7

稱　秤　緬　綽　穎

財政組織	383.41	德國文學	871.6
關係	315.167	法國詩	841.4
經濟問題		法國戲曲	842.4
經濟制度	351.8	法國散文	847.4
國際問題	388.6	法國小學	843.4
經濟學	350	經驗論	104.5
經過子午線	523.9	經義	
經藏	232.1	佛經	232.07
經書	090	聖經	252.07
經典		經常費	331.43

21945 稱

稱德	921.823
稱義	251.47
稱光	921.834

21949 秤

秤衡定量	545.3

21960 緬

緬甸	
文學	891.3
語言	409.133
佛教	239.32
地理	982.47
歷史	924.7
緬因	984.161

21946 綽

綽塞	851.23

21986 穎

佛教	232.1		
沃教	282		
神道教	291.2		
基督教	252.01		
猶太教	262		
經典派	269.1		
經費			
教育行政	331.4		
圖書館行政	022.4		
圖書館學校	028.1		
經費獨立	331		
經眼	018.1		
經院學派	121.63		
經學	090		
經學家傳記	090.097		
經學史	090.09		
經學時代			
意國文學	833.12		

川 片 豐 蠻 制 倒 劇 側 彎 任 催 兇 鼎 僑

穎花綱	575.41
22000 川	
川草科	577.71
22021 片	
片麻岩	557.42
片岩	557.43
22108 豐	
豐後國	982.166
22136 蠻	
蠻語	409.15
蠻民教育	338.09
22200 制	
制感	244.5
制度	
軍事行政	379.32
教育行政	331.2
中國國家財政	369.162
農業經濟	610.311
國家財政	369.022
國民黨	001.22
圖書館學校	028.1
勞工	354.131
22200 倒	
倒戈	371.0493
22200 劇	
劇詩	
詩	801.3
日本詩	821.7
希臘文學	831.2
劇樂	773
劇舞	792.6
22200 側	
側膜胎座綱	578.5
22207 彎	
彎曲層	553.2
22214 任	
任意法	390.005
任務	
外交	386.26
學校管理	336.1
任期	
中央政府	373.011
學校管理	336.4
任命	386.21
22214 催	
催涎劑	597.461
催述	817.738
催眠術	156.5
催馬樂	821.52
22217 兇	
兇猛獸	588.381
22227 鼎	
鼎	991.21
22227 僑	

嵩 低 岸 俘 後 變

僑工	354.256	後鰓類	583.535
僑民保護	381.826	後龜山	821.833

22227 嵩

嵩山	981.365	後涼	913.591
		後梁	914.4

22240 低

		後唐	
低音環珈琳	775.7	文學	811.714
低部法蘭克語	409.388	歷史	914.5
低部日耳曼語	409.387	後漢	914.7
低島	985.976	後志支廳	982.167
低溫	611.911	後志國	982.1672
低溫計	536.15	後燕	913.587
		後藏	981.983

22241 岸

岸	381.331	後村上	921.833
岸壁	654.35	後花園	921.834
		後革命時代	

22247 俘

俘虜		詩	861.2
國際法	381.557	散文	863.2
戰爭史	910.285	小說	867.2
俘虜交換	381.557	後趙	913.583
俘傷	930.77	後秦	913.588
		後蜀	811.718

22242 後

		後圓融	921.834
後天的適應	563.72	後獸類	588.21
後天變異	563.61	後龍	597.8117
後晉	914.6	後周	914.8
後經學時代	871.7	後小松	921.834
後科倫布時代	941.815	後光嚴	921.834
後生花	577		

22247 變

岩 嚴 循 仙 炭

變電所	657.29	變分學		515.4
變調鋼琴	776.1	變光星		523.85
變形動學	531.26	**22248 岩**		
變態		岩瘤		553.8
刑法	394.65	岩石腐化		557.7
心理學	155	岩石顯微學		557.8
婦科	598.79	岩石學		557
教育	338.96	岩石分佈		557.9
階級	313.87	岩礦分析		543.5
兒童	153.76	岩頸		553.8
變化	563.69	岩手縣		982.1626
變化論	133.65	岩代國		982.1261
變色龍類	587.855	岩極		553.4
變流器	657.48	岩梅科		589.17
變遷	134.9	岩脉		553.8
變遷時代	841.2	**22248 嚴**		
詩	841.2	嚴高蘭科		578.12
戲曲	842.2	嚴茨科		578.58
散文	847.2	**22264 循**		
小說	843.2	循環詩		801.8
變成岩	557.4	循道書		259.88
變異		**22270 仙**		
生態學	581.77	仙人		221.4
植物學	571.773	仙人掌		578.67
變異論	563.6	仙籍		220.97
變異律	563.66	**22289 炭**		
變壓機	657.43	炭疽		594.962
變質作用	551.95			

戀 乳 幾 種 崑 斷 製

炭水化物	581.498
炭酸礁岩	557.56
炭酸鈉	661.4
炭酸鉀	661.4
炭系鑛	558.12

22339 戀

戀愛	
文學	800.1897
倫理學	187.5
教育	338.9195
靜態社會學	313.342
戀愛病	155.4581

22410 乳

乳病	
生殖氣病理學	598.749
產後病學	598.861
乳糜	581.417
乳酪	615.72
乳房炎	598.861
乳熱	598.861
乳質化學	541.49

22453 幾

幾維類	587.947
幾何說	537.013
幾何級數	514.1
幾何學	517
幾何原理	517.1
幾何與三角	517.9
幾何學基礎	517.1
幾何光學	535.7

22514 種

| 種族心理 | 153.4 |

22711 崑

| 崑劇 | 783 |

22721 斷

斷代史	
西班牙史	933.8
俄國史	938.8
德國史	937.8
法國史	934.8
希臘史	931.8
羅馬史	932.8
中國史	910
印度史	923.8
美國史	941.8
斷續活動法	534.513
斷層	553.7

22732 製

製絲	616.96
製冰	655.67
製冰業	664.8
製造工業	670
製冷機械	655.6
製材	614.72
製藥學	596.6
製表法	341.4

22770 山

山
- 地質學 552.6
- 領土 381.331
- 山西省 981.64
- 山水畫 737.12
- 山形縣 982.1629
- 山歌 801.45
- 山毛櫸綱 576.65
- 山川 319.113
- 山嶽 981.36
- 山嶽崇拜 209.22
- 山梨縣 982.1637
- 山澗 593.112
- 山梗菜 579.92
- 山茶 613.87
- 山林文學 800.1893
- 山藤科 575.71
- 山茱萸科 578.95
- 山蘿蔔科 579.87
- 山茂樫綱 576.77
- 山柳科 579.11
- 山東省 981.62
- 山口縣 982.165
- 山羊草科 579.95

22770 凶

- 凶禮 319.17
- 凶殺 319.77

22770 幽

- 幽靈崇拜 209.5
- 幽默 832.82
- 幽默詩 801.6
- 幽默諷刺文學
  - 法國文學 948.2
  - 英國文學 958.2
  - 中國文學 918.2
  - 日本文學 828
  - 美國文學 868.2

22770 出

- 出庭 395.03
- 出師 319.15
- 出納 023.6
- 出血 598.943
- 出伊及記 252.212
- 出家 233.8
- 出版 010.43
- 出版自由 040.13
- 出口 362.1673

22782 嵌

- 嵌石 712.6

22900 利

- 利高里亞 983.26
- 利息 511.37
- 利溫群島
  - 西印度群島地理 984.77
  - 西印度群島歷史 947.7

利潤	359		種痘	593.2356
利未記	252.213		反種痘	593.2357
利膽劑	354.316		種族	
利益範圍	381.3194		殖民	377.2

22901 崇

崇光	921.834		種族心理	153.4
			佛學	230.19

22904 梨

梨	613.712		種族之於奴制	317.44
			種族宗教	200.07
			種族犯罪學	315.17

22904 樂

樂	095		種族問題	317.2
樂府	811.5		種子	614.482
樂音	634.7		種子植物	
樂劇	802.95		古生物學	594
樂式	770.027		植物學	569.3
樂觀論	108.1		種子分佈	571.67
樂團	779		種子消滅	581.7779
樂園	251.34		種源論	564
樂器	991.73		種苗	611.5
樂器教學法	770.077		種類	
樂與苦	151.2		經濟學	353.1
樂史	813.51		機械工程	655.272
			財政學	362.1

22913 繼

22922 彩

繼電器	657.8333		彩雲	529.66
繼續航海	381.64		彩票	367.5
繼嗣	313.387		彩色攝影	758.3

22914 種

			彩色與廣告	
種	614.77		商業	629.2

繃 移 紙 綏 緩 稻 絲 卜 外

給畫	732
彩畫	734

22927 繃
繃帶	595.814

22927 移
移民	377

22940 紙
紙	739.19
紙製品	674
紙色	010.47
紙鳶	659.49
紙質	010.47
紙類	991.76
紙幣	361.7

22944 綏
綏遠省	981.945

22947 緩
緩刑	394.55

22977 稻
稻	612.18
稻草	612.294

22993 絲
絲	
工業製造	675.4
中國音樂	770.17
服制	693.1
絲瓣鰓類	583.552
絲織品	675.4
絲狀類	582.15
絲稅	369.152
絲藻綱	573.21
絲瓜	613.26

23000 卜
卜勒浮	843.53
卜呂敦	841.84
卜呂亞士	842.46
卜筮	157.1

23200 外
外交	386
官吏	386.33
行政	386.3
治外法權	386.5
專員	386.36
歷史	930.73
外交部	
政府行政	373.052
外交	386.32
外交部長	386.32
外交行政	386.3
外交團	386.34
外交問題	386.8
外記	910.7
外部生殖器測定	565.37
外部分泌	581.446
外耳	598.441

參 僱 偏 伏 狀 代

外子目	572.26	參觀	337.195
外科	598	**23214 僱**	
病理學	598.14	僱主組織	354.61
衛生學	598.13	僱主公會	354.61
細菌學	598.12	僱工	354.11
解剖學	598.11	僱用方式	354.117
治療學	598.15	**23227 偏**	
外科敷料	598.1905	偏頭病	597.8457
外科器件	598.1901	偏僻	155.41
外債	369.182	偏射	536.48
外寄生蟲	594.973	偏光	535.37
外來字	413.9	偏光分析法	
外蒙古	981.95	定量分析法	545.7
外葉器官	591.55	定性分析法	544.7
外翅類	585.3	**23234 伏**	
外國文善本書目	019.9	伏虎	225.5
外國人地位	381.82	**23234 狀**	
外國善本	009.9	狀態(地心)	551.12
外肛類	583.83	**23240 代**	
外丹	224.5	代特	861.22
外科層	583.6	代名詞	416.2
23202 參		代表	001.243
參政	372.5	議員	373.0343
參政權	372.16	黨員	001.243
參考		代表紙券	360.32
特種書目	018.6	代表大會	
圖書館管理	023.7	國民黨	001.221
參考書用法	027.3		

愛 伐 戲 俄 鴕

國際聯盟	383.1	美國	862
代數		戲單	781.9
方程式	512.77	戲園	780
平面曲線	519.452	**23250 俄**	
函數	516.2	俄亥俄	984.175
幾何學	519.4	俄利權	982.36
級數	514.3	俄克拉何馬	984.173
曲面	519.463	俄勒阿	984.195
代數式	512.2	俄國	
代數數	512.47	文學	880
代數量之數理論	512.1	語言	480
23247 愛		建築	710.38
愛爾蘭文學	859.3	統計	354.38
23250 伐		動物	581.938
伐木	614.71	條約	387.938
23250 戲		憲法	391.138
戲劇	812	游記	985.83
戲劇表演	781	大學	338.7938
戲曲		地理	983.8
意國	833.2	地圖	980.338
西班牙	835.2	地質	550.38
俄國	882	植物	571.938
德國	872	考古	993.8
法國	842	教育	330.938
基督教	250.82	哲學	128.8
英國	852	財政	369.38
拉丁	832.2	歷史	938
日本	822	**23311 鴕**	

怠 牦 我 台 貸 秘 私 編 織 纖 縮

鴕鳥類	587.942	私家藏書	025.1
23336 怠		私運	315.183
怠業	354.84	私地	355.3
23512 牦		私地志	981.58
牦牛兒苗綱	577.85	私有郵政	636.32
23550 我		私有鐵路	633.18
我慢	241.63	私印	991.613
23600 台		**23927 編**	
台灣	921.9	編劇	781.1
23806 貸		編織用纖維	612.59
貸借	398.41	編輯部,報學	040.5
23900 秘		編目	023.4
秘訣	225.1	**23950 織**	
秘書長		織繡	
政府	373.0849	繪畫	735.7
教育	331.355	考古學	991.76
秘書		織法	675.05
地理	984.85	織品	675
歷史	948.5	織品副業	675.9
秘密社	313.63	**23950 纖**	
秘二祕		纖維作物	612.5
國民黨	001.223	纖維化學工業	668.4
國際聯盟	383.3	纖維蛇紋岩	557.48
23900 私		纖維類	547.85
私立學校	338.07	纖維植物	571.215
私立銀行	362.11	纖毛蟲類	582.4
私經濟學	350.01	**23961 縮**	
		縮小攝影	755.5

稽　綜　動

23961 稽

稽留熱	504.925

23991 綜

綜合

化學	545.9
心理學	150.175
鑛物學	558.7

24127 動

動產	369.141
動電機	657.4
動電機附件	657.48
動電學	537.3
動理演化	564.6
動能	533.11
動態社會學	312
動態中	133.61

動物

病菌	566.98
磁術	156.5
衛生	596.28
崇拜	209.28
傳染	594.96
倫理	581.708
化學	661.98
寄生	594.971

心理

比較	154.8
生態	581.701
游記	580.099
油脂	665.3
神話	580.089
地理	980.118
地質學	551.98
藥材	596.11
採集	580.075
抑制	151.36
圖畫	737.18
顯微學	566.5
彫刻	729.8
醫學	661.98
分佈	581.9
動物園	580.077
動物學	580
動物學家傳記	580.097
動作(本體論)	133.6
動字	416.2

動力

水利工程	654.12
幾何學	519.78
生態學	581.7771
物理學	531.693
心理學	150.193
地質學	551
動植物生命比較論	592.14
動嘴類	583.48
動脉	597.115

射 魁 化 先 佐 倚 佈 僞

動學	531.2

24200 射

射發學	531.698
射術	379.94
射線	535.5
射線療法	595.87
射擊	797.7

24210 魁

魁北克	984.28

24210 化

化石學	569
化理病理學	594.4
化理檢驗法	595.29
化裝舞	792.7
化學	
工業	660
平衡	541.065
變化律	541.061
動學	541.063
結晶學	559.4
藥品	596.2
靜學	541.063
成分	581.491
農藝	611.31
化學律	541.09
化學家傳記	540.097
化學表	541.09
化合物	541.03
化合力	541.067
化粧品	668.1

24211 先

先天變異	563.61
先天存在	135.71
先天揆轉	598.178
先天感覺不具	155.257
先祖遺傳	153.3
先秦哲學	111.1
先成河	552.4
先胎發育	581.695
先胎發育論	560.7
先民宗教	200.05
先知	
神學	271.2
陰陽五行	157.097
先知之僞書	252.985
先知書	252.4

24211 佐

佐渡國	982.163
佐賀縣	982.166

24221 倚

倚數	561

24227 佈

佈景	781.51
佈道	254.1

24227 僞

備 德 貘 待 彼

偽病	595.5
偽經	
佛經	232.9
聖經	252.9
偽行傳	252.993
偽福音	252.991
偽啟示錄	252.996
偽基督	251.65
偽書	018.4
偽書翰	252.995
偽足類	582.11
偽醫	593.75
偽篇	093.9

24227 備
備後國	982.165

24231 德
德謨克拉圖士	121.173
德敦	851.34
德聯	930.751
德那	861.27
德比孫	982.665
德皇時期	932.865
德島縣	982.165
德來登	
詩	851.48
戲曲	852.45
德蘭士瓦	985.74
德拉瓦	984.165

德國	
文學	870
語言	470
建築	710.37
統計	345.37
動物	581.937
條約	387.937
憲法	391.137
游記	983.7
大學	338.7937
考古	993.7
植物	571.937
地理	983.7
地圖	980.337
地質	550.37
教育	330.937
哲學	127
財政	369.37
歷史	937
德屬南非	985.72
德屬東非	985.42

24234 貘
貘類	588.348

24241 待
待宵草	578.84
待遇(教員)	336.5

24247 彼
彼得後書	252.793

彼得前書	252.792		勞工	354.4
24260 貓			休養所	593.112
貓			**24327 勳**	
畜產業	615.17		勳章	968
獸醫學	599.48		勳爵	966
貓猴類	588.81		勳位	966
貓類	588.511		**24361 鰭**	
24260 儲			鰭龍類	587.815
儲蓄銀行	362.9		**24400 升**	
24261 借			升天	
借方根	512		實踐神學	253.13
借貸			基督論	251.2958
社會救濟學	316.53		升任	336.55
銀行	362.18		升遷	354.135
24261 牆			升學	334.6
牆畫	735.1		升降變遷論	521.27
牆壁	713.4		升降機	655.36
24281 徒			**24510 牡**	
徒刑	394.513		牡丹	613.86
徒然草	827.5		**24541 特**	
24281 供			特論	301.309
供求工資說	354.311		特許狀	901.1
24290 休			特殊	
休謨	125.5		病理學	594.8
休息			函數	516.7
衛生學	593.16		紋章	965
學校管理	332.37		織品	675.6

甜 幼 裝

傳染病	593.24	服務	258.4
組織	581.24	年鑑	037.7
物質	566.15	特修	335.7
官能細菌	566.961	特洛普	853.87
演化學說	564	特式往復汽機	655.298
禱文	253.47	特藏	000
選舉制	372.523	特權	
運動官能	151.38	工業	645
存款	362.5	實業	605
橋梁	651.58	特權法	397.23
植物組織	571.17	特都里	121.622
夢	156.335	特別市	981.53
教育	338.8	特別訴訟法	395.3
青年會	256.36	特別刑法	394.6
曲面	519.47	特別法規	399
階級	313.87	特質	153.82
服裝	319.46	特質土壤	611.34
醫術	595.9	特用電燈	657.816
金屬	669.9	特性藥療法	595.77
知覺	151.175		
黨部	001.5		

24670 甜

甜菜	612.63
甜瓜	613.21

性質物	530.3
精神病	155.29

24727 幼

特種書目	018
特種材木	614.73
特種人	
教育	338.9
圖書館	025.7

幼稚園	338.13
幼稚病國際	388.57
幼里庇底士	831.23

24732 裝

裝訂	023.9

裝訂術	010.81	科里	982.661
裝潢		科羅拉多	984.187
圖書館學	010.9	科學	
美術工藝	762	中國文學	815.5
裝包	622.6	日本文學	825.5
裝置	568.14	兒童文學	805.5
裝甲邊防艦	379.665	科學的社會主義	318.5
裝置機件	655.16	科學觀心理	150.15
裝管		**24927 納**	
船舶工程	659.15	納稅	372.2
汽機工程	655.227	**24961 結**	
裝飾		結石	597.642
住宅	692	結締組織	
考古玉	991.68	解剖學	591.72
花園	615.8065	內科	597.718
24737 岐		結縷草	612.291
岐阜縣	982.1835	結婚	
24738 峽		家庭道德	183.1
峽	981.369	親屬法	397.51
24806 貨		國際民法	381.845
貨款	362.7	結晶計算法	559.11
貨樣	358	結晶形態學	559.6
貨車頭	655.272	結晶石灰岩	557.46
貨幣	361.5	結晶磁學	538.59
24900 科		結晶書法	559.13
科倫布時代	941.813	結晶顯微學	566.28
科克群島	985.974	結晶學	559
科布多	981.956	結髮	693.5

續 牛 失 生

結合膜	598.341
結節	594.994
結節草科	577.17

24986 續

續發病	594.6
續道藏	222.7

25000 牛

牛
畜產業	615.12
獸醫學	599.42

牛痘	594.913
牛酪	615.73

牛乳
化學	543.13
農業	615.71

牛類	588.335

25030 失

失語病	597.8455

失業
勞工	354.137
勞工其他問題	354.937

失神	155.7

25100 生

生	231.52
生育限制	563.57

生產
產科	598.83
經濟制度	352

人口論	349.072
生產率	349.072
生產競爭	352.5
生產論	352
生產能	562.34
生產問題	388.61
生產合作	356.71
生育遺傳	563.391
生電	657.2
生死自然論	592.1
生殖	592.6
生殖線	581.621
生殖組織	581.29
生殖細胞	591.51
生殖淘汰	563.38
生殖器崇拜	209.3
生殖器官	571.277

生殖學
動物學	581.6
生物學	561.6
植物學	571.6

生理
產科	598.85
音樂	770.012
音學	534.9
動物學	581.4
化學	592.4
生物學	561.4

心理學	153.91	生物顯微學	566.3
力學	531.32	生物學	560
植物學	571.4	生物學家傳記	560.097
農學	616.22	生物學方法	371.071
顯微學	566.92	生活要素	581.403
醫學	592	生活程度說	351.312
人類學	565.4	生活標準	317.16
光學	535.9	生活力	
生理化學		動物學	581.401
理論化學	541	醫學	592.1
動物學	581.49	生活費	317.15
生理學	592.4	生活器官之驗徵	592.17
生理特質	561.57	生活質	562.38
生態	566.925	生活原理	562.37
生態學		生活問題	
生物學	561.8	社會	317.1
動物學	581.7	勞工	354.931
植物學	571.7	生存說	354.315
農學	616.27	生存競爭	563.194
生自然性	135.9	生來	101.352
生物發生論	562.7	生機	566.921
生物化學	562.4	生長	
生物物理學	562.3	結晶學	559.63
生物心理	154	生理學	592.6
生物測定	562.6	植物學	571.45
生物考古	990.5	顯微學	566.922
生物地理	980.116	生長不均	598.176
生物力學	561.67	生長力	562.33

蜻 仲 律 佛

生長期須要食品	592.477
生髮油	668.13
生體刑	394.511
生卵	581.624
生命	
生物學	562
倫理學	180.5
財政學	368.2
民權	372.11
勞工	354.937
生命論	562.8
生命現象	562
生命刑	394.511
生命理論	562.3
生命要件	562.83
生命始原	562.7
生命救急法	593.4
生命與靈魂	592.13
生性	315.122

25127 蜻

蜻化	669.25

25206 仲

仲裁	
經濟學	382.28
國際政治	382.28
仲裁條約	387.7
仲裁院之裁決書	381.027
仲長統	111.285

25207 律

律師	392.07
律宗	239.64
律法	390
律法書	252.2
律藏	232.4
律曆	528

25227 佛

佛寺	715.3
佛西斯	983.16
佛經	232
佛經文學	232.088
佛經故事	232.081
佛經奇迹	232.082
佛經史	232.69
佛經與五明	232.085
佛經與個人	232.087
佛經與法律	232.084
佛經與其他	232.089
佛經與學術	232.08
佛特	852.62
佛爾連級數	516.82
佛克史	983.496
佛林得里群島	985.972
佛蘭斯官德	983.477
佛蘭克林	867.21
佛教	
文學	232.088

中國十進制分類法及索引 | 1175

儂 健 傳

建築	235.8
行政	235.2
制度	235
生活	238
考古	230.99
教育	237
教會	235
團體	236
財政	235.3
佛教宗派與歷史	239
佛教與文化	230.19
佛教與政治	230.13
佛教與科學	230.15
佛教與他家教	
關係	230.12
佛教與社會	230.13
佛教與教育	230.13
佛教曆	528.63
佛肛竹	612.65
佛陀論	231.2
佛陀世尊	231.22
佛學	230
佛學與倫理	230.118
佛學與心理	230.115
佛學與哲學	230.11
佛學哲學	231

25232 儂

儂語	409.126

25240 健

健康	354.114
健身所	338.639

25343 傳

傳電器	657.8331
傳誌文學	868.7
演劇	781.27
道教	220.97
歷史	970
傳記文學	828.7
傳記小說	813.827
傳說	
傳記	970.6
神學	251.293
基督教	250.84
傳說時代	
德國史	937.981
希臘史	931.81
中國史	911.1
傳電	
電氣	657.6
電學	537.27
傳狀	818.71
傳線	595.814
傳心術	
相術	157.61
陰陽五行	157.6
傳染病	593.23

使 債 侏 朱 純 積

傳染病及其他通行病	594.9
傳道	
宗教	204
基督教	253.34
傳導	
電磁	538.862
物理光學	535.31
熱學	536.41
傳力	531.9
傳奇	
中國文學	814.4
民間文學	804.4
傳奇劇	802.95
傳熱	536.4
傳教	
佛教	234
宗教	204
神道教	291.4
基督教	254
猶太教	264
回教	274
傳單廣告	629.4

25606 使

使子君科	578.8
使徒	255.51
使徒信經	251.81
使徒行傳	252.6
使徒書翰	252.79

使儀	
外交	386.27
禮俗	319.13
使權	386.25
使服	386.28
使節	386.2

25286 債

債權法	397.3
國際私法	381.843
國法	397.3
債券	366.1

25290 侏

侏羅紀	554.63

25900 朱

朱維那爾	832.827
朱伯爾	847.62
朱彝尊	817.726
朱熹	
中國文學	817.571
中國哲學	111.56

25917 純

純粹瓦斯確定法	544.41

25986 積

積聚投票法	372.528
積分	516.6
積分方程式	515.75
積分幾何學	519.4

練 白 自

積分學	515.3	白泰	409.125

25996 練

練藥	596.6	白蠟蟲	615.5
練丹		白蟻	585.35
道教	224.6	白果科	577.33
醫學	596.6	白喉	594.93
		白璧德	128.8

26000 白

白話	416.85	白髮	598.544
白雲岩	557.564	白體	811.1513
白堊	557.563	白居易	811.1458
白堊紀	554.65	白合歡	612.388
白種人	565.884	白光之分析	535.23
白化病	598.545	白光星	523.81

25000 自

白血病	566.966	自意動作	151.357
白血細胞	597.1212	自行車	659.77
白楔綱	576.55	自衛	382.21
白木耳目	573.35	自衛權	381.22
白檀科	579.35	自然主義	
白樸	812.33	哲學	107.1
白帶	598.7473	人生哲學	171
白勒	847.43	自然論	562.71
白熱電燈	657.8145	自然診斷法	595.27
白蘭佳	841.71	自然發生	561.611
白蘭地	664.55	自然動作	151.351
白蒙得	852.35	自然變異	563.69
白花菜科	577.55	自然科學	500
白楔科	576.56	自然之於人類	565.77
白翹搖	672.382	自然派	

文學	800.185	自動自行車	659.78
繪畫	736.2	自動演奏器	777.6
自然法派		自動起水機	655.37
律法	390.0194	自動車工程	659.7
國際法	381.0991	自動鋼琴	776.1
自然淘汰		自律論	173.3
種源論	564.21	自修	338.81
動態社會學	312.23	自適	563.76
植物學	571.775	自適論	562.35
自然法與平衡		自導	151.43
法時代	390.093	自著叢書	081.5
自然神學	201	自著書目	015
自然地理	980.11	自殺	
自然地質學	551	倫理學	180.59
自然喪失	381.321	心理學	155.455
自然畫	737.1	社會病理學	315.185
自然哲學	134	自來水	313.43
自然星占學	520.1	自由	251.38
自然界限	381.331	自由論	134.23
自然反應	151.51	自由競爭	351.34
自然與社會		自由形	394.513
環境之影響	153.2	自由戀愛	313.3421
自然人	397.11	自由僱用	354.117
自然美	700.18	自由權	372.13
自私	180.49	自由土黨	357.64
自動電話	657.857	自由關稅	369.1641
自動電碼電信	657.8353	自由貿易	351.53
自動傳電受信器	657.8337	自救	251.49

牌 皇 堡 伯 個 但 鬼 傀 俚 偶

自性	
二十五諦	241.61
婆羅門教	
哲學	241.1

26040 牌
牌坊	
城市風景	719.5
考古學	991.85

26041 皇
皇族	977.1
傳記	977.1
社會學	313.81
皇宮	718.2
皇室	968
皇室復興時代	921.85
皇冠	968

26104 堡
堡壘	659.31

26200 伯
伯爾尼	983.494
伯羅奔尼撒	983.17

26200 個
個別心理	153.8
個體發育	593.1
個體發生學	591.55
個人	
經濟	350.011
衛生	593.1
傳記	979
祈禱	253.23
禱文	253.45
道德	182
輔導	332.4
企業	356.21
個性教授法	337.5

26210 但
但以理	851.33
但以理書	252.45
但馬	982.164

26213 鬼
鬼怪	319.81
鬼谷子	111.195

26213 傀
傀儡戲	787
傀儡劇	802.5

26214 俚
俚諺	
文學	804.5
中國文學	814.5

26227 偶
偶然	133.4
偶然論	133.4
偶然之存在	133.4
偶然性	315.125

觸 泉 俾 得 保 鯤 鰓 卑 魏

偶像崇拜	209.8	保護貿易	357.35
偶蹄類	588.331	保耳索	842.44

26227 觸

觸	231.57	保付	364.2
觸診法	595.23	保安	315.33
觸覺	151.15	保存	
觸腳類	584.672	生物學	566.133
		圖書館學	023.9

26232 泉

泉		保葬	319.24
工程	552.5	保護色	581.75
地質學	653.14	保護國	
中國地理	981.356	殖民	377.1
泉幣	991.24	國際法	381.12

26240 俾

俾路支		保羅一世至	
語言	409.326	尼古拉一世	938.86
地理	982.58	保羅鼎	863.26
歷史	925.9	保險	368
		保險法	368.6
		保險金	354.35

26241 得

得氏波群論	530.75		

26317 鯤

鯤鯨類	588.475

得克薩斯	984.172		

26330 鰓

得數氏	512.35	鰓足類	584.863

26294 保

		鰓呼吸	581.423
		鰓氣管呼吸	581.424
保證	362.7		

26400 卑

保護	615.04	卑斯馬克群島	985.956
保護國	371.75	卑利與龍之紀略	252.96
保護關稅	364.1643		

26413 魏

吳 臭 齅 鼻 魄 和 細

魏	
韻文	811.131
中國文學	811.657
中國史	810.31
魏晉六朝隋哲學	111.3
魏司曼學說	564.33
魏了翁	817.577
魏源	817.785

26430 吳

吳承恩	813.63
吳敬梓	813.74
吳中七子	811.177
吳錫麟	817.765

26430 臭

臭虫寄生	594.974
臭化氪	597.863

26434 齅

齅感覺	151.13
齅覺	151.13

26446 鼻

鼻	597.211
鼻疽	594.963
鼻科	598.491

26613 魄

魄	157.93

26900 和

和音	534.541
和音中拍子	534.65
和音曲線	534.531
和平解決	382.2
和平與戰爭	185.8
和歌	821.2
和歌山縣	982.164
和絃法	770.025
和泉式部日記	827.35
和泉國	982.164
和聲	770.025
和約	
條約	387.4
國際法	381.58
和解	354.86

26900 細

細部構造	655.259
細勒西亞	983.796
細菌綱	572.11
細菌學	566
細菌與動物界之關係	566.96
細菌與植物之關係	566.97
細菌與無生物之關係	566.94
細胞	581.21
細胞死亡	561.59
細胞生理	581.407
細胞生理形態	592.25
細胞生理特性	592.26
細胞組織	571.13

程 穆 綿 總 線 釋

細胞化學	592.24
細胞生長	561.58
細胞核	
病理學	571.52
細胞學	561.52
細胞構造	
形態學	581.101
細胞學	561.52
細胞構成	571.117
細胞膜	571.116
細胞學	
生物學	561.5
醫學	591.71
細胞與生機	
生理學	592.2
細胞與細胞組織	571.41
細胞分裂	
生殖學	561.54
生理與構造	
植物學	571.117
細胞學	561.54

26914 程

程序法	390.007
程灝	111.541
程頤	111.542

26922 穆

穆爾	851.75
穆塞	
詩	841.74
戲曲	842.74
穆罕默德	271.29
穆里爾	842.42

26927 綿

綿火藥	663.15

26930 總

總論地租	359
總發電所	657.29
總統	373.011
總鰭類	587.471
總鰓類	587.4773
總翅類	585.37
總幹事	256.34
總則	397.1

26932 線

線	
統計法	341.5
幾何學	517.51
線刻	742.4
線狀細菌科	572.123
線流電	537.22
線束	595.813
線素幾何學	519.02
線蟲類	583.41

26941 釋

釋家傳記	231.29
釋家牟尼	231.21

緝 稷 墾 血 盤 凱 艷 龜 郵 郵

26941 緝
- 緝合語   403

26947 稷
- 稷   612.17
- 稷草   612.293

27104 墾
- 墾殖   610.317

27107 血
- 血   581.413
- 血族系統   313.383
- 血族社會   313.2
- 血循環系
  - 形態學   581.11
  - 生理學   581.41
  - 內科   597.1
- 血化學性   597.122
- 血色素   581.421
- 血液
  - 解剖學   591.75
  - 內科   597.147
- 血液循環   565.43
- 血液胞子蟲類   582.24
- 血液壓力   597.124
- 血液分析   592.29
- 血汁勞工   354.257
- 血淋巴   581.414
- 血內換氣   597.224
- 血草科   575.84
- 血素質   597.121
- 血胎   597.828
- 血管舒縮   597.128

27107 盤
- 盤城國   982.1622
- 盤振動   534.56

27110 凱
- 凱旋   319.15
- 凱旋門
  - 城市風景   719.5
  - 中國考古學   991.85

27117 艷
- 艷事
  - 中國文學   814.4
  - 民間文學   804.4
- 艷情   813.876

27117 龜
- 龜卜   157.12
- 龜類   587.817

27120 郵
- 郵金   354.35

27127 郵
- 郵票   636.4
- 郵票蒐集   636.48
- 郵務行政   636.3
- 郵務公會   636.34
- 郵務管理   636.3

歸 黎 蟹 多 佩 危 免 向

郵政		多孕	598.817
交通	636	多飛	983.498
國家財政	369.142	多毛類	583.612
郵政儲蓄銀行	362.97	多細胞構造	581.103
郵件	636.5	多源說	565.733
郵匯	636.38	多神教	200.01
郵運	636.37	多邊形	517.36

27127 歸

		多板類	583.511
歸納	143	多妻	183.2
歸先現象	563.395	多軸海綿類	582.56
歸有光	817.65	多足類	584.4
歸藏	091.9	多胚生殖	561.623

27132 黎

		多臘	841.31
黎語	409.128	多年性草花類	613.82
黎西亞士	831.842		

27210 佩

黎德		佩特拉克	833.118
英國哲學	125.63	佩戴	960.8
美國文學	861.39		

27212 危

黎俱吠陀	242.11	危地馬拉	
黎木性	983.489	中美洲各國	
黎阿第十時代	833.13	地理	984.61

27136 蟹

		中美洲各國史	946.1
蟹	584.827	危險工作	354.52

27207 多

27217 免

多立斯	983.16	免費郵件	636.51
多元論	102.5		

27220 向

多爾多內	983.492	向心力	531.696
多列藍藻科	572.173	向量解析	512.65

中國十進制分類法及索引 | 1185

御 修 角 鄉 象 像 漿 候 將

27220 御
 御風   225.2

27222 修
 修理   023.9
 修辭學
  文法   232.088
  佛經   416.8
 修行   244
 修片   755.8
 修多羅   242.15
 修身   182
 修道   258.9
 修道院   255.8
 修道會派別   259.091
 修指   693.5
 修飾   319.4
 修真   224
 修樹剪刀   610.63
 修學   018.6
 修學法   337.9
 修飾
  家政   693.5
  禮俗   319.47

27227 角
 角三分論   517.83
 角力
  游藝武術   797.6
  學校武術   338.638
 角胡麻科   579.62
 角膜   598.341

27227 鄉
 鄉土志   981.58

27232 象
 象刻   726
 象形   411.31
 象徵   145
 象徵派
  文學   800.187
  繪畫   736.4
 象牙   735.3
 象類   587.38

27232 像
 像   991.72
 像讚
  孫中山   001.192
  佛教   230.97
  傳記   970.2
 像片   781.22
 像片比較法   522.86

27232 漿
 漿果類   613.74

27234 候
 候方城   817.715
 候選   372.54

27242 將

假 侵 解 伊

將帥	910.289

27247 假

假設	141.73
假耳	598.48
假球面三角學	518.4
假借	411.35
假釋	394.57
假名草紙	823.61
假期	
教員	336.58
學年	334.37
勞工	354.46
假軟體動物	
古生物學	569.76
關節動物	583.7
假冒	315.183
假眼	598.38
假牙	598.288
假人魚草科	578.13

27247 侵

侵伐	381.551

27251 解

解僱	354.85
解瘧劑	597.466
解剖	
國家醫學	593.71
顯微學	566.81
解剖學	591
解聘	336.55
解經	253.75
解析	
心理學	150.174
算學	511.4
解析三角學	518.3
解析函數	516.1
解析幾何學	519.4
解析法	
函數	516.8
聲學	534.53
農業	610.547
解析力學	531.5
解析學	513
解析光學	535.1
解脫	241.5

27257 伊

伊庇魯斯	983.16
伊丁	982.661
伊豫國	982.165
伊利斯	983.17
伊大卡	983.16
伊勢	983.1648
伊賀	982.1648
伊里維勒內	983.461
伊爾文	
美國散文	967.23
美國小說	863.23

詹　欣　俱　條　條　冬　鮑　烏

伊豆七島	982.1611	俱舍論	239.115
伊利亞學派	121.12	俱舍宗	
伊利安學派	121.28	中國佛教	239.52
伊利阿	853.36	日本佛教	239.62
伊奧尼亞群島	983.19	**27293 條**	
伊達荷	984.196	條蟲類	583.34
伊索	831.886	**27294 條**	
伊索克雷士	831.844	條例	633.12
伊斯啓泥士	831.845	條約	
伊斯奇士	831.21	國際法	381.021
伊蘭語	409.32	普通條約	387
伊勢物語	823.32	條頓語	409.33
伊勢神宮	291.6	條頓族	
伊勢神道	291.1	地理	983.79
伊里德佛蘭薩	983.473	歷史	937.9
伊里諾亞	984.176	**27303 冬**	
伊壁鳩魯派	121.51	冬青科	578.17
伊阿華	984.178	冬青茶	612.77
伊兒	915.98	冬眠動物	592.57
27261 詹		冬瓜	613.25
詹姆士	126.4	**27312 鮑**	
詹姆斯氏時代	935.914	鮑照	811.1335
27280 欣		**27327 烏**	
欣賞	770.017	烏	737.18
27281 俱		烏台	984.192
俱樂部		烏蘇里江	981.345
建築	718.4	烏拉語	409.21
會社團體	313.65		

烏 懇 魚 身 芻 鶄 奧

烏拉圭		27400 身	
地理	984.899	身軀之成分	592.43
歷史	948.99	身心論	150.16
烏拉阿爾泰		身心交感論	150.162
文學	892	身心平行論	150.163
語系	409.2	身心動作心理	150.1917
烏托邦	371.5	身心關係	150.16
烏蜥類	587.89	身材	565.21
烏弗蘭	871.24	身材比例	565.22
27327 鳥		身材長短表	565.36
鳥	599.46	身體	
鳥取縣	982.165	社會病理學	315.185
鳥獸	811.93	國民	372.11
鳥獸保養法	619.4	身體修養	188.9
鳥類		身體清潔	
脊椎動物	587.9	外科	598.14
古生物學	569.86	學校管理	332.33
27333 懇		身體檢查	332.31
懇親會	333.8	27427 芻	
27336 魚		芻秣作物	612.3
魚	593.128	27427 鶄	
魚玄機	811.1488	鶄鴒類	587.9757
魚龍類	587.835	27430 奧	
魚鼓	770.13	奧大利	
魚梆	770.14	地理	983.795
魚類		哲學	128.5
脊椎動物	587.3	歷史	937.95
古生物學	569.83	奧爾良	841.22

獎 般 彞 船 欷 犁 物

奧羽地方	982.162
奧維德	832.12
奧治時代	937.932
奧斯騰	853.74
奧基亞	842.83
奧里亞斯	983.481
奧匹安	831.39
奧陶紀	554.53
奧義書	242.5

27430 獎

獎金	
教育行政	331.45
勞工	354.337
獎勵	377.62
獎券	367.5

27447 般

般若部	232.31

27449 彞

彞器	991.23
彞器文	990.812

27461 船

船廠	659.18
船舶	659.13
船舶設計	659.11
船舶工程	659.1
船舶裝設	659.15
船舶構造	659.11
船舶機械	659.16
船舶用具	659.17
船渠	654.31

27482 欷

欷識	010.97

27502 犁

犁	610.61

27520 物

物理	
力學	631.13
農藝	611.33
物理於植物	571.47
物理論	536.415
物理結晶學	559.3
物理特質	561.55
物理作用	
流電學	537.379
生理學	581.443
物理定律	530.5
物理基質	563.32
物理表	550.079
物理異說	530.9
物理學	530
物理關係	538.6
物理光學	535.3
物理變化	536.7
物力	531.691
物權法	397.2
物質	134.7

鵝　名　響　醬　魯　的　翻　鄱

物質不滅論	530.4	社會學	315.186
物質建設	001.157	名譽刑	394.517
物質動理	530.2	名勝古迹	
物質組織	530.1	世界類志	980.508
物質心理	150.166	中國地理	981.38
物質構造	530.11	**27601 響**	
物體		響岩	557.26
宇宙論	134.7	響板	770.16
心靈哲學	135.2	**27601 醬**	
物體光色	535.393	醬油	664.41
物墜律	531.65	**27603 魯**	
物料強度	531.41	魯	911.632
物性學	530.1	魯詩故	093.11
物權	381.842	魯干洛土	832.32
27527 鵝		魯克理細阿土	832.11
鵝		魯故	093.111
畜產業	615.2	**27620 的**	
脊椎動物	587.973	的黎玻里	985.46
獸醫學	599.45	**27620 翻**	
27600 名		翻刻本	009.12
名利	180.82	翻譯	
名色	231.59	詩	093.6
名物考	090.03	聖經	252.06
名家	111.15	佛經	232.06
名簿	372.527	書	092.6
名著	018.5	易	091.6
名譽		**27627 鄱**	
政治科學	372.11		

包 色 匈 幻 峒 島 卵 鄉

鄱陽湖	981.352	歷史	937.95

27712 包
包裹	636.6
包裹機	655.95

27717 色
色	231.61
色度分析法	
定量分析	545
定性分析	544.6
色球	523.76
色迷	155.458
色素	
生理化學	592.45
生理學	581.497
人體學	565.26
色毒變遷	598.545
色素遺傳	563.393
色素質	592.45
色素體	571.114
色界	231.82
色情狂	155.4583

27717 匈
匈奴	913.51
匈牙利	
文學	892.5
語言	409.235
地理	983.795
哲學	128.5

27720 幻
幻覺	156.1
幻燈攝影	758.8

27720 峒
峒	552.6
峒峽	981.36

27720 島
島嶼	
地面地質學	552.3
世界類志	980.503
中國類志	981.33

27727 卵
卵移動術	598.878

27727 鄉
鄉村	
職業教育	338.41
靜態社會學	313.4
國家統計	345.16
鄉村生活	313.4
鄉村計畫	313.41
鄉村衛生工程	653.6
鄉村經濟	350.024
鄉村住宅	718.7
鄉村道路	651.771
鄉村與城市之關係	313.48
鄉團	379.8

岷 祭 租 組 紐 紀 絕

鄉鎮	981.58
鄉鎮青年會	256.318

27747 岷
岷江	981.341

27901 祭
祭文	818.75
祭醮	223.5
祭祀	
家禮	319.25
婆羅門教	243
國禮	319.11
祭祖	319.25
祭典	291.3

27910 租
租借	377.1
租借地	381.3195
租界	381.3195

27910 組
組織	
基督教會	256.33
教育行政	331.31
國家財政	369.123
國民黨	001.22
組織主權	371.022
組織部	001.31
組織形態學	
形態學	561.17
生理與構造植物學	571.25
組織生理	581.408
組織系統	571.15
組織學	
動物學	581.1
生物學	561.2
植物學	571.1
醫學	591.2
組曲	779.4

27915 紐
紐約	984.164
紐芬蘭	984.28
紐蟲類	583.37

27917 紀
紀的	813.77
紀念	
孫中山傳記	001.198
禱文	253.795
歐洲史	930.78
普通學會	061.7
紀伊國	982.1646
紀念碑	
遺迹	991.85
城市風景	719.4
紀念藏	000
紀念日	334.36
紀念年刊	037.8
紀種論	563.9

27917 絕

絕症	595.4	綱球	338.635
絕對安隱	231.79	綱索鐵道	651.85
絕緣	657.67	綱走支廳	982.167
絕緣物	657.67	綱膜	598.343
絕對自由貿易	351.32		

27917 繩

27927 移

繩纜	659.17	移民	
繩索		殖民	377.6
織品	675.7	殖民移入	377.5
力學	531.93	生態學	581.767
		移動橋	651.57

27920 約

		移植	611.57
約西亞書	252.982	移植機	610.62
約耳書	252.47	移換	354.136
約伯記	252.31	移牙	598.275
約法	391.1	移民時代	937.981
約內	983.475		

27932 綠

約克縣	983.568	綠色蟲菌目	572.36
約翰	252.64	綠藻物綠	573.21
約翰孫		綠藻蟲菌目	572.37
英國文學	857.63		

27935 縫

美國文學	941.871	縫紉機	655.91

27940 叔

約翰啟示錄	252.88	叔本華	127.6
約翰第一書	252.794		

27947 級

約翰第二書	252.795	級數	514
約翰第三書	252.796		

27960 綹

翰書亞	252.22	綹緆	553.7
約拿書	252.492		

27920 綱

28100 以

以諾書	252.981
以西結書	252.44
以利沙伯時代	
英國詩	851.3
英國戲曲	852.3
英國散文	857.3
英國小說	853.3
以賽亞書	252.41
以太說	537.017
以太應力	537.11
以太構造	530.11
以斯達斯第一	252.91
以斯帖	252.92
以斯帖書	252.29
以斯拉	252.27
以弗所人書	252.75

28211 作

作夢	156.33
作法	241.5

28227 倫

倫理	020.18
倫理學	
佛學	231.18
哲學	180
倫理與心理	180.015
倫理與宗教	180.012
倫理與人生哲學	180.017
倫理與美學	180.019
倫巴底	983.26

28227 傷

傷痕	598.164
傷寒	594.926
傷熱	598.146
傷兵待遇	381.556

28227 伶

伶元	813.25

28245 併

併發病症	598.843

28240 微

微子綱	575.97
微生學	566.9
微積學	515
微積分	515
微數函數	516.6
微數幾何學	519.7
微數解析學	515.1
微分	516.6
微分方程式	515.71
微分方程式之幾何原理	519.71
微分方程式之積分	515.73
微分方程式之近似積分	519.73
微分幾何	519.7
微分學	515.2
微小畫像	737.33

28247 復

侮 儀 僧 從 徐 懲 鮮 艦 牧 犧 鹼

復生	581.697	從量	369.1677
復活		**28294 徐**	
自然神學	201.721	徐注	542.66
實踐神學	253.13	徐照	811.1575
基督論	251.25	徐陵	811.136
基督傳記	251.2957	**28334 懲**	
末世論	251.73	懲治	315.51
復籍	381.816	**28351 鮮**	
28255 侮		鮮卑	913.54
侮辱法令	395.08	**28417 艦**	
28255 儀		艦隊	379.64
儀式	243	**28540 牧**	
儀式方面	279.1	牧歌	801.1
儀式派	369.2	牧師	255.54
儀器		牧場	611.28
物理學	530.074	牧教	
學校管理	332.97	宗教	204
儀器畫法	731.7	祆教	284
儀器用法	542.2	神道教	291.4
儀器差法	522.88	基督教	254
28266 僧		猶太教	264
僧法經	249.3	回教	274
僧法派	249.3	牧教士之給養	254.3
僧法頌	249.3	牧教之撫恤	254.3
僧侶	246	**28553 犧**	
28281 從		犧牲	251.24
從刑	394.53	**28686 鹼**	
從價	369.1677		

鹼 收 稅 纖 繳 給 繪 縱 鱗 秋

鹼土金元素	546.22		給畫	151.38
鹼盾定量	545.1		給水	611.6
鹼質土壤	611.34		給資	354.32
鹼類	661.4		給資方法	354.347

28686 鹻

鹻金元素	546.21

28741 收

收益稅	369.151
收入與支出	369.125
收穫	611.8
收穫用具	610.64
收差	535.33
收歛級數	514.6

28916 稅

稅則
中國國家財政	369.161
國家財政	369.06

28940 纖

纖形科	578.93
纖形綱	578.9

28940 繳

繳費	334.15

28961 給

給資準則 354.34

28961 繪

繪畫
建築	712.1
美術	730
繪畫材料	731

28981 縱

縱波	534.33
縱振動	534.545
縱膈膜	597.218

29359 鱗

鱗	598.541
鱗莖類	613.13
鱗翅類	585.53
鱗蜥類	587.85

29980 秋

秋海棠科	578.65
秋田縣	982.1627

30101 空

空	231.313
空生動物	581.907
空軍	379.7
空軍行政	379.72
空軍電學	537.7
空中生物	561.907
空中攝影	758.2
空戰	930.765
空戰法規	381.57
空戰戰略	379.73
空間	134.4
空間解析幾何學	519.42
空間之知覺	151.1752
空間感覺	134.41
空間與時間	
宇宙論	134.43
相對論	530.71
空隊	379.74
空氣	
生物發生論	562.83
個人衛生	593.11
學校管理	332.38
公共衛生	593.27
空氣計	655.58
空氣療法	595.84
空氣制動機	655.51
空氣傳導	529.13
空氣清潔	593.115
空氣機	655.4
空氣熱動學	529.11
空氣成分	529.15
空氣與地土衛生	593.27
空氣與光線	593.11
空氣分析	543.61
空知支廳	982.167

30104 室

室樂	779.7
室內裝飾	763
室蘭	982.1674

30104 窒

窒息	593.43
窒寒	658.36

30104 塞

塞登(1719—？97)	842.57
塞那爾	985.178
塞子木綱	576.47
塞子木科	576.48
塞拜	931.833
塞來	983.562
塞內岡比亞	985.53
塞薩克斯	983.562
塞姆語系	409.5
塞姆語系文學	895
塞威勒	983.491
塞國	

宣 流 注 淮 濟 滴 蜜 淳 渡 液

地理	983.955
歷史	939.57

30106 宣
宣言	
國際交涉	386.43
國民黨	001.25
宣講	254.1
宣示	372.558
宣傳	001.26
宣傳部	001.32
宣戰	381.53
宣戰前敵對行爲	381.53
宣判	395.03

30113 流
流文岩	557.25
電流互相作用	537.33
流電動理	537.31
流電上磁石作用	538.84
流電學	537.2
流行病	593.237
流行腹瀉	594.937
流出	
液體動力學	532.53
氣體動力學	533.53
流動氣壓	529.2
流荒	338.962
流星	523.5
流星系	523.54
流體	536.72
流體説	537.011
流體硬固	567.2
流體保存	567.2
流體動學	531.27
流體運動	532.52
流年運氣	157.27

30114 注
注意	151.51
注射	595.815
注射法	567.3

30114 淮
淮水	981.347
淮南子(劉安)	111.23

30123 濟
濟士(1795—1821)	851.78

30127 滴
滴定法	545.1

30136 蜜
蜜蜂	585.58

30147 淳
淳仁	921.823

30147 渡
渡島國	982.1671

30147 液
液態	541.2
液體	

自然地質學	551.12	**30227 扁**		
物態變化	536.72	扁豆	613.3	
容量分析法	545.41	扁桃	613.763	
熱學	536.2	扁蟲類	538.3	
液體組織	581.28	**30227 窩**		
液體傳熱	536.418	窩哥律師	983.497	
液體比熱測定法	536.34	窩爾維克	983.564	
液體動力學	532.5	**30227 旁**		
液體結晶	559.31	旁聽	028.5	
液體動學	532.1	**30227 房**		
液體法	542.6	房中術	224.8	
液體速度	534.41	房屋		
液體流動	532.52	家政學	692	
液體混合	532.13	中國賦稅	369.151	
液體靜力學	532.3	房屋建築	651.3	
液體分離	532.13	房屋建築律	593.46	
30201 寧		房屋衛生工程	653.5	
寧夏省	981.67	房屋檢查	593.46	
30211 完		**30232 永**		
完數	512.41	永刑		
完口蓋頭	587.13	自然神學		
完全論	173.7	末世論	201.727	
完全變態類(內翅類)	586.5	神學末世論	251.79	
30227 扇		永生	201.79	
扇		自然神學		
手工業	688.4	末世論	251.79	
繪畫	735.6	神學末世論	201.79	
扇風機	655.53			

家 禳 穿 宿 戶

永久中立國	381.13

30232 家

家畜	615.1
家庭	
中國小說	813.86
小說	803.6
家庭電汽裝置	657.93
家庭預算	691
家庭制度	313.32
家庭紋章	963
家庭組織	313.32
家庭看護	699
家庭衛生	699
家庭生活	313.3
家庭經濟	350.013
家庭禱文	253.44
家庭道德	183
家庭祈禱	253.22
家庭起源	313.31
家庭獸學	599
家庭服務	258.2
家庭醫學	593.6
家庭簿記	691
家庭管理	691
家庭義務	183.9
家訓	188.3
家塾	338.82
家族	371.11
家族與國家起源	371.016
家譜	977.5
家政	
時種成人教育	338.913
普通家政	690
家政學	690
家傳	001.194
家憲	188.3
家法	319.2
家禮	319.2
家長	313.321
家具	763.2
家用花卉	613.8061
家禽	
畜產業	615.2
獸醫學	599.45

30232 禳

禳災吠陀	242.14

30241 穿

穿口蓋類	587.11

30261 宿

宿兵	379.34
宿命論	
自然神學	201.5
自然哲學	134.4
回教	271.4

30277 戶

戶外廣告	629.4

進 適 寒 避 寫 窰 憲 守 宇

戶外游戲	338.633
戶內廣告	629.5
戶內游戲	338.632

30301 進
進貢	369.147
進化論	
世界與人生	
價值	108.5
人生哲學	171.5
進口	369.1671

30302 適
適應	
生態學	581.77
心理學	151.53
適應論	
生態學	581.775
個體發育	563.197
演化論	563.7
適應與世代	563.77
適存論	564.23

30303 寒
寒武紀	554.52
寒帶動物	581.909
寒帶植物	571.909

30304 避
避電線	657.687
避電學	537.71
避綫	651.816
避日類	584.675

30327 寫
寫刻本	009.15
寫讀	338.138
寫字	151.38
寫實派	
文學	800.182
繪畫	736.3
寫本	010.1

30331 窰
窰業	666

30336 憲
憲政(31—後284)	
羅馬史	932.841
國家學	371.0483
憲政時代	
建國大綱	001.154
美國史(1789—1809)	941.84
憲法	
法律	391
中國憲法	391.1
中國國家財政	369.13
憲規	256.33

30343 守
守備與戰地工作	379.36

30401 宇
宇宙	523.1

安　宴　字

宇宙論		半島地理	982.43
形上學	134	印度支那	
佛學	231.144	半島歷史	924.3
婆羅門教	241.3	安南語	409.14
神學	231.144	安南文學	891.4
宇宙演化論	523.12	安土(織田)時代	
宇宙構造	523.11	(1573—82)	921.836
宇津保物語	823.34	安藝	982.165

30404 安

安石榴科	578.75	安如：	
安哥拉	985.58	賣內羅亞爾	983.461
安麗時代		安梯斯端列士	121.241
英國文學(1702—45)	851.5	安剝鳌阿	984.28
英國戲曲(1702—45)	852.5	安眠藥	597.863
英國散文(1702—45)	857.5	安慰	180.95
英國小說(1702—45)	853.5	安全工事	658.4
安利干信經	251.84	安全裝置	657.68
安利干修道	259.0918	安勞(1822—88)	
安利干會	259.3	英國詩	851.85
安山岩	557.26	英國散文	857.95

30404 宴

宴曲	821.7

30407 字

安息香	612.83	字源學	
安息香科	579.37	比較語言學	401.1
安徽省	981.76	中國語言	411
安房	982.1614	字相學	
安塞論	121.633	由其筆迹以	
安達盧西亞	983.38	占其命運	157.37
安南(中圻)			
印度支那			

中國十進制分類法及索引　1203

寓 究 突 牢 害 客 宮 富 容 審 寄

字書
　專門字書
　　應入各專類
字典
　專門字典
　　應入各專類
字母
　聲韻學　　　　　　414.1
　圖書館目錄　　　　012.6

30407 寓
寓言
　中國民間文學　　　814.3
　民間文學　　　　　804.3

30417 究
究竟原因論　　　　　134.2

30430 突
突厥語　　　　　　　409.26
突胸類　　　　　　　587.976

30502 牢
牢語　　　　　　　　409.122

30601 害
害物之天然敵　　　　611.995
害林　　　　　　　　614.5
害農　　　　　　　　611.9

30604 客
客勒比勇
　（1674—1762）　　842.52

客觀論　　　　　　　106.25

30606 宮
宮天挺　　　　　　　812.43
宮崎縣　　　　　　　982.166
宮城縣　　　　　　　982.1623
宮殿
　名勝古迹　　　　　981.381
　遺迹　　　　　　　991.82

30606 富
富山縣　　　　　　　982.163

30608 容
容顏　　　　　　　　668.16
容共　　　　　　　　001.174
容量分析法　　　　　545.4

30609 審
審計　　　　　　　　369.129
審計院　　　　　　　373.065
審問　　　　　　　　395.03
審判　　　　　　　　251.27

30621 寄
寄生病
　傳染病及其
　　他通行病　　　　594.97
　皮膚科　　　　　　598.547
寄生物之利用　　　　614.783
寄生菌綱　　　　　　572.23
寄屍細菌　　　　　　566.962

良 密 官 定 實

寄屍植物	571.71

30732 良
良心論	173.5

30772 密
密度	
液體靜力學	532.31
地球結構	551.16
氣體靜力學	533.31
密部	232.38
密爾頓(1608—74)	851.47
密砂岩	557.45
密縣	239.17
密土失比	981.171
密克羅尼西亞	
（細島）	
地理	985.96
歷史	959.6
密勒(1841—1913)	861.45
密執安	984.177
密蘇里	984.179

30777 官
官產	369.141
官爵	373.015
官能派	150.1911
官能心理	150.1911
官能交感神經病	598.747
官制	373.013
官業	369.142
官祿	373.016
官書	381.025
官吏	373.014
官吏之道	185.3
官規	373.012
官印	991.611
官營儲蓄銀行	362.94

30801 定
定本	009.31
定期交易	358
定期存款	262.5
定罪	251.2953
定量電流分析	545.51
定量電壓分析	545.53
定量心理	151.18
定量分析法	545
定影	755.4
定性定量分析	543
定性分析	544

30806 實
實證論	106.6
實元函數	516.11
實業	600
實業政策	
經濟制度	351.1
實業	601
實業經濟	601
實業法規	602

實 賽 寶

實業地理	980.15	實驗生理學	592.8
實業管理	603	實驗變異	563.67
實在論	106.1	實驗化學	542
實踐方面	253.73	實驗室	150.72
實踐佛學	233	實驗法	337.13
實踐道德	188	實驗心理學	150.71
實踐宗教	208	實驗演化	564.7
實踐神學		實驗邏輯	143
天主教	259.13	實驗與研究	150.71
袄教	283	實驗胎生	581.694
基督教	253	實驗胎生學	
猶太教	263	生殖學	561.67
回教	273	解剖學	591.58
普通宗教	203	胎生學	561.67
實際幾何學	519.1	實驗與測驗	535.392
實體	133.3	實錄	901.25
實體一元論	133.3	實錄物	823.66

30806 賓

| 賓禮 | 319.13 |

30806 賽

實體法	390.007	賽跑	338.634
實體觀念分析	133.2	賽船	338.637
實用主義	106.4	賽馬	798
實用氣象	529.7		
實驗			

30806 寶

邏輯各論	141.71	寶石	558.18
農業基礎科學	610.541	寶石彫琢術	558.181
實驗論	106.3	寶積部	232.34
實驗方面	538.45	寶器	968
實驗方法	371.073		
實驗研究	563.397		

宗

30901 宗

宗廟	319.116
宗譜	313.386
宗派	229
宗派史	259.09
宗祠	981.385
宗教	
總類	200
依題分	729.2
社會病理學	315.56
社會要素	311.2
殖民緣因	377.2
初民文化	565.792
宗教詩	801.2
宗教部	256.352
宗教建築	715
宗教劇	802.92
宗教紋章	962
宗教制度	205
宗教生活	
鄉村	313.1
宗教事業	208
宗教之於奴制	317.42
宗教心理學	158.2
宗教道德	058.5
宗教家傳記	200.97
宗教游藝	258.7
宗教教育	207
宗教華新前之帝國	
路易二世至	
馬克西米連一世	
（843—1519）	937.82
查理五世至馬總亞	
（1519—1618）	937.83
宗教地理	200.98
宗教娛樂	258.7
宗教起源	209.1
宗教考古	200.99
宗教地圖	200.98
宗教革興時代	
（1517—1789）	930.62
宗教書	737.5
宗教事業	208
宗教團體	206
宗教曆	528.62
宗教同盟	200.61
宗教與國家起源	371.017
宗教醫學	595.92
宗教舞	792.2
宗典	259.12
宗學	
基督教宗派	
與歷史	259.01
印度佛教—	
法祖宗	239.141
印度佛教—大乘	239.131

察 宋 竊 江 灑 瀝 汪 濕

宗義	
印度佛教—大乘	239.131
印度佛教—小乘	259.11
宗谷	982.167
30901 察	
察罕臺(1224—1369)	915.96
察哈爾省	981.943
30904 宋	
宋(960—1280)	
詞	811.73
史	911.633
文學	810.085
小說	813.51
宋刻本	009.111
宋玉(？前290—220)	811.312
宋代哲學	111.5
宋濂(1310—81)	817.612
宋之問	811.1414
宋遼金元(960—1368)	811.15
文別集	817.5
文學	810.5
韻文	811.15
詞	811.72
騷賦	811.35
駢散文	817.085
小說	813.5
宋遼金夏(960—1280)	915
宋鈃	111.155
30927 竊	
竊盜	155.452
31110 江	
江西省	981.75
江孫(1574—1637)	852.34
江戶時代(1653—1868)	
日本韻文	821.26
日本散文	827.6
日本史	921.84
日本小說	823.6
江河	
衛生及城市	
工程	653.14
世界類志	980.504
地面地質學	552.4
中國類志	981.34
江河工程	654.6
江湖派	811.1577
江蘇省	981.77
31111 灑	
灑落本	823.67
31111 瀝	
瀝青炭	558.124
31114 汪	
汪琬(1624—90)	817.722
31114 濕	
濕疹	598.542

濕 河 涉 馮 瀰 濾 汗 酒 潛 漂 源 福 顧 額 州

濕潤	611.333	酒色文學	800.1895
濕板	755.1	酒令	796
濕式分析法	544.1	酒精	664.55
濕氣	529.4	**31161 潛**	
31114 溉		潛水術	659.198
溉木	571.99	潛水艇	379.657
31120 河		**31191 漂**	
河	381.331	漂白	667.1
河北省	981.61	漂染工業	667
河流	614.113	**31196 源**	
河內	982.164	源氏物語	823.36
河南省	981.63	**31266 福**	
31121 涉		福音堂	259.87
涉禽類	587.974	福建省	981.81
31127 馮		福島縣	983.1621
馮延巳	811.715	福井縣	
馮特	127.78	九州地方	982.166
31127 瀰		中部地方	982.163
瀰漫	598.541	**31286 顧**	
31136 濾		顧伯(1731—1800)	851.65
濾水器	542.67	顧勒理治(1772—1834)	851.72
濾清	542.67	顧里治	941.885
31140 汗		顧炎武(1613—82)	817.713
汗腺病	598.546	**31686 額**	
31160 酒		額外給資	354.337
酒	664.51	額數	373.0345
酒瘋	155.456	**32000 州**	

測 淫 浙 澎 冰 添 袄

州廳	981.56
洲堵	981.387
洲渚	552.3

32100 測

測音器	534.99
測水器	654.18
測侯所	529.73
測定	657.442
電動機	657.407
直流電氣機械	657.442
測定法	534.511
測定器	565.31
測熱法	536.11
測地學	526
測量	
工程	650.9
水利工程	654.61
地形學	526.7
礦業工程	658.25
鐵道建築	651.811
測量求數法	517.6
測驗	330.17
心理學	150.77
思想或思維	151.88
人體測定學	565.32
普通心理學	151.68
勞工選擇	354.115
測光器	535.43

32114 淫

淫亂及其他	180.69
淫奔	313.3423
淫書	187.9
淫畫	187.9
淫慾	187.7

32121 浙

浙江省	981.78

32122 澎

澎湖	982.18
澎湖史	921.9

32130 冰

冰雹	
賑濟	316.913
肥料	611.913
冰島語	409.3824
冰島文學	879.24
冰島地理	983.7989
冰島史	937.989
冰河	551.76
冰河現象	551.76
冰湖	552.5
冰點	541.44

32133 添

添油	655.76
添附	381.311

32134 袄

涎 浮 叢 净 活 潘 褫 祈 逃 遞 近

袄教	280
袄教生活	288
袄教制度	285
袄教宗派	289
袄教事業	284
袄教團體	286

32141 涎
| 涎 | 597.321 |
| 涎腺生理 | 597.321 |

32147 浮
浮水車	655.332
浮岩	557.23
浮船渠	654.38
浮力	532.36
浮標	654.46
浮橋	651.577
浮萍科	575.55
浮世草紙	823.62
浮腫	598.942
浮體	532.36
浮體運動	532.57
浮尺	655.2255

32147 叢
叢論	087
叢論隨筆	086.9
叢書	080
郡邑	081.4

32157 净
净士宗
| 中國佛教 | 239.58 |
| 印度佛教 | 239.15 |

32164 活
活動攝影	758.7
活塞	655.259
活力論	
生理學	581.401
生命	562.32
活板	010.34
活期存款	362.7
活期款貨	362.5
活體解剖	592.8
活體解剖律	593.71
活火山	551.42

32169 潘
| 潘岳 | 811.1324 |

32217 褫
| 褫奪公權 | 394.53 |

32221 祈
| 祈禱會 | 253.28 |

32301 逃
| 逃亡 | 381.557 |

32301 遞
| 遞減發育 | 564.37 |

32302 近
| 近畿地方 | 982.164 |

透 巡 遁 割 業 心

近代國際法	381.093
近江國	982.164
近極星	523.86
近世商業	620.093
近世幾何學	519
近世化學	541
近世希臘文學	831.9
近世史	930.6
近世哲學史	100.93
近世拉丁文學	832.9
近世胞生學	561.63
近東問題	388.12

32302 透

透比	252.92
透視法	731.4
透支	364.2
透骨草科	579.68

32303 巡

巡迴圖書館	025.4

32306 遁

遁甲	157.5

32600 割

割讓	
殖民地	377.1
領土	381.315
割禾機	610.64

32904 業

業名錄	038
業報輪迴	241.4

33000 心

心	
血循環系解剖學	597.112
血循環系生理學	597.127
血循環系病理學	597.142
兒童智力發育	153.72
心痛	597.142
心塵論	150.167
心靈	
一元論	150.167
多元論	150.167
哲學	135.3
心靈研究	157.9
心靈歸宿	135.8
心靈之性質	135.2
心靈起源	135.7
心靈哲學	135
心平等根	241.68
心理	
音樂	770.015
基督教	250.11
婦女問題	313.3501
數學	510.015
圖書館學	020.15
心理建設	011.156
心理物理學	151.18

必 泌 滲 瀉 浪 淚 滅 減 治 冶 溶

心理測定	151.18
心理測驗	150.77
心理學	
佛學哲學	231.15
反省派	150.1975
普通心理學	150
心理學方法	371.075
心宗	239.56
心膜	597.141
心包	597.111
心算	510.75

33000 必
必然論	134.13
必修	335.5

33100 泌
泌尿生殖系	
病理學	597.64
形態學	581.16
手術	597.67
衛生學	597.63
生理學	597.62
解剖學	597.61
治療學	597.65
內科	597.6
藥學	597.66

33122 滲
滲透	
生理化學	581.493
液體法	542.64
液體動學	532.15
細胞學	561.55
滲透器	542.64
滲透壓	541.43
滲透分析法	544.5

33127 瀉
瀉病	594.93
瀉藥	597.362

33132 浪
浪漫派	736.6

33134 淚
淚器	598.346

33150 滅
滅諦	231.33

33150 減
減	511.12

33163 治
治療	566.85
治療學	595
治外法權	386.5
治安	315.184
治軍	399.4

33163 冶
冶金廠	669.17
冶金學	669

33168 溶

演　補　梁　對

溶度測定	542.62	日本文學	828.4
溶態	541.4	美國文學	868.4
溶解		演譯	142
溶態	541.43	演譯與歸納	142
液體	532.12	演劇	780
液體法	542.61	演劇團	333.33
固體與流體	536.713	演化	133.63
溶解法	542.61	演化論	563
溶解律	541.41	演化說	565.725
溶解表	541.42	演進心理	153
溶解與吸收	533.13	演進選輯	144
溶媒	541.46	**33227 補**	
溶點與沸點	541.64	補習教育	338.8
溶點與凝點	536.711	補修本	009.17
33186 演		補插法	341.17
演講		補牙	598.28
意國文學	833.84	補助費	331.45
西班牙文學	835.84	補助金	369.146
希臘文學	831.84	**33904 梁**	
拉丁文學	832.84	梁	
演講辯論會	333.54	文學	810.35
演講集	001.184	韻文	811.135
演講法	337.12	歷史	913.73
演講錄		**34100 對**	
文學	808.4	對位法	770.026
法國文學	848.4	對稱函數	512.71
英國文學	858.4	對稱行列式	512.31
中國文學	818.4	對外	001.172

洗 沈 淹 港 灌 滿 渤 法

對內	001.171
對數	510.23
對數函數	516.33
對數級數	514.43
對馬國	982.166

34111 洗

洗	542.69
洗衣	686
洗店衛生工程	653.7
洗濯	693.4

34112 沈

沈德潛	811.174
沈約	811.135
沈佺期	811.1414

34116 淹

淹溺救急法	593.41

34117 港

港務局	373.0828
港灣	980.503
港灣工程	654.3

34114 灌

灌溉	611.6
灌溉工程	654.8
灌溉斜槽及其水道	654.82
灌木	613.78

34127 滿

滿文特藏	009.81

滿族	
文學	819
語言	409.28
地理	981.91
國際問題	381.91
歷史	910.71
滿蒙問題	388.15

34127 渤

渤海	981.32

34131 法

法庭職員法	395.06
法庭判決	392.4
法理學	390.01
法術	225
法律	361.1
法律廢止	390.07
法律注釋	262.3
法律統一	373.0322
法律倫理學	390.016
法律解釋	
立法	373.032
法律	390.07
法律行為	
中國行政法	393.13
民法	397.15
法律派	269.3
法律心理學	390.015
法律社會化時代	390.095

法律教育學	390.017	國際私法	381.802
法律書	261.1	法典編纂	390.029
法律成熟時代	390.094	規法	
法律公布	390.07	工藝	642
法皇時期	932.863	郵政	636.1
法身	231.26	移住	377.6
法家	111.17	衣冠	319.404
法定犯	394.21	圖書館行政	
法源		與組織	022.2
國際私法	381.802	鐵路	633.11
法律	390.02	法國	
法克思	858.43	文學	834
法帖	739.13	語言	440
法權		建築	710.34
立法院	373.032	統計	345.34
國家主權	351.25	動物	581.934
法華部	232.32	憲法	391.134
法蘭西語	409.364	條約	387.934
法蘭西南部語	409.365	游記	983.4
法藥學	596.9	大學	338.7934
法相宗		地理	983.4
中國佛教	239.52	地圖	980.334
日本佛教	239.62	地質	550.37
印度佛教	239.14	考古	993.4
法事	157.7	植物	571.934
法典		教育	330.934
法律	390.029	哲學	124
國際法	381.029	財政	369.34

漆 漢 汝 波

歷史	934
法里森	409.383
法里森文學	879.3
法院編制法	396
法學家傳記	390.097
法醫學	
特別法規	399.7
國家醫學	593.8
法屬剛果	985.66
法人	397.12
法令	
教育行政	331.1
中國財務行政	369.121
國家財務行政	369.021
國學校行政	028.1
法性宗	239.13

34132 漆

漆	667.7
漆工	683
漆書科	578.15
漆畫	734.5
漆書	010.61
漆器	991.53

34134 漢

漢諾威後期	935.88
漢諾威時期	
專史	935.917
斷代史	935.87

漢水	981.341
漢志地理	982.79
漢志史	927.9
漢斯	983.562
漢賦	811.32

34140 汝

汝水	981.347

34147 波

波痕	553.3
波爾多黎各	
西印度群島史	947.5
西印度群島史地理	984.75
波亞都	983.491
波西美亞語	409.394
波形	534.37
波動論	534.2
波的亞	983.16
波之重疊	534.6
波克斯	983.562
波希米亞	983.796
波斯語	409.323
波斯文學	893.3
波斯地理	982.5
波斯教	280
波斯史	925
波斯哲學	115
波斯時代	951.82
波蘭語	409.393

洪　沐　淋　社

波蘭文學	889	**34210 社**	
波蘭地理	983.797	社論	040.5
波蘭史	937.97	社稷	319.112
波界	534.35	社約說	371.013
波羅的海各國史	939.7	社友	333.9
波羅的海沿岸		社風	319
各國地理	983.97	社會	
波里尼西亞	985.93	殖民緣因	377.2
波長	534.31	自然與社會環境	153.25
34181 洪		民國小說	813.85
洪亮吉	817.764	小說	803.5
洪水防護	654.67	社會疾病	368.6
洪德	851.79	社會病理學	315
洪澤湖	981.354	社會方法	314
洪都拉斯		社會調查	314
地理	984.63	社會主義	318
歷史	946.3	社會主義與學育	318.09
34190 沐		社會建設	001.158
沐浴		社會不安	312.29
外科	598.14	社會改造	312.8
修飾	319.47	社會改革	312.8
學校管理	332.33	社會要素	311
34190 淋		社會統計	314
淋巴		社會失虞	368.6
血循環系	581.415	社會行為	311.5
血液	591.75	社會生活	
淋巴腺	597.416	生態學	581.76
淋巴管	597.412	基督教	251.295

祛 禱 被 遠 達

社會解決	312.8	社會學	310
社會經濟之於奴制	317.43	社會民主主義	318.5
社會停滯	312.27	社會服務	258.3
社會變異	312.22	社會服務團	333.6
社會科學	300	社會風俗	319.7
社會保險	368.6	社會改良	312.8
社會保險與儲蓄	316.8	社會學派	390.0196
社會法	311.9	社會與家庭關係	351.167
社會心理	310.5	社會歷史與狀況	314
社會進步	312.25	社會問題	317
社會退化	312.27	社會義務	184.9
社會演化	312.1	社會主義派	350.097
社會進化	313.1		
社會遺傳	312.21		
社會運動	312.5		
社會道德	315.188		
社會清潔運動	317.8		
社會淘汰	312.23		
社會禮節	319.3		
社會教育	318.09		
社會地理	980.14		
社會起源	312.2		
社會救濟學	316		
社會勢力	113		
社會革命	312.6		
社會控制	311		
社會戰爭	318.09		
社會局	373.0823		

34231 祛
 祛痰劑   597.26

34241 禱
 禱文   253.4
 禱文研究會   253.49

34247 被
 被子植物
  古生物學   569.5
  植物學   575
 被圍時期   372.43
 被喉類   583.85

34303 遠
 遠志科   577.97
 遠東問題   388.14
 遠足   337.191

34303 達

違 造 遼 婆 染 冲 沸 清

達爾文學說	564.2	婆羅門教經典	242
達疴美	985.57	婆羅門教宗教	249
達爾尼加買内	983.492	婆羅門教神學	241.7
達梵科爾	982.39	婆羅門教哲學	241

34304 違
違禁戰鬥器	381.555	婆羅門教與他宗教	240.1

34904 染
染色

34306 造
造像	991.72	個體發育	563.14
造林學	614.4	漂染工業	667.2
造國學	613.9	顯微學	566.135
造兵廠	659.34	服裝	765.5
造鹽元素	546.13	染髮油	668.17
造幣律	361.1	染料	667.2
		染料作物	612.91

34309 遼
遼	811.158

35106 冲
文學	810.58	冲繩縣	982.166
詞	811.74	冲蝕防護	654.66
歷史	915.4		

35127 沸
駢散文	817.58	沸泉	551.5
小説	813.58		

35127 清
書籍刻本	009.113	清淨	231.79
遼寧省	981.911	清真寺	715.7

34404 婆
清

婆羅摩	242.16	文學	810.087
婆羅州	985.915	文學別集	810.7
婆羅門三大神	241.71	韻文	811.108
婆羅門神	241.72	詩別集	811.17
婆羅門教	240	騷賦	811.37

沸 決 漣 溝 油 漕 潰 凍 神

駢散文	817.7
曲	812.7
史	917
小説	813.7
書籍刻本	009.117
清代詞家	811.77
清代哲學	111.7
清寧至宣化	921.815
清初	
文學別集	810.71
詩別集	811.171
駢散文別集	817.71
哲學家	111.71
清道	
空氣與地土衛生	593.27
道路工程	651.79
清教派	259.84
清末	
文學別集	810.79
詩別集	811.179
駢散文別集	817.79
清晰法	614.41
清日之戰	921.863
清風藤科	578.26

35127 沸
| 沸點 | 536.721 |

35130 決
決然論	134.13
決鬥	797.2
決算	369.129
決算論	369.029

35130 漣
| 漣蟲類 | 584.821 |

35145 溝
| 溝渠污物及其處理 | 653.31 |
| 溝繁縷科 | 578.55 |

35160 油
油炭	558.123
油漆	766.5
油漆作物	612.97
油漆匠	651.17
油畫	734.7
油脂	668.6
油脂工業	665
油脂解析	665.1

35166 漕
| 漕運 | 634.6 |

35186 潰
潰瘍	
傳染病	594.941
普通外科	598.144

35196 凍
| 凍 | 611.911 |

35206 神
| 神 | 251.17 |

神童	153.765	神經系藥學	597.86
神論	201.1	神經組織	591.78
神話		神經官能病	
佛經故事	232.081	變態心理學	155.25
基督教	250.84	內科	597.845
彫刻	729.3	神經中樞	597.823
神話學	209.9	神經節瘤	597.819
神話學時代	921.811	神仙	
神鷹類	587.979	道教	220
神辯	251.19	迷信	319.81
神現顯論	251.18	神樂歌	821.51
神聖同盟	930.68	神我	241.09
神經	597.816	神秘書	262.5
神經病	597.846	神秘論	104.7
神經衰弱	597.844	神律	251.16
神經痙攣	597.846	神社	
神經系		宗教建築	715.91
形態學	581.18	神道教	291.6
生理學	581.46	神游	156.36
內科	597.8	神道	
神經系病理學	597.84	實踐神教	253.72
神經系手術	597.87	神道教	291.1
神經系生理	152.2	回教宗派與歷史	279.5
神經系生理學	597.82	神道制度	291.5
神經系衛生學	597.83	神道生活	291.8
神經系解剖	152.1	神道宗派	291.9
神經系解剖學	597.81	神道教	291
神經系治療學	597.85	神道事業	291.4

禮 袖 禎 連 迭 逮 迪

神奈川縣	982.161
神權說	371.011
神感化說	251.18
神咒	225.1
神學	
天主教	259.11
佛教	231
基督教	251
神醫	595.92
神學法派	390.019
神氣	157.33
神人論	251.28
神算	157.67
神性	251.14
神性論	201.3

35218 禮

禮	094
禮記	094.3
禮拜	
實踐神學	253.1
基督徒生活	258.1
禮拜設備	253.3
禮拜儀式	253.2
禮佛	233.2
禮佛設備	233.3
禮貌	
社會禮節	319.32
社會道德	184.2
禮俗	319
禮器	991.3
禮服	319.42
禮節	
社會道德	184.1
學校管理	332.2

35260 袖

袖章	960.4

35286 禎

禎翅類	585.33

35330 連

連歌	821.3
連山	091.9
連續組織	581.25
連續變異	563.62
連續光帶	535.443
連級數	
級數	514.9
數學	514
連帶適應	563.74
連鎖法	141.3

35303 迭

迭更士	853.83

35303 逮

逮捕	381.824

35306 迪

迪里斯	985.45

35308 遺

遺棄	397.51
遺產稅	369.151
遺棄之兒童	153.768
遺傳	
病因學	594.21
植物演化	571.771
犯罪學	315.161
小兒科	598.91
遺傳的適應	563.71
遺傳漸化	563.5
遺傳學	563.3
遺傳與環境	151.54
遺傳關係	311.17
遺物	
考古學	990.1
中國考古學	991
遺教	001.197
遺迹	
神學	251.2954
考古學	990.1
中國考古學	991.8
遺囑	
孫中山	001.197
國際民法	381.846
民法	397.6
遺民詩	811.157

35309 速

速度	
音之波及	534.41
物理光學	535.31
速記	626.8

36111 混

混雙作用	563.34
混亂時代	922.83
混合	669.21
混合建築	651.56
混合流體之凝	
結與氣化	536.74
混合土	651.765
混合國	371.63

36117 溫

溫度	
生態學	581.771
個人衛生	593.117
土壤學	611.335
地球	523.2
熱學	536.1
圖建築	024.7
月球	523.32
溫度計	536.13
溫度之變遷	534.45
溫度與輻射	529.17
溫度與壓力	533.38
溫庭筠	811.148
溫泉	551.5

渭 湯 瀑 濕 溴 澤 視 祝 褐 泉 禪 裸 迴

溫尼	982.667

36127 渭
渭水	981.342

36127 湯
湯傷	598.161
湯姆生	851.56

36132 瀑
瀑布	981.35

36133 濕
濕度	611.333
濕氣	593.114

36134 溴
溴	546.133

36141 澤
澤瀉科	575.36

36210 視
視病	598.345
視感覺	151.11
視覺	151.11
視覺病理	151.114
視覺特殊現象	151.115
視覺物理與特殊生理	151.112
視覺測驗	151.118
視學	331.7
視差法	522.81

36210 祝

祝詞	291.2

36227 褐
褐炭	558.122
褐藻植物	573.25

36232 泉
泉井	980.505

36256 禪
禪語	409.123
禪定	231.75
禪宗	
中國佛教	239.56
日本佛教	239.66
印度佛教	239.16

36294 裸
裸子植物	
古生物學	569.4
地層史學	554.63
顯花植物	574.1
裸麥	612.14
裸足類	587.66
裸頸類	583.535
裸喉類	583.84
裸體畫	700.13

36300 迴
迴射	536.46
迴線	535.35
迴折	534.47

迦 暹 邏 邊 還 盜 汎 泥 涅 沉 洞 潤 湖

36300 迦
  迦勒底文   252.051
  迦里亞語   409.371

36301 暹
  暹邏
    邏邏國雙胎   598.174
    文學   891.1
    語言   409.121
    佛教   239.33
    地理   982.48
    歷史   924.8

36301 邏
  邏輯各論   141
  邏輯學   140

36302 邊
  邊記   910.7
  邊疆   371.033
  邊沁   125.64
  邊際生產力說   354.314
  邊際效用   352.47

36303 還
  還童   581.698
  還俗   233.8

37107 盜
  盜竊   315.187

37110 汎
  汎神論
    自然神學   201.2
    婆羅門教   241.3

37111 泥
  泥炭   558.121
  泥土   557.522
  泥灰岩   557.565
  泥盆紀   554.55
  泥塑
    中國考古學   991.724
    彫刻   722

37111 涅
  涅槃   231.79
  涅槃部   232.35

37117 沉
  沉澱   551.7
  沉澱岩   557.55

37120 洞
  洞玄部   222.3
  洞庭部   981.351
  洞神部   222.4
  洞真部   222.2

37120 潤
  潤滑藥   597.367

37120 湖
  湖泊
    工程   654.5
    地理   980.505

潮 潤 渦 滑 溺 澳 漁 汲 沒 浸

地質學	552.5
中國地理	981.35
湖北省	981.78
湖沼植物	571.905
湖沼學	617.26
湖南省	981.74

37120 潮
潮夕	525.6

37120 潤
潤藥	597.367

37127 渦
渦蟲類	583.31

37127 滑
滑稽歌劇	802.2
滑稽劇	802.96
滑稽戲	785
滑稽本	823.69
滑動喇叭	774.7
滑車	531.94
滑距骨類	588.393
滑尺	510.76

37127 溺
溺死	593.41
溺河	552.4
溺嬰	
社會病理學	315.185
静態社會學	313.36
溺斃復蘇法	593.41

37134 澳
澳大利亞	
地理	985.93
歷史	959.3

37136 漁
漁船	617.6
漁業	
財政學	369.142
農業	617
漁業政策	617.1
漁業經濟	617.1
漁業問題	388.65
漁澤文學	800.1891
漁洋派	811.173
漁場	614.93
漁具	617.6

37147 汲
汲水機	655.37

37147 沒
沒收	
刑法	394.53
國家財政	369.145
沒藥	612.83

37147 浸
浸禮會	259.6
浸蝕	

澱 沿 溜 洛 凝 深 祖 冠 寇 祀 初 祠 修

森林	614.115	37214 冠	
地震學	551.7	冠禮	319.21
37147 澱		冠帽	693.3
澱粉	612.68	**37214 寇**	
澱粉工業	664.2	寇準	811.1515
澱粉作物	612.6	**37217 祀**	
澱粉類	547.83	祀孔	319.118
37161 沿		**37220 初**	
沿海河爾卑斯	983.497	初級讀本	418.5
37162 溜		初級中學	338.31
溜冰	338.637	初民風俗	
37164 洛		禮俗	319.9
洛塞諦	851.84	人類學	565.795
37181 凝		初民文化	565.79
凝結		初民物質生活	565.791
實驗化學	542.65	初民家庭生活	565.793
光學	536.728	初民社會	313.2
凝固	536.715	初民社會生活	565.795
凝汽器	655.259	初民社會游戲	565.795
凝灰岩	557.22	初民與初民關係	565.799
37194 深		初民精神生活	565.792
深海	617.57	初等婦女教育	338.914
深成岩	557.3	初等小學	338.21
37210 祖		**37220 祠**	
祖師	239.133	祠堂	991.846
祖先崇拜	209.5	**37222 修**	
祖先遺傳律	563.36	修道會歷史	259.091

逸 通 過 週 退 運

37301 逸
逸書
書 092.9
善本特藏 009.6
善本書目 019.6
逸周書 092.9
逸篇 093.9

37302 通
通商條約 387.1
通信 040.5
通信販賣 622.57
通行狀 381.5583
通告
外交 386.45
檔案 339.95
通俗著述 252.083
通過稅 369.1675
通姦 313.3423
通古斯語 409.28
通史 910.9
通則 141.75
通風
工程 658.41
家政 692
勞工 354.55
通氣
基督教 256.32
圖書館學 024.7

通知
國際法 381.025
銀行 362.5
通鑑紀事本末 910.918
通常舞 792.3

37302 過
過敏 597.8456
過產與恐慌 352.71

37302 週
週期 594.23
週期磁變 538.751
週期律 541.09
週期變化論 536.63
週期變差 529.81
週期流電 537.25
週期曲線 534.531

37373 退
退位 373.011
退化
動物學 581.696
植物學 571.777
退化論
系統與比較生物學 561.78
演化論 563.8
退熱劑 597.466

37305 運
運動
自然地質學 551.17

逢　選

動學	531.21	運河	
演化論	563.924	世界類志	980.504
內科	597.465	中國類志	981.34
本體論	133.63	領土	381.37
人類學	565.42	運河工程	654.7
分子與個體力學	531.691	運送法	398.45
普通心理學	151.3	運輸	
運動病理	151.34	實業	630
運動系	597.7	陸軍	379.58
運動系病理學	597.74	鐵路	633.5
運動系解剖學	597.71	運輸建築	717.6
運動系生理學	597.72	運輸機	655.85
運動系治療學	597.75	運輸用具	610.66
運動系藥學	597.76	運輸公司	634.3
運動系手術	597.77	運分學	515.6
運動種類	151.35	運煤機	655.86

37305 逢

逢沙	842.82

37305 選

運動生理	151.32
運動官能	151.3
運動之知覺	151.1754
運動傷	338.639
運動場及設備	
體育學校	338.639
學校管理	332.91
運動與皮膚系	581.17
運動會	
游藝	793
學校	338.634
學校生活	333.35

選種	611.5
選修	335.6
選本	418.7
選擇	151.51
選擇終止	563.195
選擇與保存	563.11
選購	023.1
選舉	
政府	373.0341

追 軍

國民	372.553	軍事訓練	332.6
國民黨	001.245	軍事行政	379.3
民權主義	001.131	軍事條約	387.4
選舉改善問題	372.58	軍事偵探	379.36
選舉票	372.55	軍事動員	379.36
選舉法	614.41	軍事佔領	381.551
選舉權	372.5	軍事法庭	379.31
選舉院	372.56	軍事家傳記	379.097
選民	251.49	軍事演習	379.36
選鑛	658.9	軍事巡哨	379.36

37307 追

追尊	319.17

軍事地理	
軍事學	379.089
地理	980.175

37506 軍

軍廠	379.377	軍事教育	379.07
軍需	379.37	軍事防禦	379.36
軍政部	373.053	軍事學	379.1
軍政時期	001.152	軍事與社會	379.019
軍縮問題	388.82	軍事與國家	379.019
軍備	379.32	軍事問題	388.8
軍備研究委員會	383.53	軍操	338.631
軍備問題	388.81	軍國主義	379.011
軍徽	379.38	軍服	
軍官	379.33	軍事學	379.393
軍官學校	379.07	禮俗	319.44
軍法	379.31	軍用飛機	386.5
軍禮	319.15	軍用信號	659.37
軍械	379.375	軍用橋	651.5027
軍械問題	388.87	軍用地質學	556.2

朗 冥 資 塗 汽 汾

軍用品	379.37	教員	336.2
軍用道路	659.36	國民黨	001.241
軍隊		資本	355
外交	386.5	資本問題	388.63
軍事學	379.54	資本金	362.4
軍令	379.31	資本主義	355
軍人生活	379.39	**38104 塗**	
軍餉	379.372	塗料	668.8
軍符	379.38	**38117 汽**	
軍糧	379.371	汽力發電	657.221
37720 朗		汽力發電所	655.23
朗詠集	821.55	汽機	
朗吉德	983.495	機車	655.274
朗格蘭	851.21	種類及構造	655.25
朗匪羅	861.31	汽機工程	655.2
37800 冥		汽機洗衣	686
冥界		汽車	
沃教	281.6	自動車工程	659.71
道教	221.6	道路	632.6
基督教	251.6	汽輪機	655.295
猶太教	261.6	汽罐	655.225
回教	271.6	汽鍋	
37806 資		船舶機械	659.163
資方手段	354.85	汽機工程	655.22
資方法權	354.16	構造種類	655.225
資治通鑑	910.915	汽筒	655.259
資格		**38127 汾**	
政府	373.0341	汾水	981.342

滋 冷 游 洋 海

38132 滋

滋賀縣	982.164
滋養	
生理化學	592.47
微生學	566.922
小兒衛生	598.93
滋養物	571.42
滋養缺乏	592.471

38137 冷

冷熱之關係	592.58

38147 游

游水類	588.47
游子	537.372
游子輻射	537.375

38151 洋

洋琵琶	775.2

38155 海

海底	637.2
海底電信	
電報	657.837
傳電	657.653
海商法	398.7
海爾投票法	372.527
海王星	523.48
海百合類	582.95
海豕類	588.42
海上衛生	593.34
海上衝突	381.73
海上自由	388.77
海上保險	
保險	368.2
海上法	381.76
海上法	381.7
海上開放	381.71
海上鎖閉	381.71
海岸工程	654.2
海岸石垣	654.2
海參類	582.94
海峽	
世界類志	980.502
中國類志	981.32
海牛類	588.4
海綿動物	582.5
海得拉巴	982.39
海象類	588.533
海豹類	588.537
海船失虞救護	381.75
海濱	593.112
海濱山澗住宅	718.8
海濱植物	571.904
海濱畫	737.11
海運	634.7
海軍	279.6
海盜	
游記	980.707

滄 涂 複

海上法	381.79	海蜘蛛類	584.63
海軍行政	379.62	海貍類	588.611
海潮利用發電	657.27	海景	737.11
海軍戰略	379.63	海因立哈	871.23
海洋		海賊	980.707
地面地質學	552.2	海戰	980.763
世界類志	980.502	海戰法規	381.56
中國類志	981.32	海驢類	588.535
捕魚	617.55	海氏量子力學	530.75
海道記	827.45	海陸軍工程	659.3
海洋生物	561.904	海陸軍衛生	593.35
海洋生活	980.707	海陸軍外科	598.195
海洋魚類學	587.49	海陸軍法	399.5
海洋冰河	551.78	海陸軍青年會	256.36
海洋地理	980.113	海關	
海洋植物	571.904	中國關稅	369.67
海洋地圖	580.306	普通關稅	369.06
海洋時代	554.2	海巴特	127.73
海洋地震	551.38	海盤車類	582.91
海洋火山	551.48	海膽類	582.93

38167 滄

滄龍類	587.851

海奈	871.75		
海斯行列式	512.24		
海地			
西印度群島史	947.4		
西印度群島地理	984.34		

38185 涂

涂瑞朵函類	516.87

38247 複

複元函數	516.13
複細胞動物	582.6
複寫板	747

海林禽類	582.98
海蕾類	582.99
海桐花科	577.75

祥　送　逆　游

複決	
立法	373.032
民權主義	001.13
複決權	372.19
複本位	361.22
複振動之解析	534.535
複振動之投射	534.537
複數論	512.61
複數範圍	519.67
複數光帶	535.447
複關	369.1615
複簧樂器	774.4

38251 祥

祥瑞	157.17

38303 送

送風機	655.53

38304 逆

逆療法	595.73
逆河	552.4
逆匯	365
逆反原理	536.64

38304 游

游記文學	
總類	808.8
法國	848.8
英國	858.8
中國	818.8
美國	868.8

游記日記	
總類	808.8
法國	848.8
英國	858.8
中國	818.8
美國	868.8
游記回憶錄	
總記	808.8
法國	848.8
英國	858.8
中國	818.8
美國	868.8
游記筆記	
英國	858.8
中國	818.8
美國	868.8
游記小記	813.828
游子遷移	539.374
游戲	
基督教青年會	256.35
兒童訓練	354.57
兒童	313.362
游戲道德	189.7
游泳	338.637
游泳池	338.639
游女	319.77
游藝	
鄉村	313.47

蒙學教育	338.134		道教與道家	220.11
普通	790		道教與其他宗教	220.12
游藝建築	717.8		道教與醫術	220.16
游藝力學	531.37		道書	222
游覽指南	980.703		道成人身	251.21
游藝會	333.3		道路	632
游擊	381.554		道路工程	651.7
			道路維持與修補	651.78
			道路種類	651.76

38306 道

道諦	231.34
道爾頓制	337.33
道德	
宗教	311.28
森林	614.125
婦女	313.3502
報學	040.18
道德薄弱	155.45
道德哲學	180
道家	111.12
道宮	227
道士	226
道藏	222
道場	223.5
道教	220
道教建築	715.2
道教與文化	220.19
道教與科學	220.15
道教與個人	220.17
道教與社會政治	220.13

38343 導

導演	
音樂演奏	760.029
戲劇表演	781.6
導管生理	581.45
導火線	663.3

38604 啓

啓示	252.01
啓示錄	252.8
啓發	337.14
啓事	339.25

39120 沙

沙摩吠陀	242.13
沙多勃良	843.65
沙漠	552.7
沙對	841.21
沙漠荒地之灌漑	654.85
沙都	842.86
沙普郎	841.44

39127 消

消元法	512.39
消化系	
生理與構造動物學	581.13
內科	597.3
消化系病理學	597.34
消化系手術	597.37
消化系衛生學	597.33
消化系生理學	597.32
消化系解剖學	597.31
消化系治療學	597.35
消化系醫學	597.36
消毒	566.968
消毒法	593.236
消費論	357
消費合作	356.73
消費與恐慌	352.72

39189 淡

淡水	617.51
淡水生物	561.905
淡水植物	571.905
淡路國	982.1645

39309 迷

迷魂符	157.75
迷迭香	612.813
迷狂病	155.252
迷狂症	597.845
迷信	319.8

40000 十

十六夜日記	827.44
十六國	913.58
十誡	262.9
十一經	090.5
十二經	090.6
十二使徒教訓	252.997
十二緣起	231.5
十二進算術	510.72
十二宮	157.23
十二支派約書	252.984
十三經	090.7
十翼	091.73
十進算術	510.71
十字軍時代（1096—1270）	
	930.57
十字花科	577.57
十字架	253.31
十七史	910.94
十史	910.93
十國（907—979）	914.9
十四行詩	801.8
十脚類	584.827
十八史	910.95

40000 X

X—光線	535.53
X 光線診斷	595.277

40000 叉

左 九 力 大

叉頭	655.259	大衍	512
叉角羚類	588.334	大衛詩篇	272.3
叉棘	681.75	大便	597.327
40011 左		大代數	512.6
左傳	096.1	大俄	983.86
左拉(1840—1902)	843.86	大彼得(俄帝)	
左思	811.1325	(1689—1725)	938.84
左羅亞斯德	281.2	大仲馬(1806—70)	843.75
40017 九		大使	386.33
九經	090.4	大和物語	823.33
九樂合奏	779.7	大和草科	577.19
九宮	157.4	大和國	982.1642
九州地方	982.166	大蟹鈞	612.275
九九表	510.211	大社	291.9
40027 力		大湖問題	388.35
力學	531	大洋洲	
40030 大		經濟史	350.95
大麻	612.52	佛教	239.9
大正(1912—26)	921.87	叢書	085
大豆	612.33	游記	980.75
大西洋諸州	984.16	地理	985.9
大粟草	612.24	歷史	959
大理岩	557.46	年鑑	037.5
大理院	373.04	類志	980.55
大乘	239.12	大喪	319.17
大乘經	232.3	大麥	612.16
大乘律	232.5	大斯馬尼亞	985.9395
大集	232.36	大戟科	577.98

太

大戴禮	094.4
大花草科	576.92
大英史	935
大翅類	585.33
大蝙蝠類	588.91
大農制	610.312
大提琴	775.6
大甲類	584.88
大衆部	239.113
大戰(世界)	930
大阪府	982.164
大區選舉制	372.526
大歷十才子	811.1451
大陸	552.1
大陸生物	561.902
大陸冰河	551.77
大陸地震	551.37
大陸火山	551.47
大腸	597.327
大隅國	982.166
大閱	319.15
大學	
特種人教育	338.917
大學教育	338.71
四書	098.1
普通圖書館	025.21
大學教育	338.7
大學教授法	337.7
大氣	
自然地質學	551.94
氣體	533.7
生理與構造動物學	581.7771
大氣高度	529.16
大氣物理學	529.1
大氣污物	653.37
大氣灰塵	529.14
大氣壓力	533.381
大氣光帶	535.47
大分縣	982.1666

40030 太

太虛	134.4
太平天國史	917.991
太平洋諸州	984.19
太平洋問題	388.19
太乙	157.5
太上道君	221.12
太上老君(老子)	221.13
太空	523.15
太空溫度	523.15
太空中天體位置	521.24
太空中軌道平面	521.21
太湖	981.353
太陽	
律曆	522.4
陰陽五行	157.211
叙述天文學	523.7

中國十進制分類法及索引

夾 友 土

太陽系	523.2	土佐國	982.165
太陽經緯	521.5	土佐日記	827.31
太陽系之太空運動	523.24	土俑	991.724
太陽系之構成	523.26	土之崇拜	209.23
太陽系固定論	523.27	土木工程	651
太陽利用發電	657.28	土壤	
太陽中心	521.2	森林經濟	614.112
太陽蟲類	582.17	人種學	565.773
太陰	157.213	分析化學	543.21
40038 夾		土壤生產力	611.35
夾板	598.1903	土壤細菌學	611.36
夾竹桃科	579.45	土壤種類	611.34
40047 友		土壤測驗	611.37
友誼	180.62	土壤學	611.3
友愛	180.62	土葬	319.24
40100 土		土地	
土	770.12	經濟學	353
土產	369.151	政治科學	371.026
土謝圖汗部	981.952	國家財政	369.141
土工術	651.14	土地主權	371.022
土耳其		土地生產與人工	353.6
文學	892.6	土地生產與自然	353.5
語言	409.26	土地生產漸減律	353.7
征服時代	931.87	土地租期	353.4
哲學	116	土地權	381.821
斯坦地理	982.59	土地局	373.0736
地理	982.6	市政	373.0822
歷史	926	縣政	373.0836

士 圭 臺 查 直 堆 境 壞

土狼類	588.514
土星	523.46
土器	
窰業	666.15
考古學	990.14
中國考古學	991.4
土器文	990.814
土屬鑛	558.16
土瓶草科	577.73

40100 士
士師記	252.23
士禮	094.2

40101 圭
圭也	983.492

40104 臺
臺北州	982.171
臺岐	982.1664
臺灣	
文學	829
地理	982.17
臺南州	981.174
臺架工事	651.135
臺東廳	082.176
臺中州	982.173
臺閣體	811.163

40106 查
查忒敦(1752—70)	851.63

40107 直

直線運動	531.221
直線投影	519.36
直流	
電動機	657.42
變壓機	656.43
直流發電機	657.446
直流電動機	657.447
直流電氣機械	657.44
直流系統	657.631
直流變壓機	657.448
直進演化	564.6
直游類	583.36
直翅類	585.31
直接交涉	382.22
直接談判	386.41
直播	614.483
直蜘蛛類	584.673
直腸	597.345
直覺	151.9
直覺論	173.5
直覺類	585.837
直知論	104.3

40114 堆
堆棧	625

40116 境
境界	981.37

40132 壞
壞疽	

培 才 麥 四 堯 獞 克 内

病理學	594.85
外科	598.145
壞血病	597.349

40161 培
培爾(1723—1842)	843.71
培根	125.1

40200 才
才子	153.9
才力測驗	150.77

40227 麥
麥爾伯蘭基	124.21
麥肯基(1715—1831)	853.65
麥塞法	675.07
麥酒釀造	664.53
麥南德	831.29
麥蕈	613.5
麥地奇(1448—92)	833.123
麥加	982.76
麥加利	983.16
麥里美(1803—70)	843.81

40210 四
| 四季風 | 529.31 |

40211 堯
| 堯典 | 092.71 |

40214 獞
| 獞 | 910.77 |

40216 克
克瓦丁	984.27
克雷明	121.624
克己論	173.4
克利西波士	121.525
克什米爾	982.38
克留斯	983.488
克汀病	594.996
克洛卜斯托克(1724—1803)	871.62
克力非蘭 (第一任)	941.876
（第二任）	941.878
克力門士(1835—1910)	863.42
克藍(1644—99)	852.43
克拉士	121.37
克陵底士	121.523

40227 内
内摩擦力	
液體	532.17
氣體	533.17
内部或組織呼吸	597.227
内部分泌	587.447
内耳	598.449
内子目	572.27
内務部	373.051
内科	597
内債	369.181

肉　布　希

內寄生蟲	594.972
內蒙古	981.94
內布拉斯加	984.182
內地稅	369.165
內華達	984.193
內葉器官	591.54
內熱反應	536.55
內戰	381.17
內明	232.085
內障	598.344
內肛類	583.81
內丹	224.1
內閣制	373.0505
內分泌心理	150.1971
內斜層	553.6
內省法	150.172
內燃機	655.43

40227 肉

肉	593.128
肉齒類	588.55
肉荳蔻科	577.44
肉相	157.35
肉體與靈體	251.37
肉胞子蟲類	582.28
肉食	694.1

40227 布

布施	231.71
布哥維亞	983.796
布大南	841.859
布郎(1771—1810)	863.22
布勒塔尼	983.461
布加利亞	
地理	983.957
歷史	939.58
布勒斯特里	
(1612—72)	861.12
布邦復辟時代	
(1814—86)	933.86
布頓安(1794—1878)	861.33
布里敦島	984.28
布氏對數	510.27
布爾佛爾	983.564

40227 希

希西阿(？前776)	831.32
希比亞士	121.223
希伯來	
地理	982.85
哲學	118.5
希伯來文	252.053
希伯來語	409.55
希伯來主日	253.191
希伯來教	260
希伯來哲學	121.66
希伯來人書	252.787
希得曼	851.12
希土金元素	546.26

有

希羅多德		有生物與無生物	562.81
（前？484—425）	831.881	有觸手類	582.771
希臘		有獎儲蓄	362.91
文學	831	有鱗類	587.85
地理	983.1	有害的	357.7
哲學	121	有害動物	581.8
歷史	121.09	[有]之自然性	133.1
歷史	937	[有]之超驗性	133.8
希臘文	252.057	[有]之觀急分析	133.2
希臘語	409.341	[有]之屬性	133.1
希臘多島	983.18	有椎類	585.58
希臘復存時期		有機方面	563.192
（1204—1453）	931.865	有機岩	557.57
希臘哲學與近世思想	121.03	有機物	593.92
希臘哲學與希臘		有機化學	547
人生之關係	121.01	有機化學藥品	661.9
希臘羅馬哲學	121.5	有機物分析	543.7
希臘法理派	390.0192	有機液態	541.21
		有機感應	151.16
40227 有		有機體說	371.014
有		有機無機物質	
佛學	231.53	比較論	592.15
哲學	133.61	有蹄類	588.33
有函類	587.2	有肺類	583.537
有孔類	582.13	[有]與其超驗	
有環類	583.6	性之區別	133.81
有瓜類	584.2	有限差法	515.5
有袋類	588.22	有關節類	588.95
有生代	554.3		

巾 南 皮

有尾類	587.67
有益動物	581.8
有益的或生產的	357.3
有劍類	585.58
有性生殖	
系統與比較生物學	561.62
生理與構造	571.63
生理與構造動物學	581.62

40227 巾
巾箱本	010.46

40227 南
南唐(933—975)	914.99
南方佛教—	
宗教與歷史	239.3
南亞語	409.17
南非地理	985.7
南北朝(420—589)	913.6
南北極	
地理	905.99
歷史	959.9
南北極光	523.57
南監本	009.17
南卡羅林納	984.168
南山宗	239.54
南俄	983.88
南島語	409.18
南涼(鮮卑)(397—414)	
	913.593
南宋(1127—1280)	
韻文	811.157
詞	911.739
南宋史	915.3
中國文學	810.57
駢散文	817.57
南澳	985.937
南冰洋	
大洋洲史	959.91
大洋洲地理	985.991
南漢(916—971)	914.96
南達科他	984.183
南海	981.32
南洋群島	
地理	985.91
歷史	959.1
南圻	924.2
南斯拉夫	939.55
南菜科	579.56
南朝(420—589)	913.7
南瓜	613.23
南美洲	
地理	984.8
歷史	948
南美有蹄類	588.39

40247 皮
皮膚滋潤品	668.12
皮爾司	941.859

皮翼類	588.81	**40331 赤**		
皮維廉(1759—1806)	858.46	赤疾	095.938	
皮膚病理學	598.54	赤化主義	318.7	
皮膚放射	592.52	赤緯表	157.25	
皮膚診斷法	595.22	赤血球	597.1211	
皮膚科	598.5	赤道	523.4	
皮膚解剖學	598.51	赤本	823.64	
皮膚生理學	598.52	赤貧	338.963	
皮膚組織		赤鐵科	579.31	
生理與構造動物學	581.23	赤光星	523.83	
解剖學	591.77	**40331 志**		
皮膚科手術	598.57	志摩國	983.1648	
皮膚科器件	598.58	志留紀	554.54	
皮膚衛生學	598.53	**40400 女**		
皮膚治療學	598.55	女童	153.775	
皮膚蒸發	592.52	女童子軍	313.67	
皮鞋	673	女傳教士	255.57	
皮革與皮革製品	673	女修道	259.0919	
皮日休(？—881)	811.1485	傳教事業	254.5	
皮脂囊腫	594.993	基督教宗派	259.0919	
皮脂腺病	598.543	女服	319.41	
皮隆(1689—1773)	842.55	女醫學校	590.078	
皮各克(1785—1866)	853.76	女陰	598.746	
皮箱	673	**40401 寺**		
40237 存		寺	235.8	
存放	398.41	寺院	991.84	
存票	362.5	**40401 幸**		
存款	362.5			

支 李 嫉 嘉 韋 難 加 古

幸福論	173.8

40407 支
支票	364.2
支配力	562.36
支派	
法相宗	239.148
法性宗	239.138
支氣管	597.213

40407 李
李	613.723
李商隱(813—858)	811.1483
李諾維	124.56
李維(前56—後17)	832.884
李白(699—762)	811.143
李溫士教(1723—90)	861.15
李存勖(885—926)	811.714
李易安(1082?—1140)	871.7391
李氏時代(1392—1910)	922.86
(後鮮朝)	
李煜	811.715

40434 嫉
嫉妬	180.67

40468 嘉
嘉立克(1716—79)	852.61
嘉禮	319.12
嘉菲爾	941.874

40506 韋

韋應物	811.1452
韋白斯特(1758—1843)	867.22
韋莊	811.717

40514 難
難解問題	517.8

40600 加
加士他牟尼	982.661

40600 古
古文	739.171
古文聖經	352.05
古文佛經	232.05
古文字學	419
語言文字學	401.9
考古學	990.8
中國語言文字學	419
史料	901.1
古玉	
石	991.31
遺物	990.13
古爾的斯丹	982.667
古瑟爾時期	
（—前59）	934.811
古刻本	
善本特藏	009.1
善本書目	019.1
古磚	991.41
古硯	991.36
古磁	991.44

吉

古代	319.409	古波斯語	409.322
古代		古淘	991.43
哲學	121.1	古柯科	577.9
歷史	100.91	古地理	
國際法	381.091	地理	980.091
日曆	528.6	中國地理	981.091
歷史	930.4	古生物學	569.1
兵器	379.9	古史	921.815
公文	901.1	古事記	291.24
古代商業	626.091	古猿類	589.51
古代動物	580.091	古典語	409.34
古代法時代	390.091	古典派	
古代基督教哲學	121.6	經濟學	350.093
古動物學	569.6	繪畫	736.5
古貘類	588.345	古里野(1772—1825)	847.63
古生代	534.5	古兵	991.26
古生物顯微學	566.29	古印	991.61
古生物學	569	古巴	947.1
古泉	991.24	西印度群島地理	984.71
古物修理	990.079	西印度群島史	947.1
古物保存	990.079	古鏡	991.27
古物採集	990.074	古普魯士語	409.369
古物學	991	古鉢	991.61
古物陳列	990.079	**40601 吉**	
古鳥類	587.91	吉爾貝群島	985.968
古寫本		吉禮	319.11
善本特藏	009.3	吉林省	981.913
善本書目	019.3	吉本(1737—94)	857.67

奢 喜 杏 奇 壽 七 袁 喪 真

吉金		七寶	764
考古學	990.12	七才子	811.166
中國考古學	991.2	七葉樹科	578.24
吉普斯語	409.318		

40604 奢

| 奢侈的 | 357.5 |
| 奢侈稅 | 369.157 |

40732 袁

袁宏道	811.167
袁枚(1716—97)	
駢文	817.762
小說	813.76

40605 喜

喜望峯眼子菜科	575.34
喜爾得布藍斯歌	871.11
喜信會	259.88
喜劇	
悲劇	782.2
戲曲	802.94
喜懼反常	155.7

40732 喪

喪失	180.93
喪禮	319.24
喪葬	253.793

40609 杏

| 杏 | 613.721 |
| 杏仁 | 613.765 |

40801 真

真	
教義	281.13
本體論	133.86
真言宗(密宗)	
中國佛教	239.57
日本佛教	239.67
真死徵	592.11
真水母類	582.73
真珠	558.188
真黏液菌綱	572.25
真偽	180.3
真德秀(1178—1235)	817.578
真細菌目	572.12
真鳥類	587.92
真空	533.37

40621 奇

奇卜察克(1238—83)	915.95
奇特	009.65
奇蹄類	588.34

40641 壽

| 壽禮 | 319.23 |

40710 七

| 七經 | 090.3 |
| 七樂合奏 | 779.7 |

中國十進制分類法及索引 | 1249

走 賣 木

真實	180.72
真空汲洞及機械	655.56
真實與謬誤	131.5
真[有]之超驗性	133.86
真鞭毛蟲類	582.31
真菌植物	573.3
真囊子菌綱	573.33
真蜘蛛類	584.65
真口類	587.47
真足類	584.3
真獸類	588.2
真與誤	141.4
真人	221.3

40801 走
走禽類	587.93

40806 賣
賣淫	187.8
賣內	983.463
賣索爾	982.39
賣藝	319.75
賣藥	596.75

40900 木
木	
香料作物	612.817
道路工程	651.75
中國音樂	770.14
木麻黃科	576.21
木工	681
木爾西亞	983.38
木工術	651.15
木耳目	573.35
木柴	663.7
木灰畫	733.1
木製品	672
木偶	991.723
木魚	
佛教設備	233.3
中國音樂	770.14
木船構造	659.114
木造	651.115
木通科	577.37
木橋	651.5015
木板	010.31
板刻	741
印本	010.31
木蘭科	577.41
木材乾溜	668.5
木星	523.45
木器	766
木匠	651.15
木彫	723
木質纖維紙	674.6
木犀科	579.41
木犀草科	577.58
木錦科	578.47
木簡	010.15

奈 索 來 柱 樟 檀 柿 樟 校

木管樂器	774	道教	221.7
木料		基督教	251.7
工程	650.45	猶太教	261.7
製造工業	670	回教	271.7

40901 奈
奈良縣	982.164

40903 索
索引	
字典	020.36
普通百科辭書	036
索引檢字法	027.9
索福客士（前？495—406）	
	831.22
索法拉	989.73
索羅內亞爾	983.475
索薪	354.32
索馬蘭	980.41
索美	983.466

40408 來
來自星球論	562.77
來布尼茲	127.1
來世	
自然神學	201.78
末世論	251.79
來世論	
自然神學	201.7
沃教	281.7
婆羅門教哲學	241.77

40914 柱
柱墩	713.2

40914 樟
樟油	665.2

40917 檀
檀香	612.817
檀香綱	576.8

40927 柿
柿樹綱	579.3

40946 樟
樟科	577.45

40948 校
校章	339.1
校產	331.6
校旗	334.83
校歌	
歌曲	771.5
學則	334.85
校務長	331.354
校刊	028.9
校外教授法	337.19
校徽	334.8
校友會	333.7

核 森 堰 壚 圬 狂 獼 帖 頗

校址	331.6
校董	331.352
校勘	
統計法	341.16
圖書學	010.97
校史	339.9
校規	
圖書館管理	028.2
學校管理	332.1
校日	
學生生活	333.41
學期	334.35
校長	331.353
校風	332.1
校服	334.87
校醫	332.3

40982 核
核	614.77
核計	369.129
核果類	613.72

40994 森
森林	
工程	614.2
地理	614.38
經濟	614.1
利用	614.7
牧場	614.92
植物學	614.3
農業	614
國家財政	369.141
顯微學	566.63
分佈	614.38
分類	614.6
森書	242.3

41114 堰
堰	654.68

41117 壚
壚坶	557.567

41127 圬
圬工	651.17

41214 狂
狂句	828.2
狂詩	828.2
狂歌	828.2

41227 獼
獼猴桃科	578.51
獼猴類	589.57

41260 帖
帖撒利	983.16
帖撒羅尼迦人後	252.782
帖撒羅尼迦人前	252.781

41286 頗
頗普（1688—1744）	
詩	851.53
散文	857.55

麵 鞭 枇 柱 極 概 桓 柯 桁 枥 樗 桿 棹 板 柘 梧 楷

41406 麵	
麵包果	613.745
麵粉製造	677
41546 鞭	
鞭毛蟲類	582.3
41910 枇	
枇杷	613.717
41914 柱	
柱德	983.491
41914 極	
極大極小論	
幾何學	517.38
微積分	515.77
大代數	512.77
極光	
氣象學	529.55
光學	535.47
41914 概	
概念	151.81
41916 桓	
桓寬	111.24
41920 柯	
柯辛	124.54
柯雷(1618—67)	851.46
柯奈耶(1606—84)	842.41
柯林士(1721—59)	851.57
柯基拉(1421—1510)	841.23
柯楓	
詩	841.85
戲曲	842.88
41921 桁	
桁樑	651.51
桁樑橋	651.51
41927 枥	
枥木縣	982.1619
41927 樗	
樗科	577.93
41940 桿	
桿秤	531.91
桿狀細菌科	572.121
41946 棹	
棹	332.93
41947 板	
板刻	740
板球	338.635
板岩	557.44
板鰓類	587.4
板畫	740
板書	010.11
41960 柘	
柘榴	613.776
41961 梧	
梧桐科	578.48
41962 楷	

標 刈 壎 獵 狐 荊 姚 妖 婚 斯

楷書	739.174
41991 標	
標記(造林)	614.45
標準	528.57
標本	
裝置	567.5
保存	567.8
採集	567.6
採集指南	567
陳列	567.7
標題音樂	779.6
標點法	416.4
標題目錄	012.4
標鎗	338.634
42000 刈	
刈草機	610.64
42131 壎	
壎	770.12
42216 獵	
獵鳥	619.2
獵獸	619.1
42230 狐	
狐猴類	589.3
42400 荊	
荊南(924—963)	914.97
42413 姚	
姚鼐(1731—1815)	817.743
42434 妖	
妖孽	157.79
妖精	157.77
妖怪	157.77
42464 婚	
婚約	313.344
法律	397.51
靜態社會學	313.314
婚姻	
講經	253.791
聖禮	253.95
制度	313.341
婚姻率	349.071
婚姻與國籍	381.813
婚體	319.22
42821 斯	
斯文本(1837—1909)	851.87
斯科夫拉病	594.995
斯時拉圖	121.43
斯多亞派	121.52
斯條亞	125.65
斯賓諾莎	128.1
斯密司(1771—1845)	857.72
斯賓塞	
文學	851.31
哲學	125.7
斯達佛	983.564
斯達埃爾夫人	

刹 札 桃 橙 橋 機

（1766—1817）	843.62
斯柏薛包士	121.33
斯忒德曼	
（1833—1908）	861.43
斯坎第那維亞	
文學	879.2
語言	409
地理	983.798
歷史	937.98
斯拉夫族	
文學	889
語言	409.39
法律	390.7
斯托德(1825—1903)	861.41
斯提爾(1671—1729)	857.53
斯氏波動力學	530.75
斯尉夫特	
（1667—1745）	853.53
斯巴達(前404—362)	931.833

42900 刹
刹洛波	983.564

42910 札
札薩克圖汗部	981.955
札幌	982.167

42913 桃
桃	613.727
桃金孃綱	578.7

42918 橙

橙	613.731

42927 橋
橋樑	
設計	651.505
工程	651.5
種類	
依形式分	651.503
依材料分	651.501
依用途分	651.502
橋墩	651.508
橋脚	651.608

42953 機
機能派	150.193
機動學	655.11
機件,用具	655.797
機遇	148
機遇游戲	795
機械	
摩擦	655.76
設計	655.13
工廠	655.7
工程	655
動學	531.29
動轉	655.12
模型	655.15
原理	655.11
附件	659.165
機械論	

楯 尤 犬 博 式 卦 求 埃 城 狘

生命	562.31
宇宙	134.1
機械藥	777
機械學	655.1
機車	
土木工程	651.814
機械工程	655.27
機車廠	655.279
機車保存與修理	655.278
機車汽鍋	655.273
機車機關	655.274
機器板	746

42964 楯

楯齒氣	587.814

43010 尤

尤侗（1618—1704）	817.727

43030 犬

犬	
家畜	615.15
獸醫學	599.47
犬儒學派	121.24
犬猿	589.57
犬類	588.516

43042 博

博雷蒙	121.35
博愛	180.4
博物院	990.079
博馬舍（1732—99）	842.58

43100 式

式威蘭	993.7987

43100 卦

卦卜	157.11

43132 求

求婚	313.343

43134 埃

埃及	
文學	896.1
語言	409.61
地理	985.1
哲學	119
歷史	951
埃甸	251.34

43150 城

城市	
職業教育	338.45
靜態社會學	313.5
住宅	718.3
經濟	350.025
生活	313.5
道路	651.773
風景	719
城郭	981.388
城寨	991.81

43250 狘

狘類	598.53

截 忒 鳶 始 載 裁 越 戴 朴 檸 栽 槭 棧

43250 截			裁縫	684
截頭類	583.32		裁軍問題	388.82
截斷術	598.1907		裁兵	379.349
截斷線論	519.04		裁判權	395.09

43300 忒
忒密斯托克士	
（前? 527—460)	831.81
忒棱士	
（前? 190—159)	832.25
忒提阿士	831.41

43327 鳶
鳶尾科	575.88

43460 始
始震旦紀	569.21
始侏羅紀	
脊椎動物	569.86
裸子植物	569.4
始寒武紀	569.71
始有魚	554.54
始有鳥	554.63
姑志留紀	569.83
始原環蟲類	583.616

43550 載
載便鐵路	633.7
載物	398.43
載人	398.44

43750 裁

43805 越
越函數	516.3
越中國	982.163
越前	982.163

43850 戴
戴震	
清代文學	817.734
清代哲學	111.75
戴復古	811.1577

43900 朴
朴素的	106.11

43921 檸
檸檬	
果類	613.737
飲料	664.66

43950 栽
栽桑	616.6
栽種機	610.62
栽種產具	610.62

43950 槭
槭	612.64
槭樹科	578.23

43953 棧

棧道	615.5023	宗教建築	715.97
棧橋	654.33	考古學	991.86

43991 棕

44104 基

棕櫚		基爾特主義	318.3
植物學	575.5	基礎	
農作物	612.66	建築構造	713.1
園藝	613.77	橋樑工程	651.508
棕櫚葉纖維	612.592	基礎工事	

44005 卅

港灣工程	654.43
道路工程	651.73
卅年戰爭時代	
（1618—48）	930.63
土木工程	651.13

44100 封

		基督	251.2
		基督論	251.2
封建國家	371.2	基督傳記	251.29
封爵	319.12	基督徒生活	258
封得乃爾		基督家庭	251.294
（1657—1757）	847.51	基督禱文	253.42
封泥	991.615	基督教	
封贈	373.018	文藝	250.8
封鎖	381.561	主日	253.195

44101 韮

		主日學校	257
韮	613.13	文化	250.19

44101 莖

		聯合會	256.1
莖	571.274	建築	715.5

44104 墓

		政治	250.14
墓誌	001.199	科學	250.15
墓碑	719.4	個人	250.17
墓地		倫理	181

宗派	259
社會	250.13
女青年會	256.4
考古	250.99
婦女聯合會	256.5
青年會	246.3
團契	256.18
歷史	250.9
勵志會	256.15
醫學	259.16
普及會	256.16
基斯塔派或完形派	150.1915
基阿那	
南美洲各國地理	984.88
南美洲各國史	949.8
基金	
教育行政	331.41
財政學	362.4
基第(1650—1712)	833.155

44104 董

董仲舒	111.215
董若雨(1620—?)	813.71
董菫菜科	578.59
董事	256.33
董事會	022.3

44106 薑

薑	613.12

44107 蓋

蓋瓦	651.16

44107 藍

藍色板攝影	756.7
藍泥爾(1842—81)	861.39
藍藻綱	572.71
藍姆(1775—1834)	857.75
藍姆女士	857.76
藍姆則(1686—1758)	851.54

44108 荳

荳蔻	612.87

44111 菲

菲爾丁(1707—55)	853.55
菲律濱群島	985.911
菲律濱問題	388.47

44111 堪

堪薩斯	984.187
堪輿	157.4

44112 地

地方	
政府	373.08
統計	345.12
行政	373.095
經濟	350.032
儲蓄銀行	362.94
生物學	561.9
組織法	393.11
法院	373.04

選舉	372.8	地理學	980
考古	991.9	地磁觀測	538.75
警察	315.323	地磁路	538.77
植物學	581.9	地磁學	538.7
目錄	013.12	地磁與地震	538.758
時計	528.58	地磁與地質構造	138.757
財政	369.19	地磁與日斑	538.753
風暴	529.39	地磁與蝕	538.754
人類學	565.9	地磁氣象	538.755
分制	331.22	地價	369.151
金石志	991.9	地線	657.652
黨部	001.4	地名表	981.031
地底鐵道	651.87	地毯	763.3
地衣類	573.4	地瀝青炭	558.127
地雷	659.32	地心	551.11
地震	316.46	地心膨脹	551.41
地震預兆	551.34	地支	157.27
地震測侯	551.34	地志	
地震學	551.3	高麗	982.25
地亞比克	982.667	俄國	983.85
地面地質學	552	法國	983.45
地形學	526	澳大利亞	983.935
地球	525	土耳其	982.65
地球形體與大小	525.1	希拉	983.15
地球物理學	525	英國	983.55
地球經緯	521.26	地土權	353.01
地球結構	551.1	地址	
地球創造說	201.4	家政	692

埼 蒲 蒟 莎 藜 蒺 薄 鼓

基督教	256.32
地板	713.6
地域	153.22
地獄	251.77
佛教	231.85
宗教	201.727
基督教	251.77
地殼	551.15
地殼破裂	551.41
地殼收縮與變遷	551.313
地勢與地境之影響	529.85
地殼始固結	554.1
地中海問題	388.25
地史學	554
地圖	
統計學	341.5
軍事學	379.098
地點	372.551
地臘	558.127
地質化學	551.95
地質由成之要素	551.9
地質顯微學	566.25
地質學	550
地質氣候	529.83
地層	553.1
地層史學	554
地氣	593.114

44121 埼

埼玉縣	982.1617

44127 蒲

蒲松齡(1630—1715)	813.73

44127 蒟

蒟蒻本	823.67

44129 莎

莎士比亞	852.33
莎草科	575.43
莎慈白利(1671—1713)	857.51

44132 藜

藜豆	612.383
藜科	579.11

44134 蒺

蒺藜科	577.91

44142 薄

薄荷	
農作物	612.85
園藝	613.4
薄情	155.4587

44147 鼓

鼓	
應鼓	770.13
音樂	777.1
晉鼓	770.13
魚鼓	770.13
軍事學	379.98
鼓詞	814.7

鼓膜	598.445

44147 坡
坡（1809—49）	863.31
坡爾弒（1776—1850）	853.75
坡利齊阿諾 （1454—94）	833.124
坡克	941.858

44147 菠
菠薐草	613.16

44161 塔
塔（浮屠）	991.843
塔立刻（1811—63）	853.82
塔索	833.14

44164 落
落窪物語	823.35
落地稅	369.153
落葵科	577.2
落花生	612.35
落葉性喬木花類	613.88
落葉性灌木花類	613.86

44181 塡
塡牙	598.277
塡築工程	654.8

44186 墳
墳墓考古	991.86

44187 茨
茨城縣	982.1616
茨藻科	575.32

44196 藻
藻菌植物	573.28
藻類植物	
地層史學	554.51
隱花植物	573.2

44201 苧
苧麻	612.53

44202 蓼
蓼綱	576.95

44207 考
考訂	010.97
考試	
五權憲法	001.139
圖書館學校	028.4
學則	334.5
民權主義	001.165
考試院	373.07
考釋	990.075
考古倫理	990.018
考古游記	990.098
考古學	990

44207 夢
夢	156.33
夢話	156.37
夢游病	156.35

44210 荒

苑 莊 花 薩 莧 梵 蘆 荷

荒地	353.19
44212 苑	
苑囿	
名勝	991.382
遺迹	991.83
44214 莊	
莊票	364.1
莊子	111.127
44214 花	
花	571.276
花癡	155.458
花語	570.083
花形虫類	582.75
花綱岩	557.33
花字	960.2
花房	610.63
花卉	613.8
花卉保存及繁殖	613.809
花卉品評	613.803
花草	719.8
花葱科	569.52
花蓮港廳	982.177
花菜類	613.17
花柳病	598.6
花椰菜	613.17
花樣	960.3
花托	610.63
花押	991.617
花捐	369.157
花園	613.8
花果	737.13
44214 薩	
薩摩	982.166
薩爾瓦多	
中美洲各國地理	984.64
中美洲各國史	946.4
薩魯斯特(前 86—34)	832.882
薩福(前？600)	831.42
薩幅克	983.566
薩克斯(1494—1576)	871.44
薩斯喀特撒溫	984.27
44216 莧	
莧科	577.13
44217 梵	
梵文	232.05
梵語	409.312
梵我	241.1
梵柏稜	941.855
44217 蘆	
蘆粟	613.62
蘆筍	613.16
蘆葦	612.594
44221 荷	
荷包牡丹科	577.53
荷蘭	

茅 芬 芮 帶 葡 繭 蕎 蘭 勸 苘 蘺 芥 蒙

德國	983.591	葡萄	613.75
條頓族	937.91	葡萄牙	
荷蘭語	409.388	文學	835
荷蘭文學		語言	435
文學	879.8	地理	983.3
地理	983.793	哲學	123
史	937.93	歷史	933
荷馬(前？900)	831.31	**44227 繭**	
44222 茅		繭	616.7
茅蒿菜科	577.65	**44227 蕎**	
44227 芬		蕎麥	612.12
芬蘭		**44227 蘭**	
文學	892.1	蘭	613.82
地理	983.91	蘭德	983.493
歷史	939.1	蘭科	575.99
芬蘭語	409.231	蘭加縣	983.567
芬蘭烏格里亞語	409.23	**44227 勸**	
芬芳植物	612.81	勸勉	244.2
芬香族	547.2	**44227 苘**	
44227 芮		苘麻	612.55
芮農		**44227 蘺**	
法國文學	847.8	蘺草	612.278
法國哲學	124.57	**44228 芥**	
44227 帶		芥子	612.88
帶水母類	582.774	**44232 蒙**	
帶狀疱疹	598.542	蒙文特藏	009.82
44227 葡		蒙穆夫	983.564

菸 狹 菱 菝 藏 蘋 蓮 芝 芍 蒸

蒙汗藥	597.861
蒙大拿	984.185
蒙古	
文學	819
語言	409.3
佛教	236.59
地理	981.93
國際問題	381.91
歷史	910.72
蒙藏委員會	373.0599
蒙旦（1533—92）	847.3
蒙學教育	338.1
蒙氣法	522.82
蒙養園	338.11
蒙鐵棱利法	337.35

44233 菸

菸	593.22
菸酒稅	369.152
菸草	612.71

44238 狹

狹衣物語	823.37
狹甲類	584.85

44247 菱

菱科	578.85

44253 菝

菝葜科	575.33

44253 藏

藏文特藏	009.84
藏經	232
藏書記	010.91

44286 蘋

蘋果	613.711

44305 蓮

蓮葉桐科	577.47

44307 芝

芝諾	
希拉羅馬哲學	121.521
古代哲學	121.125
芝諾克拉士	121.34
芝諾芬尼	121.121
芝菜科	575.35

44327 芍

芍藥	613.82

44331 蒸

蒸溜	536.727
蒸溜酒	664.55
蒸汽	
汽機蒸汽	655.21
汽車蒸汽	659.72
蒸汽生發	655.22
蒸氣傳導	655.227
蒸氣圍套	655.259
蒸氣密度	541.67
蒸氣壓	541.44

熱 蕪 燕 赫 葱

蒸熱法	542.4	熱帶醫學	593.5

44331 熱

熱		熱學	536
生物學	561.57	熱風機	655.41
醫學	597.465	熱分解	536.725
熱症	594.92	化學	541.63
熱病	592.55	物理學	536.725
熱度	523.72	熱光帶	535.45
熱療法	595.86		
熱函數	536.65		

44331 蕪

蕪菁	612.42

熱電學

熱學	536.53
光學	537.6

44331 燕

燕許	811.1418
燕饗	319.72
燕麥	612.13
燕雀類	589.976

熱彈性	536.68
熱動位	536.66
熱動力	536.67

44331 赫

赫立克(1591—1674)	851.43
赫爾普士(1817—75)	857.84
赫伯特(1593—1632)	851.38
赫德爾(1744—1803)	871.64
赫黎士(1848—1908)	863.46
赫克爾	117.76
赫斯	941.873
赫勒底亞(1842—1905)	841.86
赫拉頡利圖士	121.115
赫因(1831—86)	861.42
赫尼亞	597.344

熱動力之應用	536.69
熱動學	536.6
熱結晶學	559.36
熱化學	541.6
熱之於振動	534.58
熱河省	981.941
熱力論	536.5
熱力發電	657.22
熱力機	655.17
熱帶動物	581.908
熱帶植物	871.908

44332 葱

葱	613.13

熱帶農業	610.098

幕 惹 恭 蕁 蘚 蘇 萎 草 蕁 蕈 蔓

44333 幕
  幕府時代   921.83

44336 惹
  惹爾   983.493

44338 恭
  恭菜   612.41

44346 蕁
  蕁麻科   576.74
  蕁麻綱   576.7

44351 蘚
  蘚苔植物   569.23
  蘚類植物   573.7

44394 蘇
  蘇頲（670—727）   811.1418
  蘇瑞（1517—47）   851.28
  蘇聯共和時代
    （1917—　）   938.88
  蘇維斯忒（1806—54）   843.73
  蘇洵（1009—66）   877.513
  蘇格蘭
    文學   859.1
    語言   409.372
    地理   983.57
    歷史   935.91
  蘇格拉底派與
    反蘇格拉底派   121.2
  蘇打   664.63

  蘇軾
    韻文   811.153
    駢散文   817.514
  蘇轍（1039—1112）   817.515
  蘇撒拉傳略   252.96
  蘇丹（法屬）   985.51
  蘇門答剌   985.921

44404 萎
  萎縮演化   564.37
  萎縮   598.544

44406 草
  草   612.813
  草雙紙   823.64
  草紙   674.2
  草木   611.97
  草木崇拜   209.27
  草木犀   612.386
  草地   353.13
  草書   739.176
  草蜻蛉   585.51
  草果類   613.78

44406 蕁
  蕁麻疹   598.541

44406 蕈
  蕈菌   013.5

44405 蔓
  蔓脚類   584.87

孝 執 勃 萬 荔 募 勢 莫 葬 韓 摹 攀 華

44407 孝
 孝謙   921.823
 孝經   097
 孝德   921.821

44417 執
 執行
  修行   244.7
  國民黨   001.224

44427 勃
 勃勞理(1605—82)   857.43
 勃勞(1812—89)
  詩   851.83
  戲曲   852.8
 勃勞寧女士(1809—61)   851.82

44427 萬
 萬壽果   613.777
 萬國青年會   256.314
 萬年青   613.82

44427 荔
 荔枝   613.766

44427 募
 募兵   379.34

44427 勢
 勢能   531.693
 勢力範圍   381.3191

44436 莫
 莫干山   981.367
 莫三比克   985.44
 莫理士(1834—96)   851.86
 莫泊桑(1850—93)   843.87

44441 葬
 葬禮   319.24

44452 韓
 韓(403—233)   911.655
 韓詩   093.15
 韓詩外傳   093.15
 韓非   111.187
 韓國之亡(1908—12)   921.867
 韓愈(768—824)
  韻文   8114.154
  駢散文   817.46

44502 摹
 摹   990.076

44502 攀
 攀禽類   587.975

44504 華
 華雷斯種源論   564.31
 華爾頓(1593—1683)   857.45
 華山   981.362
 華僑統計   345.18
 華洋訴訟   381.87
 華盛頓城   984.166
 華嚴部   232.33
 華嚴宗

莓 革 靴 勒 英

中國佛教	239.53	靴墨	667.77
日本佛教	239.63	**44527 勒**	
華盛頓		勒薩日（1668—1747）	843.51
地理	984.197	**44530 英**	
歷史	984.841	英法戰爭時代	
44505 莓		（1755—63）	942.875
莓	613.78	英雄崇拜	209.4
44506 革		英格蘭語	409.383
革	770.13	英國	
革新時代		文學	850
意國文學	833.16	語言	450
瑞士史	837.945	建築	710.35
德國文學	871.4	統計	345.35
德國史	837.943	動物	581.935
英國史	935.915	條約	387.935
革命		憲法	391.135
文藝	001.98	游記	983.5
政治	001.94	大學	338.7935
種族	001.96	地理	983.05
社會	001.93	地圖	980.3305
國體	371.0491	地質	550.35
階級	001.95	哲學	125
民眾	001.99	考古	993.5
革命史		植物	571.935
法國史	934.29	教育	330.935
中國史	910.29	財政	369.35
日本史	921.29	歷史	935
44510 靴		英屬哥倫比亞	984.27

鞑 苗 茴 苜 菌 茜 菩 薔 蓄 苔 若 著 苦

英屬南非	985.71
英屬埃及蘇丹	985.17
英領洪都拉斯	
地理	984.62
歷史	946.2

44534 鞑

鞑靼語	409.2

44600 苗

苗	910.77
苗語	409.15
苗猺文	009.87
苗圃	613.808

44700 茴

茴香	613.4

44600 苜

苜蓿	612.381

44500 菌

菌蟲類	582.12
菌類植物	573.3

44601 茜

茜草綱	579.8

44601 菩

菩薩乘	231.7

44601 薔

薔薇	613.86
薔薇綱	577.7

44603 蓄

蓄音器	777.8
蓄電池	537.21
蓄水機	655.35

44603 苔

苔蘚	573.6
苔草科	575.63
苔蘚植物	573.5
苔蘚蟲類	583.8
苔類植物	573.6

44604 若

若狹國	982.163
若提子（耆那教）	249.8

44604 著

著述職業論	800.42
著者	010.41
著者目錄	012.2

44604 苦

苦	231.312
苦諦	231.31
苦行派	
基督教	259.0916
猶太教	269.5
苦力	354.255
苦木科	577.93
苦苣苔科	579.64
苦檻藍科	579.67
苦瓜	613.27
苦情	813.873

薯 蕃 荀 葫 蒔 老 蓙 世 芭 萄 葛 芸 藝

44604 薯	
薯蕷科	575.87
44609 蕃	
蕃地	982.178
蕃荅科	577.23
蕃荔枝科	577.43
蕃瓜樹科	578.63
44627 荀	
荀子	111.117
荀悅	111.283
44627 葫	
葫蘆科	579.91
葫蘆類	613.2
44641 蒔	
蒔繪	766.5
44711 老	
老衰	581.698
老死	231.51
老子	111.121
老撾(遼國)	982.46
老年	354.937
44711 蓙	
蓙花綱	575.53
44717 世	
世親	239.145
世代交番	561.625
世代生殖	571.65
世家	977.3
世界語	405
世界交通史	902.4
世界京城商埠一覽	980.033
世界主義	371.036
世界現狀	902.3
世界政治外交史	902.7
世界多數論	523.14
世界大戰	930.7
世界大同	318.9
世界戰爭史	902.8
世界與人生價值	108
世界類志	980.5
世情	737.7
44717 芭	
芭蕉	613.78
芭蕉綱	575.9
44727 萄	
萄苣	612.78
44727 葛	
葛洪	
文學	813.32
哲學	111.33
44731 芸	
芸香科	577.92
芸薹	612.42
44731 藝	

藝術上之婦女	313.3507	共和國	371.4
藝術社	700.6	共和黨或民主	
44732 蘘		共和黨	375.62
蘘荷科	575.92	共棲	581.763
44741 薛		共鳴	534.52
薛立敦		共管	381.191
文學	858.44	**44801 楚**	
戲曲	853.66	楚（907—951）	914.93
薛理（1792—1822）	851.77	楚辭	811.31
44770 甘		**44806 黃**	
甘涅底（1745—1870）	863.32	黃麻	612.54
甘蔗	612.61	黃疸病	598.944
甘薯	612.483	黃庭堅（1045—1105）	811.154
甘藷	612.41	黃玉	558.184
甘肅省	981.66	黃種	565.882
44777 舊		黃色蟲菌目	572.34
舊刻本	009.16	黃河	982.342
舊約	252.1	黃海	981.32
舊的啓示錄	252.81	黃道	522.77
舊加塞爾	983.38	黃道光	523.5
舊抄本	009.36	黃土	557.566
44801 共		黃樟	612.85
共產主義	318.7	黃熱	594.927
共變式	512.22	黃楊科	578.11
共生	581.763	黃表紙	823.64
共生植物	571.76	黃蜂	585.58
共和	571.046	黃眼草綱	575.6
		黃瓜	613.24

蕻 村 樹 材 禁 茶 菜

黃昏鳥	587.95
黃昏與黎明	525.7
黃光星	523.82
黃精鈎吻科	578.14

44886 蕻
蕻茄	597.866

44900 村
村市	371.15

44900 樹
樹液	614.76
樹木	719.7
樹木學	614.31
樹皮製造	614.75
樹皮栽培與育種	614.489
樹莓	613.78
樹脂	668.3
樹膠	668.3
樹膠與樹膠製品	676

44900 材
材料	
工程	651.71
基督教建築	256.32
材料強度與試驗	650.41
材料保護	024.2
材料搜集	341.13

44901 禁
禁虎	225.5
禁止主義	351.35
禁制	
殖民	377.63
波羅門教	244.1
禁酒	317.82
禁酒黨	375.67
禁賭	317.83
禁毀	
逸書	009.67
善本特藏	009.6
善本書目	019.6
禁食	593.124
禁食日	253.18
禁烟	317.81
禁烟委員會	373.0593

44904 茶
茶	612.72
茶科	578.52
茶稅	369.152
茶茱萸科	578.21
茶梅	613.87
茶類	664.7

44904 菜
菜蔬	
家政學	694.2
毒藥學	593.97
國家醫學	593.126
園藝	613.1

分析化學	543.25
菜田	611.23
菜園	613.1

44904 葉

葉	571.275
葉狀植物	573.1
葉狀體	571.271
葉狀類	582.15
葉適(1150—1223)	817.576
葉菜類	613.16
葉根	571.272
葉門	982.77
菜脚類	584.861

44904 藥

藥方	598.71
藥療學	595.7
藥劑	597.36
藥化學	596.4
藥物	
生物學	566.86
醫學	596.1
藥物	566.86
藥物分佈	596.099
藥物分析	543.4
藥材	596.1
藥品專賣權	593.76
藥局	396.7
藥局方	596.71
藥學	596
藥料作物	612.95
藥性	596.3
藥性學	595.71

44910 杜

杜西士(1733—1816)	842.61
杜發(1556—1621)	847.41
杜德峯(桑德)	
(1804—76)	843.82
杜仲科	578.2
杜牧(803—852)	811.148
杜滂(821—870)	841.82
杜審言	811.1417
杜威	126.7
杜甫(712—770)	814.144
杜拔里(1524—60)	841.32
杜弗勒里	
(1618—1724)	842.47
杜鵑花綱	579.1
杜鵑花科	579.15
杜鵑類	587.9755
杜光庭(850—933)	813.4

44912 枕

枕草紙	827.38

44914 桂

桂科	577.33

44914 權

權力與自由	311.57

蘿 植 蘊 椅 薪 菊 橢 模 稜 樺 桔

權柄	373.011
44914 蘿	
蘿葡	613.11
蘿摩科	579.47
44917 植	
植幼	614.487
植物	570
動物	562.85
化學藥品	661.97
自然地質學	551.97
細肥	571.11
寄生	594.978
心理學	154.7
演化	571.77
油脂	665.2
神話	570.081
地理	980.117
藥學	596.12
顯微學	566.4
器管學	571.27
彫刻	729.7
分佈	571.9
植樹	614.485
44917 蘊	
蘊藻科	578.87
44921 椅	
椅	332.93
椅科	578.6

44921 薪	
薪資比例	354.33
薪金	336.51
44927 菊	
菊	613.82
菊科	579.97
菊芋	612.485
44927 橢	
橢圓	517.44
橢圓調和	516.85
橢圓函數	516.41
橢圓幾何學	519.87
44934 模	
模型	
建築	711.3
彫刻	721.1
模仿	
生物學	563.14
社會學	311.53
模造	990.076
44947 稜	
稜龜類	587.817
44954 樺	
樺木科	576.66
樺太島	982.1679
44961 桔	
桔梗科	579.93

柑 橫 林 蒜 狆 杖 隸 樓 構 棒 槽 榛 楝 加

44970 柑
 柑橘類 613.73

44986 橫
 橫波 534.34
 橫坑道 658.35
 橫振動 534.547
 橫口類 587.41
 橫笛 774.1

44990 林
 林瑟(1490—1555) 851.26
 林政 614.15
 林肯 941.861
 林源 614.16
 林木 571.901
 林地
  經濟學 353.11
  農業農學 611.27
 林事 614.48
 林間 338.42

44991 蒜
 蒜 613.13

45206 狆
 狆語 409.127

45900 杖
 杖 394.511

45932 隸
 隸書 739.173
 隸屬 381.193

45944 樓
 樓板 713.7
 樓閣 981.383

45947 構
 構造
  幾何學 519.1
  電動機 657.407
  動物學 581
  結晶形態學 559.61
  汽機工程 655.2251
  力學 531.43
  地質學 553
  植物學 571
  圖書館學 024.3

45953 棒
 棒振動 534.55

45966 槽
 槽齒類 587.833

45996 榛
 榛子 613.763

45996 楝
 楝科 577.95

46000 加
 加諾林時期
  (752—987) 934.817
 加工 354.45

塊 埋 場 塤 帕 觀 幌 狸 猩 玀 獨 帽

加理細亞	983.796
加那列群島	983.38
加紫蘇輝長岩	557.37
加利佛尼亞	984.194
加料	579.58
加黎薩	983.36
加法	511.21
加達魯尼亞	983.37
加斯可內	983.493
加賀國	982.1633
加拉太人書	252.74
加拉馬利亞	982.662
加國魯士（前 87—54）	832.42
加羅林群島	985.961
加拿大問題	388.31

46113 塊
塊莖類	613.12

46114 埋
埋雷艦	379.661

46127 場
場地	353.15

46186 塤
塤	770.12

46200 帕
帕門尼底士	121.123
帕米爾	409.328
帕米亞語	409.234

46210 觀
觀察	141.7
觀(寺)	991.845
觀念	151.81
觀念論	106.2

46211 幌
幌菊科	579.53
幌幌木科	576.83

46214 狸
狸藻科	579.66

46214 猩
猩紅熱	594.918

46214 玀
玀玀語	409.135

46227 獨
獨立保障	381.21
獨立權	381.21
獨立國	371.71
獨占	352.6
獨斷論	105.1
獨身	187.2
獨唱	771.74
獨覺乘	231.5

46260 帽
帽	688.3
帽狀地衣	573.47

駕 想 如 娛 婢 袈 賀 相 柏 絮 架 棍 檉 楦 棉

46327 駕

 駕馳   659.194

46330 想

 想   231.63
 想像   151.7
 想像或推定元素   546.9

46400 如

 如來   231.27

46434 娛

 娛樂
  心理學   153.27
  社會學   313.47
  游藝   790

46440 婢

 婢役   313.84

46732 袈

 袈裟   233.3

46806 賀

 賀拉士（前65—前8） 832.45

46900 相

 相互關係   563.13
 相手療法   595.91
 相術   157.3
 相似   517.37
 相對論   530.7
 相神   157.33
 相關法   341.3

46900 柏

 柏塞爾函數   516.84
 柏克（1729—97） 858.42
 柏克立   125.4
 柏格森   124.7
 柏拉圖   121.31
 柏拉圖與其學院   121.3
 柏羅（1528—77） 841.33

46903 絮

 絮木科   576.61
 絮木綱   576.6

46904 架

 架構   658.37

46911 棍

 棍球   338.635
 棍棚   379.93

46914 檉

 檉柳科   578.56

46917 楦

 楦梓   613.715

46927 棉

 棉   612.51
  衣飾   693.1
  農作物   612.51
 棉稅   369.152
 棉油   665.2
 棉典棉織品   675.2

楊 櫻 帆 鶴 坎 犯 匏 砲 猛 狗 猺 超 怒 聲 朝

46927 楊
 楊愛德華（1684—1765）851.55
 楊朱 111.124
 楊士奇（1365—1444） 817.615
 楊柳綱 576.3
 楊梅綱 576.35

46944 櫻
 櫻 613.88
 櫻草綱 579.2
 櫻町（延亨二年） 921.845

47010 帆
 帆船 659.13

47127 鶴
 鶴 587.974

47182 坎
 坎拿大
  文學 869
  地理 984.2
  歷史 942

47212 犯
 犯罪學
  刑法 394.2
  社會病理學 315.1

47212 匏
 匏 770.11

47317 砲
 砲狀 598.542

47217 猛
 猛禽類 587.979

47220 狗
 狗牙根 612.271

47272 猺
 猺 910.77

47306 超
 超越數 512.47

47334 怒
 怒 180.65

47401 聲
 聲（子音） 414.2
  生理音學 534.9
  聲韻學 414.2
 聲音 597.725
 聲訓 411.13
 聲韻學 414
 聲調 534.91
 聲樂式 770.027
 聲樂附管弦樂 779.9
 聲之訓練 770.075
 聲之強度 534.533
 聲明 232.085
 聲學 534

47420 朝
 朝顏 613.81
 朝紅與夕陽 529.63

努 婦 奴 好 報

朝代叢書	081.3	運動	001.995
朝鮮文學	829	基督教	
朝覲	253.97	宗教	250.17
朝服	319.43	靜態社會學	313.352
朝舞	792.8	教訓	188.5

47427 努

努比亞	985.171
努海(挪亞)	271.22

47427 婦

婦科	598.7
婦科手術	598.77
婦科治療學	598.75
婦女	
研究	313.35
刑法	394.63
職業	313.355
聖經	313.362
政權	313.35
經濟	313.355
生殖器	
病理學	598.74
解剖學	598.71
生理學	598.72
衛生學	598.73
組織	313.356
宗教	313.352
社會	313.353
選舉	372.7

教員	336.7
教育	338.91
圖書館	025.7
國家	313.354
館員	022.5
勞工	313.355
婦女美	313.3507
婦女會	313.356

47440 奴

奴商	317.46
奴僕	354.254
奴制解放	317.48
奴制法律	317.45
奴制問題	317.4
奴草科	576.93
奴隸	
階級團體	313.85
民法	397.57

47447 好

好望角	985.77
好壞	180.1

47447 報

報章	040

靭 鞣 磬 胡 都 切 起 超 欺 期

報仇	382.32
報復	382.31
報學	040

47520 靭
靭帶	597.713

47592 鞣
鞣木科	578.16
鞣皮作物	612.93

47601 磬
磬	770.16

47620 胡
胡	910.72
中國史	
胡麻科	579.61
胡琴	770.17
胡頽子科	578.72
胡佛	941.886
胡支子	612.384
胡桃	613.761
胡桃綱	576.5
胡蘿蔔	
農作物	612.45
園藝	613.11
胡椒	612.88
胡椒綱	576.25
胡氏傳	096.4
胡笳	770.18
胡粉畫	734.2

47627 都
都市	991.81
都德(1840—97)	843.85
都伯,汝拉	983.477
都汗	983.569
都蘭語	409.2
都昔的底士	
(前 471—400)	831.882
都勒內	983.482
都鐸爾時代	
(1485—1603)	935.85

47720 切
切音	414.5
切甲類	584.86

47801 起
起石	654.63
起水灌溉	554.81
起重機	655.36
起重車	655.82

47806 超
超亡	223.5
超越曲線	519.471

47882 欺
欺詐	180.86
欺騙	155.453

47820 期
期票	364.5

楓 杞 杓 柳 桐 欄 梛 椰 鶇 橘 楊 根 橡 楔 殺

期間	367.17
期限	354.137

47910 楓
楓
花卉	613.88
農作物	612.64

47917 杞
杞柳	612.596

47920 杓
杓球	338.635

47920 柳
柳永(？1000)	811.732
柳宗元(773—819)	
韻文	811.1455
駢散文	817.47
柳葉菜科	578.83

47920 桐
桐城派	817.74

47920 欄
欄杆	651.817

47927 梛
梛子	770.14

47927 椰
椰子
農作物	612.74
園藝	613.771
椰子皮纖維	612.591

47927 鶇
鶇鶲類	587.941

47927 橘
橘	613.731

47927 楊
楊億(974—1020)	811.1511

47932 根
根	571.273
根室支廳	982.1678
根室國	982.1978
根菜作物	612.4
根菜類	613.11
根數	512.71
根足類	582.15

47932 橡
橡子木科	576.41
橡子木綱	576.4

47934 楔
楔	531.96
楔子	818.55

47947 殺
殺菌
細菌學	566.967
農藝	611.993
殺蟲	611.993
殺蛹法	616.7
殺人	155.455

穀 格 款 救 增 散 猶

47947 穀
- 穀梁傳　　　　　096.3
- 穀田　　　　　　611.21
- 穀精草科　　　　575.72

47964 格
- 格言
  - 文學　　　　　808.03
  - 法國文學　　　848.3
  - 英國文學　　　858.3
  - 中國文學　　　818.3
  - 日本文學　　　828.3
  - 美國文學　　　808.3
- 格鱗(1516—92)　852.31
- 格雷(1716—71)　851.61
- 格得運一世至二
  世(1725—96)　938.85
- 格林
  - 英國哲學　　　125.68
  - 美國文學　　　861.12
- 格蘭特　　　　　941.872
- 格羅法派　　　　381.0995

47980 款
- 款識　　　　　　990.075
- 款待
  - 家政學　　　　697
  - 社會學　　　　319.36
- 款式　　　　　　010.45

48140 救
- 救護　　　　　　659.195
- 救生船　　　　　593.487
- 救急　　　　　　658.47
- 救世論　　　　　251.4
- 救世軍　　　　　256.11
- 救贖　　　　　　251.43

48166 增
- 增一阿含　　　　232.24

48240 散
- 散文　　　　　　807
  - 西班牙文學　　835.7
  - 孫中山文集　　001.187
  - 德國文學　　　877
  - 希拉文學　　　831.7
  - 基督教文藝　　250.86
  - 拉丁文學　　　832.7
  - 美國文學　　　867
- 散熱　　　　　　592.52
- 散瞳藥　　　　　597.866

48261 猶
- 猶太
  - 傳說　　　　　262.7
  - 法律　　　　　390.4
  - 地理　　　　　982.84
  - 歷史　　　　　982.4
- 猶太教
  - 建築　　　　　715.5
  - 制度　　　　　265

驚 赦 乾 教

宗派	269	倫理	330.18
教育	267	測驗	330.17
教徒生活	268	心理學	330.15
猶大著	252.797	社會病理學	315.57
猶狄	252.92	社會學	311.3

48327 驚

驚厥	598.863	遺傳	330.13
		犯罪	330.13

48340 赦

		靜態社會學	313.3503
赦免	251.46	國家	330.12

48417 乾

		公民學	372.135
乾裂	553.3	小說	813.853
乾酪	615.74	教育部	256.353
乾船渠	654.37	行政院	373.057
乾溝	653.32	基督教青年會	256.353
乾板	755.2	教育廳	373.081
乾式分析法	544.2	教育局	373.0834
定量分析	545.2	教育家學說	330.11
定性分析	544.2	教務	336.1
乾繭法	616.7	教化與影響	235
乾旱	611.912	教律	235.4

48440 教

		教皇	259.14
教產	255.3	教皇與文化	259.149
教育	330	教皇與文藝復興	259.148
文化	330.19	教皇與帝王	259.145
建築	717.2	教皇與政治	259.144
統計	330.14	教皇與戰爭	259.146
維持稅	331.47	教業問題	336.6
行政	331	教士	255.56

嫩 斡 警

教友	255.58	神道教	291.1
教友會	259.85	道教	221
教材		猶太教	261
教育	335.1	基督教	251
圖書館學	028.5	回教	271
教授法	337	教會	
教授與職業	336.6	文化	255.09
教規		建設	255.8
佛教	235.4	行政	255.2
基督教	555.4	經濟	255.06
教員	336	制度	255
教員訓練	336.3	蠻族	255.01
教員訓練學校	338.55	個人	255.04
教員證書	336.25	法律	399.2
教員之考試問題	336.21	社會	255.03
教區	255.6	道德	255.02
教區巡視	254.2	婦女	255.04
教區團體	254.6	教育	255.07
教區會議	255.7	思想	255.09
教門		國家	255.03
制度	275	財政	255.3
生活	278	兒童	255.04
教育	277	教父學派	121.62
事業	274	**48440 嫩**	
團體	276	嫩莖類	613.14
教義		**48440 斡**	
佛教	291.1	斡旋	382.23
沃教	281	**48601 警**	

中國十進制分類法及索引 | 1285

敬 榆 櫛 松 樣 橄 梅 檜 槍 檢 狄 鞘 趙 檔 中

警庭	315.35
警章	315.31
警務	315.33
警句	960.5
警察	315.3
警規	315.31

48640 敬

敬長	319.31

48921 榆

榆科	576.71

48927 櫛

櫛水母類	582.77
櫛齒類	587.45

48930 松

松柏綱	574.4
松花江	981.345
松脂	665.2
松脂岩	557.23
松鼠類	588.613

48932 樣

樣品選取	545.3

48940 橄

橄欖岩	557.38
橄欖科	577.94

48945 梅

梅	613.88

48966 檜

檜山支廳	982.1671

48967 槍

槍戟	379.92

48986 檢

檢疫法	593.2353
檢字	036
檢字目錄	012.5
檢查注冊	377.65

49280 狄

狄洋西尼士	
（前 384—322）	831.846
狄他函數	516.47
狄戴羅	124.27

49527 鞘

鞘翅類	585.54

49802 趙

趙秉文(1159—1232)	817.583

49966 檔

檔案	
教育	339
圖書館行政	
與組織	022.9
圖書館學校	028.9

50006 中

中庸	098.2
中立論	103.7
中立法	381.6

中立國			百科全書	031
政治學	371.8		疆界	981.31
世界大戰	390.755		建築	710.1
中耳	598.444		行政	393.1
中非各國	956		經濟	350.91
文學	896		戲劇	780.1
語言	496		佛教	239.5
地理	985.6		傳記	971
歷史	956		條約	387.91
中子綱	577.1		憲法	391.1
中生代	554.6		叢書	081
中心體	571.115		法系	390.1
中葉器官	591.56		軍事	379.11
中央政府	373.01		游記	981.4
中央統計	345.11		大學	338.791
中央組織法	393.11		地圖	980.31
中央集權	331.21		地質	550.1
中央儲蓄銀行	362.94		哲學	111
中央財政	369.022		考古	991
中央黨部	001.3		植物	571.91
中毒	594.98		教育	330.91
中毒影響心理	155.259		畫	730.1
中東問題	388.13		書	739.1
中國			國家銀行	362.12
文學	810		彫刻	720.1
音樂	770.1		歷史	910
統計	345.1		財政	369.1
語言	410		學會	061

史　申　車　事　轆　推　撞　擅　抗

人口	349.1	**50006 申**	
美術	701	申不害	111.176
年鑑	037.1	申命記	252.215
中國國民黨	001	**50006 車**	
中阿含	232.22	車站	651.817
中腦	597.8115	車頭	655.27
中鳳	598.947	車輛	651.814
中學教育	338.3	車輪蟲	583.46
中學圖書館	025.23	車器	991.74
中美洲各國	946	車臣汗部	981.951
地理	984.6	車前綱	579.7
歷史	946	**50007 事**	
50006 史		事務能率	622.15
史立野(1762—94)	841.56	事務管理	622.1
史詩	801.5	**50011 轆**	
希臘文學	831.3	轆轤	610.61
拉丁文學	832.3	**50014 推**	
史記	910.911	推理法	337.15
史稿	910.085	**50014 撞**	
史劇	802.91	撞球	794
史蒂芬生		**50017 擅**	
(1850—94)	853.88	擅用財產罪	315.187
史學	900.9	**50017 抗**	
史學家傳記	900.97	抗議	386.47
史學地理	900.98	抗告	395.03
史學史	900.99	抗毒素	
史前考古學	990.9	生理化學	581.496
史鈔	910.086		

拉 夫 接 搯 擴

微生學	566.929

50018 拉
拉丁	
文學	832
語言	409.343
聖經	252.058
拉丁美洲	
地理	984.5
歷史	945
拉哥尼亞	983.17
拉比士(1815—88)	842.81
拉穆特	842.51
拉布剌多	984.28
拉封騰(1621—95)	841.45
拉伯雷斯與黎	
干得函數	
（球圓調和）	516.83
拉伯蘭	939.2
文學	892.2
語言	409.232
地理	983.92
歷史	939.2
拉梅內	124.51
拉哈普(1739—1803)	422.62
拉馬丁(1792—1869)	441.72
拉馬克學說	564.1
拉脫維亞	
語言	409.395
地理	983.97
歷史	939.73
拉美特里	124.24
拉普勒(1812—83)	841.81

50030 夫
夫勒諾(1752—1832)	861.24
夫勒拆(1585—1650)	
詩	851.37
戲曲	852.36
夫婦	
倫理	183.5
家庭	313.323
法律	397.51

50044 接
接談	
倫理學	184.3
社會學	319.35
接種防禦法	593.2355
接線(電報,電話)	657.833
接觸作用	545.57
接藻植物	572.7
接技器	610.63
接合生殖	561.621

50063 搯
搯搦	597.8447

50086 擴
擴散	
水力學	532.14

掠 晝 畫 盎 泰 蟲 蚊 青

實驗化學	542.63
氣力學	533.15
光學	536.412

50096 掠
掠奪罪	315.185

50106 晝
晝夜	525.5
晝夢	156.337
晝禽類	587.9793

50106 畫
畫像
畫繪	737.31
遺物	991.726
鋼印	991.6
畫像崇拜	209.8
畫法	731
畫法幾何學	519.3
畫品	763.1
畫眉草	612.297

50107 盎
盎格諾薩克森
語言	409.383
歷史	935.81

50132 泰
泰理士	121.111
泰山	981.361
泰福	941.882
泰布魯士	
（前？54—18）	832.43
泰蒙	121.533
泰羅(1835—78)	
伯約德	861.46
泰羅時代(美國史)	941.859
泰勞	941.857

50136 蟲
蟲害	611.94
蟲藻植物	572.4
蟲菌植物	572.3

50140 蚊
蚊虫寄生	594.974

50227 青
青空	529.62
青海	910.73
地理	981.68
歷史	910.73
青森縣	982.1626
青春心理	153.7

青年
道德	188.6
家庭	313.386
社會	317.7
團體	313.67
黨務運動	317.7

青年會
基督教	256.3

本 忠 惠 專 奏 奉 毒

學校	333.63

50230 本
本能	581.702
本能與行動	
（模仿,游戲,等）	151.37
本鄉草綱	575.4
本斯(1759—96)	851.67
本草	596.13
本若州	982.38
本罪	251.36
本質	133.22
本體論	
形上學	133
佛學	231.143
婆羅門教	241.1
本體數論	102
本體質論	103
本分	180.73
本籍	381.811
本性	315.122

50330 忠
忠順	371.029
忠島	985.951

50333 惠
惠施	111.152
惠特亞(1807—92)	861.35
惠特曼	
詩	861.38
散文	867.38
惠棟(1697—1758)	817.731
惠格黨	375.63

50343 專
專制	
政治哲學	371.9482
歐州史	932.843
專修課程	335.3
教育	335.3
圖書館學	028.5
專家教授法	337.3
專號(報章,雜誌)	040.5
專長	153.83
專門地理	980.1
專門地圖	980.308
專門圖書館	026
專門學校	338.6

50430 奏
奏議	
古文書學	901.1
公文檔案	901.23

50503 奉
奉教與反教	255.58

50505 毒
毒劑	543.49
毒彈	388.89
毒物學	593.9
毒草	611.977

轟 書 春 表 囊 責 貴 未 末

毒藥學	593.9
毒素	
生理化學	581.496
微生學	566.929
毒氣	388.87

50556 轟

轟炸	
軍器	388.87
戰法	381.553

50601 書

書庫	024.4
書店書目	011.8
書經	092
書後	818.56
書卜	157.15
書緯	092.0
書名	010.42
書名目錄	012.3
書寫	010.6
書寫電信	657.8351
書寫機	655.97
書法	739
書架	024.4
書報廣告	629.7
書翰	252.7
書本彩飾	738
書目之書目	011.1
書院	991.847

50603 春

春秋(經書)	096
春秋(772—481)	911.63
春布爾(1750—1831)	861.21

50732 表

表奏(祈願文)	223.8
表算	510.77

50732 囊

囊子地衣	573.51
囊子菌綱	573.31
囊狀鞭毛蟲類	582.37
囊鰓類	587.1

50806 責

責任	180.73
責罵	180.87

50806 貴

貴族	
政治科學	371.043
傳記	977.2
社會學	313.82
貴州省	981.87

50900 未

未見星	523.88

50900 末

末世論	
自然神學	201.7
基督教	251.7

棗 素 秦 束 柬 東 批 排

回教	271.7
末日	201.72
末腦髓	507.8118

50902 棗
| 棗 | 613.778 |
| 棗椰子 | 613.773 |

60903 素
素紙制造	674.3
素馨	612.811
素畫	733

50904 秦
秦代
哲學	111.1
歷史	911.7
春秋時代	811.636
戰國時代	911.658

50906 束
| 束腰 | 317.87 |

50906 柬
柬蒲塞(高綿)	924.4
地理	982.44
歷史	924.4

50906 東
東京
地理	982.45
歷史	924.5
東京府	982.1611

東方政策	388.11
東方哲學	110
東方朔(？160)	813.28
東晉(317—420)	913.4
東三省	981.91
東比里牛斯	983.496
東山	921.844
東俄	983.89
東魏(534—544)	913.82
東漢(25—250)	912.3
東澳	986.939
東海	981.32
東游歌	821.53
東土耳其	982.96
東羅馬帝國	
(478—1453)	932.847
東周(776—255)	911.62
東關紀行	827.45

51010 批
批評論(哲學)	105.5
批評的實在論	106.13
批發	622.54
批校本	
普本特藏	009.5
善本書目	019.5

51011 排
排水
| 工程 | 654.87 |

拒 打 振 頓 攝 拓 指 輻

農學	611.6	頓骨硬鱗類	587.474
礦業工程	658.43	**51041 攝**	
排球	338.635	攝動	521.5
排劇	781.1	攝津國	982.164
排污	313.43	攝影	
排污工事	653.3	方法	754
排除(淋巴腺)	597.42	化學	752
排簫	770.18	器具	753
51017 拒		陽攝	756
拒力	523.18	陰攝	757
51020 打		光學	751
打樂器	777	攝影板	746.7
打字		**51060 拓**	
商業實踐	626.7	拓搨(古物)	990.076
打穀機	610.65	**51061 指**	
打噎	597.26	指南	038
打胎	598.828	指力線	537.141
打針	595.815	指南針	659.192
51032 振		指猴類	589.1
振動	535.21	指事	411.32
磁學	538.17	指數函數	516.31
力學	531.87	指數級數	514.41
聲學	534.5	指數法	341.7
光學	535.21	指數表	510.25
振幅	534.31	指甲	598.59
51034 頓		**51066 輻**	
頓鰭類	587.4777	輻射	
頓體動物	583.5	能力測量	535.8

虹 蛭 蠕 甑 划 折 斬 轎 撲 抵 授 援 輜 播 插 採 蠟

化學作用	535.57
熱動學	535.58
傳導	536.4
物理學	539
輻合適應	563.75

51110 虹
虹	529.64
虹膜	598.342

51114 蛭
蛭類	583.63

51128 蠕
蠕形動物	583.1
蠕態類	583.2

51317 甑
甑	651.75

52000 划
划船	659.13

52021 折
折衷派	121.54
折衷療法	595.94
折字	157.14
折縣	983.567
折光現象	529.61

52021 斬
斬首	394.511

52027 轎
轎輿	632.2

52034 撲
撲克	795

52040 抵
抵押	362.7
抵押品	366.2

52047 授
授職	253.94
授職講道	253.75
授胎	
解剖學	591.52
內科	597.623

52047 援
援軍	381.542

52063 輜
輜重	379.58

52069 播
播磨	982.164
播種機	610.62

52077 插
插戲	802.97
插木	614.43

52094 採
採集	
動物	580.075
古物	990.074

52116 蠟
蠟畫	734.4

蜥 静 哲 刺 戈 掛 搾 挖 捕

52121 蜥
蜥龍類	587.83
蜥形類	587.7
蜥蜴類	587.853
蜥尾類	587.91

52257 静
静電計	537.077
静電學	537.1
静態社會學	313
静物畫	737.15
静力	654.11
静力學	531.61
静勢	531.63
静脉	
血循環系病理學	597.146
血循環系解剖學	597.116
静脉切開術	595.811
静脉炎	598.866
静岡縣	982.1638

52602 哲
哲斐孫	941.843
哲克孫	941.854
哲學	100
西方哲學	120
傳記	100.97
自然	530
葡萄牙	123
體系	101
哲學家傳記	100.97

52900 刺
刺	581.75
刺繡	
工藝美術	765.3
手工業	685
刺蓮花科	578.64
刺泡動物	569.73
刺激	594.27
刺激作物	612.7
刺激品	592.475
刺激與運動	571.48

53000 戈
戈爾斯密(1728—74)	851.64
詩	
散文	857.64
小説	853.64

53000 掛
掛綿	763.5
掛號郵件	636.55

53010 搾
搾擠	542.68

53017 挖
挖泥	654.63

63027 捕
捕魚	617.5
捕獲審檢所	381.565

輔 撚 挨 捰 按 拚 擦 或 蛇 蛾 成 威

53027 輔
 輔助軍艦   379.66
 輔助貿易   351.36
 輔幣   361.63

53033 撚
 撚翅類   585.56

53034 挨
 挨爾斯倫   982.666
 挨陀利亞   983.16

53034 捰
 捰傷   598.167
 捰花綱   579.4

63044 按
 按摩療法   595.98
 按工給資   354.343
 按線
  電話   657.852
  電報   657.832
 按時給資   354.345

53045 拚
 拚音讀本   418.2

53091 擦
 擦傷   598.163

53100 或
 或然   148

53111 蛇
 蛇形類   587.851
 蛇綸岩   557.47
 蛇菰科   576.87
 蛇尾類   582.92
 蛇類   587.857

53155 蛾
 蛾類   585.535

53200 成
 成文法   390.025
  種類   390.001
  法源   390.025
 成文法與不成文法   390.001
 成語   410.3
  語言文字學   401.3
  中國語言文字學   413.3
 成聖   251.47
 成仙   224
 成績展覽會   333.51
 成實論   239.114
 成漢(巴蠻)
  （304—347）   913.581
 成禮   319.26
 成油氣屬   547.12
 成人教育   338.97
 成年期須要食品   592.478

53200 威
 威廉四世   935.87
 威爾遜   941.883
 威爾滿   984.162

盛 感 戒 撓 拋 軌 拗

威爾斯(英國)		精神發育與	
文學	859.5	精神能力	153.21
語言	409.376	感覺論	104.2
地理	983.59	感覺與運動神經之差別	597.821
歷史	935.95	感情性	315.126
威信	312.65	**53400 戒**	
威儀	223	戒	231.72
威士忌	664.55	戒嚴法	372.41
威斯康星	984.177	戒嚴時期	372.41
威斯衛司(1770—1850)	851.71	戒嚴令	381.545
威地島	983.562	**54011 撓**	
威格斯衛司		撓射	536.45
(1683—1705)	861.13	撓線	535.34
威阿特(1503—42)	851.27	撓屈層	553.2
威尼		撓腳類	584.867
詩	841.73	**54012 拋**	
戲曲	842.73	拋物線	517.46
威尼西亞	983.26	拋物線幾何學	519.86
53200 盛		**54017 軌**	
盛唐		軌道	
韻文	811.142	工程	651.812
駢散文	817.42	天文學	521.3
盛應派	150.197	軌道與運動	523.33
53200 感		地球	525.3
感謝節	253.17	日球	523.73
感化所	315.7	月球	523.33
感覺		軌迹	519.44
普通心理學	151.1	**54027 拗**	

持 技 拱 蝌 蛙 蜞 蝶 井 弗 拂 扶 軼 搏 轉 抽 軸

拗扭曲面	519.463

54041 持
持統	921.821

54047 技
技能	153.83

54081 拱
拱橋	631.55

54100 蝌
蝌蚪文	739.171

54114 蛙
蛙類	587.68
水產業	617.7
動物學	587.68

54181 蜞
蜞蛛	584.63

54194 蝶
蝶類	585.531

55000 井
井	
工程	653.14
中國地理	981.357

55027 弗
弗耳特耳	
哲學	124.4
戲曲	842.56
小說	843.54
弗洛貝爾（1821—81）	843.84

弗格森	125.62

55027 拂
拂塵	611.991

55030 扶
扶南語	409.173

55030 軼
軼事	001.195
傳記	970.6
紀念藏	001.195
宗教	251.293

55043 搏
搏拊	770.13

55043 轉
轉生	201.75
轉級	334.6
轉注	411.36
轉扭力	531.85

55060 抽
抽象	151.81
抽氣機	655.52
抽籤	157.13

55060 軸
軸	
汽機工程	655.259
機械	655.74
軸承	655.75
軸動	655.74

捷 豐 蜻 慧 農

軸本	010.17	政策	351.2
55081 捷		經濟	610.3
捷克文學	889	化學	610.54
語言	409.394	動物	610.58
地理	983.796	生物	566.61
歷史	937.96	物理	610.53
55108 豐		組織	610.11
豐前國	982.166	實業	610
55127 蜻		法規	610.32
蜻蛉日記	827.34	社會	610.1
蜻蛉類	585.33	游歷	610.097
55177 慧		森林	614.91
彗星	523.6	地理	980.151
55232 農		地質	556.3
農產		機器	655.293
製造	610.8	植物	610.57
利用	610.9	農產	610.33
化學分析	543.2	數學	610.51
農礦部	373.056	田地	611.2
農礦廳	373.081	顯微	610.56
農業		時令	611.1
市場	610.358	階級	610.13
調查	610.097	財政	362.13
試驗場	610.078	學校	610.077
工程	610.6	金融	610.35
水利		公會	354.64
建築	610.6	氣象	610.52 或 529.78

慧 曲 曹 典 費 耕

銀行	610.355
簿記	610.357
農藝	611
農村	338.41
副業	610.37
生活	610.15
學校	338.41
改革	610.17
農賑	610.18
農民	
工人	001.175
遷移	610.16
運動	001.991
農奴	351.253
農民部	001.33

55337 慧

慧眼	157.63

55600 曲

曲	812
曲評	812.04
曲話	812.04
曲韻	812.03
曲譜	812.03
曲選	812.08
曲總集	812.08
歷史	812.09
曲面論	519.46
曲面體	517.55
曲線論	519.45
曲線幾何學	517.4
曲線運動	531.223
曲線曲面之微數原理	519.72
曲柄	655.259
曲拆語	403
曲折運動	531.245
曲腳類	588.385

55606 曹

曹雪芹（？1710—64）	813.76
曹植（192—232）	
詩	811.131
騷賦	811.33
駢散文	817.31
曹國（春秋時代）	911.6395

55800 典

典試委員會	373.071
典儀	332.2
典藏（圖書）	023.5
典當	362.19

55806 費

費虛奴（護持之神）	241.73
費希奈爾	127.74
費鳩諾士	121.56
費羅	121.55

55900 耕

耕種	611.4
經濟	353.64

棘 拍 規 擺 捐 揚 搨 擇 押 提 損 蜘 蝗

土地	353.41
機器	610.61

55992 棘
棘毛類	583.65
棘皮動物	582.9
古生物	569.74

56000 拍
拍子	534.63
音樂	770.027
物理學	534.63
拍賣	622.58
拍板	770.14

56010 規
規費	369.143
規則	022.6
選舉	372.551
圖書館	022.6

56011 擺
擺動	531.87
擺倫(1788—1821)	851.76
擺渡	634.5
擺温(希臘文學)	831.49

56027 捐
捐稅制度	351.35
捐贈	061.7
財政	369.146
學會	061.7

56027 揚
揚子江	981.341
揚雄	111.25
中國文學	817.25
中國哲學	111.25

56027 搨
搨本	
善本特藏	009.4
善本書目	019.4

56040 擇
擇業	620.013

56050 押
押匯	365

56081 提
提摩太後書	252.784
提摩太前書	252.783
提奧格力士	831.11
提多書	252.785
提婆	239.136

66086 損
損傷	598.16

56100 蜘
蜘蛛類	
動物	584.6
傳染病	594.975

56114 蝗
蝗蟲	314.44

螺 抱 輓 拘 捫 抒 邦 挪 掃 換 投 擔 招 摺 掘

56193 螺
  螺旋 531.97
  螺旋細菌科 572.122
57012 抱
  抱合語 403
57016 輓
  輓具 610.66
57020 拘
  拘魂 225.7
57020 捫
  捫達語 409.175
57022 抒
  抒情詩 801.4
57027 邦
  邦樂 770.1
  邦禮 319.1
  邦威爾（1820—91） 841.83
57027 挪
  挪威 937.926
    文學 879.21
    語言 409.3821
    地理 983.7986
    歷史 937.986
57027 掃
  掃雷艦 379.663
57034 換
  換補術 598.1908

57047 投
  投票 372.553
  投稿 040.5
  投資 367.1
  投機 367.3
  投機與恐慌 352.75
  投刺 319.33
  投影幾何學 519.39
  投影法 519.31
    地質學 559.13
    數學 519.31
  投降 381.5585
57061 擔
  擔子地衣 573.47
  擔子菌綱 573.35
  擔保公債 369.183
  擔振 982.1674
57062 招
  招魂 223.5
  招待 256.4354
  招徠 622.55
  招貼廣告 629.4
57062 摺
  摺橋 651.591
  摺本 010.18
57072 掘
  掘鑿法

擬 軟 探 蠅 蝦 蜂 蠍 契 齒 耙 賴 拖 挫

土工	651.143	蜂窩織炎	598.862
開鑛	658.31	蜂臘	665.4
掘足類	583.54		

57182 蠍

蠍類	584.671

57081 擬

擬瓣鰓類	583.553
擬態	563.14
動物學	581.75
進化論	563.14
擬索類	586.1
擬猴類	589.3
擬松鼠類	588.612
擬蠍類	584.676
擬足類	584.1
擬脉翅類	585.35
擬間質	547.6

57430 契

契約	
商法	398.51
工藝	642.3
實業	602.3
國際法	381.844
民法	397.4
契丹(907—1124)	
守遼金夏	915.5
邊記	910.71

57772 齒

齧齒有袋類	588.23
齧齒類	588.6
齧蟲	585.35

57082 軟

軟甲類	584.81
軟體動物	569.75
軟骨組織	591.73

57917 耙

耙	610.61

57094 探

探險記	980.707
探鑛	658.2

57986 賴

賴科夫綸	831.19

58012 拖

拖車	610.66

57117 蠅

蠅蝨類	585.57

57147 蝦

蝦	584.827

58014 挫

挫位(外科)	598.166
挫傷	598.163

57154 蜂

輸 扮 輪 撒 抍 捨 整 蛻 螠 蟻 數

58022 輸
　輸卵管　　　　598.742
　輸尿管　　　　597.611
58027 扮
　扮演　　　　　781.2
58027 輪
　輪迴論　　　　135.73
　輪生綱　　　　576.2
　輪船汽機　　　659.16
　輪迴　　　　　201.75
　輪裁　　　　　611.57
　輪藻植物　　　573.23
　輪蟲類　　　　583.45
　輪軸　　　　　531.92
　輪唱　　　　　771.72
58040 撒
　撒丁　　　　　983.28
　撒歪　　　　　983.478
　撒慕耶語　　　409.22
　撒加利亞書　　252.498
　撒母耳　　　　252.24
　撒哈拉　　　　985.47
　撒馬利亞文　　252.054
58045 抍
　抍音　　　　　414.5
58064 捨
　捨爾　　　　　983.483

58101 整
　整電　　　　　657.402
　整理　　　　　341.14
　整流器　　　　657.48
　整速論　　　　566.259
58116 蛻
　蛻膜　　　　　598.8271
58117 螠
　螠類　　　　　583.65
58153 蟻
　蟻　　　　　　585.58
　蟻培科　　　　578.86
58440 數
　數論　　　　　512.4
　　宇宙論　　　134.9
　數理　　　　　534.1
　　電學　　　　537.371
　　生物學　　　561.12
　　邏輯　　　　145
　　力學　　　　531.12
　　地理　　　　980.111
　　哲學　　　　581.011
　　熱學　　　　536.411
　　聲學　　　　534.1
　數學　　　　　510
　　商業　　　　626.1
　　統計　　　　512.95

敕 抄 口 唯 眩 暗 日

| 游戲 | 510.9 | 暗殺 | 315.185 |
| 表 | 510.2 | 暗算 | 510.75 |

58940 敕

| | | 暗光星 | 523.84 |

| 敕令 | 901.4 |

59029 抄

60100 日

日

| 抄襲 | 800.45 | 天文學 | 209.21 |

60000 口

		宗教	528.1
口		日高國	982.1674
生理學	597.321	日工	354.41
解剖學	597.311	日耳曼語言	409.38
口齒滋潤品	668.15	日爾曼法系	390.6
口號	379.38	日斑	523.75
口腳類	584.823	日球	523.7

60014 唯

		日變	538.751
唯識宗	239.52	日俄之戰（1904—05）	921.865
唯我論	106.21	日向國	982.166
唯物論	103.1	日蓮宗	239.68
唯物心理論	150.166	日冠	523.76
唯心論	103.3	日本	
唯心心理論	156.167	文學	820

60032 眩

| | | 語言 | 420 |
| 眩暈 | 597.8441 | 建築 | 710.2 |

60061 暗

		統計	345.2
暗示		動物	531.92
心理學	156.7	佛教	239.6
社會學	311.51	條約	387.92
暗室攝影	755.7	憲法	391.2
		游記	982

目 呈 里 星 墨

大學	338.792
地理	982.1
地圖	982.32
地質	550.2
哲學	112
考古	992
植物	571.92
教育	330.92
財政	369.2
歷史	921
日晷	528.59
日曆	528.6
日月	
天文	523.8
祭禮	319.114
崇拜	209.21
日間變化	529.2
日差	529.18
日蝕	523.78
日光	693.118
日光療法	595.85
日光機	595.84

60100 目
| 目的論 | 134.2 |
| 目錄學 | 010 |

60104 呈
| 呈文 | 339.24 |

60104 里

里廂內	983.486
里比利亞	
地理	985.55
歷史	955.5

60104 星
星辰	
天文	523.8
崇拜	209.21
祭禮	319.114
星論	521.7
星雨	523.53
星雲	523.81
星雲假設	523.13
星球交通學	524
星球測量法	522.8
星占	157.2
星宿	523.8
星期工作	354.46
星花休息	354.6
星期日	253.19
星蟲類	583.67
星團	523.81
星命	157.2
星命天宮圖	157.24

60104 墨
墨	739.19
墨西哥	
地理	984.4

歷史	948.4	社會學	315.19
墨西哥灣	984.48	教育	338.97
墨水	667.73	相法	315.13
墨子	111.131	**60127 蜀**	
墨家	111.13	蜀(三國)(歷史)	
墨寫	010.63	(221—263)	912.6
墨迹	729.15	**60127 蹄**	
黨義特藏	001.189	蹄兔類	588.36
美術	739.15	**60132 暴**	
墨筆量	733.7	暴動	315.184
60104 量		暴風	316.45
量度		**60147 最**	
電學	537.077	最後通牒	381.51
物理學	530.077	最後七言	251.2955
量度儀器	542.3	最小二乘法	512.93
量子論	530.7	**60150 國**	
量數度	134.9	國產稅	369.152
60107 疊		國課	315.183
疊函數	516.5	國旗	371.08
60111 罪		國歌	771.3
罪惡		國外旅行	381.828
自然神學	201.63	國外投資	367.13
神學	251.36	國債論	369.08
基督徒生活	258.57	國徽	371.08
原因	315.16	國家	381.1
罪犯		國家證券	366.5
測定	315.14	國家紋章	961
心理學	156.3359		

國家統計	345		國際調停	382.24
國家經濟	350.031		國際商法	381.85
國家道德	185		國際交涉	386.4
國家社會主義	318.2		國際調查委員會	382.26
國家財政	369		國際引渡	381.88
國家目錄—中國	013.1		國際刑法	381.88
國家學	371		國際政治	380
國家醫學	593		國際聯盟	383
國家義務	185.5		歐戰	930.753
國禮	319.1		國際平等	338.72
國內移民	377.7		國際爭議	382
國民投資	367.11		國際統一私法學院	383.63
國內貿易	351.39		國際郵政	636.8
國內匯兌	365		國際私約	387.6
國有鐵路	633.17		國際航線測量局	383.73
國花	570.087		國際航空委員會	383.75
國勢調查	345		國際經濟	350.04
國都	373.091		國際私法	381.8
國教	200.09		國際私法之編纂	381.802
國書	386.22		國際仲裁	382.1
國事犯	394.23		國際仲裁訴訟	382.45
國界			國際仲裁法庭	382.43
國家學	371.033		國際代表	386.5
國際法	381.33		國際委員會	386.38
國際問題	388.71		國際特別法	381.9
國別目錄	013		國際河	381.35
國防	369.13		國際法	381
國際訴訟法(私)	381.87		國際密約	387.6

四

國際道德	185.7	國民權利與義務	372.1
國際法之編纂	381.029	國民大會	001.176
國際法典編纂委員會	383.51	國民黨	375.12
國際法人	381.1	國舞	792.1
國際教育電影學院	383.63	國會	373.033
國際地理	980.178	國會法	392
國際救濟局	383.71	國籍法	381.81
國際警察	382.7	國籍別	349.079

60210 四

四開本	010.46
四諦(聲聞乘)	231.3
四靈	811.1575
四元	512.62
四面曲面	519.467
四面曲線	519.458
四季	
天文學	525.5
醫學	593.113
四樂合奏	779.7
四川省	981.71
四鰓類	583.571
四角號碼	012.7
四家易	091.1
四福音	252.6
四邊形	517.35
四次空間	519.63
四大汗國	915.94
四基法	511.2

國際共管	381.191
國際抗議	381.025
國際本位	361.28
國際鴉片委員會	383.56
國際關係	385
國際民法	381.84
國際問題	388
國際貿易	351.31
國際學院	383.6
國際滙兌	365
國際會議	380.6
國際智議合作學院	383.61
國際鐵路	633.19
國際常設法庭	382.41
國際勞工組織	383.8
國體	371.04
國學	070
國民	372
國民經濟學	350.04
國民教育	330.123

兄 見 罷 吊 易 胃 園 思 恩 黑

四書	098
四輔	222.5
四則	511.2
四吠陀	242.1
四肢	
解剖	591.86
測定	565.35
體質	565.25
四年制	334.4
四人合唱	771.77
四針類	582.57

60210 兄
兄弟之道	183.4

60210 見
見禮	319.34

60211 罷
罷工	354.83
罷免權	372.17

60227 吊
吊車	655.82

60227 易
易經(周易)	091
易卜拉欣(亞伯拉罕)	271.23
易緯	091.9

60227 胃
胃	597.322
胃病	597.343
胃腺	597.313
胃液	597.322
胃炎	597.343

60232 園
園藝	613
園囿	614.128

60330 思
思維	151.8
思想	
病理	151.87
政治學	372.132
心理學	151.8
哲學	131.3

60330 恩
恩庇多克士	121.16
恩惠	
倫理學	180.63
宗教	251.41

60331 黑
黑龍江(水)	981.345
黑龍江省	981.915
黑三稜科	575.25
黑種	565.881
黑德斯	982.76
黑色火藥	663.11
黑油	651.767
黑土	557.568
黑麥草	612.273

愚 團 田 早 旱 晏 曼 男 因

黑格爾	127.5
黑本	823.64
黑泰	409.125
黑點	523.75
黑曜岩	557.23
黑體輻射	535.59

60332 愚

愚童	153.766
愚笨	180.89

60345 團

團契	333.9
團體圖書館	025.6

60400 田

田麻科	578.43
田徑賽	338.634
田制	353.02
田代薯科	575.86
田納西	984.174
田作殖	543.24
田獵	619
森林	614.93
田葱科	575.77
田園文學	800.1892
詩	801.1
田園森林	614.97
田賦	369.151
田駢	111.174

60400 早

早熟禾	612.21
早生胞子類	582.26
早禱	253.26

60401 旱

旱災	316.43

60404 晏

晏子	111.193
晏幾道（? 1610）	811.734

60407 曼

曼語	409.375
曼特羅（集錄）	242.17

60427 男

男童	153.773
男生殖官能	597.621
男生殖官能病	597.645
男生殖器	597.615
男修道	254.5
男女交際	319.38
男女同校	338.918
男服	319.41
男性優勝	581.663
男性精神發育	

60430 因

因事犯	394.25
因數表	510.213
因果論	
形上學	134.11

昇 甲 畢 圍 暈 回 呂 固

佛學哲學	231.144	暈	529.65
婆羅門教	241.4	**60600 回**	
因明	231.16	回音	534.43
佛經	232.085	回文特藏	009.83
佛學哲學	231.16	回響	534.43

60440 昇

昇降橋	651.575	回想	151.84
昇降機	655.83	回教	270

60500 甲

甲斐國	982.1637	天文學	528.66
甲狀腺	597.414	建築	715.7
甲殼類	584.8	經典	272.7
甲骨	990.11	法律	390.3
文字考古	990.811	歷史	279
考古學	990.11	宗派	279
中國考古學	991.1	回回文學	819

60504 畢

畢業		語言	409.26
論文	334.74	回歸	528.3
典禮	333.45	回屬時代(997—1203)	
圖書館學校	028.4	西班牙史	933.82
畢達哥柏拉圖派	121.57	埃及史	951.85
畢達哥拉士	121.131	葡萄牙史	933.983
畢達哥拉士學派	121.13	印度史	923.82

60506 圍

圍攻工程	659.32	**60600 呂**	
圍困	381.553	呂不韋	111.197

60506 暈

		呂宋	983.912
		呂溫(772—881)	817.45
		呂祖謙(1137—81)	817.573

60604 固

固形動學	531.24

圖 暑 罰

固態	541.1	圖書史	010.9
固有法	390.002	圖書學	010
固皮目	572.53	圖書館	020
固顎類	587.4771	記備	024
固體		位置	024
變化	536.71	建築	024
比熱	536.33	行政	022
傳熱	536.417	使用法	027
速度	534.41	組織	022
運動		宣傳	022.7
在液體中	532.58	法規	022.2
在氣體中	533.57	推廣	022.7
地球結構說	551.12	目錄	012
膨脹	536.2	歷史	020.9

60604 圖

圖案		學校	028
工藝美術	762	會計	022.4
水利工程	654.42	館員	022.5
製造工業	675.02	坐落	024
紋章學	960.62	管理	023
機械工程	655.13	圖書館學	020
圖案照片	339.8	圖騰社會	313.382
圖樣	319.402	圖算	510.77

60604 暑

暑期學校	338.86
暑期學校(圖書館)	028.8

工程	651.122		
建築	711.2		
社會學	319.402		
圖畫解析	731.1		
圖書使用法	027		

60620 罰

罰款	369.145
罰金	394.515

品 晶 昆 鼉 昂 曇 囚 貝 足 異 叫 吐 畸 吶 瞞 時

60660 品
品得（前？522—？448）	831.45
品質別	349.075

60660 晶
晶基長英斑岩	557.27

60711 昆
昆士蘭	985.9391
昆布蘭	983.569
昆蟲寄生	594.974
昆蟲學	585
昆體良	832.846

60716 鼉
鼉鍵	655.259

60727 昂
昂哥拉	982.661

60731 曇
曇華科	575.83

60800 囚
囚犯	156.3359

60800 貝
貝勒（1762—1851）	852.7

60801 足
足球	338.635
足手有袋類	588.28

60801 異
異端	200.04
異位妊娠	598.821

64000 叫
叫禽類	587.977

64010 吐
吐劑	587.977

64021 畸
畸形	565.28
牙科	598.245
人類學	565.28
畸形外科	598.17
畸形學	
生物學	561.3
解剖學	591.3
植物學	571.5
畸足	598.178
畸異發育	561.75
畸胎學	591.3

64027 吶
吶喊	960.6

64027 瞞
瞞騙	315.187

64040 時
時令	611.1
時效	381.312
刑法	394.58
國際法	381.312
民法	397.18
時季	616.277

疇 噴 跗 跛 財 賄 賭 贖 睫 味 購 咖

時候分配	528.52	財產均分	359
時候差式	528.53	財務	369.13
時間		財務行政	369.12
哲學	134.5	中國國家財政	369.02
感覺	151.1753	國家財政	369.12
時會	150.162	財政部	373.054

64041 疇
疇人傳	510.097

64086 噴
噴出岩	557.2
噴泉	719.6
噴沙機	655.55
噴水	611.991

64100 跗
跗猴	589.37

64147 跛
跛行本位	361.25

64800 財
財產	
行政	373.096
保險	368.5
犯罪學	315.187
民法	397.51
財產刑	394.515
財產稅	369.151
財產法	381.842
財產權	372.12

財政廳 373.68
財政局
　市政府與行政 373.0821
　縣政府與行政 373.0832
財貨 352.3
財富 352.2

64827 賄
賄選與争選	372.57

64864 賭
賭博	315.188

64886 贖
贖罪	251.23

65081 睫
睫狀體	598.342

65090 味
味覺	151.14
味精	664.45

65845 購
購買	622.51

66000 咖
咖啡	612.73

啤 唱 咒 嚴 嬰 單 器 囂 罌 賜 咀

化學工業	664.7	單色射線取法	535.48
農業	612.73	單色彩畫	734.3

66040 啤
啤酒釀造	664.53

		單動機	655.252
		單筒機械	531.9

66060 唱
唱詩班	253.57
唱歌	338.137

		單本位	361.21
		單軌鐵道	651.84
		單口目	572.33

66217 咒
咒語	157.75

		單區選舉制	372.524
		單針類	582.57
		單簧樂器	774.3

66248 嚴
嚴羽	811.1576

66661 器
器樂	773
器官學	616.21
器械算術	510.76

66404 嬰
嬰兒霍亂	594.935

66506 單
單面動學	531.23
單一國	371.61
單一企業	356.2
單列藍藻科	572.172
單孔類	588.15
單聽	151.126
單子宮類	588.3
單子葉	569.51
單子葉植物	575.1
單毛矽藻科	572.51
單齒類	588.61
單細胞植物	571.213
單級	337.41

66668 囂
囂俄（1802—85）	
詩	841.76
戲曲	842.76
小說	843.76

66772 罌
罌粟（鴉片）	
農作病	612.75
園藝	613.81
罌粟綱	577.5

66827 賜
賜授	960.8

67010 咀

晚 明 嘲 鳴 眼 喉 吸 吹 盟 野 躑

咀嚼	597.321	喉科	598.495

67016 晚

晚生胞子蟲類	582.21
晚禱	253.26

67020 明

明諾特(1313—52)	851.19
明治(1868—1912)	921.86
明夷待訪錄	916.7
明器	991.71
明覺	151.51
明尼蘇達	984.178

67020 嘲

嘲笑	180.91

67027 鳴

鳴禽類	587.976

67032 眼

眼	
醫術	595.22
光學	535.9
眼子菜科	575.31
眼科	598.3
眼之訓練	770.074
眼鏡	
手藝	688.1
眼科	598.399

67034 喉

喉鰾類	587.4775

67047 吸

吸引	595.817
吸收	
水力學	532.15
消化生理	597.329
吸收與分散	
熱學	536.49
光學	535.38
吸收光帶	535.445
吸虫寄生	594.973
吸蟲類	583.33
吸口蟲類	583.617

67107 吹

吹管法	542.5
定量分析	545.2
定性分析	544.3

67107 盟

盟約	910.286
盟員國	383.1

67122 野

野牡丹科	578.82
野郎	319.77
野籔木科	578.74
野性	153.764

67127 躑

躑躅	613.85

路 蹂 鄂 鷺 照 鸚 鴨 吟 哈 賺

67164 路

路得記	252.23
路線	
橋樑工程	651.506
鐵道工程	651.811
路程表	
地理	980.032
中國地理	981.032
路得會	259.83
路伊斯(1775—1818)	853.71
路道	719.3
路橋	651.5021
路基	651.812
路加	252.63
路車廣告	629.4
路易斯歌	871.13
路易斯安那	984.172
路燈	653.2

67194 蹂

蹂躪	381.552

67227 鄂

鄂蘭吉自由邦	957.6
地理	985.76
歷史	957.6

67327 鷺

鷺	587.974

67336 照

照片	755.2
照像	750
照明工業	665
照會	386.45

67427 鸚

鸚鵡類	597.9751

67527 鴨

鴨	
畜產業	615.2
動物學	587.973
獸醫學	599.45
鴨茅	612.22
鴨跖草科	575.75

68027 吟

吟誦	771.73

68061 哈

哈達拉穆	982.77
哈琪利	982.667
哈該書	252.497
哈丁	941.884
哈特(1839—1902)	863.45
哈特勒	125.51
哈特曼	127.77
哈密爾敦	125.66
哈禮孫	941.856
哈禮孫便雅憫	941.877
哈巴谷書	252.495

68837 賺

敗 賒 壁 雅 臍 防 肺 膀 陪

賺工	354.256	防腐手術	598.157
68840 敗		防水法	675.08
敗血病		防禦	
產婦病	598.862	動物學	581.75
傳染病	598.947	農藝	611.994
敗醬科	579.85	防禦工程	659.33
68891 賒		防禦動物	571.74
賒賬	364.7	防波堤	654.2
70104 壁		防冷	571.73
壁蟲類		防旱	571.72
動物學	584.679	防風草	612.47
傳染病	594.975	**70227 肺**	
壁紙	763.7	肺	597
壁畫	735.11	病理	597.245
壁軸	763.6	呼吸法	597.215
70214 雅		肺魚類	587.45
雅(詩經)	093.7	肺蒸發	592.52
雅科俾	127.71	肺呼吸	
雅各書	252.791	動物	581.427
雅典	931.831	醫學	597.225
70227 臍		**70227 膀**	
臍帶	598.2277	膀胱	
臍帶脫垂	598.848	病理	597.642
70227 防		解剖	597.612
防腐		**70261 陪**	
微生學	566.968	陪音	534.541
肥料	611.993	陪審官	395.04
		陪葬	319.24

骸 譬 辟 盔 蠶 歷 腓 厄

70282 骸	
骸骨配製	567.1
70601 譬	
譬喻量	241.23
70641 辟	
辟門	983.26
71107 盔	
盔甲	379.95
盔飾	960.1
71136 蠶	
蠶豆	612.37
蠶子	616.3
蠶種	616.3
蠶牀	616.5
蠶室	616.5
蠶業	
政策	616.1
經濟	616.1
分佈	616.29
蠶體學	616.2
蠶具	616.5
71211 歷	
歷代記	252.26
歷史	900
文學	800.9
雜誌	900.5
各國史	910.950
神學	209
地理	980.19
地圖	920.3
哲學	100.9
圖畫	737.9
年表	910.092
會社	900.6
歷史上的基督	251.299
71211 腓	
腓立門書	252.786
腓得南五世與以色巴拉時代（西班牙史）（1479—1516）	933.83
腓力三世至查理四世時代（西班牙史）（1598—1808）	933.85
腓力比人書	252.76
腓尼基	928.3
語言	409.53
地理	982.83
歷史	928.3
71212 厄	
厄塞克斯	983.566
厄瓜多爾	
地理	984.869
歷史	948.69

71214 壓

壓計	533.39
壓縮律	533.36
液體	532.37
氣體	533.36
壓力	532.33
生理	581.7771
傳導	533.383
液體	532.33
減除	533.37
氣體	533.34

71210 胚

胚種	
生殖	561.64
生理	581.22
解剖	591.53
連續(遺傳)	563.33
原素(遺傳)	563.31
胎生	581.692
胚外形	591.57
胚質淘汰	563.35

71220 阿

阿摩尼亞	661.4
阿刻內尼亞	983.16
阿諛	180.92
阿爾泰語	409.25
阿列布	613.775
阿比西尼亞	
地理	985.2
歷史	952
阿肯色	
美洲地理	984.174
阿利堅	121.626
阿德	641.875
阿富汗語	
語言	409.325
地理	982.51
歷史	925.9
阿富汗帝國時代	
（印度史）	
（1205—1397）	923.83
阿波國	982.1657
阿薩密	982.36
阿塔尼西亞信經	251.83
阿根廷	
地理	984.82
歷史	984.2
阿拉	271.1
阿拉斯加	984.198
阿拉巴瑪	984.171
阿剌伯	
文學	895.1
語言	409.51
地理	982.7
哲學	117
歷史	927

隔 膈 脣 辰 脹 豚 厭 蜃 牙 肝 反

阿里	981.987	手術	598.27
阿丹	271.21	衛生	598.23
阿闍婆吠陀	242.14	解剖	598.21
阿含部	232.2	生理	598.22

71227 隔

隔離法	593.2351	治療	598.25
隔鰓類	583.557	冶金	598.286
隔絶説	563.53	器械	598.29

牙買加

地理	984.72
歷史	947.2

71227 膈

膈膜	597.217

71240 肝

肝

消化生理	597.315
消化解剖	597.325
肝卜	157.16

71227 脣

脣裂	598.172
脣形科	579.57

71232 辰

辰星崇拜	209.21

71247 反

反意字	413.4
反颶麗	529.37
反函數	516.4
反稱行列式	512.32

71232 脹

脹	597.349

反射

電磁	538.863
傳熱	536.43

71232 豚

豚	615.14
豚鼠類	588.616

71234 厭

厭世論	173.1

反線	35.32
反芻類	588.333
反宗教同盟	200.67
反對數	510.28
反轉幾何學	519.05

71236 蜃

蜃氣	523.67

71240 牙

牙科	598.2
病理	598.24

脂 階 曆 贗 願 灰 原

反數表	510.215	動物構造	581.101
反省派(心理學)	150.1975	植物組織	571.111

71261 脂
		生物細胞	561.51
脂肪族	547.1	醫學	597.721
脂肪變性	594.82	原子	541.01
脂肪體	597.318	重量	536.37

71262 階
		化學	541.01
階級		哲學學派	121.17
政治	371.066	原鯨類	588.471
倫禮	184.7	原齒類	588.11
社會	313.8	原種論	561.64

71269 曆
		原動力	655.17
曆書	528	原生動物	582.1
		古生物	569.71

71286 贗
		原生植物	572
贗造	315.187	古生物	569.21
贗器	990.077	原鰓類	583.551

71286 願
		原索動物	586
願望	151.46	原有蹄類	588.35

71289 灰
		原始宗教	209
灰泥	712.3	原始國家	371.1
灰吹法	545.2	原式機	655.251

71296 原
		原藻綱	573.21
原刻本	009.11	原素	
原形態學		化合	661.2
植物	571.23	定性	544.03
生物	561.11	哲學	133.3
原形質		原頓體類	583.51

驅 馬

原罪	251.35	馬齒莧科	577.25
原足類	584.2	馬利亞納群島	985.963
原獸類	588.1	馬利弗	

71316 驅

		(1688—1763)	643.52
驅逐艦	379.656	法國戲院	842.54
驅逐機	379.74	法國小説	843.52
驅蟲藥	597.363	馬戲	789.3

71327 馬

		馬貘類	588.346
馬	588.342	馬紹爾群島	985.967
病理	599.41	馬達加斯加島	985.78
畜牧	615.11	馬迪孫	941.851
馬痘	594.965	馬邏(1564—32)	852.32
馬諾芬時期		馬太	252.61
(法國史)		馬克斯主義	318.5
(418—752)		馬來半島	
馬可	252.62	語言	409.183
馬可黎(1800—59)	857.83	地理	982.49
馬西亞爾		歷史	924.9
(？40—120)	832.826	馬鞭草科	579.55
馬雷布		馬荼爾語	409.235
(1555—1628)	841.41	馬其頓	
馬爾内	983.471	(362—323)	931.835
馬爾也	983.488	馬力調節	655.73
馬爾薩斯人口論	349.011	馬力及其傳導	655.71
馬致遠		馬車	632.4
(？1220)	812.34	馬拉	982.77
馬術	798	馬貴斯群島	985.977
馬上比武	797.5	馬里蘭	

驃 匯 匪 區 巨 長 劉 丘 剛

哥倫比亞	984.166
馬鳴	239.134
馬尼多巴	984.27
馬兜鈴綱	576.9
馬隊	379.56
馬鈴薯	612.481
馬金烈	941.870
馬拿西祈禱書	252.96
馬金叨斯	857.71
馬錢科	579.42

71391 驃
| 驃語 | 409.171 |

71711 匯
| 匯票 | 364.4 |
| 匯兌 | 365 |

71711 匪
| 匪患 | 316.48 |

71716 區
| 區域經濟學 | 350.02 |
| 區黨部 | 001.44 |

71717 巨
巨哥斯拉夫	939.55
地理	983.935
歷史	939.55

71732 長
長頸鹿類	588.338
長形類(蚊)	585.57
長歌	821.2
長崎縣	982.166
長生	
生理	581.698
宗教	224
長鼻類	588.35
長江	981.341
長途競賽	338.636
長老會	259.5
長野縣	982.163
長阿含	232.21
長門	982.1653
長年差	529.82

72100 劉
劉歆	111.244
劉禹錫(772—842)	811.1456
劉向	111.243
劉大櫆(1698—1780)	817.742
劉基(1311—75)	817.611
劉星煒(1718—72)	817.763
劉長卿	811.1453

72102 丘
| 丘疹 | 598.541 |

72200 剛
剛果自由邦	
地理	985.65
歷史	956.5
剛愎	180.83

腫　臘　所　彫　膨　爪　瓜　脉　隱　阡　腦　盾　N

72214 腫		
腫		594.993
腫脹		561.55

72216 臘		
臘板		010.13
臘梅科		577.42

72221 所		
所得稅		369.155
所羅門詩歌		252.983
所羅門歌		252.35
所羅門群島		985.953
所羅門智慧		252.93

72222 彫		
彫刻		720
建築		712.2
木器		766.2
材料		721
技術		721

72222 膨		
膨脹		536.2

72230 爪		
爪哇		985.923

72230 瓜		
瓜水母類		582.778
瓜菜		613.2

72232 脉		
脉		
病理		597.126
診法		595.24
地質		553.8
醫學		
脉翅類		585.51
脉管組織(動物)		581.27
脉管植物		571.216

72237 隱		
隱頭類		583.615
隱名		018.3
隱色蟲菌目		572.35
隱花植物		573
古生物		569.2

72240 阡		
阡塔基		984.175

72262 腦		
腦峽		597.8116
腦神經		597.8
生理		597.823
解剖		597.811
官能病		597.844
構造病		597.843
器質病		155.23
精神病		155.24
腦膜		597.8119

72264 盾		
盾牌		379.96

72270 N

鬚 馴 驕 髮 鬣 氏 兵 質 縣 院 腔 腕 胎

N次空間	519.61	**72806 質**	
N次空間之微		質數	512.41
數幾何	519.75	質量	
N—光線	535.54	地球	525.1
72286 鬚		日球	523.71
鬚	598.59	月球	523.31
鬚鯨類	588.473	**72993 縣**	
鬚腳類	584.674	縣代表	373.6343
72300 馴		**73211 院**	
馴養	615.02	院部制	373.0506
72327 驕		**73211 腔**	
驕傲	180.81	腔液	581.411
72447 髮		腔腸動物	582.7
髮		古生物	569.72
相術	157.32	**73212 腕**	
醫學	598.59	腕足類	583.93
人類學	565.26	**73260 胎**	
髮蟲類	583.42	胎倒轉術	598.872
72716 鬣		胎生學	
鬣狗類	588.513	動物學	581.6
72740 氏		植物學	571.6
氏（304—403）	913.52	生物學	561.6
氏族社會	313.381	解剖學	591.5
72801 兵		胎息	224.2
兵庫縣	982.164	胎盤	598.8273
兵災	316.48	胎盤移動術	598.877
兵車	379.97	胎盤留滯	598.846

騙 墮 助 附 尉 陸 肋 隋

胎教	598.91	陸龜蒙(？—881)	811.486
胎附件病理學	598.827	陸奧國	982.1624
胎兒截割法	598.873	陸宰	127.75
胎兒煤素	598.174	陸運	631

73327 騙

騙拐	315.188	陸軍	379.5
		行政	379.52

74104 墮

		戰略	379.53
墮落	338.968	陸游	

74127 助

助產槓杆與鉗		韻文	811.1574
子用法	598.871	詞	811.7394
助消藥	597.365	陸克	125.3
		陸九淵(1139—92)	

74200 附

		文學	817.572
附加稅	369.1619	哲學	111.57
附感覺	151.19	陸機(261—303)	811.1322
附屬國	371.73	陸地	980.501
附着語	403	陸地地圖	980.305
		陸棲食肉類	588.51

74200 尉

		陸中	982.1624
尉拆力(1640—1715)	852.44	陸戰	930.761

74214 陸

		法規	381.55
陸雲(262—303)	811.1323	陸前	982.1624
陸賈	111.21		

74227 肋

陸行	593.481	肋鰭類	587.41
陸稻	612.18	肋骨	597.7112

74227 隋

陸生動物	581.902	隋代(581—618)	
陸生植物	571.902		
陸生蜘蛛類	584.67	文集	810.38

隨 膜 陝 陵 騏 體 胰 膿 腱 陳

詩集	811.138
哲學	111.3
歷史	813.9
騷賦	811.33
駢散文	817.3
小說	813.3

74232 隨

隨雨	225.4
隨質	597.813
隨膜	597.813
隨筆	088
隨營	025.75

74234 膜

膜翅類	585.58

74238 陝

陝西省	981.65

74247 陵

陵墓	
孫中山	001.199
名勝古迹	981.386

74381 騏

騏頓	983.16

75218 體

體育	
教育	332.5
青年會	256.355
學校	338.63
體溫	
動物	581.43
生理	592.5
體力	565.41
體裁	910.9113
體格	153.5
體操	338.631
體質人類學	565.2
體腔動物	582.8

75232 胰

胰腺	
生理	597.316
解剖	597.326

75232 膿

膿	598.143
膿潰	594.81
膿皮色狀	598.542
膿毒病	594.94

75240 腱

腱	597.716
腱囊	597.717

75296 陳

陳亮	817.575
陳設	256.32
陳那	239.146
陳子昂(656—698)	811.1415
陳代(557—589)	
文集	810.38

鼬 胭 陽 腸 腭 腺 脾 隄 隕 驛 堅 竪

詩集	811.136
哲學	111.3
歷史	911.6393
駢散文	817.3
小說	811.3
陳其年（1625—82）	817.723

75716 鼬
鼬鼠類	588.517

76200 胭
胭脂	668.16

76227 陽
陽文彫刻	721.7
陽湖派（中國文學）	817.75
陽遂足類	582.92
陽攝法	765
陽曆	528.6

76227 腸
腸	597.314
腸病	597.344
腸系膜	597.317
腸卜	157.16
腸液	597.324
腸瀉	597.344
腸熱	594.926

76227 腭
腭骨	597.7116

76232 腺
腺及淋巴系	
動物	581.14
醫學	597.4
腺系	
病理	597.44
手術	597.47
生理	597.42
解剖	597.41
治療	597.45
藥學	597.46

76240 脾
脾	597.411
脾熱	594.967

76281 隄
隄防	654.62

76286 隕
隕石	
岩石學	557.6
流星	523.51

76341 驛
驛站	632.1

77104 堅
堅證禮	253.92
堅頭類	587.63
堅果類	613.76
堅鬆	551.16

77108 竪

鬭 閩 螱 毀 肌 阻 風 鳳 尼

豎琴	775.1	作用	581.777
豎鋼琴	776.1	聲音	534.45
豎笛	774.2	農藝	611.915

77121 鬭

		氣象	529.3
鬭雞	797.1	風(詩經)	093.7

77136 閩

		風疹	594.916
閩(873—947)	914.92	風疹塊	598.541
閩江	981.348	風琴	776.7

77136 螱

		風水	157.4
螱寄生	594.974	風化	551.71

77147 毀

		風俗歌	821.54
		風俗畫	737.7
毀謗	315.186	風濕	594.991

77210 肌

		風車	655.48
肌肉	597.715	風暴	529.3
組織	591.76	風景	737.12
感覺	151.16	風箏	659.49

77210 阻

		風梨	
阻電	537.27	植物	575.73
阻力	532.56	農業	613.78

77210 鳳

天體攝動	521.57		
液體動力	532.56	鳳仙花	578.27
氣力學	533.54	鳳尾松	574.2

77210 風

77211 尼

風		尼柔蘭	
工程	650.7	條頓族	937.91
發電	657.24	地理	983.791
種類	529.31	哲學	128.1

屍 胞 尾 屋 隆 閱 覺 兒

尼耶也經	249.6
尼耶也派	249.6
尼采	127.8
尼利亞信經	251.82
尼犍子	249.7
尼治爾	
地理	982.39
歷史	923.9
尼希米書	252.28
尼加拉瓜	
地理	984.65
歷史	946.5
尼柏隆歌	871.21
尼威爾內	983.484
尼甫勒	983.484

77212 屍

屍體埋葬	593.26

77212 胞

胞子植物	569.2
胞子蟲類	582.2

77214 尾

尾	591.89
尾張國	983.1639
尾索類	586.3
尾骨腺	597.418

77214 屋

屋頂	713.5
屋内電線	657.655

77214 隆

隆鳥類	587.946

77216 閱

閱者指導	027.1
閱覽室（圖書館）	025.8
建築	024.5

77216 覺

覺官	565.45

77217 兒

兒童	
傳記	970.8
生活	
家庭	313.362
心理	153.7
保護	
家庭	313.36
國際	383.58
身體	153.71
宗教	250.17
禱文	253.46
心理	153.7
道德	188.4
權利	313.364
犯罪	315.71
教育	338.92
家庭	313.367
兒童文學	805
意國	833.5

兜 肥 颶 月 岡 同 周

俄國	885
法國	845
英國	855
中國	810
日本	825
美國	865
兒童圖書館	025.72

77217 兜
兜水母類	582.773
兜齒獸	588.37

77217 肥
肥後國	892.1665
肥皂	668.2
肥田	611.7
肥前國	882.166
肥料	
工業	668.7
化學	543.22
農業	611.7

77218 颶
颶風	529.33

77220 月
月亮	209.21
月琴	770.17
月球	523.3
月經	598.723
月經病	598.7471
月經完止	598.727
月台站	651.817
月蝕	523.38

77220 岡
岡山縣	982.165

77220 同
同意字	413.4
同一論	103.9
同形	
植物	571.217
生物	561.13
同化	377.69
同源字	413.5
同素	541.07
化學構造方	
式之不入	
541.03 者類此	
同盟絕交	354.84
同盟罷工	354.831
同學錄	339.6
同情	180.96
同情罷工	354.833
同性放射	535.25

77220 周
周敦頤	111.51
周邦彥(1060—1125)	811.737
周官	094.1
周波測定	657.18
周波與音節	534.51

胸 陶 朋 腳 膠 骨 鴉 腎

周禮	094.1	朋友團	313.66
周書	092.72	**77220 腳**	
例　洪範等		腳色	781.17
周圍神經系		**77222 膠**	
生理	597.821	膠滴菌綱	572.21
解剖	597.816	膠畫	734.5
周防國	982.1653	膠質	
77220 胸		動物生理	581.494
胸	591.84	化學	541.48
胸甲類	584.82	有機	547.93
胸膜	597.216	物理	532.7
胸膜炎	597.246	植病	572.2
胸腺	597.413	膠質海綿類	582.53
胸骨	597.7113	膠胞子蟲類	582.27
胸堂	597.7112	**77227 骨**	
77220 陶		骨刻	726
陶磁		骨牌	369.157
工藝	764	骨組織	581.26
繪畫	735.4	骨相	157.35
窰業	666.1	骨折	598.165
陶潛(365—427)		骨骼組織	591.74
韻文	811.1327	骨骼學	597.711
駢散文	817.37	**77227 鴉**	
陶土	557.521	鴉片	612.75
陶器		**77227 腎**	
建築裝飾	712.5	腎	597.611
窰業	666.11	腎病	597.641
77220 朋			

屬 爬 尿 展 限 屏 服 股 犀 降 膽 居 屠 層 眉

腎上腺	597.415
77227 屬	
屬國	281.12
77231 爬	
爬蟲類	587.8
古生物	569.85
77232 尿	
尿病	597.643
尿分析	595.29
77232 展	
展覽	018.7
衣冠	319.407
工藝	647
古物	990.079
花卉	613.8063
書目	018.7
圖	020.7
美術	700.7
77232 限	
限制僱用	354.117
限制投票法	372.528
77245 屏	
屏風	763.4
77247 服	
服制	693
服裝	
工藝	765
演劇	781.3
監獄	315.54
77247 股	
股票	366.3
股份公司	356.23
77251 犀	
犀類	588.347
77254 降	
降卒	910.285
降神	157.7
降臨	201.73
降臨節	253.11
77261 膽	
膽質	547.94
膽八樹科	578.41
77264 居	
居住	
衛生	593.15
權利	381.822
人口	349.077
居所	381.818
77264 屠	
屠宰稅	369.153
77266 層	
層向	553.5
77267 眉	
眉	157.32

尸 屈 欣 忌 驟 騷 悶 駱 關 學 丹

眉墨	668.16

77270 尸

尸佼	111.177

77272 屈

屈射	538.865
屈線	535.33
屈拆	534.45
屈原(？前310—前285)	811.311

77282 欣

欣喜	180.75

77331 忌

忌物	596.3

77332 驟

驟變	563.63

77336 騷

騷鄧(1660—1746)	852.52
騷德(1774—1843)	851.73
騷賦	811.3

77337 悶

悶死	593.43

77364 駱

駱甫雷斯(1618—58)	851.45
駱駝蟲	585.51
駱駝類	588.336

77400 關

關稅條約	387.1

77407 學

學習	151.65
學位	334.7
學徒	354.252
學生	
生活	333
履歷	334.11
學潮	332.17
學校	
建築	332.92
衛生	593.33
行政	331
出版圖書	011.3
儲蓄銀行	362.96
演劇	781
青年會	256.36
圖書館	025.5
管理	332
學期	334.32
學則	334
學院	331.32
學年	028.4
教育	334.31
圖學校	028.4
學會	060

77400 丹

丹砂	224.7
丹後國	982.164
丹波國	982.164

丹麥		閘門	651.817
文學	879.23	**77601 醫**	
語言	409.3823	醫方	595.7
地理	983.7988	醫方明	232.085
歷史	937.988	醫藥	
丹藥	224.7	牙科	598.25
丹毒	594.943	蠱	616.91
丹尼斯(1657—1734)	852.51	醫星占學	157.28
丹第(1265—1321)	833.115	醫院	593.77
77441 開		慈善事業	316.2
開方	511.5	醫學	
開戰	381.53	傳記	590.097
開學禮	334.17	心理學	158.59
開閉器	657.48	治療	595
開腹產術	598.876	道德	186
開鑛工事	658.3	顯微學	566.8
77447 段		學校	590.077
段成式(?—863)	811.1484	**77602 留**	
77503 舉		留萌支所	982.1675
舉重機	655.81	留學	338.75
77505 母		**77607 間**	
母族系統	313.384	間	521.57
母法	390.002	間腦	597.8114
母撒(摩西)		間質	547.5
上帝之言	271.25	**77717 巴**	
77506 閘		巴西	
閘	654.68	地理	984.81
		歷史	948.1

鼠 卵 印

巴爾札克(1799—1850)	843.72
巴爾幹半島	
地理	983.95
哲學	128.9
國際問題	388.21
歷史	939.5
巴比倫	
語言	409.52
地理	982.81
哲學	118.1
歷史	928.1
巴利語	409.313
巴利文一切經	232.05
巴伯(1316—95)	851.22
巴魯	252.95
巴的加雷	983.467
巴郎(1653—1729)	842.48
巴塔哥尼亞	
地理	984.829
歷史	948.29
巴勒士登	982.8
巴勒農(1834—99)	842.87
巴拉圭	
地理	984.89
歷史	984.9
巴拉馬	984.68
巴羅(1755—1812)	861.23
巴里亞利克群島	983.37

巴哈馬	
地理	984.76
歷史	946.8
巴拿馬草科	575.48
77717 鼠	
鼠疫	594.922
傳染	594.975
鼠貍類	588.343
鼠李綱	578.3
鼠類	588.615
77720 卵	
卵	
病理	598.824
生成	598.725
解剖	591.513
卵巢	598.741
卵生	581.625
77720 印	
印章	727
印度	
文學	893.1
語言	409.31
佛教	239.1
哲學	113
地理	982.3
歷史	923
印度法系	390.2
印度教	240

鷗　民　關

印度支那	
文學	891
語言	409.1
地理	982.4
歷史	924
印記	010.91
印譜	727
印形	991.63
印齒獸類	588.397
印色	991.64
印迪語	409.317
印花(漂染工業)	667.5
印花稅	369.156
印畫	769.3
印本	010.3
印質	991.62
印刷電信	657.8355
印刷板	749
印刷史	010.7
印第安納	984.176
印第安地	984.173

77727 鷗
鷗	587.973

77747 民
民主國	371.4
民族主義	001.12
民族史	931.21
民歌	771.2
民政廳	373.0811
民生主義	001.14
民衆運動	001.99
民衆教育	330.124
民衆圖書館	025.71
民約說	371.43
民俗史	932.23
民法	397
民權	372.1
民權主義	001.13
民事訴訟法	395.1
民數記	252.214
民間文學	804
意國	833.4
西班牙	835.4
俄國	884
德國	874
法國	844
日本	824
民國	814
美國	864
民間統計	345.17

77772 關
關尹子	111.122
關稅	369.16
關漢卿(？1200—85)	812.31
關東地方	982.161
關防	

門 歐 具 巽 興 輿 尺 閃 桑 監

政治	371.08
考古	990.46
史料	901.5
國民黨	001.28
美術	727
關節	597.713
關節動物	583

77777 門

門票	781.9
門窗	713.8

77782 歐

歐洲
經濟史	350.93
佛教	239.7
遊記	980.73
地理	983
地志	980.53
地圖	980.53
歷史	930
改造	930.726
年鑑	037.3

歐陽修（1007—72）
韻文	811.152
詞	811.735
駢散文	817.512

歐几里之第五
| 假定 | 519.83 |

| 歐几里士 | 121.261 |

77807 具

具保	354.115

77801 巽

巽他群島
地理	985.92
歷史	959.2

77801 興

興奮藥	597.867
興趣	354.114

77801 輿

輿論	311.54

77807 尺

尺算器械	510.76

77807 閃

閃電	529.53
閃長岩	557.36

77904 桑

桑子	613.743
桑科	576.73
桑他亞拿	126.6
桑給巴爾	985.43
桑寄生科	576.85

78107 監

監護	397.53
監理會	259.7
監督	651.127
監察院	373.06

鹽 鑒 脫 陰 隧 腹 除 駢 驗

監獄		陰影法	731.5
建築	717.4	陰曆日曆	528.6
衛生	593.36	陰陽五行	157
改革	315.5	陰陽家	157.097
勞工	354.251	陰陽眼	157.63
監獄圖書館	025.76	**78232 隧**	
監禁	381.824	隧道	658.35
78707 鹽		工程	651.6
鹽酸	661.3	鑛業	658.35
鹽膚本	612.93	**78247 腹**	
鹽化物	661.5	腹	
鹽稅	369.152	解剖	591.85
鹽業	618	消化	597.313
收入	369.14	腹孕	
鹽基定性法	544.12	病理	598.82
鹽類	661.5	生理	598.81
78109 鑒		腹毛類	583.47
鑒別板本	010.97	腹足類	583.53
78216 脫		腹膜	597.317
脫疽	598.145	腹膜炎	597.347
脫位	598.166	**78264 除**	
70232 陰		除法	511.21
陰府	251.77	除藉	381.815
陰溝	653.34	**78345 駢**	
陰道	598.745	駢文八大家	817.76
陰莖	597.617	駢散文	817
陰蔽	523.9	**78386 驗**	
陰攝法	755		

臨　騰　八　人

驗耳器	598.489	三位一體	251.17
驗力器	655.72	佛教	231.88
驗熱器	669.13	沃教	281.3
驗目器	598.39	神學	251.3
驗屍	595.29	猶太教	261.3

78766 臨

臨床程次與方法	598.835	回教	271.3
臨床醫學	595.1	人工雜種	563.52
臨終聖餐	253.98	人工生殖	561.626
臨界點	536.723	人工淘汰	571.775
臨時放款	362.7	人頭稅	369.155
臨時約法	391.1	人形論	201.33

79227 騰

騰雲	157.72	人形主義	565.012
騰寫板	747	人齒猴	589.33

80000 八

		人種學	565
八文字屋本	823.63	混合	565.73
八聖道	231.4	分類	565.8
八行詩	801.8	人生哲學	170
八仙	221.4	人物	
八出珊瑚類	582.751	繪畫	737.3
八樂合奏	779.7	彫刻	729.5
八角楓科	578.78	人名辭書	970.03
八軸海綿類	582.55	人名錄	970.3
八開本	010.46	人定界限	381.333

80000 人

		人造磁石	538.13
人文地理	980.13	人造絲	668.43
人論	251.3	人造結晶	559.7
		人造象牙	678.41
		人造寶石	

入 企

工礦	666.7	人員	636.35
礦物	558.182	人質	381.557
人造肥料	668.77	人體學	565.2
人造鑛泉	664.61	人體測定學	565.3
人道主義	107.3	人島	983.569
人壽保險		人民	371.025
數學	512.97	人民主權	371.022
財政	368.3	人民黨	375.66
人地率	349.04	人類自意動作	151.42
人猿類	589.5	人類中心論	
人格		宇宙論	107
發育	153.81	人類學	565.012
修養	153.87	人類學	
測驗	153.88	發生	565.5
權利	372.11	演化	565.71
表現	153.81	遷移	565.75
哲學	135.5	社會發生	313.1
類別	153.84	考古	565.099
人口		犯罪	315.11
殖民	377.2	自然史	565.1
環境	349.05	分化	565.74
政策	349.02	人情本	823.68
統計	349.07		
鄉村	313.42	**80000 入**	
密度	349.03	入睡之現象	156.323
限制	349.021	入學	334.1
公共衛生	593.21	入學班次	334.4
分佈	349.03	**80101 企**	
		企業聯盟	356.5

並 全 盆 益 金 鐘

企業協定	356.4

80102 並
並行論	103.5

80104 全
全頭類	587.43
全祖望(1705—55)	817.733

80107 盆
盆栽花卉	613.8061

80107 益
益林	614.5
益農	611.9

80109 金
金(朝代)	
（1115—1234)	915.7
金(音樂)	770.16
金(金屬)	546.71
金文	990.813
金言	808.3
金庫制度	369.127
金證券	361.71
金融	361
金融公司	362.16
金聖嘆(1627—65)	813.72
金仁傑(？1330)	812.46
金虎尾科	577.96
金絲桃科	578.53
金縷梅科	577.76
金魚藻科	578.32
金蓮花科	577.88
金斯黎(1819—75)	853.85
金鼓	770.16
金相學	669.7
金橘	613.733
金本位	361.21
金星	523.42
金器	768
金匯兌本位	361.26
金剛石	558.183
金丹	224.7
金屬元素	546.2
金屬製品	671
金履祥(1232—1303)	817.59
金屬板	742
金人	991.721
金鑛	558.141
採探	658.8
金鑄	725
金銀	669.91
金銀製品	671.5
金光	291.9
金類分析	543.64

80114 鐘
鐘表	
音樂	770.16
工業	671.1

錐 鏡 氫 氫 氟 鈰 翦 銥 鑲 鐺 鎌 鋅 鍍 礦

古物	991.21	**80141 鋅**	
鐘鼎文	990.812	鋅	
鐘花網	579.9	電氣冶金	669.97
80114 錐		金屬元素	546.235
錐鑽	658.32	礦物學	558.145
80116 鏡		鋅印影板	746.5
鏡與鏡被膜	598.344	**80147 鍍**	
80117 氫		鍍金	662.75
氫	546.183	鍍銀	662.75
80117 氫		**80186 礦**	
氫	546.11	礦床	
80117 氟		工業	658.21
氟	546.186	礦物	558.11
80117 鈰		礦山	369.141
鈰元素	546.26	礦泉	558.17
80132 翦		礦物	558.1
翦裁法	027.7	藥材	596.15
80132 銥		礦物學	558
銥	546.75	化學	558.4
80132 鑲		生理	558.5
鑲木	712.6	物理	558.3
鑲牙	598.28	地質	556.1
80136 鐺		顯微	566.27
鐺	546.272	分佈	558.9
80137 鎌		鑑定	558.2
鎌倉時代(1192—1333)	921.831	礦業工程	658
		電氣	658.7
		經濟	658.1

今 羌 差 兌 氪 氛 介 前 俞 斧 分

機械	658.6
鐵道與運輸	658.5
礦油	655.5
礦地	353.17
礦藏	558.11
礦毒	658.02

80207 今
今昔物語	823.38
今樣歌	821.56

80211 羌
羌(318—417)	913.55

80211 差
差異	341.3
差分學	515.5
差等與類似	
植物	571.24
生物	561.15

80216 兌
兌換銀錢	362.17
兌換券	361.73

80217 氪
氪	546.185

80217 氛
氛	546.182

80220 介
介形類	854.865
介紹	319.33

80221 前
前鰓類	583.531
前涼 漢(346—376)	913.585
前燕(鮮卑)	
(337—370)	913.584
前藏	981.981
前趙(匈奴)	
(315—329)	913.582
前秦(氐)	
(351—494)	913.586
前蜀(908—925)	914.95
前腦	597.8113

80221 俞
俞樾(1821—1906)	813.78

80221 斧
斧足類	583.55

80227 分
分工論	356.9
分水嶺	654.64
分裂	581.614
分裂生殖	561.613
分子	541.01
分子說	538.43
分子動力學	531.69
分子與固體力學	531.6
分配論	359
分配合作	356.77
分紅	354.337

舞　無

分生植物	572.1
分生藻綱	572.17
分生菌綱	572.11
分結與結核	551.99
分級教授法	337.4
分泌	597.42
分泌系	581.44
分極	538.867
分析化學	543
分權制	373.0502
分枝滴菌科	572.215
分娩	598.83
分娩病理學	598.84
分別蒸餾	541.65
分體學	517.6
分光計	535.43
分光法	535.48
分光學	535.4
分光鏡	535.41
分類	
統計	341.14
圖書	023.3
分類目類	012.1

80251 舞

舞樂	773
舞樂式	770.027
舞臺	781.5
舞草	612.385

舞曲	
游藝	792.6
日本文學	821.7
舞蹈	792

80331 無

無言劇	802.5
無病菌	566.963
無瓣類(元始花)	576.1
無脊椎動物	582
古生物學	569.7
無頭類	583.55
無水時代	554.2
無政府主義	318.4
無我	231.313
無生	349.023
無生殖能	598.775
無生代	554.2
無線電報	637.3
無線電信	657.838
無觸手類	582.777
無獎儲蓄	362.92
無組織罷工	354.835
無色界	231.83
無神論	
自然神學	201.1
婆羅門教	241.3
無法投遞之信件	636.59
無機物	593.91

念 慈 兼 尊 父 午 姜

無機物細菌	566.93	念珠藍藻科	572.174
無機化學	546	念經	233.6
無機化學藥品	661.1	念咒	157.72
無機物分析	543.6	**80333 慈**	
無機液態	541.23	慈悲	180.77
無板類	583.513	慈恩宗	239.52
無花果	613.741	慈善團	025.77
無翅類	585.1	慈善派	269.7
無患子科	578.25	慈善建築	717.3
無量壽禪	231.24	慈善事業	316
無口目	572.31	鄉村	313.46
無足類動物	587.66	慈善會	316.3
無所不能	251.143	**80337 兼**	
無所不在	251.142	兼修（圖學）	028.5
無所不知	251.141	**80346 尊**	
無體量	241.26	尊老	319.31
無關節類	583.94	尊敬	180.71
無尾類動物	587.68	**80400 父**	
無着	289.145	父族系統	313.385
無籍流民風俗	319.9	父系	313.321
無常	231.311	父母	313.322
無性生殖		父母之道	183.3
動物	581.61	父母與子女	397.52
生殖學	561.61	**80400 午**	
植物學	571.61	午禱	253.26
無烟炭	558.125	**80404 姜**	
無烟火藥	663.13	姜宸英（1628—99）	817.725

80332 念

傘 美

姜夔（？1155—1235）	811.7397

80408 傘

傘	688.5

80430 美

美	133.89
美術	700
美術上的基督	251.297
美術心理學	158.7
美術考古學	990.7
美術與技藝運動	761
美術館	700.7
美容	693.5
美塞尼亞	983.17
美洲	
百科辭書	034
經濟史	350.94
佛教	239.8
游記	980.74
地理	984
地圖	980.34
歷史	940
年鑑	037.4
類志	980.54
美濃國	982.1635
美涅憾（1582—1646）	841.42
美索波達美亞	982.668
美村	313.411
美拉尼西亞	
地理	985.95
歷史	959.5
美里瑟士	121.127
美國	
文學	860
語言	450
建築	710.41
統計	345.41
動物	581.941
條約	387.941
憲法	391.141
游記	984.1
大學	338.7941
地理	984.1
地圖	980.341
地質	550.41
考古	994.1
植物	571.941
教育	330.941
哲學	126
財政	369.41
歷史	941
美基督教委員會	256.13
美墨戰爭（1845—48）	944.85
美學	
音樂	770.017
建築	710.01
演劇	780.011

年 羊 氧 氟 義 合

哲學	190
農學	614.127
彫刻	721.01
美人蕉科	575.93
美美會	259.7

80500 年

年	528.3
年譜	001.193
年假	336.58
年齡	
病理學	594.24
心理學	153.6
年齡藥療法	595.75
年齡別	349.073
年表	910.092
年金公債	369.184
年鑑	
普通	030
圖書館	020.37

80501 羊

羊	
畜產學	615.13
獸醫學	599.43
羊齒植物	
古生物	569.24
隱花植物	573.8
羊紙皮	674.5
羊膜	598.3275

80517 氧

氧	546.151
氧元素	546.15
氧化酸化	566.927

80517 氟

| 氟 | 546.137 |
| 氟光 | 535.52 |

80553 義

義勇隊	379.8
義務	
特殊教育	338.84
倫理學	180.73
國民教育	372.2
義準量	241.24
義斯得勒馬都拉	983.36
義莊	316.6
義田	316.6

80601 合

合瓣類(後生花)	579
合調	534.67
合級	337.43
合作社	356.7
合作銀行	356.75
合資公司	398.23
合葬	319.24
合花綱	575.47
合著叢書	081.7
合著書目	016

首 普 善 曾 會

合抨	356.3
合同	
工藝	642.3
實業	602.3
合金學	669.6

80601 首

首都	981.51
首飾	671.5

80601 普

普魯達	121.57
普魯士	
地理	937.85
歷史	983.76
普魯塔士	
（前1254—184)	832.23
普洛丁諾士	121.58
普洛達哥拉士	121.222
普洛迭克士	121.225
普通法與特別法	390.003
普通教育	330.124
普郎大那時代	
（1154—1399）	935.83
普林尼（？62—114)	832.81
普帕細阿士	
（？前50—15)	832.44
普刺克立語	409.315
普救會	259.82

80605 善

善惡論	
宗教	201.6
哲學	133.88
善德	258.51
善本特藏	009
善本書目	019

80606 曾

曾子	111.1123
曾鞏（1019—83）	817.516
曾國藩（1811—72）	817.783
曾燠（1760—1831）	813.768

80606 會

會意	411.33
會話	416.7
會計	
商業	627
學校	332.7
會計年度	369.126
會議	
立法院	373.036
教育行政	331.36
國家	369.1606
圖書館	020.6
會議	
財政	362.08
會議條例	381.026
會島	985.975
會社	371.066

含 谷 命 乞 公

會社出版書目	011.6	公孫龍	111.153
會社圖書館	025.6	公理	510.3
會社團體	313.6	公司	356.23
會吏	255.55	公司條例	398.2
會長	256.33	公經濟學	350.03
會堂	715.6	公私卹貧	316.5

80607 含

含族語系		公債	369.13
文學	896	公使	386.33
語文	409.6	公債論	369.18
含液小體	571.112	公債借換	369.187
含羞草	612.387	公債募集	369.186

80608 谷

谷	552.6	公債清理	369.188
谷德倫歌	871.22	公積金	362.4
		公安	315.3

80627 命

命數法	510.5	公安體	811.167
命題	141	公安局	373.0825
命分	511.31	公法與私法	390.008
		公禱文	253.4

80717 乞

乞丐所	316.38	公禮會	259.5
		公道	180.72

80730 公

公文	339.2	公海法權	381.7
公文檔案	901.2	公式	510.3
公立學校	338.01	公地	353.2
公立銀行	362.12	公共讀書所	338.88
公函	339.22	公共建築	313.413
		建築學	717
		政府的	373.093
		鄉村的	313.413

食　養

公共衛生	593.2	生理	581.7775
公共經費	369.13	生物	562.83
公共收入	369.14	保存法	694.5
公共禮拜	253.21	家政	694
公共圖書館	025.3	田獵	616.94
公共廁所	653.35	醫學	593.121
公場	719.2	分析	543.1
公園	313.415	食品	664
建築	719.1	食物療法	595.82
社會	313.415	食滯	597.343
公曆	528.67	食禮	319.27
公民學	185.1	食肉有袋類	588.26
政治	372	食肉類	588.5
倫理	185.1	食草有袋類	588.24
教育	330.123	食蟲植物	571.75
公會	354.64	食蟲類動物	588.8
公羊傳	096.2	食品	593.12
公企業與私企業	356.1	食果有袋類	588.25
公算論	512.9	食管	597.321

80732 食

食		食管炎	597.342
民生問題	001.145	食堂	332.32

80732 養

初民生活	565.791	養生	224.3
民眾	317.12	養魚法	617.3
勞工生活	354.9312	養花	613.8
食物		養老院	316.33
病理	592.473	養老金	
蠶業	616.274	教員	336.52

貧 貪 氮 氦 氣

勞工	354.35
養蠶	616.4
養蜂	515.4

80806 貧
貧毛類	583.611
貧齒類	588.32
貧窮	352.8
貧窮收容所	316.51

80806 貪
| 貪吝 | 180.68 |
| 貪慾 | 181.68 |

80817 氮
| 氮 | 546.141 |
| 氮元素 | 546.14 |

80817 氦
| 氦 | 546.181 |
| 氦元素 | 546.18 |

80917 氣
氣球	659.44
氣球水母類	582.772
氣態	541.3
氣化	536.722
氣象	153.23
氣象電學	529.5
氣象臺	529.72
氣象力學	529.1
氣象學	529
氣象光學	529.6
氣候	565.771
生態	581.7778
森林	614.111
醫學	593.111
人種	565.771
氣候學	529.8
氣候與動物人類	529.88
氣候與植物	529.87
氣候分佈	529.89
氣液化	541.68
氣力機械	
工程	655.5
水力	533.9
氣力學	533
氣喘	597.243
氣壓機	655.55
氣壓與流動	529.2
氣壓分配	529.2
氣質	153.84
氣體	
熱學	536.2
氣力學	533
氣體比熱測定法	536.35
氣體傳熱	536.419
氣體動力學	533.5
氣體動學	533.1
氣體速度	534.41

氣體法	542.7	考古學	990.16
氣體運動	533.52	中國考古學	991.6
氣體流動	533.55	鋼印文	990.816
氣體中之電道	537.37	**81132 銾**	
氣體中流電	537.373	銾	546.255
氣體靜力學	533.3	銾鑛	558.145
氣管	597.213	**81140 鉺**	
氣管呼吸	581.425	鉺	546.271
氣管與傳導	655.57	**81143 鑀**	
80917 氘		鑀	546.295
氘	546.187	**81163 鐳**	
80917 氚		鐳	546.227
氚	669.23	鐳電診所	595.275
81120 釘		鐳體	551.12
釘十字架	251.2954	**81286 領**	
81102 銅		領空	381.38
銅	546.58	國家學	371.026
81127 鈣		國際法	381.38
鈣	546.221	領河	381.35
鈣質海綿類	582.51	領袖	312.63
鈣光	665.77	領海	381.36
81127 鎘		國家學	371.026
鎘	546.237	國際法	381.36
冶金學	669.992	領土	381.3
無機化學	546.237	國家學	371.026
81127 鋼		國際法	381.3
鋼印		領土放棄	381.323

瓶 短 頷 頌 釧 鍾 鎧 銹 銩 鏷 鎄 創 矯 矮

領土取得	381.31
領土保全	387.76
領土喪失	
政治學	371.031
國際政治	381.32
領土擴張	371.031
領事	386.6
領事裁判權	386.6
領陸	386.34

81417 瓶

瓶子草綱	577.6

81418 短

短歌	
文學	801.8
日本文學	821.2

81686 頷

頷骨	597.7116

81786 頌

頌	693.7
頌讚	
佛教	233.4
道教	223.4
頌歌	801.43
頌辭	818.45

82100 釧

釧路,河西支廳	981.1677

82114 鍾

鍾惺(1574—1624)	811.168

82118 鎧

鎧	546.219

82127 銹

銹菌目	573.35

82131 銩

銩	546.297

82135 鏷

鏷	546.67

82144 鎄

鎄	546.269

82200 創

創制	001.133
中央政府	373.0327
民權主義	001.133
創制權	372.18
創作	800.445
創作論	
生物學	562.74
自然神學	201.4
創造力	151.7
創世記	252.211

82427 矯

矯形器件	598.1903
矯質烷屬	547.11

82444 矮

矮林處置	614.47

劍 鋪 鋃 鉍 鋱 鈹 鐵 錢

82800 劍

劍術	797.4
軍事學	379.91
游藝	797.4
學校教育	338.638
劍尾類	584.66
劍舞	792.5

83127 鋪

鋪路	651.75

83132 鋃

鋃	546.265

83140 鉍

鉍	546.63

83140 鋱

鋱	546.273

83150 鈹

鈹	546.65

83150 鐵

鐵	546.35
冶金學	669.92
無機化學	546.35
鐵工	682
鐵元素	546.3
鐵船構造	659.116
鐵道	
工程	651.8
登山	651.83
建築	651.81
管理	633.3
鐵板攝影	756.3
鐵橋	651.5018
鐵樑橋	651.52
鐵軌	651.813
鐵軌鑽桿	651.813
鐵路	
交通	633
設備	651.817
政府	633.1
政策	633.1
維持	651.818
經營	633.3
外科	598.197
儲蓄銀行	362.98
修補	651.818
指南	980.703
國家財政	369.142
管理	633.3
鐵礦	
礦物學	558.13
礦業工程	658.8
鐵餅	338.634
鐵管式橋	651.53

83153 錢

錢謙益(1582—1664)	817.711
錢塘江	981.348

鉿 鎔 餓 館 針 釙 銠 鐃 鑵 鈉 鋤 鈦 鑥 鈷 錨 鋯 銷 錯 鍺 斜

錢大昕(1728—1801)	817.738
錢幣	361.6

83162 鉿
鉿	546.243

83168 鎔
鎔岩	557.21
鎔化	669.27
鎔渣	669.15
鎔鐵爐	669.11

83750 餓
餓死	593.124
餓鬼	231.86

83777 館
館務用具使用法	027.2
館員	022.5

84100 針
針指電信	657.8351

84110 釙
釙	546.57

84111 銠
銠	546.83

84111 鐃
鐃鈸	777.2

84114 鑵
鑵頭	694.5

84127 鈉
鈉	546.213

84127 鋤
鋤	610.61
鋤蟲	583.98

84130 鈦
鈦	546.261

84134 鑥
鑥	546.64

84160 鈷
鈷	546.37
冶金學	669.994
無機化學	546.37
鈷礦	558.148

84160 錨
錨	659.17

84161 鋯
鋯	546.55

84161 銷
銷	546.291

84161 錯
錯產	598.841
錯誤	151.173
錯列	511.4
錯覺	156.1
錯悟與變態	151.44

84161 鍺
鍺	546.294

84900 斜

鈍 鍵 鏤 鈾 鐯 蝕 鉑 鉬 銦 銣 銦 鋰 鑼 錦 錫 鍶 鉀 鋁 鎳

斜面	531.95
85117 鈍	
鈍腳類	588.37
85140 鍵	
鍵樂	776
85144 鏤	
鏤花	769.2
鏤鑲	766.7
85160 鈾	
鈾	546.47
85163 鐯	
鐯	546.54
85736 蝕	
蝕刻	742.8
水蝕	742.7
乾蝕	742.8
蝕論	521.8
86100 鉑	
鉑	546.73
鉑元素	546.7
86100 鉬	
鉬	546.43
86100 銦	
銦	546.275
86100 銣	
銣	546.217
86100 銣	546.277
86114 鋰	
鋰	546.215
86114 鑼	
鑼	770.16
86127 錦	
錦葵科	578.45
錦葵綱	578.4
86127 錫	
錫	546.53
冶金學	669.96
無機化學	546.53
鑛物學	558.145
錫元素	546.5
錫德尼(1554—86)	851.32
錫蘭	
印度地理	982.39
印度史	923.9
錫蘭佛教	239.31
86130 鍶	
鍶	546.223
86150 鉀	
鉀	546.211
86160 鋁	
鋁	546.274
89194 鎳	
鎳	546.39

知 羯 智 釔 鈮 釩 鈀 錳 釕 鈎 鋼 銅

冶金學	669.999
無機化學	546.39
鎳礦	558.148

86400 知
知見	018.1
知覺	151.1
知覺缺乏	155.256

86527 羯
羯(319—351)	913.53

86600 智
智	281.15
智童	153.765
智育會	333.5
智利	
地理	984.83
歷史	948.3
智力	
測驗	150.77
游戲	794
缺乏	155.47
智慧	
佛教	231.76
倫理學	180.79

87100 釔
釔	546.293

87111 鈮
鈮	546.05

87114 釩
釩	546.61
釩元素	546.6

87117 鈀
鈀	546.87

87117 錳
錳	
冶金學	669.997
無機化學	546.33
錳礦	558.146

87120 釕
釕	546.81
釕元素	546.8

87120 鈎
鈎頭蟲類	583.43

87120 鋼
鋼	669.92
鋼琴	776.1
鋼板	742.2
鋼鐵	650.48
鋼鐵術	651.18
鋼鐵製品	671.1
鋼鐵構造	651.118

87120 銅
銅	
冶金學	669.93
無機化學	546.251

鎢 銀 鍛 鍛 銘 鉛 鉻 欽 鎮

銅工	682	銀鑛	558.142
銅製品	671.3	**87147 鍛**	
銅像	991.721	鍛	546.292
銅板	742.1	**87147 鍛**	
銅本位	361.21	鍛鍊工事	669.1
銅鑛	558.143	**87160 銘**	
87127 鎢		銘	818.73
鎢	546.45	銘言	
冶金學	669.999	中國文學	818.3
無機化學	546.45	美國文學	868.3
87132 銀		銘制	991.65
銀	546.253	**87161 鉛**	
銀證券	361.71	鉛	546.241
銀元素	546.24	冶金學	669.94
銀行		無機化學	546.241
破產	362.8	鉛鑛	558.144
恐慌	352.74	鉛筆畫	733.5
制度	362.2	**87164 鉻**	
倒票	362.8	鉻	546.41
私立	362.11	冶金學	669.993
循環	362.8	無機化學	546.41
組織	362.2	鉻元素	546.4
管理	362.3	鉻鑛	558.146
銀杏	613.767	**87180 欽**	
銀杏綱	574.3	欽明	921.815
銀板攝影	756.1	**87181 鎮**	
銀本位	361.21	鎮	546.225
銀鹽陽畫	756.5		

慾 朔 鄭 鴿 欲 飢 飽 饞 飼 飲 敘 坐 笙 籃 銓 筑 鑑

87338 慾
 慾望   352.1
87420 朔
 朔拿大   779.1
87427 鄭
 鄭   911.634
 鄭珍(1806—64)   811.178
 鄭光祖   812.41
87627 鴿
 鴿傳信   639.7
 鴿類   587.972
87682 欲
 欲界   231.81
87710 飢
 飢
  生理學   592.471
  內科   597.349
 飢熱   594.923
 飢餓   593.124
87712 飽
 飽和蒸氣   536.75
87713 饞
 饞蟲   583.98
87720 飼
 飼養   615.05
 飼料   615.06
87782 飲

 飲食
  社會學   315.54
  學校管理   332.32
  醫學   598.93
 飲食病   597.349
 飲食主義   694.7
 飲料
  家政   694.4
  醫學   593.13
87940 敘
 敘述社會學   314
88104 坐
 坐法   244.3
 坐標
  近世幾何學   519.43
  地球   525.4
 坐落   024.1
88104 笙
 笙   770.11
88107 籃
 籃球   338.635
88114 銓
 銓敘部   373.075
88117 筑
 筑後   982.166
 築前   982.166
88117 鑑

鑑別	990.075	筅	770.18
88127 銻		**88220 竹**	
銻	546.62	竹	612.595
冶金學	669.991	音樂	770.18
無機化學	546.62	農作物	612.595
銻鑛	558.147	竹工	681
88134 鎂		竹取物語	823.31
鎂		竹木	
冶金學	669.995	考古學	990.15
無機化學	546.233	中國考古學	991.5
鎂元素	546.23	竹書紀年	910.913
88137 鈴		竹簡	
鈴	770.16	中國考古學	991.51
鈴蘭	613.83	圖書學	010.14
88142 簿		竹簡文	990.815
簿記	627	**88221 箭**	
88133 籤		箭齒龍	587.833
籤語	157.18	箭齒類	588.395
88161 鐟		箭根草科	575.95
鐟	546.267	箭蟲	583.98
88167 鎗		**88227 第**	
鎗	671.1	第一律	536.61
鎗礮製造	659.35	第二律	536.62
鎗斃	394.511	第三紀	554.71
88168 鉛		第四紀	554.73
鉛	546.231	第一國際	388.51
88217 篦		第二國際	388.53
		第三國際	388.55

篇 蕭 簹 篆 簇 符 箴 篠 等 笑 算

第四國際	388.57
第福(1661—1731)	853.51
第昆栖(1785—1859)	857.81

88227 篇
篇幅	010.46

88227 蕭
蕭科	577.81
蕭綱	577.8

88227 簹
簹	770.18

88232 篆
篆刻	727
篆字	739.172

88234 簇
簇葉	614.781
簇蟲類	582.22

88243 符
符牌	991.69
符契	991.69
文字考古	990.816
考古學	990.16
中國考古學	991.69
符號	770.022
符咒	157.75
符籙	157.75

88233 箴
箴言	001.183

聖經	252.33
黨義特藏	001.183

銘箴類
文學	808.3
法國文學	848.3
英國文學	858.3
中國文學	818.3
日本文學	828.3
美國文學	868.3

88294 篠
篠懸木科	577.77

88341 等
等比級數	514.2
等持	244.8
等腔類	582.51
等腳類	584.83
等差級數	514.1

88430 笑
笑話	828.2

88446 算
算術	510.7
算法式	510.6
算學	511
算學函數	512.44
算學級數	514.1
算學表	510.21
算學與代數	511.9
算命	157.27

筆 範 答 笛 答 飾 節 管

88507 筆
 筆
  製造工業   674.9
  美術   739.19
 筆記
  小說   803.3
  中國小說   813.83
 筆記法   027.8
 筆畫
  中國百科辭書   131.6
  圖書館目錄   012.8
 筆鉛   558.126

88512 範
 範圍   256.212

88601 答
 答西圖士（？ 55—117） 832.886
 答格拿士（1474—1522）851.24

88600 笛
 笛卡兒   124.1

88603 答
 答   394.511

88727 飾
 飾帶   675.7
 飾品
  禮俗   319.48
  工藝美術   762

88727 節
 節頸頓   587.45
 節理   553.4
 節制資本   001.142
 節奏   710.024
 節足動物   569.77
  動物學   584
  古生物學   569.77
 節甲犬頻   584.83
 節肢動物   584
 節令   319.71
 節會   791
 節慾   187.3

88777 管
 管水母類   582.717
 管理
  演劇   781.8
  機械工程   655.793
  圖書館學校   028.2
 管子   111.171
 管絃樂合奏   779
 管樂   774
 管家   397.55
 管皮目   572.51
 管花綱   579.5
 管藻綱   573.21
 管中瓦斯流動   655.58
 管振動   534.57
 管風琴   776.7

餘 箕 簧 簸 繁 叙 箱 鈔 銷 鐺 鍬 銤 小

88794 餘
- 餘病　　　　　　　594.6
- 餘廢利用　　　　　614.785
- 餘食　　　　　　　593.125

88801 箕
- 箕氏時代(？前—149)
  - （朝鮮）　　　　922.81

88806 簧
- 簧風琴　　　　　　776.7

88847 簸
- 簸揚器　　　　　　610.65

88903 繁
- 繁殖
  - 農藝　　　　　　611.57
  - 顯微學　　　　　566.923

88940 叙
- 叙利亞
  - 語言　　　　　　409.57
  - 地理　　　　　　982.67
  - 哲學　　　　　　118.7
  - 歷史　　　　　　928.7
  - 聖經　　　　　　252.052
- 叙述天文學　　　　523
- 叙述解剖學　　　　616.21
- 叙述顯微學　　　　566.2
- 叙述鑛物　　　　　558.1
- 叙事詩　　　　　　801.5

88963 箱
- 箱梁橋　　　　　　651.53

89120 鈔
- 鈔票　　　　　　　364.1

89127 銷
- 銷售　　　　　　　622.52

89166 鐺
- 鐺子　　　　　　　770.16

89180 鍬
- 鍬　　　　　　　　610.61

89194 銤
- 銤　　　　　　　　546.77

90000 小
- 小産　　　　　　　598.828
- 小調　　　　　　　785.8
- 小說　　　　　　　803
  - 中國小說　　　　813
- 小亞西亞　　　　　928
  - 文學　　　　　　895
  - 語言　　　　　　409.5
  - 地理　　　　　　982.8
  - 哲學　　　　　　118
  - 歷史　　　　　　928
- 小舌　　　　　　　597.312
- 小乘
  - 經典　　　　　　232.2
  - 宗派　　　　　　239.11

懷 憶 少 光

規律	232.6
小熊草科	577.19
小行	523.49
小俄	983.88
小先知書	252.49
小仲馬	842.84
小舟製作法	659.13
小麥	612.11
小戴禮	094.3
小蘗科	577.38
小蘇格拉底派	121.23
小蝙蝠類	588.95
小曲	804.7
中國小曲	814.7
小農制	610.313
小販	622.56
小阿含	232.25
小腦	597.8117
小學(語言學)	410
小學教育	338.2
小學圖書館	025.25
小兒科	598.9
小册管理法	023.8

90032 懷

懷特	851.68
懷疑論	105.3
懷疑派哲學	121.53

90036 憶

憶想書目	018.2

90200 少

少數代表制	372.528
少陽	157.215
少陰	157.217
少年刑法	394.61
少年國際	388.55

90211 光

光	
生理特質	281.11
火神教教義	561.57
光球	523.76
光環	529.65
光理學	535.1
光行差法	522.83
光齒類	588.321
光射	
地球光射	525.2
日球光射	523.72
月球光射	523.32
光結晶學	559.35
光化學	541.5
光線	535.5
工廠	354.55
住宅	692
個人衛生	593.11
青年會建築	256.32
圖書館建築	024.7

雀 肖 尚 常 黨 半 拳

學校管理	332.38
舞台光線	381.55
光線電信	657.8358
光色	
混合	535.395
消沒	535.397
感覺	535.391
光微子論	535.11
光鱗類	587.473
光波論	535.13
光帶線比較法	522.87
光帶之產生	535.45
光帶之性質與構造	535.44
光學	535
光學儀器	535.8
光鏡	522.6
光性學	535.2

90214 雀

雀斑	598.545
雀稗	612.277
雀麥	612.272

90227 肖

| 肖像 | 970.2 |
| 　孫中山 | 001.192 |

90227 尚

尚辯學派	121.20
尚書	092
尚書孔傳	092.2
尚書大傳	092.1

90229 常

常函數	516.2
常事犯	394.25
常青性喬木花類	613.87
常青性灌木花類	613.85
常關(內地稅)	369.165
常年變	538.751

90331 黨

黨旗	001.28
黨化教育	001.7
黨綱	001.21
黨徽	001.28
黨派	001.29
黨員	001.24
黨員著述	001.8
黨義特藏	001
黨籍	001.24

90500 半

半主權國	381.12
半翅類	585.38
半囊子菌綱	573.32
半擔子目	573.35
半日學校	338.85
半腦	597.8113

90502 拳

| 拳術 | |
| 　武術 | 338.638 |

學校教育	791.3	火山	551.4
90502 掌		火山岩	557.2
掌相	157.36	火災預防	354.54
90602 省		火災賑濟	316.42
省政府與行政	373.081	火傷	
省寫法	416.5	治療法	598.16
省沽油科	578.22	救急法	593.45
省略法	141.3	火燄實驗法	542.5
省會		火燄分光法	535.45
地志	981.52	火酒機	655.45
警察	315.324	火酒用法	
財產建築	373.092	自動車	659.74
省黨部	001.41	飲料	664.55
90606 當		火神教	280
當事人	395.03	火葬	319.24
當兵	372.2	火藥	663.1
90712 卷		火藥局	659.34
卷本	010.17	火成岩	557.1
卷冊	010.44	火星	523.44
卷尾猴類	589.55	火險	368.1
90800 火		火炬	665.71
火	611.917	火爐	655.223
火球		**90801 糞**	
天文學	523.52	糞便處理	653.35
光學	535.47	**90806 賞**	
火柴廠保險	368.7	賞卹	373.018
火柴製造	663.6	賞罰	332.13
		90809 炎	

米 糠 糖 恆 類 烟 粘 愷 判 燈 燻 煖 懺 燃

炎症	594.81
炎熱	611.912
炎性病	598.541

90904 米

米酒釀造	664.53

90532 糠

糠穗	612.23

91967 糖

糖尿病	597.643
糖類	
碳水化物	547.81
製糖工業	664.1
稅收	369.152
農作物	612.6

91016 恆

恆山	981.364
恆溫計	536.16
恆星	528.1

91486 類

類似論	201.31
類推	141.77
類書	031.8
類別叢書	081.8
類別書目	017
類人猿	589.7

91814 烟

烟火製造	663

91960 粘

粘土岩	557.44

42018 愷

愷撒	832.881

92500 判

判斷	151.85
判例法	390.023
判決	395.03
判別式	512.36

92818 燈

燈	665.73
燈船	654.47
燈心草科	575.81
燈塔	
旅行保護	593.482
水利工程	654.4
燈節	319.73

92431 燻

燻烘(農藝)	611.991

97847 煖

煖屋(家政)	692

93050 懺

懺禱	223.1
懺悔	253.96

93833 燃

燃燒	541.62
燃燒副料	663.8

惰 慎 煤 性 情 快 精

燃料
 蒸汽生發 655.221
 烟火製造 663.7

94027 惰
惰性 531.692

94081 慎
慎到 111.173

94894 煤
煤水車 655.275
煤炭 663.7
煤油 665.5
煤氣 661.7

95014 性
性 581.66
性認識 581.761
性僻 154.4585
性變異 563.65
性自然論 562.87
性定論
 生理學 581.661
 生物學 561.66
性之副徵 581.668
性遺傳 563.37
性道德 187
性教育
 優生學 563.55
 特種人教育 338.9191
性擇 563.17

性別
 病理學 594.25
 生理學 581.66
 生物學 561.66
 藥療法 595.76
 人口論 349.074
 精神特徵 153.1
性原論 561.66

95027 情
情詩
 希拉文 831.4
 拉丁文學 832.4
情緒 151.2
 意欲與情緒 151.31
情感
 倫理學 180.61
 心理學 151.2
情感無常 155.41
情慾 180.6
情節 781.15

95030 快
快樂 180.98
快樂論 171.1
快艇 659.13
快遞郵件 636.56

95927 精
精刻本
 善本特藏 009.2

懼 烟 燭 爆 惲 慣 耀 鄰 輝 烙 粗 糊 忤 悔 憎

善本書目	019.2
精液	591.511
精進	231.74
精神病	155.2
精神病性	155.2
變態心理學	155.4
社會病理學	315.121
精神生理	152
精神衛生	152.3
精神特徵	153.73
精神生活	313.45
精神派	150.1913
精神官能與現象	581.706
精神測驗	150.77
精神過敏	155.5
精神缺乏	155.3
精神分析	156
精抄本	009.37

96014 懼
懼怯	180.66

96800 烟
烟僻	155.457
烟酒與犯罪	315.165
烟蒸製造	678
烟火製造	663.5

96827 燭
燭	665.72

96832 爆

爆裂（化學）	541.62
爆擊飛機	379.74
爆炸（鑛業）	658.32
爆炸品	663

97056 惲
惲敬	817.751

97086 慣
慣例	381.023

97214 耀
耀焰法	534.515

97227 鄰
鄰保事業	317.88

97256 輝
輝綠岩	557.34
輝長岩	557.39

97864 烙
烙畫	769.1

97911 粗
粗石岩	557.25
粗輝綠岩	557.35

97920 糊
糊精工業	664.3

98040 忤
忤逆	180.88

98055 悔
悔罪	251.45

98066 憎

鼇 幣 鼇 炸 熁 粉 恍 憐 勞 營 燐 榮

憎惡	180.64

98214 鼇

鼇金	369.166

98227 幣

| 幣制 | 361.2 |
| 幣制與恐慌 | 352.73 |

98717 鼇

鼇類	
水產業	617.7
動物學	587.817

98811 炸

| 炸傷 | 593.44 |
| 炸藥 | 663.17 |

98827 熁

| 熁屬 | 547.2 |

98927 粉

| 粉狀胚乳綱 | 575.7 |

99015 恍

| 恍覺 | 156.15 |

99059 憐

| 憐憫 | 180.96 |

99427 勞

勞工	354
勞工種類	354.2
勞工教育	354.933
特種人教育	338.94
勞工報酬	354.3
勞工問題	388.62
勞働	354
基督教與勞働	250.17
勞資工會	354.6
勞資爭議	353.8
勞資關係	354.1
勞資糾紛之和平	
解決與預防	354.8
勞資問題	344.81

99606 營

| 營利圖書館 | 025.5 |
| 營業稅 | 369.153 |

99859 燐

| 燐光 | 535.56 |

99904 榮

榮菌科	575.23
榮蘭綱	575.2
榮典	373.018

一、形式細分表

　　Form division

二、莎士比亞文庫分類表

　　Tables of subdivisions for Shakespearian collections

三、中國歷代帝王表

　　Chronological tables of the Chinese dynasty

四、中國縣名表

　　A complete list of the Chinese Districts

附録一　Appendix I

形式細分表　Form division

.01　理論　　　　　　　　　　Theories
　1.哲學,原理,宗旨,範圍,重　　　Philosophy, principle, aim, scope,
　　要,效用,等　　　　　　　　　importance, utility, etc.
　5.心理　　　　　　　　　　　Psychology
　6.邏輯　　　　　　　　　　　Logic
　8.倫理　道德　　　　　　　　Ethics　Morals
　9.關係　影響　　　　　　　　Relations　Influence

.03　書辭　字典　　　　　　　Encyclopedias, dictionaries,
　　　術語　　　　　　　　　　lexicons, dictionary of terms
　1.書目　　　　　　　　　　　Bibliography
　2.表冊　統計　　　　　　　　Tables　Statistics
　6.索引　檢字　　　　　　　　Index
　7.年鑑　　　　　　　　　　　Yearbooks
　8.指南　業名錄　　　　　　　Directories
　9.手冊　　　　　　　　　　　Pocketbooks

.04　評論,批評,考證,　　　　Criticism, critiques, identification,
　　　集證,爭執,論　　　　　　disputation, discourses, essays,
　　　說,論文,演講　　　　　　addresses, lectures, letters,
　　　集,講義,等　　　　　　　papers, etc.

.05	期刊　雜誌　報章	Periodicals, reviews, magazines, newspapers
.06	會社,團體,協會,學會,會議,議案,紀錄,報告,等	Societies, associations, academies, congresses, conference, conventions, acts, records, reports, etc.
.07	研究,教學,教育,學校,博物院,展覽	Study and teaching, seminaries, education, schools, museums, exhibitions, etc.
	綱目,綱要,答問,等	outlines, syllabi, synopses, questions, etc.
.08	總集,彙集,全集,全書,選表,精華錄,雜集,雜著,雜錄,小册,等	Collections, polygraph, series, libraries, collected works, complete works, selections, extract, miscellany, pamphlets, etc.
.09	歷史	History

依時代分： By period:
 1.古代 1.Ancient
 2.中古 2.Medieval
 3.近世 3.Modern

依國分： By country:
 1.中國 1.China
 2.亞洲其他各國 2.Other Nations of Asia

3.歐洲各國	3.European nations
4.美洲各國	4.American nations
5.非洲大洋洲各國	5.African and oceanian nations
7.傳記	Biography
8.地理	Geography
9.古考　古迹	Archaeology Antiquities

附録二　Appendix II

莎士比亞文庫分類表
Tables of subdivisions for Shakespearian collections
其他各家文庫可仿此細分
The same scheme applies to the collections of other individual authors

852.33　Shakespeare, William (1564—1616)

Scheme of author numbers for Shakespeare's works—collections, selections, separate plays, etc.

A	1	Complete works
A	5	Selected works
A	9	All's well that ends well
A	15	Antony and Cleopatra
A	19	As you like it
C	1	Comedy of errors
C	5	Coriolanus
C	9	Cymbeline
H	1	Hamlet
H	5	Henry IV, parts 1 and 2 together
H	9	Henry IV, part 1
H	15	Henry IV, part 2
H	19	Henry V

H	25	Henry VI, parts 1,2, and 3 together
H	29	Henry VI, part 1
H	35	Henry VI, part 2
H	39	Henry VI, part 3
H	45	Henry VIII
J	1	Julius Caesar
K	1	King John
K	5	King Lear
L	1	Love's labour's lost
M	1	Macbeth
M	5	Measure for measure
M	9	Merchant of Venice
M	15	Merry wives of Windsor
M	19	Midsummer night's dream
M	25	Much ado about nothing
O	1	Othello
P	1	Pericles
R	1	Richard II
R	5	Richard III
R	9	Romeo and Juliet
T	1	Taming of the shrew
T	5	Tempest
T	9	Timon of Athens
T	15	Titus Andronicus
T	19	Troilus and Cressida
T	25	Twelfth night or what you will
T	29	Two gentlemen of Verona
W	1	Winter's tale

Lost play

    X 1   Love's labour's won

Poems

    Y 1   Collected poems

    Y 5   Selections

    Y 9   Venus and Adonis

    Y 15   Rape of Lucrece

    Y 19   Passionate pilgrim

    Y 25   Sonnets

"*Shakespeare apocryphya*"

    Z 1   Collected works

    Z 5   Selections, extracts

    Z 9   Arden of Feversham

    Z 15   Arrignment of Paris

    Z 19   Birth of Merlin

    Z 25   Bottom the weaver

    Z 29   Double falsehood

    Z 35   Edward III

    Z 39   Fair Em

    Z 45   Fifth of November

    Z 49   Locrine

    Z 55   London prodigal

    Z 59   Merry devil of Edmonton

    Z 65   Mucedorus

    Z 69   Puritan or widow of Watling street

    Z 75   Sir John Oldcastle

    Z 79   Sir Thomas More

    Z 85   Thomas, Lord Cromwell

    Z   89   Two noble kinsmen
    Z   95   Vortigern
    Z   99   rorkshire tragedy

Works on Shakespeare classified as follows:—

852.331   Theories Relations Influence
             Philosophy Esthetics
             Relations to his contemporaries
             Influence on special authors
             Influence in special countries

852.333   Dictionaries
    1   Bibliography
    2   Documents, charts
    6   Index

852.334   Criticism and interpretation, textual criticism, etc.
    1   Genius
    2   Characters   Treatment of life
    3   Technique   Dramatic art   Dramatization
    4   Plots   Stage presentation   Stage history
    5   Dramatic representation of the play
    6   Famous actors of Shakespearian parts
    7   Language, style, etc.
          Grammar: pronunciation, etc.
          Versification
          Dialect
    8   Treatment and knowlege of special subjects
    82 Religion
    83 Sociology   Economics   Politics   Law
    85 Science

     Botany, zoology, etc.

   87 Art: music, painting, etc.

   9 History of Shakespearian criticism

852.336 Authorship

   1 Manuscripts Writing Signatures

   2 Sources

   4 Forerunners, associates, followers, circle, etc.

   6 Allusions

   7 Imitations, adaptations, parodies, etc.

   8 Chronology of works

852.337 Study and teaching: Outlines, syllabi, synopses, questions, etc.

852.338 Shakespearian literature

   1 Fiction

   2 Mythology, folk-lore

   3 Prose

   4 Letter

   5 Wit and humor

   6 Quotations

   8 Curiosa and miscellany

852.339 Biography

   1. Words of Shakespeare Agrapha

   2. Chronology Iconography Portraits

   3. Narratives

   31. Early life: education

   32. Love and marriage Relation to women

   33. Public life

34. Later life
36. Homes and haunts Landmarks
4. Shakespeare's family
6. The age of Shakespeare
　　Elizabethan England
7. Death　Will
8. Anniversaries Celebrations　Memorial addresses　Birth books
9. Epitaphy　Graves　Relics

附錄三　Appendix III

中國歷代帝王表
Chronological tables of the Chinese dynasty

夏紀(前？2205—？1766) The Hsia dynasty

廟號 Dynastic title		即位 Accession	廟號 Dynastic title		即位 Accession
？大禹	The Great Yu	？前 2025	槐	Huai	2040
啟	Ch'i	2197	芒	Mang	2014
太康	T'ai K'ang	2188	泄	Hsieh	1996
仲康	Chung K'ang	2159	不降	Pu Chiang	1980
相	Hsiang	2146	扃	Chiung	1921
寒浞時代	Interregnum of forty years commencing	2118	廑	Chin	1900
			孔甲	K'ung Chia	1879
			皋	Kao	1848
少康	Shao K'ang	2079	發	Fa	1837
杼	Ch'u	2057	桀癸	Chieh Kuei	1818

商或殷紀(前？1766—？1122) The Shang or Yin dynasty

廟號 Dynastic title		即位 Accession	廟號 Dynastic title		即位 Accession
成湯	Ch'eng T'ang	？前1766	南庚	Nan Keng	1433
太甲	T'ai Chia	1753	陽甲	Yang Chia	1408
沃丁	Wu Ting	1720	盤庚	P'an Keng	1401
太庚	T'ai Keng	1691	小辛	Hsiao Hsin	1373
小甲	Hsiao Chia	1666	小乙	Hsiao Yi	1352
雍己	Yung Chi	1649	武丁	Wu Ting	1324
太戊	T'ai Wu	1637	祖庚	Tsu Keng	1265
仲丁	Chung Ting	1562	祖甲	Tsu Chia	1258
外壬	Wai Jen	1549	廪辛	Lin Hsin	1225
河亶甲	Ho Tan Chia	1534	庚丁	Keng Ting	1219
祖乙	Tsu Yi	1525	武乙	Wu Yi	1198
祖辛	Tsu Hsin	1506	太丁	T'ai Ting	1194
沃甲	Wu Chia	1490	帝乙	Ti Yi	1191
祖丁	Tsu Ting	1465	紂辛	Chou Hsin	1154

周紀(前？1122—？255) The Chou dynasty

廟號 Dynastic title		即位 Accession	廟號 Dynastic title		即位 Accession
武王	Wu Wang	？前1122	懿王	Yi Wang	934
成王	Ch'eng Wang	1115	孝王	Hsiao Wang	909
康王	K'ang Wang	1078	夷王	I Wang	894
昭王	Chao Wang	1052	厲王	Li Wang	878
穆王	Kung Wang	1001	宣王	Hsuan Wang	827
共王	Kung Wang	946	幽王	Yu Wang	781

续表

廟號 Dynastic title		即位 Accession	廟號	Dynastic title	即位 Accession
	(按年代之紀載舊說謂從茲始然六國年代總數考諸史記十二諸侯表六國年表等均各不同是舊說非也)	(Historical period commences not here)	景王	Ching Wang	544
			敬王	Ching Wang	519
			元王	Yuan Wang	475
			貞定王	Cheng Ting Wang	468
			考王	K'ao Wang	440
平王	P'ing Wang	770	威烈王	Wei Lieh Wang	425
桓王	Huan Wang	719	安王	An Wang	401
莊王	Chuang Wang	696	烈王	Lieh Wang	375
僖王	Hsi Wang	681	顯王	Hsien Wang	368
惠王	Hui Wang	676	慎靚王	Shen Ching Wang	320
襄王	Hsiang Wang	651	赧王	Nang Wang	314
頃王	Ch'ing Wang	618		於其即位之五十九年讓位秦王政	In his 59th year surrendered his dominions to the ruler of Ch'in
匡王	K'uang Wang	612			
定王	Ting Wang	606			
簡王	Chien Wang	585			
靈王	Ling Wang	571	東周君	Tung Chou Chun	255

秦紀(前 221—206) The Ch'in dynasty

廟號 Dynastic title		即位 Accession	廟號	Dynastic title	即位 Accession
始皇帝	Shih Huang Ti (First emperor) title assumed by Prince Cheng in the 26th year of his reign	前 221	二世皇帝	Erh Shih Huang Ti	209

漢紀(前202—後220) The Han dynasty
前漢或西漢(前202—後9) Former Han or Western Han

廟號 Dynastic title	即位 Accession	年號 Reign title		建元 Adopted
高祖 Kao Tsu 按高祖稱帝後五年始行即位 Claimed the Empire from B.C.206; Actually ascended the Throne at B.C.202	前202			
惠帝 Hui Ti	194			
高后 Kao Hou	187			
文帝 Wen Ti	179	後元	Hou Yuan	163
景帝 Ching Ti	156	中元	Chung Yuan	149
		後元	Hou Yuan	143
武帝 Wu Ti	140	建元	Chien Yuan	140
		元光	Yuan Kuang	134
		元朔	Yuan So	128
		元狩	Yuan Shou	122
		元鼎	Yuan Ting	116
		元封	Yuan Feng	110
		太初	T'ai Ch'u	104
		天漢	T'ien Han	100
		太始	T'ai Shih	96
		征和	Cheng Ho	92
		後元	Hou Yuan	88
昭帝 Chao Ti	86	始元	Shih Yuan	86

续表

廟號 Dynastic title		即位 Accession	年號 Reign title		建元 Adopted
宣帝	Hsuan Ti	73	元鳳	Yuan Feng	80
			元平	Yuan P'ing	74
			本始	Pen Shih	73
			地節	Ti Chieh	69
			元康	Yuan K'ang	65
			神爵	Shen Chue	61
			五鳳	Wu Feng	57
			甘露	Kan Lu	53
			黃龍	Huang Lung	49
元帝	Yuan Ti	48	初元	Ch'u Yuan	48
			永光	Yung Kuang	43
			建昭	Chien Chao	36
			竟寧	Ching Ning	33
成帝	Ch'eng Ti	32	建始	Chien Shih	32
			河平	Ho P'ing	28
			陽朔	Yang So	24
			鴻嘉	Hung Chia	20
			永始	Yung Shih	16
			元延	Yuan Yen	12
			綏和	Sui Ho	8
哀帝	Ai Ti	6	建平	Chien P'ing	6
			元壽	Yuan Shou	2
平帝	P'ing Ti	後1	元始	Yuan Shih	後1
孺子嬰	Ju Tze Ying	6	居攝	Chu She	6
			初始	Ch'u Shih	8

续表

廟號 Dynastic title	即位 Accession	年號 Reign title	建元 Adopted
新皇帝 Hsin Huang Ti 按王莽篡漢國號新朝 Wang Mang usurped the throne and established "New dynasty"	9	始建國 Shih Chien Kuo	9
		天鳳 T'ien Feng	14
		地黃 Ti Huang	20
淮陽王（帝玄）Huai-Yang Wang (Ti Hsuan)	23	更始 Keng Shih	23

後漢紀或東漢紀(25—220) The Later or Eastern Han

廟號 Dynastic title	即位 Accession	年號 Reign title	建元 Adopted
光武帝 Kuang Wu Ti	25	建武 Chien Wu	25
		中元 Chung Yuan	56
明帝 Ming Ti	58	永平 Yung P'ing	58
章帝 Chang Ti	76	建初 Chien Ch'u	76
		元和 Yuan Ho	84
		章和 Chang Ho	87
和帝 Ho Ti	89	永元 Yung Yuan	89
		元興 Yuan Hsing	105
殤帝 Shang Ti	106	延平 Yen P'ing	106
安帝 An Ti	107	永初 Yung Ch'u	107
		元初 Yuan Ch'u	114
		永寧 Yung Ning	120
		建光 Chien Kuang	121
		延光 Yen Kuang	122

续表

廟號 Dynastic title		即位 Accession	年號 Reign title		建元 Adopted
順帝	Shun Ti	126	永建	Yung Chien	126
			陽嘉	Yang Chia	132
			永和	Yung Ho	136
			漢安	Han An	142
			建康	Chien K'ang	144
冲帝	Ch'ung Ti	145	永嘉	Yung Chia	145
質帝	Chih Ti	146	本初	Pen Ch'u	146
桓帝	Huan Ti	147	建和	Chien Ho	147
			和平	Ho P'ing	150
			元嘉	Yuan Chia	151
			永興	Yung Hsing	153
			永壽	Yung Shou	155
			延熹	Yen Hsi	158
			永康	Yung K'ang	167
靈帝	Ling Ti	168	建寧	Chien Ning	168
			熹平	Hsi P'ing	172
			光和	Kuang Ho	178
			中平	Chung P'ing	184
少帝	Shao Ti	189	光熹	Kuang Hsi	189
			昭寧	Chao Ning	189
獻帝或 愍帝	Hsien Ti also styled Min Ti	189	永漢	Yung Han	189
			中平	Chung P'ing	189
			初平	Ch'u P'ing	190
			興平	Hsing P'ing	194
			建安	Chien An	196
			延康	Yen K'ang	220

三國 The Three Kindoms
蜀漢紀(221—263) The Minor Han dynasty

廟號 Dynastic title		即位 Accession	年號 Reign title		建元 Adopted
昭烈帝	Chao Lieh Ti	221	章武	Chang Wu	221
後主	Hou Chu	223	建興	Chien Hsing	223
			延熙	Yen Hsi	238
			景耀	Ching Yao	258
			炎興	Yen Hsing	263

魏紀(220—265) The Wei dynasty

廟號 Dynastic title		即位 Accession	年號 Reign title		建元 Adopted
文帝	Wen Ti	220	黃初	Huang Ch'u	220
明帝	Ming Ti	227	太和	T'ai Ho	227
			青龍	Ch'ing Lung	233
			景初	Ching Ch'u	237
廢帝 (齊王芳)	Fei Ti (Chi Wang Fang)	240	正始	Cheng Shih	240
			嘉平	Chia P'ing	249
少帝 (高貴鄉公)	Shao Ti (Kao Kuei Hsiang Kung)	254	正元	Cheng Yuan	254
			甘露	Kan Lu	256
元帝	Yuan Ti	260	景元	Ching Yuan	260
			咸熙	Hsien Hsi	264

吳紀(222—280) The Wu dynasty

廟號 Dynastic title	即位 Accession	年號 Reign title	建元 Adopted
大帝 Ta Ti	222	黃武 Huang Wu	222
		黃龍 Huaug Lung	229
		嘉禾 Chia Ho	232
		赤烏 Ch'ih Wu	238
		太元 T'ai Yuan	251
		神鳳 Shen Feng	252
廢帝（會稽王） Fei Ti (Kuei-chi Wang)	252	建興 Chien Hsing	252
		五鳳 Wu Feng	254
		太平 T'ai P'ing	256
景帝 Ching Ti	258	永安 Yung An	258
末帝（歸命侯） Mo Ti (Kuei-ming Hou)	264	元興 Yuan Hsing	264
		甘露 Kan Lu	265
		寶鼎 Pao Ting	266
		建衡 Chien Heng	269
		鳳凰 Feng Huang	272
		天册 T'ien Ts'e	275
		天璽 T'ien Hsi	276
		天紀 T'ien Chi	277

晉紀(265—420) The Chin dynasty
西晉(265—317) The Western Chin

廟號 Dynastic title	即位 Accession	年號 Reign title	建元 Adopted
武帝 Wu Ti	265	泰始 T'ai Shih	265

续表

廟號 Dynastic title		即位 Accession	年號	Reign title	建元 Adopted
惠帝	Hui Ti	290	咸寧	Hsien Ning	275
			泰康	T'ai K'ang	280
			泰熙	T'ai Hsi	290
			永熙	Yung Hsi	290
			永平	Yung P'ing	291
			元康	Yuan K'ang	291
			永康	Yung K'ang	300
			永寧	Yung Ning	301
			太安	T'ai An	302
			永安	Yung An	304
			建武	Chien Wu	304
			永安	Yung An	304
			永興	Yung Hsing	304
			光熙	Kuang Hsi	306
懷帝	Huai Ti	307	永嘉	Yung Chia	307
愍帝	Min Ti	313	建興	Chien Hsing	313

東晉(317—420) The Eastern Chin

廟號 Dynastic title		即位 Accession	年號	Reign title	建元 Adopted
元帝	Yuan Ti	317	建武	Chien Wu	317
			太興	T'ai Hsing	318
			永昌	Yung Ch'ang	322
明帝	Ming Ti	323	太寧	T'ai Ning	323

续表

廟號 Dynastic title		即位 Accession	年號 Reign title		建元 Adopted
成帝	Ch'eng Ti	326	咸和	Hsien Ho	326
			咸康	Hsien K'ang	335
康帝	K'ang Ti	343	建元	Chien Yuan	343
穆帝	Mu Ti	345	永和	Yung Ho	345
			升平	Sheng P'ing	357
哀帝	Ai Ti	362	隆和	Lung Ho	362
			興寧	Hsing Ning	363
帝奕 (海西公)	Ti Yi (Hai-hsi Kung)	366	太和	T'ai Ho	366
簡文帝	Chien Wen Ti	371	咸安	Hsien An	371
孝帝武	Hsiao Wu Ti	373	寧康	Ning K'ang	373
			太元	T'ai Yuan	376
安帝	An Ti	397	隆安	Lung An	397
			元興	Yuan Hsing	402
			隆安	Lung An	402
			大享	Ta Hsiang	402
			元興	Yuan Hsing	403
			義熙	Yi Hsi	405
恭帝	Kung Ti	419	元熙	Yuan Hsi	419

南北朝(420—589) The South and North dynasties
宋紀(劉宋)(420—479) The Sung dynasty (House of Liu)

廟號 Dynastic title		即位 Accession	年號 Reign title		建元 Adopted
武帝	Wu Ti	420	永初	Yung Ch'u	420
少帝 (營陽王)	Shao Ti (Ying-yang Wang)	423	景平	Ching P'ing	423

续表

廟號 Dynastic title		即位 Accession	年號 Reign title		建元 Adopted
文帝	Wen Ti	424	元嘉	Yuan Chia	424
孝武帝	Hsiao Wu Ti	454	孝建	Hsiao Chien	454
			大明	Ta Ming	457
廢帝	Fei Ti	465	永光	Yung Kuang	465
			景和	Ching Ho	465
明帝	Ming Ti	465	泰始	T'ai Shih	465
			泰豫	T'ai Yu	472
後廢帝 (蒼梧王)	Hou Fei Ti (Ts'ang-Wu Wang)	473	元徽	Yuan Hui	473
順帝	Shun Ti	477	昇明	Sheng Ming	477

齊紀(479—502) The Ch'i dynasty

廟號 Dynastic title		即位 Accession	年號 Reign title		建元 Adopted
高帝	Kao Ti	479	建元	Chien Yuan	479
武帝	Wu Ti	483	永明	Yung Ming	483
鬱林王	Yu-lin Wang	494	隆昌	Lung Ch'ang	494
海陵王	Hai-ling Wang	494	延興	Yen Hsing	494
明帝	Ming Ti	494	建武	Chien Wu	494
			永泰	Yung T'ai	498
東昏侯	Tung-hun Hou	499	永元	Yung Yuan	499
和帝	Ho Ti	501	中興	Chung Hsing	501

梁紀(502—557) The Liang dynasty

廟號 Dynastic title		即位 Accession	年號 Reign title		建元 Adopted
武帝	Wu Ti	502	天監	T'ien Chien	502
			普通	P'u Tung	520
			大通	Ta Tung	527
			中大通	Chung Ta Tung	529
			大同	Ta T'ung	535
			中大同	Chung Ta T'ung	546
			太清	T'ai Ch'ing	547
簡文帝	Chien Wen Ti	550	大寶	Ta Pao	550
豫章王	Yu-chang Wang	551	天正	T'ien Cheng	551
元帝	Yuan Ti	552	承聖	Ch'eng Sheng	552
貞陽侯	Cheng-yang Hou	555	天成	T'ien Ch'eng	555
敬帝	Ching Ti	553	紹泰	Shao T'ai	555
			太平	T'ai P'ing	556

陳紀(557—589) The Ch'en dynasty

廟號 Dynastic title		即位 Accession	年號 Reign title		建元 Adopted
武帝	Wu Ti	557	永定	Yung Ting	557
文帝	Wen Ti	560	天嘉	T'ien Chia	560
			天康	T'ien K'ang	566
廢帝	Fei Ti	567	光大	Kuang Ta	567
宣帝	Hsuan Ti	569	大建	Ta Chien	569
後主	Hou Chu	583	至德	Chih Teh	583
			禎明	Cheng Ming	587

北魏紀 The Northern Wei dyansty
（元魏）(386—535)(Yuan Wei)

廟號 Dynastic title	即位 Accession	年號 Reign title		建元 Adopted
道武帝 Tao Wu Ti	386	登國	Teng Kuo	386
		皇始	Huang Shih	396
		天興	T'ien Hsing	398
		天賜	T'ien Tz'u	404
明元帝 Ming Yuan Ti	409	永興	Yung Hsing	409
		神瑞	Shen Jui	411
		泰常	T'ai Ch'ang	416
太武帝 T'ai Wu Ti	424	始光	Shih Kuang	424
		神䴥	Shen Chia	428
		延和	Yen Ho	432
		太延	T'ai Yen	435
		太平真君	T'ai P'ing Chen Chun	440
		正平	Cheng P'ing	452
南安王 Nan-an Wang	452	承平	Ch'eng P'ing	452
文成帝 Wen Ch'eng Ti	452	興安	Hsing An	452
		興光	Hsing Kuang	454
		太安	T'ai An	455
		和平	Ho P'ing	460
獻文帝 Hsien Wen Ti	466	天安	T'ien An	466
		皇興	Huang Hsing	467
孝文帝 Hsiao Wen Ti	471	延興	Yen Hsing	471
		承明	Ch'eng Ming	476
		太和	T'ai Ho	477

续表

廟號 Dynastic title		即位 Accession	年號 Reign title		建元 Adopted
宣武帝	Hsuan Wu Ti	500	景明	Ching Ming	500
			正始	Cheng Shih	504
			永平	Yung P'ing	508
			延昌	Yen Ch'ang	512
孝明帝	Hsiao Ming Ti	516	熙平	Hsi P'ing	516
			神龜	Shen Kuei	517
			正光	Cheng Kuang	519
			孝昌	Hsiao Ch'ang	525
臨洮王	Lin t'ao Wang	528	武泰	Wu T'ai	528
孝莊帝	Hsiao Chuang Ti	528	建義	Chien Yi	528
			永安	Yung An	528
			更興	Keng Hsing	529
東海王	Tung-hai Wang	530	建明	Chien Ming	530
節閔帝	Chieh Min Ti	531	普泰	Chin T'ai	531
安定王	An-ting Wang	531	中興	Chung Hsing	531
孝武帝	Hsiao Wu Ti	532	太昌	T'ai Ch'ang	532
			永興	Yung Hsing	532
			永熙	Yung Hsi	532

東魏紀(534—549)The Eastern Wei dynasty

廟號 Dynastic title		即位 Accession	年號 Reign title		建元 Adopted
孝静帝	Hsiao Ching Ti	534	天平	T'ien P'ing	534
			元象	Yuan Hsiang	538

续表

廟號 Dynastic title	即位 Accession	年號 Reign title		建元 Adopted
		興和	Hsing Ho	539
		武定	Wu Ting	543

西魏紀(535—556) The Western Wei dynasty

廟號 Dynastic title		即位 Accession	年號 Reign title		建元 Adopted
文帝	Wen Ti	535	大統	Ta T'ung	535
廢帝(帝欽)	Fei Ti(Ti Ch'in)	552			
恭帝	Kung Ti	551			

北齊紀(550—577) The Northern Ch'i dynasty

廟號 Dynastic title		即位 Accession	年號 Reign title		建元 Adopted
文宣帝	Wen Hsuan Ti	550	天保	T'ien Pao	550
廢帝	Fei Ti	560	乾明	Ch'ien Ming	560
孝昭帝	Hsiao Chao Ti	560	皇建	Huang Chien	560
武成帝	Wu Ch'eng Ti	561	太寧	T'ai Ning	561
			河清	Ho Ch'ing	562
後主	Hou Chu	565	天統	T'ien T'ung	565
			武平	Wu P'ing	570
安德王	An-teh Wang	576	隆化	Lung Hua	576
			德昌	Teh Ch'ang	576
幼主	Yu Chu	577	承光	Ch'eng Kuang	577

北周紀(557—581) The Northern Chou dynasty

廟號 Dynastic title	即位 Accession	年號 Reign title		建元 Adopted
孝愍帝 Hsiao Min Ti	557			
明帝 Ming Ti	557	武成	Wu Ch'eng	558
武帝 Wu Ti	561	保定	Pao Ting	561
		天和	T'ien Ho	566
		建德	Chien Teh	572
宣帝 Hsuan Ti	578	宣政	Hsuan Cheng	578
		大成	Ta Ch'eng	579
靜帝 Ching Ti	580	大象	Ta Hsiang	580
		大定	Ta Ting	581

隋紀(581—618) The Sui dynasty

廟號 Dynastic title	即位 Accession	年號 Reign title		建元 Adopted
文帝(高祖) Wen Ti (Kao Tsu)	581	開皇	K'ai Huang	581
		仁壽	Jen Shou	601
煬帝 Yang Ti	605	大業	Ta Yeh	605
恭帝侑 Kung Ti Yu	617	義寧	Yi Ning	617
恭帝侗 Kung Ti T'ung	618	皇泰	Huang T'ai	618

唐紀(618—907) The T'ang dynasty

廟號 Dynastic title	即位 Accession	年號 Reign title		建元 Adopted
高祖 Kao Tsu	618	武德	Wu Teh	618
太宗 T'ai Tsung	627	貞觀	Cheng Kuan	627

续表

廟號 Dynastic title		即位 Accession	年號 Reign title		建元 Adopted
高宗	Kao Tsung	650	永徽	Yung Hui	650
			顯慶	Hsien Ch'ing	656
			龍朔	Lung So	661
			麟德	Lin Teh	664
			乾封	Ch'ien Feng	666
			總章	Tsung Chang	668
			咸亨	Hsien Heng	670
			上元	Shang Yuan	674
			儀鳳	Yi Feng	676
			調露	T'iao Lu	679
			永隆	Yung Lung	680
			開耀	K'ai Yao	681
			永淳	Yung Shun	682
			弘道	Hung Tao	683
中宗	Chung Tsung	681	嗣聖	Ssu Sheng	684
睿宗	Jui Tsung	684	文明	Wen Ming	684
武后	Wu Hou	684	光宅	Kuang Tse	684
武后稱制七年改唐爲周	The Empress Wu adopted the dynastic title Chou(周) in lieu of T'ang(唐) from A. D. 690		垂拱	Chui Kung	685
			永昌	Yung Ch'ang	689
			載初	Tsai Ch'u	689
			天授	T'ien Shou	690
			如意	Ju Yi	692
			長壽	Ch'ang Shou	692
			延載	Yen Tsai	694
			證聖	Cheng Sheng	695

续表

廟號 Dynastic title	即位 Accession	年號 Reign title		建元 Adopted
		天册萬歲	T'ien T'se Wan Sui	695
		萬歲登封	Wan Sui Tung Feng	696
		萬歲通天	Wan Sui Tung T'ien	696
		神功	Shen Kung	697
		聖歷	Sheng Li	698
		久視	Chiu Shi	700
		大足	Ta Tsu	701
		長安	Ch'ang An	701
中宗	Chung Tsung	705	神龍	Shen Lung	705
中宗復位改周爲唐	resumed the throne and styled T'ang in lieu of Chou		景龍	Ching Lung	707
溫王	Wen Wang	710	唐隆	T'ang Lung	710
睿宗	Jui Tsung	710	景雲	Ching Yun	710
		太極	T'ai Chi	712
		延和	Yen Ho	712
玄宗 (明皇)	Hsuan Tsung (Ming Huan)	713	先天	Hsien T'ien	713
		開元	K'ai Yuan	713
		天寶	T'ien Pao	742
肅宗	Su Tsung	756	至德	Chih Teh	756
		乾元	Ch'ien Yuan	758
		上元	Shang Yuan	760
		寶應	Pao Ying	762
代宗	Tai Tsung	763	廣德	Kuang Teh	763

续表

廟號 Dynastic title		即位 Accession	年號 Reign title		建元 Adopted
			永泰	Yung T'ai	765
			大歷	Ta Li	766
德宗	Teh Tsung	780	建中	Chien Chung	780
			興元	Hsing Yuan	784
			貞元	Cheng Yuan	785
順宗	Shun Tsung	805	永貞	Yung Cheg	805
憲宗	Hsien Tsung	806	元和	Yuan Ho	806
穆宗	Mu Tsung	821	長慶	Ch'ang Ching	821
敬宗	Ching Tsung	825	寶歷	Pao Li	825
文宗	Wen Tsung	827	太和	T'ai Ho	827
			開成	K'ai Ch'eng	836
武宗	Wu Tsung	841	會昌	Hui Ch'ang	841
宣宗	Hsuan Tsung	847	太中	T'ai Chung	847
懿宗	Yi Tsung	860	咸通	Hsien T'ung	860
僖宗	Hsi Tsung	874	乾符	Ch'ien Fu	874
			廣明	Kuang Ming	880
			中和	Chung Ho	881
			光啟	Kuang Ch'i	885
			文德	Wen Teh	888
昭宗	Chao Tsung	889	龍紀	Lung Chi	889
			大順	Ta Shun	890
			景福	Ching Fu	892
			乾寧	Ch'ien Ning	894
			光化	Kuang Hua	898
			天復	Tien Fu	901
			天祐	Tien Yu	904
哀帝 昭宣帝	Ai Ti (Chao Hsuan Ti)	904	天祐	Tien Yu	904

五代(907—960) The Five dynasties
後梁紀(907—923) The Later Liang dynasty

廟號 Dynastic title		即位 Accession	年號 Reign title		建元 Adopted
太祖	T'ai Tsu	907	開平	K'ai P'ing	907
			乾化	Ch'ien Hua	911
友珪	Yu Kuei	913	鳳曆	Feng Li	913
末帝	Mo Ti	913	乾化	Ch'ien Hua	913
			貞明	Cheng Ming	915
			龍德	Lung Teh	921

後唐紀(923—936) The Later Tang dynasty

廟號 Dynastic title		即位 Accession	年號 Reign title		建元 Adopted
莊宗	Chuang Tsung	923	同光	T'ung Kuang	923
明宗	Ming Tsung	926	天成	T'ien Ch'eng	926
			長興	Ch'ang Hsing	930
閔帝	Min Ti	934	應順	Ying Shun	934
廢帝	Fei Ti	934	清泰	Ch'ing T'ai	934

後晉紀(936—947) The Later Chin dynasty

廟號 Dynastic title		即位 Accession	年號 Reign title		建元 Adopted
高祖	Kao Tsu	936	天福	T'ien Fu	936
少帝(出帝)	Shao Ti(Ch'u Ti)	942	開運	K'ai Yun	944

後漢紀(947—951) The Later Han dynasty

廟號 Dynastic title		即位 Accession	年號 Reign title		建元 Adopted
高祖	Kao Tsu	947	天福	T'ien Fu	947
			乾祐	Ch'ien Yu	948
隱帝	Yin Ti	948	乾祐	Ch'ien Yu	948

後周紀(951—960) The Later Chou dynasty

廟號 Dynastic title		即位 Accession	年號 Reign title		建元 Adopted
太祖	T'ai Tsu	951	廣順	Kuang Shun	951
			顯德	Hsien Teh	953
世宗	Shih Tsung	954	顯德	Hsien Teh	954
恭帝	Kung Ti	960	顯德	Hsien Teh	960

宋紀(960—1280) The Sung dynasty
北宋(960—1127) The Northern Sung

廟號 Dynastic title		即位 Accession	年號 Reign title		建元 Adopted
太祖	T'ai Tsu	960	建隆	Chien Lung	960
			乾德	Ch'ien Teh	963
			開寶	K'ai Pao	968
太宗	T'ai Tsung	976	太平興國	T'ai P'ing Hsing Kuo	976
			雍熙	Yung Hsi	984
			端拱	Tuan Kung	988

续表

廟號 Dynastic title	即位 Accession	年號 Reign title	建元 Adopted
真宗 Cheng Tsung	997	淳化 Shun Hua	990
		至道 Chih Tao	995
		咸平 Hsien P'ing	998
		景德 Ching Teh	1004
		大中祥符 Ta Chung Hsiang Fu	1008
		天禧 T'ien Hsi	1017
		乾興 Ch'ien Hsing	1022
仁宗 Jen Tsung	1023	天聖 T'ien Sheng	1023
		明道 Ming Tao	1032
		景祐 Ching Yu	1034
		寶元 Pao Yuan	1038
		康定 K'ang Ting	1040
		慶曆 Ch'ing Li	1041
		皇祐 Huang Yu	1049
		至和 Chih Ho	1056
		嘉祐 Chia Yu	1056
英宗 Yin Tsung	1063	治平 Chih P'ing	1064
神宗 Shen Tsung	1067	熙寧 Hsi Ning	1068
		元豐 Yuan Feng	1078
哲宗 Che Tsung	1086	元祐 Yuan Yu	1086
		紹聖 Shao Sheng	1091
		元符 Yuan Fu	1098
徽宗 Hui Tsung	1101	建中靖國 Chien Chung Ching Kuo	1101

续表

廟號 Dynastic title	即位 Accession	年號	Reign title	建元 Adopted
		崇寧	Ch'ung Ning	1102
		大觀	Ta Kuan	1107
		政和	Cheng Ho	1111
		重和	Ch'ung Ho	1118
		宣和	Hsuan Ho	1119
欽宗 Ch'in Tsung	1126	靖康	Ching K'ang	1126

南宋(1127—1280) The Southern Sung dynasty

廟號 Dynastic title	即位 Accession	年號	Reign title	建元 Adopted
高宗 Kao Tsung	1127	建炎	Chien Yen	1127
		紹興	Shao Hsing	1131
孝宗 Hsiao Tsung	1163	隆興	Lung Hsing	1163
		乾道	Ch'ien Tao	1165
		淳熙	Shun Hsi	1174
光宗 Kuang Tsung	1190	紹熙	Shao Hsi	1190
寧宗 Ning Tsung	1195	慶元	Ch'ing Yuan	1195
		嘉泰	Chia T'ai	1201
		開禧	K'ai Hsi	1205
		嘉定	Chia Ting	1208
理宗 Li Tsung	1225	寶慶	Pao Ch'ing	1225
		紹定	Shao Ting	1228
		端平	Tuan P'ing	1234
		嘉熙	Chia Hsi	1237

续表

廟號 Dynastic title	即位 Accession	年號 Reign title	建元 Adopted
		淳祐 Shun Yu	1241
		寶祐 Pao Yu	1253
		開慶 K'ai Ch'ing	1250
		景定 Ching Ting	1260
度宗 Tu Tsung	1265	咸淳 Hsien Shun	1265
恭帝 Kung Ti	1275	德祐 Teh Yu	1275
端宗 Tuan Tsung	1276	景炎 Ching Yen	1276
帝昺 Ti P'ing	1278	祥興 Hsiang Hsing	1278

遼(契丹)紀(907—1124) The Liao (*Khitans*) dynasty

廟號 Dynastic title	即位 Accession	年號 Reign title	建元 Adopted
太祖 T'ai Tsu	907	神册 Shen Ts'e	916
		天贊 T'ien Tsan	922
		天顯 T'ien Hsien	925
太宗 T'ai Tsung	927	天顯 T'ien Hsien	927
		會同 Hui T'ung	937
		大同 Ta T'ung	947
世宗 Shih Tsung	947	天禄 T'ien Lu	947
穆宗 Mu Tsung	951	應曆 Ying Li	951
景宗 Ching Tsung	968	保寧 Pao Ning	968
		乾亨 Ch'ien Heng	978
聖宗 Sheng Tsung	983	統和 T'ung Ho	983
		開泰 K'ai T'ai	1012

续表

廟號 Dynastic title	即位 Accession	年號 Reign title		建元 Adopted
興宗 Hsing Tsung	1031	太平	T'ai P'ing	1020
		景福	Ching Fu	1031
		重熙	Ch'ung Hsi	1032
道宗 Tao Tsung	1055	清寧	Ch'ing Ning	1055
		咸雍	Hsien Yung	1066
		大康	Ta K'ang	1074
		大安	Ta An	1083
		壽隆	Shou Lung	1092
天祚帝 T'ien Tsu Ti	1101	乾統	Ch'ien T'ung	1101
		天慶	T'ien Ch'ing	1110
		保大	Pao Ta	1119

西遼紀(1124—1211) The Western Liao dynasty

廟號 Dynastic title	即位 Accession	年號 Reign title		建元 Adopted
德宗 Teh Tsung	1124	延慶	Yen Ch'ing	1124
		康國	K'ang Kuo	1131
感天后 Kan T'ien Hou	1144	咸清	Hsien Ch'ing	1144
仁宗 Jen Tsung	1151	紹興	Shao Hsing	1151
承天后 Ch'eng T'ien Hou	1164	崇福	Ch'ung Fu	1164
		皇德	Huang Teh	1164
		重德	Ch'ung Teh	1164
末主 Mo Chu	1178	天禧	T'ien Hsi	1178

金(女真)紀(1115—1234) The Ching (*Nu-chen*) dynasty

廟號 Dynastic title		即位 Accession	年號 Reign title		建元 Adopted
太祖	T'ai Tsu	1115	收國	Shou Kuo	1115
			天輔	T'ien Fu	1118
太宗	T'ai Tsung	1123	天會	T'ien Hui	1123
熙宗	Hsi Tsung	1135	天會	T'ien Hui	1135
			天眷	T'ien Chuan	1138
			皇統	Huang T'ung	1141
海陵王	Hai-ling Wang	1149	天德	T'ien Teh	1149
			貞元	Cheng Yuan	1153
			正隆	Cheng Lung	1156
世宗	Shih Tsung	1161	大定	Ta Ting	1161
章宗	Chang Tsung	1190	明昌	Ming Ch'ang	1190
			承安	Ch'eng An	1196
			泰和	T'ai Ho	1201
衛紹王	Wei-Shao Wang	1207	大安	Ta An	1209
			崇慶	Ch'ung Ch'ing	1212
			至寧	Chih Ning	1213
宣宗	Hsuan Tsung	1213	真祐	Cheng Yu	1213
			興定	Hsing Ting	1217
			元光	Yuan Kuang	1222
哀宗	Ai Tsung	1224	正大	Cheng Ta	1224
			開興	K'ai Hsing	1232
			天興	T'ien Hsing	1232
末帝	Mo Ti	1234	盛昌	Sheng Ch'ang	1156

元紀(1280—1368) The Yuan dynasty
蒙古時代(1206—1280) The Mongol period

廟號 Dynastic title		即位 Accession	年號 Reign title		建元 Adopted
太祖	T'ai Tsu	1206			
拖雷	T'o Lei	1228			
太宗	T'ai Tsung	1229			
乃馬真后	Nai Ma Chen Hou	1242			
定宗	Ting Tsung	1246			
憲宗	Hsien Tsung	1251			
世祖	Shih Tsu	1260	中統	Chung T'ung	1260
			至元	Chih Yuan	1264

統一時代(1280—1368) The period of Union

廟號 Dynastic title		即位 Accession	年號 Reign title		建元 Adopted
世祖	Shih Tsu	1280	至元	Chih Yuan	1280
成宗	Ch'eng Tsung	1295	元貞	Yuan Cheng	1295
			大德	Ta Teh	1297
武宗	Wu Tsung	1308	至大	Chih Ta	1308
仁宗	Jen Tsung	1312	皇慶	Huang Ch'ing	1312
			延祐	Yen Yu	1314
英宗	Ying Tsung	1321	至治	Chih Chih	1321
泰定帝	T'ai Ting Ti	1324	泰定	T'ai Ting	1324
			致和	Chih Ho	1328
幼主	Yu Chu	1328	天順	T'ien Shun	1328
文宗	Wen Tsung	1328	天歷	T'ien Li	1328

续表

廟號 Dynastic title		即位 Accession	年號 Reign title		建元 Adopted
寧宗	Ning Tsung	1332	至順	Chih Shun	1330
順帝(惠宗)	Shun Ti(Hui Tsung)	1333	元統	Yuan T'ung	1333
			至元	Chih Yuan	1335
			至正	Chih Cheng	1341

明紀(1368—1644) The Ming dynasty

廟號 Dynastic title		即位 Accession	年號 Reign title		建元 Adopted
太祖	T'ai Tsu	1368	洪武	Hung Wu	1368
惠帝	Hui Ti	1399	建文	Chien Wen	1399
成祖	Ch'eng Tsu	1403	永樂	Yung Lo	1403
仁宗	Jen Tsung	1425	洪熙	Hung Hsi	1425
宣宗	Hsuan Tsung	1426	宣德	Hsuan Teh	1426
英宗	Ying Tsung	1436	正統	Cheng T'ung	1436
代宗	Tai Tsung	1450	景泰	Ching T'ai	1450
英宗	Ying Tsung	1457	天順	T'ien Shun	1457
憲宗	Hsien Tsung	1465	成化	Ch'eng Hua	1465
孝宗	Hsiao Tsung	1488	弘治	Hung Chih	1488
武宗	Wu Tsung	1506	正德	Cheng Teh	1506
世宗	Shih Tsung	1522	嘉靖	Chia Ching	1522
穆宗	Mu Tsung	1567	隆慶	Lung Ch'ing	1567
神宗	Shen Tsung	1573	萬曆	Wan Li	1573
光宗	Kuang Tsung	1620	泰昌	T'ai Ch'ang	1620

续表

廟號 Dynastic title		即位 Accession	年號 Reign title		建元 Adopted
熹宗	Hsi Tsung	1621	天啟	T'ien Ch'i	1621
毅宗 (烈莊愍帝)	Yi Tsung(Lieh Chuang Min Ti)	1628	崇禎	Ch'ung Cheng	1628

清紀(1644—1912) The Ch'ing dynasty

廟號 Dynastic title		即位 Accession	年號 Reign title		建元 Adopted
世祖	Shih Tsu	1644	順治	Shung Chih	1644
聖祖	Sheng Tsu	1662	康熙	K'ang Hsi	1662
世宗	Shih Tsung	1723	雍正	Yung Cheng	1723
高宗	Kao Tsung	1736	乾隆	Ch'ien Lung	1736
仁宗	Jen Tsung	1796	嘉慶	Chia Ch'ing	1796
宣宗	Hsuan Tsung	1821	道光	Tao Kuang	1821
文宗	Wen Tsung	1851	咸豐	Hsien Feng	1851
穆宗	Mu Tsung	1862	同治	T'ung Chi	1862
德宗	Teh Tsung	1875	光緒	Kuang Hsu	1875
末帝	Mo Ti	1908	宣統	Hsuan T'ung	1908

民國(1912—) The Republic

元首 The Sovereigns		任期 Terms of office
孫文 臨時大總統	Sunyatsen, Provisional President	民國元年元旦至四月一日(1912 1 1— 4 1)
袁世凱 臨時大總統	Yuan Shih-kai, Provisional President	民國元年三月十日至二年十月六日(1912 3 10—1913 10 6)

续表

元首 The Sovereigns		任期 Terms of office
	大總統 President	民國二年十月六日至四年十二月十一日（1913 10 6—1915 12 11）
	洪憲皇帝 Claimed Emperor with the reign title Hung Hsien	民國四年十二月十一日至五年三月廿三日（1915 12 11—1916 3 23）
黎元洪 大總統	Li Yuan-hung, Presidet	民國五年六月七日至六年六月廿八日（1916 12 7—1917 6 28）
馮國璋 大總統	Feng Kuo-chang, President	民國六年八月一日至七年八月十二日（1917 8 1—1918 8 12）
徐世昌 大總統	Hsu Shih-ch'ang, President	民國七年十月十日至十一年六月二日（1918 10 10—1922 6 2）
黎元洪 復職	Li Yuan-hung resumed the presidency	民國十一年六月十一日至十二年六月十三日（1922 6 11—1923 6 13）
曹錕 大總統	Ts'ao K'un, President	民國十二年十月十日至十三年十一月三日（1923 10 10—1924 11 3）
段祺瑞 臨時執政	Tuan Ch'i-jui, Provisional Chief Executive	民國十三年十一月廿二日至十五年四月十八日（1924 11 22—1926 4 18）
蔣中正 國府主席	Chiang Chung chen, President of the National Government	民國十七年十月十日至廿年十二月十五日（1928 10 10—1931 12 15）
林森 國府主席	Lin Sen, President of the National Government	民國廿一年元旦（1932 1 1— ）

附錄四　Appendix IV

中國縣名表　A complete list of the Chinese Districts

河北省（冀）Hopei
省會 天津 PROVINCIAL CAPITAL TIENTSIN

安國縣	An-kwo	撫寗縣	Fu-ning	雞澤縣	Ki-tseh
安平縣	An-ping	邯鄲縣	Han-tan	交河縣	Kiao-ho
安新縣	An-sin	衡水縣	Heng-shui	景　縣	King Hsien
安肅縣見徐水縣		興隆縣	Hing-lung	慶雲縣	King-yun
安次縣	An-tze	雄　縣	Hiung Hsien	固安縣	Ku-an
昌黎縣	Chang-li	河間縣	Ho-kien	固城縣	Ku-cheng
昌平縣	Chang-ping	懷柔縣	Hwai-ju	鉅鹿縣	Ku-lu
長垣縣	Chang-yuan	獲鹿縣	Hwo-lu	曲周縣	Ku-chow
趙　縣	Chao Hsien	饒陽縣	Jao-yang	曲陽縣	Ku-yang
成安縣	Cheng-an	任　縣	Jen Hsien	廣昌縣見淶源縣	
正定縣	Cheng-ting	任邱縣	Jen-kiu	廣平縣	Kwang-ping
涿　縣	Cho Hsien	容城縣	Jung-cheng	廣宗縣	Kwang-tsung
房山縣	Fang-shan	開縣見濮陽縣		淶水縣	Lai-shui
肥鄉縣	Fei-siang	藁城縣	Kao-cheng	淶源縣	Lai-yuan
豐潤縣	Feng-jun	高陽縣	Kao-yang	蠡　縣	Li Hsien
阜城縣	Fow-cheng	高邑縣	Kao-yi	良鄉縣	Liang-siang
阜平縣	Fow-ping	薊　縣	Ki Hsien	臨城縣	Lin-cheng

臨榆縣	Lin-yu	深　縣	Shen Hsien	青　縣	Tsing Hsien
靈壽縣	Ling-show	深澤縣	Shen-tseh	井陘縣	Tsing-chin
樂亭縣	Lo-ting	束鹿縣	Shu-lu	静海縣	Tsing-hai
廬龍縣	Lu-lung	順義縣	Shun-yi	清豐縣	Tsing-feng
隆平縣	Lung-ping	香河縣	Siang-ho	清河縣	Tsing-ho
灤　縣	Lwan Hsien	獻　縣	Sien Hsien	清苑縣	Tsing-yuan
灤城縣	Lwan-cheng	新鎮縣	Sin-chen	遵化縣	Tsun-hwa
滿城縣	Man-cheng	新城縣	Sin-cheng	通　縣	Tung Hsien
密雲縣	Mi-yun	新河縣	Sin-ho	東光縣	Tung-kwang
南和縣	Nan-ho	新樂縣	Sin-lo	東明縣	Tung-ming
南宮縣	Nan-kung	刑臺縣	Sing-tai	磁　縣	Tze Hsien
南樂縣	Nan-lo	行唐縣	Sing-tang	完　縣	Wan Hsien
南皮縣	Nan-p'i	肅寧縣	Su-ning	宛平縣	Wan-ping
內丘縣	Nei-kiu	徐水縣	Su-shui	望都縣	Wang-tu
寧河縣	Ning-ho	大城縣	Ta-cheng	威　縣	Wei Hsien
寧晉縣	Ning-tsin	大興縣	Ta-hing	文安縣	Wen-an
甯津縣	Ning-tsing	大名縣	Ta-ming	無極縣	Wu-ki
霸　縣	Pa Hsien	唐　縣	Tang Hsien	武強縣	Wu-kiang
柏鄉縣	Pai-siang	唐山縣見堯山縣		吳橋縣	Wu-kiao
寶坻縣	Pao-ti	天津縣	Tien-tsin	武清縣	Wu-tsing
保定縣見新鎮縣		定　縣	Ting Hsien	武邑縣	Wu-yi
平谷縣	Ping-ku	定興縣	Ting-hing	堯山縣	Yao-shan
平山縣	Ping-shan	定都縣	Ting-tu	鹽山縣	Yen-shan
平鄉縣	Ping-siang	贊皇縣	Tsan-hwang	易　縣	Yi-Hsien
博野縣	Po-yeh	滄　縣	Tsang Hsien	翼　縣	Yi-Hsien
濮陽縣	Pu-yang	棗強縣	Tsao-kiang	玉田縣	Yu-tien
三河縣	San-ho	遷安縣	Tsien-an	元氏縣	Yuan-shih
沙河縣	Sha-ho	晉　縣	Tsin Hsien	永年縣	Yung-nien

永清縣　Yung-tsing

山東省(魯) Shantung
省會 濟南 PROVINCIAL CAPITAL TSINAN

安邱縣	An-kiu	黃　縣	Hwang Hsien	利津縣	Li-tsing
柞城縣	Cha-cheng	惠民縣	Hwei-ming	聊城縣	Liao-cheng
霑化縣	Chan-hwa	沂水縣	I-shui	臨朐縣	Lin-chu
章邱縣	Chang-kiu	益都縣	I-tu	臨清縣	Lin-tsing
昌樂縣	Chang-lo	日照縣	Jih-chao	臨淄縣	Lin-tze
昌邑縣	Chang-yi	榮成縣	Jung-cheng	臨沂縣	Lin-yi
長山縣	Chang-shan	高密縣	Kao-mi	臨邑縣	Lin-yi
長清縣	Chang-tsing	高唐縣	Kao-tang	陵　縣	Ling Hsien
朝城縣	Chang-cheng	高苑縣	Kao-yuan	樂安縣見廣饒縣	
招遠縣	Chao-yuan	嘉祥縣	Kia-siang	樂陵縣	Lo-ling
城武縣	Cheng-wu	膠　縣	Kiao Hsien	蒙陰縣	Meng-yin
茌平縣	Chih-ping	金鄉縣	Kin-siang	牟平縣	Mow-ping
莒　縣	Chu Hsien	邱　縣	Kiu Hsien	寧海縣見牟平縣	
諸城縣	Chu-cheng	曲阜縣	Ku-fow	寧陽縣	Ning-yang
恩　縣	En Hsien	鉅鹿縣	Ku-lu	蓬萊縣	Peng-lai
范　縣	Fan Hsien	冠　縣	Kwan Hsien	濱　縣	Pin Hsien
費　縣	Fei Hsien	觀城縣	Kwan-cheng	平度縣	Ping-tu
肥城縣	Fei-cheng	館陶縣	Kwan-tao	平陰縣	Ping-yin
福山縣	Fu-shan	廣饒縣	Kwang-jao	平原縣	Ping-yuan
海豐縣見無棣縣		萊蕪縣	Lai-wu	博興縣	Po-hing
海陽縣	Hai-yang	萊陽縣	Lai-yang	博平縣	Po-ping
菏澤縣	Ho-tseh	蘭山縣見臨沂縣		博山縣	Po-shan
桓臺縣	Hwan-tai	歷城縣	Li-cheng	濮　縣	Pu Hsien

蒲臺縣	Pu-tai	滕　縣	Teng Hsien	淄川縣	Tze-chwan
單　縣	Shan Hsien	定陶縣	Ting-tao	滋陽縣	Tze-yang
商河縣	Shang-ho	曹　縣	Tsao Hsien	濰　縣	Wei Hsien
壽張縣	Show-chang	齊河縣	Tsi-ho	汶上縣	Wen-shang
壽光縣	Show kwang	齊東縣	Tsi-tung	文登縣	Wen-teng
夏津縣	Sia-tsing	卽墨縣	Tsi-mo	武城縣	Wu-cheng
莘　縣	Sin Hsien	濟寧縣	Tsi-ning	無棣縣	Wu-ti
新城縣見桓臺縣		濟陽縣	Tsi-yang	陽穀縣	Yang-ku
新泰縣	Sin-tai	棲霞縣	Tsi-sia	陽信縣	Yang-sin
泗水縣	Sze-shui	青城縣	Tsing-cheng	掖　縣	Yi Hsien
泰安縣	Tai-an	清平縣	Tsing-ping	嶧　縣	Yi Hsien
郯城縣	Tan-cheng	鄒　縣	Tsow Hsien	鄄城縣	Yin-cheng
堂邑縣	Tang-yi	鄒平縣	Tsow-ping	禹城縣	Yu-cheng
德　縣	Teh Hsien	東阿縣	Tung-a	魚臺縣	Yu-tai
德平縣	Teh-ping	東平縣	Tung-ping	鄆城縣	Yun-cheng

河南省(豫) Honan

省會 開封 PROVINCIAL CAPITAL KAIFENG

安陽縣	An-yang	中牟縣	Chung-mow	潢川縣	Hwang chwan
長葛縣	Chang-ko	氾水縣	Fan-shui	輝　縣	Hwei Hsien
柘城縣	Che-cheng	方城縣	Fang-cheng	獲嘉縣	Hwo-kia
陳留縣	Chen-liu	封邱縣	Feng-kiu	伊川縣	I-chwan
鎮平縣	Chen-ping	扶溝縣	Fu-kow	伊陽縣	I-yang
鄭　縣	Cheng Hsien	河陰縣見廣武縣		汝南縣	Ju-nan
正陽縣	Cheng-yang	許昌縣	Hsu-chang	汝陽縣見汝南縣	
淇　縣	Chih Hsien	滑　縣	Hwa Hsien	滎澤縣見廣武縣	
河內縣見沁陽縣		淮陽縣	Hwai-yang	滎陽縣	Jung-yang

開封縣	Kai-feng	民權縣	Ming-chwan	信陽縣	Sin-yang
考城縣	Kao-cheng	南召縣	Nan-chao	修武縣	Siu-wu
汲　縣	Ki Hsien	南陽縣	Nan-yang	睢　縣	Sui Hsien
杞　縣	Ki Hsien	內黃縣	Nei-hwang	遂平縣	Sui-ping
郟　縣	Kia Hsien	內鄉縣	Nei-siang	濬　縣	Sun Hsien
經扶縣	King-fu	寧陵縣	Ning-ling	嵩　縣	Sung Hsien
確山縣	Kio-shan	寶豐縣	Pao-feng	太康縣	Tai-kang
固始縣	Ku-shih	博愛縣	Po-ai	唐河縣	Tang-ho
鞏　縣	Kung Hsien	商城縣	Shang-cheng	湯陰縣	Tang-yin
光山縣	Kwang-shan	商邱縣	Shang-kiu	鄧　縣	Teng Hsien
廣武縣	Kwang-wu	商水縣	Shang-shui	登封縣	Teng-feng
蘭封縣	Lan-feng	上蔡縣	Shang-tsai	濟源縣	Tsi-yuan
臨漳縣	Lin-chang	涉　縣	She Hsien	沁陽縣	Tsin-yang
臨汝縣	Lin-ju	陝　縣	Shen Hsien	桐柏縣	Tung-peh
臨潁縣	Lin-ying	沈邱縣	Shen-kiu	通許縣	Tung-su
林　縣	Ling Hsien	息　縣	Si Hsien	自由縣見伊川縣	
靈寶縣	Ling-pao	淅川縣	Si-chwan	洧川縣	Wei-chwan
洛寧縣	Lo-ning	西華縣	Si-hwa	温　縣	Wen Hsien
洛陽縣	Lo-yang	西平縣	Si-ping	閿鄉縣	Wen-siang
羅山縣	Lo-shan	夏邑縣	Sia-yi	武安縣	Wu-an
魯山縣	Lu-shan	襄城縣	Siang-cheng	武陟縣	Wu-chih
盧氏縣	Lu-shih	項城縣	Siang-cheng	舞陽縣	Wu-yang
鹿邑縣	Lu-yi	祥符縣見開封縣		陽武縣	Yang-wu
孟　縣	Meng Hsien	新安縣	Sin-an	葉　縣	Yeh Hsien
孟津縣	Meng-tsing	新鄭縣	Sin-cheng	郾城縣	Yen-cheng
密　縣	Mi Hsien	新鄉縣	Sin-siang	鄢陵縣	Yen-ling
泌陽縣	Mi-yang	新蔡縣	Sin-tsai	偃師縣	Yen-shih
澠池縣	Mien-chih	新野縣	Sin-yeh	延津縣	Yen-tsing

宜陽縣	Yi-yang	虞城縣	Yu-cheng	原武縣	Yuan-wu
禹　縣	Yu Hsien	尉氏縣	Yu-shih	永城縣	Yung-cheng

山西省(晉) Shansi
省會 陽曲 PROVINCIAL CAPITAL YANGKU

安澤縣	An-tze	猗氏縣	I-shih	靈石縣	Ling-shih
安邑縣	An-yi	芮城縣	Jui-cheng	樂平縣見昔陽縣	
長治縣	Chang-chih	榮河縣	Jung-ho	潞城縣	Lu-cheng
長子縣	Chang-tze	高平縣	Kao-ping	崞鄉縣見中陽縣	
趙城縣	Chao-cheng	吉　縣	Ki Hsien	寧武縣	Ning-wu
解　縣	Chieh Hsien	祁　縣	Ki Hsien	保德縣	Pao-teh
中陽縣	Chung-yang	絳　縣	Kiang hsien	偏關縣	Pien-kwan
崞　縣	Fan-sze	交城縣	Kiao-cheng	平陸縣	Ping-lu
方山縣	Fang-shan	介休縣	Kie-hsiu	平魯縣	Ping-lu
汾城縣	Fen-cheng	苛嵐縣	Ko-lan	平順縣	Ping-shun
汾西縣	Fen-si	曲沃縣	Ku-wo	平定縣	Ping-ting
汾陽縣	Fen-yang	廣靈縣	Kwang-ling	平遙縣	Ping-yao
浮山縣	Fow-shan	崞　縣	Kwo Hsien	蒲　縣	Pu Hsien
興　縣	Hing Hsien	嵐　縣	Lan Hsien	山陰縣	Shan-yin
河曲縣	Ho-ku	黎城縣	Li-cheng	神池縣	Shen-chih
河順縣	Ho-shun	離石縣	Li-shih	石樓縣	Shih-low
河津縣	Ho-tsing	遼　縣	Liao Hsien	朔　縣	Shoh Hsien
壼關縣	Hu-kwan	臨　縣	Lin Hsien	壽陽縣	Show-yang
渾源縣	Hun-yuan	臨汾縣	Lin fen	隰　縣	Si Hsien
洪洞縣	Hung-tung	臨晉縣	Lin-tsin	昔陽縣	Si-yang
懷仁縣	Hwai-jen	陵川縣	Ling-chwan	夏　縣	Sia Hsien
霍　縣	Hwo Hsien	靈邱縣	Ling-kiu	鄉寧縣	Siang-ning

襄陵縣	Siang-ling	晉城縣	Tsin-cheng	陽高縣	Yang-kao
襄垣縣	Siang yuan	沁　縣	Tsin Hsien	陽曲縣	Yang-ku
孝義縣	Siao-yi	沁水縣	Tsin-shui	翼城縣	Yi-cheng
忻　縣	Sin Hsien	沁源縣	Tsin-yuan	應　縣	Yin Hsien
新絳縣	Sin-kiang	静樂縣	Tsing-lo	岳陽縣見安澤縣	
徐溝縣	Su-kow	清源縣	Tsing-yuan	盂　縣	Yu Hsien
大寧縣	Ta-ning	左雲縣	Tso-yun	虞鄉縣	Yu-siang
大同縣	Ta-tung	屯留縣	Tun-liu	榆社縣	Yu-she
代　縣	Tai Hsien	萬泉縣	Wan-chuan	榆次縣	Yu-tze
太谷縣	Tai-ku	文水縣	Wen-shui	右玉縣	Yu-yu
太平縣見汾城縣		聞喜縣	Wen-si	垣曲縣	Yuan-ku
太原縣	Tai-yuan	五寨縣	Wu-chai	永和縣	Yung-ho
天鎮縣	Tien-chen	五臺縣	Wu-tai	永甯縣見離石縣	
定襄縣	Ting-siang	武鄉縣	Wu-siang	永濟縣	Yung-tsi
稷山縣	Tsi-shan	陽城縣	Yang-cheng		

陝西省(陝) Shensi

省會 長安 PROVINCIAL CAPITAL CHANGAN

安康縣	An-kang	鎮坪縣	Chen-ping	扶風縣	Fu-feng
安塞縣	An-sai	城固縣	Cheng-ku	府谷縣	Fu-ku
安定縣	An-ting	盩厔縣	Chow-chih	富平縣	Fu-ping
柞水縣	Cha-sbui	淳化縣	Chun-hwa	鄜施縣	Fu-shi
長安縣	Chang-an	中部縣	Chung-pu	韓城縣	Han-cheng
長武縣	Chang-wu	鳳　縣	Feng Hsien	漢陰縣	Han-yin
朝邑縣	Chao-yi	鳳翔縣	Feng siang	橫山縣	Heng-shan
鎮安縣	Chen-an	佛坪縣	Fo-ping	興平縣	Hing-ping
鎮巴縣	Chen-pa	鄜　縣	Fu Hsien	郃陽縣	Ho-yang

鄠縣	Hu Hsien	郿縣	Mei Hsien	西鄉縣	Si-siang
華縣	Hwa Hsien	米脂縣	Mi-cheh	咸陽縣	Sien-yang
華陰縣	Hwa-yin	沔縣	Mien Hsien	綏德縣	Sui-teh
懷遠縣見橫山縣		南鄭縣	Nan-chen	洵陽縣	Sun-yang
宜君縣	I-chun	寧羌縣	Ning-kiang	栒邑縣	Sun-yi
宜川縣	I-chwan	寧陝縣	Ning-shen	大荔縣	Ta-li
甘泉縣	Kan-chuan	白河縣	Pai-ho	澄城縣	Teng-cheng
高陵縣	Kao-ling	白水縣	Pai-shui	定邊縣	Ting-pien
岐山縣	Ki-shan	保安縣	Pao-an	清澗縣	Tsing-kien
葭縣	Kia Hsien	褒城縣	Pao-cheng	靖邊縣	Tsing-pien
乾縣	Kien Hsien	寶雞縣	Pao-ki	同官縣	Tung-kwan
汧陽縣	Kien-yang	邠縣	Pin Hsien	潼關縣	Tung-kwan
涇陽縣	King-yang	平利縣	Ping-li	柴陽縣	Tze-yang
嵐皋縣	Lan-kao	平民縣	Ping-ming	渭南縣	Wei-nan
藍田縣	Lan-tien	蒲城縣	Pu-cheng	武功縣	Wu-kung
醴泉縣	Li-chuan	三水縣見栒邑縣		吳堡縣	Wu-pao
臨潼縣	Liu-tung	三原縣	San-yuan	洋縣	Yang Hsien
麟游縣	Lin-yu	山陽縣	Shan-yang	耀縣	Yao Hsien
略陽縣	Lio-yang	商縣	Shang Hsien	延長縣	Yen-chang
留壩縣	Liu-pa	商南縣	Shang-nan	延川縣	Yen-chwan
洛川縣	Lo-chwan	神木縣	Shen-mu	榆林縣	Yu-lin
雒南縣	Lo-nan	石泉縣	Shih-chuan	永壽縣	Yung-show
隴縣	Lu Hsien				

甘肅省 (甘) Kansu

省會 蘭州 PROVINCIAL CAPITAL LANCHOW

安化縣見廣陽縣		安西縣	An-si	安定縣見定西縣	

漳　縣	Chang Hsien	景泰縣	King-tai	西固縣	Si-ku
張掖縣	Chang-yeh	慶陽縣	King-yang	夏河縣	Sia-ho
鎮番縣	見民勤縣	酒泉縣	Kiu-chuan	洮沙縣	Tao-sha
鎮原縣	Chen-yuan	古浪縣	Ku-lang	狄道縣	見臨洮縣
成　縣	Cheng Hsien	固原縣	Ku-yuan	天水縣	Tien-shui
正寧縣	Cheng-ning	禮　縣	Li Hsien	定西縣	Ting-si
莊浪縣	Chwang-lang	兩當縣	Liang-tang	鼎新縣	Ting-sin
伏羌縣	見甘谷縣	臨夏縣	Lin-sia	秦安縣	Tsin-an
撫彝縣	見臨澤縣	臨潭縣	Lin-tan	靜寧縣	Tsing-ning
海城縣	見海原縣	臨洮縣	Lin-tao	清水縣	Tsing-shui
海原縣	Hai-yuan	臨澤縣	Lin-tse	靖遠縣	Tsing-yuan
和政縣	Ho-chen	靈臺縣	Ling-tai	崇信縣	Tsung-sin
合水縣	Ho-shui	隴西縣	Lung-si	敦煌縣	Tun-hwang
紅水縣	見景泰縣	隆德縣	Lung-teh	東樂縣	見民樂縣
化平縣	Hwa-ping	毛目縣	見鼎新縣	通渭縣	Tung-wei
華亭縣	Hwa-ting	岷　縣	Min Hsien	渭源縣	Wei-yuan
環　縣	Hwan Hsien	民勤縣	Ming-chin	文　縣	Wen Hsien
徽　縣	Hwei Hsien	民樂縣	Ming-lo	武山縣	Wu-shan
會寧縣	Hwei-ning	寧　縣	Ning Hsien	武都縣	Wu-tu
甘谷縣	Kan-ku	寧定縣	Ning-ting	武威縣	Wu-wei
康　縣	Kang Hsien	寧遠縣	見武山縣	榆中縣	Yu-chung
皋蘭縣	Kao-lan	平番縣	見永登縣	玉門縣	Yu-men
高臺縣	Kao-tai	平涼縣	Ping-liang	永昌縣	Yung-chang
金　縣	見榆中縣	沙　縣	見洮沙縣	永康縣	見康縣
金塔縣	Kin-ta	山丹縣	Shan-tan	永登縣	Yung-teng
涇川縣	King-chwan	西和縣	Si-ho	永靖縣	Yung-tsing

寧夏省(寧) Ningsia
省會 寧夏 PROVINCIAL CAPITAL NINGSIA

中寧縣	Chung-ning	平羅縣	Ping-lo	按寧夏省區	
中衛縣	Chung-wei	平遠縣見豫旺縣		阿拉善類	
金積縣	Kin-chi	磴口縣	Teng-kow	特二旗及甘肅省	
靈武縣	Ling-wu	鹽池縣	Yen-chih	之備	
寧朔縣	Ning-sho	豫旺縣	Yu-wang		
寧夏縣	Ning-sia	蒙　旗	The Mongols		

青海省(青) Chinghai (Kokonor)
省會 西寧 PROVINCIAL CAPITAL SINING

互助縣	Hu-tsu	民和縣	Ming-ho	大通縣	Ta-tung
化隆縣	Hwa-lung	囊謙縣	Nang-chien	都蘭縣	Tu-lan
湟源縣	Hwang-yuan	碾伯縣見樂都縣		同仁縣	Tung-jen
共和縣	Kung-ho	巴燕縣見化隆縣		亹源縣	Wei-yuan
貴德縣	Kwei-teh	西寧縣	Si-ning	玉樹縣	Yu-shu
樂都縣	Lo-tu	循化縣	Sun-hwa		

四川省(川) Szechwan
省會 成都 PROVINCIAL CAPITAL CHENGTU

安　縣	An Hsien	昭化縣	Chao-hwa	忠　縣	Chung Hsien
安岳縣	An-yo	昭覺縣	Chao-kioh	中江縣	Chung-kiang
彰明縣	Chang-ming	城口縣	Cheng-kow	奉節縣	Feng-kien
長寧縣	Chang-ning	成都縣	Cheng-tu	酆都縣	Feng-tu
長壽縣	Chang-show	渠　縣	Chu Hsien	涪陵縣	Fow-ling

富順縣	Fu-shun	慶符縣	King-fu	懋功縣	Mow-kung
漢源縣	Han-yuan	邛崍縣	Kiung-lai	納谿縣	Na-chi
興文縣	Hing-wen	古藺縣	Ku-lin	南充縣	Nan-chung
合川縣	Ho-chwan	古宋縣	Ku-sung	南川縣	Nan-chwan
合江縣	Ho-kiang	筠連縣	Kun-lien	南溪縣	Nan-ki
洪雅縣	Hung-ya	珙 縣	Kung Hsien	南江縣	Nan-kiang
華陽縣	Hwa-yang	灌 縣	Kwan Hsien	南部縣	Nan-pu
會理縣	Hwei-li	廣安縣	Kwang-an	內江縣	Nei-kiang
儀隴縣	I-lung	廣漢縣	Kwang-han	寧南縣	Ning-nan
宜賓縣	I-ping	廣元縣	Kwang-yuan	峨眉縣	O-mei
仁壽縣	Jen-show	閬中縣	Lang-chung	峩邊縣	O-pien
榮 縣	Juang Hsien	雷波縣	Lei-po	巴 縣	Pa Hsien
榮昌縣	Jung-chang	理番縣	Li-fan	巴中縣	Pa-chung
榮經縣	Jung-king	梁山縣	Liang-shan	寶興縣	Pao-hing
開 縣	Kai Hsien	鄰水縣	Lin-shui	北川縣	Peh-chwan
開江縣	Kai-kiang	樂至縣	Lo-chih	彭 縣	Peng Hsien
高 縣	Kao Hsien	樂山縣	Lo-shan	彭山縣	Peng-shan
夾江縣	Kia-kiang	羅江縣	Lo-kiang	彭水縣	Peng-shui
江安縣	Kiang-an	瀘 縣	Hu Hsien	蓬安縣	Peng-an
江北縣	Kiang-peh	蘆山縣	Lu-shan	蓬溪縣	Peng-ki
江津縣	Kiang-tsing	隆昌縣	Lung-chang	郫 縣	Pi Hsien
江油縣	Kiang-yu	馬邊縣	Ma-pien	壁山縣	Pi-shan
黔江縣	Kien-kiang	眉山縣	Mei-shan	屏山縣	Ping-shan
劍閣縣	Kien-ko	綿竹縣	Mien-chu	平武縣	Ping-wu
犍爲縣	Kien-wei	綿陽縣	Mien-yang	蒲江縣	Pu-kiang
簡陽縣	Kien-yang	冕寧縣	Mien-ning	三臺縣	San-tai
綦江縣	Ki-kiang	名山縣	Ming-shan	射洪縣	She-hung
金堂縣	Kin-tang	茂 縣	Mow Hsien	石砫縣	Shih-chu

石泉縣見北川縣		太平縣見萬源縣		萬　縣	Wan Hsien
什邡縣	Shih-fang	丹稜縣	Tan-ling	萬源縣	Wan-yuan
雙流縣	Shwang-liu	德陽縣	Teh-yang	威遠縣	Wei-yuan
西昌縣	Si-chang	天全縣	Tien-chuan	汶川縣	Wen-chwan
西充縣	Si-chung	墊江縣	Tien-kiang	溫江縣	Wen-kiang
新繁縣	Sin-fan	蒼溪縣	Tsang-ki	巫溪縣	Wu-ki
新寧縣見開江縣		清溪縣見漢源縣		巫山縣	Wu-shan
新津縣	Sin-tsing	青神縣	Tsing-shen	武勝縣	Wu-sheng
新都縣	Sin-tu	井研縣	Tsing-yuan	雅安縣	Ya-an
秀山縣	Sin-shan	崇慶縣	Tsung-king	鹽邊縣	Yen-pien
敘永縣	Su-yung	崇寧縣	Tsung-ning	鹽亭縣	Yen-ting
宣漢縣	Suan-han	通江縣	Tung-kiang	鹽源縣	Yen-yuan
遂寧縣	Sui-ning	銅梁縣	Tung-kiang	營山縣	Ying-shan
松潘縣	Sung-pan	潼南縣	Tung-nan	岳池縣	Yo-chih
達　縣	Ta Hsien	東鄉縣見宣漢縣		酉陽縣	Yu-yang
大竹縣	Ta-chu	梓潼縣	Tze-tung	越嶲縣	Yueh-si
大寧縣見巫溪縣		資中縣	Tze-chung	雲陽縣	Yun-yang
大足縣	Ta-tsu	資陽縣	Tze-yang	永川縣	Yung-chwan
大邑縣	Ta-yi				

西康省（康） Sikang

省會　康定 PROVINCIAL CAPITAL KANGTING

安良縣	An-liang	恩達縣	En-ta	康定縣	Kang-ting
察雅縣	Cha-ya	河口縣見雅江縣		嘉黎縣	Kia-li
察隅縣	Cha-yu	懷柔縣見瞻化縣		科麥縣	Ko-mai
瞻化縣	Chan-hwa	義敦縣	I-tun	九龍縣	Kiu-lung
昌都縣	Chang-tu	甘孜縣	Kan-tse	貢　縣	Kung Hsien

貢噶縣	Kung-ko	石渠縣	Shih-chu	德格縣	Teh-ko
理化縣	Li-hwa	碩督縣	Shih-tu	德榮縣	Teh-jung
鑪霍縣	Lu-ho	太昭縣	Tai-chao	鄧柯縣	Teng-ko
瀘定縣	Lu-ting	丹巴縣	Tan-pa	定鄉縣	Ting-siang
寧靜縣	Ning-tsing	稻城縣	Tao-cheng	同普縣	Tung-pu
巴安縣	Pa-an	道孚縣	Tao-fu	雅江縣	Ya-kiang
白玉縣	Pai-yu	武成縣	Wu-cheng	鹽井縣	Yen-tsing

湖北省(鄂) Hupeh
省會 武昌 PROVINCIAL CAPITAL WUCHANG

安陸縣	An-lu	黃陂縣	Hwang-pei	光化縣	Kwang-huai
長樂縣見五峯縣		宜昌縣	I-chang	廣濟縣	Kwang-tsi
長陽縣	Chang-yang	宜城縣	I-cheng	來鳳縣	Lai-feng
枝江縣	Chih-kiang	宜都縣	I-tu	利川縣	Li-chwan
竹谿縣	Chu-ki	浠水縣	I-shui	禮山縣	Li-shan
竹山縣	Chu-shan	蘄春縣	Ki-chun	羅田縣	Lo-tien
鍾祥縣	Chung-siang	蘄水縣見浠水縣		麻城縣	Ma-cheng
恩施縣	En-shih	嘉魚縣	Kia-yu	沔陽縣	Mien-yang
房　縣	Fang Hsien	江陵縣	Kiang-ling	南漳縣	Nan-chang
漢川縣	Han-chwan	江夏縣見武昌縣		鄂城縣	O-cheng
漢陽縣	Han-yang	監利縣	Kien-li	巴東縣	Pa-tung
興國縣見陽新縣		建始縣	Kien-shih	保康縣	Pao-kang
興山縣	Hing-shan	京山縣	Kin-shan	蒲圻縣	Pu-chi
鶴峯縣	Ho-feng	荊門縣	King-men	石首縣	Shih-show
黃安縣	Hwang-an	穀城縣	Ku-cheng	襄陽縣	Siang-yang
黃岡縣	Hwang-kang	均　縣	Kun Hsien	孝感縣	Siao-kan
黃梅縣	Hwang-mei	公安縣	Kung-an	咸豐縣	Sien-feng

咸寧縣	Sien-ning	潛江縣	Tsien-kiang	陽新縣	Yang-sin
宣恩縣	Suan-en	崇陽縣	Tsung-yang	應城縣	Yin-cheng
隨　縣	Sui Hsien	通城縣	Tung-cheng	應山縣	Yin-shan
松滋縣	Sung-tze	通山縣	Tung-shan	遠安縣	Yuan-an
大冶縣	Ta-yeh	秭歸縣	Tze-kwei	雲夢縣	Yun-meng
當陽縣	Tang-yang	武昌縣	Wu-chang	鄖　縣	Yun-Hsien
天門縣	Tien-men	五峯縣	Wu-feng	鄖西縣	Yun-si
棗陽縣	Tsao-yang				

湖南省(湘) Hunan

省會 長沙 PROVINCIAL CAPITAL CHANGSHA

安福縣見臨澧縣		華容縣	Hwa-jung	醴陵縣	Li-ling
安化縣	An-hwa	晃　縣	Hwang Hsien	臨澧縣	Lin-li
安仁縣	An-jen	會同縣	Hwei-tung	臨湘縣	Lin-siang
安鄉縣	An-siang	宜章縣	I-chang	臨武縣	Lin-wu
茶陵縣	Cha-ling	汝城縣	Ju-cheng	零陵縣	Ling-ling
常寧縣	Chang-ning	祁陽縣	Ki-yang	瀏陽縣	Liu-yang
常德縣	Chang-teh	嘉禾縣	Kia-ho	瀘溪縣	Lu-ki
長沙縣	Chang-sha	江華縣	Kiang-hwa	龍山縣	Lung-shan
郴　縣	Chen Hsien	乾城縣	Kien-cheng	麻陽縣	Ma-yang
辰谿縣	Chen-ki	黔陽縣	Kien-yang	南　縣	Nan Hsien
城步縣	Cheng-pu	古丈縣	Ku-chang	酃　縣	Ning Hsien
芷江縣	Chih-kiang	桂東縣	Kwei-tung	寧鄉縣	Ning-siang
鳳凰縣	Feng-hwang	桂陽縣	Kwei-yang	寧遠縣	Ning-yuan
漢壽縣	Han-show	藍山縣	Lan-shan	巴陵縣見岳陽縣	
衡山縣	Heng-shan	耒陽縣	Lei-yang	寶慶縣見邵陽縣	
衡陽縣	Heng-yang	澧　縣	Li Hsien	保靖縣	Pao-tsing

平江縣	Ping-kiang	綏寧縣	Sui-ning	武陵縣見常德縣	
桑植縣	Sang-chih	大庸縣	Ta-yung	益陽縣	Yi-yang
善化縣見長沙縣		道　縣	Tao Hsien	岳陽縣	Yo-yang
邵陽縣	Shao-yang	桃源縣	Tao-yuan	攸　縣	Yu Hsien
石門縣	Shih-men	靖　縣	Tsing Hsien	沅江縣	Yuan-kiang
湘鄉縣	Siang-siang	清泉縣見衡陽縣		沅陵縣	Yuan-ling
湘潭縣	Siang-tan	東安縣	Tung-an	永興縣	Yung-hing
湘陰縣	Siang-yin	通道縣	Tung-tao	永明縣	Yung-ming
新化縣	Sin-hwa	資興縣	Tze-hing	永順縣	Yung-shun
新寧縣	Sin-ning	慈利縣	Tze-li	永綏縣	Yung-shi
新田縣	Sin-tien	武崗縣	Wu-kang	永定縣見大庸縣	
漵浦縣	Su-pu				

江西省(贛) Kiangsi

省會 南昌 PROVINCIAL CAPITAL NANCHANG

安福縣	An-fu	湖口縣	Hu-kow	吉水縣	Ki-shui
安義縣	An-i	會昌縣	Hwei-chang	建昌縣見永修縣	
安仁縣見餘江縣		宜春縣	I-chun	虔南縣	Kien-nan
安遠縣	An-yuan	宜豐縣	I-feng	金谿縣	Kin-ki
長寧縣見尋鄔縣		宜黃縣	I-hwang	九江縣	Kiu-kiang
分宜縣	Fen-i	義寧縣見修水縣		廣昌縣	Kwang-chang
豐城縣	Feng-cheng	弋陽縣	I-yang	廣豐縣	Kwang-feng
奉新縣	Feng-sin	瑞昌縣	Jui-chang	光澤縣	Kwang-tseh
浮梁縣	Fow-liang	瑞金縣	Jui-kin	貴溪縣	Kwei-ki
橫峯縣	Heng-feng	贛　縣	Kan Hsien	黎川縣	Li-chwan
興安縣見橫峯縣		高安縣	Kao-an	蓮花縣	Lien-hwa
興國縣	Hing-kwo	吉安縣	Ki-an	臨川縣	Lin-chwan

樂安縣	Lo-an	峽江縣	Sia-kiang	崇仁縣	Tsung-jen
樂平縣	Lo-ping	信豐縣	Sin-feng	崇義縣	Tung-yi
瀘溪縣	見資溪縣	新昌縣	見宜豐縣	都昌縣	Tu-chang
盧陵縣	見吉安縣	新城縣	見黎川縣	銅鼓縣	Tung-ku
龍泉縣	見遂川縣	新淦縣	Sin-kan	東鄉縣	Tung-siang
龍南縣	Lung-nan	新建縣	Sin-kien	資溪縣	Tze-ki
南昌縣	Nan-chang	新喻縣	Sin-yu	萬安縣	Wan-an
南城縣	Nan-cheng	星子縣	Sing-tze	萬年縣	Wan-nien
南豐縣	Nan-feng	修水縣	Siu-shui	萬載縣	Wan-tsai
南康縣	Nan-kang	遂川縣	Sui-chwan	武寧縣	Wu-ning
寧岡縣	Ning-kang	尋鄔縣	Sun-wu	餘干縣	Yu-kan
寧都縣	Ning-tu	大廈縣	Ta-yu	餘江縣	Yu-kiang
彭澤縣	Peng-tseh	泰和縣	Tai-ho	玉山縣	Yu-shan
平赤縣	Ping-chih	德安縣	Teh-an	雩都縣	Yu-tu
萍鄉縣	Ping-siang	德興縣	Teh-hing	鉛山縣	Yuan-shan
鄱陽縣	Po-yang	定南縣	Ting-nan	永豐縣	Yung-feng
上饒縣	Shang-jao	進賢縣	Tsin-sien	永寧縣	見寧岡縣
上高縣	Shang-kao	靖安縣	Tsing-an	永新縣	Yung-sin
上猶縣	Shang-yiu	清江縣	Tsing-kiang	永修縣	Yung-siu
石城縣	Shih-cheng				

安徽省(皖) Anhwei

省會 懷寧(安慶) PROVINCIAL CAPITAL HWEINING(ANKING)

巢　縣	Chao Hsien	全椒縣	Chuan-tsiao	阜陽縣	Fu-yang
績溪縣	Chi-ki	繁昌縣	Fan-chang	含山縣	Han-shan
滁　縣	Chu Hsien	鳳臺縣	Feng-tai	和　縣	Ho Hsien
盱眙縣	Chu-yi	鳳陽縣	Feng-yang	合肥縣	Ho-fei

懷寧縣	Hwei-ning	廬江縣	Lu-kiang	天長縣	Tien-chang
懷遠縣	Hwei-yuan	蒙城縣	Meng-cheng	定遠縣	Ting-yuan
霍丘縣	Hwo-kiu	南陵縣	Nan-ling	潛山縣	Tsien-shan
霍山縣	Hwo-shan	寧國縣	Ning-kwo	旌德縣	Tsing-teh
黟　縣	I Hsien	亳　縣	Po Hsien	青陽縣	Tsing-yang
祁門縣	Ki-men	歙　縣	She Hsien	秋浦縣見至德縣	
建平縣見郎溪縣		石埭縣	Shih-tai	桐城縣	Tung-cheng
建德縣見至德縣		壽　縣	Show Hsien	銅陵縣	Tung-ling
嘉山縣	Kia-shan	舒城縣	Shu-cheng	東流縣	Tung-liu
涇　縣	Kin Hsien	休寧縣	Siu-ning	至德縣	Tze-teh
廣德縣	Kwang teh	宿　縣	Su Hsien	望江縣	Wang-kiang
貴池縣	Kwei-chih	宿松縣	Su-sung	五河縣	Wu-ho
渦陽縣	Kwo-yang	宣城縣	Suan-cheng	蕪湖縣	Wu-hu
來安縣	Lai-an	泗　縣	Sze Hsien	無爲縣	Wu-wei
郎溪縣	Lang-ki	太和縣	Tai-ho	婺源縣	Wu-yuan
立煌縣	Li-hwang	太湖縣	Tai-hu	英山縣	Ying-shan
靈壁縣	Ling-pi	太平縣	Tai-ping	穎上縣	Ying-shang
六安縣	Liu-an	當塗縣	Tang-tu		

江蘇省(蘇) Kiangsu

南京 NANKING

省會 鎮江 PROVINCIAL CAPITAL CHENKIANG

安東縣見漣水縣		豐　縣	Feng Hsien	淮安縣	Hwai-an
常熟縣	Chang-shu	奉賢縣	Feng-sien	淮陰縣	Hwai-yin
鎮江縣	Chen-kiang	阜寧縣	Fu-ning	儀徵縣	I-cheng
啓東縣	Chi-tung	海門縣	Hai-men	宜興縣	I-hing
川沙縣	Chwan-sha	興化縣	Hing-hwa	如皋縣	Ju-kao

贛榆縣	Kan-yu	南滙縣	Nan-hwei	太倉縣	Tai-tsang
高淳縣	Kao-shun	南通縣	Nan-tung	丹徒縣見鎮江縣	
高郵縣	Kao-yu	寶山縣	Pao-shan	丹陽縣	Tan-yang
嘉定縣	Kia-ting	寶應縣	Pao-ying	碭山縣	Tang-shan
江寧縣	Kiang-ning	沛　縣	Pei Hsien	靖江縣	Tsing-kiang
江浦縣	Kiang-pu	邳　縣	Pi Hsien	青浦縣	Tsing-pu
江都縣	Kiang-tu	上海縣	Shang-hai	崇明縣	Tsung-ming
江陰縣	Kiang-yin	上元縣見江寧縣		東海縣	Tung-hai
金山縣	Kin-shan	沭陽縣	Shu-yang	東臺縣	Tung-tai
金壇縣	Kin-tan	蕭　縣	Siao Hsien	銅山縣	Tung-shan
句容縣	Ku-jung	宿遷縣	Su-tsien	吳　縣	Wu Hsien
崑山縣	Kun-shan	睢寧縣	Sui-ning	吳江縣	Wu-kiang
灌雲縣	Kwan-yun	松江縣	Sung-kiang	無錫縣	Wu-sih
溧水縣	Li-shui	泗陽縣	Sze-yang	武進縣	Wu-tsin
溧陽縣	Li-yang	泰　縣	Tai Hsien	揚中縣	Yang-chung
漣水縣	Lien-shui	泰興縣	Tai-hing	鹽城縣	Yen-cheng
六合縣	Lu-ho	太平縣見揚中縣		元和縣見吳縣	

浙江省(浙) Chekiang

省會 杭州 PROVINCIAL CAPITAL HANGCHOW

安吉縣	An-chi	諸暨縣	Chu-ki	黃巖縣	Hwang-yen
長興縣	Chang-hing	分水縣	Fen-shui	義烏縣	I-wu
昌化縣	Chang-hwa	奉化縣	Feng-hwa	仁和縣見杭縣	
常山縣	Chang-shan	富陽縣	Fu-yang	瑞安縣	Jui-an
鎮海縣	Chen-hai	海寧縣	Hai-ning	開化縣	Kai-hwa
嵊　縣	Cheng Hsien	海鹽縣	Hai-yen	嘉興縣	Kia-hing
衢　縣	Chu Hsien	杭　縣	Hang Hsien	嘉禾縣見嘉興縣	

嘉善縣	Kia-shan	紹興縣	Shao-hing	縉雲縣	Tsin-yun
江山縣	Kiang-shan	壽昌縣	Show-chang	青田縣	Tsing-tien
建德縣	Kien-teh	淳安縣	Shun-an	崇德縣	Tsung-teh
金華縣	Kin-hwa	象山縣	Siang-shan	桐盧縣	Tung-lu
景寧縣	King-ning	孝豐縣	Siao-feng	桐鄉縣	Tung-siang
慶元縣	King-yuan	蕭山縣	Siao-shan	東陽縣	Tung-yang
會稽縣見紹興縣		仙居縣	Sien-ku	慈谿縣	Tze-ki
蘭谿縣	Lan-chi	新昌縣	Sin-chang	溫嶺縣	Wen-ling
麗水縣	Li-shui	新登縣	Sin-teng	烏程縣見吳興縣	
臨安縣	Lin-an	宣平縣	Suan-ping	吳興縣	Wu-hing
臨海縣	Lin-hai	遂安縣	Sui-an	武康縣	Wu-kang
龍泉縣	Lung-chuan	遂昌縣	Sui-chang	武義縣	Wu-yi
龍游縣	Lung-yu	松陽縣	Sung-yang	樂清縣	Yo-tsing
南田縣	Nan-tien	太平縣見溫嶺縣		餘杭縣	Yu-hang
鄞 縣	Ning Hsien	泰順縣	Tai-shun	餘姚縣	Yu-yao
寧海縣	Ning-hai	湯溪縣	Tang-ki	玉環縣	Yu-hwan
平湖縣	Ping-hu	德清縣	Teh-tsing	於潛縣	Yu-tsien
平陽縣	Ping-yang	天台縣	Tien-tai	雲和縣	Yun-ho
浦江縣	Pu-kiang	定海縣	Ting-hai	永康縣	Yung-kang
山陰縣見紹興縣		錢塘縣見杭縣		永嘉縣	Yung-kia
上虞縣	Shang-yu				

福建省(閩)

省會 福州 PROVINCIAL CAPITAL FUCHOW

安溪縣	An-ki	長泰縣	Chang-tai	漳浦縣	Chang-pu
長樂縣	Chang-lo (Diongloh)	長汀縣	Chang-ting	詔安縣	Chao-an
		漳平縣	Chang-ping	政和縣	Cheng-ho

晉江縣	Chin-kiang	閩清縣	Min-tsing	霞浦縣	Sia-pu
福安縣	Fu-an	明溪縣	Ming-ki	仙游縣	Sien-yu
福鼎縣	Fu-ting	南安縣	Nan-an	松溪縣	Sung-ki
福清縣	Fu-tsing	南平縣	Nan-ping	思明縣	Sze-ming
海澄縣	Hai-teng	南靖縣	Nan-tsing	大田縣	Ta-tien
侯官縣	How-kwan	寧化縣	Ning-hwa	泰寧縣	Tai-ning
華安縣	Hwa-an	寧德縣	Ning-teh	德化縣	Teh-hwa
惠安縣	Hwei-an	甯洋縣	Ning-yang	將樂縣	Tsiang-lo
建安縣見建甌縣			(Lengyong)	清流縣	Tsing-liu
建寧縣	Kien-ning	平和縣	Ping-hwo	崇安縣	Tsung-an
建甌縣	Kien-ow	平潭縣	Ping-tan	同安縣	Tung-an
建陽縣	Kien-yang	屏南縣	Ping-nan	東山縣	Tung-shan
古田縣	Ku-tien	浦城縣	Pu-cheng	武平縣	Wu-ping
歸化縣見明溪縣		莆田縣	Pu-tien	尤溪縣	Yu-ki
連城縣	Lien-cheng	金門縣	Que-moy	雲霄縣	Yun-siao
連江縣	Lien-kong	沙　縣	Sha Hsien	永安縣	Yung-an
羅源縣	Lo-yuan	上杭縣	Shang-hang	永春縣	Yung-chun
龍溪縣	Lung-Ki	邵武縣	Shao-wu	永泰縣	Yung-tai
龍巖縣	Lung-yen	壽寧縣	Show-ning	永定縣	Yung-ting
閩　縣	Min Hsien	順昌縣	Shun-chang		(Engting)

廣東省(粵) Kwangtung

省會 廣州 PROVINCIAL CAPITAL CANTON

崖　縣	Ai Yun	昌江縣	Cheong-kong	長樂縣見五華縣	
潮安縣	Chao-an	蕉嶺縣	Chiao-ling	長寧縣見新豐縣	
潮陽縣	Chao-yang	始興縣	Chi-hing	中山縣	Chung-shan
鎮平縣見蕉嶺縣		赤溪縣	Chik-kai	化　縣	Fa Yun

花　縣	Fa Yun	連　縣	Lin Yun	遂溪縣	Sui-kai
防城縣	Fang-cheng	連平縣	Lim-ping	新豐縣	Sun-fung
佛崗縣	Fat-kong	連山縣	Lin-shan	新興縣	Sun-hing
封川縣	Fung-chun	靈山縣	Ling-shan	新寧縣見台山縣	
豐順縣	Fung-shu	陵水縣	Ling-shui	新會縣	Sun-wui
香山縣見中山縣		羅定縣	Lo-ting	信宜縣	Sun-yi
興寧縣	Hing-ning	樂昌縣	Lok-chong	徐聞縣	Su-wei
河源縣	Ho-yun	樂會縣	Lok-wui	四會縣	Sze-wui
海豐縣	Hoi-fung	陸豐縣	Luk-fung	大埔縣	Tai-pu
海康縣	Hoi-kong	龍川縣	Lung-chun	台山縣	Tai-shan
開建縣	Hoi-kin	龍門縣	Lung-moon	德慶縣	Tak-hing
開平縣	Hoi-ping	萬寧縣	Man-ning	儋　縣	Tan Yun
鶴山縣	Hok-shan	茂名縣	Mao-ming	電白縣	Tin-pak
和平縣	Hop-ping	文昌縣	Men-cheong	增城縣	Tseng-shing
合浦縣	Hop-po	梅　縣	Mui Yun	澄海縣	Tsing-hoi
惠來縣	Hwei-lai	南海縣	Nam-hoi	澄邁縣	Tsing-mai
惠陽縣	Hwei-yang	南澳縣	Nam-oa	清遠縣	Tsing-yun
饒平縣	Jao-ping	南雄縣	Nam-yung	從化縣	Tsung-fa
感恩縣	Kan-yen	吳川縣	Ng-chun	東莞縣	Tung-kun
揭陽縣	Kit-yang	五華縣	Ng-fa	東安縣見雲浮縣	
瓊山縣	Kiung-shan	安定縣	On-ting	紫金縣	Tze-kin
瓊東縣	Kiung-tung	寶安縣	Pao-on	鬱南縣	Wat-nam
高明縣	Ko-ming	平遠縣	Ping-yun	會同縣見瓊東縣	
高要縣	Ko-yiu	博羅縣	Pok-lo	欽　縣	Yam Yun
曲江縣	Ku-kong	普寧縣	Pu-ning	仁化縣	Yan-fa
廣寧縣	Kwong-ning	番禺縣	Pu-yun	恩平縣	Yan-ping
臨高縣	Lim-ko	三水縣	Sam-shui	陽春縣	Yeung-chun
廉江縣	Lin-kong	順德縣	Shun-tak	陽江縣	Yeung-kong

陽山縣	Yeung-shan	乳源縣	Yu-yun	翁源縣	Yung-yun
英德縣	Ying-tak	雲浮縣	Yun-fat		

廣西省(桂) Kwangsi
省會 邕寧 PROVINCIAL CAPITAL YUNGNING

鎮結縣	Chan-kieh	宜山縣	I-shan	龍州縣	Lung-chow
鎮邊縣	Chan-pin	融　縣	Jung Hsien	龍茗縣	Lung-ming
昭平縣	Chao-ping	容　縣	Jung Yun	龍勝縣	Lung-sheng
全　縣	Chuan Hsien	果德縣	Ko-teh	馬平縣	Ma-ping
鍾山縣	Chung-shan	恭城縣	Kung-cheng	蒙山縣	Meng-shan
崇善縣	Chung-shan	灌陽縣	Kwan-yang	明江縣	Ming-kiang
中渡縣	Chung-tu	貴　縣	Kwei Hsien	武鳴縣	Mo-ming
恩隆縣	En-lung	桂林縣	Kwei-lin	武宣縣	Mo-sun
恩陽縣	En-yang	桂平縣	Kwei-ping	武緣縣	見武鳴縣
奉議縣	Feng-i	來賓縣	Lai-pin	那馬縣	Na-ma
鳳山縣	Feng-shan	荔浦縣	Lai-po	南丹縣	Nan-tan
富川縣	Fu-chwan	雷平縣	Lei-ping	寧明縣	Ning-ming
扶南縣	Fu-nan	靈川縣	Ling-chwan	北流縣	Pak-low
興安縣	Hing-an	凌雲縣	Ling-yun	賓陽縣	Pin-yang
興業縣	Hing-yeh	柳城縣	Liu-cheng	平樂縣	Ping-lo
橫　縣	Heng Hsien	榴江縣	Liu-kiang	平南縣	Ping-nan
賀　縣	Ho Hsien	羅城縣	Lo-shing	憑祥縣	Ping-siang
河池縣	Ho-chih	雒容縣	Lo-yung	百色縣	Po-seh
信都縣	Hsin-tu	陸川縣	Lu-chwan	百壽縣	Po-show
義寧縣	I-ning	隆安縣	Lung-an	博白縣	Pok-pak
宜北縣	I-pak	隆山縣	Lung-shan	三江縣	San-kiang

上金縣	Shang-kin	思林縣	Szen-lin	同正縣	Tung-chen
上林縣	Shang-lin	思樂縣	Szen-lo	東蘭縣	Tung-lan
上思縣	Shang-sze	藤　縣	Teng-yun	懷集縣	Tai-tsar
岑溪縣	Shum-kai	天河縣	Tien-ho	萬承縣	Wan-cheng
西林縣	Si-lin	天保縣	Tien-pao	鬱林縣	Wat-lam
西隆縣	Si-lung	蒼梧縣	Tsang-wu	養利縣	Yang-li
西延縣	Si-yen	象　縣	Tseung Yun	陽朔縣	Yang-so
向都縣	Siang-tu	遷江縣	Tsien-kiang	永福縣	Yung-fu
忻城縣	Sin-cheng	靖西縣	Tsing-si	永淳縣	Yung-chun
修仁縣	Sou-yen	左　縣	Tso Yun	永寧縣見百壽縣	
綏淥縣	Sui-lu	都安縣	Tu-an	邕寧縣	Yung-ning
思恩縣	Szen-gen				

雲南省(滇) Yunnan

省會 昆明 PROVINCIAL CAPITAL KUNMING

阿迷縣見開遠縣		呈貢縣	Cheng-kung	華坪縣	Hwa-ping
安寧縣	An-ning	晉寧縣	Chin-ning	會澤縣	Hwei-tze
霑益縣	Chan-yi	中甸縣	Chung-tien	宜良縣	I-liang
昭通縣	Chao-tung	洱源縣	Erh-yuan	易門縣	I-men
車里縣	Che-li	鳳儀縣	Feng-yi	開遠縣	Kai-yuan
鎮康縣	Chen-kang	佛海縣	Fo-hai	江川縣	Kiang-chwan
鎮南縣	Chen-nan	富州縣	Fu-chow	江城縣	Kiang-cheng
鎮雄縣	Chen-siung	富民縣	Fu-ming	巧家縣	Kiao-kia
鎮沅縣	Chen-yuan	鶴慶縣	Ho-king	劍川縣	Kien-chwan
鎮越縣	Chen-yueh	河西縣	Ho-si	建水縣	Kien-shui
澂江縣	Cheng-kiang	華寧縣	Hwa-ning	景谷縣	King-ku

景東縣	King-tung	蒙自縣	Meng-tze	思茅縣	Sze-mao
邱北縣	Kiu-peh	猛丁縣	Meng-ting	大關縣	Ta-kwan
曲溪縣	Ku-ki	彌勒縣	Mi-lo	大理縣	Ta-li
曲靖縣	Ku-tsing	彌渡縣	Mi-tu	大姚縣	Ta-yao
箇舊縣	Ku-kiu	緬寧縣	Mien-ning	鄧川縣	Teng-chwan
昆明縣	Kun-ming	墨江縣	Mo-kiang	騰衝縣	Teng-tsung
昆陽縣	Kun-yang	南嶠縣	Nan-kiao	定遠縣見牢定縣	
廣南縣	Kwang-nan	寧洱縣	Ning-erh	靖江縣見綏江縣	
廣通縣	Kwang-tung	鄂嘉縣	O-kia	楚雄縣	Tsu-yung
蘭坪縣	Lan-ping	峨山縣	O-shan	通海縣	Tung-hai
瀾滄縣	Lan-tsiang	保山縣	Pao-shan	維西縣	Wei-si
滇蕖縣	Lan-chu	賓川縣	Pin-chwan	威信縣	Wei-sin
牢定縣	Lav-ting	平彞縣	Ping-i	文山縣	Wen-shan
麗江縣	Li-kiang	屏邊縣	Ping-pien	武定縣	Wu-ting
六順縣	Liu-shun	石屏縣	Shih-ping	漾濞縣	Yang-pi
羅平縣	Lo-ping	師宗縣	Shih-tsung	姚安縣	Yao-an
羅次縣	Lo-tze	順寧縣	Shun-ning	鹽豐縣	Yen-feng
祿勸縣	Lu-chuan	雙江縣	Shwan-kiang	鹽興縣	Yen-hing
祿豐縣	Lu-feng	雙柏縣	Shwan-peh	鹽津縣	Yen-tsing
陸良縣	Lu-liang	西疇縣	Si-chou	彞良縣	Yi-liang
路南縣	Lu-nan	嶍峨縣見峨山縣		玉溪縣	Yu-ki
瀘西縣	Lu-si	祥雲縣	Siang-yun	元江縣	Yuan-kiang
魯甸縣	Lu-tien	新平縣	Sin-ping	元謀縣	Yuan-mow
龍陵縣	Lung-ling	宣威縣	Suan-wei	雲　縣	Yun Hsien
馬關縣	Ma-kwan	綏江縣	Sui-kiang	雲龍縣	Yun-lung
馬龍縣	Ma-lung	尋甸縣	Sun-tien	雲南縣見祥雲縣	
蒙化縣	Meng-hwa	嵩明縣	Sung-ming	永仁縣	Yung-jen

永寧縣	Yung-ning	永平縣	Yung-ping	永善縣	Yung-shan
永北縣	Yung-peh				

貴州省(黔) Kweichow
省會 貴陽 PROVINCIAL CAPITAL KWEIYANG

安化縣見德江縣		黔西縣	Kien-si	普安縣	Pu-an
安龍縣	An-lung	金沙縣	Kin-sha	普定縣	Pu-ting
安南縣	An-nan	邛水縣見三穗縣		三合縣	San-ho
安順縣	An-shun	關嶺縣	Kwan-ling	三穗縣	San-hwei
長寨縣	Chang-chai	廣順縣	Kwang-shun	省溪縣	Sheng-ki
鎮寧縣	Chen-ning	貴筑縣	Kwei-chu	施秉縣	Shi-ping
鎮遠縣	Cheng-yuan	貴定縣	Kwei-ting	石阡縣	Shih-tsien
正安縣	Cheng-an	郎岱縣	Lang-tai	水城縣	Shui-cheng
貞豐縣	Cheng-feng	黎平縣	Li-ping	鰼水縣	Si-shui
織金縣	Chih-kin	荔波縣	Li-po	下江縣	Sia-kiang
赤水縣	Chih-shui	羅甸縣	Lo-tien	息烽縣	Sih-feng
錦屏縣	Chin-ping	鑢山縣	Lu-shan	修文縣	Siu-wen
鳳岡縣	Feng-kang	龍里縣	Lung-li	綏陽縣	Sui-yang
興義縣	Hing-i	麻江縣	Ma-kiang	松桃縣	Sung-tao
興仁縣	Hing-jen	湄潭縣	Mei-tan	思南縣	Sze-nan
后坪縣	How-ping	納雍縣	Na-jung	大塘縣	Ta-tang
黃平縣	Hwang-ping	八寨縣	Pa-chai	大定縣	Ta-ting
仁懷縣	Jen-hwai	盤　縣	Pan Hsien	台拱縣	Tai-kung
榕江縣	Jung-kiang	畢節縣	Pi-chieh	丹江縣	Tan-kiang
開陽縣	Kai-yang	平舟縣	Ping-chow	道真縣	Tao-chen
江口縣	Kiang-kow	平壩縣	Ping-pa	德江縣	Teh-kiang
劍河縣	Kien-ho	平越縣	Ping-yueh	天柱縣	Tien-chu

定番縣	Ting-fan	都勻縣	Tu-yun	婺川縣	Wu-chwan
册亨縣	Tseh-heng	獨山縣	Tu-shan	沿河縣	Yen-ho
岑鞏縣	Tsen-kung	銅仁縣	Tung-jen	印江縣	Yin-kiang
清鎮縣	Tsing-chen	桐梓縣	Tung-tze	餘慶縣	Yu-king
青溪縣	Tsing-ki	紫雲縣	Tze-yun	玉屏縣	Yu-ping
遵儀縣	Tsun-yi	威寧縣	Wei-ning	永从縣	Yung-tsung
都江縣	Tu-kiang	甕安縣	Weng-an		

遼寧省(遼) Liaoning
省會 瀋陽 PROVINCIAL CAPITAL SHENYANG

安廣縣	An-kwang	撫順縣	Fu-shun	金川縣	Kin-chwan
安圖縣	An-tu	撫松縣	Fu-sung	廣寧縣 見北鎮縣	
安東縣	An-tung	海城縣	Hai-cheng	寬甸縣	Kwang-tien
長白縣	Chang-pai	海龍縣	Hai-lung	黎樹縣	Li-shu
昌圖縣	Chang-tu	黑山縣	Hei-shan	遼中縣	Liao-chung
彰武縣	Chang-wu	興城縣	Hing-cheng	遼陽縣	Liao-yang
瞻榆縣	Chang-yu	興京縣 見新賓縣		遼源縣	Liao-yuan
鎮安縣 見黑山縣		懷仁縣 見桓仁縣		臨江縣	Lin-kiang
鎮東縣	Chen-tung	懷德縣	Hwai-teh	柳河縣	Lin-ho
承德縣 見瀋陽縣		桓仁縣	Hwan-jen	寧遠縣 見興城縣	
錦 縣	Chi Hsien	輝南縣	Hwei-nan	盤山縣	Pan-shan
錦西縣	Chin-si	義 縣	I Hsien	北鎮縣	Peh-chen
莊河縣	Chwang-ho	蓋平縣	Kai-ping	本溪縣	Pen-ki
法庫縣	Fa-ku	開通縣	Kai-tung	瀋陽縣	Shen yang
鳳城縣	Feng-cheng	開原縣	Kai-yuan	雙山縣	Shwang-shan
奉化縣 見黎樹縣		康平縣	Kang-ping	西安縣	Si-an
復 縣	Fu Hsien	金 縣	Kin Hsien	西豐縣	Si-feng

新民縣	Sin-ming	洮南縣	Tao-nan	突泉縣	Tu-chuan
新賓縣	Sin-ping	鐵嶺縣	Tieh-ling	東豐縣	Tung-feng
岫巖縣	Siu-yen	輯安縣	Tsi-an	通化縣	Tung-hwa
綏中縣	Sui-chung	靖安縣見洮安縣		通遼縣	Tung-liao
台安縣	Tai-an	清原縣	Tsing-yuan	營口縣	Ying-kow
洮安縣	Tao-an				

吉林省(吉) Kirin
省會 永吉 PROVINCIAL CAPITAL YUNGKI

阿城縣	A-cheng	依蘭縣	I-lan	舒蘭縣	Shu-lan
額穆縣	Ar-mu	依通縣	I-tung	雙城縣	Shwang-cheng
長春縣	Chang-chun	饒河縣	Jao-ho	雙陽縣	Shwang-yang
長嶺縣	Chang-ling	吉林縣見永吉縣		綏遠縣見撫遠縣	
長壽縣見延壽縣		乾安縣	Kien-an	德惠縣	Teh-hwei
珠河縣	Chu-ho	濛江縣	Meng-kiang	敦化縣	Tun-hwa
方正縣	Fang-cheng	密山縣	Mi-shan	同江縣	Tung-kiang
富錦縣	Fu-chin	穆稜縣	Mu-ling	東寧縣	Tung-ning
扶餘縣	Fu-yu	寧安縣	Ning-an	汪清縣	Wang-ching
撫遠縣	Fu-yuan	農安縣	Nung-an	葦河縣	Wei-ho
和龍縣	Ho-lung	盤石縣	Pan-shih	五常縣	Wu-chang
虎林縣	Hu-lin	寶清縣	Pao-tsing	延吉縣	Yen-ki
琿春縣	Hun-chun	賓　縣	Pin Hsien	延壽縣	Yen-show
樺川縣	Hwa-chwan	濱江縣	Pin-kiang	榆樹縣	Yu-shu
樺甸縣	Hwa-tien	勃利縣	Po-li	永吉縣	Yung-ki

黑龍江省（黑） Heilungkiang

省會 龍江 PROVINCIAL CAPITAL LUNGKIANG

璦琿縣	Ai-gun	蘭西縣	Lan-si	綏化縣	Sui-hua
安達縣	Au-ta	林甸縣	Lin-tien	綏楞縣	Sui-o
肇州縣	Chao-chow	蘿北縣	Lo-peh	綏濱縣	Sui-pin
肇東縣	Chao-tung	臚濱縣	Lu-pin	遜河縣	Sun-ho
奇克縣	Chi-ke	龍鎮縣	Lung-chen	大賚縣	Ta-lai
奇乾縣	Chi-kien	龍江縣	Lung-kiang	大通縣見通河縣	
慶城縣	Ching-cheng	明水縣	Ming-shui	泰來縣	Tai-lai
佛山縣	Fo-shan	漠河縣	Mo-ho	湯源縣	Tang-yuan
海倫縣	Hai-lun	木蘭縣	Mu-lan	鐵驪縣	Tieh-li
呼蘭縣	Hu-lan	訥河縣	No-ho	青岡縣	Tsing-kang
呼倫縣	Hu-lun	嫩江縣	Nun-kiang	通河縣	Tung-ho
呼瑪縣	Hu-ma	鷗浦縣	Ou-pu	通北縣	Tung-peh
依安縣	I-an	巴彥縣	Pa-yen	望奎縣	Wang-kwei
景星縣	King-sing	拜泉縣	Pai-chuan	烏雲縣	Wu-yun
克山縣	Ko-shan	室韋縣	Shih-wei	雅魯縣	Ya-lu

熱河省（熱） Jehol

省會 承德 PROVINCIAL CAPITAL CHENGTEH

朝陽縣	Chao-yang	開魯縣	Kai-lu	林西縣	Lin-si
承德縣	Cheng-teh	建昌縣見凌源縣		林東縣	Lin-tung
赤峯縣	Chih-feng	建平縣	Kien-ping	凌南縣	Ling-nan
豐寧縣	Feng-ning	經棚縣	King-peng	凌源縣	Ling-yuan
阜新縣	Fu-sin	灤平縣	Lawn-ping	隆化縣	Lung-hwa

平泉縣	Ping-chuan	蒙　旗	The Mongols	烏遠卓索圖二盟地方	
綏東縣	Sui-tung	按熱河省區即內蒙昭		也今皆設縣治如上	
圍場縣	Wei-chang				

察哈爾省(察) Chahar
省會 萬全 PROVINCIAL CAPITAL WANCHUAN

張北縣	Chang-peh	商都縣	Shang-tu	十縣地方也口錫林	
赤城縣	Chih-cheng	西寧縣見陽原縣		郭勒盟五部均未設縣	
涿鹿縣	Cho-lu	宣化縣	Suan-hwa	茲錄如下	
多倫縣	Do-lou	萬全縣	Wan-chuan	錫林郭勒	
懷安縣	Hwai-an	陽原縣	Yang-yuan		Silingol League
懷來縣	Hwai-lai	延慶縣	Yen-king	烏珠穆沁部	
康保縣	Kang-pao	蔚　縣	Yu Hsien		Ujamchin
沽源縣	Ku-yuan	蒙　旗	The Mongols	浩齊特部	Hochit
龍關縣	Lung-kwan	按察哈爾省區即內		阿巴噶部	Abaga
龍門縣見龍關縣		蒙錫林郭勒盟察哈		阿巴哈納爾部	
寶昌縣	Pao-chang	爾部及河北省口北			Abaganar
				蘇尼特部	Sunid

綏遠省(綏) Suiyuan
省會 歸綏 PROVINCIAL CAPITAL KWEISUI

豐鎮縣	Feng-chen	臨河縣	Lin-ho	集寧縣	Tsi-ning
興和縣	Hing-ho	包頭縣	Pao-tow	清水河縣	Tsingshui-ho
和林格爾縣	Holinkoerh	薩拉齊縣	Saratsi	東勝縣	Tung-sheng
固陽縣	Ku-yang	大佘太縣	Tashetai	武川縣	Wu-chwan
歸綏縣	Kwei-sui	陶林縣	Tao-lin	五原縣	Wu-yuan
涼城縣	Liang-cheng	托克托縣	Tokoto	蒙　旗	The Mongos

按綏遠省區即內蒙　　默特三盟及察哈爾　　今皆設縣治如上
烏蘭察布伊克昭土　　劃併之五縣地方也

新疆省（新）Sinkiang
省會 迪化 PROVINCIAL CAPITAL TIHWA

阿克蘇縣	Aksu	柯坪縣	Ko-ping	疏勒縣	Shu-leh
阿瓦堤縣	Awati	庫車縣	Ku-che	莎車縣	Su-che
額敏縣	Ar-min	呼圖壁縣	Kutupi	綏來縣	Sui-ting
博樂縣	Bo-lo	鞏留縣	Kung-liu	綏定縣	Sui-ting
昌吉縣	Chang-ki	洛浦縣	Lo-pu	塔城縣	Tah-cheng
鎮西縣	Chen-si	魯克沁縣	Luksin	迪化縣	Ti-hwa
承化縣	Cheng-hwa	輪台縣	Lun-tai	托克蘇縣	Tokosu
且末縣	Chieh-mo	麥蓋提縣	Mokaiti	托克遜縣	Tokosun
吉木乃縣	Chimunai	墨玉縣	Mo-yu	策勒縣	Tse-leh
婼羌縣	Choh-kiang	木壘河縣	Muleiho	澤普縣	Tse-pu
阜康縣	Fu-kang	寧遠縣見伊寧縣		精河縣	Tsing-ho
孚遠縣	Fu-yuan	巴楚縣	Pa-chu	吐魯番縣	Turfan
霍爾果斯縣	Gorgos	拜城縣	Pai-cheng	温宿縣	Wen-suh
哈密縣	Ha-mi	皮山縣	P'i-shan	烏什縣	Wu-shih
哈巴河縣	Hapaho	布爾津縣	Puerhtsing	烏蘇縣	Wu-su
和什托羅蓋縣		布倫托海縣	Puluntohai	葉爾羌縣	Yarkand
	Hoshtolokai	蒲犁縣	Pu-li	葉城縣	Yeh-cheng
伊寧縣	I-ning	沙灣縣	Sha-wan	焉耆縣	Yen-ki
和闐縣	Kho-tan	沙雅縣	Sha-ya	英吉沙縣	Yingkisha
奇台縣	Ki-tai	鄯善縣	Shan-shan	尉犁縣	Yu-li
伽師縣	Kia-shi	新平縣見尉犁縣		于闐縣	Yu-tan
乾德縣	Kien-teh	疏附縣	Shu-fu		

目　錄

經書分類的研究…………………………………………… 1451
中國語言文字學書籍分類的研究………………………… 1459

經書分類的研究

一　經書分類的問題

　　甲、清以前的經書分類。經書的分類自戰國至清幾是一致的以六經爲一類。所不同的祇是六經的次序，範圍，與名目不全是一樣。茲列舉五家的經書分類，做說明：

　　(1)劉歆《七略》的六藝略：《易》《書》《詩》《禮》《樂》《春秋》《論語》《孝經》《小學》。

　　(2)王儉的《七志》：《經典釋文》謂以《孝經》爲首。

　　(3)歐陽修等撰的《新唐志》：《易》《書》《詩》《禮》《樂》《春秋》《孝經》《論語》、讖緯、經解、小學。

　　(4)鄭樵的《通志・藝文略》：1.經類：《易》《書》《詩》《春秋》《孝經》《論語》《爾雅》、經解。2.禮類。3.樂類。4.小學類……

　　(5)《四庫》：《易》《書》《詩》《禮》《周禮》《儀禮》《禮記》、三禮通義、通禮、雜禮、《春秋》《孝經》、五經總義、四書、樂、小學、訓詁、字書、韻書。

　　劉歆《七略》於六經之外加入《論語》《孝經》《小學》。王儉《七志》以《孝經》居先與《七略》次序不一樣。《新唐志》六經次序與《七略》一樣，但《孝經》在《論語》之前，又加入讖緯與經解。鄭樵是第一人把禮、樂、小學列於經類之外的。《四庫》的分類與以上各家也不一樣。自來經學家、目錄學家的經書分類雖然不是完全一致，但沒有一家主張完全拆散的。

　　民國以來經書分類的三個主張。前二十年杜定友氏出版一本《世界圖書分類法》，首先打破歷代對於經書的傳統分法，主張把六經拆散分類。他的理由：《易經》是講哲理的，應當分入哲學。《書經》是史書，分入歷史。《詩經》分入文學。《禮經》分入禮俗類。《樂經》入音樂。《春秋》分入歷史。杜氏現又出版一部《三民主義分類法》，因没有看見這部書，不知他對於經書分類的主張有没有詳細的説明。

隨後劉國鈞氏在他的圖書分類法主張經書拆散分類與不拆散分類兩可説。他的理由是甚麽，因没有説明，不能臆測。

拙作《中國十進分類法》，主張經書不可拆散分類。

大概的説，民國以來經書分類的主張，有上述三種：拆散論，拆散或不拆散論，不拆散論。

二　經書不可拆散論的理由

六經成立的由來。經，班固《白虎通》訓爲"常"，劉熙《釋名》訓爲"徑"。《左傳》："夫禮，天之經，地之義，民之行也。"《中庸》："唯天下至誠，爲能經綸天下之大經，立天下之大本。"後世尊書之可以垂教萬世者曰經，如佛教稱經、律、論三藏爲經，基督教稱新、舊約爲經等是。我所説的是專指儒家的六經，或稱六藝。《莊子·天運篇》最先稱六藝爲六經，"孔子謂老聃曰：丘治《詩》《書》《禮》《樂》《易》《春秋》六經。"這是六經的名稱之所由始。太史公述六藝自序曰："孔子垂六藝之統紀於後世。"又曰："中國言六藝者，折中於夫子。"《孔子世家》贊曰："言六藝者，皆出於夫子。"這是以六經爲孔子之經。劉歆《七略》以《周官》爲周公作，鄭玄以《周官》爲三禮之首，朱熹謂《周官》非周公不能作，章學誠則謂周公集六經的大成。亦有以六經的集成不是周公、孔子者。但都把六經看作一部整個的書。

秦滅以後，六經不無散失。漢武求遺書於天下，設置五經博士。孔壁經出，係古文經。古文經云者，以孔壁諸經寫以古文也。五經立於學官的，都是今文，古文於後漢哀平之世，纔得立於學官。自是古今文之爭，千古不息，而一經說至百萬餘言矣。

靈帝因慮五經譌誤遺脱，乃於熹平四年詔諸儒正定五經，刊於石碑，即是後世所説的《熹平石經》。魏正始亦立有石經。石經有一字、三字之別。一字石經，《唐書・藝文志》稱今字石經，唐以隸爲今字也。三字石經是以古文、篆、隸三體書法寫刻者。《熹平石經》與《正始石經》，何者是一字，何者是三字，至今尚是未定之點，仍有待於將來的發現與考證。唐《開成石經》亦是一樣，恐怕年久失去五經真本，也刻石太學。《唐石經》所刻的是十二經。《孟子》之未刻入，是本陸德明《經典釋文》之例。後經乾符的修造，後梁的補刊，北宋的添注，顧炎武指正誤字甚多。《孟蜀石經》始將《孟子》刊入，是爲十三經。清乾隆所立石經，以《唐石經》爲張本。上文也都以六經爲一部整個的書，未有拆散者。再看：

乙、歷朝治經的態度。中國學術皆原於六經，自戰國已然。諸子著述，雖各趨極端，而所考信依據，論難非辯，皆以六經爲的。漢武設置五經博士，經師講授，蔚成專門學科，其所爭者，衹在今學與古學。漢儒大都今學，傳古學者僅杜、賈、馬、鄭數人，但皆博學通儒，尤以馬融、鄭玄爲最。馬融編注《九經》，爲古學之總匯。三禮三傳，皆其手定，二千年來無有變易。康成兼通古今，而以古學爲正傳。所注《周易》《毛詩》《儀禮》《禮記》《論語》《孝經》《尚書大傳》等，今古雜糅。古學得以專行，爲後世所宗者，康成之功也。漢儒治經，必守家法，且皆訓詁章句之學，兼雜災異讖緯之言。董仲舒的《春秋繁露》，鄭玄的《緯書注》都是。晉人注經，傅會鑿空益多。唐儒撰諸經義疏，而家法亡。宋以經義取士，用理學解經，盡反漢法，所以有漢學、宋學之分。宋儒疑經最勇：歐陽修之疑《十翼》，蘇軾、蘇轍之毀《周禮》，朱熹之疑《周禮》《古文尚書》《詩序》，鄭樵之疑《詩序》《左傳》，都是。尤以朱熹的三傳弟子王柏爲最甚，每以脱簡爲辭，竄改補綴經文。比方，合《舜典》於《堯典》,合《益稷》於《陶謨》,等等。元明注經均本宋學。清儒治經重考據。顧炎武、閻若璩等創導於前,惠棟、戴震承繼於後,樸學大興。戴東原校勘以識字爲本。他説:"經所以載道,所以明道者,詞也。所以明詞者,字也。學者由字以通其詞,由詞以通其道。……宋儒譏訓詁之學,而輕言語文字,是猶渡江河而忘楫也。"

民國以來以歷史的態度治經,作結賬式的整理,而以爲學術對象,一掃二千年來治經之遺習。宋朝治經方法雖不是一樣,但都以六經爲一家之學,不單是以六經爲一部整個書也,何可離析磔裂,強納近今圖書各類?兹更舉《詩經》爲例以實證經書不可拆散論。《詩經》原是一本古代詩歌的總集,從漢至清把這本書注疏成爲一本非文學的書。今分幾點來説明。

漢時説《詩》者有齊魯韓三家,其後有《毛詩》。鄭玄作《毛詩箋》,《毛詩》係專行於世。《齊詩》亡於魏,《魯詩》亡於西晉,《韓詩》亦亡,傳於世者,祗有《外傳》,而又不全。魏王肅説《毛詩》與鄭玄不同。於是朱毛、鄭、王之異同評。至宋歐陽修作《毛詩本義》,蘇轍作《詩解集傳》,都懷疑《毛詩》。鄭樵作《詩辯妄》,朱熹作《詩集傳》,王柏作《詩疑》,評擊《毛詩》特甚。至清閻若璩作《朱毛詩説》評擊《詩集傳》,要把《詩經》回復到《毛傳》《鄭箋》。魏源作《詩古微》評擊《毛傳》,要把《詩經》回復到齊魯韓的三家詩。姚際恒作《詩經通論》,從朱熹之説評擊三家詩、《毛傳》《鄭箋》。這些傳、箋、注、疏都離不了"麟趾之化""騶虞之德"的説法,而聚訟評擊,幾皆辯序之文,與《詩經》文學無涉,你能説這些書是在研究《詩經》的文學嗎?這是一點。

再看歷朝傳注《詩經》的内容是怎樣。舉例來説吧。《召南·鵲巢》一詩原文:"維鵲有巢,維鳩居之,之子于歸,百兩御之。"《毛詩序》説:"夫人之德也,國君積行累功,以致爵位,夫人起家而居有之,德如鳲鳩,乃可以配焉。"《鄭箋》説:"鵲之作巢,冬至架之,至春乃成。猶國君積行累功,故以興焉。興者,鳲鳩因鵲成巢而居有之,而有均一之德。"朱熹《詩集傳》說："南國諸侯被文王之化，能正心修身以齊其家。其女子亦被后妃之化，而有專靜純一之德，故嫁於諸侯。"他又說這首詩的意與《周南》的《關雎》一樣。這樣注釋《詩經》，是把《詩經》當作文學嗎？《漢書·儒林傳》云："六藝者，王教之典籍，先聖所以說大道，正人倫，致至治之成法也。"他們是在把六經當作修身齊家治國平天下的工具書呢。這是第二點。

還有一點，經學家不但不把《詩經》當作文學研究，像王柏還把《詩經》中最美的幾首作品刪掉。比方：《召南》的《野有死麕》，《邶風》的《靜女》，《鄘風》的《桑中》，《衛風》的《氓》，《王風》的《大車》，《鄭風》的《有女同車》等等凡朱熹認爲淫奔之詩的，全部刪掉。但是評擊他的，不是根據文學的觀點，而是以經的立場斥責他。像《四庫總目》斥他說："柏何人斯，敢奮筆而進退孔子哉。"

一部極美麗的文學書，被注疏成爲美刺王侯的道學書，難怪朱熹也不相信，《詩序》說："古人作詩，與今人作詩一般，其間亦自有感物道情，吟詠情性。幾時盡是譏刺他人。祇緣序者立例，篇篇要作美刺說，將詩人意思盡穿鑿壞了。"但他在《詩集傳·序》裏面又說："詩之爲經"，"固所以爲萬世法程而不可易者也"。歷朝經師都以經治經。治《詩經》是如此，治其他各經亦復如此。而傳注六經的書，又以千萬數。怎可不仍成經部，立爲專類嗎？

何況章學誠說六經皆史，章炳麟也以六經爲史呢。《關雎》三章，章太炎的疏解與各家特異。三家詩以《關雎》爲畢公作，刺康王之失。《毛傳》以爲正風之始，美后妃之德。《詩集傳》說不能專美后妃，而要本於文王。章氏說《關雎》歌文王與紂之事。君子指紂，淑女指鬼侯之女。獻於紂，女不喜淫，乃醢鬼侯，脯鄂侯，拘西伯。我們能聽從章氏的說法，把《詩經》分入歷史嗎？分入文學不可，分入歷史不可，分入政治、哲學、道德均不可，是則經書不可拆散分類矣。

三　經書的次序

六經的次序有：《詩》《書》《禮》《樂》《易》《春秋》與《易》《書》《詩》《禮》《樂》《春秋》二種的不同。《詩》《書》《禮》《樂》《易》《春秋》，今文學家謂孔子手定。史遷以前幾都是這個次序。今引録數家如下：

（1）《禮記·經解篇》："温柔敦厚，《詩》教也。疏通知遠，《書》教也。廣博易良，《樂》教也。絜静精微，《易》教也。恭儉莊敬，《禮》教也。屬辭比事，《春秋》教也。"

（2）《莊子·天運篇》："丘治《詩》《書》《禮》《樂》《易》《春秋》。"

（3）《莊子·天運篇》："《詩》以道志，《書》以道事，《禮》以道行，《樂》以道和，《易》以道陰陽，《春秋》以道名分。"

（4）《荀子·效儒篇》："《詩》《書》《禮》《樂》《春秋》。"

（5）《春秋繁露·玉杯篇》："《詩》《書》序其志，《禮》《樂》純其養，《易》《春秋》明其知。"

（6）史遷述六藝之序曰："《詩》《書》《禮》《樂》《易》《春秋》。"

今文學家都嚴守這個次序而不亂。

《易》《書》《詩》《禮》《樂》《春秋》這個次序始自劉歆的《七略》，爲古文學家所宗。《漢志》以下幾都是這個次序。陸德明《經典釋文》説是依六經著述早晚爲先後的。他説：《周易》雖文起周代，而卦肇伏羲，故《易》爲七經之首。古文《尚書》，既起五帝之末，理後三皇之經，故次於《易》。《毛詩》，既起周文，又兼《商頌》，故在後舜之後，次於《易》《書》。三禮：《周》《儀》二禮，并周公所制，宜次文王，《禮記》雖有戴聖所録，然忘名已久，又記二禮闕遺，次於《詩》下。《樂經》滅亡既久，今亦闕焉。《春秋》既是孔子所作，理當後於周公，故次於《禮》。左邱明受經於仲尼，公羊高受之於子夏，穀梁亦後代傳聞，三傳次第自顯。

今古文學家都嚴守各自的次序，不相引用。《中國十進分類法》類分六經之所以採用古文學家的次序的，乃爰分類依時序次之例。

今文經：《詩》止齊、魯、韓三家。《書》止《尚書》二十九卷。《禮》止高堂生十七篇。《樂》止制氏。《易》止《易經》上下二篇。《春秋經》十一卷，《春秋傳》止公、穀二家，《論語》：齊二十二篇，魯二十篇。《孝經》一篇。古文經：《易經》十二篇。《尚書》古文經四十六卷。《毛詩》。《禮》《逸禮》《周官》《禮記》（無古今文之分）。《樂》有《大司》，《樂章》與《樂記》。《春秋》古經十一篇，《春秋左氏傳》。《論語傳》二十一篇。《孝經》古孔氏一篇。

西漢以前祇有六經、五經的名稱。自《七略》列《論語》《孝經》《爾雅》爲經後，後世係有七經，九經，十經，十一經，十三經，十四經，四書五經之稱。七經之名始於《後漢書》，七經有三：1.《後漢書》：《詩》《書》《禮》《樂》《易》《春秋》《論語》。2. 宋劉敞撰《七經小傳》：《尚書》《毛詩》《周禮》《儀禮》《禮記》《公羊傳》《論語》。3. 清康熙御纂《七經》：《易》《書》《詩》《春秋》、三禮。九經之名始於馬融，九經有二：1.《易》《詩》《書》、三禮、三傳。2.《易》《詩》《書》《禮》《春秋》《孝經》《論語》《孟子》。十經之名始於《宋（劉宋）史·百官志》：《周易》《尚書》《毛詩》《禮記》《周官》《儀禮》《春秋左氏傳》《公羊傳》《穀梁傳》《論語》《孝經》（《論語》《孝經》合爲一經）。十二經之名始於唐《開成石經》：《易》《書》《詩》、三禮、三傳、《孝經》《論語》《爾雅》。十三經之名始於孟蜀《廣政石經》：加《孟子》於十二經。宋史繩祖加《大戴禮》於十三經稱十四經，四書之名始於朱熹的《四書集注》：取《禮記》的《大學》《中庸》加上《論語》《孟子》，於是有四書五經的名稱。

依據上文，經書的範圍有經，有傳，有記。六經是經，《齊》《魯》《韓》《毛》《左》《公》《穀》是傳，大、小戴《記》是記。《爾雅》原是字書，《七略》列入六藝，《唐志》《四庫》列入小學類。《中國十進》以之屬語言文字類，不列爲經，從《唐志》《四庫》也。

經書分類詳表，見《中國十進分類法》090類。本類既以經書的經，傳，記全部書籍爲對象，自無分於今古文也。

(見《説文月刊》一九四四年第四卷合訂本)

中國語言文字學書籍分類的研究

一、沿革

　　語言文字學這個名稱是晚近創制的，簡稱語文學，舊稱小學。這一類的書籍，歷代史志隸屬部居，都不相同。今列舉幾家的分類做説明。我所舉的是它們的不同點，不是原文全部。根據這些不同點，不但可以看出小學書籍分類的沿革，并可知道這些分類是否合乎今用：

　　1.《漢書·藝文志》。《七略》原書已佚，《漢志》是本據《七略》寫的。班氏自序是這樣説。鄭樵、章炳麟也都這樣説。

　　《漢書·藝文志序》曰："歆於是總群書，而奏其《七略》。……今删其要，以備篇籍。"

　　鄭樵曰："班固《藝文志》出於《七略》者也。"

　　章炳麟曰："其辭皆劉氏舊文。"

　　舉《漢志》是無異舉《七略》。《漢志》把小學書分隸經部的《孝經》與小學二類。列入《孝經》類的有：《爾雅》《小爾雅》《古今字》等。列入小學類的有：《史籀》《蒼頡》《凡將》《急就》《元尚》《訓纂》《別字》等。此外，把《弟子職》附《孝經》，八體六技入小學。

　　2.《隋書·經籍志》。《後漢書》《三國志》，與南北朝各史書原都没有藝文志，唐貞觀中長孫無忌等奉敕撰《隋書·經籍志》，把《爾雅》《廣雅》《小爾雅》《方言》《釋名》等分入經部《論語》類，經部小學類列入的有《會稽刻石文》、石經等。

3.《舊唐書·經籍志》。劉昫等撰的《舊唐書·經籍志》把《爾雅》《續爾雅》《別國方言》《釋名》《廣雅》《博雅》《小爾雅》列入經部小學類,但也把《書品》《書後品》《筆墨法》《鹿紙筆墨疏》一并列入。

4.《唐書·藝文志》。歐陽修等撰。小學類所列入的書大致與《舊唐志》同。所不同的是新加了:張參《五經文學》、唐玄度《九經字樣》等書。

5. 鄭樵《通志·藝文略》。鄭志有幾個特點是歷代史志所沒有的:甲、小學與經部分立,單獨成類。乙、石經分隸各經,不入小學。丙、小學類分細目。這都是《鄭志》獨到之處,為他書所不及。但他在經部另立《爾雅》類。小學分類把音釋:像《經典釋文》《經典集音》《群經音辨》等書籍都列入。又有法書類收入:《六文書》《四體書勢》等書。神書類收入:《蜀川鐵鑑子》《羅漢寺天篆》等書。

6. 陳振孫《直齋書錄解題》。直齋以書法的書籍入藝術;《五經文字》《九經字樣》等書入經解。

7. 焦竑《國史·經籍志》。《小學總序》曰:"……《爾雅》津涉九流,標名正物,講藝者莫不先之,於是有訓故之說。文字之興,隨世轉易,譌舛日繁,三蒼之說,始志字法,而《說文》興焉,於是有偏旁之學。五聲異律,清濁相生,孫炎、沈約始作字音,於是有音韻之學。保氏以數學教子弟……於是有算數之學。"焦氏把數學書也列入小學類矣。

8.《四庫全書總目》。《經部·小學類序》曰:"古小學所教,不過六書之類,故《漢志》以《弟子職》附《孝經》類,《史籀》等十家十五篇列為小學;《隋志》增以金石刻文,《唐志》增以書法、書品;已非初旨。自朱子作小學以配大學,趙希弁《讀書附志》遂以《弟子職》之類併入小學,又以蒙求之學相參并列,而小類益多岐矣,考訂源流,惟《漢志》根據經義,要為近古。今以論幼儀者別入儒家,以論筆法者別入雜藝,以蒙求之屬隸故事,以便記誦者別入類書。惟以《爾雅》以下編為訓詁,《說文》以下編為字書,《廣韻》以下編為韻書……"

這些史志的分類,假使歸納起來研究,那麼小學的範圍就不難劃清,它的緦屬是有它的原則在,再分目的意義又該是甚麼呢?

I 小學的範圍

《爾雅》與群雅。《漢志》把《爾雅》《小爾雅》分入《孝經》，《隋志》分入《論語》，《舊唐志》始列入小學，此後《唐志》《四庫》等多相沿用，與《唐志》《四庫》不同的有：鄭樵的《藝文略》在經部別立《爾雅》類，孫星衍的《祠堂書目》、張之洞的《書目答問》等把《爾雅》分入經部，其他雅書入小學、《爾雅》、群雅是小學書，不應列入經部。

《弟子職》，《漢志》分入《孝經》，《讀書附志》入小學，《四庫》入儒家，都不是，幼儀類的書應依類分。

書法。八體六技，《漢志》入小學，《隋志》因之，不當。《直齋》入藝術，《四庫》入雜藝，甚是。古今八體六文書法一類的書，雖是辨章書法形體與文字有關，但不是訓釋字義的書，怎可入小學？

石經。《隋志》以一字石經《周易》、一字石經《尚書》等石經列入小學，《舊唐志》以下史志多因之，不善。鄭樵始把石經分隸各經，《晁志》《文獻通考·經籍考》因之，最是。

經文字。《唐志》以張參《五經文字》、唐玄度《九經字樣》等書入小學，《直齋書錄解題》以之入經解，自較《唐志》爲善，要以分入各經纔可。

音釋。鄭樵以《經典釋文》《經典集音》《群經音辨》等音釋音義一類的書籍分入小學，《宋志》因之。以後各志，或入小學，或入經解，都不免牽強，應析入各類。

金石書。《隋志》列入小學，《郡齋讀書志》《宋志》因之。但尤袤《遂初堂書目》分入譜錄，馬端臨分入儀注。都不對，應做内容分。

數學。焦竑《國史經籍志》分入小學，黃虞稷《千頃堂書目》因之，類列失當。

蒙求。趙希弁《讀書附志》把蒙求的書籍入小學，宋明各志效法。《四庫》分隸故事與類書。蒙求一類的書籍最好依内容析入各類。

Ⅱ　小學的繫屬

1.《漢志》把小學類的書析入經部的《孝經》與小學二類。

2.《隋志》把小學類的書析入經部的《論語》與小學二類。

3.《舊唐志》《唐志》《國史經籍志》《四庫》等把小學類的書統歸入經部小學類。

4. 鄭樵把小學單獨成類，不隸屬經類，但他把《爾雅》《廣雅》《小爾雅》《釋名》《方言》《國語》（後魏夷語）、《釋梵語》等立爲《爾雅》類，以之隸屬經類，爲經類的一種。

5. 孫星衍、張之洞把小學書籍列入經部小學類，把《爾雅》一書列爲經。

這五種繫屬方法都不一樣，但大都以小學爲經部的屬類。獨鄭樵以小學自成一類與經類平行。不但打破了歷代以小學隸屬經部的謬見，并可以援引以駁正劉國鈞與美國國會分類法、布里士分類法把語文學與文學相濫爲一的不當。美國杜威法把語文學二類隔離，中國圖書館學者幾皆責難杜氏，杜氏似亦認爲錯失，乃設變通辦法補救，而不自知語言與文學分開并無不合，兩者并無合併或聯類的必然道理也。以前把小學隸入經類，大抵以小學是"習先王道"入門的學問。今把語文與文學聯類，甚或合併，其理由不外下列說法：

杜定友說：人類"抒其至情，懸其理想，發爲至善至美之文字語言，成爲可歌可泣之文章。……因列語言與文學爲第七、第八類。"劉國鈞說：文學是"使用文字以表現情感者。"所以把語文與文學合成一類。國會分類法、布里士也一樣把語文與文學合併成一語言類，說："語言包括文字與文學二者。"英國薛爾士說："語言是文學的材料，應該同是一類。"這幾位分類者的意見，頗有商榷的地方，語言與文字爲表情達意的工具，或符號，這是所有學問共同有的，不一定文學就要這樣。《胡適文存》引錄章炳麟的幾句話："文字本以代言，其用爲有獨至。""不得以感人者爲文辭，不感人者學說……"認爲很有見地，他們都承認文字"是一種代言的工具"。文辭與學說是不分的。

文學要用語文表情達意，其他學問是不是要語文發揮思想，文學需要美麗的文字，其他學問又何嘗不需要美麗的文字，東漢有文章同史的説法，《大慈恩寺三藏法師傳》還是一部至美的傳叙文學，文學講文法，而新舊約《聖經》的文法恐怕爲許多文學文所不及。吟詠文字，固是文學的一個要素，但《阿含經》不就是吟詠文字之作嗎？你説窈窕、蚩蚩、柔荑，凝脂，是文學專有的文字，別的學問也有他們的獨特術語與文字呢？即使説書寫美麗的文字，必研究語文學；那麼先儒也説過要瞭解經書就要研究小學；何爲依違取捨其間乎？説語言包括文字與文學，爲甚麼不説語言包括文字與哲理、文字與教育呢？何況語文學研究範圍與文學不同，怎可相合列爲一類。廢置錯列，没有是處。

　　總之這幾位分類學者列舉的理由，都不充足。他們把語文與文學繫連，舉不出他的必然道理來，所以鄭樵把小學獨立成類，不能不説他具有卓見。可惜他把《爾雅》列爲經之一，仍脱不了以《爾雅》爲"五經之訓故"的見解。至於他把鮮卑語一類的書也列入經類，那就不知"此何義也"。

Ⅲ. 小學的分目

　　分目始於鄭樵，《四庫》效之。鄭樵把小學書分爲八種，《四庫》分爲三類。鄭樵分目是根據一個原則的。他不滿意《七略》的"苟簡"與四庫（指舊《唐志》）的"荒唐"，是因爲《七略》，四庫不分目。他説："《易》本一類也，以數不可合於圖，圖不可合於音，讖緯不可合於傳注，故分爲十六種。《詩》本一類也，以圖不可合於音，音不可合於譜，名物不可合於訓詁，故分爲十二種。"一類的書，以研究的體例與形式不同：有的是傳注，有的是讖緯，有的是釋音，有的是考名物，不一而足，故一類之中，自應分目。他把小學類的書分爲八種：

1. 小學：《三蒼》《急就》《小學》《幼學》《千字文》《古今字詁》等。

2. 文字：《説文》《字林》《字文》《玉篇》《類篇》《五經文字》《九經字樣》《經典分毫正字》等。

3. 音韻：《聲類》《韻集》《切韻》《唐韻》《廣韻》《集韻》《禮部韻略》

《三十六字母圖》等。

　　4. 音釋：《經典釋文》《經典集音》《音訣》《群經音辨》等。

　　5. 古文：《古文官書》《汗簡》《尚書古字》《集古四聲韻》《古篆禮部韻》等。

　　6. 法書：《六文書》《四體書勢》《法書目錄》《筆墨法》《書譜》《草書雜體》《文房四譜》《法帖釋文》等。

　　7. 蕃書：婆羅門書，外國書。

　　8. 神書：《蜀川鐵鑑子》《吳國山天篆》《崆峒山石文》《合山鬼篆》《羅漢寺仙隸》等。

　　鄭氏分目的原則是對的，但他編類又不能全遵循這個原則。《蜀川鐵鑑子》《吳國山天篆》等分入道藏類；《經典釋文》《經典集音》等分入經類；《文房四譜》《法帖釋文》等分入善書術法類，這纔能說"一類之書，集在一處"。怎可以爲文字書，就把《五經文字》《九經字樣》總入小學類；正如他說："類書者，謂總衆類不可分也，若可分之書，當入甲類，且如天文有類書，自當列天文類。……豈可以爲類書，而總入類書乎。"再看小學與文字的區別是怎樣，他沒有說明。是不是說《三蒼》不是文字書，《說文》不是小學書。這樣錯列，與不分目，有何不同？

　　《鄭志》不當，《四庫》亦未見其可。茲舉例以明其編類之不成條理也。

　　小學類一訓詁有：郭璞注邢昺疏《爾雅注疏》，揚雄撰《方言》。小學類存目一又有：姜兆錫撰《爾雅補注》，陳與郊撰《方言類聚》。小學類二字書有：顏元孫撰《干祿字書》，張有撰《復古編》，楊桓撰《六書統》。小學類存目一又有：顏元孫撰《別本干祿字書》，吳均撰《增修復古編》、楊桓撰《六書鑑源》，小學類三韻書有樂韶鳳等奉敕撰《洪武正韻》，存目一也有周嘉棟撰《正韻彙編》，存目二又有楊時偉撰《正韻牋》。一類的書不舉在一處，不合分類原則。

　　學術是隨時代的輪子前進的，今日語文學的範圍已不是四庫時代的範圍了，語文雖分中外，但研究語文書的體例形式是不分中外的。

適今出版的語文書多涉專題，不限於以前的八種三類，也不限於一國了，有是一書，就得有是書的類別可歸。《四庫》原不是依照一個原則著錄的，哪能適合圖書分類之用，今日圖書館之所以另行編類，不是無因的。

二、編類

類目的設置，原是用以分類書籍，不是把書籍率意的隸入就可。這一點涉及兩個問題：一是分類法編製的問題，後文再講；一是知書的問題，這是本文要說及的。書籍分類不當，不知書是一個重要解因。鄭樵指出《漢志》把《尉繚子》列入諸子類，《崇文書目》把《刊（匡）謬正俗》列入《論語》，編類之訛，都是因爲不知書。所以編類，首先要知書。語文學的書籍，古書存留在今與新出的極多。有些書一看就可分類，有些就得細閱內容纔可。今依《四庫》小學類次序作一簡略的叙述。一書體義例明，編類繫屬，就無錯列的不當了。

I. 訓詁

王應麟《玉海》曰：“文字之學有三，其一體製，謂點畫有衡從曲折之殊，《說文》之類。其二訓詁，謂稱謂有古今雅俗之異，《爾雅》《方言》之類。其三音韻，謂呼吸有清濁高下之不同，沈約《四聲譜》及西域反切之學。”

訓詁是以“今字釋古字，雅言釋方言。”或今語釋古語，方言證雅言。陳澧《東塾讀書記》曰：“時有古今，猶地有東西南北，相隔遠則語言不通矣。地遠則有翻譯，時遠則有訓詁。有翻譯則能使別國如鄉鄰，有訓詁則能使古今如旦暮。”訓詁學現存最古的一部書是《爾雅》。《爾雅》的繫屬，各史志多不相同，已見前文。《四庫全書總目》論《爾雅》最是明審，今節錄原文如下：

“《爾雅》爲誰作，據張揖進《廣雅》稱周公著《爾雅》一篇，今俗所傳三篇，或言仲尼所增，或言子夏所益，或言叔孫通所補，或言沛郡梁文所考，皆解家所説，疑莫能明矣。"可知《爾雅》不是一時一人所作，也不專是《五經》的訓故。《四庫》謂其實綴輯《五經》《楚辭》《莊子》《列子》《穆天子》《管子》《吕氏春秋》《山海經》諸書舊文而作。自爲一書，所以編爲訓詁類。清儒研究《爾雅》的書較歷代爲多。比方，邵晉涵的《爾雅正義》，錢大昭的《爾雅釋文補》，郝懿行的《爾雅義疏》，江藩的《爾雅小箋》，徐孚吉的《爾雅詁》，都是比較著稱的書，尤以邵郝之書最是精博。輯佚的書有：馬國翰輯劉歆《爾雅注》，郭璞《爾雅音義》，顧野王《爾雅音》等等。

　　《爾雅》以後，孔鮒的《小爾雅》，揚雄的《方言》，劉熙的《釋名》，相沿繼作，大體與《爾雅》無殊，《小爾雅》本爲《孔叢子》第十一篇，或謂後人僞造。《方言》，舊題《輶軒使者絶代語釋別方言》，《舊唐志》稱《別國方言》，是揚雄未完成的一部書，文字古奥，訓義殊隱，後經明人改竄，顛倒錯亂，全失原本面目，郭璞爲之注，戴震爲之疏證，錢繹爲之筆記。劉熙的《釋名》，江聲、畢沅都有疏證，江聲又有《續釋名》，搜輯劉氏之遺佚者。

　　再後是魏張揖的《廣雅》，隋曹憲的《博雅》。《博雅》是《廣雅》的音釋，因避煬帝諱，改名《博雅》。《爾雅》以下群雅以《廣雅》最著稱，清儒的疏證，以王念孫的《廣雅疏證》最善。

　　宋有陸佃的《埤雅》，羅願的《爾雅翼》。《爾雅翼》考据較《埤雅》精審，體例也較謹嚴。

　　明有朱謀㙔的《駢雅》，張萱的《彙雅》。《駢雅》體例一依《爾雅》，駢異爲同，故名《駢雅》，《彙雅》是割裂《埤雅》，《爾雅翼》二書合爲一書的。

II. 字書

　　最早的字書是《史籀》十五篇，《漢書・藝文志》以"周宣王太史籀作大篆十五篇"。王國維著《史籀篇疏證》，説籀不是書體名，而是書名。《史籀篇》的文字是周秦間西土文字，春秋戰國時秦人作。這本書亡佚已久，今僅有馬國翰輯佚本。隋以前文字書，除《說文》《千字文》《玉篇》外，都亡佚。馬國翰《玉函山房》，黃氏《逸書考》，任大椿《小學鉤沈》，顧震福《小學鉤沈續篇》等書都收有佚書輯本。周太史籀《史籀篇》，秦李斯《倉頡篇》，漢司馬相如《凡將篇》，揚雄《訓纂篇》《三蒼》。郭顯卿《雜字指》，服虔《通俗文》，魏張揖《埤倉》《古今字詁》，吳韋昭《辨釋名》，晉呂忱《字林》，束晳《發蒙記》，葛洪《要用字苑》，梁阮孝緒《文字集略》，後魏江式《古今文字表》，隋顏之推《異字苑》，諸葛穎《桂苑珠叢》，曹憲《文字指歸》等等。張揖的《埤倉》是爲補《三倉》的缺漏作的，他的《古今字詁》是詁古今不同字體，清許瀚有考證。韋昭的《辨釋名》，是辨劉熙的《釋名》，呂忱的《字林》是補《說文》的遺闕。束晳的《發蒙記》是常識讀本。諸葛穎的《桂苑珠叢》是規正文字的著作。

《說文》

字書傳留後世的以《說文》《玉篇》二書爲最古。《玉篇》，梁顧野王撰，後經唐孫強增改，又經宋陳彭年重修，題《重修玉篇》，亦題《大廣益會玉篇》，已不是野王之書。《說文解字》，漢許慎撰，《說文》是我國字源學最有權威的著作。丁福保曰："今日尚能見古今造書之旨者，賴有此書之存也。"是書後經唐李陽冰竄改，宋徐鍇撰《袪妄篇》駁正之。李氏改本亡佚，今本《說文》最古的是徐鉉、徐鍇的大小徐本，大徐本最通行，小徐本名《說文繫傳》，二書部屬都仍許書之舊。小徐寫的《說文解字篆韻譜》，是檢閱《說文繫傳》的工具書。李燾據以撰《說文解字五音韻譜》，依《集韻》次第，起傳終甲，盡改許書舊觀。元明二代研究《說文》的書稍可者有：元周伯琦的《說文字原》與明趙宧光的《說文長箋》。許學至清最是昌盛，段桂王朱稱爲許學四大家。

段玉裁《說文解字段注》。段氏用考據校勘的方法治許書，對許書條例多有發明。王念孫序曰："千七百年無此作矣。"書未出，海内渴望幾三十年。書出後匡段，訂段，箋段，補段的著作相繼出版。匡段最力的是徐承慶的《說文解字注匡謬》。鈕樹玉的訂段的六弊，王紹蘭的《說文段注訂補》，訂是訂段的譌，補是補段的略。馮桂芬的《段注說文考正》

是段書的校勘。徐灝的《説文解字注箋》，是增段，是箋段，也是駁段。研究段氏許學的書還有桂馥的《説文段注鈔案》，朱駿聲的《説文段注拈誤》，龔自珍的《説文段注札記》，馬壽齡的《説文段注撰要》等等。

桂馥《説文義證》。桂書與段書并重一時，有段精桂博的稱呼。是書取證群書，釐訂二徐的譌錯。

王筠《説文釋例》。本許書參證金文，以求文字之源，不依旁段桂，自成一家之學。王氏又著《説文句讀》《句讀補正》《説文繫傳校録》《説文補正》《説文韻譜校》。

朱駿聲《説文通訓定聲》。朱書以聲爲系統，自創一例，説明聲義相通的道理，是聲讀的一部名著。

清以來研究許書的，除上述諸家外，其他甚多，體例形式也不一樣，今頻列如下：

1. 字源。蔣和《説文字原集注》，張行孚《説文揭原》，吳照《説文偏旁字解》等等。

2. 六書。張惠言《説文諧聲譜》，朱珔《説文假借義證》，陳立《説文諧聲孳生述》等等。

3. 經字。錢大昕撰《説文答問》，論證説文之字不見於經典中的原因，是在今之經典多後世異文，這些異文實是經典中的字。薛傳均有錢書的疏證，陳壽祺撰《説文經字考》，補錢書的漏略，郭慶藩撰《説文經字考辨正》，辨正陳書的謬誤。俞樾於錢陳二書外，復加搜輯撰《説文經字》。此外有：承培元《説文答問疏證》，邵瑛《説文解字群經正字》等等。

4. 引經，引他書。研究《説文》引經異同與體例的有：吳玉搢的《説文引經考》，吳雲蒸的《説文引經異字》，陳瑑的《説文引經考證》，雷浚的《説文引經例辨》，承培元的《説文引經證例》等等。引他書的有：程炎的《説文古語考》是研究《説文》引俗語的書，王仁俊的《説文解字引漢律令考》是研究《説文》引漢律令的書。

5. 新補字，逸字。新補字有：鈕樹玉的《説文新附考》，錢大昭的《徐氏〈説文〉新補新附考證》，鄭珍的《説文新附考》等等。逸字有：鄭珍的《說文逸字》，李楨的《說文逸字辨證》，張鳴珂的《說文佚字》，王廷鼎的《說文佚字輯説》等等。

6. 校勘。校勘大徐本的有：段玉裁的《汲古閣説文訂》，張行孚的《汲古閣説文解字校記》，鈕樹玉的《説文解字校録》等。王筠的《説文繫傳校録》是校勘小徐本，董詔的《二徐説文同異附考》是校勘二徐的同異。沈濤《説文古本考》根據《史》《漢》注、《字林》《玉篇》《經典釋文》等校訂二徐本的譌誤。嚴可均《説文訂訂》，校訂段氏的《汲古閣説文訂》。嚴可均、姚文田的《舊説文録》，録鄭玄《三禮注》，陸德明《經典釋文》，凡諸書引《説文》的都録出，亦是説文校勘重要著作。

7. 研究法。如馬叙倫的《説文解字研究法》。

8. 彙集。丁福保的《説文解字詁林》，彙集大小徐與各家諸本以及論述《説文》的文集筆記共一百八十二種，一千三十六卷。本書依許氏次第，逐字類聚衆説，是一部較詳備的著述。

9. 其他。如惠棟的《讀説文記》，葉德輝的《説文讀若字考》等。

六書

六書的名稱與次第在漢時就有左列三種的不同：

1. 班固《漢書·藝文志》：象形，象事，象意，象聲，轉注，假借。
2. 許慎《説文解字》叙：指事，象形，形聲，會意，轉注，假借。
3. 鄭玄《周禮注》：象形，會意，轉注，處事，假借，諧聲。

今日六書的名稱是從許書，次第從《漢志》。研究六書的著作，鄭樵《通志·六書略》以後頗多，《四庫全書總目》多有評論。比方：元戴侗的《六書故》分部爲九，與《説文》不同，是改變《説文》部分的第一部書。楊桓的《六書統》，以六書統諸字，故名曰《六書統》。此書大抵爲糾正戴書的錯譌作的。再是明趙撝謙的《六書本義》，本鄭樵之説論六書與《六書相生》諸圖。魏校的《六書精藴》，自序説是根據古文以正小篆的譌誤，擇小篆以補古文的闕失，但所用籀書都没有依據，不足爲訓，吳元滿的《六書總要》，承戴侗、楊桓的緒論，乖僻尤過戴楊二書。趙宧光的《六書長箋》也是疏舛支離。清初馮調鼎撰《六書準》，分象形，指事，會意，諧聲四類，雖力闡古義，但於六書本旨多有未明。六書之義乾嘉學者戴段諸人較精善，此後有江聲的《六書說》，黃以周的《六書通故》，廖平的《六書舊義》，葉德輝的《六書古微》，都是著稱之作。至專就六書之一著作的有：曹仁虎《二書轉注古書義考》，洪亮吉的《六書轉注錄》，夏炘的《六書轉注說》，宋保的《諧聲補逸》等。

偏旁與字原

《說文解字》叙曰："其建首也，立一爲耑。"《說文》分五百四十偏旁，其餘字的孳乳，都由這些偏旁生出。偏旁指部首，字原指獨體文。鄭樵謂獨體是文，合體是字。文是字原，字由文孳乳而生，偏旁是合體，所以是字。研究偏旁的有宋釋夢瑛的《偏旁字原》，研究字原的有章炳麟的《文始》。

普通字典

普通字典明代最通行的有：梅膺祚的《字彙》與張自烈的《正字通》。《字彙》以部首筆畫的多少爲分部的先後，每部之下仍以筆畫多少爲排字的次第，是今日筆數排檢的先聲。《正字通》沿《字彙》舊例編排。清《康熙字典》采《正字通》分部，"增《字彙》的闕遺，删《正字通》的繁冗。"民國以來有陸爾奎等編的《辭源》正續補編，朱起鳳《辭通》等等。

中外文字典

顏惠慶的《英華大辭典》，瞿侃、余雲岫編纂《德華大字典》等等。

III 韻書

我國音韻學分爲：古音學，根據《詩經》《楚辭》等書研究周秦古音。今音學，根據《廣韻》《集韻》《禮部韻略》等書研究六朝隋唐以來的用韻。等韻學研究反切，聲，字母等等，北音學，根據《中原音韻》《洪武正韻》研究元明音系，國音學是建立現今的音韻。

古音學。顧炎武曰："休文作譜，乃不能上據雅南，旁撫《騷》子，以成不刊之典，而僅按班張以下諸人之賦，曹劉以下諸人之詩所用之音，撰爲定本，於是今音行而古音亡，爲音學之一變。"這是說古音亡於沈約的四聲。宋以前没有古音書，至宋吳棫撰《韻補》纔有。但《韻補》多雜歐陽修，蘇軾等宋人之作，古音益是紊亂。明人古音著作有：楊慎的《古音叢目》《古音獵要》《古音餘》《古音附錄》，都是仿《韻補》體例作的。楊氏也不明古音的本真。古音學至清纔有精深的研究，王國維《周代金石文韻讀·序》曰：「古韻之學，自崐山顧氏，而婺源江氏，而休寧戴氏，而金壇段氏，而曲阜孔氏，而高郵王氏，而歙縣江氏，作者不過七人，然古音二十二部之目，遂令後世無可增損，故訓故名物文字之學有待於將來者甚多；至古韻之學，謂之前無古人，後無來者，可也。」這些古音學家的著作，以顧炎武的《音學五書》，江有誥的《音學十書》最是著名。民國以來研究古韻學者有：章炳麟，黃季剛，高本漢（瑞典），林語堂等等。研究古音的著作也有多種：楊樹達的《古聲韻討論集》，張世禄的《中國古音學》，魏建功的《古音系研究》等等。

　　今音學。我國韻書至魏晉時纔有。比方，魏李登的《聲類》，晉吕静的《韻集》，梁沈約的《古韻經》，北齊陽休之的《韻略》，隋陸法言的《切韻》都是。但原本失佚、今本都是輯佚本。僅有敦煌石室發現的《切韻》部分，王國維有考證。《切韻》傳至唐代，孫愐重爲刊定，改名《唐韻》，今僅存殘卷。《唐韻》至宋大中祥符真宗詔陳彭年、邱雍等重修，賜名《大宋重修廣韻》，是現存韻書最古的一部，莫友芝、李燾等論列頗詳。莫友之曰：「今韻書存之最古者，惟《廣韻》詳略二本，及夏竦《古文四聲韻》。此略本《廣韻》五卷，前有孫愐《廣韻序》，注文比重修本頗減。……《永樂大典》引此本皆曰陸法言《廣韻》，引重修本，皆曰宋重修《廣韻》。……考宋志載陸法言《廣韻》五卷，《玉海》引《崇文書目》有《唐廣韻》五卷，當即一書。蓋既經唐人增益，故陸書亦兼《廣韻》之名。迨後陳彭年等所定曰重修……重修本亦五卷。」李燾曰：「隋陸法言撰，唐郭知玄附益之者，時號《切韻》。天寶末，陳州司馬孫愐以《切韻》爲謬，略復加刊正，別爲《唐韻》之名。大中祥符元年改賜新名曰《廣韻》。」《切韻》《唐韻》《廣韻》雖略有參差，實是一書也。所以研究南北朝隋唐以來的音韻學稱曰《廣韻》學。稍後於《廣韻》的韻書有《禮部韻略》與《集韻》

二書。《玉海》謂景德五年《切韻》改名《大宋重修廣韻》。《廣韻》比《韻略》詳細，與《韻略》可説是一部書。景祐四年詔令丁度等改定韻窄者十三處，稱《禮部韻略》。同年詔宋祁等增修《廣韻》，改稱《集韻》，是《集韻》與《禮部韻略》爲一書的詳略二本。《禮部韻略》現存者《四庫》謂有二種：一是郭守正修的《附釋文互注禮部韻略》五卷，附貢舉條式一卷。一是毛晃增注，毛居正校勘的《增修互注禮部韻略》五卷。平水劉淵有《壬子新刊禮部韻略》（書今亡佚）定韻爲一百七部，元黄公紹的《古今韻會舉要》一百七韻就是本自劉書。毛大可説今行詩韻一百六部就是劉淵的平水韻。

邵長蘅曰："今韻宗梁沈約氏，夫人而言之：而約所譔《四聲》一卷久已亡。繼之者隋陸法言氏，而法言所譔《四聲》亦亡，嗣是有唐孫愐，而愐所譔《唐韻》五卷今亦亡。今宋元韻之存者，略可指數：《廣韻》，宋祥符間所修也。《集韻》，宋景祐間奉敕修也。《禮部韻略》，宋時列之學官者也。毛晃氏仍禮部而增益之者也。平水劉淵氏仍禮部而通併其部分者也。元黄公紹氏《韻會》仍劉韻，而廣其箋注者也。……今韻沈韻不待言，校劉韻少三千字，則今韻之非劉韻，較然易辨。"

等韻學。鄭樵《通志·藝文略》曰："切韻之學，起自西域，舊所傳十四字貫一切音。……後又得三十六字母，而音韻之道始備。中華之韻，只彈四聲矣。"《四庫全書總目》論司馬光《切韻指掌圖》曰："等韻之學，自後漢與佛經俱來。……其有成書傳世者，惟光此書爲最古。"現存的等韻書最古的還有：《韻鏡》，鄭樵《通志·七音略》，《四聲等子》，與劉鑑史《正音切韻指南》。明清等韻書較著的有：明呂坤的《交泰韻》，立切韻簡要之法。呂維祺的《音韻日月燈》，對等韻之學頗有所見。比國金尼閣著《西儒耳目資》以西文二十六字母注我國語音，等韻之學，更是淺顯。清有：潘耒的《類音》。潘氏長於音理，定五十字母，二十四韻。李光地奉敕承修的《音韻闡微》，《四庫》稱："自有韻書以來，無更捷徑於此法者，亦更無精密於此書者矣。"再有熊士伯的《等切元聲》，李汝珍的《李氏音鑑》，都是著稱之作。

等韻學研究反切，四聲，五音，字母等等。爲甚麽叫等韻？李元《音切譜》曰："反者音也，切者韻也。反惟一字，切有四等，故不曰等音，而曰等韻。"

反切。反切，古人稱反語，就是拼音的意思。用二字切出一字的音。第一字與被切的字要同紐，第二字與被切的字要同韻，同等。古代没有反切。顏之推《家訓》曰："孫叔然創《爾雅音義》。"是漢末人已知反語。陸德明、李汝珍、章炳麟都以反切起自漢末，但没有成書。齊周顒切字用紐，紐有平上去入，纔有四聲四韻。

四聲五音。唐封演《聞見記》曰："李登撰《聲類》，以五聲命之。"《魏書·江式傳》曰："呂静倣李登《聲類》之法作《韻集》五卷，宮商角徵羽各爲一篇。"四聲之説，始於南北朝沈約、周顒諸人，蓋受印度聲明學的影響者。五音，亦云七音。鄭樵《通志·七音略序》曰："七音之韻，起自西域，流入諸夏。"

字母。三十六字母，世傳元魏僧神珙所作。宋《崇文總目》祇説唐釋守温所作，不言神珙，今從此説。舊時所稱字母是指紐説的，與今日的聲母韻母不一樣。

北音學。代表元明時代北音的韻書有《中原音韻》與《洪武正韻》。元周德清的《中原音韻》是現代國語的先導。明樂韻鳳等奉敕撰的《洪武正韻》，注釋是以毛晃《增韻》爲稿本，稍以他書損益之者。二書都改革《廣韻》，歷代韻書自是而一大變。

國音學。國音就是國語的語音。民國元年讀音統一會，制定注音字母三十九個，分爲聲母二十四，韻母十五。聲母近似舊時的紐，與西文字母的子音相當，韻母近似舊時的韻，與西文字母的母音相當。聲母與韻母合拼注出一個字音。民國二十一年教育部公佈《國音常用字彙》，定北平音爲標準。若干學者對注音字母也不甚滿意，或採用國語羅馬字，羅馬字拼切漢字。或提倡簡字，或主張廢弃漢字採用萬國語。改廢漢字的最大動機之一是要語言與文字合於一。自然我國文字在字不在音，不能與歐美文字在音也在字相提并論。語言還没有統一之前，不能用切音代形，必是與歐美語文一樣統一然後可。

我國語文學還有他方面的著作。比方：

古文字學。唐代石鼓文字的研究，可説是研究古文字的開始。金文字的著述，宋時纔有。清末安陽甲骨出土後，就有契文書籍。但這三類古文字的書籍以前都是零星的考釋，也不純粹研究古文字的專著。到最近纔趨於古文字學的專門研究，有系統的古文字學書籍漸漸有了。

文法。自清初劉淇作《助字辨略》以後，直到清末纔有馬建忠的《馬氏文通》一書。《馬氏文通》是倣西文文法把我國詞類分爲九種的第一部書。清末還有章士釗的《中等國文法》。民國以來，楊樹達的《高等國文法》《詞詮》，黎錦熙的《比較文法》等等相繼出版，此外還有標點符號的著述。胡適的《請頒行新式標點符號議案》，高元的《新標點之用法》都是文法學的著作漸趨於專類的研究也漸脱離模倣而趨於自創的研究矣。

現代方言。這一類的書籍現今很多。章炳麟的《新方言》，黎錦熙的《漢語方言十二系區域表》，趙元任的《現代英語的研究》，胡以魯的《中國方言十種》，等等都是。

滿蒙藏苗等語文的研究。研究這類語文，外國學者的著述較多。比方，英人貝爾的《藏語文法》《英藏俚語字典》。法人費雅的《法儸語字典》《法苗字彙》等等。我國學者現也出版了幾種著述。

我國現代語文學的研究，一般的説，這是創始時期，學者們正在多方面從事有系統的著述，下進一步的工夫，使這個文化的工具進入燦爛光榮的時代。

三、分類法

圖書館分類的得當，知書是首要問題。不但要知書，還要有分類。祇知道書，没有分類法，圖書館就不能册繫部勒。語文分類法的編製與它類一樣有一定原則。比方，它的體例要儘可能與它國語文類齊一。圖書館界稱這一類爲形式類，因爲各國語文類目幾是一樣。此外類目的設置，不僅是根據已出版的圖書，也要顧到若干年後可能出版的圖書。再類目的分配要能利用號碼，一方面使號碼的長度減短，另方面顧及將來擴充不致有困難。又要重實用：分類法固然要以學術系統做骨幹，但它的主要目的是在乎用，所以類例雖要劃一，但更要能用，不但這樣，還包括各種要素分類表，形式細分，號碼等等，拙著《圖書分類學》都有詳細的叙述。因不在本文範圍以内，故從略。

這個分類法類列的層次與一般分類法一樣，由渾入劃，先共名，後別名，以類分，也以時次。因爲這是增改中國十進分類法語文類的，所以全部寫出，就正讀者先生。

410　中國語言文字學

一、下列.1—.9稱爲形式細分。形式細分的號碼.1—.9的前面要有零(0)，所以江恒源著《中國文字學大意》的號碼是410.0，林語堂著《言語學論叢》的號碼是410.4，伍大春撰《小學鈎沉》的號碼是410.8，胡樸安著《中國文字學史》的號碼是410.9。

二、每一個類目都可依這個形式細分。比方，胡樸安著《文字學研究法》的號碼是410.107，那麼馬叙倫著《說文解字研究法》的號碼就是411.107。顧震福撰《小學鈎沈續篇》的號碼是410.8，丁福保著《說文解字詁林》的號碼就是411.108。吳三立著《中國文字學史》的號碼是410.9，羅常培著《中國音韻沿革》的號碼就是415.09，餘類推。

三、專類文字的書依類分。比方，《五經文字》《九經字樣》分入經類。

四、古書中間有作僞，或著者尚待考證時：暫從舊說。

五、分類表中類目依朝代，或依區域細分，細分的號碼都是依中國十進分類法編的。

410.1　理論　關係
　　.2　綱要
　　.3　辭典

.4 評論
.5 雜論
.6 會社
.7 研究
.8 總集　叢書
.9 歷史

411　字源學
　.1　說文解字
　　　　依上列形式細分
　.11　字源
　　　　例　蔣和撰《說文字源集注》
　　　　　　張行孚撰《說文揭原》
　.12　六書
　　　　例　張成孫田撰《說文諧聲譜》
　.13　經字
　　　　例　郭慶藩撰《說文經字考辨證》
　.14　引經
　　　　例　柳榮宗撰《說文引經考異》
　.15　引他書
　　　　例　鄭文焯撰《說文引群說故》
　.16　逸字　新補字
　　　　例　錢大昭《說文新補新附考證》
　　　　　　張鳴珂撰《說文佚字考》
　.17　校勘
　　　　例　張行孚撰《汲古閣說文解字校記》
　.18　聲讀
　　　　例　苗夔撰《說文聲讀考》
　.19　其他

.2　段注《說文》以前注解　依朝代分

　　　例　莫友芝撰《唐寫本說文木部箋異》411.24

　　　　　徐鍇撰《說文繫傳》411.25

.3　段注《說文》

.31　研究段注《說文》的著作依作者姓氏字順排

.4　段注《說文》以後注解

　　　.41—.48 爲研究《說文》自成家派者的號碼。其他都列入

　　　.49—類目下。

.41　桂馥

　　　《說文義證》

.42　王筠

　　　《說文句讀》《說文釋例》

.43　朱駿聲

　　　《說文通訓定聲》

.44　錢坫

　　　《說文解字斠詮》

411.49　其他

　　　例　江沅撰《說文釋例》

.5　其他字源字典　依朝代分

　　　例　陶方琦輯《字林考逸補本》411.53

　　　　　司馬光撰《類篇》411.55

.6　六書

　　　研究六書的著作不限於《說文》者類此

　　　例　葉德輝著《六書古微》，高本漢著《諸聲字體的原則》

.7　偏旁　字源

　　　例　釋夢瑛撰《偏旁字源》，章炳麟著《文始》

.8　新字　外來字　俗字

　　　例　王雲五著《王雲五新詞典》，劉復著《俗字譜》

411.9　其他
412　普通字典
　　　　　依檢字法分
　　　　　專門字典分入各類
　　　　例　朱經農編《教育大辭典》分入教育類
.1　部首
　　　　例　張玉書等奉敕撰《康熙字典》
.2　字母
　　　　例　金韓孝彥撰《四聲編海》
.3　母筆
　　　　例　萬國鼎著《新橋字典》
.4　國音
　　　　例　方毅著《國音學生字彙》
.5　號碼
　　　　例　王雲五著《王雲五大辭典》
.6　筆畫
　　　　例　陸費逵編《中華大字典》
.7　基本語彙
.8　雜字
　　　　例　張揖撰《雜字》(輯佚本)
.9　成語字典
　　　　例　莊適編《國文成語辭典》。此類目包括引句，典故，外來語，等等
　　諺語分入民間文學
　　格言分入箴銘類
　　俗語，慣語，隱語分入俚語類
413　中外文字典
　　　　譯文字典(中外文對譯)依下列分

　　　　.1　漢滿，漢藏，漢蒙等文字典
　　　　　　　例　段克興改編《藏漢小字典》改訂本
　　　　.2　中日
　　　　　　　例　山口造酒與入江祝衛共編《注解和漢新辭典》
　　　　.3　中希
　　　　.4　中法
　　　　　　　例　蕭子琴等編譯《模範法華字典》
　　　　.5　中美
　　　　　　　例　顏惠慶編《英華大辭典》
　　　　.7　中德
　　　　　　　例　瞿侃，余雲岫編纂《德華大字典》
　　　　.8　中俄
　　　　　　　例　陳昌誥等編《俄華辭典》，等等
　　　　.9　其他
414　訓詁學
　　　專類的訓詁分入各類
　　　　　例　宋翔鳳撰《釋服》分入服裝類
　　　　　　　劉寶楠撰《釋穀》分入農學類
　414.1　爾雅
　　　　　　　依《說文解字》形式細分　注疏注解依朝代分
　　　　　　　郭璞撰《爾雅圖贊》(輯佚本)414.102
　　　　　　　戴震撰《爾雅文字考》414.107
　　　　　　　郭璞注邢昺疏《爾雅注疏》414.12
　　　　　　　鄭樵撰《爾雅注》414.15
　　　　　　　姜兆錫撰《爾雅補注》414.17
　　　　.19　專篇
　　　　　　　例　錢坫撰《爾雅釋地以下四篇注》
　414.2　群雅　依朝代分

　　　　　例　孔鮒撰《小爾雅》414. 21
　　　　　　　劉熙撰《釋名》414. 22
　　　　　　　張揖撰《廣雅》414. 231
　　　　　　　陸佃撰《埤雅》415. 25
　　　　　　　朱謀㙔撰《駢雅》415. 26
414. 3　同意字　反意字
414. 4　方言　研究古今方言的著作類此
　　.5　揚雄《方言》
　　.6　現代方言　依形式細分
　　　　　例　趙元任著《方言調查表格》414. 6032
　　　　　　　　　依區域分
　　　　　例　毛奇齡撰《越語肯綮錄》414. 678
　　　　　　　羅常培著《廈門音系》414. 681
　　.7　俚語
　　.8
　　.9　國語　依形式細分
　　　　　例　汪怡等編《國語字典》414. 903
　　　　　　　黎錦熙著《國語運動史綱》414. 909
　　　　　　　國語細目暫定如下
　　.91　字母
　　　　　三十六字母研究舊時的紐分入等韻學
　　.92　聲母
　　.93　韻母
　　.94　發音
　　　　　例　王怡著《國語發音學》
　　.96　重音法
　　.98　簡字
　　.99　其他

415　音韻學　專類的音韻依類分
　　　　例　毛奇齡撰《易韻》分入《易經》
　　　　　　苗夔撰《毛詩韻訂》分入《毛詩》
　.1　古音學
　　　　例　江永撰《古韻標準》，張世禄著《中國古音學》
415.2　今音學　廣韻學
　　　依朝代分
　.23　魏晉六朝隋
　.231　李登撰《聲類》
　.232　呂靜撰《韻集》
　.237　沈約撰《韻經》
　.239　陸法言撰《切韻》
　.24　唐　孫愐撰《唐韻》
　.25　宋
　.251　陳彭年，邱雍等重修《大宋重修廣韻》
　.253　丁度等改定《禮部韻略》
　.255　宋祁等增修《集韻》
　.3　等韻學
　　　　例　江有誥撰《等韻叢說》
　　　.31　字母（紐）
　　　　　　例　釋守溫撰《三十六字母》
　　　.32　切韻
　　　　　　例　劉鑑撰《經史正音切韻指南》
　　　.33
　　　.34　四聲五音
　　　　　　例　釋神珙撰《四聲五音九弄反紐圖》
　　　.35　四聲
　　　　　　例　紀昀撰《沈氏四聲考》

　　　　　.36 五音
　　　　　　　例　鄒漢勳撰《五均論》
　　　　　　　　　鄭樵撰《七音略》
　　　　　.39 其他
　　　　　.4 北音學
　　　　　　　例　趙蔭棠著《中原音韻研究》
　　　　　.5 國音學
　　　　見 414.9 國語
416　語法
　　　例　章士釗著《中等國文法》
　　　.1 言語形態學
　　　.2 名詞類
　　　　　名字，代名字，形容字，動字等等
　　　　　　　例　劉淇撰《助字辨略》
　　　　　　　　　斐學海著《古書虛字集釋》
　　　.3 章句法
　　　.4 標點法
　　　　　　　例　馬國英編《新式標點使用法》
　　　.5 省寫法
　　　.6
　　　.7 會話
　　　.8 修辭學　文章法
　　　　　　　例　喻守真編《文章體例》
　　　.81 文言
　　　.82 白話
　　　.9 其他
417　讀本
　　　研究文法的課本書類此

其關係文學方面的分入文學類
- .1 訓蒙　識字
  - 例　唐穗田著《識字新法》
- .2 拼音讀本
- .5 初級讀本
- .6 高級讀本
- .7 選本
- .8
- .9 外人用

418 古文字學
- 一、純粹研究古文字的書類此
  - 例　徐文鏡編《古籀彙編》
  - 　　唐蘭著《古文字學導論》
- 二、其文字考釋古器物的書分入考古學
  - 例　吳大澂撰《愙齋集古錄》
  - 　　王國維著《殷卜辭中所見先公先王考》
- 三、法帖，碑帖一類的書分入美術書法類
  - 例　金簡編《校正淳化閣帖釋文》
  - 　　阮元撰《華山辭考》

418.1 甲骨文字
- 例　郭沫若著《甲骨文研究》
- .3 金文字
  - 例　汪立名撰《鐘鼎字源》
- .5 石刻文字
  - 例　任兆麟撰《石鼓文考釋》
- .9 其他

419 兄弟民族語文學
這一類的語文書依下列分

例　戴穀撰《清文備考》419.1
　　佚名撰《蒙古譯語》419.2
　　佚名撰《川番譯語九種》419.3

.1　滿洲語文
.2　蒙古語文
.3　西藏語文
.4　西夏語文
.5　苗語
.6　黎語
.9　其他

（見《圖書館學報》一九四五年創刊號）